CIVIL INTERVIEWING
AND INVESTIGATING
FOR PARALEGALS
A Process-Oriented Approach

. . . .

JODI G. McMASTER, J.D.

Pearson
Prentice Hall
Legal Series

PEARSON
Prentice
Hall

Upper Saddle River, New Jersey 07458

Library of Congress Cataloging-in-Publication Data

McMaster, Jodi G.
    Civil interviewing and investigating for paralegals : a process oriented approach / Jodi G. McMaster.—1st ed.
        p. cm.
Includes bibliographical references and index.
ISBN 0-13-111891-9
1. Interviewing in law practice—United States. 2. Attorney and client—United States.
3. Legal assistants—United States. I. Title.
    KF311.M345 2006
    347.73'504—dc22

2004028432

Director of Production and Manufacturing: Bruce Johnson
Senior Acquisitions Editor: Gary Bauer
Editorial Assistant: Jacqueline Knapke
Senior Marketing Manager: Leigh Ann Sims
Managing Editor—Production: Mary Carnis
Manufacturing Buyer: Ilene Sanford
Production Liaison: Denise Brown
Production Editor: Heather Willison/Carlisle Publishers Services
Composition: Carlisle Communications, Ltd.
Senior Design Coordinator/Cover Design: Christopher Weigand

The information provided in this text is not intended as legal advice for specific situations, but is meant solely for educational and informational purposes. Readers should retain and seek the advice of their own legal counsel in handling specific legal matters.

Pearson Education Ltd.
Pearson Education Singapore Pte. Ltd.
Pearson Education Canada, Ltd.
Pearson Education—Japan

Pearson Education Australia Pty. Limited
Pearson Education North Asia Ltd.
Pearson Educación de Mexico, S. A. de C.V.
Pearson Education Malaysia Pte. Ltd.
Pearson Education, Upper Saddle River, New Jersey

ISBN 0-13-111891-9

For Brett Michael Huser: in memoriam

Pearson Legal Series

Pearson Legal Series provides paralegal/legal studies students and educators with the publishing industry's finest content and best service. We offer an extensive selection of products for over 70 titles and we continue to grow with more new titles each year. We also provide:

- online resources for instructors and students
- state-specific materials
- custom publishing options from Pearson Custom Publishing group

To locate your local Pearson Prentice Hall representative, visit www.prenhall.com

To view Pearson Legal Series titles and to discover a wide array of resources for both instructors and students, please visit our website at:

www.prenhall.com/legal_studies

CONTENTS

2

THE CLIENT: PLAINTIFF'S PERSPECTIVE 37

3

THE CLIENT: DEFENDANT'S PERSPECTIVE 75

4

THE OPPOSING PARTY

6

SPECIAL ISSUES WITH WITNESSES

7

DOCUMENTARY EVIDENCE

8

E-DOCUMENTS AND OTHER COMPUTER DISCOVERY ISSUES

9

BACKGROUND RESOURCES

10

EXPERT WITNESSES

11

REAL AND DEMONSTRATIVE EVIDENCE

12

WITNESS PREPARATION

13

ENDING THE LITIGATION

CASES

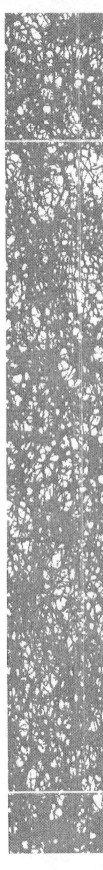

PREFACE

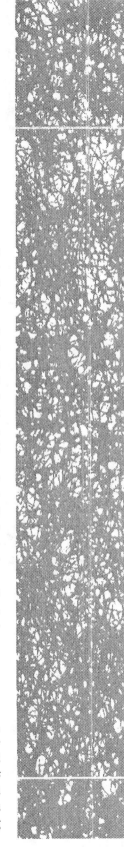

Civil Interviewing and Investigating for Paralegals: A Process-Oriented Approach is a text for students who have already completed a study of the basic substantive areas of law; it serves as a springboard for synthesizing the theoretical with the practical. Also, for students planning to take the CLA exam, the text includes coverage of the material in the official review manual, although presented in a different manner. Where the two differ, it is pointed out.

This textbook places a premium on hands-on application. It walks the student through the trial process, outlining the practical steps and introducing the evidentiary concepts that accompany each item that must be investigated. Students are addressed as though they have had the core areas of law, and knowledge of civil litigation in particular is presumed. Vocabulary terms are reviewed, in the case of core areas of law and basic legal terminology, and introduced as appropriate. Legal terms or terms of art are defined both in the chapter text and in the glossary at the end of the book. The tone is the verbal equivalent of business casual, more bar journal than law journal. And, as you'll see, it is peppered with sidebar comments with the intent of keeping students' interest and to stimulate evaluative thought processes rather than passive acceptance.

The assignments fall into two categories. The first set of exercises reviews the material presented from a recall perspective. The other exercises are application exercises to develop students' ability to practice the processes described in each chapter. The "Web Work" exercises allow students to gain proficiency in actual use of the Internet for investigative purposes. The "Brain Work" section, containing legal and problem analysis exercises, reinforces students' ability to apply new, substantive information to novel circumstances. These exercises will also reinforce the habits of analysis, thought, and practice.

The Instructor's Manual includes a sample syllabus, course competencies, the "answers" to questions based on cases, summaries of the articles listed in the "For Further Reading" section, vocabulary quizzes, and a series of questions for use in testing. The manual also includes suggested projects and classroom assessments where appropriate.

INSTRUCTOR'S RESOURCE CD-ROM

The Instructor's CD for this text includes test and quiz questions, suggestions for class activities, Word versions of the forms shown in the text, full versions of cases included in the text, and chapter by chapter PowerPoint presentations. In addition, the disk contains three digital videos. Each video features an exercise performed by a paralegal student based on the fictional case of *Haus v. Justice* used as an example throughout the book. The first is an interview of the client who is a defendant in the suit, an off-duty police officer. The second is an interview of a fact witness, a neighbor of the plaintiff. The third demonstrates an interview of an expert by a paralegal trying to evaluate her. Each video contains both positive and negative modeling, which gives the instructor an opportunity to elicit an evaluation of the videotaped students for discussion of good interviewing techniques.

This text envisions a course where the goals are to have students (1) remember legal theory from other classes, (2) analyze fact patterns appropriately, (3) practice creative problem solving, (4) develop strategic thinking, and (5) analyze the process for finding supporting evidence within legal constraints and for a given situation. Sometimes success is devising the right questions rather than finding the right answers.

ACKNOWLEDGMENTS

I have so many people to thank, it's a good thing this isn't an Oscar speech. I am indebted to all the legal secretaries and paralegals over the years who have taught me a little here and a little there, and all the lawyers I've sat listening to as they told war stories. I am also grateful to the clients and witnesses who have taught me about my profession as the years pass. A few names stand out: Daniel Diaz, Jr., Richard Copeland, Melvina Medley, and Larry Goldman. These four taught me most of the various aspects of litigation practice. Melvina, in particular, is a stellar investigator; she taught me many of the little tricks in this book.

Then there are the people who helped me with this book: Erin McAuliffe, a fellow teacher at San Antonio College, and all my students: Andrea Jackson, Mary Treviño, Frances Barfield, Matt Brzozowski, Valerie Casias, Sarah Claridge, Kathleen Dominguez, Teresa Fletcher, Ashley Garza, Kelly Hurst, Trisha Koula, Steven Lucas, Sergio Perez, Edna Rodriguez, Mario Rodriguez, M.J. Stanuga, Crystal Whitfield, and Debbie Willhite. A special thanks to Kelly Stewart, who gave me a hand with finding illustrations now that my own legal files are a thing of the past. Thanks, too, to Dr. Mary Ann Flatley, who keeps encouraging me to write—to just do it. I'm also grateful to Dr. Gail Taylor, whose sense of humor has served as a barometer for my writing choices.

I also need to thank the staff of the Huebner Oaks Starbucks, where I lived for several months while writing this. During the time I was there, I had the opportunity to meet Brett Michael Huser, a charming and friendly young man who obviously had a lot of potential. After I had completed the first draft, but before I finished the final version, Brett was killed in a car accident; the driver became distracted and drifted into the opposite lane of traffic. The tragedy served to remind me that although we must develop a certain distance and gallows humor to survive our business, the work we do deals with real people whose lives have been disrupted, sometimes in the most horrible ways. Although we should not take ourselves too seriously, the work we do *is* serious.

As always, I also want to thank my wonderful, supportive family—my husband Gary and my children David and Elyce—who took care of the house and each other during all the weekends I lived at Starbucks and who encouraged me to keep going at times when the task seemed insurmountable. I love you guys.

Special thanks to the reviewers of this text: Laura Barnard, Lakeland Community College; Sait Tarhan, Cincinnati State Technical and Community College; Robert Diotalevi, Florida Gulf Coast University.

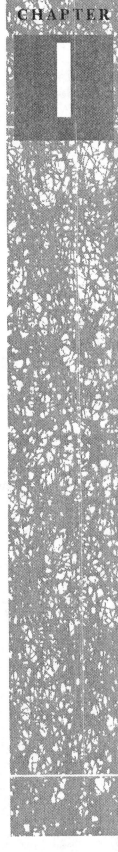

THE LAW OFFICE ENVIRONMENT

"Young lawyers attend the courts not because they have business there but because they have no business anywhere else."

Washington Irving

"It is the trade of lawyers to question everything, yield nothing, and to talk by the hour."

Thomas Jefferson

"I have come to the conclusion that one useless man is called a disgrace, that two are called a law firm, and that three or more become a congress."

Peter Stone

INTRODUCTION

Interviewing and investigating are two halves of the fact-gathering process in a lawsuit, which includes finding admissible evidence through testimony, documents, and tangible evidence and those things that will lead to admissible evidence. These terms usually refer to the informal, non-court-assisted methods, but can include formal, court-assisted discovery as well. **Interviewing** refers to the process of questioning potential witnesses; **investigating** refers to the process of obtaining tangible or documentary evidence. The **CLA. Review**, the official study guide for the national certification test given by the **National Association of Legal Assistants (NALA)**, defines interviewing as "the exchange of information between individuals, the objective of which is to elicit relevant facts based on personal knowledge, to develop leads to other witnesses who may possess relevant facts, and to elicit corroboration of facts." While performing the task of interviewing or investigating, you are acting as an investigator.

The process of interviewing and investigating does not take place in a vacuum, though. The process takes place in the context of a law office, and whether you are working as an independent paralegal or as an employee of the law office, you need to understand the dynamics of the law office to understand how you work as an investigator. Although law offices differ in culture and details, the general dynamics remain the same.

Law offices that practice litigation are high-pressure places. The work is important to the people who are there; with the general exception of adopting parents, the clients who come to see you are not there because of happy circumstances. They want answers, and the answers they get are often not the ones they want. The courtroom is not a place for simple yes or no answers; it is not where you will necessarily find truth or justice (although it does occasionally happen incidentally). I know the preceding statement sounds cynical; perhaps it is. But you must recognize the mythology or aspirations of our field are not its realities in order to be effective. In my completely unscientific survey of friends who had attended different law schools I found that not one could recall any discussions of truth or justice. Instead, we discuss theories of the evidence, interpretations, strategies, or argument. The longer you are in this field you will find that truth (and justice) are extremely elusive. But laypeople still expect those outcomes, and are dismayed to find that no one can guarantee them anything except a trial. To be a successful paralegal, you will need to recognize clients' frustrations, and empathize with each while keeping a professional manner. You are often the person who is the main contact with the client, and developing good rapport with the client through genuine interest in him and trying to understand his point of view will go a long way to building positive relations.

As a result of their unhappiness with their circumstances, clients may look for someone to blame if things go wrong. A convenient place to lay blame is the law office. Because lawyers owe clients a high degree of care, firms are easy to fault and to sue. Lawyers are also responsible for the acts of their staff. Consequently, a lawyer may be sued for professional malpractice on the basis of her own acts or on the basis of the acts of her staff. Some lawyers have difficulty seeing their own mistakes and will look at the staff's mistakes microscopically without reviewing their own; others are very good about taking responsibility for the overall outcome. Not only can you end up in litigation, but doing a bad job on a case can mean the loss of a valued repeat client or the ruin of a individual's only chance at restitution for a wrong done him. Therefore, there is a great deal of pressure for both lawyers and staff to do everything 100% right.

Being perfect is tough, particularly in an atmosphere of perpetual deadlines. Missed deadlines are the single largest reason most often cited for legal malpractice suits, according to the American Bar Association's Standing Committee on Legal Malpractice, constituting at least 20% of all malpractice suits filed. Most deadlines have to do with **discovery**, the formal process of investigating a case, although others, such as filing deadlines prior to trial or statutes of limitation, can sneak up on you, too. Often discovery requests are based on the informal interviewing and investigation, so discovery must be completed in a timely fashion, and failure to do so will cause a cascade of problems. However, all staff members are generally overworked, juggling multiple cases with multiple deadlines, and it is very easy to drop one of the many plates, balls, watermelons, and chainsaws you've got whirling around in the air.

Don't be surprised to find that you're not perfect; learn to live with it, despite the law profession's culture of intolerance for imperfection. Take time out to de-stress. In the 1990s, the legal profession topped a psychiatric list as the most depressing profession of 104 studied. Twenty to thirty-five percent of lawyers were stressed to the point of needing professional help (as opposed to 2% of the general population), and an inordinately large percentage had problems with various addictions. Don't let the lawyer's bad habits of thinking spread to you: it is, in part, this constant need to be perfect—an unobtainable goal—driving the unhappiness. A happy paralegal will find a balance between excellence and the practical realities that stand in the way of perfection and finds ways to manage the workload and relieve the stress of the workplace. Some ways to reach that balance are to be organized, to plan ahead, and to know what you have to do for any case from the beginning so that you won't be sideswiped. To some extent, every case can be planned out. Emergencies shouldn't occur unless the case has been ignored until deadlines are looming. Early planning for discovery and investigation can alleviate much stress.

In addition to being a profession and a service, a law office is a business. What the firm undertakes to do, it must do well. But it does not have to perform free work. At the outset of any case, the entire staff needs to understand the budget considerations of the client. In a perfect world, everyone would get a full investigation and equal access to experts. Interviewing and investigating takes the time of the paralegal professional, or a substitute private investigator, expert, or specialist, as well as adding attendant expenses. Hiring experts to testify is expensive. At the beginning, you must know what sort of budget you are working with and plan accordingly.

LAW OFFICE CATEGORIES

Law offices are categorized by size and by practice type. For purposes of this discussion, only litigation practices will be addressed. The other major type of practice—transactional—does not generally utilize interviewing and investigating techniques to the same degree as litigation, although all firms require paralegals to have the ability to interview clients effectively to determine their legal needs.

By Size

Sole Practitioner. A sole practitioner is a one-lawyer firm that may have many staff members. One lawyer can maximize his ability to handle cases by the wise use of paralegals and other staff, using his time solely for matters that cannot be delegated to others. This is also a place where the paralegal may find herself doing everything from the account books to the yardwork. As a result, **sole practitioners'** offices are great places to get experience because they tend to delegate more responsibility to paralegals. On the other hand, they also tend toward the sink-or-swim method of training staff.

Small Firm. A small firm has at least 2 lawyers, but there may be as many as 10. The high end of this size firm depends largely on the locale. In some areas, ten lawyers is a really big firm. At this size, staff is usually still fairly small and management is informal. After three or so, you start seeing the partner versus associate structure. The **partners** (also called **shareholders**) are the actual owners of the firm and share in the profits. The **associates** are younger lawyers who work for the partners with the expectation of eventually being asked to become a partner.

Medium-Sized Firm. A medium-sized firm is the size that is hardest to gauge. At below 20 lawyers, it tends to act more like a small firm; somewhere around that number it reaches critical mass and formal management measures must be instituted to handle the employees. At over 100, it is unquestionably large; at 50 it is probably large. Medium-sized firms still have more flexibility than large firms. Sometimes they come from a section specializing in a particular type of practice at a larger firm, as those kinds of sections have a tendency to function as smaller firms within a large firm.

Large Firms. A large firm starts at around 50 to 100, and offers great benefits and pay, but is very formal. Working at one of these forms is very much like working for a large corporations. Additional pluses are more in-house training and support. They often have satellite offices with smaller staffs, but with the large-firm pay. These firms are harder to break into unless you have a baccalaureate degree and some experience; they also are more likely to have in-house training programs.

By Practice

Personal Injury (PI) Law. Personal injury practices are firms (or sections of firms) specialize in tort-based work, often including consumer law. Get ready for a barrage of terms. **PI Lawyers** are usually plaintiff's attorneys. The PI stands for personal injury. These lawyers tend to call themselves **trial attorneys.** In tort work, the defendant's attorneys are often called insurance defense attorneys (or just **defense attorneys**—a completely different meaning than in the context of criminal law). Rather than calling themselves trial attorneys, civil lawyers for the defendants tend to use the term **litigators**. This code should let you know right away with which side of the docket a particular attorney is usually aligned.

The term **insurance defense,** another term used to refer to the firm that ordinarily represents alleged **tortfeasors**, comes from the fact that generally the person being sued is covered by some form of insurance policy that is actually paying for the defense of the claim, and the insurance company will select the attorneys. This is probably the area in which most civil interviewing and investigating takes place.

Consumer Protection. Consumer protection practices are firms (or sections of firms) specializing in cases where recovery is based on state consumer protection laws, which turn essentially contract cases into quasi-tort cases if the facts meet the criteria of the statute, which are broader than misrepresentation or fraud, the classic torts arising out of contractual relations. If the statute allows for non-pecuniary damage recovery, these firms are usually the same as the PI firms.

Commercial Litigation.   Commercial litigation practices are firms (or sections of firms) concentrating on large, complex cases that take years to go to court. All parties are businesses, and they are usually arguing over the terms of a contract. Intellectual property issues may also arise in these challenging cases. Due to the complexity and the deeper pockets of the litigants, investigations are often referred to specialists.

Family Law.   Family law practices are firms focusing on divorces, custody, and related issues. The depth of investigation depends on the ability of the client to pay for it. Family law generally relies on the parties for disclosure of important information; additional investigation is sometimes warranted, but not always affordable.

Probate Law.   These firms specialize in wills, probating wills, and will contests. Extensive informal investigation is not the norm in these firms.

Criminal Law.   These firms specialize in the defense of those charged with criminal offenses. Very few jobs in firms that practice solely criminal defense pay well.

Non-traditional Employment.   In addition to these classifications, there are paralegals working for government agencies, the state or federal attorney general, the district attorney's office (sometimes in a civil capacity), and for corporate legal counsel. The amount of investigation done in these offices also varies.

THE ROLE OF THE PARALEGAL

Although there are several competing definitions for **paralegal**, they all seem to share a common theme: performing tasks that require specialized training and education that the lawyer would otherwise have to do himself. The reason for this monumentally vague definition is that the paralegal's roles are as varied as those of the lawyer. It is my observation, and those of many paralegals of my acquaintance, that the main job of a paralegal is to keep the lawyer organized and focused. "Lawyer-wrangling" is my favorite description of the job. In keeping with this description the paralegal usually becomes responsible for making sure that whatever job has been delegated to her by the attorney is approached in a coherent fashion with the goal of using the task to help the attorney stay on track with the details he needs to attend to. Further, the attorney (particularly a sole practitioner) may expect the paralegal, without telling her, that she is responsible for making sure all the details of a case are taken care of. This is very frustrating to many novice paralegals; it's simply an accepted fact for veterans. In larger firms, the paralegal's role is sometimes more well-defined and the job narrower, but it is often difficult to get these jobs until after surviving with a sole practitioner for a while.

In terms of interviewing and investigating, exactly which tasks will be done by the paralegal and which will be done by the attorney (or associate or partner) or farmed out to a private investigator or other specialist depend on the budget, the type of case, and the preferences of the attorney. Regardless, the paralegal will be responsible for knowing what individual has responsibility for what part of the case. If there's a **baby lawyer** (the common expression for a fresh law school graduate, regardless of age) on the case, he or she may look to the paralegal for help on the nuts and bolts of investigation because that's not part of a typical law school education, which instead focuses on the theory of law and case analysis. The paralegal will be the keeper of expert files and fees, the center for contact information, and the manager of the file.

Every so often debate arises over whether paralegals acting as investigators should be licensed as claims adjusters or as private investigators. Lawyers are usually exempted from the licensing requirement by statute, but their staff members are not. It's probably more of an oversight than anything; I've never heard of a situation where an ethical paralegal was arrested or fined for violation of such a statute. That's not to say it's not possible; it's just not terribly likely. Whether you get concerned about it has more to do with risk tolerance than anything—and most lawyers tend to take the risk that their paralegals will be exempted. If you are concerned about this potential liability, you can ask for some sort of indemnification contract from your lawyer in the event of the responsible enforcement agency deciding to take you on, whether civilly or criminally, or just ask her to help you do what needs to be done to get the appropriate license.

Whether the paralegal is actually out in the street taking photographs or simply calling and telling J. J. Photoperson to take them, she must have a firm grasp of what must be done in order to adequately manage the interviewing and investigating phase of the case.

OTHER SUPPORT STAFF

To effectively manage the file, you must work with other support staff, if they are available. You may work in an office where you and the attorney are the entire office, which means you will perform all these tasks. The staff is your most important ally. If you treat them with respect and as part of your team, you will be rewarded in many ways. Some hints:

* Don't ask for favors when it's not necessary.
* Don't treat routine matters as emergencies.
* Be polite and thank staff for their help.
* Take time to think about what they do and how they contribute to the work product. Recognize it when they do their part well.
* When you have to give negative feedback, do it in private and as professionally as possible.
* Don't ask anyone to do anything you're not willing to do yourself.
* Respect the contributions of others on the legal team—and if you don't, figure out why and try to see if you can alter your perspective. If others are being paid for it, someone thinks their contribution is important.
* Don't view yourself as the most valuable member of the legal team.
* Willingly take on additional duties when necessary.
* Be a role model.

To avoid stepping on any minefields of office politics, when you first come into an office, you will do well not to commit to any particular position, loyalty, or faction. It's very difficult being new, and those of us who are talkers by nature have a really tough time with it, but the best thing is to try to listen at first and get an idea of what the underlying issues and stresses are in any particular office. In any office, there are those with nominal power (they have the job titles) and those with unofficial power—the ones who seem to really run things. The unofficial leaders may have power because they have some sort of expertise or special ability (she's the one who can always sweet-talk the district clerk into accepting late filings) or personal charisma. If you speak your mind too early in a firm or corporation, which says "tell me what you think" but means "tell me I'm wonderful," you can end up making some serious enemies early in your employment, even though you offered only legitimate constructive criticism. If you align yourself with someone early on and then decide you don't like that person, it's hard to overcome those early impressions. And if you align yourself with someone untrustworthy and he or she begins repeating or fabricating things that you have said, you're in very difficult straits. Unfortunately, perception is often more important than reality—once someone makes a decision that you are a certain way, even if it is untrue, it is very difficult to change that person's mind. Rule of thumb: watch for around six weeks. The honeymoon period will end about then, and you'll start to see people for who they really are. It probably be a bit lonely before then; try to stay involved with your work. Friendships at work can come later, although it's healthy to keep some non-legal friends in your life for balance. Other folks think we're crazy the way we talk shop constantly. Of course, it could be our work is just more interesting.

In all areas of law, it is important to develop the ability to see things from various perspectives—try to do so with other members of the staff when problems arise. They will; office politics are everywhere.

The **legal secretary** is possibly a vanishing subspecies. The main distinction between her job and that of a paralegal was the amount of typing. With the advent of computers and forms that can be saved on them, that distinction has eroded. Many individuals with the title of "legal secretary" are actually functioning as paralegals. The sidebar article from *Legal Assistant Today* discusses the distinction (and furor) between the titles **"legal assistant"** and "paralegal," noting that many legal secretaries are now moving to the "legal assistant" title, implying that a legal assistant is somehow someone less specialized than someone called a paralegal. The main distinction is paralegals (whatever you call them) perform primarily substantive legal work, whereas true legal secretaries (even if called "legal assistants") perform primarily secretarial/clerical tasks. The real question is how many people with experience still perform primarily secretarial/clerical tasks in the computer age. As you will see, there are other staff members who take up those tasks in larger offices.

A Rose by Any Other Name
by Rod Hughes

In William Shakespeare's "Romeo and Juliet," the Bard asked, "What's in a name? That which we call a rose by any other name would smell as sweet." While such romanticism might work in matters of the heart, where the law is concerned, Shakespeare has been completely undone of late.

In an online opinion poll conducted during the course of 29 days in the summer of 2002, *Legal Assistant Today* gathered 1,897 responses from legal professionals on the issue of preference between the titles of paralegal and legal assistant. The results overwhelmingly demonstrated a strong desire by some in the legal community to draw a more clear line of distinction between the two terms.

For the better part of the profession's history, the legal assistant and paralegal titles have been largely considered synonymous. However, as the legal assistant community continues to evolve, the issue of just which title smells sweeter has become hotly debated. Recently, the membership of the National Federation of Paralegal Associations voted to remove the legal assistant title from its definition of the profession, breaking with the industry standard of interchangeability of the terms (see July/August *LAT*). Additionally, paralegal-legal assistants have increasingly voiced concern regarding the trend of some legal secretaries to use the title of legal assistant in both the law firm and corporate environments.

"Numerous secretaries with no legal training and none of the responsibilities of the paralegals in our office use the title legal assistant because they don't want to be called just secretaries," according to one respondent, who mirrored the comments of a majority of poll respondents who felt the paralegal title denoted a preferred level of professionalism.

In contrast to NFPA's move on the issue of definitions, within the past year a number of associations have adopted the American Bar Association's definition of paralegals and legal assistants, which identifies the two terms as interchangeable. These associations include the National Association of Legal Assistants, the Legal Assistant Management Association and the American Association for Paralegal Education.

While the findings of the *LAT* Title Poll are not intended to represent the entire profession, the results are offered as the opinions of a representative sampling of professionals with varied experience and expertise in the field and not as the opinion or doctrine of any one particular group, James Publishing, or the staff of *LAT*.

GARDEN VARIETY PROFESSIONALS

Of the nearly 2000 legal professionals who participated in *LAT*'s online poll (at a rate of approximately 65 respondents per day), 41.7 percent reported they were college graduates. Another 22.7 percent had earned paralegal certificates, 15.9 percent had earned "some college" education, and 2.3 percent were high school graduates. A group of 17.4 percent identified their educational background as other than that of the aforementioned groups.

When asked for the primary title by which their employers identified them, 50.7 percent reported being identified as paralegals.

Those considered legal assistants by their employers comprised 26.6 percent of poll respondents, while 22.7 percent held titles in the legal profession not typically synonymous with the paralegal-legal assistant field—such as senior project manager, legal administrative paralegal, corporate compliance officer, legal investigator, notary public, and so forth. While many paralegal-legal assistants currently use such titles in the course of their legal work, many continue to use these more specific titles in addition to their preferred title of either legal assistant or paralegal.

On the low end of the poll's response rate, the average respondent reported to have worked in the legal profession in capacity or another for roughly 13.7 years. Alternatively, the average experience level for many veterans who participated in the *LAT* title Poll was approximately 20 years.

IN FULL BLOOM

The majority of those who participated in the poll (76.2 percent) reported they would choose the paralegal title in order to be recognized as legal professionals versus selecting the legal assistant designation. While there were a wide variety of reasons for choosing the paralegal title rather than the legal assistant moniker, a large number of respondents offered similar reasons for their selection. The perception that legal secretaries are encroaching on the legal assistant title; the theory that the word "assistant" denotes an air of clerical or administrative work; and a noteworthy trend in many offices of promoting legal support staff members to the position of legal assistant were all popular explanations for the preference of the paralegal title.

According to one respondent, "A title including the word assistant is too often overused and has lost its meaning as a professional title. I feel the common perception is assistant equals secretary."

In contrast, another participant stated, "I believe the word assistant is important—this is what legal assistants do—assist attorneys in whatever they need done. I think that this is a better term for the profession."

Interestingly, many respondents indicated the paralegal title seemed to denote a higher level of education and training than that of legal assistant. One respondent noted, "A paralegal title indicates that you have had additional educational instruction in the legal field, whereas the legal assistant title indicates that you have not [achieved a higher level of education]." While a large number of respondents echoed this perception, it must be noted that at press time, *LAT* was unable to confirm any known, universally discernable difference between educational standards at the national or state levels for those pursuing education options labeled for legal assistants versus those pursuing an education designed for paralegals.

Many respondents also referenced paralegal certification as a desirable element in the legal community that factored into their preferences. However, the question of what constitutes certification and by whom is an issue not settled within the profession. For instance, is a certificate of credentials of more benefit when offered by a state agency, a local community college, a state-operated university, an AAfPE-affiliated school, an ABA-accredited paralegal program or a voluntary association? And which certificate carries more weight with employers? (See January/February 2003 *LAT* for details on what employers look for in legal assistant-paralegal education credentials.)

It's also important to remember that what defines the profession in one locality doesn't necessarily transfer to other areas of the United States. For instance, California law defines the scope of paralegal assistant work (see November/December 2000 *LAT*) as well as what is required in order to identify oneself as a paralegal or legal assistant, while other states lack specific criteria regarding who can and can't use such titles, even at the state bar level. Kimberly Smith, a spokesperson for the Texas State Bar told *LAT* that at present, "The state bar has no set guidelines for defining a paralegal or legal assistant." However, Smith did note, "[The Legal Assistant Section of the bar], which is voluntary in nature, recommends paralegals or legal assistants work under the supervision of an attorney." To put it more directly, there are still areas of the country where anyone—regardless of education or experience—can legally call themselves a paralegal or legal assistant and be gainfully employed as such.

SEEDS OF DISCONTENT

When asked if it was important to make the legal assistant and paralegal titles separate and distinct, 72.2 percent of respondents indicated this was a priority, while 27.8 percent said it was not.

Again, a variety of explanations were offered, however, a common thread ran through many of the comments in support of the two titles. Respondents noted they felt the terms were no longer deemed interchangeable in the public's perception due to the apparent increase in legal secretaries using the legal assistant title. In addition, a large number of respondents pointed out that the title of legal assistant seemed too generalized and didn't appear to offer a clear picture of what role a person with that title

(continued)

played in the law office. A minority of respondents who indicated it was not a priority to distinguish the two titles argued that being identified as a legal assistant was appropriate because their work involved assisting attorneys, thereby making their roles more clear.

"When I say I'm a legal assistant, most people know I work with an attorney. If I say paralegal, some people do not know what it means," wrote one respondent who expressed a desire to see the legal assistant title as the preferred professional identifier.

Sixty percent of those who responded to the online survey noted they believed the public at large understood the difference between a legal secretary an a paralegal, while 40 percent disagreed. However, when asked if respondents believed the public could distinguish between legal secretaries and legal assistants, only 13 percent of respondents believed this was the case.

Additionally, 74.8 percent of respondents reported they believed lawyers make a distinction regarding professional ability based on professional titles, while only 25.2 percent disagreed. In the general comments provided by participants in the survey, a significant number of legal professionals noted attorneys themselves are not clear on the exact role of legal assistants-paralegals, further sowing seeds of misinformation and discontent.

A ROSE WITH MANY THORNS

Although a majority of those who participated in the survey made it clear they preferred the paralegal title to that of legal assistant, the gulf between those for and against certain titles was reduced considerably when the subject of actually making a permanent, across-the-board switch to one title or the other was raised. On the issue of the profession uniting behind either the paralegal or legal assistant title, 68.9 percent were in favor of such a move, while a healthy minority of slightly more than 31 percent reported there was not a need for a change to a single, distinct title.

"In order to focus on more important profession-related issues, I say let us put the title debate to rest once and for all," was one respondent's view. Another called the debate a distraction from the professionalism of the field. However, other respondents noted that a profession that seems divided can't move forward. Noted one respondent, "I think one title would really move this profession forward with confused legal consumers and bewildered attorneys who already don't know what to do with us." Still another asked if those in the profession can't unite behind a single and clearly defined title, how will those outside the profession "have the first clue about what we do and why we are a benefit to them?"

More than just a few legal professionals indicated in their comments that they would support either title, as long s the qualifications for attaining such a distinction were standardized throughout the United States. A minority of respondents reported they felt the legal assistant title had already been effectively "usurped by legal secretaries" and that the title should be abandoned in order to draw a clear distinction between the two fields. Still others insisted that the legal assistant title provides a broad base of authority and responsibility while succinctly indicating the professions' role as assisting lawyers and therefore clearly working under the supervision of attorneys.

Repeatedly, the interchangeability of the two titles was noted as confusing to the public at large and as such, detrimental to the professionalism of the legal assistant-paralegal community as a whole.

It's worth noting, however, that despite 72.2 percent of respondents calling the need for a title switch a priority, 57.2 percent of those same respondents noted changing to either title would not significantly change the professional status of legal assistants-paralegals, regardless of their strong feelings on the issue. Of the 57.2 percent who felt a permanent, universal title change would not effectively improve the status of the legal assistant-paralegal community, opinions ranged from the perception of adding to the general public's existing confusion on the issue to such a change addressing only enhanced self-esteem rather than professionalism.

One respondent noted that beyond adding to his or her "personal self worth," changing to one title or the other would not change the profession, or its perception in the legal community or general public.

The minority's view on the subject included the theory that using only one title would warrant increased responsibility and pay as well as drawing a needed line of distinction between the legal assistant-paralegal field and other legal support personnel.

"If the profession was defined by one title and the consumers were made aware of the parameters of the position, then either title would be sufficient and would clear up a lot of confusion that now exists," according to one respondent.

However, a number of those supporting a switch to one title repeatedly insisted that choosing one title over another would only be effective and beneficial if it was undertaken as a national effort, either through legislation or governmental regulation.

FLOWER POWER

When questions turned to the debate itself, opinions regarding its value and its impact—if any—on the profession varied.

Slightly more than 64 percent of respondents answered affirmatively that the debate regarding professional titles impacted or continues to impact the profession as a whole. Nearly 36 percent reported the debate had no impact at all on the profession itself.

Those who felt the debate regarding title preference offered no measurable advantage to the profession provided interesting insight into their reasoning. One respondent noted the debate itself served to be "something that is divisive and our attention could be better focused on more important and relevant issues that impact the profession." More than a few respondents pointed to the issues using words such as "dissention," "divisive," "wasteful," "ridiculous," and "detrimental."

Such arguments ranged from creating a divide-and-conquer mentality within the paralegal-legal assistant community, to making the profession seem less than professional by squabbling over issues that don't, on the whole, enhance the profession in a meaningful way.

One respondent wrote, "As legal assistants, we should find more important issues to consume our time. Arguing over a title is utterly ridiculous."

Offering a counterpoint, one respondent stated, "any type of professional debate or discussion, if approached with maturity and common sense, is good for the profession." And that respondent was not alone. Others noted concern over the lack of a "uniform identity" within the profession itself, asking in one instance, "if we can't decide who and what we are as a whole, how can we expect lawyers and legal consumers to make any kind of reasonable distinction?"

Still, others felt separating or distinguishing the two titles was not the paramount issue at all. There were many respondents, not statistically analyzed but clearly speaking with one united voice, who offered a theme that transcended most of the arguments regarding preferred titles, the perceived prestige of one title compared to another and the significance or value of any type of change on the subject—and that theme was the establishment of educational standards that define the available titles.

As a handful of respondents noted, many firms and corporations, in cooperation with or in spite of local bar and paralegal-legal assistant associations, classify and define those who can hold one title or another, thus handicapping the justification for debating the issue within the profession itself.

But a point that was passionately expressed—repeatedly—was the importance of establishing some universal barometer for use of both titles or just one, either through self-regulation or through state or federal legislation or licensure.

Regardless of individual positions on the issue, clearly many in the profession want to see this debate concluded in one fashion or another.

As noted on page 16 of this issue, the ABA's Standing Committee on Legal Assistants has acted to make plain its preference in the debate at hand.

According to sources within SCOLA, the proposed revisions to the official guidelines that legal assistant schools must follow to receive ABA approval include a recommendation by SCOLA to replace the legal assistant title with that of the paralegal designation in the majority of the language.

(continued)

Additionally, a number of paralegal-legal assistant associations throughout the United States, such as the Alaska Association of Paralegals, South Dakota Paralegal Association, and Sacramento Valley Paralegal Association, have all changed their names recently to demonstrate a preference of the paralegal title.

One respondent seemed to summarize the debate best by noting, "If a consensus can be reached as to what term means what, it can only help the profession. There is no universally accepted definition for a legal assistant for paralegal. The definition changes from firm to firm, and sometimes, from association to association."

Source: "A Rose by Any Other Name" by Rod Hughes

Reflections of this change in nomenclature can be seen many places in the legal community. For example, the former ABA Committee on Legal Assistants has recently changed its name to the ABA Committee on Paralegals. The **National Federation of Paralegal Associations (NFPA)** passed a resolution declaring that it no longer considered the term "legal assistant" interchangeable with "paralegal" for the same reason. The National Association of Legal Assistants is investigating (or may be offering, by the time you read this text) changing the CLA designation to a CP designation, or at least making them alternative choices. Whatever they are called, treat staff primarily concerned with clerical duties with respect; they make good allies and great sources of information.

Runners are often part-time employees, sometimes college students, whose main job is taking stacks of documents from your office to some other destination under some sort of time crunch (usually) without getting lost, losing the documents, getting into a wreck, or missing the deadline. They must know where they are going, whether they are to wait for some sort of reply, what they need to document the delivery of the documents (or whatever—it can be other things as well), and any other special instructions. A good runner can make life much easier on the paralegal, as the runner can be ready to run off to the 3:30 deposition with the one crucial document that while you told the lawyer to take, made three copies of, and he still managed to leave them all on his desk while you finish up the discovery that's due at 5:00.

The **file clerk** and the **law clerk** are two completely different creatures. Don't confuse them. The first is a hard-working, entry-level legal staff person who magically makes your papers appear in the right files and can also make them disappear forever in the reams of paper produced by your firm. The second is a law student trying to get a job, usually working part-time or temporarily—sometimes a hard worker or sometimes just doing his best trying to appear to work whenever a partner is around.

Law officer **receptionists** have the same job description as any other receptionist, although sometimes they will perform many other duties in a small or solo practice. The general procedure in a law firm is to screen calls for paralegals and attorneys; sometimes for legal secretaries too. The receptionist will find out who is calling and ask whether the professional wishes to speak to the person before telling the caller the professional is available. This allows the professional to prioritize work. Say, for example, you are working on Mrs. Jones's case, and you are waiting for a phone call from one last attorney to finish scheduling her soon-to-be-ex-husband's deposition. You're pretty sure you'll hear from the attorney within the next hour or so, and to make it work you have to send out deposition notices the moment the last attorney calls, so you're trying to get them together, just in case. Mrs. Jones calls. She's called every other day for the last two weeks, wanting to know when this deposition is. You decide she'd be better served to wait until you get the deposition notices ready and have heard from the other attorney rather than talking to her and billing her again to say, "I don't know yet, Mrs. Jones." The receptionist will help you by telling Mrs. Jones you're unavailable. (Caveat: Don't abuse this tactic to dodge annoying clients. You have to communicate with them, too.) A good receptionist can also be relied on to help you when you've been trying for weeks to get in touch with Mr. Shadow. You let her know the situation, and she can track you down—cell phone, home phone, e-mail, hairdresser—and keep Mr. Shadow happy and on the line while she does it.

The **nurse paralegal** and **legal nurse consultant (LNC)** are two different levels of the same general job category. A nurse paralegal is rather what it sounds like: a person with both nursing and legal training. These folks may be on staff at a high-volume, high-dollar, personal injury-type practice, or they may practice on a

contract basis. The most common use of a nurse paralegal within firms is to review medical records where either the dollar value of the claim warrants the expenditure or there is something out of the ordinary about it. If you work in a firm that does automobile litigation, for example, you will become very familiar with what standard "whiplash," or extension-flexion injury, records look like. You'll notice if there's something out of the ordinary, even if you don't know what it means. That's a time that you may want to ask the lawyer if he'd like to have the nurse paralegal review the records. The LNC is a more formal, recognized level of expertise in the area and generally goes far beyond simply looking for medical oddities. You can find out more about legal nurse consultants by visiting the American Association of Legal Nurse Consultants on the Internet at **http://www.aalnc.org/**.

The **legal administrator** or **office administrator** is someone you usually see only in larger offices, although sometimes smaller ones will give a senior staff member the title. In the strictest sense, this is someone with a management or other business background and has learned about the particular needs of the legal field through training or experience. This person will be knowledgeable about staffing and staffing trends, salaries, budgeting, increasing productivity and profitability, and the like. One major organization dedicated to this group of professionals is the Association of Legal Administrators, found on the Internet at **http://www.alanet.org**. A subset of this group is the **legal assistant manager**, a person whose primary duty is to supervise legal assistants. There is a professional association dedicated to this group as well, the Legal Assistant Management Association (LAMA), which has a Web page at **http://www.lamanet.org**.

Billing or bookkeeping department personnel are folks that do what it sounds like they do, bill clients and keep up with expenses. I rarely interacted with them in the firms I worked at; these poor folks always seem condemned to some inner office with no windows, huddling over long lists of numbers. If you work at a firm where you bill hours, you will hear from them if you don't turn in your time sheets by the internal deadlines imposed by the firm.

ETHICAL ISSUES

Although there are voluntary ethics rules applicable to paralegals, there are generally no ethics rules that are directly enforceable against the legal assistant. Notable exceptions are the loss of **Certified Legal Assistant (C.L.A.)** or **Certified Legal Assistant Specialist (C.L.A.S.)** status from the **National Association of Legal Assistants (NALA)** or the Texas State Board of Specialization designation for paralegals (the only state so far to institute such a program) for violations of their respective ethics rules. The **Registered Paralegal (R.P.)** designation awarded by the **National Federation of Paralegal Associations (NFPA)** can also be revoked for ethics violations, but it is not as unambiguous as the declaration of the other two entities. As various states consider mandatory regulation, this may change.

Generally, however, the main repercussions to the paralegal for ethical violations are indirect. First, lawyers are responsible for the actions of their staff, and can be disciplined by their state bars for ethical violations by their staff.

Second, ethical violations can cost the attorney a case. One situation that has caused problems is that of the new employee who formerly worked at a firm who represented an opposing party. If not handled properly, the opposing party can successfully disqualify the new employee's firm:

Phoenix Founders, Inc. v. Marshall, 887 S.W.2d 831 (Tex. 1994).

The present dispute arises from a suit brought by Phoenix Founders, Inc. and others ("Phoenix") to collect a federal-court judgment against Ronald and Jane Beneke and others. The law firm of Thompson & Knight represented Phoenix in the original federal-court suit, which began in 1990 and ended in 1991, and has also represented them in the collection suit since its commencement in 1992. The Benekes have been represented in the latter suit by the firm of David & Goodman.

In July of 1993, Denise Hargrove, a legal assistant at Thompson & Knight, left her position at that firm to begin working for David & Goodman as a paralegal. While at David & Goodman, Hargrove billed six-tenths of an hour on the collection suit for locating a pleading. She also discussed the case generally with Mark Goodman, the Benekes' lead counsel.

After three weeks at David & Goodman, Hargrove returned to Thompson & Knight to resume work as a paralegal. At the time of the rehiring, Thompson & Knight made no effort to question Hargrove in regard to potential conflicts of interest resulting from her employment at David & Goodman.

Three weeks after Hargrove had returned, counsel for the Benekes wrote to Thompson & Knight asserting that its renewed employment of Hargrove created a conflict of interest. The letter demanded that the firm withdraw from its representation of Phoenix.

Hargrove resigned from Thompson & Knight the next week, after having been given the option of either resigning with severance pay or being terminated. The firm itself, however, refused to withdraw from the case. The Benekes then filed a motion to disqualify.

After an evidentiary hearing, the trial court initially overruled the Benekes' motion, stating that it found no evidence that confidential client information was actually provided to Hargrove. On motion for reconsideration, however, the trial court granted the Benekes' motion and disqualified Thompson & Knight from further representation of Phoenix. The disqualification order states that Hargrove possesses confidential information relating to the Benekes, and that all such confidential information was imputed to the firm of Thompson & Knight at the time she was rehired.

This Court has not previously addressed the standards governing a disqualification motion based on the hiring of a nonlawyer employee. With respect to lawyers, however, this Court. . . require[es] disqualification whenever counsel undertakes representation of an interest that is adverse to that of a former client, as long as the matters embraced in the pending suit are "substantially related" to the factual matters involved in the previous suit. . . . This strict rule is based on a conclusive presumption that confidences and secrets were imparted to the attorney during the prior representation.

The Benekes argue that the standards applied to the hiring of lawyers should also apply to the hiring of paralegals. Thus, . . . the Benekes urge that the entire firm of Thompson & Knight must be automatically disqualified because of the confidences Hargrove obtained while working at David & Goodman.

We agree that a paralegal who has actually worked on a case must be subject to. . . a conclusive presumption that confidences and secrets were imparted during the course of the paralegal's work on the case. . . . This presumption serves to prevent the moving party from being forced to reveal the very confidences sought to be protected. . . . Moreover, virtually any information relating to a case should be considered confidential: the Disciplinary Rules define "confidential information" to encompass even unprivileged client information. . .

We disagree, however, with the argument that paralegals should be conclusively presumed to share confidential information with members of their firms. The Disciplinary Rules require a lawyer having direct supervisory authority over a nonlawyer to make reasonable efforts to ensure that the nonlawyer's conduct is compatible with the professional obligations of the lawyer. Tex. Disciplinary R. Prof. Conduct 5.03(a). If the supervising lawyer orders, encourages, or even permits a nonlawyer to engage in conduct that would be subject to discipline if engaged in by a lawyer, the lawyer will be subject to discipline. R. 5.03(b). Thus, to the extent that the Disciplinary Rules prohibit a lawyer from revealing confidential information, R. 1.05(b)(1), they also prohibit a supervising lawyer from ordering, encouraging, or permitting a nonlawyer to reveal such information.

The Texas Committee on Professional Ethics has considered the application of these rules in the context of a "right hand" legal secretary or legal assistant leaving one small firm and joining another that represents an adverse party. Tex. Comm. on Professional Ethics, Op. 472, 55 Tex. B. J. 520 (1992). The Committee concluded that the Rules do not require disqualification of the new law firm, provided that the supervising lawyer at that firm complies with the Rules so as to ensure that the nonlawyer's conduct is compatible with the professional obligations of a lawyer. . .

This view is consistent with the weight of authority in other jurisdictions. The American Bar Association's Committee on Professional Ethics has considered whether a law firm that hires a paralegal may continue representing clients whose interests conflict with interests of the former employer's clients on whose matters the paralegal has worked. ABA Comm. on Ethics and Professional Responsibility, Informal Op. 1526 (1988). After surveying case law and ethics opinions from a number of jurisdictions, the Committee concluded that the new firm need not be disqualified, as long as the firm and the paralegal strictly adhere to the screening process set forth in the opinion, and as long as the paralegal does not reveal any information relating to the former employer's clients to any person in the employing firm. . . . A number of courts have since relied on the ABA's opinion to allow continued representation under similar conditions. . .

Underlying these decisions is a concern regarding the mobility of paralegals and other nonlawyers. A potential employer might well be reluctant to hire a particular nonlawyer if doing so would automatically disqualify the entire firm from ongoing litigation. This problem would be especially acute in the context of massive firms and extensive, complex litigation. Recognizing this danger, the ABA concluded that "any restrictions on the nonlawyer's employment should be held to the minimum necessary to protect confidentiality of client information."

We share the concerns expressed by the ABA, and agree that client confidences may be adequately safeguarded if a firm hiring a paralegal from another firm takes appropriate steps in compliance with the Disciplinary Rules. . . . Specifically, the newly-hired paralegal should be cautioned not to disclose any information relating to the representation of a client of the former employer. The paralegal should also be instructed not to work on any matter on which the paralegal worked during the prior employment, or regarding which the paralegal has information relating to the former employer's representation. Additionally, the firm should take other reasonable steps to ensure that the paralegal does no work in connection with matters on which the paralegal worked during the prior employment, absent client consent after consultation.

Each of these precautions would tend to reduce the danger that the paralegal might share confidential information with members of the new firm. Thus, while a court must ordinarily presume that some sharing will take place, the challenged firm may rebut this presumption by showing that sufficient precautions have been taken to guard against any disclosure of confidences.

Absent consent of the former employer's client, disqualification will always be required under some circumstances, such as (1) when information relating to the representation of an adverse client has in fact been disclosed, or (2) when screening would be ineffective or the nonlawyer necessarily would be required to work on the other side of a matter that is the same as or substantially related to a matter on which the nonlawyer has previously worked. . . Ordinarily, however, disqualification is not required as long as "the practical effect of formal screening has been achieved.". . .

In reconsidering the disqualification motion, the trial court should examine the circumstances of Hargrove's employment at Thompson & Knight to determine whether the practical effect of formal screening has been achieved. The factors bearing on such a determination will generally include the substantiality of the relationship between the former and current matters; the time elapsing between the matters; the size of the firm; the number of individuals presumed to have confidential information; the nature of their involvement in the former matter; and the timing and features of any measures taken to reduce the danger of disclosure. . .

The ultimate question in weighing these factors is whether Thompson & Knight has taken measures sufficient to reduce the potential for misuse of confidences to an acceptable level. . .

Because we have modified the controlling legal standard, the writ of mandamus is denied without prejudice to allow the trial court to reconsider the disqualification motion in light of today's opinion. The stay order previously issued by this Court remains in effect only so long as necessary to allow the trial court to act.

It's possible to make a list of how to treat an incoming paralegal to make sure there's not a problem that can result in firm disqualification. From *Phoenix Founders*, first, prior to coming to work, the paralegal needs to disclose to her new employer a list of all cases on which she worked. This will allow the new firm to determine if there are any conflicts. Next, the firm needs to take the "appropriate steps" listed by the *Phoenix Founders* court. What are they?

Ethical violations by the staff may also result in litigation against the attorney. They may even result in litigation against you personally. In the following case from Arizona, the term "legal assistant" is used interchangeably with the term "paralegal."

Asphalt Engineers, Inc. v. Galusha, 770 P.2d 1180 (Ariz. Ct. App. 1989).

This is an appeal from a judgment of legal malpractice. Asphalt Engineers, Inc. and its sole shareholders, Kenneth and Winsome Mamode, filed suit . . . against Lee and Peggy Galusha, individually and doing business as Lee Galusha, Ltd. (hereinafter Galusha), and against Robert Walston, a former legal assistant in Galusha's office. . . . The jury returned a verdict against Galusha . . . and awarded compensatory damages of $22,491.01, punitive damages of $40,000, and attorney's fees of $13,130 to Asphalt Engineers. Walston is not a party to this appeal . . .

In April, 1984, the Mamodes met with Walston at Galusha's office and advised Walston that they wanted to file liens against real property involved in three construction jobs, the Maupin, Gutkin and Spillman projects, for which Asphalt Engineers had not been paid. They also requested that lawsuits foreclosing those liens be filed, if necessary. After agreeing to file the liens and collect the money, Walston requested and received a $250 retainer. At trial Winsome Mamode testified that at the time of these discussions she believed that Walston was an attorney.

Galusha filed a lien against the Spillman project. As a result, Asphalt Engineers' employers on that project paid $5,000 in settlement of the claim to Galusha's office. Galusha deducted $1,204 for attorney's fees plus court costs from the $5,000.00 collected.

In June, 1984, Walston requested and received an additional $400 retainer fee. Although Walston indicated that a lien had been filed on the Maupin and Gutkin projects, no liens were filed nor were any suits instituted to recover the monies, $2400 and $2800 respectively, which Asphalt Engineers claimed was due on those projects. The time for filing both liens expired.

Sometime after their initial visit and before they discovered that liens had not been filed, the Mamodes returned to Galusha's office and directed Walston to file a lien and foreclose against the "Northern project" for which $13,000 was owed them. No lien was filed. The Mamodes also left an $1100 two-party check made out to "Asphalt Engineers and Marty Pellegrino" with Walston with the understanding that Walston would deliver it to Pellegrino. Instead of being delivered to Pellegrino, the check was retained in the Mamodes' file in Galusha's office with "void" written on various portions of it. At trial Walston acknowledged that he had written "void" on the check but contended that he had done so at the direction of the Mamodes. The Mamodes denied directing Walston to void the check.

Pellegrino subsequently brought suit against the Mamodes, who brought a copy of the complaint to Galusha's office with the request that the check be given to Pellegrino. The check was not delivered. Although the issue was disputed at trial, there is evidence in the record that Galusha's office assumed responsibility for responding to the lawsuit. However, no answer was filed to the complaint. The result was that Asphalt Engineers suffered a default judgment in the amount of $1,635. After repeated efforts to contact Galusha and Walston, the Mamodes filed this lawsuit . . .

Although expert testimony is generally required to establish the standard of care in a professional malpractice action, it is not necessary where the negligence is so grossly apparent that a lay person would have no difficulty recognizing it . . . Asphalt Engineers asserts that the negligence shown was obvious to a lay person. We agree. The record contains ample evidence of conduct so egregious as to permit finding malpractice even in the absence of expert testimony. Galusha never met with the Mamodes. He permitted Walston, a nonlawyer, to provide them legal advice. He failed to file and foreclose liens. He billed Asphalt Engineers for time spent responding to a complaint that the Mamodes had filed against him with the Better Business Bureau. He accepted the complaint filed against Asphalt Engineers by Pellegrino. He failed to answer the complaint or to inform the Mamodes that he was not handling this case. No expert is needed to interpret this kind of evidence . . .

Expert testimony is also not required where an accused attorney acknowledges that the alleged conduct constitutes malpractice . . . Galusha testified, in part, as follows:

Q: And would you say that it wouldn't meet the standard of the profession if, in fact, a client gave an attorney's office the money to perform the service and the attorney's office did not follow through on that?

A: I would say that would not meet the standard, yes.

Q: Would you say that an attorney owes a fiduciary duty to his clients?

A: Yes, and of course, depending on whose interpretation of just what fiduciary means.

Q: And that says as an attorney that employs legal assistants to do work, you have a duty to supervise all aspects of that work?

A: Yes.

Q: And to prevent the legal assistant from actually practicing law?

A: Yes.

Q: And you would have a duty, if a client paid you or your office money to perform a certain service within a certain time limitation, you have a duty to carry out that instruction within that time limitation?

A: If it can be done, yes.

Q: And it would, in fact, be negligence if you missed the time limitations?

A: Well, not necessarily because a lot of times something is discussed and then a different decision is reached, and there's a change of game plan.

Q: In which case you would notify the client that they could not pursue what they, in fact, wanted to pursue?

A: As soon as I had the opportunity, yes. Sometime these things, decisions have to be made without an opportunity.

Expert testimony was unnecessary in light of Galusha's own acknowledgment that the alleged conduct fell below the standard of care. This testimony, coupled with the obvious nature of the negligence and the allegation of complete breach of contract, leads to the conclusion that the trial court properly submitted the issues of breach of contract and negligence to the jury without any expert testimony . . .

. . . The jury was instructed that punitive damages required clear and convincing evidence that Galusha's conduct was aggravated or outrageous and that he intentionally caused Asphalt Engineers to be damaged or pursued a course of action by which he knowingly and consciously disregarded causing a substantial risk of significant harm.

Galusha argues that there was no evidence to justify giving the instruction. We disagree. There is substantial evidence to support the instruction. Galusha's conduct in agreeing to file liens and then failing to do so and then demanding additional money to enforce a lien that he never filed was so aggravated or outrageous as to provide probable cause for criminal charges of theft. The same may be said for Galusha's conduct in billing the Mamodes for his time spent responding to their complaint against him with the Better Business Bureau.

In addition, the jury could easily have found that Galusha either intentionally caused harm to Asphalt Engineers or consciously disregarded a substantial risk of significant harm through his failure to comply with the Mamodes' instruction to release the check owed to Pellegrino and through his conduct in permitting a nonlawyer to supply the only advice given the Mamodes concerning their legal problems.

The record also supports an inference that Galusha attempted to cover-up his misconduct. In the pre-trial phase of this litigation, Galusha submitted numerous billing statements in support of his counterclaim against the Mamodes for nonpayment for legal services. The Mamodes did acknowledge receiving several dated statements. However, Galusha also submitted several undated statements which he claimed had also been sent to the Mamodes. Galusha acknowledged that the undated statements were prepared in a different format than the dated statements and included information not normally provided such as detailed recitations of conferences and telephone conversations. Galusha testified as follows:

Q: So isn't it a fact that these other statements were made up after this lawsuit was filed to try to show that things were told to the plaintiff?

A: These may have been—I know for a fact that the first one here was a retype in order to elaborate a little on just what the arrangements were. It may be that these reflect actually a retyping of what went on in an effort to furnish you with the material that you wanted.

Galusha's acknowledgment that these undated statements may have been "retypes" which "elaborate a little" on what occurred cannot be squared with his testimony that those bills were actually sent to the Mamodes, who denied ever having received them.

In summary, the record supports a conclusion that Galusha intentionally disregarded his clients' rights in an extreme fashion going beyond mere negligence. The instruction on punitive damages had ample support in the record and was not error . . .

Our supreme court has adopted the American Bar Association's 1972 Code of Judicial Conduct . . . . These seldom-cited rules govern the conduct of judges in the administration of their high office. The Code provides in part that:

A judge should report what he believes clearly to be professional misconduct of a judge or lawyer to the appropriate disciplinary agency.

Canon 3(B)(3), Code of Judicial Conduct, Rule 81. Accordingly, we are forwarding a copy of this opinion to the State Bar of Arizona for whatever action it deems appropriate.

The *Galusha* case brings up another very important issue. It is essential that clients realize your position as a paralegal and understand that you are not a lawyer. *Galusha* also underscores the importance of meeting deadlines; failure to do so can mean a loss of rights for a client. A third problem in *Galusha* was the failure to acknowledge and try to fix mistakes when they became obvious. How could the attorney have controlled the punitive damages portion of the claim against him?

Legal communities, even in very large cities, can become extremely small in some situations. If you have committed an ethical violation significant enough to have resulted in major consequences, you may find yourself without a job and a reputation that makes you virtually unemployable in the same legal community. As a result, it is a matter of self-preservation to understand and abide by the rules of ethics, because simple goodwill and honesty do not always provide a reliable guide to what to do.

In the context of interviewing and investigating, one of the most pervasive issues is that of **confidentiality**. Even laypeople are usually aware of the attorney-client privilege. There are two different aspects of the privilege: the ethical standard that governs the lawyer and the evidentiary standard that protects the information from being conveyed from the client to other persons who would like to obtain the information. Both ethical duty and privilege extend to information given to legal staff working on the file for the attorney. So what's the difference? It's a matter of whom the party is seeking the information from. If the party is seeking information from the attorney, the attorney (and her staff) looks to the broader duties imposed by the ethical duty. If the information is being sought from the client, he will have to disclose information unless it falls within the evidentiary privilege. A client can't, for instance, give the lawyer information about where he has put marital assets and then refuse to tell his spouse in divorce proceedings, claiming attorney-client privilege. That's just factual information. But if the lawyer were asked, she might not be able to tell.

The ethical rule often follows the pattern found in the American Bar Association Model Rules of Professional Conduct.

a. A lawyer shall not reveal information relating to the representation of a client unless the client gives informed consent, the disclosure is impliedly authorized in order to carry out the representation or the disclosure is permitted by paragraph (b).

b. A lawyer may reveal information relating to the representation of a client to the extent the lawyer reasonably believes necessary:

1. to prevent reasonably certain death or substantial bodily harm;
2. to secure legal advice about the lawyer's compliance with these Rules;
3. to establish a claim or defense on behalf of the lawyer in a controversy between the lawyer and the client, to establish a defense to a criminal charge or civil claim against the lawyer based upon conduct in which the client was involved, or to respond to allegations in any proceeding concerning the lawyer's representation of the client; or
4. to comply with other law or a court order.

Model Code Prof'l Cond. R. 1.6.

Technically, the work may be protected from discovery by the opposing side under one of two theories: **attorney-client privilege** or **attorney work product**. The distinction between the two is that the first protects communications between the attorney and client given for the purpose of obtaining legal assistance; the second protects the ideas, thoughts, strategy, and other work done by the attorney to provide the legal assistance to the client.

Consider this example. Juanita Alvarez calls your office and sets up an appointment. You meet her in the waiting area, take her to your office, and discuss her case. She wants to divorce her husband; they have three children. After your interview with her, you walk her out to the foyer again, and, in a burst of confidence, she tells you, "I'm not sure the youngest child is his." There are two other clients waiting in the foyer. Later, after suit is filed, the opposing party files a request for admission (a form of formal discovery that requires you to admit or deny certain statements). One of the admissions they seek from Juanita is that she is not sure the youngest child is her husband's. You start to object on the basis of attorney-client privilege. Can you?

In one sense, of course you always can object. The real question is whether if you do, the judge will sustain your objection. And in order to answer that question, you must decide whether the privilege still applies. We've seen that the attorney-client privilege extends to the lawyer's staff, so the fact that Juanita said what she did to you rather than the lawyer you work for is irrelevant. Juanita told you about the child in order to obtain legal advice and services, so her admission meets the definition. However, she said it in front of other people. Does that make it different somehow? If you think about it, the broader category here is confidentiality. Is a statement still confidential if you say it in front of someone else? What factors do you think will make a difference?

Corll v. Edward D. Jones & Co., 646 N.E.2d 721 (Ind. Ct. App. 1995).

. . . Edward D. Jones & Company ("Jones") moved to compel disclosure of the content of certain meetings the Investors had with attorneys prior to filing suit, and the Investors sought a protective order on the basis of attorney-client privilege. . .

The sole issue presented on appeal is whether the trial court abused its discretion when it granted Jones' motions to compel discovery of the content of any communications which occurred during group meetings between the Investors and counsel.

The Investors filed a class action against Jones and alleged that . . . [it] . . . misrepresented the risks involved in certain mutual funds, securities, and other investments purchased by the Investors . . . . During the course of depositions, several Investors testified that they had attended a series of group meetings held prior to the commencement of this lawsuit which were also attended by attorneys who subsequently became the Investors' counsel in the lawsuit. At those depositions, . . . the Investors were instructed by their counsel not to answer any questions regarding the substance of any conversations that took place at those meetings on the basis that the information was protected by the attorney-client privilege.

Jones filed a motion to compel discovery of both the identities of those persons who attended the meetings and also what had occurred at the meetings. The trial court summarily granted the motion. . . . In compliance with the order, and in response to an interrogatory question, the Investors provided a supplemental list of persons who had attended the meetings.

However, at a subsequent deposition, counsel for the Investors again instructed one of the plaintiffs not to answer any questions regarding conversations which had occurred during the group meetings. The Investors asserted that the court's order which compelled disclosure of the "content" of the meetings was narrow in scope and that it included only the general subject-matter of the meetings, and that any actual communications were protected by the attorney-client privilege. Jones filed a second motion to compel discovery and also moved for sanctions against the Investors. On January 25, 1994, the trial court granted Jones' second motion to compel and the request for sanctions. . .

The Investors contend the trial court abused its discretion when it denied their motion for a protective order. They assert that any communications that occurred during the group meetings between counsel and the Investors are protected by the attorney-client privilege and, thus, are not discoverable. We agree.

The scope of discovery is governed generally by Trial Rule 26(B), which provides that parties "may obtain discovery regarding any matter, not privileged, which is relevant to the subject matter of the pending action." Under Indiana law, communications between an attorney and a client are privileged and not discoverable. The attorney-client privilege provides that attorneys shall not be competent witnesses "as to confidential communications made to them in the course of their professional business, and as to advice given in such cases.". . .

The rule is that "when an attorney is consulted on business within the scope of his profession, the communication on the subject between him and his client should be treated as strictly confidential". . . . The privilege applies to all communications between the client and his attorney for the purpose of obtaining professional legal advice or aid regarding the client's rights and liabilities. . .

Our courts have never specifically addressed what the party invoking the privilege is required to show to establish that a communication is confidential. . . [O]ur supreme court. . . requir[es] the person asserting the privilege to show that (1) an attorney-client relationship existed and (2) a confidential communication was involved. . .

The record in this case reveals that on at least three occasions, several prospective plaintiffs attended meetings at the Grant County Courthouse Annex at which one or more attorneys were present. While some of the Investors were not aware what would transpire at the preliminary meetings, the purpose of those meetings was to gather those Jones investors. . . to meet with attorneys to discuss their losses.

Thus, there is no question that the purpose of each preliminary meeting was to discuss a potential lawsuit. The Investors are seeking to protect from disclosure any statements made by the Investors during the meetings and any legal advice provided by the attorneys to those in attendance. Where, as here, a group of individuals meet with attorneys concerning potential litigation, and the purpose of that consultation is to provide legal advice regarding rights and liabilities, we conclude that any communications made in furtherance of that purpose are "confidential communications" between attorney and client and carry with them an expectation of confidentiality. . . . Thus, the Investors have made a prima facie showing they are entitled to the protection of the attorney-client privilege. . .

Of course, not every communication between an attorney and a client is a "confidential communication" and entitled to a reasonable expectation of confidentiality. For example, as a general rule information regarding a client's attorney's fees is not protected by the attorney-client privilege because the payment of fees is not considered a confidential communication between attorney and client. . . . Similarly, communications which are intended to be made public are not privileged, as there is clearly no expectation of confidentiality. . . . Such is not the case here.

The fact that the Investors met as a large group and were essentially strangers to one another does not alter our conclusion that they had a reasonable expectation of confidentiality in the meeting. When two or more persons, with a common interest in some legal problem, jointly consult an attorney, "their confidential communications with the attorney, though known to each other, will of course be privileged in a controversy of either or both the clients with the outside world.". . .

Finally, Jones contends the evidence before the trial court showed that Ruth Cartwright, a newspaper reporter who was not a prospective plaintiff, was present for at least one of the meetings and, thus, that any communications which occurred were not in fact "confidential.". . .

We agree with Jones that communications made within the presence or hearing of a disinterested third person are not protected by the attorney-client privilege. . . . However, the Investors' burden is not the burden to prove a negative. That is, the party invoking the privilege need not show that disinterested third persons were not present. Where, as here, the party invoking the attorney-client privilege has shown that the consultation was for the purpose of obtaining professional legal advice, he has made the requisite prima facie showing of confidentiality for the privilege to attach to any communications made in furtherance of that purpose during such consultations. The burden then shifts to the party opposing the assertion of the attorney-client privilege to show that the communications were not protected by the privilege because the confidentiality was waived or otherwise nullified.

Here, in support of their motion for a protective order, the Investors submitted the affidavit of Ruth Cartwright. Cartwright averred that, although she helped call one of the meetings to order, she left that meeting before legal matters were discussed and did not return. Cartwright stated that she was not present during any substantive portion of any meeting between prospective plaintiffs and attorneys. In opposition to Cartwright's affidavit, Jones again directs us to the deposition testimony of three Investors who recalled that Cartwright attended at least a portion of the initial meeting but who could not recall when she left or whether she was present during all or even part of any other meeting. This testimony was at best inconclusive, and there was no evidence before the trial court which actually rebutted Cartwright's own statement that she was not present during the substantive portion of any meeting. Based on this evidence, Jones has failed to establish that the attorney-client privilege did not attach to the preliminary consultations between the Investors and their counsel. . .

. . . The discovery orders at issue here are reversed.

Now that we've established that you must be careful about who is around when you begin to discuss matters that may be confidential, let's look at what you must keep confidential. This is the part that gets even trickier. Assume that George Brandt has become a client. George is in serious financial trouble. Even he doesn't know just how bad it is: his wheeler-dealer wife, Hayley, was involved in various business dealings that she didn't tell him about. Assume that, regardless of the marital property laws of your state, they have managed their affairs in such a way that all the assets of the couple are liable. Hayley has gone off to the Andes with a German count, and George is left with all of the letters. Your assignment is to find all of George and Hayley's outstanding debt.

As a practical matter, do you think George will really want any potential creditor to know that he's gone to a lawyer for help with his money troubles? Is seeking legal counsel in itself confidential? The first thing to do, in this or any other matter of legal interpretation, is to go back to definitions. What exactly does the attorney-client privilege cover? What does attorney work product cover? Does that matter? What about your ethical duty? Do you think you'd need to identify yourself to potential creditors as George's attorney's paralegal? Why or why not? Maybe this case will help you decide.

In the Matter of D'Alessio, 617 N.Y.S.2d 484 (N.Y. Ct. App. 1994).

The issue to be decided in this case is whether an attorney can be compelled to reveal the name of an individual who consulted him regarding that individual's possible past commission of a crime. We conclude that under the circumstances of this case, where the crime, if any, has already been committed, there is no possibility of further criminal acts occurring if the individual is not identified, and the disclosure sought would expose the client to possible criminal prosecution, that the client's name is privileged information that the attorney cannot be compelled to reveal.

On the evening of December 2, 1990, Vincent Fiorito sustained critical injuries while walking in the Town of Mamaroneck, the apparent victim of a hit-and-run driver. There were no known witnesses to the incident. The following month Fiorito, who never rose from the comatose state in which he was discovered, died of the injuries he sustained. Fiorito's insurer initially indicated an unwillingness to provide uninsured motorist coverage, asserting that the driver of the vehicle that allegedly struck Fiorito was not unknown. The insurer based its disclaimer upon a newspaper article wherein it was asserted that the driver had revealed himself to an attorney.

The petitioner subsequently learned that the respondent attorney may have been contacted by an individual who may have driven the vehicle which struck the deceased. Thus she made this application pursuant to CPLR 3102 (c) for the preaction depositions of the attorney and the former Mamaroneck Police Commissioner, with whom the attorney allegedly spoke, in an effort to ascertain that individual's identity in order to commence a civil action.

. . . [T]he Supreme Court granted the petitioner's motion and directed the attorney to appear for an examination before trial. . . . The court concluded, in pertinent part, that the privilege was not applicable under the circumstances because the information sought to be revealed was the client's identity and because the purpose of the privilege would not be served by shielding an individual from the possibility of civil and criminal liability. The attorney appeals, and we reverse.

In New York State the attorney-client privilege is a creature of statute, and prohibits an attorney from disclosing a confidential communication had with his client in the course of professional employment unless the client waives the privilege. . . . Its purpose is "to ensure that one seeking legal advice will be able to confide fully and freely in his attorney, secure in the knowledge that his confidences will not later be exposed to public view to his embarrassment or legal detriment". . . . So strong is the State's regard for the confidentiality of attorney-client communications that an attorney exposes himself to possible disciplinary charges if he fails to keep confidential a communication from his client without the client's consent. . . . However, since the privilege serves to shield evidence from discovery, and thereby potentially thwart the fact-finding process, it is to be strictly construed in keeping with its purpose. . .

At bar, the information that the petitioner seeks is the identity of the individual who apparently consulted the attorney, seeking legal advice regarding his alleged involvement in a fatal motor vehicle accident. That information, according to the attorney, is privileged. "In order to make a valid claim of privilege, it must be shown that the information sought to be protected from disclosure was a 'confidential communication' made to the attorney for the purpose of obtaining legal advice or services". . . . Thus it has generally been held that the client's name, in and of itself, is not privileged, as it is considered to be neither confidential nor a communication. . . However, such "nonevidentiary information" may qualify as privileged "where disclosure might be inappropriate because inconsistent with the trust and duty assumed by an attorney.". . . This issue is one that must be resolved on a case-by-case basis. . . . Under the circumstances of this case we conclude that the client's identity does constitute a confidential communication, and therefore cannot be revealed by the attorney without the client's consent.

Initially we note that, although it clearly has been contemplated, the petitioner has not commenced a civil action against the individual whose identity she seeks to ascertain. Thus we are not faced with the situation where a litigant is seeking to learn the identity of his adversary. . . . Nor are we faced with the situation where an attorney is being asked to divulge information for the purpose of preventing a future crime, for here the client's crime, if there be one, has already been completed. . .

The case of *Matter of Grand Jury Proceeding (Cherney).* . . , while not binding upon us, is instructive. There attorney Cherney was subpoenaed by the Grand Jury to reveal the name of the individual who paid legal fees for a known individual that Cherney was defending in a narcotics conspiracy trial. Cherney refused to reveal the fee payer's identity, asserting that it constituted a confidential communication which was privileged because the payer was also allegedly involved in the drug operation and had consulted the attorney for legal advice in connection with that involvement. The Seventh Circuit agreed. ". . . Disclosure of the fee payer's identity would necessarily reveal the client's involvement in that crime and thus reveal his motive for seeking legal advice in the first place. . . . In effect, therefore, disclosure of the client's identity would expose the substance of a confidential communication between the attorney and the client.". . .

Similarly, at bar the client consulted the attorney in connection with his or her involvement in a fatal hit-and-run accident. Disclosure of his identity would reveal his possible involvement in a crime in connection with that accident, which is the precise situation for which he sought legal advice. Under these circumstances his or her identity constitutes a confidential communication, the disclosure of which is prohibited by the dictates of the attorney-client privilege. . .

"To be sure the exercise of the privilege may at times result in concealing the truth and in allowing the guilty to escape. That is an evil, however, which is considered to be outweighed by the benefit which results to the administration of justice generally". . . We conclude that the identity of the individual who allegedly was driving the vehicle which struck and killed Vincent Fiorito is privileged insofar as it was communicated confidentially to that individual's attorney. . .

As you can imagine, confidentiality is far more complicated than it may sound. The best advice is to say as little as possible about your client or your case to anyone other than those working on it with you. Keeping your client's information confidential should be a paramount concern for you.

EVIDENTIARY ISSUES

Attorney work product is a privilege that applies along the same spectrum as the ethical duty of confidentiality and the attorney-client privilege. Rather than aiming at protecting the communications between the client and legal staff, this privilege is geared toward protecting the internal workings of the legal team in preparing the case for the client. Attorney work product is divided into two categories: factual and opinion. Factual work product is the information that the legal team assembles in the course of its investigation. Opinion work product is all that which reflects what goes in the attorney's mind in the preparation of a case. This following case outlines how the two types work. (**Uncontroverted** means "undisputed or unchallenged.")

Southern Bell Telephone and Telegraph Co. v. Deason, 632 So. 2d 1377 (Fla. 1994).

We review the non-final administrative orders of the Public Service Commission (PSC). . . which direct Southern Bell Telephone and Telegraph Company (Southern Bell) to disclose certain documents to the PSC.

In February 1991, the Office of Public Counsel petitioned the PSC to investigate allegations that Southern Bell falsified information regarding its compliance with [r]ules. . . requiring rebates for the untimely repair of telephone service. The PSC, which had already begun to informally investigate similar allegations against Southern Bell, formally initiated an investigation of Southern Bell in May 1991. . .

. . . Public Counsel filed various motions to compel the production of documents from Southern Bell. Each case in these proceedings involves the discovery of a different category of information . . . Southern Bell requests this Court to quash the PSC orders compelling production and argues that the documents are protected under . . . the work product doctrine . . .

Southern Bell . . . claims that the documents which the PSC has compelled it to produce are protected by the work product doctrine. Pursuant to Florida Rule of Civil Procedure 1.280(b)(3), materials prepared in anticipation of litigation by or for a party or its representative are protected from discovery, unless the party seeking discovery has need of the material and is unable to obtain the substantial equivalent without undue hardship. The rationale supporting the work product doctrine is that "one party is not entitled to prepare his case through the investigative work product of his adversary where the same or similar information is available through ordinary investigative techniques and discovery procedures." . . . Fact work product traditionally protects that information which relates to the case and is gathered in anticipation of litigation . . . Opinion work product consists primarily of the attorney's mental impressions, conclusions, opinions, and theories . . . Whereas fact work product is subject to discovery upon a showing of "need" and "undue hardship," opinion work product generally remains protected from disclosure . . .

Although the attorney-client privilege and the work product doctrine serve separate purposes, the legal issues associated with these concepts overlap in the instant case. [T]he PSC found that the documents withheld by Southern Bell were created for a business purpose and therefore were not protected by either the attorney-client privilege or the work product doctrine. According to the PSC, Southern Bell had an independent business need to perform its own internal investigation. The PSC also argues that Southern Bell's use of the investigative materials to overhaul its telephone repair process and to discipline company employees confirms its business purpose. Southern Bell counterargues that, in light of the allegations of impropriety against it, the company had a legal motive for collecting the information now being requested for production . . .

Applying the above standards to the instant case requires separate consideration of each type of information that the PSC and Public Counsel have requested Southern Bell to produce . . .

. . . We find that the audits cannot be classified as a "communication" for the purposes of the attorney-client privilege. The audits consist of systematic analyses of data and cannot be considered the type of statement traditionally protected as a "communication." The audits do, however, fall within the definition of work product. Public Counsel argues that Southern Bell had a clear business purpose in monitoring its service quality and conducted the audits in response to a slip in customer service standards. In its order, the PSC stated:

> Internal audits are a routine vehicle for a regulated business to inform itself about its operations and to report about those operations to a regulatory agency . . . . Those business documents do not become privileged merely because non-routine developments require audits to be scheduled out of sequence or because the documents are handed over to an attorney.

Although Southern Bell regularly conducts audits for regulatory purposes and to ensure that its operations are running efficiently, the audits at issue were not conducted for either of these purposes. Rather, they were conducted at the request of counsel in direct response to the PSC's investigation. Thus, the audits were prepared in anticipation of litigation and are protected as fact work product.

Florida Rule of Civil Procedure 1.280(b)(3) permits the disclosure of work product if the party seeking discovery "has need of the materials in the preparation of the case and is unable without undue hardship to obtain the substantial equivalent of the materials by other means." Public Counsel and the PSC contend that the audits are not obtainable from any other source because the information cannot be duplicated without the use of Southern Bell's complex, integrated computer system . . . . Southern Bell points out that the audits are "analyses of information," and that Public Counsel is entitled to analyze the underlying data on which the audits are based. The underlying data consists, in part, of over 1,000,000 trouble repair reports. Although we agree with Southern Bell that it is possible to replicate the information, the standard for producing work product is not whether the replication effort is possible, but whether it causes undue hardship. We find that it would be an unduly arduous and unrealistic task to expect any party, regardless of their resources, to be able to analyze such an enormous amount of information. This is precisely the type of situation that the "undue hardship" qualification in rule 1.280(b)(3) envisioned. Therefore, Southern Bell is directed to produce the five internal audits . . .

Southern Bell argues . . . that the panel recommendations are protected as work product. Thus, once again, we reach the question of whether these materials were prepared in anticipation of litigation or whether, as Public Counsel argues, they were created for the business purpose of disciplining employees. When a corporation seeks the advice of an attorney, it is difficult to differentiate the role of a legal advisor from the role of a business advisor. In the instant case, the line between law-related communications and business communications is especially blurry.

Although it is evident that the employees' interviews with security personnel were directed by counsel in anticipation of litigation, the purpose of management personnel summarizing the results of the interviews is not as evident. The company's investigation of a legal problem led to the discovery of a potential company business problem. Southern Bell argues that the recommendations contain counsel's mental thoughts and impressions. We find Southern Bell's factual assertion to be inaccurate. The company developed information through an investigation that it memorialized in an alleged work product document. Southern Bell then took this work product, extracted information from it, and created a second set of documents—the panel recommendations. The recommendations contain the thoughts and impressions of the personnel managers based on counsel's communications to them. Although Southern Bell has proven that the employee interviews were conducted in anticipation of litigation, it has not proven that the panel recommendations were prepared for anything other than management's decision to consider whether is should discipline company employees. The disciplining of employees is a matter within the ordinary course of business even if it arises out of the PSC's investigation of Southern Bell. The fact that the panel recommendations were based on work product does not convert them into work product. Therefore, Southern Bell is ordered to produce the panel recommendations, but it is authorized to redact any notes, thoughts, or impressions of Southern Bell's counsel that are printed directly on the materials . . .

The statistical analysis was performed by Southern Bell's Assistant Vice President for Central Office Operations Support, Mr. Danny L. King. The evidence is uncontroverted that Southern Bell's Legal Department requested King to perform a statistical analysis to determine the veracity of the information obtained in the investigation and to quantify any significant deviation. According to his affidavit, King was provided with specific information and analyzed the information using a database that contained trouble histories for various years. The statistical analysis, like the internal audits at issue in case number 81,487, is not a "communication" for purposes of the attorney-client privilege. However, the nature of the document and the factual circumstances under which the analysis was created support a finding that the analysis is work product. We find insufficient any claim that the work product exception should apply to these documents and Southern Bell is not compelled to disclose the statistical analysis . . .

The second set of documents at issue . . . are statements Southern Bell employees made to Southern Bell's counsel. Applying the standards for the attorney-client privilege set forth in this opinion, we find that the employees' statements which were made directly to counsel are privileged. Statements made to security personnel, like the statements made to security that were included in the panel recommendations, are not protected by the privilege. Counsel's summaries of the employees' statements, whether the statements were communicated to counsel, to security, or to any other personnel, are protected as work product.

It is so ordered.

As you can see, the attorney work product privilege applies a little differently than the attorney-client privilege. Even if something is not privileged as an attorney-client communication, because it is between the lawyer and someone else, for instance, it can be privileged as attorney work product if the communication or work is at the behest of the attorney. You also should note the distinction made between information obtained by the lawyer and his "mental impressions, conclusions, opinions, and theories," which can otherwise be viewed as anything constituting the strategy of the legal team.

GETTING ORGANIZED

Prior to starting your investigation, you need to get organized. One of the major job requirements of the paralegal is to be able to lay hands on whatever piece of information the attorney needs in a minimal amount of time. To do so, the paralegal must have the information organized in a way that makes sense to her. Cathy Davis, an Alabama paralegal, wishes she'd been told as a new paralegal that she "didn't have to have the files the same way they'd always been done. I have lots of small files, and that makes sense to me. When I sat down and explained it to my attorney, he was okay with it, even though it was different, as long as I could find things." The nuts and bolts of how to organize may vary, but the overall organization of the files is relatively constant. You must have a way to differentiate between the parties, the friendly fact witnesses and the **hostile fact witnesses**, your experts and theirs, your documents and theirs. If you have original documents or evidence, you have to keep those separate from the copies, and keep them unaltered. You have to have the pleadings separate from correspondence, and confidential/privileged information separate from nonprivileged information. Usually legal research is separate from the rest, as well.

In order to start setting up those files and that organization, you need to know where you are going. This is where theory and the real world intersect. All of the causes of action you've learned about in various classes now must be considered in trying to decide where to go with the investigation. In the initial interview, which will be considered in detail in the next chapter, you must think through all of the possibilities and all of the defenses that may counter them.

Of course, you are not doing this alone. When you set up the file and think through the initial investigation, you will meet with your attorney and discuss the case to find out directions. But you are not simply an order-taker; you are a member of the legal team. To best serve the client, you will also be actively thinking through the facts, searching for all possible avenues. For instance, if the client has come for a divorce, and there are few marital assets, but the other spouse has substantial nonmarital assets, and there was a history of abuse, you may remember a case in which a spouse was allowed to sue in tort for assault and suggest that remedy, to the delight of your attorney, who hasn't seen that particular case. This will expand the case from just a family law case to a tort case as well, and may require additional witnesses and evidence.

Knowing the goal is important. Once you know what your causes of action are, you can start analyzing what each element is and what you need to prove it. For instance, in the case of the abused spouse, you may be trying to prove both assault for the tort cause of action and the statutory requirements to obtain the appropriate order to protect the client. To get this information, you can look at various sources: your state's pattern jury charges, *Shepard's Causes of Action* (2d ed. 1993), or *American Jurisprudence Proof of Facts* (3d ed. 1998). Your state may also have a compilation of causes of action for the jurisdiction; check with regional legal publishers. In the example given, you'd need to know, either from your attorney or from legal research, whether the tort case could all be handled within a suit for divorce, or if you'd have more than one lawsuit.

The next thing you need to do is make an **investigation plan**. The initial plan will be modified based on other information you gather as you move along in the case, and you will need to consult with the attorney as you go along. Most of the initial plan will be taken from the initial client interview and the causes of action it suggests. One of the ways to do this is to make a chart like the one shown on the next page.

In the first column, you list each element. For example, civil assault is legally defined as "apprehension of harmful or offensive contact." So first is the element of apprehension: the client realized the harmful or

Investigation Plan

Elements to Prove	Facts Client Mentions	Substantiating Sources

offensive contact would happen. The client says she saw her husband pull his hand back and then slap her across the face. Her word is evidence, but it is always better to have more evidence than simply the say-so of one of the parties. You then begin thinking of ways to back up what the client said: a medical report of bruising on her face or a police report that repeats what she said or gives the names of witnesses. In the last column, you write those possibilities. You repeat the process for each element of each cause of action you plan to claim. This will give you, in the last column, the list of items and witnesses you need to find.

Investigation Plan

Elements to Prove	Facts Client Mentions	Substantiating Sources
1. Apprehension	Saw husband about to hit her in the face	Medical records?
		Police reports?
		Witnesses? Canvass neighborhood.
2. Offensive or harmful	Hitting in face	· Medical records?
		Police reports? Check for photos ...
3. Contact	Same as element 2.	
4. Intent	He was holding her with his other hand.	Police reports?
		Check medical reports for other bruising.
		Witnesses? Other statements he has made? Canvass his work and hangouts.
	Any possible "accidental" explanation?	Talk to doctor.

You can then prioritize these items by cost and by the likelihood of each producing helpful information. This gives you a plan for investigation. In this case, medical records and police reports would seem to be your first priority. As each item is obtained, you will need to update your plan with additional information.

You would then need to set up files that would contain proof common to both the assault and family violence issues: medical records of injury, fact witnesses who heard or saw the assaults, police reports, and so forth. Then you would create the files that are needed for the family violence only: proof of the relationship and the "same domicile." You would also need a file for the assault damages claims for to document the cost of the medical care and any other economic damages (for example, prescriptions, torn or bloodied clothing, and crutches). If it will be more than one suit, you'll need to make separate files for each set of pleadings. The causes of action drive the proof, and the proof drives the organization.

Filing

There are probably as many different ways to file as there are law offices. Generally, however, there are two basic types of file systems. The first is represented by a commercial product called "The Case File," found online at **www.thecasefile.com**. This system is used by some paralegal educators to teach file organization, as it gives a well-organized, prepackaged set of checklists for client information, witness information, and such. It

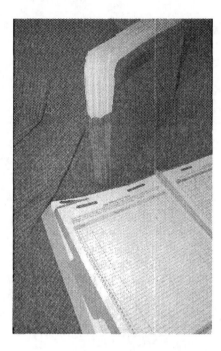

Two types of filing systems:
expandable red rope (top right)
and classified folder (bottom).

also contains a CD so that you may print forms after customizing them to your particular requirements. This is a good beginner's set if you are starting in an office with no checklists or forms and working on relatively small cases. The files used are called "Classification Files." As you can see, expansion of these files can become cumbersome, so they are only suitable for smaller cases.

The second type of filing system is in an expandable pocket, also called "red ropes" in some areas (after a particular trade name). These are good for large files because they are infinitely expandable. You simply keep adding manila folders to the file for each subdivision you need. How you subdivide the file is a matter of preference and compromise among the users of the file; however, typically there will be a correspondence file, an attorney's notes file, a pleadings file, a plaintiff's (or petitioner's) discovery file, a defendant's (or respondent's) discovery file, and files for each of the witnesses and for original documents.

A relatively recent trend in filing is the use of three-ring binders, divided with tabs that are labeled according to the needs of the particular case. Each binder is also labeled with the case name or file number and the particular function that binder fills.

Whether files of either type are legal size or letter size is also a matter of preference. Traditionally files were legal size; however, most courts have gone to letter-size paper for filing. Just make sure you have checked with the attorney, and then be consistent. Typically, the papers are two-hole punched at the top for filing.

Regardless of which system you use, the file will be kept in reverse chronological order, and there will be indexes of entries. If you are in a firm with a file clerk, the clerk will do the filing and maybe the indexing; if not, you may end up doing both. Either way, you need to understand how the file works. Reverse chronological order means that the oldest documents are filed first, nearest the bottom, and the most recent are at the top. Either at the top of the documents or on the opposite side of the file, there should be an index of any file that has a significant number of documents.

Timetables/Calendaring

The next critical step in organizing a case's development is the applicable timetable. All jurisdictions have deadlines, usually based on the trial date, as well as the deadlines imposed each time a party makes a move. For instance, if the plaintiff files suit, the defendant has a certain amount of time to file an answer. If the defendant sends the plaintiff a set of interrogatories, the plaintiff must answer them by a certain deadline. These deadlines are contained in statutes or rules of civil procedure. If you are in litigation, these rules will become your constant companion. You will learn whether you must have the answers physically to the other party by the deadline, or if mailing them on the deadline is sufficient, or if you can fax or e-mail them.

Often it is the paralegal who answers discovery requests; sometimes, however, the lawyer does so. In either case, the lawyer must at least read and sign the answers. Unfortunately, lawyers put things off. "Lawyers must go to Procrastination 101 in law school," says Cathy Davis, an Alabama paralegal. It is a major source of irritation to many paralegals that they work hard and get things done in a timely fashion and then must rush at the last minute because of the poor planning skills of the attorneys for whom they work. Part of the problem is that attorneys often end up in crisis management mode—they are constantly having to drop what they are working on and attend to the latest emergency to crop up. As one saying goes, "If it ain't on fire, it don't count." So until the discovery deadline is actually within the hour, it's not an emergency yet—it's not on fire.

One trick is to **calendar** the deadlines a day early on the lawyer's calendar. *Calendaring* is a verb in the legal world. It is the act of putting all the deadlines on the calendars of everyone who may have an interest in knowing about the case with the deadline: the legal secretary, the paralegal, the associate(s), and the partner. In some firms, the paralegal is responsible for calendaring; in others, the legal secretary performs this task. When a case comes in, you begin calendaring known deadlines, starting with the **statute of limitations**. You can also begin setting your own deadlines. Cases do not get developed unless you develop them. Do not emulate the crisis management model you see with the lawyers; it is not the best way to run an office (or your life, for that matter). Instead, set reasonable deadlines for yourself within the deadlines you cannot control.

Often you will get a **docket control order** (also called a **scheduling order**) once the case is filed and set for trial. This is an order from the court giving deadlines for certain key tasks within the case to be completed. If you had this case, you would take the order, go to the calendar of each attorney involved in the case and each paralegal and secretary for each of these attorneys, and write those deadlines on their calendars.

UNITED STATES DISTRICT COURT
FOR THE DISTRICT OF COLUMBIA

UNITED STATES OF AMERICA,
    Plaintiff,
    v.
MICROSOFT CORPORATION,
    Defendant.
	Civil Action No. 98-1232 (CKK)

STATE OF NEW YORK, *et al.,*
    Plaintiffs
    v.
MICROSOFT CORPORATION,
    Defendant.
	Civil Action No. 98-1233 (CKK)

SCHEDULING ORDER

In order to administer the above-captioned cases in a manner fair to the litigants and consistent with the Court's interest in completing this litigation in the shortest possible time, pursuant to the status hearing held on September 28, 2001, it is this 28th day of September, 2001, hereby

ORDERED that counsel for Plaintiffs and Defendant are directed to comply with each of the following directives:

(1) **COMMUNICATIONS WITH THE COURT:**

Counsel should endeavor to keep communications with chambers to a minimum. *Ex parte* communications on matters other than scheduling matters are prohibited. If counsel need to contact Chambers, it should be done jointly pursuant to a telephone conference call arranged by the parties.

(2) **MOTIONS FOR EXTENSIONS OF TIME:**[1]

Motions for extensions of time are strongly discouraged. The parties should not expect the Court to grant extensions, as they will be granted only in truly exceptional or compelling circumstances. The parties are referred to *Jackson v. Finnegan, Henderson, Farabow, Garrett & Dunner, et. al.*, 101 F.3d 145 (D.C. Cir. 1996). Motions for extension of time shall be filed at least **four** business days prior to the deadline the motion is seeking to extend. All motions for extensions **must** include the following (otherwise they will not be considered by the court):

(a) how many, if any, previous extensions of time the Court has granted to each party;
(b) the specific grounds for the motion;
(c) a statement of the effect that the Court's granting of the motion will have on all other previously set deadlines; and
(d) pursuant to LCvR 7.1(m), the moving party shall include a statement of opposing counsel's position vis-a-vis the motion.

(3) **PLEADINGS:**

(a) Every pleading shall indicate, immediately below the Civil Action No. in the caption, the next-scheduled Court deadline, such as a status conference, or pre-trial conference, or hearing date. Pleadings that do not contain such information will be, *sua sponte*, stricken from the record.
(b) Every pleading signed by an attorney shall, in conformity with LCvR 5.1(e), contain the name, address, telephone number, and bar identification number of the attorney.

(4) **DISCOVERY DISPUTES:**

Counsel are referred to LCvR 26.2 and expected to fully conform with its directives. Moreover, counsel are required, under both Fed. R. Civ. P. 26(f) and LCvR 7.1(m), to confer in good faith in an effort to resolve any discovery dispute before bringing it to the Court's attention. If, in what should be the unusual case, counsel are unable to resolve their dispute, counsel shall contact chambers in order to arrange for a telephone conference with the Court. **Counsel shall not file a discovery motion without prior consultation with opposing counsel.** Counsel are advised that if the Court is called upon to resolve such a motion, the losing **attorney** (not the principal) will be sanctioned pursuant to Fed. R. Civ. P. 37(a)(4).

(5) **DEPOSITION GUIDELINES:**

Counsel will adhere to the following guidelines when taking a deposition:

(a) Counsel for the deponent shall refrain from gratuitous comments and from directing the deponent as to times, dates, documents, testimony, and the like;
(b) Counsel shall refrain from cuing the deponent by objecting in any manner other than stating an objection for the record followed by a word or two describing the legal basis for the objection;

---

[1]The court will not entertain stipulations concerning extensions of time. The parties must file a motion when seeking an extension.

(c) Counsel shall refrain from directing the deponent not to answer any question except for reasons which conform to Fed. R. Civ. P. 30(d)(1);

(d) Counsel shall refrain from engaging in dialogue on the record during the course of the deposition;

(e) If counsel for any party or person given notice of the deposition believes that these conditions are not being adhered to, that counsel may call for suspension of the deposition and then immediately apply to the court for a ruling and remedy. When appropriate, the Court will impose sanctions;

(f) All counsel are to conduct themselves in a civil, polite, and professional manner. The Court will not countenance incivility or other behavior during the deposition demonstrating that the examination is being conducted in bad faith or to simply annoy, embarrass, or oppress the deponent;

(g) No deposition may last more than eight hours (exclusive of breaks), except by leave of the Court <u>or</u> stipulation of the parties;

(h) Fact witness depositions shall not exceed 30 for each side; and

(i) Pursuant to Fed. R. Civ. P. 30(a)-(b), the parties may take depositions upon oral examination on 10 calendar-days notice.

(6) **<u>MOTIONS FOR RECONSIDERATION:</u>**

"Motions for Reconsideration" of a prior Court ruling are strongly discouraged. Such motions shall be filed only when the requirements of Fed. R. Civ. P. 59(c) and/or 60(b) are met. If one is filed, it shall not exceed **ten** pages in length. Moreover, the Court will not entertain: (a) motions which simply reassert arguments previously raised and rejected by the Court and (b) arguments which should have been previously raised, but are being raised for the first time in the "Motion for Reconsideration." *See, e.g., National Trust v. Department of State,* 834 F. Supp. 453, 455 (D.D.C. 1995).

(7) **<u>STATUS CONFERENCE:</u>**

Counsel must be prepared at the status conference to advise the Court of the expected length of trial (in hours) and an estimate of the total number of fact and expert witnesses that each party proposes to present. Trial counsel themselves must appear at all hearings, unless excused by the Court in advance of the hearing date.

It is **FURTHER ORDERED** that:

1. Plaintiffs shall submit their proposal(s) for remedial relief not later than <u>December 7, 2001;</u>

2. Defendant shall submit its proposal for remedial relief not later than <u>December 12, 2001;</u>

3. Discovery shall commence on <u>November 2, 2001,</u> and conclude on <u>February 22, 2002;</u>

4. Interrogatories and document requests shall be served at any time after <u>November 2, 2001,</u> but not later than <u>December 14, 2001;</u>

5. Pursuant to Fed. R. Civ. P. 33, the interrogatories shall not exceed 25 in number including all discrete subparts;

6. Responses and objections to interrogatories and document requests shall be provided ten calendar days after service of such requests;

7. Plaintiffs shall provide Defendant with a preliminary witness list along with the proposal(s) for remedial relief on <u>December 7, 2001;</u>

8. Defendant shall provide Plaintiffs with a preliminary witness list along with its proposal for remedial relief on <u>December 12, 2001;</u>

9. The preliminary witness list shall be revised, supplemented, finalized, and exchanged not later than <u>February 8, 2002;</u>

10. The parties shall identify any experts and produce the appropriate reports, in conformance with Fed. R. Civ. P. 26(a)(2), not later than <u>January 25, 2002;</u>

11. Expert depositions may commence on <u>February 1, 2002,</u> and shall be completed by <u>February 22, 2002;</u>

12. Plaintiffs and Defendant shall exchange exhibit lists not later than <u>February 15, 2002</u>;
13. Joint pre-hearing statements, which will include trial briefs (in the style of a pretrial statement, as appropriate, as described in LCvR 16.5) shall be filed not later than <u>February 22, 2002</u>;
14. At the evidentiary hearing, each side shall have the opportunity to present an opening statement and a closing argument. Those statements and arguments should not exceed two hours each in length; and
15. A Status Hearing is hereby set for <u>November 5, 2001,</u> at 9 a.m. in Courtroom 11.

The Court adopts the following agreed upon provisions as set forth in the parties' Joint Status Report:

1. The terms and conditions contained in the Stipulation and Protective Order entered by the Court on May 27, 1998, shall remain in effect and continue to apply to all discovery and further proceedings in this case.
2. Service on Microsoft of any pleading or other submission filed with the Court shall be pursuant to Paragraph 5 of this Court's September 6, 2001, Order Establishing Procedures for Electronic Filing. Service on Microsoft of any pleading or other submission not filed with the Court, or responses thereto, shall be sufficient if delivered by hand, facsimile or overnight courier to (a) John L. Warden, Sullivan & Cromwell, 125 Broad Street, 31st Floor, New York, NY 10004-2498, (b) Bradley P. Smith, Sullivan & Cromwell, 1701 Pennsylvania Avenue, N.W., 7th Floor, Washington, D.C. 20006-5805, and (c) William H. Neukom, Executive Vice President – Law and Corporate Affairs, Microsoft Corporation, Building 8, One Microsoft Way, Redmond, WA 98052-6399.
3. Service on Plaintiffs of any pleading or other submission filed with the Court shall be pursuant to Paragraph 5 of this Court's September 6, 2001, Order Establishing Procedures for Electronic Filing. Service on Plaintiffs of any pleading or other submission not filed with the Court, or responses thereto, shall be sufficient if delivered by hand, facsimile or overnight courier to (a) Philip S. Beck, Esq., Bartlit Beck Herman Palenchar & Scott, Courthouse Place, Suite 300, 54 West Hubbard Street, Chicago, IL 60610, (b) Renata B. Hesse, Esq., U.S. Department of Justice, Antitrust Division, 601 D Street, NW, Suite 1200, Washington, D.C. 20530, (c) Kevin J. O'Connor, Esq., Office of the Attorney General of the State of Wisconsin, Post Office Box 7857, 123 West Washington Avenue, Madison, WI 53703-7857, (d) Jay L. Himes, Esq., Assistant Attorney General, Office of the Attorney General of the State of New York, 120 Broadway, New York, NY 10271, and (e) Blake Harrop, Esq., Office of the Attorney General of the State of Illinois, 100 West Randolph St., 12th Floor, Chicago, IL 60601.
4. Because there may be witnesses with knowledge of relevant matters residing throughout the United States, the Court finds that there is good cause to permit all parties to this action, pursuant to 15 U.S.C. § 23, to issue subpoenas to compel witnesses living outside this District to appear to testify at the remedy hearing in this matter.

Dates for the pre-hearing conference, motions *in limine*, and evidentiary hearing will be set at the final status hearing, if necessary. Additional details relevant to the evidentiary hearing will be provided at the status hearing on <u>November 5, 2001</u>. **The above-scheduled dates are firm.**

SO ORDERED.

COLLEEN KOLLAR-KOTELLY
United States District Judge

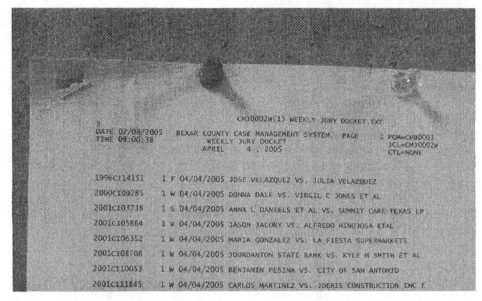

Docket posting in the hallway of the courthouse; note the lack of high tech.

To do that well, you must become familiar with both your state and local rules for notices and for counting deadlines. Make sure you know whether more than just the date of the notice is excluded, and what happens when deadlines fall on holidays or weekends.

Calendars can be physical and range from elaborate daytimers to relatively simple wirebound desk calendars. A favorite at San Antonio firms were freebies given out by court reporters. Most **malpractice carriers**, the insurance companies that insure lawyers against lawsuits, require two types of calendar systems: a physical system and a computer-based system. There are several computer programs available to help with case and time management, but make sure that you have a backup in case the computer decides to balk at giving you what you need. You never want to be in a situation where a computer crash will paralyze you.

In addition to specific dates, you need to make sure no case is ignored. When a case first arrives, there tends to be a flurry of activity, and when it's close to trial, a frenzied state recurs. To make sure things are developing correctly between the two states of affairs, the files need to be periodically reviewed. To do this, set up a **tickler system**. Such a system tickles your memory to do something about the file. It can be as simple as an index card file with months and weeks in it and an index card for every file. At the beginning of each week, pull out the new cards for the files that need to be looked at this week, have the files brought to your desk or the attorney's desk as needed, and then decide what should be done. One of the rules of ethics requires regular communication with the client. That may be all you can do at some points—simply tell the client you've done all the investigating and file development you can do until it's time to go to trial. Sometimes clients need to hear that their case hasn't been forgotten in the months that can elapse between initial informal investigation, discovery, and the actual trial.

There are certain things you have to wait for trial to do, such as proving how much your client's ongoing medical expenses are. You don't want to spend the money to do it more than once, and you want to have as much proven as possible. However, occasionally files fall through the cracks. The trial date gets close, and next to nothing has been done on a file. It's a terrifying thing in many ways for the litigation team to realize this has happened. The best plan is prevention and the best prevention is to have a good investigation plan from the beginning and to have multiple ways to follow through. A tickler system for both the paralegal and any attorneys working the file is one way to ensure that everyone is taking care of getting evidence developed for the case.

The bottom line? Make sure you have all cases scheduled with appropriate deadlines, keep up with all deadlines, and have them calendared in several places. Then make sure you and everyone else in the office pays attention to those deadlines.

Running Tallies: Costs, Damages, Billing

The practice of law is a livelihood for all those who participate, so you must not forget factors that contribute to the profitability of the firm. The costs of a case need to be tracked, the damages to the plaintiff need to be constantly reassessed as new information is received, and billing (where appropriate) needs to be kept and sent regularly.

Costs include filing fees, postage, court reporters' fees, experts' charges, copying, delivery services, process of service, and anything else that the firm either has to pay for or can think of to charge for that is not labor. In a large firm, these costs are tracked by the accounting department and by various gadgets designed for that purpose. For example, copy machines in firms often have automatic counters that have to be keyed with the file number. This way the number of copies used by any particular client is tracked by the file number and a report generated to billing. If you receive a bill, you will have to note the file number or client on it for billing purposes. In a smaller office, you will need to file such bills in the billing section of the file. The easiest way to keep track is to keep a running tally sheet on the top of the file and enter a short description and the total cost, rather like a check register. At any time during the litigation, you can then check what the total costs are on the file—an important factor for the client to know in deciding whether he or she wants to settle and for how much.

Although damages can consist of both intangible and out-of-pocket damages, in this instance you'll be tracking the monetary damages that can be proven with receipts. These damages, also referred to as "specials" in the context of tort law, need to be kept separate from bills, divided into appropriate categories (medical expenses, lost jobs, lost profits, and so on), and logged as they come in. These damages, also known as "hard damages," are often used as the beginning point for negotiations, so it is important to know what they are.

In family law, rather than damages, you'll be looking at inventories and appraisals, also known as "valuations." (Your state may have other names for them as well.) Sometimes both sides will agree on the value of the marital property; other times, they won't even agree on what marital property is. But it's these numbers that are the starting point for negotiations. Dollar totals of the realty and personalty are very important for dividing the estate and, along with income, can impact determinations of alimony (maintenance) and child support. You also need to have calculation worksheets for these items.

If you are billing a client by the hour, you will need to keep track of the hours you have used on a case. (It doesn't hurt to do track time spent on a file on contingency cases as a management tool, but that is a management decision.) Whether the client is to be billed monthly, quarterly, annually, or at the end of the case, the time will need to be calculated and billed.

When it comes time to consider a settlement offer, it is prudent to have all three types of information available to the client so that he or she can make an informed decision before accepting or rejecting the offer. If costs and attorneys fees are getting to the point where they are larger than the expected damage recovery, a plaintiff needs to think long and hard about rejecting any settlement offer. If costs and attorneys fees are still low, and the demand of a plaintiff lower than the combination of the projected remaining cost to defend a case (costs plus attorneys fees) and whatever the plaintiff is likely to recover at trial, it is usually advisable for the defendant to settle. For defendants who are "repeat players"—those who are often defendants in lawsuits by the nature of their business (insurance companies, for example)—there may be reasons other than the trial at hand, such as setting precedent, not to settle. But for the average suit, you should compare costs and take the more reasonable outcome. Or, as John Travolta's character says in the movie *A Civil Action,* "Whoever comes to his senses first, loses."

CHAPTER SUMMARY

Paralegals' function as an investigator will be determined by the type of firm for which they work. Factors influencing the degree to which a paralegal will be utilized to interview or investigate are the size of the firm and the type of law practiced. The effectiveness of a paralegal will be determined by his or her ability to work effectively with other staff members and to maintain perspective in the context of a highly demanding and stressful job. Paralegals are under pressure to perform virtually perfectly to avoid loss of job or reputation, personal liability or liability for the attorneys served, or disciplinary actions against the attorney-employers.

Confidentiality is the first duty to be concerned with when talking with clients. Paralegals must be careful not to disclose details to third parties nor discuss confidential information with the client in their presence. There is a presumption that a paralegal will have access to confidential information, so when changing employers, paralegals must take steps to avoid any contact with files upon which they have worked at another firm. The two major theories used to protect confidential information from discovery in a lawsuit are the attorney-client privilege and the attorney work product privilege.

Effectiveness is enhanced by organization and planning. Files should be designed for easy retrieval of the results of interviewing and investigation regardless of whether they are in the form of an expandable red rope, a three-ring binder, or a classification file. Plans should be made and frequently reviewed by means of a tickler system. Deadlines must be calendared for all staff and attorneys and monitored frequently for compliance. Relevant financial information, whether damages, sums owed to third parties by the client, litigation costs, or accrued attorneys fees, must be timely summarized and regularly reviewed.

FOR FURTHER READING:

American Bar Association, *The Lawyer's Desk Guide to Preventing Legal Malpractice* (1999).

Andrea Wagner, *How to Land Your First Paralegal Job* (3d ed. 2001).

Chere B. Estrin, *Paralegal Career Guide* (3d ed. 2002). This is the paralegal career bible.

Cathy D. Canny & Lesley G. Cox, R.P., *What's in a Name: Paralegal v. Legal Assistant?* National Federation of Paralegal Associations(2002) available at http://www.paralegals.org/.

Shawn T. Gaither, *The Attorney-Client Privilege: An Analysis of Involuntary Waiver,* 48 Clev. St. L. Rev. 311 (2000).

Lawrence S. Krieger, *What We're Not Telling Law Students—and Lawyers—That They Really Need to Know: Some Thoughts-in-Action Toward Revitalizing the Profession from Its Roots,* 13 J.L. & Health 1 (1998).

M. Jared Marsh, *State ex rel. Tracy v. Dandurand: Missouri Supreme Court Deals a Blow to Opinion Work Product Protection,* 70 UMKC L. Rev. 197 (2001).

Douglas R. Richmond, *The New Law Firm Economy, Billable Hours, and Professional Responsibility,* 29 Hofstra L. Rev. 207 (2000).

CHAPTER REVIEW

KEY TERMS

associate	hostile fact witness	nurse paralegal
attorney-client privilege	insurance defense	office administrator
attorney work product	interviewing	paralegal
baby lawyer	investigating	partner
billing	investigation plan	PI lawyer
calendar	law clerk	receptionist
Certified Legal Assistant (CLA)	legal administrator	Registered Paralegal (RP)
Certified Legal Assistant Specialist (CLAS)	legal assistant	runner
	legal assistant manager	scheduling order
Certified Paralegal (CP)	legal nurse consultant (LNC)	shareholder
confidentiality	legal secretary	sole practitioner
contract basis	litigator	statute of limitations
CLA Review	malpractice carrier	tickler system
defense attorney	National Association of Legal Assistants (NALA)	tortfeasor
discovery		trial attorney
docket control order	National Federation of Paralegal Associations (NFPA)	uncontroverted
file clerk		

FILL IN THE BLANKS

1. A lawyer working in a firm for other attorneys who hopes to be asked to join as an ownership member someday is a(n) _____.

2. A(n) _____ is issued by a judge to keep the case moving and to set deadlines by which certain tasks must be completed.

3. The acronym _____ is used to indicate a nurse with special credentialing that enables him or her able to function independently as auxiliary legal help.

4. The _____ is the attorney most likely to make a paralegal perform all kinds of tasks, not just those ordinarily associated with paralegalism.

5. _____ is a national organization for paralegals.

6. The term _____ was formerly interchangeable with "paralegal," but is now in flux in its usage.

7. A(n) _____ is one who may have seen or heard something related to the incident you are trying to investigate, but who does not want to cooperate.

8. A(n) _____ keeps cases from being neglected because no one has ever checked on them.

9. A(n) _____ often requires law offices to have at least two ways of ensuring that deadlines are met.

10. A(n) _____ is someone who practices civil trial work (or at least spends a good deal of time getting ready to do so).

11. In the civil context, a(n) _____ is one who represents insurance companies and their insureds.

12. The work of filing documents and delivering them to other attorneys is done by a(n) _____ in medium-sized to large law firms.

13. The work of _____ is that of finding out the facts of a particular case, in particular the documentary and tangible evidence that supports those facts.

14. _____ is the art of obtaining information from individuals.

15. A(n) _____ is the lawyer representing the plaintiff in a tort case.

16. One way to keep track of deadlines is to _____ all of them on the hard copy and computer copy of the calendar of every person associated with a particular case.

17. A good _____ can screen calls for you so that you can use your time wisely.

18. _____ is the formal, court-assisted method of obtaining information about a case.

19. An owner of a law firm may refer to himself or herself as _____ or as _____.

20. The _____ may be doing the work of a paralegal without the recognition or pay.

WEB WORK

1. Ask the Workplace Doctors: http://www.west2k.com/wego.htm

   This is a Q&A Web site where you may ask your own questions, but, please, they ask, only after you've seen what others have asked. If you scroll down to the section marked "Ask a Question," you'll see that there are highlighted links for "Search" and "Browse." Browse to see if there's a question there that you've wanted to know the answer to, but have never asked. Read the answer given. Do you believe the answer proposed is workable? Why or why not? What are the credentials of the "Workplace Doctors"? Do you think the advice is credible? Would you recommend it to anyone?

2. American Bar Association LPM Publishing: http://www.abanet.org/lpm/catalog/home.html

   Lawyers need so much help with managing their firms that the ABA had to meet the need with a publishing section of the Law Practice Management Section (LPM). Here's the online catalog. First check out *The Law Firm Guide to Client Relations for Support Staff* by Hollis Hatfield Weishar. It looks like it's free, but before you can download it, you'll have to supply the ABA with a credit card number. Now look at the list of books, either by topic or alphabetically. Are there any dealing with staff, paralegals, or, to use the ABA's preferred term for paralegals, legal assistants? If so, describe each.

3. "Real World" by Susan Howery: http://www.legalassistanttoday.com/profession/real_world.htm

   This article in *Legal Assistant Today* describes some shocks for both attorneys and student interns entering the work world. Do you forsee any of those problems for yourself? While you are at the *Legal Assistant Today* Web site, look at the archive and read another online article. What else did you learn about the real world of the law profession?

4. The Virtual Law Firm Described: http://www.lawmall.com/lm_virtu.html

   An iconoclastic alternative to the conventional law firm is described on this page. For a better idea of the clientele, look at the root directory: http://www.lawmall.com. What do you see? How would you evaluate the reliability or credibility of this site? What are your conclusions? Compare the Virtual Law Firm described with the conventional law firm. What do you think about the final comment on the Web page about the author's involvement with paralegal education?

5. Google Directory: http://www.google.com

   On the Google home page, click on the tab marked "Directory." Now choose Society>Law>Products>Practice Management>Software. All of these various programs, as well as those in the subdirectories, can help manage different aspects of the law practice. Which would be your top two choices to evaluate for managing your investigation of a case?

6. Law Tech News: http://www.lawtechnews.com

   The *American Lawyer's* online version of its best national spinoff is another resource for information on legal software and on how to use technology in the law office. The hard part is figuring out which parts are advertising and which parts are journalism. Look at the Web site and evaluate whether you believe it would be useful to you in finding and/or evaluating case management software.

7. National Federation of Paralegal Associations Regulations Web page: http://www.paralegals.org/Development/Regulations/home.html

   An area that is in a great deal of flux right now is that of paralegal regulation. NFPA keeps abreast of this area, as does *Legal Assistant Today*. Go to the NFPA Web page listed above, or, if the page has changed, to the Web site at http://www.paralegals.org and look for the "Profession Development" area. There you should find a link to the organization's page on the current status of regulation across the United States. What's happening in your state? Does that make you liable for ethics violations in more direct ways than discussed in the main text? What about in other states? Which of the schemes that have been passed make the most sense to you?

8. National Association of Legal Assistants CLA & CLAS: http://www.nala.org/cert.htm

   National Federation of Paralegal Associations RP: http://www.paralegals.org/PACE/rp_facts.htm These pages discuss the bases upon which the respective designations may be revoked. Compare the approach of the organizations to the ethical basis of revocation.

9. Cornell's Legal Information Institute: Legal Ethics: http://www.law.cornell.edu/ethics/listing.html

   Cornell's Legal Information Institute (LII) is a fabulous Web site, and this is a great section. Each state is listed with a full list of applicable rules of ethics and sites for ethics opinions. Check your state. What do you find about confidentiality? About the responsibility of the lawyer for his or her staff?

10. Another place to look for a discussion of ethics issues is http://www.LegalEthics.com, which provides both articles and links to both legal and governmental ethics. The search engine is a bit cranky, so it doesn't respond well to queries, but the site will refer you to better information. Check out your state's judicial ethics, something that can come in handy if you want to recuse a judge.

WORKING THE BRAIN

1. Soong Li comes to the office to obtain an attorney to represent her in the divorce action filed by her husband. She doesn't speak much English, so she brought a friend who is fluent in Cantonese, her native language, as well as in English, to translate. Will the discussions you have with her be privileged? Why or why not? Are there any steps you can take to make it more likely for a court to find them privileged? Try to be creative in solving the problem.

2. On September 15, 1986, Barbara McCrory leased a house from Thomas J. Johnson through his rental agent, Brad W. Houston. Under the written lease agreement, McCrory was to pay $ 600.00 a month for one year. After McCrory failed to pay part of the December rent and all of the January and February rent, Houston placed a note on her door asking her to pay rent or vacate the premises. When she did not respond, he placed a termination notice on the door requesting her to vacate the premises within 10 days. Shortly after the 10-day period expired, Houston removed all her furniture, appliances, and household items, and deposited them at a local storage facility. On April 9, 1987, Johnson filed suit for rent, late charges, and damages to his property. Barbara McCrory then counterclaimed against Johnson and his agent, Houston, claiming that they had violated the Arkansas forcible entry and detainer code provisions by removing her property from the house.

    In the midst of all of this, on March 30, 1987, Barbara McCrory complained to the Prosecuting Attorney's Office concerning the removal of her property from the house. Elizabeth Baxley, a paralegal in the prosecuting attorney's office, contacted Keith Vaughn, Houston's attorney, about the property. Baxley testified in chambers that Vaughn told her that he had advised Houston not to take the property from the leased home. Is this conversation protected under the attorney-client privilege, or should the judge allow McCrory to call Baxley to the stand?

3. Given the cases you've looked at in this chapter, do you think that unencrypted e-mail transmissions, faxes, and cell phone conversations with clients adequately safeguard client confidentiality? In other words, should you send confidential communications by these methods of transmission? Why or why not?

PUTTING IT TO WORK

1. Put together forms based on the chapter's discussions of basic tools you need, such as investigation plans, running tallies, and so forth. What strategies in organizing a form make sense to you? What sections does the form need? What would make it easy to use?

2. Assemble a basic skeleton of a file using a red rope. Make up manila folders for each section you think you would need for the internal sections: correspondence, legal research, discovery for the plaintiff, discovery for the defendant, and so forth. Make sure to include any forms prepared in question 1.

3. Find out what the rules for counting are in your jurisdiction. Get a calendar and determine when each of the following events would occur.

    a. deadline for filing responses to interrogatories 30 days from tomorrow
    b. deadline for filing supplementary responses to discovery that are due 30 days before a trial set for the same day of the month as today, but for next month
    c. deadline for filing amended pleadings seven days before the trial in part b
    d. the earliest you could depose a party if you sent notice today

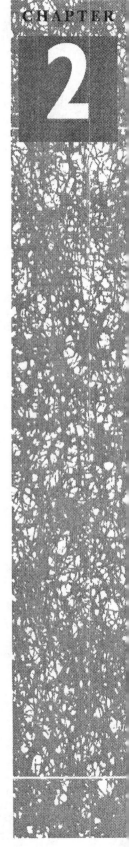

THE CLIENT: PLAINTIFF'S PERSPECTIVE

> "Client, *n.* A person who has made the customary choice between the two methods of being legally robbed."
>
> *Ambrose Bierce,* The Devil's Dictionary

INTRODUCTION

Interviewing occurs in all practices. Whenever you speak to a client and ask questions to determine what he or she needs, you are interviewing. Therefore, interviewing is an important skill regardless of the type of practice in which you end up being employed. However, the amount of detail you need, the creativity you may have to exercise, the judgment you'll have to make, and the length of an interview will be determined by the type of practice. Because the litigation context tends to be the most demanding in terms of interviewing and investigating skills, it is the one we will study, beginning with the plaintiff's point of view.

In a litigation context, you must continuously view your clients and their stories through the critical eyes of future jurors, and try to think of the questions they'd want answered after a hostile attorney has raised any possible rock under which something nasty might be hiding. As the plaintiff, you have the **burden of proof:** if it's a tie, you lose. If there's no evidence on one part of the cause of action, you lose. And, if the firm is working on a **contingency fee contract,** has advanced the costs of litigation, and only gets paid if the plaintiff wins, the firm loses not only the time of the lawyers, paralegals, secretaries, file clerks, and other staff, but the amount of money paid for filing, to court reporters, to any experts, for copies, and for other miscellaneous expenses that crop up in litigation. If you are working for the client on a **billable hour system,** every bit of time must be accounted for, and the client's budget must be considered and estimated as part of the advice given to the client when discussing litigation options.

As a result, initial interviews need to be done with a great deal of care and some measure of skepticism. Understandably, the client will tell you the story from his side, often with a complete absence of any pretense of objectivity. It's an oft-repeated truism in litigation circles that a case never looks as good as the day it walks in the door, and this is part of the reason why. The client may omit details that are crucial to understanding the case, and it is part of the interviewer's job to try to elicit these rocky details.

At the same time, you must develop rapport with the client, helping him feel that you understand the situation and his point of view. The client, in order to tell you all about the rocks and the nasty things that live underneath them, must feel secure and confident in your interest in doing the best job for him, and in the complete confidentiality of the relationship. And in order to do the best job, you must know about all those rocks, so you, your attorney, and the rest of the legal team don't fall over one. So you must elicit omitted details with finesse, doing so in a way that makes the client feel that you are asking for his own good and that you're on his side.

These two goals must be held in balance. On one hand, you must stay objective, remembering you are working for the client's legal interests as part of the team and not as a buddy. On the other hand, you have to establish an atmosphere in which the client feels comfortable telling you things that he may not have told his wife, best friend, or dog. It can be a difficult balance to maintain, and clients may try to pull you over the edge, particularly in family law, when they are emotionally vulnerable. It's a good practice to keep on hand community resources for those sorts of clients: counselors, 12-step groups, support groups, psychologists, and other trained professionals. Then when the relationship begins to teeter too far into the emotional or psychological side, you may tell the client that you appreciate what he's telling you, and wish you could help more, but you're really only trained to help with the legal side of things. "However," you say brightly, "I know this great _____" and fill in the blank with whatever professional (e.g., psychiatrist, psychologist) or group (e.g., support group for recently divorced women) you want to recommend. It saves the client money and you time.

Interviewing is an important skill, and the ability to do it well will help your career as a paralegal immensely. You may have initial interviews with clients to serve as a screening mechanism if the attorneys you work with have developed certain criteria for the types of cases they do and do not accept. If that's the case, as you are interviewing the client, the client is also interviewing you. If you make a bad impression, you may lose the firm a client. Initial interviews are also done by paralegals to allow them to weed through the client's story and get the relevant details before the client meets with the lawyer. This allows the lawyer to make more efficient use of her time with the client. Again, the paralegal is the first representative of the firm the client meets, and first impressions count.

You may also meet with the client for a detailed follow-up after the attorney has decided to accept a case after hearing the basic story. This is when you must get all the information you can for the investigation. You may, of course, call the client again, but it is far more efficient to get as much information as you can at the outset. "Checklists are how I manage," says Brenda Pruitt, a paralegal in North Carolina. "I make checklists for everything." Checklists are available commercially in most areas, but many paralegals and lawyers customize their own. As a new paralegal, you may wish to start with a checklist from a formbook, and then discuss it with the attorney you work for to get her take on what is important, what to add, and what is unnecessary.

A few shelves of
legal formbooks.

ETHICAL ISSUES

Unauthorized Practice of Law (UPL)

Initial client contact presents the first opportunity for the most pervasive ethical problem paralegals face: avoiding any appearance of (or accidental occurrence of) practicing law. One concern that should stay foremost in your mind is that if you are perceived as holding yourself out as an attorney, you can be in trouble. To head off that problem, make sure at the beginning of every interview that you introduce yourself as a paralegal and explain what a paralegal can and cannot do. For extra security, you may even want to give the client a handout or have one of the many informational videos on paralegals play in the waiting area for clients. Clients need to know, unequivocally, that you are not a lawyer. This is a protection for you, so that later they will not claim that you were engaging in the **unauthorized practice of law (UPL)**.

Conflicts of Interest

Starting to talk to a potential client also means you must make sure you don't get into any trouble with **conflicts of interest** (**COI** or **conflicts**). Conflicts of interest in the context of law offices are predicated on the idea that the lawyer and her staff owe the client a duty of loyalty. This clearly means that you will not represent one side of a case against the other. However, the duty of loyalty means more than just that. The duty is both long-term and contagious, meaning it extends past whatever matter the lawyer is originally consulted on, and the duty is owed not only by the lawyer who actually represented the client, but everyone in the firm. If there is a conflict, the firm cannot take the case. If a conflict develops after a firm has taken on a case, the firm must withdraw, or it can be disqualified from representation and its attorneys disciplined.

The basic conflict of interest rule is found in Rule 1.7.

[A] lawyer shall not represent a client if the representation involves a concurrent conflict of interest. A concurrent conflict of interest exists if:

1. the representation of one client will be directly adverse to another client; or
2. there is a significant risk that the representation of one or more clients will be materially limited by the lawyer's responsibilities to another client, a former client or a third person or by a personal interest of the lawyer.

Model Code Prof'l Cond. R. 1.7(a).

If the attorney's representation will be directly against a current client, or if it will be limited by responsibilities to another client, whether current or former, then there's a problem. Rule 1.9 further fleshes out duties to prior clients, forbidding representation of a client who would be on the other side of an issue that is materially the same as the one in which the attorney represented the former client (unless the former client consents in writing).

So far, not too tricky. It's when attorneys become responsible for what other attorneys in their firm have done that it gets to be problematic. If the firm is large, or if the caseload is large, one attorney doesn't necessarily have knowledge of what the other attorneys have done. Each firm must build in safeguards to allow all attorneys to check the names of any clients that the firm is representing to avoid such conflicts. This is done by checking potential defendants in the current case against other current or former clients, not just of this particular attorney, but of any attorney in the firm. This requirement is reasonable enough, but every attorney is also to avoid conflict with every client his former firm may have represented. This is truly difficult, but the rule does allow an out: The attorney is only responsible for knowing violations. If the opposing side wants to get rid of your firm, thinking there is a conflict, it can file a motion to disqualify, but it won't necessarily succeed.

Jaggers v. Shake, 37 S.W.3d 737 (Ky. 2001).

. . . The underlying action commenced with a complaint filed by Appellees and Real Parties in Interest, Paula Payton and Mary Blakely, against Appellant, Thomas E. Clay, and Lacey Smith for alleged professional negligence in the legal representation afforded them in a case styled *Holland Income Tax, Inc. v. Paula Payton and Mary Blakely, and Paula and Mary, Inc.*, No. 93-CI-00395, Bullitt Circuit Court. Payton and Blakely are represented by James T. Mitchell of the law firm of Conliffe, Sandmann & Sullivan. Another attorney at that law firm, Sally Lambert, represents Kevin Jaggers and his former partnership of Bolus, Jaggers, and Mayfield, P.L.L.C., in a different professional negligence lawsuit.

The reason Appellants seek disqualification is that Jaggers had previously worked for Clay as a salaried attorney and had worked on litigation involving Holland Income Tax, Inc. and several of its former franchisees, including Payton and Blakely, parties who are now adverse to Clay. Jaggers, however, did not work directly on Payton and Blakely's case while he was employed by Clay. After Jaggers left Clay's employ, however, he prepared a motion for discretionary review to this Court from the Bullitt Circuit Court case that is the basis for the Payton/Blakely negligence action against Clay, and Jaggers also advised Blakely on the phone that this motion had been filed.

Contending that Payton's and Blakely's interests were adverse to Jaggers' interests, Appellants filed a motion with the trial court seeking to disqualify Mitchell based upon the general prohibition against conflicts of interest . . . and the rule governing imputed disqualification. . . . The trial court denied the motion, reasoning that disqualification was not warranted because the two professional negligence cases had no common issues or parties and that no confidential information about the Blakely/Payton case had passed between Appellants and Mitchell or his law firm.

. . . Appellants alleged that they would suffer injury because Clay would call Jaggers as a witness in the action against Clay and that Jaggers would be subject to cross-examination by Mitchell, an associate of an attorney representing him in another action. Essentially, Appellants contend that Jaggers' testimony for his former professional associate Clay will place him in conflict with his own attorneys in other litigation, Lambert and Mitchell . . . [T]he Court of Appeals denied the requested relief, reasoning that Jaggers' position as a potential witness . . . did not constitute a showing of immediate and irreparable harm necessary for the issuance of a writ of mandamus. In so holding, the Court of Appeals noted that since the trial court's decision was interlocutory, Appellants were not foreclosed from moving the trial court to revisit the disqualification issue in the future should subsequent events make it appropriate to do so.

SCR 3.130(1.7), the general rule prohibiting representation that entails a conflict of interest, provides:

a. A lawyer shall not represent a client if the representation of that client will be *directly adverse* to another client, unless:

1. The lawyer reasonably believes the representation will not adversely affect the relationship with the other client; and

2. Each client consents after consultation.

b. A lawyer shall not represent a client if the representation of that client may be materially limited by the lawyer's responsibilities to another client or to a third person, or by the lawyer's own interests, unless:

1. The lawyer reasonably believes the representation will not be adversely affected; and

2. The client consents after consultation.

(emphasis added). SCR 3.130(1.10), the imputed disqualification rule, provides in relevant part,

a. While lawyers are associated in a firm, none of them shall knowingly represent a client when any one of them practicing alone would be prohibited from doing so by Rule 1.7.

Thus, for purposes of Rule 1.10, Mitchell, an associate of Lambert, is considered to represent Jaggers. He also represents Payton and Blakely in this case against Clay and Smith, and Mitchell owes a duty of loyalty to both sets of clients.

In applying Rule 1.7 to the instant case, the threshold issue is whether Mitchell's representation of Payton and Blakely is "directly adverse" to Lambert's representation of Jaggers as is required for disqualification under section (a) of the rule. In elucidating the meaning of "directly adverse," the Commentary to Rule 1.7 explains,

As a general proposition, loyalty to a client prohibits undertaking representation directly adverse to that client without that client's consent. . . . Thus, a lawyer ordinarily may not act as advocate against a person the lawyer represents in some other matter, even if it is wholly unrelated. On the other hand, simultaneous representation in unrelated matters of clients whose interests are only generally adverse, such as competing economic enterprises, does not require consent of the respective clients.

Accordingly, Mitchell, in his representation of Payton and Blakely, is not acting as an advocate against Jaggers. Although Jaggers was associated with Clay during the time of the alleged professional negligence by Clay, and Jaggers will testify to subsequent events, he is not a party to that action. Thus, Mitchell's representation of Payton and Blakely is not directly adverse to that of Jaggers, and disqualification is not required under section (a) of Rule 1.7.

Disqualification is likewise not required by section (b) of Rule 1.7. Section (b) prohibits representation if it will be "materially limited" by the lawyer's responsibilities to other persons. Here, the two legal malpractice lawsuits are completely unrelated matters. Appellants have failed to show that Lambert's representation of Jaggers in the legal malpractice suit against him will be hindered by Mitchell's representation of Payton and Blakely in their lawsuit against Clay.

Appellants further contend that even absent an actual conflict of interest, Mitchell should be disqualified because his representation of Clay brings about an impermissible appearance of impropriety. This Court announced its adherence to the "appearance of impropriety" standard as a separate reason for disqualification in *Lovell v. Winchester* . . . In *Lovell*, an attorney consulted with a potential client regarding a claim and retained documents relating to the claim. The attorney subsequently declined to represent the client and returned the documents. Sometime later, the attorney took on representation of the opposing side, and the first party sought to disqualify the attorney based upon a conflict of interest. Although the attorney had returned the relevant documents and claimed that he could not remember the initial consultation with the first party, this Court held that there was an appearance of impropriety and disqualified the attorney from the case.

No similar circumstance exists here. Payton and Blakely have expressly waived any conflict and the mere fact of two attorneys in the same firm representing a party on the one hand and being adverse to that person as a witness in another case on the other hand is too attenuated to create an appearance of impropriety.

For the foregoing reasons, the judgment of the Court of Appeals is affirmed.

You may have to graph out these relationships to follow the Kentucky Supreme Court's reasoning in this case, because some of the statements made by the court seem a little strange.

Ethical or Chinese Wall

There are some significant exceptions to the COI rules. Government attorneys are allowed to quit and bring suit against their former employer; they just can't work on any cases with which they were formerly involved. What is commonly called a **Chinese wall** (after the Great Wall of China) or an **ethical wall** must be built around the attorney, and procedures must be instituted to make sure that the attorney has nothing to do with any such case. Some people find the Chinese wall term to be not politically correct, and prefer to use **ethical wall**. "I never much minded lawyers saying 'build a Chinese Wall' to refer to limiting access to confidential materials for ethical reasons. 'Chinese Wall' refers to an object with a specific cultural reference, but it has no subtext . . . 'Chinese fire drill' is just downright puzzling to me. I have no idea why teenagers who stop their car at an intersection, all jump out, run around, and jump in again, having switched seats, would make anyone think of Chinese or fire drills."[1] Whatever you call it, it is also required of staff. If legal staff worked on a case at a former legal employer, they must not have anything to do with the case at the new firm, and the same Chinese wall procedure must be employed.

Potential conflicts are issues that need to be uncovered in the initial interview and will be known after gathering information about potential defendants.

---

[1] Frank H. Wu, *Yellow: Race in America Beyond Black and White*, 23 (2002).

EVIDENTIARY ISSUES

Attorney-Client Privilege

As mentioned in the last chapter, attorney-client privilege applies to communications between you and the client as well as the client and the attorney. To stay confidential, communications must not be divulged (given out) to any third party. When you meet the client in the waiting area, which is usually a common area, make sure that any discussion is strictly small talk: How are you? Did you have any problem finding the office? Did you have any problem parking? That sort of thing.

Attorney Work Product

In addition, your notes and plans are covered by the privilege of attorney work product, with the same caveat. Don't leave your notes where they are easily seen by others. Don't take them other places; file them as soon as you are done with them. You may not want to trash them; they may turn up useful, but putting them in the file is the safest place for them.

Make sure the client is made aware of the two evidentiary rules. Don't advise; simply inform.

AN INITIAL CLIENT CALL

This is not a real phone call, but it could be. Imagine yourself sitting at your desk. It's covered with paper, either in neat stacks or in messy piles, depending on how you work. The receptionist buzzes you, says your name, and continues.

"I've got a potential client here that says she was arrested when she shouldn't have been."

"Did you tell her we don't do criminal law?" you reply.

"Yeah, but she said that's all over," says the receptionist.

"Oh. Well, what does she want, then?" you ask.

"She wants to sue the policeman," says the receptionist.

"Oh, geez," you say.

"No, really," says the receptionist, "I think you need to listen to her."

"Okay." You then take the call and introduce yourself. Patty Haus is on the line.

"So, Ms. Haus, what can we do for you?" you ask her, after explaining that you are not a lawyer.

"I want to sue the sonovabitch," says Patty.

"I see," you say. "Well, Ms. Haus, who is it you want to sue and why do you believe you can?"

"That %$%*%$# policeman that works at the apartment, that's who."

You wait for your ears to stop burning and calmly reply, "And why is it, again, you believe you have a lawsuit against this officer?"

"I was driving my boyfriend's pickup into the driveway to our apartment, the brakes went out and I hit the apartment building."

"Okay . . . " you encourage her to go on.

"And this, this—" Patty sputters a bit.

"Yes?"

"He said I did it on purpose! He called some of his buddies and had me arrested. I spent two days in jail for it. Two days!" She is yelling by the end of this conversation. Your mind begins to click through possible causes of action. Before you make the appointment, though, you think quickly. Has the firm ever represented an apartment complex before? A police officer? You're pretty sure the answer to the first question is no, but you're not too sure about the second. You ask Ms. Haus to give you the names of all people involved just to be sure.

"Ms. Haus, I'd like to have an opportunity to discuss this with you further. Can we make an appointment?" you ask.

Now, in real life, when you make a date with someone on the phone, that's the end of it. However, in the legal world, you must begin learning to paper your steps. So, before you get off the phone with the client—Ms. Haus in this example—you will need to get her address and phone number. If there is enough time before you meet with her, which there probably will be, you will send her a letter that confirms the time and place you are meeting. Ordinarily you will meet at your firm's office. However, circumstances may require you to meet in other places: the client may be disabled or ill, work odd hours, or lack transportation, for example. You will want to set the meeting, if at all possible, for a time at which your attorney is available in the office so you can have access to him if necessary. You should include in the **confirmation letter** instructions about how to get to the office and a map as well. You may want to use **www.mapquest.com** or **www.randmcnally.com** for the map.

[Date]

Patty Haus
3434 Broken Bow Ave
Big City, Confusion 99999

Re: Incident at Vista Libre Apartments

Dear Ms. Haus:

Thank you for contacting us. This letter confirms your appointment with me on [Month Day], [day of the week], at [time] to gather more information for evaluation by the attorney.

Our offices are located at 100 Years War Lane, Suite 1412, Big City, Confusion 99999, near [landmark—it's a good idea to give people a general idea of the area]. For your convenience, here is a map showing how to get here from your home.

[Insert map from www.mapquest.com or www.randmcnally.com]

If you have any of the following items, please bring them with you.

* a copy of the police report
* a copy of your apartment lease
* any documents regarding repairs to your boyfriend's truck before the incident
* any document showing that the brakes failed at the time of the incident
* any pictures of damages to the apartment or of the condition of the brakes at the time of the incident
* any documents relating to your arrest and time in jail

If you have any questions, please call. I look forward to seeing you.

Sincerely,

Sarah Miller
Paralegal for Ms. St. Joan

Then you'll do a **conflict check** to avoid conflicts of interest. Conflict checks are usually done first by computer, by making sure that there are no matches between any of the people you think you might be suing and the people you have ever represented. Then there may be a list passed around the attorneys and staff to make sure that no one who has joined the firm who used to work at another law office has ever worked for the defendants. If there are no matches, then there is no conflict of interest, and you are good to go with your meeting. If there is a match, you will have to call Ms. Haus and tell her that you have discovered a conflict of interest, apologize, and suggest some other attorneys. Send a letter to confirm the cancellation and to document that your firm is not representing her. Make sure it is clear that the cancellation in no way reflects any opinion upon the merits of her claim.

After you send the letter, you must calendar the meeting. Recall from Chapter 1 that, in legalese, *calendar* is a verb as well as a noun, and refers to the process of putting a time-sensitive event on the physical and computer calendars of any individuals to whom the event is relevant. In this case, you would put the meeting on your calendar (of course), on your secretary's calendar, on your supervising attorney's calendar, and on your supervising attorney's secretary's calendar. In each case, you would put the event on both the hard copy and electronic calendar.

You hope this is the beginning of a beautiful relationship, and not the first sign of a nightmarish case. At this point, you'd try to analyze it according to the chart discussed in Chapter 1. What are your possible causes of action? After you'd guessed at a few, you'd stop your supervising attorney, George, and mention this potential client to him.

"George, I got an interesting call from a potential client today."

"Oh, really?" says George, half listening as he reads through the papers you've given him to sign. After you summarize, he looks up at you, and thoughtfully chews the end of the pencil.

"Hmmm. Possible § 1983 action, false imprisonment, conspiracy, malicious prosecution—got the police officer, the police department, and the apartment complex as defendants. Maybe even the car manufacturer; I can't remember what they are liable for if there's not any physical injury. Guess that depends on whose fault the brakes were. Could be good if it checks out. Let me know what she's like."

"She's coming in a week from today."

"Do you know where I'll be then?" asks George.

"Yes, George. You've got a depo set here," you remind him. "In the Turner case."

"Good, let me know if you think I should meet her."

Now you've got the causes of action listed by the attorney and you can look them up to decide what to do.

THE INITIAL INTERVIEW

"[T]he heart of good listening is authenticity . . . Authenticity means that you are listening because you are curious and because you care, not just because you are supposed to. The issue then, is this: Are you curious? Do you care?"[2]

Objectives

The initial interview is extremely important. You want to get as full a report as possible and also get a feel for the client as a person and as a witness. You need to assess the client's strengths and weaknesses. You have to start developing investigatory leads. You will need to determine the potential value of the case if it is taken on a contingency basis. And you need to develop rapport with the client so that he or she feels safe enough to trust you with secrets often never spoken aloud. There's a lot to deal with. As a result, you need to be sure that you have clear objectives in mind and are prepared enough to be ready to listen. Most of this is applicable to any witness, not

---

[2]Douglas Stone, Bruce Patton, and Sheila Heen, *Difficult Conversations: How to Discuss What Matters Most*, 168 (1991).

just the client; distinctions involve the duties owed to the witness, the privileges that cover the discussions, the paperwork generated, the goals of the discussion, and the paperwork involved. Preparation, manner, techniques, and observation and evaluation of the witness are universal to any interview of any witness, not just the client.

Preparation

One of the best ways to help listen to the client is to prepare **intake forms.** An intake form, similar to what doctors use, will ensure that you get the basic information you need. It can also be a springboard for additional discussion. Often law firms send the intake form to the client with confirmation of the appointment and directions to the office, so if there are papers the client needs to bring along, he'll know up front. You'll need contact information, including people that don't reside with the client, and social security number for any office. It may surprise you how often clients move and don't tell their lawyers; it's a rough day if you have to produce your client and you can't find her.

SOL _____

CLIENT INFORMATION SHEET

Background Information _____

NAME _____

Address _____

Telephone Number (home) _____

Age _____ Date of Birth _____ Soc. Sec. No. _____

EMPLOYER _____

Address _____

Telephone Number (work) _____

Occupation _____ Worked there how long? _____

Immediate Supervisor _____

Supervisor's Phone Number _____

SPOUSE'S NAME _____

Address _____

Telephone Number (home) _____

Spouse's Employer _____

Employer's Address _____

Telephone Number (work) _____ Occupation _____

Age _____ Date of Birth _____ Soc. Sec. No. _____

CHILDREN

Name(s)/Age(s) _____

_____

_____

How many children are living with you now? _____

(continued)

EMERGENCY CONTACT (Not listed above and not living at same address)

Name _____

Relationship _____

Address _____

City _____ State _____ Zip _____

Telephone Number _____

EDUCATION

High School/G.E.D. _____ Year of Graduation _____

Technical School _____

College/University _____ Years & Degree _____

Any other relevant education _____

_____

_____

EMPLOYMENT HISTORY

Employer _____ Position _____

Duties _____

_____

Employer _____ Position _____

Duties _____

_____

Employer _____ Position _____

Duties _____

_____

Employer _____ Position _____

Duties _____

_____

Incident Information

Why are you seeking legal assistance? _____

_____

_____

_____

_____

_____

When and where did the incident described take place? _____

_____

_____

Who are the individuals and/or businesses you believe to be responsible for the situation that brought you here?

1. NAME & ADDRESS _____

_____

_____

Telephone Number (_____)_____

Role in the Situation _____

_____

_____

_____

_____

_____

2. NAME & ADDRESS _____

_____

_____

Telephone Number (_____)_____

Role in the Situation _____

_____

_____

_____

_____

_____

3. NAME & ADDRESS _____

_____

_____

Telephone Number (_____)_____

Role in the Situation _____

_____

_____

_____

_____

_____

POTENTIAL WITNESSES

1. NAME & ADDRESS _____

_____

_____

Telephone Number (_____)_____

Relationship (work acquaintance, personal friend, relative, supervisor, bystander, etc.)

_____

What do you believe this person will be able to testify to? _____

_____

(continued)

2. NAME & ADDRESS _____

_____

_____

Telephone Number (_____) _____

Relationship (work acquaintance, personal friend, relative, supervisor, bystander, etc.)

_____

What do you believe this person will be able to testify to? _____

_____

3. NAME & ADDRESS _____

_____

_____

Telephone Number (_____) _____

Relationship (work acquaintance, personal friend, relative, supervisor, bystander, etc.)

_____

What do you believe this person will be able to testify to? _____

_____

Relationship (work acquaintance, personal friend, relative, supervisor, bystander, etc.)

_____

What do you believe this person will be able to testify to? _____

_____

Damages Information

A. Have you had any financial losses? _____ If not, skip to section **B.**
Please describe. _____

_____

_____

_____

What papers do you have to show these losses? _____

_____

_____

_____

B. Were you physically injured in this situation? _____ If not, skip the next section.
Please describe. _____

_____

_____

_____

Did you go to the hospital? _____

Which hospital? _____

Admitted or Out Patient? _____

If admitted, release date _____

X-Rays taken? _____ Were you taken by ambulance? _____

Are you under the care of a physician now? _____

LIST DOCTORS

1. Name _____

   Address _____

   _____

   Telephone Number _____

   When did you last see the doctor? _____

   When will you see the doctor again? _____

   Are you receiving physical therapy? _____

   Current balance on medical bills _____

2. Name _____

   Address _____

   _____

   Telephone Number _____

   When did you last see the doctor? _____

   When will you see the doctor again? _____

   Are you receiving physical therapy? _____

   Current balance on medical bills _____

3. Name _____

   Address _____

   _____

   Telephone Number _____

   When did you last see the doctor? _____

   When will you see the doctor again? _____

   Are you receiving physical therapy? _____

   Current balance on medical bills _____

PRESCRIPTIONS: BRING IN ALL RECEIPTS, BILLS, ETC. NOTE USE OF CERVICAL COLLAR, CASTS, WALKER, CRUTCHES, ETC. HAVE CLIENT BRING IN FOR EVIDENCE WHEN FINISHED USING, OR WHEN CAST IS REMOVED.

Miscellaneous Information

1. Have you seen any other lawyers regarding this incident? _____ If yes, please give the name, address, and outcome of the discussion with the other lawyer. _____

_____

_____

_____

_____

2. Have you had any prior lawsuits? _____ If yes, please give the circumstances and outcome of each. _____

_____

_____

_____

_____

(continued)

49

3. Do you have any conditions, mental or physical, that require constant medication? _____ If yes, please list each medication and the dosage. _____

_____

4. Do you require any special accommodations (e.g., translators, wheelchair or walker access, large print)? _____

_____

5. Have you had any convictions in the past, including any tickets? _____ If yes, explain the charges and approximate date of the offense. _____

_____

The rest of the information you need will depend on the type of case. If it's litigation, as it probably would be in an investigation, you'd need criminal background information. In torts, you want to find out about any prior injuries, prior suits, and work history. In family law, you also want the client's work history, current wages, and everything the client and the soon-to-be-ex have. So the exact content will vary greatly. You may have several different intake sheets for use in different situations.

If you don't send the paperwork ahead to the client, you may wish to have her fill it out while she's waiting in the reception area. Or you may wish to fill it out together as a format for the meeting. It's your choice.

For the interview, you will have a list of questions based on the initial phone call from the client. How detailed the list is will depend on how much information was gathered from the initial phone call. In the case of Patty Haus, you had enough information to guess at the defendants and possible causes of action. You have a pretty good idea of what follow-up questions you need.

If you have the client fill the form out ahead of time, you may want to have the receptionist bring it to you before you have the client come in. This will give you a chance to review the information to fine tune your preparation for the interview.

Preparation for any interview is important, and applies to interviewing a plaintiff, defendant, or any other type of witness. There are two ways to prepare for the topics you want to discuss. One way is to write out line-by-line questions; the other is to designate areas of exploration. Generally, you begin as an interviewer with the first and as you become more comfortable move to the second, only writing specific questions when it is extremely important that a particular question is asked and you are afraid you might otherwise forget. Make sure you cover the journalistic questions, also known as the five Ws: who, where, when, what, and why. In any case, make sure you leave yourself plenty of room for notes.

Before you meet with the client, make sure the room is ready. It sounds trivial, but it's important. First impressions matter, and you want to leave the client with the impression that the firm is organized and on top of things. So you need to have whatever area you plan on meeting the client in prepared appropriately. Have paper ready for the client in case she needs to draw anything, make a list, or take notes. Have a fresh notepad ready for yourself as well. Have things neat and organized. Neat and organized doesn't particularly bother those of us who work messy, but messy work spaces drive neatniks nuts.

On the subject of first impressions, the *CLA Review* has the 1980s dress-for-success mentality (dark clothes, sensible pumps, small earrings, few rings, etc.). That advice is somewhat dated. Most businesses have gone to at least casual Fridays, and many are casual all the time. What you wear will be dictated by the culture of your locale, your firm, and your clients. Some firms operate in nice jeans and shirts when not in court; others are strictly suit-and-tie sorts of places. There is no one-rule-fits-all. The only caveat is to avoid being "out there"—you don't want to scare clients away with anything that is a little avant garde, like piercings, tattoos, and such, even though they are becoming more accepted. One criminal lawyer I know is an unrepentant left-over hippie with a grey ponytail to his waist and a beard to his collarbones who goes to court in jeans with a jacket over them. I'm quite sure he's scared a few prospective clients away, despite the fact that he's quite good at what he does. The idea is that you want to make the client comfortable with you and, to some extent, you may have to dress according to her expectations. On the other hand, the television version of the well-coiffed, designer-dressed, drop-dead-gorgeous lawyer may have a real-life counterpart, but she is far from the norm, as is her companion, the Italian suit-wearing guy with the perfect smile. Don't even try to compete with that image; just be yourself. Sincerity goes a long way.

The room for your interview should be private and comfortable. The *CLA Review* says it should be "conservatively furnished"; I'm not sure I agree with that. Depending on your definition of *conservative,* it could be very uncomfortable. What is important is that the room is conducive to a good interview—that there are enough comfortable furnishings to relax and talk, but not so much that the interviewee's attention wanders. Have tissues on hand regardless of the gender of the client; I've had big, tough men cry on me in interviews. A pitcher of water and glasses are always a nice touch, and most firms have some sort of refreshments available for clients. Remember to offer them at the beginning of the interview and at any point you think you or the client need a minute to regroup. Instruct the receptionist that you are not to be disturbed during the interview.

Think about how you want to sit. Often the client and anyone with him will look to you to seat them, as if you are the hostess at a very formal party. A table or desk between you and the client is formal and helps if you have an aggressive or overly talkative client over whom you need to assert some control. Sitting next to each other at a table is a cozy arrangement, and will relax the nervous client, although you should make sure you have enough distance so you do not impinge upon her personal space. If the client shows up with a significant other, try to figure out if the other is there as a protector or a supporter. Protectors should be seated between you and the client; supporters on the other side of the client. Other seating arrangements will make them antsy. If you can't tell, just tell them to sit down anywhere as you indicate where you will be sitting. The trick is to arrange seating that will result in the most productive interview.

Manner

Treat the client with good manners and courtesy. Again, this applies to anyone you are interviewing. Greet the client formally when meeting him in the reception area; seeing a lawyer is a relatively formal occasion. Introduce yourself and address the client by the last name. Unless you are in an extremely traditional area, address a woman as "Ms."; aside from public schools, that appears to be the norm. If you are in a very conservative area, use the "Miss/Mrs." form of address. Shake hands with persons of either gender, but don't simply place your hand in theirs like a dead mackerel. Grasp the other person's hand firmly (but not with a death grip), shake once or twice, and release. It's not difficult, but many people seem to mismanage a relatively simple convention and make a poor impression in the bargain.

You now must begin making the client comfortable and building rapport. Begin while escorting the client to the conference room by asking questions that allow the client to talk about himself in a positive way, but stay away from the case until you have the privacy necessary to preserve confidentiality. Allow him to express opinions on matters about which he has expertise, or on which anyone can have a legitimate opinion: sports, movies, music, or other aspects of popular culture. As long as you are courteous and interested, you should have a positive response.

Your manner must be one of respect for the client, regardless of your personal feelings. Clients will tell you things that may make you want to bolt from the room, hit them, or simply shake your head at their stupidity. But none of those reactions can surface in your treatment of them. Your job is to be the professional listener. If you have a strong visceral reaction, then it's possible the jury will, too, and you need to share that reaction with your attorney, but not with the client.

Occasionally it becomes extremely difficult to be respectful of a client. I've found that clenching my teeth and swallowing three times deliberately helps me get my voice under control before I start trying to ask more questions about statements like that when what I really want to do is start yelling at the guy and throw him out of the office. When you feel like you are about to lose control, make up an excuse to leave the meeting room. Take a couple of minutes to walk out of the office and vent in a corner somewhere until you regain professional distance. If you work in an office where this happens frequently, you need to consider a different area of law.

The easiest way to keep that distance is to maintain an attitude of genuine curiosity. If you are always trying to understand why people act the way they do, it becomes a little easier to deal with some of the incredible idiocy you will run into in the law office. The man who hit his daughter did it out of ignorance and frustration—he had never beaten her before. She was 16 and had gotten involved in drugs and was at the end of his rope (sorry—probably a bad choice of words). The preacher at his church did a "spare the rod, spoil the child" spiel on him, so he tried this to try to make her afraid enough of him not to do drugs anymore. He had gone to a psychologist afterwards and regretted the incident.

Whenever you start getting frustrated with your clients' behavior, remember that their shortcomings mean job security for you.

The Don'ts of Interviewing
* Don't "talk down" to a client.
* Don't accuse a client of lying (even when you know he is).
* Don't tell a client he has a bad case.
* Don't tell a client he has a great case.
* Don't express your personal opinions.
* Don't act surprised, shocked, or disgusted by something your client has done (even when you are).
* Don't argue with a client about the case.
* Don't get caught up in legalese—use everyday terms.
* Don't give the client legal advice.

The lawyer gets to sort out the problematic things. Often clients truly believe what they say, despite the fact that all the evidence is against them. And some are liars, some whiners, some disturbed. Your job is to get the information, evaluate it, and present it to the attorney, not to "fix" the client. Remember, your role is not that of psychologist, psychiatrist, or counselor, but of legal paraprofessional. Sometimes your client will need the services of a mental health professional as well as a lawyer, and it is a good idea to collect a list of referrals to send clients to. Occasionally it is difficult not to slip into patronizing a client, particularly if she has difficulty grasping legal concepts. Always remember that there was a time that you didn't know any of this and that, even if it came to you easily, there are some things that are difficult for you that may be a breeze for the client. Each individual has different strengths and weaknesses—keeping that in mind may help you keep from slipping into a superior attitude. If you really do think you are smarter than your clients, or have difficulty dealing with the average client because of his intellect or education, you need to reconsider the area of law in which you are working. That feeling will communicate itself to your clients and be a liability to you and to your firm.

The Do's of Interviewing
* Do explain your role as a paralegal first.
* Do listen carefully.
* Do make the client feel accepted and respected.
* Do act respectful of the client's point of view.
* Do be professional and formal.
* Do be discreet.
* Do expect the client to treat you professionally as well.
* Do take your time to obtain all pertinent information.
* Do take notes and ask the client to repeat exact quotes.

Just as lawyers don't get Paralegal 101 in law school, the rest of the world doesn't get a short course on paralegals in the law office, and most clients will be a little fuzzy on the concept. Not a semester goes by that someone doesn't call my office wanting to hire a paralegal "just to do the paperwork" on a will or divorce. I trot out my sternest tone of voice and explain that my doing so would be a violation of law and unauthorized practice of law, and that we cannot do that. The public perception of what a paralegal can and cannot do is fairly inaccurate, so you need to be prepared with a short disclaimer at the beginning of the interview about not being a lawyer, and you need to clearly define your role in the case.

To make sure that you don't get rushed or pressured and make the client feel unimportant, allot more time than you think you'll need for the interview, and then add a little more. Include time to write up or dictate your interview summary after the interview.

Techniques

There are basically two things to consider when you are thinking about techniques in interviewing: the questions you're going to ask and the listening you're going to do. Good interview techniques apply whether interviewing a plaintiff, a defendant, a fact witness, or an expert. Two different kinds of questions are the open-ended and closed. An **open-ended question** is one like "What did you do today?" which calls for a narrative (story) answer. A **closed question** is one that calls for a short or yes/no answer: "Did you have a good day today?" With both questions, you may intend to elicit something about the person's day, but the first one is inherently designed to do so.

Both types of questions have their place. The open-ended question is often good for getting people started, unless, of course, you have the inarticulate, shy sort sitting across from you. Then it may be like trying to get a balky engine to turn over: you might have to ask several pointed, closed questions until the interviewee finally starts talking on his own. Silence can also be an effective tool, although some closed-mouth clients are quite comfortable with silence. Ask an open-ended question, and when the interviewee gives an incomplete answer, wait. Watch the client and nod encouragingly or sympathetically, whichever is appropriate. Let the silence drag on a bit. Often the pressure to offer more information will build, and the client will. After five minutes, give up. A client who can hold out that long is probably immune to open-ended questions.

The other problem personality you might encounter is the gregarious "motor-mouth" who won't stay on topic. This client might be charming in another context, but time is money in a law office (as in many other places), and you need to keep him on task. Starting with open-ended questions and then reigning in the compulsive talker with pointed questions will help redirect him to the topics in which you're interested. Let's say Patty is one of those kinds of clients.

"Now, Ms. Haus, could you tell me what you were doing before the accident occurred?" you ask. This is an open-ended question, because the question does not limit the number of answers possible.

"Well, first I went to the grocery store, where they had a great sale on detergents. I hate paying so much for cleaners, but you have to have them, you know, and I really like the kind that smell April fresh. And then I went to the dry cleaners to pick up some laundry. I have to go through every piece of laundry they give me because they can't ever get the cleaning done right: either they scorch something or lose a button or miss a stain or something. Or they don't have my whole order. Once I spent three weeks arguing with them over a blue shirt that was my absolute favorite. It had silver buttons that looked like pesos, you know, from Mexico, and it was missing two of them, and they were there when I dropped it off, and—"

"So you were running errands?" you jump in. This is a closed question. The only choices are yes or no. This keeps the client from going farther afield on the favorite blue shirt. You don't really need to know the details, just the general character of what she was doing: nothing unusual, illegal, immoral, or something that would increase her chances of getting in an accident. This kind of question also serves to recapitulate and summarize the client's remarks, showing her that you are paying attention to the gist of what she is saying.

Another way to guide the discussion with either the quiet client or the chatty Cathy is to use the "Could you tell me a little more about X?" approach. This is a formulation of an open-ended question that is nonthreatening and reflects a sincere desire to know rather than containing any particular agenda.

The phrasing of your questions is very important. First, you do not want to ask **leading questions.** A leading question is one that suggests its own answer, such as, "Were you going to the mall?" instead of, "Where were you going?" Some questions are not leading in the most obvious way, but the wording can influence what the witness will say. Human memory can be easily manipulated, even unintentionally. There is a place for colorful language describing your client's case, like *smashed, shattered,* or *devastated,* but that place is not in the initial interview. Consider this comment from John S. Applegate, a professor at Harvard Law School, in his article about ethics in witness preparation (cited in full in Chapter 6):

> Studies of interrogation techniques have uniformly demonstrated the distorting effects of suggestive questioning. Recollection is largely in the control of the pretrial interrogator, who can determine the areas of memory that will be called upon and suggest the contents of that memory. Distortion can occur along two axes: the substantive content of the memory and the certainty with which the memory is held. The second is as dangerous as the first. If the facts are in dispute, their resolution may be much easier if witnesses on one side recognize and communicate the uncertainty of their recollections. Presuppositions or assumptions in questions, even if entirely baseless, are remarkably successful in creating new, false recollections. For example, using "the" instead of "a" in the question "Did you see the train?" can induce entirely false recollections of the train's existence or increase the certainty of related details. Similarly, use of the word "smashed" instead of "hit" can increase the reported speeds of colliding automobiles. A "memory" created in this way can become permanent, and the witness may strongly believe that it is absolutely true, making successful cross-examination far more difficult.

As you can see, Applegate attributes most of the changes in memory to "the pretrial interrogator," which would be you. You can affect both what the witness remembers and how certain she is she remembers it with suggestive questions or with a failure to ask questions to offset those that sound one-sided. For instance, if the witness says, "I think I got to the restaurant at noon," instead of confirming it with, "So, you got to the restaurant at noon. What happened then?" you would ask, "What makes you unsure?" or "Can you work backwards from when you left to figure out when you got there?" Such questions do not assume a fact of which the client isn't certain. Avoiding reinforcement of uncertain opinions with certainty will aid in the prevention of a client becoming dead certain of a fact that turns out to be conclusively wrong. It may also get in the way of getting to the real facts. Researchers believe memory and imagination may be closely linked in the brain, which would account for many a funky dream and the wishful rewrites of memory nostalgia brings. Because of this, the theory goes, there is a possibility that these false memories overlie the real memory, making it difficult to get past the false memory into the true. Scientists researching this theory believe the original memory is still there, but has been distorted by the later overlay that has occurred and that interferes with memory retrieval. So your questioning must not only be suited to the kind of response you want to get—limited or free-flowing—but must also be worded as neutrally toward the facts as possible.

When the interviewer controls the interview using open-ended and closed questions after establishing rapport with the client, it is referred to as a **structured interview.** Psychologists have suggested another approach based on the way we store memory. When an event occurs, we remember it primarily in images, not in the concepts or words we use to describe them. A way to approach this memory retrieval is called **cognitive interviewing.** The strategy for cognitive interviewing is to have the client (or other witness) first recall the context of the event you are interested in: how she was feeling emotionally, what the weather was like, how she was feeling physically, what smells were present, and so on. Then you have the client visualize the scene, telling her to close her eyes if that is helpful. The client is then told to "report everything" she sees. Probing closed questions are used to follow up.

The cognitive interviewing process also can transfer control of the interview process to the witness, something legal folks are probably loathe to do. Otherwise, the two techniques are fairly similar except for the use of context and imaging. Keep these techniques in mind for clients who have a hard time expressing themselves or who are unsure of details. Visual memory may be stronger for them, and taking the time to allow them to put themselves in the right place and time may prove valuable.

The kind of listening you should strive for is **active listening.** Many books on the market discuss active listening, and many Web sites are devoted to the concept. The idea is that rather than being focused on yourself as interviewer, you focus on understanding the speaker, trying to avoid distractions, and seeing things from the speaker's point of view. Not only that, you need to communicate to the speaker this empathic approach. As the speaker finishes expressing ideas, you **recapitulate** those ideas, summarizing what you think he has said back to him. In our work, this gives the client the opportunity to correct any misunderstandings or to elaborate on any information about which we may be fuzzy. You also can stop the speaker at various times and say something like "What I think I hear you saying is . . . ." You must make sure that the client does not believe you are looking for a particular answer or that a particular answer will have a certain outcome. End your summary with, "Please correct me if there's anything I said that isn't right or if there's anything in this about which you are unsure." Another important thing to discern is what the client wants from legal services so that you can assess whether your firm can do what he wants. This is particularly important in areas such as family law. If what the client really wants is *not* to be divorced, well, under no-fault, that's not an option, and he needs to be told.

Many fact situations may turn on location issues. If that is the case, have the client make a diagram with stick figures. It is amazing how much miscommunication is avoided by the simple use of a diagram showing how an intersection is laid out, where a water fountain was, which direction a speaker was facing, or where the window was on the wall. Use of arrows to indicate directions vehicles are moving or people are walking or looking or other relevant directions will help clarify the drawing when reviewed later. In a follow-up interview, it can be effective and relatively inexpensive to take the client to a particular location and videotape his perspective. One case in which this was a particularly effective strategy involved a rear-end highway accident. The driver of the rear vehicle, at this point a defendant in a lawsuit, claimed he was not at fault because he could not see the vehicle stopped in front of him until he had cleared a ridge, at which point there was no time for him to stop even if traveling at a reasonable speed. The frame of mind of the plaintiff and his legal team was, "You're in back; you're responsible." A paralegal went with the defendant for a drive over the accident scene with the defendant and a videocamera. She videotaped the defendant's point of view by holding the videocamera on the top of the dashboard over and to the right of the driver, and as he drove the area, he announced where he was and where the accident occurred. It was clear from the videotape that the defendant could not see anything to warn him of the impending impact until topping the ridge, just as he had claimed. The case settled the week after the plaintiff's attorneys received the tape.

Content

Interview content will vary depending on the needs of the client. Content of the questions will be determined by the causes of action that are implied by the occurrence that has compelled the client to come to the office. However, there are typical items that must be completed. If the client has come for a divorce, then all the assets of the family need to be listed; if for a personal injury case, the damages; if for a will, the estate's assets; if for a contract dispute, the contract; and so forth. Remember not to get so wrapped up in completing your questions that you don't listen to answers and ask additional questions that may be needed because of the answers the client gives. You need to be flexible enough to explore new avenues as they arise; that is part of the point of active listening.

Make sure you obtain all basic personal information about the client, such as her name, address, social security number, date of birth, every phone number she has, the name and number of the emergency contact not living with her (this is to track down a missing client), and the name and number of an alternative contact other than the emergency contact. (This is a fallback in case the emergency contact doesn't lead you to the client.) Also obtain the client's employment information, educational background, and criminal record (ask her to list anything that is not a simple traffic ticket, although most people don't realize that past traffic tickets are technically a criminal record). Ask about any current health issues, any medication she is taking, and her use of alcohol or illegal drugs at any time relevant to the occurrence that is the basis of the lawsuit. This sort of information can be covered in a questionnaire; you will still need to review all the information listed—from the employment information to the end of the form—with the client during the interview.

> What was the name of the officer at your
>   complex?
> What was the last conversation you had
>   with the officer prior to the incident? When?
> When was the last time you had any
>   conflicts with the officer?
> Had he ever made any threats?
> Did you ever complain about him to the
>   apartment manager? If so, when?

In your preparation, you will have created the list of questions you want to ask. You may want to use the computer to make your list, or you may want to do it by hand—it's a personal preference. Refer to your questions to make sure you have covered everything, but if discussion drifts to an area planned in the middle, move to that section and finish it and then return to your preplanned order. The client will be more comfortable if the interview proceeds like an ordinary conversation rather than a question-and-answer session, so you will need to be flexible about the order in which you obtain information.

If you need a moment to check something, ask the client if you can take a short break and let her know where the bathrooms are. If you are in your office rather than a meeting room, take her to the lobby area so that there is no question of any breach of confidentiality of any other client's information. (Bored clients who are waiting can become very interested in the contents of the papers on your desk.) Make sure someone checks about getting her a drink, water if nothing else. Usually what you'll want to check is a question about some area of law that the client has raised that is outside the guidelines for accepting cases or for which you need more information in order to interview her appropriately. The best course of action is to find your supervising attorney and see if he wants to handle it or if he wants to give you some guidelines for proceeding.

The release or releases that need to be explained and signed are routine paperwork. In most cases, you will need the client to consent to a **release** of information form for the law firm to receive confidential records directly from the pertinent record keeper. Depending on the type of case, the release may be addressed to any or all of the following agents.

* the client's employer's personnel or human resources department to obtain employment records
* the mortgage company the client has dealt with in order to obtain all records dealing with a real estate transaction
* the client's bank or other financial institution in order to obtain all records dealing with the client's financial records
* the Internal Revenue Service or the Social Security Administration to obtain information about the client's tax records or social security contributions (you'll have to use the forms required by these entitites)
* a former attorney to release files dealing with the current or related litigation or transactions

This list is not meant to be exhaustive; it is merely a sample.

Caveat   Some states have very specific rules about what needs to be in releases. Make sure you have the right forms. Federal law governing health information privacy, commonly referred to as **HIPAA** (pronounced like *hippo* but ending in an *uh* sound), also affects release forms, and is making some health care providers extremely nervous about what form to use to the point that they will only accept their own.

To: _____
    _____
    _____

AUTHORIZATION FOR RELEASE OF INFORMATION

RE: Patty Haus

I, Patty Haus, Social Security Number 111-22-3333, have authorized Lisa St. Joan to obtain and copy any and all information, documents, statements, recordings, and/or reports that you may have in your possession regarding me, including all confidential information, and also including, but not limited to, letters written to or from me, statements taken from me or any other information that you may have concerning me. I further authorize any person that Lisa St. Joan may designate to obtain such items from you.

You are further authorized to disclose any oral reports and/or narratives to Lisa St. Joan or her representative.

Please treat this information as confidential and do not furnish it in any form other than directed in this authorization without written authorization from me. Thank you in advance for your cooperation.

Date _____

_____
Patty Haus

MEDICAL AUTHORIZATION RELEASE FORM

To: Dr. Lotta Payne

I, Patty Haus, SSN 111-22-3333, DOB 02/03/74, hereby authorize Dr. Lotta Payne, who treated me for the time period from August 12, 1999 until the present, to release any and all records in your custody, including office records, medical reports, charts, x-rays, and bills concerning my physical or mental condition to Lisa St. Joan.

The purpose for this release of information is to assist me and my attorney in anticipated or pending litigation.

A copy of this authorization has the same force and effect as an original. This authority will remain in effect for a period of 90 days from the date hereon or until I revoke same in writing.

I understand that I have the right to revoke this authorization by providing you with a written request to revoke this authorization. I further understand that revocation will not be effective to the extent that Dr. Lotta Payne has taken action in reliance upon this authorization prior to receipt of the revocation.

I understand that information that is disclosed or used under this authorization may be disclosed by Lisa St. Joan and no longer protected by the privacy provisions of the Health Insurance Portability and Accountability Act of 1996, 45 C.F.R. Section 164.508(c).

_____
Patty Haus

_____
Date

If you have been instructed by the attorney to accept cases under certain guidelines, and you have determined that the case meets these guidelines, you will probably have the client sign a contract. This is a potential violation of the National Association of Legal Assistants, Inc.'s Code of Ethics and Professional Responsibility Canon 3(B), which states, "A legal assistant must not . . . establish attorney-client relationships . . . [or] set fees." The *CLA Review Manual* goes on to opine that even if there are guidelines, they are usually not concrete, and that the lawyer must be the one to set the fees in any given case. I've been unable to find case law one way or the other on this issue (which, as anyone familiar with legal research knows, doesn't necessarily mean that it isn't out there somewhere), and there's nothing in the Model Rules for Lawyers that indicates that these responsibilities cannot be delegated, so this seems to be simply a policy position on NALA's part. On the other hand, there is a crucial distinction between "setting fees" and merely quoting those which the lawyer has set. However, if you are a member of NALA, you should not, as you are bound by NALA's Code.

You will need to explain the contract to clients, preferably the way your supervising attorney tells you to. To explain something, you need to understand how it works. Remember, if you are working on the plaintiff's side of a personal injury case and will be using a contingency fee contract, you need to see what the damages are, and fairly soon in order to determine whether the case is worth pursuing. If this is an hourly billing case, you'll be looking for the client to come up with a retainer. Regardless, there will be a fee agreement of some kind entered into. Although only contingency fee contracts must be in writing, as a matter of practice, the vast majority of attorneys put all of their contracts in writing. If the client decides to retain the services of the attorney, you will need to go over the contract with the client.

Virtually all attorney contracts have a clause that allows them to fire their clients under rather broad circumstances. Why? Although clients may fire an attorney at any time for any reason, lawyers do not have that option. We are bound by various versions of ABA Model Rule 1.16:

[A] lawyer may withdraw from representing a client if:

1. withdrawal can be accomplished without material adverse effect on the interests of the client;
2. the client persists in a course of action involving the lawyer's services that the lawyer reasonably believes is criminal or fraudulent;
3. the client has used the lawyer's services to perpetrate a crime or fraud;
4. the client insists upon taking action that the lawyer considers repugnant or with which the lawyer has a fundamental disagreement;
5. the client fails substantially to fulfill an obligation to the lawyer regarding the lawyer's services and has been given reasonable warning that the lawyer will withdraw unless the obligation is fulfilled;
6. the representation will result in an unreasonable financial burden on the lawyer or has been rendered unreasonably difficult by the client; or
7. other good cause for withdrawal exists.

Model Code Prof'l Cond. R. 1.16.

Additionally, once suit is filed, the court must grant permission for **withdrawal.** On top of all that, the withdrawing attorney is in a bind. If he gets stuck with the client, he will not want to tell opposing counsel why he wants out; however, he needs to tell why so he can get out. Thus, a contract with many reasons and a catchall phrase like "other good cause" is very useful; the withdrawing attorney can say "the client is in breach of contract" without specifying whether it is a noncooperation breach, a lying breach, a fraud breach, a moving-without-forwarding-address breach, or whatnot. Unless reason exists for the court to view the motion to withdraw as an excuse to delay (or the attorney has managed to really annoy the judge), the motion is usually granted. However, the closer a case is to trial, the greater chance there is that the motion will not be granted. Moreover, in some jurisdictions mere nonpayment of fees is insufficient for withdrawal.

Contingency Fee Contracts

In order for a contingency fee to be enforceable, it must be in writing in most states and usually must conform to the state version of ABA Model Rule of Professional Conduct 1.5(c).

ATTORNEY CONTINGENCY FEE CONTRACT

THIS AGREEMENT is made on January 16, 2004, in Big City, Confusion between Patty Haus ("Client"), and the Law Office of Lisa St. Joan, of Big City, Texas, ("Attorney").

The Client retains and employs the Attorney to negotiate, settle, compromise, sue for and recover all damages and compensation to which may arise out of the incident that occurred on or about [date] at 2000 Washington Avenue, Big City, State of Confusion, when the Client was arrested after accidentally colliding with the sign in front of the Vista Libre Apartments.

In consideration of services by the Attorney in connection with this matter, the Client agrees to pay to Attorney the following amounts on the total settlements, monies, judgments or other consideration which have or may be paid on this legal matter:

> 33 and 1/3 percent prior to the filing of a lawsuit,
>
> 40 percent if collected after said filing of a lawsuit,
>
> and 45 percent if an appeal is required to a higher court.

The Client conveys and assigns to the Attorney an interest to the Client's claim and cause of action, and in any action, compromise, settlement, judgment, payment of services, profits or recovery to the extent of the Attorney's fees and expenses.

The Attorney is hereby authorized to enter into any and all settlement negotiations on behalf of those whom Attorney represents as the Attorney deems appropriate. This includes, but is not limited to, the Attorney's prerogative to pursue cash or structured payment settlement negotiations.

Client grants the Attorney a power of attorney to handle negotiations and settlement discussions regarding the obtaining of possession of any and all monies or other things of value subject of the matter due to the Client under this claim as fully as the Client could do so in person.

No settlement of any nature shall be made for any of the claims of the Client without the approval of the Client, nor shall the Client obtain any settlement without the approval of the Attorney.

It is understood and agreed that **the Attorney cannot warrant or guarantee the outcome of the case and the Attorney has not represented to the Client that the Client will recover all or any of the funds so desired.** The Client has also been informed that obtaining a judgment does not guarantee that the opposing party will be able to satisfy the judgment. _____ initial

All reasonable expenses incurred by the Attorney in the handling of this project shall be deducted from the gross settlement proceeds at the time the case is settled or resolved. _____ initial

The expenses contemplated above, include but are not limited to **any and all out of pocket expenses incurred in connection with this case, including but not limited to the following expenses:** filing fees, court costs, certified copies of documents, pleadings, orders etc., transcripts, depositions, duplication costs, postage, office supplies, photographs, trial exhibits, long distance phone and fax calls, appraisal fees, consultants, expert witnesses and other fees associated with preparation and trial testimony, investigation fees, delivery charges, overnight mail/parcel services, parking, toll road and mileage expenses, out of town expenses including travel expense, air fare, hotels, meals, and any other expense incurred in connection with the matter. _____ initial

The Client shall keep the Attorney advised of the Client's whereabouts at all times, and provide the Attorney with any changes of address, phone number or business during the time period which Attorney's services are required, and shall comply with all reasonable requests of the Attorney in connection with the case. _____ initial

The Attorney may, at his option, withdraw from the case and cease to represent the Client **for any reason.** _____ initial

The Attorney may, at the sole discretion and expense of the Attorney, associate any other attorneys in the representation of the aforesaid claims of the Client. _____ initial

The rights set forth in this agreement are subject to the professional responsibility requirements which regulate attorneys.

TAX DISCLOSURE AND ACKNOWLEDGMENT:

THE CLIENT IS ADVISED TO OBTAIN INDEPENDENT AND COMPETENT TAX ADVICE REGARDING THESE LEGAL MATTERS SINCE LEGAL TRANSACTIONS CAN GIVE RISE TO TAX CONSEQUENCES.

THE UNDERSIGNED LAW OFFICE AND ATTORNEY HAVE NOT AGREED TO RENDER ANY TAX ADVICE AND ARE NOT RESPONSIBLE FOR ANY ADVICE REGARDING TAX MATTERS OR PREPARATION OF TAX RETURNS, OR OTHER FILINGS, INCLUDING, BUT NOT LIMITED TO, STATE AND FEDERAL INHERITANCE TAX AND INCOME TAX RETURNS.

FURTHERMORE, THE CLIENT SHOULD OBTAIN PROFESSIONAL HELP REGARDING THE VALUATION AND LOCATION OF ALL ASSETS WHICH MAY BE THE SUBJECT OF A LEGAL MATTER INCLUDING BUT NOT LIMITED TO PENSIONS, EMPLOYMENT BENEFIT AND PROFIT SHARING RIGHTS THAT MAY BE CONTROLLED BY ANY OTHER PARTY TO THE LEGAL MATTER.

I certify and acknowledge that I have had the opportunity to read this Agreement. I further state that I have voluntarily entered into this Agreement fully aware of its terms and conditions.

Signed on this _____ day of _____, 2005.

_____
Patty Haus

Signed on this _____ day of _____, 2005.

Law Office of Lisa St. Joan
BY: _____

Lisa St. Joan
100 Years War Lane, Suite 1412
Big City, Confusion 99999
(888) 555-0987
(888) 555-0986 (telefax)
State of Confusion Bar No.
0987676

The prohibited areas under (d) are criminal law and family law. Contracts where payment is contingent upon recovery of certain items of family property are not universally prohibited, although fairly universally frowned upon. It's an area that will draw scrutiny from the court, at any rate, if there isn't a flat prohibition in your state. In some states, once the contingency fee contract is signed, it automatically creates a lien on the recovery. This interpretation of the contract is to prevent a client from letting the attorney do all the work until just before settlement and then firing him so that the client can collect the entire settlement without having to pay attorney's fees. In other states, the contract must create the lien by its terms. In order to avoid paying the attorney after dismissing him, the client must get a release of lien.

[A] lawyer may withdraw from representing a client if:

1. withdrawal can be accomplished without material adverse effect on the interests of the client;
2. the client persists in a course of action involving the lawyer's services that the lawyer reasonably believes is criminal or fraudulent;
3. the client has used the lawyer's services to perpetrate a crime or fraud;
4. the client insists upon taking action that the lawyer considers repugnant or with which the lawyer has a fundamental disagreement;
5. the client fails substantially to fulfill an obligation to the lawyer regarding the lawyer's services and has been given reasonable warning that the lawyer will withdraw unless the obligation is fulfilled;

6. the representation will result in an unreasonable financial burden on the lawyer or has been rendered unreasonably difficult by the client; or

7. other good cause for withdrawal exists.

Model Code Prof'l Cond. R. 1.5(c).

In other states, the legal theory used to protect the attorney for the time spent on a contingency fee file when a client fires him near or after settlement or verdict is *quantum meruit,* an equitable theory used in contract law that allows one who provides a service to recover the value of services when the failure to do so would result in unjust enrichment of the other party.

If there is no written contract (which, you'll note, is preferred, not required), the court will set the client's fee pursuant to the guidelines set forth in the ethical rules, which are usually variations on the ABA's Model Rule of Professional Conduct 1.5, which states, in part:

a. A lawyer shall not make an agreement for, charge, or collect an unreasonable fee or an unreasonable amount for expenses. The factors to be considered in determining the reasonableness of a fee include the following:

1. the time and labor required, the novelty and difficulty of the questions involved, and the skill requisite to perform the legal service properly;

2. the likelihood, if apparent to the client, that the acceptance of the particular employment will preclude other employment by the lawyer;

3. the fee customarily charged in the locality for similar legal services;

4. the amount involved and the results obtained;

5. the time limitations imposed by the client or by the circumstances;

6. the nature and length of the professional relationship with the client;

7. the experience, reputation, and ability of the lawyer or lawyers performing the services; and

8. whether the fee is fixed or contingent.

b. The scope of the representation and the basis or rate of the fee and expenses for which the client will be responsible shall be communicated to the client, preferably in writing, before or within a reasonable time after commencing the representation, except when the lawyer will charge a regularly represented client on the same basis or rate. Any changes in the basis or rate of the fee or expenses shall also be communicated to the client.

Model Code Prof'l Cond. R. 1.5(a),(b).

A contingency fee contract (which must be in writing, remember) is simple in concept: attorneys fees are a percentage of the client's recovery. However, it is common for the attorney to also advance expenses: filing fees, court costs, postage, copying, expert expenses, and other miscellaneous expenses. These expenses can add up to some rather large bills.

Take, for example, a client who enters into a contingency fee contract where the attorney will take 1/3 of the gross recovery (the amount before expenses are deducted) and who settles for $12,000.

Settlement	12,000
Attorney's fees	<4,000>
	8,000

Now suppose the client had $3,000 in expenses fronted by the attorney.

Settlement	12,000
Attorney's fees	<4,000>
	8,000
Expenses	<3,000>
	5,000

The attorney will retain $7,000 from the settlement and the client $5,000. The client now believes the attorney came out with more than he did, even though only $4,000 of it was for the work the attorney did. The $3,000 was to pay back the "loan" the attorney had given the client—interest free—to bring the lawsuit, and for which there would be no repayment had there been no recovery. The $4,000 was the amount the attorney loaned, and was less than the $5,000 the attorney cleared. Although clients may understand this when they walk out the door, they often forget by the time they get to their car. All they remember is that the attorney got a check for $7,000 and theirs was only $5,000. As a result, many plaintiffs' attorneys will reduce their fees to avoid this appearance of greed, even though they are taking a risk every time they "loan" their clients money for trial.

Hourly Billing and Retainers

In other cases, such as family law, the customary contract is an hourly contract with a **retainer.** Retainers are fees clients pay as a deposit to keep or "retain" the lawyer's services. There are three basic types of retainer. They vary in terms of whether the retainer is refundable or not and whether it applies toward future legal services. The first type is a nonrefundable, nonapplicable retainer. This means that the client simply pays the retainer as a fee to the lawyer to get started; the retainer does not pay for any work the lawyer does. The second type is a nonrefundable, applicable retainer. In this situation, the client will not get back any portion of the retainer. It will be credited toward legal work done, and the client will not be billed for any attorney's fees until enough work has been done to equal the retainer fee. The third type of retainer, the refundable retainer, allows a refund of any unearned retainer. As you might guess, it's a fairly rare type of billing arrangement.

Imagine that Frank Cheatham is an attorney charging a $5000 retainer who also charges $100 per hour. He has worked 9 hours on a case and is finished. The following would be the final billing under each type of contract.

Nonrefundable, nonapplicable	Nonrefundable, applicable	Refundable, applicable
Client owes $900	Client owes nothing; attorney owes nothing	Attorney owes Client $4100.

As you might guess, nonrefundable, applicable contracts appear to be the most common.

RETAINER CONTRACT

Patty Haus ("Client") hereby employs the Law Office of Lisa St. Joan ("Attorney") to represent Client in all matters regarding the incident that occurred on or about [date] at 2000 Washington Avenue, Big City, Confusion, when the Client was arrested after accidentally colliding with the sign in front of the Vista Libre Apartments.

By execution of this agreement, Client also appoints Attorney as her agent and lawful attorney-in-fact in connection with this matter.

The rates charged by the Attorney are as follows:

Lisa St. Joan	$150.00
Paralegals	$ 75.00

These rates will be billed in minimum increments of 1/10 of an hour. These fees are collectively referred to as attorney's fees.

Responsibility to provide legal services will be accepted and work will begin when Attorney receives a nonrefundable deposit of $2500 ("retainer fee") to be credited against attorney's fees.

In addition to legal fees, Client also agrees to pay all reasonable expenses incurred by Attorney in this matter, including but not limited to, postage, copies, long distance telephone calls, travel and filing fees, etc.

Attorney is authorized to employ other persons or firms deemed necessary for the proper handling of this matter, at Client's expense, but shall not obligate Client for any expense in excess of $1500 without Client's prior approval.

Client shall be billed upon the first day of each month. Unpaid legal fees and expenses, if not paid within ten (10) days from the statement's date, shall accrue interest at the rate of 10 percent per annum until paid.

Should Attorney find it necessary to resort to litigation in order to collect the attorney's fees and expenses owed pursuant to this Agreement, the Client shall be liable for reasonable attorney's fees, costs, and expenses thereby incurred. Venue for any action shall be in Big City, Dux County, Confusion.

Attorney has the right to cease legal work and withdraw from representing the Client and keep the retainer and/or all funds received for legal services and expenses if Client does not make payments as requested by Attorney. Client has the right to dismiss the Attorney at any time, but any sums owing the Attorney are still an outstanding legal debt.

Any sums collected on behalf of the Client, when received by Attorney, shall be first credited against Client's obligation to Attorney.

No promise or guarantee has been made as to the outcome of this matter. The Client acknowledges that the course of legal matters is uncertain and that any estimate of overall cost may be substantially affected by future events and that it is not possible to give an accurate accounting of the overall cost at this time and that any estimates given are in good faith based on the information given by the Client to the Attorney at this time.
_____initial

The Client acknowledges that the Attorney may engage other attorneys to work on my case or the Attorney may refer my case to another law firm and receive a referral fee from the other attorney. _____initial

TAX DISCLOSURE AND ACKNOWLEDGMENT:

THE CLIENT IS ADVISED TO OBTAIN INDEPENDENT AND COMPETENT TAX ADVICE REGARDING THESE LEGAL MATTERS SINCE LEGAL TRANSACTIONS CAN GIVE RISE TO TAX CONSEQUENCES.

THE UNDERSIGNED LAW FIRM AND ATTORNEY HAVE NOT AGREED TO RENDER ANY TAX ADVICE AND ARE NOT RESPONSIBLE FOR ANY ADVICE REGARDING TAX MATTERS OR PREPARATION OF TAX RETURNS, OR OTHER FILINGS, INCLUDING, BUT NOT LIMITED TO, STATE AND FEDERAL INHERITANCE TAX AND INCOME TAX RETURNS.

FURTHERMORE, THE CLIENT SHOULD OBTAIN PROFESSIONAL HELP REGARDING THE VALUATION AND LOCATION OF ALL ASSETS WHICH MAY BE THE SUBJECT OF A LEGAL MATTER INCLUDING BUT NOT LIMITED TO PENSIONS, EMPLOYMENT BENEFIT AND PROFIT SHARING RIGHTS THAT MAY BE CONTROLLED BY ANY OTHER PARTY TO THE LEGAL MATTER.

Client has read this Agreement and agrees to each of the terms and conditions stated in it.

SIGNED AND ACCEPTED this _____ day of _____, 2004.

_____
Patty Haus

However, some jurisdictions do not allow nonrefundable retainers, reasoning that the client will be less likely to fire an attorney, even though the client has a right to, if there is a nonrefundable retainer, and that there should not be any barrier to the client disposing of an attorney with whom she is not pleased.

Wrapping It Up

At the end of the initial interview, make sure the client knows the next step. Often clients are left at the end of this first meeting without a clue about what happens next; make sure your client knows. Some law offices have prepared new-client handouts to help clients understand the life of a case and the roles of the office personnel—not a bad idea. You need to make sure the client understands that although you believe her, you still must produce proof for the jury, and that means finding additional information to confirm her story. If there are people she has mentioned as witnesses whom she has contact with, have her give them your name and tell them that you will be in contact with them. Assure her that corroboration is normal and necessary. If there are documents you need from her, reiterate the list before she leaves, and make sure that she has written it down or write it down for her. Calendar a date a week or so ahead to make sure the information has been received (this is sometimes called a "tickler," as it will tickle your memory); if not, then call or write and remind her of the things that need to be sent.

If the client has not yet met the lawyer, and you have either already signed a contract or want to, you need to make an appointment for the client before the client leaves. If the client's case is not one the firm you work for will take, you may either refer the client to another attorney's office or send him on his way. To make sure there is no misunderstanding (and to create a paper trail), you should always send a letter confirming the outcome of the meeting, whether positive or negative. **Letters of nonrepresentation** are very important. You should always prepare a letter stating that the firm is declining representation, thank the client for his time, tell him the nonrepresentation is not a comment on the evidence, and tell him to look for a new lawyer before the statute of limitations runs. If any new potential defendants have arisen, you'll need to run another conflicts check on these new defendants.

January 16, 200-

Ms. Patty Haus
3434 Broken Bow Ave.
Big City, CF 99999

RE: Legal representation of Patty Haus, regarding on or about [date] at 2000 Washington Avenue, Big City, Confusion.

Dear Ms. Haus:

I have had the opportunity to review your case, and I regret to inform you that I will not be able to represent you in this matter. I will take no further action on your claim.

Please understand that my actions are in no way a comment on the factual or legal validity of your claim or as to the likelihood of a recovery or nonrecovery in your claim. IF YOU WISH TO PURSUE THIS MATTER FURTHER, **IMMEDIATELY OBTAIN LEGAL REPRESENTATION.** Your rights are limited in time, and may be **cut off if appropriate actions are not taken by [date SOL runs].**

To find an attorney to represent you, you may contact any lawyer of your choice, or try the Bar Association's Lawyer Referral Service, which will refer you to competent attorneys who may be able to take your case.

Thank you for the opportunity to discuss this case with you.

Sincerely yours,

Lisa St. Joan

jgm:LSJ

Whether the interview results in acceptance of the case, rescheduling for the attorney to meet the client, or a rejection of the case, the paralegal should escort the client back out of the office. This helps the client avoid the embarrassment of getting lost and protects the office from accidental breaches of confidentiality. It's also just another practice of courtesy.

You are not done once the client leaves the office. You will now need to start thinking carefully about the file. First you'll want to prepare a memo to the file or to your supervising attorney regarding your interview of the client. This memo will detail the information you got from the client as well as her physical appearance, her age, race, gender, and information relevant to her likely effect on a jury. Do this immediately after the interview; after awhile, the clients all start running together. Make the memo as detailed and factual as possible: "Three visible tattoos on the upper left shoulder may bother more conservative jurors"; "Client stuttered on words beginning with 'st' "; "Client has a deep, gravelly voice that makes him sound intimidating even when he does not intend to" and so on. You do not have to share jurors' biases to recognize them and you do clients a disservice if you do not. For example, if you represent a gay couple as plaintiffs in a very conservative town, you need to note that because it may affect the jurors' view of both the plaintiffs' credibility and damages. You must be aware of the shortcomings of potential juries and what factors may trigger them to judge a client negatively. Often the paralegal is the one to explain some of the "fixable" items to a client ("No, Mimi, you cannot wear that much makeup to court if you want to have a chance to win") to prepare the client for court appearances. Remember, though, to keep your memo as factually based as possible—and written in such a way that it would not embarrass you or your attorney if read to a jury if, for some unforeseen reason, the client decided to sue the firm later.

Memo

To: Lisa St. Joan

From: Jennifer Edwards

Date: Today

RE: *Patty Haus v. John Justice and Vista Libre Apartments*

I met with the client Patty Haus today. Ms. Haus is a 32-year-old white female of average height and medium build. She has brown eyes, is deeply tanned, and has brassy red hair that appears to be artificial. She is slightly overweight, but not obese. She has eight piercings on her left ear and six on her right and a large rose tattoo on her upper right arm with the bloom on the shoulder and the stem and leaves curling around her bicep to just above her elbow. She was attired in black jeans, a neon orange form-fitting tank top and cowboy boots when I met with her. She is a heavy smoker, and has the beginnings of the lines around her mouth and hollows in her cheek, as well as nicotine stains on her fingers which are indicative of smoking and might indicate that practice to an alert observer.

On the date of the incident in question, Ms. Haus had been at the house of a friend of hers, Roxanne Spur. She and Ms. Spur had not been doing anything in particular, just "watching TV and talking" on that Friday night. She thinks they might have consumed "a couple of beers." Ms. Haus denies having had any medications that day. She states that alcohol does not make her combatative. She was using Geronimo "Jerry" Smoker's 1990 Ford 150 pickup truck for transportation that night because her car was in the shop. Jerry was off fishing that weekend with a friend. She left Ms. Spur's home at approximately 10:15 P.M.—she said it was halfway through the evening news, before sports came on. Ms. Spur lives at the Empire Apartments, only a few blocks from her so she is sure that she was home at the Vista Libre Apartments no later than 10:30 P.M.

When she came home, she was coasting down the hill to turn right into the apartment complex and had reduced speed substantially. However, as she applied her brakes going into the turn, the brakes did not respond, and she began to fishtail. When she tried to straighten out, she overcompensated, driving directly into the large brick sign for the Vista Libre apartment complex in the traffic island. She was not injured, although she says she "was in shock."

She states that John Justice, the off-duty Big City Police Officer who lives at the Vista Libre complex and takes care of their security, came to the scene in plainclothes before she was able to get out of the pick-up. She states that he did not ask her whether she was injured, but simply began shouting obscenities at her: "You f_ _ _ _ _ _ bitch! You did that on purpose! You and that f_ _ _ _ _ _ asshole boyfriend of yours! I'll get you!" and that he started banging on the pick-up door and yelling "Get out! You aren't hurt, you lazy bitch!" She said that she was then afraid to get out and that she didn't get out until he walked away. Once he left the pick-up and walked back to his apartment, she left the vehicle and went to her own apartment and locked herself in. She called a wrecker to haul off the pick-up.

She said that about an hour later, two uniformed police officers knocked on her door with Officer Justice, who was still in plainclothes. They asked her about the accident, and she told them the story. She said that the two officers walked off a little ways with Justice, and that they appeared to be arguing. After about five minutes, they came back and arrested her for criminal mischief. She was able to get out on a PR bond, but she had to go down to the station and get booked. She has a prior police record for public intoxication and domestic violence. She states that the domestic violence was a "revenge thing" because she had first "called it on him." "Him" was her ex-live-in at the time, Ford Fontana, whereabouts unknown. That incident was over 10 years ago.

She says that the shop where they had the pick-up towed to says the brakes failed. They didn't explain why. She states she does not know why Justice was convinced she'd done it on purpose, although she says he's had run-ins with her live-in, Mr. Smoker before over being "too loud or too rowdy," but that Justice "overreacts."

If Ms. Haus could be persuaded to modify her appearance somewhat, she would make an average witness. As is, she would probably make a below-average witness.

After preparing and sending your memo, you should determine your preliminary **causes of action** and the applicable **statutes of limitation.** It is amazing how often clients manage to come in the week before the statute of limitations runs. In Patty's case you already had a list; now, after the interview, you have a date. You can then find the shortest statute of limitations among the various possible causes of action and use that as your applicable limitations deadline. That is the latest date upon which you may file suit. You may want to calendar the deadline at least two weeks before that. This will give you a last window of opportunity to settle prior to filing suit. It also gives you some time to nag your attorney to get her to prepare and/or sign the appropriate documents. Be extremely mindful of the statute of limitations; failure to meet it is, in most years, the single most frequent reason for malpractice cases.

With the preliminary causes of action in hand, you can also begin to make your investigation plan, discussed in Chapter 1. Begin making lists of potential witnesses. Witnesses may be divided into two subgroups: **fact witnesses,** those who are somehow involved in this particular incident, and **expert witnesses,** those who can, through special education or training, help explain what happened. The first people you'll want to contact are the fact witnesses so you can get their story while it is still relatively fresh in their minds. You'll also want to calendar any other relevant items, such as notice deadlines if there's a governmental entity involved.

INITIAL WITNESS LIST

Witness Name	Role	Contact Info	Areas to Investigate
Roxanne Spur	Friend client was with before accident	(800) 555-9393	Client's mental and physical state, any knowledge of incidents between client and Justice
Jerry Smoker	Live-in, owner of vehicle	unknown	Last repairs to vehicle and brakes issues, relationship with Justice, incidents involving him and client that were part of eviction
Jim Tweedledee	Arresting officer	(800) 555-0911	Circumstances surrounding arrest
Tim Tweedledum	Arresting officer	(800) 555-0911	Circumstances surrounding arrest
Missy Loess	Apartment manager	(800) 555-4663	Complaints about client, Smoker, or Justice
Names Unknown	Neighbors of client	Vista Libre Apts.	Complaints about client, Smoker, Justice, or apartment complex; accident and arrest of client
John Justice	Apt. security guard	(800) 555-0911	Complaints about client, Smoker, Justice, or apartment complex; accident and arrest of client

CLIENT CONTACT

One of the professional ethical requirements is to keep the client informed. This is probably the second largest area of client complaint in litigation. The legal team knows that there are periods of intense activity followed by waiting periods; the client doesn't always realize that and feels forgotten. For ethical and business-building reasons, it is good practice to make sure that the client regularly receives information about the case status. When writing a letter on the case, send a copy to the client, often referred to cc:-ing the client ("cc:" comes from carbon copy back before copy machines). When you file a document, send the client a copy. Make sure you've got the case on a diary so that you can periodically send the client an updated status report even when nothing much is going on, simply along the lines of "No new offers from defendant, and we don't want to bid against ourselves" or "Nothing to do until the proximity of trial begins to pressure the opposing party."

Return calls from clients promptly; it's their case and they need to know the news, good or bad. I've had clients who have had other lawyers before me thank me for being straight with them early on rather than putting them off to avoid giving them bad news—they appreciate a coherent, prompt answer. If the client mentions a significant event—a major anniversary, a child's graduation—in a conversation, make note of it and mention it in the next conversation. This technique builds trust and rapport, as well as having the additional benefit of creating a greater likelihood of referrals or repeat business. However, making a special call to the client about a significant event might be perceived as overkill.

Sometimes you will have the obsessive-compulsive client who calls six times a day on her contingency fee case. This is problematic, because she has no disincentive for calling, as she is not being billed for each phone call. If the number of calls is excessive and unreasonable for the case, they will prevent you from doing work that needs to be done. What you will first need to do is get the attorney on your side. Over a week or two, document the times the client calls and how long each call lasts. Take the information to the attorney and describe how work was disrupted or time wasted. He may have some ideas about how to handle the problem. However, it is always better to go to the boss with a solution as well as with the problem, so be prepared to suggest possible ways of dealing with the client.

The attorney may want to bring the issue to the client's attention, taking the approach that he is concerned about her stress levels over the case, and recommending a mental health care professional to help her deal with her anxiety. As paralegal, you should continue to keep track of the client's calls. If the mental health care recommendation does not take care of the problem, then the three of you can meet and review the time spent on the phone with the client and negotiate what you believe is a reasonable amount of client contact per week. Draft an agreement and have it signed by the client: such an agreement might state that any calls in excess of the negotiated amount of time shall not be returned except in extraordinary circumstances which she must articulate on voice mail and which must be proven to be true or she will owe attorneys fees at some agreed-upon rate. If the signed agreement doesn't work, then you'll have to look at the value of the case and see if it's worth keeping the client.

BACKGROUND CHECKS

Not surprisingly, clients may have ulterior motives when they seek legal advice. Some may have heard all the press about the "legal lottery" and mistakenly believe that it's easy to get some quick cash from an unwitting corporate defendant if they simply brazen out a good story. Some are victim personas who are always on the short end of the stick. Others are in need of psychiatric help. Some are just ordinary people trying to make themselves look a little better. Regardless of the motivation, it is incumbent upon the legal staff to make sure that they find as many landmines as quickly as possible prior to filing suit.

One major area of attack is a prior criminal record, so a client's prior record should always be checked. In the initial intake, the county of residence is known, so county records should be checked for possible criminal convictions, even if the client denies any. In most states, conviction information, which is public (except for juvenile records), is organized by county, so you must check at each county courthouse separately. Much of this information is now becoming available online or through dial-up modem services in metropolitan counties; you usually still have to go to the actual courthouse in rural locales. If there are no records of conviction on a client, fine. If there are some and the client denied having any, it may be time to drop the client. Firing the client is, of course, the attorney's call; you just need to bring all the relevant facts to her attention.

In tort cases, you also need to see if the client has filed prior tort claims against other defendants. Again, this will be listed by county or district courts. If there are no previous filings, no problem. If there are prior filings, you may or may not have a problem. If the client omitted them, it could be a problem; it will depend on the age, severity, and number of prior filings. Those same factors will also determine how much of a problem it will be for the case, as well as how close a relationship the injuries in the prior case(s) have to the current problem. If there are numerous cases, it would be easy to make the client out to be a professional plaintiff, and that is the kiss of death to even a good case: you've now got the little boy who cried wolf as a client.

You'll also need to obtain prior medical records to see if this is a preexisting condition. Although a plaintiff can recover for an aggravation of a preexisting condition, if your client did not tell you about a preexisting condition and represented that this accident was the first time whatever body part was injured, you again have a problem with whether the client is telling you the truth. When clients are not truthful with their own legal team, it often foretells trouble down the line. Tell the lawyer; let her decide whether she thinks the client has told a lie or just made a mistake and whether she wants to deal with the client under those circumstances.

FINDING POTENTIAL DEFENDANTS

Now that you've got the case, how do you find whom to sue? Lots of resources are at hand. First, if you've got a corporate name, you'll check your state's **secretary of state.** That office handles all corporate filings. If the corporation is incorporated in your state, they have to pay their franchise tax there. If they are incorporated from another state, they have to file paperwork indicating that they are incorporated in another state with the state in which they are doing business. The secretary of state keeps records of all that, and requires that each of these corporations has an agent for service of process, the person you need to contact about any pending lawsuits. Most state secretaries of state are now online; the National Association of Secretaries of State maintains a Web site with a map of the capitals and their Web sites at **http://www.nass.org/UnitedStates_file/ United_States.htm**. Charitable entities, once immune from suit, can now be sued in most states, and usually can be found listed at the secretaries of state as well. As a tactical matter, though, the firm usually thinks very carefully before suing the Poor Sisters of Charitable Works—it's not good politics with the jury unless the Poor Sisters have been very, very bad.

Even if a business is not incorporated, if it is doing business under a business name, it is ordinarily required to file an **assumed name certificate.** The place for filing these is usually the county; check your state statutes to be sure. The proper county section will keep records in which you can look up the business name and find the owner's name and address. Of course, not every business owner follows this requirement of filing the assumed name certificate, so it may take some additional searching to track down the name of the owner. Check for advertisements or business news for clues as to who owns the business, go to the place of business and look for business cards, or call and ask the employees. Just tell them you need to send some paperwork to the owner and you needed the name and address. You'll be surprised how often they'll give it to you, particularly in small businesses. When you sue this individual, it will be under his name doing business as the assumed name: Joe Lee **d.b.a.** (doing business as) Lee's Lies.

If you have an address of a property, you can find the owner of the property by checking the deed records or the tax records. Sometimes deed records are only filed under legal descriptions, but usually tax records are under both legal description and street address. Again, this is public information. If you go to the county or district tax assessor, you can look up the records under the address and find the owner of record of the property. If the owner is leasing the property to someone else and that is the person you need to be suing rather than the owner, owners tend to be fairly quick about giving you the information you need.

What about suing an individual? If there is no insurance available or if the occurrence is not the kind covered by insurance, you will need to do an asset check unless the case is something like family law, where you are not seeking money damages. There is no point in suing someone for money damages in order to simply obtain a worthless piece of paper. If your state does not allow **garnishment** of wages for a money judgment, you will have to find out what assets are **exempted** from **attachment** to satisfy a judgment (usually listed in the state property code), figure out what kind of assets might be left over, and then determine if the defendant has any such assets. To find those assets, you would again check the county records, where any real estate filings would be, as well as filings under the Uniform Commercial Code (UCC) Chapter Nine provisions for **purchase money security interest** (PMSI) filings. Again, you can also check newspapers and various commercial sources. Lexis-Nexis ran an ad touting its service because someone ran a search on Nexis and found a defendant had a string of racehorses—not something you'd pick up in an ordinary search, but something that came up through running the man's name in the newspapers. They were attachable and the firm was able to collect for its client.

Of course, if you are involved in a family law or other status matter, collectibility is not an issue. You may need to engage in **skip trace** methods to find your defendant. "Skip trace" just refers to the fact that your person has "skipped" and now you have to trace her. This search can be done by a private investigator or in-house investigation. Attorneys and their staff have some rules that keep them from engaging in some of the tactics that private investigators sometimes use, but many of the same strategies can be taken care of in-house, and will be discussed later. It simply depends on what is more cost-effective for the firm.

Suing the government is another option, but a tricky one. The presumption is that governmental entities cannot be sued; you must find an exception. Usually the exception is found under a **tort claims act** of some sort or a theory that the governmental entity is acting in a **proprietary function;** that is, that the city (usually) is doing something that could be done just as well by a private corporation that is not necessarily governmental in nature. Suits against governmental entities often have short statutes of limitation or quick notice requirements (like six months), very limited grounds for recovery, and only a limited amount of money that may be recovered. If you checked out a § 1983 action, you'll have seen that there are specific requirements to be met before you may hold a governmental entity liable.

Just because you've found whom you'd sue doesn't mean you'll file suit immediately. If the statute of limitations runs within the next month, you probably will. However, if not, you will probably do some investigation first and then send a demand letter instead. Why? It is far less time-consuming for you and less expensive for the defendant, and there are no public records of the claim. It is therefore an attractive time to settle if the parties can agree upon the value of the suit. For purposes of this text, we will continue as though the suit had to go directly on to litigation, but in the real world, if you work for a plaintiff's firm, particularly in personal injury, you will often skip to the informal investigation steps, prepare a **demand letter,** and then settle the case without ever dealing with an opposing attorney, only with an adjuster from the defendant's insurance company.

[Today's Date]

Ronald Trump
Vista Libre Apartments, Inc.
3333 Jefferson Street, Suite 612
Big City, Confusion

      RE: Name: *Patty Haus v. John Justice and Vista Libre Apartments*
          Date of Accident: [incident date]

Dear Mr. Trump:

I represent Patty Haus in a claim for injuries and damages received by Ms. Haus due to the actions of your employee on [incident date].

    John Justice, an employee of Vista Libre Apartments, maliciously and intentionally caused Ms. Haus to be prosecuted for a crime she did not commit. Further, he slandered Ms. Haus by falsely accusing her of crimes to the apartment manager of Vista Libre Apartments, Missy Loess. Further, Mr. Justice deprived my client of her civil rights in his treatment of her after an accident.

    Ms. Haus suffered damages to her mental health which required therapy. We anticipate that Ms. Haus's treatment will continue in the future. As a direct result of the accident on [incident date], Patti Haus has incurred expenses totaling $750 to date. She has also lost her home, her reputation, and has a loss of earning capacity.

    In an effort to settle this claim without further legal action, we hereby make demand upon you for tender of $35,000 in settlement of this case. I ask that you give consideration to this offer.

    I look forward to hearing from you very soon. Should you have any further questions or require anything else to assist you in your evaluation of this claim, please do not hesitate to contact me.

                          Sincerely yours,

                          Lisa St. Joan

LSJ/jgm

cc: Patty Haus

Once you have determined your defendant or defendants, you are ready to prepare the original complaint for your attorney's signature. Once that is finalized, you will prepare it for the appropriate form of service, make the appropriate number of copies, and file the suit along with the appropriate filing fee. You then must arrange for the suit to be served to the defendant or defendants. Once the suit is served, calendar the deadline for the defendant to answer. At that point, the ball is in the defendant's court.

CHAPTER SUMMARY

When representing the plaintiff, you must evaluate what the plaintiff can reasonably receive from a jury if she were to go to trial. The plaintiff is one of the most important witnesses for or against her own case, so you must listen carefully to her and decide what kind of witness she would make as well as how you could prove the case to a jury. No matter how convinced the client is of the justice of her cause, unless there is some evidence in addition to her testimony and some remedy the court can render, there is no point to going to court, and it is your firm's duty to point that out. You must find out as much as you can from the client by interviewing her effectively and using techniques such as open-ended and closed questions, active listening, recapitulation, and diagrams. If a decision is made to reject the client, a letter of nonrepresentation should be sent. If a decision is made to accept the client, a contract should be signed as well as releases to obtain the necessary information. The interviewer needs to then make a summary of the initial interview and prepare an initial investigation plan. The firm should do at least a preliminary background check for prior criminal cases against the client as well as prior civil cases filed by the plaintiff. If there is enough time before the statute of limitations runs, the firm should informally investigate the claim and make a settlement demand prior to filing suit. If no settlement can be reached, or if it is too close to limitations, then suit will be filed.

FOR FURTHER READING

Clark D. Cunningham, *Evaluating Effective Lawyer-Client Communication: An International Project Moving from Research to Reform*, 67 Fordham L. Rev. 1959 (1999).

Andrew J. DuBrin, *Human Relations: Interpersonal, Job-Oriented Skills* (7th ed., 2000).

Stephen Ellmann, *Symposium Case Studies in Legal Ethics: Truth and Consequences*, 69 Fordham L. Rev. 895 (2000).

Michelle S. Jacobs, *People from the Footnotes: The Missing Element in Client-Centered Counseling*, 27 Golden Gate U.L. Rev. 345 (1997).

Raven Lidman, *The Power of Narrative: Listening to the Initial Client Interview*, 22 Seattle Univ. L. R. 17 (1998).

Amina Memon, Linsey Wark, Angela Holley, Ray Bull, & Gunter Koehnken, *Eyewitness Performance in Cognitive and Structured Interviews*, 5 Memory 639 (1997).

Linda F. Smith, *Interviewing Clients: A Linguistic Comparison of the "Traditional" Interview and the "Client-Centered" Interview*, 1 Clinical L. Rev. 541 (1995).

Douglas Stone, Bruce Patton, & Sheila Heen, *Difficult Conversations: How to Discuss What Matters Most* (1991).

CHAPTER REVIEW

KEY TERMS

active listening	cognitive interviewing	exempt
assumed name certificate	confirmation letter	expert witness
attachment	conflict check	fact witnesses
billable hour system	conflict of interest (COI)	garnishment
burden of proof	contingency fee contract	HIPAA
cause of action	d.b.a.	intake forms
Chinese wall	demand letter	leading questions
closed question	ethical wall	letter of nonrepresentation

open-ended question

proprietary function

purchase money security interest
    (PMSI)

recapitulate

release

retainer

secretary of state

skip trace

statute of limitations

structured interview

tort claims act

unauthorized practice of
    law (UPL)

withdrawal

FILL IN THE BLANKS

1. It is always a good idea to send a(n) _____ for any appointment or agreement to avoid misunderstandings, and if one occurs, to show diligence on your part.

2. To avoid charges of _____, you must always introduce yourself as a paralegal, make sure you do not give legal advice, enter into a contract with a client only under the guidelines set forth by your supervising attorney, and make sure you sign all correspondence designating yourself as a paralegal.

3. An interview based on questions and answers only is a(n) _____ interview.

4. Property that you can keep regardless of your debts is considered _____ and listed by state statute.

5. _____ are used to get basic information that will be needed in every case.

6. A(n) _____, in the context of the type you have signed during an initial interview, is one for gathering information, and can be used to obtain medical or employment information.

7. The time period you have from the time a cause of action accrues until you must file suit or lose the right to do so under the enacted law is called the _____.

8. Once a client is in litigation and the attorney or firm representing him wishes to quit, rather than "quitting" it is called a(n) _____.

9. When suing an individual doing business under an assumed name, you use the shorthand designation _____.

10. The portion of money that is a down payment for the attorney's services is called a(n) _____.

11. A question that requires only a yes-or-no response is a(n) _____.

12. A question that requires a narrative answer is a(n) _____.

13. Witnesses who can testify as to what occurred are _____.

14. Witnesses who can testify as to why things happened and give opinions are _____.

15. When a municipality is doing something that a private corporation might do rather than a traditional governmental function, it is exercising a(n) _____.

16. A search for a witness or defendant who has disappeared is called a(n) _____.

17. When selling an expensive piece of merchandise on credit, the seller may use the merchandise as collateral if it files for a(n) _____.

18. Asking "What do you think went wrong to cause the accident?" is an example of the use of a(n) _____.

19. The federal act governing health information privacy, _____, affects medical release language.

20. A(n) _____ is philosophically justified by the fact that it enables injured parties who would not otherwise be able to afford an attorney and it induces the attorney to take the risk of not recovering any fees.

21. The process of looking through current and past clients to make sure that representing a potential new client would not violate any duty to the existing ones is called a(n) _____.

22. The legal requirement to produce the requisite weight of believable evidence for the cause of action or affirmative defense is the _____.

23. A set of facts that constitutes a pattern upon which a court can grant a remedy is a(n) _____.

24. In order to make sure that you are clear about what the client has said, and to let the client know you are listening, you _____, or sum up, what the client has been saying.

25. When you focus on the speaker, give him feedback, recapitulate what he says, and evince a caring attitude, it is called _____.

26. When you have a judgment against someone who has not paid voluntarily, you will need to have some property of hers legally designated as yours to fulfill the debt, which is called a(n) _____.

27. Family law matters should always be conducted under a fee agreement that provides for _____.

28. _____ is a form of debt recovery that allows the person owed money to get a share of the debtor's paycheck.

29. If after a meeting with a potential client the attorney decides not to take the case, you should always send a(n) _____.

30. The work generated by an attorney that reflects her reasoning, strategy, thoughts, and plans is privileged under _____.

31. The generic term for legislation allowing personal injury claims against governmental entities is _____.

32. Before filing suit, if there is time, it is better to send a(n) _____ to try to settle the case without the additional cost of litigation.

33. Most states require individuals conducting business in a name other than their own to file a(n) _____.

34. If you ask your client a(n) _____, you will have suggested the answer you want and be less likely to get the truth.

35. The executive officer of state government responsible for maintaining records about corporations and other business entities required to file with the state is the _____.

36. The Latin word for warning, _____, is frequently used in legal contexts.

WEB WORK

1. Has your state adopted the ABA Model Rules of Professional Conduct? Find out at http://www.abanet.org/cpr/mrpc/alpha_states.html.

   If so, when? If not, is it using the old ABA Model Code of Professional Responsibility?

2. Some of the concepts of active listening are more applicable to the legal field than others, and active listening has been adapted to a variety of contexts. Read the article found at http://crs.uvm.edu/gopher/nerl/personal/comm/e.html and see what comments or directives you think are appropriate or inappropriate for the legal context. Why? Using a search engine, like Google (www.google.com), run a search for "active listening" and see the various contexts to which the concept has been applied. Then try adding "law" as a search term. You'll see that active listening is often used as a quasi-counseling technique; it does work to build trust, as it often convinces the speaker that you understand and care about him or her.

3. HIPAA compliance is something that anyone working with health information needs to be aware of, and our friends in the federal government have been nice enough to give us a Web site with basic information: http://www.hhs.gov/ocr/hipaa/. Check it out and make a list of at least five things you must do to protect the integrity of health information.

4. Using http://www.nass.org/UnitedStates_file/United_States.htm, find your state's secretary of state. What information can you access online? What is free and what requires fee payment?

5. "Active listening" is a concept used in education, counseling, business, leadership studies, and so on and is applicable to almost any field's mode of communication. Run a search for "active listening" and see how many hits the search engine comes up with. Browse through some of the sites and look for suggestions that you think are helpful. Make a list of at least five.

WORKING THE BRAIN

1. You may hear some experienced lawyers say, "Some cases just have to be tried." What circumstances do you think are most likely to end up classified this way?

2. You have an ethical responsibility to keep your client's communications confidential. What if your client admits to child abuse, which is not the subject of the litigation? Would any child abuse reporting laws in your state supersede the attorney-client privilege?

3. What if the client can afford to pay by the hour, but the attorney wants a contingency fee contract? Is that ethical? What would the parameters be?

4. Under what is known as the English Rule, the loser must always pay the attorney fees of the winner, something that only happens under certain situations in American law, and usually only at the discretion of the court. There are those who advocate the adoption of the English Rule in the United States. What would be the advantages and disadvantages of such a rule? Whom would it tend to benefit?

5. What sort of questions do you think would work best with a shy person? A compulsive talker? What strategy would you use if the potential client were condescending to you because "you're not the lawyer, after all"?

PUTTING IT TO WORK

1. Using the fact situation assigned for you, prepare for and interview another student role-playing the client after writing a confirmation letter for the interview to take place at the next class meeting. Write the memo of the interview to the file and make a recommendation to the supervising attorney about whether you believe the case should be accepted or not, explaining why. Draft an initial discovery action plan and a demand letter to the defendant.

2. Using the file you prepared in Chapter 1, file all the materials you have generated in the assigned case. If you do not have appropriate manila folders to file them in, make some.

3. Assume you are not going to accept the case of the plaintiff you interviewed. Draft a letter of nonrepresentation.

THE CLIENT: DEFENDANT'S PERSPECTIVE

> "I don't know as I want a lawyer to tell me what I cannot do. I hire him to tell me how to do what I want to do."
>
> *J.P. Morgan (1925)*

INTRODUCTION

The defendant's firm always begins with an immediate deadline: the **answer**. The very first thing a paralegal must do is figure out when the answer is due and calendar it, as failure to answer on time may result in a default judgment against the defendant. The case screening is usually done by phone because answer deadlines are far shorter than statutes of limitations: three weeks, give or take a week or so, depending on the jurisdiction. The phone call will generally consist of the questions "When were you served?" and "What are you being sued for?" on the part of the firm. The answer to the first question will tell you if the potential client has called too late; the second will tell you if it's the sort of case your firm handles. The next part of the call is telling the client the retainer charged for this type of case. Because there is no recovery to invest in, defense cases are virtually always charged on an hourly basis with a retainer. Most firms have an established fee schedule depending on the type of case if this is a called-in, one-time individual client. (If you are dealing with a client who potentially will have repeat business, the attorney will be dealing with the client from the beginning, and it will be evident from the beginning that the caller is a "somebody.") If the caller is satisfied with the retainer and the firm is satisfied with the type of case, the defendant has representation. Taking a new client is a transaction most common in a family law case.

When the firm is defending an established client, the defense may not even see its client before filing an answer. How's that? With an established client, the attorney-client relationship is already in existence; depending on the **pleading requirements** of the jurisdiction, the firm may be able to file an answer just from the receipt of the complaint (called a *petition* in some jurisdictions). It all depends on the type of case and the relationship with the client.

Clients of the defense firm tend to be a little different in mind-set than those of the plaintiff firms. There are two general groups: the first is comprised of unsophisticated auto insurance, family law, dogbite, other homeowner claims, and occasional small claims clients; and the second is comprised of sophisticated professional and business clients. The one thing all clients have in common is they think they're being cheated in some way. It is rare to have a client come in who says, "I'm sorry, I'm responsible, and the other guy is completely justified in the amount he is asking for." Usually clients don't think they did anything wrong (even the drunk driver who blew a .23) and think the plaintiff is asking for a ridiculous amount of money (even the quadriplegic asking for $150,000 when his future medicals are over one million).

The difference between the two types of client is that unsophisticated clients, while more suspicious in some ways because they don't really understand what is going on, are more willing to go along with what is advised because they really don't have any viable alternatives. On the other hand, it can take an inordinate amount of time to explain what it is you need them to do or get for you to get your job done, and can be quite frustrating. However, if you gain their trust and they sense you really are trying to help them the best you can, you will get their best effort as well.

Sophisticated clients, on the other hand, will usually neither be as bad nor as good as the unsophisticated ones. They tend to understand the rules of the game, but because of that understanding are immune to some of the usual appeals to help. They may understand real deadlines, but they often treat their own deadlines as more important than yours—unless they're paying the legal fees. The dreaded client in this group is the demanding **CEO**. He will think he has bought your firm's time exclusively, and that you should be able to work miracles in defiance of all legal timetables. He will call up and expect your boss to be available at his every whim, and then blast you personally for your boss's inexcusable absence. If you have corporate clients, find out if you have one of this species among them, and see if your boss will allow you to fax his itinerary to the CEO's executive assistant whenever you have a hot case going with the dreaded man. That may circumvent at least a little bit of his hostility. And then get flame retardant sealant for the earpiece of your phone!

Another lovely thing that may happen in defense firms is that some clients that you are obliged to take may hand you cases where the answer is already overdue. A **default judgment** may have been entered. At this point, a careful study has to be made to see if the judgment is final and whether you can still make a **Motion for New Trial**. If the deadline for a Motion for New Trial has passed (usually something along the lines of 30 days or so), you should check your state's rules for **process of service** and check the **return of service** against the **pleadings**. Because of the constitutional requirements of notice, the rules for service are generally fairly strict and unusually hypertechnical. If the name and address on the return and the pleadings do not match, and there is nothing to indicate that the rules for process of service were not followed to account for the mismatch, there was no service, there is no **personal jurisdiction** for the judgment, and the judgment is a nullity. You would be amazed at how often this turns out to be the case; I haven't found any statistics on it, but I'm sure the rate is high.

ETHICAL ISSUES

The thorniest issues on the defense side arise in the context of **insurance defense**. An insurance defense firm is one that is paid by insurance companies to defend its **insureds**. For example, if a person is responsible for an automobile accident, his insurance company pays for an attorney to represent him in any lawsuit resulting from the accident. These insured defendants may be individuals, professionals, or businesses. As part of the insurance contract, the **insurer** has the right to decide when to settle and to control the litigation in exchange for the duty to pay for the defense of the insured. In large corporations or corporations that have numerous small claims (referred to, along with insurers, as **repeat players** because of their frequent visits to the courthouse), the corporate defendant may be self-insured for a rather large amount and have much more to say in the litigation, even if the insurance company technically has this sort of control. In insurance defense cases, the firm will usually receive an investigation file along with the complaint, giving them a head start on the case.

Dual Representation

What makes this tricky is the question of "Who is the client?" In some jurisdictions, the answer to that question is based on the general principle that you represent a particular interest unless all parties agree— even if some other party is paying the bill. You make certain disclosures to the insurance company due to the contractual relationship between the insurer and the insured, but it has nothing to do with to whom the

PRIVATE PROCESS

"The State of Texas" NO. 283590

WILSON PENNYPACKER AND NEGEM LLP
Plaintiff
vs.

RYAN GRANT ANDERSON
Defendant

Citation Directed to: RYAN GRANT ANDERSON
108 ANTELOPE
SAN ANTONIO, TX 78232-2102

IN THE COUNTY COURT AT

LAW NO. 3

BEXAR COUNTY, TEXAS

NOTICE

"You have been sued. You may employ an attorney. If you or your attorney do not file a written answer with the clerk who issued this citation by 10:00 a.m. on the Monday next following the expiration of twenty days after you were served this citation and petition, a default judgment may be taken against you." Said petition was filed on the 3RD day of June , 2003 .
ISSUED UNDER MY HAND AND SEAL OF SAID COURT ON THIS 5TH DAY OF June A.D., 2003 .

GERRY RICKHOFF
County Clerk of Bexar County, Texas
Bexar County Courthouse
San Antonio, Texas 78205

KIM M PETTIT
Attorney/PLAINTIFF
address 411 HEIMER RD
SAN ANTONIO, TX 78232-4854

By: _Elliott Jointer_ Deputy
ELLIOTT D. JOINTER

OFFICER'S RETURN

Came to hand 6 day of June , A.D. 2003 , at 11:00 o'clock A .M.
and executed the 11 day of June , A.D 2003 , in Bexr
at 9:10 o'clock A.M. by delivering to Ryan Grant Anderson
in person a true copy of this citation together with the accompanying copy of plaintiff's
petition. Served at 745 E McLeberry , San Antonio Tx
+ Request For Disclosure, Admission, Production, Interrogatories, Disclose
I traveled miles in the execution of this citation. fees: Serving citation
$ 44 Mileage Total $
IS 0519072
_____ County, Texas

By _____

The State of Texas

NON - PEACE OFFICER VERIFICATION

VERIFICATION OF RETURN (IF NOT SERVED BY PEACE OFFICER)

SWORN TO this 11 day of June 2003 ,

German Marty
NOTARY PUBLIC, STATE OF TEXAS

283590
(DKC001)

GERMAINE MARTINEZ
Notary Public, State of Texas
My Commission expires
January 14, 2007

RETURN TO COURT

duty is owed. This way of looking at things makes the attorney and his staff owe all ethical duties to the defendant insured by the liability policy. The other major school of thought is that the insurance defense firm engages in **dual representation**, representing the interests of both insurer and insured, but may not touch any issue in which there is a conflict between the two. However, the attorney has a duty to notify both sides of potential conflicts. In many jurisdictions, the legal answer to "Who is the client?" is not all that clear. Any way you go, there's always a potential for problems.

From the business point of view, the client is the insurance company. It's the insurance company reps who are wined and dined, the insurance company who sends you repeat business, the insurance company for whom you do seminars. So a firm that has a substantial amount of business in insurance defense work has a vested interest in keeping its insurance company contacts happy. However, it also has a vested interest in keeping one's bar license and not getting hit with a big legal malpractice claim.

Most insurance defense firms that get into trouble do so by failing to keep insured/defendant clients informed. They don't generally have trouble with sending status reports to the insurance company, however. Failure to communicate often gets attorneys in trouble, and is an area that can potentially blow up for insurance defense attorneys.

The reason insurance defense attorneys do not get in trouble for failure to communicate with clients as often as their peers is because the insured usually has no damages as a result of their failure to do so. If the insurance company settles, the case is over and the insured doesn't have to pay anything. If the insurance company fails to settle and the case goes to court, the jury will either fine an amount for more or less than the limits of the policy. If less than the **policy limits**, the insurance company will pay, and the insured doesn't have to pay anything; if more than the policy limits, the amount the insurance company pays generally depends on whether a good faith demand was made within the limits of the policy before trial (check your jurisdiction to verify). If a demand was made and rejected by the insurance company, it will have to pay the entire amount of the jury verdict. If no offer was made, then the insured would possibly have basis for a suit only if he could prove that being aware of something not disclosed to him by the attorney would have resulted in a different outcome. You find out the policy limits from the **Declarations Page**, often referred to as the Dec Sheet, of the policy.

The group that usually balks most at not being told anything about settlement offers is professionals: doctors, accountants, engineers, and others. They feel that settling reflects on their competence, and are most likely to resist settlement because they want their "good names cleared." Unfortunately, the professionals most often sued are those with the poorest people skills, so they are the ones the jury is most likely to dislike and therefore most likely (if they find that the facts are fairly evenly weighted) to find against (a process called "**resolving doubt against**"). Although the following case does not represent the usual finding—that the physician has no legal gripe about the settlement of the case—it does illustrate the problem very nicely, and still appears to be the law of Illinois.

Dual representation arises in other contexts as well. Similar to the insurance context is the **indemnification agreement**. An indemnification agreement is one in which one party agrees to be legally responsible for another's actions in a certain context, such as a police department for any actions of a police officer while she is on duty. Like the insurance context, the situation is muddied by the existence of a contract and how it governs the relationship of the two parties.

Less complicated situations arise without contracts. In family law, it arises in the plaintiff's office when the couple wanting a "friendly" divorce comes in. An attorney may do so with the written consent of both parties, but it is rare that a divorce stays friendly, and as soon as there is a conflict, the attorney must not represent either client. It's far easier to say up front that you'll only represent one regardless of where the money is coming from. It is also a good idea to have the spouses sign a waiver stating that the firm has informed them that only one is represented and that the other one has the right (and has been advised) to seek other counsel.

Concerns related to dual representation also emerge in cases involving businesses, when the firm may represent a corporation and its agents. Again, as long as there is no conflict between them, there is no problem. But when interests diverge, life gets interesting. Your role will mostly be to alert the attorney if you notice a conflict and to ask the attorney what sort of **diary** he wants each client on for status reports. In this context, a diary is not a notebook of innermost thoughts; it is a system for reviewing files. "Putting a file on a diary" means to schedule a file for review every specified number of days or weeks. At those times, the file will be pulled from the shelf and given to the lawyer or paralegal to review. Usually all members of the legal team diary the file in order to make sure that nothing is missed and that the client is contacted regularly for status reports.

Renewal of Number

No. sample

**TEXAS PERSONAL AUTO POLICY
DECLARATIONS**

Named Insured and Mailing Address (No., Street, Apt., Town or City, County, State, Zip Code)

Policy Period: From: To:

  12:01 A.M., Standard Time at the address of the named insured as stated herein.

The Auto(s) or Trailer(s) described in this policy is principally garaged at the above address unless otherwise stated:

(No., Street, Apt., Town or City, County, State, Zip Code)

Coverage is provided where a premium and a limit of liability are shown for the coverage.

COVERAGES		LIMITS OF LIABILITY		PREMIUMS		
				Auto 1	Auto 2	Auto 3
A LIABILITY COVERAGE	Bodily Injury Liability	$ each person $ each accident		$	$	$
	Property Damage Liability	$ each accident		$	$	$
	Combined Bodily Injury & Property Damage Liability	$ each accident		$	$	$
B MEDICAL PAYMENTS COVERAGE		$ each person		$	$	$
B PERSONAL INJURY PROTECTION COVERAGE		$ each person		$	$	$
C UNINSURED/ UNDERINSURED MOTORISTS ($250 DEDUCTIBLE APPLICABLE TO P.D. LIABILITY)	Bodily Injury Liability	$ each person $ each accident		$	$	$
	Property Damage Liability	$ each accident		$	$	$
	Combined Bodily Injury & Property Damage Liability	$ each accident		$	$	$
D COVERAGE FOR DAMAGE TO YOUR AUTO	Other than Collision	Auto 1 Auto 2 Auto 3 Actual Cash Value unless otherwise stated $ $ $ Less Deductible $ $ $		$	$	$
	Collision	Auto 1 Auto 2 Auto 3 Actual Cash Value unless otherwise stated $ $ $ Less Deductible $ $ $		$	$	$
3 TOWING AND LABOR COST		$ Per Disablement		$	$	$
Form numbers for endorsements attached to policy at date of issue				$	$	$
			Sub Total Premium	$		
			Total Premium	$		

Description of auto or trailer.				F.O.B. List Price or	
Year of Model	Trade Name	Body Type/Model	Identification Number	Delivered Price at Factory	Class & Rating Symbol
A U T O 1 2 3					

A U T O	Any loss under Part D is payable as interest may appear to the named insured and (include name and address)
1 2 3	

We agree to make available to you an installment payment plan as described in Rule 14 of the Texas Automobile Rules and Rating Manual, except when an installment payment plan is prohibited by other rule or by statute.

A sample dec sheet.

Rogers v. Robson, Masters, Ryan, Brumund and Belom, 407 N.E.2d 47 (Ill. 1980).

Plaintiff, James D. Rogers, M.D. . . . alleged that he had been named as a party defendant in an action alleging that a postoperative wound infection was due to [his] negligence . . . ; that discovery depositions taken by defendants, the attorneys employed by plaintiff's insurance company, showed that there was no negligence on the part of plaintiff; that despite that fact and contrary to plaintiff's wishes and instructions conveyed to the defendants, a settlement was negotiated in the malpractice action. The complaint alleged damages suffered by plaintiff.

Defendants' motion for summary judgment shows that at the time of the alleged negligent acts out of which the malpractice action arose plaintiff was insured by Employer's Fire Insurance Company, and that defendants negotiated a settlement with the plaintiff in the malpractice action and, upon execution of a covenant not to sue, paid $1,250 and effected dismissal of the action as to plaintiff. The policy under which plaintiff was insured provided that the written consent of a former insured was not required before the insurer made any settlement on any claim or suit "even if such claim or suit was made, preferred or alleged while such former insured was an insured under this policy."

In an affidavit filed in opposition to the motion for summary judgment plaintiff stated that during the pendency of the malpractice action he repeatedly informed one of the partners in the defendant law firm that he would not consent to the settlement of the action, that he was assured that the action would be defended, and that at no time was he advised that defendants intended to settle the malpractice suit . . . .

. . . Although defendants were employed by the insurer, plaintiff, as well as the insurer, was their client (*Thornton v. Paul* [1978], 74 Ill. 2d 132; *Maryland Casualty Co. v Peppers* [1976], 64 Ill. 2d 187) and was entitled to a full disclosure of the intent to settle the litigation without his consent and contrary to his express instructions. Defendants' duty to make such disclosure stemmed from their attorney-client relationship with plaintiff and was not affected by the extent of the insurer's authority to settle without plaintiff's consent. We need not and therefore do not consider the question whether plaintiff's insurance carrier was authorized to settle the malpractice action without his consent.

Further, since no disclosure was made and plaintiff was not given the opportunity to elect what course to pursue, we need not speculate what recourse, if any, plaintiff had under the terms of the insurance policy. Nor need we reach the question whether plaintiff can prove damages which are the proximate result of the breach of the duty to make a full disclosure of the conflict between defendants' two clients. It cannot be determined from this record what damages, if any, plaintiff can prove. We decide only that this record does not preclude the possibility that some damage to plaintiff may have flowed from defendants' alleged failure to make the requisite disclosure.

EVIDENTIARY ISSUES

The same evidentiary issues apply for plaintiffs and defendants. In addition to those issues covered in Chapters 1 and 2, one must keep in mind two separate types of evidence in terms of its use: discoverable versus admissible. **Discoverable evidence** is any evidence that may lead to admissible evidence. **Admissible evidence** is that evidence that the judge will allow the jury to hear or see. Although the term *discoverable* really refers to evidence found through the formal channels of discovery, it is also a good guideline for thinking about informal investigation: What can I look for that will lead me to something I can show the jury? If it won't get you there, it isn't worth the time, because even if all you spend is time, it still costs the firm money.

Rule 403

The governing principle of admissibility is **relevancy**. How relevant is the evidence when weighed against other considerations? Thirty-eight jurisdictions have adopted the Uniform Rules of Evidence, similar to the Federal Rules of Evidence, which were themselves a compilation of common law practices of evidence, and the pertinent rules state the general rule of admissibility of relevant evidence as follows:

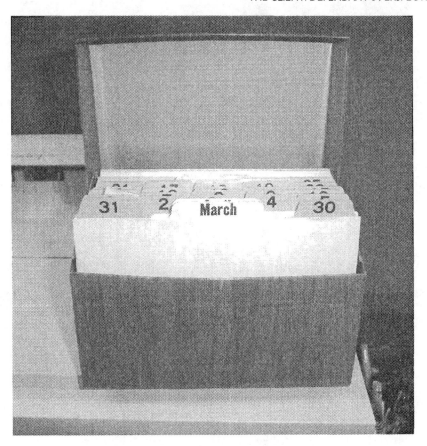

A typical
diary system.

"Relevant evidence" means evidence having any tendency to make the existence of any fact that is of consequence to the determination of the action more probable or less probable than it would be without the evidence.

All relevant evidence is admissible, except as otherwise provided by the Constitution of the United States, by Act of Congress, by these rules, or by other rules prescribed by the Supreme Court pursuant to statutory authority. Evidence which is not relevant is not admissible.

Fed. R. Evid. 401, 402.

If you stopped here, you might be tempted to believe that any relevant information gets to the jury. But fear not, gentle reader: it is not so, or we legal folk would not be nearly so valuable and juries might actually have all the facts before them. Rule 403 is the provision battles are fought over, and trials often turn on the judge's decision on how to apply this one:

Although relevant, evidence may be excluded if its probative value is substantially outweighed by the danger of unfair prejudice, confusion of the issues, or misleading the jury, or by considerations of undue delay, waste of time, or needless presentation of cumulative evidence.

Fed. R. Evid. 403.

Even if relevant, evidence may be kept out if its persuasive (**probative**) value is overwhelmed by (1) danger of **unfair prejudice**; (2) confusion of the issues; (3) misleading the jury; (4) undue delay; (5) waste of time; or (6) cumulative evidence. The last three are easy to explain: the judge can keep relevant evidence out when she's ready to move along. So once you've got plenty of evidence on one aspect of a case, it's time for you to move along in your investigation.

The first reason, unfair prejudice, needs to be examined carefully. *Prejudice,* in this context, has no connotations of racial prejudice, associations the word has acquired in this country in our time. Instead, the term means any idea or inclination that prevents a person from being objective. Of course, the whole idea of advocacy is to incline the jury to your way of thinking, to make the jury see matters from your side, so simple prejudice is not enough. Just because evidence makes the jury believe you is no reason for the judge to exclude it. The key is that the evidence be "unfairly" prejudicial, that it persuade jurors to side with one party to a degree not really warranted by the evidence. A classic example is gory photographs. The introduction of images of body parts on the side of the road has a tendency to make a jury really want someone to be responsible, and make them less worried about being wrong. Such photographs can constitute "unfair" prejudice, and are often excluded by judges. On the other hand, these evidentiary rulings are discretionary, meaning that the judge is given wide latitude to make a decision either way, and unless the decision is clearly wrong or the judge ignored all law, it usually will not be reversed on appeal, as Ms. Steger found out.

Steger v. General Electric Co., 318 F.3d 1066 (11th Cir. 2003).

Elizabeth Steger . . . claimed that, during the course of her employment, GE . . . violated the Equal Pay Act, 29 U.S.C. § 206(d), by paying her differently than her male colleagues. On appeal, she argues that GE failed to meet its burden of persuasion on her age and gender claims. . . . Because we find . . . that the district court did not err in its challenged rulings . . . we AFFIRM . . .

GE moved to preclude Steger from referencing or introducing evidence "of sexist comments or discrimination." . . . GE cited Steger's deposition testimony that she believed that Player's "alleged comment about her having the old southern charm" was sexist . . . and argued that such evidence was irrelevant because she was not "pursuing a claim of sexual discrimination," . . . and that Player's comment was remote in time, unrelated to the termination of her employment, and unfairly prejudicial. Steger responded that Player's comments were relevant to the Equal Pay Act claim because they showed that "gender was something . . . on Mr. Player's mind." . . . When the district court inquired about Player's role in setting Steger's pay, and GE responded that, although "there was no decision-making process" when the employees were first hired for CASO, Player subsequently made recommendations about the pay of the employees that he supervised. . . . However, GE argued that the comments were irrelevant and unfairly prejudicial because they did not relate to Steger's pay. Steger countered that Player's comment to her that she had "a husband to take care of [her]" related to her pay . . . . The district court granted GE's motion finding that Player's "thoughts or biases" were not relevant because he was not a decision maker involved in setting Steger's pay when she was initially employed in CASO . . .

Steger argues that the district court erred in precluding Player's sexist comments because they were admissible as evidence of pretext. She contends that her proffer of testimony addressed Player's comment to Steger that she did not need a raise because she had a husband who would care for her. To rebut an employer's legitimate nondiscriminatory reasons for its adverse action, the employee must produce evidence which directly establishes discrimination or which permits the jury to reasonably disbelieve the employer's proffered reason . . . . Any believable evidence which demonstrates a genuine issue of fact regarding the truth of the employer's explanation may sustain the employee's burden of proof . . . . A decision maker's discriminatory comment which may not qualify as direct evidence of discrimination may constitute circumstantial evidence which could assist a jury in disbelieving the employer's proffered reasons for the adverse action. . . . Although a decision maker's statement regarding an employee's "family man" status can serve as evidence of discrimination . . . "statements by non-decision makers, or statements by decision makers unrelated to the decisional process" at issue will not satisfy the employee's burden . . .

Evidence is relevant and, therefore, admissible, if tends "to make the existence of any fact that is of consequence to the determination of the action more probable or less probable that it would be without the evidence." Fed. R. Evid. 401 & 402. "Relevancy . . . exists only as a relation between an item of evidence and a matter properly provable in the case." Rule 401 advisory committee notes. Evidence is inadmissible if it is not relevant, Rule 402, and excludable "if its probative value is substantially outweighed by the danger of unfair prejudice, confusion of the issues, or misleading the jury." Rule 403. "'Unfair prejudice . . . means an undue tendency to suggest decision on an improper basis, commonly, though not necessarily, an emotional one.'" . . . The district court did not abuse its discretion in precluding evidence of Player's sexist comments because they were not relevant to Steger's Equal Pay Act claim, Player was not a decision maker, and the comments may have unfairly prejudiced GE . . .

Although a different judge may have decided differently, this judge was upheld on the basis that the comments "may" have unfairly prejudiced the defendant. Evidentiary decisions are in the judge's hands, and that's a frightening thought. If you are in a jurisdiction where the judge is assigned well ahead of trial, which is true in most places, you have some chance of predicting the outcome of evidentiary battles. In the few places where you don't know your judge until the day of trial, the risk factor is indeed a worrisome matter.

"Confusion of the issues" and "misleading the jury" are usually conflated. If the issues get confused, the jury will be misled, and vice versa, some of the thinking goes, even though they are separate grounds. Basically, if the evidence starts wandering afield and brings in causes of action not alleged or parties not before the court, even if part of the evidence is relevant, it may be excluded from the jury's consideration. And if you come across evidence that is confusing, you probably want to ignore it and keep investigating. Jurors are average people. The juror is *you*. What kind of story would *you* like to hear? What kind of story would *you* follow? What kind of story would *you* believe? If you can't summarize the story or explain it clearly to yourself or a secretary in the office, it probably needs work, because that's what you're doing: putting together the client's story to tell the jury.

Hearsay

Because we're focusing on interviewing here, we should begin considering the **hearsay rule**. I often cringe when I hear laypeople discuss hearsay, because they're usually very far off the mark. It's kind of like nails on a blackboard once you know how it really works. To put the problem with the definition of hearsay in perspective, let me quote a judge I once heard while sitting in court and waiting for my case to be called: "There is no such thing as the hearsay rule. There are only lawyers too stupid to get around it." Although I don't completely agree with this judge, I understand his point of view. The hearsay rule has 2 to 4 exclusions in its definition, 24 exceptions (give or take, depending on the jurisdiction) regardless of the availability of the witness, and 4 more if the witness is unavailable. Most of the evidence that actually ends up excluded under the hearsay rules could be taken care of under Rule 403.

Therefore, as you interview people, beginning with your own client, remember that things your client said or says other people said may be admissible. Don't reject those statements out of hand as hearsay; if the statement is good for you, it may get in. If the statement is bad for you, don't rely on hearsay to get you out of trouble. On the other hand, some of the psychological studies done on hearsay suggest that jurors, probably rightly, assign less weight to hearsay statements if the person who originally made the statement is unavailable for cross-examination, and it is worthwhile to try to get the same information elsewhere if at all possible.

The definition of hearsay tends to give law students headaches, and it has made all my paralegal students cross-eyed. Don't spend an inordinate amount of time delving into its mysteries; the only reason it's here is to keep you from wondering what it is. The main thing you will need to concern yourself with in real life is the exclusions and exceptions. Here, in all its glory, is the definition: *Hearsay* is an out-of-court statement offered in evidence to prove the truth of the matter asserted.

Most people are fine with this definition until they get to "truth of the matter asserted." Before we discuss that, look at the phrase "out-of-court statement." Note that this is not limited to oral statements. Written documents are covered by this as well. Hearsay can encompass any kind of record: medical, personnel, checks, letters, financial statements, and the like.

"Truth of the matter asserted" is the concept that typically presents the most difficulty. Say June Curves was suing Marty Maple for sexual harassment. June's attorney wants to present testimony that June's co-worker, May, called Marty a "pig with 25 hands" in front of his boss. Now that is definitely an out-of-court statement! "Being offered to prove the truth of the matter asserted" means that the statement is supposed to show the jury that whatever the speaker said was true. Did May mean Marty was a deformed barnyard animal? Is that what the lawyer wants to prove? Or is that a slang statement that would prove he is a sexual predator, and is that the truth that the attorney wants to prove to the jury? Or does the attorney want to prove simply that the boss was given notice that Marty was a possible problem and did nothing? If this last interpretation is the case, then the statement is not being offered to prove the truth of the matter asserted (that what the speaker said was true) but for another purpose, and may be admissible because it is not hearsay under those circumstances. Don't worry about it if it doesn't make sense to you at first; you're not alone.

James McElhaney, the author of the litigation column in the *ABA Journal* (which should be regular reading for anyone in litigation, even though it is aimed primarily at lawyers and some of it may not apply to you), suggests a completely different test. He recommends simply looking for whomever it is you'd like to cross-examine. If it's not the person on the stand, then you're probably dealing with hearsay. That still doesn't mean there's not an exception to the rule, but it helps with the definition.

Party-Opponent Admissions

The first non-hearsay hearsay to keep in mind is what is sometimes referred to as the *party-opponent rule* or -**party-opponent admissions** or **admission by a party-opponent**. This rule is enshrined in Rule 801(d)(2).

A statement is not hearsay if—

1. *Admission by party-opponent.* The statement is offered against a party and is
   a. the party's own statement, in either an individual or a representative capacity or
   b. a statement of which the party has manifested an adoption or belief in its truth, or
   c. a statement by a person authorized by the party to make a statement concerning the subject, or
   d. a statement by the party's agent or servant concerning a matter within the scope of the agency or employment, made during the existence of the relationship, or
   e. a statement by a coconspirator of a party during the course and in furtherance of the conspiracy.

Fed. R. Evid. 801(d)(2).

This is not an exception. These statements are simply not considered hearsay under the definition. Although the strict definition is that whatever was said has to be something one of the parties said (or the other situations described) and it is "against" the party (hurts the party in some way), the real-life effect is that basically anything any party has said is usually admissible unless one of the other rules of evidence can be used against it. So finding out what everyone said at any time the parties had contact is very important.

Other important hearsay exceptions have to do with what people said at the time of the incident. This cluster of exceptions is sometimes referred to generically as **res gestae** exceptions under the common law theories, which tends to conflate the various specific exceptions under newer evidentiary rules. *Res gestae* is a Latin term meaning (very roughly) "the beginning of related parts of the thing," and the phrase refers to the events that gave rise to the litigation. The word *res* is used often in law for "legal thing"; the idea here is that some things are admissible because the words spoken were part of the event. The relevant part of the rule follows.

The following are not excluded by the hearsay rule, even though the declarant is available as a witness:

1. Present sense impression. A statement describing or explaining an event or condition made while the declarant was perceiving the event or condition, or immediately thereafter.
2. Excited utterance. A statement relating to a startling event or condition made while the declarant was under the stress of excitement caused by the event or condition.

3. Then existing mental, emotional, or physical condition. A statement of the declarant's then existing state of mind, emotion, sensation, or physical condition (such as intent, plan, motive, design, mental feeling, pain, and bodily health), but not including a statement of memory or belief to prove the fact remembered or believed unless it relates to the execution, revocation, identification, or terms of declarant's will.

Fed. R. Evid. 803(1)-(3).

The "declarant" is the person who made the out-of-court statement. These statements are allowed because it is thought that under these circumstances fabrication is less likely; the statements are more likely to be reliable. So a statement by a witness describing what happened made at the scene of an accident, or about one of the parties, or an outburst, or what anyone thought or felt, is admissible unless it violates one of the other rules of evidence.

Christensen v. Economy Fire & Casualty Co., 252 N.W.2d 81 (Wisc. 1977).

At about 6:25 A.M. on July 12, 1972, a head-on crash of a pick-up truck and a carry-all van occurred resulting in the deaths of both drivers, each of whom was the sole occupant of his vehicle. There were no eyewitnesses. One driver died immediately but the other, David Wroblewski, survived approximately forty-five minutes after the mishap. During the time Wroblewski was at the site waiting for an ambulance he spoke with James Horsens, a motorist who happened onto the scene shortly after the accident. Wroblewski's statements during that conversation concerned, among other things, the cause of the crash, and these statements form the basis for this appeal.

The issue before the court is whether the trial court properly excluded the testimony of James Horsens who would relate the words of David Wroblewski. It is conceded that Horsens' repetition of Wroblewski's statements is hearsay and is not admissible except as specially provided by rule. . .

At the trial, the court held an in camera hearing to evaluate the offer of proof made by Economy Fire and Casualty Company concerning Horsens' testimony to determine whether the testimony would be admissible under one of the exceptions to the hearsay rule. . . . The witness stated that he arrived on the scene while water and steam were still spewing from each vehicle. After determining that the other driver was unconscious he went to Wroblewski's van and, in response to a plea for help, unpinned him from inside it. At this point Wroblewski asked Horsens, "Why did it happen to me, what could I do, the guy was coming at me." He also asked about the condition of the other driver, whom he was told was unconscious but all right, and he continued to wonder out loud why the accident had happened to him and what else he could have done to avoid it since the other guy was coming at him.

Horsens testified that Wroblewski was coughing, spitting blood and gurgling. Unable to lie down because of his pain, the victim sat up with his arms crossed over his chest. He expressed fear of dying and he repeatedly asked why the ambulance was taking so long to arrive. Horsens continued the conversation, reassuring Wroblewski that he would not die and responding to his questions in general to keep his mind off the pain. . .

The question of admissibility is one of law which is determined by the judge. We have held on numerous occasions that the decision on the admissibility of a hearsay statement is within the discretion of the trial court. . . . Such discretion will not be reversed unless it is abused or is premised upon an erroneous view of the law. The term discretion contemplates a process of reasoning which depends on facts that are of record or reasonably derived by inference from the record and a conclusion based on a logical rationale founded on proper legal standards. The record should show that the discretion was in fact exercised and the basis of that exercise. . . .

From an examination of the record in the instant case we believe that the judge had a mistaken view of the law and that to the extent he was exercising his discretion, it was exercised on improper grounds. The trial court improperly determined that Horsens' testimony, admittedly hearsay insofar as it relates to Wroblewski's statements, was not admissible under sec. 908.03(2), Rules of Evidence, the excited utterance exception.

The excited utterance exception, which was formerly part of the res gestae exception. . . is based upon spontaneity and stress which endow such statements with sufficient trustworthiness to overcome the reasons for exclusion of hearsay. In determining whether a statement qualifies as an excited utterance, the important factors for the judge's consideration are timing and stress. [A] case no less applicable because it concerned the older res gestae exception:

"It must be shown that the statement was made so spontaneously or under such psychological or physical pressure or excitement that the rational mind could not interpose itself between the spontaneous statement or utterance stimulated by the event and the event itself. The psychological basis for the res gestae exception is that people instinctively tell the truth but when they have time to stop and think they may lie. . . . "

. . . The significant factor is the stress or nervous shock acting on the declarant at the time of the statement. The statements of a declarant who demonstrates the opportunity and capacity to review the accident and to calculate the effect of his statements do not qualify as excited utterances. . . . Conversely, statements of declarants whose condition at the time of their declarations indicates that they are still under the shock of their injuries. . . or other stress due to special circumstances. . . will be admitted under this exception. It is the condition of excitement that temporarily stills the capacity for reflection which is the significant factor assuring trustworthiness, assuring that the declarant lacked the capacity to fabricate. The court must assess the "special circumstances in which the statement is made [that] make it reliable and trustworthy." . . .

It is clear from the record that Horsens arrived on the scene within minutes of the impact. Despite massive front-end damage, both vehicles were still spouting water and steam. Wroblewski was in pain, spitting blood, gurgling, coughing and concerned about dying. The record does not show that the court considered either the short time lapse between the event and the declaration or the extent of the victim's injuries which contributed to his shock and stress. Instead the court stressed the self-serving nature of the declaration and its suspicion that the statement was made with a view to later litigation. The court felt that "in such a situation no one would admit he was at fault," noting that after the accident the declarant "ended up on the wrong side of the road." The court's decision overemphasizes the self-serving nature of the statement and the fact that the other driver was not alive to refute the testimony.

The issue for the judge is whether the special circumstances existed. . . which make the statement reliable and trustworthy. Here, the trial court in refusing to admit the statement stressed its visceral reaction to the untrustworthiness of the statement rather than the objective circumstances. . . that will lead the court to the conclusion that the statements are or are not trustworthy. The judge did not state the facts or inferences therefrom upon which he reached his conclusion that the statements are not trustworthy. . . . While the court's statements on trustworthiness are adjunctively relevant, they do not import a correct view of the law or an exercise of judicial discretion on permissible grounds. . .

For these reasons, we conclude that the court erred in its determination to exclude Horsens' testimony. . .

By the Court. — Judgment reversed and cause remanded for a new trial.

According to this case, which is representative of the general outlook, the judge is not to look at the rationale for the exception, but at the objective standards within the rule in making a determination as to the applicability of any particular hearsay exception.

THE INITIAL INTERVIEW

The first steps of the defendant's initial interview are the same as the plaintiff's. It begins with a phone call to the office.

"Good morning. This is Dewey, Cheatham, and Howe. I'm Mr. Howe's paralegal. May I help you?"

"I don't think so. I need a lawyer."

"Mr. Howe's in court right now. If you tell me what your situation is, maybe I can help you find out what Mr. Howe can do for you. My job is to assist Mr. Howe and his clients—what a nurse is to the doctor."

"Oh. Okay. Well, how much does it cost to talk to Mr. Howe?"

"Well, sir, that all depends. Right now, talking to me isn't costing you anything. Why don't you tell me what you need a lawyer for and let's go from there."

"I got papers from this guy this morning saying I was being sued. And when I got to work and had a chance to look at them, I find out my wife is saying that I can't support her so she wants a divorce!"

"Oh. Sir, did the petition say that the marriage had become 'insupportable'?"

"Yeah. That's what I said."

"Sir, that's legalese for a no-fault divorce. It only means that she wants a divorce, but it's nobody's fault."

There's usually a silence about this point while the caller digests this information.

"Oh. Well. Do I need a lawyer?"

"Well, sir, whenever legal rights are being decided, having a lawyer is always the safest thing. But as a paralegal I can not give you legal advice."

Note how the paralegal didn't tell the caller specifically what to do. It's probably safe enough to recommend to someone that he get an attorney, but in family law matters, if there are no children and no property, there may be no reason to get an attorney, and you don't want to have told someone to pay the money for no good reason. On the other hand, in a quick conversation it is difficult to ascertain potential issues, so many commentators maintain that you should always advise someone to seek an attorney when legal rights are at stake.

The conversation will go on to address when the answer is due and what the retainer and hourly rate of the attorney is. If the fees are acceptable to the client, you run a conflict check, make an appointment with the caller, and generate a confirmation letter. In addition, you would request the client to fax or deliver the original divorce petition to the office prior to the initial meeting. You would also almost surely send an intake form with the confirmation letter, as family law matters require an exhaustive accounting of assets.

After that, the interview would take on the same characteristics described in Chapter 2: preparation (more later about the specifics in the defense context), making the client feel comfortable, treating the client professionally, making sure the client understands your role as a paralegal, and use of questioning and active listening techniques. After the interview, you will need to write a memo to the file summarizing the interview and taking note of any observations you made. In addition, you need to take into consideration body language, something that applies to the interviewing of plaintiffs or any other witness.

Emotional Baggage and Venting

Before we discuss nonverbal communication, one other issue deserves to be addressed, and being aware of this issue may help you sort credibility issues from other emotional stress. Expression of emotion is different than acting out. It is fine to express emotions; it is not okay to behave poorly. You will probably have to deal with a certain amount of venting on the part of the defendant (or the plaintiff). Being sued is a scary experience for most people, repeat players excepted. Defendants are afraid, and fear affects people in funny ways. Some of your clients will express their fear through anger; some will be simply nervous. Some are fearful of the unknown; some may erroneously believe they can go to jail in a civil case. Some are righteously indignant—the small businessman who spent his life building a small fortune "will declare bankruptcy" before letting a plaintiff "get a penny of it," even when the injury is legitimate and the liability relatively clear. You should confront these emotional issues at some point, not to fix the client, but to allow the client to name and express the emotions, and it is better to do so before you get to the meat of the case.

The suit may challenge one or more aspects of the client's **identity issues**. The client may wonder, "Am I a good person?" or "Am I competent?" Or the client may be concerned about the question, "What will people think about me if they know I've been sued?" or "How will this affect my business/job/marriage/life?" Some may blame themselves for events or circumstances that are not their fault, like the battered wife who is being divorced.

One of the things you can do is simply give the client information—information, not advice. Just explain the process. Give the client statistics about how often cases actually go to trial, somewhere around 4 to 6 percent of all cases filed. Assure him that you and the attorney are there to help him and will answer his questions. Explain that you can help with information—"What happens?" types of questions—and that the attorney will answer advice questions—"What do I do?" types of questions. When explaining processes, avoid legal jargon and make sure that the client is with you at each step of the discussion.

If necessary, take a minute or so to let the client **vent**. There are various ways to facilitate this. My personal favorite is to say something along the lines of, "If I were in your position, I think I would feel. . . " and then describe those feelings. Usually a remark like that will elicit a reaction, whether agreement or denial; regardless, it gets the other person talking about what he feels. Do not tell the client, "I know how you feel" or "You feel X." This approach tends to evoke a completely different response than you want; the client is more likely to be angry at you for thinking you know him or his situation well enough to know how he feels. Other clients react defensively to statements along those lines and decide the speaker is arrogant. These clients will often stop talking.

For example, say Mr. Grant Marido, the caller who thought he was being divorced because he couldn't support his wife to her satisfaction, comes in. After you've introduced yourself by name and as a paralegal, the following conversation might occur.

"I'm glad to meet you, Mr. Marido, although I'm sorry it's under these circumstances."

"What? My wife stabbing me in the back with a divorce? Why should you be sorry?"

"If I were in your situation, I think it would make me very sad."

"Me? I'm not sad. She's the one who's gonna be sad. She can't never be happy with nothing. I worked hard to get her everything. She didn't have nothing when I married her, and she won't have nothing when I'm done with her."

"So was she unhappy with your financial situation?"

"Oh, she never had enough money. I got a big house, nice car for her and me, good little plumbing business I built up from nothing, she has clothes and those whatchacallem fingernails and gets her hair done every week, and that's still not good enough for her."

"Is she your first wife?"

"My only."

At this point, the tone may change. At any rate, the rants usually expires of their own accord; if not, the use of closed questions to redirect the conversation can move it away from the emotional when enough time has elapsed. However, you still need to be sensitive to the emotional state of your client or it can get in the way of your case. (It's also the humane thing to do.) You might reassure the client that what he is feeling is normal or common under the circumstances, but do so diplomatically: some clients want to believe their suffering is unique; others feel comforted knowing they are not alone.

There are some people you can't talk about feelings with, though, and you should be sensitive to that. They may be too guarded, suspicious, or reserved to be comfortable exposing themselves in that way, and their point of view must be respected. You will not build a trust relationship with such clients with an attempt to coax feelings out of them; they will usually become even more guarded.

Nonverbal Communication

What makes us decide whether someone is telling the truth or not? Many people can't explain why they believe one person and not another; trust is often given or withheld on the basis of **nonverbal cues**. Our tone of voice is far easier to control than those unruly muscles in our face or our twitchy hands. Sensitivity to your body language will help you gain the trust of your client or communicate when you do not believe him without actually saying so. Because nonverbal communication is so powerful, is very important to have a face-to-face interview with a client—a telephone interview just will not give you a fair assessment of client credibility.

First of all, to communicate to a client that you are ready to listen, you need to have an open posture. This means that your arms are not crossed in any way (even if that is more comfortable for you) and that you lean slightly toward the client. Keep eye contact with the client, but not to an unnatural degree so that he feels your eyes boring into him. While you are in the midst of the interview, avoid clock watching or any other glances away that indicate to the client that you are disinterested. Nod when appropriate. Leaning back may be understood as a signal that you have stopped listening and may slow down someone who has gone off on a tangent. Your standing signals that the meeting is over. These few nonverbal cues, used judiciously, may help you control the interview.

Not everyone will respond to these cues. Mild forms of **autism** have proliferated in the population and have as a defining characteristic the inability to read or react appropriately to nonverbal cues. This type of client needs to be recognized, as his inability to appropriately react to nonverbal cues will either need to be explained, worked on, or recognized as a deficiency in the case.

The goal of much research on nonverbal communication has been to find a way to determine when an individual is lying. The problem is that any behavior that indicates lying may also indicate something else. The reason? Such behaviors actually indicate anxiety or stress. So what causes the anxiety? Lying? Or a fear of not being believed? Or just anxiety because of the situation? The subjective reasons, despite their intrinsic interest, are not really the point in the legal context, despite the complaints of legal scholars who want jurors to stop judging credibility on facial tics and movements. Your problem is to discover whether those behaviors exist, because you must make note of them and realize that the jury may put the worst possible interpretation on them: that is, your client is lying. If you are delegated the task of dealing with these behaviors, you might take this approach: "I understand that you are telling the truth, Mr. Client. But if you have your hand over your mouth while you talk, there's a good chance the jury will think you are lying."

The *CLA Review* has a rather interesting take on lying. Its position (and the correct answer for purposes of its exam) is that if a witness lies to you during an interview, you are to stop immediately and consult with your supervising attorney. Every litigator/trial attorney I've mentioned this to has expressed some variation of my own reaction: frown, furrowed brow, rapid eye blinks, and "What?" From an admittedly limited number and nonscientific poll, the consensus is that this is a bad idea. Telling the supervising attorney it is correct insofar as you should let the attorney decide how to handle the issue, but that's as far as it goes.

First of all, you usually don't really know for sure if a witness is lying while you are talking to her. Often you're pretty certain, because you recall some sort of conflicting testimony given by the client or conflicting evidence. However, in practice you will be dealing with a number of cases, and you cannot accuse a witness—a client in particular—of lying until after you have had a chance to verify everything in the files. This includes accusations directed to the supervising attorney. Stopping an interview to go rummaging through the files is a poor use of time, particularly if you happen to be in error. If you are correct, stopping signals to the witness, "Ah-ha! I've caught you!"—a message that may not be a good choice strategically. And finally, not all lies are significant. Some will make the attorney who uses them look like a bully; others will be considered mere slips of memory or white lies. The ones you want to use are the ones that will knock someone down, the ones that no one will mistake for anything but an obvious attempt to mislead the jury in the search for the truth in this case. Therefore, interrupting an interview to talk to an attorney about a lie that doesn't matter will simply disrupt the rapport you've been trying to build (since the witness will probably realize why you just left) for no good reason. It's far better to be discreet; you can always make an issue about a possible lie later.

At any rate, a party's body language is under scrutiny not only when he testifies, but during the entire trial. In a slip and fall trial I participated in, one juror commented that the reason he voted to hold the defendant responsible was that the defendant would smile at odd times, times the juror thought were inappropriate. "It was like the guy was smirking, like he wasn't taking it seriously," said the juror. The jury in that case awarded $150,000 to the plaintiff for a herniated disk in his back, around double the typical award for that type of injury with those facts in that particular locale at that time. The outcome of that case was largely due to the juror's perception of the "smirk" on the face of the defendant during the trial.

One interesting study conducted a number of years ago and published by research psychologists indicated that in criminal trials involving date rape, older women absolutely disbelieved the victim if she refused to meet the eyes of the accused rapist. Considering the number of other possible reasons—fear, feeling naked under his eyes for instance—that could explain this behavior, it was interesting how consistently women in a particular age group felt this way. You have to work against entrenched belief systems to present your client's position in the best possible light.

Other studies have consistently shown that "confidence in one's ability to detect lies is unrelated to the actual accuracy of the statements" (Jeremy Blumenthal, *A Wipe of the Hand, A Lick of the Lips,* 72 Neb. L. Rev 1157, 1961 [1993]). When asked to judge whether a speaker is telling the truth based on body language, most people tested cannot. All of the behaviors usually associated with lying have more to do with perception of untruth than actual attempts at deception. Research has indicated that changes of vocal pitch, speech hesitations, speech errors, and mismatches between voice and facial communication are far more likely to occur during deception than behaviors typically associated with lying.

Having said all that, it is true as well that nonverbal and other behavioral communications are more reliable than verbal ones, and that if your client (or any other witness, for that matter) is displaying cues that indicate anxiety (such as those listed in the following figure), it is possible—perhaps even probable—that he is being deceptive, even if not intentionally. One particular gesture or posture may be simply an idiosyncrasy of the client and thus may not be significant, but if you see several of these behaviors, then it probably means something. If certain cues are present, note them and explore the areas again in other ways to see if there are things you have missed or to see what weaknesses there are in the information you have been given.

Demeanor Likely to Be Interpreted as Being Untruthful	Demeanor Likely to Be Interpreted as Being Truthful
Slouching in chair	Upright but not rigid posture
Unnaturally rigid or immobile	Aligned to face the interviewer
Overly anxious	Spontaneous
Evasive	Open
Defensive	Sincere
Overly polite	Leans forward when answering questions
Guarded	Smooth posture changes
Complaining	"anti-gravity" gestures—raising up toes, coming up on the balls of the feet, raising eyebrows (tend to be absent during deceptive statements)
Licking lips	
Stuttering	
Failure to align body frontally with interviewer	Normal rate of eye contact (30–60% of the time between two people)
Hiding behind barriers	
Moving chair away from interviewer during key questions	
Cutting eyes down before answering question	
Putting hands in front of mouth	
Jerky posture changes	
Sweaty hands	
Change in rate of head and hand movements	
Touching the face while talking	**Demeanor More Likely to Indicate Deception**
Abnormally high or low rate of eye contact	Change in pitch of voice
Eyelash flutter/rapid blinking before an untruth	Mismatch of tone and expression
Rubbing hands together constantly	Speech hesitation
Shrugs	Speech errors

In addition to these behaviors, there are facial responses that are universal to every human on the planet. In some cultures, such responses are rapidly suppressed, but they reveal underlying emotions. These emotions are on our faces at least briefly and are given the same interpretation regardless of culture. Dr. Paul Ekman at the University of California Medical School at San Francisco is the leading researcher in this area, and has written several books and articles on the subject, including training materials on how to look for cues in people's faces that reveal emotions: anger, repulsion, fear, and so on. These cues can lead to more accurate assessments as to what may be driving any anxiety behaviors. You can check out his Web site at http://www.paulekman.com for more information.

To train yourself to recognize these nonverbal behaviors, it may be advantageous to use a checklist. This checklist may be one you refer to before and after, rather than during, the interview. Why? You never know what the client may be able to read from her point of view. If the client were to see this checklist, it could affect her responses, as a list like this tends to make one self-conscious. If you decide to keep it available during the interview, try to keep it covered, although don't do so in a way that attracts attention.

There is also a theory, not widely accepted by academics, called "neuro-linguistic programming" based on the idea that there is a standard relationship between eye movement and cognition. This theory has been represented in the area of investigation as a proven fact, which is not quite accurate. The standard rendition of the theory is that when visualizing memories, people look up; when remembering sounds, they look to the side; and, when reflecting on feelings, they look down and to the left. In some circles, this formulation has morphed into look up—remember; look down—feel, look sideways—lying. Other versions equate abruptly broken eye contact with lying—not necessarily the case, although this nonverbal behavior probably does indicate stress associated with whatever was concurrently said, and should be investigated further.

Behaviors/Expressions	Frequency			Context
	1x	2–5x	5 + x	
Hands near mouth				
Tapping				
Learning away				
Learning forward				
No eye contact				
Hands touching face				
Anger				
Repulsion				
Fear				
Fidgeting with hands of clothes				
Slouching				
Changes in voice pitch				
Inappropriate reactions				
Leg or foot tapping				
Using barriers				
Blinking too much				
Not blinking at all				
Body turned away				

Although one application of knowledge of nonverbal behavior is to note and judge the credibility of the client, there is another to keep in mind. When questioning the client, ask her to describe the body language or facial expressions of the plaintiff or witnesses. These descriptions are valid testimony. Specifics are far more credible than conclusions: to say that someone smelled of beer, was slurring his words (particularly saying "sh" instead of "s"), almost missed the steps that were clearly marked and lit, kept blinking his eyes to focus, and was having trouble standing up straight is far more convincing than simply saying he was drunk. To say someone paced back and forth, crossed and uncrossed her arms, frowned constantly, looked at her watch repeatedly, tapped her foot, and yelled as she got into the vehicle is far more convincing than simply saying you think she was mad when she got into the car. Any specifics you can elicit on nonverbal communication—whether from your client or any other witness—will prove valuable.

Using the Complaint

Up until this point, the interviewing process has been the same for the defendant as for the plaintiff. Where it deviates is at the point of the **complaint**. The defendant has some notice of what the issues are. If you have had an opportunity to see the complaint prior to meeting with the defendant, you will be able to check and see if any specific **affirmative defenses** can be raised in this particular context.

In the past, insurance defense firms primarily used associates to initially meet with clients to develop a sense of the case. Insurance companies have been insisting on lower and lower attorney fees, so it may be that in some locales, firms are or will be utilizing paralegals to perform this function. In cases involving established non-insurer clients, who conducts the initial meeting will depend on the firm's relationship with the client and the client's preferences for cost-effectiveness versus ego massaging. (Some clients feel they are getting "first-class treatment" in being served by a lawyer rather than a paralegal.) With family law clients, paralegals will probably do most of the work of client contact and case development in order to maximize the attorney's effectiveness.

In any case, going over the complaint is a good place to start. Asking the defendant what he agrees and disagrees with factually is important, particularly in jurisdictions that require the defendant to specifically deny factual allegations rather than allowing a blanket **General Denial**. It will be up to the legal team to decide the applicability of any particular cause of action, as well as determine the value of the case. In addition, ask the defendant for witnesses and any other information that will help support the defendant's version of the facts as well as any that support the plaintiff's. Ask general questions about the defendant's criminal background and any other pertinent background information. Make sure you have enough information to draft and file the appropriate answer for the client, including any applicable affirmative defenses. Keep in mind that this information may also help later with **stipulations** and **admissions**.

Affirmative defenses are "So-what?" defenses: Even if everything horrible you say about me is true, so what? I win anyway because of X. The classic example of an affirmative defense is the statute of limitations: Even if I am the rotten scoundrel you say I am, and I swindled you out of all your money, too bad. You took too long to file suit, so I win.

Other Examples of Affirmative Defenses Are
* governmental (or sovereign) immunity—the government can not be sued absent legislation to the contrary;
* parental immunity (not universal)—children can not sue their parents, or may do so only very limited circumstances;
* res judicater—can't sue the same person for the same situation more than once;
* collateral estoppel—an issue has already been established as a matter of law in another proceeding;
* statute of frauds—certain kinds of contracts must be in writing to be enforceable;
* spousal immunity (largely eroded in most jurisdictions)—spouses can not sue each other except under limited circumstances;
* charitable immunity (almost extinct)—non-profit benevolent organizations can not be sued; and
* official immunity—government officers can not be sued while in the course of their duties, particularly when those duties are discretionary.

Whenever you are working on the defense side, you must actively consider any possible affirmative defenses you can assert on the part of the defendant. You must also remember to include these defenses when drafting the defendant's answer; in most jurisdictions, failure to specifically plead an affirmative defense results in a waiver of that defense.

THE PAPERWORK

Contracts on the defense side are almost always going to be on an hourly basis and should be completed during the initial meeting if there is not an ongoing relationship with the client or some other entity that is paying the defense costs. Again, you must explain the portions of the contract to the client clearly. After the interview is concluded, you will, as in the case of the plaintiff, write a memo detailing the interview as discussed in Chapter 2. You will diary the deadline for the client to send you any follow-up documents so you can contact the client if he fails to do so.

Remember that the discovery plan will need to be reviewed and updated each time you add new evidence to the case file. Early in the case, you and the lawyer should talk about what the key facts are and what the story you want to tell is. Every case is a story. It may be a story about lost opportunities, about failure of middle management, about secrecy, about someone's taking advantage of a little old lady—but whatever it is, it is a story. There should be a beginning, a goal for your protagonist (your client), and adversaries to face. The jury's resolution of the facts is the climax. Although you must add evidentiary details to the story to make it more than a fantasy, some facts usually grab your attention early in the case and make you believe your client. These are the salient facts. Facts from the other side that bother you are also facts to worry about. You will need to figure out the "other guy's" story, too, and be prepared to counter it.

Once you've figured out your story and theirs, you'll know how to prioritize your discovery. The areas that will best support yours and undermine theirs are the first priority. Due to the legal requirement for evidence for each element of a **cause of action** or affirmative defense, you will have to make sure you have something for every part upon which you have the burden, but once you have covered those legal requirements, your emphasis in fact finding will be on capturing evidence that supports the story you want to tell.

As evidence is assembled, you must evaluate each piece. Will the jury believe it? Or are the facts not supporting your story? The best lawyer in the world can be confounded by bad facts; the worst has to work at losing if she's got good facts. You have to be objective enough to see what attacks may be generated against each piece of testimony. What are the holes? Where does the logic not hold up? What is missing?

When reviewing your client's story, you need to figure out what assumptions your client is making. Do not make the same assumptions. For instance, Mr. Marido assumed that the reason his wife was divorcing him was dissatisfaction with their financial status. Don't assume he is correct. He well may be, but there may be more to the case than that. Depending on what is at stake (child custody, large alimony payments, or the disposition of property), you may need to look past that and see if there is something else motivating the break-up that may be relevant to the case.

In addition, you need to sort out fact from opinion. In your interview with Mr. Marido, he may have told you his wife had "trampy friends," (an opinion) and given you the facts of their names, addresses, and phone numbers. He may have told you that she "never spent any time with the children," but was unable to give much in the way of detail about the weekday activities of his wife vis-à-vis his children because he was at work, only knowing that on weekends he took care of them the entire time. Mr. Marido has personal knowledge of the facts concerning his care of the children on the weekend; those are facts that need to be corroborated if possible, but they are still facts. His opinion of her care of the children during the week is just an opinion; you do not know if it is true. The best strategy is to treat the client as though you agree he is accurate in his assessments, but let him know that you'll have to prove the truth of his perceptions to the judge or jury. To do this, you'll have to get information from the daycare (yep, that'll require a release) to get the check-in and check-out times for the kids and to talk to the daycare workers. The opinions of the client are not going to help his case; facts will. You must separate these and then determine whether his opinions can be substantiated. That is the core of investigation—verifying the information given by the parties.

The investigation plan, as it is being created, needs to have specific goals. On the plaintiff's side, because of the burden of proof, the elements of the cause of action drive the process, but on either side, you need to establish a theme, an idea of what the story will be from the beginning based on the attitudes of the parties and the facts of the case. What makes sense to you now and will make sense to a jury when you present it? Legal professionals do best with a story line—as the movie folks know, easy-to-follow action films make the big bucks, not ambiguous character studies that are dear to the hearts of actors and critics.

Perhaps the client you met with was the off-duty police officer, John Justice, in the Patty Haus case described in Chapter 2. He told you that Haus and her live-in boyfriend were constant troublemakers, that he had been forced to have her boyfriend arrested several times, and that the last two times she had threatened to "get even" with him and the apartment complex owners, who were instituting eviction procedures against the two.

After consultation with the lawyer, you agree your story is "Vengeful girlfriend appears to be fulfilling promise. What else was officer to think?" This is not an affirmative offense, so you have no burden of proof and no legal requirement to put on any particular pieces of evidence. You will be looking for things that support your version of events.

What are the holes in Patty's story? How would she know if the brakes were out at the time? Was she going fast enough that applying the brakes wouldn't have helped? Were there other places she could have run her car up against besides the apartment complex? Was there any motivation she could have had for damaging the vehicle? What was the cause of the brake malfunction? Is it possible that the event was planned?

From the discussion with the police officer, you can make an **investigation action plan (i.p.)**. It will look a little different from the earlier version.

INVESTIGATION ACTION PLAN

Theory to Prove	Areas to Investigate	Possible Leads
Vengeful girlfriend	Prior arrests of boyfriend	Police reports?
"	Threats	Friends; deposition of plaintiff?
"	Eviction proceedings	JP court in district
"	Vandalism rate of ex-tenants	Insurance company claims history?

As each specific piece of evidence (police report, other apartment residents, court records, crime statistics) is investigated, it needs to be checked off. An **investigation plan summary** should be provided that shows your results.

INVESTIGATION PLAN RESULTS SUMMARY

Theory to Prove	Areas Investigated	Evidence Found
Vengeful girlfriend	Prior arrests of boyfriend	Police reports of 8/22, 8/31, 9/05, 9/17, 9/19, 9/25, 10/01, 10/15, and 10/31 of year of incident
"	Threats	Admitted by plaintiff
"	Eviction proceedings	Cause No. 12345 in the 1st Precinct J.P. court
"	Vandalism rate of ex-tenants	Not obtained yet; ask insurance company for claims history.

Then you should have a more detailed list of the important parts of each piece of evidence you have listed on the summary. If you do this as you go along, you will have a major section of a **trial notebook** completed by the time you need it. You'll also have managed your time far better and accrued billing for it as it comes in rather than waiting for a trial that may not come. Every time you complete an investigation task, update each section of this evidentiary notebook and plan.

INVESTIGATION DETAILS

Theory to Prove	Areas Investigated	Evidence Found
Vengeful girlfriend	Threats	Admitted by plaintiff

Result Details

Admission of threat to "get even" with Justice after first arrest of boyfriend; deposition of Patty Haus, page 34, line 14.

Admission of threat to "tear this place apart" with reference to apartment complex; deposition of Patty Haus, page 37, line 05.

Admission of threat to "take everything that isn't nailed down, and then everything that is;" deposition of Patty Haus, page 37, line 20.

Admission of threat to "shove a tailpipe up your ass" to Justice; deposition of Patty Haus, page 38, line 18.

Admission of threat to "key his car" with reference to Justice; deposition of Patty Haus, page 40, line 06.

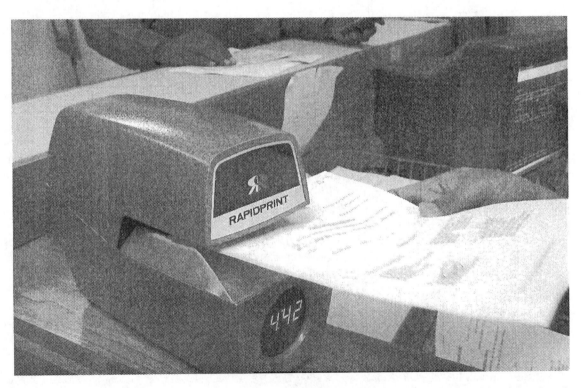

This machine stamps the copies with date and court with a definite clacking sound. Note the digital display which was the time: 4:42 P.M.

FOLLOW-UP

You've got one immediate task with a deadline and another that needs to get done to get your investigation moving. You must draft the defendant's answer (or give the information to the attorney so he can do so) and get any information you can based on the releases and leads given to you by your client.

Once you have drafted the defendant's answer, and had it reviewed and signed by your supervising attorney, you will need to file it. When the answer is filed, you will ask for **conformed copies**, also known as **file-stamped copies**. These are copies that the clerk at the courthouse stamps with a time/date stamp, usually automated (I would say all but there may still be an old courthouse out there somewhere still using a hand stamp). You always take (or send) an original, a copy for opposing counsel, one for your files, and one for your client(s). You don't have to file stamp the copy for opposing counsel; however, the clerk usually stamps all the copies you hand her. This stamp is proof that the original was filed on that time and date, handy when the courthouse mislays your original—something that happens from time to time.

Now that the original parties have done their dance, everyone launches into the investigation mode, trying to find the evidence that will support the story the client wants to tell.

CHAPTER SUMMARY

The defendant's legal team begins with an imminent deadline: the answer date. The complaint and service must be checked to find out when that deadline is and, if it has already passed, to determine if a default judgment has been rendered. The procedure for accepting a client will depend on whether the client is a new one or an established one. In insurance defense work, the legal team needs to be aware of the issues of who the client is and to whom various duties are owed. If the client is new, a conflict of interest check must be performed. An interview needs to be scheduled as soon as possible, but in states where a general denial is possible, that interview may not be held until after the answer date.

When interviewing, the interviewer needs to be looking for both relevant evidence and information that could lead to relevant evidence. Relevant evidence may be excluded, however, if it is unfairly prejudicial, confuses the issues, misleads the jury, causes undue delay or wastes time, or is simply cumulative evidence. Although hearsay evidence is excluded, the paralegal shouldn't worry overmuch about hearsay issues because of the large number of hearsay exclusions, including the party/opponent admission rule and the *res gestae* exception.

The interview process is much the same on the defense side: the paralegal needs to identify herself and consider the place, manner, and questioning techniques to be used in the interview. The paralegal will often need to allow the client to vent before she is able to elicit valuable information from him. Additionally, the interviewer should take into account nonverbal cues, whether from defendant or plaintiff, to assess how the jury will determine the client's credibility. The interviewer should also use the complaint as a guide in asking the client about specific allegations. After escorting the client out of the office, the interviewer needs to prepare a client interview report, an investigation action plan and summary, and (if not already done) an answer. The answer will need to be filed and conformed copies made for the office and for the client.

FOR FURTHER READING:

Debra Lyn Bassett, *Three's a Crowd: A Proposal to Eliminate Joint Representation*, 32 Rutgers L.J. 387 (2001).

Janet Bavelas & Nicole Chovil, *Visible Acts of Meaning*, 19 J. Lang & Soc. Psych 163 (2000).

Jeremy A. Blumenthal, *A Wipe of the Hands, A Lick of the Lips: The Validity of Demeanor Evidence in Assessing Witness Credibility*, 72 Neb. L. Rev. 1157 (1993).

Paul Ekman & Wallace V. Friesen, *Nonverbal Leakage and Clues to Deception*, 32 Psychiatry 88 (1969).

George Fisher, *The Jury's Rise as Lie Detector*, 107 Yale L.J. 575 (1997).

Steven I. Friedland, *On Common Sense and the Evaluation of Witness Credibility*, 40 Case W. Res. 165 (1990).

J. S. Pail, *How Far Should the "No Contact" Rule Go to Protect Governmental Employees?* 20 J.L. & Com. 129 (2000).

Charles Silver & Kent Syverud, *The Professional Responsibilities of Insurance Defense Lawyers*, 45 Duke L.J. 255 (1995).

Eleanor Swift, *Abolishing the Hearsay Rule*, 75 Calif. L. Rev. 495 (1987).

William C. Thompson & Maithilee K. Pathak, *How Do Jurors React to Hearsay Testimony? Empirical Study of Hearsay Rules: Bridging the Gap Between Psychology and Law*, 5 Psych. Pub. Pol. and L. 456 (1999).

Olin Guy Wellborn III, *Demeanor*, 76 Cornell L. Rev. 1075 (1991).

CHAPTER REVIEW

KEY TERMS

admissible evidence	dual representation	personal jurisdiction
admission by a party-opponent	General Denial	pleading requirements
admissions	file-stamped copies	pleadings
affirmative defense	hearsay rule	policy limits
answer	identity issues	probative
autism	indemnification agreement	process of service
cause of action	insurance defense	relevancy
CEO	insured	repeat players
complaint	insurer	*res gestae*
conformed copies	i.p. (investigation plan)	return of service
Declarations Page	investigation plan summary	stipulations
default judgment	Motion for New Trial	trial notebook
diary	nonverbal cues	unfair prejudice
discoverable evidence	party-opponent admissions	vent

FILL IN THE BLANKS

1. A firm that is hired by an insurance company on behalf of a driver who had an accident does _____ work.

2. Sometimes you should allow witnesses to _____, or express their emotions freely.

3. The maximum dollar amount an insurer will pay, regardless of damages, is the _____, and the specific amount is based on the contract between the insurer and the insured.

4. _____ is required under due process before a court has the power to enter any judgment or order against any individual, and the individual over whom the order is sought must be given notice and service in accord with the statutes governing service.

5. All deadlines must be _____ for all members of the legal team involved in meeting them.

6. The head of a large corporation is often referred to as a(n) _____.

7. _____ is that which the judge will allow to form a part of the official record and be presented to the jury.

8. After the court has entered a judgment in an action, the first move to make is ordinarily a(n) _____, in which you explain why you think there's a problem with the judgment as it stands and why the judge should change it.

9. The defendant's official document, a part of the pleadings, is his _____.

10. The national certification test given by the National Association of Legal Assistants leads to a(n) _____ designation.

11. A(n) _____ is a system for file review.

12. A(n) _____ can be used between contractors and subcontractors, for example, where the subcontractor may agree to take responsibility for all legal actions against the contractor as a result of the subcontractor's work.

13. _____ serve as your proof that a document was filed at the courthouse on a particular date and time.

14. The court clerk will usually give you _____ if you bring extra copies of what you file with the court.

15. For some reason, the term _____ is used frequently in evidentiary law, rather than its more commonly used equivalent, *persuasive*.

16. A(n) _____ organizes how the investigation will take place.

17. A(n) _____ organizes how the investigation has been accomplished to date.

18. An attorney representing two clients with mutual interests is engaged in _____, and will probably have to withdraw if a conflict arises between the two.

19. The consumer who pays for the insurance policy (as well as certain others, depending on the type of insurance) is the _____.

20. A(n) _____ is the document filed with the court in which the process server indicates whom, when, where, and how he served.

21. The _____ consist of all the documents containing the official position statements of the parties along with their legal theories and requests for relief.

22. The _____ prevents the admission of out-of-court statements offered for the truth of the matter asserted.

23. The events surrounding an occurrence giving rise to a lawsuit are sometimes referred to as the _____, and statements made at that time are referred to in a like manner.

24. The insurance company is also known as the _____.

25. _____ vary from state to state; some want specific facts spelled out and others only require sufficient facts to give the parties notice of the case against them.

26. Tone of voice, posture, gestures, and expression are all _____.

27. A(n) _____ begins legal proceedings and sets forth the facts, legal position, and damages sought by the plaintiff.

28. Failure to appear in court by the designated deadline after service results in a(n) _____.

29. The documents reflecting how a defendant was given notice of the lawsuit or the action of giving notice are the _____.

30. The basic rule for admissibility of evidence is _____, which means that it must tend to prove or disprove a fact material to the case.

31. Preparation for trial may include a(n) _____, which organizes all the key pieces of evidence and notes needed by the attorney (and her paralegal if attending trial with the attorney).

32. A(n) _____ is one that excuses the defendant, not because he did not act as alleged, but for some other legally recognized excuse.

33. A congenital disease, _____, interferes with an individual's ability to relate normally to other people, and its symptoms range from complete withdrawal from others to poor interpretation and use of nonverbal signals.

34. Certain businesses and insurance companies are _____ in the legal system, meaning they are frequently involved in litigation.

35. Evidence that will inflame the jury creates _____.

36. _____ are excluded from the definition of hearsay, even if they meet the definition.

37. Although not all _____ will be allowed before the jury, it includes anything that may lead to information that can be.

WEB WORK

1. Go to the Nonverbal Dictionary by David B. Givens at http://members.aol.com/nonverbal2/diction1.htm#The%20NONVERBAL%20DICTIONARY and click on "Entries." Click on "Deception Cue" and read the explanation there, clicking on each of the links. Do you have any of the habits that are described as indicators of deception? Do you do those things when you are lying, or only when you are nervous for some other reason?

2. Check at http://www.law.cornell.edu/uniform/evidence.html to see if your state has adopted the Uniform Rules of Evidence. If not, chances are that the law is not much different, as the Rules are essentially a codification of the common law of evidence.

3. Go to Paul Ekman's site at http://www.paulekman.com/ and follow the links to find the table of contents and sample chapter of his book about deception recognition. Do you think it would be useful for your purposes? Why or why not?

4. Peter Tillers at Cardozo Law School has a different method of organizing facts for a case, which he explains in his paper at http://tillers.net/fi-course/fpaper.html. What are the pros and cons of his methodology?

5. Using your favorite search engine, run a search with the terms "interviewing" and "nonverbal." Do you find many sites? Many useful sites? How do you think you could modify the search to make it more productive?

WORKING THE BRAIN

1. A human resources manager writes in a memo regarding a meeting about a potential lawsuit:

   All the facts point to one issue, harassment or possibly sexual harassment. The supervisor commented that from Chris's (the alleged harasser's) perspective, this is a much different issue than from the perspective of the alleged victim, Teresa. This has a much higher level of importance to Teresa. In addition, when you are out of the plant representing the Company, you have to consider the perception of your actions vs. what is received. All of your actions can put the Company in jeopardy.

   The supervisor stated, "Chris, I think you made some bad judgments, going out and getting drunk is not in the best interest of anybody, particularly when you are in a supervisory role. We must prevent this from ever happening again. I'm not sure you realize how serious this could have been. You and the company both could have been sued and still could be sued."

   Do you think the memo meets the definition of an admission of a party-opponent?

2. An insurance company hires an attorney for the insured to defend him in an automobile accident. The insured wants to file a counterclaim for his damages because he was injured; the insurer doesn't want to pay for the attorneys fees attached to the counterclaim and wants it dismissed. Is this a conflict? How may the issue be resolved?

3. If psychological and/or sociological tests have shown that jurors are using "folk wisdom" to determine credibility that is not justified by science, should those experts be allowed to testify to what the proper ways to determine credibility are? Or how should we determine credibility? Who should determine the credibility of witnesses if not the jurors?

4. Would evidence of pre-divorce spousal abuse be unfairly prejudicial in trying to determine whether a child was afraid to visit with the allegedly abusive spouse a year and a half after the divorce? Why or why not?

5. A plaintiff's expert specialized in emergency medicine and had practiced emergency medicine for 25 years. The defendant's counsel asked the doctor whether he was board-certified in emergency medicine. The doctor answered that he was not, saying, "The reason is that I was the first president of the Board of Emergency Medicine and was instrumental in development of the examination, and then served for many years as the editor of both the written and the oral exam." He followed up with: "The opinion of legal counsel was that there may be a conflict of interest if I [had taken] the exam [because it would have been perceived] that I knowed [sic] all the answers." The defendant contended that this was hearsay; the plaintiff argued it was not. Who do you think is right and why?

PUTTING IT TO WORK

1. Finish the discovery action plan started in the chapter. Be creative and try to think of as many sources as you can, whether people, documents, or things.

2. Interview a "defendant" in the fact situation provided by your instructor. Prepare a file to contain the case before meeting with the defendant, and make sure you have as much information as you can. Prepare a fee agreement, an answer, a discovery action plan, and write a memo to your supervising attorney reporting the meeting with the client and your view of the theory of the case (what the story is).

4

THE OPPOSING PARTY

"A common law trial is and always should be an adversarial proceeding. Discovery was hardly intended to enable a learned profession to perform its functions either without wits or on wits borrowed from the adversary."

Robert H. Jackson, Solicitor General (1947)

"No one means all he says, and yet very few say all they mean, for words are slippery and thought is viscous."

Henry B. Adams (1907)

"The wise learn many things from their enemies."

Aristophanes (414 BCE)

INTRODUCTION

The parties to the litigation are the ones whose credibility matters most. As a result, you will want to find out anything that may **impeach** (undermine the jury's belief in the opposing party as a believable witness) him, her, or it. (When you have a corporate defendant, you have an "it," although it will act through various people.) If possible, you'd like to find evidence that the opposing party is a liar, but that's not always possible. To claim the party is a liar doesn't mean, by the way, that the person was mistaken on some small detail. That argument won't fly. You'll need to show that he (1) has established a pattern of being mistaken on small details; (2) always has to explain away things; or (3) has lied about serious matters where there is no explanation but that he *did* lie. The civil trial of O. J. Simpson is instructive in all of these areas. The plaintiffs' attorney, Daniel Petrocelli, did an excellent job of cross-examining Simpson using all of these techniques to convince the jury that Simpson was lying, resulting in a liability verdict.

143

26   Q.   (BY MR. PETROCELLI) If Mr. Taft

27   testified in his deposition that you had that injury

28   on your fourth finger when you were at the police

144

1   station, would he be correct or incorrect?

2   A.   He'd be incorrect.

3   Q.   And was he there with you?

4   A.   He was there with me just about every

5   day.

6   Q.   So was Howard Weitzman, your lawyer?

7   A.   That's correct.

[. . .]

26   Q.   You see that cut up there, Mr. Simpson?

27   A.   Show me.

28   Q.   You don't see that injury up there on the

151

1   top part of your finger?

2   A.   I see something there that doesn't

3   comport with the earlier picture that I saw with the

4   side angle thing.

5   Q.   Where did you get that, Mr. Simpson?

6   A.   I don't think that's a cut. I think

7   that's—

[. . .]

15   Q.   (BY MR. PETROCELLI) Where did you get

16   that injury?

17   A.   I don't know.

[. . .]

26   Q.   (BY MR. PETROCELLI) Where did you

27   sustain these injuries, sir?

28   A.   Who knows.

153

1   Q.   You don't know?

2   A.   No.

3   Q.   Did you have them when you came back from

4   Chicago?

5   A.   If I did, they're so small I don't think

6   I would have noticed.

7   Q.   So you could have had those injuries?

8   A.   They could have been there.

9   Q.   And you could have had them—sustained

10   them on the evening of June 12, right?

11   A.   I wouldn't have any idea why they would

12   have been there, so—if you look at the wrinkles on

13   your hand, and you look at those, they're so small, I

14   wouldn't have noticed it, like if it would have

15   happened like a week before.

16   Q.   You don't dispute that those injuries

17   would—could have occurred on the evening of June

18   12, do you?

19   A.   No.

20   Q.   If you got them after you came back from

21   Chicago, you cannot tell the jury how you got them,

22   true?

23   A.   That's correct.

[. . .]

21   Q.   When you were in the Chicago hotel room

22   packing up, Mr. Simpson, you checked around and looked

23   for any blood?

24   A.   No.

25   Q.   And it is true, sir, that there was not

26   any blood anywhere in that hotel room except for a

27   small stain on a hand towel, true?

28   A.   I don't know.

   156

1   Q.   You did not see any blood anywhere else

2   except on a hand towel, true?

3   A.   I don't even know if I saw it on that.

4   Q.   Okay.

[. . .]

   157

1   Q.   (BY MR. PETROCELLI) That's the hand

2   towel that you believe that you used at some point?

3   A.   I don't know. I would assume so.

4   Q.   Well, don't assume anything.

5   A.   Okay.

6   Q.   Is that the only time you saw blood, was

7   on that hand towel?

8   A.   I don't recall if I even saw blood on

9   that hand towel.

[. . .]

26 Well, before we get downstairs, you made

27   three phone calls from your hotel room in Chicago to

28   this man Jim Merrill, right?

   163

1   A.   I would think at least three.

[. . .]

12 When you first called him, you asked him
13   to come back to pick you up and take you to the
14   airport, right?
15   A.   I told him I had to go.
16   Q.   And you called him at his cell phone
17   number, right?
18   A.   I don't—I'm pretty sure I called him
19   at his house.
20   Q.   Right.
21 And he lived 45 minutes away in the
22   suburbs, didn't he, sir?
23   A.   No. He told me he lived pretty close is
24   what he told me.
25   Q.   He lived 30 to 45 minutes away; did he
26   not tell you that?
27   A.   No. He told me he lived relatively
28   close.

        164

 1 And I said, are you coming?
 2 And he said, yeah, I should be there—I
 3   thought he said in a half-hour.
[. . .]
 5   Q.   Now, you called Merrill once; you called
 6   Merrill twice; you called Merrill three times from
 7   your hotel room, right?
 8   A.   Yes.
 9   Q.   The second time, Mr. Merrill told you on
10   the telephone, he goes: "Look, I'm pretty far away
11   and you probably should get some alternative
12   transportation," true?
13   A.   No, that's not true.
14   Q.   So if he testified under oath to that in
15   his deposition, he would be lying; is that true?
16   A.   That's correct.
[. . .]
20   Q.   And the truth of the matter is,
21   Mr. Simpson, that the reason you were so anxious to
22   get Mr. Merrill back to your hotel room is not because
23   you needed a ride, but because he had your golf clubs,
24   right?
25   A.   No, that's not correct.
26   Q.   And in that golf club bag—you put that
27   other bag over near the Bentley, right?
28   A.   I suppose it was still in there, yes.

        166

 1   Q.   And that's why you really wanted Mr.
 2   Merrill back, right?

3   A.   No. I could have waited and took the

4   10 o'clock plane that Cathy had arranged, but I didn't

5   want to, so I took a 9:15 flight that I had arranged.

[. . .]

21   Q.   And then, while you were waiting for a

22   cab, you're sitting on a bench outside, right?

23   A.   Yes.

24   Q.   And a Hertz colleague of yours drove up,

25   a man named Jack Johnson, right?

26   A.   That's right.

27   Q.   And you told Jack Johnson that you were

28   going to—you were waiting to catch a cab to the

168

1   airport, right?

2   A.   I think I told him, can somebody take me

3   to the airport.

4   Q.   And he had with him an employee by the

5   name of Raymond Kilduff, right?

6   A.   I have no idea.

7   Q.   And this fellow that was with Mr. Johnson

8   ended up taking you to the airport, right?

9   A.   Yeah.

10   Q.   Okay.

11   And you told Mr. Johnson, before leaving

12   for the airport, that you wanted to make sure you got

13   your golf clubs back, didn't you?

14   A.   No, I don't think that's correct. I may

15   have mentioned that Mr. Merrill was coming, and I was

16   waiting for him, and if he can get to that—I think

17   we tried to call him from the car, to tell him that we

18   were on our way to the airport and for him to, if he

19   went to the airport—just what flight I was on, if

20   he wanted to put them on that flight.

21   Q.   If Mr. Kilduff said that, he would be

22   mistaken, true?

23   A.   I think in substance, possibly no. But

24   what I just said to you, I think, is more accurate.

25   Q.   If Mr. Kilduff testified in his

26   deposition that before leaving the airport, you told

27   Mr. Johnson, in his presence, that you wanted to make

28   sure your golf clubs got back, Mr. Kilduff would not

169

1   be telling the truth?

2   A.   No.

[. . .]

6   Q.   You recognize the photos here as the

7   interior of your house?

8   A.   Yes.

9   Q.   And now, you see—let's take these two

10   photos in the lower left-hand corner of the bathroom

11   floor, right?

12   A.   Yes.

13   Q.   Okay.

14 Now, that's your bathroom floor, right?

15   A.   Yes.

16   Q.   You have any explanation, sir, how blood

17   found on the bathroom floor, that matched your blood,

18   was found there?

19   A.   Well, one, I don't know if they ever

20   determined it matched my blood. That's where I shave

21   and that's where I do all my—do—

22   Q.   Did you bleed on the bathroom floor on

23   the evening of June 12, yes or no?

24   A.   I don't know.

25   Q.   Didn't you testify previously in this—

26   in this courtroom, that the only time that you saw

27   blood on the evening of June 12, 1994, for that matter

28   any time that day, was in the kitchen?

      209

1   A.   Yes.

2   Q.   Okay.

3 So you did not see any blood on the

4   bathroom floor; is that what you're saying?

5   A.   That's correct.

6   Q.   You have no explanation for how your

7   blood got there?

8   A.   If it's my blood. I don't know if they

9   ever tested it. I would assume it could have happened

10   any time that I shaved in my bathroom.

11   Q.   You would assume that?

12   A.   Yes.

13   Q.   But you don't know?

14   A.   Correct.

[. . .]

8   Q.   You saw those Bruno Magli shoes that were

9   discussed in court, right?

10   A.   Yes.

11   Q.   And you heard the testimony that those

12   Bruno Magli shoes, size 12, left the footprint at

13   Bundy, right?

14   A.   Yes.

15   Q.   And you wear size 12, right?

16   A.   At times, yeah, among other shoes. Yes,

17   anywhere from 11, 12, 13.

18   Q.   Including size 12?

19   A.   That's right.

20   Q.   Those Reeboks are size 12?

21   A.   I don't know.

22   Q.   The ones you gave to Lange?

23   A.   I don't know. But they probably were.

24   Q.   They probably were?

25   A.   They could have been.

26   Q.   Okay. Now, your deposition was taken in

27   this case in January of 1996, sir?

28   A.   I don't know. I don't recall.

    234

1   Q.   You do recall, though, that your

2   deposition was taken at a time before the photograph

3   of you wearing those shoes appeared in the National

4   Enquirer, sometime in March or April, correct?

5   A.   I don't recall that, no.

6   Q.   You wouldn't dispute that if the dates

7   bore that out, right?

8   A.   No.

9   Q.   Okay.

10   And you recall that I asked you if you

11   ever owned the Bruno Magli shoes, Bruno Magli shoes,

12   size 12, the type that you were shown in court, as of

13   June 12, 1994?

14   Do you recall what your answer was?

15   A.   Yes.

[. . .]

27   Q.   (BY MR. PETROCELLI) I'll read it.

28   Page 1305, starting at line 10:

    235

1   "Q.   Did you ever buy shoes that

2   you knew were Bruno Magli shoes?

3   "A.   No.

4   "Q.   How do you know that?

5   "A.   Because I know. If Bruno

6   Magli makes shoes that look like the shoes

7   that he had in court that are involved in

8   this case, I would have never owned those

9   ugly-ass shoes.

10   "Q.   You thought those were

11   ugly-ass shoes?

12   "A.   Yes.

13   "Q.   Why were they ugly-ass shoes?

14   "A.   Because in my mind, they

15   were.

16   "Q.   What about them was ugly,

17   Mr. Simpson?

18   "A.   The look of them, the style."

19   Do you recall giving that testimony?

20   A.   Yes.

21   And the color of them.

22   Q.   Now, after that deposition testimony,

23   this picture of you appeared in the National Enquirer,

24   right?

25   A.   Yes.

26   Q.   And that is you, Mr. Simpson, is it not?

27   A.   It looks like me.

28   Q.   And you did attend a football game at

      236

1   Rich Stadium in Orchard Park, New York, on September

2   26, 1993, correct?

3   A.   I could have, yes.

4   Q.   What do you mean, you could have?

5   Did you or did you not?

6   A.   I don't know.

7   Q.   Do you remember being there?

8   A.   I don't know the dates, but I certainly

9   attended a lot of games in Buffalo.

10   Q.   Well, how's this for refreshing your

11   recollection? The last time that you saw the Bills

12   play the Dolphins at Rich Stadium?

13   A.   I don't recall when that was.

14   Q.   That would have been that game, correct?

15   A.   I went to two or three games, sometimes,

16   a week, so I wouldn't know.

17   Q.   There's two in a season; there's one at

18   Buffalo, there's one at Miami. That was the last

19   season before Nicole's death that you did football

20   games, true?

21   A.   If you say that is that game, I'll accept

22   that. I'm just—.

23   Q.   Thank you.

24   A.   —telling you, I don't remember what

25   dates what games were played.

26   Q.   Okay.

27   And you don't remember much about the

28   games, sir?

237

1   A.   No, not really.

2   Q.   You know who won?

3   A.   I hope Buffalo.

4   Q.   But you don't remember, do you?

5   A.   No.

6   Q.   And your routine was to get there before

7   the game and, you know, do some pregame interviews and

8   that sort of thing?

9   A.   Yes.

10 Q.   And you recognize what part of the

11   stadium you're walking in there, sir?

12 A.   It appears to be the end zone.

[. . .]

21 Q.   (BY MR. PETROCELLI) Now, Mr. Simpson you

22   are wearing Bruno Magli shoes, size 12, in that

23   photograph?

24 A.   That photograph depicts that, but I

25   don't—I wouldn't—wasn't wearing Bruno Magli

26   shoes.

27 Q.   Well, are you saying those are not Bruno

28   Magli shoes?

238

1   A.   They look like Bruno Magli shoes, yes.

2   Q.   But you're not wearing them; is that what

3   you're saying?

4   A.   I'm—that's what I'm saying.

5   Q.   How can that be, sir?

6   A.   I don't know.

7   I saw a picture of Mark Fuhrman and I

8   playing golf together, and I know I never, ever played

9   golf with him, either.

10 Q.   What does this have to do with Mark

11   Fuhrman?

12 A.   I don't know.

13 You asked me how can that be. I'm no

14   expert on pictures, but I saw a picture of Mark

15   Fuhrman and me playing golf, together in a golf cart.

16 Q.   What you're saying to the jury is, that

17   picture is a fraud?

18 A.   I believe so, yes.

19 Q.   What do you mean, you believe so. Is it

20   or is it not?

21 A.   I would say it is.

[. . .]

3   Q.   Okay.

4 What part of that picture is fraudulent?

5   A.   I couldn't tell you exactly. But

6   anything that below my—I have—I had a tie sort

7   of like that tie, I know.

8 As I've told you in a deposition, the

9   coat, I can't really tell. I've worn all kinds of

10   sports coats. It looks like a nice sports coat. The

11   collar on the shirt is definitely a collar that I've

12   had shirts that look like that.

13 The belt, I can't really tell.

14 The pants look a little big on me.

15 And the shoes, I don't know, weren't my

16   shoes.

17   Q.   You're absolutely positive about the

18   shoes?

19   A.   I'm pretty sure.

20   Q.   Pretty sure?

21   A.   Well, I am sure.

22   Q.   There is no doubt in your mind, is there,

23   sir?

24   A.   No, there's not.

25   Q.   There's no doubt?

26   A.   I said no.

27   Q.   None, right?

28   A.   For the third time, no.

    240

1   Q.   And give us your definitive opinion: Are

2   those pants yours or not? Yes or no?

3   A.   I couldn't tell you. They're gray pants.

4   They look big on whoever that might be.

5   Q.   Is your answer you can't tell us?

6   A.   I can't tell you.

7   Q.   They could be your gray pants?

8   A.   I own gray pants, and I've owned pants

9   with cuffs, yes.

10   Q.   You have any reason to believe those

11   pants are not yours?

12   A.   Only the shoes lead me to believe that

13   those are not my pants.

14   Q.   Forget the shoes, focusing on the pants,

15   are the pants yours?

16   A.   I don't know.

17   Q.   You don't know?

18   A.   They look a little big in the legs.

19   Q.   Let's go to the belt.

20   Is the belt yours?

21   A.   I can't tell.

22   Q.   You don't know?

23   A.   I can't tell.

24   Q.   Is the jacket yours?

25   A.   I mean, I've owned plenty of—if—I

26   can't tell from here if it's a double-breast or

27   single-breast blue or black jacket. I've owned plenty

28   of them, yes.

     241

1   Q.   Is the jacket yours?

2   A.   I don't know.

3   Q.   You don't know?

4   A.   It looks like it could be my jacket.

5   Q.   You're saying you can't tell if that's

6   your jacket or not?

7   A.   It looks like that's my jacket, yes.

8   Q.   Is that your opinion, that it is your

9   jacket?

10   A.   That would be my opinion, yes.

11   Q.   And the tie?

12   A.   I know I had a tie that looked like that,

13   yes.

14   Q.   And that tie is yours, right?

15   A.   I had a tie like that, so I would say

16   yes.

17   Q.   And the white shirt. Is that your white

18   shirt?

19   A.   By the collar of the shirt, I knew I had

20   shirts that looked like that, yes.

21   Q.   And the hands and the upper torso, that's

22   all you, right?

23   A.   Yeah. Yes, I would say so.

24   Q.   So it's basically the shoes that you

25   question, right?

26   A.   Yes. The pants somewhat, too.

[. . .]

16   Q.   (BY MR. PETROCELLI) Is that the same

17   jacket, tie, and shirt, Mr. Simpson?

18   A.   It looks the same, yes.

19   Q.   Okay.

20 And that's—you don't have any reason
21   to think that those are not your items that you're
22   wearing there, is there?
23 A. From what I could see.
24 Q. Is that where it ends?
25 A. Yes. I'm trying to see the colors.
26 Yeah, that still looks like—
27 Q. And that's TV footage from the same game,
28   right?

    243

1   A. I would assume so, yes.
[. . .]
9
10 MR. PETROCELLI: Same exhibit. This is the
11   same game.
12 Now, stop it there.
13 Q. (BY MR. PETROCELLI) Now, you see you're
14   wearing these same belt and gray pants and shirt
15   there, Mr. Simpson?
16 A. I can't really tell, but they are gray
17   pants, and I can't really tell what the belt is.
18 Q. You can make out the tie there, can't
19   you?
20 A. Yes.
21 Q. Same tie, same shirt, right?
22 A. That's right.
23 Q. You can see that the pants there are
24   gray, can you?
25 MR. PETROCELLI: You can't blow that up, can
26   you, Steve?
27 We finally found something you can't do?
28 A. I would say that the pants were gray

    244

1   pants, yeah.
2   Q. (BY MR. PETROCELLI) So, basically
3   everything is there. Is it—you can see it there,
4   right?
5   A. Yes.
6   Q. Same belt, same pants, same everything,
7   right?
8   A. No. The coat is obviously a raincoat.
9   Q. Well, that's a different coat you put on,
10   right?
11 A. Yes.

12   Q.   So, that changes your mind a little bit on
13   the pants, makes you sure that those pants were
14   genuine?
15   A.   No.
16   Q.   That the—that the pants you're wearing
17   here are the same pants depicted here?
18   A.   No, that didn't change my mind.
19   Q.   Doesn't change your mind, seeing it on
20   the video?
21   A.   No. I'm sure I wore gray pants that day
22   because I normally wear gray pants.
23   Q.   Do you think the video is a fraud too?
24   A.   Not at all.
25   Q.   Okay.
[. . .]
 7   Q.   (BY MR. PETROCELLI) And that's a picture
 8   of you interviewing Keith Byers?
 9   A.   It appears to be, yes.
10   Q.   Who was then on the Miami Dolphins?
11   A.   That's correct.
12   Q.   And again, that's before game time,
13   right?
14   A.   I don't know. Could have been after.
15   Q.   And there you're wearing the same outfit
16   depicted in the picture of you walking through the end
17   zone, right?
18   A.   From the waist up, yes.
19   Q.   The same tie, shirt, and jacket?
20   A.   Appears to be, yes.
21   Q.   Now, is it your opinion that picture's a
22   fraud?
23   A.   Well—
24   Q.   Yes or no?
25   A.   I would say no.
26   Q.   Not a fraud?
27   A.   Yes.
[. . .]
 4   Q.   You're not able to produce those shoes in
 5   court that you're wearing in that photograph, are you?
[. . .]
10   You cannot bring to this courtroom the
11   shoes depicted in that photograph?
12   A.   The shoes depicted in this photograph,
13   no.

14   Q. And by the way, you still think those

15   shoes are ugly-ass shoes that you're wearing there?

16   A. Not as ugly as the ones in the courtroom.

17 I don't think those are attractive shoes,

18   No.

As you can see, the line of questioning includes testimony in which Simpson is positive about details that will help him, but he equivocates constantly on other related details. He does not know what clothes belong to him; he says the other person is lying, but not him, as in the discussion regarding the golf clubs, and makes claims that look like rather big lies (for example, not wearing the clothes he appears to be wearing at the game). These are the sorts of facts you look for in trying to find ways to demonstrate that a witness is lying.

You won't be able to prove every witness is a liar. Other ways to make juries dislike a party or be more inclined to discredit their testimony is to show that the party exaggerates (a whiner as a personal injury plaintiff, for instance), is a bad person, is biased in some way, or has some disability that prevents her from being able to evaluate things clearly. This last bit has to be handled sensitively; you don't want to beat a little old lady over the head for being hard of hearing or practically blind, but you do need to bring it up if what she heard or saw forms the basis of the suit. The "bad person" part has limitations that will be discussed below, but if you can get the evidence admitted, it is strategically advantageous to show that the party is a felon or other sort of lowlife, as the jury will be less worried about being fair to her.

This concern for fairness is an important consideration because you don't want the jury to perceive the attorney as being a bully—and if the "bad acts" are not significant, that can happen. In one case I was involved in, the plaintiff was clearly a naïve woman. The defense attorney began to badger her about details on her tax return to attack her claim of damages. She had no clue—she'd used a tax preparer. The attorney made the mistake of continuing to ask her questions after she had explained that she had no idea, and it made him look like he was bullying the poor woman—or so said the jurors after he lost the case.

One of the other characteristics of the Simpson testimony is his flippant attitude during questioning—not something that goes over well when people have been brutally murdered. The attorney also tried to show that Simpson was not terribly upset when he "learned" of his wife's murder by showing that he was more concerned about his golf clubs. In omitted testimony, the plaintiff's attorney also mentioned that Simpson was signing autographs and smiling at folks on the plane when he supposedly had just found out about Nicole's death. These attitudes are not shown by summary; in other words, you can't just say, "Mr. Simpson, you didn't care that your ex-wife was killed, did you?" and be successful. You establish this with the jury fact by fact. You obtain these facts by interviewing and investigating.

ETHICAL ISSUES

No Contact Rule

You may not speak to a represented party. Model Code Prof'l Cond. R. 4.2. Once someone has an attorney, you must go through the attorney to obtain any information. **Pro se** (or **pro per**) folks—those who represent themselves—you can talk to, but they will try to get you to give them advice. You also are under an ethical duty to make sure they understand you are on the other side and that you are not a lawyer. Model Code Prof'l Cond. R. 4.3. Sometimes you can get information from them, but usually you'll get more out of lawyers who know how the game is played. The tricky part of representation arises when **corporations** are involved.

Representation of Corporations

Because corporations are not natural persons, no single human represents the entity. As a result, there is a question as to which people the attorney represents. The ethical rules have not done a good job of delineating who is represented in the corporate context. This is important for the investigator to know, as you ordinarily may speak to employees of the corporation who are not represented, but not those who are. In the past, it was clear that you could speak to former employees with no problem, but not current employees. Now the ABA has taken the position that when a former employee had the power to bind the corporation, it may be unethical to talk to that employee as well. Aside from checking the ethics opinions in your state, which you should do and adhere to if such opinions are available, you can look to general principles of law to try to resolve your ethical dilemma as to whom you may speak. There are two different issues to review here: who is represented and to whom attorney-client privilege applies.

Representation may be determined by the **control group test**, by the **authority structure**, or by the **framework of dealing.** The control group test is one that looks at the persons in the corporation who have the power to direct the litigation. The reasoning is that those persons will be the ones to need the protection of the privilege because they are the ones with whom the attorney will communicate and the ones who will know the strategies of the corporation. By this test, only a limited number of corporate employees are represented by the attorney.

The authority structure approach looks at the official corporate structure of the entity and extends representation to those with formal decision-making authority as evidenced by the documents of incorporation. This would generally be the officers and board of the corporation.

The framework of dealing is a hybrid approach that takes into account both the day-to-day operators and any upper management actually involved in the chain of authority for litigation. Advocated by some commentators, this is a minority approach.

Properly, attorney-client privilege is an evidentiary issue rather than an ethics one, but it needs to be discussed here to help shed light on the anti-contact rule. States have adopted different tests for determining whom attorney-client privilege extends to: the control group test (the same one discussed above), the **subject matter test,** or some variation on these two.

Not surprisingly, the subject matter test focuses on the subject of the litigation. The persons connected with the matters being litigated will be afforded the protection of attorney-client privilege, generally a larger number of people.

The most likely compromise between the two is the *Upjohn* test, named for the United States Supreme Court decision that follows.

Upjohn Co. v. United States, 449 U.S. 383 (1981).

We granted certiorari in this case to address important questions concerning the scope of the attorney-client privilege in the corporate context and the applicability of the work-product doctrine in proceedings to enforce tax summonses . . . . With respect to the privilege question the parties and various *amici* have described our task as one of choosing between two "tests" which have gained adherents in the courts of appeals. We are acutely aware, however, that we sit to decide concrete cases and not abstract propositions of law. We decline to lay down a broad rule or series of rules to govern all conceivable future questions in this area, even were we able to do so. We can and do, however, conclude that the attorney-client privilege protects the communications involved in this case from compelled disclosure and that the work-product doctrine does apply in tax summons enforcement proceedings.

I

Petitioner Upjohn Co. manufactures and sells pharmaceuticals here and abroad. In January 1976 independent accountants conducting an audit of one of Upjohn's foreign subsidiaries discovered that the subsidiary made payments to or for the benefit of foreign government officials in order to secure government business. The accountants so informed petitioner Mr. Gerard Thomas, Upjohn's Vice President, Secretary, and General Counsel. Thomas is a member of the Michigan and New York Bars, and has been Upjohn's General Counsel for 20 years. He consulted with outside counsel and R. T. Parfet, Jr., Upjohn's Chairman of the Board. It was decided that the company would conduct an internal investigation of what were termed "questionable payments." As part of this investigation the attorneys prepared a letter containing a questionnaire which was sent to "All Foreign General and Area Managers" over the Chairman's signature. The letter began by noting recent disclosures that several American companies made "possibly illegal" payments to foreign government officials and emphasized that the management needed full information concerning any such payments made by Upjohn. The letter indicated that the Chairman had asked Thomas, identified as "the company's General Counsel," "to conduct an investigation for the purpose of determining the nature and magnitude of any payments made by the Upjohn Company or any of its subsidiaries to any employee or official of a foreign government." The questionnaire sought detailed information concerning such payments. Managers were instructed to treat the investigation as "highly confidential" and not to discuss it with anyone other than Upjohn employees who might be helpful in providing the requested information. Responses were to be sent directly to Thomas. Thomas and outside counsel also interviewed the recipients of the questionnaire and some 33 other Upjohn officers or employees as part of the investigation.

. . . On November 23, 1976, the Service issued a summons pursuant to 26 U. S. C. § 7602 demanding production of:

". . . written questionnaires sent to managers of the Upjohn Company's foreign affiliates, and memorandums or notes of the interviews conducted in the United States and abroad with officers and employees of the Upjohn Company and its subsidiaries."

The company declined to produce the documents . . . on the grounds that they were protected from disclosure by the attorney-client privilege and constituted the work product of attorneys prepared in anticipation of litigation . . . [T]he Court of Appeals for the Sixth Circuit . . . agreed that the privilege did not apply "[to] the extent that the communications were made by officers and agents not responsible for directing Upjohn's actions in response to legal advice . . . for the simple reason that the communications were not the 'client's.'". . . The court reasoned that accepting petitioners' claim for a broader application of the privilege would encourage upper-echelon management to ignore unpleasant facts and create too broad a "zone of silence." Noting that Upjohn's counsel had interviewed officials such as the Chairman and President, the Court of Appeals remanded to the District Court so that a determination of who was within the "control group" could be made. . .

II

Federal Rule of Evidence 501 provides that "the privilege of a witness . . . shall be governed by the principles of the common law as they may be interpreted by the courts of the United States in light of reason and experience." The attorney-client privilege is the oldest of the privileges for confidential communications known to the common law. . . . Admittedly complications in the application of the privilege arise when the client is a corporation, which in theory is an artificial creature of the law, and not an individual; but this Court has assumed that the privilege applies when the client is a corporation . . . and the Government does not contest the general proposition.

The Court of Appeals, however, considered the application of the privilege in the corporate context to present a "different problem," since the client was an inanimate entity and "only the senior management, guiding and integrating the several operations, . . . can be said to possess an identity analogous to the corporation as a whole.". . . The first case to articulate the so-called "control group test". . . reflected a similar conceptual approach:

> Keeping in mind that the question is, Is it the corporation which is seeking the lawyer's advice when the asserted privileged communication is made?, the most satisfactory solution, I think, is that if the employee making the communication, of whatever rank he may be, is in a position to control or even to take a substantial part in a decision about any action which the corporation may take upon the advice of the attorney, . . . then, in effect, *he is (or personifies) the corporation* when he makes his disclosure to the lawyer and the privilege would apply. (Emphasis supplied.)

Such a view, we think, overlooks the fact that the privilege exists to protect not only the giving of professional advice to those who can act on it but also the giving of information to the lawyer to enable him to give sound and informed advice. . . . The first step in the resolution of any legal problem is ascertaining the factual background and sifting through the facts with an eye to the legally relevant. . .

In the case of the individual client the provider of information and the person who acts on the lawyer's advice are one and the same. In the corporate context, however, it will frequently be employees beyond the control group as defined by the court below—"officers and agents . . . responsible for directing [the company's] actions in response to legal advice"—who will possess the information needed by the corporation's lawyers. Middle-level—and indeed lower-level—employees can, by actions within the scope of their employment, embroil the corporation in serious legal difficulties, and it is only natural that these employees would have the relevant information needed by corporate counsel if he is adequately to advise the client with respect to such actual or potential difficulties. This fact was noted in *Diversified Industries, Inc.* v. *Meredith*, 572 F.2d 596 (CA8 1978) (en banc):

> In a corporation, it may be necessary to glean information relevant to a legal problem from middle management or non-management personnel as well as from top executives. The attorney dealing with a complex legal problem "is thus faced with a 'Hobson's choice'. If he interviews employees not having 'the very highest authority', their communications to him will not be privileged. If, on the other hand, he interviews *only* those employees with 'the very highest authority', he may find it extremely difficult, if not impossible, to determine what happened." . . .

The control group test adopted by the court below thus frustrates the very purpose of the privilege by discouraging the communication of relevant information by employees of the client to attorneys seeking to render legal advice to the client corporation. The attorney's advice will also frequently be more significant to noncontrol group members than to those who officially sanction the advice, and the control group test makes it more difficult to convey full and frank legal advice to the employees who will put into effect the client corporation's policy. . .

The communications at issue were made by Upjohn employees to counsel for Upjohn acting as such, at the direction of corporate superiors in order to secure legal advice from counsel. As the Magistrate found, "Mr. Thomas consulted with the Chairman of the Board and outside counsel and thereafter conducted a factual investigation to determine the nature and extent of the questionable payments *and to be in a position to give legal advice to the company with respect to the payments*." (Emphasis supplied.) . . . The communications concerned matters within the scope of the employees' corporate duties, and the employees themselves were sufficiently aware that they were being questioned in order that the corporation could obtain legal advice. The questionnaire identified Thomas as "the company's General Counsel" and referred in its opening sentence to the possible illegality of payments such as the ones on which information was sought . . . A statement of policy accompanying the questionnaire clearly indicated the legal implications of the investigation. The policy statement was issued "in order that there be no uncertainty in the future as to the policy with respect to the practices which are the subject of this investigation." It began "Upjohn will comply with all laws and regulations," and stated that commissions or payments "will not be used as a subterfuge for bribes or illegal payments" and that all payments must be "proper and legal." Any future agreements with foreign distributors or agents were to be approved "by a company attorney" and any questions concerning the policy were to be referred "to the company's General Counsel." *Id.*, at 165a–166a. This statement was issued to Upjohn employees worldwide, so that even those interviewees not receiving a questionnaire were aware of the legal implications of the interviews. Pursuant to explicit instructions from the Chairman of the Board, the communications were considered "highly confidential" when made . . . and have been kept confidential by the company. Consistent with the underlying purposes of the attorney-client privilege, these communications must be protected against compelled disclosure.

The Court of Appeals declined to extend the attorney-client privilege beyond the limits of the control group test for fear that doing so would entail severe burdens on discovery and create a broad "zone of silence" over corporate affairs. Application of the attorney-client privilege to communications such as those involved here, however, puts the adversary in no worse position than if the communications had never taken place. The privilege only protects disclosure of communications; it does not protect disclosure of the underlying facts by those who communicated with the attorney:

> [The] protection of the privilege extends only to *communications* and not to facts. A fact is one thing and a communication concerning that fact is an entirely different thing. The client cannot be compelled to answer the question, "What did you say or write to the attorney?" but may not refuse to disclose any relevant fact within his knowledge merely because he incorporated a statement of such fact into his communication to his attorney.

... Here the Government was free to question the employees who communicated with Thomas and outside counsel. Upjohn has provided the IRS with a list of such employees, and the IRS has already interviewed some 25 of them. While it would probably be more convenient for the Government to secure the results of petitioner's internal investigation by simply subpoenaing the questionnaires and notes taken by petitioner's attorneys, such considerations of convenience do not overcome the policies served by the attorney-client privilege. As Justice Jackson noted in his concurring opinion in *Hickman* v. *Taylor*, 329 U.S., at 516: "Discovery was hardly intended to enable a learned profession to perform its functions . . . on wits borrowed from the adversary."

Needless to say, we decide only the case before us, and do not undertake to draft a set of rules which should govern challenges to investigatory subpoenas. Any such approach would violate the spirit of Federal Rule of Evidence 501. . . . While such a "case-by-case" basis may to some slight extent undermine desirable certainty in the boundaries of the attorney-client privilege, it obeys the spirit of the Rules. At the same time we conclude that the narrow "control group test" sanctioned by the Court of Appeals in this case cannot, consistent with "the principles of the common law as . . . interpreted . . . in the light of reason and experience," Fed. Rule Evid. 501, govern the development of the law in this area.

III

Our decision that the communications by Upjohn employees to counsel are covered by the attorney-client privilege disposes of the case so far as the responses to the questionnaires and any notes reflecting responses to interview questions are concerned. . . .

Accordingly, the judgment of the Court of Appeals is reversed, and the case remanded for further proceedings.

It is so ordered.

Commentators have characterized this decision as a "subject matter-like" decision, but it is not as broad nor does it specifically state that as the test, despite the similarity of approach. The court analyzes the privilege in terms of what is necessary for the attorney to do his job. The court does not, however, discuss who is covered by the privilege in terms of whom the attorney represents; the case simply addresses what communications are privileged. Can a person who receives a privileged communication not be represented as well? It's just not clear.

EVIDENTIARY ISSUES

Propensity Evidence and Prior Bad Acts

In looking for information that will categorize the opposing party as a liar or otherwise bad person, it is helpful to know what kind of evidence is admissible. Two types exist: evidence that is admissible in order to make your case, and evidence that is admissible for purposes of impeachment. The first kind is evidence that the attorney plans to put before the jury as part of the trial presentation. The second, impeachment, is only allowed before the jury after the witness has made a statement contrary to the impeachment evidence. Often you ask a party questions hoping he'll lie so you can bring in the impeachment evidence up as an impeachment issue. For instance, let's say you ask a plaintiff in a deposition if he has ever been investigated for fraud. If he says no, and he actually has, you may address the issue in court because the plaintiff has now lied under oath. If the plaintiff admits the fraud investigation in the deposition, however, it will probably not be admissible. Why? Because of the rules governing the admission of crimes and **prior bad acts.**

The first rule to consider is Federal Rule of Evidence 404.

a. Character evidence generally

Evidence of a person's character or a trait of character is not admissible for the purpose of proving action in conformity therewith on a particular occasion, except:

. . .

3. Character of witness—Evidence of the character of a witness, as provided in rules 607, 608, and 609.

b. Other crimes, wrongs, or acts

Evidence of other crimes, wrongs, or acts is not admissible to prove the character of a person in order to show action in conformity therewith. It may, however, be admissible for other purposes, such as proof of motive, opportunity, intent, preparation, plan, knowledge, identity, or absence of mistake or accident . . .

Fed. R. Evid. 404.

Say what? It always amuses me when people say they're willing to be "character witnesses." As you can see, the first statement says that evidence of character is generally not admissible. What is this rule addressing? It is addressing planned evidence admitted to establish elements of your cause of action or defense, not impeachment evidence. And it is saying that you cannot buttress your case by adding evidence of what a great person you are all the time to prove you were a great person this time. There are, of course, exceptions. The first two are under criminal circumstances, so we need not address them here. The exceptions referred to in (a)(3) are the rules for impeachment. It is also important to note subsection (b), which addresses "crimes, wrongs, or acts." So you can't talk about "bad stuff" the other party has done in the past just to show she'd do it again now; this is called **propensity evidence.** But you can talk about the bad stuff if it's for a different reason.

For example, one of the things auto adjusters used to get excited about when I was working as counsel in an insurance company was finding out a driver on the other side had a history of driving while intoxicated (DWI, or driving under the influence, DUI, as your state may characterize it). Knowing this rule, I would look at them rather cynically, I'm afraid, and say, "Why is that helpful?"

"Well, it was late and there were drinks at the restaurant, so maybe he was drinking."

"Mmm. So you want to use the fact that he's been drunk and driving in the past to prove that he did it this time?"

The adjuster would usually give me a "Well, *duh*" kind of look at this point. I'd have to then explain that unlike in real life, where we use past experience with people to explain the present, the rules of evidence specifically prohibit doing that.

I'd usually then ask the adjuster, "Who owns the car the DWI was driving?" Most of the time it would be the drunk himself. But once in a while, someone else owned the vehicle. "Now you can use that information," I'd tell the adjuster. She would look at me with a puzzled expression.

"You can use it to show not that the guy was driving drunk that night, but to show that the owner of the vehicle was negligent in letting him drive the car since he knew or should have known about the DWI convictions."

"Ooooohhhh." If evidence of prior bad acts is admitted as something other than as propensity evidence, then you're back to the relevancy versus prejudicial effect argument rather than a flat prohibition. And subsection (b) gives you some idea of what other reasons for admission might be: proof of motive, opportunity, intent, preparation, plan, knowledge, identity, or absence of mistake or accident. It's not a complete list, but it's a start.

However, the more frequent way for information to come before the jury is through impeachment. The Federal Rules of Evidence governing bad acts and impeachment are as follows.

Rule 607. Who May Impeach

The credibility of a witness may be attacked by any party, including the party calling the witness.

Rule 608. Evidence of Character and Conduct of Witness

a. Opinion and reputation evidence of character. The credibility of a witness may be attacked or supported by evidence in the form of opinion or reputation, but subject to these limitations:

1. the evidence may refer only to character for truthfulness or untruthfulness, and
2. evidence of truthful character is admissible only after the character of the witness for truthfulness has been attacked by opinion or reputation evidence or otherwise.

Fed. R. Evid. 607, 608.

The reputation part of this rule ordinarily comes into play only if a person's reputation has something to do with the cause of action, such as in a defamation case. The opinion part doesn't come up all that often, and it is not something that would probably be admissible in most instances because of a concept not stated in the rules. This concept is that opinion evidence is not allowed when it bears on an ultimate issue that the jury should decide. Overall opinions of credibility of the parties (and other witnesses) are the reason juries try cases, and something they weigh by listening to and observing them in the courtroom. One area of expert witness testimony that has consistently been rejected by the courts is the psychiatric proof (well documented, by the way) that eyewitnesses to crisis situations are notoriously unreliable as a result of the effect the crisis has on their perceptions. However, you may bring up how truthful a party is after it has been attacked "otherwise."

b. Specific instances of conduct.

Specific instances of the conduct of a witness, for the purpose of attacking or supporting the witness' credibility, other than conviction of crime as provided in rule 609, may not be proved by extrinsic evidence. They may, however, in the discretion of the court, if probative of truthfulness or untruthfulness, be inquired into on cross-examination of the witness

1. concerning the witness' character for truthfulness or untruthfulness, or

2. concerning the character for truthfulness or untruthfulness of another witness as to which character the witness being cross-examined has testified.

The giving of testimony, whether by an accused or by any other witness, does not operate as a waiver of the accused's or the witness' privilege against self-incrimination when examined with respect to matters which relate only to credibility.

Fed. R. Evid. 608(b).

This is where you can work in that prior DWI (presuming it is a misdemeanor) or whatever if the opposing party is foolish. When the deposition is taken, your attorney will ask a list of "Have you ever. . . ?" questions. If the opposing party admits these "bad acts," there won't be a problem. His attorney will address the issues in a motion in limine and she will probably be successful. However, if he lies about the prior DWI (or whatever), then, when trial comes, your attorney may impeach the witness like this.

Q: Do you remember when we got together before the trial and I asked you a lot of questions?

A: Yes.

Q: And do you remember that you took an oath to tell the truth?

A: Yes.

Q: Just like the one you took today?

A: Yeah.

Q: And do you remember that I asked you if you had ever had a DWI?

A. MmHmm.

Q: I'm sorry; I don't know if the court reporter could get that. Could you repeat your answer? Do you remember me asking you if you ever had a DWI?

A: Yes.

Q: And what did you say?

A: I don't remember.

Q: Well, I have a copy of the deposition right here. Would you like to look at it?

A. Ummm. Okay. [reads] I said, "No."

Q: And is that the truth?

A: [long pause] Yes.

Q: [handing him a piece of paper] Take a look at this. Can you tell the jury what this is?

A: [mumbles inaudibly]

Q: I'm sorry; I didn't hear that.

A: It's a certified copy of the order convicting me.

Q: Convicting you of what?

A: DWI.

Q: And was that before or after the accident?

A: Before.

Q: No further questions.

So even if the evidence can't be used up front, it still may come in handy later.

Rule 609. Impeachment by Evidence of Conviction of Crime

a. General rule.

   For the purpose of attacking the credibility of a witness,

   1. evidence that a witness other than an accused has been convicted of a crime shall be admitted, subject to Rule 403, if the crime was punishable by death or imprisonment in excess of one year under the law under which the witness was convicted, and evidence that an accused has been convicted of such a crime shall be admitted if the court determines that the probative value of admitting this evidence outweighs its prejudicial effect to the accused; and

   2. evidence that any witness has been convicted of a crime shall be admitted if it involved dishonesty or false statement, regardless of the punishment.

b. Time limit.

   Evidence of a conviction under this rule is not admissible if a period of more than ten years has elapsed since the date of the conviction or of the release of the witness from the confinement imposed for that conviction, whichever is the later date, unless the court determines, in the interests of justice, that the probative value of the conviction supported by specific facts and circumstances substantially outweighs its prejudicial effect. However, evidence of a conviction more than 10 years old as calculated herein, is not admissible unless the proponent gives to the adverse party sufficient advance written notice of intent to use such evidence to provide the adverse party with a fair opportunity to contest the use of such evidence.

c. Effect of pardon, annulment, or certificate of rehabilitation.

   Evidence of a conviction is not admissible under this rule if (1) the conviction has been the subject of a pardon, annulment, certificate of rehabilitation, or other equivalent procedure based on a finding of the rehabilitation of the person convicted, and that person has not been convicted of a subsequent crime which was punishable by death or imprisonment in excess of one year, or (2) the conviction has been the subject of a pardon, annulment, or other equivalent procedure based on a finding of innocence.

d. Juvenile adjudications.

   Evidence of juvenile adjudications is generally not admissible under this rule . . .

e. Pendency of appeal.

   The pendency of an appeal therefrom does not render evidence of a conviction inadmissible. Evidence of the pendency of an appeal is admissible.

Fed. R. Evid. 609.

As you can see, the rules for impeachment are a little broader. If you wish to attack the credibility (trustworthiness or believability) of the witness, you may use a felony conviction less than 10 years old of an adult or any misdemeanor conviction that involves "dishonesty or false statement." Such misdemeanors may include theft by check, perjury, some insurance frauds, and securing documents by deception. Some states add "moral turpitude" to the rule's list of permissible crimes you may use to impeach, which seems to mean stuff that is morally abhorrent but not quite a felony; you pretty much have to check case law to find out what misdemeanors have made the cut. Once the conviction is entered, even if it is not final pending an appeal, it is admissible. If there is an appeal in process, the party with the conviction may make the jury aware of that fact in an attempt to undermine the effectiveness of the evidence of the conviction. For most jurors, though, a trial court's entry of a conviction is good enough for them to believe the convict is a bad person. A pardon, annulment, or certificate of rehabilitation will make the conviction inadmissible.

Habit Evidence

One other type of evidence to consider is habit evidence. Habit occurs when an individual—or more frequently, a business—always performs a specific act the same way: "We always time stamp documents when they arrive"; "We always send green cards"; "We always keep our messages." When you can honestly and believably assert that an individual always does something in exactly the same way, make sure you consider this approach. In one case, a cyclist routinely went down a particular hill where an accident occurred. There was a dispute as to whether he stopped at a sign midway down the hill. He was able to put in evidence to show that he stopped every single time he traveled that route because the attorney was able to convince the judge that repeated behavior on the part of the cyclist amounted to habit.

INFORMAL INVESTIGATION

Informal investigation is any investigation that does not go through the court system. Because of the anti-contact rule, there isn't much you can ask the opponent directly to find out about her. Background investigation is something you'll do on every opponent, however, and on significant witnesses when the value of the case warrants it. That means you'll want to check for a criminal record at the very least, if not also for prior lawsuits and any financial and personal information available at the courthouse. For each person investigated, you'll need to make up a checklist. You'll end up with your own shorthand for sources and jurisdictions, such as "Bex." for Bexar County or "DMV" for the Department of Motor Vehicles. You can even make up a sheet for others to decipher your code, just like they have in Shepard's. That's how these things get started, you know.

Surveillance

One method favored indiscriminately by inexperienced adjusters and gung-ho security types is **surveillance.** They fancy capturing the plaintiff in the wheelchair throwing it aside and dancing wildly in the street. That happens only once in a long while, although it does—admittedly—happen. However, surveillance should be used judiciously because it may "blow up" in the careless user's hands. Why? Well, in some jurisdictions, photos and videotapes are discoverable regardless of what sort of privilege you may be able to arguably assert for them, so surveillance tapes will always be discoverable in those jurisdictions. This is not so in federal courts, which largely have considered surveillance videotapes as attorney work product, but other courts have taken the view that (1) videotapes and photos are always discoverable or (2) surveillance is a form of party statement.

If surveillance is ordered by a defendant or her insurer, and nothing comes of it, it looks like bullying and an invasion of privacy, and tends to make the jury angry at the defendant who uses it to try to prove that a plaintiff is lying. Rather than undermining the plaintiff, it bolsters the plaintiff's story and makes the defendant look contemptible. So although a successful surveillance tape is a slam-dunk for the defendant, as it will win the civil suit and usually expose the plaintiff to criminal prosecution for insurance fraud, surveillance must be used only after careful consideration of the risks and a firm foundation of fact gathering that substantially supports a successful outcome.

Another potential problem with surveillance is the risk of committing the tort of invasion of privacy against the plaintiff while following him in hopes of an indiscretion. Although generally one cannot invade privacy so long as all the surveillance is of the party when she is in public, there are occasions when what constitutes "public" can become a close enough call that it can cost the client (or the private investigator) quite a bit of money.

Client _____   **File No.** _____

Cause No. _____

Witness Name _____

Criminal Record

Date Checked _____ Jurisdiction(s) Checked _____

Prior Lawsuits

Date Checked _____ Jurisdiction(s) Checked _____

Prior Injuries [in a tort suit]

Date Checked _____ Sources Checked _____

Prior Addresses

Date Checked _____ Sources Checked _____

Other Impeachment Evidence

I.C.U. Investigations, Inc. v. Jones, 780 So.2d 685 (Ala. 2000).

A jury found in favor of Charles R. Jones on his invasion-of-privacy claim, awarding him $100,000 against the defendant I.C.U. Investigations, Inc. ("ICU"). ICU appeals, arguing that the court erred in denying its motion for a judgment as a matter of law on that claim.

Jones was employed by Alabama Power Company ("APCo") as a groundman and winch-truck driver. While working on February 26, 1990, he suffered an electric shock and fell from the bed of the truck, dislocating and fracturing his left shoulder. Following his injury, he underwent five operations for problems with his shoulder, neck, back, and ribs. Jones sued APCo for workers' compensation benefits; APCo disputed the extent of his disability.

In preparation for the workers' compensation trial, APCo hired ICU, an investigation firm, to watch Jones's daily activities. ICU was owned and operated by Kevin Hand. Hand and another investigator for ICU, Johnson Brown, went to Clay County to monitor Jones's activities. ICU investigated Jones for 11 or 12 days during February and March 1998 . . . Jones lived in a mobile home at the intersection of Highway 77 and County Road 79; the front of his residence faced County Road 79. Jones testified that his mobile home was approximately 200 yards from Highway 77 and a "lot closer" to County Road 79. The front yard was visible from both Highway 77 and County Road 79. When watching Jones at his home, Hand would videotape from a motor vehicle parked on the shoulder of Highway 77 or County Road 79 . . .

Neither Hand nor Brown entered onto Jones's property. When Hand or Brown recorded Jones's activities in the nearby town of Wadley, they filmed from a vehicle parked on a public street or in a parking lot.

On at least four occasions, Hand taped Jones urinating in his front yard. Hand testified that when he videotaped Jones's activities, he often watched with his naked eye; thus, he said only once had he suspected that Jones was urinating. At the end of each day's surveillance or soon thereafter, Hand copied the tapes and sent the copies to APCo's attorney.

When Jones learned that Hand had videotaped him urinating in his yard, Jones filed another lawsuit against APCo, adding as defendants ICU and Hand. He alleged that APCo and ICU had been negligent or wanton in hiring and supervising their employees, and he alleged that all three defendants had invaded his privacy. APCo, ICU, and Hand each moved for a summary judgment. The court granted APCo's motion, but denied ICU and Hand's motions. Jones later dismissed Hand.

After Jones rested his case, ICU moved for a judgment as a matter of law ("JML") on the invasion-of-privacy claim. The trial court denied the motion. ICU renewed its motion for a JML at the close of all the evidence. The motion was again denied. At the close of all the evidence, the judge, the jury, and the attorneys for each side visited Jones's property to view the location of the videotaping; they then returned to the courtroom for closing arguments and the trial judge's oral charge. The trial court submitted only the invasion-of-privacy claim to the jury. The jury returned a verdict in favor of Jones on the invasion-of-privacy claim, awarding him $75,000 in compensatory damages and $25,000 in punitive damages . . .

"This Court recognizes that the wrongful intrusion into one's private activities constitutes a tort known as the invasion of privacy . . . This Court . . . set out the 'four distinct wrongs' of the tort of invasion of privacy:

" '1) the intrusion upon the plaintiff's physical solitude or seclusion; 2) publicity which violates the ordinary decencies; 3) putting the plaintiff in a false, but not necessarily defamatory, position in the public eye; and 4) the appropriation of some element of the plaintiff's personality for a commercial use.'

. . .

"The tort of invasion of privacy may occur both where there is a public and commercial use or publication and where there is a wrongful intrusion into one's private activities or solitude or seclusion . . . There are two standards the Court uses to find whether there has been a tort of invasion of privacy:

" '1) If there has not been public or commercial use or publication, then the proper standard is whether there has been an "intrusion upon the plaintiff's physical solitude or seclusion," or a "wrongful intrusion into one's private activities in such manner so as to outrage or to cause mental suffering, shame or humiliation to a person of ordinary sensibilities"; and 2) if there has been public or commercial use or publication of private information, then the proper standard is whether there has been "unwarranted publicity," "unwarranted appropriation or exploitation of one's personality," publication of private affairs not within the legitimate concern of the public, an intrusion into one's "physical solitude or seclusion," the placing of one in a "false but not necessarily defamatory position in the public eye," or an "appropriation of some element of [one's] personality for commercial use.' "

. . . Like Johnson, this case requires that we first determine the purpose for the investigation and whether 'the thing into which there is intrusion or prying [is], and [is] entitled to be, private.'. . . [T]his Court noted, with approval, that plaintiffs making personal-injury claims " 'must expect reasonable inquiry and investigation to be made of [their] claims and [that] to this extent [their] interest in privacy is circumscribed.'"

The key issue in Jones's workers' compensation case was the extent of his injury. Jones, therefore, should have expected a reasonable investigation regarding his physical capacity. In fact, Jones testified that he was aware that APCo might investigate the validity of his workers' compensation claim and that the investigation might involve surveillance. We conclude that the purpose for the investigation was legitimate; thus, we must consider whether the means used in the investigation was offensive or objectionable . . .

Hand watched Jones and taped his activities while Jones was outside his home, in his front yard, where he was exposed to public view. Indeed, Jones's front yard was located at the intersection of two public roads. At no time did Hand enter or tape activities conducted inside Jones's own home. Because the activities Jones carried on in his front yard could have been observed by any passerby, we conclude that any intrusion by ICU into Jones's privacy was not "wrongful" and, therefore, was not actionable.

The trial court should have granted ICU's motion for a JML on Jones's invasion-of-privacy claim. The judgment is reversed and a judgment is rendered for the defendant ICU.

REVERSED AND JUDGMENT RENDERED. . .

COOK, Justice (dissenting) [with whom Johnstone, J., joins.]

I respectfully dissent from the majority's holding that the intrusion by ICU Investigations, Inc. ("ICU"), into Jones's privacy was not "wrongful" and, therefore, not actionable. Jones lives in a mobile home on 41 acres of land, his only neighbor living 250 yards away. ICU's employee, Hand, was told to videotape Jones doing activities, with the tape to be used as evidence against Jones at his workers' compensation trial. However, Hand videotaped Jones urinating in his front yard and submitted the tape to the lawyer for Alabama Power Company, Jones's employer. Clearly, a videotape of Jones urinating in his yard served no legitimate purpose in Jones's workers' compensation case. Although Jones was in his front yard, the matter was clearly personal in nature.

Although the evidence was undisputed that Jones was urinating in his front yard, I conclude that, given the distance from the highway, and the layout of his property, a disputed issue existed as to whether Jones's activities were public. In addition, a factual issue existed as to whether the means used to videotape Jones was improper, offensive, and unreasonable. The trial court and the jury reviewed the videotapes and went to the scene where the video was filmed. The trial court and the jury inspected the property and the area where Hand testified that he was positioned when he filmed the video. The jury could have determined that Hand was in fact not on public property when he videotaped Jones conducting an act that Jones intended to be private. Because a factual question existed as to whether the means used was unreasonable, offensive, or improper, the trial court properly submitted the claim to the jury. Apparently, after viewing the scene, the jury found the means used by ICU to be unreasonable, objectionable, and offensive. Therefore, I would affirm the judgment based on the jury verdict in favor of Jones and against ICU.

This case was a direct action against the parties conducting the surveillance and generated a second dissenting opinion not included here. It was a close call, and might come out differently in another jurisdiction. Imagine the impact that such a videotape would have had in the underlying litigation if the plaintiff had shown it as part of what the defendant was doing to try to discredit him. The plaintiff would not have to allege an invasion of privacy for the videotape to affect the verdict. The defendant would have to hope that the trial court judge would keep out the videotape on a Rule 403 decision and that it would be upheld on appeal.

Aside from gathering information from parties other than the actual opposing party and surveillance of the opposing party's actions, very little informal investigation of the opposing party can be conducted. However, the information you gather from those sources will drive some of the formal discovery you do.

Discovery

Discovery refers to court-aided investigation. The methods and rules are prescribed under statute or court rules, with penalties (called **sanctions**) for failure to comply. These penalties range from fines to the "**death penalty**" **sanction**—striking the offending party's pleadings. If the judge takes out one party's pleadings—the plaintiff's complaint or the defendant's answer—she has effectively taken away that party's case, hence the term "death-penalty." Therefore, cooperating with discovery is important as well as the ethical response.

Discovery has several purposes. First, it limits the scope of litigation. The parties will have to commit to a particular story, which limits the extent of questions to those relevant to the version of the facts each espouses. Further, rules or questions require disclosure of all witnesses prior to the date of trial, usually no later than 30 days. In some circumstances, or jurisdictions, disclosure may be required even earlier. Second, discovery provides leads for further investigation. Each step of discovery provides new details to corroborate or undermine. Third, discovery provides avenues to obtain information which would otherwise not be available. For instance, it is the only way to compel the opposing party to give you documents in its possession. Fourth, discovery is a source of gamesmanship: there are rules (beyond the scope of this text) involved in it that you must be aware of that can be used to block and harry an opponent.

Each time you receive a response to discovery, you need to inspect it for what it can tell you about new witnesses, new causes of action, new areas of impeachment, new documentary evidence, and new tangible evidence.

Discovery for Parties Only

Interrogatories (rogs) are limited sets of written questions sent only to parties to the litigation that must be answered within a set amount of time, often 30 days. Interrogatories are ordinarily the first form of discovery used in litigation. Depending on the jurisdiction, there may be required disclosures that must be made regardless of the questions asked by the parties (as in federal courts); in other states, you only have to disclose information in response to the questions asked. Interrogatories will almost always ask for basic identifying information about the opposing party: legal name, prior names, social security number, date of birth, driver's license number, marital status, and number of children (unless, of course, this information must be provided under a disclosure rule). Interrogatories are then crafted with an eye to the specifics of the litigation and may include questions relating to witnesses with knowledge of the events, witnesses with knowledge of the injuries alleged in the pleadings, information about employment history, past convictions, any similar or related incidents, information about medical history, information about the damages claimed, knowledge of any other possible parties to the lawsuit, and where documents and tangible pieces of evidence are located.

Care must be taken in how interrogatories are worded because inartfully drafted interrogatories will draw objections. First, if you ask for information in a way that could be construed as requiring privileged information in order to respond completely, an objection will often follow. Better firms will go ahead and provide anything that is not actually privileged; they may not even actually have anything privileged, but feel they owe it to their clients to object in case anything surfaces that is privileged. However, because in many (if not most) jurisdictions objections have to be made by a certain deadline or the objection is waived, the attorney will make the objection in advance to avoid any future problems.

Another common problem is interrogatories that are not limited in time or scope. Consider the following interrogatory, sent to a 45-year-old female plaintiff with a neck injury:

> 3. List all health care providers from whom you have sought care, including the provider's name, address, and phone number, and the reason for which you sought care from each.

This interrogatory, as written, appears to require the plaintiff to provide the name, address, and phone number for every illness since birth, and would include things that had nothing to do with her neck, such as gynecological care. This interrogatory would almost certainly draw an **objection** for being overly broad. Of course, if the opposing side is not paying attention, you might get by with it, but for the most part, you are simply wasting time and effort. That may be a strategy that your attorney wants to use, but if so, you should be doing so knowingly, not by accident. If your attorney wants to use that strategy, she may be accused of using Rambo tactics, a charge that has resulted in sanctions against lawyers across the country, depending on the degree to which she plays that game.

A better, nonobjectionable version of the interrogatory would be the following:

> 3. List all health care providers from whom you have sought care in the last five years [for any strain, pain, or similar ailment in the upper half of your torso], including the provider's name, address, and phone number, and the reason for which you sought care from each.

PATTY HAUS	§	IN THE DISTRICT COURT
Plaintiff,	§	
	§	
v.	§	225TH JUDICIAL DISTRICT
	§	
JOHN JUSTICE AND VISTA LIBRE	§	
APARTMENTS	§	
Defendants	§	DUX COUNTY, CONFUSION

DEFENDANT'S REQUEST FOR DISCLOSURE

TO: Patty Haus, Plaintiff, by and through Plaintiff's attorney of record, Lisa St. Joan

Pursuant to the Confusion Rules of Civil Procedure, you are requested to disclose, within 30 days of service of this request, the information or material as set forth below in Exhibit A. A response to a request is due according to the Confusion Rules of Civil Procedure.

The disclosure must be signed in accordance with Confusion Rules of Civil Procedure, Rule 191.3, and delivered to the attorney of record for the Defendant. If you fail to comply, the Court may order sanctions against you in accordance with the Confusion Rules of Civil Procedure.

Respectfully submitted,

By: _____
Thomas Battle
Confusion Bar No. 1234567
2020 Slaughter Lane
Big City, Confusion 99999
(888)555-1230
Fax(888)555-1231
Confusion Bar No. 2020201

Attorney for Defendant
John Justice

CERTIFICATE OF SERVICE

I certify that on [date] a true and correct copy of Defendant's Request for Disclosure was delivered to Lisa St. Joan Attorney for Patty Haus, by personal service at 100 Years War Lane, Suite 1412, Big City, Confusion 99999.

_____
Thomas Battle

EXHIBIT A

REQUESTS FOR DISCLOSURE

1. State the correct names of the parties to the lawsuit.

2. State the name, address, and telephone number of any potential party.

3. State the legal theories and, in general, the factual basis for your claims or defenses.

4. State the amount and method of calculating any economic damages.

5. State the name, address, and telephone number of persons having knowledge of relevant facts. Include a brief statement of each identified person's connection with the case.

6. For any testifying expert, state:

    1. the expert's name, address, and telephone number;

    2. the subject matter on which the expert will testify;

    3. the general substance of the expert's opinions and a brief summary of the basis for them, or if the expert is not retained by, employed by, or otherwise subject to your control, documents reflecting such information;

    4. if the expert is retained by, employed by, or otherwise subject to your control:

        A) produce all documents, tangible things, reports, models, or data compilations that have been provided to, reviewed by, or prepared by or for the expert in anticipation of the expert's testimony; and

        B) produce the expert's current resume and bibliography.

7. Produce any indemnity and insuring agreements.

8. Produce any settlement agreements relating to this cause.

9. Produce any witness statements.

10. If this is a suit alleging physical or mental injury and damages, produce all medical records and bills which will be claimed or, in lieu thereof, an authorization permitting the disclosure of such medical records and bills.

11. If this is a suit alleging physical or mental injury and damages, produce all medical records and bills obtained by you through an authorization furnished by Defendant.

NO. <u>05-CI-101010</u>

PATTY HAUS	§	**IN THE DISTRICT COURT**
Plaintiff,	§	
	§	
v.	§	**225TH JUDICIAL DISTRICT**
	§	
JOHN JUSTICE AND VISTA LIBRE	§	
APARTMENTS,	§	
Defendants	§	**DUX COUNTY, CONFUSION**

<u>DEFENDANT'S INTERROGATORIES TO</u>
<u>PLAINTIFF PATTY HAUS</u>

TO: Patty Haus, Plaintiff, by and through Plaintiff's attorney of record, Lisa St. Joan

Pursuant to the Confusion Rules of Civil Procedure, Defendant John Justice serves the attached interrogatories to propound to Plaintiff Patty Haus.

You are instructed to answer the following interrogatories separately, fully, in writing, and under oath if required by the Confusion Rules of Civil Procedure. The responses shall be served on the Defendant's counsel within 30 days after the service of these interrogatories.

Your failure to make timely answers or objections may subject you to sanctions as provided in the Confusion Rules of Civil Procedure.

Furthermore, demand is made for the supplementation of your answers to these interrogatories as required by the Confusion Rules of Civil Procedure.

Respectfully submitted,

By: _____

Thomas Battle
Confusion Bar No. 1234567
2020 Slaughter Lane
Big City, Confusion 99999
(888)555-1230
fax(888)555-1231
Confusion Bar No. 2020201

Attorney for Defendant
John Justice

CERTIFICATE OF SERVICE

I certify that on [DATE] a true and correct copy of Defendant's Interrogatories was delivered to Lisa St. Joan, Attorney for Patty Haus, by personal service at 100 Years War Lane, Suite 1412, Big City, Confusion 99999.

_____

Thomas Battle

DEFINITIONS AND INSTRUCTIONS

1. As used herein, the terms "you" and "your" shall refer to Patty Haus, Patty Haus's attorneys, agents, and all other natural persons or business or legal entities acting or purporting to act for or on behalf of Patty Haus, whether authorized to do so or not.

2. As used herein, the term "documents" shall mean all writings of every kind, source and authorship, both originals and all nonidentical copies thereof, in your possession, custody, or control, or known by you to exist, irrespective of whether the writing is one intended for or transmitted internally by you, or intended for or transmitted to any other person or entity, including without limitation any government agency, department, administrative, or private entity or person. The term shall include handwritten, typewritten, printed, photocopied, photographic, or recorded matter. It shall include communications in words, symbols, pictures, sound recordings, films, tapes, and information stored in, or accessible through, computer or other information storage or retrieval systems, together with the codes and/or programming instructions and other materials necessary to understand and use such systems. For purposes of illustration and not limitation, the term shall include: affidavits; agendas; agreements; analyses; announcements; bills, statements, and other records of obligations and expenditures; books; brochures; bulletins; calendars; canceled checks, vouchers, receipts and other records of payments; charts or drawings; check registers; checkbooks; circulars; collateral files and contents; contracts; corporate bylaws; corporate charters; correspondence; credit files and contents; deeds of trust; deposit slips; diaries; drafts; files; guaranty agreements; instructions; invoices; ledgers, journals, balance sheets, profit and loss statements, and other sources of financial data; letters; logs, notes, or memoranda of telephonic or face-to-face conversations; manuals; memoranda of all kinds, to and from any persons, agencies, or entities; minutes; minute books; notes; notices; parts lists; papers; press releases; printed matter (including books, articles, speeches, and newspaper clippings); purchase orders;

records; records of administrative, technical, and financial actions taken or recommended; reports; safety deposit boxes and contents and records of entry; schedules; security agreements; specifications; statements of bank accounts; statements; interviews; stock transfer ledgers; technical and engineering reports, evaluations, advice, recommendations, commentaries, conclusions, studies, test plans, manuals, procedures, data, reports, results, and conclusions; summaries, notes, and other records and recordings of any conferences, meetings, visits, statements, interviews or telephone conversations; telegrams; teletypes and other communications sent or received; transcripts of testimony; UCC instruments; work papers; and all other writings, the contents of which relate to, discuss, consider, or otherwise refer to the subject matter of the particular discovery requested.

3. In accordance with the Confusion Rules of Civil Procedure, a document is deemed to be in your possession, custody, or control if you either have physical possession of the item or have a right to possession of the item that is equal or superior to the person who has physical control of the item.

4. "Person": The term "person" shall include individuals, associations, partnerships, corporations, and any other type of entity or institution whether formed for business purposes or any other purposes.

5. "Identify" or "Identification":
(a) When used in reference to a person, "identify" or "identification" means to state his or her full name, present or last known residence address, present or last known business address, and telephone number.
(b) When used in reference to a public or private corporation, governmental entity, partnership or association, "identify" or "identification" means to state its full name, present or last known business address or operating address, the name of its Chief Executive Officer, and telephone number.
(c) When used in reference to a document, "identify" or "identification" shall include statement of the following:
(i) the title, heading, or caption, if any, of such document;
(ii) the identifying number(s), letter(s), or combination thereof, if any; and the significance or meaning of such number(s), letter(s), or combination thereof, if necessary to an understanding of the document and evaluation of any claim of protection from discovery;
(iii) the date appearing on such document; if no date appears thereon, the answer shall so state and shall give the date or approximate date on which such document was prepared;
(iv) the number of pages and the general nature or description of such document (i.e., whether it is a letter, memorandum, minutes of a meeting, etc.), with sufficient particularity so as to enable such document to be precisely identified;
(v) the name and capacity of the person who signed such document; if it was not signed, the answer shall so state and shall give the name of the person or persons who prepared it;
(vi) the name and capacity of the person to whom such document was addressed and the name and capacity of such person, other than such addressee, to whom such document, or a copy thereof, was sent; and
(vii) the physical location of the document and the name of its custodian or custodians.

6. "Settlement": as used herein, means:
(a) an oral or written, disclosed or undisclosed agreement, bargain, contract, settlement, partial settlement, limited settlement, arrangement, deal, understanding, loan arrangement, credit arrangement, contingent settlement, limitation on the amount of liability or judgment, or a promise by or between plaintiff and any defendants or between any defendants herein whereby plaintiff or defendants have in any way released, compromised, in whole or in part, directly or indirectly, or agreed to do so in the future, any of the matters in controversy in this lawsuit whether before,

after, or during trial or before or after any jury verdict is returned herein or a judgment is entered or rendered herein.

   (b) any resolution of the differences between the plaintiff and defendants by loan to the plaintiff or any other device which is repayable in whole or in part out of any judgment the plaintiff may recover against defendants.

7. Unless a specific date or dates is set forth in any specific question herein, you are directed that each question shall be answered for the period of time up to and including the present date.

INTERROGATORIES

1. State the full name, telephone number, address, and your immediate supervisor for your employers for the last five (5) years. Please indicate if you have held any ownership interest in this (these) business(es).

ANSWER:

2. State whether you were acting within the course and scope of any employment, service, or agency at the time of the collision, and describe the relationship of the persons involved.

ANSWER:

3. State the Style, Court, and Cause number of any lawsuit to which you have been a party and the final disposition of said suit.

ANSWER:

4. Please state any and all traffic violations you have had in the five (5) years preceding the accident described in the pleadings of this action. Please indicate if you have had your driving license revoked due to any of these violations and the period of time your license was revoked.

ANSWER:

5. Please state whether you have had any other motor vehicle accidents in the past five (5) years. If so, please list the date and location of such accident, the parties involved and a factual description of the accident.

ANSWER:

6. List all criminal arrests and/or charges against you by giving the cause number; identities of all accused; court of jurisdiction; description of criminal charges; date and place of arrest; plea made; date of trial and/or plea bargain; whether or not convicted and on what charges; time served; date of release from confinement; whether or not granted pardon or parole, and if so, date pardon granted or parole was or will be successfully completed.

ANSWER:

7. State in detail what intoxicating beverages, if any, you had consumed and what drugs and/or medications, whether prescribed or over-the-counter, you had taken for the 24-hour period prior to the collision.

ANSWER:

8. State the make and model of the vehicle you were driving at the time of the collision.

ANSWER:

9. Give the date of the last inspection of the vehicle you were driving at the time of the collision and the name of the inspection station giving the inspection and the date the inspection was given.

ANSWER:

10. Please state where you had been just prior to the collision, where you were going at the time of the collision, and the purpose of the trip.

ANSWER:

11. Describe the road or street surface conditions at the time of the collision.

ANSWER:

12. What was the posted speed limit on the roadway or street on which the vehicle involved in this collision were traveling at the time of the collision in question?

ANSWER:

13. Do you contend that there were any obstructions to visibility for you? If so, indicate what the obstructions were immediately before the collision and how the obstructions contributed to the collision in question.

ANSWER:

14. Please give a detailed description of how the collision made the basis of the lawsuit occurred. Please indicate in your description the speed or estimated speed that the vehicle was traveling at the time of the incident. On the back of this sheet, please draw a diagram to indicate the location of the accident and the direction that the vehicle was traveling at the time of the collision.

ANSWER:

15. Describe any defect that you believe, or have reason to believe, was present in the vehicle described in response to Interrogatory 8 that either caused or contributed to the collision in question.

ANSWER:

16. Please identify by name, address, phone number(s), Internet address, and email address, any and all persons who provided service, maintenance, or repairs for the vehicle involved in the incident made the basis of the lawsuit.

ANSWER:

17. Please describe your relationship with or to Geronimo "Jerry" Smoker at the time of the incident made the basis of the lawsuit and for five (5) years before that date, including the legal status of the relationship, beginning and ending dates, and any dates that there was no relationship or when there was separation of any period.

ANSWER:

18. List all criminal arrests and/or charges against Geronimo "Jerry" Smoker by giving the cause number; identities of all accused; court of jurisdiction; description of criminal charges; date and place of arrest; plea made; date of trial and/or plea bargain; whether or not convicted and on what charges; time served; date of release from confinement; whether or not granted pardon or parole, and if so, date pardon granted or parole was or will be successfully completed.

ANSWER:

19. Please identify (by title, author, editor, edition, publisher, date of publication, section, portion, and page) every published treatise, periodical, or pamphlet on a subject of history, medicine, or other science or art that you may offer to use in the trial of this case under Rule 803(18) of the Confusion Rules of Evidence.

ANSWER:

20. Please describe your communications with or to Vista Libre Apartments, including all documents, contracts, correspondence, or oral discussions, including the dates and times of the communications.

ANSWER:

21. Please describe your communications with or to John Justice, including all documents, contracts, correspondence, or oral discussions, including the dates and times of the communications.

ANSWER:

22. Please describe your communications with or to any law enforcement officer regarding the incident made the basis of the lawsuit, whether during the incident or thereafter, including all documents, contracts, correspondence, or oral discussions, including the dates and times of the communications.

ANSWER:

VERIFICATION

STATE OF CONFUSION	§
	§
COUNTY OF DUX	§

BEFORE ME, the undersigned authority, personally appeared Patty Haus, who stated, upon oath, that the statements made in the foregoing instrument are within her personal knowledge and are true and correct.

_____
Patty Haus

SUBSCRIBED AND SWORN TO BEFORE ME on _____,
by _____.

_____
Notary Public, State of Confusion

This wording limits the interrogatory in time and scope, although many lawyers would omit the part in brackets as overkill and include it only if required to by a judge.

You may also spend considerable time with clients answering interrogatories. These are sent to the client immediately, and because they are written in the forked tongue of lawyers, most real people have trouble with the language, and need an interpreter. That would be you. Often it takes more than one try at the answers to get them right, but remember: it is the client who swears to the answers, not you and not the lawyer. Make sure the client knows what he is swearing to because his answers can be used to impeach him later. The answers will have to be notarized. (Helpful hint: Get a notary's license; doing so will save you ever so much hassle. Make your boss pay for the bond; there's not much else to it.) Make your reservations with your clients early.

PATTY HAUS	§	IN THE DISTRICT COURT
Plaintiff,	§	
	§	
V.	§	225TH JUDICIAL DISTRICT
	§	
JOHN JUSTICE AND VISTA LIBRE	§	
APARTMENTS	§	
Defendants.	§	OF DUX COUNTY, CONFUSION

<u>PLAINTIFF'S RESPONSE TO</u>
<u>FIRST SET OF INTERROGATORIES</u>
<u>OF DEFENDANT JOHN JUSTICE</u>

To: **John Justice, Defendant, by and through Defendant's attorney of record, Thomas Battle**

Patty Haus, Plaintiff, responds to this Set of Interrogatories propounded by John Justice pursuant to Rule 197 of the Confusion Rules of Civil Procedure.

Respectfully submitted,

By: _____

Lisa St. Joan
100 Years War Lane, Suite 1412
Big City, Confusion 99999
(888) 555-0987
(888) 555-0986 (telefax)
State of Confusion Bar No. 0987676
Attorney for Plaintiff
Patty Haus

ANSWERS TO INTERROGATORIES

1. State the full name, telephone number, address, and your immediate supervisor for your employers for the last five (5) years. Please indicate if you have held any ownership interest in this (these) business(es).

<u>ANSWER:</u>

OBJECTION: The discovery request asks for information that is not relevant and is not reasonably calculated to lead to the discovery of admissible evidence. Plaintiff does not seek any damages for loss of income or loss of earning capacity.

2. State whether you were acting within the course and scope of any employment, service or agency at the time of the collision, and describe the relationship of the persons involved.

<u>ANSWER:</u>

OBJECTION: Patty Haus is unable to comply with the discovery request because it is vague, ambiguous, and overly broad, and cannot determine with reasonable specificity the information requested.

Subject to this objection and without waiver thereof, no.

3. State the Style, Court, and Cause number of any lawsuit to which you have been a party and the final disposition of said suit.

ANSWER:

OBJECTION: The discovery request is overly broad, lacks definition, or is not reasonably limited in scope or time. Further, the discovery request calls for information that is privileged under contractual agreement.

Subject to this objection and without waiver thereof, the Plaintiff was one of three plaintiffs in a products liability suit in Bloomington, Indiana which ended in settlement; plaintiff does not have the information regarding the style of the case and the attorney who represented her has since died.

4. Please state any and all traffic violations you have had in the five (5) years preceding the accident described in the pleadings of this action. Please indicate if you have had your driving license revoked due to any of these violations and the period of time your license was revoked.

ANSWER:

OBJECTION: The discovery request asks for information that is not relevant and is not reasonably calculated to lead to the discovery of admissible evidence. There is no pleading or suggestion that any other individual is vicariously liable for the actions of the plaintiff, therefore her prior driving record is not within the realm of permissible discovery.

5. Please state whether you have had any other motor vehicle accidents in the past five (5) years. If so, please list the date and location of such accident, the parties involved, and a factual description of the accident.

ANSWER:

OBJECTION: Patty Haus is unable to comply with the discovery request because it is vague and ambiguous, and cannot determine with reasonable specificity the information requested. Further, the discovery request potentially requires the disclosure of privileged communication between an attorney and client. Further, the discovery request asks for information that is not relevant and is not reasonably calculated to lead to the discovery of admissible evidence.

6. List all criminal arrests and/or charges against you, by giving the cause number; identities of all accused; court of jurisdiction; description of criminal charges; date and place of arrest; plea made; date of trial and/or plea bargain; whether or not convicted and on what charges; time served; date of release from confinement; whether or not granted pardon or parole, and if so, date pardon granted or parole was or will be successfully completed.

ANSWER:

OBJECTION: The discovery request is overly broad, and is not reasonably limited in scope or time. Further, the discovery request asks for information that is not relevant and is not reasonably calculated to lead to the discovery of admissible evidence.

7. State in detail what intoxicating beverages, if any, you had consumed and what drugs and/or medications, whether prescribed or over-the-counter, you had taken for the 24-hour period prior to the collision.

ANSWER:

Advil.

8. State the make and model of the vehicle you were driving at the time of the collision.

ANSWER:

   1999 Ford 150 Pick-up Truck.

9. Give the date of the last inspection of the vehicle you were driving at the time of the collision and the name of the inspection station giving the inspection and the date the inspection was given.

ANSWER:

   The discovery request asks for information, or for documents or other tangible things, that are not within the possession, custody, or control of Patty Haus.

10. Please state where you had been just prior to the collision, where you were going at the time of the collision, and the purpose of the trip.

ANSWER:

   Prior to my arrival at 2000 Washington I was at my friend's house and I was on my way home.

11. Describe the road or street surface conditions at the time of the collision.

ANSWER:

   Dry.

12. What was the posted speed limit on the roadway or street on which the vehicle involved in this collision was traveling at the time of the collision in question?

ANSWER:

   45 mph on Washington Street

13. Do you contend that there were any obstructions to visibility for you? If so, indicate what the obstructions were immediately before the collision and how the obstructions contributed to the collision in question.

ANSWER:

   OBJECTION: The discovery request potentially requires disclosure of attorney work product and communications subject to the attorney client privilege.

   Subject to this objection, and without waiver thereof, no.

14. Please give a detailed description of how the collision made the basis of the lawsuit occurred. Please indicate in your description the speed or estimated speed that the vehicle was traveling at the time of the incident. On the back of this sheet, please draw a diagram to indicate the location of the accident and the direction that the vehicle was traveling at the time of the collision.

ANSWER:

   OBJECTION: Patty Haus is unable to comply with the discovery request because it is vague and ambiguous, and cannot determine with reasonable specificity the information requested.

   Subject to this objection, and without waiver thereof, the vehicle was traveling at approximately 30 mph when the brakes failed, at which time the Plaintiff collided with the large brick sign at the entrance of the Vista Libre Apartments.

ANSWER:

> OBJECTION: This interrogatory is unnecessarily cumulative and has already been answered.
>
> Subject to this objection, and without waiver thereof, see the answer to Interrogatory 14.

15. Describe any defect that you believe, or have reason to believe, was present in the vehicle described in response to Interrogatory 8 that either caused or contributed to the collision in question.

ANSWER:

> OBJECTION: The discovery request potentially requires disclosure of attorney work product and communications subject to the attorney client privilege.
>
> Subject to this objection, and without waiver thereof, the brakes did not work.

16. Please identify by name, address, phone number(s), Internet address, and email address, any and all persons who provided service, maintenance, or repairs for the vehicle involved in the incident made the basis of the lawsuit.

ANSWER:

> OBJECTION: The discovery request asks for information, or for documents or other tangible things, that are not within the possession, custody, or control of Patty Haus. The vehicle in question was owned by Geronimo Garcia, and he has all information relating to its service, repair, and maintenance.
>
> Subject to and without waiving the foregoing, Plaintiff does not know but believes the vehicle was serviced within three weeks of the incident made the basis of the lawsuit.

17. Please describe your relationship with or to Geronimo "Jerry" Smoker at the time of the incident made the basis of the lawsuit and for five (5) years before that date, including the legal status of the relationship, beginning and ending dates, and any dates that there was no relationship or when there was separation of any period.

ANSWER:

> OBJECTION: Patty Haus is unable to comply with the discovery request because it is vague and ambiguous, and cannot determine with reasonable specificity the information requested. Further, the discovery request is overly broad and lacks definition. Further, the discovery request is an invasion of the Plaintiff's right to privacy.
>
> Subject to this objection and without waiver thereof, Patty Haus and Geronimo Smoker entered into a romantic relationship three years prior to the incident made the basis of the lawsuit and started cohabiting two years and eight months prior to the incident made the basis of the relationship. The relationship ended the day after the incident made the basis of the relationship.

18. List all criminal arrests and/or charges against Geronimo "Jerry" Smoker by giving the cause number; identities of all accused; court of jurisdiction; description of criminal charges; date and place of arrest; plea made; date of trial and/or plea bargain; whether or not convicted and on what charges; time served; date of release from confinement; whether or not granted pardon or parole, and if so, date pardon granted or parole was or will be successfully completed.

ANSWER:

> OBJECTION: The discovery request is overly broad and is not reasonably limited in scope or time. Further, the discovery request asks for information, or for documents or other tangible things that are not within the possession, custody, or control of Patty Haus.

Subject to this objection and without waiver thereof, Plaintiff is aware that Geronimo Smoker was arrested approximately six times during the period when they were residing at the Vista Libre Apartments but only convicted twice of misdemeanor charges.

19. Please identify (by title, author, editor, edition, publisher, date of publication, section, portion, and page) every published treatise, periodical, or pamphlet on a subject of history, medicine, or other science or art that you may offer to use in the trial of this case under Rule 803(18) of the Confusion Rules of Evidence.

ANSWER:

OBJECTION: The discovery request potentially requires disclosure of information subject to the attorney work product and communications subject to the attorney client privilege.

Subject to this objection, and without waiver thereof, Plaintiff will supplement when this information is available.

20. Please describe your communications with or to Vista Libre Apartments, including all documents, contracts, correspondence, or oral discussions, including the dates and times of the communications.

ANSWER:

OBJECTION: The discovery request is overly broad, lacks definition, or is not reasonably limited in scope or time.

Subject to this objection and without waiver thereof, Plaintiff was served with a suit for entry and detainer by Vista Libre Apartments and had a contract with Vista Libre Apartments.

21. Please describe your communications with or to John Justice, including all documents, correspondence, or oral discussions, including the dates and times of the communications.

ANSWER:

OBJECTION: The discovery request is overly broad, lacks definition, or is not reasonably limited in scope or time.

Subject to this objection and without waiver thereof, Plaintiff had many oral discussions with John Justice over the course of her residency at Vista Libre Apartments at the rate of approximately three times per week. Plaintiff has no written documents exchanged between herself and John Justice with the exception of those filed in this action.

22. Please describe your communications with or to any law enforcement officer regarding the incident made the basis of the lawsuit, whether during the incident or thereafter, including all documents, contracts, correspondence, or oral discussions, including the dates and times of the communications.

ANSWER:

OBJECTION: The discovery request is overly broad, lacks definition, or is not reasonably limited in scope or time. The discovery request potentially requires disclosure of information subject to the attorney work product and communications subject to the attorney client privilege.

Subject to this objection and without waiver thereof, there were discussions with the arresting officer and the other officer who arrived at the scene and the officers who were at the booking area and those who were at the jail during her period of incarceration.

VERIFICATION

STATE OF CONFUSION	§
	§
COUNTY OF DUX	§

BEFORE ME, the undersigned authority, personally appeared Patty Haus, who stated, upon oath, that the statements made in the foregoing instrument are true and correct.

_____

Patty Haus

SUBSCRIBED AND SWORN TO BEFORE ME on

_____, by _____.

_____

Notary Public, State of Confusion

CERTIFICATE OF SERVICE

I certify that on [DATE] a true and correct copy of Plaintiff's Responses to Interrogatories was served by facsimile transmission on Thomas Battle at (888)555-1231.

_____

Lisa St. Joan

Requests for production (RFP) work the same way as interrogatories and have similar time limits, except that instead of asking for answers to questions, you are asking for documents. It depends on the type of litigation as to whether the RFP will be sent contemporaneously with the interrogatories; the more unusual the case, the less likely the two types of discovery will be sent together. Requests will be for documents relating to the opposing party and the litigation; these documents should be examined for leads to investigate further. Although the typical form asks for an opportunity to copy documents, usually copies are provided rather than allowing opposing counsel into the area to make copies. The same issues in drafting are involved; poorly worded requests will draw objections on the basis of privilege or overbreadth.

An additional issue that arises in requests for production is cost, particularly when the request is made to a large corporate defendant. The way the plaintiff needs documents is not necessarily the way the defendant stores them, and if the documents are stored electronically, the defendant may encounter several expensive obstacles to extracting them, which will draw an objection. This is not reason to forebear from asking for documents you need, but a reason to think about what you want carefully so that you can pick your battles and stand firm on what you have to have rather than using a shotgun effect that scatters a wider amount but won't penetrate and simply annoys the target.

Overall, these forms of discovery constitute a game of Go Fish disguised behind big words and lots of rules.

You can make other discovery requests as well. **Requests for admissions** are what they sound like: you ask the other side to admit that certain things are true. Ordinarily you do so to dispense with matters that are not really in controversy. You can also use them to prove up records; I've seen some plaintiff's attorneys use them as a low-budget way of getting medical bills established. They will attach the bills as an Exhibit, and then ask the defendant to admit that the Exhibit is the reasonable and necessary medical bills from Dr. Goodhealth incurred as a result of the incident made the basis of the lawsuit. The best objection is to say, "I have no personal knowledge of that," since the defendant doesn't know this information on a firsthand basis. Such a response is somewhat **specious**, as the legal team *will* know, and as the defendant's agent, the knowledge will be **imputed** to the defendant. (Did you get that? *Specious* and *imputed*? *Specious* in this context is about the same as *lame;* and *imputed to* is approximately the same as *substituted for.*)

Another useful discovery mechanism is a **request for an independent medical exam (IME).** If you suspect that the treating physician is biased, ask for an examination by another doctor. You can make this request for both physical and psychological ailments. You will have to set up the examination with the other doctor, make the appointment, and confirm the appointment in writing with everyone. It is particularly important to get this appointment confirmed when you have had to get a court order to enforce this right; if the opposing party shows up and the doctor's office has no idea about the appointment or its purpose, the opposing party will have fulfilled the court order without you gaining what you were supposed to.

You may also want a **request for inspection of tangible evidence;** this is the same as a request for production in some jurisdictions. This could be used for things like looking at the remains of an allegedly defective vehicle in the possession of the plaintiff. The request requires the opposing party to set up an appointment to look at the tangible evidence, and may include a request to take a small portion of that evidence for testing by your experts or for the experts to conduct tests there. Testing must, of course, be non-destructive to ensure that the evidence may be preserved for trial.

If the opposing side has identified an expert, you can make a **request to reduce opinions to writing.** Get the other side's expert to give you theories. If you don't know what the expert is going to attack, it's hard to prepare. Sometimes opposing sides (or your own) will drag their feet because they're hoping to settle rather than spend any more time and money on the case, but delaying will only cause a stressful pile-up later on.

DEPOSITIONS: DISCOVERY FOR EVERYBODY

Depositions come in two types: **oral depositions** and **depositions by written questions.** If the form is not specified, an oral deposition is usually what is meant. Depositions can be used for any witness—not just parties—and are very flexible. A deposition by written questions is a device to obtain documents; it will be discussed in a later chapter.

The oral deposition of the opposing party is a very important step in the litigation. This is the opportunity for your attorney to get a sense of the type of witness she will make and the story she will tell, to set up any potential impeachment traps, to prove up evidence, and to find out about witnesses, possible sources of documentary and tangible evidence, and additional possible areas of impeachment. That's a lot to keep track of. You can help the attorney prepare by making sure the details have been taken care of.

Before you start, find out about any local rules or customs that may affect how you should handle things. For instance, in my local jurisdiction, we cannot count the day we give notice or the day of the deposition in figuring adequate notice, and three days' notice is required. If you just heard three days and didn't know how a jurisdiction like mine counts, you might set up a Friday deposition after giving notice on Wednesday, counting Wednesday, Thursday, and Friday as your three days. You'd be wrong because of our weirdness in counting. These little local tidbits are sometimes in writing, and sometimes they are custom that carries incredible weight. Ask your boss or a more experienced paralegal or legal secretary about local customs or rules. There is absolutely nothing wrong with asking; it's far better than trying to fix a problem that has resulted from a failure to ask. And local rules can vary substantially, so knowing one set is not good enough—you need to know them for every court with which you deal.

First, if you are the one noticing the deposition, find out if there is anything that the opposing party should bring along. If so, you'll need to add a **subpoena duces tecum** to the deposition notice describing anything else you want to look at that is in the possession of the opposing party. This is helpful if there's something you've found out about since sending the request for production that you'd like to get directly from the opponent. Also, consider whether you want to videotape the deposition. Ordinarily, parties' depositions (and those of fact witnesses) are not videotaped; the only depositions that are routinely videotaped are those of expert witnesses so as to avoid the cost of paying them to testify twice. There might be a strategy reason to videotape the opponent, such as to discomfit him or to force him to take it seriously, in specific circumstances, but ordinarily, you would not do so. If you do choose to have the deposition videotaped, that information usually must be included in the notice and separate arrangements must be made to have a videographer in addition to the court reporter. In some jurisdictions there has been some discussion regarding whether solely a videographer is sufficient for admissibility; I wouldn't count on admissibility unless the rule is crystal clear. Otherwise, play it safe and always have both. There's also some question whether you must have a third party videotape. Again, lawyers tend to play it safe, so the question has generally remained unanswered.

Second, review the investigation plan. See what things you can prove through the opponent. Make sure your attorney is aware of those areas. She may prefer you to make up questions or simply make a list of the areas that need to be covered.

Third, make a list of areas in which the opponent is vulnerable to impeachment and make sure your attorney is made aware of them. She can use her knowledge of these areas to trap the opponent in a lie.

If you are preparing the question list for your attorney, you need to consider whether you want the questions to be in an organized format. Sometimes you need the questions to appear jumbled so that the opposing party cannot see where you are going. If the questions proceed in a logical fashion, he'll know the direction the line of questioning is heading and be able to prepare. If the questions are not as linear, the opposing party will be less able to anticipate both the questions and what the attorney is digging for. This inability to anticipate is more likely to result in inconsistencies if the party is lying. It's as if someone were to try to lie about his age. First, you ask how old the person is. Then, later, after talking about various other things, you ask him his date of birth. If the two figures do not match up, you've caught him in a lie. However, if you ask those questions consecutively, regardless of order, you substantially diminish your opportunity to trap him in the lie.

Once the deposition is over, review it for new leads and key pieces of information. Are there any new people mentioned that were not disclosed in other discovery? Are there any references to other documents or places that ordinarily keep documents? If so, you may want to add them to the list of people or things you need to check out. Is there anything that indicates a new cause of action, defendant, or defense? If so, you may consider adding them to the pleadings after consultation with your attorney. The process of investigating is recursive; that is, each step requires you to look back over prior steps and refine and/or update them. Update your investigation plan documents.

FOREIGN OPPOSING PARTIES

What do you do when the opposing party is from a foreign country? The short answer: If a foreign party has been served and appeared in court, the party is probably subject to the discovery rules of that court. The federal courts formerly stated that discovery would be limited to the extent that it was allowable in the foreign country, but that does not seem to be the law in most states any more.

The trick is to serve the foreign national or corporation. If you're lucky, the foreign corporation has a domestic agent for service of process, and then you simply proceed as you would against anyone else. If not, you will have to serve the foreign corporation in its own country. That may be done under the rules of the Inter-American Convention or the Hague Service Convention if the country is one of the 17 signatories to the former or one of the 38 signatories to the latter. As you may imagine, this can be a complicated task, but there is a simplified approach. If you wish to serve someone under either convention, you have to prepare letters rogatory in the language of the defendant and transmit them to the defendant through the U.S. Department of Justice (DoJ). The DoJ will then send them to the appropriate agency in the desired defendant's country, who will attempt to serve the defendant under that country's rules of service. Once served, a certificate of service will be transmitted back to the DoJ from the foreign country's agency and then sent on to the court. It's a tedious process, but worthwhile in cases where a foreign corporation has ongoing contacts with the United States.

1   are no good.

2   Q.   So if you don't get payment, that's an

3   indication of improper coding?

4   MS. GEIS: Objection. Form.

5   THE WITNESS: I can tell you that the

6   CPT codes that I've been using have been the same CPT

7   codes now for about—I would say a good ten years.

8   Q.   (BY MR. MOWERY) My question was if you do

9   not get paid, is that one indication of possible

10 improper coding?

11   A.   It hasn't happened to me, so I wouldn't know.

12   Q.   How do you document your service? I want to

13 start out as if a jury is hearing this for the first

14 time. Let's say you get a call to perform a service.

15 Does the documentation process start then?

16   A.   The way I was doing it before, way prior

17 before—I'm not doing surgery anymore. Kayla would

18 call, the girl from Santa Rosa. She'd say you have a

19 surgery on Wednesday and she would give me the

20 patient's name and the doctor. That's all I need. I

21 show up at that time, I go and I go to holding, go

22 greet the patient. The patient's demographics is in

23 there, the patient's information surgery. I introduce

24 myself to the patient, have them sign a consent saying

25 that they're allowing me to do the billing and

Sample page
from a
deposition.

Death by Discovery: How Much Knowledge Can Your Client Afford?
by Jim McCormack

My client approached me in our last encounter with the bizarre insight that I had clients other than her. She let me off the hook for less than immediately returned phone calls and said that she understood that I couldn't always meet with her at a moment's notice. My client even volunteered to have more realistic expectations about my responsiveness to her requests. In short, she agreed *sua sponte* to stop acting like a normal client. I pondered what other surprises my completely abnormal client might have for me. And I didn't have to ponder long.

> **Client:**   It occurs to me that you are working too hard on my case. I need for you to slow down.
>
> **Me:**   I didn't hear you clearly. I thought you said that I was working too hard on your case.
>
> **Client:**   You heard me right.
>
> **Me:**   Pardon me if I say that no client ever has said that to a lawyer in the history of Anglo-American jurisprudence. I have to work hard on your case. Remember that little matter of a fiduciary duty that I owe to you as your attorney. And not to mention little things called "negligence" and "malpractice lawsuit" if I don't work hard enough on your case.
>
> **Client:**   I should explain. I appreciate your hard work. I need your best effort. But more than that, I need the benefit of your true professional judgment about what is really needed so that I won't go broke from paying for all of your hard work on my behalf. You're planning to take the depositions of two dozen people, copying thousands of pages of documents and reviewing boxes of documents I didn't know existed. The expenses are mounting. Could you please work a little less for me?
>
> **Me:**   I think we have been over this ground before. . . .

A client asking a lawyer to work less. Now, that's novel. But a client worrying about how much all that work—particularly discovery work—is costing, well, that I get. And to understand how we reached the point of nearly bankrupting our clients with exhaustive discovery, a small history lesson may help.

TRIAL BY AMBUSH

Discovery of information from the opposing party through a formal process is a relatively modern development. If you went back in a time machine 30 or 40 years ago, litigation mostly could be summarized in three short words: trial by ambush. That's right: zero formal discovery, as we know it today. No interrogatories, no requests for admission, no requests for production, and no depositions. Also, of course, not much in the way of discovery fights—which, from a trial judge's perspective, must have been heaven on earth.

If you wanted to find out something about the opposing party, you did it the old-fashioned way: You went around talking to people or called them on the phone and begged them to talk to you about the facts of your case. If they had some documents, you begged them for the chance to look those over. If you received any information at all from the opposing party, it was either an act of genius on your part or sheer dumb luck. The result? Lots of cases went to trial in the prediscovery days that would likely settle today because the litigants had such limited information.

Still, having tried at least a couple of cases without any discovery, I am here to testify that trial by ambush can be extremely fun if you are lucky and don't mind a little terror and uncertainty in not knowing what cards your opponent is holding. But most lawyers and clients today don't like terror and uncertainty all that much. And the chief consequence of not liking those things is lots of knowledge—some of it useful and some of it not—and mountains of expenses.

Of one thing I am certain: The drafters of modern discovery rules had no comprehension of how expensive justice was going to become with all this reform. The drafters dwelt on one main goal for these new discovery rules: With more information available to the litigants, more cases would settle because lawyers and clients could better evaluate the strengths and weaknesses of their cases. The unimagined downside: A litigant could go broke paying a lawyer to use all of these discovery techniques. As ol' Darth might say, "Don't be so proud of this technological terror you've created."

Today, working hard for your client often means engaging in exhaustive discovery. This concept is well established in the profession for at least three superb reasons: 1. the legitimate reasons the drafters had in mind; 2. it is a useful thing to point to at your malpractice trial; and 3. it has made suits at least 10 times more expensive. In some firms, there are legions of lawyers and paralegals who do nothing but sort through mounds of documents to be produced or which were received in discovery. Vast contingents of other lawyers camp out in conference rooms—drinking lots of black coffee—taking depositions of everybody and everybody's mother. And all of it, gloriously billable time.

For Pete's sake, what do clients want from all this? Less discovery, more terror? Lower costs, but more uncertainty? Perfect knowledge at any cost? You have to ask. But first you have to inform. Clients need to know what you think about how much discovery is likely to be enough and what the risks are—financial and otherwise—of engaging in too much versus too little discovery. Clients need the benefit of the lawyer's true professional judgment about what is absolutely essential about discovery in their case and what is a luxury to be indulged, if the client can afford it. To do this well, the lawyer has to be clear-eyed about his or her own fears of failure. For the best discovery is the right mix of what the client truly needs and truly can afford.

Source: Originally published on July 8, 2003 in the *Texas Lawyer.* Copyright 2003 ALM Properties, Inc. Reprinted by permission.

WORKING WITH OPPOSING COUNSEL AND STAFF

You will find that even in a large metropolitan area the legal world becomes relatively small. You will have to work with the same attorneys and paralegals on the other side over and over, so your reputation is important. Your initial reputation will be colored by the firm or attorney you work for: If you work for an honorable attorney, you will be given a little more trust than if you work for one of those that no one will turn his back on. If you are trustworthy, if your word is good, you will find that your work life will be immeasurably eased as you build that personal reputation.

There are deadlines galore when dealing with opposing counsel. There have been instances where paralegals have gotten extensions from notoriously no-budge-on-deadline firms because the paralegal has developed a good working relationship with the firm. You do not do favors for opposing counsel to the detriment of your client, but you do make deals on procedural issues often because everyone runs into trouble from time to time. A favor of extending a deadline for two weeks now will result in a favor of an extension for you later.

However, if you say you will give an **extension,** you must do so. Do not offer what you cannot deliver. Usually the recipient of the favor is the one to send a written confirmation for signature; it is always better to have the agreement in writing, so even if you do not receive something, make some sort of note to the file that you have agreed to whatever. As someone once told me, you should always document the file so that if you went into a coma in the next 10 minutes, anyone in the office could pick up the file and be able to figure out exactly what was going on and take up where you left off. A dismal thought, but a good guideline for how much you need to make sure makes it into the file.

You may have to schedule depositions, inspections, and hearings with opposing counsel. I say "may" because in my experience it's not just varied from firm to firm, but even from attorney to attorney whether the paralegal or legal secretary takes care of this task. If you are talking to the opposing party's legal team regularly

LAW OFFICES

JESSE H. OPPENHEIMER
REESE L. HARRISON, JR.
STANLEY L. BLEND
JOHN H. TATE II
J. DAVID OPPENHEIMER
RICHARD N. WEINSTEIN
TAYLOR S. BOONE
OLEN A. YALE
RAYMOND W. BATTAGLIA
BRUCE M. MITCHELL
CHERYL K. FREED
KIRK L. JAMES
DAVID P. STANUSH
DOUGLAS W. SANDERS
MARTIN I. ROOS
JEROME B. COHEN
DIANA M. GEIB
ELIZABETH A. COPELAND
BARBARA S. DE MARIGNY
KATHLEEN QUIROZ

PAUL D. BARKHURST
BRADLEY T. BORDEN
JEFFREY T. CULLINANE
RUSSELL L. DENNIS
LISA T. DUNDAS
JOE R. HINOJOSA
M. CHERYL KIRBY
LAURA C. MASON
JULIE C. PEREZ
ROXANNA L. OLVERA
ANGELA M. SANCHEZ
GREGORY S. STIEG
W. RICHEY WYATT

OF COUNSEL:
KENNETH M. GINDY
RICHARD I. MANAS

OPPENHEIMER, BLEND, HARRISON & TATE, INC.

711 NAVARRO

SIXTH FLOOR

SAN ANTONIO, TEXAS 78205-1796

210/224-2000

FAX 210/224-7540

December 1, 2003

Estella Deans   **VIA FACSIMILE**
c/o Ron D. Ross
11722 Raindrop
San Antonio, Texas 78216

RE: Cause No. 20003-CI-0600; *Sleep Diagnostic Services, Inc., et al. v. Frank Kuwamura, M.D.*, et al.; In the 224th Judicial District Court; Bexar County, Texas.

Dear Mr. Ross:

This letter will serve as our agreement, pursuant to Tex. R. Civ. P. 11, that Estella Deans' deadline to respond to Defendants, Frank Kuwamura, M.D. and Ellen Duncan, M.D.'s Subpoena to Non-Party Estella Deans to Produce Documents served in the above-referenced cause is extended to **December 3, 2003**. The documents responsive to said Subpoenas will be produced by 5:00 p.m. at the law offices of Oppenheimer, Blend, Harrison & Tate, Inc., by said date.

Please sign below to evidence that the foregoing accurately reflects our agreement.

Very truly yours,

JOE R. HINOJOSA

_____
Ron D. Ross

_____
Date

JRH:am

cc: Randal A. Mowery – Via First-Class Mail
       Kim M. Petit – Via First-Class Mail
       Pascual Madrigal – Via First-Class Mail

144

about this stuff, you need to be honest about when and where. You'll learn quickly which firms are horsey about something as simple as scheduling a deposition and which ones will work with you.

You will find that in some cases you'll be talking to other paralegals and in others, attorneys. Be professional, courteous, and nonconfrontational. Leave the arguing to your boss. You will be the bridge of communication between the firms to smooth necessary interactions. There will be times where the attorneys have a serious degree of antipathy or disrespect for each other that goes far beyond the present case. Those personal feelings cannot get in the way of taking care of the client, and you may have to be the objective professional who mediates or who reminds your attorney of that fact.

There's also a selfish reason for getting along with opposing counsel. Some paralegals have advanced their careers that way. Several of my former students have been offered jobs by attorneys who met them by way of a case where they were opposing counsel. The attorney was impressed with their abilities and offered each a job. One received a $6 per hour raise plus medical and retirement benefits. To twist the saying a bit, luck comes to the prepared paralegal.

CHAPTER SUMMARY

Informal investigation of opposing parties is limited due to the anti-contact rule, which prevents an attorney from talking to a represented party without the presence of counsel. When a corporation is involved, whether an investigator may speak to current employees of the corporation (and which ones) is determined by the test used by the jurisdiction. However, the investigator will do a background check on the opposing party, even knowing that it may be of limited value because of the evidence rules governing prior bad acts. Most of the information from the opposing party will be gathered using various discovery tools: interrogatories, requests for production, requests for admission, requests for inspection, requests for independent medical evaluation, and depositions. The paralegal drafting discovery needs to take care in drafting discovery to avoid objectionable language so that the discovery can be answered expeditiously. In the process of discovery, the paralegal will have contact with the opposing party's counsel, and should take care in maintaining a professional demeanor and integrity with the opposition in order to assist the smooth proceeding of the case.

FOR FURTHER READING

Susan J. Becker, *Conducting Informal Discovery of a Party's Former Employees: Legal and Ethical Concerns and Constraints*, 51 Md. L. Rev. 239 (1992).

Brian Patrick Bronson, *Comment: Pennsylvania's Common Law Right to Privacy Inadequately Protects the Rights of Individual Workers' Compensation Claimants from Harassment Caused by Video Surveillance*, 40 Duq. L. Rev. 523 (2002).

Phillip A. Buhler, *Transnational Service of Process and Discovery in Federal Court Proceedings: An Overview*, 27 Mar. Law. 1 (2002).

Donna Denham and Richard Bales, *The Discoverability of Surveillance Videotapes Under the Federal Rules*, 52 Baylor L. Rev. 753 (2000).

James A. George, *The "Rambo" Problem: Is Mandatory CLE the Way Back to Atticus?*, 62 La. L. Rev. 467 (2002).

Brian E. Hamilton, *Conflict, Disparity, and Indecision: The Unsettled Corporate Attorney-Client Privilege*, 1997 Ann. Surv. Am. L. 629 (1997).

Chris William Sanchirico, *Character Evidence and the Object of Trial*, 101 Colum. L. Rev. 1227 (2001).

Andrea M. Seielstad, *Unwritten Laws and Customs, Local Legal Cultures, and Clinical Legal Education*, 6 Clinical L. Rev. 127 (1999).

William H. Simon, *Whom (Or What) Does the Organization's Lawyer Represent?: An Anatomy of Intraclient Conflict*, 91 Calif. L. Rev. 57 (2003).

Stephen N. Subrin, *Discovery in Global Perspective: Are We Nuts?*, 52 DePaul L. Rev. 299 (2002).

CHAPTER REVIEW

KEY TERMS

authority structure

control group test

corporation

"death penalty" sanction

deposition

deposition by written questions

discovery

extension

framework of dealing

impeach

imputed

interrogatories (rogs)

objection

oral depositions

prior bad acts

pro se/pro per

propensity evidence

request for an independent
    medical exam

request for inspection of tangible
    evidence

requests for admissions

requests for production

request to reduce opinions to
    writing

sanctions

specious

subject matter test

subpoena duces tecum

surveillance

FILL IN THE BLANKS

1. A(n) _____ is a formal protest to providing information based on a privilege or a rule of evidence.

2. _____ are sent to the opposing party to obtain documents.

3. In order to create an artificial person who is separate from its owners for purposes of liability, there are laws governing the creation of a(n) _____, which endures perpetually.

4. Courts rarely impose the _____, usually only for repeated and egregious abuses of discovery rules.

5. A corporation's _____, or formal hierarchy, determines who has the right to make decisions that bind the corporation.

6. _____ are one way to obtain documents from non-parties under oath.

7. Always confirm in writing when you've granted opposing counsel a(n) _____ to answer discovery.

8. Determining attorney representation of corporate employees by considering both day-to-day operations and the formal structure of the corporation is the minority approach called _____.

9. A person representing himself is called _____ or _____.

10. _____ can be an excellent tool when used with thought and care, but has significant dangers when used without consideration for the potential consequences.

11. _____ may be taken of anyone, but are conducted in front of all the parties' lawyers, a court reporter, and under oath.

12. Under the _____, employees involved in the facts of litigation will be covered by the attorney-client privilege.

13. _____ is that which is introduced to show that an individual acted in accordance with his usual inclinations.

14. Although it can refer to both written and oral, the term _____ standing alone usually refers to the oral version.

15. A(n) _____ is a set of questions sent to the opposing party.

16. When you are suspicious about the accuracy of a party's medical records, you may want to file a(n) _____.

17. To look at physical evidence in the possession of the other party, file a(n) _____.

18. Many different approaches can be taken to _____ an opposing party, including showing that he is lying, whining, or incapable of knowing what happened.

19. When you want the opposing party's expert's opinions, file a(n) _____.

20. The _____ affords attorney representation to anyone who is one of the persons who are part of the group making day-to-day decisions affecting the litigation.

21. The correct document to send when you want someone to bring documents along to the deposition is a(n) _____.

22. _____ request the opposing party to admit or deny the truth of particular statements.

WEB WORK

1. Look at the Pro Se Resource Center at http://www.legalfreedom.com/prc/ and evaluate whether it is in violation of any UPL principles or whether it is a benefit to potential pro se litigants. Find similar Web sites and compare.

2. Relatively few corporations post their organizational charts online so that you can see their official structure, but a few do. To see how such corporations work, visit the following.

   http://www.chinaoil.com.cn/english/view/organization.asp
   http://www.citation.net/suppliers-orgchart.html
   http://telecom.fm/corporate/chart.htm
   http://www.mdarchives.state.md.us/msa/mdmanual/25ind/priv/html/medc.html
   http://www.miratekcorporation.com/organization.htm

   Are they helpful? Would you know who to go to if you had a client with a problem?

3. Go to your favorite search engine and run "private investigator surveillance." Look at five different sites. Is there anything on each site that lets you know that they are reliable? How would you go about selecting one of the five to work for you? How would you know if they had good sense about how to conduct a surveillance?

4. Go to www.google.com and run "sex offender" along with the name of your state. That is one background check that is very easy to do online.

5. To find out the kinds of services court reporters offer, try a search on court reporters via your favorite search engine. What do you find?

WORKING THE BRAIN

1. A hospital sued for malpractice loses part of the medical records involved in the case, but the lawyer has a copy of the lost records from the insurer, who did a risk analysis at the time of the injury to the patient. When the interrogatories are received, they ask for information about all parties with knowledge of the existence of the missing records. What objections should be made? Will they stand?

2. An employer is sued for negligent hiring because of the criminal record of an employee that it failed to check. Is that inadmissible propensity evidence, or is there a reason that it would be admitted?

3. A problem that faces the legal profession is the incivility of some attorneys. An example is found in the case of *Carroll v. Jaques*, 926 F. Supp. 1282 (E.D. Tex. 1996), *aff'd*, 110 F.3d 290 (5th Cir. 1997), in which the objectionable behavior is exhibited by the lawyer as deponent.

   On February 1, 1996, counsel for Plaintiff conducted the deposition of Leonard Jaques. Over the course of the deposition, Jaques refused to answer questions and verbally abused counsel for Plaintiff with profanity. After a barrage of profanity by Jaques, counsel for Plaintiff terminated the deposition. The court regrets having to repeat Jaques's profanity in this opinion, but the court must explain the necessity for drawing on its inherent power to control a party's conduct in a case before the court. Although the court ultimately sanctions Jaques for particular profane words, it is important to put the words in a "question and answer" context so that the transcript fairly represents Jaques's contumacious behavior at the deposition. As referenced in the deposition transcript, Plaintiff's counsel is questioning Jaques ("THE WITNESS"), and Defendants' counsel represents Jaques. While the transcript contains many other instances of Jaques's abusive behavior, the court will repeat only a portion. The deposition transcript reads:

[PLAINTIFF'S COUNSEL]:   Do you want to make your objection now?

[DEFENDANTS' COUNSEL]:   Please. I object to the form of the question, and it is argumentative and calls for a legal conclusion from the witness. Let me take a short break.

THE WITNESS: More than that, it's not relevant to any issue of this cause. I mean it is stupid. It is out of order. *Only an ass would ask those questions.*

* * *

Q. Well, do you think you wrote Mr. Carroll a letter and told him that the judge had dismissed his case on Forum on Nonconvenience [sic] in 1982?

A. I'm not thinking.

[DEFENDANTS' COUNSEL]:   Excuse me. Excuse me. Excuse me. This is repetitious. He's already told you that he doesn't recall.

A. Let him go on. Just let him go on. *He's an idiot.* Let him go on.

* * *

Q. So, this is the document that constitutes your authority? I mean you would be wrong to go file suit for a man or to do something for him if you didn't have the authority to represent him under your state laws and, I assume. That would be s [sic] right?

A. Well, you took ethics, too. And is that your understanding of legal ethics?

Q. Are you telling me that I'm right?

A. *I'm telling you you're an ass to ask me such a question.*

* * *

Q. And the place to look for the answer if there is one would be again in the firm's file?

[DEFENDANTS' COUNSEL]:   Excuse me.

(By [Plaintiff's counsel])

Q. Correct?

[DEFENDANTS' COUNSEL]:   I object to form of the question, misleading, assumes facts not in evidence.

A. *Isn't that an asinine question?*

Q. We would have to look in the file, wouldn't we? There is no place else that you would look for it, is there?

[DEFENDANTS' COUNSEL]:   Nonresponsive.

A. *Isn't that an asinine question?*

* * *

Q. So, you knew you had Mr. Carroll's file in the—

A. (Interrupting) *Where the f_ _ _ is this idiot going?*

Q. — winter of 1990/91 or you didn't?

[DEFENDANTS' COUNSEL]:   Nonresponsive. Objection, objection this is harassing. This is . . .

THE WITNESS: He's harassing me. *He ought to be punched in the goddamn nose.*

* * *

Q. How about your own net worth, Mr. Jaques? What is that?

[DEFENDANTS' COUNSEL]:   Excuse me. Object also that this is protected by a—

THE WITNESS: (Interrupting) *Get off my back you slimy son-of-a-bitch.*

[PLAINTIFF'S COUNSEL]:   I beg your pardon, sir?

THE WITNESS: *You slimy son-of-a-bitch* [Shouting].

[PLAINTIFF'S COUNSEL]:   You're not going to cuss me, Mr. Jaques.

THE WITNESS: *You're a slimy son-of-a-bitch* [Shouting].

[PLAINTIFF'S COUNSEL]: You can cuss your counsel. You can cuss your client. You can cuss yourself. You're not going to cuss me. We're stopping right now.

THE WITNESS: You're damn right.

[PLAINTIFF'S COUNSEL]: We'll resume with Judge Schell tomorrow. Thank you.

THE WITNESS: Come on. Let's go.

[PLAINTIFF'S COUNSEL]: Good evening, sir.

THE WITNESS: *F_ _ _ you, you son-of-a-bitch. . . .*

Jaques Depo. Tr. dated Feb. 1, 1996 (emphasis added). Considering Jaques's shocking and uncivilized conduct at his deposition, counsel for both parties are to be commended for the way they conducted themselves under such difficult circumstances. . . . The court finds that the appropriate sanction in this case to deter such behavior by Jaques is a fine payable to the United States Treasury . . . [T]he court finds that a fine of $7,000 is appropriate to deter Jaques from engaging in abusive behavior . . . While the court's fine addresses Jaques's abusive behavior at the deposition as a whole, the court arrived at the $7,000 figure by focusing on Jaques's most egregious language. The $7,000 amount was calculated by assessing fines of: $500 for each of the four times Jaques referred to Plaintiff's counsel as either an "idiot" or an "ass"; $1,000 for Jaques's suggestion during the deposition that Plaintiff's counsel "ought to be punched in the goddamn nose"; $1,000 for each of the three times Jaques called Plaintiff's counsel a "slimy son-of-a-bitch"; and $1,000 for Jaques's parting words to Plaintiff's counsel, which were "F_ _ _ you, you son-of-a-bitch."

Carroll v. Jacques, 926 F. Supp 1282, 1284–1293 (E. D. Tex. 1996), *aff'd* 1107.3d 290 (5th Cir. 1997).

How would you handle an abusive client, witness, or opposing counsel? What steps could you take to protect yourself or to document such abuse?

4. Various reasons are advanced for the ugliness and lack of professionalism reflected in the example cited in question 3, including the emphasis on law firms as a business rather than a profession or calling, the advances of technology that have increased time pressures, and the economics of firms that have raised the average case load and decreased attorney satisfaction. Others point to modern society as a whole. Do you think the legal profession has something to be concerned about, or is it just catching up with the rest of the world? Should the legal profession be different from other areas of work?

5. What other forms of impeachment can you look for other than dishonesty, exaggeration, "badness," or physical inability for what the opposing party claims to have happened? What forms of bias exist that you can look for as reasons to disbelieve a party?

PUTTING IT TO WORK

1. Prepare interrogatories and requests for production for each of your cases and present them to the opposing side. When you receive interrogatories and requests for production, meet with your client to answer them. File the originals and the answered set appropriately in the files. Make sure you file copies with the "court" as required.

FACT WITNESSES

> "Perhaps the most fatuous of all notions solemnly voiced by learned men who ought to know better is that when legal rules are 'clear and complete' litigation is unlikely to occur. . . . Such writers surely cannot be unaware that thousands of decisions yearly turn on disputes concerning the facts; i.e., as to whether clear-cut legal rules were in fact violated. It is the uncertainty about the 'facts' that creates most of the unpredictability of decisions."
>
> *Ricketts v. Pennsylvania R.R.,* 153 F.2d. 757, 761-762 (2d Cir. 1946) (Frank, J., concurring)

> "When I took courses on Evidence in law school, the explanation given for this giant collection of rules was simply that Juries were stupid."
>
> *Gordon Tullock,* The Logic of the Law (1971).

INTRODUCTION

Fact witnesses are what they sound like: witnesses who have personal knowledge of the facts of the case, whether of the incidents pertaining to liability or of the outcomes that make up damages. Fact witnesses may be neutral, having no particular allegiance to any party to the litigation, or they may be aligned with one of the parties. **Neutral witnesses** are people who just happened to be at the scene, observed what happened, but have no particular interest in the outcome in the case, no relationship with the parties, and no overt reason to tailor their story toward one particular side. Neutral witnesses tend to take on heightened importance in the jurors' eyes even though they may be as flawed in their perception as any aligned witness, so a neutral witness who is damaging to your client's case needs to be evaluated for potential areas of impeachment.

A subset of neutral witnesses (even if they aren't actually neutral) is comprised of **official witnesses:** police officers, fire fighters, arson investigators, health and safety inspectors, and the like. These witnesses are particularly influential because they have both personal contact with the case and a certain air of expertise mixed with an air of neutrality. To preserve this neutrality, police officers in some jurisdictions will not engage in ex parte communications with legal staff; they will only speak in response to a subpoena at a deposition so that both sides are present. This is by no means a universal rule; find out what custom prevails in your jurisdiction. As it is a custom, not a rule, it is subject to exceptions; befriend a few officers and you may find a way to get around the problem.

Aligned fact witnesses have their own issues. Those witnesses who are friends or family of a party, or who have financial or other significant interests similar to a party such that they are inclined to favor that party, are referred to as **friendly witnesses.** Friendly witnesses may try too hard and end up coming off as untrustworthy as a result, or set themselves up for impeachment. They may not mean to lie, but exaggeration in the service of a friend is as good as a lie if done under oath and exposed by opposing counsel in front of a jury. The jury may not become angry at a friend for doing so and may not penalize the party in terms of the damages awarded, but jurors will discount the testimony of that friend accordingly, and it will not have assisted the party at all.

Hostile witnesses are usually close to impossible to speak to without a deposition, hence the modifier "hostile." One form of hostile witness is the kind aligned with the other party. Look for the same problem with these witnesses that you worry about with your own friendly witnesses: exaggerating on behalf of their friends and allies. Another type of hostile witness is the person who simply does not want to have anything to do with the litigation, either from a desire to be left alone or from a fear of repercussions (e.g., illegal aliens, criminal records, warrants). The final kind of hostile witness is the kind who takes an instant personal dislike to you or your attorney. These are rare, but you will encounter them. You might try to send someone else to the deposition in your firm, but once an individual gets it in his head that he isn't going to help you because you are somehow "bad," in some way, he likely won't assist you indirectly through someone else. If the problem is a simple personality conflict, and the person is generally willing to cooperate but you're just not getting anywhere with him, sending someone else to talk to the witness may fix it.

Everyone runs into people with whom there is a mutual rub-the-wrong-way vibe going on; don't worry too much about it unless it's happening to you on a regular basis. If it happens more than once or twice a year, you need to think through your method and manner and see if there's something you are unconsciously doing to alienate witnesses. If you can't figure it out for yourself, either videotape an interview (mock or real) or have someone sit in on one of your interviews and give you feedback. A combination of the two is probably the most effective because then you can *see* the behavior that might be the cause of the problem.

The best kind of fact witnesses can be those who testify against their expected alignment, for example, the mother who testifies against her son having custody of his child, or the boss who testifies against corporate policies. These are admittedly rare, but highly effective if they testify for the right reason: the call of conscience. Now, if you are facing that kind of damaging testimony, you want to look for a not-so-honorable reason: revenge, collusion, some sort of monetary or other gain, or something else along those lines.

ETHICAL ISSUES

Disclosure

One of the first things newcomers to the profession think to do when they can't get a witness to talk to them is to just not tell the witness who they are. You've seen it in the movies; it works in real life, too. Just show up somewhere the witness hangs out, strike up a conversation, and lead it to what you want to discuss. This is a problem. Why? Check out these rules.

It is professional misconduct for a lawyer to:

a. violate or attempt to violate the Rules of Professional Conduct, knowingly assist or induce another to do so, or do so through the acts of another;

. . .

b. engage in conduct involving dishonesty, fraud, deceit or misrepresentation . . .

Model Rules of Prof'l Cond. R. 8.4.

Because the attorney cannot engage in conduct involving dishonesty or deceit, neither can you. What about private investigators? As long as they are operating within the parameters of their license and their ethics codes, deception may not be a problem. Why? Because private investigators are usually independent contractors, not direct employees, and therefore the lawyer does not have the same level of responsibility for their behavior. However, if the lawyer knows that a particular private investigator engages in unethical behavior, such as snagging mail out of mailboxes of the persons he's investigating, then he would be liable for the behavior. Furthermore, once the private investigator is caught and impeached for doing so, he's useless as a witness, for that one instance may be brought up in later trials for impeachment purposes.

Tape Recording

Another issue that comes up in interviewing fact witnesses is the question of whether one may properly use a concealed tape recorder. First you must check the law generally governing the use of a recorder in those circumstances. In many states, as long as one party to the conversation knows that the conversation is being recorded (you), it is perfectly legal. In some states, specific rules exclude attorneys or their agents from doing so. Absent these statutes, regulations, or rules, where do you look for guidance?

Ward v. Maritz Inc., 156 F.R.D. 592 (D.N.J. 1994).

Presently before the Court is the motion by defendants Maritz Inc. and Maritz Marketing Research Inc. (collectively "Maritz"), to compel the production of certain tape recordings and testimony and for sanctions . . .

BACKGROUND

On September 2, 1993, plaintiff filed a complaint against defendants alleging sexual harassment and constructive discharge from her employment with Maritz. The present motion arises from defense counsel's deposition of plaintiff on April 13, 1994. According to Ms. Ward's deposition testimony, she secretly tape-recorded telephone conversations in late 1993 with two American Telephone and Telegraph ("AT&T") employees (Linda Bauer and Lori Jakubek) and a former Maritz employee (Rasha Proctor). The conversations apparently related to "the working environment in the offices where [Ward] had been employed.". . . Ward placed the calls from her attorneys' office consulting with counsel. Plaintiff's counsel advised Ward that "it would be helpful to her case to obtain statements from witnesses who were familiar with" the aforementioned working environment . . . Furthermore, plaintiff and her counsel "discussed the categories of information that would be of most value and observed also that it would be best to contact witnesses who would be willing to testify openly in court.". . . Neither Bauer nor Jakubek was aware of the recording or consented to it . . .

Both Jakubek and Bauer have requested from plaintiff's counsel a copy of the their [sic] tape-recorded conversations with plaintiff. These requests were contained in letters dated April 4 and April 6, 1994, respectively. Plaintiff's counsel has not complied with such requests.

Defendants' motion to compel seeks the production of the tapes themselves as well as deposition testimony as to the content of the tapes and the circumstances under which they were created . . .

It is fundamental under the Federal Rules of Civil Procedure that the work product doctrine offers a qualified protection for documents and tangible things prepared in anticipation of litigation or for trial by or for a party or by or for the party's representative, such as an attorney . . . Such materials are discoverable only where the moving party demonstrates a substantial need for the materials and is unable without undue hardship to obtain their substantial equivalent by other means. Nevertheless, Rule 26 requires that even where such a showing has been made, the Court protect against disclosure the mental impressions, conclusions, opinions or legal theories of an attorney with respect to the litigation . . .

The work product doctrine is "qualified" in another sense: Protection may be vitiated by the unprofessional or unethical behavior of an attorney or a party . . .

In [the] *Parrott* [case] plaintiff's counsel clandestinely recorded telephone conversations that he had with two witnesses to the circumstances surrounding the death of plaintiff's son. The Eleventh Circuit held that whatever work product protection might have applied to the tapes was vitiated by the attorney's secretive recording of the conversations.

. . . [I]t must be emphasized that the present motion involves the work product doctrine as applied to a party's secret, one-sided recordings of conversations with third persons. Statements of witnesses taken by attorneys, with such witnesses' full knowledge, clearly constitute work product . . . Such knowledge was lacking in this case, however.

The case of *Bogan v. Northwestern Mutual Life Insurance Co.*, 144 F.R.D. 51 (S.D.N.Y. 1992), is directly on point. In *Bogan*, the plaintiffs tape-recorded conversations with certain witnesses without their consent. The plaintiffs claimed that the recordings were made in preparation of litigation. Nonetheless, the *Bogan* court ordered the production of the tapes to opposing counsel.

The court articulated a myriad of concerns with respect to the continued secrecy of the tapes. First, the court stated that "known, claimed or suspected contents of such tapes in the hands of one party might lead to distortion of witnesses' testimony because of concern over how the tapes might be used.". . . The court observed that "even if the tapes were prepared in connection with the litigation, attorney involvement in encouraging taping of this type raises questions of legal ethics justifying, at the least, provision of the tapes to the adversary so that any relevant issues can be explored.". . . The Bogan court also commented that one-sided, surreptitious taping of potential witnesses without discovery could produce an unfairly prejudicial effect in that witnesses could be subjected to surprise introduction of tapes at trial or potential blackmail . . .

The court explained that the "extremely mild remedy of discovery" would not interfere with the right of the plaintiffs or their counsel to interview witnesses, except where secret taping without the consent of the interviewee is involved. The *Bogan* court concluded that where unconsented, secret tape recording has occurred, the use of the tapes for litigation purposes should not be approved without discovery absent "special circumstances.". . .

In addition to *Bogan*, several other cases have addressed this issue. In *Haigh v. Matsushita Elec. Corp. of America,* 676 F. Supp. 1332 (E.D. Va. 1987), the plaintiff, acting on his own initiative and absent directives from his counsel, tape-recorded conversations with fifty-eight individuals without their knowledge. Plaintiff provided the tapes to his counsel within a day or two following each conversation, and the contents of the tapes were reviewed by counsel and used to prepare the complaint and discovery requests.

While finding that the tapes constituted work product, the *Haigh* court determined that the protections of the work product doctrine had been vitiated by the conduct of plaintiff's counsel. The court stated that, rather than merely passive and noncommittal acquiescence, counsel's actions comprised "active encouragement and affirmative support" for plaintiff's secret tape recording . . . The *Haigh* court found that such conduct vitiated the work product protection.

Similarly, in *Wilson v. Lamb,* 125 F.R.D. 142 (E.D. Ky. 1989), plaintiff and his counsel recorded a meeting with two defense witnesses without their knowledge or consent. The witnesses certified that they would not have participated in the meeting had they known that it was being recorded. The Wilson court "assumed" that the tape constituted work product . . . Relying upon *Parrott, Moody* and *Haigh,* the court determined that the conduct of plaintiff and his counsel vitiated the work product protection that otherwise would have attached to the tapes. *See also Chapman & Cole v. Itel Container Int'l B.V.,* 865 F.2d 676, 686 (5th Cir.), *cert. denied,* 493 U.S. 872 (1989) (failure to reveal clandestinely recorded tape of conversation between defense counsel and witness waives work product protection as contravention of ABA Model Rules of Professional Conduct).

Finally, two other cases merit attention. The first is *In re Hunter Studios, Inc.,* 164 Bankr. 431 (Bankr. E.D.N.Y. 1994), in which an attorney tape-recorded a conversation between himself and a purchaser without the latter's consent or knowledge. The conversation occurred three years before the attorney became engaged in the matter. Relying upon Formal Opinion 337 of the American Bar Association Committee on Ethics and Professional Responsibility, the *Hunter Studios* court determined that a recording is not inadmissible solely because it is created by an attorney . . . The bankruptcy court articulated a series of rationales for the proscription against an attorney obtaining a secret recording while engaged in a matter: the appearance of surreptitiousness; the decrease in public confidence in the bar and the public's desire to speak openly; and, the enticement for attorneys to "create" evidence . . .

The other case that merits scrutiny is *H.L. Hayden Co. of New York, Inc. v. Siemens Medical Sys., Inc.,* 108 F.R.D. 686 (S.D.N.Y. 1985). In *Hayden,* the principal of the plaintiff corporations secretly recorded telephone conversations with a former employee of the defendant corporation. The defendant moved to compel the plaintiffs to produce the tapes. The *Hayden* court began its analysis by speculating that the tapes constituted work product, although the court noted that the parties had not sufficiently addressed that issue. In denying the motion to compel, the court reached a practical resolution. Noting that defense counsel and the former employee were "on friendly terms" in that counsel represented the former employee at his deposition, the *Hayden* court commented that defense counsel "can, and almost certainly already has," learned about the recorded conversations from the former employee . . . The court further noted that the defendant could obtain the tapes by having the former employee request them from the plaintiffs pursuant to Fed. R. Civ. P. 26(b)(3).

While resolving the motion to compel on the particular facts present in the case, the *Hayden* court, in a footnote, addressed the very issue that is presently before this Court. The *Hayden* court remarked: "The entire situation raises a concern in the court's mind which may have to be addressed at a later time: the ethical ramifications of an attorney, who is not himself permitted to record a conversation with a third party without that party's consent, directing his client to do so and the effect of such a circumstance on work product protection.". . . It appears that such "later time" has arrived in this district by means of the present application by defendant Maritz.

The threshold inquiry in any case involving the work product doctrine is whether the given materials comprise work product as defined in Rule 26(b)(3). In this case, the circumstances surrounding the tape recordings reveal that the tapes were created in preparation for trial. The recordings occurred after the complaint was filed. The idea of the recordings appears to have been first proposed by plaintiff's counsel. Counsel advised Ward as to the type of statements that would be most beneficial to her case. Ward placed the calls from her counsel's office, although the attorneys were not present during the conversations. These facts clearly demonstrate that the recordings were prepared for litigation or trial purposes and, thus, constitute work product under the Federal Rules . . .

The discrete issue in this regard is whether the method used by plaintiff and her counsel, i.e., secret tape recording, to obtain the statements of the three witnesses should defeat the protection of the work product doctrine. In answering this question, the Court has examined the cases discussed above as well as various ethics opinions on the subject of secret, one-sided tape recording. It is important to distinguish between two areas of concern: the issue of whether certain conduct is ethical or unethical and the issue of whether certain conduct vitiates the work product rule. Conduct that is deemed "ethical" or permissible under prevailing standards of professional responsibility may nevertheless abrogate the work product doctrine and result in the discoverability of the materials.

As an initial matter, it should be noted that no opinion of a New Jersey ethics committee has been cited or found relating to the present issue. ABA Formal Opinion 337, dated August 10, 1974, is the genesis of the tape recording issue as far as ethics opinions are concerned. Opinion 337 determined that, with certain exceptions, "no lawyer should record any conversation whether by tapes or other electronic device, without the consent or prior knowledge of all parties to the conversation." The Opinion maintained that the conduct involving dishonesty, fraud, deceit or misrepresentation proscribed by Disciplinary Rule 1-102(A)(4) encompassed secret recording by an attorney of conversations with any persons.

Plaintiff argues that because New Jersey has adopted the Rules of Professional Conduct ("RPC") rather than the Code of Professional Responsibility upon which Opinion 337 was based, the Opinion and its interpretive caselaw, such as *Parrott*, should be discounted. This suggestion is unavailing, however. The RPC contain the exact proscription against "conduct involving dishonesty, fraud, deceit or misrepresentation" upon which Opinion 337 relied. See RPC 8.4(c). Clearly, the message is the same whether it is expressed in the RPC or the Code of Professional Responsibility, and there is no reason to dismiss these valid interpretations.

Additionally, plaintiff points to Opinion 696 of the New York County Lawyer Association's Committee on Professional Ethics as "rejecting" Opinion 337. Ward Opposition Brief, at 8. Noting that "normative standards change over time," Opinion 696 held that "[a] lawyer may secretly record telephone conversations with third parties, provided one party to the conversation consents and the recording does not violate any applicable law or specific ethical rule." Nevertheless, Opinion 696 declared that "a lawyer may not use recorded statements out of context or in an otherwise misleading way." The Opinion also warned that "it would be ethically improper . . . for an attorney to record or cause to be recorded any conversation with an adverse party or witness represented by counsel without that party's consent or prior knowledge." It is significant for purposes of the present motion that the New York Opinion anticipated that "a lawyer may be creating discoverable evidence" where he records a telephone conversation with a client or between a client and a third party. The Opinion observes that "this may result in an accompanying duty not to suppress such evidence."

A variant of this latter situation occurred in this case. In short, plaintiff herself secretly recorded conversations with potential witnesses immediately after consultation with her attorneys. Also, plaintiff denied to at least one of these persons that she was recording their conversation . . . While such conduct may not be deemed unethical under the recent New York Opinion 696, the Court notes that this Opinion is not controlling in this district. More importantly, this Opinion explicitly stated that discoverable evidence may be created by secret tape recording. Thus, Opinion 696 recognized the distinction between the issue of ethics and the issue of discoverability.

Accordingly, regardless of whether the conduct of plaintiff's counsel violated the RPC, the Court finds that the secret tape recording vitiated the work product rule. The unprofessional behavior of plaintiff's attorneys in counseling Ward to surreptitiously record conversations, during one of which she denied that the recording was taking place, should abrogate the protection of the work product doctrine . . .

In conclusion, the Court finds that the work product doctrine has been vitiated by plaintiff's secretive recording of her conversations with the three witnesses. The tapes shall be produced to defense counsel within 15 days of the date of the accompanying Order . . .

Maritz also seeks to compel further deposition testimony as to the circumstances surrounding the making of the recordings. The work product doctrine protects against the disclosure of protected documents or communications, not the underlying facts . . . Consequently, it does not contravene the work product rule for an attorney to question an opposing party as to the information contained in protected documents . . .

The Court believes that it is permissible and appropriate for defense counsel to further depose plaintiff as to the circumstances surrounding the tape recordings. The facts contained on the tapes are not protected by the work product doctrine. Nor, for that matter, are the facts relating to how, when and why the recordings were made. Plaintiff shall appear for further deposition with respect to these foundation questions . . .

Finally, there is the issue of fees and sanctions. While it is certainly within the Court's discretion to award costs to defense counsel the Court does not believe that such an award is mandated in this case. The position taken by plaintiff's counsel at the deposition was not so contrary to law that sanctions are required.

An appropriate Order will be entered.

In the end, this court skirted the ethics issue. The court implied taping was unethical, said it was bad enough to require the plaintiff to turn over the tapes despite the fact they were privileged, but wouldn't actually hold the behavior unethical. Why? To leave the ethics issue open for the appropriate enforcement body to investigate and punish. The rules require lawyers and judges to immediately report known ethics violations to the appropriate ethics enforcement body in the state bar. This court would be required under the ethics rules to do so. If the court held that the behavior of the attorney violated the ethical rules, it could arguably tie the hands of the ethics committee, who might then be required to find that a violation existed, even if they disagreed, because it now had the force of law. This way, the bar could work through the ethics issue rather than having it decided by the court. It was a very politic decision, if not terribly helpful for those of us looking for an answer.

Another problem that sometimes arises is the issue of payment. A fact witness may want to be paid for his or her time and trouble. It is unethical to pay a fact witness for testimony, as rather obliquely stated in the Model Rules.

A lawyer shall not . . . offer an inducement to a witness that is prohibited by law.

Model Rules of Prof'l Cond. R. 3.4(b).

However, a fact witness may be paid for actual out-of-pocket expenses (including lost wages) incurred for testifying as long as there is no indication that the payment was made to induce the witness to testify a certain way. As a practical matter, you won't want to make it look as though a fact witness was paid off, either, as the jury will discount the testimony accordingly. Usually reimbursement for such expenses is not offered except in extraordinary circumstances; it more often occurs when demanded by a witness.

EVIDENTIARY ISSUES

Privileges

People who know about the opposing party or the facts of the incident may possess information that is **privileged.** This means that you cannot use the information at trial; you also cannot seek such information because the communication between the party and the witness is protected from disclosure. However, if the privilege is waived, or if there is some sort of exception to the privilege, then the information can be used. In some states, privileges are statutorily prescribed; in others, you must search case law to find them all.

The most common are **attorney-client, physician-patient, psychotherapist-patient,** and **priest-penitent.** Each of these can be more broadly stated, as the attorney-client privilege extends to any agent working on behalf of the attorney, the physician-patient privilege covers most health care professionals, the psychotherapist-patient often covers any mental health care professional, and the priest-penitent has been extended to cover any religious leader and his or her flock. You may wonder what happened to the husband-wife communications privilege: that one ordinarily exists only in criminal law.

Exceptions to Privileges

For each privilege, there are exceptions. Waiver by the patient/client/penitent is one. If the mental or physical condition of the patient is in issue, the privilege is waived, but only to the extent that you may use discovery methods to obtain the information; **ex parte communications** are not allowed without the express consent of the patient. If the patient is your client, you will have gotten that consent in the initial interview. If the patient/client/penitent sues the physician/psychotherapist/attorney/priest, the privilege is waived as well. As the courts are wont to say, the person to be protected by the privilege can't turn the shield into a sword by making accusations and then saying that the other party can't use any of their conversations to rebut the accusations because the information is privileged.

The **crime-fraud exception** to attorney-client privilege is found in Rule 1.6(b)(1).

> b. A lawyer may reveal information relating to the representation of a client to the extent the lawyer reasonably believes necessary:
>
> 1. to prevent reasonably certain death or substantial bodily harm.
>
> Model Rules of Prof'l Cond. R. 1.6(b)(1).

If the lawyer "reasonably believes" that it is "reasonably certain" that a client will cause death or substantial bodily harm, he or she "may" reveal information. Some states have made disclosure under these circumstances mandatory, but the two "reasonables" still apply: When do you believe a client is going to certainly harm someone? Such a decision is tough in family law, unless your client has a history of abusing his spouse. The weasel language is there to protect the privilege, not the third party that might be harmed. Is that right? It's hard to say. In the easy cases, such as an abusive husband who has put his wife in the hospital three times before and tells his lawyer that he's gotten ammo for his gun and knows his wife is hiding at her sister's house and that he's going over there tonight at 7:00 to off them both, then yes, it's clear that the moral choice is to forget about client confidentiality and warn the women. However, when you have an angry man in your office who simply says, "I wanna kill that bitch" (something you hear every day), and he makes good his threat, you can't berate yourself by thinking, *I should have said something.* How could you have known? Can you tell every wife of every man that has said that in a fit of anger? It's cases like that that make it necessary to have the double "reasonable" in the rule. Notice, too, that the rule only applies to future crimes. Once it's over, you cannot disclose the acts of the client. Otherwise, no one who is actually liable or guilty of anything would have any confidence in telling the attorney the truth.

What about other types of crimes? There is another rule that prohibits lawyers from helping clients commit fraud.

> d. A lawyer shall not counsel a client to engage, or assist a client, in conduct that the lawyer knows is criminal or fraudulent, but a lawyer may discuss the legal consequences of any proposed course of

conduct with a client and may counsel or assist a client to make a good faith effort to determine the validity, scope, meaning or application of the law.

Model Code Prof'l Cond. R. 1.2(d).

This does not actually waive the attorney-client privilege, but that does happen in many jurisdictions by judicial action.

Olson v. Accessory Controls and Equipment Corp., 757 A.2d 14 (Conn. 2000).

This certified appeal raises two principal issues. First, we must determine the extent to which the attorney-client privilege applies to communications between counsel for a company and an environmental consulting firm retained by counsel to assist in responding to an order issued by the department of environmental protection. Second, we must determine whether, if privileged, the communications fall within the crime-fraud exception to the attorney-client privilege . . . We conclude . . . as a matter of first impression, that communications otherwise covered by the attorney-client privilege lose their protected status when they are procured with the intent of furthering a civil fraud. Under the facts of this case, however, we conclude that the plaintiff did not meet his burden of establishing that the exception applies . . .

The record discloses the following relevant facts. In December, 1981, the plaintiff was employed by the defendant as an engineering technician in the defendant's Windsor plant. The defendant manufactured, among other products, air conditioning equipment, jet air starters and ground power units for airplanes. By 1985, the plaintiff, who had been promoted to plant manager, was responsible for the manufacturing operations. The plaintiff held this position at all times relevant to the present case.

On October 11, 1989, the state department of environmental protection (department) conducted an on-site inspection of the defendant's Windsor plant. The department documented its findings in an inspection report that identified two areas of concern regarding hazardous waste discharge and storage activity . . .

. . . On or about June 7, 1990, [the consultant hired to deal with the hazardous waste issue by the defendant's attorney Briggs] issued a preliminary report to . . . the defendant concerning waste contamination at the Windsor plant. A copy of that report, which is referred to by the parties as the Diaz report, was sent to the plaintiff in his capacity as plant manager. The Diaz report also contained information about areas of the plant that had not been identified in the department's inspection report . . . The June 7, 1990 Diaz report was never submitted to the department.

As stated by the Appellate Court, "thereafter, and according to the plaintiff's complaint, the defendant [Teleflex Lionel-DuPont S.A. (Teleflex)], a French corporation, acquired an ownership interest in [the defendant]. In February, 1992, Teleflex' representatives, Francois Calvarin and Alex Reese, visited the Windsor plant as part of a postacquisition review of [the defendant's] operations. While there, Calvarin and Reese questioned the plaintiff about [the defendant's] prior practices with regard to the storage and disposal of toxic and hazardous waste at the plant. Calvarin and Reese encouraged the plaintiff to cooperate with their investigation by promising the plaintiff that his communications with them would be confidential and would not be shared with [the defendant's] management. They further assured him that his communications with them would not be the subject of reprisal or other negative employment action.

"Relying on Calvarin and Reese's assurances, the plaintiff disclosed to them that there had, in fact, been improper storage and disposal of toxic and hazardous waste at the Windsor plant. The plaintiff further advised them of the existence of the June 7, 1990 Diaz report . . . The plaintiff asserts that despite their assurances, Calvarin and Reese communicated to senior management [of the defendant] the information that the plaintiff had provided them.

"According to the plaintiff, upon learning of his disclosures to Calvarin and Reese, [the defendant] commenced a campaign of retaliation against the plaintiff with the apparent goal of forcing him to resign or, in the alternative, to provide [the defendant] with a justification for dismissing him. On February 12, 1993, following the unsuccessful campaign to force him to resign, [the defendant] dismissed the plaintiff under the pretext that his position had been eliminated." . . .

Following his termination, the plaintiff commenced this action . . . alleging that his dismissal constituted wrongful termination and retaliatory discharge. In particular, the plaintiff claimed that he had been discharged for having reported to Teleflex representatives potential violations of the state environmental laws and regulations governing waste storage and disposal at the defendant's plant.

Before trial , . . . the defendant moved for a protective order seeking to preclude the plaintiff and his attorneys from disclosing, inter alia, oral and written communications that had occurred between the defendant and Briggs, which the defendant claimed had been made for the purpose of conveying legal advice. The defendant also sought the return from the plaintiff of all documents containing such communications. The trial court granted the defendant's motion for a protective order concluding that the documents were protected by the attorney-client privilege and that the crime-fraud exception was not applicable under the facts of the case . . .

The defendant then filed a motion in limine, asking the trial court to adopt the earlier protective order and to exclude from trial any information previously found to be protected by the attorney-client privilege. In granting the defendant's motion, the trial court adopted the factual findings contained in the earlier protective order and prohibited any use of, or reference to, the Diaz report . . . or the information contained therein. The defendant then moved to dismiss the action, claiming that, in light of the trial court's evidentiary ruling to exclude from disclosure the information contained in the protective order, the plaintiff would be unable to present a prima facie case. The plaintiff joined in the defendant's motion. The trial court granted the defendant's motion, and rendered judgment dismissing the plaintiff's complaint . . .

We conclude that the attorney-client privilege covers the communications at issue in this case. We conclude further that, under the crime-fraud exception, otherwise privileged communications may be stripped of their privileged status if the communications have been procured with the intent to further a civil fraud. Finally, we conclude that, under the circumstances of this case, the plaintiff has failed to meet the requisite burden to establish the applicability of that exception. We therefore affirm the judgment of the Appellate Court . . .

At the outset, we recite the standard governing the review of a trial court's decision on a discovery motion. We have long recognized that "the granting or denial of a discovery request rests in the sound discretion of the [trial] court," and is subject to reversal "only if such an order constitutes an abuse of that discretion." . . . "It is only in rare instances that the trial court's decision will be disturbed." . . .

With these standards in mind, we address the issues before us. On numerous occasions we have reaffirmed the importance of the attorney-client privilege and have recognized the "long-standing, strong public policy of protecting attorney-client communications." . . .

As a general rule, "communications between client and attorney are privileged when made in confidence for the purpose of seeking legal advice." . . . "A communication from attorney to client solely regarding a matter of fact would not ordinarily be privileged, unless it were shown to be inextricably linked to the giving of legal advice." . . . Moreover, although we have acknowledged that "statements made in the presence of a third party are usually not privileged because there is then no reasonable expectation of confidentiality"; . . . we have recognized that "the presence of certain third parties . . . who are agents or employees of an attorney or client, and who are necessary to the consultation, will not destroy the confidential nature of the communications." . . .

Appropriately, the attorney-client privilege "extends to interpreters, and to clerks and agents employed by the attorney . . . in the business committed to his [or her] charge."

. . . In the present case, the parties do not dispute that [the consultant] was hired by Briggs to assemble the Diaz report for the defendant for ultimate submittal to the department. Therefore, the issue of agency is uncontested. Our inquiry distills to whether the Diaz report was made in confidence, and whether the communications were "'inextricably linked to the giving of legal advice'" so as to bring them within the attorney-client privilege . . .

The plaintiff contends that the department's order was a mandate to the defendant to submit a broad environmental audit of its entire Windsor facility. According to the plaintiff, the Diaz report was merely a response to the department's order and, therefore, it "was not created for the purpose of giving legal advice." The plaintiff concedes that Briggs' role as the defendant's attorney was "to provide [the defendant] with legal assistance in dealing with the facts," but argues that "creation of the facts," that is, compiling the facts concerning potential sources of contamination on the plant property in the Diaz report, "falls outside of the attorney-client privilege." The plaintiff urges that, because the Diaz report is a "nonlegal, technical report," mandated by the department, . . . it . . . cannot be privileged.

The defendant maintains that the department's order was negotiable and ultimately subject to appeal in the Superior Court. The defendant contends that it reserved the right to appeal the nonbinding order and that its purpose in soliciting the Diaz report and corresponding with the department was "in the nature of a voluntary effort to agree on a resolution" to the problems concerning the areas of contamination that the department had identified. The defendant argues that Briggs' sole purpose in engaging Environmental Management was to compile the Diaz report, and thus the only reason for the subsequent communications between Briggs and Environmental Management was to "enable counsel to advise [the defendant] on its legal responsibilities in responding to the administrative order." We agree with the defendant.

Drawing the line between technical, factual information that is necessary for legal advice and technical information that is not essential to such advice requires a fact-specific inquiry. This is particularly true in the context of reports compiled by outside consultants.

In *United States* v. *Kovel,* 296 F.2d 918, 922 (2d Cir. 1961), the court addressed the extent to which confidential communications made by a client to an accountant, who had been hired by the client's tax attorney, were protected from disclosure before a grand jury. The accountant had been engaged to assist the attorney in rendering tax advice to the client. Id. In extending the attorney-client privilege to the communications, the court recognized that "the privilege must include all the persons who act as the attorney's agents" when the assistance of the agent is "indispensable" to the attorney's work . . . The court cautioned, however, that "if what is sought is not legal advice but only accounting service . . . or if the advice sought is the accountant's rather than the lawyer's, no privilege exists" . . .

Courts have been reluctant, however, to extend the privilege to reports compiled by third parties absent a clear indication that the information was submitted confidentially by an agent to the attorney for legal advice. For example, in *United Postal Service* v. *Phelps Dodge Refining Corp.,* 852 F. Supp. 156, 161 (E.D.N.Y. 1994), the court refused to apply the privilege to communications made by two environmental consultants to the defendants and their in-house counsel. The consultants had been retained to conduct environmental studies and to develop a remedial program for cleaning up the defendants' property in connection with a request from the New York state department of environmental conservation . . . The court refused to extend the attorney-client privilege because "neither consultant [could] be considered an agent [of the attorney] encompassed by the privilege.". . . The court noted that the consultants "were not employed by [the defendants'] attorneys specifically to assist them in rendering legal advice . . . [but] were hired by [the] defendants to formulate a remediation plan acceptable to the [state agency] and to oversee remedial work at the property.". . . Although the court stated that "factual data can never be protected by the attorney-client privilege" because scientists and engineers rarely would be considered agents of the attorney, its ultimate conclusion rested on a review of the documents themselves . . . The court found that "none of the documents revealed any confidential communications by the defendants or their attorneys to the consultants," and concluded that the notations on the documents by the attorneys did not amount to legal advice . . .

These cases do not support a bright line rule that would deem all technical or factual reports compiled for eventual submittal to a governmental agency as outside the attorney-client privilege in all circumstances . . .

In the present case, the trial court concluded that the Diaz report [was] covered by the privilege as communications necessary for legal advice. The trial court determined that the department's order was nonbinding and that it imposed no duty on the defendant to submit the entire Diaz report . . .

[T]he trial court reasonably found that the Diaz report was connected intimately to the rendering of legal advice, and hence, properly extended the attorney-client privilege to . . . the Diaz report . . .

We next address the plaintiff's argument concerning the crime-fraud exception to the attorney-client privilege . . . We consider this a suitable case in which to adopt the fraud exception, as a matter of law, but conclude that it does not apply to the facts of this case . . .

"[E]xceptions to the attorney-client privilege should be made only when the reason for disclosure outweighs the potential chilling of essential communications.". . .

"It is the purpose of the crime-fraud exception to the attorney-client privilege to assure that the seal of secrecy . . . between lawyer and client does not extend to communications made for the purpose of getting advice for the commission of a fraud or crime.". . .

We previously have limited this exception by permitting its application only to situations wherein the communications enveloped by the privilege "are made to counsel in respect to the commission of some intended crime."...

The trial court determined that the plaintiff's failure to identify a criminal statute precluded the application of the crime exception. The trial court, however, did analyze the civil fraud issue "on the added assumption that our appellate courts will extend the exception to the privilege to civil fraud." With respect to the plaintiff's allegations of fraud, the court concluded that "the fraud involved here is really alleged to be an attempt to mislead [the department] by false representations about the conditions at [the defendant's] plant."

We see no principled distinction between communications made to counsel with respect to the commission of some intended crime, and communications made to counsel with respect to the commission of some intended fraud. We therefore adopt an exception to the attorney-client privilege when the privileged communications are made with the intent to further a crime or civil fraud. See footnote 6 of this opinion. Because we are embracing a decidedly new doctrine in Connecticut, it is necessary to delineate the contours of the crime-fraud exception ...

[W]e determined that, in order for the crime exception to lie, the party seeking to abrogate the privilege must offer "reasonable evidence of ... guilty intent." So too, the fraud exception requires some quantum of proof by the party seeking to pierce the privilege. "It would be absurd to say that the privilege could be [eliminated] merely by making a charge of fraud."...

According to the Second Circuit Court of Appeals, proper application of the crime-fraud exception requires the court to determine that "there is probable cause to believe that a crime or fraud has been attempted or committed and that the communications were in furtherance thereof."... Expounding on the probable cause requirement, the Second Circuit has determined that the exception "requires that a prudent person have a reasonable basis to suspect the perpetration or attempted perpetration of a crime or fraud, and that the communications were in furtherance thereof."...

We consider the standard applied by the Court of Appeals for the Second Circuit to be an appropriate enunciation of the exception. We therefore also adopt the standard as our own. As articulated by the Second Circuit, the crime-fraud exception permits abrogation of the attorney-client privilege solely upon a determination by the trial court that there is probable cause to believe that the privileged communications were made with the intent to perpetrate a civil fraud and that the communications were made in furtherance of that fraud ...

In conclusion, the Appellate Court properly affirmed the trial court's decision to extend the attorney-client privilege to the report compiled by the environmental consultant and to the related communications because they were made in confidence for the purpose of obtaining legal advice. We also conclude that the trial court properly deemed the fraud exception inapplicable to the facts of the present case. That exception requires a showing of probable cause to believe that the proponent of the privilege intended to commit a fraud and that the communication was made in furtherance of the fraud. On the basis of the evidence presented by the plaintiff, he has failed to meet this burden and, therefore, the fraud exception was properly held inapplicable.

Other privileges may exist as well, created by statute or even out of constitutional right. One that is often contested is that of a reporter and his or her source. The viability of that privilege varies from state to state, since the United States Supreme Court has not come down with a definitive answer on the subject, only saying that there may be a qualified privilege. At least half of the states have adopted some sort of statute with some sort of protection of reporter's sources; the other half, to the extent those states have addressed it, have generally mimicked the United States Supreme Court. Here's the decision that has been the basis of all the discussion.

Branzburg v. Hayes, 408 U.S. 665 (1972).

The issue in these cases is whether requiring newsmen to appear and testify before state or federal grand juries abridges the freedom of speech and press guaranteed by the First Amendment. We hold that it does not ...

The writ of certiorari ... brings before us two judgments of the Kentucky Court of Appeals, both involving petitioner Branzburg, a staff reporter for the *Courier-Journal*, a daily newspaper published in Louisville, Kentucky.

On November 15, 1969, the *Courier-Journal* carried a story under petitioner's by-line describing in detail his observations of two young residents of Jefferson County synthesizing hashish from marihuana, an activity which, they asserted, earned them about $ 5,000 in three weeks. The article included a photograph of a pair of hands working above a laboratory table on which was a substance identified by the caption as hashish. The article stated that petitioner had promised not to reveal the identity of the two hashish makers . . . Petitioner was shortly subpoenaed by the Jefferson County grand jury; he appeared, but refused to identify the individuals he had seen possessing marihuana or the persons he had seen making hashish from marihuana . . .

The second case involving petitioner Branzburg arose out of his later story published on January 10, 1971, which described in detail the use of drugs in Frankfort, Kentucky. The article reported that in order to provide a comprehensive survey of the "drug scene" in Frankfort, petitioner had "spent two weeks interviewing several dozen drug users in the capital city" and had seen some of them smoking marihuana. A number of conversations with and observations of several unnamed drug users were recounted. Subpoenaed to appear before a Franklin County grand jury "to testify in the matter of violation of statutes concerning use and sale of drugs," petitioner Branzburg moved to quash the summons; the motion was denied, although an order was issued protecting Branzburg from revealing "confidential associations, sources or information" but requiring that he "answer any questions which concern or pertain to any criminal act, the commission of which was actually observed by [him].". . .

Branzburg press[es] First Amendment claims that may be simply put: that to gather news it is often necessary to agree either not to identify the source of information published or to publish only part of the facts revealed, or both; that if the reporter is nevertheless forced to reveal these confidences to a grand jury, the source so identified and other confidential sources of other reporters will be measurably deterred from furnishing publishable information, all to the detriment of the free flow of information protected by the First Amendment. Although the newsmen in these cases do not claim an absolute privilege against official interrogation in all circumstances, they assert that the reporter should not be forced either to appear or to testify before a grand jury or at trial until and unless sufficient grounds are shown for believing that the reporter possesses information relevant to a crime the grand jury is investigating, that the information the reporter has is unavailable from other sources, and that the need for the information is sufficiently compelling to override the claimed invasion of First Amendment interests occasioned by the disclosure . . . The heart of the claim is that the burden on news gathering resulting from compelling reporters to disclose confidential information outweighs any public interest in obtaining the information . . .

We do not question the significance of free speech, press, or assembly to the country's welfare. Nor is it suggested that news gathering does not qualify for First Amendment protection; without some protection for seeking out the news, freedom of the press could be eviscerated. But these cases involve no intrusions upon speech or assembly, no prior restraint or restriction on what the press may publish, and no express or implied command that the press publish what it prefers to withhold. No exaction or tax for the privilege of publishing, and no penalty, civil or criminal, related to the content of published material is at issue here. The use of confidential sources by the press is not forbidden or restricted; reporters remain free to seek news from any source by means within the law. No attempt is made to require the press to publish its sources of information or indiscriminately to disclose them on request.

The sole issue before us is the obligation of reporters to respond to grand jury subpoenas as other citizens do and to answer questions relevant to an investigation into the commission of crime. Citizens generally are not constitutionally immune from grand jury subpoenas; and neither the First Amendment nor any other constitutional provision protects the average citizen from disclosing to a grand jury information that he has received in confidence . . . The claim is, however, that reporters are exempt from these obligations because if forced to respond to subpoenas and identify their sources or disclose other confidences, their informants will refuse or be reluctant to furnish newsworthy information in the future. This asserted burden on news gathering is said to make compelled testimony from newsmen constitutionally suspect and to require a privileged position for them.

It is clear that the First Amendment does not invalidate every incidental burdening of the press that may result from the enforcement of civil or criminal statutes of general applicability. Under prior cases, otherwise valid laws serving substantial public interests may be enforced against the press as against others, despite the possible burden that may be imposed. The Court has emphasized that "the publisher of a newspaper has no special immunity from the application of general laws. He has no special privilege to invade the rights and liberties of others.". . . [T]he Associated Press, a news-gathering and disseminating organization, was not exempt from the requirements of the National Labor Relations Act . . . [T]he Court rejected the claim that applying the Fair Labor Standards Act to a newspaper publishing business would abridge the freedom of press guaranteed by the First Amendment . . . Likewise, a newspaper may be subjected to nondiscriminatory forms of general taxation.

The prevailing view is that the press is not free to publish with impunity everything and anything it desires to publish. Although it may deter or regulate what is said or published, the press may not circulate knowing or reckless falsehoods damaging to private reputation without subjecting itself to liability for damages, including punitive damages, or even criminal prosecution . . . A newspaper or a journalist may also be punished for contempt of court, in appropriate circumstances . . .

It is thus not surprising that the great weight of authority is that newsmen are not exempt from the normal duty of appearing before a grand jury and answering questions relevant to a criminal investigation. At common law, courts consistently refused to recognize the existence of any privilege authorizing a newsman to refuse to reveal confidential information to a grand jury . . . In 1958, a news gatherer asserted for the first time that the First Amendment exempted confidential information from public disclosure pursuant to a subpoena issued in a civil suit, *Garland* v. *Torre,* 259 F.2d 545 (CA2), cert. denied, 358 U.S. 910 (1958), but the claim was denied, and this argument has been almost uniformly rejected since then, although there are occasional dicta that, in circumstances not presented here, a newsman might be excused . . . These courts have applied the presumption against the existence of an asserted testimonial privilege . . . and have concluded that the First Amendment interest asserted by the newsman was outweighed by the general obligation of a citizen to appear before a grand jury or at trial, pursuant to a subpoena, and give what information he possesses . . .

A number of States have provided newsmen a statutory privilege of varying breadth . . . , but the majority have not done so, and none has been provided by federal statute. Until now the only testimonial privilege for unofficial witnesses that is rooted in the Federal Constitution is the Fifth Amendment privilege against compelled self-incrimination. We are asked to create another by interpreting the First Amendment to grant newsmen a testimonial privilege that other citizens do not enjoy. This we decline to do . . .

The preference for anonymity of those confidential informants involved in actual criminal conduct is presumably a product of their desire to escape criminal prosecution, and this preference, while understandable, is hardly deserving of constitutional protection. It would be frivolous to assert—and no one does in these cases—that the First Amendment, in the interest of securing news or otherwise, confers a license on either the reporter or his news sources to violate valid criminal laws . . .

Thus, we cannot seriously entertain the notion that the First Amendment protects a newsman's agreement to conceal the criminal conduct of his source, or evidence thereof, on the theory that it is better to write about crime than to do something about it. Insofar as any reporter in these cases undertook not to reveal or testify about the crime he witnessed, his claim of privilege under the First Amendment presents no substantial question. The crimes of news sources are no less reprehensible and threatening to the public interest when witnessed by a reporter than when they are not.

There remain those situations where a source is not engaged in criminal conduct but has information suggesting illegal conduct by others. Newsmen frequently receive information from such sources pursuant to a tacit or express agreement to withhold the source's name and suppress any information that the source wishes not published. Such informants presumably desire anonymity in order to avoid being entangled as a witness in a criminal trial or grand jury investigation. They may fear that disclosure will threaten their job security or personal safety or that it will simply result in dishonor or embarrassment.

The argument that the flow of news will be diminished by compelling reporters to aid the grand jury in a criminal investigation is not irrational, nor are the records before us silent on the matter. But we remain unclear how often and to what extent informers are actually deterred from furnishing information when newsmen are forced to testify before a grand jury. The available data indicate that some newsmen rely a great deal on confidential sources and that some informants are particularly sensitive to the threat of exposure and may be silenced if it is held by this Court that, ordinarily, newsmen must testify pursuant to subpoenas . . . but the evidence fails to demonstrate that there would be a significant constriction of the flow of news to the public if this Court reaffirms the prior common-law and constitutional rule regarding the testimonial obligations of newsmen . . .

Accepting the fact, however, that an undetermined number of informants not themselves implicated in crime will nevertheless, for whatever reason, refuse to talk to newsmen if they fear identification by a reporter in an official investigation, we cannot accept the argument that the public interest in possible future news about crime from undisclosed, unverified sources must take precedence over the public interest in pursuing and prosecuting those crimes reported to the press by informants and in thus deterring the commission of such crimes in the future.

We note first that the privilege claimed is that of the reporter, not the informant, and that if the authorities independently identify the informant, neither his own reluctance to testify nor the objection of the newsman would shield him from grand jury inquiry, whatever the impact on the flow of news or on his future usefulness as a secret source of information . . .

We are admonished that refusal to provide a First Amendment reporter's privilege will undermine the freedom of the press to collect and disseminate news. But this is not the lesson history teaches us. As noted previously, the common law recognized no such privilege, and the constitutional argument was not even asserted until 1958. From the beginning of our country the press has operated without constitutional protection for press informants, and the press has flourished. The existing constitutional rules have not been a serious obstacle to either the development or retention of confidential news sources by the press . . .

Finally, as we have earlier indicated, news gathering is not without its First Amendment protections, and grand jury investigations if instituted or conducted other than in good faith, would pose wholly different issues for resolution under the First Amendment. Official harassment of the press undertaken not for purposes of law enforcement but to disrupt a reporter's relationship with his news sources would have no justification. Grand juries are subject to judicial control and subpoenas to motions to quash. We do not expect courts will forget that grand juries must operate within the limits of the First Amendment as well as the Fifth.

So the press does not have quite the privilege it would like to have under the Constitution; the **reporter's privilege,** such as it exists, is granted under state law.

There is one other common statutory privilege that you should be aware of, and that is the **peer review committee privilege.** These are committees that may be formed within hospitals or by state agencies to ascertain the quality of the medical services performed by doctors, chiropractors, or nurses; the documents produced by these committees, as well as the discussions within them, are usually privileged from any sort of disclosure. Even if you happen to get your hands on anything the peer review committee wrote about a doctor you're suing, you probably can't use it, although the contents may guide you to usable information.

FINDING WITNESSES

Witnesses have a nasty habit of disappearing. By the time you start investigating, two years or more may have passed since the incident underlying the lawsuit. In an automobile accident, for example, you may have the name, address, and phone number of a witness on a police report that no one ever bothered to talk to, and that witness is no longer at that address or phone number. Imagine further that this is a red light swearing match—both plaintiff and defendant swear the other one ran the red light—and that the plaintiff has significant damages. This witness is potentially the key to the outcome of the case. Finding him is important. What do you do?

First, try going by the location. If it's an apartment, see if the apartment manager knows anything about what happened to the witness or if he was friends with anyone still at the apartment complex. Get as much information as you can about whether there are friends or family members in the area who may know where the potential witness is. Also check with the neighbors to find out what they know.

The Courthouse

If the witness (or his family) has lived in the area for a significant amount of time, your county courthouse is a wonderful source of information. Get to know it and its quirks well. Treat its personnel well. I have always found courthouse folks very helpful as long as they are treated with respect. Too often lawyers and their staff treat courthouse employees like peons, and that treatment is remembered and dealt with accordingly. If the golden rule doesn't motivate you, maybe self-interest will; being nasty, short, rude, or arrogant with courthouse staff will guarantee you bad service at the courthouse as well as a bad reputation with the judges. They do talk to each other. Take the opposite tack. Get to know the courthouse staff; try to remember their names. You don't have to be a brown-noser; just be friendly and interested.

Now take a minute to think about everything that has to be filed at the courthouse. Everything that has to be filed there is indexed and available for public review, with a few limitations. Deeds, divorces, voter registrations, marriage licenses, tax records, criminal and civil actions, powers of attorney, wills, as well as other odds and ends—in ranching states, cattle brands—are all to be found at your friendly county courthouse. In some locales, the duty is split between registrars—the county clerk and the recorder—but they still are related and somewhat centrally located (usually). Some courthouses are putting the indexes to many of these records online, so you may be able to check them out without leaving your office. In some places (like California) the legislature has passed statutes protecting privacy in such a way as to make it difficult to place the information online; other jurisdictions are looking at the information as a way to raise cash, so making it available for free online is not in their best interest. Some courthouses have dial-up services with fairly reasonable set-up or annual fees. If you are doing a high volume of background checks and skip traces, it will be worth the time savings (and parking fees, in some places) to pay for a dial-up contract.

By now you already know whether the witness lived in a house or apartment, so you'll know whether to check deed records. Deed records can tell you whether the witness owned the house in which he was living. If so, the deed and mortgage documents may disclose another address, a full legal name, a spouse's name, a social security number, or other potential leads. You can also check back tax records and see if you can come up with a social security number—one of the things you need to run a commercial search for the witness. If the witness did not own the house, you can identify someone else to contact who may be able to give you some information about the witness.

Access to birth certificates is limited as a result of problems with identity theft. If your witness registered to vote, voter's registration information will give you a date of birth, which is also necessary in running searches in various commercial databases. A marriage license gives you a spouse's name as an alternative person to look for. A divorce petition will give you everything you need; you simply have to look up the document. The indexes will give you a cause number; somewhere in the courthouse will be a physical file containing all the papers filed in the action. You will need to get the physical file and look through it to find the information you need. If there were minor children in the marriage, the child support office should have a current address. If there were no children, you can look up the ex-wife in the phone book and see if she's listed. Give her a call; it's amazing how often former spouses who "never want to see" their exes again know exactly where they are and what they're doing.

If the witness has been convicted of a crime, it's good news and bad news. You've got a good chance of finding him; on the other hand, his credibility is damaged. Of course, you don't yet know what he's going to say, so maybe the damage to his credibility is a good thing. You should be able to track down where the witness is by checking the **State Identification Number (SID)** assigned to him. Your state may call it something slightly different; the concept's the same. If the person you're looking for is in the county jail, go there and ask to speak to him; you'll need the SID number. If he's in the state system, you'll ordinarily need to contact the state's central system, and with the SID number, the prison system will let you know where the witness is incarcerated. Then you get to take a field trip. If the witness has been or is a prisoner in the federal system, the Bureau of Prisons will have assigned him an eight-digit **registration number.** The last three digits indicate the district in which he was convicted. If the witness is paroled, you'll have to find the parole officer in the county or district where he was convicted. The parole officer should know how to find your witness.

Inst 2000038835
Book: 1820
Pages: 1823 - 1824
Filed & Recorded
05/10/2000 02:12:08 PM
JAMES C. WATKINS
CLERK OF CIRCUIT COURT
LAKE COUNTY
RECORDING $ 9.00
TRUST FUND $ 1.50
DEED DOC STAMP $ 56.00

Parcel I.D. # 46-18-24-0000-008-00400

THIS WARRANTY DEED, Made this 9th day of May, 2000, by RONALD ZIMMER AND ELAINE ZIMMER, HUSBAND AND WIFE, hereinafter referred to as "Grantor", to PETER GOUGH AND ANITA GOUGH, HUSBAND AND WIFE, whose post office address is 2 GRAIG PARK ROAD, MALPAS NEWPORT, MOMMOUTHSHIRE NP96HB, SOUTH WALES, UNITED KINGDOM, hereinafter referred to as "Grantee":

Book 1820 Page 1823

(Wherever used herein the terms "Grantee" include all the parties to this instrument and the heirs, legal representatives, and assigns of individuals, and the successors and assigns of corporations, wherever the context so admits or requires.)

WITNESSETH, That the Grantor, for and in consideration of the sum of $10.00 and other valuable considerations, receipt of which is hereby acknowledged, hereby grants, bargains, sells, aliens, remises, releases, conveys and confirms unto the Grantee all that certain land, situate in LAKE County, State of Florida, viz:

SEE EXHIBIT "A" ATTACHED HERETO AND MADE A PART HEREOF.

TOGETHER with all the tenements, hereditaments and appurtenances thereto belonging or in anywise appertaining. TO HAVE AND TO HOLD, the same in fee simple forever.

AND the Grantor hereby covenants with said Grantee that the Grantor is lawfully seized of said land in fee simple; that the Grantor has good right and lawful authority to sell and convey said land, and hereby warrants the title to said land and will defend the same against the lawful claims of all persons whomsoever; and that said land is free of all encumbrances, except taxes accruing subsequent to December 31, 1999.

IN WITNESS WHEREOF, the said Grantor has signed and sealed these presents the day and year first above written.

Signed, sealed and delivered in the presence of:

Witness Signature
Printed Name JANNA HARRIS

Witness Signature
Printed Name KIMBERLY E. PRICE

RONALD ZIMMER
38834 LAKEVIEW DRIVE
LADY LAKE, FL 32159

Witness Signature
Printed Name JANNA HARRIS

Witness Signature
Printed Name KIMBERLY E. PRICE

ELAINE ZIMMER
38834 LAKEVIEW DRIVE
LADY LAKE, FL 32159

STATE OF FLORIDA
COUNTY OF LAKE

I hereby certify that on this day, before me, an officer duly authorized to administer oaths and take acknowledgments, personally appeared RONALD ZIMMER AND ELAINE ZIMMER, known to me to be the person(s) described in and who executed the foregoing instrument, who acknowledged before me that they executed the same. Said person(s) provided the following identification: drivers license.

WITNESS my hand and official seal in the County and State last aforesaid this 9th day of May, 2000.

Notary Signature

Janna L. Harris
My Commission CC772082
Expires October 24, 2002

Warranty deed from Florida. Note all the addresses it shows.

DEED OF TRUST

Return To:
Beneficiary

PIN:
0812-16-94-4487

Prepared By:
David A. Swanson
714 Ninth Street
Durham, NC 27705

BRIEF DEFINITION FOR THE INDEX: Lot 3, Block 3, Hester Heights

This DEED of TRUST made this 17th day of **July, 2003**, by and between:

Grantor

**JOHN MOORE
and JOANNE DAHILL (for marital interest only)
2902 Hillsborough Road
Durham, NC 27705**

Trustee

DAVID A. SWANSON

Beneficiary

**THE MUSIC LOFT
7923 Morrow Mill Road
Chapel Hill, NC 27516**

The designation Grantor, Trustee, and Beneficiary as used herein shall include said parties, their heirs, successors, and assigns, and shall include singular, plural, masculine, feminine or neuter as required by context.

WITNESSETH, That whereas the Grantor is indebted to the Beneficiary in the principal sum of **Ninety-one thousand, eight hundred and 00/100------------------------Dollars ($******91,800.00)**, as evidenced by a Promissory Note of even date herewith, the terms of which are incorporated herein by reference. The final due date for payment of said Promissory Note, if not sooner paid, is **August 1, 2023.**

NOW THEREFORE, as security for said indebtedness, advancements and other sums expended by Beneficiary pursuant to this Deed of Trust and costs of collection (including attorneys fees as provided in the Promissory Note) and other valuable consideration, the receipt of which is hereby acknowledged, the Grantor has bargained, sold, given, granted and conveyed and does by these presents bargain, sell, give, grant and convey to said Trustee, his heirs, or successors, and assigns, the parcel(s) of land situated in the City of **Durham,**   Township, **Durham**   County, North Carolina, (the "Premises") and more particularly described as follows:

> BEING all of Lot 3, Block 3 of HESTER HEIGHTS PROPERTY as shown on the plat recorded in Plat Book 5 at page 50, Durham County Registry, to which reference is hereby made for a more particular description of same, save and except therefrom that portion conveyed to the City of Durham for the purpose of a sidewalk as shown in Deed Book 179 at page 514.

Property Address: **2902 Hillsborough Road, Durham, NC 27706**

Warranty deed from North Carolina. Again, notice the addresses, which include a lead to a business.

TO HAVE AND TO HOLD said Premises with all privileges and appurtenances thereunto belonging, to said Trustee, his heirs, successors, and assigns forever, upon the trusts, terms and conditions, and for the uses hereinafter set forth.

If the Grantor shall pay the Note secured hereby in accordance with its terms, together with interest thereon, and any renewals or extensions thereof in whole or in part, all other sums secured hereby and shall comply with all of the covenants, terms and conditions of this Deed of Trust, then this conveyance shall be null and void and may be cancelled of record at the request and the expense of the Grantor. If, however, there shall be any default (a) in the payment of any sums due under the Note, this Deed of Trust or any other instrument securing the Note and such default is not cured within ten (10) days from the due date, or (b) if there shall be default in any of the other covenants, terms or conditions of the Note secured hereby, or any failure or neglect to comply with the covenants, terms or conditions contained in this Deed of Trust or any other instrument securing the Note and such default is not cured within fifteen (15) days after written notice, then and in any of such events, without further notice, it shall be lawful for and the duty of the Trustee, upon request of the Beneficiary, to sell the land herein conveyed at public auction for cash, after having first giving such notice of hearing as to commencement of foreclosure proceedings and obtained such findings or leave of court as may then be required by law and giving such notice and advertising the time and place of such sale in such manner as then be provided by law, and upon such and any resales and upon compliance with the law then relating to foreclosure proceedings under power of sale to convey title to the purchaser in as full and ample manner as the Trustee is empowered. The Trustee shall be authorized to retain an attorney to represent him in such proceedings.

The proceeds of the Sale shall after the Trustee retains his commission, together with reasonable attorneys fees incurred by the Trustee in such proceeding, be applied to the costs of sale, including, but not limited to, costs of collection, taxes, assessments, costs or recording, service fees and incidental expenditures, the amount due on the Note hereby secured and advancements and other sums expended by the Beneficiary according to the provisions hereof and otherwise as required by the then existing law relating to foreclosures. The Trustee's commission shall be five percent (5%) of the gross proceeds of the sale or the minimum sum of $_____, whichever is greater, for a completed foreclosure. In the event foreclosure is commenced, but not completed, the Grantor shall pay all expenses incurred by Trustee, including reasonable attorneys fees, and a partial commission computed on five percent (5%) of the outstanding indebtedness or the above stated minimum sum, whichever is greater, in accordance with the following schedule, to-wit: one-fourth (1/4) thereof before the Trustee issues a notice of hearing on the right to foreclosure; one-half (1/2) thereof after issuance of said notice, three-fourths (3/4) thereof after such hearing; and the greater of the full commission or minimum sum after the initial sale.

And the said Grantor does hereby covenant and agree with the Trustee as follows:

1.   **INSURANCE.** Grantor shall keep all improvements on said land, now or hereafter erected, constantly insured for the benefit of the Beneficiary against loss by fire, windstorm and such other casualties and contingencies, in such manner and in such companies and for such amounts, not less than that amount necessary to pay the sum secured by this Deed of Trust, and as may be satisfactory to the Beneficiary. Grantor shall purchase such insurance, pay all premiums therefor, and shall deliver to Beneficiary such policies along with evidence of premium payment as long as the Note secured hereby remains unpaid. If Grantor fails to purchase such insurance, pay premiums therefor or deliver said policies along with evidence of payment of premiums thereon, then Beneficiary, at his option, may purchase such insurance. Such amounts paid by Beneficiary shall be added to the principal of the Note secured by this Deed of Trust, and shall be due and payable upon demand of Beneficiary. All proceeds from any insurance so maintained shall at the option of Beneficiary be applied to the debt secured hereby and if payable in installments, applied in the inverse order of maturity of such installments or to the repair or reconstruction of any improvements located upon the property.

2.   **TAXES, ASSESSMENTS, CHARGES.** Grantor shall pay all taxes, assessments and charges as may be lawfully levied against said Premises within thirty (30) days after the same shall become due. In the event that Grantor fails to so pay all taxes, assessments and charges as herein required, then Beneficiary, at his option, may pay the same and the amounts so paid shall be added to the principal of the Note secured by this Deed of Trust, and shall be due and payable upon demand of Beneficiary.

3.   **ASSIGNMENTS OF RENTS AND PROFITS.** Grantor assigns to Beneficiary, in the event of default, all rents and profits from the land and any improvements thereon, and authorizes Beneficiary to enter upon and take possession of such land and improvements, to rent same, at any reasonable rate of rent determined by Beneficiary, and after deducting from any such rents the cost of reletting and collection, to apply the remainder to the debt secured hereby.

4.   **PARTIAL RELEASE.** Grantor shall not be entitled to the partial release of any of the above described property unless a specific provision providing therefor is included in this Deed of Trust. In the event a partial release provision is included in this Deed of Trust, Grantor must strictly comply with the terms thereof. Notwithstanding anything herein contained, Grantor shall not be entitled to any release of property unless Grantor is not in default and is in full compliance with all of the terms and provisions of the Note, this Deed of Trust, and any other instrument that may be securing said Note.

5.   **WASTE.** The Grantor covenants that he will keep the Premises herein conveyed in as good order, repair and condition as they are now, reasonable wear and tear excepted, and will comply with all governmental requirements respecting the Premises or their use, and that he will not commit or permit any waste.

6.   **CONDEMNATION.** In the event that any or all of the Premises shall be condemned and taken under the power of eminent domain, Grantor shall give immediate written notice to Beneficiary and Beneficiary shall have the right to receive and collect all damages awarded by reason of such taking, and the right to such damages hereby is assigned to Beneficiary who shall have the discretion to apply the amount so received, or any part thereof, to the indebtedness due hereunder and if payable in installments, applied in the inverse order of maturity of such installments, or to any alteration, repair or restoration of the Premises by Grantor.

7.   **WARRANTIES.** Grantor covenants with Trustee that he is seized of the Premises in fee simple, has the right to convey the same in fee simple, that title is marketable and free and clear of all encumbrances, and that he will warrant and defend the title against the lawful claims of all persons whomsoever, except for the exceptions hereinafter stated. Title to the property hereinabove described is subject to the following exceptions:

Easements and Restrictions of record.

2003 ad valorem taxes.

8.   **SUBSTITUTION OF TRUSTEE.** Grantor and Trustee covenant and agree to and with Beneficiary that in case the said Trustee, or any successor trustee, shall die, become incapable of acting, renounce his trust, or for any reason the holder of the Note desires to replace said Trustee, then the holder may appoint, in writing, a trustee to take the place of the Trustee; and upon the probate and registration of the same, the trustee thus appointed shall succeed to all rights, powers and duties of the Trustee.

☐   **The following paragraph, 9. Sale of premises, shall not apply unless the block to the left margin of this sentence is marked and/or initialed.**

9.   **SALE OF PREMISES.** Grantor agrees that if the Premises or any part thereof or interest therein is sold, assigned, transferred, conveyed or otherwise alienated by Grantor, whether voluntarily or involuntarily or by operation of law [other than: (i) the creation of a lien or other encumbrance subordinate to this Deed of Trust which does not relate to a transfer of rights of occupancy in the Premises; (ii) the creation of a purchase money security interest for household appliances; (iii) a transfer by devise, descent, or operation of law on the death of a joint tenant or tenant by the entirety; (iv) the grant of a leasehold interest of three (3) years or less not containing an option to purchase; (v) a transfer to a relative resulting from the death of a Grantor; (vi) a transfer where the spouse or children of the Grantor becomes an owner of the Premises; (vii) a transfer resulting from a decree of a dissolution of marriage, legal separation agreement, or from an incidental property settlement agreement, by which the spouse of the Grantor becomes the owner of the Premises; (viii) a transfer into an inter vivos trust in which the Grantor is and remains a beneficiary and which does not relate to a transfer of rights of occupancy in the Premises], without the prior written consent of Beneficiary, Beneficiary, at its own option, may declare the Note secured hereby and all other obligations hereunder to be forthwith due and payable. Any change in the legal or equitable title of the Premises or in the beneficial ownership of the Premises, including the sale, conveyance or disposition of a majority interest in the Grantor if a corporation or partnership, whether or not or record and whether or not for consideration, shall be deemed to be the transfer of an interest in the Premises.

10.   **ADVANCEMENTS.** If Grantor shall fail to perform any of the covenants or obligations contained herein or in any other instrument given as additional security for the Note secured hereby, the Beneficiary may, but without obligation, make advances to perform such covenants or obligations, and all such sums so advanced shall be added to the principal sum, shall bear interest at the rate provided in the Note secured hereby for sums due after default and shall be due from Grantor on demand of the Beneficiary. No advancement or anything contained in this paragraph shall constitute a waiver by Beneficiary or prevent such failure to perform from constituting an event of default.

11   **INDEMNITY.** If any suit or proceeding be brought against the Trustee or Beneficiary or if any suit or proceeding be brought which may affect the value or title of the Premises, Grantor shall defend, indemnify and hold harmless and on demand reimburse Trustee or Beneficiary from any loss, cost, damage or expense and any sums expended by Trustee or Beneficiary shall bear interest as provided in the Note secured hereby for sums due after default and shall be due and payable on demand.

12.   **WAIVERS.** Grantor waives all rights to require marshalling of assets by the Trustee or Beneficiary. No delay or omission of the Trustee or Beneficiary in the exercise of any right, power or remedy arising under the Note or this Deed of Trust shall be deemed a waiver of any default or acquiescence therein or shall impair or waive the exercise of such right, power or remedy by Trustee or Beneficiary at any other time.

13.   **CIVIL ACTION.** In the event that the Trustee is named as a party to any civil action as Trustee in this Deed of Trust, the Trustee shall be entitled to employ an attorney at law, including himself if he is a licensed attorney, to represent him in said action and the reasonable attorney's fee of the Trustee in such action shall be paid by the Beneficiary and added to the principal of the Note secured by this Deed of Trust, and bear interest at the rate provided in the Note for sums due after default.

14.   **PRIOR LIENS.** Default under the terms of any instrument secured by a lien to which this Deed of Trust is subordinate shall constitute default hereunder.

15.   **OTHER TERMS.**

IN WITNESS WHEREOF, the Grantor has hereunto set his hand and seal, or if corporate, has caused this instrument to be signed in the corporate name by its duly authorized officers and its seal to be hereunto affixed by authority of its Board of Directors, the day and year first above written.

(Corporate Name)	*John Moore* (SEAL)
By: _____	**John Moore**
_____ President	*Joanne Dahill* (SEAL)
ATTEST:	**Joanne Dahill**
_____ Secretary (Corporate Seal)	_____ (SEAL)

State of <u>NORTH CAROLINA</u>
County of <u>DURHAM</u>

   I, the undersigned Notary Public of _____ <u>DURHAM</u> _____ County and the
State of <u>NORTH CAROLINA</u> _____, do hereby certify that ___ <u>JOHN MOORE AND WIFE JOANNE DAHILL</u>
personally appeared before me this day and acknowledged the due execution of the within Deed of Trust.

   Witness my hand and official seal this the ____ <u>17th</u> ____ day of ____ <u>July</u> _____, 2003.

(Notary seal: DAVID A. SWANSON NOTARY *** PUBLIC DURHAM COUNTY, N.C.)

Notary Public *DAVID A. SWANSON*
My commission expires: _____ My Commission Expires 01-30-06

State of _____
County of _____

   I, the undersigned Notary Public of _____ County and the
State of _____, do hereby certify that _____
personally appeared before me this day and acknowledged the due execution of the within Deed of Trust.

   Witness my hand and official seal this the _____ day of_____. 2003.

                                  _____
                                  Notary Public
                                  My commission expires: _____

State of _____
County of _____

   I, the undersigned Notary Public of _____ County and the
State of _____, do hereby certify that _____
personally appeared before me this day and acknowledged that _____ he is _____
Secretary of _____ a North Carolina corporation, and that by authority
duly given and as an act of the corporation, the foregoing instrument was signed in its name by its
President, sealed with its corporate seal and attested by _____ as its _____
Secretary.

   Witness my hand and official seal this the _____ day of_____, 2003.

                                  _____
                                  Notary Public
                                  My commission expires: _____

Last page of the same North Carolina deed. If you needed them, this would provide signature exemplars.

WILLIE L. COVINGTON
REGISTER OF DEEDS , DURHAM COUNTY
DURHAM COUNTY COURTHOUSE
200 E. MAIN STREET
DURHAM, NC 27701

****

Filed For Registration:	07/18/2003 10:53:33 AM
Book:	RE 4007 **Page:** 195-199
Document No.:	2003043917
	D-T 5 PGS $23.00
Recorder:	SHARON DAVIS

****

State of North Carolina, County of Durham

The foregoing certificate of DAVID A. SWANSON Notary is certified to be correct. This 18TH of July 2003

WILLIE L. COVINGTON , REGISTER OF DEEDS

By: _____

Deputy/Assistant Register of Deeds
****

2003043917

Certificate for the same North Carolina deed. This seal should fulfill the requirements for self-authentication of the public record.

Mail to: Secretary of State
Corporations Section
1560 Broadway, Suite 200
Denver, CO 80202
(303) 894-2251
Fax (303) 894-2242

951016543 $10.00
SECRETARY OF STATE
02-09-95 10:56

CERTIFICATE OF
ASSUMED OR TRADE NAME

LL 941137129

_____ McDonald Properties LLC *NC/GS* _____ , a corporation,
limited partnership or limited liability company under the laws
of ____ Colorado _____ , being desirous of transacting a
portion of its business under an assumed or trade name as
permitted by 7-71-101, Colorado Revised Statutes, hereby
certifies:

1. The location of its principal office is:

    6078 Fox Hill Drive
    Longmont, Colorado 80501

2. The name, other than its own, under which business is carried
on is:

    Sweetgrass Company LLC ✓

3. A brief description of the kind of business transacted under
such assumed or trade name is: building construction, real estate
acquisition and management and other investments.

Limited Partnership or Limited Liability Companies complete this section.	Corporations complete this section
Name of Partnership or Company	Name of Corporation
by Margaret McDonald	by_____
Title, ~~General Partner~~, Manager	Its_____
Margaret McDonald	Title
Title, ~~General Partner~~, or Manager	

COMPUTER UPDATE COMPLETE

This Colorado assumed-name certificate provides you with a local franchise contract and would help
you determine residency of the corporation.

NO. 2003-CI-00907

IN THE MATTER OF	§	IN THE DISTRICT COURT
THE MARRIAGE OF	§	
	§	
TAMMIE GALE PUGH	§	JUDICIAL DISTRICT
AND	§	
TRUMAN CHARLES PUGH	§	BEXAR COUNTY, TEXAS

INVENTORY AND APPRAISEMENT OF TAMMIE GALE PUGH

Tammie Gale Pugh, Petitioner, submits this Inventory and Appraisement of all assets and liabilities, community and separate estates, as follows:

Community Estate of the Parties

1. **Real Property** (include any property purchased by contract for deed, such as Texas Veterans Land Board property, property purchased in recreational developments, and time-shares)

    1. Street address: 519 Breathless View, San Antonio, Bexar County, Texas 78260

        Description of improvements, if any: 2-story, 4 bedroom, 3 bath stucco house containing approximately 2,749 square feet situated on about 1.01 acres

        Legal description: Lot 46 and Lot 47, Block 9, Timberwood Park, nit 2, Bexar County, Texas, according to plat thereof recorded in Volume 8000, Pages 212–216, Deed and Plat Records of Bexar County, Texas.

        Current fair market value (as of March 5, 2003): $211,240.00 per Bexar Appraisal District; Box & Associates Appraisal Report, dated August 16, 2001, showed a fair market value of 184,000.00

        Name of mortgage company and account number: Ohio Savings Bank, account number 7172465

        Current balance of mortgage (as of March 5, 2003): $166,201.69

        Other liens against property: None

        Current net equity in property: $45,038.31 (estimated)

2. **Mineral Interests** (include any property in which the parties own the mineral estate, separate and apart from the surface estate, such as oil and gas leases; also include royalty interests, working interests, and producing and nonproducing oil and gas wells) **NONE**

3. **Cash and Accounts with Financial Institutions** (include cash, traveler's checks, money orders, and accounts with commercial banks, savings banks, credit unions, and funds on deposit with attorneys and other third parties; exclude accounts with brokerage houses and all retirement accounts)

    1. Cash on hand (as of March 5, 2003): $20.00

    2. Traveler's checks (as of March 5, 2003): $0

    3. Money orders (as of March 5, 2003): $0

Family law documents are particularly rich in information. Not only do they give you the names of ex-spouses and children, but detailed property information you can use to help you determine whereabouts and personal worth.

4. Name of financial institution: Bank of America, N. A.

   Account name: Truman Pugh
   Account number: 0057 7721 9378
   Type of account: checking account
   Name(s) on withdrawal cards: Truman Pugh
   Current account balance (as of December 27, 2002): $16,708.44

5. Name of financial institution: Bank of America, N. A.

   Account name: Truman Pugh
   Account number: 0057 7722 1395
   Type of account: regular savings account
   Name(s) on withdrawal cards: Truman Pugh
   Current account balance (as of March 5, 2003): $Unknown

6. Name of financial institution: Randolph Brooks Federal Credit Union

   Account name: Tammie G. Pugh
   Account number: 98587-2
   Type of account: savings account
   Name(s) on withdrawal cards: Tammie G. Pugh
   Current account balance (as of March 5, 2003): $50.00

7. Name of financial institution: Randolph Brooks Federal Credit Union

   Account name: Tammie G. Pugh
   Account number: 98587-2
   Type of account: checking account
   Name(s) on withdrawal cards: Tammie G. Pugh
   Current account balance (as of March 5, 2003): $300.00

8. Name of financial institution: Bank of America, N. A.

   Account name: Truman Pugh
   Account number: 0047 7492 2164
   Type of account: money market account
   Name(s) on withdrawal cards: Truman Pugh
   Current account balance (as of March 5, 2003): $Unknown

4. **Brokerage/Mutual Fund Accounts**   **NONE**

5. **Publicly Traded Stocks, Bonds, and Other Securities** (include securities not in a brokerage account, mutual fund, or retirement fund)   **NONE**

6. **Stock Options** (include all exercisable nonexercisable, vested, and nonvested stock options, regardless of any restrictions on transfer)   **NONE**

7. **Bonuses**

   1. Name of company: Specialty Hospital Group (Husband's employer)
          Date bonus expected to be paid: March 2003
          Anticipated amount of bonus: $30,000–$40,000

8. **Closely Held Business Interests** (include sole proprietorships, professional practices, corporations, partnerships, limited liability companies and partnerships, joint ventures, and other nonpublicly traded business entities)   **NONE**

9. **Retirement Benefits**   **NONE**

10. **Other Deferred Compensation Benefits** (e.g., worker's compensation, disability benefits, other "special payments," and other forms of compensation)   **NONE**

This page of the Inventory and Appraisement gives you the husband's bank information, his employer, and a sense of his net worth.

11. Insurance and Annuities

A. *Life Insurance*   **NONE** personally owed by either party. Term life insurance is supposedly provided to each party by their respective employer. Amounts of coverage are not known.

B. *Annuities*   **NONE**

12. Motor Vehicles, Boats, Airplanes, Cycles, etc. (including mobile homes, trailers, and recreational vehicles; exclude company-owned vehicles)

1. Year: 2002
   Make: Chevrolet
   Model: Avalanche
   Name on certificate of title: Truman Charles Pugh
   In possession of: Truman Charles Pugh
   Vehicle identification number: 3GNEK 13T52G191903
   Name of creditor if loan against vehicle: Randolph-Brooks FCU
   Current balance (as of January 22, 2003): $30,160.05
   Current net equity in vehicle: $<5,235,05>

2. Year: 2002
   Make: Chevrolet
   Model: Suburban
   Name on certificate of title: Truman Charles Pugh
   In possession of: Truman Charles Pugh
   Vehicle identification number: 3 GNEC16Z12G246781
   Name of creditor if loan against vehicle: Randolph*Brooks Federal Credit
   Current balance (as of January 22, 2003): $34,037.93
   Current net equity in vehicle: $<7,787.93>

3. Year: 1985
   Make: Itasca
   Model: Winnebago
   Name on certificate of title: Truman Charles Pugh
   In possession of: Truman Charles Pugh
   Vehicle identification number: Unknown
   Name of creditor if loan against vehicle: None
   Current balance (as of January 22, 2003): $0
   Current net equity in vehicle: $800–1,000

4. Year: 2000
   Make: BMW
   Model: K1200LT
   Name on certificate of title: Truman Charles Pugh
   In possession of: Truman Charles Pugh
   Vehicle identification number: 1B10555A2YZD72978
   Name of creditor if loan against vehicle: BMW Financial Services NA., Inc.
   Current balance (as of December 22, 2002): $14,820.67
   Current net equity in vehicle: $<5,000.00>

5. Year: 2000
   Make: Yamaha
   Model: Jet Ski/Wave Runner
   Name on certificate of title: Truman Pugh and Tammie Pugh
   In possession of: Truman Charles Pugh
   Vehicle identification number: UNKNOWN
   Name of creditor if loan against vehicle: None
   Current balance (as of March 5, 2003): $0.00
   Current net equity in vehicle: $5,000.00

This page gives you a second financial institution you could subpeona for information.

6. Year: 2002
   Make: Yamaha
   Model: YZ426FP
   Name on certificate of title: Truman Charles Pugh
   In possession of: Truman Charles Pugh
   Vehicle identification number: UNKNOWN
   Name of creditor if loan against vehicle: None
   Current balance (as of March 5, 2003): $0
   Current net equity in vehicle: $3,000.00

7. Year: 2001
   Make: Yamaha (minicycle/dirt bike)
   Model: TTR90N
   Name on certificate of title: Truman Charles Pugh
   In possession of: Truman Charles Pugh
   Vehicle identification number: UNKNOWN
   Name of creditor if loan against vehicle: UNKNOWN
   Current balance (as of March 5, 2003): $0
   Current net equity in vehicle: $1,000.00
   This vehicle was sold by Husband for an unknown amount

8. Year: 2002
   Make: Yamaha (minicycle/dirt bike)
   Model: TTR125LP
   Name on certificate of title: Truman Charles Pugh
   In possession of: Truman Charles Pugh
   Vehicle identification number: UNKNOWN
   Name of creditor if loan against vehicle: UNKNOWN
   Current balance (as of March 5, 2003): $0
   Current net equity in vehicle: $1,300.00
   *Husband sold this vehicle on January 20, 2003 for $1,500.00

9. Year: 2001
   Make: Flatbed motorcycle trailer
   Model: Unknown
   Name on certificate of title: Truman Charles Pugh
   In possession of: Truman Charles Pugh
   Vehicle identification number: UNKNOWN
   Name of creditor if loan against vehicle: None
   Current balance (as of March 5, 2003): $1,200.00
   Current net equity in vehicle: $1,000.00

10. Year: 2002
    Make: Yamaha (motocross)
    Model: YZ250FP
    Name on certificate of title: Truman Charles Pugh
    In possession of: Truman Charles Pugh
    Vehicle identification number: UNKNOWN
    Name of creditor if loan against vehicle: UNKNOWN
    Current balance (as of March 5, 2003): $0
    Current net equity in vehicle: $2,500.00

13. **Money Owed to Me or My Spouse** (include any expected federal or state income tax refund but do not include receivables connected with a business)   **NONE**

14. **Household Furniture, Furnishings, and Fixtures**

    1. In possession of husband: **See Exhibit "A"**
    2. In possession of wife: **See Exhibit "B"**

15. **Electronics and Computers**

    1. In possession of husband: **See Exhibit "A"**
    2. In possession of wife: **See Exhibit "B"**

16. **Antiques, Artwork, and Collections** (include any works of art, such as paintings, tapestry, rugs, and coin or stamp collections)

    1. In possession of husband: **NONE**
    2. In possession of wife: **NONE**

17. **Miscellaneous Sporting Goods and Firearms**

    1. In possession of husband: **NONE**
    2. In possession of wife: **NONE**

18. **Jewelry and Other Personal Items**

    1. In possession of husband: **NONE**
    2. In possession of wife: **NONE**

19. **Livestock** (include cattle, horses, and so forth)

    1. In possession of husband: **NONE**
    2. In possession of wife: **NONE**

20. **Club Memberships NONE**

21. **Travel Award Benefits** (include frequent-flyer mileage accounts)

    1. Name of airline: Southwest Airlines
    Account number: UNKNOWN
    Current number of miles (as of March 5, 2003): UNKNOWN
    Current value (if any): UNKNOWN

    2. Name of airline: America West Airlines
    Account number: UNKNOWN
    Current number of miles (as of March 5, 2003): UNKNOWN
    Current value (if any): UNKNOWN

22. **Miscellaneous Assets** (include intellectual property, licenses, crops, farm equipment, construction equipment, tools, leases, cemetery lots, gold or silver coins no part of a collection described elsewhere in this inventory, estimated tax payments, tax overpayments, loss carry-forward deductions, lottery tickets/winnings, stadium bonds, stadium seat licenses, seat options, and season tickets)

    1. In possession of husband: **NONE**
    2. In possession of wife: **NONE**

23. **Safe-Deposit Boxes**   **NONE**

24. **Storage Facilities**   **NONE**

25. **Community Claim for Reimbursement**   **NONE**

26. **Equitable Interest(s) of Community Estate**   **NONE**

27. **Contingent Assets** (e.g., lawsuits by either party against a third party)   **NONE**

28. **Community Liabilities**

    A. *Credit Cards and Charge Accounts*

        1. Name of creditor: Conn's Appliances
        Account number: 2316487
        Name(s) on account: Truman Charles Pugh
        Balance as of December 14, 2002: $2,613.64
        Current balance (as of 1/17/2003): $0.00

This page lists a creditor—another potential source of information.

2. Name of creditor: Circuit City
    Account number: 4104130007303573
    Name(s) on account: Truman Charles Pugh
    Balance as of December 14, 2002: $2,141.65
    Current balance (as of December 26, 2002): $0.00

3. Name of creditor: Randolph-Brooks Mastercard
    Account number: 5449 7417 6087 7743
    Name(s) on account: Truman Pugh and Tammie Pugh
    Balance (as of December 9, 2002): $2,001.26
    Current balance (as of March 5, 2003): $1,450.00 (estimate)

4. Name of creditor: Lerners
    Account number: 951 079 490
    Name(s) on account: Tammie Pugh
    Current balance (as of March 5, 2003): $0.00

5. Name of creditor: WalMart
    Account number: 6032 2030 8429 3330
    Name(s) on account: Tammie Pugh
    Current balance (as of March 5, 2003): $70.00 (estimate)

6. Name of creditor: Bealls
    Account number: 040 88 478 3
    Name(s) on account: Tammie Pugh
    Current balance (as of March 5, 2003): $300.00 (estimate)

7. Name of creditor: AT&T Universal Card
    Account number: 5491 1303 3510 7520
    Name(s) on account: Truman Pugh
    Balance as of December 20, 2002: $7,959.00
    Current balance (as of March 5, 2003): $Unknown

8. Name of creditor: Sears
    Account number: 80 60507 88339 1
    Name(s) on account: Truman Pugh
    Balance as of December 21, 2002: $50.70
    Current balance (as of March 5, 2003): $Unknown

9. Name of creditor: Mervyn's
    Account number: 6322-1796-415
    Name(s) on account: Truman Pugh
    Balance as of December 21, 2002: $314.94
    Current balance (as of March 5, 2003): $Unknown

10. Name of creditor: Target Visa
    Account number: 4352-3733-6675-7703
    Name(s) on account: Truman C. Pugh
    Balance as of November 30, 2002: $805.77
    Current balance (as of March 5, 2003): $Unknown

11. Name of creditor: Providian Visa
    Account number: 4559-9067-2818-3737
    Name(s) on account: Truman Pugh and Paulette Pugh
    Balance as of December 14, 2002: $1,581.46
    Current balance (as of March 5, 2003): $Unknown

Here we have a bonanza of creditors.

12. Name of creditor: Discover
Account number: 6011 0009 7650 0151
Name(s) on account: Truman Pugh and Paulette Pugh
Balance as of December 15, 2002: $12,107.39
Current balance (as of March 5, 2003): $Unknown

13. Name of creditor: Concesco
Account number: 7074 5001 0164 5856
Name(s) on account: Truman Pugh
Balance as of December 14, 2002: $4,189.38
Current balance (as of March 5, 2003): $Unknown

14. Name of creditor: Citi Platinum Select
Account number: 5424 1801 7543 4551
Name(s) on account: Truman Pugh
Balance as of December 26, 2002: $1,551.15
Current balance (as of March 5, 2003): $Unknown

15. Name of creditor: Direct Merchants
Account number: Unknown
Name(s) on account: Truman Pugh
Balance as of December 26, 2002: $Unknown
Current balance (as of March 5, 2003): $Unknown

16. Name of creditor: Mobil
Account number: Unknown
Name(s) on account: Truman Pugh and Paulette Pugh
Balance as of December 26, 2002: $Unknown
Current balance (as of March 5, 2003): $Unknown

B. *Federal, State, and Local Tax Liability*

1. Amount owed in any previous tax year: <$0>
2. Amount owed for current year 2003: $Unknown

C. *Attorney's Fees in This Case*

1. Husband (as of March 5, 2003): <$Unknown>
2. Wife (as of March 5, 2003): <$1,800.00> (estimate)

D. *Other Professional Fees in This Case*

1. Husband (as of March 5, 2003): <$Unknown>
2. Wife (as of March 5, 2003): <$0.00>

E. *Other Liabilities Not Otherwise Listed in This Inventory* (e.g., loans, margin accounts, if not previously disclosed)

1. Name of creditor: Allen Gordon
Account number: None
Party incurring liability: Truman Pugh
Is loan evidenced in writing? Yes
Current balance (as of January 22, 2003): $48,515.86
Current balance (as of March 5, 2003): <$Unknown>
Security, if any: creditor is listed as a beneficiary on Mr. Pugh's life insurance policy.

F. *Reimbursement Claims against Community Estate*

1. Reimbursement claim by husband's separate estate: **NONE**
2. Reimbursement claim by wife's separate estate: For use of her premarital retirement funds in the approximate amount of $15,000.00 as a down payment for the community home identified above.

And yet more creditors.

G. Equitable Interest Claims against Community Estate

　　1. Equitable interest due to financial contribution of wife's separate property community estate: For use of her premarital retirement funds in the approximate amount of $15,000.00 as a down payment for the community home identified above.

　　　Basis of claim: See above
　　　Amount of claim (as of March 5, 2003): $15,000.00 (estimate)

H. *Pledges (include charitable, church, and school related)* - **NONE**

　　1. *Contingent Liabilities* (e.g., lawsuit against either party, guaranty either party may have signed) - **NONE**

Separate Estates of the Parties

29. Separate Assets of Husband (generally defined as assets owned before marriage or assets acquired during marriage by gift or inheritance or as a result of personal injury) - **See Exhibit "C"**

　　1. Husband's separate reimbursement claim against community estate: **NONE**
　　　Value (as of March 5, 2003): $0

30. Liabilities of Husband's Separate Estate

　　1. Community estate's reimbursement claim against husband's separate estate: **NONE**
　　2. Equitable interest claim due to financial contribution of community property to husband's separate estate: **NONE**

31. Separate Assets of Wife (generally defined as assets owned before marriage or assets acquired during marriage by gift or inheritance or as a result of personal injury) - **See Exhibit "D"**

　　1. Wife's separate reimbursement claim against community estate: For use of her premarital retirement funds in the approximate amount of $15,000.00 as a down payment for the community home identified above.
　　2. Equitable interest claim due to financial contribution of wife's separate estate to community estate: For use of her premarital retirement funds in the approximate amount of $15,000.00 as a down payment for the community home identified above.

32. Liabilities of Wife's Separate Estate

　　1. Community estate's reimbursement claim against wife's separate estate: **NONE**

Trust and Estate Assets

33. Assets Held by Either Party for the Benefit of Another (include formal and informal trusts): **NONE**
34. Assets Held for the Benefit of Either Party as a Beneficiary (include formal and informal trusts) - **UNKNOWN**

VERIFICATION

I, Tammie Gale Pugh, state on oath that, to the best of my knowledge and belief, this Inventory and Appraisement contains-

1. a full and complete list of all properties that I claim belong to the community estate of me and my spouse, with the values thereof;

2. a full and complete list of all properties in my possession or subject to my control that I claim or admit are my or my spouse's separate property and estate, with the values thereof; and

3. a full and complete list of the debts that I claim are community indebtedness.

Any omission from this inventory is not intentional but is done through mere inadvertence and not to mislead my spouse. There may be other assets and liabilities of which my spouse is aware, and the omission of those items from this inventory should not be construed as a waiver of my interest in them.

TAMMIE GALE PUGH

STATE OF TEXAS   §
COUNTY OF BEXAR   §

SIGNED under oath before me on _March 6_____, 2003.

Kelly M. Stewart
Notary Public, State of Texas

KELLY MARIE STEWART
MY COMMISSION EXPIRES
APRIL 19, 2004

The gravy—if you wanted to use this document to impeach the wife, it would be no problem as it was signed under oath.

NO. 2003-CI-00907

IN THE MATTER OF	§	IN THE DISTRICT COURT
THE MARRIAGE OF	§	
	§	
TAMMIE GALE PUGH	§	JUDICIAL DISTRICT
AND	§	
TRUMAN CHARLES PUGH	§	BEXAR COUNTY, TEXAS

EXHIBIT "A"
Items in Possession of Husband

1. Asset: Sony Computer
   Value: $1,700.00

2. Asset: 2002 Chevy Avalanche
   Value: $24,925.00

3. Asset: 2002 Chevy Suburban
   Value: $26,250.00

4. Asset: 1980 Itasca Motor home
   Value: $5,500.00

5. Asset: 2002 Yamaha YZF426 Motorcycle
   Value: $24,500

6. Asset: 2002 Yamaha YZF250 Motorcycle
   Value: $3625.00

7. Asset: 2002 Yamaha TTR 125L Motorcycle
   Value: $1500

8. Asset: 2001 Yamaha TTR 90 Motorcycle
   Value: $ 980.00

9. Asset: Motorcycle Accessories
   Value: $ 500.00

10. Asset: Motorcycle Trailer
    Value: $1,000.00

11. Asset: 2000 BMW K1200LT Motorcycle
    Value: $12,485

12. Asset: Clothing Belonging to Truman
    Value: $ _____

13. Asset: Motorcycle Parts
    Value: $100.00

14. Asset: Folding Chairs/Stool
    Value: $100.00

15. Asset: Fondue Pot
    Value: $ _____

16. Asset: Sewing Machine
    Value: $ _____

17. Asset: Majority of Power Tools
    Value: $ _____

18. Asset: Majority of Misc. Tools
    Value: $ _____

NO. 2003-CI-00907

IN THE MATTER OF	§	IN THE DISTRICT COURT
THE MARRIAGE OF	§	
	§	
TAMMIE GALE PUGH	§	JUDICIAL DISTRICT
AND	§	
TRUMAN CHARLES PUGH	§	BEXAR COUNTY, TEXAS

Exhibit "B"
Items in Possession of Wife

1. Asset: Pool Table
   Value: $250.00

2. Asset: Texas Bookshelf
   Value: $100.00

3. Asset: Decorations on Texas Shelf
   Value: $100.00

4. Asset: Texas Flag Picture
   Value: $150.00

5. Asset: Pool Table Accessories
   Value: $75.00

6. Asset: Metal Star Wall Hanging
   Value: $75.00

In an enforcement or bankruptcy case, these exhibits would be valuable in trying to trace these assets. The asset lists often continue for several pages.

7. Asset: Rodeo Gear
   Value: $50.00

8. Asset: Metal Sculpture - Roper
   Value: $125.00

9. Asset: Trunks
   Value: $50.00

10. Asset: Texas Flag Throw
    Value: $50.00

11. Asset: DVD Player
    Value: $250.00

12. Asset: Receiver/Surround Sound Speakers
    Value: $250.00

13. Asset: Leather Love Seat
    Value: $375.00

14. Asset: End Tables
    Value: $_____

15. Asset: Table Lamps (2)
    Value: $50.00

16. Asset: Metal Star Bookends
    Value: $75.00

17. Asset: Limestone Rock/Stand
    Value: $200.00

18. Asset: DVDS
    Value: $200.00

19. Asset: Pot & Pan Set
    Value: $150.00

20. Asset: Texas Dishes
    Value: $60.00

21. Asset: Kitchen Items
    Value: $300.00

22. Asset: Microwave
    Value: $100.00

23. Asset: Roaster
    Value: $50.00

24. Asset: Computer
    Value: $200.00

25. Asset: Computer Desk
    Value: $50.00

26. Asset: Television
    Value: $50.00

27. Asset: Television
    Value: $75.00

28. Asset: Computer
    Value: $200.00

29. Asset: Computer Desk
    Value: $50.00

30. Asset: Sofa Sleeper
    Value: $500.00

31. Asset: Dart Board
    Value: $65.00

32. Asset: Computer
    Value: $200.00

33. Asset: Big Screen Television
    Value: $2836.00

34. Asset: Computer Desk
    Value: $50.00

35. Asset: Bed w/ Mattress
    Value: $150.00

36. Asset: Foosball Table
    Value: $50.00

37. Asset: Television
    Value: $75.00

38. Asset: Pillow Top Mattress
    Value: $500.00

39. Asset: Towel Rack
    Value: $45.00

40. Asset: Clothing Belonging to Tammie
    Value: $_____

41. Asset: Riding Mower
    Value: $500.00

42. Asset: Minimal Amount of Power Tools
    Value: $_____

43. Asset: Minimal Amount of Misc. Tools
    Value: $_____

44. Asset: Turkey Cooker
    Value: $60.00

45. Asset: Canoe
    Value: $25.00

46. Asset: Freezer
    Value: $450.00

47. Asset: Tent
    Value: $150.00

48. Asset: Easy Up Cover
    Value: $ 150.00

49. Asset: Universal Gym
    Value: $300.00

50. Asset: Folding Chairs/Stool
    Value: $100.00

51. Asset: Sony Digital Camera
    Value: $350.00

52. Asset: Epson Color Printer
    Value: $150.00

IN THE MATTER OF	§	**IN THE DISTRICT COURT**
THE MARRIAGE OF	§	
	§	
TAMMIE GALE PUGH	§	**JUDICIAL DISTRICT**
AND	§	
TRUMAN CHARLES PUGH	§	**BEXAR COUNTY, TEXAS**

EXHIBIT "D"
Separate Property of Wife

1. Asset: Rocking Chair
   Value: $100.00

2. Asset: Kitchen Table/Chairs
   Value: $300.00

3. Asset: Hutch
   Value: $150.00

4. Asset: Refrigerator
   Value: $_____

5. Asset: Washer/Dryer
   Value: $_____

6. Asset: Queen Bed/Mattress
   Value: $_____

7. Asset: VHS Movies
   Value: $_____

8. Asset: Small Desk
   Value: $_____

9. Asset: 19" Color TV
   Value: $_____

10. Asset: VCR
    Value: $_____

11. Asset: Dining Table
    Value: $_____

12. Asset: Recliner
    Value: $_____

13. Asset: Tools
    Value: $_____

14. Asset: Cedar Chest
    Value: $_____

15. Asset: Sheets, Blankets, Linens
    Value: $_____

16. Asset: Dishes
    Value: $_____

17. Asset: Family Memorabilia
    Value: $_____

18. Asset: Bunk Bed w/Mattress
    Value: $250.00

STATE OF FLORIDA
MARRIAGE RECORD
TYPE IN UPPER CASE
USE BLACK INK
This license not valid unless seal of Clerk,
Circuit or County Court, appears thereon.

(STATE FILE NUMBER

CFN 2004036543
Bk 02529 Pg 1472; (1pg)
DATE: 03/22/2004 09:01:08 AM
JAMES C. WATKINS, CLERK OF COURT
LAKE COUNTY
RECORDING FEES 8.88

2004 ML 000364
(APPLICATION NUMBER)

APPLICATION TO MARRY

1 GROOM'S NAME (First, Middle, Last)			2 DATE OF BIRTH (Month, Day, Year)
CLARENCE WILSON			05/04/1930

3a RESIDENCE - CITY, TOWN, OR LOCATION	3b COUNTY	3c STATE	4 BIRTHPLACE (State or Foreign Country)
EUSTIS	LAKE	FL	WV

5a BRIDE'S NAME (First, Middle, Last)		5b MAIDEN SURNAME (If different)	6 DATE OF BIRTH (Month, Day, Year)
NAOMI G MOBLEY		JOHNSON	05/24/1925

7a RESIDENCE - CITY, TOWN, OR LOCATION	7b COUNTY	7c STATE	8 BIRTHPLACE (State or Foreign Country)
EUSTIS	LAKE	FL	MI

WE THE APPLICANTS NAMED IN THIS CERTIFICATE, EACH FOR HIMSELF OR HERSELF, STATE THAT THE INFORMATION PROVIDED ON THIS RECORD IS CORRECT TO THE BEST OF OUR KNOWLEDGE AND BELIEF, THAT NO LEGAL OBJECTION TO THE MARRIAGE NOR THE ISSUANCE OF A LICENSE TO AUTHORIZE THE SAME IS KNOWN TO US AND HEREBY APPLY FOR LICENSE TO MARRY

9 SIGNATURE OF GROOM (Sign full name using black ink)	10 SUBSCRIBED AND SWORN TO BEFORE ME ON (DATE)
	March 9, 2004
11 TITLE OF OFFICIAL	12 SIGNATURE OF OFFICIAL (Use black ink)
JAMES C. WATKINS, CLERK OF COURT	BY: D.C.
13 SIGNATURE OF BRIDE (Sign full name using black ink)	14 SUBSCRIBED AND SWORN TO BEFORE ME ON (DATE)
Naomi G. Mobley	March 9, 2004
15 TITLE OF OFFICIAL	16 SIGNATURE OF OFFICIAL (Use black ink)
JAMES C. WATKINS, CLERK OF COURT	BY: D.C.

LICENSE TO MARRY

AUTHORIZATION AND LICENSE IS HEREBY GIVEN TO ANY PERSON DULY AUTHORIZED BY THE LAWS OF THE STATE OF FLORIDA TO PERFORM A MARRIAGE CEREMONY WITHIN THE STATE OF FLORIDA AND TO SOLEMNIZE THE MARRIAGE OF THE ABOVE NAMED PERSONS. THIS LICENSE MUST BE USED ON OR AFTER THE EFFECTIVE DATE AND ON OR BEFORE THE EXPIRATION DATE IN THE STATE OF FLORIDA IN ORDER TO BE RECORDED AND VALID

17 COUNTY ISSUING LICENSE	18 DATE LICENSE ISSUED	18a. DATE LICENSE EFFECTIVE	19 EXPIRATION DATE
LAKE	03/09/2004	03/12/2004	05/08/2004

20a SIGNATURE OF COURT CLERK OR JUDGE	20b TITLE	20c BY D.C.
JAMES C. WATKINS	CLERK OF CIRCUIT COURT	

CERTIFICATE OF MARRIAGE

I HEREBY CERTIFY THAT THE ABOVE NAMED GROOM AND BRIDE WERE JOINED BY ME IN MARRIAGE IN ACCORDANCE WITH THE LAWS OF THE STATE OF FLORIDA

21 DATE OF MARRIAGE (Month, Day, Year)	22 CITY, TOWN, OR LOCATION OF MARRIAGE
03-20-04	2400 KURT ST. EUSTIS, FLORIDA 32726
23a SIGNATURE OF PERSON PERFORMING CEREMONY (Use black ink)	23c ADDRESS (Of person performing ceremony)
Tim Jensen	1933 CORNEZIA DR., EUSTIS, FL 32726
23b NAME AND TITLE OF PERSON PERFORMING CEREMONY (Or notary stamp)	24 SIGNATURE OF WITNESS TO CEREMONY (Use black ink)
TIM JENSEN PASTOR - HAINES CREEK BAPTIST	Jessie Johnson
	25 SIGNATURE OF WITNESS TO CEREMONY (Use black ink)
SEAL	Bessie Cline

This Florida marriage license provides dates of birth, always useful in obtaining information from other sources, and contacts (a pastor and witnesses who often will know family members if not specifics about the person you are trying to locate).

CFN 2004025550
Bk 02514 Pgs 1302 - 1304; (3pgs)
DATE: 02/27/2004 02:04:39 PM
JAMES C. WATKINS, CLERK OF COURT

DURABLE POWER OF ATTORNEY

LAKE COUNTY
RECORDING FEES 13.00
TRUST FUND 2.00

BY THIS DURABLE POWER OF ATTORNEY, I, **SARA S. WARREN**, of Lake County, Florida, appoint as my Attorney In Fact to manage my affairs my daughter, **MOLLIE CONNOR DAVIS**, or if she is unable or unwilling to act, my grandson, **CONRAD B. MELANCON**. By execution of this Power of Attorney, I specifically revoke any and all prior Powers of Attorney heretofore executed by me.

This Durable Power of Attorney shall not be affected by any physical or mental disability that I may suffer except as provided by statute, and shall be exercisable from this date. All acts done by my Attorney In Fact pursuant to this power shall bind me, my heirs, devisees and personal representatives. This Durable Power of Attorney is nondelegable.

All of my property and interests in property are subject to this Durable Power of Attorney.

Without limiting the broad powers conferred by the preceding provisions, I authorize my Attorney In Fact to:

1.   Collect all sums of money and other property that may be payable or belonging to me, and to execute receipts, releases, cancellations or discharges.

2.   Settle any account in which I have any interest and to pay or receive the balance of that account as the case may require.

3.   Enter any safe deposit box or other place of safekeeping standing in my name alone or jointly with another and to remove the contents and to make additions, substitutions and replacements.

4.   Borrow money on such terms and with such security as my Attorney In Fact may think fit and to execute all notes, mortgages and other instruments that my Attorney In Fact finds necessary or desirable.

5.   Draw, accept, endorse or otherwise deal with any checks or other commercial or mercantile instruments, specifically including the right to make withdrawals from any checking account, savings account, building and loan deposits, retirement plans, individual retirement accounts, and pension or profit sharing plans.

6.   Redeem bonds issued by the United States Government or any of its agencies, any other bonds and any certificates of deposit or other similar assets belonging to me.

7.   Sell, transfer or pledge bonds, shares of stock, warrants, debentures, or other assets belonging to me, and execute all assignments, pledges and transfers and other

Prepared By:

ROBERT F. VASON, JR., P.A.
ATTORNEYS AT LAW
101 EAST FIFTH AVENUE
MOUNT DORA, FLORIDA 32757
TELEPHONE: (352) 383-4151
WWW.VASONLAW.COM

This Florida power of attorney provides you with the names and relationships of family members.

IN THE CIRCUIT COURT OF THE F   A
JUDICIAL CIRCUIT, CRIMINAL DIVISION,
IN AND FOR LAKE COUNTY

CASE NO.: _2003 CF 360_
STATE OF FLORIDA
VS.
DEFENDANT: _Andres Hilario Cardenas_
ADDRESS: _____

SOCIAL SECURITY NO.: _593 43 0271_
DATE OF BIRTH: _____
DEFENDANT'S SIGNATURE: _Andres Cardenas_

CFN   2004036519
Bk 02529 Pg 1413; (1pg)
DATE: 03/22/2004 08:48:01 AM
JAMES C. WATKINS, CLERK OF COURT
LAKE COUNTY
RECORDING FEES 0.00

RECORDING SPACE

ORDER ASSESSING ADDITIONAL CHARGES, COSTS, AND FINES AND ENTERING FINAL JUDGMENT (IF INDICATED) TO BE RECORDED

The defendant is hereby ordered to pay and a judgment is hereby entered on behalf of Lake County Clerk of the Court, PO Box 7800, Tavares, Florida 32778 and the State of Florida in the following sums (if indicated).

MANDATORY

1. $ 40.00 ᴅᴴ Indigent Criminal Defense Trust Fund [§27.52] (Public Defender's Application Fee, if not previously paid)
2. $ 6.00   Recording Fee [§28.24]
3. $ 3.00   Additional Court Cost Clearing Trust Fund [§ 938.01]
4. $ 50.00   Crimes Compensation Trust Fund [§938.03]
5. $ 200.00   Local Government Criminal Justice Trust Fund [§938.05]
6. $ 20.00   Crime Stoppers Trust Fund [§938.06]
7. $ 2.00   Additional Criminal Justice Education by Municipalities and Counties [§ 938.15; Lake County Code, §9-1)]
8. $ 550.00 ᴅᴴ Public Defender's Fees and Costs [§ 938.29; F.R.Cr.P. 3.720(d)(1)] (Defendant shall be liable to pay in full after judgment of conviction becomes final. Notice of the accused's right to a hearing to contest the lien amount shall be given.)
9. $ _____ Felony DUI [§ 316.193(2)(b)] (Mandatory for fourth or subsequent DUI. Shall not be less than $1,000)
10. $ _____ Criminal Wildlife Violation [§372.7015] ($250 if wildlife offense committed while violating Ch. 810)
11. $ _____ Crimes Compensation Trust Fund [§§938.04, 960.21] (5% surcharge on all fines)
12. $ _____ DUI/BUI Assessment [§938.07] ($135 for any violation of §316.193 or §327.35)
13. $ _____ Additional Cost Domestic Violence [§938.08] ($201 for §784.011 asslt, 784.021 agg /asslt, 784.03 batt, 784.041 fel batt, 784.045 agg batt, 784.048 stalk, 784.07 asslt/batt leo, 784.08 asslt/batt 65, 784.081 asslt/batt spec off/emp. 784.082 asslt/batt jail, 784.083 asslt/batt inspector, 784.085 batt child , 794.011 sex batt, 741.28 dv)
14. $ _____ Additional Cost Rape Crisis Centers [§938.085] ($151 for §784.011, 784.021, 784.03, 784.041, 784.045, 784.048, 784.07, 784.08, 784.081-083, 784.085, 794.011)
15. $ _____ County Alcohol and Other Drug Abuse Trust Fund [§938.13; Lake County Code, §9-10) ($15 for a misdemeanor involving unlawful use of drugs or alcohol)
16. $ 50.00 Prosecution/Investigative Costs [§ 938.27]
17. $ Assessed Probationary Costs of Supervision [§948.09] ($50 per month payable to Department of Corrections)

DISCRETIONARY

18. $ _____ Fines [§ 775.083] (Up to $15,000 for life felony; $10,000 for 1st or 2d degree felony; $5,000 for 3ʳᵈ degree felony) Includes additional mandatory fines for trafficking offenses, if any. [Chapter 893]
19. $ _____ Alcohol and drug abuse programs [§938.21] (Court cost up to the amount of the fine may be imposed for violation of chapters 562, 567, 568, 893, or s.316.193, 856.011, 856.015–but may not be imposed unless defendant has ability to pay the fine and the cost and will not be prevented thereby from rehabilitation or from making restitution.)
20. $ _____ Operating Trust Fund of the FDLE [§938.25] ($100 for any criminal violation of §893.13)
21. $ _____ Assessment of additional court costs for court facilities [§939.18] (Cost not to exceed $150; may be imposed if court finds defendant has ability to pay and will not be prevented thereby from paying restitution or child support)
22. $ 1.00   1ˢᵗ Step Program [§948.03] (Payable to Department of Corrections)
23. $ _____ Other: _____

The foregoing charges, costs, and fines shall be assessed as to each case number shown above.

DONE AND ORDERED in open court in Lake County, Florida,

this _15_ day of _March_ _2004_.

_____
CIRCUIT COURT JUDGE

The quality of this image
is equivalent to the quality
of the original document.

CERTIFICATION SPACE

DOCKETED BY D. HODGE

FELONY 16 July 2003

This criminal order provides a social security number and indicates that the individual has a felony conviction.

UCC FINANCING STATEMENT
FOLLOW INSTRUCTIONS (front and back) CAREFULLY

A NAME & PHONE OF CONTACT AT FILER [optional]

CFN 2004037396
Bk 02530 Pgs 1973 - 1974; (2pgs)
DATE: 03/23/2004 09:51:49 AM
JAMES C. WATKINS, CLERK OF COURT
LAKE COUNTY
RECORDING FEES 9.00
TRUST FUND 1.50

B SEND ACKNOWLEDGMENT TO (Name and Address)

Union Federal Bank of Indianapolis
7500 W. Jefferson Boulevard
Fort Wayne, IN 46804
Preparer Dave Depodesta

The quality of this image
is equivalent to the quality
of the original document.

THE ABOVE SPACE IS FOR FILING OFFICE USE ONLY

1 DEBTOR'S EXACT FULL LEGAL NAME - insert only one debtor name (1a or 1b) - do not abbreviate or combine names

1a ORGANIZATION'S NAME			
1b INDIVIDUAL'S LAST NAME	FIRST NAME	MIDDLE NAME	SUFFIX
Janssen	Clyde	Eric	
1c MAILING ADDRESS	CITY	STATE	POSTAL CODE	COUNTRY
32709 Highland Lakes Road	DeLand	FL	32720	U.S.

1d TAX ID# SSN OR EIN	ADD'L INFO RE ORGANIZATION DEBTOR	1e TYPE OF ORGANIZATION	1f JURISDICTION OF ORGANIZATION	1g ORGANIZATIONAL ID#, if any
591-05-6107				☐ NONE

2 ADDITIONAL DEBTOR'S EXACT FULL LEGAL NAME - insert only one debtor name (2a or 2b) - do not abbreviate or combine names

2a ORGANIZATION'S NAME			
2b INDIVIDUAL'S LAST NAME	FIRST NAME	MIDDLE NAME	SUFFIX
2c MAILING ADDRESS	CITY	STATE	POSTAL CODE	COUNTRY
32709 Highland Lakes Road	DeLand	FL	32720	U.S.

2d TAX ID# SSN OR EIN	ADD'L INFO RE ORGANIZATION DEBTOR	2e TYPE OF ORGANIZATION	2f JURISDICTION OF ORGANIZATION	2g ORGANIZATIONAL ID#, if any
				☐ NONE

3. SECURED PARTY'S NAME (or NAME of TOTAL ASSIGNEE of ASSIGNOR S/P) - insert only one debtor name (3a or 3b) - do not abbreviate or combine names

3a ORGANIZATION'S NAME			
Union Federal Bank of Indianapolis			
3b INDIVIDUAL'S LAST NAME	FIRST NAME	MIDDLE NAME	SUFFIX
3c MAILING ADDRESS	CITY	STATE	POSTAL CODE	COUNTRY
7500 W. Jefferson Boulevard	Fort Wayne	IN	46804	U.S.

4 This FINANCING STATEMENT covers the following collateral

See Attached Exhibit "A"

5 ALTERNATIVE DESIGNATION [if applicable]	☐ LESSEE/LESSOR	☐ CONSIGNEE/CONSIGNOR	☐ BAILEE/BAILOR	☐ SELLER/BUYER	☐ AG LIEN	☐ NON-UCC FILING

6 ☒ This FINANCING STATEMENT is to be filed [for record] (or recorded) in the REAL ESTATE RECORDS Attach Addendum [if applicable]	7 Check to REQUEST SEARCH REPORT(S) on Debtor(s) [ADDITIONAL FEE] [optional]	☐ All Debtors	☐ Debtor 1	☐ Debtor 2

8 OPTIONAL FILER REFERENCE DATA
2258486
Janssen

FILING OFFICE COPY - NATIONAL UCC FINANCING STATEMENT (FORM UCC1) (REV 07/29/98)
WZ82 12/01   65945716

UCC financing statements for PMSIs provide addresses and creditor information.

Reviewing SEC Disclosures Can Yield Dividends
by V. John Ella

Public companies must, by law, disclose current financial and other information to the Securities & Exchange Commission ("SEC"). This information is available to anyone, not just shareholders, and it can be especially useful to attorneys wishing to learn more about a particular company. Before filing suit against any publicly held entity, therefore, it makes sense to review its annual report and other disclosures. Some attorneys refer to this as "opposition research" or "informal" discovery and maintain a separate sub-file for SEC filings.

The Internet is now the best practical source for obtaining SEC filings, which can be used in conjunction with other business information available on the Internet, including data from various Secretary of State Web sites. This article is a brief guide to finding, reading, and understanding 10-K's, 10-Q's, and related information available online.

USING THE INFO

The type of information in public disclosures can be useful in a wide variety of cases. For example, in a recent case brought under the WARN Act, which may hinge on whether a company was seeking to raise capital or whether it faced "unforeseen business circumstances," the author used the defendant's SEC disclosures to help establish the timing of recent financial transactions. Employment attorneys can use these disclosures to view the actual employment, severance, and noncompete agreements of the primary officers, directors, and other executives. They can also use SEC information to determine whether a "change in control" has occurred in order to invoke a golden parachute.

Collection and bankruptcy attorneys can track major financial events to determine the company's ability to sustain a large judgment or to trace preferential payments. Transactional attorneys can review recent mergers and acquisitions. Securities fraud/class action attorneys can view what representations were made and when.

Competitors and their counsel can learn about the history of the company, its product line, where it is located and incorporated, who the primary officers and directors are, and a host of other information.

SEC disclosures are especially interesting to litigators because public companies are required to list and describe any "material" lawsuits that could affect the company's bottom line. This has prompted a theory—often voiced, although probably exaggerated—that public companies may wish to settle lawsuits in an effort to avoid the necessity of public disclosure through SEC filings, which in turn might have a negative effect on the value of the stock.

SEC filings can provide other information as well, such as:

* a general history of the company over the last year;
* who it uses as general counsel; and
* recent transactions, expansions, purchases, acquisitions, sales, and personnel changes.

ONLINE REPORTS

One of the Internet's most valuable and often-used resources has been **www.freeedgar.com,** which was run by a private company and provided access to SEC filings and other useful information. (EDGAR is an acronym for "Electronic Data Gathering Analysis and Retrieval.")

The SEC used to provide disclosure information on its own Web site, but in December 2001, the SEC announced that it signed a contract with EDGAR to handle all of its online access to this information, free of charge. As of April 2001, however, EDGAR is not always "free," at least for some purposes. Forms can still be accessed without cost from **www.freeedgar.com,** but premium service is also available from **www.edgar-online.com,** for a fee. The subscription fee, depending on your means, may be worth the money for improved formatting, easier searching and additional information.

Another popular site that offers SEC documents online, and is preferred by some securities law attorneys for formatting reasons, is **www.10kwizard.com.** Attorneys practicing ERISA law can download Form 5500's, which are filed with the Department of Labor for various pension plans, without cost—after obtaining a password—from **www.freeERISA.com.**

Finally, never overlook the company's own Web site, which often has a link to at least the most recent annual report, as well as other miscellaneous information that might not be in any publicly filed document but may be helpful in the informal discovery process.

PASSWORD PANDEMONIUM

Many Web sites charge a subscription fee, or at least require a password, in order to obtain certain information online. Examples include **www.westlaw.com, www.lexis.com,** most newspapers and news magazines, as well as the Minnesota Secretary of State's office, **www.sos.state.mn.us,** which offers more extensive information for paid subscribers, including Uniform Commercial Code (UCC) filing information.

Keeping track of all of these passwords can be confusing, and law firms may want to keep this information consolidated, along with clear instructions for paralegals, law clerks and associates regarding what types of searches incur costs beyond the flat fee or subscription amount.

PUBLIC COMPANIES

According to the Securities & Exchange Acts of 1933 and 1934, a public company is generally defined as one having registered its securities for sale to the public, or one required to register as a result of having over 500 shareholders and more than $10 million in assets. The definition thus includes all companies listed on public stock exchanges such as the New York Stock Exchange, the American Stock Exchange and NASDAQ, regardless of their assets or number of shareholders.

Public companies are not all Fortune 500 companies. They also include companies which are not traded on an exchange but whose shares are tradable in the over-the-counter (OTC) or pink sheet markets. Minnesota has hundreds of public companies, most of which are not household names.

Privately held companies, of course, are not required to publicly disclose information and some of these companies can be quite large, such as Cargill, which is one of the largest privately held companies in the world.

Once a company becomes large enough, or decides to raise capital in the public marketplace, it begins the journey of becoming a public company by filing either a registration statement or a Form 10. These disclosures are extremely comprehensive and are intended to include all material information about the company, which is kept current with periodic additional filings.

There are more than 50 different forms that public companies may file with the SEC. This article, however, focuses on just a few key documents that can be obtained either from the SEC directly or through the Internet.

ANNUAL REPORT v. 10-K

Most lawyers and investors are familiar with the glossy annual reports published by publicly held companies. Shareholders' annual reports are not exactly the same as a Form 10-K, however.

The 10-K is the annual report filed with the SEC. It must contain significantly more detailed information than the annual report and does not include color photographs or fancy charts. To be truly thorough, one should obtain a copy of both the shareholders' annual report and the 10-K, although some of the information will overlap.

The main components of a 10-K are organized as follows:

Part I

- Item 1. Business (A thorough discussion of the history and nature of the company's business, as well as its current status, its competition, research and development, personnel, subsidiaries, etc.)

(continued)

- Item 2. Description of Property (A description of the company's real estate, including cost, rents, leases, etc.)
- Item 3. Legal Proceedings (A disclosure of all material lawsuits.)
- Item 4. Submission of Matters to a Vote of the Security Holders (A description of any matter submitted to a vote of shareholders during the preceding calendar quarter.)

Part II

- Item 5. Market for the Company's Equity and Related Stockholder Matters (Describes recent sales of equity securities.)
- Item 6. Selected Financial Data (A summary of the company's financial position.)
- Item 7. Management Discussion and Analysis of Financial Conditions and Results of Operations (Management's explanation of financial changes, trends and results on a comparative basis.)
- Item 7A. Quantitative and Qualitative Disclosures About Market Risk (Generally applies to companies holding or trading market-sensitive instruments, such as derivatives, forward contracts or foreign currency.)
- Item 8. Financial Statements and Supplementary Data (The company's audited financial statements.)
- Item 9. Changes In and Disagreements with Accountants on Accounting and Financial Disclosures

Part III

- Item 10. Directors and Executive Officers of the Company (Who they are.)
- Item 11. Executive Compensation (Amount of money they made, including stock options and perks.)
- Item 12. Security Ownership of Certain Beneficial Owners and Management (Equity holdings by officers, directors and shareholders owning 5 percent or more of the stock.)
- Item 13. Certain Relationships and Related Transactions (Transactions between the company and members of management or significant shareholders, including family members.)
- Item 14. Exhibits (Includes contracts, employment agreements, transaction documents, loan agreements, etc.)

To get an accurate picture when reviewing a 10-K and an accompanying annual report, which can be quite voluminous, focus on the numbers and hard data rather than relying on statements from the chairman of the board. Do not overlook the importance of footnotes and remember that the exhibits can be a valuable source of information and usually include copies of actual agreements and contracts.

THE 10-Q

Form 10-Q is similar to the 10-K but the "Q" in this case stands for "quarterly" and is simply a smaller, more streamlined report filed with the SEC three times a year—after the end of each quarter, unless it is at the end of a fiscal year. Form 10-Q's are different from 10-K's in that they provide a continuing view of the company's financial position during the year, rather than a comprehensive, overall summary of the big picture as provided in the 10-K.

THE PROXY STATEMENT

Proxy statements are sent out and filed with the SEC about six weeks in advance of a company's annual meeting and state where and when the meeting will be held. The form, known as Form 14A, is designed to inform shareholders of issues that may be passed upon in the meeting, including the election of directors. For this reason, proxy statements usually contain a "Summary Compensation Table" which states how much the CEO and the four highest paid executives earned annually over the past three years in salary, bonus, stock options and any other compensation.

Form 14As also include a section labeled "Options, Grants in the Last Fiscal Year" which lists what options were issued and at what price, along with a table that estimates what options grants are worth, based on various assumptions.

Other sections to look for include "Election of Directors," "Certain Relationships," "Director Compensation," and "Related Party Transactions," which lists all payments nonemployee directors received for extra services—such as helping to broker a transaction or selling insurance to the company.

There may be other important filings as well, depending on the financial health of the company and what type of activity it is engaged in. For example, any significant occurrence, defined as an "unscheduled material event," including a bankruptcy, merger or acquisition, the resignation of directors, or a change in the fiscal year, requires the filing of a Form 8-K.

Also, individuals with "insider" status must file certain documents, starting with a Form 3. Any insider trading activity must be reported within 30 days on a Form 4, and at the end of the year all such activity is reported on a Form 5. A list of other SEC forms and an explanation of what they are is available at **www.edgar-online.com/formdef.asp.**

Hopefully this guide will help attorneys take advantage of the large amount of data public companies must disclose and other information available online.

Source: Originally published by The Minnesota Lawyer (Minneapolis, MN) March 25, 2002. Copyright 2002 Dolan Media Newswires. Reprinted by permission.

* * * * * * * * * * * * * * * * * * *

If, in your visit to the witness's neighborhood, you happened to find out about some elderly relatives, you might want to look up their names in the wills division of the county courthouse, ordinarily referred to as probate. If you find them, and your witness, in the will, you will also find the names of other family members. These are people who are much more likely to know where your witness is.

Reunions are also a great source of information. If you know that an individual went to a particular high school, talk to the reunion organizer. You can find out what year by looking through old yearbooks of that school, which most high schools retain. The organizer may have an address, or know someone who knows someone who knew your witness. The high school acquaintance is likely to have leads, such as the names of other family members or spouses, or where the family moved to, and so forth even if the acquaintance doesn't know the witness's current address.

The DMV

Your state department of motor vehicles (or whatever the driver's licensing authority in your state is called) is often an excellent place to find a current address. Because most people have driver's licenses, and because the law requires current addresses for these licenses, this agency often has the information you are seeking. In many states, a simple form and a low fee is all it takes to get all the addresses of a person who has ever held a driver's license in that state: it's public information. You can also get a list of all prior accidents from the DMV; it's not particularly useful in locating witnesses, but it's handy for finding out about prior accidents that opposing parties may have had.

The Internet

The Internet has become a very handy tool for finding people. First, you can simply run names on the various search engines. Some people who have unlisted phone numbers may have their names listed on institutional, business, governmental, news, educational, or other Web sites. You can contact the entity with the Web site to find your witness or to find out how to contact your witness. Second, there are many phone book Web sites. One particularly good one is **www.anywho.com,** AT&T's Web site. It allows you to look up names by state, and also has a **reverse look-up.** If you just have a phone number, you can insert the number and find out who

APPLICATION FOR COPY OF DRIVING RECORD

The availability of records is subject to the provisions of the Uniform Motor Vehicle Records Disclosure Act.

If filing this request in person, be prepared to furnish us with proof of identification. If filing this request through the mail, your signature must be notarized and the appropriate fees included or the request will be returned to you unprocessed.

PLEASE PRINT	**--FORM *MUST* BE COMPLETED IN FULL--**	**$3.00 Per Record**

Name (as it appears on driver's license): _____

Date of Birth: _____ Nebraska Driver's License Number _____

Name and Date of Birth OR Name and Nebraska Driver's License Number must be supplied before a record check can be done.

For what purpose will this record be used? (See reverse side for additional information)_____

_____

Please Print Your Name:_____

Business Name (if applicable):_____

Address: _____

City, State, Zip:_____

Under penalty of law, the undersigned certifies that the information contained on the driving record being purchased will be used as authorized by the Uniform Motor Vehicle Records Disclosure Act. The undersigned hereby acknowledges that this request is made with the understanding that any person requesting disclosure of personal information from the Department of Motor Vehicles who misrepresents his or her identity, misrepresents the purpose for which the information requested will be used, or otherwise makes a false statement on the application shall be guilty of a class IV felony.

Signature:_____ Date: _____

(Signature must be notarized in Box 1 below, if filing this request through the mail.)

The Department of Motor Vehicles is prohibited from disclosing the information on the record you are requesting unless the purpose indicated above is for an exempt use (see reverse side for a list of exempt uses) or you have obtained the **notarized** written consent of the record holder on this form as provided below.

I _____ hereby authorize _____ to obtain a copy of my driving record as described above.

Signature of Record Holder: _____

(Signature must be notarized in Box 2.)

Box 1 State of_____	**Box 2** State of_____
County of_____	County of_____
The foregoing signature of the **requestor** was acknowledged before me this_____ day of _____, _____ .	The foregoing signature of the **record holder** was acknowledged before me this_____ day of _____, _____ .
_____ Notary or Designated County Official	_____ Notary or Designated County Official
Seal	Seal

Submit this application with $3.00 fee per record requested to:

Nebraska Department of Motor Vehicles
Driver and Vehicle Records Division
301 Centennial Mall South
PO Box 94789
Lincoln, NE 68509-4789

Make Checks Payable to: Department of Motor Vehicles

A STAMPED SELF-ADDRESSED ENVELOPE IS REQUIRED FOR ALL MAIL-IN REQUESTS.

For questions regarding this application please contact this office at (402) 471-3918.

Revised 7/2002

Nebraska's official form for obtaining driving records.

The exempted uses permitted under the Uniform Motor Vehicle Records Disclosure Act are as follows:

1. Use by any federal, state, or local governmental agency, including any court or law enforcement agency, in carrying out its functions, or by any private entity acting on behalf of an agency in carrying out their functions.

2. Use in connection with vehicle or driver safety and theft; vehicle emissions; vehicle product alterations, recalls or advisories; performance monitoring of vehicles, vehicle parts, and dealers; motor vehicle market research activities and survey research; and removal of nonowner records from the original owner records of motor vehicle manufacturers.

3. Use in normal course of business by a legitimate business to verify accuracy of information submitted by an individual or business; or to obtain correct information if the above is not correct or no longer correct, for the purpose of preventing fraud, pursuing legal remedies against or recovering on a debt or security interest against the record holder.

4. Use in connection with a civil, criminal, administrative or arbitral proceeding in any federal, state or local court, government agency, or self-regulatory body, including service of process, investigation in anticipation of litigation, and execution or enforcement of judgment; or pursuant to an order of a federal, state, or local court, an administrative agency, or a self-regulatory body.

5. Use in research activities and statistical reports, as long as personal information is not published, redisclosed or used to contact individuals.

6. Use by any insurer/insurance support organization or by a self-insured entity in connection with claims investigation activities, anti-fraud activities, rating or underwriting.

7. Use in providing notice to owners of abandoned, towed or impounded vehicles.

8. Use by a private detective, plain clothes investigator, or private investigative agency licensed under Neb.Rev.Stat. 71-3201 to 71-3213 for purposes permitted under this act.

9. Use by an employer, employer's agent or insurer, to obtain or verify information of a Commercial Driver's License holder.

10. Use in connection with the operation of private toll transportation facilities.

11. Any use if requestor has notarized consent of the record holder and has provided proof of such consent to the Department, as indicated on the front of this form.

12. Use, including redisclosure through news publication, for a member of a medium of communication as defined in Neb.Rev.Stat. 20-145, in connection with news involving motor vehicle or driver safety or vehicle theft.

13. Any use if the request for the record is made by the record holder.

Redisclosure

A recipient of a motor vehicle record may only resell or redisclose the information obtained if for one of the uses permitted under the Uniform Motor Vehicle Records Disclosure Act. You shall make and keep for 5 years, records identifying each person to whom you redisclosed the information and the permitted purpose for which it was redisclosed. These records shall be made available for inspection and copying by a representative of the Department of Motor Vehicles upon request.

Revised 7/2002

The fine print for requesting a driving record. Number 4 is your reason; track its language when filling out the previous page.

REQUESTS FOR NATIONAL
DRIVER REGISTER (NDR) RECORD CHECKS

Who may obtain an NDR record check

Any person may ask to know whether there is an NDR record on him or her and may obtain a copy of the record if one exists. Requests from individuals require Form NDR-PRV.

Employers of drivers and locomotive engineers may also obtain NDR record checks. *Every driver or operator on whom an NDR file check is requested is entitled to review the NDR report(s) provided to the employer.* The results of the NDR check will be mailed only to the current or prospective employer or third party service provider. If no employer is named on the form or it is changed, the request will not be processed.

The following authorization applies to Railroad Company requests:

> **NDR Check Authorization:** The U. S. Department of Transportation, Federal Railroad Administration, in accordance with 49 CFR, Part 240.111, requires that I hereby request and authorize the National Highway Traffic Safety Administration (NHTSA) to perform an NDR check of my driving record for a 36-month period prior to the date of this request including license withdrawal actions open at the time of file check. I hereby authorize the NDR to furnish a copy of the results of this NDR check directly to the railroad company identified on this inquiry form.

What NDR Records Contain

NDR results for employers will contain only the identification of the state(s) which have reported information on the driver to the NDR and only information reported within the past 3 years from the date of the inquiry. Driver control actions initiated prior to that time, even if still in effect, will not be included.

Detailed information to confirm identity or to describe the contents of the driver record can be obtained only from the state(s) listed when probable matches are reported. The name and address of the driver licensing official will be provided for each state listed.

How to request and NDR record check

The Request for National Driver Register File Check on Current or Prospective Employee form, may be completed by either the current or prospective employer or the current or prospective employee, **(1) the driver must authorize the request by his or her signature or mark as witnessed; (2) the driver must certify his or her identity; and (3) the request must be to the state where the driver is licensed.**

All NDR record check request **must be notarized** to certify identity unless the request is presented in person to the National Driver Register, Nassif Building, 400 7th Street, Washington, DC. Employer/employee record checks may be mailed directly to the NDR or to:

> Department of Motor Vehicles
> Public Operations—G199
> P. O. Box 944247
> Sacramento, CA 94244-2470

Individual requests for NDR checks must be submitted directly to the NDR by the individual (subject of the request) and will only be released to the individual.

Location of NDR Records

Requests for NDR record checks by individuals may be presented in person during regular working hours at 7:45 am to 4:15 pm, each day except, Saturdays, Sundays, and Federal legal holidays. The address for requesting record information in writing directly from the NDR or for making requests in person is:

> National Driver Register
> Nassif Building
> 400 7th Street, SW
> Washington, DC 20590

INF 1301A (NEW 8/95) **WWW Form**

This national register is open to "any person" and will provide information from any state which has reported to NDR.

STATE OF CALIFORNIA
DEPARTMENT OF MOTOR VEHICLES
A Public Service Agency

REQUEST FOR NATIONAL DRIVER REGISTER (NDR) FILE CHECK
ON CURRENT OR PROSPECTIVE EMPLOYEE

Current or Prospective Employer to Receive the NDR Search Results: ☐ Driver Employer ☐ Railroad Company
Fee: $5 per request. DO NOT send cash. Enclose check/money order payable to DMV.

EMPLOYER OR AGENCY NAME

TO THE SPECIFIC ATTENTION OF: BUSINESS TELEPHONE
                                                                     (   )

MAILING ADDRESS (NUMBER AND STREET)

CITY, STATE AND ZIP CODE

TYPE OR PRINT PLAINLY (Avoid delays. Inquiries that cannot be read will not be processed.)

FULL LEGAL NAME (FIRST, MIDDLE, LAST)

OTHER NAMES USED (MAIDEN, PRIOR NAME, NICKNAME, PROFESSIONAL NAME, OTHER)

MAILING ADDRESS (NUMBER AND STREET WITH APARTMENT OR RURAL ROUTE/CARRIER AND BOX NUMBER)   HOME TELEPHONE (OPTIONAL)
                                                                                            (   )

CITY, STATE, AND ZIP CODE   WORK TELEPHONE (OPTIONAL)
                                                                                            (   )

DRIVER LICENSE NUMBER AND STATE (DRIVER MUST BE LICENSED IN THE STATE INITIATING THE SEARCH) SOCIAL SECURITY NUMBER (OPTIONAL)

MONTH, DAY, AND YEAR OF BIRTH | SEX | COLOR OF EYES | HEIGHT | WEIGHT

EMPLOYEE UNDERSTANDING: I understand that the National Driver Register (NDR) search will result in a printed report which will be sent only to the employer or regulatory agency listed above on this form. The report will indicate either (1) that the NDR does **not** contain a record matching my identification or (2) that the NDR has a probable identification (match) from one state (or more) which will be named on the report. A separate check of state files would be required (1) to verify the identification or (2) to obtain the driving record. It is the responsibility of the listed employer to obtain the state driver records and to determine or veryify records which apply to me. Under the Privacy Act, I have the right to request record(s) pertaining to me from the NDR. I also understand that if convictions, suspensions or revocations of mine are found which I have not shown on my applications or interviews, I might not be hired as a driver or could lost my job as a driver, and the State where I am licensed may also take action on my driver license including suspension, cancellation, or revocation. I hereby, with my signature, authorize a one-time file search of the NDR and any resulting reports to be sent to the employer or agency on this form.

DRIVER'S SIGNATURE (PLEASE READ INFORMATION ON BACK BEFORE SIGNING)   DATE

OFFICIAL USE ONLY

DATE RECEIVED	DATE SENT	INTERNAL CONTROL

TYPE OF IDENTIFICATION:
☐ Valid Photo Driver License   ☐ Birth Certificate
☐ State-issued Photo ID   ☐ Valid Passport
☐ Military Discharge Papers   ☐ Valid Military
☐ Other (specify) _____

EMPLOYEE VERIFYING APPLICANT IDENTIFICATION (PRINT NAME)

SIGNATURE

NOTARIZATION
The employee's signature must be notarized or the request will be returned unprocessed.

Sworn to and ascribed before me this

DAY	OF	YEAR

IN THE CITY/COUNTY OF

STATE OF

Notary Public Seal or Stamp

WWW Form INF 1301A (NEW 8/95)

195

Motor Vehicle Division
ADOT
46-4416 R08/03   www.dot.state.az.us

Mail Drop 504M
Records Unit
Motor Vehicle Division
PO Box 2100
Phoenix AZ 85001-2100

MOTOR VEHICLE RECORD REQUEST

The manner in which the Motor Vehicle Division (MVD) may release information from its driver license or motor vehicle records is regulated by the Federal Driver's Privacy Protection Act (or DPPA), 18 USC 2721-2725 and Title 28, Chapter 2, Article 5 of the Arizona Revised Statutes. It is the responsibility of the individual or entity making a request to gain knowledge of all state and federal laws which govern access to and use of MVD records, and to determine eligibility under these laws.

Anyone who knowingly obtains, discloses, or uses personal information from an MVD record for a use not permitted under 18 USC 2721, and anyone requesting the disclosure of personal information who misrepresents their identity or makes a false statement in connection thereto with the intent to obtain such information in a manner not authorized by law, is subject to civil and/or criminal penalties.

Driver Record — All three criteria are required by state law, unless exempt (see below)

Record Type □ Uncertified 39-Month □ Certified 5-year	1. Licensee Full Name (first, middle name or initial, last, suffix)
2. Arizona Driver License Number □ Has not applied for license □ License is suspended or revoked	3. Date of Birth or license expiration date (month/day/year)

Vehicle Record — All three criteria are required by state law, unless exempt (see below)

Record Type □ Uncertified □ Certified	1. Owner Full Name (first, middle name or initial, last, suffix)
2. Arizona License Plate Number □ No plate has been issued	3. Vehicle Identification Number

Requester Information — proof of identification required

Requester Name (first, middle, last, suffix)	Driver License Number or Other ID	Daytime Phone Number ( )
Mailing Address	City	State Zip
Representing (name of business or other organization)		
Reason For Record Inquiry		

—— This form must be signed and notarized on the back and under federal law at least one permissible use must be checked. ——

Exemptions — I am entitled to the following exemption from the requirement to provide all three criteria (proof required):

☐ Licensed private investigator

☐ Financial institution or enterprise under the jurisdiction of the Arizona Banking Department or a federal monetary authority

☐ Federal, state, or local government agency or persons acting for the agency (no fee required)

☐ Attorney registered with State Bar of Arizona (Record requested must be relevant to a pending or potential court proceeding.)

☐ Motor vehicle dealer, licensed and bonded by MVD, or a state organization of licensed and bonded motor vehicle dealers

☐ Motor vehicle insurer under the jurisdiction of the Arizona Insurance Department (39-month record only. Must provide 2 of the 3 criteria.)

☐ A person involved in an accident or the owner of a vehicle involved in an accident (May receive record of any vehicle involved or of any person operating a vehicle involved. Proof of involvement required. Must also complete form # 46-0200.)

☐ Applicant for a bonded Arizona title, in order to contact the registered owners of the vehicle (Must provide MVD vehicle inspection document.)

☐ Your driver record – Must provide full name and date of birth.

☐ Your vehicle record – Must provide full name and plate or vehicle identification number.

Fees (per record or document)

	Uncertified	Certified		Uncertified	Certified
Over-the-Counter (while you wait)	$3.00	$5.00	Drop-off	$2.00	$5.00
Mail-in (must be notarized)	$3.00	$5.00	Supporting microfilm documents	$3.00	$5.00

MVD Use

Record Located □ Yes □ No	Amount Paid	Check Number	Customer Number	Date Paid	MVD Agent

This Arizona MVD request exempts attorneys from providing complete information about either the driver or the vehicle.

Permissible Uses

I understand that the DPPA requires me to have a "permissible use" for requesting and receiving an MVD record which contains personal identifying information (e.g., a person's driver license photograph/image, social security number, driver license number, name, address and medical/disability information). Based on the specific use(s) checked below, I hereby certify that I am entitled to obtain the requested record under the authority of 18 U.S.C. 2721:

☐ I am requesting a copy of my own record.

☐ I have obtained the written consent of the individual whose record is being requested. (You must attach a signed and notarized Consent to Release Motor Vehicle Record, form # 96-0276.)

☐ I am acting on behalf of a federal, state or local government agency (as named on the reverse side) and the record will be used to carry out the official functions of that agency.

☐ I am an attorney licensed to practice law in this state or a licensed private investigator, and the record will be used in connection with a civil, criminal, administrative or arbitral proceeding in federal, state or local court, or a proceeding held before a government agency or self-regulatory body (such permissible use may include the service of process, investigation in anticipation of litigation, and the execution or enforcement of judgments and orders, or other actions taken pursuant to a court order). Attach copy of relevant court order or judgment, if applicable.

Professional License Number	Court Name and Case Number (if available)

☐ I am an employer or its agent or insurer, and the record will be used to obtain or verify information relating to a holder of a commercial driver license.

☐ I am an owner or an authorized agent, employee or contractor of an insurance company, insurance support organization or self-insured entity (as named on the reverse side) and the record will be used by such company, organization or entity in connection with its claims investigation activities, antifraud activities, rating or underwriting.

> Unless a request is made for one or more of the above permissible uses, the record released by MVD will not contain the person's driver license photograph/image, social security number or medical/disability information.

☐ I am an owner or an authorized agent, employee or contractor of a legitimate business (as named on the reverse side) and the record will be used in the normal course of that business, but only 1) to verify the accuracy of the personal information submitted to the business by the individual whose record is being requested, and/or 2) to obtain correct information about this individual for purposes of preventing fraud, pursuing legal remedies or collecting a debt or security interest against the individual.

Federal Tax Identification/Vendor or Professional License Number	Applicable Licensing Agency

☐ The record will be used in connection with matters of motor vehicle or driver safety and theft; motor vehicle emissions; motor vehicle product alterations, recalls, or advisories; performance monitoring of motor vehicles, motor vehicle parts and dealers; motor vehicle market research activities, including survey research; and removal of non-owner records from the original owner records of motor vehicle manufacturers.

☐ The record will be used in performing research activities and for use in producing statistical reports, but will not be published, redisclosed or used to contact individuals.

☐ The record will be used in providing notice to the owners of towed or impounded vehicles.

☐ I am an owner or authorized representative of a licensed private investigative agency or licensed security service (as named on the reverse side) and the record will be used only for one of the permissible uses listed above or below. (You must indicate a second permissible use in accordance with the DPPA).

☐ The record will be used in connection with the operation of a private toll transportation facility.

☐ The record will be used for a purpose specifically authorized by ARS 28-450 relating to a vehicle accident, bonded title, self-storage vehicle foreclosure sale or motor vehicle dealer. If a request is being made for any other use that is specifically authorized by law and is related to the operation of a motor vehicle or to public safety, you must specify both, the reason for your request and the law. A request made on this basis must also be reviewed and approved by MVD management before any record is released.

Certification

I hereby certify, under penalty of perjury, that any records or information obtained pursuant to this request will be used solely for the use(s) indicated on this form, and for no other use. I understand that I am prohibited from selling or disclosing the personal information set forth in these records, except in accordance with applicable law. I further acknowledge that the Motor Vehicle Division, by giving me access to the requested record information, is relying on the truth of the representations contained on this form, and I am intending that MVD so rely. I therefore agree to defend, hold harmless and indemnify MVD and any of its officers, employees, agents or contractors, from all actions brought or damages alleged by reason of the negligent, improper or unauthorized use or dissemination of the information provided to me by MVD.

Requester Name (first, middle, last, suffix)		Requester Signature	
	Acknowledged before me this date.	Notary or MVD Agent Signature	
Date	County	State	Commission Expires

The back side of the Arizona request lists your reason fourth.

APPLICATION FOR COPY OF DRIVER RECORD

Mail to: Driver Records Bureau, Texas Department of Public Safety, Box 149246, Austin, Texas 78714-9246
MAKE CHECK or MONEY ORDER PAYABLE TO: TEXAS DEPARTMENT OF PUBLIC SAFETY
Any questions regarding the information on this form should be directed to Customer Service at 512/424-2600. Allow 2-3 weeks for delivery

CHECK TYPE OF RECORD DESIRED   **FEE**

☐ 1. Name - DOB - License Status - Latest Address. $ 4.00
☐ 2. Name - DOB - License Status - List of Accidents/Moving Violations in Record within Immediate Past 3 Year Period. $ 6.00
☐ 2A. CERTIFIED version of #2. This Record Is Not Acceptable for DDC Course. $ 10.00
☐ 3. Name - DOB - License Status - List of ALL Accidents and Violations in Record. **Furnished to Licensee ONLY.** $ 7.00
☐ 3A. CERTIFIED version of #3. **Furnished to Licensee ONLY and is Acceptable for DDC Course.** $ 10.00
☐ Other: (Original Application, DWLS, etc.)_____ (If Required) $ ____

MAIL DRIVER RECORD TO: Requestor's Name _____ DL Number_____
(PLEASE TYPE OR PRINT)

                                Address _____

                                City, State, Zip Code _____ Telephone # _____

If requesting on behalf of a business, organization, or other entity, please include the following:

        Name of business, organization, entity, etc._____

        Your Title or Affiliation with above_____

        Type of business, organization, etc. _____
                                            (i.e. Insurance provider, towing company, private investigation firm, etc.)

INFORMATION REQUESTED ON:

Texas Driver License #_____ Date of Birth (Month/Day/Year)_____

Last Name_____ First Name_____ Middle/Maiden_____

INDIVIDUAL'S WRITTEN CONSENT FOR *ONE TIME* RELEASE TO ABOVE REQUESTOR

(Requestor, if you do not meet one of the exceptions listed on the back of this form, please be advised that without the written consent of the driver license/ID card holder, the record you receive will not include personal information.)

I, _____, hereby certify that I grant access on this one occasion to my Driver License/ID Card record, inclusive of the

personal information (name, address, driver identification number, etc.), to _____

_____   _____
Signature of License/ID Card Holder or Parent/Legal Guardian   Date

---

State and federal law requires requestors to agree to the following:

In requesting and using this information, I acknowledge that this disclosure is subject to the federal Driver's Privacy Protection Act (18 U.S.C. Sect. 2721 et seq.) and Texas Transportation Code Chapter 730. False statements or representations to obtain personal information pertaining to any individual from the DPS could result in the denial to release any driver record information to myself and the entity for which I made the request. Further, I understand that if I receive personal information as a result of this request, it may only be used for the stated purpose and I may only resell or redisclose the information pursuant to Texas Transportation Code §730.013. Violations of that section may result in a criminal charge with the possibility of a $25,000 fine.

I certify that I have read and agree with the above conditions and that the information provided by me in this request is true and correct. If I am requesting this driver record on behalf of an entity, I also certify that I am authorized by that entity to make this request on their behalf. I also acknowledge that failure to abide by the provisions of this agreement and any state and federal privacy law can subject me to both criminal and civil penalties.

_____   _____
Signature of Requestor   Date

If you are not requesting a copy of your own record or do not have the written consent of DL/ID holder, you must provide the information requested on the reverse.

DR-1 (Rev. 9/01)

The Texas Department of Public Safety may disclose personal information to a requestor without written consent of the DL/ID holder, on proof of their identity and a certification by the requestor that the use of the personal information is authorized under state and federal law and that the information will be used only for the purpose stated and in complete compliance with state and federal law.

You must meet one or more of the following exceptions if you do not have written consent of the DL/ID holder to be entitled to receive personal information on the above named individual. Please _initial_ each category that applies to the requested driver record.

_____ 1. For use in connection with any matter of (a) motor vehicle or motor vehicle operator safety; (b) motor vehicle theft; (c) motor vehicle emissions; (d) motor vehicle product alterations, recalls, or advisories; (e) performance monitoring of motor vehicles or motor vehicle dealers by a motor vehicle manufacturer; or (f) removal of nonowner records from the original owner records of a motor vehicle manufacturer to carry out the purposes of the Automobile Information Disclosure Act, the Anti Car Theft Act of 1992, the Clean Air Act, and any other statute or regulation enacted or adopted under or in relation to a law included in the above.

_____ 2. For use by a government agency in carrying out its functions or a private entity acting on behalf of a government agency in carrying out its functions.

_____ 3. For use in connection with a matter of (a) motor vehicle or motor vehicle operator safety; (b) motor vehicle theft; (c) motor vehicle product alterations, recalls, or advisories; (d) performance monitoring of motor vehicles, motor vehicle parts, or motor vehicle dealers; (e) motor vehicle market research activities, including survey research; or (f) removal of nonowner records from the original owner records of motor vehicle manufacturers.

_____ 4. For use in the normal course of business by a legitimate business or an authorized agent of the business, but only to verify the accuracy of personal information submitted by the individual to the business or the authorized agent of the business and to obtain correct information if the submitted information is incorrect to prevent fraud by pursuing a legal remedy against, or recovering on a debt or security interest against the individual.

_____ 5. For use in conjunction with a civil, criminal, administrative, or arbitral proceeding in any court or government agency or before any self regulatory body, including service of process, investigation in anticipation of litigation, execution or enforcement of a judgment or order, or under an order of any court.

_____ 6. For use in research or in producing statistical reports, but only if the personal information is not published, redisclosed, or used to contact any individual.

_____ 7. For use by an insurer or insurance support organization, or by a self insured entity, or an authorized agent of the entity, in connection with claims investigation activities, antifraud activities, rating or underwriting.

_____ 8. For use in providing notice to an owner of a towed or impounded vehicle.

_____ 9. For use by a licensed private investigator agency or licensed security service for a purpose permitted as stated on this page.

_____ 10. For use by an employer or an authorized agent or insurer of the employer to obtain or verify information relating to a holder of a commercial driver license that is required under 49 U.S.C. Chapter 313.

_____ 11. For use in connection with the operation of a private toll transportation facility.

_____ 12. For use by a consumer-reporting agency as defined by the Fair Credit Reporting Act (15 U.S.C. §1681 et seq.) for a purpose permitted under the Act.

_____ 13. For any other purpose specifically authorized by law that relates to the operation of a motor vehicle or to public safety.

Please state specific statutory authority _____

_____ 14. For use in the preventing, detecting, or protecting against identity theft or other acts of fraud. The Department prior to release of personal information may require additional information.

The back side of the Texas form lists your reason as number 5.

MISSISSIPPI DEPARTMENT OF PUBLIC SAFETY
DRIVER RECORDS REQUEST   **DRIVER SERVICES POLICY: 6-9(A**

DRIVER NAME: _____ DL NO: _____ DOB:

I HEREBY REQUEST THE FOLLOWING RECORDS RELATING TO THE ABOVE-NAMED PERSON:

Record Requested: _____   MVR Summary
                       _____   Other Record (must be specified)

CHECK THE FOLLOWING APPLICABLE STATEMENT:

_____   I am the person named in the record sought.
        Type ID Shown _____   Authorized Agent
_____   I am requesting the information on behalf of the current owner (written authorization from record owner required).
_____   The information is to be used by a legitimate business or its agents, employees or contractors for use in the normal course of business only:
        1.   To verify the accuracy of personal information submitted by the individual to the business or its agents, employees.
        2.   If such information as submitted is not correct, or no longer correct, to obtain the correct information for the sole purpose of preventing fraud by pursuing legal remedies against, or recovering on a debt or security interest against the individual.
_____   The information is to be used in conjunction with a civil, criminal, administrative or arbitral proceeding in a federal, state or local court or agency or before any self-regulatory body, including service of process, investigation in anticipation of litigation and the execution or enforcement of a judgment or order, or pursuant to an order of any court.
_____   The information is to be used by an insurer or insurance support organization, or by a self-insured entity, or its agents, employees or contractors in connection with the claims investigation activities, anti-fraud activities, rating or underwriting.
_____   I represent a license private investigative agency or licensed security service and the information will be utilized for one of the above listed permitted purposes.
_____   For use by an employer or its agency or insurer to obtain or verify information relating to a holder of a commercial driver's license that is required under the Commercial Motor Vehicle Safety Act of 1986 (49 U.S.C. App. 2710, et seq.).
_____   For use in connection with the operation of private toll transportation facilities.
_____   For use by a government agency, court or law enforcement agency in carrying out its functions.
_____   For use in connection with matters of motor vehicle or driver safety and theft, motor vehicle omissions, recalls, performance monitoring and the like.
_____   For use in the normal course of business by a legitimate business to verify accuracy of personal information submitted by the individual to the business and if the information is incorrect, to obtain the correct information, but only for fraud prevention or recovering debts from the individual.
_____   For use in connection with any civil, criminal or administrative proceeding in any federal, state or local court or agency for service of process or enforcement of judgments.
_____   For use in research activities so long as the personal information is not published, redisclosed or used to contact the individual.
_____   For use by an insurance company for claims investigation, rating or underwriting.
_____   For use in notifying owners of towed or impounded vehicles
_____   For use by any licensed private investigator for any purpose permitted under the DPPA.
_____   For use by an employer to obtain or verify information relating to the holder of a commercial driver license.
_____   For use in connection with the operation of private toll transportation facilities.
_____   For any other use authorized by state law, if the use relates to motor vehicle operation or public safety.

I understand the personal information furnished is confidential under Federal and State law and is being released to me only for the reason I have indicated above and that it is unlawful for me to furnish the information to an unauthorized person or entity.

Printed Name of Individual: _____ Signature: _____ Date

Representing
Printed Name of Company: _____ Address:

City: _____ State: _____ Zip: _____

DPPA-3

The Mississippi DPS form lists your reason fourth. Note how the language has been similar in most of these forms.

200

it belongs to, unless the number is unlisted. This function is also served by Criss-Cross Directories, cumbersome print books which tend to be more complete than the Web site, but it's much faster and more accessible to use the Internet version.

The United States Postal Service (USPS)

Don't overlook the post office in a search for a new address. If the witness filed a change of address form with the post office, the USPS will automatically forward mail for up to a year. If you go to one of its fee-based services, you can get address changes for up to two years after someone has moved. The downside to this service is that it is designed for bulk mailers and may not really meet your needs unless you are dealing with a fairly high volume of people you are mailing on a regular basis.

Paying for Help

Your firm may pay the fees to obtain credit reports from either the large companies who maintain these records or a local or regional company maintaining credit reports. These companies, like Equifax and Dun and Bradstreet, will issue a credit report on whomever you request if you have paid their fees and if you have a name and social security number. These reports can help you find current addresses. If you are trying to determine if a defendant has assets, the reports will also give you an idea of what assets the witness may possess. Various companies do commercial background checks as well. These companies buy data from county courthouses across the country and enter it into their database to build a comprehensive national database. For a fee, these companies will run your witness through their databases if you present name, social security number, and/or date of birth of that witness. You'll then receive information from multiple jurisdictions from one vendor.

You can also enlist the services of a private investigator or an information broker, who will perform various parts of these tasks for you. Investigators and brokers may have invested in databases that you are not willing to spend the money on, like the Social Security Administration's Death Master File, which gives the address of the last payment to any person receiving Social Security benefits, and which has a regular updating service. (Doesn't "Death Master" sound like a new video game?) The subscription price for this lovely service is a hefty $6,900—not exactly a bargain for an occasional-use item. However, there are genealogical services, such as Family Search, that will let you have relatively inexpensive access to information online on a monthly basis. The only problem with using this service is that you need to know the state where an individual's social security number was issued, not the state of last residence, in order to access information. If someone has moved since then (not unlikely), you'll have to check numerous states in order to get a hit.

INTERVIEWS

Once you've located the witness, you need to interview him or her. The best interview occurs in person; that way, you can get a feel for the person's nonverbal signals. Even a witness who says he knows nothing must be followed up if there is discovery that indicates the contrary. I am too paranoid for that; I don't trust witnesses to mean it when they say they know nothing without something in writing to verify that.

Occasionally you have no choice but to have a telephone interview, but that should be your last choice. Some writers advocate using the telephone for interviewing because it is far more economical, and it is, but the loss of quality seems too great to make up for the savings in dollars unless the witness is truly insignificant. The more witnesses you can get in your office, the better your time management. But occasionally you simply must get out and go meet the witnesses where they are.

Regardless, you will usually make your first contact with a witness by telephone; approach him by requesting his help. Coming off as demanding will alienate someone who has no driving necessity to be a part of the litigation. Instead, acknowledge that the interview is an inconvenience to the witness and that she is doing you a great service as well as performing a civic duty by explaining what happened, and that you will meet her where and when it is convenient for her. Unfortunately, that's the way it works; you have to work around the witness's schedule—not your own. Once you've established the place and time, send a confirmation letter, just as you would with a client. Calendar the meeting with all legal staff involved in the case.

Just as in the interviews of clients, you must be well-prepared. Be familiar with the appropriate interview techniques and with nonverbal communication. However, there is a key difference between interviewing a client and interviewing a witness: you do not and will not have an ongoing relationship with a fact witness that creates rights, duties, and/or obligations between you and the witness. You have to be honest up to a point, but you also cannot reveal any client confidences, and you have to be discreet about what you do say. Further, you can't promise to keep anything a witness says confidential. On the other hand, the witness owes you nothing, either, and has little incentive to go out of her way to talk to you. Although you can threaten a witness with a subpoena, that's not really a good way to get her to cooperate in a friendly way. The nice thing about civil cases is that people are a little less afraid to testify, as they're not testifying about someone who they believe is likely to try and get even. On the other hand, witnesses often don't want to "waste their time" on someone else's problem.

The exceptions are so-called "friendly" witnesses: the friends and family of the plaintiff, the boss or co-workers of the defendant, and so on. The problem with these guys is that they are *too* helpful; they have a tendency to overstate the facts in favor of whichever party they are aligned with and therefore make themselves less credible. The opposing party simply has to prove one of the exaggerations, and the jury will discount everything the witness has said. It's not that the jury will blame them or dislike them for it; they just know that it's hard to be objective under those circumstances. Think about what you'd think if you were sitting in the jury box listening to this trial on sexual harassment.

Q: So you've known the defendant for 25 years?

A: Yes.

Q: And you're telling the jury that he never had any romantic or sexual relationship other than with his wife?

A: Yes.

Q: Never?

A: That's right.

Q: Not one exception?

A: That's what I'm telling you.

Q: And you would know if there was an exception?

A: Yes, sir. I know pretty much all there is to know about Bill.

Q: That's pretty remarkable, wouldn't you say, for 25 years?

A: He's a remarkable person.

Q: And he and his wife met in high school?

A: Yes. Their junior year. And got married right after graduation.

Q: And you two were on the football team together at Dinky College?

A: Yes, sir.

Q: Then I guess you could explain to me how he got the nickname of "Rubbers" McGraw.

A: [after prolonged choking fit] Uh. . . uh. . . uh. . . well. . . —

So friends are only as good as their willingness to tell the truth, warts and all. Most friends and family members don't really want to be that honest. If you're talking to one of them, you have to explain the pitfalls. Even if the witness is honest, jurors may discount her testimony on the basis of the relationship, figuring that bias on the behalf of the friend or relative tainted the testimony.

Strangers don't have that problem, so they are usually the preferred witnesses if you can get them. However, if a stranger is eager to testify, beware: he may have an agenda. Find out what that ulterior motive is before he gets on the witness stand.

Practical Considerations

Because witnesses are not obligated to talk to you short of a subpoena, and you don't want to alienate them or scare them with the court order, you need to meet at the convenience of the witness. Going out of the office to meet a client is sometimes referred to as a **field interview.** Meeting for coffee or lunch to talk sometimes works; there's nothing unethical about buying a meal while you talk and it sometimes makes the inconvenience of the discussion go down a little easier. Twenty-four hour coffee shops are great places: no one usually cares if you stay at a table for a long time, and if you ask, waitpersons will often give you one larger than you really need for two people. Meet at a location convenient to the witness but one where you feel comfortable as well.

Why at a restaurant? Your personal safety. You have no idea who the witness is, what kind of person he or she is, or who he or she lives with, or anything else yet. It is far safer for you to meet in a well-lit, public place, particularly if you are meeting at an odd time of day or night. It also reassures the witness. How bad can the interview be if you're meeting at an IHOP? A neutral location grants neither person the upper hand in a psychological sense, and gives the witness the sense that he can leave at any time.

Another possibility is to meet at the location where the incident on which the lawsuit is based occurred. Using a digital video camera, you can record the conversation on the audio and get a clear fix on what the witness is describing. You can also pick out any stills you may want later. In places where there is a great deal of background noise, make sure you have adequate microphone capacity to pick up the witness's voice and not just the ambient noise. Taping gives you the additional advantage of showing the witness to the attorney if you think there are any particular issues regarding his credibility, good or bad. Conveying how really great a witness is who is going to kill your case is as important as describing one who is helpful.

Make sure you schedule enough time to talk. An hour may be enough for an automobile case; however, for a more complicated situation, you may need more time. Take everything you might need. That means not only your business cards, writing pad, pens, and pencils, but any photographs or documents you may need to reference or may want the witness to authenticate. If there's a location you'll want the witness to describe, have him draw it, and have him sign and date the drawing. That way, if he wants to deny knowledge later, he'll also have to deny his signature. Take any documents you might want him to sign. Take your calendar, in case you have to schedule a second meeting.

It makes sense in today's technological world to take a laptop computer, a printer, and a portable scanner to the interview. That way you can take any statements you need, edit any documents you need to for the witness to sign, and make copies of any documents the witness brings along as well as providing copies of anything the witness has prepared for her to take with her. It also makes it easier to add witnesses to your database later if you are storing all of your client's information electronically. Unless you've got one of those nifty laptops that let you take notes on the cover, though, I'd take notes on paper. An open laptop puts a barrier between you and the witness that makes it harder to talk.

Ask the witness if you can record the conversation, but note that many witnesses will become more stilted and less open if the conversation is recorded. Remember, too, that you should not record the conversation without your attorney's prior approval. Fortunately, this initial hesitation often fades as the conversation ensues, but make sure that you have recorded the witness's permission as the conversation begins and ends, using something along the lines of the following script that models a suggested approach.

Paralegal: This is Paula Paralegal and I am interviewing William Witness at the International Hut of Pasta, in Littleton, New Bigstate, on November 3, 2004, at 12:30 P.M. Mr. Witness, do I have your permission to record this interview?

Witness: Yes.

✷ ✷ ✷ ✷ ✷ ✷

Paralegal: This is Paula Paralegal and this concludes the interview of William Witness on November 3, 2004, at 2:10 p.m., in Littleton, New Bigstate. Mr. Witness, did you freely give your permission to record this interview?

Witness: Yes.

Rather than using one of the magnetic tapes or even digital recorders that are prone to run out before you are done, beginning another period of awkwardness, use one of the newer technologies developed for music storage. I like Creative Labs Nomad Jukebox, which allows you to record from a table microphone or over the phone if you have the right attachment.

What to Tell

You should, of course, explain (again) that you are a paralegal and not an attorney. This precaution avoids problems of holding yourself out as an attorney when you are not one. Give the witness a card. If suit has been filed, tell the witness that you are investigating the facts of the lawsuit between the parties, and name them. Identify the attorney and client for whom you work. Make sure the witness understands you want the truth, and that you are not there to be told what the witness thinks you want to hear. Don't tell the witness any more than you need to in order to identify the occurrence so that she can understand how her information is relevant. Your reticence serves two purposes: first, it avoids planting ideas in the mind of the witness and second, it protects you from disclosing confidential information.

What to Ask

The flippant answer to "What do I ask?" is "Everything," but that's not terribly helpful. Here are the basic items you should always cover:

- contact information of the witness
- date of birth and SSN of the witness (sometimes the witness will be reluctant to give that information; explain that in case the trial takes a while and the witness moves, you'll use the information to find him later)
- the relationship of the witness to each party
- if the witness observed a certain event, what she was doing immediately prior to the incident and factors that may have affected her point of view
- if the witness has been a part of an ongoing situation, her beliefs or points of view that may affect testimony
- if the witness is a damages witness, the basis of opinions about damages: frequency of observation, before and after, etc.

Have your questions prepared ahead of time, just as you would for a client interview, making sure you know what issues are at stake and what story you are trying to tell. Review the file carefully enough to be familiar with any contested facts. Listen to the witness's answers closely enough to be ready to pursue an unforeseen area of discussion that deviates from your preparation. If the witness says something you don't quite understand, review the information until you do understand it: Don't be afraid to not know something; knowledge is what you are trying to gain here. Make sure you cover the journalistic who, what, when, where, how, and why questions.

How to Ask

In discussing initial client interviews, open-ended questions, closed questions, cognitive interviewing, and nonverbal cues were addressed. The way that leading questions and even the wording of questions could suggest answers was also addressed.

Suggestibility and certainty are issues that need to be explored a bit more. When you talk to a witness, you want to get as much out of the witness as possible, and you want it to be accurate. It serves no one's purpose for a witness to make statements that will later be irremediably impeached. The better interviewer will strive not to suggest things to the witness, but to help the witness clarify matters for himself.

To figure out how best to do that, let's examine the reasons witnesses have **false memories** or otherwise change their answers (not all psychologists believe that the change is a result of a false memory). First, psychologists point to the problem of "expert pressure." If a witness feels pressure from an authority figure or expert (such as the paralegal in the context of these interviews) that he is not testifying "well" or "correctly," he may change his answers to try to please the expert. If a quantitative question is phrased in a way that implies no limit, the amounts tend to be higher than if there is a limit. The longer the time lapse between the event and the testimony, the more error there is likely to be in the witness's testimony (not a real surprise to anyone). Different psychological types appear to be more prone to suggestions from investigators as well. One study indicated that introverted people—those who gather information indirectly and through reflection rather than from their observations—are far more susceptible to suggestion than those who are extroverts—those who interact directly with the world around them.

If the event upon which the litigation is based was traumatic, the witness may have suffered from **weapons focus,** in which he concentrated solely on the threat to the exclusion of details surrounding it. If the witness was preoccupied or anxious before the event, he may not have taken in all the details. In either of these situations, the mind tends to fill in the gaps or missing parts, just as you can see faces in woodgrain: our minds are made to recognize patterns. People will often think they have seen things because they can't quite deal with the blank. In filling in the blank, they often resort to the familiar, which will lead to misidentification of people and other sorts of incorrect recollections.

So, to start, you need to take several measures. Reassure the witness that it is okay not to remember every detail; you are simply asking to see if he does. Use the cognitive interviewing technique of letting the witness place himself in time through recalling sensory and mood details. Let the witness start with a broad recollection of his own before you pose any questions. Be supportive, not judging. When you do begin to probe, phrase questions as neutrally as possible. Don't ask, "Was the car going north?" which suggests it was; ask "Which way was the car going?" If you suspect the witness is filling in details he does not know with certainty, ask about his mental state immediately before and during the incident. See if you can get an admission that he was preoccupied or fixated on the threat. In short, do everything you can to undermine the psychological tendencies of a witness to unknowingly fabricate his statement.

The Witness Who Knows Nothing

Sometimes you may try to establish contact with a witness who will keep dodging you. When you finally do speak with him, he might say, "I don't know anything about it." The answer to this is not to say "Oh. Thanks," and then to leave him alone. The answer is to say, "Well, sir, I understand that and I'd like to arrange it so you won't be bothered anymore. The problem is that you've been identified as someone who has knowledge, so I need something to say you don't. Would you mind signing something for me that says that you don't have any knowledge of the incident?" Often the witness will agree to do so. In that case, take an affidavit to your meeting with him; he can sign this statement, which basically says he knows nothing relevant.

It's quite possible that the witness may know more than he's letting on, but you need to protect yourself from a surprise appearance by this guy later. If he signs the affidavit and later shows up to give a lengthy story about what happened, and his statement hurts your client, you can use the affidavit to impeach him.

> **Q:** So, Mr. Mann, you are telling us here today that you have perfect recall of all these events that happened over two years ago?
>
> **A:** Oh, yes.
>
> **Q:** Would you agree, Mr. Mann, that events are remembered most clearly right after they occur?
>
> **A:** [suspiciously] Uh, yeah.
>
> **Q:** So what someone remembers, oh, a year after an event is probably clearer than two years after?
>
> **A:** [slowly] Probably.
>
> **Q:** And six months after, even clearer?
>
> **A:** I would think so, yeah.
>
> **Q:** I'm handing you what's been marked Plaintiff's Exhibit #22. Do you recognize the signature?
>
> **A:** [resigned] It's mine.
>
> **Q:** And what did you sign?
>
> **A:** An affidavit that I didn't know anything about this case.
>
> **Q:** And you signed that only 8 months after the event, isn't that right?
>
> **A:** Umm, yeah.
>
> **Q:** No further questions.

The affidavit can be very helpful. Don't forget to obtain one.

State of Confusion   §
County of Dux   §

AFFIDAVIT

Walt Witness appeared in person before me today and stated under oath:

"My name is Walt Witness. I am competent to make this affidavit and am over the age of 18. The facts stated in this affidavit are within my personal knowledge and are true and correct.

"I reside at 2001 Washington Avenue, Big City, Confusion 99999. I have been contacted by the attorneys for Patti Haus to give information regarding the incident which occurred at Vista Libre Apartments, 2000 Washington Avenue, Big City, Confusion on [date]. I have no knowledge of the incident or of any circumstances relating to the incident. I am not connected to John Justice, Vista Libre Apartments, or Patti Haus in any way.

"I have not been contacted by any other person or entity involved in this incident."

Further, Affiant sayeth not.

_____

Walt Witness

State of Confusion   §
County of Dux   §

SIGNED under oath by Walt Witness before me on [date].

_____

Notary Public, State of Confusion

A sample affidavit. It would usually appear in Courier type.

WITNESS STATEMENTS

At times you will need **witness statements.** These are sometimes valuable in support of various motions, such as ex parte protective orders or motions for summary judgment. Witness statements should be drafted in a particular format and with some magic words, but the rest of the wording should be as close to the witness's language as possible. The magic words are usually "I have personal knowledge of these facts," "these facts are true and correct," and "I am over the age of 18." You may also want a witness statement to memorialize the witness's testimony if she has said something important that you do not want to lose or have her word differently before you can get her deposed. Although the form is not as prescribed in this instance, it's better practice to follow the same format you would if you were going to file the statement as an affidavit.

Caption the affidavit as you would any other document filed in the case, with the cause number, parties, and court information. Head the affidavit as "Affidavit of" and then fill in the name of the witness. The paragraph should begin with the following boilerplate (or something similar—your jurisdiction's customs may require slightly different wording):

On this the _____ day of Month, in Big City, Medium County, State, came [Winnifred Witness] and under oath avowed and averred the following:

"My name is [Winnifred Witness] and I am [22] years of age. I have personal knowledge of all the facts stated in this affidavit.

Each paragraph thereafter should start with a quotation mark. State what of importance the witness has to say. When you come to the last paragraph, close with quotation marks, and have the final paragraph read "Further affiant sayeth not," without quotes. The witness should sign on a signature line after being put under oath. Include a notary's line that indicates that the witness stated all the foregoing under oath before you—assuming, of course, that you are a notary public. It is difficult to take care of these field interviews without

State of Confusion   §
County of Dux   §

AFFIDAVIT

Ethel Cartwright appeared in person before me today and stated under oath:

"My name is Ethel Cartwright. I am competent to make this affidavit and am over the age of 18. The facts stated in this affidavit are within my personal knowledge and are true and correct.

"I reside at 2000 Washington Avenue, Apartment 212, Big City, Confusion 99999. I live next door to Patti Haus and Jerry Smoker in the Vista Libre Apartments, who lived in Apartment 214. On many occasions I have had to contact the police because of disturbances in their apartment.

"I have heard Mr. Smoker threaten to injure or kill Ms. Haus on several occasions. I have also heard him say that he would get revenge on John Justice, the security officer at Vista Libre, whom I have asked on several occasions to escort me to my car or to my apartment because I was afraid of Mr. Smoker.

"I have not seen Mr. Smoker at the apartment since [day after occurrence]. Ms. Haus was crying that day, and she told me that it was Mr. Justice's fault that Mr. Smoker broke up with her."

Further, Affiant sayeth not.

_____
Ethel Cartwright

State of Confusion   §
County of Dux   §

SIGNED under oath by Ethel Cartwright before me on [date].

_____
Notary Public, State of Confusion

Another affidavit for the *Haus v. Justice* case.

being one; often the firm you work for will pick up the bill for your becoming one. (Now I'm past hinting—underline this and ask your boss to take care of it.)

WITNESS SUMMARIES

Just as you prepared a summary of your meeting with the client, you will summarize your meeting with each witness. Not only do you need to recount what the witness had to say, you need to analyze her importance as both an asset and a liability; you must also assess her credibility. Do so by detailing specific facts about the witness's appearance and nonverbal communication. Complete this as quickly as possible after meeting the witness, while all the details are still fresh. Again, update all your investigation plan documents to reflect the new information you've received and decide if the plan needs any modification.

COST CONSIDERATIONS

The costs you generally take into consideration for fact witnesses are costs of your time and any outlay for finding them. As a rule, you do not pay for any costs associated with fact witnesses, although you may cover their expenses in some circumstances, such as when a witness must travel from out of state. Remember: the ethical constraint is that you may not pay a fact witness so as to induce her to testify in a particular way, but you may

MEMORANDUM

To: Thomas Battle

From: Frances Morehead

Date: [Today]

Re: *Haus v. Justice & Vista Libre Apartments*, Cause No. 05-CI-101010, 225th Dist. Court

Today I met with Ethel Cartwright, the next-door neighbor of the Plaintiff, at her home. She lives at 2000 Washington Avenue, Apartment 212, Big City, Confusion 99999. Patti Haus and Jerry Smoker lived in Apartment 214. She is a petite lady in her 80s with short white-gray hair. She was dressed in a lime green polyester pantsuit—the kind common in the 1960s. She was very alert, and had no difficulty hearing or understanding what I was saying. She recently had a fall and broke her ankle, so she has difficulty getting around.

Mrs. (she was quite emphatic about that) Cartwright remembers the plaintiff and her former live-in boyfriend, Jerry Smoker, quite well. She described each of them very accurately. She was not aware that Mr. Smoker's real name was Geronimo. She said that she was very afraid of Mr. Smoker, but had called the police several times when she heard crashing and yelling next door. She said she had often seen Ms. Haus with bruises after one of these incidents, but that every time the police showed up, Ms. Haus would plead with them not to take them away, and then "curse them roundly" whenever they did arrest Mr. Smoker. She could not give specific dates or the number of times she had called the police, but believed it was "almost every couple of weeks" in the four months the couple lived there.

Mrs. Cartwright also said that she had heard Mr. Smoker threaten to injure or kill Ms. Haus on several occasions, mostly through the wall of the apartment. She also heard Mr. Smoker say that he would "get revenge on John Justice," the security officer at Vista Libre. She stated that Mr. Justice often had intervened in situations before the police officers showed up, but that it was okay because "he's a police officer, too." She said that Mr. Justice was not in uniform any of the times she saw him get involved in the situation. She would watch through the window for the police to arrive any time she reported the disturbances. Because she was also afraid of retaliation, although she had never heard Mr. Smoker threaten her, she asked Mr. Justice to escort her to her car or to her apartment on several occasions.

Mrs. Cartwright heard Ms. Haus "crash into the entrance sign," but was too far away to hear any of the conversation that night. She saw Ms. Haus get out of the pick-up and then saw Mr. Justice run up to her. She said there was lots of arm-waving by Ms. Haus, and that Mr. Justice left for a moment, and then returned with something in his hand. At that point she stopped watching.

Mrs. Cartwright reports that she has not seen Mr. Smoker at the apartment since the day after the accident with the pick-up truck and the entrance sign. She said that Ms. Haus was crying that day, and told her it was Mr. Justice's fault that Mr. Smoker broke up with her.

I believe Mrs. Cartwright would make an above average witness. She was thoughtful, but not unsure, about her answers, and had no difficulty answering any question with "I don't know" when necessary.

A typical witness summary.

defray expenses. Regardless of what type of billing arrangement you have with your client, the number of witnesses and the extent of your time spent on each will be governed by the value of the case. It doesn't make sense to spend $10,000 worth of your time on a case that's only worth $10,000 if the jury gives you everything you ask for. On the other hand, $10,000 is a fairly small amount to spend on a case worth $1,000,000. In a family law case, where there may not be money at stake (in child custody disputes, for instance), the client's budget must be taken into consideration. How much investigation can the client really afford? Can you track down every single possible lead? You must, of course, check out all that are reasonable under the circumstances, but it is not necessary—or even possible—to turn over every available rock.

CHAPTER SUMMARY

Fact witnesses may be neutral, friendly, hostile, or official. They all share the basic trait of having personal knowledge of the facts of a case. You must be straight with them; you cannot record their conversations without their knowledge or pretend to be someone else. You have to inform a fact witness that you are a paralegal and explain whom you represent and obtain information before recording them. Some potential witnesses will not be able to talk to you without a release or court order because their knowledge about the case is gained through privileged communications with the opposing party: the doctor, the psychologist, the priest or clergyman, a reporter, or a former attorney. To find a witness, you may have to go through court records, tax records, the DMV, the USPS, the state correctional system, private credit databases, or a private investigator. Once you find a witness, you need to set up an interview much like one with a client, but you are constrained from discussing anything with the witness that may possibly expose any confidential matters to him. You do not owe the witness any duties, although you must act ethically. You will need to prepare according to whether you are meeting in the office (which would be the same as for a client) or going to a field interview. Field interviews should always be held in public in a location conducive to your asking questions about the incident. Appropriate questions need to be prepared after review of the file, and should be asked in such a way as to avoid creating false memories in those individuals susceptible to suggestion. A witness statement may be generated after the interview; a witness summary for the attorney always will. In deciding how and how many witnesses to interview, costs must be taken into consideration, and although face-to-face interviews are preferred and optimal, client budget issues may necessitate telephone interviews from time to time.

FOR FURTHER READING

Marguerita B. Dolatly, *Note and Comment: Creating Evidence: Ethical Concerns, Evidentiary Problems, and the Application of Work Product Protection to Audio Recordings of Nonparty Witnesses Secretly Made by Attorneys or Their Agents*, 22 Rutgers Computer & Tech. L.J. 521 (1996).

Chad Horner, *Note: Beyond the Confines of the Confessional: The Priest-Penitent Privilege in a Diverse Society*, 45 Drake L. Rev. 697 (1997).

Thomas J. Lipscomb, Hunter A. McAllister, and Norman J. Bregman, *Bias in Eyewitness Accounts: The Effects of Question Format, Delay Interval, and Stimulus Presentation*, 119 J. of Psych. 207 (2001).

Kathleen M. Maynard, *1997 John M. Manos Writing Competition on Evidence: The Psychotherapist-Patient Privilege: A Rational Approach to Defining "Psychotherapist,"* 45 Clev. St. L. Rev. 405 (1997).

Carol A. Remler, *Note: Academic Freedom Privilege: An Excessive Solution to the Problem of Protecting Confidentiality*, 51 U. Cin. L. Rev. 326 (1982).

Rachel Roper and David Shewan, *Compliance and Eyewitness Testimony: Do Eyewitnesses Comply with Misleading "Expert Pressure" During Investigative Interviewing?* 7 Leg. & Crim. Psych. 155 (2002).

Brenda V. Thompson, *Comment: Corporate Ombudsmen and Privileged Communications: Should Employee Communications to Corporate Ombudsmen Be Entitled to Privilege?* 61 U. Cin. L. Rev. 653 (1992).

Roger A. Ward and Elizabeth F. Loftus, *Eyewitness Performance in Different Psychological Types*, 112 J. of Gen. Psych. 191 (1985).

Euphemia B. Warren, Notes, *She's Gotta Have It Now: A Qualified Rape Crisis Counselor-Victim Privilege*, 17 Cardozo L. Rev. 141 (1995).

CHAPTER REVIEW

KEY TERMS

attorney-client privilege	hostile witness	psychotherapist-patient privilege
crime-fraud exception	neutral witness	registration number
ex parte communications	official witness	reporter's privilege
fact witnesses	peer review committee privilege	reverse look-up
false memories	physician-patient privilege	State Identification Number (SID)
field interview	priest-penitent privilege	weapons focus
friendly witness	privilege	witness statements

FILL IN THE BLANKS

1. One type of _____ is one who is friendly to the other side.
2. Not only confessions, but also discussions between a Protestant pastor and a member of his congregation are protected from discovery under the _____.
3. If you have a phone number but no address, you can use a(n) _____ to find where the call came from.
4. _____ is a technique of interviewing that is witness-centered, allowing her to begin at a point before the event started and giving her control over the process.
5. A(n) _____ is a sworn written statement taken before a notary.
6. A legal right not to disclose certain communications or types of information is called a(n) _____.
7. A(n) _____ is one with personal knowledge of facts relevant to the litigation or those calculated to lead to relevant facts.
8. A question that suggests the answer is a(n) _____.
9. You ask _____ that can be answered yes or no either to control an interview or to mop up some details.
10. There is no constitutional _____; it is only granted by state statute.
11. The evidentiary privilege that attaches to communications between counsel and clients is the _____ privilege.
12. To find someone with a criminal record, you need his _____.
13. A _____ has nothing to gain from litigation and is not aligned with any party.
14. Tone of voice, facial expression, and body movement constitute _____.
15. To memorialize what the witness said, you may want to take a(n) _____ under oath and have the witness sign it.
16. A witness can develop _____ if they are suggested to him and he is vulnerable to suggestion.
17. The discussion between a patient and his therapist (mental, not physical) is protected by the _____.
18. The discussions between a patient and her doctor are protected by the _____.
19. _____ invite the witness to elaborate freely on the subject.
20. Although _____ often refers to one side communicating with a judge, it can refer to any communication by one party without the other's presence.
21. _____ protects the records of a hospital's procedure of examining a doctor's background to allow her to practice medicine at its facility.
22. A(n) _____ is usually perceived as neutral, and his position often gives him increased stature in the eyes of the jury.
23. A fact witness aligned with your side is referred to as a(n) _____.
24. Talking to a witness outside the office is sometimes called a(n) _____.
25. The _____ allows attorneys to breach confidentiality when they are reasonably certain a client is going to do something that is reasonably certain to cause serious harm or death.

WEB WORK

1. Go to www.usps.com/nationalpremieraccounts/manageprocessandaddress.htm and see the requirements for using the address updating services. Would it be worthwhile for a small firm to use the U.S. Post Office's service?

2. Go to www.co.washoe.nv.us/recorder/ and click on the icon indicated to access the deed records. Register as a new user; it's free. When you get to the search page, enter your last name in the Query by Name space; note that the instructions tell you to enter last name first and to use no comma. How many hits do you get? What sorts of documents? What information can you access about any particular individual you locate? Try some other common names and see what you can find.

3. Go to www.countyclerk.bexar.landata.com/ and click on the Assumed Names button. Choose the option of searching by Business Name and enter "Taco Cabana." What do the documents tell you about that business (at least in the past)? As long as you're at this Web site, try the UCC filings. Figure out how to use this site and determine what you can find out from it.

4. Go to www.asr.co.pima.az.us/apiq/index.cfm and type in "Salazar" as the taxpayer. What do you find? Try your last name. Do you find anyone there with your name? A place to look for other tax assessor offices online is http://www.pulawski.com/, which divides them by state and indicates those with search features in bold. It doesn't seem to be comprehensive, but it is at least one reference to check out.

5. Go to www.anywho.com and click on the reverse look-up. Enter your telephone number and those of people you know. Did the addresses come up? If not, why not?

WORKING THE BRAIN

1. The privilege protecting communications to clergy is rooted in the First Amendment's free exercise clause. However, when there is a statute that requires anyone who knows of a crime (such as child abuse) to report it, there is a conflict between privilege and the constitutional right. How should that conflict be resolved: in favor of keeping the communication private, or in favor of reporting the crime?

2. Several reasons were given for unconscious fabrication of witness statements. Can you think of more? How would you test your hypothesis? Why would a non-party consciously fabricate testimony?

3. Do you think the stated policy reasons for the various privileges are legitimate? Do you think society would be better served by limiting or abolishing any of them? Which ones? Do you think additional ones should be created? Why? Which ones?

4. If you were preparing for a meeting with a witness at a public location, what would you do to ensure that you had all the materials you needed? What methods besides those mentioned in the text would you use to organize and prepare for the meeting?

5. How do you feel about the prohibition against hidden tape recorders during interviews? How do you feel about the prohibition against your pretending you are someone else in order to find witnesses who are hiding? Do you think it is a good idea that legal staff can't do that, or do you think it is unfair because private investigators use the same techniques regularly? Why is a distinction made, do you think? Is the distinction justified?

PUTTING IT TO WORK

1. Visit your local courthouse and locate where the various materials discussed in the chapter are filed. Determine how to access them. Go to the local DMV and find out what forms you have to fill out to get driving history or driver's license information. Go to the tax assessor to find what you need to do to use those resources. At each of these places, find out how much information anyone could obtain about you. You may be surprised at how easily a stranger could find out a good deal of information that you think is private or personal.

2. Pick four non-celebrities out of the local daily newspaper. See how much you can find out about them from your county courthouse and any online resources you have available.

SPECIAL ISSUES WITH WITNESSES

> "Grown-ups never understand anything for themselves, and it is tiresome for children to be always and forever explaining things to them."
>
> *Antoine de Saint-Exupéry (1943)*
>
> "It is easier for eight or nine elderly men to feel their way towards unanimity if they are not compelled to conduct their converging maneuvers under the microscopes of the press, but are permitted to shuffle about a little in slippers."
>
> *Herbert A. L. Fisher (1921)*
>
> "Common sense is not so common."
>
> *Voltaire (1764)*
>
> "It is more of a job to interpret the interpretations than to interpret the things."
>
> *Michel de Montaigne (1595)*

INTRODUCTION

Some witnesses present particular problems that must be addressed carefully but directly. You cannot afford to ignore problems with a witness; you must bring such problems out in the open. How you do so will greatly influence how the problem is resolved. These problems are not those they are coming to have resolved by the legal team, but those issues that relate to who the client is: age, disability, language, culture, and race. These attributes of a client or witness may or may not present a problem, but any time the client is not the average Joe or Jane Citizen the attribute must be reviewed for potential problems.

ETHICAL ISSUES

A client is in charge of his or her legal interests per Rule 1.2, which states in the pertinent part that "a lawyer shall abide by a client's decisions concerning the objectives of representation."

However, when you have a client who is acting against what he has expressed as his desires for a long period of time, after aging or some traumatic brain injury or disabling neurological disorder or similar disease, what is the ethical course of action? Take, for example, the client who has always expressed the desire to live in his home until the day he dies and then leave it to his wife so "she can live her days out in comfort." One day he shows up in the office wanting to give himself a life estate in the house and make his cat the remainderman. Is it ethical to carry out the client's wishes? If you don't, will another lawyer simply do it, not knowing the history of the client? Say you ask questions and find out that the client's relationship with his wife is fine; he's just concerned about the welfare of the cat because it's been a great comfort to him, and no one else in the family really cares about it. Is that a reason to worry? And if you decide that there is reason for concern for the client's competency, what measures can you take without violating confidentiality?

Client Wishes and the Incompetent Client

If the client is clearly incompetent, unable to make any coherent, reasonable decisions in regard to serious issues with knowledge of possible risks and benefits, the rules do have an out. (Any of us is arguably incompetent in some area—most of us act irrationally in some area of our lives, so the rules to find someone incompetent or lacking **capacity** are fairly stringent.) Model Rule 1.14 allows a lawyer who reasonably believes her client cannot act in his own interest to seek the appointment of a guardian or take "other protective action." This leaves an awful lot of wiggle room. "Reasonable belief" is a rather slippery standard to begin with, and how does one determine whether someone "cannot" act "in his own interest"? There are those who have perfect comprehension of who their loved ones are, but no idea of their finances. What interests are we speaking of? The lawyer's? Granted, it is helpful to have someone else responsible for those determinations, and if the client has a spouse, that may avoid problems down the line. Here's the Restatement (Third) of Law Governing Lawyers (2000) summary of what is supposed to be the law (but may not be):

1. When a client's capacity to make adequately considered decisions in connection with the representation is diminished . . . the lawyer must, as far as reasonably possible, maintain a normal client-lawyer relationship with the client and act in the best interests of the client as stated in Subsection (2).

2. A lawyer representing a client with diminished capacity . . . and for whom no guardian or other representative is available to act, must, with respect to a matter within the scope of the representation, pursue the lawyer's reasonable view of the client's objectives or interests as the client would define them if able to make adequately considered decisions on the matter, even if the client expresses no wishes or gives contrary instructions.

3. If a client with diminished capacity . . . has a guardian or other person legally entitled to act for the client, the client's lawyer must treat that person as entitled to act with respect to the client's interests in the matter, unless:

   a. the lawyer represents the client in a matter against the interests of that person; or

   b. that person instructs the lawyer to act in a manner that the lawyer knows will violate the person's legal duties toward the client.

4. A lawyer representing a client with diminished capacity . . . may seek the appointment of a guardian or take other protective action within the scope of the representation when doing so is practical and will advance the client's objectives or interests as stated in Subsection (2).

Restatement (3d) of Law Governing Lawyers § 24 (2000).

Bottom line: If you suspect a client may be incompetent, you need to alert the attorney as soon as possible. Before you jump to any conclusions, be sure that you have asked questions whose answers might explain the odd changes, comments, or behavior that have elicited your concern. **Dementia,** the symptom identified with Alzheimer's disease (the most common disease process causing dementia in the elderly) requires the symptoms listed on the next page for a clinical diagnosis.

When it is diagnosed, however, even Alzheimer's does not automatically render someone incompetent to handle her affairs. Instances of temporary dementia also make it difficult to declare incompetency for legal purposes. How long the dementia will last and whether it is reversible depends on its causation,

---

DIAGNOSTIC CRITERIA FOR DEMENTIA

1. Demonstrable evidence of impairment in short- and long-term memory
2. At least one of the following:

   Impairment in abstract thinking
   Impaired judgment
   Other disturbances of higher cortical function, such as aphasia, apraxia (inability to carry out motor activities despite intact comprehension and motor function), agnosia (failure to recognize or identify objects despite intact sensory function), and "constructional difficulty" (e.g., difficulty copying a geometrical figure)

3. Personality change
4. The above disturbances significantly interfere with work or usual social activities or relationships with others
5. Not occurring exclusively during the course of delirium

DSM-IV lists the elements of dementia.

so even if you have a client meeting all of the criteria presented earlier, more investigation is necessary before undertaking anything as drastic as a guardianship proceeding. Even when a family member wants a guardianship proceeding, things can get ugly, and you must keep up with the current status of the client, as the following case illustrates.

Colorado v. Bottinelli, 926 P.2d 553 (Colo. 1996) (per curiam).

This is a lawyer discipline case . . . The charges of misconduct against him all arise from the respondent's participation as counsel in a probate case . . . for the guardianship and conservatorship of Ruth Claire Otterpohl . . . In 1990, then seventy-four-year-old Ruth Otterpohl was diagnosed by her treating physicians as suffering from depression and dementia. Otterpohl's only daughter, Kathleen Jenson, hired attorney Robert Fisher, in May 1990, to petition the El Paso County Probate Court for guardianship and conservatorship of her mother. Before filing the petition, Kathleen Jenson had placed her mother in a nursing home.

The probate matter was originally assigned to Commissioner (now Magistrate) E. David Griffith. The commissioner appointed Tristan Bonn as the guardian ad litem. Commissioner Griffith initially recused himself when he became aware that Kathleen Jenson's lawyer, Robert Fisher, was associated as counsel for the plaintiff in a personal injury case in which Griffith was a defendant. The probate case was reassigned to El Paso County Court Judge Rebecca Bromley, who routinely handled probate matters as acting district court judge when necessary. Jenson later became dissatisfied with Fisher, discharged him, and hired the respondent.

The respondent filed a motion for continuance of the competency hearing, which was set for September 1990, since the setting was less than thirty days away when he was retained. At the hearing on the motion for continuance, Otterpohl's lawyer, Jack Scheuerman, called Jenson's former lawyer, Fisher, to testify. Scheuerman and Fisher had previously discussed that Fisher would be called. At the hearing, Fisher passed a note to Scheuerman and sat beside Otterpohl's granddaughter Karen Constantini, who was opposing her mother on the issue of Otterpohl's competency. Judge Bromley denied the respondent's motion for continuance, and the hearing on Otterpohl's competency remained set for September 24–26, 1990.

The probate court had appointed Arthur Roberts, M.D., to evaluate Otterpohl, and on or about June 14, 1990, Dr. Roberts issued a written report to the probate court, stating that in his opinion Otterpohl was doing significantly better and was no longer incompetent. The respondent sought a second medical evaluation by one of Otterpohl's treating physicians, but Judge Bromley instead appointed Scott Sickbert, M.D., to conduct a second evaluation on behalf of the court. Dr. Sickbert also found Otterpohl competent.

Because Fisher had withdrawn, the underlying reason for the commissioner's disqualification no longer applied, so the case was again assigned to Commissioner Griffith, who presided at the September 24–26, 1990, hearing. During the hearing, Dr. Sickbert examined Otterpohl again and testified that she was competent, as did Dr. Roberts.

The respondent questioned Otterpohl regarding statements she had made to Dr. Roberts concerning the size of her estate. Commissioner Griffith interrupted the proceedings and chastised the respondent in chambers for what the commissioner believed was an attempt to trick the elderly woman. During the respondent's questioning of Otterpohl, he also showed her a teddy bear which had a very strong emotional significance for her.

At the conclusion of the hearing, Commissioner Griffith found Otterpohl competent, and the case was continued until December 1990 to determine the reasonable attorney fees to be paid by the Otterpohl estate and to address certain other matters, including whether Jenson should restore to Otterpohl any property or funds taken from her accounts. [A special guardian ad item] also recommended that the court assess fees against the respondent and his client Kathleen Jenson for maintaining frivolous and groundless positions in the proceedings . . .

During the course of the proceedings, the respondent filed numerous motions alleging a conspiracy among Commissioner Griffith, Judge Bromley, El Paso County District Court Judge Donald Campbell, and various Colorado Springs lawyers, against his clients.

On or about June 19, 1991, District Court Judge Campbell found that the respondent and his clients, the Jensons, had resisted the efficient closing of the Otterpohl estate.

. . . [T]he hearing board found that the respondent repeatedly made false accusations of judicial misconduct against Commissioner Griffith, Judge Bromley, and Judge Campbell. For example, the respondent filed a motion in the probate proceeding entitled, "Motion for Stay of Order Dated February 5, 1991, and for Stay of Hearing Scheduled for April 11, 1991, Pending Application for Writs Pursuant to C.A.R. 21, to the Colorado Supreme Court, and Order of Stay." In the motion, the respondent alleged that Kathleen Jenson's efforts to protect her Mother from being falsely imprisoned and undly [sic] influenced by Karen Constantini have been thwarted by repeated acts of judicial misconduct by the Honorable Donald E. Campbell, the Honorable Rebecca Bromley, and Commissioner E. David Griffith, including the participation by all said judges and commissioner in approximately fifteen ex parte meetings with attorneys opposed to Kathleen Jenson in the instant cause. . . .

At the disciplinary hearing, Commissioner Griffith and Judges Bromley and Campbell testified that they did not engage in ex parte conversations with any of the lawyers or litigants in the probate matter, except for a few scheduling discussions the hearing board determined were not improper and which provided the respondent with no basis for the charges in his motion.

The respondent also filed a "Petition for Relief in the Nature of Mandamus, Prohibition and Habeas Corpus Pursuant to C.A.R. 21" in *Jenson v. District Court*, No. 91SA65 (Colo. filed Feb. 21, 1991). The petition claimed that "members of [a forensic] network conspired to deny Kathleen Jenson a fair trial."

The respondent also alleged the appearance of "a common scheme between [sic] Jack Scheuerman, Tristan Bonn, Clifton Kruse, Robert Fisher, Michael Gross, the Honorable Rebecca Bromley, Commissioner E. David Griffith, and the Honorable Donald E. Campbell, to oppose the petition of Kathleen Jenson for guardianship and conservatorship over her Mother's person and affairs." Moreover, the petition stated, "As offensive as Robert Fisher's role has been in this matter, it is pale in comparison to the judicial misconduct of Commissioner E. David Griffith." The board summarized the respondent's allegations concerning Commissioner Griffith "as allegations that Commissioner Griffith was orchestrating the outcome" of the proceeding.

According to the respondent's petition, Judge Campbell "appears to be attempting to conceal the misconduct of Commissioner Griffith and Judge Bromley." Also:

> The order [by Judge Campbell] then affirmed all prior orders in effect in this case and ignored the judicial misconduct which is replete in this matter. The Honorable Donald E. Campbell has therefore ignored a duty he has as Chief Judge to supervise judges and commissioners who work under him, and to discipline them for misconduct. The respondent also alleged in the petition that the "conspirators," including the judicial officers, had "commenced a campaign to slander the integrity of Kathleen Jenson, Kenneth Jenson and their family as a diversion to conceal the conspirators' misconduct."

. . . The hearing board specifically found that all of the above "accusations of collusive, conspiratorial conduct, of a cover-up, of a forensic network and the like were untrue, and that [the respondent] had no basis in fact to make any of these allegations." The respondent thereby violated DR 1-102(A)(4) (a lawyer shall not engage in conduct involving dishonesty, fraud, deceit, or misrepresentation); DR 1-102(A)(5) (a lawyer shall not engage in conduct prejudicial to the administration of justice); DR 1-102(A)(6) (a lawyer shall not engage in conduct that adversely reflects on the lawyer's fitness to practice law); DR 7-102(A)(5) (in representing a client, a lawyer shall not knowingly make a false statement of law or fact); and DR 8-102(B) (a lawyer shall not knowingly make false accusations against a judge or other adjudicatory officer).

. . . Two members of the hearing board recommended that the respondent be suspended for two years. The presiding officer recommended that the respondent be disbarred, as did the hearing panel . . . A number of factors persuade us that disbarment is warranted.

Were this the first time that the respondent had engaged in this type of misconduct, a period of suspension might be appropriate . . . The respondent, however, has engaged in such conduct before, and has been suspended for it, with no apparent effect on his subsequent behavior . . . [T]his same respondent was suspended for six months for similar misconduct. The respondent falsely represented in pleadings to a district court and in a letter to the grievance committee that a lawyer on the opposing side in a civil case had withdrawn because of a conflict of interest . . . He also misrepresented facts in a pleading by charging that an opposing lawyer had assaulted him and had stolen documents from him, when he knew that the charges were not true . . . He also attempted to acquire information about an opposing party's sexual conduct, religious habits, and personal acquaintances through two sets of interrogatories, and, after the trial court had ruled that such issues were not relevant, he filed two affidavits alluding to the other party's personal relationships and alleged promiscuity . . .

The similarities between the misconduct that was the subject of the two disciplinary proceedings are striking. Following the six-month suspension, and less than three months after being reinstated to the practice of law on June 5, 1990, the respondent entered his appearance in the Otterpohl probate matter. ABA Standards 8.1(b) provides that, in the absence of mitigating circumstances, disbarment is appropriate when a lawyer "has been suspended for the same or similar misconduct, and intentionally or knowingly engages in further acts of misconduct that cause injury or potential injury to a client, the public, the legal system, or the profession.". . .

It is hereby ordered that Gary Alan Bottinelli be disbarred and that his name be stricken from the list of attorneys authorized to practice before this court[.]

EVIDENTIARY ISSUES

Witness Competency

When you have children or mentally ill witnesses (whether due to psychosis of some sort or old age dementia), you also have potential evidentiary issues. The federal rules have gotten away from any limitations or declaration of certain witnesses as **incompetent;** under the current federal rules, all witnesses are considered competent except jurors or judges in the action. Fed. R. Evid. 601. Many states have joined this trend; check your state's laws to see if yours is among them. This approach allows the jury to listen to all testimony and simply weigh the credibility of what has been said; in other words, rather than the judge keeping out "bad" fact witnesses, the jury can sort through which ones are not believable because of age or infirmity of whatever kind. However, even when the general rule is that all witnesses are competent, opposing counsel can claim that a particular witness—usually a minor or someone with some kind of mental deficit—is not, as occurred in the following case.

Tennessee v. Gass, No. M2000-02008-CCA-R3-CD, 2002 Tenn. Crim. App. LEXIS 30 (Tenn. Crim. App. at Nashville, January 9, 2002).

The defendant, Steve Gass, was indicted on two counts of rape of a child and two counts of aggravated sexual battery . . . He was convicted of one count of rape of a child, one count of aggravated sexual battery, and one count of attempted rape of a child. The trial court ordered sentences of 21 years, 9 years, and 11 years, respectively . . . The judgments of the trial court are affirmed . . .

The defendant . . . claims that the trial court erred by finding that the victim, age seven at the time of the trial, was competent to testify. Competency of a witness is controlled generally by Tennessee Rule of Evidence 601, which provides that "every person is presumed competent to be a witness except as otherwise provided in these rules or by statute." "Virtually all witnesses may be permitted to testify: children, mentally incompetent persons, convicted felons." Tenn. R. Evid. 601, Advisory Commission Comment (emphasis added). Tennessee Rule of Evidence 603 provides as follows:

> Before testifying, every witness shall be required to declare that the witness will testify truthfully by oath or affirmation, administered in a form calculated to awaken the witness's conscience and impress the witness's mind with the duty to do so.

The common law rule is that if the child "understands the nature and meaning of an oath, has the intelligence to understand the subject matter of the testimony, and is capable of relating the facts accurately," he or she is deemed competent to testify. *State v. Ballard*, 855 S.W.2d 557, 560 (Tenn. 1993)...

Through direct questioning, the trial court determined that the victim knew the difference between the truth and a lie. She stated that a lie placed her "in trouble" and that the truth did not. Although she could not define the term "oath," she understood the term "promise" and promised to tell the truth. When the defense argued that the victim's degree of competence fell short of the requirements of Rule of Evidence 603, the trial court imposed additional questions:

> **Q:** I may have used some words that you didn't understand. If I do, would you tell me that you don't understand them?
>
> **A:** Yes.
>
> **Q:** Okay. Then we'll go back to this question. Do you know what a lie is?
>
> **A:** Yes.
>
> **Q:** Okay. And do you know what the truth is?
>
> **A:** Yes.
>
> **Q:** All right. Do you promise to tell the truth?
>
> **A:** Yes.
>
> **Q:** And what happens if you tell a lie?
>
> **A:** You'll get in trouble.
>
> **Q:** Okay. . . . As to the questions that are asked of you, will you tell nothing but the truth?
>
> **A:** Yes.

The determination of the competency of a minor witness is properly a matter within the discretion of the trial judge, who has the opportunity to observe the witness first-hand. The decision of a trial judge will not be overturned absent a showing of abuse of that authority . . . In our view, the record demonstrates that the victim understood the nature of her oath.

. . . Accordingly, the judgments of the trial court are affirmed.

In states where **competency** is an issue, the rules may take a couple of different approaches. New Jersey, for instance, uses flexible exceptions.

> Every person is competent to be a witness unless (a) the judge finds that the proposed witness is incapable of expression concerning the matter so as to be understood by the judge and jury either directly or through interpretation, or (b) the proposed witness is incapable of understanding the duty of a witness to tell the truth, or (c) except as otherwise provided by these rules or by law.

N. J. R. Evid. 601.

The "except otherwise provided" is the provision that jurors and judges cannot testify in the trial upon which they sit; that's a universal prohibition. Other states categorize the types of witnesses as incompetent to testify, such as in Georgia.

> . . . [P]ersons who do not have the use of reason, such as idiots, lunatics during lunacy, and children who do not understand the nature of an oath, shall be incompetent witnesses.

Ga. Code Ann. § 24-9-5 (2002).

Mental disabilities and childhood are the usual grounds for witness incompetency. Rather than measuring the individual ability of the witness and allowing the jury to take into consideration the age of the child or the mental disability of the witness, the rules simply bar the witness as incompetent. Many of these states have some types of exceptions in the case of child abuse, particularly of a sexual nature, Georgia included. Often the child is not actually in the courtroom in a sexual abuse case: the child's story is recorded outside of the adversarial setting so as to protect him or her.

If you have evidence that needs to be presented, but it is only available through a witness who is considered incompetent, you will have to look for another way to get the evidence in. Experts are allowed to rely on evidence "commonly used in their field," even if it is not something that would usually be admissible. In addition, a specific hearsay exception exists for statements made to obtain medical treatment. So if the expert uses the testimony for her work, it may come in through this back door, as it did in this case (**sub judice** means "under judgment").

West Virginia v. Shrewsbury, 582 S.E.2d 774 (W. Va. 2003) (per curiam).

This is an appeal by Artie Gene Shrewsbury (hereinafter "Appellant") from a November 6, 2001, order of the Circuit Court of Mercer County sentencing him to four consecutive terms of one to five years in the penitentiary and five years probation upon his conviction of seven counts of first degree sexual assault and four counts of first degree sexual abuse. The Appellant contends that the lower court erred in admitting the testimony of the children's play therapist regarding statements made by the alleged victims of abuse. Upon thorough review of the record and the arguments of the parties, we disagree with the Appellant's contentions and affirm the lower court . . .

On October 11, 2000, the Appellant was indicted for seven counts of first degree sexual assault and four counts of first degree sexual abuse. The indictment alleged that, from November 1996 through November 1999, the Appellant had engaged in sexual intercourse with his step-nephews, J.C., a minor under the age of eleven years, and R.S., the younger brother of J.C. . . .

. . . [T]he children's mother scheduled counseling with Phyllis Hasty, a children's counselor and play therapist at Southern Highlands Community Mental Health Center. At trial, Ms. Hasty testified that she engaged in several forms of child-directed play therapy with the boys, including activities such as workbooks, drawing pictures, letter writing, painting, and hitting an "anger bop bag" to express feelings. Ms. Hasty testified that the children had talked to her about Artie touching and fondling them, as well as requests from Artie that the children also touch him. Ms. Hasty also testified that the children informed her that oral sex was involved, with J.C. offering the statement that "he didn't understand about the white stuff that comes out of Artie's thing." Ms. Hasty explained that the children had told her that they witnessed each other being abused. R.S. related an incident to Ms. Hasty in which Artie had attempted to penetrate R.S. while J.C. watched . . .

. . . The Appellant . . . attacks the admissibility of the statements in the present case based upon the alleged absence of reliability . . .

. . . [T]he United States Supreme Court clarified that hearsay evidence that falls under a firmly rooted exception to the hearsay rule or alternatively, when such evidence is accompanied by "particularized guarantees of trustworthiness," is admissible without any affront to the Confrontation Clause . . .

The following [is] . . . not excluded by the hearsay rule, even though the declarant is available as a witness: . . . (4) Statements for Purposes of Medical Diagnosis or Treatment. Statements made for purposes of medical diagnosis or treatment and describing medical history, or past or present symptoms, pain, or sensations, or the inception or general character of the cause or external source thereof insofar as reasonably pertinent to diagnosis or treatment. W.Va.R.Evid. 803(4). . .

The two-part test set for admitting hearsay statements pursuant to W.Va.R.Evid. 803(4) is (1) the declarant's motive in making the statements must be consistent with the purposes of promoting treatment, and (2) the content of the statement must be such as is reasonably relied upon by a physician in treatment or diagnosis.

The issue of reliability and reliance upon Rule 803(4) was also raised in [a similar case.] In that case, this Court affirmed the lower court's finding that Ms. Hasty's testimony . . . was reliable because it fell within the medical diagnosis or treatment exception to the hearsay rule . . . The . . . Court . . . determined that the statements made to Ms. Hasty by the children regarding the sexual abuse were made in a therapeutic context. Her sole involvement with [the children] was diagnosis and treatment. Also, the statements were such that they were reasonably relied upon by Ms. Hasty in her diagnosis and treatment. Ms. Hasty's testimony was properly admitted at trial . . .

When a social worker, counselor, or psychologist is trained in play therapy and thereafter treats a child abuse victim with play therapy, the therapist's testimony is admissible at trial under the medical diagnosis or treatment exception to the hearsay rule . . . if the declarant's motive in making the statement is consistent with the purposes of promoting treatment and the content of the statement is reasonably relied upon by the therapist for treatment. The testimony is inadmissible if the evidence was gathered strictly for investigative or forensic purposes.

We find no legitimate basis upon which to distinguish the circumstances of the present case . . . We consequently conclude that the statements of the children to the therapist fall within the medical diagnosis or treatment exception to the hearsay rule and thereby possess sufficient indicia of reliability to satisfy the reliability requirement of the Confrontation Clause. We affirm the decision of the lower court in this regard . . .

We conclude that the lower court did not abuse its discretion in admitting testimony in the Appellant's trial. We consequently affirm the decision of the lower court.

Affirmed.

CHILDREN

When children come into the courtroom, problems can arise. Testimony from children, when allowed, must be approached very carefully. Small children, in particular, are easily impeachable because of their perceived impressionability, although research suggests that children make no worse witnesses than adults but for their difficulty in finding words to describe the events they have experienced. When sexual abuse is the issue, jurors as a whole tend to be in denial. If evidence is not preserved at the outset of the case, as opposed to after therapy, the testimony of a young child is almost always irretrievably tainted by the therapist's interventions. Even when children are questioned (usually on videotape) upon first contact with any investigator, the questions must be carefully phrased so as not to suggest any answers. This same problem pervades all interaction with children. When you are trying to get information from a child, you are fighting with whatever developmental issues are facing the child, or you may be dealing with a preverbal client. If you need any extensive information from a child, the best course of action is to hire an expert in child psychology and receive reports from her. Of course, to meet the requirements of the rule, the expert cannot merely be evaluating the child, but must also provide treatment.

Children come to civil court in a variety of ways. Children under the age of 18 are not able to institute a suit on their own behalf, so their interests are usually brought before the court by a "Next Friend" unless in a family law case, where the suit affecting the child is brought under the style of "In the Matter of Child, a minor." Problems come up when the child's interests are in conflict with those of the next friend or the adults in their lives who are supposed to be looking out for them. In those cases, the court should appoint a **guardian ad litem (GAL)** or **attorney ad litem** (or both) to look out for the child's interest independent of the adults involved, including their parents and their lawyers.

Another option available in some locales in the context of child welfare cases is the appointment of a **Court Appointed Special Advocate (CASA).** These specially trained laypeople are a godsend in these cases; the acronym stays the same although the specific name of the organization may change in different venues (e.g., Child Advocates San Antonio—but still CASA). This is a chain of nonprofit affiliates that screens, trains, and provides volunteers to the family courts to follow a particular child or children in a family where the child protective services (whatever they may be denominated in your neighborhood) have become involved to make factual recommendations as to what is in the best interest of the child.

The difference between an attorney ad litem and a guardian ad litem is that a guardian ad litem has a broader range of duties to the child: she must look out for the child's total interests, whereas an attorney ad litem is only responsible for the legal interests of the child. Not all states have the attorney ad litem option, and lawyers appointed will become responsible for more than the legal interest of the child. The following case discusses the issues, although it doesn't do much for clarifying the **nomenclature** (naming system).

In re Care of Georgette, 785 N.E.2d 356 (Mass. 2003).

These cases . . . concern . . . decrees and judgments that placed two . . . daughters (Georgette and Lucy) in the permanent custody of the Department of Social Services (department) . . . and . . . an order denying Georgette and Lucy's motion for a new trial . . . The Appeals Court affirmed the decrees, judgments, and order . . . We granted Georgette and Lucy's application for further appellate review solely to consider the order. The motion asserted that trial counsel appointed for the children . . . had provided Georgette and Lucy with ineffective assistance of counsel. The claim noted that [Georgette and Lucy indicated they wanted to return to their father] and that trial counsel had advocated that Georgette and Lucy not be returned to their father's custody in direct contravention of their wishes and in circumstances constituting an actual conflict of interest. We affirm the order.

. . . The conclusions that the father has grievous shortcomings, and that his unfitness was . . . "clearly, convincingly, and decisively established,". . . are beyond contention . . . The factual predicates, therefore, for the entry of the decrees and the judgments are conclusively established.

Since the release of the Appeals Court's opinion, Georgette . . . has turned eighteen years of age. Because she is no longer a minor, Georgette's appeal from the order is moot, leaving Lucy . . . as the sole challenger to the order . . . Although Lucy informed the Appeals Court that she no longer wanted her appellate counsel to act on her behalf . . . she apparently instructed him to proceed with her application for further appellate review, and, presumably, this appeal . . .

Georgette and Lucy's motion for a new trial presented two aspects of alleged substandard performance by their trial counsel, namely that their trial . . . did not represent their expressed custodial preference, that is, advocate for their return to their father's custody . . . On the point with which we are concerned—whether trial counsel for Georgette and Lucy was ineffective—the Appeals Court . . . applied the familiar two-part test set forth in *Commonwealth v. Saferian*, 366 Mass. 89, 96, 315 N.E.2d 878 (1974). That test inquires, first, whether the "behavior of counsel [fell] measurably below that which might be expected from an ordinary fallible lawyer," and, if so, "whether [counsel's conduct] has likely deprived the defendant of an otherwise available, substantial ground of defence." [sic] . . . The *Saferian* test for evaluating the effectiveness of counsel is an appropriate standard to apply in care and protection proceedings . . . The Appeals Court . . . ultimately rested its decision that Georgette and Lucy should not obtain relief under the motion because no prejudice had been shown based on the overwhelming proof of the father's unfitness which no measure of zealous advocacy could have overcome . . . As for trial counsel's conduct of "'advocating against [Georgette and Lucy],' taking positions 'diametrically opposed to' theirs, and 'setting himself squarely against . . . [their] goals and objectives,'" the Appeals Court stated that this "were it true, would be deemed misconduct under our ethical standards.". . .

We essentially agree with the Appeals Court's reasoning. We note that, even if Lucy's trial counsel had advocated against her . . . she has failed to demonstrate any prejudice based on the overwhelming proof of the father's unfitness. As explained by the Appeals Court:

> The trial judge was well aware of Georgette's and Lucy's stated (if intermittent) desires regarding their father (through testimony, presentations by their now-maligned trial counsel, and lobby conferences). Given the overwhelming evidence of the father's unfitness (as well as the clear and convincing evidence of the two girls' special problems and needs in substantial consequence thereof), which persuaded both the trial judge and the motion judge that it was not in Georgette's and Lucy's best interests to be returned to his care, it is implausible that the most zealous and impassioned arguments by any trial counsel to give their custody to the alcoholic and unrepentant father who had neglected and had physically or sexually abused them would have realistically accomplished any change in the result.

. . . The failure to show prejudice, which constituted the Appeals Court's holding on the new trial issue, is correct, and for that reason, among others, the order will be affirmed . . .

. . . This leaves the larger issue: what are the obligations of trial counsel in circumstances such as the present when counsel represents siblings of various ages, competency, and understanding; faces a care and protection or termination of parental rights case (or other proceeding in which a change of custody as a result of State intervention is contemplated or sought) that presents compelling evidence demonstrating parental unfitness and the likely risk of harm to the children if returned to the unfit parent; and one or more of the clients (the children) want counsel to advocate for return to the parent. There is no question that the children are entitled to counsel, that their autonomy and rights to be heard on issues affecting their interest should be respected, and that their positions, based on mature expression, are entitled to weight in custody proceedings (although not determinative)... Nonetheless, we have noted that, "even where it is undisputed that a child and her attorney disagree, the law is unclear as to whether the attorney is always bound by her minor client's decision when the attorney feels that the child's decision is not in her own best interests."... In that decision, we felt "particularly hesitant to conclude that a difference of opinion between what a young child ... expresses as her wish and the position of her attorney necessarily suggests a conflict of interest."... We also pointed out that, "the notion that an attorney might zealously advocate for a result opposed by the client clearly sets the representation of children apart from the normal context in which attorneys operate."...

The issue creates serious problems: tension as to trial counsel's ethical duties... doubt on what counsel should do when a client (or clients) lacks maturity, understanding, or competence; and concern about when to request intervention by the judge, perhaps to ask for appointment of a guardian ad litem or other independent examiner (and how to preserve client confidences in the process). This description of problems is by no means exhaustive. The issue also raises challenges for the judge: should the judge press counsel to explain the problem; should new counsel be appointed for some children based on disagreement between them and counsel (thereby necessitating delay...)... should the judge examine the children in camera; is a guardian ad litem necessary; and where, in a time of shrinking resources and budgets, does the judge find funds to provide the necessary assistance. Again, this list of problems is not exhaustive.

When an attorney may deviate from seeking the objectives of a minor client has been the subject of considerable comment and the expression of various standards. Under the Massachusetts Rules of Professional Conduct, which became effective on January 1, 1998, a few months before this trial, a lawyer is obligated to, "as far as reasonably possible, maintain a normal client-lawyer relationship with the client" even when the "client's ability to make adequately considered decisions in connection with the representation is impaired, whether because of minority, mental disability, or for some other reason."... Departure from the "normal client-lawyer relationship" is permitted by our rule when "a lawyer reasonably believes that a client has become incompetent or that a normal client-lawyer relationship cannot be maintained ... because the client lacks sufficient capacity to communicate or to make adequately considered decisions in connection with the representation, and if the lawyer reasonably believes that the client is at risk of substantial harm, physical, mental, financial, or otherwise."... When either of these circumstances is present, "The lawyer may take the following action. The lawyer may consult family members, adult protective agencies, or other individuals or entities that have authority to protect the client, and, if it reasonably appears necessary, the lawyer may seek the appointment of a guardian ad litem, conservator, or a guardian, as the case may be. The lawyer may consult only those individuals or entities reasonably necessary to protect the client's interests and may not consult any individual or entity that the lawyer believes, after reasonable inquiry, will act in a fashion adverse to the interests of the client. In taking any of these actions the lawyer may disclose confidential information of the client only to the extent necessary to protect the client's interests."...

The Committee for Public Counsel Services (CPCS) has ... promulgated performance standards that apply to appointed counsel in State intervention cases.

... The... standards provide (excluding commentary):

a. Child's counsel should elicit the child's preferences in a developmentally appropriate manner, advise the child and provide guidance.

b. If counsel reasonably determines that the child is able to make an adequately considered decision with respect to a matter in connection with the representation, counsel shall represent the child's expressed preferences regarding that matter.

c. If a child client is incapable of verbalizing a preference, counsel shall make a good faith effort to determine the child's wishes and represent the child in accordance with that determination or may request appointment of a guardian ad litem/next friend to direct counsel in the representation.

d. If a child can verbalize a preference with respect to a particular matter, but counsel reasonably determines, pursuant to paragraph (b) above, that the child is not able to make an adequately considered decision regarding the matter and if representing the child's expressed preferences does not place the child at risk of substantial harm, then counsel shall represent the child's expressed preferences.

 If the child is not able to make an adequately considered decision regarding the matter and if counsel determines that pursuing the child's expressed preferences would place the child at risk of substantial harm, counsel may choose one of the following options:

   i. represent the child's expressed preferences regarding the matter;

  ii. represent the child's expressed preferences and request the appointment of a guardian ad litem/investigator to make an independent recommendation to the court with respect to the best interests of the child;

 iii. inform the court of the child's expressed preferences and request the appointment of a guardian ad litem/next friend to direct counsel in the representation; or

 iv. inform the court of the child's expressed preferences and determine what the child's preferences would be if he or she was able to make an adequately considered decision regarding the matter and represent the child in accordance with that determination" (emphasis in original).

CPCS Assigned Counsel Manual, Standard 1.6 of the Performance Standards Governing the Representation of Children and Parents in Child Welfare Cases (1999) (1999 CPCS Standards).

On the national level, there are various advisory standards, including the American Bar Association (ABA) Standards of Practice for Lawyers Who Represent Children in Abuse and Neglect Cases (1996) (ABA Standards). . . and the standards articulated by the American Law Institute in the Restatement (Third) of the Law Governing Lawyers § 24 (2000). . . The National Association of Counsel for Children (NACC) provides an overview of various standards, or so-called models of representation, and with respect to the ABA Standards, has "carved out a significant exception" to ABA Standard B-4 . . . "where the client cannot meaningfully participate in the formulation of his or her position.". . . In such cases, the NACC's exception "calls for a GAL [guardian ad litem] type judgment using objective criteria. Additionally, the NACC's version requires the attorney to request the appointment of a separate GAL, after unsuccessful attempts at counseling the child, when the child's wishes are considered to be seriously injurious to the child" (emphasis in original). . .

Fordham University School of Law hosted a conference on ethical issues in the legal representation of children and published various recommendations of the conference's working groups. The Fordham Recommendations provide that "[a] lawyer appointed or retained to serve a child in a legal proceeding should serve as the child's lawyer. The lawyer should assume the obligations of a lawyer, regardless of how the lawyer's role is labelled [sic], be it as guardian ad litem, attorney ad litem, law guardian, or other. The lawyer should not serve as the child's guardian ad litem or in another role insofar as the role includes responsibilities inconsistent with those of a lawyer for the child.". . . In circumstances where a child lacks capacity to direct the representation, the Fordham Recommendations contain standards that "limit the permissible discretion that lawyers for children may exercise on behalf of their clients"; suggest that lawyers for children employ a process that identifies the child's "legal interest," which "begins and ends with [an analysis of] the child-in-context"; and requires lawyers for children to present evidence in court on all of the options existing for the child . . .

Finally, standards have been articulated in Guidelines for Public Policy and State Legislation Governing Permanence for Children from Adoption 2002: The President's Initiative on Adoption and Foster Care (rev. 2001) (President's Initiative Guidelines). Those guidelines provide, as far as relevant here, that (1) "if a child lacks capacity to articulate a preference, the attorney should determine and advocate the child's legal interests," and (2) "if the child's attorney not only believes that the child's expressed preferences are contrary to his/her opinion of the child's best interests, but also could place the child at considerable risk of severe injury or harm, the lawyer may request appointment of a separate guardian ad litem. In this case, the attorney would continue to represent the child's expressed preference, unless the child's position is prohibited by law or without any factual foundation. The child's attorney shall not reveal the basis of the request for appointment of a guardian ad litem that would compromise the child's position." Guideline VII-15A of the President's Initiative Guidelines.

These various expressions have met with criticism. For example, in commentary to standard 1.6 of the 1999 CPCS Standards, CPCS criticizes our rules of professional conduct, stating that the rules only provide "some limited guidance." The Children's Law Center of Massachusetts, Inc., rejects several approaches reflected in the 1999 CPCS Standards, specifically, standard 1.6. The Massachusetts Citizens for Children recommends the adoption of an approach similar to that enacted by statute in Michigan that has been explained as follows:

"The Michigan statute codifies two roles for the child's legal advocate—a client-directed attorney role and a best interests lawyer-guardian ad litem role. The statute . . . requires appointment of a lawyer-GAL in every child protection case, but permits the court to appoint an attorney for the child, in addition to the lawyer-GAL, where the child and lawyer-GAL are in conflict about identification of the child's interests. The statute also establishes aggressive duties for the lawyer-GAL, provides for attorney-client privilege, requires the lawyer-GAL to present the wishes of the child even if inconsistent with the lawyer-GAL's views of best interests, and requires the lawyer-GAL to weigh the child's wishes in making the best interests determination according to the age and maturity of the child.". . .

. . . The same author also criticizes the ABA Standards, NACC Standards, and Fordham Recommendations, pointing out that these models "actually contain within themselves serious opportunities for lawyers to exercise unfettered and unreviewed discretion in representing children.". . .

In summary:

There is considerable ongoing discussion among lawyers, judges, and other children's advocates about the appropriate role for a lawyer to assume when representing child clients. In particular, a range of views exist about the extent to which lawyers should take direction from their child clients. For the most part, States have provided inadequate guidance to lawyers for children about their proper role and, as a result, each lawyer makes her or his own decision. This ad hoc approach produces confusion among clients, other involved individuals, and the courts. It also has the effect, overall, of reducing the quality of legal representation. In order for children to be well served by the court process, it is essential that each State clearly articulate the role the child's lawyer is expected to play.

Commentary to guideline VII-14 of the President's Initiative Guidelines.

. . . We are persuaded from the array of conflicting standards that the subject needs clarification. Without expression of views by those involved in these cases, we are reluctant to pick one set of standards over another (or to formulate guidelines from a mixture of standards). We conclude that the matter is best resolved, as recommended by the department, by reference to our standing advisory committee on the rules of professional conduct for the committee's study and the formulation of suitable standards which can be expressed (in the committee's choice) in new or revised rules, commentary thereto, or guidelines derivative of the rules.

The order denying Georgette and Lucy's motion for a new trial is affirmed.

Nice punt by the court to a committee, but probably well-advised under the circumstances. Too often the various supreme courts try to fashion a rule without the long consideration experience gives those who deal with the issue regularly. Balancing the distorted view of reality held by abused and neglected children, held ransom by fear and feelings of worthlessness, against the problematic issue of how to prevent arbitrary application of personal standards of best interest of the child by the attorney representing the child is tricky. Worst-case scenarios are often presented—not the norm, certainly, but one that makes everyone twitchy, such as "What if the problem is spanking at an inappropriate age and the kid wants to go back but the ad litem thinks that any corporal punishment is child abuse?" That's why the insertion of objective standards is important.

The responsibility of a GAL is a heavy one, and many well-meaning attorneys become overwhelmed by it. As a result, some jurisdictions have gone to specific licensing requirements prior to allowing an attorney to be appointed as a GAL. Others prefer the use of specially trained laypersons, such as those in the various affiliates of the CASA program. Still others use a combination of these solutions. In any case, it is advisable for someone involved in these cases to research the details of the developmental needs specific to the child's age, the psychological issues involved in the specifics of the case, and any relevant health issues. Although difficult, the GAL cannot simply use her values as a guide for "best interest of the child." Instead, she must have some objective basis for evaluating the best interest. The paralegal can help by providing the GAL with informative materials to read and by keeping tabs on the topic if her attorney is in a practice that tends toward child advocacy.

Sometimes problems arise when the ad litem is suggested by one of the attorneys in the case, as is the norm in a friendly suit. Friendly suits are cases filed by parties solely to gain the approval of the court for a settlement involving a minor that has already been agreed upon by the parties. Because the minor's parents have a duty to pay for their child's necessities, including medical, they are allowed to recover medical costs incurred during the child's minority. All other recovery is the property of the child, and usually goes into a trust that cannot be touched without the court's permission. Any recovery by the minor and relinquishment of all future claims must be approved by the court. The ad litem is usually appointed after the settlement has been made, and some lawyers expect her to function as a mere rubber stamp. Doing so fails the duty the ad litem owes the child.

Whether this is a delegable duty is in doubt, but if you are asked to review the file and compile an initial evaluation, you must get a sense of what kind of physical and psychological problems the child has had in the past, is still having, and is likely to continue to have. The ad litem (or you, if your attorney has tasked you with it) should meet with the child and evaluate whether the settlement is fair to the child. This meeting should not take place in the lawyer's office. To evaluate a child, you must see the child in her own surroundings. You must be aware of the appropriate developmental stage for the child. You must see if his actions in his environment seem appropriate to that developmental stage. Is he happy? Content? Comfortable? Interacting appropriately with other family members? Who is the child particularly attached to? It is better to visit more than once; children, particularly very young children, can have very fussy and very good days. It's better to try to get a good sampling to get a more complete view.

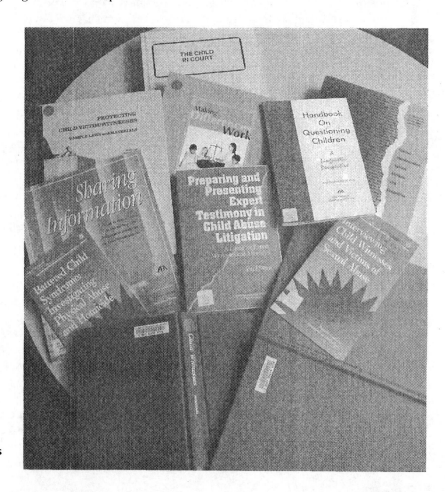

There are many resources available to prepare for child witnesses, as this array of books demonstrates.

Talking to the child's doctor is a good idea; you'll probably have to give her a copy of the order appointing you the ad litem. You may even have to obtain an order specifically authorizing the doctor to speak with you, as the child cannot authorize the release of her records or a discussion of her medical state.

A more difficult problem arises when you realize, in the course of your representation of one of the parties to the divorce, that the children need their own representation. Although some would argue that it is some sort of violation of confidentiality, a simple request for an ad litem does not give any information away but does allow for a competent attorney to begin looking into the situation. In cases where the state is involved from the beginning because of suspected abuse, ad litems for the children are appointed as a matter of course. This way, someone outside the debate of whose fault it was becomes involved. Regardless of which parent, step-parent, boyfriend, girlfriend, other family member, or friend is at fault, the issue of the child's safety will be kept separate and in the forefront of at least one attorney's mind. The same rules apply for an investigating ad litem here as in a friendly suit or any other litigation: you must have an idea of what the child needs and is about, particularly when he is unable to articulate his needs and desires.

A problem you face in both situations is the need to speak to represented parties. To get an idea about the child, you need to talk to the parents and/or other caretakers. At the point the ad litem comes into the litigation, anyone who holds that position is already represented by counsel. You will have to either get a waiver from the lawyers of the parents or caretakers, or ask them to be present for the interview, or set a deposition, or be short some important information about the child. In a family law situation, where the costs may come back to the parents and/or caretakers, they have some incentive to go along with one of the cheaper alternatives.

Questioning children requires special attention. Researchers recommend the following guidelines for gearing the interview for a child, although these recommendations are helpful for any witness.

- Use active rather than passive voice.
  e.g.: Who drove the car?
  NOT: Who was the car driven by?
- Avoid negatives and double negatives.
  e.g.: Was your mother with you?
  NOT: Wasn't your mother not there?
- Include only one query per question.
  e.g.: Was the other car going north? Who was the driver?
  NOT: Who was driving the other car and was it going north?
- Use simple words.
  e.g.: big
  NOT: humongous
- Use simple phrases.
  e.g.: Was that the first thing that happened?
  NOT: Did the events you described in foregoing answer precede all other occurrences?
- Use the child's terms.
  e.g.: If the child calls the other vehicle a "big red truck," you refer to it in the same way.
- Watch for signals that the child is having difficulty understanding the questions.

Nancy Walker, *Forensic Interviews of Children: The Components of Scientific Validity and Legal Admissibility*, 65 Law & Contemp. Problems 149, 165 (2002).

In particular, children need to be asked more open-ended questions, with the interviewer encouraging the child to keep explaining without reformulating the information into adult terms. You should also make sure the child knows (1) that she may say she doesn't understand the question, (2) that the interviewer's asking a question more than once doesn't mean that she answered incorrectly, (3) that she should correct the interviewer if he inaccurately paraphrases her story, and (4) that she will be the one doing most of the talking, not the adult.

What to do about the child once you have finished your investigation is an area of contention among lawyers advocating for children, as indicated in the Massachusetts case of *In re: Care of Georgette*, supra. How do you determine what is in the best interest of the child? If the child is old enough to state his desires, are those desires necessarily in his best interest? These questions are easier to answer in the context of the friendly suit, where the attorney merely needs to evaluate the value of the case independently of the other lawyers and determine if the settlement is appropriate given the usual jury awards for similar cases in the jurisdiction. The questions in family law are far more difficult—and values based. You need to note what the child wants, what psychologists recommend, what any school folks recommend, and what anyone else who has commented or is relevant to the case thinks.

So how do you prepare a child for trial? If you are in a state where children are considered incompetent, their views and testimony will come in through other witnesses, so there is no need to prepare them. (We refer to evidence as "coming in" because it is a matter of coming before the jury—the attorneys already know about most of the facts, which are disclosed during discovery.) In states where children are not incompetent to testify, judges often ask a preliminary set of questions to make sure the child is capable of testifying. As you saw in *Tennessee v. Gass*, the questions usually start simply:

What is your name?

How old are you?

Do you go to school?

Where do you live?

[If appropriate:] What parent do you live with?

Can you tell me what a lie is?

And so on until the judge is satisfied. If this is an interview in chambers for the judge to have input from the child on the custody question, it will ordinarily be with the attorneys present but not the parents. The child needs to know ahead of time that there is no way that the lawyers can promise to keep what he says "a secret" from his parents or caretakers. Although you still will encourage the child to say what he really thinks, explain how important it is for the child not to lie, and explain the consequences of lying, the child will often have problems making this kind of choice. Another problem that you need to try to head off is the possibility of the child's fantasy of using the interview in chambers as an opportunity to reunite his parents. This wishful thinking can distort the testimony of the child. You might tell him: "Johnny, I know that what you really want is for your mom and dad to give up this whole divorce thing and to just live together again. I hope that it can happen for you, although I don't think it will. But your talk with the judge will not stop it, so for the time you talk to him, at least pretend that they are going to stay apart, and tell him the truth for that situation." You can't really deprive a child of that hope; he must come to that realization in his own time. On the other hand, you have to have the child's cooperation for the term of the judge's interview for his own benefit. And, like any other witness, you need to explain to the child what the process is, and make sure he knows that he is in no danger of going to jail.

For child testimony, the choices, in order of ordinary preference, are to have an expert testify on behalf of the child, to have the child testify in chambers to the judge (**in camera**), or to have the child take the stand. Sometimes finances of the parties will preclude the expert option and the judge will preclude the in camera option.

Excerpt from Leigh Goodmark, *From Property to Personhood: What the Legal System Should Do for Children in Family Violence Cases*, 102 W. VA. L. REV. 237, 284-316 (1999) (footnotes/citations from original omitted).

My worst experience as a trial lawyer involved a five-year-old child who was forced to testify during a restraining order hearing. The child, who was living with her grandmother, told her grandmother that her father hit her during a visit. The grandmother filed for protection on behalf of the child and came to me for assistance. The child later repeated the story to me: when she asked her father for money for her school pictures, her father punched her in the stomach. She was absolutely clear about what had happened, and I was convinced that she was telling the truth.

Prior to the restraining order hearing, the child and I discussed what would happen in the courtroom: that she would have to talk to the judge, that she should tell the truth. She was very worried that her father would be in the courtroom, but we talked about how she could look at other people and how he couldn't harm her anymore. Once in court, we attempted to introduce the testimony of the child through the grandmother. The hearsay objection was sustained. Before her testimony, I asked the court to allow the child to testify *in camera*, out of the scrutiny of her father. Denied. I asked the court to modify the courtroom setting so that the child was not forced to sit on the witness stand, where her father could glare at her. Denied. And so the child took the witness stand. With the judge sitting above her and to her left on the bench, wearing his black robe, with her father sitting directly across from her, I began to ask her questions. I asked her about whether she understood what the truth was and whether she could tell the truth. I then took her through the day when her father punched her. Opposing counsel cross-examined the child, who never changed the substance of her story—that her father had punched her after she asked for money.

The judge, after hearing all of the evidence, ruled for the father. His ruling, he explained, was based almost completely on one factor: he didn't believe the child because she hadn't looked him in the eye during her testimony. He found that the child could have been manipulated into saying that her father hit her. And when I went to get her at the day care center, where she'd gone after her testimony, her first question was whether her father was going to get her. Ultimately, he did: he took her from the grandmother's home, where she had lived her entire life, and continued to emotionally and physically maltreat her.

That experience raised a number of questions about how children are treated when they serve as witnesses in court hearings. Children are more and more frequently called to court to testify to violence against them, to violence against a parent, and/or to the impact of the violence on them. This section considers whether children can be witnesses, whether they should be witnesses, and suggests ways that the legal system could change both substantive law and courtroom procedures in order to make the process of being a witness an easier one for children.

A. Can Children Testify?

"Judges and attorneys who question children in court often have apprehensions about young witnesses." One commentator describes a preliminary hearing in a child sexual abuse case where, after considering all of the testimony, "the judge refused to bind the case over for trial and made the following statement: 'I'm not going to ruin the life of this fifty-year-old man on the testimony of a five-year-old.'" Although the legal system has long been skeptical about the utility of the testimony of child witnesses, modern social science research refutes the characterization of children's testimony as unreliable. Research shows that children can testify effectively in court, are not "necessarily less reliable than adults," and, in fact, are more capable witnesses than most adults believe. A child's ability to testify is certainly different than that of an adult, but "these differences should not obscure the fact that even very young children have demonstrated a remarkable ability to provide both relevant and reliable information to decision makers."

1. Memory

Does a child have the capacity to observe an occurrence and remember it sufficiently to testify? Children develop the skills necessary to "witness" incrementally; age, therefore, is the dominant variable in considering the ability to witness. Because children retain and retrieve more information as they get older, they are less able to access distant experiences than adults. Developmental immaturity may make children less able to encode and retrieve information, two of the central memory processes.

Despite these differences, research shows that children can recall experiences accurately and describe them effectively in court. Very young children can accurately recall historical events, although they are not as proficient as adults at responding to open-ended questions calling for free recall. As age decreases, children recall less information spontaneously and must be assisted in recalling what they know. When cues and prompts are used to trigger retrieval, young children's memory substantially improves.

For "single stimulus tasks" like basic identification, children aged three have reliable memories, and children aged four and a half years old have skills almost comparable to adults. Young children can recall basic temporal order, understand the actual frequency of events, and sort out actions involving several individuals. Whether a child will notice and recall detail turns on the salience of the detail—the importance of the object or action to the child. Like an adult witness, a child encodes more detail when

(continued)

she realizes the importance of the event or is made aware of the importance by someone else's reaction to it. Children's memory is especially resilient when recalling the central details or main action of events, personally significant events, and events in which the child directly participated.

The passage of time has a significant impact on children's memory. Delay between the occurrence of an event and the relation of the event can cause memory distortion. Children forget significantly more information than adults, and young children forget more than older children. But while young children's memories may fade more quickly than adults, the child is likely to remember the salient features of the event. And "as long as the child is asked to use recognition or recall memory soon after the event to be remembered, reliability risks are minimal and no greater than for adult testimony."

Children, like adults, do make mistakes in memory. Like adults, children are more likely to give an incorrect report about peripheral details. Neither children nor adults retain peripheral detail well. When children make errors in recollection, they are more often errors of omission (failure to include information) than errors of commission (including false or fabricated information). Moreover, "there is nothing in the scientific literature that proves that if a child incorrectly remembers one aspect of an event, she will be incorrect about everything else as well." Both children and adults use "stored memories," memories of previous events that fit into the event being recalled, to fill in gaps in an account.

2. Conceptual Issues

Certain conceptual problems that affect testimony are unique to children because of their developmental immaturity. "Young children appear to be more 'data-bound,' more faithful to what they actually saw or heard or smelled and less prone to make assumptions about details that might have been present." Children therefore may have difficulty with questions that require them to make abstract inferences. Moreover, while children as young as four can provide reliable descriptive data about colors, identifying characteristics and basic object characterizations, the ability to make time and distance categorizations is acquired at least four years later.

The social science research supports the position that children have sufficient memory capacity to testify. The next question, then, is whether children are so susceptible to suggestibility that their testimony is worthless.

3. Suggestibility

Suggestibility, or the tendency to accept and incorporate false or misleading information into one's memory, has become one of the prime topics for social science researchers interested in children's memory. The research leans toward the conclusion that children are more suggestible than adults, although the question is still being debated within the scientific community.

Research has shown that young children (under the age of five) are disproportionately more vulnerable to suggestibility than school-aged children or adults, and are highly likely to accept misleading information in certain circumstances. By the time children reach the ages of ten to twelve years, they are no more suggestible than adults. Suggestibility should not, however, be seen as a memory failing peculiar to children. Adults' memories, too, can be influenced, changed, or distorted by suggestive factors.

Suggestibility in children is overwhelmingly a result of the influence of adults' beliefs and interview techniques on children's memories. Erroneous suggestions put forth by adults, usually in the context of interviews or therapy, can overwrite the child's original memory. "Children's inaccurate reports or allegations do not always reflect a confusion of events and details of an experience, but may at times reflect the creation of an entire experience in which the child did not participate." Misinformation repeated across interviews is incorporated into the child's memory both directly (children repeat the same language that they heard) and indirectly (children draw inferences based on the misinformation). When children are repeatedly asked to create mental images of fictitious events, over time they will increasingly begin to believe that the events have occurred and may be reluctant to relinquish that belief.

The manner in which a child is questioned is the key to whether the child's memory will be tainted by suggestibility. The accuracy of a child's report decreases when the child is interviewed in leading or suggestive ways by investigators who are not open to considering theories other than those they seek to support through the interview. If the initial interview of the child is neutral, it helps to protect the child's memory against later suggestive interviews.

Young children are not invariably suggestible. Children are much less likely to be misled about central information than they are about peripheral detail. It is harder to mislead children when the events are fresh than when their memories have faded. And some children are unwilling to accept suggestion at all. "These children's resistance is an indication of how difficult it sometimes is to use suggestive techniques to capture and change the memories and reports of some young children who steadfastly refuse to relinquish their accurate memories."

4. Lies.

By the age of four, children can distinguish between reality and fantasy. At least as early as age six, children can lie, and do lie when the motivation to lie is strong enough. Motivations to lie include avoiding punishment, gaining an otherwise unattainable material benefit, protecting themselves or others from harm, protecting friends from trouble, winning the admiration of others, avoiding awkward social situations, avoiding embarrassment, maintaining privacy, demonstrating authority, sustaining a game, or keeping a promise.

But there is a difference between lying and making mistakes. Young children are commonly inconsistent across several interviews: "What looks like inconsistency may actually be a product of the child's comfort with the interviewer, the interviewer's developmental insensitivity, or the child's ability to retrieve relevant information at a given moment in time." In the absence of suggestive influences, children's inconsistency should not be equated with unreliability or untruthfulness, as children regularly provide and omit detail over time. Similarly, as noted above, children have difficulty with time and measurement; problems with misordering the sequences of events or dates do not mean that the child is fabricating central facts. And occasionally children (like adults) simply give bizarre answers—without leading questions or motivations to distort the facts.

How can we determine when a child's testimony is truthful? While there is no definitive answer, some factors are telling. A child witness' testimony is likely to be accurate when it conveys the central information about an event; when the event was relatively extended over time, allowing ample opportunity for observation; when the assailant is familiar to the child; when the event has been repeated; and when no highly suggestive questioning of the child has occurred. Stories that include unexpected complications, unusual details and superfluous details are probably being recalled from memory. Also, a child who makes spontaneous corrections or additions to her story is probably recalling an actual event, as is a child who is willing to admit that she has forgotten elements of the story. Ultimately, the responsibility is with the trier of fact to ensure that a child who testifies understands her obligation to tell the truth.

The social science research indicates that although they have certain deficiencies, children can serve as witnesses to events and provide probative information. The next section asks whether children should serve as witnesses in our current adversarial system, and looks for alternatives permitting the inclusion of the testimony of children who should not.

B. Should Children Have to Serve as Witnesses?

1. Emotional and Psychological Factors

The answer to the question posed in this section is no, according to Dr. Albert J. Solnit, former director of the Yale Child Study Center. Dr. Solnit has suggested that children be kept out of courtrooms altogether—that it is never in a child's best interest to be a witness. Few other experts take quite so decisive a stance. Some believe that testifying can be beneficial for children; "for many children, testifying in court often helps them to feel empowered and to heal." Some children want to share their experiences, to describe the impact of the violence and their fears, risks they perceive and their preferences on custody. Especially in cases where the parents cannot afford expert witnesses or the child

(continued)

is not represented, the judge will have no other means of hearing "the testimony of those who may be most affected by the family court decisions." Children who are not permitted to participate in the legal process may become angry; "such anger causes the child more stress than if he or she had testified in court." Moreover, testifying may help children recover from the psychological trauma of the underlying events. At least one study shows that children who testified in juvenile court resolved their psychological trauma more quickly than children who did not testify.

Nonetheless, testifying can be incredibly stressful for some children. The way that the child reacts to testifying depends on the child's personality and ability to handle new and stressful situations, the severity of the underlying event, and how the child was affected by the event. The courtroom setting in and of itself can be stressful. Children have little idea of what to expect from court; what little they do know comes from the media and television and often causes "intense fear and anxiety." They believe that they could go to jail for giving a wrong answer or that the defendant will be permitted to "get" them or yell at them. Added to those fears are the pressures of speaking in front of an audience, being cross-examined, and being separated from a support person. Simply being in the same room as the defendant can be incredibly traumatic. The atmosphere of the courtroom can be "threatening," "frightening," or "confusing" for children. Questioning a child in an intimidating environment like a courtroom can increase a child's stress; it can also undermine the quality of the information obtained. While the effects of stress on memory and the reliability of child witnesses are still unclear, researchers have posited that stress can prompt memory retrieval problems, can make children more suggestible, and can cause them to become more easily confused, leading to a loss of confidence in their testimony.

"Testifying is difficult for most children, and it is not surprising when young witnesses respond in childlike ways," including whispering, crying and refusing to speak. Some children simply cannot testify in open court. Case law describes children who:

—were rendered inarticulate by intimidating court surroundings;

—were frightened by the jury, the defendant and the court setting, unable to answer any but neutral questions, and left the court clutching the mother and crying hysterically;

—suffered from guilt, fear and anxiety, and faced potential long-term problems including nightmares, depression, eating, sleeping, and school problems, and behavioral difficulties, including acting out.

Children who do testify may perform poorly, undermining their credibility. A traumatized child may refuse or be physically unable to testify in front of the defendant. A young child coping with the anxiety of testifying might avoid questions or fail to fully disclose, especially when they've been told not to tell anyone about the event. The child's reticence may lead judges to discredit a "frozen, inarticulate child," damaging the child's confidence. Moreover, children who are grappling with psychiatric issues like attentional deficits, psychic numbing, social withdrawal, and feelings of hopelessness, self-hatred or helplessness "can appear to be highly reluctant, uncooperative witnesses who provide little information."

2. The Adversarial Legal System

The adversarial legal system is not well-equipped to accommodate child witnesses. "For some children, testifying in the traditional manner interferes with the child's ability to answer questions, thus undermining the very purpose of the trial—discovery of the truth." For a number of reasons, the time-honored methods of direct and cross-examination are not the best means of gleaning the truth from child witnesses. As discussed above, children do not always give complete information when asked the type of free-recall, open-ended questions that are common during direct examination. Moreover, children are "emotionally and linguistically ill-equipped for the rigors of cross-examination and are easily confused." During cross-examination, attorneys confuse children by using double negatives, difficult sentence constructions and complicated words. The accusatory manner of cross-examination can be intimidating for the child. Because children have difficulty remembering peripheral events and the sequence of events, questions about those details can undermine the child's confidence and render her testimony less effective.

Additionally, "suggestibility theory itself suggests that a lawyer may be able to lead a child witness to statements advantageous to the defendant." Children are, as discussed above, susceptible to suggestion through leading questions. Moreover, children are motivated by a desire to please adults, and may tailor their answers to reflect what they believe the adult wants to hear, even if that answer is inconsistent with their own knowledge of the event. "In fact, children are so accommodating of adult questioning that they will struggle against all odds to bring order out of confusion, to make sense of questions, and to provide answers to adults' seriously stated inquiries." Finally, children, when asked the same question more than once, often change their answers, assuming that because they have been asked again, the original answer must have been incorrect. Children are especially likely to change their answers to specific or leading questions—precisely the type of situation that a lawyer conducting cross-examination is likely to exploit. The combination of susceptibility to suggestion, confusion about language, desire to please adults and tendency to change answers makes children singularly unsuited to undergo cross-examination. "In sum, many factors point to the conclusion that, if the goal is to determine the truth, the adversary process may not be the best means of obtaining the truth from children."

3. Intrafamily Cases

Testifying in a case involving family violence presents unique problems for the child witness; while he may be the only eyewitness to the violence, "the child may suffer great trauma from testifying." The stakes for children and families are particularly high in family violence cases. "Intrafamily offenses are especially problematic because even young children can foresee the havoc truthfulness can invite." Child victims and witnesses often feel responsible for the abuser's actions, especially when a family member is committing the abusive acts. Children are pressured by their parents to testify/not to testify, fear physical retribution if they do testify, and often don't want to take sides. Children become "informational pawns, caught between two beloved parents and facing catastrophic loss no matter how they choose" to testify.

Testifying about family violence, especially where custody determinations are involved, requires the child to divide his loyalties and potentially to make derogatory statements about a parent with whom the child wants a long-term relationship . . . [C]hildren may side with the abusive spouse and request that they be placed in the custody of the abuser. "Outright fear" can "determine a child's testimony."

To alleviate the pressure on children to testify in domestic relations proceedings, some states have begun to restrict the ability of parties in these matters to call children as witnesses. Florida Family Law Rule of Procedure 12.407 states that a minor child cannot serve as a witness without the permission of the court, granted on good cause shown, except in emergency proceedings. Prior to the inception of the Rule, "parents were bringing children to meet with [attorneys] to tell various things that would be 'helpful' to our cases and . . . the parents wanted the kids to testify to these events and to their desires as to parenting in court." The Rule was designed to limit children's involvement to cases of absolute necessity and to create disincentives to parents manipulating or burdening the child. The Rule does not take the position that children should never come to court or that child testimony is "inherently unreliable;" it simply seeks to dissuade parents from manipulating their children and to control the manner in which the testimony will occur if such testimony is deemed necessary. Requiring advance notice that a child will testify allows the court to adjust courtroom procedure to protect the child's best interest—by appointing a *guardian ad litem*, requiring that the child be brought to court by a neutral third party, setting limits on the nature, manner and extent of questioning, and deciding whether the parents should be present during the testimony.

California's Family Code incorporates a similar provision. California Family Code § 3042 allows the court to "preclude the calling of the child as a witness where the best interests of the child so dictates. . . ." Section 3042 is designed to protect children from the emotional damage of testifying by preventing a child from being called as a witness where the value of the testimony is outweighed by the potential emotional damage to the child. Like the Florida rule, the California statute does not prevent the child from testifying when the child expresses a desire to testify, but seeks to protect children from the emotionally damaging consequences of forced testimony.

(continued)

Although children have the capacity to serve as witnesses, not all children are emotionally or cognitively prepared to testify in family violence cases. Provisions such as those in place in Florida and California remove the decision from the hands of the interested parties, who may have motives for urging the child witness to testify entirely separate from concerns about the well-being of the child, and put them in the hands of neutral finders of fact. If properly enforced by judicial officers, such provisions could protect children who are not equipped to testify without enacting a blanket proscription against children's testimony.

Another means of allowing the child to be heard without causing undue harm to the child is through out-of-court statements made to another party. The next section will discuss how the creative use of hearsay exceptions can ensure that the child is heard in court without the collateral damage of testifying.

C. Alternatives to In-Court Testimony

Often a child's experience or opinion will be relevant, and even probative, in deciding cases involving family violence. But when testifying is too difficult for the child, that perspective is often lost. This section will discuss introducing child hearsay statements and will propose modifications to and new applications for the child hearsay exclusions becoming common in child sexual abuse cases.

1. Use of Current Hearsay Exceptions

Hearsay evidence is "evidence of a statement made outside of the proceedings in which it is being offered to prove the truth of the matter asserted in the statement." Such evidence is generally inadmissible, but hearsay statements may be admitted under a number of exceptions to the hearsay rule when both the trustworthiness of and the necessity for the statement can be established. The hearsay exceptions permit the court to consider the out-of-court declarations "of any witness, including a child."

Social scientists have determined that "lacking empirical data that children's volunteered out-of-court statements are inherently less reliable than adults', we may safely continue the traditions of more than three hundred years of the hearsay rule development." Similarly, some courts have found that the hearsay rules and exceptions properly cover children's declarations, in part to protect children from the harm of testifying.

Historical analyses of the arcane judicial rules concerning hearsay and competency that have developed over the centuries in cases involving adults, whether civil or criminal in nature, are of little assistance in proceedings designed only to determine how to best safeguard the welfare of children of extremely tender years. Such children may be totally incapable of treating with the abstractions that underlie testimonial competency, yet are quite capable of observing and reporting on specific events to which they are privy.

Hearsay statements are objectionable largely because they cannot be tested through cross-examination, deemed "the greatest legal engine ever invented for the discovery of truth." But this adage may not hold true in cases involving children's testimony. In fact, a child's out-of-court statement may be more reliable than her in-court testimony. The reliability of the child's statement may be enhanced because it is spontaneous and unrehearsed, because it is not the product of extended questioning, and because it is free of the stress caused by the courtroom setting. Moreover, certain hearsay statements avoid the problem of memory fade. "Testimonial memory-fade, which is a greater risk for children than adults, is certainly less of a problem when hearsay statements are offered that were made closer in time to the child's experience." Hearsay testimony is crucial in cases where, although the child has the cognitive ability to do so, she simply cannot testify or her testimony is ineffective.

A number of hearsay exceptions are commonly used to admit the statements of child witnesses. They include the exceptions for excited utterances or spontaneous exclamations; statements for the purpose of medical diagnosis or treatment; statements of existing mental, emotional or physical condition; and the residual hearsay exception.

a. Excited Utterances/Spontaneous Exclamations

The excited utterance exception applies to a statement made as a result of a shocking or exciting event, if the event is still affecting the child at the time the statement is made and the statement is made during or immediately following the event, before there is time for reflection. Advocates for children should take special note of statements made to police, hospital staff, teachers, doctors and day care workers, all of whom may interact with the child near the time of an incident of family violence.

Courts differ as to how close in time the statement must be to the exciting event to be admissible. Some courts allow statements made after days or weeks; others disallow statements made only a few minutes or hours after the exciting event. Statements made at the "first safe opportunity" or during a period of "rekindled excitement" may be admissible despite the passage of time. Such statements may be admitted after significant time has passed because courts recognize that a child witness may not have immediate access to the person he will tell about the frightening event. But the willingness to allow for the passage of time has prompted some critics to argue that courts have "distorted the hearsay rule."

b. Statements for the Purpose of Medical Diagnosis or Treatment

Statements made to medical professionals for the purpose of diagnosing or treating an ailment are also admissible as an exception to the hearsay rule. Statements for the purpose of diagnosis or treatment are admitted under two rationales. First, the patient's interest in receiving appropriate medical care suggests that patients will give reliable information to their doctors. Second, the exception allows only for the admission of statements that would be reasonably relied upon by doctors, based on the assumption that doctors can separate accurate from inaccurate information. States vary on the question of whether statements to mental health professionals are admissible under this exception.

Commentators have suggested that children's statements to physicians are not sufficiently reliable to be admitted under this exception. They argue that children do not understand the importance of reporting accurate information and therefore do not have the same sense of self-interest in conversations with doctors. They may try to evade the doctor's questions, believing that doctors are "being mean" when they provide treatment. But doctors who regularly treat children, including pediatricians, child psychiatrists and child psychologists, are trained to explain the importance of accurate reporting, especially when a child is withdrawn or frightened.

c. Then Existing State of Mind/Emotion/Sensation/Physical Condition

A statement that is otherwise hearsay is admissible for the truth of the matter asserted when it describes the existing state of mind, emotion, sensation or physical condition experienced at the time the statement was made. The child's state of mind is uniquely relevant in family violence cases, where the impact of the violence on the child and the ramifications for custody and visitation determinations are being considered. "In child custody and visitation litigation . . . the child's feelings, fears, likes, and dislikes are central to the child's best interest. The child's state of mind is in issue in such litigation, and the child's hearsay statements revealing the state of mind are admissible." The most probative evidence of the child's opinion may lie in statements to others rather than in the child's testimony in open court. Such statements may also be admissible for non-hearsay purposes; for example, a child's statement about violence perpetrated by the father might be admitted not to prove that the violence occurred, but rather to show the child's fear of the father.

d. Residual Exception

Some states and the Federal Rules of Evidence have adopted a residual hearsay exception. The exception permits the admission of statements that do not satisfy the requirements of traditional hearsay exceptions but nonetheless have sufficient indicia of trustworthiness that admission is warranted. The residual exception has been widely used in child sexual abuse cases where a child's statements were not admissible under any other exception. Although the flexibility of the residual exception makes it an attractive option, courts' willingness to employ it has varied widely. In part, the courts' reluctance may

(continued)

stem from the lack of guidance as to "what constitutes 'sufficient indicia of reliability.'" Factors used to determine whether the statement is sufficiently reliable include the age of the child; the nature of the event; physical evidence of the event; the relationship of the child to the defendant; the contemporaneity and spontaneity of the assertions in relation to the event; the reliability of the assertions; and the reliability of the testifying witness. Other indicia of reliability could include the child's physical or mental condition; the circumstances of the statement; how the child was questioned; the consistency of the child's statements; the affect of the child; whether the child used age-appropriate language; whether the child had a motive to fabricate; whether the statement was overheard by more than one person; whether the statement was taped; the child's level of certainty; and whether any corroborating evidence existed.

e. Creative Use of Hearsay

Given the difficulty of eliciting useful testimony from children in an adversarial system, a child's hearsay statement may be the most reliable piece of evidence that a court will receive. Many statements made by children fit squarely within traditional hearsay exceptions. Children make excited utterances to police officers and domestic violence advocates after incidents of family violence. Statements for the purpose of diagnosis or treatment are made when children are the unintended victims of abuse. Children describe the impact of the violence to teachers, social workers, doctors and others, evidence that goes directly to the child's state of mind. Advocates should offer and judges should be open to admitting statements that fit within these exceptions in lieu of requiring the child to testify where doing so would be harmful for the child. Moreover, judges and advocates should employ the residual hearsay exception where traditional hearsay exceptions are inapposite and where the statements have sufficient indicia of reliability. Inclusion of such statements, if deemed reliable, could relieve numerous children of the burden of testifying in formal court proceedings.

In some situations, however, neither the traditional hearsay exceptions nor the residual exception will permit the inclusion of a child's out-of-court statement. To address this problem, a number of states have passed special child hearsay statutes, largely in the context of child sexual abuse cases. The next section examines those statutes and proposes a hearsay statute available to child witnesses in family violence cases.

2. Child Hearsay Exceptions

The purpose of child abuse hearsay exceptions is to admit into evidence statements regarding child abuse that do not fit within the existing hearsay exceptions. As the court explained in *In re Carmen O.*, which established California's child dependency hearsay exception:

> A child will be afraid publicly to accuse his or her father; the child may be cowed by the formal setting of the court; he or she may be intimidated by adverse counsel and cross-examination. Hence we often have occasion to seek means of admission of obvious hearsay statements, and we appear to achieve our objective by straining traditional hearsay concepts.

In a majority of the states, legislatures responded to this "strain" by enacting child abuse or child sexual abuse hearsay statutes. While all of the statutes are designed to permit the admission of children's out of court statements, their components differ. Some statutes apply only to criminal cases; others to both criminal and civil cases. Some cover only child sexual abuse, while others allow statements regarding all forms of child abuse. Some statutes require either that the child testify or that the child be unavailable to testify. A child's inability to testify due to psychological trauma constitutes unavailability in a number of states. Unavailability can also be established where "parents do not allow their child to testify because of fear of causing the child emotional distress, although there would be insufficient evidence of emotional trauma to satisfy the unavailability requirement." The majority of the states require corroborating evidence when the child is unavailable to testify. Most also require that the court hold a hearing to determine whether the statement is reliable prior to its admission at trial. Although the statutes vary, essentially all "child hearsay exceptions are simply residual exceptions for children's out-of-court statements." The factors used to assess reliability are the same under the residual exception and the child hearsay exception, and neither is a "firmly rooted" hearsay exception.

All of these exceptions require that the statement pertain to an act of abuse or neglect perpetrated against a child. The goal, in part, is to spare the child from the trauma of testifying. But "the same compassion oddly enough has not been extended to every child who becomes enmeshed as a witness in any proceeding . . . . All children deserve special consideration when they serve as witnesses." Therefore, "there is no reason why child sexual abuse hearsay statutes cannot be used as models for a special hearsay exception that is generally applicable to any proceeding in which a child is a witness." Lucy McGough therefore proposes a child hearsay statute that would cover all children's testimony. The legislature would enumerate the factors to be considered in determining trustworthiness and "the proponent would ultimately have the burden of demonstrating that, in light of all the enumerated factors, the hearsay carries substantial guarantees of trustworthiness and special evidentiary value that cannot be recaptured by in-court testimony." In determining trustworthiness, the court would consider the age and maturity of the child; the child's opportunity to form an accurate impression; corroborating evidence; the interval between the experience and the report; the relationship between the child and the perpetrator; the content of and language used in the report; and whether any subsequent conflicting reports existed. McGough's proposed statute mandates that the child either testify at the trial or that the child be found unavailable to testify. Finally, McGough's proposed statute requires the court to probe the biases of the adult to whom the statement is made.

While McGough's proposal has much to recommend it, some of its provisions are problematic. For example, if child hearsay statutes are designed to spare children from the trauma of testifying, why should the child have to be "unavailable" before the statement can be used? Moreover, given the empirical data that children's reports are often inconsistent, not because they are lying but because of the function of children's memory, why should the existence of subsequent "conflicting" reports be a negative factor?

One strength of McGough's proposal, however, is its consideration of the bias of the adult listener. As she notes, "The hidden hook in the receipt of all hearsay is the nature of the relationship between declarant and listener, a hook of real danger for the reliability of children's hearsay." This is especially true in family violence cases, where both parents have a motive to distort children's statements. Rather than simply relying on the court to judge the bias of such parties, a model statute should take the approach used by Maryland and Rhode Island's child hearsay statutes. The Maryland statute allows the admission of statements made by a child to physicians, psychologists, nurses, social workers, principals, vice principals, or school counselors acting "in the course of the individual's profession when the statement was made." Similarly, Rhode Island permits courts to consider statements made to a person to whom the child would normally turn for "sympathy, protection or advice." Narrowing the range of persons to whom a statement can be made confronts the problems with the bias of the adult witness.

I propose a model hearsay statute that incorporates many of the elements of McGough's, but with a few pertinent changes. First, admission of the statement would require neither that the child testify nor that the child be found unavailable. Secondly, the court would be required to consider a range of factors surrounding the "time, content and circumstances" of the statement, including but not limited to the age and maturity of the child; the child's opportunity to observe the event described; corroborating evidence; the interval between the experience and the report; the relationship between the child and the perpetrator; and the appropriateness of the language used in the report. Third, the child's statements could be introduced through any adult with whom the child has a relationship of trust, with the exclusion of parties to the action. Although other family members or friends might be tempted to skew their testimony to support one of the parties, removing the parents (who are most often the parties in family violence cases) from the equation both helps to keep the child from being made a pawn in litigation and decreases their incentive to manipulate the child.

Employing a hearsay exception like the one described above balances the needs of the child against the importance of the child's testimony. But a hearsay exception will not meet the needs of all children. Some may not have made out-of-court statements; others have the desire to testify in open

(continued)

court. What can be done, then, to improve conditions for children who either have to or want to testify? The next section addresses that question.

D. Improving the Testimonial Experience

"It is peculiar to the domestic relations area that strict adherence to concepts of procedural due process must also be tempered by the need to afford protection to the child whose interests are also at stake, though she is not a party to the action." In civil family violence cases, because there is no Sixth Amendment right to confrontation, courts have greater latitude to adjust courtroom procedures to accommodate child witnesses. This section will suggest ways that the legal system can do just that.

1. Education and Preparation

Children have a very limited understanding of the court system, its participants and conventions; as a result, the experience of testifying can be frightening if children are not adequately prepared. And "in fact, why shouldn't unprepared children be frightened by the courtroom experience? They are asked to enter a formal-looking enclosure, face the American flag and an authority figure in a black gown, and submit themselves to intense and often prolonged questioning from strangers in front of an audience of grown-ups." One way to alleviate these fears is to ensure that a child is comfortable with the courtroom setting long before the child's testimony begins.

a. What Do Children Understand About Court?

Although comprehension of the legal system improves as children get older, most young people believe that court is a "bad" place where only "bad" people go. Children understand very little of the legal system and its players, rules, procedure and language. What little they do know is too often based on misperceptions and inaccuracies.

Children between the ages of three and seven have a visual image of the judge, but don't understand his role. They have little or no idea of what lawyers do. The majority of these children do not understand the role of witnesses in a trial, and think that all witnesses tell the truth and are always believed. Between the ages of eight and eleven, children begin to understand the concept of rights and recognize the court's role in settling disputes. Nonetheless, they remain confused about what actually happens in court. At about the same age, children are more likely to say that court is neither good nor bad; towards adolescence, children begin to develop positive perceptions of the court system. Comprehension of the court system is not aided by television or school lessons, which tend to depict it in overly simplistic terms.

b. Preparation to Testify

Preparation prior to testimony can help children to alleviate the stress born of their confusion and misperceptions. A child who is going to testify should be introduced to the court and its processes. Education about courtroom procedures and courtroom figures is one way of providing such an introduction. Court schools in several cities provide children with an overview of the court process and their role in it, familiarizing the children and their families with the court's physical environment, the court's procedures and practices, and what is expected of them as witnesses. Because children are literal, concrete thinkers, taking the child to the courthouse and letting the child sit in the witness chair, touch and use the microphone, and observe where others will sit in the courtroom can also help to alleviate the child's stress. Similarly, arranging a face to face meeting between the child and a judge prior to the child's testimony can eliminate the fear of the unknown and help the child to understand that the judge is a "real person."

Preparation can help to enhance the quality of a child's testimony. Children can improve the accuracy of their testimony by being trained to provide complete responses, to resist misleading questions and to handle questions that they do not understand by asking the questioner to rephrase the query. One of the most important things to teach a child prior to testifying is that answering "I don't know," "I don't remember," or "I don't understand the question," is not only permissible, but preferable.

Perhaps the most important thing to tell children, however, is that they are not responsible for the outcome of the case and that they cannot control the judge's decision.

Education and preparation prior to trial help to alleviate the child witness' fear of the unknown. But that fear does not end when the child enters the courtroom; in fact, just the opposite is true. Steps must be taken to make the courtroom itself a friendly space for the child witness. Those steps are discussed in the next section.

2. The Courtroom Setting

Accommodating the needs of the child witness by reconfiguring courtroom space is firmly within the discretion of the trial judge. Allowing the child to testify in chambers and/or modifying the physical setting in the courtroom are two options open to the trial judge.

a. In Camera v. Open Court

Testifying in the courtroom (as opposed to a less formal setting) can have a direct impact on the child's ability to testify accurately. Children testifying in a courtroom setting are more likely to claim no knowledge of something about which they have personal knowledge and are less likely to accurately recall information than children testifying in a small private room outside of the presence of the perpetrator. One study divided children into two groups; some were interviewed at school and others at court. The children who were interviewed at school (considered a more familiar, less threatening setting) recalled more information correctly through free recall than children interviewed at court. The children interviewed at court were more likely to provide incorrect information to leading questions; the children interviewed at school made fewer errors in response to misleading questions. The children at court perceived their experience as more stressful, and the more stressful the child perceived the setting, the fewer correct answers the child provided through free recall.

The decision whether to meet with a child in chambers is generally within the discretion of the trial court. Concerns about stress and about a child's unwillingness to divulge certain information in front of her parents can be alleviated by a "nonadversarial inquiry *in camera* . . . . " Some states have provided judges with guidelines for conducting *in camera* hearings.

But many judges are reluctant to meet with children in chambers. The judges' discomfort stems from their lack of training as well as the lack of sufficient time to spend with the child.

Like attorneys, judges vary in their level of comfort in talking to children—particularly young children—because they do not believe they are sufficiently skilled in talking with children about difficult issues. Other judges avoid talking to children because they do not want the children to feel pressured or to feel that they will be the ones to decide whom they will live with.

One judge stated that given his discomfort with interviewing children, he would have the child evaluated by a mental health professional if the child's insight into the proceedings was needed.

Should the judge choose to speak with the child in chambers, certain precautions should be taken prior to beginning the interview. First, the court should delineate the subject matter of the interview and make the goal of the interview clear to counsel, the parties, and most importantly, the child. If the information provided in the interview is not going to be kept confidential, the child must know. The court should also articulate guidelines for evaluating the child's testimony.

b. Modifying the Physical Layout

Removing the child from the courtroom altogether is not the only option available to judges and advocates seeking to make testimony less traumatic for a child. Rather, the courtroom itself can be modified in order to facilitate the child's testimony. As one court explained, "The courtroom need not be made to appear a place of horrors and is not required, by law, to have any particular configuration. It may look like a playroom, a school room, a family room or living room, so long as the necessary persons are present." Another court concurred: "So long as the seriousness of the proceeding is not compromised, there is no objection to alterations which accommodate children." Courts have permitted children to testify from

(continued)

child-sized tables, joined by the judge and counsel, brought child-sized chairs into the courtroom, and allowed children to testify from underneath the prosecutor's table. Courts could require that attorneys question children from a single, neutral place. Laws in some states specifically provide for alterations to the courtroom setting.

3. Conduct of Proceedings

Altering the courtroom setting is one way of facilitating child testimony. Restructuring the way that proceedings are conducted based on the presence of a child witness is another.

a. Questioning Child Witnesses

"When children and the justice system in this country collide, language gets in the way." A number of linguistic issues make testimony difficult for child witnesses. In questioning children, lawyers use vocabulary that children don't understand and complicate their questions with confusing word orders, double negatives, and ambiguous words or phrasing and by including a number of ideas in a single question, leaving the child unsure of which part of the question she should answer.

Children misunderstand adults' questions because they don't often comprehend the concepts involved; adults misunderstand children's responses because they don't use language as a child would. To alleviate this confusion, actors within the legal system need to understand how to elicit information from children. For children under the ages of seven or eight, questions and sentences should be short and should contain only one query per question. Grammatical constructions should be simple, using the active voice. Counsel and the court should use simple words and phrases and the common meaning of terms (and possibly have the child define and use the term to show that she understands it). Children do not develop the ability to tell time until about seven or eight years old: they should not be asked questions about time before they understand the concept.

Many of these problems are exacerbated by the arcane and unconventional use of language within the legal system. "It is virtually never safe to assume that children understand legal terms." Children will understand and use the common meaning for a term that may have a different denotation within the legal system. A court is a place to play basketball. Charges are what you do with a credit card. Hearing is what you do with your ears, and parties are a place for getting presents. Swearing is like cursing, and something that you would never do with your parents sitting in the courtroom because you'd be in trouble. Moreover, legal words may sound similar to other, more familiar words, causing confusion for children. "Jury" can sound like "jewelry." "allegation" like "alligator."

Children are capable of testifying accurately, but only when questioned age-appropriately. Otherwise, they will try to answer questions that they do not understand, and they will not ask for clarification. Responsibility for ensuring that children understand what they are being asked lies with adults: in a courtroom setting, with individual counsel, and most importantly, with the judge. When a judge fulfills this responsibility, the ultimate purpose of a trial, the finding of truth, becomes much more likely.

The judge's responsibility to manage the trial includes a duty to control the manner in which counsel question a child witness. The judge must ensure that the child understands the questions. In doing so, the court increases the likelihood that the child's answer will accurately reflect the child's knowledge, and will provide the information which the child wished to convey.

Judges can set a number of ground rules that will enhance the reliability of children's testimony. Age-appropriate language should be used in questioning. Attorneys should not raise their voices when questioning children or when making objections during the child's testimony. The court can limit the scope of cross-examination, precluding attorneys from asking embarrassing, marginally relevant or collateral, developmentally inappropriate, repetitive or confusing questions. Courts can also prevent counsel from harassing child witnesses and from asking questions designed to elicit inadmissible evidence.

A number of states have recognized the enormous importance of using appropriate language with child witnesses and have specifically empowered judges to ensure that children are questioned in an age-appropriate manner. California's evidence code provides as follows:

> With a witness under the age of 14, the court shall take special care to protect him or her from undue harassment or embarrassment, and to restrict the unnecessary repetition of questions. The court shall also take special care to insure that questions are stated in a form which is appropriate to the age of the witness. The court may in the interests of justice, on objection by a party, forbid the asking of a question which is in a form that is not reasonably likely to be understood by a person of the age of the witness.

Many of these state laws apply only to criminal cases or to child abuse cases. But as with the hearsay exceptions discussed earlier, children in all types of cases face similar problems with language and questioning. Judges certainly have the discretion to protect children in their courtrooms, and advocates could voluntarily be more sensitive to the needs of child witnesses. But to ensure that children are questioned in an appropriate manner, states should expand their language legislation to encompass all cases where children are witnesses, and should certainly apply them to cases likely to cause children significant trauma as witnesses—family violence cases.

b. Breaks

Sitting and concentrating for long periods of time can be difficult for children. The child, however, will not monitor his own needs and may be afraid to ask the court to recess. Again, adults must be responsible for ensuring that the child's needs are met. Children need regularly scheduled, frequent breaks during testimony. The court should also recess whenever the child seems fatigued or displays signs of a loss of attention or unmanageable stress.

c. Supportive Persons

Research indicates that for some children, the presence of a supportive adult increases their ability to testify (both on direct and on cross-examination). The presence of supportive adults, therefore, can also enhance the truth-finding process. Moreover, having a supportive person present during testimony can help to ease the child's fears, especially if the child is testifying against someone he previously trusted. The adult support person can simply be present in the courtroom, or can sit at counsel table or stand by the child during his testimony. The child could even testify while sitting on the supportive person's lap.

Courts have the discretion to allow supportive persons to be present during testimony in any of the guises described. A number of states and the federal government have specifically authorized judges to permit the presence of supportive persons during child witness testimony. Utah's statute is slightly different, allowing the court to appoint an advisor for the child to be present during the testimony and to assist a child aged thirteen or younger in understanding counsel's questions.

Unfortunately, the majority of these statutes apply only in criminal cases or in cases of child abuse, depriving the child witness in a family violence case (or other type of case) of their protection. Again, states should recognize that testifying in any type of case can be traumatic for a child, and extend the provisions allowing the presence of supportive persons to all child witnesses. In the interim, courts should use their discretion to allow children to be accompanied during their testimony.

* * * * * * * * * * * * * * * * * * *

If the child will be testifying in open court, make sure a motion is made to modify the court for the benefit of the child. Ask to bring in a table and chair sized appropriately for the child and request permission for a trusted adult to sit near the child for assurance. When questioning the child in your offices, in her home, or when in court, have the adult sit slightly behind the child so that the child is unable to read the body language of the adult; this way, there is less chance of the child's modifying what she says to please the adult. If possible, take the child to the court (after any requested modifications are made) prior to her appearance so that she may become familiar with the physical surroundings. These precautions will assist the child in testifying more accurately and perhaps result in less trauma from the experience.

The most difficult children to deal with are those who are preverbal: infants and toddlers. Neonatal doctors sometimes refer to their practice as "veterinary practice" because children cannot give any feedback past reaction. Just as issues with intelligent animals spawn a spectrum of opinions, all passionately held, so do preverbal children in a family law court. The child cannot communicate desires, needs, hurts, or feelings past a very primitive level. The best interest of the child in these circumstances is more vulnerable to the subjective views of the attorneys and judge than in any other circumstances because there is no evidence of what this child feels. Each adult has a tendency to project his own feelings or values into the situation. Especially in the case of preverbal children, it is essential that the attorneys involved consult objective standards and try to step back from their own ways of doing things to look at what would be best for this particular child.

ELDERLY CLIENTS OR WITNESSES

In an elder law practice, or any time you have occasion to deal with an elderly person in the course of a suit, you must be aware of the special issues posed when dealing with the elderly. Even when the older client or witness is competent and healthy, an aging body still forces its needs upon the client. Issues such as impaired vision and hearing are more common, although certainly not limited to the elderly, and will be dealt with at length in the next section. You'll also need to check on the mobility status of elderly clients and witnesses. Are they fully ambulatory? Do they use a walker, cane, or wheelchair? Regardless, make sure you let the client know where the elevators are in your building if you are not on the first floor.

First concern yourself with the comfort of the client or witness. It is usually better to interview the older person in her own home. As the body grows frailer, each person learns to make her own accommodations. Rather than trying to know exactly what needs to be done for each elderly individual, you can go to where those needs have been taken care of; doing so will also help reduce anxiety levels. Depending on the age of the individual, there may be increased stress in dealing with visiting the law office that is related more to age than legal issues: What if I need my medications? How will I get there? What if I get lost? Will I need my glasses? What documents will I need? Due to their experience, the elderly are more aware that there will be things required of them; due to fixed incomes, they are also concerned with maximizing the "bang for their buck."

If you cannot have the conference with the elderly person in her home, then make it as easy as possible for her. Schedule the meeting at a time when medications are least likely to make the individual groggy and when she doesn't have to eat or such to make sure the meds don't bother her. If she is driving herself, schedule the appointment for a low-traffic time so that there are fewer hazards to deal with (elderly people are more at risk for automobile accidents). If someone else is driving her, make contact with the driver to confirm arrangements.

Be sure you have pillows and throws available in the office or conference room where you meet. Poor circulation can make the elderly person more susceptible to chills, and law offices are often too cold for them. Pillows can help settle an older client into a chair that otherwise would become unbearable for her, but you want to start with a hard chair that is easy to get in and out of rather than one of those cushy chairs that you can sink into (sometimes even younger people need a crane to get out of the worst of these things). Whether in the office or the client's home, be prepared to take frequent breaks as needed. Patience, patience, patience. Do not rush them.

With older clients, be more formal: "Yes, ma'am," "No, sir," "Mr. Smith," and "Mrs. Jones" will go a long way here. Think of the strictest teacher you ever had, and act accordingly. As a rule, elderly clients come from a more formal generation than you and will appreciate your respect. Don't patronize them, but do make sure you pace yourself at their pace, not yours. Response time slows in all ways as one ages, but slower doesn't always mean less intelligent. Remember, you'll be there too someday, unless you meet a less palatable alternative.

A significant challenge with many elderly people is getting them to discuss the very information you need to know. The generation begins gapping quite significantly at this point: it is only recently that people have been encouraged from youth to discuss important issues like family conflict or other people's problems openly—and particularly with total strangers. The information you may want—financial, medical, family problems, conflict—goes against a lifetime's habit of concealment. Sometimes sharing other stories similar to the interviewee's can help the person open up; sometimes sharing the goal can. Incentive or shared goals and

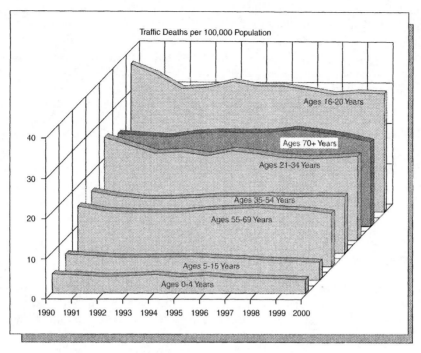

As this graph from the NHTSA shows, the elderly are the second-largest age group killed in traffic accidents.

Source: DOT HS 809 328, U.S. Department of Transportation, National Highway Traffic Safety Administration, page 2

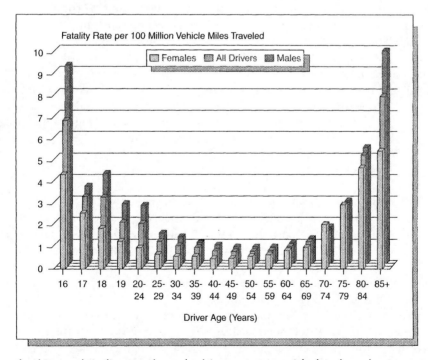

As this graph indicates, the only drivers at more risk than brand-new 16-year-olds are those 85 and older.

Source: DOT HS 809 328, U.S. Department of Transportation, National Highway Traffic Safety Administration, page 3

a sense of belonging or trust are important in any case, but they may need to be made a little more explicit in the case of the elderly client or witness.

If the elderly client or witness is going to someone else's office, as in the case of a deposition, or to trial, you need to scout out any potential issues and make sure accommodations are made. Inform opposing counsel's office of the issues and offer to have the deposition in your office, as the individual is already familiar with it. Be aware, however, that your offer may not fly because of the customs and power plays associated with having a client or affiliated witness in the office of the lawyer of his choice. Meet somewhere in advance of the deposition or trial so that you can accompany the client or witness to the designated spot; there is a greater tendency for the elderly to become disoriented, and you don't need the individual to become more stressed or flustered when testifying than the experience is already going to be. Make sure you have brought along anything needed to make the client or witness more comfortable. In the new surroundings, position the individual in such a way as to make him most comfortable and to have the greatest potential for clear communication.

DISABLED OR IMPAIRED CLIENTS OR WITNESSES

You may deal with clients or witnesses who are hearing or vision impaired, have mobility issues, or have serious injuries or illnesses that inhibit their communication skills. With any such individuals, you must develop sensitivity to their challenge, learn about how people cope with this challenge, and act accordingly.

Hearing Impairments

Hearing loss is fairly common, and ranges from moderate to severe. If you have a client with hearing loss in one ear, move your chair to the side of the good ear. Make sure that you have eliminated as much **ambient noise** as possible (close the door, turn off anything that makes noise that you don't need to have on); most people with hearing loss have difficulty in noisy environments. Speak more slowly and clearly than you ordinarily would. Enunciation is more important than volume; distinguishing "g" from "k," for example, is more of a trick than you'd suppose. Many people with poor hearing unconsciously lip read; others do it consciously. Regardless, make sure you face the person when you speak and stop speaking if you have to turn away.

In cases of severe to complete hearing loss, you may need a sign language interpreter if you do not speak sign language. You may even need more than one. Why? Because it is common for sign language interpreters to become incapacitated from working too long at a stretch. You may be thinking, well, I can just hand them all the documents; they're written out in English. Well, yes, but the deaf community regards English as a second language. There is a culture based on **American Sign Language (ASL)** as its primary language, and if you do not treat it as such, you very well may alienate a deaf client or witness.

Vision Impairments

Another common disability is **vision impairment.** Magnifying glasses or squares should be available for clients with vision issues to review documents, particularly those which you did not produce and cannot reprint in larger font. For those you do print, prepare the client's or witness's copies in very large font so that they are of use to the person. As with the good ear, find out where the person's vision is best, and then sit in the vision cone and place documents or objects for her review in that area. When navigating through the office or other unfamiliar territory, offer the sight-impaired person your arm. If there are any changes in height or texture of the ground surface, inform the sight-impaired person.

If your client is totally blind, you will have some additional issues to deal with. Mobility concerns are greater than for the nearly blind; you'll need to deal with the client in nearly the same way as you would a mobility-impaired client. You will, of course, have to read every document for the client, and tape recording or making computer audio files of the documents will be necessary for her copy. Ask in advance what format is best for the client. If the client reads Braille, ask if she has a place that she would like to have all documents sent to for transcription. Lighthouse for the Blind, which has offices in most regions of the country, is a wonderful resource.

Mobility Impairments

When you deal with a mobility-impaired witness or client, you need to be aware of the extent of the impairment and prepare accordingly. Again, it may be easier to meet with individuals with severe disabilities in their own homes because they will have already modified them to serve their needs. Although the Americans with Disabilities Act (ADA) has been in effect for a long while, your firm may not actually be in compliance—check to make sure a wheelchair can clear the aisles and enter the room in which you wish to meet. Find out what time constraints may be imposed on the interview as a result of care requirements for the client or witness because the individual may tire easily.

Transportation is often an issue for persons with mobility impairment. Many individuals cannot drive and many do not have appropriately modified vehicles, so they must rely on various publicly available transportation for the handicapped. In my experience, these services can be wildly unreliable. For important matters, if the client or witness does not have available transportation, arrange for appropriate private transport. It will add days to your life span because of the stress relief.

General Issues

Don't get flustered when dealing with the disabled. Don't freak out if you say "See you later" to a blind client. (I know of a man with an amputated leg who talks about jumping in with both feet.) I have found that being openly interested in the person as a whole, including the disability, has made it fairly easy to discuss the needs that the disability imposes. It will depend on the individual, of course, as to his or her reaction. I've been met with fury, acceptance, and humor when we have to discuss the disability directly if it bears on the legal issue. Be prepared and try not to take it personally if it goes bad.

When going on field trips with the disabled client or witness, such as depositions and trials, follow the guidelines used with the elderly. Make sure you advocate for them to be where they can hear or see best, for better lighting, for reduced ambient noise, for the side of the questioning attorney on which the better ear resides, and so on. And I do mean *advocate*. These details often escape your attorney. These are not legal issues; these are human issues. You may ask for necessary accommodations from opposing counsel or the judge unless specifically asked not to do so by your attorney. Although this consideration for the client or witness will have an impact on her ability to testify, it will not be perceived as a purely calculated tactical move when you do it, as it would be if the lawyer did it, no matter how well motivated he might be.

You must also be alert for issues that the disability poses for the testimony of the disabled person. If a hearing impaired person testifies to something that everyone else became aware of because of a sound, such as a car crash, why would this individual have noticed it? You'll need to confront these issues head on, because if you don't, someone else will. A gracious way to do it is to introduce it with, "I need to clarify something because if I don't, the other side's attorney may try to make an issue with you about this, and if we know all the details, we can try to protect you from that." Of course, not everyone takes it well. A young man who wore braces (not the kind on your teeth) and propelled himself by use of clip-on arm braces and had a specially equipped car was in a wreck where it appeared he was at fault. I told him that he needed to be able to explain very clearly how the equipment worked because jurors would be likely to blame devices that are complicated and might blame him for the accident because of the extra tasks he had to do because of his disability. He became explosively angry at me and at the world, and stomped out of the office, hitting the walls with his crutches as he left. It was good to know how he would deal with any suggestion of blame on that basis as his response would have worked against him—angry, bitter man blaming the rest of the world for his condition = aggressive driver = liability. It doesn't have to be true to be believable to a jury, and that is what I try to get across to clients and witnesses: "I don't [necessarily] believe it, and you know what the truth is, but it's a matter of what the jury can be made to believe in the courtroom."

If you haven't seen the movie *Chicago*, it is worthwhile (despite Richard Gere's complete lack of dancing or musical talent [okay, it's just my opinion]), for the clever idea behind "Razzle-Dazzle Them," a musical number in which the entire trial is made out to be a song and dance show to distract the judge and jury from the real issues. When I saw it for the first time, I felt vindicated in my point of view that the trial is theatre. If you can make the client or witness see it that way—that some of the witnesses are actors and some are not, but the jury can't necessarily tell the difference because of the special effects—it may help them feel less judged.

LANGUAGE BARRIERS

There are many linguistic minorities in the United States, encompassing various Spanish-speaking groups to various Arabic-speaking communities to groups who communicate in Chinese dialects to those who speak various languages from the African continent. Old World communities still speak European languages from west to east of the continent. The 2000 census listed over 30 specific languages spoken in the United States, with several blanket categories like "other Indo-European Languages" to account for the rest. According to the census, approximately 5% of United States residents do not speak English or do not speak it well. In the 2002 Annual Report of the Director of the Administrative Office of the Federal Courts, the director stated:

> In fiscal year 2002, there was a 3.8 percent decrease in the number of events requiring the use of interpreters in the courts. District courts reported that they used interpreters in 174,405 events, compared to 181,303 events reported in fiscal year 2001. The number of languages requiring interpretation increased from 88 in 2001 to 102 in 2002. Spanish remains the most used language for interpreters in the courts, accounting for 93.6 percent of all reported events (163,344 events), followed by Arabic (1,692 events). Other frequently used languages in fiscal year 2002 were Mandarin (1,266 events), Russian (732 events), Vietnamese (643 events), Korean (636 events), Cantonese (628 events), Haitian Creole (551 events), French (403 events), and Punjabi (309 events).

If your client has difficulties with English, you are usually faced with a family member acting as an unofficial interpreter at the beginning of the case. This may be fine at the outset, but you will have to find an interpreter who is acceptable to the court to interpret at depositions and trial testimony. Sometimes it is necessary to find one earlier because the family member isn't much better than the client at speaking English, or the vocabulary you need interpreted is too highly specialized.

Finding and choosing interpreters is a tricky process. You must find an interpreter whose understanding of nuances is the same as your client's, for interpretation is more than simply a vocabulary exercise, despite the suggestions of computerized translators. Consider, for example, the multiple uses of the word *snow*. Its ordinary meaning refers to that cold white stuff that falls from the sky in winter unless you live in the southernmost part of the United States. However, you can "snow" someone, having nothing to do with the frosty stuff, but everything to do with misleading her. Or you can obtain some "snow," which, although white and powdery, is neither freezing nor legal. In the far south, however, some amusement parks obtain snow in the sense of the frozen stuff for a winter attraction. If a witness says, "I got some snow," you'd have to know the context. In any language, the proper interpretation of a word can depend on context.

Sarcasm and irony also present problems. We often say the opposite of what we mean, but everyone understands because of the way it is said or the nonverbal communication accompanying our words. A typical example is "Right," which, when said by Dr. Evil of the *Austin Powers* movies, means anything but "correct." Therefore, an appropriate interpreter for your witness is one who understands not only the words, but the context and the culture's intonation patterns and nonverbal communications.

One way to check out the interpreter before the deposition is to have the witness, the family member who acts as interpreter, and the proposed official interpreter meet together to talk. You will have to meet with the witness and unofficial interpreter first to prepare them for the meeting. Caution the witness, particularly if she is your client, that because this person will be considered an officer of the court, she should not say anything to the interpreter that she wouldn't want to say to the judge. In the meeting, have the witness explain what you have agreed upon to the proposed interpreter and have the interpreter interpret it for you while the unofficial interpreter takes notes. When the meeting is over, thank the interpreter, and then meet with the witness and family member. Have the family member relay what the interpreter said, and see if he believes the interpreter is accurately translating what the witness says. If the answer is yes, you've got yourself an interpreter. If no, keep looking.

If you don't have a good interpreter, weird things can happen. I've had witnesses whose English was actually quite good argue with the interpreter over how he or she worded what the witness said. In San Antonio, Texas, which has a high number of speakers of the so-called "Tex-Mex" dialect, a plaintiff testifying in Spanish was being translated by a woman from South America. Frequently during her translation, the plaintiff and the Spanish-speaking jurors, lawyers, and judge would start shaking their heads at the inaccuracy of the translation. The idiosyncrasies of the local dialect escaped her, and nuances were lost on anyone in the courtroom who spoke English only or any other form of Spanish. This problem elevated the Spanish-speaking jurors to a position of knowing more about the case than the other jurors, giving a small group an expert power that most lawyers try to avoid in the jury pool.

Make sure that the interpreter meets any state or local court rules for interpreters and that there are no objections to the interpreter from opposing counsel before engaging the interpreter for depositions. Once you've gotten a good interpreter, hold on to the information and save it in multiple locations to safeguard against loss; good ones are hard to find.

In addition to making sure about the standards for the interpreter, make sure you know when the interpreter is needed. Different jurisdictions have different standards about when the right to an interpreter attaches; following is one court's view about the importance of an interpreter.

Figueroa v. Doherty, 707 N.E.2d 654 (Ill. Ct. App. 1999).

St. Joseph Hospital and Home Health Care Center fired Walter Figueroa on January 22, 1996. A referee for the Illinois Department of Employment Security (IDES) denied Figueroa's claim for benefits. The Board of Review and the circuit court affirmed the referee's decision. Figueroa appeals.

Figueroa began working in the hospital's food service department in 1977. On January 15, 1996, Maria Sandoval, another hospital employee, called Figueroa at work. Figueroa left the department a few minutes later. A coworker, Tom Barliss, went to the supervisor, Ray Rees, to report that he saw Figueroa take some lemons from the refrigerator. Rees found Figueroa and Sandoval in the hallway. Sandoval held a bag of lemons. Rees notified security. The hospital fired Figueroa one week later.

Figueroa applied for unemployment benefits. The hospital faxed to the claims adjudicator a statement of its contention that Figueroa stole the lemons. Figueroa denied the charge. The hospital did not permit the adjudicator to contact Sandoval. The adjudicator ruled Figueroa eligible for benefits and the local office upheld the decision. On the hospital's appeal, the referee held a hearing de novo.

Figueroa, appearing without counsel, brought an interpreter to the hearing to translate the proceedings into Spanish for him. At the outset of the hearing the referee asked Figueroa four questions in English about his address and social security number. Figueroa responded "Yes" to all four questions. After introduction of the parties and swearing of the witnesses, including Figueroa, the referee said:

"You seem to understand what I am saying.

[Figueroa]: A little.

Referee: A little yeah. Okay if you understand what's going on then just listen if you don't understand what they're saying indicate to your interpreter that you don't understand it, and I will let you whisper in his ear. I don't want to go back and forth okay. We don't have the time for that. *** If there is any real problem we'll stop and let you go."

The hospital presented an affidavit from Barliss, who swore he saw Figueroa take "a handful" of lemons from the refrigerator. The affidavit does not clarify whether he saw whole lemons or lemon slices. Rees testified that when he found Figueroa and Sandoval in the hall he asked where she got the lemons. She said they were hers. He asked Figueroa where he put the lemons he took from the refrigerator. Figueroa showed Rees a container holding 8 to 10 lemon wedges. The hospital's attorney asked Rees a series of questions to clarify the testimony and establish that taking lemons violated hospital rules.

The referee then asked the interpreter to ask whether Figueroa had any cross-examination for Rees. After a brief discussion in Spanish between Figueroa and the interpreter, the transcript shows the following:

"R: He has no questions.

INTERP: She asked a couple of questions, but he is not sure that she understood everything that is going on. So he INAUDIBLE.

R: Okay you might just very briefly explain to him Mr. Rees has testified to the fact that there was a witness that saw him take out 5 lemons from the refrigerator and give them to another employee. *** Okay just briefly tell him what the jest [sic] of his testimony."

While Figueroa was still stating his question in Spanish, the hospital objected that he seemed to be testifying rather than questioning. The transcript shows that the interpreter answered:

"He is saying ah that what based on what he could understand ah, there are several INAUDIBLE at this point of what Mr. Rees says that at one point he sold Mr. Figueroa 5 lemons, and INAUDIBLE there was a handful and another person ah, there was 5 or 6 left in a plastic bag. He is saying and wondering why he was able to count the lemons since they were inside a plastic bag.

R: Alright that's his question.

***

How were you able to count the lemons if they were in a bag?"

The referee asked no questions of either witness about Figueroa's statement that Rees had sold him the five lemons. Figueroa began his testimony in Spanish. The transcript shows the following:

"R: Okay will you just say what he says.

INTERP: Okay.

R: And summarize it.

INTERP: He says that ah, ah he received a phone call from a spanish [sic] speaking lady that they should name for it. Ah that she wants to see him because she asks him to go out for ride that day and that's why he went to see this spanish [sic] speaking lady. Mr. Rees has no proof whatsoever that he actually gave her any lemons."

Figueroa then presented a notarized document from Sandoval stating that Figueroa never sold or gave her any lemons. The interpreter added:

"He said some other things but I don't know if I have to say them or not.

R: Are they, you summarized them right?

INTERP: Okay in another words he says that the reason he took the lemons was because another person that he never mentioned in this problem his name Martha asked Mr. Figueroa for the lemons previously. She works in the preparation room and that's why he was in the area. Part of his work to deal with who prepares the salads and cuts lemons."

The referee asked no questions to clarify Figueroa's testimony. The hospital's attorney summarized the hospital's views and then the interpreter translated Figueroa's summary as follows:

"In anther [sic] words he is going back to the person saying that, that ah, the reason that he was there was because that's were he had worked for the last 17 years. He had a reason to be there. That was assignment area of work. INAUDIBLE and he is also wondering if they believe that every piece of food that comes out of the hospital is considered INAUDIBLE. Ah he believes that Mr. Rees doesn't know ah, the different customs of people. Spanish people have lemons with everything, with tea, with fish ah, it is a common thing for spanish people to take the lemons to work or bag of tea or anything else. So he argues that every piece of food INAUDIBLE.

*** For 17 years he has never had a problem whatsoever ah, you know, in any manner and that he is not dumb enough to go and take 5 lemons ***.

Okay he is saying that at no time and there is not record of it security confronted Mr. Figueroa outside the cafeteria. He said he never took anything outside the hospital."

The referee sought no clarification of Figueroa's testimony or argument. Although Figueroa seemed to think he had been accused of entering an area where he did not belong, the referee did not clarify the charges for Figueroa or ask him any questions concerning his insistence that he belonged in the area where Rees met him. The referee found that Barliss saw Figueroa take five lemons from the refrigerator and Figueroa gave the lemons to Sandoval. The referee decided that this constituted unauthorized removal of hospital property, a kind of misconduct that disqualified Figueroa from receiving benefits.

Figueroa appealed from the referee's decision, arguing that the referee "did not allow enough time to present my side of the case. The first thing that the Referee expressed was that he was running half an hour behind his scheduled."

After he filed the appeal, an attorney prepared a brief on Figueroa's behalf.

The Board of Review held that the "record adequately sets forth the evidence so that no further evidentiary proceedings are deemed necessary." The Board found that the hospital lost the use of five lemons, so it affirmed the referee's decision. The circuit court upheld the findings and decision of the Board. The court found that the transcript of the hearing did not support Figueroa's argument that he needed an interpreter, so the interpreter's failure to translate all proceedings word for word did not deprive Figueroa of a fair hearing.

On appeal Figueroa again argues that the referee did not give him a fair hearing. IDES counters that Figueroa waived all due process claims by failing to raise them before the Board of Review. Figueroa, somewhat informally, described the inadequate procedures as a basis for his appeal to the Board. We find that Figueroa adequately preserved the issue . . . Moreover, "the general rule that an appellate court should confine itself to issues raised in earlier proceedings is not a rigid or inflexible one, and, where injustice might otherwise result, a reviewing court may consider questions of law not passed upon by an administrative agency.". . . Figueroa's claims that IDES did not provide him a fair hearing warrant consideration even if he has waived them.

The Unemployment Insurance Act provides that a "Referee *** shall afford the parties reasonable opportunity for a fair hearing.". . . The hearing must accord with fundamental principles of due process . . . Fundamental due process rights may require a court to permit an interpreter to translate courtroom proceedings. "This is so because inherent in [the] nature of justice is the notion that those involved in litigation should understand and be understood." . . .

In *United States ex rel. Negron v. New York*, 434 F.2d 386 (2d Cir. 1970), the court held:

"*** Not only for the sake of effective cross-examination, however, but as a matter of simple humaneness, [a defendant] deserve[s] more than to sit in total incomprehension as the trial proceed[s]."

Negron, 434 F.2d at 389-90 . . .

Here, the referee permitted an interpreter to accompany Figueroa, although Figueroa appeared to understand some English. Because the referee did not want to spend the time required for full translation, he specifically directed the interpreter to translate, by whispering in Figueroa's ear during the testimony, only when Figueroa had a specific question about the testimony. The referee told the interpreter to summarize Figueroa's testimony, rather than translate it word for word. And the referee directed the interpreter to translate for Figueroa a specific, one-sentence summary of Rees' testimony. Rees' testimony takes up 7 pages out of the 15-page transcript of the entire hearing.

Although Figueroa answered some questions in English, the questions were simple and none of Figueroa's answers showed any facility with English. Figueroa's extended discussions with the interpreter demonstrate that he is far more capable of understanding and expressing himself in Spanish.

In *People v. Starling*, 21 Ill. App. 3d 217, 315 N.E.2d 163 (1974), the trial court appointed an interpreter to translate the testimony of the complaining witness from Spanish into English. The defendant objected to the interpreter's summarizing of the testimony without a verbatim translation. The appellate court held:

"It is obvious the interpreter was not fully, completely or accurately translating the questions and answers. When an interpreter is employed, that practice must be strictly followed; otherwise the possibility of editing, and error, rests solely with the interpreter. Due process rights of persons charged with crimes cannot be short-cut by avoiding the ritual of translating each question and answer ***." *Starling*, 21 Ill. App. 3d at 222.

Similarly, in *People v. Alfaro*, 227 Ill. App. 3d 281, 592 N.E.2d 1117, 170 Ill. Dec. 437 (1992), the defendant alleged that the interpreter provided only synopses of the testimony. The appellate court remanded for hearing on the allegations, because a failure to provide a full translation of proceedings "goes to the heart of constitutional due process of law." *Alfaro*, 227 Ill. App. 3d at 285. Thus, even reasonably accurate summaries of testimony do not suffice to protect a litigant's due process rights . . .

The summary of the testimony the referee instructed the interpreter to translate is more egregious than the summaries involved in *Starling* and *Negron*, because the summary here is wrong. The referee told Figueroa, through the translator, that a witness saw him take five lemons from the refrigerator and give them to an employee. Barliss swore he saw Figueroa take "a handful" of lemons. The referee, like Rees, may have interpreted the number taken as five because that is the number of lemons Sandoval held. More importantly, no one saw Figueroa hand anything to Sandoval. The incorrect summary left Figueroa thinking he needed to rebut evidence not presented . . .

The referee also instructed the interpreter not to translate Figueroa's testimony word for word, but to provide only a summary. The instruction effectively denied Figueroa the right to testify on his own behalf . . .

Finally, "as part of the referee's duty to afford a fair hearing, he must assure that the record in cases involving pro se parties is fully developed.". . . The referee has a duty to ascertain all pertinent facts surrounding a claim, and he breaches that duty if he fails to ask a pro se claimant questions needed to clarify and complete the statement of the claimant's position . . . Here . . . the referee failed to develop the record fully, as the record contains only a nearly indecipherable statement of Figueroa's argument, and the referee asked no questions and made no effort to clarify the testimony.

The failure to provide a complete translation of all proceedings deprived Figueroa of his right to a fair hearing that he understood and at which he would be understood . . . That failure became more egregiously prejudicial when the referee instructed the interpreter to translate for Figueroa a not merely incomplete, but also highly inaccurate, summary of the evidence against him. The referee further breached his duties by failing to fully develop Figueroa's position in a clear, comprehensible record. In view of the largely incomprehensible record, we elect not to decide what results may be permissible in hypothetical factual situations. Although "a court may simply reverse the agency" in appropriate circumstances, "where the record of the hearing is clearly inadequate, the case should be remanded to the agency.". . . The case is remanded for rehearing before a referee who will provide a fair hearing for Figueroa's claim.

Reversed and remanded.

I love cases where you can read between the lines and see that the court is really annoyed. In this one, note the comment in the last full sentence. It's clear that the court doesn't think the first referee is capable of providing a fair hearing. In addition, there's that lovely word *egregiously*. **Egregious,** in any form, means horrendously, awfully, inarguably, obviously bad. When you see that word in a court opinion, the court is very much displeased.

In addition to arranging for foreign language interpreters, you may have to arrange for American Sign Language (ASL) interpreters if you have deaf or hearing-impaired witnesses or clients. These interpreters usually insist on teams; long periods of translating have caused injury that has forced some interpreters to retire. A relatively new area is **facilitated communication** for people with autism. In facilitated communication, a patient with autism is taught to type on a computer or alphabet board with the physical support of a facilitator, who ideally will reduce his support until the patient functions independently of him. In the early stages, the facilitator may be assisting the typing by placing his hands over the patient's hands, so there is some concern over the validity of the information. The facilitor as interpreter will generate challenges from an expert witness point of view, as there has been debate over the validity of the method. You will also have to illustrate the facilitator's competence as an interpreter.

CULTURAL BARRIERS AND RACISM

Cultures vary in customs in ways that can lead to serious misunderstandings in intent and discomfort between people. Psychologists, sociologists, linguists, ethnologists, and other behavioral scientists have studied issues of nonverbal communication, personal space, vocabulary usage, and other markers in differences in behavior or custom. It has become a marketable consulting area in business to assist with cross-cultural negotiations or service transactions, as the problems inherent in failing to recognize cultural differences becomes evident even when the language barrier is overcome.

Paralegals should strive to be culturally sensitive. Characteristics of a culturally sensitive paralegal include the following.

* An awareness and sensitivity to her own cultural heritage and to valuing and respecting differences
* An awareness of her own values and biases, and how they may affect clients with differing value systems
* Comfort with differences that exist between herself and her clients in terms of race and beliefs
* An awareness of her own prejudiced attitudes, beliefs, and feelings

The difficulty is achieving awareness, particularly if you are white. White Americans do not always perceive the racism or prejudice that is evident to others. It is just assumed that "things are done that way," and there is little challenge to those value systems. In "White Privilege: Unpacking the Invisible Knapsack," Peggy McIntosh of the Wellesley College Center for Research on Women, McIntosh states that "whites are carefully taught not to recognize white privilege." She lists 26 conditions that she believes attach somewhat more to skin-color privilege than those based on class, ethnicity, status, or geographical location. The list is thought-provoking, and will probably start some arguments, but it does at least begin the process of heightened awareness of assumptions and privileges held by the majority culture of the United States. Here are a few of the conditions McIntosh lists:

- I can swear, or dress in secondhand clothes, or not answer letters, without having people attribute these choices to the bad morals, the poverty, or the illiteracy of my race.
- I can go home from most meetings of organizations I belong to feeling somewhat tied in, rather than isolated, out-of-place, outnumbered, unheard, held at a distance, or feared.
- I can be pretty sure that if I ask to talk to "the person in charge," I will be facing a person of my race.

Although McIntosh's article was written in 1988, there is still merit to her observations and some of them reflect problems continuous in our society. Depending on your locale, you may have greater or lesser degrees of intercultural hostility, but to figure out your client's story or the witness's perspective, you will have to start challenging your assumptions of the world.

Sociolinguistics, an area of linguistics that focuses on language differences based on gender, culture, class, and so on, has looked at this problem of cross-cultural miscommunication for years. One legal situation drew the interest of sociolinguistics internationally: the 1988 case of a young Aboriginal woman named Robyn Kina. After suffering three years of abuse by her live-in, she stabbed the non-Aboriginal man in the chest as he came at her with a chair when she attempted to defend her 15-year-old niece (who was living with them) from his threat to rape her. Kina did not discuss the history of abuse with her lawyers, and was convicted for murder in an extremely short trial. A few years later, in a television documentary, Kina told her story to reporters. Outrage over her conviction followed, and the Australian legal profession wanted to know why Kina would talk to the press but not her lawyers. It was the sociolinguists who answered the question.

Kina was communicating "in an Aboriginal way," and the reporters could communicate with her on that basis. Her lawyers, on the other hand, found her difficult to talk with. The reason for this was that, in Aboriginal culture, one does not ask direct questions; privacy is respected. Instead, if you want information, you volunteer some of your own and hint at what you want to know, using these hints to direct the conversation and allowing silence and space for the speaker to relate the story. Such an approach is completely different from the interrogation style usually employed by English speakers, which failed completely in Kina's case.

Kina's story illustrates how you must become sensitive to cultural differences when you have clients or witnesses from a non-majority background. Realize you may have to think through your assumptions about how people communicate. Although generalities may not apply to any given person from an ethnic group, you need to be sensitive to the fact that they may. Find out what you can about communication styles and non-verbal communication in that culture. Find out what makes folks uncomfortable in the culture of your witness. When in doubt, ask if something is a problem or makes the witness uncomfortable; it's better to demonstrate a concern for the other person's sensitivities than to ignore them completely. Whenever you have a witness from a different culture, you also need to find out what you can about the negative stereotypes that prevail. You do not have to share prejudices to recognize them, and if they exist, you will have to take them into account when evaluating how the jury will perceive your witness.

In the *Kina* case, a sociolinguist testified in subsequent legal proceedings to obtain Kina's freedom. Similarly, a relatively new concept has been the use of a **cultural defense** to mitigate against intent; it has created an uproar because, as commentators quite reasonably point out, the intent to commit the act is still the same, regardless of whether the perpetrator considered it a criminal act, and the primary negative impact is on women and children.

Customs can be key in understanding behavior, timing of communication, interaction between people, and all sorts of small details that can loom large in litigation. However, is it possible to use an expert to explain cultural issues in a civil case? The Ninth Circuit didn't think it was a problem.

Vang v. Xiong, 944 F.2d 476 (9th Cir. 1991).

Vang Xiong Toyed ("Xiong") appeals from a judgment entered after a jury verdict against him in a suit pursuant to 42 U.S.C. § 1983 (§ 1983). Plaintiffs, along with their spouses, brought this action against Xiong, a Washington State employee, asserting he raped them during the course of his employment. Appellant . . .

argues the trial court erroneously admitted the testimony of three expert witnesses and that such testimony was prejudicial. We have jurisdiction under 28 U.S.C. § 1291 and affirm.

The parties in this case are Hmong refugees from Laos. Appellee Yia Moua ("Moua") moved with her family to Spokane, Washington in 1979. In 1981 she sought employment and was referred to Xiong who was employed by the Washington State Employment Security office. Xiong was responsible for interviewing and finding refugees suitable employment. Moua apparently filed an application and was interviewed by Xiong, but was unsuccessful in obtaining a job.

In 1983 Moua contacted Xiong to assist her in learning to drive and in passing the Washington driver's license test. Moua alleged that sometime between January and March 1983 Xiong picked her up and told her he was going to take her some place where she could study for the driver's exam. The two drove to a motel where, Moua charges, Xiong raped her.

In 1983 appellee Maichao Vang ("Vang") moved with her family to the Spokane area from a refugee camp in Thailand. Vang testified she eventually contacted Xiong to assist her in obtaining employment and that at various times Xiong drove her to sewing clubs to apply for work. On one occasion Xiong insisted that she accompany him to Idaho to deliver a letter to a Hmong family. Instead, Xiong drove Vang to a motel where he raped her twice.

Later, Xiong contacted Vang regarding a possible job. After she joined him for the interview, he raped her. Vang testified that Xiong raped her at least sixteen times and on each occasion he relied on the pretext of a potential employment opportunity. On one occasion Xiong raped Vang when he was supposed to be helping her obtain her driver's license.

Eventually each plaintiff revealed the rape to her husband and the couples filed a complaint under § 1983 against Xiong . . . The trial resulted in a verdict in favor of the plaintiffs for $ 300,000 . . .

Xiong . . . challenges the trial court's admission of three experts' testimony.

Prior to trial, Xiong challenged the testimony of Marshall Hurlich, an epidemiologist with the Seattle Department of Public Health. Hurlich described Hmong culture and explained the behavior of the plaintiffs in this case within that cultural context. The trial court granted Xiong's motion in limine in part and denied it in part. Hurlich was permitted to testify "generally as to the Hmong culture, but [he was precluded from testifying] as to his opinion regarding the specifics of this case, such as whether there was a rape or why these particular plaintiffs did not report the rape."

At trial, Hurlich explained that Hmong women are generally submissive, and are raised to respect and obey men. He described the role of Hmong women in marriage; their attitudes towards sex, discussion of sex, and extramarital affairs. Most significantly, Hurlich explained that upon fleeing from Laos, Hmong refugees were reliant on government officials for their needs and would not survive in the United States without government assistance. Because of this reliance on government assistance, the Hmong have developed an awe of persons in government positions.

Plaintiffs' counsel attempted to elicit testimony from Hurlich regarding: the likelihood that a Hmong woman would accuse a man of rape; the likelihood that a Hmong woman would travel with a man who was not her husband; and the ability of Hmong women to articulate feelings and memories and to testify in court. The court rejected these questions as violative of the pretrial order.

Xiong argues that Hurlich's testimony should have been excluded because it was not relevant . . . Hurlich's testimony was not relevant, in appellant's view, because plaintiffs did not testify they feared Xiong because he was a government official. On the other hand, the testimony was prejudicial because it supported plaintiff's claim that they had trusted and relied on Xiong because he was a government official . . . and painted unsupported ethnic stereotypes which engendered compassion for the plaintiffs and bolstered their credibility . . .

The district court in this case did not abuse its discretion in deciding that Hurlich's testimony, which the court limited to a general explanation of Hmong culture and the role of women in that culture, was relevant. In a hearing that preceded the evidentiary ruling the court said "Hurlich is . . . the only expert that either side has located who can explain to the trier of fact who these people are, where they came from, and *why they have responded the way they have in these various functions and various relationships.*" The testimony was relevant to assist the trier of fact to understand certain behavior of the parties here that might otherwise be confusing. . . and to explain the cause, effect and nature of long term Hmong reliance on governmental agencies for support. The testimony was prejudicial to Xiong because it supported plaintiffs assertions that he raped them. It was not, however, *unduly prejudicial* because of its limited scope and its direct relevance to the issues in the case . . .

The judgment of the district court is AFFIRMED.

When the culture needs explanation to help the jury understand things that could be a problem for them, which in the *Vang* case would be the late reporting and a continued relationship with Xiong after the initial rapes, it is within the discretion of the court to allow this kind of testimony. As a practical matter, if there is something that might sound odd to a jury made up of people who are not of the ethnic group represented by a key witness or the client, and cultural differences can explain the oddness away, think very seriously about getting an expert. But you'll have to do your homework first: find out how that particular group communicates, what behaviors are expected, and how common behaviors are interpreted differently than the American or local standard. (I live in Texas, and people who would not dream of saying the same thing about any other ethnic group will offer, "Well, you have to make allowances for Soandso; he is a Yankee, you know." The rest of the group will all intone "Ohhh," in a that-explains-it sort of way. Cultural differences can be regional as well as foreign.) Start your study as soon as you know that there is an ethnic divergence that may count.

CHAPTER SUMMARY

Although all witnesses and clients present unique opportunities, there are classes of clients and/or witnesses that carry issues the paralegal should be aware of in preparing for and conducting the interview. Clients with competency issues pose problems in ethics, as the duty to allow the client to control legal representation can be in conflict with what the attorney believes is in the best interest of the client. When a paralegal believes there may be issues of competency or capacity, she should alert the attorney. When dealing with children, the age of the child and the attorney's position in the case will make the difference in how the case is approached. In setting up meetings with children, it is best to see them in their own environment, and have significant adults situated behind them. The elderly are particularly vulnerable to dementia, a condition that makes them unable to make sound decisions. The paralegal must also consider elderly clients' (or witnesses') hearing and vision impairments, mobility issues, generational concerns, comfort needs, and pace. In dealing with persons with various disabilities, the paralegal should be acquainted with the specific needs of the client or witness and make the necessary accommodations and advocate as needed. In the case of children, the elderly, or the disabled, the paralegal should visit the courtroom or other location that a client or witness will have to visit and prepare both the visitor and the location as much as possible for the visit. For non-English speaking clients, the paralegal should find an interpreter who speaks the same regional version of the client's language. For clients or witnesses from a different culture, whether they speak English or not, the paralegal should acquaint herself with the culture, particularly with regard to differences in communication, and be ready to ask questions to clarify those differences. She should be ready to challenge her own assumptions about persons of other races and ethnicities.

FOR FURTHER READING

Annette R. Appell, *Decontextualizing the Child Client: The Efficacy of the Attorney-Client Model for Very Young Children*, 64 Fordham L. Rev. 1955 (1996).

Emily Buss, *Confronting Developmental Barriers to the Empowerment of Child Clients*, 84 Cornell L. Rev. 895 (1999).

Gerard F. Glynn, *Multidisciplinary Representation of Children: Conflicts Over Disclosures of Client Communications*, 27 J. Marshall L. Rev. 617 (1994).

Susan J. Hemp and Cheryl Rae Nyberg, *Elder Law: A Guide to Key Resources*, 3 Elder L.J. 1 (1995).

Jan Ellen Rein, *Clients with Destructive and Socially Harmful Choices—What's an Attorney to Do? Within and Beyond the Competency Construct*, 62 Fordham L. Rev. 1101 (1994).

Robert P. Roca, *Determining Decisional Capacity: A Medical Perspective*, 62 Fordham L. Rev. 1177 (1994).

Lisa Carol Rogers, *Child Custody: The Judicial Interview of the Child*, 47 La. L. Rev. 559 (1987).

Franklyn P. Salimbene, *Court Interpreters: Standards of Practice and Standards for Training*, 6 Cornell J. L. & Pub. Pol'y 645 (1997).

Ramon Valle, *A "Culture-Fair" Approach to Bioethical Advocacy in Dementing Illness*, 35 Ga. L. Rev. 465 (2001).

Helen L. Westcott, *Children, Hearsay, and the Courts: A Perspective from the United Kingdom*, 5 Psych. Pub. Pol. and L. 282 (1999).

CHAPTER REVIEW

KEY TERMS

ambient noise
American Sign Language (ASL)
attorney ad litem
capacity
competency
Court Appointed Special Advocate (CASA)

cultural defense
dementia
egregious
facilitated communication
guardian ad litem (GAL)
hearing loss

in camera
incompetent
nomenclature
sub judice
vision impairment

FILL IN THE BLANKS

1. Literally meaning "in secret," the phrase _____ refers to when a judge reviews documents or other items in private so that confidentiality is not breached before a ruling is made on privilege but to avoid an ex parte hearing.

2. The primary language for the deaf is _____; persons communicating in this language often consider English a second language.

3. Technically, a(n) _____ represents an incapacitated or incompetent person only to the extent of the person's legal interests; he is not responsible for determining what is in that person's best interest.

4. The _____ for the spectrum of ad litems varies.

5. A(n) _____, or member of a group with the same acronym, _____, is a specially trained layperson who will investigate and determine the needs of a child in child welfare litigation.

6. _____ and _____ are often used interchangeably; both are used to refer to someone's ability to make coherent legal decisions for herself in a mature way, knowing the risks and benefits that may result.

7. The Latin phrase for "under judgment" is _____.

8. Although often associated with Alzheimer's, _____ can be experienced in a range of illnesses and injuries.

9. Older clients are more likely to suffer from _____, so having magnifying glasses available and printing documents for their review in larger print is advisable.

10. _____, although a new and promising way for people with autism to communicate, faces problems of acceptance in the courtroom.

11. A(n) _____ often has conflicting duties as to his incompetent clients, needing both to take care of their best interests and to advocate their wishes to the extent they can express them—a distinct problem when children are involved.

12. The relatively new concept of _____ is under attack to the extent that it may excuse criminal acts under the guise of diversity or sensitivity.

13. Once someone is formally declared _____, the guardian will make determinations of what is in the best interest of the individual.

14. An individual who has experienced _____ all her life is more likely to identify herself as a member of the _____ because all of her interactions are based on ASL rather than English, even though ASL itself is based on English.

15. Persons who have _____ often have more difficulty understanding what is being said when there is a lot of _____.

16. Not allowing an interpreter for a litigant who does not speak English is a(n) _____ violation of someone's rights.

WEB WORK

1. The Cross-Cultural Communication Strategies Web site from the International Online Training Program on Intractable Conflict presented by the Conflict Research Consortium at the University of Colorado is focused on a different type of conflict resolution, but the articles there are still relevant and useful: http://www.colorado.edu/conflict/peace/treatment/xcolcomm.htm. Scan the linked articles and determine which ones would be most useful to you in your area.

2. The Pew Charitable Trusts have some useful research; the Pew Forum on Religion and Public Life is no exception. One area of its Web site addresses issues facing Muslims in light of post-9/11 America: http://pewforum.org/news/display.php?NewsID=2437. Do you think these measures will be helpful? Do any of the articles dispel any concerns you have or that you believe a potential juror might have?

3. To prepare American students to go overseas to school, Studyabroad.com has a short primer on cultural differences at http://www.studyabroad.com/handbook/cultdiff.html. It is particularly enlightening to find out how other cultures perceive Americans. Check out the American stereotypes. Do you think there is a legitimate basis for them?

4. The Michigan Deaf and Hard of Hearing Organization has an informational page at http://www.michdhh.org/asl_deaf_culture/ on deaf culture. In what ways does it differ from mainstream American culture? In what ways does it seem the same?

5. The National Clearinghouse on Child Abuse and Neglect Information, a service of the Children's Bureau in the U.S. Department of Health and Human Services, provides numerous publications on issues related to child welfare, which are indexed at http://www.calib.com/nccanch/pubs/index.cfm. Would any of these be helpful in preparing yourself or your witnesses?

BRAIN WORK

1. On the whole, court interpreters are loosely regulated. Draft a statute for court interpreters that would take into consideration the problems raised in the chapter.

2. How would you define *culture* generally? What is your personal cultural background? How does it shape your worldview? Can an understanding of cultural differences assist you as a paralegal? How?

3. Which of the proposals discussed in *In re the Care of Georgette* makes sense to you? Do you think one's moral sense solves the ethical problem posed? Explain your answer.

4. Do you think the explanation of the sociolinguist in the *Kina* case was warranted? Would you have reversed the case based on that information? Why or why not?

5. In a negligence case, what would be the argument to exclude cultural testimony on behalf of a defendant? Hint: Think about how we determine duty and breach of duty in civil law versus criminal law. Would the outcome be the same in a case based on an intentional tort? Why or why not?

PUTTING IT TO WORK

1. In the *Haus* case, one of the neighbors who lives next door to Patty is an elderly woman who is hard of hearing. She can only hear in her left ear. She is relatively healthy, but must take medication for high blood pressure. She is rumored to have some knowledge of the relationship between the three major players: Patty, the police officer, and the boyfriend. Prepare to interview her, including preliminary research, question list, letter to confirm an appointment, and a to-do list for yourself of reminders on how to handle the interview.

2. Among the witnesses for your cases are a child, an elderly or disabled person, and a person who faces problems resulting from language or cultural barriers. Prepare to interview each with their issues in mind (including set-up and confirmation of the interview), interview each, and prepare an interview summary for your attorney. Your summary should include concerns raised by the special issues of each witness and the extent to which you confronted them. Also include your recommendations to the attorney for depositions and trial.

DOCUMENTARY EVIDENCE

"People in general have no notion of the sort and amount of evidence often needed to prove the simplest matter of fact."

Peter Mere Latham (c. 1875)

"Take nothing on its looks; take everything on evidence. There's no better rule."

Charles Dickens (1861)

"I pass with relief from the tossing sea of Cause and Theory to the firm ground of Result and Fact."

Sir Winston S. Churchill (1898)

"Facts are stubborn things."

Alain René Lesage (c. 1735)

INTRODUCTION

Juries tend to take things in print more seriously than the things people say in court, so written evidence taken down at the time of the incident made the basis of the lawsuit, or documents that shed light on the parties' relationship, claims, or credibility, will be very important pieces of evidence to obtain and review. If the documents will hurt your client, the legal team needs to know that and take it into consideration; if they will help, you need them to make your case.

The types of documents used in any particular case are determined largely by the subject matter of the case. If you have a tort case, you will certainly have medical records and perhaps some psychologists' records as well. If you are working a family law or wills case, you may have tax returns, pay stubs, bank statements, deeds, real estate valuations, corporate records of a closely held company, stocks, and various valuations of any valuable personal property. In addition, for a family law case, you may also have social studies and school records if custody is an issue. A contract dispute will involve the contract and any correspondence between the parties, subcontracts, receipts, liens, or brochures. An employment discrimination case will require corporate policy manuals on discrimination and harassment, the records of discipline for the parties, the complaint rates for the company, any complaints made against the parties, and any documents alleged to create a hostile environment. These lists are not comprehensive or exhaustive; they are simply examples of the minimum number of document types you would need. The idiosyncrasies of each case drive it and require specific documents to satisfy its requirements.

Even so, certain types of documents are fairly common, and you need to learn what to look for in them. Reading accident reports by police officers, medical records by health care professionals, and tax returns by litigants with an eye toward discovering evidence in a civil litigation context is much different than reading them for criminal law, health care, or tax liability. Knowing those basics certainly gives you a leg up, but it is the ability to apply your legal knowledge to the data that makes you a valuable member of a legal team.

ETHICAL ISSUES

Rambo Litigators

One problem that arises is the continuation of the idea of the duty to **zealously represent** the client, language that came in the first ABA Model Code of Professional Responsibility Canon 7 and still persists in case law. This language has been deleted from the model rules (although it is briefly mentioned in the preamble), but the idea is still around, and has, for some attorneys, been transformed into a justification for the "win at any cost" mind-set. This attitude is often referred to as "Rambo litigation," and it usually manifests in unnecessary fights over discovery, or at least that seems to be the primary symptom. **Rambo litigators** also tend to go back on their word or at least will interpret the agreements they've made in ways that no one would have expected. They will force you to court over every reasonable discovery request, objecting to everything, and make it difficult even to schedule a deposition. They make practicing law unpleasant, for there are enough real issues to fight over. They also do their clients a disservice by inflating legal costs, alienating judges, and losing credibility with other attorneys, even those they are aligned with. Unfortunately, many clients think that these lawyers are doing a good job because they're "tough" and don't let the other side "get by with anything," when in reality they usually drive the cost of the case up and don't necessarily change the outcome by much, just the stress level.

The problem is that lawyers have three different duties they must juggle. First, they are obliged to represent the client to the best of their ability. On the other hand, an attorney is also an officer of the court, and is sworn to uphold the integrity of the judicial system, and lies or misrepresentations are inconsistent with that oath. Finally, the attorney is charged to be fair to opposing counsel or unrepresented opposing parties. If all three of these duties were held in balance by all attorneys, justice might actually occur. Unfortunately, there is a tendency for lawyers to become unbalanced.

Certain unethical practices often crop up in the course of obtaining documentary evidence. The first is the problem of missing pages. You will find there are some firms that omit pages that damage their client from records requested in proper requests for production. As you can imagine, this is a violation of the rule requiring fairness to your opponent. Despite this, very few firms involved in such violations are ever brought before disciplinary boards for this nasty little practice because it is difficult to prove that the firm did it on purpose. However, you will notice that it seems to happen awfully regularly with particular firms. Keep records and documentation if you suspect such a thing is happening; if you can establish a practice of omissions consistently occurring in response from a particular law firm, you may be able to **sanction** the firm for **discovery abuse,** if your attorney will allow it.

Although there is an ethical rule that requires lawyers to turn in other lawyers (Rule 8.3), in practice it rarely occurs. Why? Because we all have to live together, and lawyers don't . . . personal enemies lightly. If you turn in a fellow attorney for an ethics violation, it will become personal, and God help you if the same thing happens to you. No one would consider turning another attorney in for "oops" types of violations, like failing to contact clients on a regular basis. However, an attorney will start thinking about calling the ethics committee about the sleazy stuff. The questions that immediately arise and begin to make the attorney's resolve waver are (1) Can I prove it? and (2) What will be the consequences if I rat someone out to the grievance board? As your boss begins to imagine the glares and whispers as she walks by, she may become less interested in turning in the other attorney, even if you do have all the documentation. It just depends on how important the goodwill of other lawyers is to her and her practice, and the reputation and degree of influence of the attorney she would be taking on.

You also must be careful of monitoring documents when you are providing discovery; you can accidentally turn over a document that is covered by attorney-client privilege, attorney work product, or some other privilege fairly easily when you are in a time crunch. These accidental disclosures are definitely potential malpractice claims, as you've now handed evidence over to the other side—evidence the opposition is not entitled to.

EVIDENTIARY ISSUES

Business Records Exception

Documents are out-of-court statements, so they are subject to a hearsay objection, something that comes as a surprise to many. As you might guess, there's an exception that applies. The most commonly used exception is the **business records exception (BRE),** found in Rule 803.

> Records of regularly conducted activity. A memorandum, report, record, or data compilation, in any form, of acts, events, conditions, opinions, or diagnoses, made at or near the time by, or from information transmitted by, a person with knowledge, if kept in the course of a regularly conducted business activity, and if it was the regular practice of that business activity to make the memorandum, report, record or data compilation, all as shown by the testimony of the custodian or other qualified witness, or by certification that complies with Rule 902(11), Rule 902(12), or a statute permitting certification, unless the source of information or the method or circumstances of preparation indicate lack of trustworthiness. The term "business" as used in this paragraph includes business, institution, association, profession, occupation, and calling of every kind, whether or not conducted for profit.

Fed. R. Evid. 803(6).

The business records exception, when you slim it down to the bone, comes out to the following elements:

1. A record of some sort,
2. made at or near the time the information recorded occurred,
3. by or from a person with knowledge of the information,
4. if the records are kept in the regular conduct of business,
5. it was the regular practice of the business to make records of that kind, and
6. the **custodian** of the records or "other qualified witness" can testify to 1–5.

Any witness you want to use to prove up the BRE must be able to answer all of these questions, although the fourth and fifth items often throw them, just because they're worded in a way that seems odd to laypeople. All those criteria mean that the business usually both makes and keeps the kind of record you're trying to admit, as opposed to the record being something unusual either to record or to preserve. The idea behind this exception and all hearsay exceptions is the fact that circumstances make this category of out-of-court statements reliable enough to let in. In other words, because these records are made and kept routinely and the information is stored near the time it is known by someone with knowledge, it is likely that the records can be relied on without necessarily having to cross-examine every person involved in the process of recording and storing the records.

This exception is used constantly for medical records. Doctors, of course, always write down what happens in an examination—or at the very least, dictate it (regular practice). This is done either while the doctor is meeting with the patient or immediately thereafter (made near or at the time). The doctor has knowledge of the information—she actually met with the patient and spoke to him and evaluated the patient. It is a part of a medical practice to keep all medical records on all patients (regular conduct)—there's no special reason in this particular patient's case that the records are kept. So it is possible to have either the doctor or "the custodian of records" testify that all these elements are met. The custodian of records is usually a particular individual in a doctor's office (or any other office, for that matter) who is responsible for record maintenance. Doctors who deal with litigators on a regular basis are usually familiar with the process, and someone in the office will have a clue about what you need.

The exception to the exception is "unless the source of information or the method or circumstances of preparation indicate lack of trustworthiness." So if there is something in who or how the information is contained in the records that indicates the records are unreliable, or if the method of preparation is untrustworthy, or there's something wrong with the preparation of the records, the BRE may not be applied. If there is a record that harms a client and you want to keep it out of evidence, you need to look for these kinds of problems. Find out how the information was obtained and who obtained it. Is there reason to believe that it (or he or she) is untrustworthy? Nail matters down with more investigation. Sometimes one person's record is filed with another's. If your client swears something in a record was never said or never happened, see if you can figure out a good reason to support the client's story. If you can find some proof to support the story (aside from "I never said that," which is unlikely to impress the judge), you have given your attorney ammunition for the battle for admissibility as well as for weight if the admissibility fight is lost.

Not all states, of course, adhere to the federal rules model of doing things. California, for example, flips the burden of establishing trustworthiness.

Taggart v. Super Seer Corp., 40 Cal. Rptr. 2d 56 (Cal. Ct. App. 1995).

Plaintiff Edward L. Taggart (Taggart), a police officer, was thrown from his motorcycle during training. Afterwards, he developed symptoms which were eventually diagnosed as epilepsy. Taggart and his wife Sarah (collectively plaintiffs) then filed this action against Super Seer Corporation (Super Seer). . . the manufacturer of the helmet Taggart had been wearing when he fell from the motorcycle, alleging causes of action for products liability, negligence, and loss of consortium. The jury found for Super Seer. Plaintiffs filed a motion for judgment notwithstanding the verdict or new trial, which was denied. Plaintiffs filed a timely notice of appeal. . .

In 1976 or 1977, Taggart joined the San Bernardino police force. In 1985, he transferred from patrol to the motorcycle division. On Wednesday, June 12, 1985, as part of his motorcycle training, Taggart was practicing a "decel" (rapid deceleration) maneuver. On one attempt, he braked too hard and was thrown, rolling or tumbling, off the motorcycle. He struck the ground with his right hip, then rolled or slid along the pavement, shredding his shirt and scraping skin from his back, shoulders, and arms. He ended up in a sitting position. Taggart did not remember hitting his head; the back of his helmet, however, was scraped.

Taggart was taken to a doctor's office, examined, and treated. He did not think he was seriously injured. He went back to work the following Monday and completed his motorcycle training. In the days and weeks following, however, he experienced headaches, confusion, forgetfulness, and irritability. Muscles in his right leg twitched . . .

Some months after the accident, Taggart's twitching turned into involuntary muscular contractions involving his whole body. On October 17, 1985, the neurologist told Taggart he could never resume work as a policeman. Around December 1985 or January 1986, Taggart learned from other doctors that he had brain damage. They agreed that he could not resume police work. In May 1986, he was involuntarily retired on medical grounds.

On June 24, 1986, Taggart was given an electroencephalogram. As a result, he was diagnosed as having epilepsy. His involuntary muscular contractions were deemed seizures. He had to take both anticonvulsive medication and pain medication. Medication, however, did not completely prevent him from having seizures. There was evidence that his epilepsy was caused by the motorcycle accident.

The motorcycle helmet Taggart was wearing when his accident occurred had been manufactured by defendant Super Seer in 1981. It consisted of a fiberglass outer shell and a polyurethane energy-absorbing liner.

Federal Motor Vehicle Safety Standard (FMVSS) 218, promulgated by the DOT, prescribes performance standards for motorcycle helmets . . . Helmet manufacturers must comply with FMVSS 218. Under FMVSS 218, helmet performance is measured by, among other things, an "impact attenuation test": a helmet, mounted on a "headform" containing instrumentation, is repeatedly dropped onto a hard surface under controlled conditions. A helmet fails the impact attenuation test if the instrumentation registers any of the following: (1) more than 400 g's of acceleration; (2) acceleration of more than 200 g's for more than 2 milliseconds; and (3) acceleration of more than 150 g's for more than 4 milliseconds. A helmet's performance in an impact attenuation test is related to how well it protects against head injury.

In 1981 and 1984, Southwest [a testing service] performed impact attenuation tests on Super Seer helmet model 1602. Taggart's helmet was model 1608. Model 1602 and model 1608 differed only as to harness shape and visor; they had the same outer shell and polyurethane liner. The helmet failed every time. Sixteen drops onto a flat surface were required in every test; it failed on at least three out of sixteen and as many as eight out of sixteen drops.

Super Seer's helmet expert, Dr. James Newman, testified that the helmet was "compatible with the state of the art." It had sound basic design principles, a good, solid, strong shell, and an energy-absorbing liner.

Dr. Newman had found Southwest's test data to be unreliable.

[Robert] Smith [the president of Super Seer], testified that in 1981, the DOT had sent Southwest's test reports to Super Seer. The DOT indicated that it was considering recalling Super Seer's helmets, and asked Super Seer to respond. Later in 1981, Super Seer sent the DOT additional information, including results of tests performed by an independent testing laboratory, Hauser Research Laboratories, which indicated that its helmets complied with FMVSS 218. In response, the DOT told Super Seer it was closing its files with respect to Super Seer helmet models 1602, 1604, and 1608 . . .

Counsel for plaintiffs stated that Southwest had refused to respond to a subpoena calling for its test reports. He had asked the DOT to produce records pertinent to the helmet; in response, the DOT had sent copies of the Southwest test reports. Once the DOT produced the copies, Southwest agreed to have its custodian of records look at the DOT's copies, confirm that they were true copies of its reports, and supply a declaration to that effect. Southwest duly returned such a declaration, together with the copies, in a sealed envelope, pursuant to sections 1560 and 1561 of the Evidence Code . . .

Super Seer then moved *in limine* to exclude any evidence that the helmet was defective due to failure to comply with FMVSS 218. It noted that plaintiffs' helmet expert had never tested the helmet himself; any opinion on his part that the helmet had failed to pass impact attenuation tests would be based entirely on the Southwest reports, which, it argued, were inadmissible hearsay. Plaintiffs filed a written opposition in which they argued that the Southwest reports were admissible under the business records exception to the hearsay rule (§ 1271).

In connection with the hearing on the motions *in limine,* the trial court opened the sealed envelope. It reviewed the Southwest reports and the custodian's declaration. Super Seer then objected that the custodian's declaration failed to demonstrate that the reports were admissible under the business records exception, because the custodian did not testify to the identity or mode of preparation of the documents. The trial court overruled this objection; it found that the "declaration meets the requirements of Evidence Code [s]ection 1271." It therefore held that one page of each report, showing the numerical test results, was admissible under the business records exception, and that plaintiffs' expert witness could "us[e] those numbers as a basis of his opinion." It held the remainder of the reports inadmissible because they contained opinions that were not admissible under the business records exception . . .

Along with the records, the custodian must also send an affidavit which states that: (1) "[t]he affiant is the duly authorized custodian of the records or otherwise qualified witness and has authority to certify the records," (2) "[t]he copy is a true copy of all the records described in the subpoena" and (3) "[t]he records were prepared by the personnel of the business in the ordinary course of business at or near the time of the act, condition, or event." . . . The affidavit is admissible as evidence of these matters. (§ 1562.) Moreover, "[i]f the original records would be admissible in evidence if the custodian had been present and testified to the matters stated in the affidavit, and if the requirements of section 1271 have been met, the copy of the records is admissible in evidence." . . .

Section 1271 embodies the business records exception to the hearsay rule. It provides that: "Evidence of a writing made as a record of an act, condition, or event is not made inadmissible by the hearsay rule when offered to prove the act, condition, or event if:

(a) "The writing was made in the regular course of a business;
(b) "The writing was made at or near the time of the act, condition, or event;
(c) "The custodian or other qualified witness testifies to its identity and the mode of its preparation; and
(d) "The sources of information and method and time of preparation were such as to indicate its trustworthiness."

It will readily be seen that a custodian's declaration may state all the matters it is required to state under section 1561, yet fail to provide a sufficient foundation for admission of the records under section 1271 . . . Most significantly, the custodian's declaration is not required to state the "identity" or "mode of preparation" of the records. As a result, it will usually fail to show that "[t]he "sources of information and method and time of preparation" of the records indicate their trustworthiness.". . . Therefore, in the face of a hearsay objection, the affidavit of the custodian, made pursuant to [section] 1561, does not satisfy the requirements of the business-records exception to the hearsay rule set forth in [section] 1271(c)–(d), and the copy of the business record, produced pursuant to [sections] 1560–1561, is inadmissible hearsay."

Here, the custodian's declaration conformed meticulously to section 1561. However, it contained no evidence as to what the Southwest reports were, how they were prepared, or what sources of information they were based on. It offered no evidence that the Southwest reports were trustworthy . . . The reports therefore failed to qualify for admission as business records under section 1271 . . .

. . . Thus, a declaration in compliance with sections 1560 and 1561 is insufficient to guarantee that the records produced will be admissible. The proponent also must comply with the additional requirements of section 1271.

We are aware that this construction of section 1560 et seq. lessens their usefulness as a low-cost way to obtain documentary evidence for use at trial. Nevertheless, our construction is compelled by the fact that the Legislature has expressly made admissibility under section 1562 conditional on satisfying the business records exception of section 1271. We conclude that the Legislature did so intentionally, to prevent the wholesale admission of hearsay lacking any guarantees of reliability or trustworthiness. A contrary construction would create a hole in the business records exception big enough to drive a truckload of hearsay through; the proponent of a business record who could not show how it was prepared, or who knew that the way it was prepared would indicate that it was untrustworthy, could nevertheless introduce the record into evidence.

The Legislature's wisdom is demonstrated by what occurred in this case: not only did plaintiffs fail to show that the records were trustworthy, but Super Seer had no opportunity to show that the records were *un*trustworthy, or *un*reliable. Normally, where the proponent of evidence invokes the business records exception, the opponent can test the applicability of the exception by cross-examining the custodian of the records. Here, however, Super Seer had no opportunity to depose and cross-examine either the custodian or the Southwest employees who actually prepared the reports . . . More importantly, as Southwest was not within the jurisdictional range of the subpoena power . . . Super Seer had no opportunity to subpoena the custodian for trial. The custodian's declaration enjoyed an irrebuttable and conclusive effect on the admissibility of the records.

The trial court was on the right track when it recognized that, despite the custodian's declaration, the Southwest reports had to satisfy the requirements of the business records exception. Thus, it refused to admit those portions of the Southwest reports which it found constituted opinion rather than "a record of an act, condition, or event.". . . It erred, however, when, over Super Seer's objection, it held that the custodian's declaration satisfied all the other prerequisites of the business records exception and ruled that numerical test results in the reports would be admissible. It corrected its own error by reversing itself at the close of trial and refusing to admit the numerical test results. Even assuming that its reason for doing so was erroneous, the result was not. We review only the trial court's ruling, not its reasoning . . . Because plaintiffs failed to lay a foundation for the admission of the Southwest reports under the business records exception, the trial court properly excluded the reports in their entirety . . .

The judgment is affirmed in its entirety. Super Seer shall recover costs on appeal against plaintiffs.

Authentication

All documents must be proven to be what legal teams states they are, a requirement known as **authentication.** You must have a witness who somehow proves that the document is authentic, the basis of the term. It's really nice if you don't have to make someone show up in court to do that—it aggravates people to come to the courthouse just to say "Well, yeah, that's what that paper is." So certain types of documents can be authenticated by some additional papers (or other items) within the document itself, referred to as *self-authenticating.* One of the ways to **self-authenticate** a document is set forth in Rule 902(11).

The original or a duplicate of a domestic record of regularly conducted activity that would be admissible under Rule 803(6) if accompanied by a written declaration of its custodian or other qualified person, in a manner complying with any Act of Congress or rule prescribed by the Supreme Court pursuant to statutory authority, certifying that the record

a. was made at or near the time of the occurrence of the matters set forth by, or from information transmitted by, a person with knowledge of those matters;
b. was kept in the course of the regularly conducted activity; and
c. was made by the regularly conducted activity as a regular practice.

A party intending to offer a record into evidence under this paragraph must provide written notice of that intention to all adverse parties, and must make the record and declaration available for inspection sufficiently in advance of their offer into evidence to provide an adverse party with a fair opportunity to challenge them.

Fed. R. Evid. 902(11).

You must provide "a written declaration . . . certifying" records of the business, but there isn't a whole lot of guidance as to what constitutes certification; and you must give notice "sufficiently in advance of its offer," which doesn't really tell you just how long before trial is meant. According to the Notes of Advisory Committee on 2000 amendments, "A declaration that satisfies 28 U.S.C. § 1746 would satisfy the declaration requirement of Rule 902(11), as would any comparable certification under oath." This answers the first question, at any rate, although it would have been nice if the Committee had simply included that in the rule.

§ 1746. Unsworn declarations under penalty of perjury

Wherever, under any law of the United States or under any rule, regulation, order, or requirement made pursuant to law, any matter is required or permitted to be supported, evidenced, established, or proved by the sworn declaration, verification, certificate, statement, oath, or affidavit, in writing of the person making the same (other than a deposition, or an oath of office, or an oath required to be taken before a specified official other than a notary public), such matter may, with like force and effect, be supported, evidenced, established, or proved by the unsworn declaration, certificate, verification, or statement, in writing of such person which is subscribed by him, as true under penalty of perjury, and dated, in substantially the following form:

1. If executed without the United States: "I declare (or certify, verify, or state) under penalty of perjury under the laws of the United States of America that the foregoing is true and correct. Executed on (date).
   (Signature)."
2. If executed within the United States, its territories, possessions, or commonwealths: "I declare (or certify, verify, or state) under penalty of perjury that the foregoing is true and correct. Executed on (date).
   (Signature)."

28 U.S.C. § 1746 (2000).

The issue of what constitutes "sufficiently in advance" does not appear to have been litigated (or at least not published) at the time of writing in a civil context of this rule; however, the following criminal case is instructive.

United States v. Bledsoe, 70 Fed. Appx. 370, 2003 U.S. App. LEXIS 13312 (7th Cir. 2003) (unpublished opinion).

Steven Bledsoe was convicted by a jury of conspiring to possess and distribute cocaine and conspiring to launder money. He appeals arguing . . . that the district court erred in admitting business records offered pursuant to the self-authentication provision in Federal Rules of Evidence 902(11) because he was not given adequate notice and opportunity to review the records and certifying affidavits. We find . . . that the district court did not err in admitting the business records. We therefore affirm Bledsoe's conviction . . .

Steven Bledsoe and James Rounds were grammar school classmates who reunited in 1996 and agreed to distribute cocaine together. Under their arrangement, Bledsoe would acquire the drugs from his source, give the drugs to Rounds to distribute to his customers or sub-distributors, and Bledsoe and Rounds would split the profits equally. In the process, Rounds enlisted several individuals, including David Merritt, Frank Duffy, and Charity Melton, to distribute the drugs to individual purchasers. To further their arrangement, Bledsoe opened private mailboxes under the names of several fictitious businesses in order to receive cash from Rounds (or from Merritt, Duffy, and Melton directly). Bledsoe would use the money to purchase the cocaine, which he would then deliver to Rounds or one of the others in California or ship to them in Indiana. Bledsoe typically shipped the cocaine to Rounds or the others at private mailboxes that they had opened under fictitious company names, otherwise he would send the drugs to them under fictitious personal names at various private residences. Bledsoe and Rounds frequently used Western Union money orders to send each other their half of the profits that flowed from Bledsoe's purchase and/or Rounds's subsequent sale of the cocaine. When Rounds and his customers traveled to California to transact business with Bledsoe, they would sometimes meet as a group at Bledsoe's apartment, and Rounds was given a key to the apartment and permission by Bledsoe to use it "to take care of business."

During trial, the government introduced certified business records relating to the distribution scheme, including hotel records, phone records, shipment records, mailbox rental agreements, and apartment rental information. The government had provided this material to Bledsoe during discovery. Bledsoe objected to the introduction of these records at trial because he believed them to be hearsay and because he had received only four-days notice that the records would be introduced with certifying affidavits pursuant to Federal Rules of Evidence 803(6) and 902(11). The district court found that Bledsoe had waived his objection to these records by failing to object prior to trial, when a continuance could have been granted, and further found the argument lacking merit because the documents had sufficient guarantees of trustworthiness. Also during trial, Bledsoe testified that while he had supplied cocaine to Rounds, he was unaware that there was a distribution ring and asserted that he only had a buyer-seller relationship with Rounds. On this basis he moved for judgment of acquittal on the drug conspiracy count at the close of evidence. After the jury returned guilty verdicts on both counts, the district court denied his motion . . .

Federal Rule of Evidence 803(6) provides that business records may be introduced "without foundation testimony from the record custodian so long as the records are authenticated according to Fed. R. Evid. 902(11)." . . . Under Rule 902(11), "a party may authenticate a business record through a written declaration by a qualified custodian that the record meets the necessary foundational requirements," . . . but the party intending to offer the record must "provide written notice of that intention to all adverse parties, and . . . make the record and declaration available for inspection sufficiently in advance of their offer into evidence to provide an adverse party with a fair opportunity to challenge them." . . . Bledsoe contends that the district court abused its discretion in admitting business records because he was not given sufficient advance notice and opportunity to review the records and certifying affidavits, as required in 902(11). The district court found that Bledsoe waived his right to object on this ground by failing to present that argument before trial and also found that the documents were reliable. We agree. Assuming, however, that there was no waiver, Bledsoe has not shown how he was prejudiced by the government's notice . . .

Bledsoe argues that he was prejudiced because the business records were damaging to his case on the merits. That may be true, but it misunderstands the prejudice that he is required to show. The purpose of giving notice and an opportunity to review, under Rule 902(11), is for the adverse party to have the opportunity to verify, and challenge if necessary, the accuracy and reliability of the records and/or certifying affidavits. Therefore, the prejudice associated with the lack of notice that Bledsoe must show is his inability to adequately review and/or challenge the documents on either of these bases due to insufficient time. Bledsoe did not make that argument before the district court . . . and he concedes on appeal, after having months to review both sets of documents, that they are neither defective nor otherwise unreliable . . . We therefore find no error in the district court's evidentiary ruling admitting the business records.

We further believe that Bledsoe received adequate notice. The government informed him four days before trial that it intended to introduce the business records, which Bledsoe admits he received during discovery over one year before trial, with certifying affidavits as authorized by Rules 803(6) and 902(11). And Bledsoe's counsel reviewed the records and certifying affidavits three days before trial. Under the circumstances, this was sufficient time to determine whether an objection needed to be made or more time was needed for an adequate review . . . .

In states following the wording of the federal rule, you need to find any notes, statutes, or cases fleshing out the parameters of these terms. Beyond consulting the law books or legal database, you need to consult your local rules as to what constitutes sufficient notice and what is accepted as a certified record. Although

---

NO. 05-CI-101010

PATTY HAUS	§	IN THE DISTRICT COURT
Plaintiff,	§	
	§	
V.	§	225TH JUDICIAL DISTRICT
	§	
JOHN JUSTICE AND VISTA LIBRE	§	
APARTMENTS	§	
Defendants.	§	OF DUX COUNTY, TEXAS

AFFIDAVIT FOR ADMISSION OF BUSINESS RECORDS

BEFORE ME, the undersigned authority, on this day personally appeared Tess Duberville, who, being by me duly sworn, deposed as follows:

"My name is Tess Duberville, I am of sound mind, capable of making this affidavit, and personally acquainted with the facts herein stated:

"I am the custodian of the records of Dr. Eloise Payne. Attached hereto are 43 pages of records from Dr. Eloise Payne. These said 43 pages are kept by Dr. Eloise Payne in the regular course of business, and it was the regular course of business of Dr. Eloise Payne for an employee or representative of Dr. Eloise Payne, with knowledge of the act, event, condition, opinion, or diagnosis, recorded to make the records or to transmit information thereof to be included in such records; and the records were made at or near the time or reasonably soon thereafter. The records attached hereto are either the originals or the exact duplicates of the originals."

SIGNED on _____, 2004.

_____
Tess Duberville, Affiant

SUBSCRIBED AND SWORN TO BEFORE ME on _____,
by _____.

_____
Notary Public, State of Texas

Texas BRE affidavit for self-authentication of records falling within the business records exception to the hearsay rule.

you may meet the state's standard according to case law, you may find that the local custom is stricter, and, to paraphrase Mark Twain, custom can be more binding than law.

The self-authentication of documents admissible under the business rule exception is also allowable in many states, with some variations on the federal rule. Texas is one such state, allowing for self-authentication of business records under Texas Rules of Evidence 902 (10) if:

* the records would be admissible under the BRE exception
* an affidavit meeting the BRE exception is filed along with the records with the clerk of the court at least 14 days before trial
* copies must be served on all opposing counsel and notice given at least 14 days before trial

The rule also includes a form for the **affidavit** on the previous page. Nice, bright lines; we know exactly what to do and how many days to do it within. In jurisdictions where the rules provide you with a form, don't be clever and original. Slavishly follow the form; this is one area in which creativity is not rewarded. Just copy the form and fill in the blanks as appropriate for your case.

Why would you do this rather than just prove up the documents in trial? Imagine asking all these questions in front of a jury. Watch their eyes glaze, their eyelids droop. It's boring. It's absolutely necessary to lay the legal basis to admit the records, but it is still deadly dull. It also reduces the number of things you have to worry about during the trial. The records are not yet admitted, but they are in admissible form. You can go straight to admitting them as soon as you are ready to. Because you have so many details to track during trial, it is beneficial to eliminate any you can ahead of time. All it takes in these jurisdictions is filing the correct pieces of paper on time.

Another common documentary detail you can take care of ahead of time is establishing that medical bills are **reasonable and necessary.** For medical expenses to be recoverable in a personal injury suit, or any other conceivable suit where a physical injury would be part of the damages, the plaintiff ordinarily must establish that the medical bills are both reasonable in amount for medical care of that type and necessary for the injuries sustained as a result of the incident that is the basis of the cause of action. As you can imagine, any doctor who treated the plaintiff will state that the bills for the medical care he supplied were both reasonable and necessary. Further, as you might anticipate, it is rare to find another doctor willing to swear that those bills are *not* reasonable and necessary. As a result, it is unusual for there to be a dispute over that particular aspect of the case. However, it is still incumbent on the plaintiff to prove this detail; failure to do so will result in the legal elimination of those damages from the plaintiff's recovery, either through **directed verdict** or a **judgment non obstante veredicto.**

To avoid a surprise attack on the bills, and to keep from wasting everyone's time, some jurisdictions allow plaintiffs to prove up medical bills in a form similar to the self-authentication rule. Texas, for instance, does both, and provides for the proof of "reasonable and necessary" medical bills (as well as any other professional bill) in the Texas Civil Practice and Remedies Code § 18.001.

a. This section applies to civil actions only, but not to an action on a sworn account.

b. Unless a controverting affidavit is filed as provided by this section, an affidavit that the amount a person charged for a service was reasonable at the time and place that the service was provided and that the service was necessary is sufficient evidence to support a finding of fact by judge or jury that the amount charged was reasonable or that the service was necessary.

c. The affidavit must:

   1. be taken before an officer with authority to administer oaths;
   2. be made by:
      a. the person who provided the service;

      or

      b. the person in charge of records showing the service provided and charge made; and
   3. include an itemized statement of the service and charge.

d. The party offering the affidavit in evidence or the party's attorney must file the affidavit with the clerk of the court and serve a copy of the affidavit on each other party to the case at least 30 days before the day on which evidence is first presented at the trial of the case.

e. A party intending to controvert a claim reflected by the affidavit must file a counteraffidavit with the clerk of the court and serve a copy of the counteraffidavit on each other party or the party's attorney of record:

   1. not later than:

      a. 30 days after the day he receives a copy of the affidavit; and

      b. at least 14 days before the day on which evidence is first presented at the trial of the case; or

   2. with leave of the court, at any time before the commencement of evidence at trial.

f. The counteraffidavit must give reasonable notice of the basis on which the party filing it intends at trial to controvert the claim reflected by the initial affidavit and must be taken before a person authorized to administer oaths. The counteraffidavit must be made by a person who is qualified, by knowledge, skill, experience, training, education, or other expertise, to testify in contravention of all or part of any of the matters contained in the initial affidavit.

Tex. Civ. Prac. & Rem. Code Ann. § 18.001 (Vernon 2002).

This statute also provides a sample affidavit, an example of which is on the next page.

Plaintiffs in states like Texas may both self-authenticate and prove the necessity and reasonableness of the medical bills prior to trial, checking off those requirements. They will also know if the defendant intends to make an issue over the amount or relatedness of the medical bills. Some firms routinely object to this; I would contend that if there is a pattern of doing so with nothing but a tenuous basis, it is a form of Rambo litigation. If you suspect a firm of doing this, check its prior records, compile a list, and ask for sanctions. On the other hand, if you are on the defendant's side and have good reason to contest the amount of medical bills, do so and make sure you do it in the allotted amount of time.

INFORMAL METHODS

Finding the documents you want can be miraculously easy to horrendously difficult. It all depends on finding the persons who have the documents in their possession and how badly they want to protect them. You will need to think through the kinds of transactions that ordinarily produce documents to think about what documents to look for and who might have them. Is there a transaction that would generate a bill, check, contract, or order? Is there an incident that would generate an official report, emergency call, towing charge, press coverage, e-mails, letter-writing, interoffice memos, new procedures, announcements, or any other sort of dissemination of the information? Would the incident spur some sort of investigation from a governmental body? Does anyone connected with the litigation keep a diary or journal? Is this the kind of situation for which logs or other sorts of daily charts would be applicable? Would the time clock or any other type of automatic check-in system be important? Who would be likely to have access to or a copy of these records? Is this someone you can talk to, or does the **no contact rule** apply to him?

If the documents are not subject to any privilege, you can simply ask whoever has them to allow you to make copies. If they are privileged, you will have to jump through a few hoops first.

Releases and Other Requests

At the initial interview, you will have asked your client for releases or for copies of pertinent documents. If you received releases, you will send the releases to the relevant entities: the client's doctor, the client's employer, the client's psychologist, and so on. This will require a simple transmittal letter. The response to this request will provide you with the records, which you then must read and understand. You may have to pay a copying fee; in some doctor's offices, it is cheaper to have the patient request the records than for you to do so. The problem, of course, is making sure that the client complies. If you tell the client to request records, send a follow-up letter to remind him to do so. Explain that you will be glad to pay for records now, but the increased cost will be billed to him either at the end of litigation out of his share or as a portion of attorney's fees.

No. _____

JOHN DOE	§	**IN THE** _____ **COURT**
(Name of Plaintiff)	§	
V.	§	_____ **DISTRICT**
JOHN ROE	§	
(Name of Defendant)	§	_____ **COUNTY, TEXAS**

AFFIDAVIT

BEFORE ME, the undersigned authority, personally appeared _____ (NAME OF AFFIANT) _____, who, being by me duly sworn, deposed as follows:

My name is _____ (NAME OF AFFIANT) _____. I am of sound mind and capable of making this affidavit.

On _____ (DATE) _____, I provided a service to _____ (NAME OF PERSON WHO RECEIVED SERVICE) _____. An itemized statement of the service and the charge for the service is attached to this affidavit and is a part of this affidavit.

The service I provided was necessary and the amount that I charged for the service was reasonable at the time and place that the service was provided.

_____
Affiant

SWORN TO AND SUBSCRIBED BEFORE ME on the _____ day of _____, 20 ___.

My commission expires:

_____

_____
Notary Public, State of Texas

Notary's printed name:

_____

Affidavit for proving special damages are reasonable and necessary when the affiant is the actual person providing services.

NO. _____

JOHN DOE	§	**IN THE _____ COURT**
(Name of Plaintiff)	§	
V.	§	
JOHN ROE	§	**_____ COUNTY, TEXAS**
(Name of Defendant)	§	

AFFIDAVIT

    BEFORE ME, the undersigned authority, personally appeared _____ (NAME OF AFFIANT) _____, who, being by me duly sworn, deposed as follows:

    My name is _____ (NAME OF AFFIANT) _____ I am of sound mind and capable of making this affidavit.

    I am the person in charge of records of _____ (PERSON WHO PROVIDED THE SERVICE) _____. Attached to this affidavit are records that provide an itemized statement of the service and the charge for the service that _____ (PERSON WHO PROVIDED THE SERVICE) _____ provided to _____ (PERSON WHO RECEIVED THE SERVICE) _____ on _____ (DATE) _____. The attached records are a part of this affidavit.

    The attached records are kept by me in the regular course of business. The information contained in the records was transmitted to me in the regular course of business by _____ (PERSON WHO PROVIDED THE SERVICE) _____ or an employee or representative of _____ (PERSON WHO PROVIDED THE SERVICE) _____ who had personal knowledge of the information. The records were made at or near the time or reasonably soon after the time that the service was provided. The records are the original or an exact duplicate of the original.

    The service provided was necessary and the amount charged for the service was reasonable at the time and place that the service was provided.

_____
Affiant

    SWORN TO AND SUBSCRIBED BEFORE ME on the _____ day of _____, 20___.

My commission expires:

_____

_____
Notary Public, State of Texas

Notary's printed name:

_____

Affidavit for proving special damages are reasonable and necessary when the affiant is the custodian of records,

October 24, 200-

Eloise Payne, Ph.D.
711 Freud Tower Circle, Suite 1313
Big City, Confusion 99999

RE: Patty Haus, SSN 111-11-1111, DOB 04-01-1972

Dear Dr. Payne:
 Enclosed please find the original of the HIPPA conforming release from Ms. Haus. We would like copies of all her medical records in your custody and will be glad to pay reasonable copying costs.
 Please send the copies to the undersigned in the self-addressed, stamped envelope enclosed for your convenience.
 If you have any questions regarding this matter, please contact me at (888) 555-0987.

 Sincerely yours,

 Melanie Flores
 Paralegal to Lisa St. John

LSJ/jgm
Enclosure
cc: Patty Haus

Letter for enclosing medical release.

MEDICAL AUTHORIZATION AND RELEASE TO DISCUSS MEDICAL CONDITION WITH LAW FIRM

RE: Name: Patty Haus
 SSN: 111-11-1111
 DOB: April 1, 1972

TO: Dr. Eloise Payne
 I, Patty Haus, have retained Lisa St. Joan, (hereinafter referred to as "ATTORNEY"), as my representative. ATTORNEY and ATTORNEY's agents and representatives are hereby authorized to receive from Dr. Max Payne any and all information for the period five years preceeding this date including, but not limited to, office records, medical reports, charts, x-rays, and bills concerning my physical or mental condition.
 Furthermore, Lisa St. Joan and Lisa St. Joan's agents and representatives are authorized to discuss my physical and mental condition with ATTORNEY and ATTORNEY's agents and representatives.
 The purpose for this release of information is to assist me and my attorney in anticipated or pending litigation.
 A copy of this authorization has the same force and effect as an original. The authority granted herein remains in effect for a period of five years from the date hereon or until I revoke same in writing.
 I understand that I have the right to revoke this authorization, except to the extent that Lisa St. Joan has taken action in reliance thereon, by providing you with a written request to revoke this authorization.
 I understand that information that is disclosed or used under this authorization may be disclosed by Lisa St. Joan and no longer protected by the privacy provisions of the Health Insurance Portability and Accountability Act of 1996, 45 C.F.R. Section 164.508(c).
 Signed on _____, 200-.

 _____
 Patty Haus

A typical HIP release. Note the reference to the statute in the last line. Is it accurate?

Sometimes these records will make references to other conditions or doctors, and you will need to obtain those records as well. You can rest assured opposing counsel will, and you need to know what landmines may be buried within them. It may be a preexisting condition, it may be a completely different causation, or it may be nothing at all, but if you do not know, you will not be prepared to respond. If you had a blank release at the beginning, you will not need an additional release for each additional doctor. Call your client at some point and ask about the other doctors; see what her explanation is. This is one of those points at which you can find out just how straight your client is being with you. If your client tells you something contrary to what the records say, tell the attorney. She may wish to withdraw or, if there are numerous doctors, sit and talk with the client to see if there is a genuine mistake or if the client is trying to hide something.

FOIA

The federal **Freedom of Information Act (FOIA)** is repeated on the state level in similar acts. Under this act and acts like it, any government agency will disclose any reasonably described document unless it is one of the following.

1. (A) specifically authorized under criteria established by an Executive order to be kept secret in the interest of national defense or foreign policy and (B) are in fact properly classified pursuant to such Executive order;
2. related solely to the internal personnel rules and practices of an agency;
3. specifically exempted from disclosure by statute (other than section 552b of this title), provided that such statute (A) requires that the matters be withheld from the public in such manner as to leave no discretion on the issue, or (B) establishes particular criteria for withholding or refers to particular types of matters to be withheld;
4. trade secrets and commercial or financial information obtained from a person and privileged or confidential;
5. inter-agency or intra-agency memorandums or letters which would not be available by law to a party other than an agency in litigation with the agency;
6. personnel and medical files and similar files the disclosure of which would constitute a clearly unwarranted invasion of personal privacy;
7. investigatory records compiled for law enforcement purposes, but only to the extent that the production of such records would (A) interfere with enforcement proceedings, (B) deprive a person of a right to a fair trial or an impartial adjudication, (C) constitute an unwarranted invasion of personal privacy, (D) disclose the identity of a confidential source and, in the case of a record compiled by a criminal law enforcement authority in the course of a criminal investigation, or by an agency conducting a lawful national security intelligence investigation, confidential information furnished only by the confidential source, (E) disclose investigative techniques and procedures, or (F) endanger the life or physical safety of law enforcement personnel;
8. contained in or related to examination, operating, or condition reports prepared by, on behalf of, or for the use of an agency responsible for the regulation or supervision of financial institutions; or
9. geological and geophysical information and data, including maps, concerning wells.

Any reasonably segregable portion of a record shall be provided to any person requesting such record after deletion of the portions which are exempt under this subsection.

5 U.S.C. § 552(b) (2000).

The section you need to be most concerned about is 5 U.S.C. § 552(b)(7) because this exclusion is more likely to show up in a specific record you are seeking in a particular case. However, if you wait until after any potential criminal proceedings, as is customary in civil actions, you probably will avoid the proscriptions here, as most every concern will be eliminated or can be redacted so as to address those concerns.

All that is necessary to make an FOIA request is a letter. The letter needs to describe what you want with reasonable specificity—of course, that is kind of like writing a good request for production. You need to make

March 28, 200–

HEALTH & HUMAN SERVICES DEPARTMENT
Director, FOIA/Privacy Division
Rm. 645F, HHH Bldg.
200 Independence Ave., S.W.
Washington, DC 20201
(202) 690-7453
fax (202) 690-8320

RE: FOIA REQUEST

Dear FOIA Officer:

Pursuant to the federal Freedom of Information Act, 5 U.S.C. § 552, I request access to and copies of any documents referencing activity by Vista Libre Apartments.

I agree to pay reasonable duplication fees for the processing of this request in an amount not to exceed $250. However, please notify me prior to your incurring any expenses in excess of that amount.

If my request is denied in whole or part, I ask that you justify all deletions by reference to specific exemptions of the act. I will also expect you to release all segregable portions of otherwise exempt material. I, of course, reserve the right to appeal your decision to withhold any information or to deny a waiver of fees.

I look forward to your reply within 20 business days, as the statute requires.

Thank you for your assistance.

Sincerely,

Lisa St. Joan

A typical FOIA release. Is it specific enough?

the request broad enough to capture any documents you want, but not so broad that the agency can reject it. The search is free; the copying is not. There are, of course, some tricky bits, mostly knowing which agency to go to usually a perusal of the agency's description will give you a clue. To limit the amount of the copy cost, you may put in the letter a maximum amount you wish to pay and ask to be notified if the costs will run in excess of the amount. For an excellent primer on the FOIA, check out the American Civil Liberties Union's Web site.

One of the reasons for rejecting an FOIA request that may need a little explanation (and that may arise) is 5 U.S.C. § 552(b)(5), discussed at length in the *Winterstein* case.

Winterstein v. United States Department of Justice, 89 F. Supp. 2d 79 (D.D.C. 2000).

Proceeding *pro se,* plaintiff brought suit challenging the decision of the Department of Justice to withhold a single document he had sought under the Freedom of Information Act, 5 U.S.C. § 552. The matter is currently before the Court on defendant's motion to dismiss or for summary judgment. Because defendant filed a declaration along with its motion, the Court will treat the motion as one for summary judgment under Rule 56 of the Federal Rules of Civil Procedure. See Rule 12(c), Fed. R. Civ. P. Defendant's motion will be granted . . .

On October 14, 1997, plaintiff filed a Freedom of Information Act request with the United States Department of Justice seeking the release of a single document, referred to as "the Prosecution Memorandum, dated 4-21-83, from Neal Sher to Mark Richard; consisting of 51 pages, concerning the *Rudolph* case." Compl. Ex. 1 (plaintiff's FOIA request). This memorandum was prepared during the course of an investigation conducted by the Department of Justice, Office of Special Investigations ("OSI"), into the wartime conduct of one Arthur Rudolph. Mr. Rudolph served as Operations Director of a V-2 rocket production facility at the Mittelwerke complex near Niedersachswerfen in Centeral Germany . . . Allegations had been made that Mr. Rudolph participated in atrocities perpetuated on slave laborers used by the Nazi regime.

After World War II, Mr. Rudolph relocated to the United States, became a citizen and participated in this country's space exploration effort, assisting in the design of the Saturn V rocket and earning the National Aeronautics and Space Administration Distinguished Service Medal. After the allegations against him were made and he was under investigation by OSI, Mr. Rudolph voluntarily renounced his U.S. citizenship and returned to Germany in 1984. He resided there until his death last year. Believing that Mr. Rudolph was ill-treated by the Justice Department, plaintiff conducted a private investigation of the allegations of wartime misdeeds. Toward this end, and with the explicit permission of Mr. Rudolph, plaintiff filed the FOIA request at issue in this case . . .

On February 17, 1998, the Justice Department informed plaintiff that it had located one record responsive to his request, referred to as "Prosecution Memorandum 4-21-83 Neal Sher, Acting Director, Office of Special Investigations, to Mark Richard, Deputy Assistant Attorney General, Criminal Division; 49 pages." . . . The Department advised plaintiff that it was withholding the entire document pursuant to FOIA Exemption 5, and parts of the document pursuant to Exemptions 6 and 7(C) . . . On March 2, 1998, plaintiff appealed this decision, and on October 28, 1998, the Justice Department's Office of Information and Privacy informed plaintiff that it was the final determination of the Department to withhold the document in its entirety pursuant to the previously stated exemptions . . . Plaintiff subsequently filed this action seeking full disclosure of the document in question . . .

An agency may withhold documents responsive to a FOIA request only if the responsive documents fall within one of nine enumerated statutory exemptions. See 5 U.S.C. § 552(b). The agency bears the burden of justifying the withholding, and the court reviews the agency claims of exemption de novo . . . To enable the Court to determine whether documents are properly withheld, the agency must provide a detailed description of the information withheld through the submission of a so-called "Vaughn Index," sufficiently detailed affidavits or declarations, or both . . . Furthermore, the FOIA requires that "any reasonably segregable portion of a record shall be provided . . . after deletion of the portions which are exempt." 5 U.S.C. § 552(b). "Non-exempt portions of a document must be disclosed unless they are inextricably intertwined with exempt portions." . . . To withhold the entirety of a document, the agency must demonstrate that it cannot segregate the exempt material from the non-exempt and disclose as much as possible . . .

The Court may award summary judgment to a government agency solely on the basis of information provided in affidavits or declarations when the affidavits or declarations describe "the documents and the justifications for nondisclosure with reasonably specific detail, demonstrate that the information withheld logically falls within the claimed exemption, and are not controverted by either contrary evidence in the record nor by evidence of agency bad faith." . . . An agency must demonstrate that "each document that falls within the class requested either has been produced, is unidentifiable, or is wholly [or partially] exempt from the Act's inspection requirements." . . .

There is no dispute in this case as to the identity of the document in question, or whether the Department of Justice fulfilled its duty in locating the information requested by the plaintiff. The Court therefore must decide whether the Department was correct in withholding the entire document under Exemption 5 or portions of the document under Exemption 6 or 7(C). . . .

FOIA Exemption 5 protects from disclosure "inter-agency or intra-agency memorandums or letters which would not be available by law to a party . . . in litigation with the agency." 5 U.S.C. § 522 (b)(5). This provision "exempt[s] those documents, and only those documents, normally privileged in the civil discovery context," including those covered by the "attorney's work-product privilege . . . Protection for attorney work product has also been recognized as important in the criminal arena . . . Indeed, "its role in assuring the proper functioning of the criminal justice system is even more vital." . . . The privilege protects the adversarial process by "ensuring that lawyers can prepare for litigation without fear that opponents may obtain their private notes, memoranda, correspondence, and other written materials." . . .

While the work-product privilege is a qualified privilege, Congress intended Exemption 5 of the FOIA to allow disclosure of only those materials "which would 'routinely be disclosed' in private litigation" and to exclude from disclosure "memoranda prepared by an attorney in contemplation of litigation which set forth the attorney's theory of the case and his litigation strategy." . . . Under Exemption 5, the attorney work-product privilege does not end with the litigation, but exempts protected material from mandatory disclosure "without regard to the status of the litigation for which it was prepared." . . .

Here, the government has invoked Exemption 5 to protect a single document, a 49-page prosecution memorandum prepared by Neal Sher, Acting Director of OSI, claiming that it is the kind of attorney work-product traditionally protected because it was prepared in anticipation of litigation . . . While in some cases a court must determine whether the withheld records were prepared for the purpose of a specific claim or defense in order to enjoy work-product protection, that is not the case here. There is no question that the memorandum sought by plaintiff in this case was prepared for the purpose of pursuing a specific claim— namely, the contemplated prosecution of Arthur Rudolph . . .

The declaration submitted by Linda J. Joachim, a litigation attorney in the Freedom of Information Act/Privacy Act Unit of the Office of Enforcement Operations, Criminal Division, United States Department of Justice, . . . represents that the memorandum contains "a discussion of the major points and allegations concerning the *Rudolph* case and reflects the attorney's legal analysis, theory of the case, thoughts, impressions, opinions, and assessments of facts and issues upon which an attorney could evaluate the case"—materials traditionally protected as attorney work product . . . Ms. Joachim also states that she discussed the matter with the attorney who prepared the memorandum for OSI and that, even sixteen years after the memorandum was prepared,

> there are sufficient connections between the *Rudolph* case and still pending investigations to warrant concern about disclosure. To reveal the information in question would inhibit the candid, internal discussion and evaluation necessary for efficient and proper litigation preparation in such a sensitive and complex area of law enforcement. Furthermore, disclosure would provide insight into the agency's general strategic and tactical approach to investigating and prosecuting such cases . . .

Although Ms. Joachim's declaration contains many statements that are better characterized as conclusions of law than reportage of facts, this language is surplusage. The Court finds that her factual assertions are specific enough to provide notice to the requestor and to give the Court an adequate foundation to review the Department's position and to conclude on the basis of the declaration that the Department was justified in withholding the document under Exemption 5 . . .

In his responsive filings, plaintiff argues that disclosure of this document is necessary in the public interest . . . Plaintiff relies generally on the purpose of the FOIA, to get at information that "sheds light on an agency's performance of its statutory duties." . . . Plaintiff's reliance on the public interest fails on two grounds.

First, when Congress enacted the FOIA to throw open the workings of government, it purposefully provided specific exemptions to disclosure under the Act. The exemptions reflect Congress' judgment as to what is in the public interest and "represent the congressional determination of the types of information that the Executive Branch must have the option to keep confidential, if it so chooses." . . . It is only necessary therefore to consider whether a particular document is of the type that Congress has determined should be disclosed or exempt from disclosure—in other words, whether a particular exemption applies.

Second, Congress recently examined the issue of documents maintained by the Office of Special Investigations in connection with its investigations of alleged Nazi war criminals. While Congress, in the Nazi War Crimes Disclosure Act, directed the government to release classified materials relating to Nazi war crimes and instructed that FOIA requests for such material be expedited, Section 4 of the Act specifically identifies the type of document at issue here as expressly exempt from disclosure:

> This [Act] shall not apply to records—(A) related to or supporting any active or inactive investigation, inquiry, or prosecution by the Office of Special Investigations of the Department of Justice; or
> (B) solely in the possession, custody, or control of that office.

Nazi War Crimes Disclosure Act, Pub. L. 105-246, 112 Stat. 1859 (October 8, 1998) (codified at 5 U.S.C. § 552 note).

The government has asserted, without contradiction, that the requested document was found in the Office of Special Investigations, and that it was and is connected to past and ongoing investigations . . . The Court therefore cannot help but conclude that the memorandum that plaintiff seeks is squarely within that class of documents the withholding of which Congress has deemed to be in the public interest. The Court finds that the Department of Justice acted properly in withholding the prosecution memorandum.

Because the Department of Justice acted properly in withholding the entire document sought by plaintiff, the Court need not decide whether it would also have been appropriate to withhold the names in the memorandum under Exemptions 6 and 7(C). Having determined that the prosecution memorandum was protected attorney work-product and therefore exempt from disclosure under Exemption 5 of the FOIA, the Court concludes that the defendant is entitled to summary judgment.

An appropriate Order will issue this same day.

An FOIA request may help you receive some helpful information and leads, but a response will not be forthcoming if a criminal matter is pending. Additionally, you will not receive any documents that may be construed as attorney-work product, and some of the information on documents may be blacked out. On the other hand, you sometimes obtain information about additional witnesses, new facts, and governmental findings that make the entire process worthwhile.

FORMAL METHODS

The formal methods are those found in the applicable rules of discovery. They are supported by the court and failure to comply with the rules may result in sanctions. This makes them very effective; on the other hand, most are costly because of the inclusion of additional players, such as court reporters.

Request for Production

A **request for production** is inexpensive, but it has two main drawbacks: it may only be sent to other parties and it has no mechanism for proving up any of the documents so produced. It also may be subject to more objections than other types of discovery because the parties are far more likely to assert privileges than nonparties, since non-parties usually do not seek legal counsel in the course of civil discovery.

Asking for documents is relatively easy. First, look at your investigation action plan. Consider the investigation action plan you drew up in the defense of the *Haus v. Justice* case.

Which of these documents are likely to be in the possession of the plaintiff? Which would you like to show that the plaintiff had to prove she knew about them? A document involving crime statistics would not be one that she'd be likely to have, so that's not something to request. The threats weren't in writing, so that's no good. The plaintiff might have copies of the police reports, and you would want to show she was aware of the eviction proceedings, so you would ask for those, as well as any documents relating to the actual incident and her damages. However, although a request for production gets the documents to you, and proves the plaintiff had them, it does not **prove up** the documents. You'll have to try something else for that if, once you get the documents and review them, you decide you want the documents in admissible form.

INVESTIGATION ACTION PLAN

Theory to Prove	Areas to Investigate	Possible Leads
Vengeful girlfriend	Prior arrests of boyfriend	Police reports?
"	Threats	Friends; deposition of plaintiff?
"	Eviction proceedings	JP Court in district
"	Vandalism rate of extenants	Insurance company claims history?

NO. <u>05-CI-101010</u>

PATTY HAUS,	§	**IN THE DISTRICT COURT**
Plaintiff	§	
	§	
V.	§	**225TH JUDICIAL DISTRICT**
	§	
JOHN JUSTICE AND VISTA LIBRE	§	
APARTMENTS,	§	
Defendants	§	**DUX COUNTY, CONFUSION**

<u>DEFENDANT'S FIRST REQUESTS FOR PRODUCTION</u>
<u>TO PLAINTIFF PATTY HAUS</u>

TO: Patty Haus, Plaintiff, by and through Plaintiff's attorney of record, Lisa St. Joan

Please take notice that request is hereby made by John Q. Justice, pursuant to the Confusion Rules of Civil Procedure, that Plaintiff, Patty Haus, produce or permit the undersigned attorney, Thomas Battle, to inspect and copy or reproduce the items hereinafter designated on Exhibit "A" attached hereto.

Within 30 days after service of these Requests for Production, you must serve a written response to the undersigned attorney at Thomas Battle, 2020 Slaughter Lane, Big City, Confusion 99999-9999, including the items requested or stating with respect to each request that an inspection and copying or reproduction will be permitted as requested.

In the event a request is objected to, please specifically state (a) the legal or factual basis for the objection, and (b) the extent to which you refuse to comply with the request. Pursuant to the Confusion Rules of Civil Procedure, a party must comply with as much of the request to which the party has made no objection unless it is unreasonable under the circumstances to do so before obtaining a ruling on the objection.

Respectfully submitted,

Dewey, Cheatem, and Howe

By: _____
Thomas Battle
Confusion Bar No. 88888888
2020 Slaughter Lane
Big City, Confusion 99999-9999
Tel. (888) 555-1234
Fax. (888) 555-1235
Attorney for Defendant
John Justice

<u>CERTIFICATE OF SERVICE</u>

I certify that on [date] a true and correct copy of Defendant's First Request for Production of Documents to Patty Haus was served to each person listed below by the method indicated.

_____
Thomas Battle

Lisa St. Joan	X Certified mail,
Attorney for Patty Haus	return receipt requested
100 Years War Lane, Suite 1412	_____ Personal delivery
Big City, Despair 99999-9999	_____ Private delivery
TEL: (888) 555-0987	_____ Facsimile transfer
FAX: (888) 555-0986	

The cover page for a request for production. The meat of it is found in the attached exhibit.

DEFINITIONS AND INSTRUCTIONS

1. As used herein, the terms "you" and "your" shall mean Patty Haus, and all attorneys, agents, and other natural persons or business or legal entities acting or purporting to act for or on behalf of Patty Haus, whether authorized to do so or not.

2. As used herein, the term "documents" shall mean all writings of every kind, source and authorship, both originals and all nonidentical copies thereof, in your possession, custody, or control, or known by you to exist, irrespective of whether the writing is one intended for or transmitted internally by you, or intended for or transmitted to any other person or entity, including without limitation any government agency, department, administrative, or private entity or person. The term shall include handwritten, typewritten, printed, photocopied, photographic, or recorded matter. It shall include communications in words, symbols, pictures, sound recordings, films, tapes, and information stored in, or accessible through, computer or other information storage or retrieval systems, together with the codes and/or programming instructions and other materials necessary to understand and use such systems. For purposes of illustration and not limitation, the term shall include: affidavits; agendas; agreements; analyses; announcements; bills, statements, and other records of obligations and expenditures; books; brochures; bulletins; calendars; canceled checks, vouchers, receipts and other records of payments; charts or drawings; check registers; checkbooks; circulars; collateral files and contents; contracts; corporate bylaws; corporate charters; correspondence; credit files and contents; deeds of trust; deposit slips; diaries or drafts; files; guaranty agreements; instructions; invoices; ledgers, journals, balance sheets, profit and loss statements, and other sources of financial data; letters; logs, notes, or memoranda of telephonic or face-to-face conversations; manuals; memoranda of all kinds, to and from any persons, agencies, or entities; minutes; minute books; notes; notices; parts lists; papers; press releases; printed matter (including books, articles, speeches, and newspaper clippings); purchase orders; records; records of administrative, technical, and financial actions taken or recommended; reports; safety deposit boxes and contents and records of entry; schedules; security agreements; specifications; statements of bank accounts; statements or interviews; stock transfer ledgers; technical and engineering reports, evaluations, advice, recommendations, commentaries, conclusions, studies, test plans, manuals, procedures, data, reports, results, and conclusions; summaries, notes, and other records and recordings of any conferences, meetings, visits, statements, interviews or telephone conversations; telegrams; teletypes and other communications sent or received; transcripts of testimony; UCC instruments; work papers; and all other writings, the contents of which relate to, discuss, consider, or otherwise refer to the subject matter of the particular discovery requested.

3. In accordance with the Confusion Rules of Civil Procedure, a document is deemed to be in your possession, custody or control if you either have physical possession of the item or have a right to possession of the item that is equal or superior to the person who has physical control of the item.

4. "Person" or "persons" means any natural persons, firms, partnerships, associations, joint ventures, corporations and any other form of business organization or arrangement, as well as governmental or quasi-governmental agencies. If other than a natural person, include all natural persons associated with such entity.

5. Any and all data or information which is in electronic or magnetic form should be produced in a reasonable manner.

Lawyers worry about leaving weasel room for the other side, so they often include lengthy definitions such as these.

USE OF DEFINITIONS

The use of any particular gender in the plural or singular number of the words defined under paragraph "I", "Definitions" is intended to include the appropriate gender or number as the text of any particular request for production of documents may require.

TIME PERIOD

Unless specifically stated in a request for production of documents, all information herein requested is for the entire time period from five years prior to the date of the incident which is the basis of this lawsuit, through the date of production of documents requested herein.

EXHIBIT A
DOCUMENTS TO BE PRODUCED

1. All photographs that pertain to this lawsuit in the possession, custody, or control of Patty Haus, Patty Haus's attorney, or anyone acting on Patty Haus's behalf.

2. All photographs taken of Patty Haus which may be in the possession, custody, or control of Patty Haus, Patty Haus's attorney, or anyone acting on Patty Haus's behalf.

3. All written statements made by Patty Haus that pertain to this lawsuit in the possession, custody, or control of Patty Haus, Patty Haus's attorney, or anyone acting on Patty Haus's behalf but not including those made to her attorney for the purpose of obtaining legal advice and not disclosed to any third party.

4. All oral statements made by Patty Haus that pertain to this lawsuit which were either recorded or taped on an electronic device or recorder which are in the possession, custody, or control of Patty Haus, Patty Haus's attorney, or anyone acting on Patty Haus's behalf.

5. A copy of all documents filed with any state, county, city, federal, or governmental agency, institution, or department containing information about Patty Haus which are in the possession, custody, or control of Patty Haus, Patty Haus's attorney, or anyone acting on Patty Haus's behalf.

6. A copy of all medical records, doctor or hospital records, and reports or medical documents of any kind containing information about Patty Haus and/or concerning the medical or physical condition of Patty Haus which are in the possession, custody, or control of Patty Haus, Patty Haus's attorney, or anyone acting on Patty Haus's behalf.

7. All written reports of inspection, tests, writings, drawings, graphs, charts, recordings, or opinions of any expert who has been used for consultation in connection with this lawsuit and whose work product was reviewed in whole or in part by an expert who is to be called as a witness.

8. A curriculum vitae or resume for any consulting expert whose mental impressions or opinions have been reviewed by a testifying expert.

9. Copies of any and all liability insurance policies held by Patty Haus.

10. Copies of any and all books, documents, or other tangible things which may be used at the time of trial of this lawsuit.

11. Copies of any and all tangible things whose production has not been requested previously in this or other requests which Patty Haus may use as demonstrative evidence at trial.

12. Copies of any and all police reports, business cards, or other similar memoranda produced in connection with any arrests or investigations of Geronimo "Jerry" Smoker.

13. Copies of any and all documents in the possession of Patty Haus relating to her residence in Vista Libra Apartments, including, but not limited to, the eviction proceedings in the months prior to the incident made the basis of the suit.

The actual request for documents. Are any of them objectionable?

Depositions

Although the formal term is **oral deposition,** unless "by written questions" follows the word *deposition,* it is assumed that you mean an oral deposition when you say "deposition," or, more informally, **depo.** Because depo testimony is the evidentiary equivalent of court testimony, it can be used to prove up documents. If you and your attorney have decided that a particular document needs to be proved up, use depos as a way to accomplish that particular task. For instance, say you are representing the plaintiff and have gotten all the police records for the plaintiff's former live-in, Jerry Smoker, in response to the request for production you sent the defendant. When you depose one of the other officers, you send a **deposition notice** with a subpoena duces tecum asking him to bring along copies of these same reports.

The next step is to remind the attorney on the date of the deposition of the need to prove up those documents unless she has changed her mind. The best way to do this is to attach copies of the documents to a reminder memo that you put wherever you want to make sure the attorney sees it before she goes to the deposition. In the various offices I worked at, the you-must-read-now place to set things was in the attorney's chair—we would all definitely notice that, even if we had to sit on it first. The attorney will then ask the **deponent** the necessary questions to prove it up: first the authentication questions (what is this and how do you know this is what you say it is) and then the hearsay exception questions. You may want to give baby attorneys a cheat list of the requisite questions. It's really nerve wracking to be in a depo and know there are four things you have to ask for the BRE and only be able to come up with three of them. You really love your paralegal when you see she gave you that little note just in case you became brain dead mid-depo.

When the deposition comes back, you have your evidence proved up; you just have to keep track of it so you don't have a conniption just before the trial or cost your client extra money to prove it up twice. Lots of attorneys prove up the same piece of evidence several different ways. Part of that is necessary, because you should always have a back-up plan in case an unanticipated attack arises, but there is such a thing as overkill. Even if the attorney is fronting expenses in a contingency fee case, a point will come when you will have to account for the money you've spent on behalf of the client. Each subpoena duces tecum costs money to serve. Each deposition cost is based on the amount of time it takes, so the extra time to prove up documents directly affects the amount the deposition costs. And if the settlement or verdict is low and expenses are high, it will look as if the attorney has made much more out of the case than the client, even though it is, in essence, the repayment of an interest-free loan. So keep track of each item once it is proved up, and prove it up again for a reason, not just because you forgot it had been done once, or you'll end up with unnecessary expenses.

Deposition by Written Questions

A deposition by written questions is a nifty time-saving device, but not the cheapest route to go. You simply call the court reporter's office, fill out a form, and they do the rest. Usually you check off a box for whether you want a document authenticated and for the court reporter to include the business record exception questions. The court reporter sends the form to the proper keeper of records, puts that person under oath, and assembles everything in a nice little comb-bound or spiral-bound book for you and files the original with the court. The opposing counsel is given an opportunity to ask cross-questions, but must pay the court reporter for the privilege and her copy of the records. Some attorneys will try to get the results of the depositions by written question by sending a request for production asking for them after they are returned; it's an open question as to whether that's appropriate. Again, check your locale. It may be no big deal or it may subject you to sanctions, depending on how your local judge(s) feel about it, but it appears to be enough of a discretionary matter not to be the subject of appeal.

The downside of depositions by written questions (outside of the fact that there is no short slang for it that I'm aware of—oh, yeah, and that expense thing) is that if you are requesting records from an office that is not familiar with the process and the weirdness of the BRE, they may not understand the questions and fail to prove up the record. Now you have the custodian of records stating under oath that the documents you want do not fit one (or more) of the elements of the business record exception. Generally you can clear up problems of comprehension in oral depositions or trial testimony, but there's no chance of that kind of communication in this form of discovery. If you try to clean it up by calling the custodian to testify at trial, you'll still have to deal with the custodian's contradictory testimony, which usually can be explained away and which the jury usually doesn't hold against you. However, it's one more hassle to have to resolve during trial.

NO. <u>05-CI-0012345</u>

PATTY HAUS **Plaintiff,**	§	**IN THE DISTRICT COURT**
	§	
	§	
V.	§	
	§	
JOHN Q. JUSTICE AND GLOBAL	§	**1313TH JUDICIAL DISTRICT**
INTERNATIONAL MONEY MAKERS,	§	
INC. D/B/A VIVA LIBRE	§	
APARTMENTS	§	
Defendants.	§	**OF DUX COUNTY, CONFUSION**

NOTICE OF INTENTION TO TAKE ORAL DEPOSITION

TO: Officer Charlie Garcia, at 360 Nueva Ley Ave, Big City, Confusion 99999-9999

Please take notice that on December 19 at 2:00 pm and continuing thereafter from day to day until complete, Plaintiff, Patty Haus, will take the oral deposition of Officer Charlie Garcia, pursuant to Rule 199 of the Despair Rules of Civil Procedure, at 333 Martyr Towers, Suite 100, Big City, Texas 99999-9999.

Please take further notice that in connection with the taking of this deposition, and pursuant to the Confusion Rules of Civil Procedure, the deponent shall produce at the commencement of the taking of the deposition the documents described in Exhibit "A" which is attached hereto and incorporated by reference for all purposes as if written verbatim herein.

Your attention is directed to the penalties set forth in the Confusion Rules of Civil Procedure for failure of the deponent to appear and/or comply with the discovery requested.

Other parties are invited to attend and examine the witness.

Respectfully submitted,

By: _____
Lisa St. Joan
State Bar No. 0987676
333 Martyr Towers, Suite 100
Big City, Texas 99999-9999
Tel. (888) 555-0987
Fax. (888) 555-0986
Attorney for Plaintiff
Patty Haus

CERTIFICATE OF SERVICE

I certify that on October 24, 200– a true and correct copy of Plaintiff's Notice of Oral Deposition was served to each person listed below by the method indicated.

_____
Lisa St. Joan

Larry Lorenzo
Attorney for John Q. Justice
666 Attorney Plaza, Suite 999
Big City, Confusion 99999-9999
TEL: (888) 555-1234
FAX: (888) 555-1235

   X   Certified mail,
return receipt requested
_____ Personal delivery
_____ Private delivery
_____ Facsimile transfer

A notice of deposition requesting documents. This document could have a page break before the certificate of service if desired.

Eve Smith
Attorney for Global International
Money Makers, Inc. d/b/a Vista
Libre Apartments
5117 Marx Center, Suite 200
Big City, Confusion 99999-9999
TEL: (888) 555-4567
FAX: (888) 555-4568

<u> X </u> Certified mail,
return receipt requested
_____ Personal delivery
_____ Private delivery
_____ Facsimile transfer

DEFINITIONS AND INSTRUCTIONS

    1. As used herein, the terms "you" and "your" shall mean Officer Charlie Garcia, Officer Charlie Garcia's attorneys, agents, and all other natural persons or business or legal entities acting or purporting to act for or on behalf of Officer Charlie Garcia, whether authorized to do so or not.

    2. As used herein, the term "documents" shall mean all writings of every kind, source and authorship, both originals and all nonidentical copies thereof, in your possession, custody, or control, or known by you to exist, irrespective of whether the writing is one intended for or transmitted internally by you, or intended for or transmitted to any other person or entity, including without limitation any government agency, department, administrative, or private entity or person. The term shall include handwritten, typewritten, printed, photocopied, photographic, or recorded matter. It shall include communications in words, symbols, pictures, sound recordings, films, tapes, and information stored in, or accessible through, computer or other information storage or retrieval systems, together with the codes and/or programming instructions and other materials necessary to understand and use such systems. For purposes of illustration and not limitation, the term shall include: affidavits; agendas; agreements; analyses; announcements; bills, statements, and other records of obligations and expenditures; books; brochures; bulletins; calendars; canceled checks, vouchers, receipts and other records of payments; charts, drawings; check registers; checkbooks; circulars; collateral files and contents; contracts; corporate bylaws; corporate charters; correspondence; credit files and contents; deeds of trust; deposit slips; diaries, drafts; files; guaranty agreements; instructions; invoices; ledgers, journals, balance sheets, profit and loss statements, and other sources of financial data; letters; logs, notes, or memoranda of telephonic or face-to-face conversations; manuals; memoranda of all kinds, to and from any persons, agencies, or entities; minutes; minute books; notes; notices; parts lists; papers; press releases; printed matter (including books, articles, speeches, and newspaper clippings); purchase orders; records; records of administrative, technical, and financial actions taken or recommended; reports; safety deposit boxes and contents and records of entry; schedules; security agreements; specifications; statement of bank accounts; statements, interviews; stock transfer ledger; technical and engineering reports, evaluations, advice, recommendations, commentaries, conclusions, studies, test plans, manuals, procedures, data, reports, results, and conclusions; summaries, notes, and other records and recordings of any conferences, meetings, visits, statements, interviews or telephone conversations; telegrams; teletypes and other communications sent or received; transcripts of testimony; UCC instruments; work papers; and all other writings, the contents of which relate to, discuss, consider, or otherwise refer to the subject matter of the particular discovery requested.

    3. In accordance with the Confusion Rules of Civil Procedure a document is deemed to be in your possession, custody or control if you either have physical possession of the

Another example of lawyerly attempts to limit loopholes through definitions.

item or have a right to possession of the item that is equal or superior to the person who has physical control of the item.

4. "Person" or "persons" means any natural persons, firms, partnerships, associations, joint ventures, corporations and any other form of business organization or arrangement, as well as government or quasi-governmental agencies. If other than a natural person, include all natural persons associated with such entity.

5. Any and all data or information which is in electronic or magnetic form should be produced in a reasonable manner.

USE OF DEFINITIONS

The use of any particular gender in the plural or singular number of the words defined under paragraph "1", "Definitions" is intended to include the appropriate gender or number as the text of any particular request for production of documents may require.

EXHIBIT A
DOCUMENTS TO BE PRODUCED

1. The police and/or arrest reports, including, but not limited to, any supplemental reports, generated in connection with the arrest of Geronimo "Jerry" Smoker on or about August 22 [of the year of the incident made the basis of the suit].

2. The police and/or arrest reports, including, but not limited to, any supplemental reports, generated in connection with the arrest of Geronimo "Jerry" Smoker on or about August 31 [of the year of the incident made the basis of the suit].

3. The police and/or arrest reports, including, but not limited to, any supplemental reports, generated in connection with the arrest of Geronimo "Jerry" Smoker on or about September 5 [of the year of the incident made the basis of the suit].

4. The police and/or arrest reports, including, but not limited to, any supplemental reports, generated in connection with the arrest of Geronimo "Jerry" Smoker on or about September 17 [of the year of the incident made the basis of the suit].

5. The police and/or arrest reports, including, but not limited to, any supplemental reports, generated in connection with the arrest of Geronimo "Jerry" Smoker on or about September 19 [of the year of the incident made the basis of the suit].

6. The police and/or arrest reports, including, but not limited to, any supplemental reports, generated in connection with the arrest of Geronimo "Jerry" Smoker on or about September 25 [of the year of the incident made the basis of the suit].

7. The police and/or arrest reports, including, but not limited to, any supplemental reports, generated in connection with the arrest of Geronimo "Jerry" Smoker on or about October 1 [of the year of the incident made the basis of the suit].

8. The police and/or arrest reports, including, but not limited to, any supplemental reports, generated in connection with the arrest of Geronimo "Jerry" Smoker on or about October 15 [of the year of the incident made the basis of the suit].

9. The police and/or arrest reports, including, but not limited to, any supplemental reports, generated in connection with the arrest of Geronimo "Jerry" Smoker on or about October 31 [of the year of the incident made the basis of the suit].

As in the request for production, the exhibit is where you find the good stuff. Are any of these requests subject to a valid objection?

SUBPOENA DUCES TECUM

THE STATE OF CONFUSION §
COUNTY OF DUX §

Style of suit: *Haus v. Justice*
Cause No.: 05-CI-0012345
Court: 1313TH Judicial District Court, Dux County, Confusion

Party Issuing Subpoena: Patty Haus
Party's Attorney of Record: Lisa St. Joan
To: Officer Charlie Garcia

You are commanded to attend and give testimony at a deposition in the above-styled case on December 19 at 2:00 PM at 333 Martyr Towers, Suite 100, Big City, Confusion 99999-9999. You must remain there until discharged by the court or the party summoning you.

You are further commanded to produce and permit inspection and copying on December 19 at 2:00 PM at 333 Martyr Towers, Suite 100, Big City, Confusion 99999-9999, of the following documents or tangible things in your possession, custody, or control: the police and/or arrest reports, including, but not limited to, any supplemental reports, generated in connection with the arrest of Geronimo "Jerry" Smoker on or about August 22 [of the year of the incident made the basis of the suit]; the police and/or arrest reports, including, but not limited to, any supplemental reports, generated in connection with the arrest of Geronimo "Jerry" Smoker on or about August 31 [of the year of the incident made the basis of the suit]; the police and/or arrest reports, including, but not limited to, any supplemental reports, generated in connection with the arrest of Geronimo "Jerry" Smoker on or about September 5 [of the year of the incident made the basis of the suit]; the police and/or arrest reports, including, but not limited to, any supplemental reports, generated in connection with the arrest of Geronimo "Jerry" Smoker on or about September 17 [of the year of the incident made the basis of the suit]; the police and/or arrest reports, including, but not limited to, any supplemental reports, generated in connection with the arrest of Geronimo "Jerry" Smoker on or about September 19 [of the year of the incident made the basis of the suit]; the police and/or arrest reports, including, but not limited to, any supplemental reports, generated in connection with the arrest of Geronimo "Jerry" Smoker on or about September 25 [of the year of the incident made the basis of the suit]; The police and/or arrest reports, including, but not limited to, any supplemental reports, generated in connection with the arrest of Geronimo "Jerry" Smoker on or about October 1 [of the year of the incident made the basis of the suit]; the police and/or arrest reports, including, but not limited to, any supplemental reports, generated in connection with the arrest of Geronimo "Jerry" Smoker on or about October 15 [of the year of the incident made the basis of the suit]; and the police and/or arrest reports, including, but not limited to, any supplemental reports, generated in connection with the arrest of Geronimo "Jerry" Smoker on or about October 31 [of the year of the incident made the basis of the suit].

FAILURE BY ANY PERSON WITHOUT ADEQUATE EXCUSE TO OBEY A SUBPOENA SERVED UPON THAT PERSON MAY BE DEEMED A CONTEMPT OF THE COURT FROM WHICH THE SUBPOENA IS ISSUED OR A DISTRICT COURT IN THE COUNTY IN WHICH THE SUBPOENA IS SERVED, AND MAY BE PUNISHED BY FINE OR CONFINEMENT, OR BOTH.

Date: October 24, 2004

_____
Lisa St. Joan

RETURN

I certify that I personally served Officer Charlie Garcia with a copy of this subpoena on _____ at _____. I also tendered to the witness the witness fees required by law at the time the subpoena was delivered.

_____
[Process Server's Printed Name]

A subpoena duces tecum.

S 3POENA DUCES TECUM
THE STATE OF TEXAS

COUNTY OF BEXAR

To the Sheriff, Constable or any other person authorized to serve and execute a Subpoena as provided in Rule 176, T.R.C.P.

Greetings,

You are hereby commanded to Subpoena and Summon the following witness:

Custodian of MEDICAL & BILLING Records for : DR. J. MICHAEL GRAHAM

to be and appear before a commissioned Officer of the State of Texas, a Notary Public with L.O.R.R. RECORD RETRIEVAL, 2318 SAN PEDRO, SUITE 1, SAN ANTONIO, TEXAS or their designated agent on _____ at_____AM / PM, AT THE OFFICE OF THE CUSTODIAN, or at another agreed upon time as the Officer may designate, then and there to give evidence by Deposition by Written Questions.

The witness is also to produce for inspection and photocopying (to be attached to the Deposition):

ANY AND ALL MEDICAL RECORDS AND ITEMIZED BILLING STATEMENTS FROM OCTOBER 27, 1998 TO THE PRESENT

pertaining to: JULIE H. STIRMAN, DOB: , -SS-AN:

This Subpoena is being issued at the instance of the PLAINTIFF in that certain Cause No. 2000-CI-15834 pending on the docket of the DISTRICT COURT OF THE 408TH JUDICIAL DISTRICT OF TEXAS, BEXAR County, Texas, Styled:

JULIE H. STIRMAN   VS   WILLIAM BROCK AND CAROLYN BROCK

and there to remain from day to day and time to time until discharged by me according to Law. T.R.C.P. Rule 176.8(a) states: Enforcement of Subpoena. (a) Contempt. Failure by any person without adequate excuse to obey a subpoena served upon that person may be deemed in contempt of the court from which the subpoena is issued or a district court in the county in which the subpoena is served, and may be punished by fine or confinement, or both.

This subpoena is issued in accordance to Rule 201 and Rule 176, T.R.C.P.

REQUESTED BY: E.B. BARRETTO

MICHELLE EASTON
NOTARY PUBLIC STATE OF TEXAS
COMMISSION EXPIRES:
MARCH 31, 2007

ATTORNEY FOR THE PLAINTIFF

Witness my hand on this, the 22nd day of May , 2003

Officer of the State of Texas
As provided in Rule 201 and 178, T.R.C.P.

Officer's Return

CAME TO HAND 22nd day of May, 2003 and executed the 22nd day of May, 2003 by delivering to _____ a true copy of this subpoena together with the accompanying deposition by written questions, and tendering the lawful witness fee of $ 1.00

Authorized person under Rule 178 of T.R.C.P.
as provided in Rule 201 and 176, T.R.C.P.

25517   DW

A completed duces tecum. The missing text at the top is from the two-hole punch used to put documents in the court file.

JULIE H. STIRMAN	IN THE DISTRICT COURT FOR
VS	BEXAR COUNTY, TEXAS
WILLIAM BROCK AND CAROLYN BROCK	408TH JUDICIAL DISTRICT

NOTICE OF INTENTION TO TAKE DEPOSITION
BY WRITTEN QUESTIONS

TO: RICHARD R. STORM, JR.

You will take notice that after 20 days from the service of a copy hereof with attached questions, a deposition by written questions will be taken of the CUSTODIAN OF MEDICAL & BILLING RECORDS FOR:

DR. J. MICHAEL GRAHAM
17270 RED OAK DR. SUITE 260
HOUSTON, TX 77339

at the offices of LORR ,or at another agreed upon time and/or place before a Notary Public, an Officer of the State of Texas and employee of LORR, 2318 San Pedro Avenue, Suite 1, San Antonio, Texas 782 or their designated agent. Which deposition, with attached questions, may be used in evidence upon the trial of the above styled and numbered cause pending in the above named Court.

Notice is further given that request is here made as authorized under Rule 200, Texas Rules of Court, to the Officer authorized to take this deposition to issue a SUBPOENA DUCES TECUM and cause to be served on the witness to produce for inspection an photocopying:

ANY AND ALL MEDICAL RECORDS AND ITEMIZED BILLING STATEMENTS FROM OCTOBER 27, 1998 TO THE PRESENT

pertaining to JULIE H. STIRMAN, DOB: , SSN: and turn all such records over to the Officer authorized to take this deposition for inspection and photocopying, the same may be made by him and attached to said deposition.

E.B. BARRETTO
SBID NO. 01816350
SINKIN & BARRETTO, P.L.L.C.
105 W. WOODLAWN,
SAN ANTONIO, TX 78212
Phone 2107326000 Fax 2107362777
ATTORNEY FOR THE PLAINTIFF

CERTIFICATE OF SERVICE

I certify that a true and exact copy of the foregoing Notice of Intention to Take Deposition by Written Questions was provided to the respective parties or attorneys of record, pursuant to Rule (21a), by registered mail, postage prepaid, hand delivered or telephonic document transfer.

Date: 5-20-0_   By: _E.B. Barretto_
                              E.B. BARRETTO

19893   25517   DW

This notice for deposition on written questions includes a subpoena duces tecum.

The BRE affidavit is like a bastard stepchild of the deposition by written questions. Rather than having a court reporter take the oath, we let a notary public take an oath and verify a signature, and, depending on the circumstances, we may require some other entity to "certify" the records. The same problem can arise with the affidavit as with the deposition in written questions: some people don't understand what is being said in the BRE. However, when you draft it and send it, if the recipient doesn't understand it, she will usually phone you and ask, just as you should request in the cover letter. This gives you a chance to translate legalese. Note that this communication is an instance of legal information, not legal advice, and it is perfectly legitimate to tell the prospective **affiant.**

Calling Witness at Trial

You may, of course, always call the custodian as a witness at trial. This is probably the absolute cheapest way to prove up your record. So why don't people do it more often? Because you annoy the custodians. No one wants to go to court to testify. And it sure seems that the worse your relationship is with a particular medical office or whatever other common keeper of records, the more likely you will have to deal with that office in the future—another corollary to Murphy's rule. If you call the custodian of records for your metropolitan area's major trauma center, and you annoy this custodian of records by doing so because she has had to come downtown and fight traffic and pay an exorbitant amount for parking and then sit for hours in the hall before she could testify when she has real work to do back at the hospital, and she was given a hard time by her boss for having to go, and—well, you get the idea. You will not be her favorite person, and when the day comes that you need a favor from her, she won't be taking your call.

There are times that there is no choice. Sometimes something related to the case will come up less than 14 days before trial, and you will need the custodian to come down and testify. Sometimes something arises that you didn't anticipate, either legally (e.g., a new case invalidating the testimony of the kind of witness you used to prove up the documents) or factually (the witness that proved up the documents was just convicted for fraud involving document scams). In those cases, call the custodian and explain. Don't give an involved explanation of your predicament, but let the custodian know you weren't simply caught with your pants down. Custodians who frequently release information will know that you should have done something sooner, and unless you have already established a reputation with them and they know you are generally on top of things, they won't be terribly sympathetic. If the custodian has not testified at trial before, explain why she will have to sit in the hall. Ask whether it will be better for her to be subpoenaed or not. Some people do not like to have a subpoena sent, as it involves some sort of official service and they think it looks bad. Others want the official notice to impress upon their superiors that it is absolutely necessary for them to appear or in order to be paid for their absence. In any case, do everything you can to minimize the amount of time the witness will be there, and if you have staff available, pick up the witness. Offer to pay for the witness's parking; that is not an ethics violation.

AUTOMOBILE ACCIDENT REPORT

One of the most common sorts of records you will have to look at is the police automobile accident report. If you nose around the materials that the state licensing agency for police officers has, you'll probably find a "how-to" booklet about how to fill one out. This can be useful if you have a report that is unfavorable.

Accident reports are public records, so anyone can get them. Reading an automobile accident report seems self-explanatory. The report tells you where, who, when, and how; it also lists witnesses. The officer marks down contributing factors, and that's it, right? Sure. And a contract is any promise written on paper and nothing else. (I hope you've learned enough law by now to know that the last statement is patently false.)

If you like the police report, you probably don't want to look for holes, but you want to be prepared for any attacks on the report. Police officers tend to be influential with the jury if the case is about the auto accident itself or if some fact about the accident is of significance to the case. The reason is that the police officer is viewed as an expert of sorts (whether justified or not) and a neutral: he is not paid by either party to be there—it's just part of his job. It shouldn't make a bit of difference to him who he says is at fault—although, of course, police officers are like anybody else and not exempt from biases and mistakes.

TEXAS PEACE OFFICER'S ACCIDENT REPORT

MAIL TO: ACCIDENT RECORDS, TEXAS DEPARTMENT OF PUBLIC SAFETY, PO BOX 4087, AUSTIN TX 78773-0001

PLACE WHERE ACCIDENT OCCURRED

COUNTY **BEXAR**

CITY OR TOWN **SAN ANTONIO**
SHOW CITY IF INSIDE CITY LIMITS
☐ ☐ ☐ ☐

IF ACCIDENT WAS OUTSIDE CITY LIMITS, INDICATE DISTANCE FROM NEAREST TOWN **N/A** MILES NORTH S E W OF **N/A**
CITY OR TOWN

LOC. NO

DO NOT WRITE IN THIS SPACE

DPS NO.

ROAD ON WHICH ACCIDENT OCCURRED
BLOCK NUMBER   STREET OR ROAD NAME   ROUTE NUMBER OR STREET CODE

CONSTR. ZONE ☐ YES ☐ NO   SPEED LIMIT

INTERSECTING STREET OR RR X'ING NUMBER
BLOCK NUMBER   STREET OR ROAD NAME   ROUTE NUMBER OR STREET CODE

CONSTR. ZONE ☐ YES ☐ NO   SPEED LIMIT

NOT AT INTERSECTION _____ ☐ FT. ☐ ☐ ☐ ☐ OF
☐ MI. N S E W

LOC.

CODE

SEVERITY

FAT. REC.

DR. REC.

DATE OF ACCIDENT _____ 20 ___   DAY OF WEEK _____   HOUR _____   ☐ A.M. ☐ P.M.   IF EXACTLY NOON OR MIDNIGHT, SO STATE

UNIT NO. 1 – MOTOR VEHICLE

VEH IDENT NO _____   IF BODY STYLE = VAN OR BUS, INDICATE SEATING CAPACITY

YEAR MODEL _____   COLOR & MAKE _____   MODEL NAME _____   BODY STYLE _____   LICENSE PLATE _____
YEAR STATE NUMBER

DRIVER'S NAME _____
LAST   FIRST   MIDDLE   ADDRESS (STREET, CITY, STATE, ZIP)

PHONE NUMBER _____

DRIVER'S LICENSE _____
STATE   NUMBER   CLASS/TYPE

DOB _____
MONTH DAY YEAR

☐ W ☐ B ☐ H
RACE ☐ I ☐ A ☐ M   SEX _____   OCCUPATION _____

SPECIMEN TAKEN (ALCOHOL/DRUG ANALYSIS) 1-BREATH 2-BLOOD 3-OTHER 4-NONE 5-REFUSED ☐

ALCOHOL/DRUG ANALYSIS RESULT _____

PEACE OFFICER, EMS DRIVER FIRE FIGHTER ON EMERGENCY? ☐ YES ☐ NO

LESSEE ☐
OWNER ☐

LIABILITY INSURANCE ☐ YES ☐ NO
(NAME (ALWAYS SHOW LESSEE IF LEASED, OTHERWISE SHOW OWNER))   ADDRESS (STREET, CITY, STATE, ZIP)
INSURANCE COMPANY NAME   POLICY NUMBER

VEHICLE DAMAGE RATING _____

UNIT NO. 2   MOTOR VEHICLE ☐   TRAIN ☐   PEDALCYCLIST ☐
TOWED ☐   PEDESTRIAN ☐   OTHER ☐   VEH IDENT NO _____   IF BODY STYLE = VAN OR BUS, INDICATE SEATING CAPACITY _____

YEAR MODEL _____   COLOR & MAKE _____   MODEL NAME _____   BODY STYLE _____   LICENSE PLATE _____
YEAR STATE NUMBER

DRIVER'S NAME _____
LAST   FIRST   MIDDLE   ADDRESS (STREET, CITY, STATE, ZIP)

PHONE NUMBER _____

DRIVER'S LICENSE _____
STATE   NUMBER   CLASS/TYPE

DOB _____
MONTH DAY YEAR

☐ W ☐ B ☐ H
RACE ☐ I ☐ A ☐ M   SEX _____   OCCUPATION _____

SPECIMEN TAKEN (ALCOHOL/DRUG ANALYSIS) 1-BREATH 2-BLOOD 3-OTHER 4-NONE 5-REFUSED ☐

ALCOHOL/DRUG ANALYSIS RESULT _____

PEACE OFFICER, EMS DRIVER FIRE FIGHTER ON EMERGENCY? ☐ YES ☐ NO

LESSEE ☐
OWNER ☐

LIABILITY INSURANCE ☐ YES ☐ NO
(NAME (ALWAYS SHOW LESSEE IF LEASED, OTHERWISE SHOW OWNER))   ADDRESS (STREET, CITY, STATE, ZIP)
INSURANCE COMPANY NAME   POLICY NUMBER

VEHICLE DAMAGE RATING _____

DAMAGE TO PROPERTY OTHER THAN VEHICLES
OBJECT   NAME AND ADDRESS OF OWNER   PROPERTY FROM CODE $ _____   DAMAGE ESTIMATE

LIGHT CONDITION ☐
1-DAYLIGHT
2-DAWN
3-DARK-NOT LIGHTED
4-DARK-LIGHTED
5-DUSK

WEATHER ☐ ☐
1- CLEAR   6-SMOKE
2-RAINING   7-SLEETING
3-SNOWING   8-HIGH WINDS
4-FOG   9-OTHER
5-BLOWING DUST

SURFACE CONDITION ☐
1-DRY
2-WET
3-MUDDY
4-SNOWY/ICY
5. OTHER

TYPE ROAD SURFACE ☐
1-BLACKTOP
2-CONCRETE
3-GRAVEL
4-SHELL
5-DIRT
6. OTHER

DESCRIBE ROAD CONDITIONS (INVESTIGATOR'S OPINION)
_____
_____

IN YOUR OPINION, DID THIS ACCIDENT RESULT IN AT LEAST $1000.00 DAMAGE TO ANY ONE PERSON'S PROPERTY?   ☐ YES ☐ NO

CHARGES FILED
NAME _____   CHARGE _____   CITATION NO. _____
NAME _____   CHARGE _____   CITATION NO. _____

TIME NOTIFIED OF ACCIDENT _____   ☐ A.M. ☐ P.M.   HOW _____
DATE   HOUR

TIME ARRIVED AT SCENE OF ACCIDENT _____   ☐ A.M. ☐ P.M.
DATE   HOUR

TYPED OR PRINTED NAME OF INVESTIGATOR _____   DATE REPORT MADE _____   IS REPORT COMPLETE ☐ YES ☐ NO

SIGNATURE OF INVESTIGATOR _____   ID NO. _____   DEPARTMENT **San Antonio Police Department**   DIST./AREA _____

ST-3 Rev. (07-03)

A blank police report for a traffic accident.

285

First check the report for internal inconsistencies. Then look at the report's style. It should be an investigation: He said; she said; damage was here; debris was there; and so on. Unless the report is based on the extremely unusual situation where the officer actually witnessed the accident, it can be attacked if it is written in such a way as to suggest that the officer knew firsthand what occurred. Many officers do not write tickets as a result of the fact that they did not witness the accident, so too much cannot be made of the fact that no tickets were issued unless that is not brought out in deposition.

If your client's testimony was omitted—which can happen—it is something to raise. Ideally, your client would ask to have the officer file a supplemental report immediately after the accident, but that's unlikely, and won't help if the officer has made the accident seem to be the client's fault. If the officer is not an expert, such as a member of a special unit trained in accident reconstruction, then you have another out. When you get a witness statement from the officer, or in the questions prepared for the attorney's deposition, ask if the police officer relied on the statements of other people in making his determinations as to the cause of the accident. If he says "Yes," use the reasoning of this case to exclude both his testimony and his report.

Neno v. Clinton, 772 A.2d 899 (N.J. 2001) (per curiam).

Plaintiffs sustained serious injuries after being hit as they walked across a highway intersection by a truck owned by defendant Gilsonite Music Industries, Inc. (Gilsonite). Plaintiffs filed suit against Gilsonite and Derek Clinton (Clinton), the driver of the truck. The jury found that Clinton was negligent, but that his negligence was not a proximate cause of the collision, and the Law Division entered judgment for defendants . . .

In January 1995, plaintiffs Joao Neno and Helder Neno were working at a construction site that straddled both sides of Route One in Plainsboro. On the day in question, they and several other workers had to walk across the intersection of Route One, a four-lane highway, and Scudders Mill Road, to reach another part of the site. There are no pedestrian crosswalks at that intersection. The workers began to walk through the first two lanes of Route One south when the traffic light facing them was green. They walked in front of a truck stopped in the right lane without incident. Another worker who was slightly ahead of Joao and Helder successfully crossed the left southbound lane, but when plaintiffs stepped into that second lane the Route One traffic light turned green. Plaintiffs were hit by a truck heading southbound on Route One in the left lane driven by defendant Clinton. Just prior to the collision, the driver of the truck stopped in the right-hand lane, William Burnett, saw Clinton look away from the road and into Burnett's driver's side mirror, a fact that Clinton did not dispute. Clinton accelerated prior to reaching the intersection, and was traveling thirty to thirty-five miles per hour at the time of the collision. Both plaintiffs suffered severe injuries.

Officer Kelly, the primary investigating officer, arrived on the scene after the accident but before Joao and Helder were taken away by ambulance. He interviewed Burnett and Mark Meyer, another driver who witnessed the accident as he approached the intersection driving his vehicle in the opposite, northbound direction.

Kelly testified that Meyer told him that the light facing Meyer's vehicle, which was headed northbound, was green when defendant's truck struck plaintiffs. Meyer's statement established the fact that the light also was green for defendant Clinton as he entered the intersection from the opposite, southbound direction. Officer Kelly also testified that Burnett, the truck driver stopped at the light, told him that the traffic light was green when defendant's truck entered the intersection. The trial court allowed Kelly to testify to the content of the statements of the two eyewitnesses over plaintiffs' objection, concluding that Kelly's testimony was admissible because both Burnett and Meyer would be testifying later in the trial.

The trial court also permitted Kelly to testify, over objection, that in his opinion plaintiffs were at fault because they continued to cross the road against a red light. Officer Kelly's testimony included the following opinion:

> [B]ased on all the statements and the investigation that I did at the accident—of this accident[,] the pedestrians failed to properly cross the intersection. The sequence of events suggests the pedestrians began to cross the roadway after the [Scudders] Mill Road signal turned red and before US Route 1 signal turned green. A slight delay of approximately 4 seconds is utilized where all signals are red. This allows the intersection to clear prior to US Route 1 receiving a green signal.

. . . The court explicitly refused to qualify Kelly as an expert, instead allowing him to offer his opinion as a lay witness. Kelly based that opinion testimony on his investigation of the scene after the accident and on the eyewitness statements given to him by Burnett and Meyer.

At the conclusion of the trial, the jury returned a verdict of no cause for action, finding that although defendant Clinton was negligent, his negligence was not a proximate cause of the accident.

Plaintiffs challenge two evidentiary rulings concerning Officer Kelly's testimony. First, they contend that the trial court improperly allowed Kelly to testify to the substance of statements made by Burnett and Meyer at the scene. Second, they assert that the trial court improperly allowed Kelly to testify to his opinion regarding who was at fault in the accident. We address each ruling in turn.

"'Hearsay' is a statement, other than one made by the declarant while testifying at the trial or hearing, offered in evidence to prove the truth of the matter asserted.". . . The hearsay prohibition "ensures the accuracy of the factfinding process by excluding untrustworthy statements, such as those made without the solemnity of the oath, and not subject to cross-examination . . . or the jury's critical observation of the declarant's demeanor and tone." . . .

One possible exception to the hearsay bar . . . allows admission of statements "offered to rebut an express or implied charge against the witness of recent fabrication or improper influence or motive.". . . The scope of the exception encompasses prior consistent statements made by the witness before the alleged "improper influence or motive" to demonstrate that the witness did not change his or her story . . . A court cannot admit a prior consistent statement unless it falls within the parameters of that hearsay exception.

More importantly, "[a] prior consistent statement offered [solely] to bolster a witness' testimony is inadmissible.". . .

Burnett's and Meyer's statements, as testified to by Kelly, were undoubtedly hearsay. Kelly testified that Burnett told him that he was stopped at a red light that turned green just prior to the collision. The statement was offered for the substantive truth of the matter, i.e., that the light facing Burnett was initially red, but turned green just before the collision (and therefore that plaintiffs were crossing when faced with a red light). Similarly, Kelly testified that Meyer, the driver approaching the intersection from the opposite direction, told the officer that Meyer had a green light at the time of the accident. The statement was offered to prove Meyer's light was green, and tended to establish that defendant Clinton, who was traveling in the opposite direction from Meyer, also had a green light. As to both Burnett and Meyer, Kelly was permitted to testify to out-of-court statements that were introduced exclusively to prove the truth of those statements. Thus, the trial court improperly admitted those statements because there was no charge of improper influence or motive in this case. The prior consistent statement exception is not applicable to either statement. The fact that Burnett and Meyers were scheduled to testify later in the trial, a fact relied on by the trial court to admit Kelly's opinion, does not render admissible their hearsay statements.

The next question is whether the trial court properly admitted Officer Kelly's lay opinion regarding the cause of the accident, based on the hearsay statements of the eyewitnesses Burnett and Meyer. We conclude, as did the dissent below, that lay opinion based primarily on hearsay statements is inadmissible. Accordingly, the trial court improperly admitted the testimony.

. . . If a witness is not testifying as an expert, the witness' testimony in the form of opinions or inferences may be admitted if it (a) is rationally based on the perception of the witness and (b) will assist in understanding the witness' testimony or in determining a fact in issue.

In a variety of circumstances, New Jersey courts have concluded that an investigating officer's lay opinion may be admissible. *State v. Locurto*, 157 N.J. 463, 471–72, 724 A.2d 234 (1999) (allowing officer to testify that car was speeding); *State v. Haskins*, 131 N.J. 643, 649, 622 A.2d 867 (1993) (permitting officer to testify about measurements made between site of alleged drug transaction and school property); *State v. Johnson*, 120 N.J. 263, 295, 576 A.2d 834 (1990) (allowing officer to testify about footprint because "footprint identification is an area in which lay-opinion testimony is acceptable") . . . *Trentacost v. Brussel*, 164 N.J. Super. 9, 20, 395 A.2d 540 (App. Div. 1978), *aff'd*, 82 N.J. 214, 412 A.2d 436 (1980) (permitting officer to offer opinion on high-crime nature of neighborhood); *State v. Perez*, 150 N.J. Super. 166, 169, 375 A.2d 277 (App. Div.), *certif. denied*, 75 N.J. 542, 384 A.2d 521 (1977) (permitting officer to offer opinion on voice comparison of defendant). . . . This case, however, adds the additional element of hearsay to the testifying officer's opinion . . .

At least one other jurisdiction has expressly concluded that a testifying police officer cannot proffer a lay opinion about the cause of an accident when that opinion is based on hearsay statements from eyewitnesses. *Calhoun v. Chappell*, 117 Ga. App. 865, 162 S.E.2d 300, 301 (Ga. 1968) ("A police officer may not testify on the trial of a tort action resulting from a motor vehicle collision as to the manner in which the collision occurred where his testimony is based merely on statements of what the parties told him, since this is hearsay."). . . . [I]n most jurisdictions, lay opinion testimony that relies on inadmissible hearsay ordinarily is itself inadmissible.

We conclude . . . that a police officer cannot provide an opinion at trial when that opinion is based primarily on the statements of eyewitnesses. Any other conclusion would allow an officer to subvert the prohibition against hearsay and pass along the essence of those hearsay statements to the jury even when the officer is not permitted to testify to the substance of the witness's statements under the hearsay rule. Further, the fact that those statements were the basis for Kelly's lay opinion will not render them admissible because to do so would defeat the purpose of the hearsay rule . . . . A lay witness's opinion cannot rely on the inadequate support of inadmissible hearsay without the benefit of an exception. Consequently, a police officer cannot advance an opinion when it is primarily based on the hearsay statement of an eyewitness . . .

. . . Officer Kelly testified prior to Burnett's and Meyer's testimony, giving the jury an opportunity to hear the substance of their statements from a police officer before hearing their own accounts. A jury may be inclined to accord special respect to such a witness. Deference to a police officer in turn may have enhanced the credibility of the statements of Burnett and Meyer. It is safe to say that Officer Kelly's testimony created improper bolstering . . .

We therefore conclude that admission of the investigating officer's lay opinion based on the witnesses' hearsay statements and his recitation of those statements was error . . .

Reversed and remanded for further proceedings consistent with this opinion.

Will you be able to talk to the officer about the report? Depends on the jurisdiction. If not, you might try to determine some of the customs in your area. For instance, in many places, there is a convention of placing the driver the officer believed to be at fault as Driver #1. Find out if that's true in your area: even if the officer did not actually assign blame, you'll know whom the officer believed to be more responsible, even if only by a hair, and have an idea of what to expect in the officer's deposition.

If the officer made a mistake, such as failing to run a breathalyzer when someone was clearly intoxicated, find out what the department's standard operating procedures are or what the department's general manual has to say. Often these documents are available for public perusal at the municipal or county library.

MEDICAL RECORDS

If you have any type of physical injury in the case, you'll have medical records. These will necessitate a certain level of understanding of medical terminology so that you will know when to take notice of something unusual. There are certain terms and issues to be alert for. First of all, most lawsuits involve **traumatic** injuries: some sort of injury that occurred at a given point in time and caused by a given circumstance, such as a fractured pelvis in a catastrophic vehicular accident. So words indicating **degenerative, chronic,** or **congenital** conditions are probably antithetical to a contention that a particular condition or injury is caused by whatever incident is claimed. The term **"acute,"** on the other hand, indicates something of recent origin (it does not necessarily relate to the degree of the injury, as is often supposed).

The second thing to look for are signs of alcohol or drug use, whether legal or illegal. Because of numerous possible side effects, intended or unintended, expected or unexpected, this area is a potential gold mine or minefield, depending on your point of view. If your client is the sweet little old lady whom you don't want to be mean to, you can just blame those nasty ol' drugs that give those horrible side effects that make it hard for her to judge distances or tell exactly where she is all the time. The accident may still be her fault, but you didn't have to be ugly to her.

The first few times you read medical records will be an ordeal. With practice, it gets easier, and you'll find that you read the same kinds of records depending on the area of practice you're in. If you are in the area of worker's compensation, you tend to read about L-4, L-5, and S-1 back injuries. In this context, L refers to the **lumbar** region, or the lower part of the small of the back. The spine is divided into regions, and in each region, the vertebrae are numbered. In between each vertebra is a disk—roughly the size, shape, and consistency of a hockey puck—with gel inside. If it is punctured, or **herniated,** the "gel" can press on the nerves in the spine and cause pain, numbness, and even paralysis **(radiculopathy)** in the related sections of the body, usually the arms and legs (the **extremities**). The S section is the **coccyx,** or tailbone; it's not C because that letter refers to the **cervical** spine—the neck. That's what you'll read about if you do automobile accidents. The other major section of the spine is the **thoracic,** the ribcage, but it is stabilized well because of the ribs and is rarely the focus of an injury case. When it is, there's probably either something very odd or very serious going on.

In the area of back injury, for instance, you may see reference to *spondylolisthesis,* a forward dislocation of one vertebra over the one beneath it, producing pressure on spinal nerves, and *spondylolysis,* a degeneration of a portion of the vertebrae. The terms are very similar, but the first is consistent with traumatic injury while the second isn't. So you must watch carefully for which term the doctor uses. Whatever report you're reading, look for references to other reports, other doctors, and other testing, and make sure you have gotten all of those records as well. The opposing party or the client may hide a doctor or two, but their colleagues won't.

The term **ETOH** is what you will see on a report, particularly an emergency room report, to indicate that the patient had been using alcohol when brought in. ETOH is short for ethanol, the biochemical component of alcohol that makes it an intoxicant. (Don't ask me why it's not ETHO or some other abbreviation that corresponds to the order of the letters in the word it shortens.) The report also includes a place for the patient to indicate any medications she is taking. Various reference books can tell you about the side effects of any prescription drug, but *The Physician's Desk Reference,* almost universally referred to as the PDR, an annual reference book, is probably the most commonly used. Most drug side effects occur within the first two weeks of first use or dosage adjustment, so there needs to be some close questioning if that is suspected. A lapse in filling a prescription or in taking medications also should be explored if you are dealing with someone who has been taking a particular medication with no apparent problem who is now suspected of having some responsibility due to the medication's side effect—anything that would be unusual that could affect the biochemistry of the drug. You also need to explore what the patient knew about the side effect, if the patient had any similar side effects from the medication, and so on if the patient is your client. If the patient is not your client, include these issues for your attorney to explore.

If you have a claim of a toxic tort, you definitely want to have a medical review of all the records. Other conditions and medications can cause symptoms that mimic toxic torts. I had a case where a woman was obtaining Xanax, an anti-anxiety medication with addictive properties, from several different doctors while claiming working at our client's facility had caused non-A non-B hepatitis. The doctor reviewing her files immediately pinpointed the problem.

"There's nothing wrong with her except that she's a Xanax addict," said the doctor. "That's what's causing all of her liver function studies to come out abnormal."

"Oh," said I. The case was over within 24 hours of that phone call.

And then there's the code word for "faking it." Doctors are not ordinarily going to come out and say that they think the patient is a malingerer or a whiner; instead, the doctor will make a comment about **secondary gains.** This means that the patient has some motivation other than alleviating the problem for seeking medical care. In the absence of a lawsuit, the phrase can refer to people who are seeking attention. In a lawsuit, it can mean trouble for the plaintiff. The appearance of "secondary gains" is definitely something to note and have explained so that the problem can be resolved, whether by early settlement, dropping the client, or some other strategy selected by the plaintiff's attorney; or by deposition, mediation, or lowered offer, for example, by the defendant's attorney.

Once you've gotten all your documents in, remember to update your investigation action plan and investigation summary so you know where to go next. Along with the police reports and medical records, you'll need to figure out what the rest of this stuff means.

Patient:	Stirman, Julie	Physician:	Allen Chu M.D., Ph.D.
Sex:	Female	Test Date:	08/09/01
Age:	43		
Height:	66 inches		
Weight:	178 lbs		**FAXED**
I.D.#:	071458		
PCP:			AUG 1 3 2001
Ref. M.D.	Dr. Michael Graham		

INTERPRETATION:

There is neurophysiologic evidence of cervical radiculopathy at C5/C6 on the right. The denervation changes on C5/C6 myotomes were mild.

Bilateral median neuropathy at the wrist (carpal tunnel syndrome) of moderate severity, right worse than left.

There is no neurophysiologic evidence of C5-T1 cervical radiculopathy on the left. No evidence of ulnar neuropathy/ radial neuropathy/ musculocutaneous neuropathy/ brachial plexopathy on either side.

Thank you for your referral.

Allen Chu M.D., Ph.D.

Motor Nerve Study

Median Nerve

Rec Site: APB	Lat (ms)		Dur (ms)		Amp (mV)		Area (mVms)		Dist (mm)		C.V. (m/s)	
STIM SITE	L	R	L	R	L	R	L	R	L	R	L	R
Wrist	3.6	4.6	4.9	5.5	11.7	11.4	34.0	33.4	65	65		
Elbow	7.7	9.0	5.3	5.5	11.4	11.0	34.5	32.9	220	230	53.9	52.1

(normal value median distal latency < 4.5 ms)

Ulnar Nerve

Rec Site: ADM	Lat (ms)		Dur (ms)		Amp (mV)		Area (mVms)		Dist (mm)		C.V. (m/s)	
STIM SITE	L	R	L	R	L	R	L	R	L	R	L	R
Wrist	2.6	2.3	5.4	5.1	11.5	13.9	36.7	37.9	65	65		
B.Elbow	6.2	5.9	5.9	5.4	10.8	12.8	34.4	37.3	210	220	58.6	61.4
A.Elbow	7.8	7.7	5.9	5.7	10.6	12.4	34.0	37.4	100	100	63.2	57.1

Med/Ul motor Nerve

Rec Site: Lumbri/inter	Lat (ms)		Dur (ms)		Amp (mV)		Area (mVms)		Dist (mm)		C.V. (m/s)	
STIM SITE	L	R	L	R	L	R	L	R	L	R	L	R
M Wrist	3.5	4.3	4.8	5.2	4.8	3.4	14.4	11.0	80	80		
U Wrist	2.8	2.8	3.6	3.6	5.9	6.1	10.2	10.0	80	80		

(Normal values: Med/Uln difference < 0.5 ms)

This EMG report was filed as part of a court record. See if you can interpret the interpretation.

NORTHWEST SPINE CENTER

RECONSTRUCTIVE SPINAL SURGERY & ORTHOPAEDIC SURGERY

J. Michael Graham, M.D., Ph.D.
Diplomate of the American Board of
Orthopaedic Surgery

August 9, 2001

Philip Leggett M.D.
800 Peakwood #6B
Houston, TX 77090

Re: Julie Stirman

Dear Dr. Leggett:

Thank you for referring Julie Stirman for consultation.

As you know, Ms. Stirman is a healthy 43 year old woman with chronic cervical pain. She occasionally has numbness and tingling in both of her hands. Other than these complaints she claims to be in good health. There is no history of recent trauma, although she was injured in a severe motor vehicle accident three years ago. Bowel and bladder function are normal. The past medical history, social history, family history and review of systems were reviewed and are found to be unremarkable and non-contributory.

As you know, it was recently recommended to her by a neurosurgeon in San Antonio that she undergo a multi-level cervical decompression and fusion. She seeks another opinion with regards to this suggestion.

The exam today showed no focal neurological deficits in the upper or lower extremities and all deep tendon reflexes were symmetric and within normal limits.

A recent MRI scan was reviewed. The scan shows a significantly degenerative and herniated disc at C4-C5 with posterior spondylosis. This causes focal spinal stenosis at C4-C5 with flattening of the spinal cord.

My assessment is that she may have a mild cervical radiculopathy and that she has cervical spinal stenosis. I suspect that the cervical operation was recommended in order to decompress the spinal cord and to prevent a spinal cord injury in the event that she has an accident.

However, if she were to have surgery, I would limit it to a one-level anterior cervical discectomy and fusion at C4-C5. I have also recommended EMG testing to confirm the presence of a cervical radiculopathy.

Thanks again for referring Ms. Stirman for consultation.

Best regards,

J. Michael Graham, M.D., Ph.D.
Dictated but not proof read
JMG/as

Another doctor's report, this one sent to the treating physician who referred the patient to an orthopedic surgeon.

Some typical resources used to decipher medical records.

CHAPTER SUMMARY

Obtaining and using documentary evidence, whether traditional hardcopy or newer e-documents, requires the paralegal to understand privilege rules, evidentiary rules, discovery rules, ethical limitations, specialized knowledge of other fields, local custom, and attorney reputation. You may get a privileged document informally through a proper request and release; your attorney may have to get a court order otherwise. Some documents may be available from the government through an FOIA request; however, you must be ready to wait. No matter what kind of document is involved or who it is from, it must be analyzed for more information, summarized for the information it contains, and organized for later retrieval.

FOR FURTHER READING

Stanley Hoppenfeld, *Physical Examination of the Cervical Spine & Extremities* (Pren. Hall 1976). (This text has wonderful pictures and detailed explanations of standard orthopedic examinations.)

Edward A. Tomlinson, *Use of the Freedom of Information Act for Discovery Purposes*, 43 Md. L. Rev. 119 (1984).

CHAPTER REVIEW

KEY TERMS

acute	custodian	Freedom of Information Act (FOIA)
affiant	degenerative	
affidavit	depo (see oral deposition)	herniated
authentication	deponent	judgment non obstante veredicto
business records exception (BRE)	deposition notice	lumbar
chronic	directed verdict	no contact rule
cervical	discovery abuse	oral deposition
coccyx	ETH	prove up
congenital	extremities	radiculopathy

Rambo litigators   sanction   thoracic

reasonable and necessary   secondary gains   traumatic

requests for production   self-authenticate   zealously represent

FILL IN THE BLANKS

1. The person giving a sworn statement, or _____, is called the _____. These statements are often prepared by the paralegal.

2. The most commonly used hearsay exception to introduce documents is the _____ for records maintained in the usual course of business.

3. The magic words that you need to prove up specific expenses related to a cause of action are _____.

4. The person responsible for maintaining records is referred to as the _____.

5. The need to prove that a document or other piece of evidence is what you claim is called _____.

6. When the judge enters a verdict prior to jury deliberation, based on an issue of law, it is a(n) _____. But when the judge changes the jury's verdict after they have deliberated based on an issue of law, it is a(n) _____.

7. The ethical prohibition from talking to a person represented by counsel is called the _____.

8. You have to _____ your evidence, or to put it another way, obtain it in an admissible form.

9. "The backbone's connected to the tailbone" is medically known as the _____.

10. The medical term for something that is protruding into another area where it doesn't belong is _____.

11. The formal mechanism for getting documents from other parties is a(n) _____.

12. A notation of _____ means the doctor believes something other than a medical condition is causing the patient's complaints.

13. A legal right not to disclose certain communications is a(n) _____.

14. The federal version of the acts that require the government to disclose information within its records is the _____.

15. A condition that has been with a person since birth is _____.

16. Certain types of documents _____, which means that you do not have to have any special testimony to have them authenticated.

17. A condition that comes on suddenly is referred to as _____, as opposed to one that has been ongoing for sometime, which is referred to as _____.

18. "The headbone's connected to the neckbone" is medically known as the _____ spine.

19. An injury caused by accident rather than illness is labeled _____.

20. Symptoms from one region that radiate to another, particularly seen in spinal injuries, are referred to as _____.

21. "The ribcage is connected to the lower backbone," is known medically as the _____ spine.

22. A condition that gets worse with age is _____.

WEB WORK

1. Go to the National Association of Investors Corporations Online at http://www.better-investing.org/articles/web/5017 and read the article about how to read an annual report's financial statements. What information would be important to pay attention to if a stockholder was claiming that the board of directors was defrauding the stockholders?

2. Using your favorite search engine, run a search using the terms "tax return" and "hidden assets." What documents would you want to look at based on the articles you find? What sorts of things would you look at in those articles?

3. Using your favorite search engine, find either a copy of or a reference to a handbook for writing police reports. What search terms did you use? If your search was not successful, go to the Web site of a college or university in your state that offers criminal justice or police certification training and visit their library's Web page. Search the library catalog to see if they have a similar manual available. Were you more successful there?

4. Check out the National Highway Traffic Safety Administration's FOIA request list at http://www.nhtsa.dot.gov/nhtsa/whatsup/foia/requests/Index.cfm and see which law firms have made FOIA requests. What do you suppose the requests are for?

5. Go to www.swacha.com, the SouthWestern Automated Clearing House Association's Web site. This organization is an affiliation of banking institutions that provides members with information about the industry. Explore the site—what does it tell you about the requirements for obtaining information about financial accounts? How would a firm benefit from joining this organization? Based on what you learn about this organization, try to locate one in your area. Were you successful?

WORKING THE BRAIN

1. Under what circumstances can you imagine challenging the BRE affidavit?

2. What kinds of cases do you think are most likely to use FOIA requests? Why? Hint: Think about all the various governmental agencies out there. *Caveat:* Some agencies' employees and reports are explicitly excluded from use in court proceedings, such as the Environmental Protection Agency. Check the Code of Federal Regulations for restrictions on the use of reports from any particular agency.

3. In *Taggart v. Super Seer Corp,* the court makes a reference to a benchbook. What do you think that is and why would it have any significance to anything? Is it something you would want to find out about?

4. Each of the cases set forth in the text discussed evidence. What ideas can you get from the evidence discussed, aside from the particular evidence highlighted, about what sort of leads should be followed up on and developed? In other words, what is the scope of the evidence presented in each type of trial? Is there anything you would not have thought of?

5. If your boss were failing to disclose information required under the discovery rules, or needlessly requiring hearings for clearly discoverable material, or otherwise seeming to participate in discovery abuse, how would you handle it?

PUTTING IT TO WORK

1. Think about the Haus side of the *Haus v. Justice* case. What documents would Patty want from Justice or the apartment owners? Prepare the appropriate request for admissions. What would she want from a third party? Prepare the request for deposition by written questions, using any local entity or person that would be appropriate.

2. Review the police report. What would you do to attack the report? Write a memo to the attorney outlining the vulnerabilities of the report.

3. Review the medical report. Summarize the findings in plain English. Make note of any other records you would want to obtain after reading this report, and write a memo to that effect. To whom would you address it? You can send it to the attorney, asking for authority to obtain the records, or you can write a memo to the file (some people address it to themselves) outlining your plan of action and diary the file for two weeks in the future.

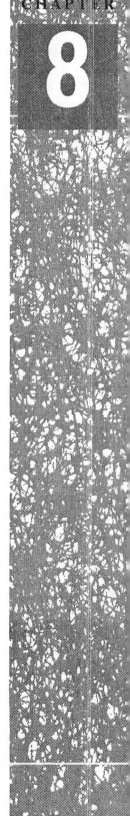

E-DOCUMENTS AND OTHER COMPUTER DISCOVERY ISSUES

> "Computers are like Old Testament gods; lots of rules and no mercy."
>
> *Joseph Campbell*
>
> "The big corporations are suddenly taking notice of the web, and their reactions have been slow. Even the computer industry failed to see the importance of the Internet, but that's not saying much. Let's face it, the computer industry failed to see that the century would end."
>
> *Douglas Adams*
>
> "A computer lets you make more mistakes faster than any invention in human history—with the possible exceptions of handguns and tequila."
>
> *Mitch Ratcliffe*

INTRODUCTION

Electronic documents (e-documents) and the rest of the information stored in a computer is generally treated the same way and with the same evidentiary and ethical issues as ordinary paper documents. However, given the fact that the information is written in code in the bowels of the computer, there are practical considerations that are somewhat different when considering how to frame requests for and find the information. For the information to be usable, it must be transformed into a paper-based document. However, simply clicking on the print icon will not always get you all the information the computer has stored about a document.

Not only should you consider how to get e-documents from opposing parties, you need to have your own clients look into the possibility of damning evidence being within their own computers.

METADATA

The supposedly paperless society we have entered into, while not devoid of paper, certainly does keep an enormous amount of information stored in computers. Businesses and individuals correspond more and more by e-mail and may have documents that have gone back and forth without ever actually being committed to paper. Moreover, and what is very important to the process of litigation, the computer stores **metadata,** that is, information about the information you see—how many drafts, what the prior drafts were, and so forth. It also stores information that you may want to have, although it does not ordinarily access the information in the way you need it.

For instance, a corporation may issue checks electronically and require that each check be assigned a category number. Among the category numbers is one that reflects litigation expenses and settlements. The checking system will also show who requests the checks. Although the corporation has no central way of tracking how many cases it has had regarding a particular product or manager, and it usually does not use the checking system to cross-check these two items, it is theoretically possible that this could be done with the correct programming language.

A hard drive contains deleted items even after they have been deleted, even if you cannot directly access them any longer. Many child pornographers, for example, have thought they dumped all their laptop obscenity, and have been distressed to find that the police were able to retrieve the deleted files from the computer's hard drive.

As a result, you need to be aware of the kinds of information available and the kinds of cases in which you should utilize a data recovery service in order to find out this kind of information in a case. You also need to know the special discovery issues that arise in the context of electronic information, which are neither traditional documents nor tangible physical evidence.

First of all, the courts have recognized that electronic records are more than what they print out, as this case illustrates.

Armstrong v. Executive Office of the President, 1 F.3d 1274 (D.C. Cir. 1993) (per curiam).

This consolidated appeal presents us with important questions of federal agencies' statutory obligations to manage electronic records . . .

In the flagship portion of the appeal, defendants-appellants—the Executive Office of the President ("EOP"), the Office of Administration, the National Security Council ("NSC"), the White House Communications Agency, and Trudy Peterson, Acting Archivist of the United States—challenge the district court's conclusion that EOP and NSC guidelines for managing electronic documents do not comport with Federal Records Act ("FRA" or the "Act") requirements. More specifically, these government agencies and officials contend that, contrary to the court's ruling, they have, in the past, reasonably discharged their FRA obligations by instructing employees to print out a paper version of any electronic communication that falls within the statutory definition of a "record" and by managing the "hard-copy" documents so produced in accordance with the Act. We reject the government's argument on this score. The government's basic position is flawed because the hard-copy print-outs that the agencies preserve may omit fundamental pieces of information which are an integral part of the original electronic records, such as the identity of the sender and/or recipient and the time of receipt . . .

Federal agencies' records creation, management, and disposal duties are set out in a collection of statutes known collectively as the Federal Records Act. See 44 U.S.C. §§ 2101 et seq., 2901 et seq., 3101 et seq., 3301 et seq. The FRA, Congress informs, is intended to assure, among other things, "accurate and complete documentation of the policies and transactions of the Federal Government," "control of the quantity and quality of records produced by the Federal Government," and "judicious preservation and disposal of records." 44 U.S.C. § 2902(1), (2), (5) . . . Moreover, under the Act, agency chiefs must also "establish and maintain an active, continuing program for . . . economical and efficient [records] management," id. § 3102, and "establish safeguards against the removal or loss of records [the agency head] determines to be necessary and required by regulations of the Archivist." Id. § 3105 . . .

Besides assigning specific duties to agency heads, the FRA prescribes the exclusive mechanism for disposal of federal records. See 44 U.S.C. § 3314 (no records may be "alienated or destroyed" except in accordance with the FRA's provisions). For these purposes, "records" are defined as all books, papers, maps, photographs, machine readable [*i.e.*, electronic] materials, or other documentary materials, regardless of physical form or characteristics, made or received by an agency of the United States Government under Federal law or in connection with the transaction of public business and preserved or appropriate for preservation by that agency . . . as evidence of the organization, functions, policies, decisions, procedures, operations, or other activities of the Government or because of the informational value of data in them. Library and museum material made or acquired and preserved solely for reference or exhibition purposes, extra copies of documents preserved only for convenience of reference, and stocks of publications and of processed documents are not included.

. . . Since the mid-1980s, the NSC and the EOP have utilized electronic communications systems to improve their operational efficiency . . . These systems allow employees to create and share electronic appointment calendars as well as to transfer and edit word processing documents, but it is their electronic mail (or "e-mail") capacity that has racked up the most mileage. The 1,300 federal employees with access to the EOP and NSC electronic mail systems can, and apparently do, utilize them to relay lengthy substantive—even classified— "notes" that, in content, are often indistinguishable from letters or memoranda. But, in contrast to its paper cousin, e-mail can be delivered nearly instantaneously at any time of the day or week. And, in contrast to telephone conversations, e-mail automatically creates a complete record of the exact information users send and receive.

Other attributes of the EOP and NSC electronic mail systems are also relevant here. First, these systems give recipients the option of storing notes in their personal electronic "log." After receiving a message, a user may instruct the computer to delete the note; otherwise, it will be stored in her log for later use. Second, both the recipient and the author of a note can print out a "hard copy" of the electronic message containing essentially all the information displayed on the computer screen. That paper rendering will not, however, necessarily include all the information held in the computer memory as part of the electronic document. Directories, distribution lists, acknowledgements of receipts and similar materials do not appear on the computer screen—and thus are not reproduced when users print out the information that appears on the screen. Without this "non-screen" information, a later reader may not be able to glean from the hard copy such basic facts as who sent or received a particular message or when it was received. For example, if a note is sent to individuals on a distribution list already in the computer, the hard copy may well include only a generic reference to the distribution list (*e.g.*, "List A"), not the names of the individuals on the list who received the document. Consequently, if only the hard copy is preserved in such situations, essential transmittal information relevant to a fuller understanding of the context and import of an electronic communication will simply vanish. A final relevant fact here is that the individual note logs are not the only electronic repositories for information on the e-mail system. The defendant agencies periodically create backup tapes—snapshots of all the material stored on these electronic communications systems at a given time—that can be used later for retrieval purposes.

. . . [T]he district court first addressed whether the communications stored in these electronic communications systems constituted federal records. Because the FRA's definition of "records" includes material "regardless of physical form or characteristics," the court concluded that substantive communications otherwise meeting the definition of federal "records" that had been saved on the electronic mail came within the FRA's purview. *See id.* at 340–41.

The court then found that the defendants' current practices for electronic records management were deficient in two key respects. First, assuming *arguendo* that the defendant agencies unequivocally informed their staffs to print out all on-screen information of any electronic note that qualified as a federal record (an assumption that the plaintiffs have vigorously contested throughout this litigation), that instruction was not adequate to meet the FRA's requirements because the "electronic material . . . [is] qualitatively different than a copy printed out in paper form." . . . The district court emphasized that unless employees also printed out the transmittal information stored in the computer but not appearing on screen, the hard copies preserved in the paper files would not necessarily contain all the important items retained in the electronic system . . . Specifically, data "regarding who has received the information and when the information was received" might well be omitted from the paper versions . . .

The court found a second flaw in the agencies' records management practices: they failed to provide for any supervision of agency employees' electronic recordkeeping practices. Noting that (1) the National Archives Records Management Handbook provided that only "records officers" should determine the status of FRA records and (2) the defendant agencies supervise staffers' management of paper, but *not* electronic, records, the court concluded that the defendants' failure to supervise employees' electronic recordkeeping was arbitrary and capricious . . .

[The district court] enjoined all the defendants "from removing, deleting, or altering information on their electronic communications systems until such time as the Archivist takes action . . . to prevent the destruction of federal records, including those records saved on backup tapes." *Id.* In response to an emergency motion by the defendants, this court stayed this last requirement to the extent of allowing the agencies to "remove, delete, or alter" information so long as it was preserved elsewhere in *identical* form . . .

Our analysis is a straightforward one. We begin with the apparently undisputed proposition that the EOP and NSC electronic communications systems can create, and have created, documents that constitute federal records under the FRA. The FRA contemplates that documents qualifying as records may be stripped of that status only if they are "extra copies of documents preserved only for convenience of reference." 44 U.S.C. § 3301. Applied to this case, that means that the mere existence of the paper print-outs does not affect the record status of the electronic materials unless the paper versions include all significant material contained in the electronic records. Otherwise, the two documents cannot accurately be termed "copies"—identical twins—but are, at most, "kissing cousins." Since the record shows that the two versions of the documents may frequently be only cousins—perhaps distant ones at that—the electronic documents retain their status as federal records after the creation of the paper print-outs, and all of the FRA obligations concerning the management and preservation of records still apply. *See, e.g., id.* § 3105 (requiring agency heads to "establish safeguards against the removal or loss" of "records"); *id.* § 3314 (stating that "records" may only be "alienated or destroyed" in accordance with FRA provisions, *i.e.*, with the approval of the Archivist).

To qualify as a record under the FRA, a document must satisfy a two-pronged test. It must be (1) "made or received by an agency of the United States Government under Federal law or in connection with the transaction of public business" and (2) "preserved or appropriate for preservation by that agency . . . as evidence of the organization, functions, policies, decisions, procedures, operations, or other activities of the Government or because of the informational value of data in [it]." *Id.* § 3301. The appellants do not contest the fact that many, if not all, of the communications relayed over the electronic system satisfy the "public transaction" element of this test. At oral argument, the government appeared to acknowledge that the "preserved or appropriate for preservation" criterion was satisfied as well for some documents on the system . . .

Our refusal to agree with the government that electronic records are merely "extra copies" of the paper versions amounts to far more than judicial nitpicking. Without the missing information, the paper print-outs—akin to traditional memoranda with the "to" and "from" cut off and even the "received" stamp pruned away—are dismembered documents indeed. Texts alone may be of quite limited utility to researchers and investigators studying the formulation and dissemination of significant policy initiatives at the highest reaches of our government . . . In our view, as well as the district judge's, the practice of retaining only the amputated paper print-outs is flatly inconsistent with Congress' evident concern with preserving a *complete* record of government activity for historical and other uses . . . Perhaps that is why, in this court, the appellants seem to have abandoned their former heavy reliance on this theory.

To recap: We affirm the district court's decision that the EOP and NSC electronic records management guidelines violate the FRA . . .

So ordered.

When talking to your clients, ask about the metadata their computers have (if they know). With corporate clients, talk to the folks in their IT (Information Technology) section or their vendors. The software programmers should know what metadata is available. Ask clients about drafts of important documents—and whether any other relevant documents have been deleted. Make sure you make them aware that they should not delete any electronically created information in their possession as of the date the litigation began so that they do not expose themselves to discovery sanctions.

E-MAIL

As you might imagine, e-mail is something you should request in discovery to look for a "smoking gun." People often take correspondence by e-mail lightly, forgetting that it might some day be read to a jury, and they say some things that sound very bad when read aloud in a courtroom. And, as the *Armstrong* case indicates, the metadata can tell you more than just what the sender said. It can tell you when the correspondence was composed, when it was sent, how many drafts were made, who received it, and, if you have the electronic file, whether a hard drive or tape, you can find any discarded messages in the same thread. The reason is that the delete command simply tells the computer that the space taken up by the e-mail may be written over when needed. If there is a large amount of space on the system, or if new information comes in slowly, it may be a long while before the e-mail actually disappears. Even if the e-mail is overwritten, "ghost" data often can be retrieved with the proper expertise and software.

Instruct your clients not to delete e-mails received prior to the date litigation began. Have any backed-up data files set aside rather than written over. Check them out yourself for any "smoking guns"—it's better that you find them than the opposing party. If you find one that is going to hurt your client, bring it to the attention of your attorney immediately so that a damage control plan can be put into action. Either they can choose to settle before producing the document or try to figure out a **colorable** legal protection for it.

COST ISSUES

Oddly enough, a corporation will take exception to your asking to start rummaging through its employee's personal computer's hard drive. And they won't be excited about spending the money to write a subroutine just to give you ammunition for your case. So what are the guidelines? It depends on the court. Some courts will look at e-mail pursuit as just another expense of doing business and won't bat an eye at making a defendant spend $50,000 to $70,000 to produce relevant e-mails, as occurred in *In re Brand Name Prescription Drugs Antitrust Litigation*, C.A. No. 94C897, MDL No. 997, 1995 WL 360526 (N.D. Ill. June 15, 1995). Others will find it overly burdensome and will require the requesting party to pay the potential costs. Still others will follow the newer trend illustrated by the balancing test set down in the following case.

Rowe Entertainment, Inc. v. William Morris Agency, Inc.,
205 F.R.D. 421 (S.D.N.Y. 2002).

Too often, discovery is not just about uncovering the truth, but also about how much of the truth the parties can afford to disinter. As this case illustrates, discovery expenses frequently escalate when information is stored in electronic form.

The plaintiffs are black concert promoters who contend that they have been frozen out of the market for promoting events with white bands by the discriminatory and anti-competitive practices of the defendants. The defendants fall into two categories: some are booking agencies that represent white artists and allegedly steer their clients away from the plaintiffs; others are promoters like the plaintiffs, but they purportedly collude with the booking agency defendants to monopolize the concert industry.

During discovery in this action, each defendant has responded to the plaintiffs' requests by permitting inspection of its concert files, which contain documents relating to the promotion of concerts. Four sets of defendants, however, have now moved . . . for a protective order relieving them of the obligation of producing electronic mail, commonly known as e-mail, that may be responsive to the plaintiffs' discovery requests.

Background

A. The Discovery Demands

The plaintiffs' document demands are sweeping. For example, they demand production of all documents concerning any communication between any defendants relating to the selection of concert promoters and bids to promote concerts . . . Similarly, the plaintiffs have requested "all documents concerning the selection of concert promoters, and the solicitation, and bidding processes relating to concert promotions." . . . They have also demanded "all documents concerning market shares, market share values, market conditions, or geographic boundaries in which any . . . concert promoter operates." . . . These are but three examples of the 35 requests made in the plaintiffs' first document demand.

B. The Defendants' Motions

Each of the moving defendants contends that it should be relieved of the obligation of producing e-mail responsive to the plaintiffs' requests because the burden and expense involved would far outweigh any possible benefit in terms of discovery of additional information. If production is nevertheless required, the defendants ask that the plaintiffs bear the cost. Because the burden to each defendant depends upon the specific structure of its e-mail retention and on the related means for retrieving and producing responsive e-mails, each defendant's position will be outlined separately.

1. William Morris Agency

The William Morris Agency, Inc. ("WMA"), one of the booking agency defendants, argues that the chances are small that a search of its e-mails would turn up responsive documents. According to its Senior Vice President, WMA's music agents have historically conducted business by telephone and fax and have been slow to utilize e-mail . . . Moreover, to the extent an e-mail was deemed important, it would likely have been printed and saved in the appropriate concert file—files that have been produced for inspection by the plaintiffs . . .

WMA further contends that the production of its e-mails would be exorbitantly expensive and, to some extent, a technical impossibility. Prior to May 1998, WMA's Music Division had utilized Quickmail for Macintosh for its e-mail communications . . . The e-mail files were backed up using a software program called Retrospect that is no longer commercially available . . . Consequently, WMA has neither the computer hardware nor the software to read these tapes . . . And, although WMA has given them to an outside vendor for examination, that vendor has thus far been unable to recover enough data to determine what is stored on the tapes . . .

In May 1998, WMA's Music Department converted to Lotus Notes for e-mail communications . . . It backs up its e-mail files along with other electronic files such as word processing and spreadsheet documents five times each week, using a software program called Arcserve . . .

The plaintiffs agreed, at least as a first cut, to limit their discovery demands to e-mail generated or received by 56 WMA employees located in the defendant's New York and Beverly Hills offices . . . Likewise, they proposed an initial search limited to a sample of one back-up session for each quarter of 1998 and 1999, for a total of eight sessions . . . According to WMA, in order to comply with this request, it must engage in a three-step process: cataloguing, restoring, and processing . . . Cataloguing involves identifying the tapes that contain the mailbox files of the designated employees and marking them for restoration . . . Restoration consists of saving all e-mails from the identified files to a master database and then removing all duplicates . . . Finally, each file must be processed so that it is not only readable on a computer screen, but also may be printed and Bates-stamped . . . Where an e-mail contains an attached file such as a word processing document, WMA proposes converting the attachment into a Tagged Image File Format or "TIFF" file . . . According to WMA, this would be necessary in order to make any redactions . . .

WMA obtained an estimate from Fios, Inc., a computer consultant, of the cost of such an undertaking . . . Fios projects that the cost for eight selected back up sessions would include $7,864 for cataloguing, $8,960 for restoration, and $379,120 for processing, for a total of $395,944 . . . If the e-mails on all of the back-up tapes were produced instead of a sample of eight sessions, the total cost would mushroom to almost $9,750,000 . . .

2. Monterey Peninsula Artists

Like WMA, Monterey Peninsula Artists, Inc. ("Monterey") is a booking agency. It currently employs nine agents, each of whom is supplied with a personal Macintosh computer . . . The agents' personal computers use a variety of different e-mail programs, so that all files cannot be reviewed by a single search program . . . In total, there are almost 200,000 e-mails stored on the hard drives of these computers . . .

According to the President of Monterey, the company still does ninety percent of its business by means other than e-mail, including telephone and fax . . . It is estimated that fifty to seventy percent of the use of e-mail consists of alerting agents about telephone calls received by a receptionist . . . In addition, some portion of the e-mail relates to advice of counsel . . . Significant e-mails may be printed as hard copy and placed in the relevant files . . .

Monterey Computer Corporation ("MCC") has provided three alternative cost estimates for producing the e-mail of Monterey's agents. First, a computer operator could be employed to retrieve and print all e-mails from each personal computer . . . This is a labor-intensive option estimated to cost $84,060 . . . Alternatively, a programer could archive all e-mails on the computer in which they are located and then print them more efficiently in "batch" mode . . . MCC projects that this option would entail approximately $57,860 in costs . . . Finally, an information systems analyst could import all of the agents' e-mail into a single common format, creating a single database. The entire database could then be reviewed using one search engine . . . Assuming that all of the e-mails would nevertheless be printed, MCC estimates the cost of this third option to be $43,110 . . . None of the alternatives proposed by MCC require the creation of TIFF files . . .

Monterey has also proffered an estimate of the cost involved in reviewing the e-mails for privilege. By using paralegals to review the production at the rate of two e-mails per minute at fees of $150 per hour, it is estimated that the privilege analysis would cost approximately $247,000 . . .

3. Creative Artist Agency

The third moving defendant, Creative Artist Agency, LLC ("CAA"), is also a booking agency. It currently employs approximately 50 music agents and assistants . . . These personnel use Microsoft Exchange software for e-mail . . . Since January 1999, CAA has backed up its corporate electronic data including e-mails on a daily basis, using either Backup Exec or Omniback II software . . . It has accumulated a total of 523 back-up tapes for this period, of which 261 have been catalogued and contain e-mails. The remaining 262, ten of which may predate 1999, have not been catalogued and may or may not include e-mails . . .

Prior to 1999, CAA's computer system went through a series of transformations. From 1993 through March 1996, CAA used a Mac OS-based system . . . From March 1996 through August 1997, the company converted to a Windows NT 4.0 system . . . CAA first acquired access to the Internet and external e-mail capacity in February 1996 . . . Until January 1999, CAA backed up its corporate data on a daily basis but only saved the last week of each month for archival purposes . . . CAA has located 376 back-up tapes from its Mac system and 64 digital audio tapes ("DAT's") with pre-1999 back up data, of which 18 contain e-mails . . . The remaining 46 DAT's and the other back-up tapes have not been catalogued and may or may not contain e-mail data . . .

As with WMA, production of the e-mail would require cataloguing the tapes for which this has not been done, then restoring and retrieving the e-mails . . . CAA's Director of Information Technology estimates for the period from 1999 on, this process would cost $187,500 to $237,500 for labor and $48,000 for necessary hardware and software and would take two and one-half years to complete . . .

With respect to the pre-1999 period, it would cost $25,000–$31,000 to retrieve the e-mails from the DAT's and $78,500 to restore them from the Mac back-up tapes . . . CAA thus estimates that its total cost would be a minimum of $395,000 . . .

In addition, like Monterey, CAA has calculated the cost of conducting a privilege review. It estimates that one employee earning $60,000 per year would take two years to complete the task, for a total cost of $120,000 . . .

4. SFX and QBQ

The last group of moving defendants consists of QBQ Entertainment, a booking agency, along with twenty-two concert promoters, collectively referred to as "SFX." . . . The e-mails for this group are contained in SFX's exchange server, 23 back-up tapes for SFX's exchange server, 24 back-up tapes for the exchange server of Contemporary Productions, Inc., and the personal computers of 126 e-mail users . . .

Ontrack Data International, Inc. ("Ontrack") provided an estimate of the cost of retrieving the e-mail from these sources. The total estimate, including printing costs, management fees, and travel expenses, comes to over $403,000 . . . Of this, approximately $126,000 is attributable to the cost of creating TIFF files, based on the assumption that 10,000 pages would be retrieved for each of the 126 e-mail users . . .

C. The Plaintiffs' Response

The plaintiffs argue first that the discovery of e-mail is critical to their case. They dispute the assumptions that little business is conducted by the defendants through e-mail and that important e-mails would have been reduced to hard copy in any event . . . Furthermore, the plaintiffs maintain that the paper discovery taken to date supports their claims that the defendants have engaged in discriminatory and anti-competitive practices. For example a CAA memorandum refers to how the head of its music department kept the "black promoter issue" "under control" in connection with a tour by Janet Jackson in 1998 . . . The plaintiffs interpret this to mean that CAA deterred black promoters from participating in the tour by imposing on them more onerous financial terms than were offered to white promoters . . . Similarly, the plaintiffs argue that a letter by Beaver Productions, a white-owned promotion company, advocating that the City of Memphis should not enter into an exclusive contract with a black promoter, illustrates the collusive relationship between white promoters and white booking agencies . . .

The plaintiffs also contend that the defendants' cost estimates are wildly inflated. In general terms, the plaintiffs propose to reduce the expense of e-mail production by: (1) identifying key personnel rather than retrieving the e-mail of all employees; (2) restoring only a portion of the archival tapes, based on date restrictions and sampling; (3) producing e-mail in electronic rather than paper form; and (4) conducting automated searches for privilege and responsiveness . . . The plaintiffs would also forego the use of TIFF files, which they argue is unnecessary and unduly expensive . . . According to one of the plaintiffs' consultants . . . TIFF files are not themselves searchable, since they are merely graphic depictions of electronic text . . . Because they are not searchable, they do not facilitate the removal of duplicate documents from a file . . . And, as an image of an electronic document, the TIFF version contains less information than the original document . . . These principles underlie the plaintiffs' cost estimates with respect to production by each of the moving defendants.

1. WMA

The plaintiffs agree to limit production of WMA's e-mails to a sample of eight sessions of the archive tapes for 30 e-mail accounts . . . By also eliminating conversion to TIFF files, they estimate that WMA could provide responsive e-mails at a cost ranging from $24,000 to $87,000 depending upon assumptions about the volume of e-mail and the amount of duplication . . .

2. Monterey

The plaintiffs' second expert . . . proposes to create a "mirror image" of the hard drive of each personal computer at Monterey . . . The plaintiffs would then identify potentially responsive directories and files, convert them to a common format, and create a single database that could be searched for privilege and responsiveness . . . [The plaintiffs' expert] estimates the cost for this project to be $10,000–$15,000 . . .

3. CAA

By engaging again in a sampling process, the plaintiffs estimate that they could reduce the cost of production of CAA's pre-1999 e-mail to $20,000 . . . Likewise, by limiting production for 1999 to quarterly samples for 30 e-mail accounts, they project costs of $40,000–$50,000 . . . Thus, the plaintiffs' total cost estimate for production by CAA is $60,000–$70,000 . . .

4. SFX and QBQ

Apparently, the plaintiffs are willing to forego any review of the back-up tapes of SFX and QBQ. Instead, they propose to work from the hard drives of approximately 60 users who store e-mail on their individual computers . . . As with Monterey, the plaintiffs would take an image of the hard drive and create a database of potentially responsive files. They estimate that this would cost $64,000 . . .

Discussion

A. Discoverability and Relevance

The plaintiffs have successfully demonstrated that the discovery they seek is generally relevant. Although the defendants vigorously contest the plaintiffs' interpretation of the documents that have already been produced . . .

those documents are plainly pertinent to the plaintiffs' claims. To the extent that the defendants' e-mails contain similar information, they are equally discoverable. Electronic documents are no less subject to disclosure than paper records . . .

Nor are the defendants' claims that the e-mail is unlikely to yield relevant information persuasive. General representations by WMA and Monterey that their employees do little business by e-mail are undocumented and are contradicted by data proffered by these same defendants. Monterey, for example, estimates that its eight computers contain 198,000 e-mail messages . . . while WMA's figures lead to the conclusion that each of its agents sent or received about 43 e-mails per day . . . It is probable that some significant portion of this traffic related to the conduct of business.

Furthermore, the supposition that important e-mails have been printed in hard copy form is likewise unsupported. In general, nearly one-third of all electronically stored data is never printed out . . . Here, the defendants have not alleged that they had any corporate policy defining which e-mail messages should be reduced to hard copy because they are "important." Finally, to the extent that any employee of the defendants was engaged in discriminatory or anti-competitive practices, it is less likely that communications about such activities would be memorialized in an easily accessible form such as a filed paper document.

The defendants' concern about privacy is also unavailing. To the extent that the corporate defendants' own privacy interests are at issue, the[y] are adequately protected by the confidentiality order in this case. To the degree the defendants seek to assert the privacy concerns of their employees, those interests are severely limited. Although personal communications of employees may be appear in hard copy as well as in electronic documents . . . the defendants made no effort to exclude personal messages from the search of paper records conducted by plaintiffs' counsel. Moreover, an employee who uses his or her employer's computer for personal communications assumes some risk that they will be accessed by the employer or by others . . .

Thus, there is no justification for a blanket order precluding discovery of the defendants' e-mails on the ground that such discovery is unlikely to provide relevant information or will invade the privacy of non-parties.

B. Cost-Shifting

The more difficult issue is the extent to which each party should pay the costs of production. "Under [the discovery] rules, the presumption is that the responding party must bear the expense of complying with discovery requests" . . . Nevertheless, a court may protect the responding party from "undue burden or expense" by shifting some or all of the costs of production to the requesting party . . . Here, the expense of locating and extracting responsive e-mails is substantial, even if the more modest estimates of the plaintiffs are credited. Therefore, it is appropriate to determine which, if any, of these costs, are "undue," thus justifying allocation of those expenses to the plaintiffs.

1. Production

One line of argument, adopted by the plaintiffs, holds that the responding party should bear the costs of producing electronic data since "if a party chooses an electronic storage method, the necessity for a retrieval program or method is an ordinary and foreseeable risk." . . . But even if this principle is unassailable in the context of paper records, it does not translate well into the realm of electronic data. The underlying assumption is that the party retaining information does so because that information is useful to it, as demonstrated by the fact that it is willing to bear the costs of retention. That party may therefore be expected to locate specific data, whether for its own needs or in response to a discovery request. With electronic media, however, the syllogism breaks down because the costs of storage are virtually nil. Information is retained not because it is expected to be used, but because there is no compelling reason to discard it. And, even if data is retained for limited purposes, it is not necessarily amenable to discovery . . .

Because of the shortcomings of [a] bright-line rule, courts have adopted a balancing approach taking into consideration such factors as: (1) the specificity of the discovery requests; (2) the likelihood of discovering critical information; (3) the availability of such information from other sources; (4) the purposes for which the responding party maintains the requested data (5) the relative benefit to the parties of obtaining the information; (6) the total cost associated with production; (7) the relative ability of each party to control costs and its incentive to do so; and (8) the resources available to each party. Each of these factors is relevant in determining whether discovery costs should be shifted in this case.

a. Specificity of Requests

The less specific the requesting party's discovery demands, the more appropriate it is to shift the costs of production to that party . . . Where a party multiplies litigation costs by seeking expansive rather than targeted discovery, that party should bear the expense . . .

b. Likelihood of a Successful Search

. . . Here, there is a high enough probability that a broad search of the defendants' e-mails will elicit some relevant information that the search should not be precluded altogether. However, there has certainly been no showing that the e-mails are likely to be a gold mine. No witness has testified, for example, about any e-mail communications that allegedly reflect discriminatory or anti-competitive practices. Thus, the marginal value of searching the e-mails is modest at best, and this factor, too, militates in favor of imposing the costs of discovery on the plaintiffs.

c. Availability from Other Sources

Some cases that have denied discovery of electronic evidence or have shifted costs to the requesting party have done so because equivalent information either has already been made available or is accessible in a different format at less expense . . .

In the instant case there has been no showing that the defendants' e-mails are generally available other than by a search of the defendants' hard drives or back-up tapes. The representations that "important" e-mails were probably printed out are entirely speculative. Accordingly, this consideration favors requiring the defendants to produce the e-mails at their own expense.

d. Purposes of Retention

If a party maintains electronic data for the purpose of utilizing it in connection with current activities, it may be expected to respond to discovery requests at its own expense . . .

Conversely, however, a party that happens to retain vestigial data for no current business purposes, but only in case of an emergency or simply because it has neglected to discard it, should not be put to the expense of producing it. In this case, the back-up tapes clearly fall into this category. There is no evidence that the defendants themselves ever search these tapes for information or even have a means for doing so. Cost-shifting is therefore warranted with respect to the back-up tapes . . .

The same is true of e-mails which, although deleted from the user's active files, remain on the hard drive . . . Just as a party would not be required to sort through its trash to resurrect discarded paper documents, so it should not be obligated to pay the cost of retrieving deleted e-mails . . . Thus, since there has been no showing that the defendants access either their back-up tapes or their deleted e-mails in the normal course of business, this factors tips in favor of shifting the costs of discovery to the plaintiffs.

e. Benefit to the Parties

Where the responding party itself benefits from the production, there is less rationale for shifting costs to the requesting party . . . Such a benefit could come in one of two forms. First, the process of production could have collateral benefits for the responding party's business. For example, a computer program created to conduct a search for purposes of discovery could also be useful in the regular activities of the business. Second, the responding party may benefit in litigation from the review of its own records.

Neither circumstance is present here. Since the computer data at issue is not regularly used by the defendants, cataloguing or searching it would have little business value to them. Similarly, recovery of e-mail will not benefit the defendants in this litigation since the e-mails are not relevant to any issue on which the defendants bear the burden of proof . . . the absence of any benefit to the defendants makes cost-shifting more appropriate.

f. Total Costs

If the total cost of the requested discovery is not substantial, then there is no cause to deviate from the presumption that the responding party will bear the expense . . . Here, the costs of the proposed discovery would be substantial by any definition. Even the plaintiffs project that the costs for WMA would be between $24,000 and $87,000, for Monterey between $10,000 and $15,000, for CAA between $60,000 and $70,000, and for SFX and QBQ approximately $64,000. The magnitude of these expenses favors cost-shifting.

g. Ability to Control Costs

The plaintiffs have professed an ability to limit the costs of discovery of e-mails to a much greater extent than defendants. Of course, this factor alone does not dictate cost-shifting; the defendants could be required to pay the bill for the less expensive methodologies proposed by the plaintiffs. However, where the discovery process is going to be incremental, it is more efficient to place the burden on the party that will decide how expansive the discovery will be . . . The plaintiffs here will be able to calibrate their discovery based on the information obtained from initial sampling. They are in the best position to decide whether further searches would be justified . . . This consideration, then, also militates in favor of cost-shifting.

h. The Parties' Resources

Finally, the ability of each party to bear the costs of discovery may be an appropriate consideration . . . In some cases, the cost, even if modest in absolute terms, might outstrip the resources of one of the parties, justifying an allocation of those expenses to the other. But in this case, all parties have sufficient resources to conduct this litigation. Although the plaintiffs argue that the defendants are some of the most powerful players in the concert promotion business, the plaintiffs purport to be able to compete with them in the marketplace. The relative financial strength of the parties, then, is at most a neutral factor.

The relevant factors thus tip heavily in favor of shifting to the plaintiffs the costs of obtaining discovery of e-mails in this case . . . The protocol to be followed will be addressed below.

2. Privileged and Confidential Documents

Beyond the cost of isolating and producing the requested e-mails, the defendants argue that the expense of reviewing these documents for privilege and confidentiality would be enormous . . . However, the sanctity of the defendants' documents can be adequately preserved at little cost by enforcement of the confidentiality order and by the additional elements of the protocol described below, including requirements that the e-mails be reviewed on an attorneys'-eyes-only basis and that review of attorney-client documents shall not be deemed a waiver of the privilege . . .

Even with such protections, however, the disclosure of privileged documents cannot be compelled . . . Apparently, the defendants retained privileged or confidential documents in electronic form but failed to designate them to specific files. This situation is analogous to one in which a company fails to shred its confidential paper documents and instead leaves them intermingled with non-confidential, discoverable papers. The expense of sorting such documents is properly borne by the responding party, and the same principle applies to electronic data. Accordingly, if any defendant elects to conduct a full privilege review of its e-mails prior to production, it shall do so at its own expense.

C. Protocol

The protocol set forth here for the defendants' production of e-mails is necessarily only a set of guidelines, and the parties are free to add detail and otherwise modify the protocol by agreement.

Initially, the plaintiffs shall designate one or more experts who shall be responsible for isolating each defendant's e-mails and preparing them for review. The defendants shall have the opportunity to object to any expert so designated. The expert shall be bound by the terms of this order as well as any confidentiality order entered in the case.

With the assistance and cooperation of the defendants' technical personnel, the plaintiffs' expert shall then obtain a mirror image of any hard drive containing e-mails as well as a copy of any back-up tape. The plaintiffs may choose to review a sample of hard drives and tapes in lieu of all such devices.

Plaintiffs' counsel shall formulate a search procedure for identifying responsive e-mails and shall notify each defendant's counsel of the procedure chosen, including any specific word searches. Defendants' counsel may object to any search proposed by the plaintiffs.

Once an appropriate search method has been established, it shall be implemented by the plaintiffs' expert. Plaintiffs' counsel may then review the documents elicited by the search on an attorneys'-eyes-only basis. The plaintiffs may choose the format for this review; they may, for example, view the documents on a computer screen or print out hard copy. Once plaintiffs' counsel have identified those e-mails they consider material to this litigation, however, they shall provide those documents to defendants' counsel in hard copy form with Bates stamps. The plaintiffs shall bear all costs associated with the production described thus far.

However, the defendants shall pay for any procedures beyond those adopted by the plaintiffs, such as the creation of TIFF files.

Defendants' counsel shall then have the opportunity to review the documents produced in order to designate those that are confidential and assert any privilege. Any purportedly confidential or privileged document shall be retained on an attorneys'-eyes-only basis until any dispute about the designation is resolved. The fact that such a document has been reviewed by counsel or by the expert shall not constitute a waiver of any claim of privilege or confidentiality.

Should any defendant elect to review its database prior to production, it shall do so at its own expense. In that event, the defendant shall review those hard drives and back-up tapes selected by the plaintiffs and shall create copies from which privileged or confidential and unresponsive material has been deleted. The defendant shall then provide plaintiffs' counsel with each "redacted" hard drive or tape, together with a privilege log identifying the documents removed. The process would then continue as described . . .

Conclusion

For the reasons discussed here, the defendants' motion for a protective order is denied insofar as it sought to preclude altogether the discovery of e-mail. It is granted to the extent that the plaintiffs shall bear the costs of production, though the defendants shall continue to be responsible for the expense of any review for privileged or confidential material . . .

SO ORDERED.
JAMES C. FRANCIS IV
UNITED STATES MAGISTRATE JUDGE

Dated: New York, New York
January 15, 2002

This case gives a detailed example of how to analyze the issues and how to go about the process of disclosing the data. You may want to use it to model any motions on as well as citing it as persuasive precedent. Shepardize it as well; as of this writing, *Rowe* has already garnered citations in several jurisdictions, so it may have **progeny** in yours.[1]

Interestingly, though, *Rowe* is no longer the law in its own jurisdiction. It was modified in the following case.

Zubulake v. UBS Warburg LLC, 217 F.R.D. 309 (S.D.N.Y. 2003).

The world was a far different place in 1849, when Henry David Thoreau opined (in an admittedly broader context) that "the process of discovery is very simple." . . . That hopeful maxim has given way to rapid technological advances, requiring new solutions to old problems. The issue presented here is one such problem, recast in light of current technology: To what extent is inaccessible electronic data discoverable, and who should pay for its production?

I. INTRODUCTION

[I]t is now beyond dispute that "broad discovery is a cornerstone of the litigation process contemplated by the Federal Rules of Civil Procedure." . . . The Rules contemplate a minimal burden to bringing a claim; that claim is then fleshed out through vigorous and expansive discovery . . .

---

[1] By the way, the *Rowe* case is still, as of this writing, fighting discovery battles, with an opinion spawned on September 23, 2003, with a witness claiming that attorneys and paralegals were also in on the discriminatory practices.

In one context, however, the reliance on broad discovery has hit a roadblock. As individuals and corporations increasingly do business electronically[5]—using computers to create and store documents, make deals, and exchange e-mails—the universe of discoverable material has expanded exponentially . . . The more information there is to discover, the more expensive it is to discover all the relevant information until, in the end, "discovery is not just about uncovering the truth, but also about how much of the truth the parties can afford to disinter." . . .

This case provides a textbook example of the difficulty of balancing the competing needs of broad discovery and manageable costs. Laura Zubulake is suing UBS Warburg LLC, UBS Warburg, and UBS AG (collectively, "UBS" or the "Firm") under Federal, State and City law for gender discrimination and illegal retaliation. Zubulake's case is certainly not frivolous[8] and if she prevails, her damages may be substantial.[9] She contends that key evidence is located in various e-mails exchanged among UBS employees that now exist only on backup tapes and perhaps other archived media. According to UBS, restoring those e-mails would cost approximately $175,000.00, exclusive of attorney time in reviewing the e-mails . . . Zubulake now moves for an order compelling UBS to produce those e-mails at its expense . . .

II. BACKGROUND

A. Zubulake's Lawsuit

UBS hired Zubulake on August 23, 1999, as a director and senior salesperson on its U.S. Asian Equities Sales Desk (the "Desk"), where she reported to Dominic Vail, the Desk's manager. At the time she was hired, Zubulake was told that she would be considered for Vail's position if and when it became vacant.

In December 2000, Vail indeed left his position to move to the Firm's London office. But Zubulake was not considered for his position, and the Firm instead hired Matthew Chapin as director of the Desk. Zubulake alleges that from the outset Chapin treated her differently than the other members of the Desk, all of whom were male. In particular, Chapin "undermined Ms. Zubulake's ability to perform her job by, inter alia: (a) ridiculing and belittling her in front of co-workers; (b) excluding her from work-related outings with male co-workers and clients; (c) making sexist remarks in her presence; and (d) isolating her from the other senior salespersons on the Desk by seating her apart from them." . . . No such actions were taken against any of Zubulake's male co-workers.

Zubulake ultimately responded by filing a Charge of (gender) Discrimination with the EEOC on August 16, 2001. On October 9, 2001, Zubulake was fired with two weeks' notice. On February 15, 2002, Zubulake filed the instant action, suing for sex discrimination and retaliation under Title VII, the New York State Human Rights Law, and the Administrative Code of the City of New York. UBS timely answered on March 12, 2002, denying the allegations. UBS's argument is, in essence, that Chapin's conduct was not unlawfully discriminatory because he treated everyone equally badly. On the one hand, UBS points to evidence that Chapin's anti-social behavior was not limited to women: a former employee made allegations of national origin discrimination against Chapin, and a number of male employees on the Desk also complained about him. On the other hand, Chapin was responsible for hiring three new females employees to the Desk.

B. The Discovery Dispute

Discovery in this action commenced on or about June 3, 2002, when Zubulake served UBS with her first document request. At issue here is request number twenty-eight, for "all documents concerning any communication

---

[5] See Wendy R. Liebowitz, Digital Discovery Starts to Work, Nat'l L.J., Nov. 4, 2002, at 4 (reporting that in 1999, ninety-three percent of all information generated was in digital form).

[8] Indeed, Zubulake has already produced a sort of "smoking gun": an e-mail suggesting that she be fired "ASAP" after her EEOC charge was filed, in part so that she would not be eligible for year-end bonuses. See 8/21/01 e-mail from Mike Davies to Rose Tong ("8/21/01 e-Mail") . . .

[9] At the time she was terminated, Zubulake's annual salary was approximately $500,000. Were she to receive full back pay and front pay, Zubulake estimates that she may be entitled to as much as $13,000,000 in damages, not including any punitive damages or attorney's fees . . .

by or between UBS employees concerning Plaintiff." The term document in Zubulake's request "includes, without limitation, electronic or computerized data compilations. . . " On July 8, 2002, UBS responded by producing approximately 350 pages of documents, including approximately 100 pages of e-mails.

UBS agreed unconditionally to produce responsive e-mails from the accounts of five individuals named by Zubulake: Matthew Chapin, Rose Tong (a human relations representation who was assigned to handle issues concerning Zubulake), Vinay Datta (a co-worker on the Desk), Andrew Clarke (another co-worker on the Desk), and Jeremy Hardisty (Chapin's supervisor and the individual to whom Zubulake originally complained about Chapin). UBS was to produce such e-mails sent between August 1999 (when Zubulake was hired) and December 2001 (one month after her termination), to the extent possible.

UBS, however, produced no additional e-mails and insisted that its initial production (the 100 pages of e-mails) was complete. As UBS's opposition to the instant motion makes clear—although it remains unsaid—UBS never searched for responsive e-mails on any of its backup tapes. To the contrary, UBS informed Zubulake that the cost of producing e-mails on backup tapes would be prohibitive (estimated at the time at approximately $300,000.00). . .

Zubulake objected to UBS's nonproduction. In fact, Zubulake knew that there were additional responsive e-mails that UBS had failed to produce because she herself had produced approximately 450 pages of e-mail correspondence. Clearly, numerous responsive e-mails had been created and deleted[19] at UBS, and Zubulake wanted them.

C. UBS's E-Mail Backup System

In the first instance, the parties agree that e-mail was an important means of communication at UBS during the relevant time period. Each salesperson, including the salespeople on the Desk, received approximately 200 e-mails each day. . . Given this volume, and because Securities and Exchange Commission regulations require it. . . UBS implemented extensive email backup and preservation protocols. In particular, e-mails were backed up in two distinct ways: on backup tapes and on optical disks.

1. Backup Tape Storage

UBS employees used a program called HP OpenMail, manufactured by Hewlett-Packard,. . . for all work-related e-mail communications. . . With limited exceptions, all e-mails sent or received by any UBS employee are stored onto backup tapes. To do so, UBS employs a program called Veritas NetBackup. . . which creates a "snapshot" of all e-mails that exist on a given server at the time the backup is taken. Except for scheduling the backups and physically inserting the tapes into the machines, the backup process is entirely automated.

UBS used the same backup protocol during the entire relevant time period, from 1999 through 2001. Using NetBackup, UBS backed up its e-mails at three intervals: (1) daily, at the end of each day, (2) weekly, on Friday nights, and (3) monthly, on the last business day of the month. Nightly backup tapes were kept for twenty working days, weekly tapes for one year, and monthly tapes for three years. After the relevant time period elapsed, the tapes were recycled.[25]

Once e-mails have been stored onto backup tapes, the restoration process is lengthy. Each backup tape routinely takes approximately five days to restore. . . Because each tape represents a snapshot of one server's hard

---

[19] The term "deleted" is sticky in the context of electronic data. "'Deleting' a file does not actually erase that data from the computer's storage devices. Rather, it simply finds the data's entry in the disk directory and changes it to a 'not used' status—thus permitting the computer to write over the 'deleted' data. Until the computer writes over the 'deleted' data, however, it may be recovered by searching the disk itself rather than the disk's directory. Accordingly, many files are recoverable long after they have been deleted—even if neither the computer user nor the computer itself is aware of their existence. Such data is referred to as 'residual data.' ". . . Deleted data may also exist because it was backed up before it was deleted. Thus, it may reside on backup tapes or similar media. Unless otherwise noted, I will use the term "deleted" data to mean residual data, and will refer to backed-up data as "backup tapes."

[25] Of course, periodic backups such as UBS's necessarily entails the loss of certain e-mails. Because backups were conducted only intermittently, some e-mails that were deleted from the server were never backed up. For example, if a user both received and deleted an e-mail on the same day, it would not reside on any backup tape. Similarly, an e-mail received and deleted within the span of one month would not exist on the monthly backup, although it might exist on a weekly or daily backup, if those tapes still exist. As explained below, if an e-mail was to or from a "registered trader," however, it may have been stored on UBS's optical storage devices.

drive in a given month, each server/month must be restored separately onto a hard drive. Then, a program called Double Mail is used to extract a particular individual's e-mail file. That mail file is then exported into a Microsoft Outlook data file, which in turn can be opened in Microsoft Outlook, a common e-mail application. A user could then browse through the mail file and sort the mail by recipient, date or subject, or search for key words in the body of the e-mail.

Fortunately, NetBackup also created indexes of each backup tape. Thus, [UBS] was able to search through the tapes from the relevant time period and determine that the e-mail files responsive to Zubulake's requests are contained on a total of ninety-four backup tapes.

2. *Optical Disk Storage*

In addition to the e-mail backup tapes, UBS also stored certain e-mails on optical disks. For certain "registered traders," probably including the members of the Desk,[26] a copy of all e-mails sent to or received from outside sources (i.e., e-mails from a "registered trader" at UBS to someone at another entity, or vice versa) was simultaneously written onto a series of optical disks. Internal e-mails, however, were not stored on this system.

UBS has retained each optical disk used since the system was put into place in mid-1998. Moreover, the optical disks are neither erasable nor rewritable. Thus, UBS has every e-mail sent or received by registered traders (except internal emails) during the period of Zubulake's employment, even if the e-mail was deleted instantaneously on that trader's system.

The optical disks are easily searchable using a program called Tumbleweed . . . Using Tumbleweed, a user can simply log into the system with the proper credentials and create a plain language search. Search criteria can include not just "header" information, such as the date or the name of the sender or recipient, but can also include terms within the text of the email itself. For example, UBS personnel could easily run a search for e-mails containing the words "Laura" or "Zubulake" that were sent or received by Chapin, Datta, Clarke, or Hardisty . . .

III. LEGAL STANDARD

. . . Rule 26(b)(1) specifies that,

> Parties may obtain discovery regarding any matter, not privileged, that is relevant to the claim or defense of any party, including the existence, description, nature, custody, condition, and location of any books, documents, or other tangible things and the identity and location of persons having knowledge of any discoverable matter. For good cause, the court may order discovery of any matter relevant to the subject matter involved in the action. Relevant information need not be admissible at the trial if the discovery appears reasonably calculated to lead to the discovery of admissible evidence . . .

In turn, Rule 26(b)(2) imposes general limitations on the scope of discovery in the form of a "proportionality test":

> The . . . extent of use of the discovery methods otherwise permitted . . . shall be limited by the court if it determines that . . . the burden or expense of the proposed discovery outweighs its likely benefit, taking into account the needs of the case, the amount in controversy, the parties' resources, the importance of the issues at stake in the litigation, and the importance of the proposed discovery in resolving the issues . . .

Finally, "under [the discovery] rules, the presumption is that the responding party must bear the expense of complying with discovery requests, but [it] may invoke the district [court]..to grant orders protecting [it] from 'undue burden or expense' in doing so, including orders conditioning discovery on the requesting party's payment of the costs of discovery." . . .

---

[26] In using the phrase "registered trader," Behny referred to individuals designated to have their e-mails archived onto optical disks. Although Behny could not be certain that such a designation corresponds to Series 7 or Series 63 broker-dealers, he indicated that examples of registered traders include "equity research people, [and] equity traders type people." . . . He admitted that members of the Desk were probably "registered" in that sense . . .

The application of these various discovery rules is particularly complicated where electronic data is sought because otherwise discoverable evidence is often only available from expensive-to-restore backup media . . . By and large, the solution has been to consider cost-shifting: forcing the requesting party, rather than the answering party, to bear the cost of discovery.

By far, the most influential response . . . was given by United States Magistrate Judge James C. Francis IV . . . in *Rowe Entertainment*. Judge Francis utilized an eight-factor test to determine whether discovery costs should be shifted. Those eight factors are:

> (1) the specificity of the discovery requests; (2) the likelihood of discovering critical information; (3) the availability of such information from other sources; (4) the purposes for which the responding party maintains the requested data; (5) the relative benefits to the parties of obtaining the information; (6) the total cost associated with production; (7) the relative ability of each party to control costs and its incentive to do so; and (8) the resources available to each party . . .

Both Zubulake and UBS agree that the eight-factor *Rowe* test should be used to determine whether cost-shifting is appropriate . . .

IV. DISCUSSION

A. Should Discovery of UBS's Electronic Data Be Permitted?

. . . Zubulake is entitled to discovery of the requested e-mails so long as they are relevant to her claims . . . which they clearly are. As noted, e-mail constituted a substantial means of communication among UBS employees. To that end, UBS has already produced approximately 100 pages of e-mails, the contents of which are unquestionably relevant . . .

Nonetheless, UBS argues that Zubulake is not entitled to any further discovery because it already produced all responsive documents, to wit, the 100 pages of e-mails. This argument is unpersuasive for two reasons. First, because of the way that UBS backs up its e-mail files, it clearly could not have searched all of its e-mails without restoring the ninety-four backup tapes (which UBS admits that it has not done). UBS therefore cannot represent that it has produced all responsive emails. Second, Zubulake herself has produced over 450 pages of relevant e-mails, including e-mails that would have been responsive to her discovery requests but were never produced by UBS. These two facts strongly suggest that there are e-mails that Zubulake has not received that reside on UBS's backup media . . .

B. Should Cost-Shifting Be Considered?

Because it apparently recognizes that Zubulake is entitled to the requested discovery, UBS expends most of its efforts urging the court to shift the cost of production to "protect [it] . . . from undue burden or expense." . . . Faced with similar applications, courts generally engage in some sort of cost-shifting analysis, whether the refined eight-factor *Rowe* test or a cruder application of Rule 34's proportionality test, or something in between . . .

The first question, however, is whether cost-shifting must be considered in every case involving the discovery of electronic data, which—in today's world—includes virtually all cases. In light of the accepted principle, stated above, that electronic evidence is no less discoverable than paper evidence, the answer is, "No." The Supreme Court has instructed that "the presumption is that the responding party must bear the expense of complying with discovery requests" . . . Any principled approach to electronic evidence must respect this presumption . . .

Courts must remember that cost-shifting may effectively end discovery, especially when private parties are engaged in litigation with large corporations. As large companies increasingly move to entirely paper-free environments, the frequent use of cost-shifting will have the effect of crippling discovery in discrimination and retaliation cases. This will both undermine the "strong public policy favoring resolving disputes on their merits," . . . and may ultimately deter the filing of potentially meritorious claims.

Thus, cost-shifting should be considered only when electronic discovery imposes an "undue burden or expense" on the responding party . . . The burden or expense of discovery is, in turn, "undue" when it "outweighs its likely benefit, taking into account the needs of the case, the amount in controversy, the parties' resources, the importance of the issues at stake in the litigation, and the importance of the proposed discovery in resolving the issues." . . .

Many courts have automatically assumed that an undue burden or expense may arise simply because electronic evidence is involved . . . This makes no sense. Electronic evidence is frequently cheaper and easier to produce than paper evidence because it can be searched automatically, key words can be run for privilege checks, and the production can be made in electronic form obviating the need for mass photocopying . . .

In fact, whether production of documents is unduly burdensome or expensive turns primarily on whether it is kept in an accessible or inaccessible format . . . [I]n the world of electronic data, thanks to search engines, any data that is retained in a machine readable format is typically accessible . . .

Whether electronic data is accessible or inaccessible turns largely on the media on which it is stored. Five categories of data, listed in order from most accessible to least accessible, are described in the literature on electronic data storage:

1. **Active, online data:** "On-line storage is generally provided by magnetic disk. It is used in the very active stages of an electronic records [sic] life—when it is being created or received and processed, as well as when the access frequency is high and the required speed of access is very fast, i.e., milliseconds." . . . Examples of online data include hard drives.
2. **Near-line data:** "This typically consists of a robotic storage device (robotic library) that houses removable media, uses robotic arms to access the media, and uses multiple read/write devices to store and retrieve records. Access speeds can range from as low as milliseconds if the media is already in a read device, up to 10–30 seconds for optical disk technology, and between 20–120 seconds for sequentially searched media, such as magnetic tape." . . . Examples include optical disks.
3. **Offline storage/archives:** "This is removable optical disk or magnetic tape media, which can be labeled and stored in a shelf or rack. Off-line storage of electronic records is traditionally used for making disaster copies of records and also for records considered 'archival' in that their likelihood of retrieval is minimal. Accessibility to off-line media involves manual intervention and is much slower than on-line or near-line storage. Access speed may be minutes, hours, or even days, depending on the access-effectiveness of the storage facility." . . . The principle difference between near-line data and offline data is that offline data lacks "the coordinated control of an intelligent disk subsystem," and is, in the lingo, **JBOD** ("Just a Bunch Of Disks") . . .
4. **Backup tapes:** "A device, like a tape recorder, that reads data from and writes it onto a tape. Tape drives have data capacities of anywhere from a few hundred kilobytes to several gigabytes. Their transfer speeds also vary considerably . . . The disadvantage of tape drives is that they are sequential-access devices, which means that to read any particular block of data, you need to read all the preceding blocks." . . . As a result, "the data on a backup tape are not organized for retrieval of individual documents or files [because] . . . the organization of the data mirrors the computer's structure, not the human records management structure." . . . Backup tapes also typically employ some sort of data compression, permitting more data to be stored on each tape, but also making restoration more time-consuming and expensive, especially given the lack of uniform standard governing data compression . . .
5. **Erased, fragmented or damaged data:** "When a file is first created and saved, it is laid down on the [storage media] in contiguous clusters . . . As files are erased, their clusters are made available again as free space. Eventually, some newly created files become larger than the remaining contiguous free space. These files are then broken up and randomly placed throughout the disk." . . . Such broken-up files are said to be "fragmented," and along with damaged and erased data can only be accessed after significant processing . . .

Of these, the first three categories are typically identified as accessible, and the latter two as inaccessible . . . The difference between the two classes is easy to appreciate. Information deemed "accessible" is stored in a readily usable format. Although the time it takes to actually access the data ranges from milliseconds to days, the data does not need to be restored or otherwise manipulated to be usable. "Inaccessible" data, on the other hand, is not readily usable. Backup tapes must be restored using a process similar to that previously described, **fragmented data** must be de-fragmented, and erased data must be reconstructed, all before the data is usable. That makes such data inaccessible . . .

The case at bar is a perfect illustration of the range of accessibility of electronic data. As explained above, UBS maintains e-mail files in three forms: (1) active user e-mail files; (2) archived e-mails on optical disks; and (3) backup data stored on tapes. The active (HP OpenMail) data is obviously the most accessible: it is online data that resides on an active server, and can be accessed immediately. The optical disk (Tumbleweed) data is only slightly less accessible, and falls into either the second or third category. The e-mails are on optical disks that need to be located and read with the correct hardware, but the system is configured to make searching the optical disks simple and automated once they are located. For these sources of e-mails—active mail files and e-mails stored on optical disks—it would be wholly inappropriate to even consider cost-shifting. UBS maintains the data in an accessible and usable format, and can respond to Zubulake's request cheaply and quickly. Like most typical discovery requests, therefore, the producing party should bear the cost of production.

E-mails stored on backup tapes (via NetBackup), however, are an entirely different matter. Although UBS has already identified the ninety-four potentially responsive backup tapes, those tapes are not currently accessible. In order to search the tapes for responsive e-mails, UBS would have to engage in the costly and time-consuming process detailed above. It is therefore appropriate to consider cost-shifting.

C. What Is the Proper Cost-Shifting Analysis?

In the year since *Rowe* was decided, its eight-factor test has unquestionably become the gold standard for courts resolving electronic discovery disputes . . . But there is little doubt that the *Rowe* factors will generally favor cost-shifting. Indeed, of the handful of reported opinions that apply *Rowe* or some modification thereof, all of them have ordered the cost of discovery to be shifted to the requesting party . . .

In order to maintain the presumption that the responding party pays, the cost-shifting analysis must be neutral; close calls should be resolved in favor of the presumption. The *Rowe* factors, as applied, undercut that presumption for three reasons. First, the *Rowe* test is incomplete. Second, courts have given equal weight to all of the factors, when certain factors should predominate. Third, courts applying the *Rowe* test have not always developed a full factual record.

1. The Rowe *Test Is Incomplete*

a. A Modification of Rowe: Additional Factors

Certain factors specifically identified in the Rules are omitted from *Rowe*'s eight factors. In particular, Rule 26 requires consideration of "the amount in controversy, the parties' resources, the importance of the issues at stake in the litigation, and the importance of the proposed discovery in resolving the issues." . . . Yet *Rowe* makes no mention of either the amount in controversy or the importance of the issues at stake in the litigation. These factors should be added. Doing so would balance the *Rowe* factor that typically weighs most heavily in favor of cost-shifting, "the total cost associated with production." The cost of production is almost always an objectively large number in cases where litigating cost-shifting is worthwhile. But the cost of production when compared to "the amount in controversy" may tell a different story. A response to a discovery request costing $100,000 sounds (and is) costly, but in a case potentially worth millions of dollars, the cost of responding may not be unduly burdensome.[65]

Rowe also contemplates "the resources available to each party." But here too—although this consideration may be implicit in the *Rowe* test—the absolute wealth of the parties is not the relevant factor. More important than comparing the relative ability of a party to pay for discovery, the focus should be on the total cost of production as compared to the resources available to each party. Thus, discovery that would be too expensive for one defendant to bear would be a drop in the bucket for another.[66]

---

[65] A word of caution, however: in evaluating this factor courts must look beyond the (often inflated) value stated in the ad damnum clause of the complaint.

[66] UBS, for example, reported net profits after tax of 942 million Swiss Francs (approximately $716 million) for the third quarter of 2002 alone . . .

Last, "the importance of the issues at stake in the litigation" is a critical consideration, even if it is one that will rarely be invoked. For example, if a case has the potential for broad public impact, then public policy weighs heavily in favor of permitting extensive discovery. Cases of this ilk might include toxic tort class actions, environmental actions, so-called "impact" or social reform litigation, cases involving criminal conduct, or cases implicating important legal or constitutional questions.

b. A Modification of Rowe: Eliminating Two Factors

Two of the *Rowe* factors should be eliminated:

First, the *Rowe* test includes "the specificity of the discovery request." Specificity is surely the touchstone of any good discovery request . . . requiring a party to frame a request broadly enough to obtain relevant evidence, yet narrowly enough to control costs. But relevance and cost are already two of the *Rowe* factors (the second and sixth). Because the first and second factors are duplicative, they can be combined. Thus, the first factor should be: the extent to which the request is specifically tailored to discover relevant information.

Second, the fourth factor, "the purposes for which the responding party maintains the requested data" is typically unimportant. Whether the data is kept for a business purpose or for disaster recovery does not affect its accessibility, which is the practical basis for calculating the cost of production . . .

Of course, there will be certain limited instances where the very purpose of maintaining the data will be to produce it to the opposing party. That would be the case, for example, where the SEC requested "communications sent by [a] broker or dealer (including inter-office memoranda and communications) relating to his business as such." Such communications must be maintained pursuant to SEC Rule 17a-4 . . . But in such cases, cost-shifting would not be applicable in the first place; the relevant statute or rule would dictate the extent of discovery and the associated costs . . . Cost-shifting would also be inappropriate for another reason—namely, that the regulation itself requires that the data be kept "in an accessible place."

c. A New Seven-Factor Test

Set forth below is a new seven-factor test based on the modifications to *Rowe* discussed in the preceding sections.

1. The extent to which the request is specifically tailored to discover relevant information;
2. The availability of such information from other sources;
3. The total cost of production, compared to the amount in controversy;
4. The total cost of production, compared to the resources available to each party;
5. The relative ability of each party to control costs and its incentive to do so;
6. The importance of the issues at stake in the litigation; and
7. The relative benefits to the parties of obtaining the information.

2. The Seven Factors Should Not Be Weighted Equally

Whenever a court applies a multi-factor test, there is a temptation to treat the factors as a check-list, resolving the issue in favor of whichever column has the most checks . . . But "we do not just add up the factors." . . .

Weighting the factors in descending order of importance may solve the problem and avoid a mechanistic application of the test. The first two factors—comprising the marginal utility test—are the most important. These factors include: (1) The extent to which the request is specifically tailored to discover relevant information and (2) the availability of such information from other sources.

The second group of factors addresses cost issues: "How expensive will this production be?" and, "Who can handle that expense?" These factors include: (3) the total cost of production compared to the amount in controversy, (4) the total cost of production compared to the resources available to each party and (5) the relative ability of each party to control costs and its incentive to do so. The third "group"—(6) the importance of the litigation itself—stands alone, and as noted earlier will only rarely come into play. But where it does, this factor has the potential to predominate over the others . . . Finally, the last factor—(7) the relative benefits of production as between the requesting and producing parties—is the least important because it is fair to presume that the response to a discovery request generally benefits the requesting party. But in the unusual case where production will also provide a tangible or strategic benefit to the responding party, that fact may weigh against shifting costs.

D. A Factual Basis Is Required to Support the Analysis

Courts applying *Rowe* have uniformly favored cost-shifting largely because of assumptions made concerning the likelihood that relevant information will be found . . .

But such proof will rarely exist in advance of obtaining the requested discovery. The suggestion that a plaintiff must not only demonstrate that probative evidence exists, but also prove that electronic discovery will yield a "gold mine," is contrary to the plain language of Rule 26(b)(1), which permits discovery of "any matter" that is "relevant to [a] claim or defense." . . .

Requiring the responding party to restore and produce responsive documents from a small sample of backup tapes will inform the cost-shifting analysis laid out above. When based on an actual sample, the marginal utility test will not be an exercise in speculation—there will be tangible evidence of what the backup tapes may have to offer. There will also be tangible evidence of the time and cost required to restore the backup tapes, which in turn will inform the second group of cost-shifting factors. Thus, by requiring a sample restoration of backup tapes, the entire cost-shifting analysis can be grounded in fact rather than guesswork.[77]

IV. CONCLUSION AND ORDER

In summary, deciding disputes regarding the scope and cost of discovery of electronic data requires a three-step analysis:

First, it is necessary to thoroughly understand the responding party's computer system, both with respect to active and stored data. For data that is kept in an accessible format, the usual rules of discovery apply: the responding party should pay the costs of producing responsive data. A court should consider cost-shifting only when electronic data is relatively inaccessible, such as in backup tapes.

Second, because the cost-shifting analysis is so fact-intensive, it is necessary to determine what data may be found on the inaccessible media. Requiring the responding party to restore and produce responsive documents from a small sample of the requested backup tapes is a sensible approach in most cases.

Third, and finally, in conducting the cost-shifting analysis, the following factors should be considered, weighted more-or-less in the following order:

1. The extent to which the request is specifically tailored to discover relevant information;
2. The availability of such information from other sources;
3. The total cost of production, compared to the amount in controversy;
4. The total cost of production, compared to the resources available to each party;
5. The relative ability of each party to control costs and its incentive to do so;
6. The importance of the issues at stake in the litigation; and
7. The relative benefits to the parties of obtaining the information.

Accordingly, UBS is ordered to produce all responsive e-mails that exist on its optical disks or on its active servers (i.e., in HP OpenMail files) at its own expense. UBS is also ordered to produce, at its expense, responsive e-mails from any five backups tapes selected by Zubulake. UBS should then prepare an affidavit detailing the results of its search, as well as the time and money spent. After reviewing the contents of the backup tapes and UBS's certification, the Court will conduct the appropriate cost-shifting analysis.

Just because the federal Southern District of New York changed its rule, other courts that have adopted *Rowe* did not automatically change to the *Zubulake* rule. Either case can be argued in jurisdictions not having addressed the issue.

As the *Zubulake* court indicated, it is important to know what kind of storage system the party from whom information is sought has. Find out early exactly how your clients store data and consider asking the opposing party this question in interrogatories when seeking data.

The courts are making it clear that printed information based on computer data is insufficient in response to a specific request for the electronic data. There's a very good reason for insisting on the data, and

---

[77] Of course, where the cost of a sample restoration is significant compared to the value of the suit, or where the suit itself is patently frivolous, even this minor effort may be inappropriate.

not just the results: you want your expert to analyze how the data were analyzed and calculated. Just listen to a statistician sometime—you'll find that manipulating numbers to say things the way you want them to be said is not that difficult. The problem for the number-impaired (like me) is that it is not transparent when the numbers have been cooked. Numbers and statistics make a solid thunk sound in my brain and I, like many of us in the scientific age, am easily dazzled by numbers and automatically assign them more persuasive (or pro-bative) value unless someone can give me a clear idea of how to look at them critically.

So if you have a litigant who is not giving you the electronic data you want, keep pushing for it. Here's how it paid off for one employment discrimination plaintiff.

Zhou v. Pittsburg State University, 2003 U.S. Dist. LEXIS 6398 (D. Kan. February 5, 2003).

Pending before the Court is Plaintiff's Motion to Compel . . . More specifically, Plaintiff seeks to compel Defendant to produce computer-generated documents—instead of typewritten documents compiled by hand already produced—reflecting the salaries of faculty working within Defendant's music department from Fall semester 1997 through Spring semester 2000.

Relevant Background

Plaintiff worked for Defendant as an Assistant Music Professor from Fall semester 1997 through Spring semester 2000. In this lawsuit, Plaintiff alleges Defendant discriminated against him in the terms and conditions of his employment.

During the course of discovery, Plaintiff propounded an interrogatory to Defendant requesting information from 1996 to 2002 with respect to salaries of faculty working within Defendant's music department. On November 4, 2002, Defendant responded to this interrogatory by compiling a typewritten document setting forth the information requested in table format. Defendant asserts the salary information provided to Plaintiff was pulled from the Pittsburg State University Human Resource computer system, which allegedly is the most accurate payroll system available to Defendant.

On November 29, 2002, Plaintiff filed a Motion to Compel seeking the underlying computer-generated data used to compile the salary table provided to Plaintiff on November 4, 2002. On December 12, 2002, the Court ruled on Plaintiff's Motion to Compel and ordered Defendant to "produce copies of any original documents showing faculty salary information during the time period in which Plaintiff was employed by PSU, to the extent any such original documents exist.". . .

In response to the Court Order, Defendant produced two documents entitled "Departmental Budget Recommendations," which reflect computer-generated salary information for fiscal years 1998–1999 and handwritten recommendations from the Vice-President for Academic Affairs to the Human Resources department regarding salary adjustments for the succeeding years. Defendant asserts it did not provide 1997 "Departmental Budget Recommendations" because Defendant only maintains documents for a period of five years.

On January 3, 2003, Plaintiff filed another Motion to Compel, this time seeking not only the computer-generated data used by Defendant to compile the salary table provided to Plaintiff on November 4, 2002, but also the computer-generated data reflecting whether or not the handwritten salary adjustment recommendations were implemented. In response to this current Motion to Compel, Defendant states

> Defendant has provided all information relating to the salaries of the Pittsburg State University and complied with the Court Order relating to the salary information. The Court stated that the Defendant shall produce copies of any original documents that exist. The Defendant has complied with this Order, and cannot produce copies of documents that do not exist . . .

Discussion

Fed. R. Civ. P. 34 describes both the scope of documentary discovery and the procedure by which litigants may obtain that discovery. Rule 34(a) allows any party to serve on any other party a request to produce and permit the party making the request, or someone acting on the requestor's behalf, to inspect and copy, any designated documents . . . or to inspect and copy, test, or sample any tangible things which constitute or contain matters within the scope of Rule 26(b) and which are in the possession, custody or control of the party upon whom the request is served[.]

The Notes to the 1970 Amendment to Rule 34 include the following explanation with regard to the definition of "document":

. . . It makes clear that Rule 34 applies to electronic data compilations from which information can be obtained only with the use of detection devices, and that when that data can as a practical matter be made usable by the discovering party only through respondent's devices, respondent may be required to use [its] devices to translate the data into usable form. In many instances, this means that respondent will have to supply a print-out of computer data . . . Similarly, if the discovering party needs to check the electronic source itself, the court may protect respondent with respect to preservation of [its] records, confidentiality of nondiscoverable matters, and costs.

As used by the advisory committee, "computerized data and other electronically-recorded information" includes, but is not limited to: voice mail messages and files, backup voice mail files, e-mail messages and files, backup e-mail files, deleted e-mails, data files, program files, backup and archival tapes, temporary files, system history files, web site information stored in textual, graphical or audio format, web site log files, cache files, cookies, and other electronically-recorded information. . . . Simply put, the disclosing party must take reasonable steps to ensure that it discloses any backup copies of files or archival tapes that will provide information about any "deleted" electronic data.

Adhering to these directives, the Court hereby grants Plaintiff's Motion to Compel to the extent that Defendant shall, **within ten (10) days from the date of this Order,** disclose all data compilations, computerized data and other electronically-recorded information as specifically defined in this Order that reflect the salaries of faculty working within Defendant's music department from Fall semester 1997 through Spring semester 2000, including but not limited to the computerized data and other electronically-recorded information used by Defendant to compile the salary table provided to Plaintiff on November 4, 2002 (reflecting information from FY 1997 through FY 2000) and the handwritten salary adjustment recommendations provided to Plaintiff in December 2002. If Defendant does not disclose, or believes it is unable to disclose, this information to Plaintiff, then Defendant shall **show cause to the Court within ten (10) days of this Order why it did not comply with this Order and shall specifically describe the efforts it made to comply with this Order;**

It is further ordered that the parties shall preserve evidence that they know, or should know, is relevant to the ongoing litigation, including preservation of all data compilations, computerized data and other electronically-recorded information as specifically defined in this Order.

As will be discussed again in the context of animation in demonstrative evidence, a problem arises when graphics are introduced **ostensibly** for illustration. If any part of the graphics is automatically generated by the computer based on the entry of data, someone must testify as to the accuracy of the technique or software program in doing so, as discussed at length in the following case.

New Mexico v. Tollardo, 77 P.3d 1023 (N.M. App. 2003).

Trial lawyers are acutely aware that one picture is worth a thousand words. Studies show that jurors retain more information from visual presentations or presentations that are both verbal and visual than from verbal presentations alone . . . A witness can illustrate his or her testimony by drawing diagrams on paper for a jury, as long as the diagram is not misleading . . . This case concerns the use and admission into evidence of images generated by a computer, rather than drawn by a person. We hold that under the circumstances of this case, the trial court correctly required the proponent of the images to establish the validity of the computer programs used to generate the images. We further hold that the trial court did not abuse its discretion in determining that the programs were valid. Thus, we affirm . . .

The events that were the subject of the trial took place in the early morning hours of July 20, 2000, near Taos, New Mexico. Shortly after midnight, Rosalee Kisto, Robert Miera, and Jeremy Trujillo went to Miera's mobile home in a mobile home park outside of Taos. What happened at the mobile home was disputed at trial . . . However, it was undisputed that Defendant, Kisto, and Trujillo argued loudly, that Miera joined them at some point, and that Miera and Kisto moved away from Defendant and Trujillo. Ultimately, Defendant retrieved a gun from Kisto's car and shot Trujillo and Miera. Both victims died as a result of their wounds. The testimony at trial indicated that at least four shots were fired in rapid succession.

At some point before trial, the State contacted the Federal Bureau of Investigation (FBI) for assistance. Carl Adrian, a visual information specialist examiner in the Investigative, Prosecutive and Graphic Unit, which is part of the FBI laboratory, was assigned to the case. Using information gathered by others investigating the case and computer programs described in more detail below, Adrian set out to determine whether, given the physical evidence found at the scene, a shooter in a fixed location could quickly fire three shots that would create the wounds found in Trujillo's chest, in Miera's chest, and in Miera's thigh. The result was a series of computer images that showed three figures against a checked background. Two of the figures represented the victims, with dotted lines through their bodies indicating the trajectory of the bullets that caused the three wounds. The third figure was a shooter holding a gun. The computer programs allowed Adrian to move the figures of the victims so that the dotted lines of the bullet trajectories intersected with the muzzle of the gun. Using these images, Adrian determined that a person standing in one place could have fired all three shots. Because the images were to scale and were shown against a checked background in which each check represented a square foot, the images also showed the relative distances between the figures. In addition, the images showed Trujillo was crouched down and facing forward and that Miera was turning at the time they were hit by the bullets.

Before trial, Defendant filed a motion in limine asking the trial court to exclude the images. Among other things, Defendant argued that the computer-generated images did not meet the standards of validity and reliability . . . for the admission of scientific testimony.

The trial court held an evidentiary hearing on Defendant's motion. At the hearing, Adrian testified in detail and was subject to cross-examination concerning the information he used to construct the images shown on the exhibit, the nature and accuracy of the application programs he used to create the images, and the process he went through to create the images. At the close of the hearing, the State argued that the images were demonstrative evidence that would be used as visual aids to assist the jury in understanding the evidence. Therefore, in the State's view, the images were not scientific evidence . . . [The trial court] held that Adrian's testimony was sufficient to establish the validity of the programs used to generate the images. Accordingly, the trial court held that the exhibit could be admitted into evidence and the images on it shown to the jury during Adrian's testimony, subject, of course, to the requirement that the State lay a proper foundation for the admission of the evidence . . .

The State's last witness was Adrian. Adrian was recognized as an expert in several areas. First, Adrian was recognized as an expert in crime scene reconstruction, or, as Adrian calls it, "reverse engineering of crime scenes." Reverse engineering of crime scenes involves using known information, such as the locations of objects at the scene or the trajectory of a bullet as described in an autopsy report, to determine unknown information. Adrian was also recognized as an expert in Computer Assisted Design (CAD) programs, a program referred to as MAYA, and in three-dimensional bullet trajectory analysis in computer systems. Defendant did not object below and does not challenge Adrian's expertise on appeal.

The jury convicted Defendant of voluntary manslaughter for the killing of Miera, and murder in the second degree for the killing of Trujillo. Defendant appeals. On appeal, Defendant argues . . . that the trial court erred in admitting the exhibit into evidence and allowing the images to be shown to the jury. The use and admission into evidence of computer-generated images is an issue of first impression in New Mexico . . .

Defendant and the State dispute the nature of the evidence and the standard used to determine its admissibility. Defendant argues that the images were not demonstrative evidence but real evidence used to prove his guilt. The State argues that the images were simply demonstrative evidence used to illustrate Adrian's testimony . . .

Evidence used in court is generally broken into three broad categories: testimonial evidence, documentary evidence, and demonstrative evidence . . . New Mexico cases define demonstrative evidence, also sometimes referred to as real evidence or evidence by inspection, as "such evidence as is addressed directly to the senses of the court or jury without the intervention of the testimony of witnesses, as where various things are exhibited in open court." *Holloway v. Evans,* 55 N.M. 601, 607, 238 P.2d 457, 460–61 (1951), quoting 32 C.J.S., Evidence, § 601 (internal quotation marks omitted). When used in this broad sense, demonstrative evidence includes a wide variety of things. *See, e.g., State v. Nelson,* 63 N.M. 428, 434, 321 P.2d 202, 206 (1958) (clothing and other personal effects); *Mott v. Sun Country Garden Prods., Inc.,* 120 N.M. 261, 269–70, 901 P.2d 192, 200–01 (Ct. App. 1995) (trailer involved in vehicular accident); *State v. Gallegos,* 115 N.M. 458, 459, 853 P.2d 160, 161 (Ct. App. 1993) (tattoos on a person's body). There is no question that the images are demonstrative evidence in this sense.

The fact that something is demonstrative evidence in this sense does not, however, determine the standards for admitting the evidence because "not all tangible exhibits are offered for the same purpose or received on the same theory." 2 *McCormick on Evidence* § 212, at 3. In this case, Defendant argues that the images were used as substantive evidence, while the State contends that the images were simply visual aids used to illustrate Adrian's expert opinion. The State points out that visual aids are often used to illustrate the trajectory of a bullet fired into the human body . . . Moreover, courts in other jurisdictions have affirmed the use of mannequins and dowel rods as visual aids to illustrate the trajectory of a bullet . . .

Both parties direct our attention to decisions of other courts that have considered the admissibility of computer-generated evidence. Some courts divide computer-generated exhibits into two categories: computer animations and computer simulations. An "animation" is a computer-generated exhibit that is used as a visual aid to illustrate an opinion that has been developed without using the computer. On the other hand, a "simulation" is a computer-generated exhibit created when information is fed into a computer that is programmed to analyze the data and draw a conclusion from it. *See, e.g., State v. Farner,* 66 S.W.3d 188, 208 (Tenn. 2001); *Clark v. Cantrell,* 339 S.C. 369, 529 S.E.2d 528, 535 n.2 (S.C. 2000); *People v. Cauley,* 32 P.3d 602, 606–07 (Colo. Ct. App. 2001). When the image is used as a visual aid, the courts do not require a showing that the exhibit was produced by a scientifically or technologically valid method . . . Instead, the critical issue is often whether the visual aid fairly and accurately represents the evidence or some version of the evidence. On the other hand, before admitting a simulation, in which the computer has been used to analyze data, the courts require proof of the validity of the scientific principles and data . . .

The State asserts that the computer-generated evidence in this case was used merely to illustrate Adrian's opinion and thus should be treated as an animation. However, as we understand the testimony, Adrian used the computer to help him form his opinions, not simply to illustrate opinions reached in another manner. On the other hand, the testimony also indicated that the computer did not "analyze" data fed into it; instead it created a visual image based on the same data that would have been used to create paper and pencil drafts on a drafting board. Thus, it does not fall squarely into either category espoused by those cases.

Nevertheless, we think those cases are helpful because they focus attention on the central question: who (or what) is the source of the opinion. When the computer-generated evidence is used to illustrate an opinion that an expert has arrived at without using the computer, the fact that the visual aid was generated by a computer probably does not matter because the witness can be questioned and cross-examined concerning the perceptions or opinions to which the witness testifies. In that situation, the computer is no more or less than a drafting device . . . However, when an expert witness uses the computer to develop an opinion on the issue, the opinion is based in part on the computer-generated evidence. *See, e.g., Pierce v. State,* 718 So. 2d 806, 808 (Fla. Dist. Ct. App. 1997) (indicating that when an expert uses a computer to develop an opinion, the courts require that the technique be shown to be reliable under the applicable test); *Kudlacek v. Fiat S.p.A.,* 244 Neb. 822, 509 N.W.2d 603, 617–18 (Neb. 1994) (discussing admissibility of expert opinion when expert used a computer program to reconstruct the path of the vehicle on the roadway). In that situation, the proponent of the evidence must be prepared to show that the computer-generated evidence was generated in a way that is scientifically valid . . .

In this case, Adrian used the computer to help him supply missing information based on the physical evidence available. Thus, the images were not visual aids used to illustrate an opinion developed by other means. Instead, they were used to develop the opinion to which Adrian testified.

. . . [O]ur Supreme Court, following the lead of the United States Supreme Court in *Daubert,* adopted a new test for determining the admissibility of expert opinion evidence under Rule 11-702 NMRA 2003. . . Thus, the focus of the inquiry shifted from general acceptance in a particular field to "the validity and the soundness of the scientific method used to generate the evidence." *Id.* In making this determination, the Court indicated that in addition to considering whether the technique was accepted in a particular field, the courts should examine the relationship between the technique used to generate the evidence and established scientific techniques and the availability of specialized literature addressing the validity of the technique . . . [The Court] defined validity as "the measure of determining whether the testimony is grounded in or a function of established scientific methods or principles, that is, scientific knowledge." . . .

In this case, we are concerned with the techniques used to generate computer images. We agree with the trial court that computer-generated images are more properly characterized as technical rather than scientific . . . However, the critical inquiry is whether the method used to generate the images is a valid application of the principles of computer technology.

In the trial court, Defendant argued that the computer applied the laws of physics to the data entered into it. Adrian specifically testified that this was not the case. Thus, the fact that Adrian was not qualified as an expert in physics does not matter. Adrian, however, was qualified as an expert in the use of both computer programs involved as well as an expert in three-dimensional analysis of bullet trajectories using a computer.

Defendant argues that Adrian was not competent to establish the validity of the computer programs he used to create the images. We disagree. As the trial court observed, we are long past the days when computers and computer programs were outside the ordinary experience of jurors. This is particularly true for the types of programs at issue here. We think many jurors have had experience with CAD programs used to design a house, a room, a landscape, or a host of other things. Indeed, at least one court has held that crime scene reconstruction through computer-generated images has become so common that it should be considered generally accepted . . . Computer-generated figures that move the way a human being moves are also common.

In this case, Adrian used two "off-the-shelf" programs, meaning programs that can be purchased by anyone with the money to buy them and a computer capable of running them. The first was a CAD program. Adrian testified that he had used CAD programs for many years. CAD programs have generally replaced hand drafting. The CAD programs that Adrian uses, Auto-CAD and GES, are accurate within 1/100,000 of an inch. Indeed, CAD programs generally are more accurate than drafting by hand. The second off-the-shelf program is referred to as MAYA. MAYA includes a feature called kinemation, which is the feature that Adrian used to animate the figures and move them around. MAYA was developed by the film industry and has been widely used to generate animated figures and special effects. Adrian testified that he had found some discrepancies in other facets of the MAYA program and so he cross-checked the MAYA images against the CAD images. We think this was all that was necessary to establish the validity of the method used to generate the images. Thus, we hold the trial court did not abuse its discretion in determining that the methods used to generate the images were valid uses of computer technology.

CONCLUSION

In summary, we hold that the trial court correctly determined that computer-generated images were required to meet the standard of validity. We further hold that in the circumstances of this case, the testimony of Adrian was sufficient to establish the validity of the computer programs used to generate the images . . .

Defendant's convictions are affirmed.

PROTECTIVE ORDERS AND SPOLIATION

There is also a potential problem of alteration of data in a computer, which can be followed if you have access to the hard drives themselves. Experts in this area are often referred to as "data recovery specialists." When should you suspect alteration of data and ask for access to the computer or drives themselves? What legal grounds do you have? You can always move for protection of the data and expedited discovery. This is a different type of protective order than found in family law; it simply directs a party to take particular steps to protect the evidence. Even if you don't have any reason to believe that the other side is purposely going to change the evidence, if you believe this is a case in which you will need substantial amounts of evidence contained in computers, you should get a protective order requiring the company not to dispose of any **back-up tapes**. Most corporations back up all electronic data on a particular schedule and dispose of older back-ups on a particular schedule. This back-up gives a snapshot of what the computer system of a company looked like at a particular time. If you want it unaltered, ask to have back-ups of a certain date range to be kept rather than overwritten. If there are particular individuals whose computers you want to investigate, ask to have their computers placed under similar protective orders.

The amount and quality of evidence you'll have to have to get the protective order will depend on the jurisdiction. Some courts will grant them routinely, some courts will issue orders if the attorney asking for them has sufficient credibility with the court, and others will require a full-blown evidentiary hearing. Find out what is customary for your locale.

Once you obtain the protective order, get the information you need and go about your business unless you have very good evidence that there truly is a problem that deserves sanctions. *Gates Rubber Co.* is a good example of the pursuit of sanctions gone bad.

Gates Rubber Co. v. Bando, 167 F.R.D. 90 (D. Colo. 1996).

. . . This order addresses the sanctions which have been sought by Gates Rubber Company (Gates) for what the attorneys for Gates have called chronic and continuous destruction of evidence by the defendants. These sanctions proceedings began almost four years ago on July 22, 1992, with the filing by Gates of its first motion for defendants to show cause as to why sanctions should not be imposed . . .

At this stage of the proceedings, the defendants have been reduced to four main groups: (1) Bando American, Inc., Bando Manufacturing of America, Inc., and Bando USA, Inc. (Bando) These entities are all American corporations, and they are the primary defendants in this case. (2) Bando Chemical Industries, Ltd. (Bando Chemical), is a Japanese company, and it is the parent company of the other Bando entities. The only two individuals who remain in the lawsuit as defendants with potential liability are (3) Steven R. Piderit (Piderit) and (4) Ron Newman (Newman). For ease of reference, when defendants are referred to collectively, they may be referred to simply as "the defendants," or as Bando.

Sanctions are not being sought, or are not available, against some of the defendants. The only parties against whom sanctions may be obtained are Bando (the American entities) and Ron Newman. Claims for sanctions against Steven Piderit and Bando Chemical were dismissed by me at the conclusion of Gates' case-in-chief at the sanctions hearing . . .

Gates and Bando are both involved in the manufacture of industrial belts. Although they compete against one another in the industrial belt market, Gates is clearly the dominant force. Gates enjoys a market share of approximately 38 percent, while Bando's market share is approximately 7 percent.

This case began when Gates accused Bando of stealing trade secret information. The trade secrets which were initially at issue consisted of two computer programs which were contained on computer disks, or floppy disks. Gates called the programs "Design Flex 4.0" and "Life in Hours."

Design Flex is a program which assists Gates' technicians and sales staff to determine the belt size which would be appropriate for a customer's machinery. Ordinarily, engineers are required to do a complicated set of computations involving numerous variables. The engineers at Gates developed Design Flex, which simplifies the process. With this program, sales personnel from Gates could plug in the information which was supplied by the customer, and the computer would make the necessary calculations to arrive at the proper belt size. Gates held a copyright on Design Flex. Life in Hours performs a similar function in the calculation of the number of hours of life which can be expected from a particular industrial belt.

Several of the named individual defendants are former employees of Bando [sic]: Allen Hanano, who left Gates to become chief executive officer for Bando American, and Piderit and Newman, engineers who were hired away from Gates by Hanano in 1988. In June of 1989, Gates learned that persons associated with Bando had demonstrated a computer program called "Chauffer" at a trade convention. This program appeared to emulate exactly the functions of Design Flex, and Gates suspected that the former employees had stolen Design Flex, copied it and were now using it in competition with Gates. The former employees had signed written, non-competition fiduciary agreements. Gates therefore filed this present action on January 4, 1992, charging unfair competition, misappropriation of trade secrets, infringement of copyright, and breach of contract. At various hearings, Gates' lawyers have stated that they believe that the value of their claims is "tens of millions," and even "hundreds of millions" of dollars.

During the discovery process for these proceedings, Gates learned that Newman had allegedly destroyed files on his computer, and had modified his computer menu program to delete any reference to Life in Hours, one of Gates' computer programs. Gates filed a motion on September 15, 1992, in which it asked the court to grant to Gates expedited discovery pursuant to the provisions of Fed. R. Civ. P. 34. Gates argued that there was evidence which suggested that Bando was engaged in a process of destroying evidence and erasing computer files, and that irreparable harm would result if Gates was not permitted to enter upon the premises of Bando's various entities for the purpose of copying files and records in order to preserve them from destruction.

Following oral argument on September 25, 1992, I granted the motion of Gates for expedited discovery, and I signed the written order which is now called the "Site Inspection Order." This order permitted the lawyers for Gates to take various technicians to all of Bando's facilities for the purpose of locating and copying materials, including all computer records, which Gates wished to preserve from the alleged destruction. It directed Bando and its employees to destroy no records.

The discovery procedures were supervised by a Special Master who was appointed by Judge Sparr. Under the directions of the Special Master, any identified and copied materials were to be placed in escrow, such as in a vacant room in a warehouse, and were to be released only subject to appropriate motions and orders for discovery. The goal of the Site Inspection Order was to provide a means by which to preserve materials from the alleged destruction, while simultaneously protecting the rights of Bando to object to the production of certain materials under the usual rules of discovery.

Within days of the signing of the Site Inspection Order, Gates began the process of preservation. Teams of lawyers and technicians, from both Gates and Bando, appeared at Bando's various factories and offices. All computer records were copied. Efforts were made to duplicate the hard drives of every computer, and efforts were made to determine for every computer what matters ever had been erased from any Bando computer. Every file cabinet, closet and desk drawer was explored, and, where desired, the contents of files and drawers were removed and taken to a commercial copying establishment. Gates was provided with the unprecedented opportunity to copy at will any materials which the lawyers believed may be relevant to the purposes of their inquiry.

During the site inspections, the lawyers for Gates observed things and events which led them to suspect that Bando had engaged in a deliberate effort to destroy documents and records which were relevant to the claims which Gates had filed against Bando. Gates then began the process of filing motions, amended motions and supplemental motions, all of which argued much the same thing: Bando had destroyed relevant materials; Gates' ability to prosecute its case was impaired; and Bando should be sanctioned by the entry of a default judgment.

Discovery on the merits of the case was put aside, and over the next several years the parties engaged in what has been called "sanctions discovery." All discovery was limited to obtaining testimony, evidence and materials which were relevant to the various claims for sanctions which Gates had alleged. No discovery was started or conducted on the merits of Gates' claims until after the last written argument on sanctions had been provided to me in February of 1995.

On May 23, 1993, in an effort to narrow and clarify the evidence and issues for the sanctions hearing itself, I entered a "Prehearing Order." In that order, I eliminated from consideration certain of Gates' complaints surrounding the theft and misuse of their computer programs. I found that many of Gates' complaints were not appropriate matters for sanctions. Instead, they were related to credibility issues which had been addressed, implicitly, by Judge Sparr in the order which he issued at the conclusion of the injunction hearing. Gates had received its "remedy" for any lies or thefts in Judge Sparr's findings that defendants had "willfully and maliciously" stolen trade secrets, and in the injunction which granted Gates the relief it sought. Other issues were related not to sanctions, but to damages, which could be addressed at the conclusion of any trial which may occur in this case. I directed the attorneys for Gates to focus their efforts only on allegations of destruction which they claimed would impair their ability to fully and fairly prepare their case for trial.

The sanctions hearing itself consumed a total of six weeks of evidence and testimony, and the hearing was conducted in several sections over a period of a year. I viewed countless hours of segments of video deposition testimony, covering approximately 20 witnesses; I listened to testimony from 20 witnesses who were called to court to testify live; and I received thousands of pages of pleadings, exhibits, documents and deposition excerpts. These materials were presented to me in 3-ring binder notebooks, and by the conclusion of the sanctions hearing I had received 50 of them. As of the time of the writing of this order, there are over 1,500 docket entries in the clerk's office, the vast majority of the entries relating to the sanctions proceedings . . .

Gates is seeking sanctions because of what it alleges to be various acts of destruction of evidence by the defendants. Destruction of evidence, or spoliation, is a discovery offense, and in order for Gates to demonstrate that it is entitled to sanctions for defendant's alleged actions it must present evidence which meets or satisfies the elements of the offense. The case law presents various discussions on these elements, but an excellent summary is provided in a volume entitled *Destruction of Evidence:*

> Although the elements establishing a basis for imposition of discovery sanctions are not settled, the prevailing consensus of courts is that sanctions are appropriate when a party (1) destroys (2) discoverable matter (3) which the party knew or should have known (4) was relevant to pending, imminent, or reasonably foreseeable litigation.

J. Gorelick et al., *Destruction of Evidence*, § 3.8, p. 88 (Wiley 1989).

Determining whether a party has committed actions which satisfy the elements of the offense only begins the inquiry. In conjunction with this determination, judges must explore and weigh other factors. The Tenth Circuit summarized these factors in *Ehrenhaus v. Reynolds*, 965 F.2d 916, 920 (10th Cir. 1992):

> . . . [A] court should ordinarily consider a number of factors, including "(1) the degree of actual prejudice to the defendant; (2) the amount of interference with the judicial process; . . . (3) the culpability of the litigant," [and] (4) whether the court warned the party in advance that dismissal of the action would be a likely sanction for noncompliance. . . .

Two of the factors which are discussed in *Ehrenhaus* . . . have taken on greater importance in most of the cases on sanctions for spoliation: (1) the culpability of the offender, or the alleged mental state which gave rise to the destruction of evidence, and (2) the degree of prejudice or harm which resulted from the actions of the offender. A review of the cases reflects that the two factors of "mental state" and "harm" are intertwined, and one of them can hardly be discussed without a simultaneous examination of the other . . .

The cases generally are unanimous in declaring that a dispositive sanction may be imposed only when the failure to comply with discovery demands is the result of willfulness, bad faith, or some fault of a party other than inability to comply . . . A "willful failure" is defined as " 'any intentional failure as distinguished from involuntary noncompliance. No wrongful intent need be shown.' " . . .

Where no willfulness, bad faith or fault is shown from the evidence, a dispositive sanction would be improper . . .

On the other hand, serious sanctions are warranted in cases where the judge finds willfulness or bad faith. This is so because actions which are found to be deliberate and purposeful ought to be punished accordingly . . . Where materials, documents or records are destroyed with conscious and deliberate intent, a judge can presume that the suppressed evidence would have damaged the nondisclosing party's case . . .

In the usual case, a party's loss of evidence through carelessness might not result in the imposition of a dispositive sanction. Where misconduct is not willful or intentional, there is less reason to presume that the loss of evidence flowed from a consciousness that the materials would hurt a party's case . . . Even so, in some circumstances, it would not be improper for a court to order dispositive sanctions for negligent conduct . . . In order to determine the appropriateness of certain sanctions, whether dispositive or otherwise, judges need to balance the degree of misconduct evidenced by a party's mental state against the degree of harm which flows from the misconduct.

The second factor of significant importance is that of the degree of prejudice which has been caused by the conduct of the alleged offender. Prejudice from the destruction of evidence can range from serious to modest. In some cases, there may be no harm at all as a result of an opponent's loss or destruction of evidence. In weighing and determining the appropriateness and severity of sanctions, judges should examine the materiality and value of the suppressed evidence upon the ability of a victim to fully and fairly prepare for trial . . . On the one hand, where the destruction of evidence results in substantial impairment to a party's abilities to prepare for trial, serious sanctions might be warranted.

. . . On the other hand, "concealed evidence may turn out to be cumulative, insignificant, or of marginal relevance." . . . In such circumstances, dispositive sanctions would undoubtedly constitute an overreaction, but sanctions of less severity would perhaps be appropriate . . .

Gates has pointed out on numerous occasions that the dilemma of lost evidence is that the aggrieved party can never know what it was, and can therefore never know the value that it may have had to the aggrieved party's case. To a certain extent, this is a compelling argument. However, before any sanctions would be appropriate, a judge must at least be satisfied that the lost materials had, or would have had, some relevance and materiality to the proceedings.

Gates is correct when it argues that destruction of evidence may give rise to a presumption of prejudice. However, any such presumption is rebuttable . . . and the presumption must be one which is warranted, or which naturally flows from the nature of the material or documents which have been destroyed . . . Although judges must be alert to the potential for harm when evidence is destroyed, judges must be wary when parties seek to prove too much from the absence of evidence . . .

Sanctions have a number of purposes. Two important purposes to be served in a case where allegations of destruction of evidence are asserted are punishment and deterrence.

. . . Other functions include compensation of the victims of evidence destruction and the promotion of accuracy of the fact-finding process . . . Finally, judges have recognized the role which sanctions play in the management of cases on a crowded docket . . .

On the one hand, judges must be careful to tailor the remedy to the problem, and "take pains neither to use an elephant gun to slay a mouse nor to wield a cardboard sword if a dragon looms . . . The sanction to be applied needs to be one which is " 'appropriate to the truth-finding process, not one that . . . serve[s] only further to suppress evidence.' " . . .

I conclude that the burden of proof for sanctions should be as stringent as the circumstances require. If a judge intends to order a dismissal or default judgment because of discovery violations, the judge should do so only if the judge is impressed to do so by evidence which is clear and convincing.

When the party has alleged the destruction of evidence, as Gates has alleged in this case, the party may be assisted by a presumption or inference that the destruction of the material was prejudicial to its case.

The purpose of the sanctions hearing was to determine whether or not any of the defendants had violated any discovery obligations, and, if so, to determine what sanctions would be appropriate for each violation. The lawyers for Gates argued continuously that the conduct of people associated with Bando was sufficiently serious that the most extreme sanction of default judgment was warranted. I do not agree.

Two former employees of Gates, Newman and Piderit, have been found by Judge Sparr to have stolen certain of Gates' computer programs, and to have utilized them in their activities at Bando. The facts which underlie this finding by Judge Sparr were not disputed by Bando during the sanctions proceedings. The lawyers for Gates attempted to persuade me that the actions of Newman and Piderit were a reflection of a grand conspiracy among all of the employees of the Bando corporations to conceal or destroy evidence. I am not persuaded.

The lawyers for Gates deposed numerous individuals associated with Bando. The lawyers have argued that every one of these individuals is a liar. With the possible exceptions of Newman and Piderit, I did not find this to be the case. For the most part, I found the employees of Bando to be ordinary people who were thrust into an extremely difficult set of circumstances by my Site Inspection Order, and did the best that they could toward interpreting and understanding the requirements of that order. Neither Newman nor Piderit testified at the sanctions hearing.

Viewing the evidence as a whole, there is overwhelming evidence to support Bando's point that Gates received full and complete cooperation from Bando employees during the site inspection. One of Gates' lawyers, Stephen Craig, noted in an affidavit that literally "millions of pages of documents" were produced for review, inspection and copying. The lawyers for Gates argue that I should ignore this massive production of material, some of it revealing the very core of Bando's manufacturing processes, and focus instead on the relatively few pages which Gates claims have been concealed or destroyed. In the circumstances of this case, that argument represents a reversal of priorities.

The lawyers for Gates have delayed this case for the better part of three and one-half years over an exaggerated concern with minutiae. They had little idea what they were looking for during the site inspection. They copied very little of the type of materials which they now complain were destroyed by the defendants. They admit that they have not examined any of the large quantity of boxes of documents which they did copy and preserve. In fact, the lawyers for Gates have argued vociferously that they have not yet even started discovery on the merits of this controversy. Harm from the alleged destruction of documents must be measured in light of what is produced, as well as what is not produced . . . Gates has no idea what has been produced . . .

In the omitted portion of the case, which goes on for some length, the magistrate details all the types of computer files at issue, which include overwritten hard drives, a laptop computer that was disposed of, spreadsheets, deleted word processing files, shredders, and "wiped" hard drives. As you can see, when the party alleging spoliation brought forth their concerns and evidence, the court made orders to address the concern, requiring segregation of the appropriate computer-based evidence. The problem was that the party didn't know when to let it go. Three and a half years of discovery and a six-week trial for discovery sanctions is a bit much, even in a multimillion dollar case, when you don't ever really get a smoking gun. Settling would have been much more to the party's benefit.

However, these kinds of "ex-employee" cases can be as emotional and personal as a divorce case, and an aggressive attorney and an angry, betrayed employer who is also a take-no-prisoners type of businessman can egg each other on into some wasteful litigation: wasteful in the sense of wasting the client's money, wasteful in the sense of unnecessarily prolonging the life of the lawsuit, wasteful of the court's resources (which the judge will let you know about, as this one did, making Gates pay the attorney's fees for Bando), and wasteful of the emotional energy of the litigants, witnesses, and legal staff.

As this court articulated, the requirements for sanctions for **spoliation** will depend on what kind of sanction you are seeking. A **dispositive** sanction is one that will dispose of the case because it automatically hands the case over to the opposing party either in fact (as in a summary judgment) or in effect (striking pleadings, which, although it does not directly give an order or judgment, will result in a judgment). The two factors are the intent of the party destroying the evidence and the effect it has on the ability of the other party to present its case. If the sanction is dispositive, the moving party must prove its case with clear and convincing evidence. This is only one approach to spoliation; some states approach it differently. Another approach will be addressed in the discussion of physical evidence.

DEATH PENALTY SANCTIONS

Dispositive orders are the worst of sanctions, the so-called **death penalty sanctions,** and are only imposed after a history of **discovery abuse** within the same case. This is somewhat annoying when you identify firms that are always on the verge of sanctions, but have enough of a sense of self-preservation not to fall off the edge, and therefore never seem to get sanctioned for the same sort of objectional behavior demonstrated in case after case. Judges are aware that these attorneys play these games, but they are required to justify a death penalty sanction, not through showing a pattern of behavior by the lawyer, but a pattern in the case. Why? Because the death penalty sanction mostly punishes the client—not the lawyer—by depriving the client of his opportunity to have the case tried on the merits (on the substance of the case rather than procedurally).

Here's one case where the court finally decided it was time to send the case to the guillotine for misbehavior on the part of both the lawyers and the clients. The judge takes care to explain that there's a difference between plain ol' weirdness in the discovery process and lies and refusal. In the midst of all the problems, try to focus particularly on what happens with regard to electronic evidence. The case also makes several references to compliance discovery, which refers to additional formal investigation to determine whether the parties had complied with her orders. To follow the chain of events in this extraordinarily lengthy case, you may want to make a flow chart or timeline, but stick with it—the cumulative effect of all the things that happened in the case make it a prime example of lawyers behaving badly.

Metropolitan Opera Association, Inc., v. Local 100, Hotel Employees and Restaurant Employees International Union, **212 F.R.D. 178 (S.D.N.Y. 2003).**

"A lawsuit is supposed to be a search for the truth," . . . and the tools employed in that search are the rules of discovery. Our adversary system relies in large part on the good faith and diligence of counsel and the parties in abiding by these rules and conducting themselves and their judicial business honestly.

The judicial system prefers to resolve controversies on the merits . . . In the ordinary course, lawsuits should not be resolved based on who did what to whom during discovery. Indeed, a result driven by discovery abuse is justified only on the rarest of occasions and then only after the miscreant has demonstrated unquestionable bad faith and has had a last clear chance to comply with the rules.

Some judges come to the bench from academia, some from government service, some from private practice. Because I came to the bench from private civil practice, I am familiar with the hurly-burly of the discovery process in a hotly-contested civil case, with the existence of sharp elbows, speaking objections, rude responses and with the ever-popular, much-cited Rambo litigation tactics. I am certainly familiar, both from practice and from my time on the bench, with discovery disputes that devolve into arguments about which child threw the first spitball.

The discovery process in this case, however, transcended the usual clashes between adversaries, sharp elbows, spitballs and even Rambo litigation tactics. This case was qualitatively different. It presented the unfortunate combination of lawyers who completely abdicated their responsibilities under the discovery rules and as officers of the court and clients who lied and, through omission and commission, failed to search for and produce documents and, indeed, destroyed evidence—all to the ultimate prejudice of the truth-seeking process. As confirmed by discovery into the Union's and its counsel's compliance with the Met's discovery requests, both the lawyers and the clients exhibited utter and complete disregard for the rules of the truth-seeking process in civil discovery . . .

Though perhaps technically sufficient for relief under one or the other of the rules or statutes forming the basis of the Met's motion, any one of these discovery failures, standing alone, would not ordinarily move a court to impose the most severe sanction . . .

. . . I am cognizant of the relatively lengthy discussion in the Union's papers about discovery failings by the Met, the Met's motivations on this motion and the like.[1] As the referee on the ground in this engagement, however, I reject the Union's . . . justification that the Met and its counsel participated in the same type of conduct that is the basis of the motion. To the extent that there were failings by the Met or its counsel, they were well within the normal hurly-burly of the discovery process and, in any event, were promptly addressed. The conduct of the Union and its counsel, on the other hand, transcended the hurly-burly into gross negligence, recklessness, willfulness and lying . . .

II. THE ALLEGATIONS IN THE ACTION

In this action, the Met alleges that the Union used "the Met's name and prestige . . . as a weapon" in both Local 100's dispute with RA and in Local 100's larger campaign to promote

> membership and power by installing the Union as the collective bargaining representative of workers, both at the [Met] and elsewhere, without having to undergo a statutorily-approved, NLRB-supervised, secret-ballot election.

. . . According to the Met, since 1999, Local 100 continuously has sought to unionize the RA employees working on the Met's premises by way of a "card check" process, which is a non-statutory recognition procedure . . . To further this goal, Local 100 allegedly attempted to induce the Met, through fraudulent and coercive means, "to abandon its neutral stance in the existing dispute between Local 100 and RA over the method used for recognition." . . . According to the Met, its refusal to side with the Union prompted Local 100 "to harass, intimidate, threaten, defame, and injure the Met, and thereby coerce the Met to support the Union's card check procedure against RA's proposed secret-ballot election procedure." . . . .More specifically, the Met asserts that Local 100 has: distributed false, misleading and defamatory leaflets and letters about the labor dispute and the Met's involvement in it; attempted to extort the support of Met officers, employees, donors,

---

[1]In light of the obvious seriousness of the allegations in the Met's moving papers on this motion, it is remarkable that Marianne Yen, the Herrick Feinstein associate primarily responsible for the Union's document production and the only lawyer who submitted an opposing affidavit for the time period comprising the bulk of discovery, devotes three paragraphs of her responsive declaration . . . to discovery on her watch and fifteen paragraphs to the Met's perceived failings and its motivations . . .

patrons, and directors by threatening to involve them in the dispute; encouraged Met employees, donors, and patrons to boycott the Met and withhold monetary contributions; interfered with public funding of the Met; and violated court orders by demonstrating and holding rallies in and around the Met . . . Furthermore, Local 100 allegedly has "willfully and unlawfully traded on the Met's name to obtain economic benefits for themselves [sic], to garner unwarranted publicity for their [sic] actions, and otherwise to trade on the Met's status, reputation, name and mark for their [sic] own gain." . . .

III. THE COURSE OF DISCOVERY

A. Discovery on Lynett's Watch[6]

1. The Met's First Document Request

The Met served its First Document Request with the Complaint on May 2, 2000, and asked for . . . all documents that (a) "concerned communications which concern the Met;" (b) were communicated to or intended to be communicated to the Met or any patron, donor, potential patron or donor, Board member, or agent of the foregoing (listing names); (c) concerned any of the foregoing; (d) concerned use or application of pressure on the Met or any of the foregoing persons; and (e) concerned the Union "candlelight vigil" of March 30, 2000, the rally of May 11, 2000, or any other rally or similar event planned to occur through September 30, 2000 . . . Joseph Lynett, who was the Union's in-house counsel at that time and soon after became an associate at Herrick Feinstein on May 15, 2000, was counsel of record . . . At about that time, Lynett gave a copy of the Complaint and the First Document Request to Brooks Bitterman, Local 100's Research Director, and William Granfield, who at the time was the Union's Secretary/Treasurer and is now its President . . . Bitterman is not a lawyer, and there is no indication in the record that Granfield is a lawyer.

On May 4, 2000, Justice Kapnick of the New York Supreme Court issued a TRO after a hearing, and on May 12, the Union removed the case to this Court. At a pretrial conference on May 18, I ordered the Union to produce documents on an expedited basis because the Preliminary Injunction and Contempt Hearing ("PI Hearing") was scheduled to commence on May 24, 2000.

On May 23, 2000, the day before the PI Hearing, I held a teleconference with counsel and directed the parties to produce documents to each other that day. The Met received defendants' expedited production of approximately 500–600 pages, which consisted largely of leaflets that had been disseminated by the Union and form letters that the Union had sent to donors and directors of the Met . . . According to the Met, there were virtually no internal Local 100 documents, and Local 100 neither made objections to the First Document Request nor provided a written Rule 34 Response . . .

At the commencement of the PI Hearing on May 24, 2000, Deborah Lans, counsel for the Met, told the Court, "I have a concern about the completeness of the document production that was made to us." . . . Specifically, she noted that no letters or other communications that the Union had sent out subsequent to May 1 had been produced, even though the Met knew the Union had sent several because the Met had obtained them from third parties. When I questioned Lynett at the hearing, he said he believed that a search had been made and that all letters had been produced. . . . adding, "The union's records aren't kept in that great of order, but I have Mr. Bitterman here and I can consult with him," to which I responded, "I presume it was not he who was going to search the files," . . .

In his deposition testimony of March 22, 2002, Lynett recalled meeting with Bitterman, Granfield, and Diaz in May 2000 regarding the document demands and providing them with copies of the Met's First Document Request. . . Lynett "instructed [Bitterman] to alert all [Local 100] staff that all Met-related documents

---

[6]Lynett appeared as Union counsel at the outset of the case in federal court and generally presided over the Union's response to the Met's First Document Request . . . ("Well, you have to understand something that I was not really involved much in discovery after that initial production on May 23rd" [2000]); 37 (no other role regarding discovery); 49–50 (never doubled back after injunction hearing to assure completeness of production); 64 (had no conversations with his successor as in-house counsel to the Union, Jamin Sewell, or with the Union's later-retained outside counsel, Michael Anderson, about the Union's discovery obligations). Lynett did not submit an affidavit in connection with this motion.

must be retained." . . . Passing for the moment what a "Met-related" document is, Bitterman failed to follow this instruction in that he only alerted some Union employees, certainly not all of those who were likely to have relevant documents. Lynett also recalled that he conducted a search of Bitterman's, Diaz's, and Granfield's file cabinets for responsive documents on or about May 20, 2001 . . . and that Bitterman and Granfield also must have done a search because they provided him with documents around that time . . . Lynett, however, could not specifically recall discussing with Bitterman, Granfield, or Diaz what types of documents would be responsive . . . and there is no indication in the record that Lynett ever discussed with Bitterman or anyone else at the Union, inter alia, that a "document included all drafts and non-identical copies and electronically-stored documents." Lynett never doubled back after the PI Hearing to assure the completeness of the Union's expedited document production . . . and had no conversations about discovery compliance with those who replaced him, Jamin Sewell and Michael Anderson . . .

Two days later at the PI Hearing, on May 26, 2000, Lans again raised the issue of defendants' lack of production, citing particular items in the Met's First Document Request of May 2, 2000 . . . Lynett stated, "Your Honor, we have turned over every document that we have except for privileged documents . . . I am representing that we conducted a search, a thorough search on this matter" . . . The colloquy continued:

> **MS. LANS:** I think what he is saying to you, your Honor, is he may have given me—done his best to give me the things you ordered him to give me a day early, last week—I don't believe he means to say he has responded to my discovery request.
>
> **THE COURT:** Counsel, have you produced every responsive document [sic]?
>
> **MR. LYNETT:** Yes, your Honor, we have produced all documents responsive to that request.

. . . Despite Lynett's having been presented with a last clear chance to remedy the situation by Lans' calling attention to the failures of production on May 24, compliance discovery confirmed not only that these representations in open court were false but also that a thorough search, albeit on an expedited basis, had not been conducted and, therefore, that there was no basis whatsoever for the representation.

B. Discovery on Anderson's Watch[7]

1. The Met's Duplicate Document Request to Bitterman

In early August 2000, the Met served a notice for the deposition of Brooks Bitterman and attached thereto another document request addressed solely to Bitterman, which merely repeated the requests made on May 2 . . . On August 25, 2000, defendants produced documents that they said were, together with the production made in May, "all the nonprivileged documents responsive to the requests for documents served upon Brooks Bitterman and a privilege log [which]. . . covers all documents in the Union's possession." . . . Some of those documents had been generated subsequent to May, but many others predated the First Document Request . . . Thus, Lynett's May 26 representation of full production proved to be false, and there was no explanation of why the earlier-produced documents had not been produced in a timely fashion. In any event, this August 25 representation of full production was also false and without basis.

Michael T. Anderson had assumed responsibility for supervising discovery for the defendants in August 2000 . . . Anderson's firm, Davis Cowell & Bowe LLP, filed a notice of appearance in this case on August 21, 2000 . . . According to Anderson, "Bitterman was the most logical choice to act as custodian of records because he and the researchers he supervises generated and maintained virtually all of the documents that were called for in the Met's first two sets of document requests." . . . Anderson never visited the Union's office but contented himself with talking on the telephone to Bitterman about Met-related issues . . .

On February 2, 2001, Met attorney Vincent Pentima wrote to Anderson "regarding the sufficiency and propriety of the Defendants' response to Plaintiffs' First Request for the Production of Documents dated May 2, 2000 . . . in an effort to resolve matters prior to seeking the Court's intervention." . . . Pentima stated that,

---

[7] In his Declaration dated April 25, 2002 . . . Anderson states that he "does not specialize in trial work or in discovery litigation," . . . that he came into the case in June of 2000 and commenced discovery activity in August of 2000 . . . He states that he "transitioned" out of the case by the end of July 2001 . . . Anderson never withdrew as Union counsel.

although defendants maintained that all responsive documents had been produced, the evidence showed that was not the case. He cited various types of documents which Union representatives had testified about at the PI Hearing in May 2000, but which had never been produced. He noted specifically that, although the First Document Request was a continuing one, no documents more current than May 2000 had been produced,[8] no notes or drafts of any kind had been produced, and no documents to, from and/or about RA which mentioned the Met (except the leaflets and letters) had been provided. He requested that defendants "conduct a thorough search and both provide written responses to our requests and a full production of documents." . . .

Anderson responded by letter of February 6, 2001, stating that he had reviewed, with his client, Pentima's letter and the categories of documents referenced therein and that defendants would supplement their production to include "all new documents generated since our production in August." . . . Anderson indicated that Bitterman would search the Union records for certain responsive documents . . . On February 16, 2001, Anderson wrote to Pentima and indicated that he would provide the Met with "new [Union] documents generated since our [last] production" and any other documents referenced on February 6 . . .

On February 22, 2001, Anderson made a "supplemental production" which he said included "all responsive non-privileged documents generated to date since the Union's production in May 2000, as well as any further responsive documents you inquired about in your February 2, 2001 letter." . . . He also noted that "a file drawer of publicly available documents relating to the Met and various directors and donors" would be made available at Herrick Feinstein for inspection . . . Compliance discovery confirmed that Anderson's February 22 representation of full production was false and was without basis.

Pentima responded on March 22, 2001 "concerning defendants' still inadequate document production." . . . He wrote, "Once again, I call upon defendants to provide us with a complete production of their documents" and he noted as an example of what "plainly" had not been provided that no e-mails had been produced . . . He further noted, "It would appear that only a smattering of notes, messages and the like have been provided and we question the search made by defendants." . . . Again, he demanded a written document . . . to the Met's First Document Request that had been served almost one year before . . .

Anderson responded by letter on April 10, 2001 . . . together with a formal Response to the Met's First Document Request and a "supplemental production of documents generated since our last production in February," which only included documents from February 2001 to April 2001 . . . With respect to e-mails, he noted two that had been produced earlier and six more that were included in the current production and he represented that these were "all [the] responsive emails stored by the Union." . . . That this representation was without basis is demonstrated by Anderson's Declaration which notes no discussion of e-mails until after May 25 . . . Of the eight e-mails, six contained the same text, simply an advertisement by the Union of its "Workers' Rights Hearing." . . . The two pre-2001 e-mails were two that had simply come into the Union's internet site; there was not one e-mail sent by anyone at the Union . . . With respect to Pentima's comment about the lack of notes, messages, etc., Anderson again stated, "We have produced all non-privileged written documents in the Union's records responsive to your request." . . . The formal Response to the Met's Request was signed by Anderson and represented that "Defendants have produced all non-privileged documents responsive to [questions 1, 4-6] throughout the course of this litigation."[9] Compliance discovery has also confirmed that the April 10 representations of full production were false and without basis.

2. The Met's Second Document Request

On May 25, 2001, the Met served a Second Request for Documents, which was intended to encompass all that had been covered by the First Request but to be more specific so that, to the extent defendants had been interpreting the word "responsive" in a narrow way, there could be no question of what had been requested . . . Also on that date, Charles Stillman, counsel for the Met, wrote to Anderson . . . He stated, "We are troubled by Defendants' failure to produce whole categories of responsive documents," giving examples of "all internal communications concerning the Met," "all e-mails concerning the Met," "the thousands of letters sent by

---

[8] Pentima was not precisely correct, because a handful of documents included in the August 2000 production had been generated since May.

[9] . . . No Response was ever made to the Met's Fourth Request.

defendants to Met directors, officers, employees, donors and patrons," "the drafts of all documents created by defendants concerning the Met," and "the responses by RA employees at the Met to the 'Survey of Working and Living Conditions.' ". . .

Anderson reviewed Stillman's May 25 letter with Bitterman, "questioned [Bitterman] about all issues raised there, and reviewed with [Bitterman] what documents (subject to objections) were responsive to the Met's Second Request." . . . Bitterman believed that only two flyers and "a handful of responses" had been sent or received by e-mail . . . Anderson "instructed the Union to search its files for any notes relating to the Met, [and] to construct a log showing what people on the Union's mail-merge list received the letters in the record . . . including any documents sent by e-mail." . . . Passing again the meaning of "notes relating to the Met," there is no indication that Anderson (or anyone else) made inquiry to assure this instruction was carried out.

On May 30, 2001, the Union made a supplemental production of documents which consisted almost entirely of form letters sent in April and May 2001 by the Union to colleagues and fellow board members of boards other than the Met on which Met board members also sat . . . However, no other documents were produced, and Stillman received no response to his May 25 letter . . . Stillman wrote again on June 28, 2001, noting Anderson's lack of response and informing him that, unless the Met received assurance that the deficiencies in production would be corrected by July 10 (the date for response to the Met's Second Document Request), the Met would seek appropriate sanctions with the Court . . .

Anderson responded on July 10, 2001, enclosing defendants' Responses and Objections to the Met's Second Document Request . . . Because a pretrial conference with the Court was scheduled to be held on July 18, Anderson and Stillman agreed to meet on July 17 to discuss discovery matters . . . In his July 10 letter, Anderson stated that the Union had compiled documents in response to the Met's Second Document Request, as well as further documents responsive to the First "ongoing" Request that would be made available to the Met on July 12 at Herrick Feinstein's office . . . Anderson also responded to some of the examples of inadequate production listed in Stillman's May 25 letter . . . Except for specific categories of items the Met's letter had mentioned, however, nothing in Anderson's letter indicated that a thorough search had been made or that any document production had been supervised or conducted by an attorney.

In its Response to the Met's Second Document Request, signed by Anderson, the Union objected to the production of clearly relevant information, apparently taking the position that unless material specifically "concerned the Met," it was outside the scope of the pleadings . . . Thus, for example, it deemed all communications with New York City Council members (whom the Met alleged the Union had importuned to withhold money from the Met and from the Lincoln Center Redevelopment Project because of the RA situation at the Met) and communications concerning the food and beverage service at Lincoln Center facilities (all of which are run by Restaurant Associates and, except for the Met, unionized by Local 100) as not relevant . . . In response to a request for documents concerning the Union's retention, storage, or deletion of e-mails or of communications or drafts thereof, defendants objected . . . giving no further information . . . Coming as it did after repeated questions by Met counsel about the Union's document retention procedures, especially relating to e-mails and counsel's early admission that "the Union's records aren't kept in that great of order" . . . this response, although technically correct, is wholly inconsistent with counsel's obligations to conduct discovery in good faith.

When Met counsel went to inspect the items made available at the Herrick Feinstein office on July 12 and received the production to which Anderson had referred, they found that many documents were being produced that were clearly responsive to the Met's First Request served 15 months earlier . . . The production contained documents dating from 1999 to the then-current date, and the Met received no information as to which Union files they had come from or why they had not been produced earlier.[10] On July 12, defendants also produced the e-mail log that Anderson had directed the Union to reconstruct in May.

Counsel for both sides scheduled a meeting on July 17 to discuss these matters, but as soon as the July 17 meeting began, Anderson informed Met counsel that defendants were obtaining "new" attorneys and, therefore, he would not speak about the Union's document production because that would be up to the "new"

---

[10] In fact, the Met later learned that Brooks Bitterman had created subject-oriented files for the purpose of the production . . .

attorneys . . . Anderson would not discuss matters further, stating that he believed the Union's production was complete and that Met counsel could raise any problems with the Court the following day. That supposedly new counsel were to appear did not, however, prevent Anderson from discussing what he viewed as deficiencies in the Met's production of documents.

At the conference with the Court the following day, the Union introduced its new attorneys at Herrick Feinstein, the firm that had been the attorneys of record for the Union before Anderson's first contact with the case in June 2000 and had continued, together with Anderson, as the attorneys of record . . . Met counsel began to explain the inadequacies in defendants' discovery compliance, but Anderson stated that he could no longer speak to the point, and the Herrick Feinstein lawyers stated that they were not yet familiar with the situation. While perhaps warranted in situations where genuinely new counsel are substituted, . . . here where the Herrick Feinstein firm had been counsel of record throughout, such cat-and-mouse conduct is not consistent with counsel's obligation to engage in discovery in good faith.

3. Electronic Documents

During the July 18 conference, I overruled essentially all of the defendants' objections to specific document requests. Anderson stated that he had not specifically instructed the Union not to delete computer files and that no retention procedure had been put in place. Met counsel also explained that, apparently, no attorney had conducted or supervised the Union's document production and, three months before the then-fixed close of discovery, the Met was unable to take depositions and develop its case because of defendants' failure to make proper disclosure. In response to the Met's concerns about how document discovery had been conducted, defendants' counsel stated that they would look into it. I directed defendants' counsel to clarify immediately with their clients that all documents relevant to the Met's document requests must be preserved, expressly making the order applicable to all work done on computers and all information sent out or received through computers . . . In that conference, Union counsel undertook that all of the Union's ISPs would be contacted in an effort to retrieve deleted electronic documents . . . Compliance discovery later revealed that some but not all ISPs were contacted.

At that time, Anderson "mistakenly believed that e-mails are always automatically stored on the user's server" and he "had not specifically focused on e-mails in [his] original [instructions to his client]." . . . After the July 18 conference, Anderson asked Bitterman whether e-mails were automatically stored, and Bitterman directed Anderson to check with Union staff members Dahlia Ward and Michelle Travis . . . On July 20, Anderson called Ward and Travis, learned that the Union's staff's servers did not store e-mail after 30 days and "instructed them and Brooks Bitterman to ensure that all staff immediately made all possible adjustments to save e-mail" or to print out hard copies of responsive e-mails and to reconstruct information about e-mails that had not been saved on a log . . . Between July 18 and 30, Anderson "repeatedly" asked Bitterman, Travis, and Ward whether there were responsive internal e-mails among them or to other researchers and "emphasized" that any such e-mails must be either produced or disclosed as lost . . . Anderson further "directed that all Union staff make hard copies of all responsive incoming and outgoing e-mails, and place them in a box for production" and he "repeated the scope of discovery obligation to include all documents, drafts, e-mails and other materials defined in Plaintiff's Document Requests." . . . Although Anderson states that he "repeated" these instructions, he nowhere states where, when and to whom he gave the initial instruction.

On July 23, Anderson wrote to Met counsel concerning these issues stating, "At my instruction, the Union staff have now gone through their computers to see if any e-mails had been overlooked, and to compare the hard copies in our production to identify any missing e-mails." . . . Furthermore, Anderson wrote, "My clients understand that they have a duty to retain all Met-related documents. To date, my instructions have been communicated to the Union staff through Brooks Bitterman. He has asked all staff to forward copies of all Met-related documents to be placed in a box for our periodic rolling production." . . . He additionally stated:

> Some of the union staff's servers have not been programmed to automatically retain e-mails indefinitely. All staff will now make the necessary adjustments to reprogram their servers to retain all e-mails on the server automatically.

. . . He further explained that the Union had "retrieved" most of the deleted e-mails—that is, to the extent Union staff knew of e-mails they had sent, they contacted the recipients and asked for copies which the recipients might have retained . . . In other words, he explained, where mass mailings had occurred of notice of the May 11 and September 25 rallies the Union held against the Met and the Union had the "mail-merge" list of addresses, it contacted those addressees. Anderson understood that the Union would be contacting its ISPs to see whether e-mails could be retrieved from their servers . . . Although Anderson took some steps to follow up on his various instructions concerning e-mails and other electronic documents . . . he ended his involvement in the case in July, and the remaining follow-up fell between the cracks. For example, Bitterman contacted some but not all of the Union's ISPs.

On July 26, 2001, Stillman wrote to defendants' counsel and pointed out certain problems with the response given in the July 23 letter . . . Among these were the meaning of Met-related documents as opposed to documents requested and relevant to the case, the failure to address computer files other than e-mails, and the failure to explain adequately the e-mail situation and to comply with the Court's ruling . . . Anderson responded on July 30 . . . stating that with regard to the term "Met-related documents," his instructions to his clients "encompass Plaintiff's First Set of Document Requests and the further documents memorialized in your July 18 letter," . . . Anderson did not clarify what he told his clients constituted "Met-related documents;" he referred to the Met's First Document Request, but not the Second, and he referred to the Met's July 18 letter which only identified a few specific categories of documents that had been addressed by the Court at the conference that morning . . . With respect to e-mails, Anderson said that only one Union staff member, Dahlia Ward, had an Internet account that retained e-mails. He further stated:

> The Union found the e-mails of Dahlia Ward and Michelle Travis when counsel Michael Anderson directly contacted Union staff about e-mails last week. Prior to last week, this inquiry had been conducted by Brooks Bitterman. Bitterman had overlooked Ward in asking union staff about e-mails. Michelle Travis recalled rally notices from May and September, 2000 and a small number of other e-mails, and realized they had not been retained nor produced in the last production.

> ***

> The Union has retrieved missing e-mails by contacting the known addressees. It has also contacted the internet service providers, who to date have advised that deleted e-mails cannot be recovered.

> ***

> My clients understand that their obligation extends to documents created on computer, whether at the Union office or elsewhere. The Union has provided all responsive information in its hard copy files and in its computers.

. . . Compliance discovery confirmed that this representation was also false in that, inter alia, all ISPs had not been contacted, all Union computers had not been searched, all responsive documents had not been produced, and all files had not been searched . . .

In late July and early August 2001, the Union produced more documents, including "retrieved" e-mails . . . Local 100 produced additional documents later in August and in September. The documents dated back to 1999 and, except for a small number of recent ones, should have been produced earlier.[11]

C. Discovery on Moss' and Yen's Watch

In mid-October 2001, Marianne Yen, an associate who had just joined the Herrick Feinstein firm, learned that she would be assisting James A. Moss, a partner at the firm, with completing discovery and preparing for trial . . . Moss' and Yen's watch extended through the present motion.

1. The Met's Third Document Request—Benefits

The Met's Third Document Request dated October 2, 2001, requested documents "concerning the benefits which Local 100 provides or has provided to its members or their families, including but not limited to health benefits, life insurance, disability benefits, and pension and/or savings plans." . . . In a response dated

---

[11] Because none of the Union's productions was organized in accordance with Fed. R. Civ. P. 34(b), which requires the production of documents either as they are kept in the ordinary course of business or by document request . . . the Met could not know which files had been searched, who the custodian of a particular document had been, or whether a proper search had yet been made.

October 26, 2001, signed by Moss, the Union stated that "there are no responsive documents." . . . In her Declaration, Yen reiterated that "this category of documents does not exist, because benefits are paid not by Local 100, but rather by the employers" . . . Yen also stated that she "personally questioned each employee of Local 100, including the receptionist, and all have stated unequivocally that they have not seen any documents such as the Met has requested, nor have they maintained any such documents in their files. [She] searched various file drawers of Local 100's office where these documents might theoretically be kept and did not discover any." . . .

. . . [O]ther discovery responses demonstrate that the representations that there are no responsive documents are untrue . . . [D]ocuments that have been produced refer to discussions, inquiries and meetings between and among Local 100 personnel concerning benefits . . . These Minutes refer, for example, to Report of New Benefits (10/23/99), Local 100 Welfare Fund Meeting to be run by Tamarin discussing changes to medical, dental and pension benefits (3/4/00), report reviewing new/improved benefits (7/12/00), discussion of new pension plan (8/22/00), announcement of meeting with GHI (healthcare provider) (10/31/00), discussion of pension benefits and GHI (1/22/01), report concerning benefits and funds (1/30/01). There is no explanation by Moss of the basis for the untrue response he signed stating that there were no responsive documents.[12]

D. The Met's Fourth Document Request

The Met's Fourth Document Request dated October 23, 2001 was never responded to because one associate was transitioning out of the case and another transitioning in . . . Moss, the partner in charge during that period, is silent.

1. Depositions

The Met began depositions six weeks before the scheduled discovery deadline, when it believed it had obtained enough information to do so.

a. Granfield

On October 16, 2001, the Met deposed William Granfield, the Union's soon-to-be President (as of October 27, 2001). At the deposition, Granfield explained that Bitterman had the responsibility for searching for and producing documents pursuant to the Met's requests . . . Granfield testified that he was shown the Met's Document Requests (although not given copies) and that he turned over his file "with respect to the campaign at the Met." . . . He did not turn over some of his other files, which included, for example, those containing media materials and correspondence with the International Union . . .

The following day, Met counsel sent a letter to defendants' counsel . . . identifying files that Granfield had withheld, noting once again that no files apparently had been reviewed for production by an attorney, and stating:

> All of these files appear likely to contain responsive material. Furthermore, we can only assume that if Mr. Granfield was allowed to withhold files from review, other officers and/or employees may have acted similarly.
>
> In order to bring the union in compliance with its discovery obligations, please review all of the Union's files to determine if they contain responsive documents.

. . . On November 2, 2001, Yen responded, stating that Granfield's files had not been produced "because a review of those files revealed no relevant documents" but not responding to counsel's complaint that no attorney had reviewed the Union's files . . . On November 7, 2001, Met counsel responded, noting that Granfield had testified that as of the date of his deposition on October 16, those files had not been reviewed to determine if they contained responsive documents . . . Second, the letter noted again,

---

[12] The Met's Third Request instructed that if a responsive document was withheld from production or had been destroyed, the circumstances thereof should be explained . . . The Union's response did not indicate that responsive documents were being withheld or had been destroyed . . .

After Mr. Granfield admitted that all of his files had not been examined, we asked your firm to review all of the Union's files to bring the defendants into compliance with their discovery obligations. Your letter does not state whether a Union-wide review of files by an attorney has taken place. Please confirm that, subsequent to October 16, 2001, such a review has been conducted.

. . . Yen responded on November 13, 2001, . . . disputed the content of Granfield's testimony and then confirmed that Granfield had been asked to review those files after his deposition and found no documents responsive to the Met's Document Requests. Yen said nothing, however, about whether there had been a review of the Union's files in any organized way or under the supervision of any attorney . . .

b. Travis

On November 8, the Met deposed Michelle Travis, a Union researcher. Travis testified that Local 100 holds regular weekly or bi-weekly staff meetings . . . She said this case, including the meaning of the Court's injunction, and the Union's campaign against the Met were discussed at such staff meetings . . . No minutes or notes of such meetings had been produced, even though Travis testified that she, for one, sometimes took notes . . . In addition, Travis was told at some point to print out e-mails and turn them over to Bitterman for this case but had no recollection of when she was told to do so . . . She turned them over to Bitterman when he asked, which he did perhaps about every two weeks . . . In any event, although Travis said she was instructed to turn over e-mails, she admitted she had "forgotten" about it . . . She was never told to set her computer to save any e-mails until the Summer of 2001 (presumably as a result of the July 18 court conference), so e-mails were not retained unless Travis happened to print them out . . . At some point prior to the Summer of 2001, her computer crashed, and she got a new one . . . When testifying about e-mails that were received in response to Local 100's campaign against the Met on Local 100 websites, Travis explained that her computer is not connected to a printer, so when she finally went to produce such e-mails, she cut and pasted them into a Word document, put the new document on a disk and went to another computer to print it out . . . When asked, "You could have hooked your computer up to a printer though, right?," she answered, "Yeah, but I have not done that yet." . . . Further, although Travis sent many letters out, she did not think she was required to keep copies of the actual signed letters, as long as she had a master "form" letter . . . For example, in the space of two days in March 2001, letters signed by Tamarin and personally addressed to each recipient were sent out to members of the New York City Council's Parks, Cultural Affairs, Finance and Labor committees, but no copies of these letters were made. Thus, when the Met asked Travis to whom the letters were sent, Travis relied solely on her memory and on notes Bitterman had written on top of the letters when they were produced based on Travis' recollection . . . Travis testified that "hits" to the Union's three websites, lincolncenterwatch.com metoperacritic.org and metoperawatch.com, could be obtained from the site host (Yahoo) only by Local 100. The Union simply had to request the data from Yahoo . . . Apparently, that request was never made.

c. Diaz

(i) Weekly Reports

On November 15, 2001, the Met deposed Dennis Diaz, Lead Organizer of the Union and an individual defendant in this action, about "Weekly Reports." Weekly Reports show the daily activity of every Union employee, with the sole alleged exception of Bitterman . . . The employees record their activities on a daily basis indicating when they meet with Restaurant Associates workers, leaflet (and the locations thereof), lobby politicians, hold rallies and demonstrations, draft speeches and so forth. In the case of Granfield, the reports (which, it was later learned, he sent to the International Union office because it paid him directly) also track, on a weekly basis, the number of RA workers at the Met who have signed "cards"—a figure used frequently in defendants' challenged leaflets as a supposed measure of worker support . . .

Several of plaintiff's document requests called for production of the reports . . . However, these reports were never produced or otherwise made known in document production or deposition testimony. Contrary to the later-revealed facts just noted, at Granfield's first deposition, held October 16, 2001, he stated:

Q: In the period from January 1999 to the present have you or Mr. Tamarin provided any written reports to your knowledge to the International with respect to your activities?

A: I haven't provided any written reports. I don't know about Henry [Tamarin].

. . . Granfield also testified:

Q: Are there pieces of paper that are in your files that would indicate that you tally up what the vote would look like from time to time?

A: No.

Q: Is that the job of any organizer to do?

A: No.

. . . On July 11, 2001, Diaz, in sworn testimony before the NLRB in a proceeding the Union brought against Lincoln Center, stated:

Q: Do you keep a diary?

A: No.

Q: Do you keep a calendar of your appointments?

A: A calendar of what's going on, yes. But I don't save them.

Q: Do you log what you do on a day-to-day basis? Your activities on behalf of Local 100.

A: No.

. . . Exhibit 57 to the Lans Declaration is Diaz's Weekly Report for the week ending July 14, 2001. In his deposition on November 15, 2001, however, Diaz testified with regard to the Weekly Reports as follows:

Q: Do you see to the left of where it says cafeteria it says report?

A: Yes.

Q: What does it mean?

A: Could be, had to do with my reports, my daily reports. I can't remember –

Q: What are your daily reports?

A: Office reports that we fill in at each week we fill out reports.

Q: What are those reports about?

A: The weekly work that was done.

Q: What do those reports look like? Have we seen any of them today?

A: No.

Q: Are they on a form? Is that a form that you fill in?

A: It is a weekly report. Legal paper.

Q: Do you give it to somebody?

A: Yes.

Q: Who do you give it to?

A: To one of the secretaries from the office that is in charge.

Q: Whose name is?

A: Mary. I forgot what her last name is.

Q: Are you trying to remember Mary's last name?

A: No, I can't remember her last name.

***

Q: Do the research people prepare weekly reports and give them to Mary?

A: I think so, yes.

Q: Do you know whether Mr. Granfield before he became president made weekly reports?

A: I think so, yes.

Q: Does Mary keep all of those in a file together? Is that the idea?

A: Yes.

. . . On the record immediately following Mr. Diaz's revelation, Lans stated:

MS. LANS: . . . Needless to say, Ms. Yen, those would have been called for by any number of our document requests. We've never seen them and I would call for their immediate production.

MR. MOSS: We'll put them on the list of things for us to discuss with respect to immediate production.

MS. LANS: You can say what you want to say. I think that from—

MR. MOSS: And we have. And we have.

MS. LANS: —from May of 2000 they are documents that should have been produced to us.

. . . In his March 25, 2002 deposition, after the existence of the Weekly Reports was revealed,[13] Granfield testified:

Q: Mr. Granfield, the first question is simply are Exhibits 18, 19 and 20 all reports that you prepared and provided to the International on an essentially weekly basis during 1999, 2000 and 2001?

A: Yes.

Q: They're reports on your activities?

A: Yes.

. . . With copies of his Weekly Reports in front of him, displaying that he submitted a weekly tally of worker cards as part of those reports, Granfield testified:

Q: Now, can you turn to the second page of that week? There's a form there, it's a box, it's headed specific activity and then there's a box below that that's called organizing campaigns in representation cases.

A: Yes.

Q: In each of the weekly reports that you prepared was there an entry made with respect to any organizing campaign or representation case that was active in this box?

A: Yes.

Q: Now, is the information that's reported in this box called organizing campaigns and representation cases on a weekly basis information about each of your active organizing campaigns, the number of workers at the unit, the number of committee members at the unit and the number of authorization cards that have been signed at the unit?

A: Yes.

Q: In order to provide this information each week and in particular I mean with respect to the Met Opera which if you were to look at this report page after page you would see you supplied information on every week, did you take a tally of the number of authorization cards that have been signed each week?

A: I would ask the organizer.

Q: So every week you would have a conversation with the organizer about how many cards have been signed?

A: Most weeks, yes.

. . . In attempting to explain his apparently perjurious testimony denying that he provided written reports to the International with respect to his activities, Granfield stated: "the transcript reveals at most that Ms. Lans . . . and I were not on the same wavelength concerning the scope of the questions she asked." . . . Granfield does not consider his weekly time records to be "written reports to the International with respect to [his] activities.". . . Rather, the reports instead account for his time "using general phrases or words to explain where [he] has been during each day of a pay period." . . . When he was deposed, Granfield said, he thought that

---

[13] Exhibit 56 to Lans' Declaration is Granfield's Weekly Report for the week ending Saturday, October 20, 2001, which Granfield signed on October 20, and which the Met received from defendants' counsel on December 28, 2001 . . . Under the heading calling for listing of "current active campaigns," the first page of the Weekly Report shows the "vote" of the workers that week, and the second page shows Mr. Granfield's activities each day of that week . . .

Lans was "seeking to ascertain whether [he] ever sent substantive reports about [his] Union activities to the International." . . . Moreover, the "tally" that the Union kept merely was to record the number of RA workers at the Met who supported the card check process by signing authorization cards . . . By signing the cards, the workers were not voting in an NLRB election and, according to Granfield, the tally therefore did not have anything to do with projecting votes in an NLRB election . . . On November 21, the day after Granfield's first deposition session, Met counsel wrote to Union counsel, stating, "We write to voice our grave concern that defendants continue to withhold documents that are clearly responsive to our discovery requests" . . . The Met asked for immediate production of the Union staff's Weekly Reports and asked, again, for a review of the Union's files by Union counsel . . . The Met further stated:

> Based on Mr. Granfield's failure to turn over files for review that likely contained responsive documents, and based on the revelation at Mr. Diaz's deposition that Mr. Diaz and other Local 100 officers create "weekly reports" of their activities that have never been turned over to the Met, we have serious concerns about the completeness of the entirety of defendants' production. Although this is the third time that we have written you about this matter, you still have not provided us with any assurance that an attorney has reviewed all the Union's files to determine if they contain documents responsive to the Met's discovery requests.

. . . In a letter to the Court responding to one of defendants' letters, Met counsel, after addressing the issues raised by defendants, informed the Court that the Met had a number of issues about defendants' continued noncompliance with their discovery obligations:

> The most troublesome . . . is defendants' continuing failure to comply with simple blackletter discovery obligations . . . [D]efendants, over one year after the start of this litigation and service of our discovery requests, had never made a proper search and were routinely deleting responsive documents from their computers. We have since been informed by defendants that many deleted files cannot be recovered. It is undisputed that relevant information was thus lost to us. Since depositions of Union principals and employees began about a month ago, we have now learned of additional critical documents that continue to be destroyed as well as of the existence of an untold number of potentially critical documents that were never produced due to defendants' counsel's failure still to do a proper search and otherwise comply with their obligations under the law.

***

> For example, defendant Dennis Diaz, lead organizer of the Union, testified last week that each Union organizer and researcher working on the campaign against the Met wrote weekly reports of his or her activities. These have gone unreviewed by defendants' counsel and unproduced.

. . . In response to the various letters, I directed counsel to confer and report to me in writing on November 27. On November 27, the parties sent separate letters to the Court. Met counsel wrote:

> Defendants have refused to certify that a complete search of the Union's records has been made by counsel for documents responsive to the Met's various document requests.
>
>   This refusal is profoundly troubling to the Met. Some examples of our problem were brought to light at recent depositions of Local 100 employees. The Met learned of the existence of "weekly reports" that organizers and researchers of the Union's campaign against the Met are required to submit to the Union, as well as whole files not reviewed or produced. The problem appears to be the defendants' method of "searching" for documents—without the benefit of the Met's documents requests themselves, certain of Local 100's lay-employees were asked to search their own files and select what was to be given to counsel; other employees apparently were not even asked to review their files. We were thus told last evening, for example, that the "weekly reports" were in the Union's payroll department, which was not searched. It goes without saying that simply allowing lay-employees to select what to provide to counsel is not adequate compliance.

In a footnote Met counsel informed the Court that defendants had now agreed to produce the "Weekly Reports," although they continued to claim that they were not relevant or responsive to any Met document request.[14] The Met asserted that defendants' position of the Reports' nonrelevance "raises further concern about the completeness of defendants' production." . . .

The Stillman & Easterly Letter also provided a last clear chance to the Union and its counsel on benefits. . . . Stillman and Easterly note that while the Union maintained that no benefits documents . . . exist, "minutes of local 100 Executive Board Meetings specifically reference both meetings about member benefits and efforts by Local 100 to improve these benefits." . . . No responsive documents were ever produced.

When the Union only produced Diaz's and Hoffman's Weekly Reports and an updated privilege log on November 26, 2001 . . . Met counsel wrote a letter to defendants stating, "Your failure to produce all of the weekly reports created by Local 100 officers and employees (and your vacillating responses to our request for these documents) is inconsistent with a good faith effort to comply with your discovery obligations," . . . The Met further listed specific requests to which the reports were responsive . . .

In response, instead of looking to whether the Weekly Reports were or were not responsive to any outstanding document request, Yen stated that defendants believed that the reports had not been previously asked for because "they conceivably could be considered a 'schedule' and thus such reports were produced for the particular employees from whom schedules were sought and who submitted these weekly reports." . . . As was later learned, Yen decided, apparently unilaterally and certainly without informing Met counsel, not to produce all the Weekly Reports regarding the Met campaign on this narrow, stilted basis. Nevertheless, Yen stated that the Union would produce the Weekly Reports "for Local 100 employees who worked on the Met Opera campaign." . . . Compliance discovery confirmed that even this last clear chance was rejected, and such production was never completed.

Easterly wrote to Yen on December 4, 2001, noting that the Met had not yet received any further production and that the Weekly Reports should be produced immediately for all Local 100 employees who participated in any way in the campaign against the Met . . . and on the same day Easterly told Yen that, in addition, monthly reports were required to be submitted by Local 100 to the International, yet none of those had ever been produced . . . On December 5, defendants produced some additional Weekly Reports.

Easterly wrote letters to Yen on December 10 and December 11 regarding several specific areas in which the defendants had failed to produce documents . . . Among Easterly's written and previously telephoned requests were those documents concerning Tamarin, whose deposition was scheduled for December 11. On December 10, Easterly wrote:

> . . . [T]he weekly reports submitted by Local 100 officers and employees to the Union are clearly covered by document requests dating back to May 2000. Nevertheless, the weekly reports for Mr. Diaz and Mr. Hoffman were not produced until November 26, 2001, after their non-production was exposed at Mr. Diaz' deposition. Weekly reports for Dahlia Ward, Michelle Travis and Amanda Ream were not produced until December 5, 2001, and only after we reminded you, once again, of your discovery obligations. Today you informed me for the first time that Mr. Bitterman and Mr. Granfield filed activity reports with the International Union and that they are "trying" to obtain copies of these reports. You also stated that you did not know if Mr. Tamarin filed such reports with HEREIU. Needless to say, defendants should have kept copies of the reports submitted to the International Union as they are clearly responsive to a number of our document requests. Moreover, these reports should have been produced (and subsequently updated) in response to our initial document requests and in response to our subpoena to the International. Finally, at this stage in the game, you should know whether Mr. Tamarin filled out such reports when he was President of Local 100. Please produce these reports immediately. As with the agendas and minutes referenced above, Mr. Tamarin's reports should be produced before his deposition begins . . .

---

[14]Union counsel's position that the Weekly Reports were not responsive or relevant is wholly without merit. One need only compare the first request in the Met's First Rule 34 Request, "documents concerning communications that concern the Met," . . . to a Weekly Report . . . For example, page one of Granfield's Weekly Report form asks for a listing of "current active campaigns" and, as to each, the " # of signed cards." Page two asks for a daily listing of activities, including "campaign planning re:" or "meetings re:". Any mention of the Union's then-ongoing campaign against the Met would likely have made the document responsive.

d. Tamarin

Despite this clear request, however, no further production was made, and the Met deposed Tamarin on December 11 without his Weekly Reports and the other documents the Met had requested . . . At that deposition, the Met asked Tamarin whether he had ever filed Weekly Reports, and he responded affirmatively . . . When asked what kinds of activities he reported on those forms, he answered, "whether you had meetings, if so what kinds of meetings, organizing campaigns, house visits on organizing campaigns, if any, grievances, . . . negotiations." . . . The deposition continued:

Q: Have your counsel in this case asked you to provide them with copies of those reports?

A: Yesterday evening.

Q: Yesterday evening?

A: Yes.

Q: Have your counsel in this case ever asked you to provide them with your files relating to Restaurant Associates, the Metropolitan Opera, card check neutrality agreements or the like?

A: Not prior to yesterday evening.

Q: Did you ever provide your files so far as they relate [to] the Met, RA, the activities at the Met, card check agreements?

A: I believe I was asked last year and provided whatever I had at that time.

Q: Asked by whom?

A: It was either Joe Lynett or Brooks Bitterman.

***

Q: You stated last year, so you're talking about some time in 2000?

A: I believe so.

Q: . . . Between last year and last night were you asked for anything?

A: I don't have a recollection.

Q: Last night were you asked for anything other than your weekly reports?

A: No.

. . . Thus, after a month of activity surrounding Weekly Reports, which should have been produced in response to the Met's First Document Request in May of 2000, and after a specific plea by Met counsel the day before Tamarin's deposition for production of his Weekly Reports, not only were they not produced in time for the deposition, but Union counsel did not even ask him for them until the night before his deposition. Such conduct is wholly inconsistent with counsel's obligation to conduct discovery in good faith.

(i) Subsidies

Later in the deposition, Tamarin was questioned about a letter of February 28, 2001 that he had written relating to a subsidy to Local 100 from the International, which responded to a letter from the International. He also testified to a written request for a subsidy renewal that he had sent the International. When asked if he had any idea why neither of those had been provided to the Met, he responded, "No."

It appears that there are other responsive documents relating to subsidies, shown by other discovery to have existed, that have not been produced . . . In explaining the production of documents from his files, Tamarin stated that he was given a list, which might have been only a verbal list, of files and documents to look for. He did some of it personally and delegated the rest to Bitterman. Tamarin had no record of what he or Bitterman looked at. He did not believe he had looked at any files in his office in Chicago which he had occupied since November 1999 and from which he dealt with the Union's campaign against the Met. He had no recollection of looking through any files to turn over to his lawyers for possible production from the time he did so in 2000 until the night before his deposition, other than his date books. He then remembered that he was also asked the night before his deposition about a letter he signed to cultural venues in Chicago. Although this correspondence had taken place close to a year earlier, in January 2001, and included documents defendants created after the commencement of this case and long after the Met's document requests had been served, the Union had produced only a draft and had not looked through Tamarin's Chicago files to see if the finalized letter still existed. When Tamarin was asked if he had copies, he said, "Well, I don't know. We're looking." . . .

On December 13, two days after the deposition, Yen sent a letter to Easterly, enclosing Tamarin's letter to the International and stating that she was looking for the other specific documents that had been revealed as never having been produced . . .

On December 17, 2001, defendants wrote to the Court requesting an extension of time beyond the December 31, 2001 discovery deadline to take the depositions of certain non-party witnesses who were unavailable in December . . . In a lengthy letter to the Court dated December 18, 2001, Met counsel stated that the defendants "have remained willfully ignorant of their obligations, failed to retain responsive documents, failed to conduct meaningful searches of the documents actually in their possession, and failed to produce wholesale categories of documents" and outlined the events of the discovery process from May 2000 to that point . . . The Met requested permission to take discovery on the issue of defendants' discovery compliance and to re-depose certain key witnesses whom the Met had deposed earlier without the benefit of the bulk of documents produced after such depositions. The Met further stated:

> Finally, although we cannot at this point determine how much prejudice has been suffered by the Met due to the improper destruction and withholding of critical evidence, if, upon deposing the people knowledgeable about defendants' document retention, production and lack thereof, we learn that it is necessary, we will move for preclusion or judgment against defendants. We sincerely believe that defendants' willful failure to comply with their obligations is of the severest nature and may demand that remedy once we learn the full extent of the prejudice thereby imposed on the Met.

. . . Yen responded by letter stating that she was prepared to explain her review of Local 100's document production . . .

During a December 18 teleconference with the Court, there was also discussion of the Weekly Reports. Met counsel stated that they still had no Weekly Reports for Tamarin, Granfield or Bitterman. Yen asserted that these reports were maintained for payroll purposes and said the reports did not matter because the employees' calendars showed the same information. Yen also maintained that because these three witnesses' Weekly Reports were submitted to and kept on file at the offices of the International Union, she should not have to obtain them because the International was not a party . . . I again ordered that the reports be produced. Defendants still have not fully complied with that order . . .

e. Ream

(i) Payroll Department

On December 20, the Met deposed Amanda Ream, a Research Analyst at Local 100 who was hired in September 2000 to work on the campaign against the Met and continues to do so. Ream testified that "to her knowledge" there is no separate "Payroll Department" at Local 100's office . . . Although it had been represented to Met counsel and to the Court that the Weekly Reports were kept "in the Payroll Department" and that Department was not searched because it was thought it would not have any responsive documents, Ream testified that the "Payroll Department" was a secretary who sat with everyone else in the open office structure . . . Ream testified that it is a "very small office" and that each staff member simply gives his or her Weekly Report to this secretary, who shows them to Granfield and then puts them in a file cabinet in the open office with all the other files.

Although Ream showed all the files in her area to Bitterman, various materials, which were clearly responsive and quite relevant to the Met's case, had not been produced to the Met. She also testified that drafts of documents created on computers were not saved by Local 100 employees, even those that related to the Met campaign, unless an individual staff member decided, based on his or her own understanding, that a document should be turned over for production to the Met. Even finished documents, computer-generated or otherwise, were not routinely retained . . . Even those documents that were put into a box for review by Bitterman—for his determination as to whether such documents should be given to the Union's counsel for possible production to the Met—were not necessarily retained on the computer . . . So, if an employee was incorrect as to what was required for production and did not print out a hard copy of a document, or Bitterman (himself a non-lawyer) decided that it was not responsive, there was no way to retrieve it because the Union had no retention policy . . .

2. Interrogatories Regarding Affirmative Defenses

. . . [F]our interrogatories sought the basis . . . of the affirmative defenses . . . in defendants' Amended Answer:

2. Set forth the factual basis for the claim . . . that "Plaintiff has commenced this action in retaliation against defendants' lawful conduct permitted by Federal labor laws" and identify any documents supporting this claim.

   Response: Defendants object to this Interrogatory on the ground that it cannot be answered as framed. Subject to and without waiving the above General Objections, Defendants refer Plaintiff to the Amended Complaint in this action, the Affidavit of James H. Naples in support of motion for injunctive relief, the testimony of Sharon E. Grubin at the preliminary injunction hearing; the deposition transcript and exhibits of Joseph Volpe; information contained in documents bates [sic] numbered HF 000001-2347, HF 003365-3974, HF 006944-8329, HF 008899-9144; and knowledge and information possessed by witnesses already deposed in this action and witnesses yet to be deposed in this action.

3. Set forth the factual basis for the . . . that "the alleged statements of facts made by defendants are true" and identify any documents supporting this claim.

   Response: Defendants object to this Interrogatory on the ground that it cannot be answered as framed. Subject to and without waiving the above General Objections, Defendants refer Plaintiff to the deposition transcripts and exhibits of Brooks Bitterman, Michelle Travis and Amanda Ream; information contained in documents bates numbered HF 000001-2347; HF 003365-3974, HF 006944-8329, HF 008899-9144; ME 100638-662; the testimony of Bruce Crawford at the preliminary injunction hearing; and knowledge and information possessed by witnesses already deposed in this action and witnesses yet to be deposed in this action.

4. Set forth the factual basis for the claim . . . that "Plaintiff's culpable conduct has contributed to any damages it has sustained" and identify any documents supporting this claim.

   Response: Defendants object to this Interrogatory on the ground that it cannot be answered as framed. Subject to and without waiving the above General Objections, Defendants refer Plaintiff to information contained in documents bates numbered HF 000001-2347; HF 006944-8329, HF 008899-9144; ME 100638-662; Plaintiff's website, brochures, programs, letters and other publications; and knowledge and information possessed by witnesses already deposed in this action and witnesses yet to be deposed in this action.

5. Set forth the factual basis for the . . . that "Plaintiff is estopped from claiming relief for statements that plaintiff makes about itself" and identify and documents supporting this claim.
   Response: Defendants object to this Interrogatory on the ground that it cannot be answered as framed. Defendants further object to this Interrogatory insofar as it seeks a factual explanation of a principle of law. Subject to and without waiving the above General Objections, Defendants refer Plaintiff to information contained in documents bates numbered HF 000001-2347; HF 006944-8329, HF 008899-9144; ME 199537 [sic]-662; Plaintiff's website, brochures, programs, letters and other publications; and knowledge and information possessed by witnesses already deposed in this action and witnesses yet to be deposed in this action.

. . . Thereafter, Lans communicated with Yen about the insufficiency of the responses . . . but Yen insisted that her answers had been appropriate and never supplied any further information . . . In response to clear, narrow interrogatories, counsel's wholesale reference to literally hundreds of pages of documents and to "knowledge and information possessed by witnesses already deposed in this action and witnesses yet to be deposed in this action" signals their continuing contempt for the discovery process and their preference for gamesmanship over their obligations as officers of the Court . . .

3. Compliance Discovery

On December 18, 2001, I conducted a lengthy teleconference with counsel wherein I granted the Met's application to serve discovery compliance interrogatories on defendants, who were required to answer promptly, rather than in 30 days; to depose persons with respect to discovery compliance; and to re-examine witnesses on the merits only with respect to topics raised by documents it had obtained after the witnesses had been deposed.

Compliance discovery proceeded initially through interrogatories inquiring into the system the Union and its counsel used in responding to the Met's discovery requests and then proceeded to depositions of individuals at the Union and several of their lawyers who were involved (or, as seemed to be the case with some, not involved) in the discovery process.

On this motion, two Union lawyers submitted declarations in opposition discussing discovery matters: Anderson, who was attorney of record from August of 2000 through the present but who "transitioned out" of the case in July of 2001 . . . and Yen, who was assigned to the case in mid-October 2001 and remained through compliance discovery in the Spring of 2002.[15]

a. Interrogatories

On December 28, 2001, the Met served interrogatories concerning defendants' discovery compliance on the named defendants—Local 100, Tamarin, and Diaz—which were to be answered on January 4 . . . Yen wrote to the Met on January 4 stating that she would be unable to provide any responses that day . . . On Monday, January 7, counsel attended a conference with the Court at which discovery issues were addressed . . . Met counsel asked the Court to direct that interrogatory answers be provided on a date certain. Yen said that she had been working very hard on them but because she had to talk to each of the lawyers who had represented defendants since the case began to find out what occurred with respect to document production, it was taking some time. Met counsel pointed out that Herrick Feinstein had represented the Union in the case from its inception, so it was difficult to understand why Yen was only then piecing together information from her colleagues' memories in order to answer that a complete document search had been made. I agreed, noting that Yen's review of the correspondence file should have provided the information she needed and stated: "If it didn't, then, you know, we have a greater cause for concern than that these folks have to search their memories at this point." . . . Compliance discovery has confirmed that there is indeed more to worry about.

On January 9, Yen wrote to the Court saying it was not possible for her to respond that day and requesting an extension to Monday, January 14 . . . Yen stated that she had requested consent from Met counsel, who had refused . . . Yen stated, "In light of the Court's explicit direction to me during the January 7 conference to provide 'a serious response on behalf of defendants' . . . I cannot in good faith submit by the end of business today Answers to Interrogatories signed by me before I have had the chance to exhaust my interviews and investigation." . . . Met counsel assert that they received Yen's letter by fax at 7 P.M. . . . That night, Easterly sent a letter to the Court in response, stating:

> Defendants have had ample time to gather the information needed to respond to these Interrogatories—which simply ask the defendants to outline what they did to search for and produce documents responsive to each of the Met's five sets of document requests. Indeed, given defense counsel's repeated assurances to the Met over the past six months that defendants were in full compliance with their obligations, it should not be necessary at this late date to gather any information at all. They are merely being asked to set forth what they have already done.
>
> If, however, Ms. Yen is saying that she must (only now that she is obligated to sign her name to a legal document . . .) determine whether her law firm complied with its discovery obligations, then her letter proves what the Met has always feared—that counsel for defendants has failed to provide adequate supervision, instruction and guidance to defendants in the discovery phase of this lawsuit, resulting in what we have continuously maintained is an inadequate and faulty production.
>
> ***
>
> The Met has already been prejudiced in having to take depositions and plan its case based on incomplete information. Every additional day that defendants withhold information further prejudices the Met in our efforts to prepare for trial within the Court's schedule. Accordingly, we

---

[15] Lynett, who represented the Union from the outset through the PI Hearing, did not submit an opposing declaration, but his deposition was taken in the course of compliance discovery. As is noted below, Moss also did not submit an opposing declaration.

Jamain Sewell, an in-house attorney at Local 100, also submitted a declaration, but it was directed to proceedings before the NLRB. Sewell did not represent the Union in any phase of the litigation . . .

respectfully request that Your Honor order defendants to submit immediately their responses to these Interrogatories and provide the other information due so that the Met can move on.

. . . The Met received the interrogatory responses on Monday, January 14.[16]

At the January 7 conference, Met counsel raised other problems with defendants' discovery, and I made certain rulings . . . With regard to the production of Weekly Reports, Met counsel explained that although some had recently been produced, production was not complete, pointing out, as an example, that no reports for Bitterman had been produced . . . Yen repeated that defendants had not "realized" that "anything in the payroll or expense department was called for," . . . despite my having rejected that explanation before and having ordered production. Moreover, at that conference, Yen stated that Bitterman did not generate any Weekly Reports, which was contrary to what the Court and Met counsel had been told by Union counsel orally and in writing . . . Yen explained:

> . . . a box arrived from the International Union containing Mr. Tamarin's, Mr. Granfield's, Mr. Bitterman's for a three year period of their weekly reports and expense reports or, you know, whatever they had. I have no reason to doubt they have given me everything.

> **THE COURT:** If it is now the defendants' position that there are no more, then you better put in a response to that effect and then we are finished with it. But now plaintiffs are sitting here telling me they don't have them.

> **MS. LANS:** And I'm actually not clear whether Ms. Yen has had a chance asking [sic] the International whether there are any reports. . . .

> **THE COURT:** How are we going to find out the answer to this question?

> **MS. YEN:** I can make one last inquiry of the people at the International who would know and then ascertain that everything they gave me is everything that is in their possession relating to weekly reports or expense reports of all these individuals.

> **MS. GRUBIN:** Which individuals?

> **THE COURT:** I actually do recall the discussion of Mr. Bitterman's reports having been sent to Chicago. I don't, as I sit here, remember what the instructions are in the document requests, but at least get out a response so that if plaintiffs are going to take some more steps they can do it promptly. All right?

. . . Further, Met counsel expressed their concern that a thorough search of the Union had not been conducted, specifically with respect to the Weekly Reports:

> **MS. GRUBIN:** . . . I don't want it focused on the specific individuals. We are entitled to weekly reports of anybody at this Union who had anything to do with this, and now we—

> **THE COURT:** By "this," of course, you mean the campaign?

> **MS. GRUBIN:** The campaign against the Met. Yes.

> **THE COURT:** Whatever the document request says it says. If that's what it says, then that's what you are entitled to.

> **MS. GRUBIN:** The document request says all the documents.

> **THE COURT:** Ms. Yen is going to put a response in.

> **MS. GRUBIN:** No. But the document request asks for all documents relating to the Met and the campaign against the Met. That's one document request. The problem is we found out that these weekly reports existed during one of the depositions that we took.

> **THE COURT:** I remember all this.

> **MS. GRUBIN:** So now we are focused on that. But my problem is when we say what else hasn't been produced, we only know what we found out what hasn't been produced, and from what I'm hearing from Ms. Yen's answer as to whom she has to talk to, as to what kind of search was made and—

***

---

[16]Yen's difficulty in responding to an interrogatory essentially inquiring as to the system established by the Union and its counsel to respond to the Met's requests for documents foreshadowed the conclusion I reach today that there was no system.

MS. LANS: I think the weekly reports are an example of the problem we are having. We sent off a letter on Friday that related to document requests and interrogatory answers and the inadequacies of those. We sent a letter this morning with respect to other document issues. I think the point here is, we will, I believe, want to redepose some witnesses.

THE COURT: But that is not today's problem.

MS. LANS: But I think we first need to get to the bottom of complete discovery, paper discovery, I think.

THE COURT: Absolutely. And I don't think anybody is objecting. We are going to get the answers to the interrogatories the end of the day the 9th. It sounds like we ought to get the Rule 34 response at the same time, if not before that . . .

(i) Subsidies

The conversation then turned to the Met's specific document request concerning subsidies received by Local 100 from the International:

MS. EASTERLY: We received partial documents. For example, we received a letter, I believe, it was dated February 28 from Mr. Tamarin, the former president—

THE COURT: February 28?

MS. EASTERLY: Of 2001, from Mr. Tamarin to John Wilhelm, who is the president of the International Union. In that letter Mr. Tamarin refers to correspondence from Mr. Wilhelm from earlier in the month. So we said, well, we want that letter, too, please produce that letter. We got that letter. That letter refers to an earlier letter in January from Mr. Tamarin.

      We feel we are being nickel and dimed. We would like the defendants to produce all correspondence, all documents that relate to the subsidy that they are receiving. Notably, we have not received any correspondence concerning the subsidy of the year 2000, yet the Form 990s of the Union shows there was a subsidy.

THE COURT: Ms. Yen, what do you say?

MS. YEN: I don't know why they need the subsidy number of the International to Local 100. What has that to do with defamation or in the Lanham Act?

THE COURT: Is this in the nature of an objection to the request?

MS. YEN: Yes. I think at this point I would object given—

THE COURT: But it is too late now.

MS. YEN: Not under my watch. But documents have been produced and I think now they are getting very far afield in wanting more and more documents on this particular subject, which I don't find has anything to do with what they have to prove at trial.

THE COURT: But the request was out there for some time now apparently unobjected to. Am I wrong?

. . . At that point Moss interjected:

MR. MOSS: No, no. This is the interpretation of a **blunderbuss** request for all documents relevant. This is now the plaintiffs' [sic] refinement of that request as they go along and they say now we want this and we want that and we want the other thing.

THE COURT: What was the request?

MS. EASTERLY: The request was for all documents—I can get it for you specifically. But I object to the characterization that it is a refinement of the request. When you have received one piece of correspondence that clearly responds to the request and that references a prior piece of correspondence that it is responding to, one would think that the whole part and parcel, the whole parcel of correspondence is responsive to the request. But let me find it for you.

MS. GRUBIN: There was a specific request. Ms. Moss [sic] before you read it, what was the date of the request?

MS. EASTERLY: This is dated October 23. We asked for all documents or communications concerning HEREIU's subsidy, reimbursement or other financial support of Local 100's organizing activities, staff and/or operating or administrative expenses.

THE COURT: It doesn't sound blunderbuss to me. Produce them by the 10th.

. . . Yen's and Moss' responses in this interchange were typical of their approach to discovery in this action. At a conference where Met counsel raised a discovery item previously discussed with Yen and Moss, as to which no response had theretofore been received, Yen manufactured an objection on the spot. When that was rejected as being too late, Moss objected (clearly without stopping and thinking about the legitimacy of his objection) that the request was a "refinement" of a "blunderbuss request," only to be directed to the specific narrow request seeking precisely the documents under discussion. Piecemeal production (or in the words of Met counsel, "nickel and diming"), obstruction and delay remained the order of the day. Union counsel also continued their tactic of responding to the Met's fortuitous identification of a particular document rather than assuring that a complete search for all responsive documents had been conducted.

(ii) Benefits

The other specific document request discussed at that conference was one for documents concerning benefits paid to Union workers, which, as noted above, had been the subject of the Met's Third Document Request to which defendants' Rule 34 Response, signed by Moss, stated, "there are no responsive documents." . . . As also noted above, however, defendants' witnesses and documents showed that could not be the case. After a lengthy discussion, in which Yen related what she had been told by Union officers as to the nonexistence of such documents, the following transpired:

MS. GRUBIN: Maybe I'm off the mark, but isn't it counsel's responsibility to do the search and then tell us there aren't any documents, rather than say, well, Mr. Granfield testified that they are not in writing?

***

THE COURT: Ms. Yen, the question is, is that a response on behalf of defendants and officers and the like, or is that a response from Mr. Tamarin? If the answer on behalf of defendants is no such documents, then I don't know why we are discussing it. But it doesn't sound like the inquiry has been made.

MS. YEN: I can make one last inquiry of everyone in the office. I mean, we asked the people who are in the know—

THE COURT: Okay. But there has to be a response made in a proper Rule 34 manner. Let's do it. Same thing. January 9. Next.

MS. EASTERLY: . . . I would just like to say, we would like the court to direct the defendants to make a Union wide search by attorneys of the documents that are in defendants' possession. And that seems to be sort of the root of the problem here, is that the lawyers involved have not conducted the search, they have relied on representations by lay people and that's part of why we have been receiving documents piecemeal.

THE COURT: I thought that that's what we are doing with the follow-up depositions now, the interrogatories and the like.

MS. GRUBIN: Yes.

MS. EASTERLY: I think we are getting more information about what occurred in the past, but I think prospectively, I guess we can wait for that response.

THE COURT: I think Ms. Yen has the point here. Ms. Yen, I said I think you have the point. Yes?

MS. YEN: Yes. . . .

. . . As discussed above, Yen did not timely complete the interrogatories. In addition, the Met did not receive any of the documents ordered to be produced on January 9 or 10 . . . With respect to the Rule 34 Responses, the Met received by fax at 9 P.M. on January 10 a letter from Yen, in which she responded to specific questions that had been asked in the Met's prior correspondence, and then stated:

Additionally, this serves as a Rule 34 response that (1) there are no weekly reports for Brooks Bitterman at either the International Union or at Local 100 and all expense reports submitted by Mr. Bitterman to the International Union for the period requested have been produced; (2) as to Request 28, I have personally questioned Mr. Tamarin, Mr. Granfield and each employee of Local 100 who may have knowledge, and I have reviewed Mr. Granfield's file, and I am satisfied that there are no documents in defendants' possession reflecting "communications with its members or internally among its employees about these benefits plans" or "documents that might show that Local 100 members have complained that they don't get their benefits." . . .

. . . Thus, the Rule 34 Responses were limited to only the Weekly Reports of Bitterman (previously represented by Yen to have been sent to Chicago to the International) and not those of other Union employees. On January 11, Yen sent a letter enclosing what she said were all documents responsive to the Met's Request concerning subsidies from the International which had not previously been produced . . . She also provided a day planner kept by organizer Dahlia Ward, explaining that although she had previously questioned all Local 100 employees and thought that Ms. Ward had informed her she had no day planner, she learned upon questioning employees on January 10 that she did have one . . .

. . . Easterly questioned Yen about her January 10 letter. With respect to the Weekly Reports, Easterly wrote:

> We understand your response to mean that Mr. Bitterman did fill out weekly reports (as did all the other officers and employees of Local 100), but that these reports simply cannot be found at either the offices of the International Union and Local 100. Please clarify: whether Mr. Bitterman filled out weekly reports, and, if so, where these reports were filed and what efforts have been undertaken to locate them. Also, please clarify whether, aside from Mr. Bitterman, you have produced all the weekly reports for all the union employees or officials who worked on the campaign against the Met.

To date, the Met has never received a response from defendants as to whether all Weekly Reports which reflect work on the campaign against the Met have been produced by Union officials and employees . . .

Easterly also pointed out to Yen that her representation that she had produced all subsidy documents appeared incorrect, specifying to Yen what was still missing . . . Easterly's third letter was sent to the International regarding its "patently incomplete" production concerning subsidies and other requested documents . . .

On January 15, Easterly again wrote to Yen:

> Finally, we note that we are still waiting to receive from you a number of documents as well as responses to discovery challenges. Your attempt to dismiss as "peripheral" documents still withheld by defendants is disingenuous. But more importantly, your assessment of their importance is irrelevant and immaterial given that the Court ordered you to produce specific categories of documents by dates certain last week and ordered you to produce all documents responsive to the Met's document requests by last Thursday, January 10.

. . . In a letter of January 18, Easterly gave Yen a compilation of numerous (although not all), long-standing discovery items on which defendants were still in default . . . Weekly Reports that clearly did exist had not been produced; . . . Bitterman's expense reports had been produced only for scattered dates and that no expense reports from other Union personnel had been produced for July 2001 to the present; . . . the representation concerning the completeness of Peter Ward's documents was patently incorrect; and . . . the Met was still awaiting a response as to why the documents concerning subsidies from the International . . . had still not been produced . . . Yen never responded . . .

Met counsel sent additional letters during February and March seeking other long-requested items, among them those that defendants had agreed to provide during depositions of their witnesses but had never provided. In a response confirming defendants' clear purpose of delay and obfuscation, Yen responded to most of these letters that discovery had "closed" on December 31 . . .

On March 26 and 28 and April 1, the Met sent additional letters . . . to Yen concerning various items, including the numerous Weekly Reports that have still not been produced. On April 2, Yen sent her response, ignoring all but two specific inquiries—one concerning a transcript and the other concerning the Union's privileged documents . . . She also stated: "I have earlier stated to you in writing that discovery has been closed for some time and we will not respond to new demands." . . .

b. Depositions

In March of 2002, the Met took depositions relating to the defendants' discovery compliance and went for a "walk-through" of Local 100's office.[18] The Met deposed Bitterman, Granfield, Lynett, Rimmelin and Yen on the subject of discovery compliance . . . All witnesses agree there was no filing system at Local 100 and no policy or practice as to how files should be kept. Rather, each person just kept (or did not keep) his or her own files. It is also agreed that there has never been any policy or practice regarding retention or destruction of documents . . .

(i) Granfield

Granfield testified that he remembered a conversation when this action was commenced with Lynett (who was Local 100's in-house lawyer at the time) in which Lynett told him about the lawsuit and said defendants were required to turn over some documents. He said Lynett showed him a "list" (which was a copy of the Met's First Document Request) and told him he should look through his own files . . . He does not remember Lynett's telling him anything beyond that. He was not provided with copies of any of the Met's other Document Requests in this action . . . He told Lynett that Bitterman, Diaz and Dahlia Ward might also have relevant documents because they worked on the Met campaign . . . Granfield then looked through his "Met Opera organizing file" and nothing else . . . Lynett did not discuss with him what a "document" was. He does not recall Lynett's ever telling him that e-mails, for example, or drafts of documents were required. He does not recall whether Lynett talked to him about non-identical copies of a document being required or of any discussion of calendars or day planners. He did not have any conversation with Lynett about what any of the document requests meant or what the scope was of the documents encompassed by the requests . . . He gave his "organizing file" to Lynett, which was the only thing he did with respect to document production in this case until over a year later in July 2001 . . .

Granfield does not recall Lynett's telling him to look for documents saved on computers or to save documents relating to the Met on his computer . . . In fact, he did not check any computers for documents until much later. When Granfield did search computers, he searched two of the three computers that were maintained in Local 100's "shared" computer room . . . When Granfield searched the two computers, he did so by looking only at the titles of documents in the computer's "My Documents" folder or its hard drive; he did not remember which. What he looked for were document titles "that would say Met Opera." . . . Although he knows how to use the computer's "Find" tool, he did not do so. He only looked at the names the documents had been given on the drive. He does not remember if he found any documents for production as a result of this "search." He explained, however, that he himself does not save any documents on the computer. Whatever documents he wants to save he has always put on a diskette . . . He only maintains one diskette—when it is full, he simply deletes items and saves the new ones on it . . . He has no record of every item that has been deleted from his diskette . . . He has never provided his diskette to any of the Union's counsel . . . He never told Yen that he deleted items from his diskette, and she has never asked.

Granfield had no conversations with Anderson concerning discovery. He has never talked to Jamin Sewell (Lynett's replacement as the Union's in-house counsel as of mid-June 2000) generally about retention of documents or discovery obligations (although they did discuss the fact of new document requests) . . . The first time he spoke to either Moss or Yen about discovery was when he was prepared for his deposition in October 2001 . . . When Yen went to the Local 100 office on January 10 (to interview people to answer the Met's compliance interrogatories), he provided his files to her. January 10, 2002—after the close of discovery— was the first time since May of 2000 that any lawyer had come to the Local 100 office to look at the contents of Granfield's file cabinets . . .

Granfield had put Bitterman in charge of document production . . . He is not aware of any request ever being made by Bitterman or by any of the lawyers to any of the staff in writing concerning document discovery. Finally, when asked at the end of his deposition if he would articulate what documents responsive to

---

[18] The Union had initially objected to a walk-through, and, in an effort to avoid it, Yen produced a floor plan of the Union's offices . . . She argued that production of the floor plan obviated the need for a walk-through. In light of that argument, it was astounding to learn, in subsequent depositions, that the floor plan was admitted to be inaccurate . . .

the Met's requests are, he stated—after a speaking objection by Yen on the basis that there are over 69 separate requests—that they are "documents that talk about the Met or are used in relationship to the Met RA campaign." . . .

At this deposition on March 25, it was learned that the three computers the Met had seen in the shared computer room at the time of the Met's walk-through on March 15 were brand new. When asked when the three computers that had been there for several years were replaced with these new ones, Granfield said, "About two weeks ago." . . . [I]t was two weeks earlier, on March 11, in a teleconference, that Met counsel asked for permission to have a forensic computer expert examine defendants' computers. Granfield did indicate that the old computers are still around Local 100's office.[20] In response to the Met's present motion, Rimmelin explained that the new computers had been ordered prior to the Met's mention of a forensic computer expert . . . Even accepting that statement as true, for the Union and its counsel to permit the computers in use during the relevant period to be dismantled without notice to Met counsel in the face of a year of protest by Met . . . court orders to preserve and retrieve electronic documents and the Met's announcement that it might engage a forensic computer expert is a willful disregard of their discovery obligations.

(ii) Bitterman

Bitterman confirmed at his deposition that he was the person generally in charge of assuring defendants' compliance with discovery obligations. However, he could not remember what he had done specifically in making his search or when. Bitterman spoke to Anderson . . . and Lynett . . . but cannot recall what they said. He . . . asked those people whom he thought would have responsive documents to give him whatever they had. He did not remember how he described what the documents were that should be provided. Bitterman knew of the existence of Weekly Reports at least since the inception of this action . . . He did not always check each individual's files himself; rather, he sometimes left it up to the individual to do his or her own search. He does not recall what he did to search for e-mails . . . and he personally searched only his own laptop and the computer that was located closest to him . . . He spoke to people about the document requests but he did not recall ever giving anyone copies of the Met's requests . . . He never put any instructions in writing to others as to what was required, and he never received any written instructions from defendants' counsel as to what he was supposed to do. He created no checklist, and there is no other document from which one could ascertain the steps he took to assure compliance with discovery requests . . .

(aa) The Union's Storage Facility

At the Met's walk-through on March 15, there were several boxes against a wall that, it turned out, were being sent to Local 100's storage facility . . . The deposition testimony of Local 100's office manager, Margaret Rimmelin . . . and of Lynett . . . reveals that every year to year-and-a-half there is a weekend in which files in the office are reviewed. Some are thrown away, and others are sent to storage . . . No one has ever looked in the storage facility . . . in connection with document production in this case. Although Rimmelin has an inventory of what is in storage, she has no recollection of a lawyer's or Bitterman's ever asking to look at it.

(iii) Rimmelin

Rimmelin has been at Local 100 since its inception in 1983. Mary Myhre works under Rimmelin. Myhre keeps the office's contract files, posts dues, keeps the Weekly Reports file and types letters. The letters she types on her computer are whatever is placed in her "basket" by organizers or others at the office. Myhre also "purges" files as needed . . . and keeps a file of Weekly Reports . . .

Rimmelin maintains files on membership meetings, including sign-in sheets which she gets from Granfield . . . She is in charge of documents that are sent to storage and keeps an inventory of what is in storage, although she currently still has in the office about the last two years of documents . . . The individual organizers keep their own files and do not send them to storage through Rimmelin . . . She and Granfield put together the draft budget for last year. Her computer has Internet access and e-mail.

---

[20]The Met explored retention of such an expert, but (apart from the significant cost thereof) was told that because of the time period involved and the manner of Local 100's usage of computers, the likelihood that material could be retrieved was not high . . .

Rimmelin was involved in document production in this case on two occasions. The first was in January 2002—after the close of discovery—when she was asked to provide telephone records,[21] and the other was about a "month ago," (i.e., February of 2002), when she was asked to provide the Union's by-laws, its documents relating to its subsidy for the Met campaign from the International and certain other financial records.[22] The only attorney she has ever spoken to about document production in this case is Yen, who called her once on the phone at the end of 2001 or beginning of 2002 about some specific documents and then came to the office on January 10, 2002 . . . Yen had not looked at her files prior to January 10, 2002 . . . Rimmelin has never had a conversation with Bitterman or Granfield about keeping documents or document retention for purposes of this case, although she knows Bitterman had a basket someplace where people were putting copies of documents for the case . . . She has no understanding of what documents are supposed to go into that basket and has never put any there herself . . .

(iv) Lynett

Lynett's only responsibility for document discovery in this case was with respect to the Met's First Document Request in May 2000 . . . As he had told the Court in May 2000 and as he stated in his deposition, after producing the documents to the Met on May 23, the night before the PI Hearing, he never went back to Local 100's office to confirm that a full search had been made because he was satisfied that what had been produced on May 23 was complete . . . As is clear from . . . the testimony of the Union employees . . . there was no basis for Lynett's belief. Lynett was also asked about the storage facility:

Q: Are you aware that Local 100 has a storage facility of some kind?

A: I think they have one.

Q: Have you ever been there?

A: God, no. I think I'd remember it. Having been to storage facilities are memorable events. Now that you mention it I think they do.

Q: Do you have any idea what's in the storage facility?

A: I imagine a lot of paper.

Q: Right. Do you have any knowledge of who is responsible for the maintenance of the storage facility?

A: I don't know if anybody would be.

Q: Do you know if there's an inventory of what's in storage?

A: I have no idea . . .

(v) Yen

In her deposition, Yen said she had been to Local 100's office three (maybe four) times. She went for the first time in November 2001, just to look it over and meet some of the staff. The next time was on January 10, 2002—after the close of discovery—when she went there to be able to respond to the Met's discovery compliance interrogatories by reviewing with employees what they had produced. The only additional time she remembers was on March 15 when she accompanied Met counsel on the walk-through . . . Aside from providing the document request, Yen has never given written instructions to anyone at Local 100 concerning their obligations with respect to document retention or production . . .

As noted above, when Yen finally agreed to produce the Weekly Reports, she decided (but did not inform Met counsel) that she would produce them only for those people for whom the Met had requested day planners and calendars: Diaz, Tamarin, Bitterman, Granfield and Hoffman . . . In addition, she decided that because Tamarin, Granfield, and Bitterman were paid directly by the International and all their reports were sent by them to the International's offices, she would not obtain the reports because the International was a "non-party." . . . It was only after the Court ordered her to do so that she obtained those

---

[21] I ordered these to be produced in July 2001.

[22] These were all documents requested by the Met's Fourth Document Request, served October 23, 2001.

reports.[23] Yen acknowledged that she had not known of the existence of "Weekly Reports" . . . until the Diaz deposition but she took no steps to produce them even then because she did not think they were relevant to any document request except, perhaps, the one requesting calendars, day planners and so forth. Yen testified:

> **Q:** Now, when you first learned about the weekly reports did you go back and review the various document requests that had been made in the case to see whether the reports were encompassed by any of those requests?
>
> **A:** Yes.
>
> **Q:** It was your view that there was no request except possibly the request for calendar and related material which encompassed the weekly reports?
>
> **A:** That's right.
>
> **Q:** So, for example, it was your view that request Number 19 . . . which is promulgated as part of our second request which were dated May 25th, 2001 which reads all documents and communications concerning any past or future leafletting, [sic] publicity or other scheduled activity directed in whole or in part to the Met, potential donors to or patrons of the Met including without limitation any public or private gathering, meeting, demonstration, rally, protest or any communication in a public or private place concerning the Met that that request, for example, did not encompass the weekly reports?
>
> **A:** I don't recall now, but at the time I may have looked to see if we objected to the scope of this particular request or to the broadness or vagueness or over inclusiveness of this request. But yes, I still believe that weekly reports done so that they can collect their paychecks would not be in the contemplation of this document request.

. . . Despite Met counsel's constant clamoring for a complete file search supervised by an attorney, Yen never made a search of any files at Local 100 prior to January 10, 2002 during compliance discovery. On January 10, she spent about seven hours at the office, approximately three of which she spent looking at certain files, although she did not actually review the documents contained in most of them . . . She sat at one of the fourteen computers and asked Dahlia Ward to pull up the list of her e-mails . . . Yen found two e-mails that had not been produced and provided them to the Met the following day but she did not look at anyone else's e-mails and at no other time did she look at the contents of any Local 100 computer. She has never asked anyone at Local 100 which ISPs they used and she does not recall if she asked anyone about having computers at home that they used for work . . . She is not aware of any other lawyer for defendants having looked at the contents or an inventory of any Local 100 computer . . .

Yen was then asked about records of "house visits" in connection with the Met campaign . . . House visits are trips made by Union personnel to the homes of RA workers. Reports of visits by Union personnel to RA workers in connection with the Union's campaign to organize workers at the Met would be responsive to . . . Plaintiff's First Document Request . . . The Weekly Reports indicate that Union personnel made many house visits to the individual RA workers to solicit their support for the Union. However, the only report or notes of the results of any of those visits produced by defendants are two pages from one day in 1998 and some scribbled notes. The 1998 records were made on a form entitled "Housecalling Sheets." . . . Referring to a Weekly Report of Dahlia Ward for the week ending January 29, 2000 . . . Lans asked Yen:

> **Q:** . . . on the Wednesday of that particular week Ms. Ward makes an entry which says calling Met, and there's a word that I can't read. Then it says and filling out house . . . and something is cut off and then it says house visit report sheets. Do you see that?
>
> **A:** I see it, but I'm trying to determine what it says.
>
> **Q:** Well, you see the reference to house visit report sheets?
>
> **A:** Yes.
>
> **Q:** And to filling them out?
>
> **A:** Yes.

---

[23] The Met received Tamarin's and Granfield's Weekly Reports on December 28, three days before the close of discovery. There were significant gaps even in that production.

Q: Have you ever asked Ms. Ward or anyone else at Local 100 about house visit reports or report sheets that they maintain concerning visits to Met workers?

A: I've never asked them about, quote, unquote, house visit report sheets, but I've had conversations with the organizers about materials or notes, if any, in connection with house visits. . . .

Q: Has either Mr. Diaz or Ms. Ward or any other organizer told you that they have completed from time to time any sort of a form whether they've called it a house visit report sheet or not concerning their visits?

A: No.

Q: Did you ask them whether they completed any sort of form or kept any sort of record of their house visits?

A: Not in that way. I would say do you bring anything on your house visits and the answer was no. Do you take notes? The answer was no. I'm not sure if I asked him specifically do you keep reports as such.

Q: So, in any event, insofar as your conversations with the organizers including Mr. Diaz and Ms. Ward, were you left with the impression from what they told you that they did not keep any form of written record of who they visited, when they visited and what occurred on a visit?

A: Yes.

. . . Then, referring to the two pages of the 1998 "Housecalling Sheets," . . . Lans asked:

Q: Have you ever brought either of the two documents that I've given you as Exhibit 7 to the attention of Ms. Ward or Mr. Diaz and asked them what they are?

A: No.

Q: Have you ever had any conversation with either of them or any other organizer of Local 100 about what those documents are, what type of documents they are?

A: No . . .

THE WITNESS: I want to note for the record that these documents were produced by Local 100 at the inception of the litigation. That probably goes back to August of 2001.

. . . Yen's comment typifies the lawyers' attitude toward discovery in this case; instead of shouldering the responsibility imposed by the Rules to conduct a good faith search for responsive materials—which would have yielded the obviously-responsive Housecalling Sheets—defense counsel seeks to impose on Met counsel the burden of identifying with specificity documents in the Union's files that are responsive and have not been produced. The Union's lawyers have it seriously backwards.

Yen has never been to the Local 100 storage facility and does not know what is stored there. She has never looked at an index or inventory of the items. In fact, Yen did not even know the Union had a storage facility until the Met's walk-through when Met counsel asked about certain boxes in the office:

Q: Do you remember when it was that you talked to Ms. Rimmelin about materials that were being sent to storage?

A: I think it was on the date of the inspection.

Q: Okay. That's last Friday [March 15, 2002]?

A: Yeah.

. . . Yen never gave either of Tamarin's secretaries (in New York or Chicago) copies of the document requests for review, even though Mr. Tamarin types none of his own letters . . . She never spoke to or reviewed files of organizers who had participated in rallies, leafleting and RA team meetings, such as (but not limited to) Robert Demand, Gilbert Palacios, Cliff Fried, Juan Galan and Miguel De La Rosa . . . As noted earlier, when—just after the depositions—the Met attempted to obtain defendants' voluntary compliance with many of these production defaults, defendants responded that discovery was "closed." . . .

Stepping back for a moment to view the big picture, I note Yen complains in the May 22 surreply that "the Met treats the [Lans Declaration] as if it were a pleading, and contends that all statements not specifically denied are somehow deemed admitted by the defendants" and then points out that in her declaration she "does in fact deny each and every allegation of misconduct that the Met claims supports an order of judgment and sanctions." . . . Again, Yen is technically correct, but the inference she wishes to draw is substantively wrong. The Lans Declaration was lengthy and extremely detailed. As noted above, after preliminarily reviewing it and hearing defendants' views, I found the motion (and thus the declaration) not to be frivolous. In her opposing declaration, Yen does in fact "declare that each and every allegation of perjury, obstruction, destruction, and spoliation of evidence, made by the Met against defendants, me, my colleagues at the law firm of Herrick Feinstein and co-counsel Michael T. Anderson is untrue." . . . [E]ven the first person conclusory denial is of little effect in countering the specific, detailed evidentiary material proffered by the Met.

Moss, the . . . partner in charge of the case during the bulk of the discovery proceedings and involved in the court appearances and discovery conferences from early fall 2001 to the present, submitted no declaration in opposition to the motion. Thus, it is not clear whether Yen, a young associate, . . . was wholly unsupervised in her conduct of discovery from October 2001 through compliance discovery or whether she was subject to Moss' (or someone else's) supervision and acquiescence. Even if Moss failed to supervise Yen actively, . . . such a failure by the partner in charge in the face of Met counsel's constant complaints of no adequate search and demonstrations of inadequate production rises far above carelessness to willfulness. Of course, if Moss did supervise Yen and acquiesce in her actions (and non-actions), the result is the same—a willful failure to engage in discovery responsibly. Either way, Moss' silence is deafening.

V. THE MET'S MOTION FOR SANCTIONS REGARDING THE SUBPOENA OF THE MET DIRECTORS AND WARD'S DEPOSITION

A. The Met Directors

On November 26, 2001, I held a teleconference with the parties regarding defendants' intention to depose six Met Directors as third-party witnesses. Despite the Met's objections to these depositions, I allowed them to go forward on a limited basis and I directed the Met to produce certain documents on an expedited basis. Because the discovery deadline at the time was December 31, the Directors were also ordered to conduct an expedited document search and to make themselves available in December; some of them rearranged their holiday and vacation schedules to comply . . . As such, the Directors and Met counsel spent approximately two weeks scheduling these depositions and preparing the witnesses . . . On December 13, the Met confirmed that the Directors would be deposed on December 18, 19, 20, 27 and 28 . . .

On December 12, the Union issued a subpoena to Grubin requiring her to appear for a deposition on December 27 . . . The next day, Grubin and Lans met with two of the Directors to prepare for their depositions . . . Shortly after these meetings, however, they learned that the Union's counsel had informed Easterly that afternoon that they no longer wished to depose five of the six Directors noticed . . . In addition, the Met learned that the Union had served another subpoena on an employee of the Met Opera Guild to take her deposition on December 31 . . . As a result, the Met filed an application seeking the Met's attorneys' fees incurred in preparing for the depositions that were cancelled and that the newly-noticed depositions be precluded.

. . . According to Yen, the defendants issued subpoenas to the six Met Directors, with copies to Met counsel by regular mail, on November 20, 2001, for various dates in December . . . Before the subpoenas had been successfully served, the Met's attorneys had received them and moved to quash . . . As previously noted, a teleconference was held on November 26, and I directed that the depositions proceed . . .

As Yen collected documents relating to the Directors and reviewed testimony from the PI Hearing, she "became focused on the fact that Grubin had testified to conversations at a board meeting relating to defendants' activities and had testified to receiving instructions from the Board" and Yen therefore "came to believe that Ms. Grubin waived any attorney client privilege as to her conversations with Met directors on the subject." . . . On November 27, Moss deposed the Met's General Manager, Joseph Volpe, and learned facts that led Union counsel to doubt the Met's previous assertion of an attorney-client privilege and therefore that additional ground could be explored . . . Defendants also deposed James Naples, the Met's House Manager, on December 7 . . . After speaking with a nonparty on December 10 and reviewing Naples' deposition testimony, Moss and Yen decided on December 12 that it was more important to depose other individuals related to the Met than the Directors . . . Accordingly, on the afternoon of December 12, Yen began drafting sub-poenas for these new individuals, which were finalized on December 13 . . . "Given the previous difficulty in serving the Met's directors," Moss and Yen waited to get confirmation of service before formally cancelling the Directors' depositions . . . When Easterly called Yen on December 14, Yen told Easterly that the defendants intended to cancel all except one of the Directors' depositions . . .

B. Ward's Deposition

On December 5, the Met served a subpoena on Peter Ward for a deposition on Friday, December 21, then—in the rush to conclude discovery—the only date available to all counsel for a deposition . . . Despite the fact that counsel had been in contact on a daily basis throughout December about the discovery schedule, it was not until December 14—nine days after Ward's subpoena—that Yen informed Met counsel that Ward's deposition had to be rescheduled to mid-January because he was going on vacation and his flight was leaving the morning of December 22 . . . Met counsel offered to depose Ward on December 21 or 22 prior to his departure, but Union counsel refused . . . When Union counsel informed Met counsel that Ward was unavailable on any day during the week of December 17, Met counsel wrote to the Court requesting that Ward appear on the 21st, the previously-scheduled date, or on the 19th or 20th . . . In a teleconference with the Court on December 18, Yen represented to Met counsel that Ward was "gonna be on an airplane" on the 21st, despite having previously stated that Ward was leaving on the 22nd . . . When Met counsel suggested that Ward could take a plane on the 22nd (and presumably be deposed on the 21st), Yen replied "He's going away with his family, come on. It's Christmas vacation." . . . After more discussion between counsel and in light of Yen's representation that Ward would be "getting on a plane" on the 21st and the discovery cut-off and impending trial, I ordered that Ward be deposed for three hours prior to his departure and, if necessary, that the deposition be completed upon his return.

Moss requested a teleconference on the morning of December 19 (without consulting with Met counsel) . . . In that teleconference, Moss stated that Ward's vacation was to begin on the 20th (not the 22nd or the 21st, as Yen had represented seriatim) and that it would be "impossible" for Ward to be deposed prior to his departure. I reiterated my prior ruling of December 18 that Ward sit for three hours of his deposition before leaving. Instead of immediately contacting Ward and then promptly informing Met counsel when he could sit for his court-ordered deposition, (as Union counsel had undertaken to do . . .), Yen called Grubin at 3:45 P.M. on December 19 to say that Ward would be available for his deposition at 4:00 P.M., that is, fifteen minutes later . . . When Grubin stated that she might not be able to contact Lans (who Yen knew was to take the deposition) and that, even if she could, it was unlikely Lans could physically arrive at the Herrick Feinstein office on fifteen minutes notice, Yen replied that "her 'marching orders' were to get a court reporter and notify [Met counsel] that Mr. Ward would be available at 4:00." . . . Grubin was not able to reach Lans until an hour later, and at that time, Met counsel were told that it was too late for Ward . . . Following these developments, another teleconference was held, and, based on Ward's supposed vacation plans, I ordered that his deposition proceed on January 7.[26]

On December 20, Moss and Lans agreed to start the Ward deposition on January 7 at 9:30 A.M., but on December 21, during a conference call, Moss requested that Ward's deposition be rescheduled to January 10 because of "long-scheduled meetings." . . . I refused defendants' request and directed Ward to be deposed on January 7 or 8, but after much discussion, it was agreed that Ward would be deposed on January 11 for the entire day . . . On January 10, Moss called Easterly and stated that the deposition could not begin at 9:30 as scheduled because Ward had a pre-operative appointment but that Ward would be there at 11:00 and stay as late as necessary. Ward arrived around noon . . .

---

[26]As noted, Ward testified that he had been called that morning and told to "drop everything" and appear for his deposition and that he "went over to Mr. Moss' offices and had been told after sitting there for almost two hours that the other side had decided they weren't prepared to go forward that day. . . ." . . . Moss and Yen have not explained why they waited until 3:45 to notify Met counsel of Ward's newly-discovered availability. Indeed, in surreply papers on this issue, Moss remained silent, and Yen omitted any reference to the lack of adequate notice. In what can most charitably be described as a less than complete response, Yen stated only that "after Met counsel insisted in a conference call with the Court that Mr. Ward be produced forthwith, he appeared on December 19, 2001 for his deposition, only to be told that Ms. Lans was not prepared to begin the deposition." . . .

A few minutes into the deposition, Ward and Moss took a short recess to discuss whether or not Moss was representing Ward. They determined that he was. The deposition continued:

Q: You were on vacation this winter in December at some point?

A: Yes, I was.

Q: Where did you go?

A: Where did I go?

Q: Yes.

THE WITNESS: Is that something I need to discuss at this deposition?

Q: Yes. You had a deposition scheduled and we had a great deal of difficulty which the judge is privy to in terms of scheduling it and I'm just trying to understand where you went and what dates you went.

A: I don't think I'm going to get into that with you.

Q: What dates were you on vacation?

A: I don't recall the exact dates. It was over the holiday.

Q: Do you have a date book?

A: Not with me.

Q: You have one in your office?

A: I do.

Q: Does it reflect the dates that you were out on vacation?

A: I'm quite certain it does.

Q: I'm going to ask you to provide us with the pages that show that.

MR. MOSS: And we will take that under advisement.

Q: Now, when did you first tell Mr. Moss that you had a doctor's commitment this morning?

A: I don't recall.

Q: Yesterday?

A: Yesterday or the day before.

Q: When did you first learn that we were going to take your deposition today? Was it some weeks ago?

A: It was—I believe this date was agreed to prior to when I went on vacation.

Q: Okay. Were you told at the time that you learned of this date that it was an 11 o'clock deposition or a 9:30 deposition?

A: I wasn't given a time.

Q: You weren't given a time?

A: No, not that I recall.

Q: Were you advised about the date in writing or over the telephone?

A: I don't recall.

***

Q: Were you ever told that the deposition was going to be on January 7th?

MR. MOSS: You're asking him about communications with counsel or outside?

MS. LANS: I don't think this would be a privileged communication, Jim, whether it was from counsel or otherwise. The scheduling of a deposition is hardly a privileged matter.

MR. MOSS: I'm going to advise, ask the witness not to respond to any question that calls for him to discuss matters that he and I have spoken about.

MS. LANS: Even the scheduling of this deposition?

MR. MOSS: Right.

MS. LANS: You regard that as confidential?

MR. MOSS: Yes.

MS. LANS: Okay. We'll deal with it.

Ward later stated that he had to leave at 4:30, and Moss "insisted that the Court had ordered that the deposition be limited to three hours." . . . The parties agreed to continue the deposition on January 28. On January 16, Moss requested that it be rescheduled to January 31. On January 31, Lans noticed that Ward's date book had a notation about a Giants football game on December 23. When Lans asked him whether he had spent his vacation in New York, Ward refused to respond, counsel called the Court, and I directed Ward to respond. Ward then testified that he spent his vacation at home in New York from December 21 through January 6 . . . In that recorded teleconference during his deposition, Ward stated that he never told anyone that he was getting on a plane . . .

VI. DISCUSSION

A. Applicable Legal Standards

The Met now moves for judgment, attorneys' fees, and further relief pursuant to Rules 26 and 37 of the Federal Rules of Civil Procedure, 28 U.S.C. § 1927, and the Court's inherent power.

Rule 26(g)(2) provides that:

> Every discovery request, response, or objection made by a party represented by an attorney shall be signed by at least one attorney of record in the attorney's individual name, . . . [which] constitutes a certification that to the best of the signer's knowledge, information, and belief, formed after a reasonable inquiry, the request, response, or objection is:
>
> (A) consistent with [the Federal Rules] and warranted by existing law or a good faith argument . . . ;
> (B) not interposed for any improper purpose . . . ; and (C) not unreasonable or unduly burdensome.

. . . Rule 26(g) imposes on counsel an affirmative duty to engage in pretrial discovery responsibly and "is designed to curb discovery abuse by explicitly encouraging the imposition of sanctions." . . . Furthermore, the Rule

> provides a deterrent to both excessive discovery and evasion by imposing a certification requirement that obliges each attorney to stop and think about the legitimacy of a discovery request, a response thereto, or an objection. The term "response" includes answers to interrogatories and to requests to admit as well as responses to production requests.

. . . Rule 37 addresses a variety of discovery failures that are without justification and not harmless, including failure to obey a discovery order and failure to comply with Rule 26(e) obligations (supplementing responses). Like Rule 26, Rule 37 is intended to encourage and enforce strict adherence to the "responsibilities counsel owe to the Court and to their opponents," . . . [It] authorizes a court to impose a variety of sanctions, including default judgment . . . Like Rule 26, Rule 37 authorizes imposition of sanctions for negligence or tactical intransigence as well as willful or intentional wrongs . . .

In *Residential Funding Corporation v. DeGeorge Financial Corporation,* 306 F.3d 99 (2d Cir. 2002), the Court of Appeals recently reviewed some of the procedures set forth in Rule 37 for sanctioning discovery misconduct and emphasized that a court has "broad discretion in fashioning an appropriate sanction." . . . Courts have also noted Rule 37 sanctions may be applied both to penalize conduct that warrants sanctions and "to deter those who might be tempted to such conduct in the absence of such a deterrent." . . . In Rule 37 cases, intentional behavior, actions taken in bad faith, or grossly negligent behavior justify severe disciplinary measures . . . The *Residential Funding* court also recalled earlier holdings that in determining whether evidence was made unavailable by a party with a culpable state of mind, the sanction of an adverse inference instruction was also available for negligent conduct . . . It makes little difference to the party victimized by the destruction of evidence whether that act was done willfully or negligently. The adverse inference provides the necessary mechanism for restoring the evidentiary balance. The inference is adverse to the destroyer not because of any finding of moral culpability, but because the risk that the evidence would have been detrimental rather than favorable should fall on the party responsible for its loss . . .

There are no specific requirements for the imposition of sanctions under Rule 37 . . . Over time, however, courts have identified relevant considerations to assist in deciding whether discovery abuse warrants the entry of judgment, including: "'(a) willfulness or bad faith of the noncompliant party; (b) the history, if any, of noncompliance; (c) the effectiveness of lesser sanctions; (d) whether the noncompliant party had been warned about the possibility of sanctions; (e) the client's complicity; and (f) prejudice to the moving party.'". . .

Pursuant to 28 U.S.C. § 1927:

> any attorney or other person admitted to conduct cases in any court of the United States who so multiplies the proceedings in any case unreasonably and vexatiously may be required by the court to satisfy personally the excess costs, expenses, and attorneys' fees reasonably incurred because of such conduct.

. . . Under that statute, a party must show bad faith, which is satisfied when "the attorney's actions are so completely without merit as to require the conclusion that they must have been undertaken for some improper purpose such as delay." . . .

. . . "[E]ven in the absence of a discovery order, a court may impose sanctions on a party for misconduct in discovery under its inherent power to manage its own affairs." . . . Like sanctions under § 1927, sanctions under the Court's inherent power require a finding of bad faith. Unlike § 1927, however, where a court may only sanction attorneys, under its inherent power, a court may impose sanctions on an attorney, a party, or both . . .

B. Sanctions Are Warranted in This Case

At the outset, I recognize the Court of Appeals' instruction that the entry of judgment against a defendant or "dismissal with prejudice is a harsh remedy" that should be used "only in extreme situations . . . , and then only when a court finds willfulness, bad faith, or any fault on the part of [the litigant]." . . . Nevertheless, a court "'should not shrink from imposing harsh sanctions where . . . they are clearly warranted . . . In addition, "unless Rule 37 is perceived as a credible deterrent rather than a 'paper tiger,' the pretrial quagmire threatens to engulf the entire litigative process." . . .

1. Rule 26

As is apparent from the lengthy factual recitation above,[27] Union counsel's participation in and supervision of discovery in this case was in no way "consistent with the spirit and purposes of Rules 26 through 37," and mandatory sanctions under Rule 26(g) must be imposed . . . Counsel had an affirmative duty under Rule 26(g) to make a reasonable inquiry into the basis of their discovery responses and to "stop and think about the legitimacy of [those responses]." . . . Instead, as is crystal clear in hindsight, counsel's responses to the Met's discovery requests, in formal responses, in letters . . . and to the Court—particularly counsel's repeated representations that all responsive documents had been produced—were made without any real reflection or concern for their obligations under the rules governing discovery and, in the absence of an adequate search for responsive documents, without a reasonable basis . . . Especially troubling, and of great weight in my decision to impose the most severe sanction, is that counsel's conduct was not merely negligent but was aggressively willful. Union counsel's repeated representations of full production were made in response to Met counsel's continuing high-decibel allegations of failure to make adequate inquiry and repeated demonstrations of incomplete compliance and non-compliance with discovery requests. Met counsel's questions began soon after discovery commenced and continued unabated throughout the case. Union counsel were given numerous last clear chances to comply with their discovery obligations. That, in response, Local 100's counsel continually . . .

---

[27] Despite the length of the factual recitation, it is far from a complete catalog of the discovery failures perpetrated by the Union and its counsel. Exhibit 60 to the Lans Reply Declaration is a copy of the Lans Declaration, the factual recitation upon which the Met's motion is primarily based, marked to indicate which statements were or were not contested in the Union's opposing papers. A review of that document demonstrates that the lengthy, detailed statements in the Lans Declaration setting out innumerable discovery failures by the Union and its counsel are, for the most part, uncontested. (Defendants have not challenged Lans' markings as to which items were and were not contested). In this Opinion, in an obviously futile effort toward brevity, I have only set out representative examples of the failures demonstrated . . .

professed full compliance—falsely and, as confirmed by compliance discovery, without making a reasonable inquiry—constitutes such gross negligence as to rise to intentional misconduct . . .

Counsel's primary defense . . . is to assert that there is no requirement that counsel "personally supervise every step of the discovery process" and that "counsel is expected to rely on the client's initial document production." . . . While, of course, it is true that counsel need not supervise every step of the document production process and may rely on their clients in some respects, the rule expressly requires counsel's responses to be made upon reasonable inquiry under the circumstances . . . Here, there is no doubt whatsoever that counsel failed to comply with that standard in that . . . counsel (1) never gave adequate instructions to their clients about the clients' overall discovery obligations, what constitutes a "document" or about what was specifically called for by the Met's document requests; (2) knew the Union to have no document retention or filing systems and yet never implemented a systematic procedure for document production or for retention of documents, including electronic documents; (3) delegated document production to a layperson who (at least until July 2001) did not even understand himself (and was not instructed by counsel) that a document included a draft or other non-identical copy, a computer file and an e-mail; (4) never went back to the layperson designated to assure that he had "established a coherent and effective system to faithfully and effectively respond to discovery requests," . . . and (5) in the face of the Met's persistent questioning and showings that the production was faulty and incomplete, ridiculed the inquiries, failed to take any action to remedy the situation or supplement the demonstrably false responses, failed to ask important witnesses for documents until the night before their depositions and, instead, made repeated, baseless representations that all documents had been produced. Indeed, given the almost complete disconnect between counsel (who had the document requests but knew nothing about the documents in the Union's possession other than that the files were in disarray and there was no retention system) and defendants (who had the documents but were entirely ignorant of the requirements of the requests), there is simply no way that any discovery response made by counsel could have been based on a reasonable inquiry under the circumstances . . .

Defendants' brazen assertion that looking at "comprehensive productions . . . there was no reason for any of [the Union's] counsel to question the completeness of the production," . . . betrays their willful disregard of their discovery obligations. Certainly when counsel learned that their clients, for over a year after the commencement of the litigation, had not understood that e-mails were called for and had not retained electronic documents or drafts, they should have had "reason to question" the completeness of defendants' productions (and the adequacy of their own supervision) . . . Yet counsel persisted in ignoring, indeed belittling, the Met's inquiries concerning the patent lack of production of e-mails, computer files and drafts until July 18, 2001 when I told them—fourteen months after the start of this litigation—that their failure to search for and to have instructed their clients to save computer-generated documents was inexcusable and directed them to inquire of their clients and to comply with their discovery obligations forthwith . . . Even then, counsel's disregard for their obligations continued, and no attorney performed any significant review of Union files until January 10, 2002—after the close of discovery and then only in order to respond to discovery compliance interrogatories.[31] Incredibly, that lawyer still failed to search numerous files, failed to interview several Union employees and conducted only the most superficial review of major files. . . In addition, counsel never inquired about the contents of the Union's document storage facility . . .

Through counsel's oversight, the Union never responded to the Met's Fourth Document Request at all . . . Even the responses to discovery compliance inquiries could not have been based on reasonable inquiry. For example, in response to Interrogatory No. 4 seeking the details of steps taken to respond to the Met's document requests, the Herrick Feinstein firm responded, in part, that in response to the Met's first document request, Lynett "searched Local 100's files, including all researchers' files and any other files that might contain responsive documents." . . . At his subsequent deposition, however, Lynett testified that the only files he looked at were materials Granfield and Bitterman had assembled, some files and a file cabinet next to Bitterman's desk, a file cabinet next to Granfield's desk and a file cabinet next to Diaz's desk . . . In addition . . .

---

[31] As noted in the factual recitation, Mr. Lynett did review some files in three file cabinets prior to the PI Hearing. It is undisputed, however, that no attorney attempted anything more extensive or anything like a general review until January 10, 2002.

scores of clearly responsive documents (some of which, like Weekly Reports, were expressly ordered to be produced) have never been produced.

. . . [I]t is plain that Union counsel failed in their duty "to explain to their client what types of information would be relevant and responsive to document requests and ask how and where relevant documents may be maintained.". . . Instead they "simply reacted to [Met counsel's] fortuitous discovery of the existence of relevant documents by making disjointed searches, each time coming up with a few more documents, and each time representing that that was all they had." . . . Sometimes they did not even go to the trouble of making a disjointed search but just stated that no responsive documents exist when that representation was demonstrably false . . .

Finally, Union counsel's attitude toward their discovery obligations is perhaps best reflected in several of their Spring 2002 responses. As I have noted repeatedly, Met counsel began questioning the adequacy of defendants' document search and document production almost from the outset of the case. By July of 2001, it was apparent that at least some electronic documents had not been preserved. As set out above, because of the continuing, serious questions about defendants' compliance with their discovery obligations, I permitted the Met to propound discovery requests in early 2002 regarding defendants' compliance. It was in this context that Met counsel wrote to Union counsel yet again seeking production of long-requested, oft-promised documents. Instead of complying or taking some other action consistent with their discovery obligations, counsel demonstrated their utter contempt for their discovery obligations by mischaracterizing Met counsel's requests as new and responding that discovery had "closed" on December 31 . . . There can be no doubt that counsel's repeated representations that all responsive documents had been produced were not the result of a reasonable inquiry, that counsel failed to stop and think about their responses, and that counsel did not engage in discovery responsibly—all in violation of Rule 26 . . . [T]he Union and its counsel failed "to establish a coherent and effective system to faithfully and effectively respond to discovery requests . . . [Instead, they] employed an unconscionably careless procedure to handle discovery matters, suggesting a callous disregard for [their] obligations.

2. Rule 37

Sanctions are also appropriately imposed here under Rule 37, and the factors considered under that Rule also inform my judgment regarding sanctions under 28 U.S.C. § 1927 and the Court's inherent power.

a. Willfulness or Bad Faith

. . . [T]here is ample evidence of willfulness and bad faith on the part of both counsel and the Union. First . . . counsel's continuing representations of full compliance with the Met's discovery requests in the face of constant questions being raised by Met counsel about inadequate inquiries and inadequate production were so lacking in a reasonable basis as to rise to the level of bad faith.

Second, despite defendants' arguments to the contrary . . . defendants have failed to comply with several court orders, also constituting willfulness and bad faith. Two examples relate to e-mails and the Weekly Reports . . . As to my oral ruling at the July 18, 2001 conference regarding the retention of all documents, including electronic documents . . . Yen states that "defendants' counsel understood the Court to direct an investigation into the retention and production of Local 100's e-mails and to correct any deficiencies going forward" . . . Even assuming that was the extent of the order, it was not complied with. Among other things, there is no indication that all of Local 100's computers were searched . . . Granfield's supposed search was only superficial . . . and Bitterman did not contact all of the Union's ISPs, as Anderson had represented he would . . . In any event, as noted above, all responsive e-mails have never been produced . . . Also, Granfield, the Union's current president, admitted that he failed to save documents and deleted documents from his diskette right up until his discovery compliance deposition . . . He never gave the diskette to counsel . . . and Yen never asked about it.

With regard to the Weekly Reports, at a recorded teleconference on January 7, 2002, I ordered the Union to produce those Reports that had not already been produced . . . While the parties dispute the scope of the order, it is clear that, at a minimum, the Reports for Tamarin, Granfield and Bitterman were to be produced. Although the existence of Bitterman's Reports remains in dispute . . . complete production has still not been made of the Reports for Tamarin and Granfield . . . Accordingly, there is no doubt that the defendants remain in violation of valid court orders . . .

Third, the falsehoods uttered by individual defendants and by Union counsel as to simple but material factual matters also constitute willfulness and bad faith requiring severe sanctions. For example, in his October 16, 2001 deposition, Granfield denied providing any "written reports. . . to the International with respect to [his] activities," . . . and denied that there were any "pieces of paper in [his] files that would indicate that [he] tallied up what the vote would look like from time to time" . . . In his November 15, 2001 deposition, however, Diaz testified that he and . . . Granfield filled out reports of "the weekly work that was done." . . . In his March 25, 2002 discovery compliance deposition, Granfield admitted that he prepared weekly "reports on [his] activities" that were sent to the International during 1999, 2000 and 2001 . . . and that the reports provided "a tally of the number of authorization cards that had been signed each week" . . . Although Granfield explains by affidavit essentially that he misunderstood the questions, his explanation is incredible in light of the clarity of the question asked. ("In the period from January 1999 to the present, have you or Mr. Tamarin provided any written reports to your knowledge to the International with respect to your activities?" . . .) The Weekly Reports were called for in the Met's first document request . . . and were of obvious relevance in documenting activities that are the subject of this action. That Granfield falsely denied their existence and that all such reports have to date not been produced is ample evidence of bad faith by the Union.

(i) The Ward Deposition

The machinations surrounding the deposition of Peter Ward further illustrate the bad faith with which defendants' counsel approached the discovery process and the Court's orders. As is set out above, these events occurred in December of 2001, less than a month before the discovery cut-off date. Despite the push to complete discovery (or perhaps because of it), Union counsel were tardy in informing Met counsel of Ward's supposed unavailability on account of his holiday vacation. . . .

In response to the Met's motion, Yen says that she does "not even have a vague recollection of what precise words were said in the various telephone conversations that [she] had with the Met's counsel in December 2001" but that she does "remember exclaiming something along the lines of 'come on, it's Christmas vacation.'". . . Yen also asserts that there was no "suggestion that this Court was in any way misled," . . . and, in typical hindsight, much-ado-about-nothing fashion, that "there was never any urgency to take Mr. Ward's deposition before Christmas, and there has been no prejudice to the Met from the fact that his deposition occurred in January instead," . . . Yen nowhere denies having represented that Ward was "getting on a plane."

. . . Here, the discovery deadline was less than a month away, including the holidays, and as set out above, long-sought documents had still not been produced so numerous depositions remained to be completed as the deadline loomed. Thus, the pressure to complete discovery was . . . intense . . . [T]he present record can only be read as reflecting deliberate falsehood and willful and deliberate delayed notice aimed at frustrating a court-ordered deposition.

Yen's statement to the Court that Ward was "getting on a plane" was crystal clear. In light of (1) Grubin's assertion that the statement was made, (2) Ward's testimony that he never told anyone that he was getting on a plane, (3) Yen's lack of recollection as to whether she represented Ward was getting on a plane, failure to deny that she did so represent and silence about whether Ward did or did not say he would be getting on a plane, and (4) the absence of an affidavit from Moss, the only inference that can be drawn is that Yen's statement was a deliberate falsehood intended to delay the court-ordered deposition . . . Yen's assertion that the Court was not misled is patently untrue. Had I known the true facts about Ward's presence in the New York area in late December of 2001, I would have viewed the situation entirely differently. There is no doubt that I was misled by Yen's false representation.

In the same recorded conference during his deposition, Ward testified that he "was called the morning [of December 19] and told to drop everything [he was] doing and make [himself] available for a deposition" and that he "went over to Mr. Moss' office and had been told after sitting there for almost two hours that the other side had decided they weren't prepared to go forward that day". . . Moss gave Yen "marching orders" to give Met counsel fifteen minutes notice of Ward's deposition on December 19, 2001. Because neither Moss nor Yen disputes Ward's testimony that he was called in the morning and "sat around" for some two hours in Moss' office before being told that Met counsel could not attend, the only inference to be drawn is that Moss instructed Yen to delay giving Met counsel notice in order to frustrate my order that Ward's deposition be started before Ward left on vacation.

Contrary to Yen's attempts to minimize those falsehoods and machinations, it is beside the point that, in her view, there was no urgency to the Ward deposition and no prejudice to the Met from taking the deposition in January, not December. The point is that under the circumstances, counsel's conduct was not "merely discourteous" but rather a breach of their responsibility to opposing counsel and the Court . . . to engage in discovery in good faith, comply with court orders and, more fundamentally, to tell the truth . . . There is no doubt that the circumstances surrounding the Ward deposition demonstrate bad faith by Moss and Yen. Accordingly, the Met's motion for sanctions based on Union counsel's behavior as to the Ward deposition is granted.

b. The History of Non-Compliance

As is set forth at length above, the Union and its counsel have failed to comply with their discovery obligations from the very outset of this action . . . [D]efendants' non-compliance and failure to make an adequate search has continued to the present in the face of continuing complaints from Met counsel. This factor weighs heavily in favor of the most severe sanctions.

c. The Client's Complicity

. . . [T]he discovery abuses evidenced here cannot be laid solely at counsel's door. Although the degree of the Union's complicity cannot be measured accurately on this record, that it was significant cannot be doubted. For example, the Union's failure to produce Weekly Reports proceeded initially from Granfield's false testimony that he prepared no log of his activities on behalf of the Union and that there were no documents reflecting the Union's view of the current vote tally.

The Union's failure to set up an adequate system for document production resulted primarily from the glaring omissions of Bitterman. Granfield put Bitterman, the Union's head researcher, in charge of assembling documents. . . Bitterman, however, has no record or recollection of what steps he took to do so. He did not create a checklist or any other written record of what he did . . . He did not give written instructions regarding document production to anyone and does not recall giving copies of the Met's document requests to anyone . . .

Bitterman also made less than a good faith effort to produce documents that were responsive.[35] For example, although Bitterman knew throughout the case that Weekly Reports were maintained by most nonclerical employees of the Union . . . and he testified that he looked through the file cabinet maintained by Myhre in which the Weekly Reports are kept . . . he never suggested to counsel that they might be responsive, for example, as communications relating to communications about the Met . . . Also, although Bitterman testified that he understood after July of 2001 that computers were to be searched for documents and he knew that e-mails were to be requested from ISPs, he has no memory of what he did with respect to certain computers . . . and personally looked only at his laptop and the computer nearest to him . . . Also, he admittedly failed to contact all of the Union's ISPs.

Perhaps most indicative of Bitterman's lack of good faith effort is that he never checked back with the few employees he did speak with to be sure they were complying with his instructions, such as they were . . . A review of . . . the entirety of Bitterman's compliance deposition convinces me that his document production efforts were purposely scattershot, intended only to go through the motions.

Such a haphazard effort at collecting responsive documents is insufficient. More is required—even of an inadequately instructed layperson. Bitterman failed to communicate with all Union employees who were likely to have relevant documents, including such obvious persons as Rimmelin, the office manager and keeper of the storage facility inventory. He failed to execute specific, narrow instructions, such as contacting all the Union's ISPs, and failed overall to put into place any organized method of collecting responsive documents, instead assuming that those employees he did speak to would remember to put "Met-related" documents in the designated box. . . Even adjusting for Bitterman's lay status, he, and thus the Union, failed "to

---

[35] Granfield, the then-incoming Union president, also reflects the Union's less than good faith approach to document discovery . . . Tamarin, the then-outgoing Union president, was also grossly inadequate in his own document search. For example, he never even looked at the documents in his Chicago office . . .

establish a coherent and effective system to faithfully and effectively respond to discovery requests." . . . Instead, the Union, through Bitterman, "employed an unconscionably careless procedure to handle discovery matters, suggesting a callous disregard for its obligations as a litigant." . . .

. . . The Union's complicity in the discovery failures weighs in favor of sanctions against the Union itself.

d. Prejudice

First, the Union's assertion that the Met must show prejudice before a sanction may be ordered under Rule 37 is without merit . . . The Union is wrong on the law.

Second, in any event, the Met has demonstrated that it has been prejudiced by the Union's discovery failures. Because of counsel's failure to instruct their clients properly about discovery obligations, the Union's haphazard search and both the Union's and counsel's failure to check that an adequate search was made, it is beyond peradventure that many documents have been destroyed that related directly to events taking place during the most critical time period in this action, that is, when the Union planned its campaign against the Met, decided what its leaflets, letters and other public statements would say and on what basis . . . Those documents, from that most critical period, have not been retrieved. Moreover, the documents that have been produced were often produced in an untimely, disorganized fashion, after numerous letters and telephone calls were exchanged and court conferences held and after the depositions of the relevant witnesses. The Met was not only denied the opportunity to prove its case but was denied the opportunity to plan its strategy in an organized fashion as the case proceeded . . .

. . . [M]any important documents were produced after the depositions of key witnesses. All of these obstructions prevented the Met from adequately planning and preparing its case; it was forced to proceed with depositions before relevant documents were produced, it was no doubt hampered . . . in preparing for trial. The Union's continued reference to the large number of pages it has produced is irrelevant in the face of conclusive evidence that at least a year's worth of electronic documents from the time period most critical to the action have been destroyed while Met counsel continually called attention to the failure . . . This factor weighs in favor of a severe sanction.

e. Effectiveness of Lesser Sanctions

Finally, I find that lesser sanctions, such as an adverse inference or preclusion, would not be effective in this case. I acknowledge the judicial system's preference for resolving cases on the merits . . . [T]he Union's wholesale destruction of documents, by omission or commission, has made that preferred path impossible . . . There is no indication that lesser sanctions would bring about compliance, and "there is no meaningful way in which to correlate [defendants'] discovery failures with discrete issues in the case."

Finally, because of the egregiousness of the conduct at issue and because it continued in the face of repeated, documented examples of non-compliance and repeated inquiries by Met counsel and the Court, a lesser sanction would not be adequate to penalize the Union and its counsel here or to deter others from similar misconduct in the future . . . Thus, this factor also counsels the most severe sanctions. Accordingly, all of the factors generally considered under Rule 37 call for imposition of the most severe sanction.

3. 28 U.S.C. § 1927

. . . I have found that Union counsel's failures to comply with their discovery obligations and their unreasonable obstruction and delay of discovery to be "so completely without merit as to require the conclusion that they must have been undertaken for some improper purpose such as delay." . . . The factual recitation leaves no doubt that counsel's conduct multiplied the proceedings "unreasonably and vexatiously." The time and effort spent on discovery follow-up letters and conferences with counsel and the Court was far beyond what is normal, even in a contentious, hard-fought litigation, and . . . the compliance discovery well beyond normal parameters. Accordingly, sanctions are also appropriate under § 1927.

Defendants incorrectly argue that they are required to have received an explicit warning that they might be sanctioned. To the contrary, "parties and counsel have no absolute right 'to be warned that they disobey court orders at their peril,'" . . .

4. The Met Directors' Depositions

Perhaps of particular relevance under § 1927 is Moss' and Yen's behavior with respect to the Met Directors' depositions . . . I ordered limited depositions of six Met Directors, over Met counsel's objections, together with expedited document production from those individuals. With both the discovery deadline and the holidays approaching, Met counsel spent time over approximately a two-week period preparing the six witnesses and finalizing December 18, 19, 20, 27 and 28 as the dates for their depositions. On December 13, the Thursday before the first scheduled Tuesday deposition, Union counsel informed Met counsel that . . . the Union no longer wished to pursue the Directors' depositions. By way of explanation, Yen explains essentially that she and Moss changed their strategy and determined that it would be more advantageous to depose other Met-related individuals than the Directors and that they delayed notifying Met counsel of their decision because of the "previous difficulty in serving the Met's directors."

Although Moss' and Yen's delay in notifying Met counsel of their decision to cancel the Met Directors' depositions was rude and costly, both in fees and in precious time during the holiday season just before the close of discovery, I cannot say with confidence that counsel's conduct was so lacking in merit as to constitute bad faith. Accordingly, the Met's motion for fees for cancellation of the Met Directors' depositions is denied under § 1927 and, because it also requires a finding of bad faith, the Court's inherent power. Although bad faith is not required under Rules 26 and 37, the motion is also denied under those rules in light of counsel's explanation of their tactical reasons for the delay in notice.

5. The Court's Inherent Power

. . . [N]ecessary to the Court's conducting judicial business in our adversary system is the inherent power to sanction those who deviate from the standards of good faith . . . Equally necessary to continuing to conduct judicial business is actually exercising that power . . . [D]efendants and their counsel are squarely in this category [of deviating from standards of good faith]. To fail to use the Court's inherent power to sanction on the facts presented here would diminish the Court's authority and the adversary system and would serve as a license, encouraging similar behavior. Accordingly, the Met's motion for sanctions pursuant to the Court's inherent power is also granted.

VII. CONCLUSION

Plaintiff's motion for judgment as to liability against defendants and for additional sanctions in the form of attorneys' fees necessitated by the discovery abuse by defendants and their counsel . . . is granted against defendants and their counsel.

Had the attorneys done their job and made it clear to the clients what was expected and followed up with the issues, and, probably even more important from the judge's point of view, not lied to the court and consistently evaded their responsibility to comply with discovery (or at the very least make a good-faith attempt), the responsibility would have been placed solely on the clients. As the opinion reads, the judge was fed up with the actions of the attorneys and was not giving them any wiggle room. I get the impression that she was condemning the manner in which the Union's attorneys dealt with their clients, and I wouldn't want to be in their shoes if the Union decided to file a malpractice claim. The firms involved also now have their practices publicly disclosed to all their friends and neighbors in the legal community, who will probably be glad to cite the case should they try to repeat this behavior. The case may also be used to impeach any of the involved parties if they testify in the future, as it deals with their credibility.

I hope you only deal with spitballs, but when you are dealing with a pattern of evasion for both electronic and traditional documents, you will need extensive notes about any discussions you've had with the other side's paralegal or attorney. Because you won't know initially that you are dealing with a situation of this magnitude, you can't simply take notes on an **ad hoc** basis. You need to keep track of what you said, to whom you said it, and when. The same goes for talking to your own clients about disclosure. The judge in *Metropolitan Opera Ass'n* was clearly unimpressed with bald assertions by counsel that they discussed discovery matters "repeatedly" when these details were not available. If there's a problem with responsiveness of discovery, you want to be able to show the court a good-faith effort on your part.

In *Metropolitan Opera Ass'n* there was a problem of missing or destroyed e-mail. To avoid falling into this trap, make sure you explain to clients that they should not destroy any e-mail that is in any way related to the litigation. Clients are often tempted to simply withhold or destroy damaging information, particularly when it is as seemingly **ephemeral** as e-mail. As the case illustrates, it is sometimes suprising how much the other side will become aware of in the litigation: not everyone will realize that some fishy things have been going on and, bless their hearts, they tell the truth. The perpetual liars, on the other hand, lose track of their stories and sometimes slip up and get caught. The *Metropolitan Opera Ass'n* case is a good primer on how you should *not* behave in discovery, which is what makes it worth reading such a long case.

It's amazing what a small world it is and how often someone knows someone who knows someone who is somehow connected to the information in litigation. The following is an example of a related sort of connection that did not link two opposing firms with informal sources of information, but was nonetheless crucial to the case. On National Public Radio's *Talk of the Nation* on March 29, 2004, a caller responded to the show's request for former jurors to discuss their experience. He told a story about hearing a friend describe a particular doctor as being shady upon learning that the caller was serving on a civil jury—and it was one of the doctors testifying in the trial upon which he sat. In violation of the rules, the juror shared the information with the rest of the jurors, which resulted in the loss of the case for the plaintiff. Had counsel found out about it, this action on the part of the juror could have resulted in a mistrial; no one from either side discussed the case with the juror afterwards.

CHAPTER SUMMARY

Electronic documents are a special area of concern because of the data that is encoded in them. Electronic files and computers themselves should be inspected to enable the parties to fully assess the information contained therein. Any revisions to the material often can be recovered by an expert in the data recovery field. The allocation of expenses may be done in a way so as to protect defendants from having to bear all the cost, but e-mails are still a problem because of the relative flippancy with which they are drafted. Following rules about how to avoid problems in e-mail and transmitting those rules to clients is important. Trying to cover up, destroy, avoid, or otherwise impede discovery of electronic documents (as well as regular documents) can result in serious sanctions to the client or her attorneys.

FOR FURTHER READING

Comment, Michael Marron, *Discoverability of "Deleted" E-Mail: Time for a Closer Examination*, 25 Seattle Univ. L. R. 895 (2002).

Devin Murphy, *The Discovery of Electronic Data in Litigation: What Practitioners and Their Clients Need to Know*, 27 Wm. Mitchell L. Rev. 1825 (2001).

Martin H. Redish, *Electronic Discovery and the Litigation Matrix*, 51 Duke L.J. 561 (2001).

Mark D. Robins, *Computers and the Discovery of Evidence—A New Dimension to Civil Procedure*, 17 J. Marshall J. Computer & Info. L. 411 (1999).

CHAPTER REVIEW

KEY TERMS

ad hoc	discovery abuse	metadata
backup tapes	dispositive	ostensibly
blunderbuss	ephemeral	progeny
colorable	fragmented data	spoliation
death penalty sanctions	JBOD	

FILL IN THE BLANKS

1. When data are stored in _____, it mirrors the way the computer stores things, not the way people would look for information.

2. _____ on the part of clients and attorneys when discovery responses are straightforward leads to trouble with the court. Even when these individuals are not actually sanctioned, the behavior is noted and may result in unfavorable treatment from the judge in discretionary matters.

3. Information without a program or other organizing principle is referred to by the acronym _____.

4. E-mail seems _____ since it comes and goes so easily, but it actually can persists in the hard drive of your computer.

5. Data that has been pulled apart and stored in various bits around the computer is called _____.

6. Rather than using _____ procedures, it is better to have a plan of how to supervise the client's disclosure of information in response to discovery requests.

7. A motion or order that takes care of all the issues before the court is _____.

8. A party who destroys evidence within his control will be subject to a claim of _____, which may be handled in a variety of ways, depending on the jurisdiction.

9. The term for a punishment for not acting according to the established rules of procedure is a(n) _____.

10. Some lawyers or legal assistants prepare discovery in such a way as to be simply hoping to get something in a broad or vague request; this _____ approach (also called a "fishing expedition") is objectionable.

11. _____ will do "anything" to win and believe that approach constitutes _____ of their clients, instead of balancing their duties to the court and to the opposing side. (They also run up their clients' legal fees).

12. The offspring of a particular case is known as its _____.

13. Information about the information residing in a computer is _____.

14. Data left over after deleting are _____.

15. Storage that is easily available, such as that in a hard disk, is _____.

16. When a party _____ is complying with discovery requests, but it later turns out that he was not, sanctions may be proper.

17. Things that end at the same place are _____.

18. Information stored in a medium placed in a reader, such as a floppy disk, is _____.

19. Using the discovery process to harass the other side and to make unreasonable demands is called _____.

20. Stored and/or shelved information outside the computer is called _____.

21. A sanction that results in the automatic loss of the case by the sanctioned party is referred to as a(n) _____.

WEB WORK

1. Go to Kroll Ontrack at http://www.krollontrac.com and check out its Law Library and Legal Tools. There's good stuff there about electronic evidence (eEvidence) and discovery rules as well as sample forms.

2. CNT has white papers on the legal requirements for record retention in the financial industry at http://www.cnt.com/literature/documents/PL731.pdf. You'll need Adobe Acrobat Reader for this, available free at www.adobe.com. If the specific address doesn't work, try www.cnt.com and use the links to find it.

3. CBL Data Recovery Technologies has some information about the process of digital evidence collection. Use the link to Data Forensics from their home page at http://www.cbltech.com.

4. Go to the Web site of the software provider that was used in the *Zubulake* case: www.veritas.com. Look for information about the Veritas NetBackup program.

5. Go to Google and run "metadata" and then click on the link to News results. Take a look at the stories published on the topic.

WORKING THE BRAIN

1. Should e-discovery be treated any differently than any other kind? Why or why not?

2. What should the Union's legal firm in *Metropolitan Opera* have done differently in terms of client contact? Do you think that there is some sort of SOP (standard operating procedure) that should be adopted to avoid the problems in that case?

3. It's easy to get lost in all the verbiage of *Rowe*, and that's just the edited version. Go through the opinion and make a flow chart of its test for determining how to allocate costs. Do you come up with the same factors *Zubulake* did?

4. Do you think the *Zubulake* factors will have the intended effect?

5. What advice do you think should be given to clients regarding e-mails? When and how should this advice be relayed? What are potential pitfalls in sharing this advice?

PUTTING IT TO WORK

1. Draft a motion to allocate costs based on the *Rowe* test, using the facts attributable to one of the parties in that case.

2. Make a checklist of instructions and/or procedures to use to assist clients in compliance with discovery.

3. Draft a motion for sanctions based on just one of the complained of actions in *Gates Rubber* or *Metropolitan Opera*.

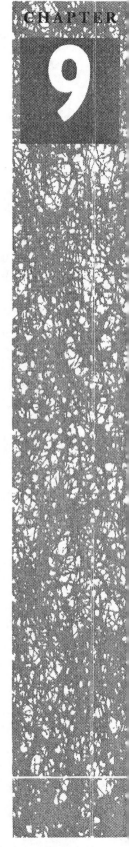

BACKGROUND RESOURCES

> "Knowledge may give weight, but accomplishments give luster, and many more people see than weigh."
>
> *Philip Dormer Stanhope, Earl of Chesterfield (1750)*
>
> "Learn, compare, collect the facts!"
>
> *Ivan Petrovich Pavlov (1936)*
>
> "A little learning is a dangerous thing; drink deep, or taste not."
>
> *Alexander Pope (1711)*
>
> "Books are the treasured wealth of the world . . . Their authors are a natural and irresistible aristocracy in every society, and, more than kings or emperors, exert an influence on mankind."
>
> *Henry David Thoreau (1849)*

INTRODUCTION

Some sources you will use to understand the documents you have gathered in your investigation or to establish certain facts that have a bearing on your case are not documents that your client, your expert, or anyone on your legal team will produce or create. These facts may or may not be in contention; they often are simply facts that must be established to link various events or facts together or that must be established because you have the burden to do so, even if the fact is not in contention. These sources can also help establish generally accepted **standards of care** for tort work as benchmarks for the jury to compare with the actions of the defendant. Some of these are from sources used regularly because they are easy to obtain, reliable, and easy to have admitted into evidence. These sources may contain information from reference books, maps, and governmental agencies, or may be reference books, maps, or publications of governmental agencies. You may also want to find data from services or organizations ordinarily used by a particular industry to establish things like ordinary costs, typical accident rates, average salaries, model policies, and so on. Finding these types of written evidence is simply a matter of knowing to look for them.

Perhaps your case involves an employment discrimination claim based on disparate impact, which requires the plaintiff to prove that a policy of the employer has made it harder for a particular ethnic group to be hired or promoted. The plaintiff is a Japanese-American. Regardless of whom you represent, you need to find out the overall population of Japanese-Americans in your area to see if there is a chance of the plaintiff's prevailing: you will need to compare that ethnic group's population in the locale to their representation in the defendant employer's company. Reports may vary from year to year, but overall these percentages are usually not a major basis of dispute, barring a sudden influx of immigrants.

This type of information—that which is not specific to the individuals involved in the case or that which is publicly available—is the focus here.

ETHICAL ISSUES

The main issue of ethics in this context is one that has been highlighted in the previous two chapters: the duty of fairness to opposing counsel and honesty to the court. You must disclose the sources as necessary under the relevant discovery requests and you must use these sources in good faith. At any time you become aware that a source is no longer reliable, you must withdraw it. *Reliable* in this sense does not mean that no one disputes it; often reports are disputed even though they are reliable. Instead, *reliable* in this sense refers to the instance where, for example, the report is replaced by a revised version or an editorial correction is issued by a publisher.

EVIDENTIARY ISSUES

In matters that are covered by common sources, you may ask the court to take **judicial notice** of the evidence. This process relieves the attorney of the cumbersome process of asking a witness the appropriate foundation questions for admission—a tedious line of questions that makes jurors' attention wander—and instead allows the attorney to have the evidence admitted early and easily.

The operative parts of the federal rule governing judicial notice are as follows.

Rule 201. Judicial Notice of Adjudicative Facts

b. Kinds of facts.

A judicially noticed fact must be one not subject to reasonable dispute in that it is either

1. generally known within the territorial jurisdiction of the trial court or
2. capable of accurate and ready determination by resort to sources whose accuracy cannot reasonably be questioned.

c. When discretionary.

A court may take judicial notice, whether requested or not.

d. When mandatory.

A court shall take judicial notice if requested by a party and supplied with the necessary information.

e. Opportunity to be heard.

A party is entitled upon timely request to an opportunity to be heard as to the propriety of taking judicial notice and the tenor of the matter noticed. In the absence of prior notification, the request may be made after judicial notice has been taken.

f. Time of taking notice.

Judicial notice may be taken at any stage of the proceeding.

g. Instructing jury.

In a civil action or proceeding, the court shall instruct the jury to accept as conclusive any fact judicially noticed . . .

Fed. R. Evid. 201.

Thus, three requirements are in place for a party to obtain judicial notice of a fact: (1) it must be a fact that is not subject to reasonable argument; (2) the judge must be given the information when the request to take notice is made; and (3) timely notice should be given to opposing counsel. Although the rule does provide for a way around the third requirement, the better practice is to have a motion to take judicial notice prepared to file and serve along with a motion in limine. This way, preliminary evidentiary issues will be dispensed with at the same time. What is a little frightening is that the judge may take judicial notice of facts **sua sponte.** Although it's not clear how often this happens in the trial courts, it appears to be happening in the appellate courts, which adds a bit of evidence to the trial outside the control of the parties. This independent fact-finding could add a wildcard to the outcome of any particular case. For instance, in the dissenting opinion *United States v. Brown*, 159 F.3d 147 (3d Cir. 1998), Judge Rendell's disagreement with the majority opinion is based on his own check of the facts. The case involves the stop-and-frisk of a defendant "one block over" from a shooting location. The relative locations were established by the testimony of the police officer. The judge's check on Mapquest (**www.mapquest.com**) found the search location to be farther away than a block. If the trial judge had made the same search and announced it to the jury during a trial where that proximity was in issue, it could destroy the prosecution's case. Moreover, the defense attorney should have come up with it on his own during his investigation of the case.

In the following termination case, the court made a blanket statement about judicial notice in family law cases. It may be hard to follow exactly what was judicially noticed.

In re Interest of L.H. v. D.H., 487 N.W.2d 279 (Neb. 1992).

. . . After a long series of dispositional hearings, the juvenile court terminated appellant's parental rights in the children. D.H. appeals the orders of the juvenile court. We affirm.

. . . On March 6, 1985, the State filed a petition . . . alleging that D.H.'s oldest child, L.H. was a juvenile [who] lacked proper parental care by reason of the faults or habits of her mother. The State specifically alleged:

a. On or about February 18, 1985, said child was placed in protective custody because the whereabouts of [D.H.] were unknown.
b. On numerous occasions, said child has been left with relatives and non-relatives by [D.H.], for prolonged periods, without making prior arrangements, and her whereabouts are unknown during said absences.
c. [D.H.] suffers from a dependence upon alcoholic beverages which impairs her ability to provide the necessary parental care, protection and supervision required by said child.

. . . At the adjudication hearing on June 27, 1985, D.H. admitted the allegations . . .

At a dispositional hearing held on August 14, 1985, attended by D.H. and her counsel, the court received four exhibits: a report containing a rehabilitation plan, a foster care report, a chemical dependency evaluation, and a home evaluation of D.H.'s uncle and aunt, who wanted to provide a home for L.H. . . .

A further hearing was held on February 14, 1986. The court concluded at the hearing that D.H. had not fully complied with the rehabilitation plan; she did not enter the inpatient alcoholism treatment program, but instead involved herself in outpatient counseling; she had not maintained full-time employment; she had not provided for adequate housing; and she had not entered the Mother's Support Group . . .

At the next review hearing on August 20, 1986, . . . D.H. still did not comply with the plan. She failed to visit L.H., to participate in the alcohol counseling, and to maintain stable housing. She had attended the Mother's Support Group only twice since the previous review hearing . . .

On December 16, 1987, the court became aware of some domestic violence that occurred between D.H. and W.D., her boyfriend and L.H.'s father. In addition, the court noted that D.H. had started drinking again . . .

At the hearing on May 13, 1988, the court took notice of the facts that the D.H. did not maintain stable housing, that there had again been some physical abuse between her and W.D., and that D.H. had not attended the domestic violence groups. The court ordered D.H. and W.D. to enter into chemical dependency and codependency treatment . . .

During the next review hearing, on February 13, 1989, the court noted that D.H. still had not complied with the visitation orders, had not participated in the chemical dependency and codependency programs, and had not gone to the domestic violence counseling. The court ordered D.H. to attend relinquishment counseling.

On March 28, 1989, the county attorney filed a petition . . . alleging that D.H.'s other three children, A.H. . . . W.H. . . . , and T.H. . . . , were juveniles [exhibiting] lack of care by reason of the faults or habits of their mother . . .

A detention hearing regarding A.H., W.H., and T.H. was held on April 19, 1989, with the mother and her counsel present. D.H. did not resist the children's detention, and the court entered an order placing temporary custody of the three children with DSS. The court ordered a foster placement for T.H., and placed A.H. and W.H. in the physical custody of their mother.

On November 14, 1989, the court held an adjudication hearing regarding A.H., W.H., and T.H. D.H.'s aunt testified that on about January 27, 1989, D.H. asked her to babysit A.H., W.H., and T.H. for a weekend. D.H. returned 15 days later. Her aunt had not known where she was. D.H. had not provided her aunt with enough supplies for the children. Her aunt also did not know the whereabouts of W.D. A babysitter testified that D.H. brought T.H. over to her house in March 1989 and asked her whether she could take care of the baby for one night. D.H. brought her baby supplies for one day. D.H. did not return for her baby, and the babysitter was not aware of her whereabouts. D.H. never called to ask about her baby. The babysitter turned the baby over to the police on March 13, 1989. D.H. testified that she left her children with her aunt because she wanted "some space to try to find myself." She stated that she did not intend to leave for two weeks. She spent her time away cleaning the house, buying a bed for the children, and talking to friends. She testified that she was working as a nurse's aide. She admitted leaving T.H. at the babysitter's house. She denied having a habit of leaving her children at other people's houses . . .

A disposition hearing was held on December 20, 1989, concerning A.H., W.H., and T.H. The record indicates that D.H. had not made herself available to the probation officer and CPS.

Another review hearing was held for L.H. on June 13, 1990. The evidence shows that D.H. and W.D. still failed to fully comply with the court orders.

On July 15, 1990, the State took protective custody of A.H., W.H., and T.H. . . . and the court ordered detention of the children because continuation of the children in their home would be contrary to their welfare. Apparently, the mother again left her children with her aunt and other caretakers for extended periods of time, which resulted in D.H.'s conviction for child abuse on July 16, 1990. The record also shows a shooting incident between D.H. and W.D.

On December 5, 1990, the State filed a motion for termination of the parental rights between D.H. and her four children, L.H., A.H., W.H., and T.H. . . .

A hearing on the motion to terminate the parental rights was held on May 9, 1991, with D.H. present in person and with counsel. The testimony shows that D.H. had not successfully completed the chemical dependency and codependency treatment; she had lived in 18 different residences since 1985; she had never fully participated in the domestic violence group, despite the fact that there was much violence between D.H. and W.D.; she had not maintained a stable income; she had attended AA meetings on only an irregular basis and had not always provided proof of attendance; she had left her three youngest children at other people's residences for extended periods of time and was charged with three counts of child abuse as a result of that; she had not provided her children with adequate care and supervision; she had not kept in contact on a regular basis with officers assigned to the case; and she had often not made scheduled visits to L.H. In her own defense, D.H. testified that she had lived at seven or eight locations, not 18.

The court terminated D.H.'s parental rights to all four children on May 15, 1991 . . .

D.H. argues that the juvenile court, during the termination hearing, erred in taking judicial notice of exhibits offered at the August 14, 1985, hearing. From D.H.'s argument, it appears this error is based on a claim that the August 14 dispositional hearing did not take place; consequently, the four exhibits were not properly a part of the record and a part of the State's motion for judicial notice, and therefore, the mother did not have an opportunity to either object to or cross-examine the authors of the exhibits, amounting to a denial of her due process rights.

Concerning the alleged August 14, 1985, hearing, the bill of exceptions for that date includes only the four exhibits, with one exhibit bearing the typed notation: "No Hearing was held. Reports submitted." The transcript includes a signed court order of a hearing held on August 14, 1985, attended by D.H. with counsel;

it shows that the exhibits were received into evidence and that the court entered a rehabilitation order with terms, which order was subject to review in 6 months.

The bill of exceptions shows that reference was made during the February 14, 1986, hearing to a hearing held on August 14, 1985.

We assign no verity to the typed notation on the exhibit, and conclude that a dispositional hearing was held on August 14, 1985, attended by D.H. with counsel, and that the four exhibits were part of the court records and therefore exhibits in case No. S-91-598.

At the consolidated termination hearing, attended by D.H. with counsel, the State moved the court to take judicial notice of the court's own records, exhibits, and orders . . . No objection being made, the court agreed to the motion.

At issue here are the following four summarized exhibits . . . . : (1) a report to the court, dated August 2, 1985, and drafted by Anna Foster, a DSS service officer; Burton, the CPS worker; and David Stickman, the guardian ad litem, which report proposed a rehabilitation plan that was generally adopted at the hearing; (2) a printed form, dated July 9, 1985, of a foster care case plan review with recommendations by Burton; (3) a chemical evaluation of D.H., dated July 16, 1985, by Barbara Preston, counselor; and (4) a home evaluation, dated June 17, 1985, concerning the home of D.H.'s aunt and uncle in Omaha, Nebraska, prepared by Linda Hruska of DSS. All these exhibits were clearly hearsay evidence and subject to objection if promptly made . . .

The concept of judicial notice of disputed allegations has no place in hearings to terminate parental rights . . . "[In] proceedings to terminate parental rights, reports may not be received in evidence for the purpose of that proceeding, nor otherwise relied upon by the court, unless they have been admitted without objection" . . .

Since the failure of D.H.'s counsel to object to the judicial notice motion constituted a waiver of her rights to cross-examine the authors of the exhibits, the court did not commit a procedural error in granting the motion to take judicial notice of the documents. Absent a showing to the contrary, it is presumed that the trial court disregarded all incompetent and irrelevant evidence . . .

In this case, the court took judicial notice of its record, even though the evidence within it could have been held inadmissible. Generally, a court may take judicial notice of its own proceedings, including any documents within those proceedings. It cannot, on the other hand, take judicial notice of disputed facts contained within the records. D.H.'s attorney blew it twice. First, at the August hearing, he should have objected to the reports if he had a problem with them. The reports involved were authored variously by Department of Social Services officers, the guardian ad litem, Child Protective Services officers, and a counselor. Most of them could have been admitted under the proper hearsay exclusion, as you'll see below. Second, the attorney failed to object to the State's motion for judicial notice, so he waived any argument to that motion. I wonder if this case was the subject of a motion for judicial notice when D.H. took her lawyer to task for these two omissions.

If evidence does not come in through judicial notice, you can still have it entered. Remember, though, that documents are also hearsay, so you have to make sure you have the proper exception to cover the item you wish to admit. If your documents are from a governmental entity, you can see if either of these exceptions apply.

8. Public records and reports. Records, reports, statements, or data compilations, in any form, of public offices or agencies, setting forth
   a. the activities of the office or agency, or
   b. matters observed pursuant to duty imposed by law as to which matters there was a duty to report, excluding, however, in criminal cases matters observed by police officers and other law enforcement personnel, or
   c. in civil actions and proceedings and against the Government in criminal cases, factual findings resulting from an investigation made pursuant to authority granted by law, unless the sources of information or other circumstances indicate lack of trustworthiness.
9. Records of vital statistics. Records or data compilations, in any form, of births, fetal deaths, deaths, or marriages, if the report thereof was made to a public office pursuant to requirements of law.

Fed. R. Civ. P. 803(8), (9).

In civil cases, you must establish that there was a duty imposed by law for the observations or legal authority for an investigation for factual findings to admit a public record or report. This includes police reports, reports by the Occupational Safety and Health Administration (OSHA), and other agencies. Often no one objects to the police report even though it's available; that's a tactical matter for the attorney to decide. If you are finding this kind of information, you want to make sure that you have the statutes that indicate the governmental entity had the authority or duty to make the report your client potentially will need introduced into evidence. Also be sure there are no regulations restricting the use of such reports. The same considerations apply to vital statistic records.

Interestingly, though, there is a line of cases that allow for an attack on the admissibility of police reports which can be used if you would like to exclude a problem police report. These cases are contrary to what was discussed in the earlier chapter about police reports, and, if followed, could render most police reports inadmissible. This New Hampshire case is illustrative of the principle used to keep out those reports.

Worster v. Watkins, 669 A.2d 212 (N.H. 1995).

The plaintiff, Philip Worster, appeals from a jury verdict finding the defendant, Mark Watkins, not liable for damages resulting from injuries sustained by the plaintiff during a fight at the defendant's house. The plaintiff argues that the [trial court] erred when it ruled that two out-of-court statements were inadmissible at trial. We affirm.

On August 10, 1991, the defendant held a bachelor party in his home. The plaintiff attended the party and became involved in a fight between the groom and another guest. During the fight, a fourth person, Stephen Fowlie, joined the altercation and struck the plaintiff in the jaw with either a tire iron or a wrench. The blow fractured the plaintiff's jaw.

On October 22, 1991, more than two months after the party, Fowlie was arrested and charged with assault in connection with his attack on the plaintiff. While in custody, Fowlie gave Detective Ted Curtis of the Merrimack Police Department a written confession in which he said that the defendant wanted him to attend the bachelor party to prevent guests from fighting and to act as a designated driver. Detective Curtis filed a supplementary investigation report following his interview with Fowlie, summarizing what Fowlie had told him.

Armed with Fowlie's confession and the police report, the plaintiff filed suit against the defendant. The plaintiff alleged that Fowlie was acting as the defendant's agent when the assault occurred and, therefore, that the defendant was liable for damages.

Prior to trial, the defendant moved in limine to exclude Fowlie's written confession and the supplementary investigation report filed by Detective Curtis. The defendant argued that both out-of-court statements were hearsay. The plaintiff countered by arguing that the documents could be introduced under specific exceptions to the hearsay rule . . .

On May 18, 1994, the jury returned a verdict in favor of the defendant. The plaintiff appeals on the ground that the trial court erred in granting the defendant's motion in limine . . .

The plaintiff first challenges the trial court's refusal to admit Stephen Fowlie's written confession into evidence. The plaintiff concedes that the confession is hearsay, but he argues that it should have been admitted under New Hampshire Rule of Evidence 804(b)(3). Rule 804(b)(3) provides an exception to the hearsay rule for a statement which was, at the time it was made, contrary to the declarant's penal or pecuniary interest. Such a statement is admissible because "one does not make [a] statement that would damage oneself unless the statement is true." . . .

Before such a statement can be admitted into evidence, however, the party introducing it must prove that the declarant is "unavailable" to testify at trial . . . A declarant is "unavailable" for trial if he satisfies any of the conditions listed in Rule 804(a). The only condition relevant here is found in Rule 804(a)(5), which states that a declarant is unavailable if he "is absent from the hearing and the proponent of [his] statement has been unable to procure [his] attendance (or in the case of a hearsay exception under subdivision (b)(2), (3), or (4), [his] attendance or testimony) by process or other reasonable means." N.H. R. Ev. 804(a)(5).

The plaintiff attempted to locate Fowlie in an effort to secure his attendance at trial. When efforts to locate Fowlie produced only two addresses—one in Maine and one in Florida—the plaintiff concluded that he was unable, by process or other reasonable means, to bring Fowlie to New Hampshire to testify. Therefore, he argues, Fowlie was unavailable for purposes of Rule 804(a)(5).

Rule 804(a)(5), however, requires a more rigorous showing of unavailability than the one made by the plaintiff. Even assuming the plaintiff demonstrated that Fowlie could not be forced to attend the trial, the parenthetical clause in Rule 804(a)(5) required the plaintiff to show that he could not procure Fowlie's "testimony" for trial. N.H. R. Ev. 804(a)(5). We interpret that clause to mean that the plaintiff had to demonstrate that he was unable to depose Fowlie . . . Jurisdictions examining the corresponding federal rule have concluded that Congress intended to adopt an "attempt to depose" standard . . . Because New Hampshire's version of Rule 804(a)(5) is identical in every important respect to the federal rule, we find those cases persuasive in our interpretation of the New Hampshire rule . . .

In this case, the trial court found that the plaintiff made no effort to depose Fowlie before trial and therefore ruled that he was not unavailable for purposes of Rule 804. We see no reason to overturn the trial court's ruling. We will assume for purposes of this case that the plaintiff's duty to depose Fowlie did not arise until he learned that Fowlie was not going to appear at trial in response to the subpoena sent to his last known address in New Hampshire. After learning that Fowlie would not appear to testify, the plaintiff made no effort to contact Fowlie in Maine or Florida—or to request a continuance to give him time to do so—despite having specific information about his location. We conclude, therefore, that the trial court reasonably held that the plaintiff failed to meet the requirements of Rule 804(a)(5) . . .

The plaintiff next challenges the trial court's refusal to admit Detective Curtis' supplementary investigation report into evidence. According to the plaintiff, the report was admissible under . . . the public records . . . exception . . . to the hearsay rule. We disagree.

The public records exception is codified in Rule 803(8). It provides that the following records are not excluded by the hearsay rule:

> Records, reports, statements or data compilations, in any form, of public officers or agencies, setting forth . . . (B) matters observed pursuant to duty imposed by law as to which matters there was a duty to report . . . or (C) in civil actions . . . factual findings resulting from an investigation made pursuant to authority granted by law, unless the sources of information or other circumstances indicate lack of trustworthiness.

N.H. R. Ev. 803(8). According to the plaintiff, Detective Curtis' report should have been admitted into evidence under both Rule 803(8)(B) and (C). He argues that the report contained both visual and auditory "observations" about Fowlie and "factual findings" about Fowlie's criminal behavior. We disagree.

Detective Curtis' supplementary investigation report is a summary of statements made by Fowlie during their interview. In that sense, the report contains "auditory observations" made by Detective Curtis. Rule 803(8)(B), however, was not meant to cover this type of observation. The contents of a witness' statements to a police officer are not matters observed by the officer for purposes of Rule 803(8)(B) . . . Therefore, we conclude that Detective Curtis' report is not admissible under Rule 803(8)(B).

Detective Curtis' report also does not contain "factual findings" based on his own investigation and cannot be admitted under Rule 803(8)(C) . . . The report's language, which refers to what Fowlie "stated" and "indicated" during the interview, demonstrates that Detective Curtis was simply recording what Fowlie told him. He made no effort to evaluate Fowlie's credibility and reached no independent conclusions based on Fowlie's testimony. As a result, his report lacked the typical characteristics of a factual finding . . .

Cases from several jurisdictions indicate that when a police report simply records a witness' statement, the report cannot be admitted under Rule 803(8)(C) . . . We find those cases persuasive and conclude that the supplementary investigation report was not admissible under Rule 803(8)(C) . . .

This case dealt specifically with a confession that was key to the plaintiff's case. However, the reasoning can be applied when the officer has nothing to base his report upon except testimony of a single witness and the report is simply a record of one party's complaint. Also note the discussion of the "admission against interest" hearsay exception; it is only available when a nonparty **declarant** is unavailable, and the proof for unavailability must be obtained in advance of trial. Plan ahead.

For non-governmental reports that "everyone in the business" uses, two other possible hearsay exceptions apply.

17. Market reports, commercial publications. Market quotations, tabulations, lists, directories, or other published compilations, generally used and relied upon by the public or by persons in particular occupations.

18. Learned treatises. To the extent called to the attention of an expert witness upon cross-examination or relied upon by the expert witness in direct examination, statements contained in published treatises, periodicals, or pamphlets on a subject of history, medicine, or other science or art, established as a reliable authority by the testimony or admission of the witness or by other expert testimony or by judicial notice. If admitted, the statements may be read into evidence but may not be received as exhibits.

Fed. R. Evid. 803(17), (18).

Compilations of factual data that are relied on by particular occupations or published items used by experts are admissible. For the "market report" exception to apply, you will have to find at least one witness who will be able to say "yes" to the following two questions:

1. Is [Market Report I desperately want to admit] generally used in [witness's occupation]?
2. Is [Market Report I desperately want to admit] relied upon by the public or by people in [witness's occupation]?

These questions, which address a requirement for admission into evidence, are called **foundation questions,** and the process of asking them is referred to as **"laying a foundation."** When all the questions for the foundation have been asked and answered in a way that the court will accept them, such as in deposition testimony, whether written or oral, the evidence is said to be "proved up." Even when the exception is properly used, though, it is still vulnerable to attack on the basis of Rule 403, as occurred in the following case.

Tire Shredders, Inc. v. ERM-North Central, Inc., 15 S.W.3d 849 (Tenn. Ct. App. 1999).

Defendants ERM-North Central and ERM-Enviroclean-North Central (collectively "ERM") appeal from a jury verdict requiring ERM to pay $1,300,000.00 as damages to Plaintiff Tire Shredders, Inc. ("TSI") for the negligent destruction of a shredding machine owned by TSI. For the reasons set forth below, we uphold the jury verdict and affirm the challenged evidentiary rulings of the trial court . . .

ERM entered into a contract with Nissan Industrial Equipment Company ("Nissan") under which ERM agreed to destroy and dispose of some fiberglass boats at Nissan's facility in Memphis . . . [Along with other subcontractors] TSI agreed to provide a shredding machine . . . and personnel to operate the machine. TSI shipped its shredding machine to the Nissan facility in Memphis and began performing under its subcontract with ERM. The Nissan project was scheduled to last approximately four weeks. On the thirteenth day of the project, however, a fire occurred at the Nissan facility that completely destroyed TSI's shredding machine . . .

. . . TSI filed a negligence action against ERM . . . After a trial on TSI's claims against ERM . . . the jury found that TSI had sustained a total of $1,300,000.00 in damages and that ERM was 100% responsible for these damages. ERM subsequently filed a motion to set aside the jury verdict or, in the alternative, for a new trial. The trial court denied ERM's post-trial motion. This appeal followed . . .

. . .

ERM . . . argues that the trial court erred in excluding from evidence certain trade journals[7] containing advertisements for the sale of shredding machines. The trial court ruled that these materials were inadmissable

---

[7] These trade journals include publications entitled "Waste Age," "Resource Recycling," "Scrap Processing and Recycling," and "The Management of World Wastes."

hearsay. ERM contends, however, that these trade journals are admissible under an exception to the hearsay rule. Rule 803 of the Tennessee Rules of Evidence provides in pertinent part as follows:

The following are not excluded by the hearsay rule:

17. Market Reports and Commercial Publications. Market quotations, tabulations, lists, directories, or other published compilations, generally used and relied upon by the public or by persons in particular occupations.

T.R.E. 803 (17). The parties disagree regarding whether trade journals qualify as published compilations within the meaning of Rule 803(17).

We are aware of only one case in Tennessee discussing the requirements of Rule 803(17). In *Frakes v. Cardiology Consultants, P.C.*, 1997 Tenn. App. LEXIS 597, No. 01- A-01-9702-CV-00069, 1997 WL 536949 (Tenn. App. Aug. 29, 1997), the trial court permitted the defendant's attorney to question various witnesses using a guidelines table from a brochure that was produced by the American College of Cardiology and the American Heart Association . . . With respect to the applicability of Rule 803(17), this Court stated as follows:

The guidelines table is neither a market report nor a commercial publication, and despite the fact that all the expert witnesses agreed that cardiologists relied upon it we do not agree that it is the type of list that comes within paragraph 17 of Rule 803.

. . . There are cases from other jurisdictions, however, wherein items similar to the trade journals in the instant case were held to be admissible under a rule identical to Rule 803(17). *See United States v. Cassiere*, 4 F.3d 1006, 1018-19 (1st Cir. 1993) (monthly report listing properties sold, the sales prices, and the dates on which the sales were closed); *United States v. Grossman*, 614 F.2d 295, 297 (1st Cir. 1980) (catalog displaying pictures of and listing prices of Colibri cigarette lighters); *United States v. Johnson*, 515 F.2d 730, 732 n.4 (7th Cir. 1975) (publication entitled "Red Book" listing average values of certain automobiles); *Henry v. Serey*, 46 Ohio App. 3d 93, 546 N.E.2d 474, 476 (Ohio Ct. App. 1989) ("N.A.D.A. Official Used Car Guide" and other magazines containing advertisements for used automobiles), *overruled in part on other grounds, Dunn v. Westlake*, 1990 Ohio App. LEXIS 1755, * 8, No. C-880422, 1990 WL 59262, at * 4 (Ohio Ct. App. May 9, 1990); *Ohio v. Stickles*, 1985 Ohio App. LEXIS 8094, * 11, No. 85 AP-06, 1985 WL 10321, at * 4 (Ohio Ct. App. June 13, 1985) (magazine entitled "Old Cars Price Guide"). Consistent with the rationale of these cases, we think that trade journals qualify as published compilations and thus are admissible under Rule 803(17) as an exception to the hearsay rule.

Despite our conclusion that the trade journals in the instant case are not excludable under the hearsay rule, we find that the trial court could have excluded these items under Rule 403 of the Tennessee Rules of Evidence . . .

[W]e think this evidence is of little probative value. Additionally, we think that the admission of this evidence would have resulted in undue delay, waste of time, and needless presentation of cumulative evidence.

[C]onsequently, this evidence was excludable under Rule 403 . . .

A foundation must be established to admit a **learned treatise** as well. Learned treatises include reference books, scholarly articles, and texts that everyone in a given profession refers to. Notice that in Rule 803(18), one of the ways that the foundation for a learned treatise may be established is by judicial notice; however, the book, article, or pamphlet is not actually given to the jury. Under this rule, it is only to be used when questioning an expert, usually in an impeachment context, not as a substitute for an expert for a cheap way to get expert testimony.

The distinction between using Rule 803(18) and the use of references in judicial notice is that you may ask a judge to judicially notice facts from a learned treatise; in Rule 803(18), the reference's commentary and conclusions—not just facts—are allowed in after the publication is judicially noticed as a learned treatise. Aside from judicial notice, the way to prove up a learned treatise is to ask the expert the following question: Is [*Everything About the Universe* by The Greatest Expert] a reliable authority?

If everyone uses it, there may be a follow-up question along the lines of, "And isn't it one of the standard references in the field?" This is not necessary for admissibility, but it helps with the weight of the reference before the jury.

Of course, the admissibility of learned treatises, as everything you find in your investigation, is subject to the discretion of the judge, as the plaintiff in the following case learned.

Greathouse v. Rhodes, 618 N.W. 2d 106 (Mich. Ct. App. 2000).

In this medical malpractice action, plaintiff appeals . . . from the jury's verdict. Plaintiff challenges the trial court's ruling . . . denying her request to use learned treatises to question her expert witnesses on direct-examination in order to establish that their opinions were supported by "peer review publications" . . . We affirm . . .

In December 1994, decedent Robert Greathouse began to experience episodes of severe chest pain. Decedent sought treatment from his regular physician, Dr. Charles Rhodes, whom decedent had seen regularly for the last five years. Dr. Rhodes prescribed medication and referred decedent for a cardiac stress test. Another doctor conducted the stress test and, after reviewing the results and decedent's symptoms, instructed decedent to immediately consult a cardiologist. Dr. Rhodes referred decedent to cardiologist Dr. John Duge, who prescribed a different type of medication and scheduled an angiogram. Decedent, however, suffered a fatal heart attack six days before the scheduled procedure.

On May 13, 1996, plaintiff filed an amended complaint against Drs. Rhodes and Duge, alleging that their failure to properly diagnose and treat decedent's unstable angina caused his death . . .

Before plaintiff presented her standard of care experts at trial, the trial court . . . heard arguments regarding her plans to question them with learned treatises on the diagnosis and treatment of unstable angina. Plaintiff wanted to use excerpts and enlarged graphs taken from a federal Department of Heath and Human Services publication entitled *Unstable Angina and Management Clinical Practice Guideline* and similar guidelines approved by the American Heart Association. Defendants argued that the materials were hearsay and inadmissible under MRE 707 (use of learned treatises for impeachment) because plaintiff was not using them to impeach her own witnesses. Plaintiff responded that she was not using the materials as substantive evidence, but rather to establish . . . that her experts' opinions about the standard of care and defendants' failure to comply with that standard were based on accepted scientific standards. The trial court ruled that plaintiff could not use the material for this purpose because [the statutory basis the plaintiff argued] applied only to "scientific opinions" and issues concerning the standard of care, unlike those pertaining to proximate cause, did not involve scientific opinion . . .

Plaintiff also argues that the trial court erred in refusing to allow her to use treatise evidence to question her standard of care experts on direct examination in order to establish that their opinions were supported by "peer review publications" . . . We disagree . . .

The Legislature enacted [the statute in question] in an apparent effort to codify the United States Supreme Court's holding in *Daubert v. Merrell Dow Pharmaceuticals, Inc,* 509 U.S. 579; 113 S. Ct. 2786; 125 L. Ed. 2d 469 (1993). The plain language of the statute establishes the Legislature's intent to assign the *trial court* the role of determining, pursuant to the *Daubert* criteria, whether proposed scientific opinion is sufficiently reliable for jury consideration. Contrary to plaintiff's position, the statute is devoid of language suggesting that it is a rule of evidence, that it displaces the rules of evidence, or that it allows a party to establish her own witnesses' reliability through criteria the statute requires the trial court to employ . . . We therefore conclude that a party may not use [the statute] as a basis to admit treatise evidence at trial, and a party's attempt to establish the reliability of its experts before the jury must be accomplished through, and in a manner consistent with, the rules of evidence.[1] Accordingly, irrespective of whether plaintiff's experts' proposed evidence constituted "scientific opinion," the trial court's decision not to allow plaintiff's proposed line of questioning . . . was proper . . .

Evaluating the trial court's ruling under the rules of evidence, we hold that it did not abuse its discretion in excluding the evidence in question . . . Plaintiff's only apparent purpose in offering the angina guidelines

---

[1] Plaintiff was not attempting to place her evidence of reliability before the trial court but, instead, sought to use § 2955 as a vehicle to bolster her experts' testimony with corroborative medical evidence on direct examination—a use not contemplated by the statute.

was to corroborate her experts' testimony that decedent's stress test results required immediate hospitalization, thereby constituting inadmissible hearsay. MRE 801(c). Furthermore, the treatise materials were not admissible under MRE 707, which permits parties to introduce statements contained in published treatises, periodicals, or pamphlets "for impeachment purposes only." Plaintiff did not plan to impeach her own witnesses' testimony with the contested materials and sought instead to use them to bolster their testimony on direct examination.

Because we find plaintiff's issues to be without merit, we affirm the trial judgment for defendants.

The **weight of the evidence** refers to the relative importance assigned to it by the jurors. "Weight" is often used to contrast "admissibility," as in the oft-repeated phrase, "That goes to the weight, not the admissibility." The phrase usually means that the speaker believes the jury will get to hear it (it is admissible), but that the jury will have to take the argument under discussion into account in deciding whether to give the evidence any consideration in their decision.

One more evidentiary concept needs to be considered before discussing the sources themselves: that of authentication. How do you prove that the pieces of paper you are handing the court are, in fact, the pieces of paper you claim they are? In other words, how can the court tell that something really is, say, the police report? Before the advent of copy machines, this was much more of a problem. Now, since everyone has a copy of everything, if there is anything that doesn't match, one of the lawyers will stand up and shout if anyone tries to pass something fake off as evidence. However, every piece of evidence still must be proven to be what you say it is.

Stotz v. Shields, **696 A.2d 806 (Pa. Super. Ct. 1997).**

John Phillip Stotz appeals from the judgment entered in the Court of Common Pleas of Indiana County on May 13, 1996, after a jury rendered a verdict of $18,750 in his favor. For the reasons set forth below, we are constrained to reverse and to remand for a new trial.

The procedural history of this case may be summarized as follows. On October 2, 1992, after commencing the action by writ of summons, appellant filed a complaint against Margaret Shields which sought damages arising from an automobile accident. Twelve days later, Ms. Shields answered the complaint by admitting negligence, denying appellant's allegations regarding damages, and setting forth numerous defenses. In the years that followed, the parties engaged in extensive litigation over the admissibility of certain evidence including testimony by army physician Lee A. Pietrangelo and documents which both contained Dr. Pietrangelo's medical opinions and indicated that appellant's post-accident discharge from the Ohio National Guard was medical in nature. The trial court ultimately ruled that the challenged evidence was inadmissible since the doctor apparently had never examined appellant or reviewed reports submitted by appellant's private physicians.

Trial on the matter commenced on February 20, 1996. During the course of that proceeding, appellant presented evidence which established the following. On June 7, 1992, a vehicle driven by Ms. Shields struck appellant. Although appellant tried to avoid injury by jumping onto the hood, he was pinned against a church building. He sustained a fractured left ankle, two fractures of his right foot, and two dislocated right toes. Although appellant spent several weeks in casts and has attempted to rebuild his strength gradually, he continues to have persistent and debilitating left ankle pain. According to Dr. Paul Burton, appellant suffers from post-traumatic arthritis and his condition may never improve.

Although he had been fairly active prior to the accident, appellant's ankle pain has affected his ability to engage in sports adversely. Several months after the accident, appellant, who knew that he could not complete the necessary two-mile run, failed to take the annual physical fitness test required of all National Guard members. Consequently, appellant was subjected to a mandatory physical examination which led to his involuntary discharge from the service. As he had served in excess of two years in the military before sustaining his injuries . . . appellant focused much of his claim for damages on benefits lost as a result of the discharge including tuition assistance, loan repayment subsidies, pay for time that he would have spent on duty, and the pension which would have been available to him after twenty years of service. Employment rehabilitation expert Jay Jarrell valued the lost service benefits and other economic damages sustained by appellant at in excess of $180,000.

Ms. Shields attempted to impeach appellant by asking him whether he had sought permission to take an alternate fitness test. Appellant, who objected to this line of questioning on the ground that it was unsupported by the necessary evidentiary foundation, indicated that he was not aware that an alternate fitness test existed . . . Later, despite another foundational objection, the trial court admitted four photocopied pages which set forth matters relating to the physical fitness test and to an alternate testing procedure . . . Finally, Ms. Shields attempted to counter appellant's medical evidence by presenting Dr. W. Scott Nettrour, an orthopedic surgeon, who testified that he examined appellant and could find no physical support for appellant's complaints of pain . . .

Appellant raises several evidentiary claims related to the admission of the documentation evidencing the alternate fitness test and to the exclusion of both the testimony of Dr. Pietrangelo and the materials indicating the medical nature of National Guard discharge. Keeping in mind that questions concerning the admission and exclusion of evidence are within the sound discretion of the trial court whose decisions thereon will not be disturbed in the absence of an abuse of discretion, . . . we consider the appropriateness of the former decision.

Generally, two requirements must be satisfied for a document to be admissible: it must be authenticated and it must be relevant. In other words, a proponent must show that the document is what it purports to be and that it relates to an issue or issues in the truth determining process . . . The establishment of those two requirements is known as laying a foundation . . .

In the present case, our review of the record demonstrates that appellant objected to the admission of the alternate fitness test materials on the basis that Ms. Shields had failed to present any foundational evidence . . . Consequently, he clearly asserted in the trial court that Ms. Shields had neither authenticated that evidence nor demonstrated its relevance. While appellant now characterizes his argument as relating only to the issue of authentication, he questions the relevance of the materials by pointing out that no proof established they were in existence at the time that he was being evaluated or that they applied to him. . . . We will address both aspects of appellant's claim.

Specific evidentiary rules relate to the authentication of documentary evidence. A document may be authenticated by direct evidence such as an admission . . . A document also may be authenticated via circumstantial evidence relating to a myriad of considerations including its appearance, contents, and substance . . . Acknowledged writings, public records, and under Federal Rule of Evidence 902, documents purporting to be issued by public authority, are self-authenticating . . . Consequently, they are admissible into evidence without further proof of genuineness . . .

As discussed previously, our review of the record reveals that appellant never admitted the authenticity of the contested materials and that Ms. Shields failed to introduce any foundational testimony regarding them. In addition, an examination of the contested materials demonstrates that they discuss army policy regarding physical fitness, the mandatory physical fitness test, and the availability of alternate test activities in the event that the soldier has either a temporary or permanent disability. While the materials cite various regulations, they contain no indication that they were printed or issued by governmental authority. Thus, even if we assumed that the principle embodied in the federal rule permitting self-authentication of official publications reflects our law . . . we would not find the contested materials self-authenticating. See 5 Christopher B. Muller and Laird C. Kirkpatrick, Federal Evidence § 543 (2d ed. 1994) (self-authentication rule regarding official publications does not apply to the reproduction of official pronouncements in the absence of an official nexus). Accordingly, we find that Ms. Shields failed to authenticate the contested evidence.

We also believe that Ms. Shields neglected to demonstrate that the evidence was relevant. Even if the materials in question actually set forth army regulations regarding physical fitness testing and the various alternative activities available for injured or disabled personnel, those regulations are relevant only to the extent that they existed at the time that appellant was being tested and were applicable to him. Since Ms. Shields presented no evidence regarding the materials, and appellant specifically denied any knowledge of the existence of an alternate testing procedure, the record is devoid of any evidence satisfying that basic issue.

As our analysis demonstrates, the trial court admitted the alternate testing evidence without requiring Ms. Shields to provide the requisite evidentiary foundation. In doing so, the court permitted Ms. Shields to circumvent our basic rules of evidence and thus, committed an abuse of discretion. Moreover, the court's erroneous decision to admit the contested evidence undoubtedly could have impacted upon the jurors' determination as to appellant's ability to remain in the National Guard despite his ankle injury, a key issue in light of the fact that appellant's primary claim for damages concerned matters arising from his discharge. Accordingly, we are constrained to reverse the judgment and to remand the case for a new trial. In light of this decision, we need not address the remaining issues raised by appellant, which concern Ms. Shields' failure to disclose her intention to utilize the alternate testing materials in a timely fashion and the admissibility of certain evidence indicating that appellant's discharge was medical in nature.

Judgment reversed. Case remanded for a new trial . . .

As you can see from this case, rules governing authentication must be observed. Rule 902 lists self-authenticating documents, that is, documents that do not require anyone to identify the document specifically and testify that it is an accurate copy.

Rule 902. Self-authentication

Extrinsic evidence of authenticity as a condition precedent to admissibility is not required with respect to the following:

. . .

4. Certified copies of public records. A copy of an official record or report or entry therein, or of a document authorized by law to be recorded or filed and actually recorded or filed in a public office, including data compilations in any form, certified as correct by the custodian or other person authorized to make the certification, by certificate complying with paragraph (1), (2), or (3) of this rule or complying with any Act of Congress or rule prescribed by the Supreme Court pursuant to statutory authority.

5. Official publications. Books, pamphlets, or other publications purporting to be issued by public authority.

6. Newspapers and periodicals. Printed materials purporting to be newspapers or periodicals . . .

8. Acknowledged documents. Documents accompanied by a certificate of acknowledgment executed in the manner provided by law by a notary public or other officer authorized by law to take acknowledgments . . .

Fed. R. Evid. 902 (4)-(6), (8).

Ms. Shields failed to submit either certified copies of public records or "official publications," and produced photocopies instead, so she did not have a chance of arguing that her documents evidencing the existence of alternative testing were self-authenticating. Documents in the forms specified by Rule 902 do not require someone to testify that the document is what the lawyer says it is in order to have it admitted into evidence. Ordinarily, the first question about a document (or a photograph, for that matter) is "Do you recognize this?" and the second, "Can you tell me what it is?" This is how evidence is authenticated—using a witness with reason to know whether the document is the real deal. If you plan on using a particular witness to authenticate evidence that you want admitted, make sure the witness does in fact recognize it.

SOURCES

What source you choose is based on what you need it for. Are you trying to educate yourself or your attorney in the area of the litigation? You will find that law can be a never-ending education in the oddest areas. If you are trying to get the big picture in order to know what to ask a witness or what documents to look for, you may be looking for different sources than when you are looking for statistics, public records, and learned treatises. For self-education, the best places to go are either continuing legal education materials focused on the area of litigation you are working or where the folks in the area originally got their information: textbooks.

Continuing legal education notebooks may not be pretty, but they can be great sources for practical information. Remember, though, they are not updated, so use the most recent material available.

The major textbook publishers have their catalogs available online. You can browse their wares and find descriptions of books that seem most likely to help you. Here's a sampling from Prentice Hall's available books about which I thought, gee, I wish I'd had that book when I was working the suchandsuch case. Even though Prentice Hall is the publisher of this book, this was my idea, and I don't get anything for plugging these books (although maybe I should mention that to my editor . . . hmmm):

- Sundberg, Winebarger, and Taplin, *Clinical Psychology: Evolving Theory, Practice, and Research* (4th ed.). Why did I like this book? First, Chapter 4 gives the whole basis of assessment in psychology—how psychologists approach interviewing, what they look for, what tests they give, and what the point is. Chapter 5 discusses report writing—something you'll want to know so you can read the blasted things. Chapter 10 discusses working with older adults—and it's one of the various places I confirmed my experiences with the elderly client to make sure that I was addressing universal, and not individual, realities of dealing with the older client.

- Thorndike, *Measurement and Evaluation in Psychology and Education* (6th ed.). This psychology book is a great reference. It's not as user friendly as some clinical psychology texts, as it's written in a prolix style (weighty language to impress upon you the importance of the topic), but it has scads of useful information. Virtually any standardized test you need to find out about is listed in this book. Appendix 4 alone is worth the price of the book. You want to know what an MMPI is? Look it up in Appendix 4—there it is: the Minnesota Multiphasic Personality Inventory Revised, and it gives you a cross-reference in the text. If you go to Chapter 11, you find the entry on the MMPI that gives you a history, the basics, and, to warm the cockles of any legal person, criticisms—what is wrong with the test. That's the paydirt in this book. Because social studies in family law will include psychological tests, and anyone who wants to make a decent claim at mental anguish needs to see a psychologist, you'll come across some form of psychological testing at some point. In severe head trauma cases, a battery of these tests is often done to determine the level of post-accident functioning (although if you don't have anything pre-accident to compare to, it's only somewhat useful). After arm-wrestling case law, you should be ready for this guy. Just get aspirin for the math bits.

- Saferstein, *Criminalistics: An Introduction to Forensic Science* (7th ed.). Criminal investigation is a completely different field than civil. The rules are different because the playing field is so, well, not level. The prosecution runs way uphill; the defense just has to poke holes in the prosecution because of the burden of proof. The kinds of issues that arise relatively frequently in criminal law are somewhat rare in the civil world because they are too expensive for private litigants to be involved in, particularly given the fact that most criminal defendants are judgment-proof. However, there are areas of overlap, particularly in family law, and it can be worth your while to learn a little bit about what forensic scientists do.

On the one hand, if you watch the forensics shows like those on the Discovery Channel, you may be aware of all the cool things out there. On the other hand, be aware that all of those nifty tools are not available everywhere and they are not used routinely. So don't be surprised if no one took up microfibers at the crime scene on your subsequent criminal case.

Saferstein's book has very nice overviews of the various areas of forensic study, but the things that come up most often in my life are DNA issues (molestation, paternity, etc.) and document verification. Chapter 13 is all about DNA evidence, a primer to get you started so you can figure out what the fuss is all about—why are there experts out there who get huffy about whether DNA tests are good enough? It was good enough for one little blue dress. It's a very technical subject, and the explanation is quite good and very thorough.

Chapter 16 is a good discussion of document and voice examination. You have a tape that sounds suspect? Bring in an examiner, because although Saferstein makes it easy to understand, it takes practice and the right equipment to make any determinations about suspect tapes (or documents, for that matter).

- Fuller, *Robotics: Introduction, Programming, and Projects* (2d ed.). The only reason I chose this one is because it struck me as being off-the-wall. I can visualize an injury at the hands of a robot in a factory setting, resulting in a products case. Tah-dah! The beginner's guide to robots, complete with a list of experts inside. It even has chapters on Robot Maintenance (standard of care?), Robotics and Safety—including "How Robots Injure People" (foreseeability?), and, of course, information about what all those bits and pieces are called.

That's it. Just a few. The list should be enough to get you thinking about what you might want to look for in the textbook catalog.

Government Sources

The federal government is a wealth of information. You can find all sorts of lovely pamphlets, reports, statistics, and other helpful information for your case from Uncle Sam, and he's been good enough to put much of it on the Web. To find a list of online federal agencies, go to **http://www.infoctr.edu/fwl/**, the Federal Web Locator, which organizes the vast array of agencies and their underlings for you. The nice thing about the federal sources is that they have a tendency to run the gamut from documents that the average citizen can comprehend to information only for experts, so there's a rich variety of information and potential demonstrative evidence to work with.

Any agency of the federal government is a good target for research. Got a case involving an injury at a place of business? Check out **Occupational Safety and Health Administration (OSHA)** at **http://www.osha.gov/** and see what goodies they have. You'll soon find the publications Web page, which has documents entitled Respiratory Protection, Stairways and Ladders, Working Safely with Video Display Terminals, and Protecting Whistleblowers, just to name a few. Even if you are representing someone who is not a worker, if you have a person who fell at a job site on a stairway that was not in compliance with the OSHA book on stairways, you've got some nice evidence of a standard that a reasonably prudent person could find easily—and the publication is available for free on the Web. Following is a case in which an OSHA issue was key.

Six Flags Over Georgia II, L.P. v. Kull, 576 S.E.2d 880 (Ga. 2003).

We granted certiorari to the Court of Appeals in *Kull v. Six Flags Over Georgia*, 254 Ga. App. 897, 564 S.E.2d 747, (2002), to determine whether O.C.G.A. § 9-11-43 (c) requires written notice of intent to rely on federal OSHA law. We answer in the negative and reverse a contrary ruling in *Kull* . . .

Kull's employer, Mahalo Advertising, was under contract to repair and maintain an electrical scoreboard located on a softball field on property owned by Six Flags . . . Kull, who was a technician for Mahalo, was injured while changing a lightbulb in the Six Flags scoreboard. Kull brought suit against Six Flags and others, alleging that his injuries resulted from negligence on the part of the defendants. Six Flags sought and was granted summary judgment. On appeal, Six Flags argued in part that Kull's actions constituted negligence per se because he violated OSHA guidelines. The Court of Appeals rejected the OSHA claim, sua sponte reasoning that Six Flags had not given proper notice under O.C.G.A. § 9-11-43 (c) of its intent to rely on federal OSHA regulations . . .

O.C.G.A. § 9-11-43 (c) provides in pertinent part: "A party who intends to raise an issue concerning the law of *another state or of a foreign country* shall give notice in his pleadings or other reasonable written notice." (Emphasis supplied.) Where the language of a statute is plain and unambiguous, judicial construction is not only unnecessary but forbidden . . .

By its terms, the statutory notice requirement of O.C.G.A. § 9-11-43 (c) applies only to the introduction of "law of another state or of a foreign country," not to the law of the United States such as the OSHA provisions relied upon by Six Flags. The purpose of the notice requirement "is to give the court and parties adequate preparation time to litigate the foreign law issue.". . . There is a vast distinction between the treatment of foreign laws, which have no force in Georgia except on principles of comity, O.C.G.A. § 1-3-9, and federal law which is inherently binding on the states by virtue of the Supremacy Clause, Art. VI, of the United States Constitution . . . Because federal laws of general application are "capable of immediate and accurate demonstration by resort to easily accessible sources of indisputable accuracy,". . . an adverse party is not disadvantaged by lack of notice of intent to rely on such authority. Accordingly, we hold that O.C.G.A. § 9-11-43 (c) does not require notice of intent to rely on federal law. To the extent that *Kull* . . . states a contrary rule, it is hereby reversed.

Because the Court of Appeals erroneously determined that lack of notice prevented Six Flags from relying on its OSHA defense, that court failed to reach the question of whether OSHA regulations apply to this litigation, and if so whether the evidence compels a finding that Kull was contributorily negligent per se. This issue must be decided in order to determine whether the grant of summary judgment was appropriate. Accordingly, the judgment of the Court of Appeals is reversed and the case is remanded for further proceedings not inconsistent with this opinion. Judgment reversed. All the Justices concur.

Another agency to check is the **National Transportation Safety Board** (**NTSB**) at **http://www.ntsb.gov/**, particularly its publications page. In products liability cases against automobile manufacturers, it can help you establish notice and work for you on the punitive damages side—or if the case comes out well for the manufacturer, help exonerate your client. You can also find administrative appeals opinions later than mid-1992 on the Web site.

The **Census Bureau** can give you overall statistics about population, broken down by state, county, and metropolitan area. The National Weather Service will give you the official weather report for any given day for any given place in the United States, as well as the conditions of any bodies of water. The National Center for Educational Statistics **http://nces.ed.gov/** is a subdivision of the U.S. Department of Education and does what the name implies: keeps educational statistics. GovStats **http://govinfo.kerr.orst.edu/**, hosted by Oregon State University, keeps statistics "not available elsewhere on the internet," mostly demographic information by county, on commerce, and on agriculture. The Department of Energy's Office of Environmental Safety and Health, **http://www.eh.doe.gov/portal/home.htm,** posts various health and safety warnings related to energy sources, and, for a reason that escapes me (although I'm sure there is one) posts information dealing with illnesses. The Department of Justice maintains a Bureau of Justice Statistics, on the Web at **http://www.ojp.usdoj.gov/bjs/**, helpful when you are working on a premises security case, among others.

Both the Department of Energy and the Department of Health and Human Services have extensive materials for experts. The Department of Energy has multiple labs under its auspices, most quite prestigious, dealing with physics, computer science, waste management, nuclear energy, genetics, and environmental studies, to name a few. The Department of Health and Human Services maintains the well-respected **National Institutes of Health** (**NIH**) and the **Centers for Disease Control** (**CDC**). The NIH's subdivisions all provide factbooks on the particular diseases or conditions they specialize in that may make wonderful exhibits. One of the things often needed, a mortality table to calculate how long a person could have been expected to live, is found at the CDC Web site in the National Center for Health Statistics section. Ordering information is found there as well if the judge will not take judicial notice of Internet-generated information. In the following case, the CDC information netted the defendant a summary judgment from the trial court, even though it was reversed on appeal. It's still good evidence, even if the defense team now has to sell it to a jury, always a problem with this kind of case, where the plaintiffs are very sympathetic.

Allison v. Merck and Co., 878 P.2d 948 (Nev. 1994).

The trial court entered summary judgment against appellant Jo Ann Allison and her son Thomas, who are suing the Merck pharmaceutical company ("Merck") and the Clark County Health District ("Health District") because they claim that a Merck-manufactured measles, mumps and rubella vaccine (the MMR II) administered by the Health District caused then seventeen-month-old Thomas to contract encephalitis and to suffer from consequent blindness, deafness, mental retardation and spastic contractures . . . We conclude that Merck may be liable to Thomas Allison by reason of its strict liability as manufacturer if Thomas can prove that the vaccine in question is the cause of his disabilities . . . In addition, we conclude that Merck may be liable to Thomas and Ms. Allison for failing to provide a proper warning regarding the vaccine. Accordingly, we reverse the summary judgment in favor of Merck and remand to the trial court for a trial on Thomas' strict liability claim and on Thomas' and Ms. Allison's failure-to-warn claims . . .

We have already considered the meaning of the word "defect" in connection with strict products liability. "[Definitions of defect] rest upon the common premise that those products are defective . . . because they fail to perform in the manner reasonably to be expected in light of their nature and intended function.'". . . If Thomas can establish that the vaccine caused him to suffer permanent brain damage, then surely the vaccine failed to perform in the manner reasonably to be expected "in light of [its] nature and intended function." The nature and intended function of this vaccine, of course, is to create an immunity to measles, mumps and rubella without attendant blindness, deafness, mental retardation and permanent brain damage . . .

Under the law of strict liability in this state, responsibility for injuries caused by defective products is properly fixed wherever it will most effectively reduce the hazards to life and health inherent in defective products that reach the market. Although manufacturers are not insurers of their products, where injury is caused by a defective product, responsibility is placed upon the manufacturer and the distributor of the defective product rather than on the injured consumer . . .

Unless we are going to abandon long-standing public policy grounds for holding manufacturers and distributors of defective products responsible for injuries caused by manufactured products that prove to be defective, Thomas must be given an opportunity to prove that a malfunctioning vaccine caused his injuries . . . A vaccine that causes blindness and deafness is a defective product. Causation is a factor yet to be determined by a factfinder . . .

Merck claims that it is free from strict manufacturer's liability by virtue of the dictum stated in comment k to section 402A of the Restatement (Second) of Torts . . . This comment suggests that a drug manufacturer should not be held liable for "the unfortunate consequences attending" the use of its drugs if: (1) the manufacturer supplies "the public with an apparently useful and desirable product, attended by a known but apparently reasonable risk," (2) the drug is "properly prepared and marketed," and (3) "proper warning is given."

It is not easy to divine just why the framers of the comment thought that a drug manufacturer should be excused in cases in which it manufactured a drug that was "known" to be dangerous. The whole idea behind strict tort liability is that the manufacturer, not the consumer, should bear the responsibility for injuries, even when the product is ostensibly properly prepared and marketed and when the plaintiff is not in a position to prove the origin of the defect . . .

What the question in this case really gets down to is whether an exception should be made in a case in which a drug manufacturer injures a consumer with a drug that it knows is dangerous, but not too ("unreasonably") dangerous. That is to say, should a drug manufacturer be allowed to profit with impunity from the distribution of a drug that it knows is capable of resulting in physical injury, so long as the drug can somehow be certified as not being unreasonably dangerous? We answer that question in the negative and say that a drug manufacturer should, under the strict liability jurisprudence of this state, be held liable in tort even when the drug is "properly prepared and marketed" (that is to say, non-negligently) and even when the known danger inherent in the drug may be what the comment calls "reasonable."

The apparent rationale of comment k in relieving drug manufacturers from liability is that where the manufacturer . . . produces a product that is "incapable of being made safe," the manufacturer should not be responsible for injuries resulting from use of the drug. The comment itself gives as an example of such an "unavoidably unsafe" drug—the Pasteur treatment of rabies "which not uncommonly leads to very serious and damaging consequences when it is injected." We would note, however, that the reason why serious and damaging consequences of the Pasteur rabies treatment do not result in tort liability is not because of the "unreasonably dangerous" doctrine proposed by comment k, but, rather, because the victim chooses to be injected with a drug having known "damaging consequences" rather than to die from rabies. It is the voluntary choice to take the antirabies serum that eliminates tort liability and not the serum's being said to be unavoidably or reasonably dangerous. There is no need to make an exception to the rules of strict liability such as that suggested by comment k in the rabies example because the rabies victim waives tort claims by accepting what the victim knows to be the necessary risk involved in the treatment . . .

Speaking of "unavoidable" danger or fault-free infliction of harm, or speaking of reasonable (and therefore acceptable) risk of harm, is very much alien to strict liability theory and should have no place in the Restatement provisions relating to strict liability. Mixing concepts of fault-free ("unavoidable") manufacture and "reasonable risk" into the context of non-negligent, strict liability is entirely inconsistent with our products liability cases and with the law established in this state for almost thirty years.

. . . Merck, not Thomas Allison, must, if the Merck product did in fact cause Thomas' overwhelming misfortune, bear the "burden of the accidental injuries caused by products intended for consumption." Restatement (Second) of Torts, § 402 A, cmt. c (1965). . .

. . . Merck appear[s] to be arguing that if Merck were to be held liable for statistically infrequent injuries such as the one at bar, society would be the worse because Merck and other drug manufacturers would be fearful and retarded in the development of new and greatly needed immunological products. If Merck were to have to pay for what its vaccine has done to Thomas, this would, Merck says, necessarily inhibit the development and marketing of immunological products which are helpful to many and "unfortunately" devastating to others.

Although, on policy grounds, Merck might talk some legislative body into immunizing it from liability, it would be certainly inappropriate for the court to make such a radical change in our well-established products liability law. Further, one would think that if a legislature were going to give such special benefits to drug manufacturers, most certainly the resultant legislation, to be just, would have to afford some kind of compensation or relief to the victims of "unavoidably unsafe" drugs. If, for example, a legislature provided that automobile manufacturers would be held to a standard of strict liability for manufacturing defects, even if injuries caused by a given defect are statistically infrequent and perhaps "unavoidable," and at the same time immunized drug manufacturers from liability for injuries caused by their vaccines, the legislature would, as mentioned, very probably and properly include in such discriminatory legislation some kind of no-fault victim compensation plan to set off the advantage given to drug manufacturers over other kinds of manufacturers . . .

In summary, this court cannot, under our law, read comment k as giving immunity to liability in cases such as the present one . . .

. . . [E]ven if . . . we were to accept Merck's interpretation of comment k in this case, Thomas and his mother would still be entitled to a trial. A factfinder could find in this case that the product here, if not defective or dangerous "per se," was "unreasonably dangerous as marketed.". . . "[I]n terms of the user's interests, a product is 'unreasonably dangerous' only when it is 'dangerous to an extent beyond that contemplated by the ordinary consumer.' " . . . Citing to comment k, the . . . court thus held that even an "unavoidably" unsafe vaccine may be defective if marketed without an adequate warning . . . Accordingly . . . even under the broadly exculpatory interpretation of comment k espoused by Merck, liability cannot be avoided by a drug manufacturer and distributor in the marketing of a vaccine unless the vaccine is "accompanied by proper directions and warning.". . .

It would appear that a factfinder in this case could reasonably conclude that the vaccine given to Thomas Allison was not accompanied by a proper warning . . . Although Merck does not admit that this vaccine can cause disastrous central nervous system disorders, it announces in its MMR II package circular (which is not distributed to vaccinees) that "significant central nervous system reactions such as encephalitis and encephalopathy occurring within 30 days after vaccination, have been temporally associated with measles vaccine approximately once for every million doses.". . . In dealing with the mass consumers of the vaccine, the Health District revised this information when it issued its "Important Information" (not a "Warning") flyer prepared by the Center for Disease Control ("CDC"). The "Important Information" flyer is a revision of Merck's package circular, and it contains a much less dissuading statement, namely, that, "although experts are not sure," there might be a very remote possibility—a chance in a million—that takers of the vaccine "may have a more serious reaction, such as inflammation of the brain (encephalitis)." The gist of the faulty warning aspect of liability in this case is that none of the prospective vacinees was warned of the actual possibility of permanent brain damage. Rashes, yes; sore throats, yes; "inflammation of the brain," yes; but permanent blindness, deafness, and mental retardation, no . . .

Further, there is evidence in the record that Merck underestimated the incidence of serious central nervous system involvement caused by or "temporally associated with" the vaccine.[15] Whether the incidence data be true or not, the information that was ultimately conveyed to Jo Ann Allison could be seen by a factfinder as being slanted and insufficient; and the only information that was actually made available to Ms. Allison was that there was a one in one million [not four in one million] chance that her son "may" have a more serious reaction to the vaccine "such as inflammation of the brain." At no time was Ms. Allison ever made aware that the vaccine might result in her son's becoming an invalid.

Accordingly, there is certainly an issue of fact as to whether the warning in this case was "proper"; and, in fact, there appears to be substantial evidence in this case from which a jury could find that the vaccine in question was not "'accompanied by proper directions and warning,'". . . Consequently, even if we were to accept Merck's version of comment k, the Allisons would still be entitled to a trial on the merits . . .

Merck claims that since it contracted with the government to provide the necessary warnings to accompany this vaccine, the government, and not Merck, should be liable for any faults in the warning process . . . Merck wants to be relieved of any responsibility for these faulty warnings because it contracted-out its duty to warn of the dangers inherent in this vaccine.

Merck claims in its brief that it did not participate in the preparation of the "Important Information" form, but does not deny knowing of its contents. Merck puts the "legal question in this case" to be "whether it was negligent for Merck to rely on the Center for Disease Control—the foremost authority in the world on the subject." A jury could definitely conclude that the answer to this question is, "yes." Almost anyone who reads the Important Information handout should be able to see immediately that it does not warn of the possible risks of blindness, deafness and permanent brain damage. As discussed in the preceding section, a jury could find that the warning given was inadequate and that Merck knew that the warning that was being promulgated with its vaccine was inadequate. This fact accompanied by Merck's admitted knowledge of the Center for Disease Control's bias and concern "that manufacturers would overwarn of the risk of the vaccine,". . . tells us that a jury could have properly found that Merck was marketing a substance which it knew was (albeit, "unavoidably") "unsafe," and did so knowing that the accompanying written warnings were inadequate. Thus

---

[15] There is considerable controversy in this case as to whether encephalitis and disabling brain damage is caused by (or "temporally associated" with) use of the vaccine one in one million times or four in one million times, or more, or less. The incidence of catastrophic sequelae of the vaccine is disputed; still, we cannot see how it would make the slightest bit of difference to Ms. Allison in accepting the vaccination whether the chances that her son would be brain damaged were one in one million or four in one million or ten or twenty in a million. She was not told that the kind of injury suffered by her son was even a possibility. The only information that she might have had (assuming that she read the two page information sheet furnished to her by the Health District) was this "blurb":

Although experts are not sure, it seem (sic) that about 1 out of a million children who get measles or mumps vaccines may have a more serious reaction, such as inflammation of the brain (encephalitis).

Whether one out of a million or four out of a million children, or more children "have a more serious reaction, such as inflammation of the brain," is not of any great consequence unless Ms. Allison had been informed that inflammation of the brain might mean deafness, blindness, mental retardation and permanent brain damage.

a jury could reasonably conclude that Merck was negligent in purveying this dangerous vaccine when it was unaccompanied by an adequate warning.[17]

The only question here, as we see it, is whether Merck can free itself from any liability simply by delegating that duty and by contracting out that duty to a third party—in this case the Center for Disease Control . . . Since failure to give proper warning, under all legal theories, renders a product "defective," we conclude that although a manufacturer may decide to assign its duty to warn of the unsafeness of its product to others, a manufacturer cannot be relieved of ultimate responsibility for assuring that its unsafe product is dispensed with a proper warning. Although there is authority to go either way, it seems to us to be far the better rule that Merck should not be allowed to walk away, on summary judgment, from its duty to warn users of the dangers of its vaccine, especially when there is evidence from which a jury could find that the warning actually given was faulty . . .

Viewing the facts in the light most favorable to the Allisons, Thomas is entitled under Nevada law to pursue an action against Merck under a strict tort liability theory . . .

We reverse the summary judgment in favor of Merck on Thomas Allison's strict liability claim and on Thomas' and Ms. Allison's failure-to-warn claims and remand for trial. We affirm the judgment in all other respects.

The Department of Health and Human Services is also responsible for the Agency for Toxic Substances and Disease Registry, a helpful place for checking out what those chemicals are and what diseases they may cause. An example of one of the articles on the Web site at **http://www.atsdr.cdc.gov/** is an "Interaction Profile for Persistent Chemicals Found in Breast Milk," which lists the chemicals, the outcomes from exposure, the typical reasons for the chemicals, and what levels scientists have found. This can be important information in initial investigation when your attorney is trying to decide whether there's a case before spending money on an expert.

A great central place for technical publications is the National Technical Information Service Web site **http://www.ntis.gov/index.asp**. The site sells print publications and CDs covering topics of all kinds. The military has several sites for researchers and investigators: the Department of Defense's Publication site, which also includes a link to the Court Martial Manual and the USCMJ **http://www.defenselink.mil/pubs/**; the Air University Press **http://www.maxwell.af.mil/au/aul/aupress/**, and the U.S. Army Publishing Directorate **http://www.apd.army.mil/**.

State and local governments keep statistics, too, and they can also be useful. State comptrollers offices, secretaries of state, public universities and colleges, county clerk offices, and municipalities all provide useful information. Any state agency, local branch of a federal agency, local branch of a state agency, county-run entity, or city-run entity will have reporting requirements keep tabs on various numbers. Much of the reporting is for the agency (or whatever) to justify its existence and to show why it needs money. In the process, the agency may gather information important to you. The agency may also be created to govern an area in which you need information for your case, and it may have educational pamphlets and information sheets for you to use. Local governments often store their materials in the local city library; contact the reference librarian there for information about the collections.

---

[17] One possible explanation why no proper warnings were given to the Allisons or other vaccinees is revealed in the affidavit of Dr. Dull, which has been offered by Merck. Dr. Dull is a retired Center for Disease Control physician, who testified that the CDC had a policy of offering to prepare product information sheets for vaccines because the government feared that otherwise "vaccine manufacturers would overwarn potential vaccinees and thus discourage the use of vaccines." Given the CDC's admitted biases against "discouraging the use of vaccines," a jury could conclude that Merck knew or had reason to know that the CDC was not going to provide the truth about Merck's product and did not, in fact, give proper warning. If a jury were to conclude that Merck had such knowledge, Merck should not, in fairness, be allowed to insulate itself from tort liability simply by saying that it contracted with the CDC to take over all of Merck's responsibility for warning about its "unavoidably unsafe" product. If Merck decided to let the CDC go fast and easy on the warnings in order that people would not be reluctant to take the Merck-manufactured vaccines, Merck, while accepting the financial gain, should not be freed from financial responsibility for the untoward consequences suffered by the Allisons by reason of Thomas' taking the vaccine, especially in light of the possibility that Merck fully realized how inadequate the warning really was.

Government Sources: FOIA Reading Rooms

As part of the Federal Freedom of Information Act, the various agencies have been instructed to make responses to FOIA requests available at physical reading rooms and, since 1997, online. If you are doing research on ADA compliance, for instance, you very well may want to check out the Civil Rights Reading Room, which has a list of various opinions and rulings on equal access requirements that may prove helpful. The Department of Justice has a very nice central site for links to many reading rooms, and the various handbooks can be helpful for setting standards for various entities.

Market Reports and Other Commercial Publications

The first list of commercial publications to look at would be from your client, if she's in a particular business and the business is part of the issue you are investigating. If not, you can start with a visit to both your local college and public libraries and see what magazines, indexes, reports, and references each carries in the particular business. See what is quoted by the *Wall Street Journal, Forbes, Fortune,* or *Money Magazine.* Find out what they publish and what it means.

For example, you'll hear about the Dow Jones frequently on financial news. What is it? When would it be useful? You could go to its Web site at **http://www.dowjones.com/** and read up on the company, but doing so probably won't help you with the reference. When the reference is made to "the Dow Jones," it is about the **Dow Jones Industrial Average.** You can find an explanation about the Dow Jones Industrial Average, which is an index of how the stock market is doing. The Dow Jones is figured by taking various successful stocks in a wide range of industries and then averaging out the change in price. When would such data be useful? To establish what the market was like generally if you were trying to show that a particular stock was being manipulated or that the company was mismanaged. It would be more useful to show what stocks in similar industries were doing: selling well or losing money. However, Dow Jones also has indexes of specific markets; you just have to look a little harder to find them. The Dow Jones Industrial Average comes up in the following case; what relevance does it have here such that the court mentions it?

In re The Walt Disney Co., 825 A.2d 275 (Del. Chancery 2003).

In this derivative action filed on behalf of nominal defendant Walt Disney Company, plaintiffs allege that the defendant directors breached their fiduciary duties when they blindly approved an employment agreement with defendant Michael Ovitz and then, again without any review or deliberation, ignored defendant Michael Eisner's dealings with Ovitz regarding his non-fault termination. Plaintiffs seek rescission and/or money damages from defendants and Ovitz, or compensation for damages allegedly sustained by Disney and disgorgement of Ovitz's unjust enrichment . . .

. . . [P]laintiffs' new allegations give rise to a cognizable question whether the defendant directors of the Walt Disney Company should be held personally liable to the corporation for a knowing or intentional lack of due care in the directors' decision-making process regarding Ovitz's employment and termination. It is rare when a court imposes liability on directors of a corporation for breach of the duty of care, and this Court is hesitant to second-guess the business judgment of a disinterested and independent board of directors. But the facts alleged in the new complaint do not implicate merely negligent or grossly negligent decision making by corporate directors. Quite the contrary; plaintiffs' new complaint suggests that the Disney directors failed to exercise *any* business judgment and failed to make *any* good faith attempt to fulfill their fiduciary duties to Disney and its stockholders. Allegations that Disney's directors abdicated all responsibility to consider appropriately an action of material importance to the corporation puts directly in question whether the board's decision-making processes were employed in a good faith effort to advance corporate interests . . .

As mentioned, this case involves an attack on decisions of the Walt Disney Company's board of directors, approving an executive compensation contract for Michael Ovitz, as well as impliedly approving a non-fault termination that resulted in an award to Ovitz (allegedly exceeding $140,000,000) after barely one year of employment . . . [P]laintiffs used . . . a request for books and records . . . to obtain information about the nature of the Disney Board's involvement in the decision to hire and, eventually, to terminate Ovitz . . . The facts set forth hereafter are taken directly from the new complaint and, for purposes of the present motions, are accepted as true. Of course, I hold no opinion as to the actual truth of any of the allegations set forth in the new complaint; nor do I hold any view as to the likely ultimate outcome on the merits of claims based on these asserted facts. I determine here *only* that the facts, if true, arguably support all three of plaintiffs' claims for relief, as asserted in the new complaint, and are sufficient to excuse demand and to state claims that warrant development of a full record . . .

Michael Eisner is the chief executive officer ("CEO") of the Walt Disney Company. In 1994, Eisner's second-in-command, Frank Wells, died in a helicopter crash. Two other key executives—Jeffrey Katzenberg and Richard Frank—left Disney shortly thereafter, allegedly because of Eisner's management style. Eisner began looking for a new president for Disney and chose Michael Ovitz. Ovitz was founder and head of CAA, a talent agency; he had never been an executive for a publicly owned entertainment company. He had, however, been Eisner's close friend for over twenty-five years.

Eisner decided unilaterally to hire Ovitz. On August 13, 1995, he informed three Old Board members—Stephen Bollenbach, Sanford Litvack, and Irwin Russell (Eisner's personal attorney)—of that fact. All three protested Eisner's decision to hire Ovitz. Nevertheless, Eisner persisted, sending Ovitz a letter on August 14, 1995, that set forth certain material terms of his prospective employment. Before this, neither the Old Board nor the compensation committee had ever discussed hiring Ovitz as president of Disney. No discussions or presentations were made to the compensation committee or to the Old Board regarding Ovitz's hiring as president of Walt Disney until September 26, 1995.

Before informing Bollenbach, Litvack, and Russell on August 13, 1995, Eisner collected information on his own, through his position as the Disney CEO, on the potential hiring of Ovitz. In an internal document created around July 7, 1995, concerns were raised about the number of stock options to be granted to Ovitz. The document warned that the number was far beyond the normal standards of both Disney and corporate America and would receive significant public criticism. Additionally, Graef Crystal, an executive compensation expert, informed board member Russell, via a letter dated August 12, 1995, that, generally speaking, a large signing bonus is hazardous because the full cost is borne immediately and completely even if the executive fails to serve the full term of employment . . . Neither of these documents, however, were submitted to either the compensation committee or the Old Board before hiring Ovitz. Disney prepared a draft employment agreement on September 23, 1995. A copy of the draft was sent to Ovitz's lawyers, but was not provided to members of the compensation committee.

The compensation committee, consisting of defendants Ignacio Lozano, Jr., Sidney Poitier, Russell, and Raymond Watson, met on September 26, 1995, for just under an hour. Three subjects were discussed at the meeting, one of which was Ovitz's employment. According to the minutes, the committee spent the least amount of time during the meeting discussing Ovitz's hiring. In fact, it appears that more time was spent on discussions of paying $250,000 to Russell for his role in securing Ovitz's employment than was actually spent on discussions of Ovitz's employment. The minutes show that several issues were raised and discussed by the committee members concerning Russell's fee. All that occurred during the meeting regarding Ovitz's employment was that Russell reviewed the employment terms with the committee and answered a few questions. Immediately thereafter, the committee adopted a resolution of approval.

No copy of the September 23, 1995 draft employment agreement was actually given to the committee. Instead, the committee members received, at the meeting itself, a rough summary of the agreement. The summary, however, was incomplete. It stated that Ovitz was to receive options to purchase five million shares of stock, but did not state the exercise price. The committee also did not receive any of the materials already produced by Disney regarding Ovitz's possible employment. No spreadsheet or similar type of analytical document showing the potential payout to Ovitz throughout the contract, or the possible cost of his severance package upon a non-fault termination, was created or presented. Nor did the committee request or receive any information as to how the draft agreement compared with similar agreements throughout the entertainment industry, or information regarding other similarly situated executives in the same industry.

The committee also lacked the benefit of an expert to guide them through the process. Graef Crystal, an executive compensation expert, had been hired to provide advice to Disney on Eisner's new employment contract. Even though he had earlier told Russell that large signing bonuses, generally speaking, can be hazardous, neither he nor any other expert had been retained to assist Disney regarding Ovitz's hiring. Thus, no presentations, spreadsheets, written analyses, or opinions were given by any expert for the compensation committee to rely upon in reaching its decision. Although Crystal was not retained as a compensation consultant on the Ovitz contract, he later lamented his failure to intervene and produce a spreadsheet showing the potential costs of the employment agreement.

The compensation committee was informed that further negotiations would occur and that the stock option grant would be delayed until the final contract was worked out. The committee approved the general terms and conditions of the employment agreement, but did not condition their approval on being able to review the final agreement. Instead, the committee granted Eisner the authority to approve the final terms and conditions of the contract as long as they were within the framework of the draft agreement. Immediately after the compensation committee met on September 26, the Old Board met. Again, no expert was present to advise the board. Nor were any documents produced to the board for it to review before the meeting regarding the Ovitz contract. The board did not ask for additional information to be collected or presented regarding Ovitz's hiring. According to the minutes, the compensation committee did not make any recommendation or report to the board concerning its resolution to hire Ovitz. Nor did Russell, who allegedly secured Ovitz's employment, make a presentation to the board. The minutes of the meeting were fifteen pages long, but only a page and a half covered Ovitz's possible employment. A portion of that page and a half was spent discussing the $250,000 fee paid to Russell for obtaining Ovitz. According to the minutes, the Old Board did not ask any questions about the details of Ovitz's salary, stock options, or possible termination. The Old Board also did not consider the consequences of a termination, or the various payout scenarios that existed. Nevertheless, at that same meeting, the Old Board decided to appoint Ovitz president of Disney. Final negotiation of the employment agreement was left to Eisner, Ovitz's close friend for over twenty-five years . . .

Ovitz was officially hired on October 1, 1995, and began serving as Disney's president, although he did not yet have an executed employment agreement with Disney. On October 16, 1995, the compensation committee was informed, via a brief oral report, that negotiations were ongoing with Ovitz. The committee was not given a draft of the employment agreement either before or during the meeting. A summary similar to the one given on September 26, 1995, was presented. The committee did not seek any further information about the negotiations or about the terms and conditions of Ovitz's agreement, nor was any information proffered regarding the scope of the non-fault termination provision. And, as before, no expert was available to advise the committee as to the employment agreement.

Negotiations continued among Ovitz, Eisner, and their attorneys. The lawyers circulated drafts on October 3, October 10, October 16, October 20, October 23, and December 12, 1995. The employment agreement was physically executed between Michael Ovitz and the Walt Disney Company on December 12, 1995. The employment agreement, however, was backdated to October 1, 1995, the day Ovitz began working as Disney's president. Additionally, the stock option agreement associated with the employment agreement was executed by Eisner (for Disney) on April 2, 1996. Ovitz did not countersign the stock option agreement until November 15, 1996, when he was already discussing his plans to leave Disney's employ. Neither the Old Board nor the compensation committee reviewed or approved the final employment agreement before it was executed and made binding upon Disney . . .

The final version of Ovitz's employment agreement differed significantly from the drafts summarized to the compensation committee on September 26, 1995, and October 16, 1995. First, the final version caused Ovitz's stock options to be "in the money" when granted. The September 23rd draft agreement set the exercise price at the stock price on October 2, 1995, the day after Ovitz began as president. On October 16, 1995, the compensation committee agreed to change the exercise price to the price on that date (October 16, 1995), a price similar to that on October 2nd. The agreement was not signed until December 12, 1995, however, at which point the value of Disney stock had increased by eight percent—from $56.875 per share on October 16th to $61.50 per share on December 12th. The overall stock market, according to the Dow Jones Industrial Average, had also increased by about eight percent at the same time. By waiting to sign the agreement until December, but not changing the date of the exercise price, Ovitz had stock options that instantly were "in the money.". . . This allowed Ovitz to play a "win-win" game at Disney's expense—if the market price of Disney stock had fallen between October 16 and December 12, Ovitz could have demanded a downward adjustment to the option exercise price; if the price had risen (as in fact it had) Ovitz would receive "in the money" options.

Another difference in the final version of Ovitz's employment agreement concerned the circumstances surrounding a non-fault termination. The September 23rd draft agreement stated that non-fault termination benefits would only be provided if Disney wrongfully terminated Ovitz, or Ovitz died or became disabled. The October 16th draft contained a very similar definition. These were the only two drafts of which the compensation committee was made aware. The final version of the agreement, however, offered Ovitz a non-fault termination as long as Ovitz did not act with gross negligence or malfeasance. Therefore, instead of protecting Ovitz from a wrongful termination by Disney, Ovitz was able to receive the full benefits of a non-fault termination, even if he acted negligently or was unable to perform his duties, as long as his behavior did not reach the level of gross negligence or malfeasance. Additionally, a non-compete clause was not included within the agreement should Ovitz leave Disney's employ.

The employment agreement had a term of five years. Ovitz was to receive a salary of $1 million per year, a potential bonus each year from $0 to $10 million, and a series of stock options (the "A" options) that enabled Ovitz to purchase three million shares of Disney stock at the October 16, 1995 exercise price. The options were to vest at one million per year for three years beginning September 30, 1998. At the end of the contract term, if Disney entered into a new contract with Ovitz, he was entitled to the "B" options, an additional two million shares. There was no requirement, however, that Disney enter into a new contract with Ovitz.

Should a non-fault termination occur, however, the terms of the final version of the employment agreement appeared to be even more generous. Under a non-fault termination, Ovitz was to receive his salary for the remainder of the contract, discounted at a risk-free rate keyed to Disney's borrowing costs. He was also to receive a $7.5 million bonus for each year remaining on his contract, discounted at the same risk-free rate, even though no set bonus amount was guaranteed in the contract. Additionally, all of his "A" stock options were to vest immediately, instead of waiting for the final three years of his contract for them to vest. The final benefit of the non-fault termination was a lump sum "termination payment" of $10 million. The termination payment was equal to the payment Ovitz would receive should he complete his full five-year term with Disney, but not receive an offer for a new contract. Graef Crystal opined in the January 13, 1997, edition of *California Law Business* that "the contract was most valuable to Ovitz the sooner he left Disney.". . .

Ovitz began serving as president of Disney on October 1, 1995, and became a Disney director in January 1996. Ovitz's tenure as Disney's president proved unsuccessful . . .

Ovitz wanted to leave Disney, but could only terminate his employment if one of three events occurred: (1) he was not elected or retained as president and a director of Disney; (2) he was assigned duties materially inconsistent with his role as president; or (3) Disney reduced his annual salary or failed to grant his stock options, pay him discretionary bonuses, or make any required compensation payment. None of these three events occurred. If Ovitz resigned outright, he might have been liable to Disney for damages and would not have received the benefits of the non-fault termination . . . Eisner agreed to help Ovitz depart Disney without sacrificing any of his benefits . . .

. . . Neither the New Board of Directors nor the compensation committee had been consulted or given their approval for a non-fault termination. In addition, no record exists of any action by the New Board once the non-fault termination became public on December 12, 1996.

. . . [A] December 27th letter stated that Ovitz's termination would "be treated as a 'Non-Fault Termination.'" . . . This differed from the December 12th letter, which treated Ovitz's termination "as though there had been a 'Non-Fault Termination.'" . . . It also made the termination of Ovitz's employment and his resignation as a Disney director effective as of the close of business on December 27th, instead of on January 31, 1997, as in the December 12th letter. Additionally, it listed the amount payable to Ovitz as $38,888,230.77, and stated that the "A" options to purchase three million shares of Disney vested on December 27th, instead of January 31, 1997, as in the December 12th letter. Both Eisner and Litvack signed the letter. Again, however, neither the New Board nor the compensation committee reviewed or approved the December 27th letter. No record exists of any New Board action after the December 27th letter became public, nor had any board member raised any questions or concerns since the original December 12th letter became public.

. . . Disney's bylaws required board approval for Ovitz's non-fault termination . . . No documents or board minutes currently exist showing an affirmative decision by the New Board or any of its committees to grant Ovitz a non-fault termination. The New Board was already aware that Eisner was granting the non-fault termination as of December 12, 1996, the day it became public. No record of any action by the New Board affirming or questioning that decision by Eisner either before or after that date has been produced. There are also no records showing that alternatives to a non-fault termination were ever evaluated by the New Board or by any of its committees . . .

. . . These facts, if true, do more than portray directors who, in a negligent or grossly negligent manner, merely failed to inform themselves or to deliberate adequately about an issue of material importance to their corporation. Instead, the facts alleged in the new complaint suggest that the defendant directors *consciously and intentionally disregarded their responsibilities,* adopting a "we don't care about the risks" attitude concerning a material corporate decision. Knowing or deliberate indifference by a director to his or her duty to act faithfully and with appropriate care is conduct, in my opinion, that may not have been taken honestly and in good faith to advance the best interests of the company. Put differently, all of the alleged facts, if true, imply that the defendant directors *knew* that they were making material decisions without adequate information and without adequate deliberation, and that they simply did not care if the decisions caused the corporation and its stockholders to suffer injury or loss. Viewed in this light, plaintiffs' new complaint sufficiently alleges a breach of the directors' obligation to act honestly and in good faith in the corporation's best interests for a Court to conclude, if the facts are true, that the defendant directors' conduct fell outside the protection of the business judgment rule.

. . . Although the strategy was economically injurious and a public relations disaster for Disney, the Ovitz/Eisner exit strategy allegedly was designed principally to protect their personal reputations, while assuring Ovitz a huge personal payoff after barely a year of mediocre to poor job performance. These allegations, if ultimately found to be true, would suggest a faithless fiduciary who obtained extraordinary personal financial benefits at the expense of the constituency for whom he was obliged to act honestly and in good faith. Because Ovitz was a fiduciary during both the negotiation of his employment agreement and the non-fault termination, he had an obligation to ensure the process of his contract negotiation and termination was both impartial and fair. The facts, as plead, give rise to a reasonable inference that, assisted by Eisner, he ignored that obligation . . .

It is of course true that after-the-fact litigation is a most imperfect device to evaluate corporate business decisions, as the limits of human competence necessarily impede judicial review. But our corporation law's [sic] theoretical justification for disregarding honest errors simply does not apply to intentional misconduct or to egregious process failures that implicate the foundational directoral obligation to act honestly and in good faith to advance corporate interests. Because the facts alleged here, if true, portray directors consciously indifferent to a material issue facing the corporation, the law must be strong enough to intervene against abuse of trust. Accordingly, all three of plaintiffs' claims for relief concerning fiduciary duty breaches and waste survive defendants' motions to dismiss.

The practical effect of this ruling is that defendants must answer the new complaint and plaintiffs may proceed to take appropriate discovery on the merits of their claims. To that end, a case scheduling order has been entered that will promptly bring this matter before the Court on a fully developed factual record.

IT IS SO ORDERED.

The Dow Jones reference shows that when Ovitz came on board with Disney, Disney's stock was increasing at the same rate as the market as a whole. What was not mentioned—and would be interesting to know, and a potential measure of damages—is what the stock was doing at the time Ovitz bailed on Disney. If it had a history of tracking with the Dow Jones until then, and after Ovitz took over as president it started a downward trend out of sync with the Dow Jones Industrial Average, that would be a persuasive piece of evidence that Disney was off its standard financial returns during that period as a result of all of the shenanigans with Ovitz's compensation package and poor job performance.

What about another reference, **Dun and Bradstreet?** That's a company that provides credit reports, establishes credit references for new businesses, and owns Hoover's, a business intelligence manual.

Aside from financial markets, there are other markets. What about the automobile market? *The Blue Book,* or the NADA report, is used by banks, auto dealers, and just plain folks to figure out the going price for a particular vehicle. As indicated in the case, that would be the type of publication envisioned by the hearsay exception for market reports and commercial publications. Accident rates, theft rates, and repair costs are reported by the Consumer Union and by automobile insurers, and these also influence the market. Are they market reports or commercial publications? If you can get a witness to say so and a judge to accept it. Real estate sales for a particular area from the real estate agent's reports is another report commonly relied on by persons in the business for the valuation of real estate.

Also take a look at what the **National Association of Legal Investigators (NALI)** has up on its links site. NALI **www.nalionline.org** is an association that requires members to prove at least two years of active practice in doing investigation for lawyers prior to acceptance. The organization offers a **Certified Legal Investigator (CLI)** designation, which requires five years of practice, presentation of a paper on an area of investigation, and passage of a test. On NALI's helpful Web site is a prodigious links page, which includes links to corporate sources.

To sum up, anything with a chart, graph, and numbers is a good candidate for acceptance in the market reports category. The key thing is to keep your eyes open and to be curious. Look around the Internet, the library, the local bookstore. Talk to people in the business. It's amazing what helpful facts you run across if you pay attention to what is going on around you.

Reference Books and Other Learned Treatises

Dictionaries, maps, and atlases are the first reference books that come to mind. When the meaning of a statute or a contract is at issue in a case, the first thing to consider is the "plain meaning" of the word. An ordinary dictionary can supply you with this plain meaning. For example, according to Samuel A. Thumma and Jeffrey L. Kirchmeier, the United States Supreme Court referred to *Webster's Third New International Dictionary* in 102 opinions in the 1997–1998 term, taking judicial notice to do so. Therefore, it doesn't hurt to have a dictionary on hand as needed, whether Webster's or another general usage dictionary.

Maps and atlases are helpful as well. Depending on the type of case, you may want a close-up of a particular area, so you may want a detailed map of a city, or you may need a textured topographical map. So long as the map or atlas is produced by a reputable and recognizable company, there should be no problem having the court take judicial notice of it.

Other learned treatises or reference material will be specific to the particular area of practice. If you are interested in a particular area of medicine, check out what standard texts are used for training doctors in that area. For psychology and psychiatry, the reference that everyone uses is the *Diagnostic and Statistic's Manual, Fourth Edition (DSM-IV).* This book lists all the recognized psychiatric diagnoses, what the symptoms of each are, and various treatments. For pharmacology, doctors typically use the *Physician's Desk Reference (PDR),* which lists drugs by brand and generic name, has pictures of the various drugs, and gives the uses, doses, contraindications, and warnings for each. *Gray's Anatomy* is still a classic on human anatomy, regularly revised to keep it in line with current research.

This is another time to look at the American Association for Whatsits. The various National Associations, American Associations, Associations of Professional Doohickeys, Federations of Professional Thingamajigs, and so on, may have statements of purpose, goals, papers, books, journals, and other publications that will be considered "learned treatises." For example, The American Society of Mechanical Engineers (ASME, Web site at **http://www.asme.org/**) has a section on codes and standards that cover boiler pressures, surface materials, and a host of other matters. The New York State Education Department maintains a Web site listing various professional organizations at **http://www.op.nysed.gov/national.htm**, a good place to go for a pre-screened list of legitimate organizations, ranging from acupuncture to veterinary professionals. Using the link to the National Academy of Opticianry, you could find a list of books and videos on contact lenses and how to fit them. If that were the subject of the litigation, a video from the professional organization could be a very nice piece of evidence to present, depending on whether it helps or harms your client. The New York State Education Department's site is not an exhaustive list, though, so if you do not find the area for which you are searching, don't give up. There are still more organizations out there.

Another example of a prestigious group is the **American Medical Association (AMA)**, an organization that a judge would probably take judicial notice of as being authoritative. The AMA has come up with guidelines for interviewing and standards for various types of abuse and neglect, available online at **www. ama-assn.org/ama/pub/category/3548.html** and also available in published form. Not only do the guidelines help you prepare for initial interviews when you suspect, for example, elderly abuse, the printed version can help establish for the jury what constitutes "abuse."

. . . .

Using the Phone to Gather Information
by Risa Sacks

In the information field, our goal is to solve each problem in the optimum way possible—most efficient, most complete, fastest, cheapest, most reliable, etc. In order to meet this goal, it's important to use the research tool, or combination of research tools, best suited to each individual situation. With the constantly expanding array of new technologies available, it's easy to forget the unique and important advantages of the telephone as a research tool.

This article asks you to re-evaluate the usefulness of the telephone as a research tool and to consider reintegrating it into your research.

In re-evaluating the telephone, we'll examine questions such as

Why bother with the phone at all?

When might the telephone be your most appropriate research tool?

How does the telephone fit in with your other research tools?

How to find whom to phone

How to plan and make the phone call

How to follow up after the phone call

And (being realistic to the last) what to do if you still really detest the telephone.

With this basis, let's begin . . . in praise of telephones.

WHY PHONE?

The telephone has a number of advantages as a research tool. Here are just a few, to get you reconsidering.

It's interactive, direct and exact. Let's look at each factor separately, although in fact these three interrelate.

Interactive—One of the best things about the telephone is that communication can be an immediate two-way street. If you're not sure you understand something, it's easy to say, "Let me see if I have this straight. You're saying that . . . " And if you don't have it straight, you can catch the problem and clarify it right there. You can keep modifying and refining as you go along—"How would a resurgence of tuberculosis change the situation?" You can keep expanding as you need: "Would this also apply to . . . "

Direct—With the telephone, you can, in effect, go to the source's mouth. For example, you can call the person who conducted a particular study. The answer you need may exist in the researcher's original data, even though it was not one of the published conclusions of the study.

Exact—With techniques such as online, library, or archives research, you can find information only on questions that other people have chosen to answer. With the telephone, you can find the answer to the exact question you need answered. I once needed to find the number of stolen rental cars involved in injury accidents in California from 1987 through the present. If you think that no database had that statistic, you're absolutely right. Speaking to experts directly, however, I was able to find the numbers that let us extrapolate the answer.

Want more (of the many additional) points in the telephone's favor? It's fast—dial the number, and there you are. It's immediate and as real time as possible—when you talk to someone, you are not getting information that was updated yesterday or last week. If something happened the minute before you called, or even while you're on the phone, you can be told about it.

It's cheap—there is virtually no initial cost for equipment, the costs of calls even around the world continues to decrease, and special phone packages available from a number of carriers reduce the prices even further. Local calls and toll-free numbers save your budget even more. Almost everyone has a telephone and you don't have to learn any unique language, commands or codes to use one.

The rapid spread of fax machines gives yet another important dimension to telephone research. In the past, after speaking to someone on the phone, it could take days or weeks for documents that they had to reach you. Today, with the proliferation of fax machines, documents are in your hands in seconds.

(continued)

I recently conducted a search for a toll or instrument that could identify the sizes of metal rebars that were totally encased in concrete. I didn't know if there was such a thing, let alone what to call it. Three local phone calls, two toll-free calls and 15 minutes later I had faxes in my hands with pictures, graphs, specifications, prices and explanations for a range of pachometers that could do the job to various levels of specificity.

Many of the points listed in the previous discussion are advantages, however, only in the right situations: Cheaper? Well, sometimes? Faster? That depends on what you need. The next section introduces the issues of when to phone and how to integrate the telephone with other research techniques.

WHEN TO PHONE

There are no hard, fast rules about when to choose the telephone and how to integrate the telephone with your other research techniques. As you proceed, you'll find the mix that works best for you. There are, however, some rules of thumb that you might find useful.

You can think of many of these as the "too" rules: for instance, "too" wide, complex, narrow, specialized, new, or old. That is, the telephone is especially useful when your topic or desired answer is "too" something for online or library research to easily provide the answer, or the whole answer. Let's look at some examples.

Too wide/too complex—Using online sources, you might be able to find the effect of a drought on a set of crops for a specific country. You might not, however, be able to find the effect of that same drought on six specific crops in four neighboring countries. If you speak to an expert in the field, he may have that data at his fingertips, or be willing to think about it and actually synthesize the answer for you.

Too narrow/too specialized—At the other end of the wide-narrow spectrum, if the answer you need applies to a very narrowly defined or specific situation, online may not offer the best solution. "Stolen rental cars involved in injury accidents" was definitely too narrow, or too specialized. Data were available from traditional sources, for example, on stolen cars, but not stolen rental cars. Putting that answer together required talking to people from several different disciplines in three states and two countries. Other examples might include information that applies only to a specific community, or area within a city, or a special subgroup, or that crosses several subgroups—single working mothers of children with disabilities. As the number of individual descriptors pile up (stolen—rental car—injury accident—California), remember to consider the telephone.

Too old/too new—If something just occurred today (or developed very recently), there may not have been time for all of the data to appear in print or to be available online. At the other end of the spectrum, online sources frequently go back only a certain length of time. In one search related to the death of a doctor in Virginia, the online full text records for the Richmond Times/Dispatch went back to 1989, while the death occurred in 1963. I called the newspaper; they referred me to their research librarian; within the hour, she found and faxed the obituary.

In addition to the "too" rules, some inherent restrictions in online searching might make you consider the telephone. The inability to obtain visuals is one example of an inherent restriction.

For example, a DIALOG reference indicated that a relevant article contained a set of graphs depicting market shares. Unfortunately, even full text did not provide these key visuals. I called the author's office and the person I spoke with was happy to fax me the visuals as we talked!

Terminology is another example of inherent restriction or difficulty with online searching. Computers give you exactly what you ask for, which can lead to two different but related terminology problems. First, you may not know the correct or technical name for something. Second, there can be many terms or names for the concept you want.

The pachometer search is a good example of the first type of terminology problem. I didn't know if there was such a thing, let alone what to call it. While there are ways I could have searched using keywords and descriptors such as "rebars" and "measurements," this may have produced a mass of extraneous information. Being able to talk to a person and ask, "Is there something that maybe does this and sort of does that?" produced more time- and cost-efficient results for me.

The second terminology problem relates to multiple terms for a single concept—for example, "thesis," "dissertation," "Ph.D.," and "doctorate." This can be a problem particularly when dealing with more than one database and newly invented terms and vocabulary (neural networks, cybernetics, cyberspace). Where controlled vocabulary or identifiers have not yet been updated, there can be holes in synonyms, thesauri or descriptor listings. Because of this, you may omit the exact term used in a particular reference, and miss that reference. A person on the other end of the telephone is likely to give you the information, even if your terminology is slightly off (a good example of what the Doonesbury cartoon referred to as "User friendly live-ware.")

As the previous paragraphs indicate, there are a number of ways to integrate the telephone with other research methods, including:

Use online to find relevant articles, then the phone to obtain the visuals.

Use online to learn the general facts on a topic, then telephone to find how it applies to your specific situation.

Use the phone to help define the terms of the problem, then use other methods to gather additional information.

The next section further highlights the interdependence of research techniques.

WHOM TO PHONE

The big challenge is to find the first name and number to call. Once you have a person to call, he or she can provide the next contact and you're on your way.

There are innumerable sources for that first number. In this section we'll touch on some of the most common ones.

Online—Begin with online research and go from there. Online can provide you with articles that reference experts in the area you want. In addition, you'll know the author of the article and the name and location of the publication. Look up the phone number for the publication, and call the author. Authors are wonderful resources—they know the subject and are generally willing to talk. Authors are frequently gold mines of further information, such as phone numbers for people they referenced in their articles and additional references they never mentioned in the article.

CD-ROM—If CD ROM is available, that can provide a cost-effective means of obtaining reference names. For example, check the Social Sciences Citation Index for relevant experts. This index even offers author addresses, if available.

Yellow Page/Phone Books/Information—Because we're so used to having phone books around, it's easy to overlook them as a source for research information. In my pachometer search, I began with the Yellow Pages to find the number of a local, very-full-service hardware store. Yellow Pages frequently have additional indices to help you find what you want. My local Yellow Pages, for example, has a Subject Index (Automotive, Health and Well-being, etc.), a Brand Name Index, and an Alphabetical Index. The white pages are full of useful information such as phone numbers for libraries, government offices, and individual departments for local universities. If you need an expert in a given field, speaking to someone from a relevant department of the nearest university can be a useful starting point. For numbers in other towns, states and countries, your local library may have "foreign" phone books, or call the telephone information operator for that location. Toll-free phone books can provide numbers that save your budget even more.

Directories—There are directories for everything—even directories. The Directory of Directories (now titled "Directories in Print," sometimes referred to as the "DOD," published by Gale Research Company) lists over "10,000 business and industrial directories, professional and scientific rosters, directory databases and other lists and guides of all kinds." The DOD has a title, keyword, and subject

(*continued*)

index. The listing for each directory shows the publisher's name, address and phone numbers as well as information about the directory. It's a good bet that a publisher of the "Awning Manufacturers Directory" or of the "Who's Who in Canvas and Industrial Fabrics" could supply you with information in that field, or give you the name of an expert to call.

Associations—There are associations for everything. In fact, you'll find the "Encyclopedia of Associations" listed in the "Directories in Print." Geriatric Assessment, Dentistry, Education, Nutrition, Ophthalmology, Psychiatry and Research each have their own association. Each association listing shows address, phone and the names of the key persons in the organization along with their titles. With a name, a phone number and a title, you're on your way. Some associations will only provide information to their own members, but all associations know other organizations or key personnel in their special fields.

Publications—Just like directories and associations, there are publications for everything. There are a number of sources for information of publications, including "Gale Directory of Publications and Broadcast Media," "Newsletters Directory," and "Periodical Directories and Bibliographies." The Standard Rate and Data Service (SRDS) publications are designed to present advertising rates, but for the researcher, they provide names, addresses and phone numbers for personnel on thousands and thousands of publications. You can find business publications, for example, organized by subject area and local newspapers organized by city within state.

These are just a sampling of resources for your first phone number, but we need to move on to "How to Phone."

HOW TO PHONE

There are a number of ways you could look at the phone call process, but for purposes of this article we'll break the process into preparing, opening, interviewing and closing.

Preparing—In many ways, what you do before the phone call is the most important part of the call. If there's one single recommendation, it's DO YOUR HOMEWORK. When you call people and ask to take up their valuable time, there is a tacit understanding that you are not asking that person to do your work for you—you've already done your work and are asking for help where you need it.

Preparation may involve many things, including the following:

Do your preliminary research—find out as much information as possible on your own. If there are articles available, read them; if someone in your office has basic information on a topic, talk to that person for background and terminology.

Clearly formulate your questions, needs, and purposes for the call. Know and be ready to state in as few words as possible what you need and why you need it. Be clear in your own mind what you already know and what gaps you hope this person will help you with.

Have all your materials ready before you call. Nothing is so counterproductive as having to search for pen, paper, prepared questions or other names you wanted to ask about while you have a contact on the phone.

I recommend preparing a separate sheet for each person you are going to call. At the top of the sheet, list the name, position/organization and phone number (especially if someone referred you, be sure to include that reference).

List the major questions and points you want to cover. You might consider an outline format, or just major headings; or use file cards or legal pads—whatever you find lets you be both most organized and most flexible during the actual interview.

Leave plenty of room for notes about each point as well as for other information that may surface. Have extra paper at hand in case your notes go on to several pages. As a suggestion, only write on the front side of each page. It's too easy to lose or overlook information if you're flipping from the front to back sides of pages.

Another place to seek information is the card catalogue of your local libraries. Most libraries have gone online these days, so you can check through their holdings over the Internet. Look at what is available under a particular subject heading, particularly in the library's reference section. These volumes may be particularly profitable. If you have a college or university nearby that offers a major in the field of expertise in which you are looking for sources, zero in on that library first, as it will be more likely to collect reference materials to support students in the program than other libraries. Such libraries may also have professional journals available, either in hard copy or via a database accessible from their library. If it appears that there are sufficient resources there to warrant a visit, take a trip to the library to see what you can get.

CHAPTER SUMMARY

Whether for use as background information, substantive evidence, demonstrative evidence, learned treatises, or sources for experts, general authoritative sources can be extremely helpful. Selecting and finding the appropriate materials is important, and you may be able to use judicial notice, an expert, the learned treatise, public report, or market report exceptions to admit these materials into court. Don't overlook textbooks or publications of state or federal agencies in your search.

FOR FURTHER READING

Casenote, *Admission of Statistical Surveys Under Learned Treatise Exception to Hearsay Rule,* 40 Tenn. L. Rev. 759 (1973).

John F. Shampton, *Statistical Evidence of Real Estate Valuation: Establishing Value Without Appraisers,* 21 S. Ill. U. L. J. 113 (1996).

Samuel A. Thumma and Jeffrey L. Kirchmeier, *The Lexicon Has Become a Fortress: The United States Supreme Court's Use of Dictionaries,* 47 Buffalo L. Rev. 227 (1999).

Dennis J. Turner, *Judicial Notice and Federal Rule of Evidence 201—A Rule Ready for Change,* 45 U. Pitt. L. Rev. 181 (1983).

CHAPTER REVIEW

KEY TERMS

American Medical Association (AMA)
Census Bureau
Centers for Disease Control (CDC)
Certified Legal Investigator (CLI)
declarant
Diagnostic and Statistics Manual, Fourth Edition (DSM-IV)
Dow Jones Industrial Average

Dun & Bradstreet
foundation questions
Gray's Anatomy
judicial notice
laying a foundation
learned treatise
National Association of Legal Investigators (NALI)
National Institutes of Health (NIH)

National Transportation Safety Board (NTSB)
Occupational Safety and Health Administration (OSHA)
Physician's Desk Reference (PDR)
standard of care
sua sponte
weight of the evidence

FILL IN THE BLANKS

1. When a court acts of its own accord, without a request from either party, it is referred to as _____.

2. Two major business resources are the _____, which gives background information on various businesses, and the _____, which gives stock market indicators.

3. Before evidence can be entered, the person offering it must lay a _____ by asking _____ questions.

4. _____ must be established in order to decide whether a defendant has acted as a reasonably prudent person.

5. A classic source on anatomy is _____.

6. The relative value assigned to a particular item of evidence by the jury is referred to as the _____.

7. The court's ability to simply recognize certain easily ascertainable facts is called _____.

8. The federal government has an alphabet soup of acronyms of helpful agencies, including _____, the agency responsible for investigating aviation, highway, and marine accidents, and _____, the agency responsible for setting standards for workplace safety.

9. A(n) _____ is a resource commonly relied on by experts in the field.

10. The _____ is the most common pharmaceuticals resource for doctors.

11. The person who made the hearsay statement is the _____.

12. The _____ exception to the hearsay rule applies to reports commonly relied on in a particular area of business.

13. The _____ is a tool used by mental health care professionals to make diagnoses.

14. _____ offers a certification test for professionals specializing in investigations for lawyers and legal matters that results in a(n) _____ designation.

15. The _____ exception to the hearsay rule applies to reports generated by governmental agencies.

WEB WORK

1. Go to www.google.com. Enter "market reports" as a search term. Name four different kinds of markets for which you find references. How useful was this as a search term?

2. Go to www.altavista.com. Enter "commercial publications" as a search term. Name four different areas of commerce for which you find references. How useful was this as a search term?

3. Go to www.dogpile.com. Enter "reference books" as a search term. Name four different areas of specific knowledge for which you find books. How useful was this as a search term?

4. Go to www.yahoo.com. Enter "learned treatise" as a search term. How useful was this as a search term for finding the references? What did you find?

5. Go to http://www.lib.umich.edu/govdocs/ and see what local government sites apply to you. What documents are available about which you were unaware?

WORKING THE BRAIN

1. What information do you think you would need to fully understand the factual issues discussed in *In re Interest of L.H. v. D.H.*? What resources would best help you do so?

2. What information do you think you would need to fully understand the factual issues discussed in *Stotz v. Shields*? What resources would best help you do so?

3. What information do you think you would need to fully understand the factual issues discussed in *Six Flags Over Georgia II, L.P. v. Kull*? What resources would best help you do so?

4. What information do you think you would need to fully understand the factual issues discussed in *Allison v. Merck and Co.*? What resources would best help you do so?

5. What information do you think you would need to fully understand the factual issues discussed in *In re The Walt Disney Co.*? What resources would best help you do so?

PUTTING IT TO WORK

1. What background research would you want to do to prepare for the *Haus* case? Where do you think you would find resources appropriate to that research? Start making a list of possible resources and what hearsay exceptions they would fall under.

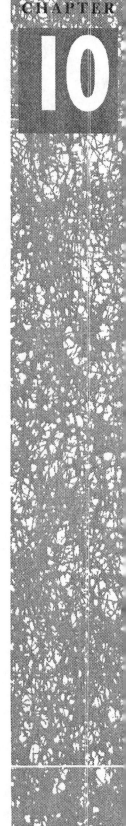

EXPERT WITNESSES

> "Expert opinion . . . is only an ordinary guess in evening clothes."
>
> *Earl M. Kerstter, Inc. v. Commonwealth, 171 A.2d 163 (Pa. 1961)*

> "In response to the question: 'Is that your conclusion that this man is a malingerer?' Dr. Unsworth responded: 'I wouldn't be testifying if I didn't think so, unless I was on the other side, then it would be a post-traumatic condition.'"
>
> *Ladner v. Higgins, 71 So.2d 242 (La. Ct. App. 1954)*

> "Gentlemen of the jury, there are three kinds of liars: the common liar, the damned liar, and the scientific expert."
>
> *Anonymous trial lawyer, 1897*

INTRODUCTION

Expert witnesses are often a key part of explaining how things happened. In some types of cases, a plaintiff cannot prevail without one, such as in medical malpractice, where you must have a doctor testify that the defendant doctor failed to meet the required standard of care. A good expert witness can help your side figure out the case, offer advice on questions to ask, and deflate "their" expert. A good expert witness will also tell you the truth, not just what he or she knows you'd like to hear. There are strategies to use in how you choose an expert, when you retain an expert, and what you tell an expert. None of the expert's help comes for free, and you have to be careful how you use it.

Experts are pervasive in trials. According to one source, there were over a million tenders of expert psychiatric evidence per year in the United States as of 1988. A poll of jurors conducted by the *National Law Journal* in 1993 revealed that 89% believed that paid experts were believable; 71% stated that the expert contributed to the outcome of the trial. Some types of evidence require experts, such as whether medical damages were caused by a particular incident; other situations are simply made more understandable by the presence of experts.

The bottom line: You will rarely go to trial these days without at least one expert, even if it is only a treating physician.

ETHICAL ISSUES

Anecdotal evidence makes experts, and the use of experts, seem shady and suspect, as this story related by George C. Harris illustrates.

> The incentives for shaped or slanted expert testimony in civil cases, where experts often receive substantial fees for helpful testimony, are certainly no less than in criminal prosecutions. One doctor, Houston hematologist Robert Lewy, examined more than 4,700 women with breast implants, most referred by lawyers, and found illness in ninety-three percent of them. He set up a foundation called Breast Implant Research, Inc. and saw his income rise in one year from $300,000 to $2 million, primarily as a result of his expert services to breast implant plaintiffs. Both a national panel of court-appointed independent experts and the Institute of Medicine of the National Academy of Sciences subsequently concluded that there was no credible evidence that breast implants cause disease; not, however, before numerous plaintiffs had received multiple millions as a result of jury verdicts and settlements.

> George C. Harris, *Testimony for Sale: The Law and Ethics of Snitches and Experts,* 28 Pepp. L. Rev. 1 (2000) (footnotes omitted).

At this time, the majority rule is that the hired expert has the right to payment and answers (almost) exclusively to the party hiring her. The minority view is that the expert is just another witness, and may be contacted by any party. But the concerns that are raised by the story quoted above are the subject of many calls for reform.

The concerns are not just for the more egregious situations, but also for the ethical experts who try to be objective. Payment to a witness is generally not allowed; paying experts is an exception. Even the most ethical expert can be subtly swayed by the fact of who is paying the bills. Additionally, the information the expert receives tends to be filtered because lawyers often believe that advocacy means winning at any cost—and if that includes not telling the expert everything in order to obtain a slanted opinion, so be it. Many ethical experts realize this, and resent lawyers who do not tell them everything. Or maybe it's more ego than ethics, because the expert does not like to look an idiot because his opinion is not correct under the real facts and he based it on the edited facts from the attorney. Because of the cost of sitting through all the testimony, it is unlikely that the lawyer will pay for the expert to be there for the entire trial, and it is equally unlikely the expert will volunteer to be there. But he may find out additional facts later from a colleague that alter his view and embarrass him professionally.

Reformers have various proposals, including (1) disclosure of all experts, whether testifying or not; (2) equal access to all experts, regardless of who retains the expert; (3) court-appointed experts whose cost is spread among the parties; and (4) court-regulated fees for experts.

If you want to uphold the highest ethics, choose experts with integrity (or at least a good deal of professional pride) and give them the unvarnished truth.

EVIDENTIARY ISSUES

As you may suspect, there is a rule to govern experts.

> Rule 702. Testimony by Experts

> If scientific, technical, or other specialized knowledge will assist the trier of fact to understand the evidence or to determine a fact in issue, a witness qualified as an expert by knowledge, skill, experience, training, or education, may testify thereto in the form of an opinion or otherwise, if (1) the testimony is based upon sufficient facts or data, (2) the testimony is the product of reliable principles and methods, and (3) the witness has applied the principles and methods reliably to the facts of the case.

> Fed. R. Evid. 702.

The first hurdle, then, is to establish that the witness will help the jury (or judge, if it's a **bench trial**) understand the evidence. If the witness doesn't add to the jury's understanding, in the opinion of the judge, the expert will not be allowed in. Experts have been excluded because the judge decided that the expert would just be telling the jury something it already knew ("that's just common sense")—an opinion that is often used to exclude certain types of psychiatric testimony.

The second hurdle is that the expert must be qualified. To do that, the opposing counsel will "take the expert on **voir dire.**" This means that before the expert is allowed to make any comments on the case, his status as an expert will be determined. The list found in the rules—sufficient facts or data, reliable principles and methods, and reliable application of those principles and methods—have been further explained in two major United Supreme Court case decisions: *Daubert* and *Kumho.* We'll take them chronologically.

The *Daubert* case came first, addressing the concerns that many had about "**junk science.**" Prior to this case, the federal standard for "novel" science, which required general acceptance by the scientific community, made it difficult to introduce new scientific evidence. The *Daubert* case, which ostensibly loosened the standard, has actually made the introduction of expert evidence more stringent.

Daubert v. Merrell Dow Pharmaceuticals, Inc., 509 U.S. 579 (1993).

JUSTICE BLACKMUN delivered the opinion of the Court.

In this case we are called upon to determine the standard for admitting expert scientific testimony in a federal trial.

Petitioners Jason Daubert and Eric Schuller are minor children born with serious birth defects. They and their parents sued respondent . . . alleging that the birth defects had been caused by the mothers' ingestion of Bendectin, a prescription antinausea drug marketed by respondent . . .

[R]espondent moved for summary judgment, contending that Bendectin does not cause birth defects in humans and that petitioners would be unable to come forward with any admissible evidence that it does. In support of its motion, respondent submitted an affidavit of Steven H. Lamm, physician and epidemiologist . . . Doctor Lamm stated that he had reviewed all the literature on Bendectin and human birth defects—more than 30 published studies involving over 130,000 patients. No study had found Bendectin to be a human teratogen (i.e., a substance capable of causing malformations in fetuses). On the basis of this review, Doctor Lamm concluded that maternal use of Bendectin during the first trimester of pregnancy has not been shown to be a risk factor for human birth defects.

Petitioners did not (and do not) contest this characterization of the published record regarding Bendectin. Instead, they responded to respondent's motion with the testimony of eight experts of their own . . . These experts had concluded that Bendectin can cause birth defects. Their conclusions were based upon "in vitro" (test tube) and "in vivo" (live) animal studies that found a link between Bendectin and malformations; pharmacological studies of the chemical structure of Bendectin that purported to show similarities between the structure of the drug and that of other substances known to cause birth defects; and the "reanalysis" of previously published epidemiological (human statistical) studies.

The District Court granted respondent's motion for summary judgment . . .

We granted certiorari . . . in light of sharp divisions among the courts regarding the proper standard for the admission of expert testimony . . .

Rule 702, governing expert testimony, provides:

"If scientific, technical, or other specialized knowledge will assist the trier of fact to understand the evidence or to determine a fact in issue, a witness qualified as an expert by knowledge, skill, experience, training, or education, may testify thereto in the form of an opinion or otherwise."

. . . [The change brought about by] the Rules of Evidence does not mean, however, that the Rules themselves place no limits on the admissibility of purportedly scientific evidence . . . Nor is the trial judge disabled from screening such evidence. To the contrary, under the Rules the trial judge must ensure that any and all scientific testimony or evidence admitted is not only relevant, but reliable.

The primary locus of this obligation is Rule 702, which clearly contemplates some degree of regulation of the subjects and theories about which an expert may testify . . . The subject of an expert's testimony must be "scientific . . . knowledge.". . . The adjective "scientific" implies a grounding in the methods and procedures of science. Similarly, the word "knowledge" connotes more than subjective belief or unsupported speculation . . . Of course, it would be unreasonable to conclude that the subject of scientific testimony must be "known" to a certainty; arguably, there are no certainties in science . . . Instead, it represents a process for proposing and refining theoretical explanations about the world that are subject to further testing and refinement". . . But, in order to qualify as "scientific knowledge," an inference or assertion must be derived by the scientific method. Proposed testimony must be supported by appropriate validation—i.e., "good grounds," based on what is known. In short, the requirement that an expert's testimony pertain to "scientific knowledge" establishes a standard of evidentiary reliability . . .

Rule 702 further requires that the evidence or testimony "assist the trier of fact to understand the evidence or to determine a fact in issue." This condition goes primarily to relevance . . . [S]cientific validity for one purpose is not necessarily scientific validity for other, unrelated purposes . . . The study of the phases of the moon, for example, may provide valid scientific "knowledge" about whether a certain night was dark, and if darkness is a fact in issue, the knowledge will assist the trier of fact. However (absent creditable grounds supporting such a link), evidence that the moon was full on a certain night will not assist the trier of fact in determining whether an individual was unusually likely to have behaved irrationally on that night. Rule 702's "helpfulness" standard requires a valid scientific connection to the pertinent inquiry as a precondition to admissibility.

That these requirements are embodied in Rule 702 is not surprising. Unlike an ordinary witness . . . an expert is permitted wide latitude to offer opinions, including those that are not based on firsthand knowledge or observation . . . Presumably, this relaxation of the usual requirement of firsthand knowledge—a rule which represents "a 'most pervasive manifestation' of the common law insistence upon 'the most reliable sources of information,'". . . is premised on an assumption that the expert's opinion will have a reliable basis in the knowledge and experience of his discipline.

Faced with a proffer of expert scientific testimony, then, the trial judge must determine at the outset, pursuant to Rule 104(a), . . . whether the expert is proposing to testify to (1) scientific knowledge that (2) will assist the trier of fact to understand or determine a fact in issue . . . This entails a preliminary assessment of whether the reasoning or methodology underlying the testimony is scientifically valid and of whether that reasoning or methodology properly can be applied to the facts in issue. We are confident that federal judges possess the capacity to undertake this review. Many factors will bear on the inquiry, and we do not presume to set out a definitive checklist or test. But some general observations are appropriate.

Ordinarily, a key question to be answered in determining whether a theory or technique is scientific knowledge that will assist the trier of fact will be whether it can be (and has been) tested. "Scientific methodology today is based on generating hypotheses and testing them to see if they can be falsified; indeed, this methodology is what distinguishes science from other fields of human inquiry.". . .

Another pertinent consideration is whether the theory or technique has been subjected to peer review and publication. Publication (which is but one element of peer review) is not a sine qua non of admissibility; it does not necessarily correlate with reliability . . . and in some instances well-grounded but innovative theories will not have been published . . . Some propositions, moreover, are too particular, too new, or of too limited interest to be published. But submission to the scrutiny of the scientific community is a component of "good science," in part because it increases the likelihood that substantive flaws in methodology will be detected . . . The fact of publication (or lack thereof) in a peer reviewed journal thus will be a relevant, though not dispositive, consideration in assessing the scientific validity of a particular technique or methodology on which an opinion is premised.

Additionally, in the case of a particular scientific technique, the court ordinarily should consider the known or potential rate of error . . . and the existence and maintenance of standards controlling the technique's operation . . .

Finally, "general acceptance" can yet have a bearing on the inquiry. A "reliability assessment does not require, although it does permit, explicit identification of a relevant scientific community and an express determination of a particular degree of acceptance within that community . . . Widespread acceptance can be an important factor in ruling particular evidence admissible, and "a known technique which has been able to attract only minimal support within the community,". . . may properly be viewed with skepticism.

The inquiry envisioned by Rule 702 is, we emphasize, a flexible one . . . Its overarching subject is the scientific validity—and thus the evidentiary relevance and reliability—of the principles that underlie a proposed submission. The focus, of course, must be solely on principles and methodology, not on the conclusions that they generate.

Throughout, a judge assessing a proffer of expert scientific testimony under Rule 702 should also be mindful of other applicable rules. Rule 703 provides that expert opinions based on otherwise inadmissible hearsay are to be admitted only if the facts or data are "of a type reasonably relied upon by experts in the particular field in forming opinions or inferences upon the subject." Rule 706 allows the court at its discretion to procure the assistance of an expert of its own choosing. Finally, Rule 403 permits the exclusion of relevant evidence "if its probative value is substantially outweighed by the danger of unfair prejudice, confusion of the issues, or misleading the Jury . . . " Judge Weinstein has explained: "Expert evidence can be both powerful and quite misleading because of the difficulty in evaluating it. Because of this risk, the judge in weighing possible prejudice against probative force under Rule 403 of the present rules exercises more control over experts than over lay witnesses.". . .

We conclude by briefly addressing what appear to be two underlying concerns of the parties and amici in this case. Respondent expresses apprehension that abandonment of "general acceptance" as the exclusive requirement for admission will result in a "free-for-all" in which befuddled juries are confounded by absurd and irrational pseudoscientific assertions. In this regard respondent seems to us to be overly pessimistic about the capabilities of the jury and of the adversary system generally. Vigorous cross-examination, presentation of contrary evidence, and careful instruction on the burden of proof are the traditional and appropriate means of attacking shaky but admissible evidence . . .

Petitioners and, to a greater extent, their amici exhibit a different concern. They suggest that recognition of a screening role for the judge that allows for the exclusion of "invalid" evidence will sanction a stifling and repressive scientific orthodoxy and will be inimical to the search for truth . . . It is true that open debate is an essential part of both legal and scientific analyses. Yet there are important differences between the quest for truth in the courtroom and the quest for truth in the laboratory. Scientific conclusions are subject to perpetual revision. Law, on the other hand, must resolve disputes finally and quickly. The scientific project is advanced by broad and wide-ranging consideration of a multitude of hypotheses, for those that are incorrect will eventually be shown to be so, and that in itself is an advance. Conjectures that are probably wrong are of little use, however, in the project of reaching a quick, final, and binding legal judgment—often of great consequence—about a particular set of events in the past. We recognize that, in practice, a gatekeeping role for the judge, no matter how flexible, inevitably on occasion will prevent the jury from learning of authentic insights and innovations. That, nevertheless, is the balance that is struck by Rules of Evidence designed not for the exhaustive search for cosmic understanding but for the particularized resolution of legal disputes . . .

As you can see, *Daubert* doesn't only apply to new science; it applies to all science. The four factors have been applied by judges to expert testimony prior to allowing experts to testify before the jury. If the expert cannot address these factors, the expert will not be allowed to testify. Many states have adopted the **Daubert standard**; Texas, for instance, looked at the *Daubert* factors and said, "If four is good, eight would be better," and added four more factors to its state test.

After a while, though, lawyers found something to make a problem over. What is scientific and what is not? Is beekeeping scientific? There is certainly some science to the study of bees, but someone who keeps them is not going to be publishing peer studies.

You may wonder why the beekeeper keeps popping up. It's not original; it came from a Sixth Circuit case decided before *Kumho*, which illustrates the dilemma in states that have followed *Daubert*, but not *Kumho*.

Berry v. City of Detroit, 25 F.3d 1342 (6th Cir. 1994).

RALPH B. GUY, JR., Circuit Judge.

. . . On June 23, 1987, Lee Berry, Jr. (Lee), who was employed in a family moving business, was driving the company van in rush-hour traffic to the family residence in Detroit. According to the testimony of Lee's sixteen-year-old brother, Dwayne Berry, and his eight-year-old nephew, David Askew, both of whom were in the van, Lee committed several misdemeanor traffic violations during this journey. The infractions consisted of running a red light, driving on the wrong side of the road, and passing three cars that were stopped for a red light.

These traffic offenses attracted the attention of Officer Joseph Hall, a seventeen-year veteran of the Detroit Police Department. Exactly what happened immediately thereafter, however, is a matter of some dispute. On the witness stand, Hall testified—in contrast to the testimony of the surviving occupants of the van and in partial contradiction of his earlier deposition testimony—that the violations prompted a dangerous, high-speed chase involving the police. Dwayne and David, on the other hand, offered a markedly different account of what transpired. They testified that Lee had not been speeding, had not attempted to flee from arrest, and had not committed any traffic violations other than those described above.

Moments after the van arrived at the Berry family home, Hall arrived on the scene. Hall confronted Lee Berry and a struggle then ensued, during which Hall shot Lee in the back from a distance estimated as being between three and ten feet . . . Although no eyewitnesses observed the shooting, David, Dwayne, and several bystanders stated that Hall, upon his arrival at the Berry home, used profanity, threats, and physical force in attempting to effect an arrest. Hall, however, claimed that Lee attacked him; that the gun fired accidently when Lee, during their struggle, attempted to wrestle the pistol away from him; and that he continued to fire at Lee while Lee was fleeing because the firearm was set on "automatic" and because his (Hall's) vision had been impaired by blood. Plaintiff's expert witnesses opined that Lee had not touched Hall's revolver because Lee was several feet away from the gun when it fired, that Hall had not been blinded by blood, and that Hall's service revolver lacked any type of "automatic" firing mechanism.

Shortly after the incident, the police department conducted an investigation that exonerated Hall. No criminal charges were brought against him and no sanctions were imposed upon him. At the time of trial, Hall remained a member of the Detroit Police Department on disability retirement with full pension benefits.

Plaintiff initiated this suit against Hall and the City . . . under 42 U.S.C. § 1983. Plaintiff's complaint also listed several state law causes of action. Plaintiff claimed that the City pursued a deliberate policy of failing to . . . discipline adequately its police officers in the proper use of deadly force, which failures caused the violation of Lee's constitutional rights under the Fourth and Fourteenth Amendments. At the conclusion of the trial, the jury returned verdicts against both Hall and the City in the amount of six million dollars.

Both Hall and the City appealed from the denial of their motions for j.n.o.v. or for a new trial. While this appeal was pending, the parties settled Hall's appeal and jointly moved for an order remanding that appeal for consideration of the settlement. As a result of this settlement, the City's obligation under the judgment was reduced to two and one-half million dollars. The only question before this court is the issue of municipal liability for Lee Berry's death . . .

. . . Any discussion of municipal liability under § 1983 begins with *Monell v. Department of Social Services,* 436 U.S. 658, 56 L. Ed. 2d 611, 98 S. Ct. 2018 (1978). In *Monell,* the Supreme Court held that municipalities can be sued directly under § 1983 where the action of the municipality itself can be said to have caused the harm, as when "the action that is alleged to be unconstitutional implements or executes a policy statement, ordinance, regulation, or decision officially adopted and promulgated by that body's officers." . . . Municipal liability for the actions of employees may not be based on a theory of *respondeat superior. Monell* went on to clarify that municipal liability may be predicated upon grounds other than explicit expressions of official policy.

Moreover, although the touchstone of the § 1983 action against a government body is an allegation that official policy is responsible for a deprivation of rights protected by the Constitution, local governments, like every other § 1983 "person," by the very terms of the statute, may be sued for constitutional deprivations visited pursuant to governmental "custom" even though such a custom has not received formal approval through the body's official decision-making channels . . .

The . . . problem . . . stems from the nature of the "expert" testimony offered by plaintiff. There are two facets to this problem. First, we have grave concerns about the qualifications of plaintiff's witness, Frederick Postill, to opine as he did. As we have now defined the issue on appeal, Postill's testimony must have provided the basis for the jury to determine that the alleged failure of the Detroit Police Department to discipline properly officers other than Hall was the proximate cause of Hall shooting Lee Berry. As we view the record, Postill did not have the qualifications to testify as an expert on this question, and, if he did, no proper foundation was laid for his ultimate opinion.

In order not to be simply conclusory on this point, a detailed review of Postill's credentials must be undertaken. Postill received a degree in sociology in 1971, and a master's degree in education in 1976. He also took courses in criminal justice, but how many and what kind was never revealed. His law enforcement career started when he received an appointment as a deputy sheriff in 1966, a position for which, Postill admits, *no* qualifications were required. Equally important, however, is that he did not receive formal training. Postill simply started and worked with more experienced officers. The only information conveyed by the record as to what he did or learned as a deputy sheriff is the following:

Q: All right. During your tenure as a deputy sheriff, could you tell us what types of duties you were involved in?

A: Basically, general patrol, investigation work, riding a black and white, responding to calls.

Q: Were you ever certified to instruct as a deputy sheriff other members of—of the Sheriff's Department?

A: I was an instructor there in the Department. I taught defensive tactics, things of that nature.

Q: What do you mean by "defensive tactics"?

A: Physical control of subjects that you would be arresting.

Postill also admits that he was fired twice during his two-year stint as a deputy, apparently as a result of trying to organize the deputies into a labor union against the wishes of the incumbent sheriff. Postill's disagreement with the sheriff culminated in his decision to run against the sheriff in the 1972 election. Although his election bid was successful, the electorate decided to retire him four years later. Interestingly, not one question was asked during trial to elicit what Postill did or learned during his four years as sheriff, a job for which the only necessary qualification is the ability to get elected.

Postill's testimony as to what he did after being deposed as sheriff illustrates the problem that courts and juries have with expert testimony, particularly of the type offered here. If an expert has a degree in electrical engineering, there are some assumptions that safely can be made relative to his general training, since all electrical engineers receive similar training. In this same vein, if an electrical engineer says his first job was designing generator motors, there is some notion of what that job entails. But when a sociologist cum sheriff is allowed to testify as to all manners of police practices and procedures, the slopes become slippery indeed.

Postill's next job after being sheriff was to work for four years for the Justice Department where he "developed the training criteria to train sheriffs and managers of large sheriffs['] departments." Since up to this point in time he had had little or no training himself, exactly why he got this assignment is difficult to understand.

From 1981 to the present, Postill appears to have conducted seminars in police management techniques; taught; formed a one-man corporation called "Criminal Justice Consultants"; testified in court; and purchased a hunting and fishing resort in Canada, where he spends five months a year. The fact that some of this would sound impressive to a jury is its vice not its virtue. The fault lies not with Postill but, rather, with the system. The courts have had a difficult time in appropriately cabining the opinion testimony of "scientific" experts. At least with scientific testimony there is some objective criteria to look to and there is some basis for evaluating a given expert's testimony against the scientific norm on the subject about which an opinion is offered. The problem that "junk science" has caused in the courtrooms has not gone unnoticed . . . The Supreme Court recently revisited the controversy that has swirled around expert testimony for the last several years. In *Daubert v. Merrell Dow Pharmaceuticals, Inc.*, 125 L. Ed. 2d 469, 113 S. Ct. 2786 (1993), the Court made a number of clarifying pronouncements. These holdings, however, are in the context of scientific evidence, and thus are only of limited help in the instant case . . . It would appear obvious, however, that evidentiary problems are exacerbated when courts must deal with the even more elusive concept of non-scientific expert testimony, as is the case here.

The distinction between scientific and non-scientific expert testimony is a critical one. By way of illustration, if one wanted to explain to a jury how a bumblebee is able to fly, an aeronautical engineer might be a helpful witness. Since flight principles have some universality, the expert could apply general principles to the case of the bumblebee. Conceivably, even if he had never seen a bumblebee, he still would be qualified to testify, as long as he was familiar with its component parts.

On the other hand, if one wanted to prove that bumblebees always take off into the wind, a beekeeper with no scientific training at all would be an acceptable expert witness *if* a proper foundation were laid for his conclusions. The foundation would not relate to his formal training, but to his firsthand observations. In other words, the beekeeper does not know any more about flight principles than the jurors, but he has seen a lot more bumblebees than they have.

Carrying this example into the instant case, it is clear that Postill's testimony, if admissible at all, would have been from the viewpoint of the beekeeper, not the aeronautical engineer. If there is some formal training that would allow one to testify from a scientific standpoint on how failure to discipline officer "A" would impact on the conduct of his peer, officer "B," it is clear that Postill does not have such training. Thus, for this kind of testimony to be admissible, a foundation would have to have been laid based upon the witness's firsthand familiarity with disciplining police officers and the effect of lax discipline on the entire force. To the degree one might be tempted to argue that "everyone knows that if discipline is lax more infractions occur," this argument proves too much. If everyone knows this, then we do not need an expert because the testimony will not "assist the trier of fact to understand the evidence or to determine a fact in issue. . . ." Fed. R. Evid. 702.

If, for example, Postill had testified that when he became sheriff there were "x" number of incidents involving alleged excessive force, but two years after he instituted a training program, there were "$x - y$" incidents, we would have a starting point. If he then said that after the training program was in place, he increased the regularity and severity of discipline for infractions and incidents fell to "$x - y2$," then at least there would be some basis for his opinions. Here, however, the only discipline experience referenced was the discipline imposed *upon* Postill.

Although, as indicated, *Daubert* dealt with scientific experts, its language relative to the "gatekeeper" function of federal judges is applicable to all expert testimony offered under Rule 702. "Under the Rules the trial judge must ensure that any and all . . . testimony or evidence admitted is not only relevant, but reliable.". . .

In providing guidance as to how a court should carry out its gatekeeping function, the Court in *Daubert* indicated that one of the first inquiries should be whether the "theory or technique . . . can be (and has been) tested.". . . As pointed out earlier, there is no indication of any testing of Postill's discipline theory.

Second, the Court noted that "another pertinent consideration is whether the theory or technique has been subjected to peer review and publication." *Id.* at 2797. There certainly is no testimony as to any peer review of Postill's theory, and, as to publication, the record reveals the following:

Q: Mr. Postill, what articles have you written regarding police—any aspect of police procedure or policy, whatever?

A: I don't know I've written any specific articles on police procedure or policy. I've written articles and—I co-authored a textbook on jail administration.

Q: You wrote a textbook on jail administration?

A: That's correct.

Q: Did you bring that with you today?

A: No.

Q: You were asked at the deposition—it was April 28th—about the articles and—and asked to supply us with copies. Did you bring any of your articles that you've written with you today in court?

A: No.

Q: Okay. Did you bring that alleged textbook that you wrote?. . .

A: No, I didn't.

If there were any relevant publications, the jury was left in the dark as to what they were.

The Court in *Daubert*, concludes the gatekeeper discussion by indicating that "general acceptance" still has a bearing on the inquiry . . . Here again we know nothing about whether the discipline theory offered by Postill was other than his own.

The *Daubert* Court's final observation is also pertinent here: "The Rules of Evidence—especially Rule 702—do assign to the trial judge the task of ensuring that an expert's testimony both rests on a reliable foundation and is relevant to the task at hand." 113 S. Ct. at 2799. Although *Daubert* was decided after the trial in the instant case, earlier decisions of our court have provided guidance relative to expert testimony and its admission. . . . [T]his court counseled against putting some general seal of approval on an expert after he has been qualified but before any questions have been posed to him . . . The issue with regard to expert testimony is not the qualifications of a witness in the abstract, but whether those qualifications provide a foundation for a witness to answer a specific question . . .

In the case at bar, after the qualifying questions were asked of the expert, plaintiff's attorney stated:

Mr. Mateo: Your Honor, at this point in time I would offer Mr. Frederick Postill as an expert so that he may render opinion testimony as to appropriate police policies and practices.

Unfortunately, the trial judge in the case at bar replied to the proffer by stating:

The Court: Very well. The Court will accept the qualifications of the witness as an expert in the field of proper police policies and practices, based upon the testimony as to his background and experience in that—in that field.

The danger in doing what the trial judge did here is that there is no such "field" as "police policies and practices." Any witness, like our hypothetical beekeeper, may be allowed to opine based on observation and experience if a proper foundation is laid. But here, there was no foundation at all for discipline testimony, even though it would fall under the general label of "police policies and practices." This term, however, is so broad as to be devoid of meaning. It is like declaring an attorney an expert in the "law." A divorce lawyer is no more qualified to opine on patent law questions than anyone else, and it is a mistake for a trial judge to declare anyone to be generically an expert.

With all due respect to Mr. Postill, his credentials *as set forth in the record* do not qualify him to know any more about what effect claimed disciplinary shortcomings would have on the future conduct of 5,000 different police officers than does any member of the jury. Among other things, Postill's testimony assumes that all 5,000 police officers would know enough about the facts of each *claimed* event to evaluate the sufficiency of the discipline . . . and that the officers would formulate their future course of conduct accordingly. It also assumes, without any basis in fact or logic, that police officers will be extravagant in their use of deadly force if they know discipline will not be severe if a shooting occurs. We are not talking about cheating on overtime here, or some other minor peccadillo; we are talking about the taking of the life of another person.

Additionally, Postill's methodology was as suspect as his conclusions . . . Postill analyzed the "shots fired" reports from the Detroit Police Department for 1982 through 1987. These annual reports consist of statistical information of all shooting incidents for that year summarized in a one-page report. Postill concluded that the 636 incidents covered in the reports, involving the discharge of 1,538 shots, fired at an average distance of 30 to 35 feet from the officers' "opponents," represented a "fairly frequent" use of fatal force by Detroit police officers. Postill opined that the frequency of the incidents could not be justified by "self-defense," a term listed for 502 of the incidents.

Postill also testified that 277 of the 636 incidents included shootings at burglary suspects. Postill then testified that even prior to the Supreme Court's decision in *Tennessee v. Garner,* 471 U.S. 1, 85 L. Ed. 2d 1, 105 S. Ct. 1694 (1985), the Detroit Police Department had a policy requiring officers to exhaust all reasonable means before shooting at a burglar. Again, it should be emphasized that Postill's statistics were taken from the one-page summary sheet of shooting incidents for each year. Postill did not review the underlying facts in these cases to determine, among other things, whether the suspect was armed. Pursuant to *Garner,* fatal force may be used when an officer has reason to believe that a felon poses a danger to himself or to others.

Postill also testified concerning his review of the actual records of 161 of the 636 incidents. In his opinion, 78 of these incidents were "unjustifiable" on the basis of "existing law and Detroit City policy." Postill concluded that out of these 161 incidents only 15 officers were disciplined and, in seven of these cases, the disciplinary action was held in abeyance. Postill then described 13 incidents in which he thought police officers should have been disciplined. In one of these incidents, the officer fired his weapon, accidently hitting a bystander, only after the officer already had been shot twice. Postill still felt that the officer should have been disciplined. The fact that the officer fired only after having been shot twice was not volunteered by Postill and was only revealed upon cross-examination.

After describing these 13 specific cases, Postill concluded that "the department tolerates this kind of reckless use of firearms. They either get no discipline or a slap on the wrist." It was his "opinion that their failure to direct and discipline and train their officers not to use improper deadly force constitute a pattern of gross negligence." Postill equated "gross negligence" with "deliberate indifference" and defined it as "conscious knowledge of something and not doing anything about it.". . .

This latter testimony was particularly suspect. It was carefully couched in the precise language used in case law, either indicating a keen awareness by Postill of the direction in which he had to head, or else careful coaching prior to his testimony. "Gross negligence" is not enough to ground liability according to the Supreme Court, so Postill testified that gross negligence equates to "deliberate indifference." We apparently now have an etymology expert testifying.

We also believe this testimony was received in violation of the Federal Rules of Evidence . . . The expert can testify, if a proper foundation is laid, that the discipline in the Detroit Police Department was lax. He also could testify regarding what he believed to be the consequences of lax discipline. He may not testify, however, that the lax discipline policies of the Detroit Police Department indicated that the City was *deliberately indifferent* to the welfare of its citizens.

It would have been easy enough for the drafters of the Federal Rules of Evidence to have said that a properly qualified expert may opine on the ultimate question of liability. They did not do so. When the rules speak of an expert's testimony embracing the ultimate issue, the reference must be to stating opinions that suggest the answer to the ultimate issue or that give the jury all the information from which it can draw inferences as to the ultimate issue. We would not allow a fingerprint expert in a criminal case to opine that a defendant was guilty (a legal conclusion), even though we would allow him to opine that the defendant's fingerprint was the only one on the murder weapon (a fact). The distinction, although subtle, is nonetheless important.

Furthermore, "deliberate indifference" is a legal term, as the questioning of Postill indicated. It is the responsibility of the court, not testifying witnesses, to define legal terms. The expert's testimony in this regard invaded the province of the court.

. . . If the rule were other than [this], we would soon breed a whole new category of "liability experts" whose function would be to tell the jury what result to reach—exactly what the expert did here . . . .

The jury verdict against the City of Detroit is REVERSED, and the case is REMANDED for an entry of judgment as a matter of law in favor of the City of Detroit.

As this case presages, *Kumho v. Carmichael,* 526 U.S. 137 (1998), extended the *Daubert* standard to all experts, concluding that the trial judge was a gatekeeper that needed to determine whether the expert's testimony rested on a reliable foundation and was relevant to the case. Further, the four specific factors are to be used flexibly as is appropriate to each case.

FINDING EXPERTS

Often it is the paralegal who keeps the file for experts and who is responsible for finding the appropriate expert for a particular case. Each case presents its own challenges; for instance, if you have a products liability case where a little boy was burned while asleep in bed, you'll want to find an expert on the burn rates for mattresses or fabric to test whatever materials are left over to say whether these materials met the prevailing standards. The mere fact the child was burned is not enough to establish liability; you must prove either that someone breached a duty or that there was a defective product. An expert can help.

So how do you find this burn expert? There are several methods. One way is to simply network. Ask if any other paralegals have used an expert of this sort. Local paralegal groups may sponsor an electronic bulletin board or e-mail group for this sort of thing. The problem with these groups is that if there is much traffic on them, busy paralegals will begin to sign off the group because they don't want the e-mail, and then queries on the list or bulletin board won't elicit much response when you ask the question.

Another route is by checking verdict reports for similar cases. The **VerdictSearch** in Texas, New York, California, New Jersey, and Florida is available in paper by weekly subscription; it lists the experts who testified, their field of expertise, and with which party they were aligned. You can also search nationally online at **www.verdictsearch.com**, a relatively inexpensive and simple proposition. Once you have found a prospective expert, note his name, the name of the firm that used him, the name of the case, and the firm's client.

NORTHEAST

EMPLOYMENT

Partnership Agreements — Contracts — Breach of Contract

Claiming to be partner, fired worker wanted share in profits

VERDICT (P)	$1,240,349
CASE	Jessica L. Ellis v. D. Craig Walker, The Profit Group, Inc. and Athens Trust, No. 01-4676-I
COURT	Dallas County District Court, 162nd, TX
JUDGE	Bill Rhea
DATE	11/14/2003
PLAINTIFF ATTORNEY(S)	Michael P. Lynn, Lynn & Tillotson, Dallas, TX
	Basheer Ghorayeb, Lynn & Tillotson, Dallas, TX
	Mark E. Torian, Lynn & Tillotson, Dallas, TX
DEFENSE ATTORNEY(S)	William L. Wolf, Law Offices of William L. Wolf, Dallas, TX
	Barton Reeder, Law Offices of William L. Wolf, Dallas, TX

FACTS & ALLEGATIONS In November 1997, plaintiff Jessica Ellis, a paralegal in her 50s, began working with D. Craig Walker of Dallas on his real estate investment deals. Walker owned two companies, The Profit Group Inc. and Athens Trust, both also based in Dallas. Ellis had experience in real estate, and although the terms of their business arrangement were later disputed, they worked together until she was terminated in 2002.

Ellis sued Walker and both companies for breach of contract. Ellis alleged that she and Walker had reached a partnership agreement under which she was to receive a 10% net profits participation interest. She alleged that Walker terminated her because they were about to close some major deals.

Ellis also contended that Athens Trust was an alter ego of Walker. She sought a declaratory judgment that she had been denied profits from it.

Walker denied that there was a partnership agreement or any contract similar to that described by Ellis. He contended that Ellis had merely been an employee. He also denied that Athens Trust was an alter ego or that the company had denied her due compensation.

INJURIES/DAMAGES Ellis claimed approximately $2.2 million in damages.

RESULT The jury found that no partnership existed, but did find a contract under terms alleged by Ellis. They awarded her $1,240,349.

The court refused to find that Athens Trust was an alter ego of Walker, but did rule that Ellis should have received profits from it. The plaintiff's attorney estimated that she would receive about an additional $1 million as a result.

TRIAL DETAILS	Trial Length: 6 days
	Jury Deliberations: 2 days
	Jury Poll: 12-0
	Jury Composition: 3 male, 9 female
PLAINTIFF EXPERT(S)	Mark Werbner, attorney fees, Dallas, TX
	Jim Penn, valuation, Fort Worth, TX
DEFENSE EXPERT(S)	Robert Dohmayer, valuation, Dallas, TX

EDITOR'S NOTE The attorneys for the defendants did not contribute to this report.

–Kirk Sowell

DENTON COUNTY

PREMISES LIABILITY

Invitees — Animals — Dangerous Condition

Cable worker leaped and fell when charged by Rottweiler

VERDICT (P)	$2,500
CASE	Keith Riedner, plaintiff, and Trinity Insurance Company, intervenor v. John Gotcher and Clarissa Gotcher, No. 2002-20155158
COURT	Denton County District Court, 158th, TX
JUDGE	Jake Collier
DATE	8/4/2003
PLAINTIFF ATTORNEY(S)	Kim R. Thorne, Thorne, Skinner & Thorne, Grand Prairie, TX (Keith Riedner)
	M. Sheppard Sands, The Carpenter Law Firm, Plano, TX (Trinity Insurance Company (intervenor))
	John Thorne, Thorne, Skinner & Thorne, Grand Prairie, TX (Keith Riedner)

A sample page from a verdict reporter. Note the information regarding the experts.

When you use the verdict reporters, you will have to contact the firm that used the expert for contact information. Use *Martindale-Hubbell* to find the firm. The firm will probably have the information listed by client. When you find out the contact information, make sure you chat a little more about the case and the expert. Get a sense of how the legal team felt about the expert's performance. Even if there was a favorable jury verdict, it may not have been due to the expert; it may have even been in spite of him or her. It's always best not to assume. You can also ask for contact information and for an estimate of the fee structure, which may also influence your decision whether to contact the expert.

The last strategy is to find an expert with no lead from similar trials or cases. *Martindale-Hubbell* has an experts section, the various *American Lawyer* publications have expert advertising sections as well as annual directories of expert witnesses and consultants, as do **Findlaw** and numerous other online sources, including Martindale-Hubbell's Internet site.

Another approach is to find an expert by checking the authors or review boards of authoritative sources or articles in relevant professional journals, or by looking at the Web sites of relevant professional organizations for members of the board or committees. You can also see if there is a state, regional, or local chapter of the Professional Society/Association of Whatevers in which to look for an expert. The problem with this approach is that it gives you no sense of the expert's performance in a real-life situation; word of mouth or a verdict search will yield a more focused context in which to evaluate the expert's ability.

These methods will give you a name and a way to find contact information. Once you contact the expert, you'll need to ask for his **curriculum vitae (C.V.),** a **fee schedule,** and whether the expert's schedule is free for you to schedule depositions before any discovery deadlines and for trial. Regardless of how you find your expert, you should always ask for several references and make sure you check them. Ask for a copy of a videotaped deposition, if the expert or any references has one available; copying a videotape shouldn't be

The book version of the
Martindale–Hubbell Law Directory.

onerously expensive and will allow you an independent assessment. You'll probably want to contact a few experts (three is always a good number to start with) to choose among.

EVALUATING EXPERTS

Once you've checked the expert's references and reviewed her C.V., fee schedule, references, and videotaped depositions, how do you decide whether she is the right expert for you?

First, you must look at the *Daubert* standard, if it applies in your jurisdiction, and to the appropriate rules standard if it does not. Does this expert have the requisite experience, training, and knowledge to be qualified to testify on the specific areas about which you will need her to testify? If not, you need to keep looking. If so, you've passed the threshold test; you'll need to talk to the expert to see if she can testify that the evidence she wants to give is based on methodology or theory subject to testing; if it has been published or peer reviewed; what the known or potential rate of error is; if standards regarding the method or test are maintained (if they exist); and whether the method or theory has generally been accepted by the pertinent expert community.

Next, look at the expert's prior experience. Does she only testify for one side of the bar? If so, she's open to charges of bias. How often does her side win? The expert is obviously not the only factor, but if she's always on the losing side, you'll want to make sure she's not contributing to the outcome. What about her credentials? Credentials tend to mean more to judges and lawyers than to juries. Juries need to be able to understand the expert without feeling as if she is condescending or patronizing. If the expert speaks over their heads, she might as well not testify at all; if she talks down to them, they won't like her and will be less receptive to her message. You need enough credentialing to make it by the judge, but after that, the effect of the expert on the jury is far more important than whether her credentials would win favor in the world of academia. She needs to be able to articulate her theories and findings to the jury in a clear and credible manner.

Prior experience isn't the only consideration, though. An expert who is clearly comfortable with his field and willing to state his opinions confidently is a find. The risk you take is that the expert won't actually be able to handle the pressure under hostile questioning. Cathy Davis, a paralegal in Montgomery, Alabama, found and used an expert who turned out to be the turning point in a major case. "Most of the time I look for someone who has testified a lot," she says. "But one of the best experts I ever had never testified before in his life." The case went to the Alabama Supreme Court and has been cited over a hundred times.

State Farm Fire & Casualty Company v. Slade, **747 So.2d 293 (Ala. 1999).**

LYONS, Justice.

. . . In March 1992, the Slades undertook construction of their home in Montgomery. The Slades paid approximately $650,000 for the construction. During the construction of their home, the Slades' next-door neighbors commenced construction of a home and removed a substantial amount of soil from their lot. The soil removal created a severe drop-off between the neighbors' property and the Slades' property. This drop-off required the Slades to construct a retaining wall on the property line, along the drop-off, to prevent erosion and soil movement. This retaining wall was attached to the Slades' home.

On January 16, 1993, the Slades purchased a State Farm "Homeowner's Extra" policy. This policy was in effect at the time of the occurrence of the events later made the basis of the Slades' insurance claim. On August 4, 1993, the retaining wall collapsed when lightning struck it during a severe storm. The collapse of the wall caused the ground around the Slades' backyard pool to give way; this resulted in extensive damage to the pool area. State Farm paid for the repairs to the Slades' pool and for the replacement of the wall and of the soil that was washed away during the storm. Soil was replaced up to three feet from the corner of the Slades' home, but no soil was replaced under the slab area of the home.

In October 1993, the Slades noticed cracking in the ceilings and in the interior and exterior walls of their home. They informed State Farm of this cracking on November 8, 1993 . . . The Slades believed that the damage was covered by the terms of their policy, which covered damage directly caused by lightning . . .

The jury found in favor of the Slades on the claims of fraud and bad faith in the adjustment of the Slades' insurance claim, but against the Slades on the breach-of-contract claim. The jury awarded the Slades $668,850 in compensatory damages, but reduced that award by $301,500, the amount of the pro tanto settlement. The jury also awarded the Slades $301,500 in punitive damages. The trial court entered a judgment in favor of the Slades in the amount of $668,850 ... The court also awarded costs, in the amount of $21,753.83, to the Slades, including the costs incurred to secure the testimony of the Slades' experts ...

The Slades attempted to prove that a lightning strike either directly or indirectly caused the damage to their home and that, according to the terms of their policy with State Farm, the damage was a loss that State Farm should have covered ... [T]he Slades maintain that the following section of their policy provides coverage for their loss:

"SECTION I - LOSSES INSURED
"COVERAGE A - DWELLING

"1. We cover:
"a. the dwelling used principally as a private residence on the residence premises shown in the Declarations. This includes structures attached to the dwelling.
"....
"We insure for accidental direct physical loss to the property described in Coverage A, except as provided in SECTION I - LOSSES NOT INSURED.
"COVERAGE B - PERSONAL PROPERTY
"We insure for accidental direct physical loss to property described in Coverage B caused by the following perils, except as provided in SECTION I - LOSSES NOT INSURED.
"1. Fire or lightning."

(Emphasis in original.) The Slades contend that they produced substantial evidence indicating that lightning caused "direct physical loss," i.e., the cracking in their home. They argue that this evidence consists of expert testimony and investigative reports that state that lightning caused the damage to their home.

The Slades rely on the same three theories that they say they presented to the jury ...

The Slades say that their third theory was supported by their lightning expert, Richard Kithill, who testified at trial. Mr. Kithill testified that, in his opinion, the lightning struck the Slades' retaining wall and then traveled through the ground and into the metal rebar used to strengthen the concrete in the Slades' home. From there, Kithill said, the lightning caused "explosions due to water in [the concrete], and leading to the degradation of the ability of the slab to act as a foundation to the house and support the house." Kithill based his opinion on his scientific knowledge that saturated ground often acts as a conductor of lightning. He also based his opinion on a study that he had conducted for the federal government in which he had found similar damage that had occurred to underground concrete bunkers with metal rebar, bunkers that had also been struck by lightning....

We now turn to State Farm's third contention: that it was entitled to a preverdict JML on the Slades' third theory, i.e., that their loss was covered because lightning moved through the saturated ground and struck the slab of their home. State Farm attempts to discredit Kithill's testimony by calling it "science fiction." However, State Farm does not argue that Kithill's testimony was improperly admitted. We conclude that Kithill's testimony created a factual question as to whether the lightning directly struck the Slades' home, and that the portion of the Slades' contract claim based upon Kithill's testimony was properly submitted to the jury ...

An insurer can be liable for the tort of bad faith when it fails to properly investigate the insured's claim ... Here, the Slades produced substantial evidence, in the form of expert testimony, indicating that the term "dwelling" did include their retaining wall. They also presented substantial evidence indicating that State Farm did not investigate their claim properly. The Slades produced evidence indicating that State Farm never, in the course of its investigation, sent to their home someone who was qualified to conduct a lightning investigation. The Slades presented evidence indicating that State Farm never interviewed any of the witnesses present on the day lightning struck their retaining wall. The Slades presented expert testimony indicating that these omissions amounted to an improper investigation, on the basis that an investigation of a claim such as the Slades made required the use of a lightning expert. The Slades also presented evidence indicating that

State Farm did not investigate lightning as a cause. The Slades produced evidence indicating that State Farm told its engineer, Buck Durham, to investigate a "possible soil problem" and that it did not tell Durham about the lightning strike. This evidence conflicted with State Farm's "Good Faith Claims Handling" video, which was admitted into evidence and which contained a statement that State Farm's claims-handling policy was to attempt to find coverage.

This evidence, the Slades say, shows that State Farm never investigated the possibility that lightning directly struck their dwelling, a fact, which if proven, would negate the application of the earth-movement exclusion. The Slades maintain that this failure created a question of fact as to whether State Farm properly investigated their claim, and, therefore, that the trial court properly submitted this portion of their bad-faith claim to the jury. We agree.

Furthermore, State Farm's argument on this point, i.e., that it cannot be held liable because it believes it properly investigated noncovered events and found evidence that noncovered events caused the Slades' loss, is unacceptable. An insurance company's duty to investigate does not extend only to those events that are not covered . . . [A]n insurance company has a "responsibility to marshal all . . . facts" necessary to make a determination as to coverage "before its refusal to pay.". . . This duty must include a duty to investigate a covered event that an insured claims has caused his loss. Otherwise, the duty to properly investigate, imposed by the law regarding the tort of bad faith and recognized in *Barnes*, supra, would be meaningless. Therefore, we reject State Farm's contention, and we hold that this portion of the Slades' bad-faith claim was properly submitted to the jury . . .

Richard Kithill was the first-time expert in this case, and Cathy Davis believes he made the difference. The moral, she says, is "Don't write off somebody because they haven't testified before." She thinks that he was effective because he didn't have anything to prove; he was the head of a lightning research center and just had his opinions to give and offered them honestly. "You take a case that you think is going to be an ordinary case," she says now. "It shows you can't tell which ones may end up being important and that people will see what you did."

COST CONSIDERATIONS

Experts are costly. They charge for their time like lawyers charge for theirs, although often at a much higher hourly rate. Usually there are different rates for research, reviewing files, writing reports, testifying at a deposition, and testifying at trial; the fee schedule will detail each of these items. As you might imagine, the rates for testifying are the highest, with trial testimony being the most expensive. As a result, you must manage both the number of experts used in any particular trial and the amount of time you utilize the expert based on the trial budget, which is based on the value of the case and/or pocketbook of your client.

Pierce Couch Hendrickson Baysinger & Green v. Freede, 936 P.2d 906 (Okla. 1997).

. . . The plaintiff in this case is the law firm of Pierce, Couch, Hendrickson, Baysinger & Green (law firm), and the defendant is Dr. Henry J. Freede, a client of the law firm. The law firm represented Dr. Freede in a case filed in federal court against Texas Oil & Gas Corporation (TXO) (case I). The appeal now before this Court (case II) involves the litigation costs incurred by the law firm on behalf of Dr. Freede while representing him in the TXO case (case I). An understanding of the disputes involved in this appeal is dependent on the facts regarding the plaintiff's and defendant's agreements in the TXO case (case I) and their unusual professional relationship.

Dr. Freede was a close friend of Mr. Couch and Mr. Hendrickson, two of the partners in the law firm. Also Dr. Freede's daughter worked for the law firm . . .

Through his daughter, Dr. Freede invited the law firm to take the TXO case (case I) . . . Dr. Freede believed TXO was not paying him as much money as they should for his interest in certain wells operated by TXO. The law firm agreed to represent Dr. Freede . . . [T]he agreement was oral.

Mustang Production Company (Mustang) had interests in these same wells and believing that it, like Dr. Freede, had not received the full amount to which it was entitled, wished to enter the suit between Dr. Freede and TXO. The law firm sent Mustang a letter stating that it would represent Mustang on a contingent fee arrangement for one-third of the recovery after expenses and that Mustang would have to share in the cost of the suit if allowed to enter even if there was no recovery. Mustang countered with a letter setting out the following terms . . . In exchange for the firm representing Mustang and for Dr. Freede allowing Mustang to enter the case, the costs would first be paid from any recovery, then the firm would receive one-third of the remainder of the recovery, and the remaining two-thirds would be divided 70.14 percent to Mustang and 29.86 percent to Dr. Freede . . . If the recovery were insufficient to cover the costs, Mustang would pay 70.14 percent of the costs of the litigation. Dr. Freede, a representative of Mustang, and a representative of the law firm signed the letter agreement. The agreement did not state what would happen should one of the plaintiffs settle, leaving the other as the sole remaining plaintiff.

In December 1988, Mustang settled with TXO for what is believed to be $75,000. The firm, without consulting Dr. Freede, accepted Mustang's payment of $25,000. Of the payment, $10,481.04 was applied to expenses, and the firm retained the remaining $14,518.96 as attorney fees. Dr. Freede did not receive any funds from the settlement. On December 20, 1988, after Mustang settled, the firm sent Dr. Freede a statement showing costs of $10,481.04. At the time, Dr. Freede did not dispute any of this bill.

Before the statement of December 20, 1988, the firm had requested Dr. Freede pay a bill of $7,926.08 directly to Waterman & Company Oil and Gas Consultants for expert witness and consulting fees. Without protest, Dr. Freede paid this bill on February 19, 1988. This expense was not included in Dr. Freede's statement of December 1988, in the calculation of expenses prior to Mustang's settling, or in the calculation of Mustang's share of the expenses.

The only costs that Dr. Freede questioned before being sent the final statement was that of Ken Manes, a consultant. Sometime before July 22, 1991, Dr. Freede requested that the law firm dismiss Ken Manes because Dr. Freede thought his testimony was duplicative. The law firm did not dismiss Mr. Manes. The costs for Mr. Manes after the date that Dr. Freede sought his dismissal were $1,000 and $1,800 for a total of $2,800. Other than this request, Dr. Freede did not question or protest the costs while they were being incurred.

The litigation continued with only Dr. Freede as the plaintiff. The matter went to trial in federal court. After the evidence was presented, the law firm requested the judge lift the cap on the punitive damages. The trial judge refused. Until this refusal both Dr. Freede and the law firm anticipated the recovery of substantial punitive damages. In fact, plaintiff's exhibit 5, which is plaintiff's response to Dr. Freede's interrogatories, shows TXO offered Dr. Freede $85,000 to settle the case. The attorneys for TXO stated they would recommend $100,000 as a settlement to TXO. In anticipation of a large punitive damage recovery, Dr. Freede countered with an offer of $250,000. TXO did not respond to this counteroffer. The matter went to trial, and the jury found for TXO, resulting in no recovery by Dr. Freede.

There was a great deal of discovery after Mustang was dismissed from the suit including 27 depositions. During this time, the law firm rented a "war room" at a cost of $560.00. About one year and nine months after the close of the litigation, the firm billed Dr. Freede $26,285.54 for the costs of the litigation incurred after Mustang settled. These costs were in addition to the $21,956.42 . . . which Dr. Freede had paid directly to the providers without protest.

When presented with a statement from the law firm for costs incurred by them, Dr. Freede refused to pay, arguing he was responsible for only 29.86 percent of the costs . . .

The first issue to be addressed is the terms of the contract between the law firm and Dr. Freede in the TXO case (case I). Both parties agree that the letter agreement of February 5, 1988, is a binding contract but dispute the construction of the contract. Dr. Freede argues that, under the contract, he was obligated to pay only 29.86 percent of the expenses incurred until the end of trial. The law firm argues that Dr. Freede was obligated to pay 29.86 percent of the expenses prior to Mustang's settlement of and dismissal from the case and 100 percent thereafter . . .

. . . Considering the contract as a whole, it is clear that the parties intended that Mustang's obligation for the costs would extend only until recovery or settlement and that Mustang did not intend to pay expenses incurred solely on behalf of Dr. Freede after Mustang settled. Likewise, had Dr. Freede settled his claim leaving Mustang as the sole plaintiff, it is clear that he did not intend to be obligated to pay 29.86 percent of the expenses incurred solely on behalf of Mustang . . . On several occasions, both before and after the settlement, the law firm requested that Dr. Freede pay 100 percent of several bills directly which he did without protest. Only after Dr. Freede was sent a bill for the balance of costs did he complain. The actions of the parties after the settlement show that the parties did not intend for either Mustang or Dr. Freede to be responsible for expenses incurred entirely for the benefit of the other after one party settled . . .

The reasonableness of expenses is reviewed under the abuse of discretion standard . . . The trial judge corrected the expenses to reflect the payments Dr. Freede made directly to providers before Mustang's settlement. Thus, the trial judge determined Dr. Freede was entitled to a credit of $2,429.71. The judge also deducted $560.00 for the cost of renting the "war room". The judge then entered judgment for the law firm for $23,295.83.

At the hearing, a legal assistant testified that they charged $.20 a page for copying. There was also testimony that the number of pages of in-house copies was the cost divided by the $.20 per page charge. The December 20, 1988 statement reflected a charge of $610.40 for a total of 3,052 copies at $.20 a page. The final statement shows the in-house costs of the copies after Mustang settled was $4,655.70 at $.20 a page. The exhibits reflect that outside printing costs were $.06 and $.07 a page except those of the United States District Court for the Western District of Oklahoma which included a retrieval fee. Section 942(4) of title 12 of the Oklahoma Statutes limits the award of costs for copying to $.10 a page. Although this statute is not controlling in recovering costs from a client, we determine $.10 a page to be a reasonable cost, especially in light of the fact that outside copying cost $.06 to $.07 a page. Thus, Dr. Freede should have been given credit for the excessive charges for copies . . .

The testimony was that Dr. Freede told the law firm that he wanted Ken Manes, a consult, dismissed before his next to last bill. Dr. Freede thought that his services were duplicative. However, the law firm did not dismiss Ken Manes upon Dr. Freede's request. Given these facts, it was unreasonable for the law firm to have incurred the additional expenses. Thus, Dr. Freede should have been given credit in the amount of $2,800 for these costs.

Dr. Freede argues that expenses were unreasonable given the belief that the actual damages were thought to be $20,000. As discussed above, both the attorneys and Dr. Freede believed the punitive damages would be much more. In fact, Dr. Freede rejected a settlement offer of $100,000 and countered with an offer of $250,000. Given that the attorneys and Dr. Freede thought the punitive damages to be substantial, the costs were not excessive except as modified herein . . .

At the close of trial in the case at bar (case II), the law firm filed a motion for an award (1) of attorney fees in the amount of $16,095.00, (2) of legal assistant, intern, and law student fees in the amount of $9,346.50, (3) of costs in the amount of $1,001.57, and (4) of prejudgment interest. Dr. Freede contests the reasonableness (1) of the hourly rate for the legal assistants, (2) of the number of hours for the attorney, legal assistants, legal intern, and the law student . . .

The law firm presented an expert witness who testified that the number of hours and the hourly rate requested by the law firm were reasonable. Dr. Freede cross-examined this witness but did not offer a witness in support of his position. The trial judge reduced the amounts . . .

Dr. Freede argues that several of the hours spent by the attorney and the legal assistants were not recoverable. For example, he argues that legal assistant's time spent notifying the law firm's errors and omissions company was not work that would otherwise have to be performed by an attorney. We agree with Dr. Freede that the 4.2 hours spent by the legal assistant to notify the law firm's errors and omissions company was not substantive legal work and is not recoverable . . .

The trial judge correctly determined that the law firm was entitled to collect the reasonable costs of the TXO case (case I) incurred before December 20, 1988, from appellant, Dr. Freede, at a rate of 29.86 percent and thereafter at a rate of 100 percent of reasonable costs. However, the trial court erred in calculating the reasonable amount of copying and consulting and expert witness expenses and . . . in calculating the reasonable legal assistant fees for costs incurred in the present case (case II) . . .

AFFIRMED IN PART AS MODIFIED, REVERSED IN PART.

As you can see, experts aren't the only things that get expensive. The expert that the client and the firm argued about charged the firm $2800 for his time, which the firm was not able to recover—because the firm did not listen to the client when he said to get rid of him. So you must keep in mind that your client does have the last word, particularly when he is ultimately responsible for the bill.

One way to manage the use of the expert's time is to make sure you understand the basics of the expert's field. Sometimes the attorney will do the background research herself; sometimes you have to do it. To do so, you will have to educate yourself in whatever area the expert will be testifying. If your expert is testifying on burn rates of mattresses, you'll go find out what you can about the standards for burn rates, how they are tested, who maintains the standards, and so on.

To do this, you'll use the general documentary sources discussed in Chapter 9. You'll write up what you find in a memo to the attorney, and use the expert to fill in the blanks and explain specific problems in the case rather than using him for easily obtained information. Some tasks will become routine. If you are in the personal injury area, you will learn to read common medical records, use standard medical reference books, and know when something unusual comes up to send to an expert for review. If you are in the family law area and work with wealthy clients, you'll learn to read tax returns for evidence of assets; your expert will actually value the asset.

USE OF EXPERTS

As has been noted, experts are used to help the jury understand some aspect of the case. Experts will explain principles of science, accounting, valuation, economics, mechanics; customs of industries; psychiatric profiles; illnesses and traumas; and all manner of other interesting things. They will also help you prepare for the deposition of the other side's expert. Some cases are referred to as **"dueling experts"** cases because the main dispute in the case is an issue to which the experts are testifying. Some attorneys believe those cases are won or lost on the credibility of the expert; others (myself included) believe that hired experts tend to cancel each other out in the jurors' minds (unless one is clearly unintelligible) and the case will hinge more on the credibility of the parties. That doesn't mean you don't have to have an expert; you absolutely must in order to neutralize the effects of the other side's expert. The question is simply whether it is the experts that make the difference or the litigants that make the difference. In the following case, decide for yourself which was more important.

T. K. v. Simpson County School Dist., 846 So. 2d 312 (Miss. Ct. App. 2003).

T. K., through her guardian and next friend, brought suit against the Simpson County School District (District) . . . alleging that she had been sexually assaulted by two male classmates, claiming the District was liable for damages because of its failure to properly supervise students on the campus of Magee Middle School. Following a bench trial, the Circuit Court of Simpson County entered a judgment for the defendants denying all recovery sought.

T. K. appeals asserting that the circuit court erred by . . . requiring her to prove she had been sexually assaulted . . . [and] allowing expert testimony of a psychometrist who stated T. K. did not display characteristics of a rape victim during an interview . . .

On September 22, 1997, school dismissed at its regular time of 3:15 P.M. Most students left the campus by 3:25 on school buses. However, due to a shortage of bus drivers, students on at least one bus route had to wait for a bus to complete a route, and return to take them home. Consequently, some students were left waiting at the school until approximately 4:00 P.M. T. K. was among these students.

T. K. testified that, at some point in time while she waited, she entered the school to use the restroom. She used the restroom and was walking down a hallway to return outside, when two male students forced her into the boy's restroom. One student removed her undergarments and attempted to rape her, but was unsuccessful. The other male then raped her. The males left the restroom. T. K. returned to the girl's restroom and washed her face. She then went outside where she looked for a teacher to report the attack, but could not find one. Another classmate testified that T. K. was crying and upset. At the time, T. K. was eleven years old, and the male students were twelve and thirteen years old.

T. K. did not initially report the attack to her grandmother, but that same evening, a classmate telephoned and told her grandmother that the boys had "went with her." Her grandmother questioned T. K., but she would not tell her grandmother what happened. The next day, September 23, 1997, T. K. told both her grandmother and her uncle, a Magee police officer, that she had been sexually assaulted. On September 24, 1997, they sought medical attention, but this examination was inconclusive except to show that at some unascertainable time prior to the examination, T. K. had experienced some sexual contact. T. K. and her family then reported the allegation to Ernest Jaynes, the school principal . . .

This case involves the issues of cause in fact and proximate cause. To recover in tort, a plaintiff must show both causation in fact as well as proximate cause . . .

The circuit court found no causation in fact because T. K. failed to show that she had been sexually assaulted. There was no physical evidence that T. K. was raped, nor does it appear any criminal charges were brought. Rather, T. K. asserts that she declined to pursue criminal remedies because the District sought to avoid publicity. T. K. testified to the assault, but on at least one occasion prior to trial, she recanted her charges. Her classmate confirmed that T. K. appeared upset at the time the assault was alleged, and her grandmother and uncle testified to what she had told them. T. K. also called two expert witnesses who testified that T. K.'s failure in reporting the charges immediately, and offering different versions of events, was consistent with victims of sexual assault. The District, in its turn, called the two male students, whom T. K. alleged assaulted her, and they denied any sexual activity. The District also called its own expert witness, who stated T. K.'s demeanor in an earlier interview was not consistent with victims of sexual assault. The school principal, Ernest Jaynes, testified that after interviewing the students, he believed that "something" happened in the bathroom. While he did not believe an actual rape occurred, neither did he believe T. K. was making false accusations, so he was unable to determine exactly what did occur in the boy's bathroom.

Based upon this evidence, the circuit court found as fact that T. K. failed to prove she had been assaulted. Factual findings will not be reversed if supported by credible evidence . . . The trial court's decision is supported by T.K.'s recanting her allegations on at least one occasion and the absence of any physical evidence of an assault. The alleged attackers denied the attack, and an expert witness testified that T. K.'s behavior was inconsistent with that of a victim. Based upon this record, we cannot say the circuit court manifestly erred. . . .

Paul Davey was a master's level psychometrist and licensed counselor, whose practice included counseling in sexual abuse cases. He was accepted as an expert pertaining to investigations of sexual abuse allegations. He testified, **inter alia**, that a videotape of T. K. showed her answering questions without evidencing the "trauma" abuse victims typically evidenced. Admittedly, he never interviewed her in person.

At first glance, the reason for admitting this testimony is questionable. T. K. testified and people to whom she made the allegations testified. So, it would seem the circuit court had evidence upon which to base its determination of credibility, without resort to expert testimony. However, T. K. gave differing accounts and recanted her charges at one time. To remedy this defect in the case, T. K. called two experts to testify that her actions were consistent with sexual abuse. To counter that testimony, the District called Davey. Consequently, this case involved dueling experts.

T. K.'s argument goes to the credentials of Davey, not the subject of his testimony. Davey testified that he had "seen" over 2800 children who had been sexually abused, and had testified in an unspecified number of trials involving child sexual abuse. The standard of review for a trial court's determination of whether an expert witness is qualified to testify on the grounds for which his testimony is offered is abuse of discretion . . . There was a credible basis for accepting Davey as an expert in the area pertaining to exhibited characteristics of sexually abused children. There is no merit to this argument . . .

THE JUDGMENT OF THE SIMPSON COUNTY CIRCUIT COURT IS AFFIRMED. COSTS ARE ASSESSED TO THE APPELLANT.

Hired experts are always impeached on the basis of the fact that they are paid. It's almost a "So what?" impeachment, but everyone wants to establish which expert is paid by which party. The jurors realize that the experts are hired guns; there's a spectrum as to how much they believe being paid for an opinion influences that opinion. The jury's assessment of bias based on financial motives is often more dependent on how personable the expert is than on credentials or plausibility in any higher sense. However, any expert who is

Resources for preparation
for expert witnesses.

perceived as neutral (read "unpaid") is given extra weight. A **court-appointed expert** is generally listened to more carefully. For example, a police officer's opinion—if admitted because the officer has sufficient qualifications—as to speed and causation of an accident the officer investigated will be accorded extra weight by the jury. These "neutral" experts must be carefully undermined by your expert if they testify against the interest of the client. To know what the weaknesses in their testimony are, the expert will review the reports or depositions of these experts and give an opinion.

Of course, the opinion of court-appointed experts aren't always adopted by the jury. The following case is over the value of property taken by the government for public use. To refresh your memory, the **condemnor** is the governmental entity taking (and paying for) the property; the **condemnee** is the property owner. **Condemnation** is the process; **eminent domain** is the power. The lower number may be a result of the fact that the money paid here comes out of taxes and not out of a corporate treasury.

Carlson v. Underwood Equipment, Inc., 44 P.3d 439 (Kan. 2002).

This condemnation appeal raises [the] question[:] . . . Was it reversible error for extraneous documents included in an exhibit which were admitted into evidence pursuant to the condemnee's request and over the condemnor's objection to be considered by the jury? We answer . . . in the negative and affirm the trial court.

The Kansas Department of Transportation (KDOT) initiated an eminent domain action against Underwood Equipment, Inc. (Underwood) to acquire 1.01 acres of a 10.6-acre track to improve an interchange at I-35 and K-68 highways in Franklin County, Kansas. The court-appointed appraisers awarded Underwood $145,000 for the taking.

KDOT was dissatisfied with the award and filed the present action to have a jury determine the just compensation that should be awarded . . .

At trial, KDOT presented testimony of expert Bernie Shaner that the values before and after the taking were $490,000 and $445,000, respectively, with total compensation of $45,000 due. The other KDOT expert, Tom Frey, opined the values before and after were $436,800.30 and $402,739.04, respectively, with total compensation of $34,061.26 due.

Glenn Underwood testified that the values before and after were $2,260,000 and $1,965,000, respectively, with total compensation of $295,000 due. David Webb, an expert for Underwood, testified that the values before and after were $1,610,000 and $1,366,246, respectively, with total compensation of $243,754 due.

The testimony of all witnesses included computation of the reduction in value of the property due to loss of the 1.01 tract acre as well as damages relating to moving and replacing various fixtures on the property such as the sewer system, fencing, a tree, and large rocks bordering the property, generally referred to as "costs to cure."

At trial, during KDOT's cross-examination of Webb, his appraisal report was marked for identification. The report was used for the limited purpose of showing a discrepancy between Webb's definition of fair market value and that of other authoritative sources. Webb identified the exhibit as a copy of his appraisal report that he had brought to court that day. After cross-examination was complete, Underwood moved to introduce the report into evidence. KDOT objected, contending the entire report should not be admitted but only relevant portions. The trial court admitted the entire report.

The instructions submitted by Underwood as to the measure of compensation for the partial taking consisted of PIK Civ. 3d 131.04 divided into three separate instructions. There was no objection by KDOT, and the instructions were given as Underwood requested.

During deliberations, the jury returned with the following question: "What County thinks its worth [sic] (During Mr. Frey's testimony)?" The parties were unclear as to the meaning of the question. KDOT's counsel questioned whether the jury was asking for the county appraised value of the entire property or merely the improvements. KDOT admitted that Frey had testified concerning the county's appraisal of the improvements, but argued the appraised value for the entire property was not part of the record. During this colloquy, Underwood's expert witness, Webb, stated it was his belief that the value of the county's overall appraisal was part of the record because it was included within his appraisal report. The court and KDOT's counsel indicated they did not realize these documents were included in the exhibit. The court requested that exhibit be taken from the jury room, and the additional documents were found to be contained in the exhibit.

KDOT's counsel argued the documents should not be permitted to return to the jury because he did not know that at the time exhibit 31 was introduced, it was anything other than an exact duplicate of Webb's appraisal report. Underwood argued that it would be error to delete the documents since they had already gone to the jury room. The court found that the documents had in fact been admitted into evidence and allowed them to return to the jury.

The jury returned a verdict . . . which found the values of the property before and after the taking occurred to be $490,000 and $426,000, respectively. The total amount awarded for just compensation was $64,000. This resulted in a $81,000 reduction from the amount awarded by the court-appointed appraisers . . .

It was Underwood who moved for admission of this exhibit over KDOT's objection. It was Underwood's expert who included the documents within the report and advised the court of their presence when the jury's question was being considered.

While Underwood states that "both counsel" did not know the extra information was in exhibit 31, the record reflects that it was the court and KDOT's counsel who expressed lack of knowledge of the included documents. KDOT objected to the documents being allowed to be considered. Underwood's counsel contended the documents needed to remain with the jury and now complains about a ruling it requested below . . .

The trial court's ruling was correct. The documents had been admitted into evidence and were properly returned to the jury . . .

The trial court is affirmed.

It is never good form to ask for something and then complain that you got it.

All of the information available from an expert gives the legal team a better handle on the case for purposes of negotiation and settlement. It is not enough to know the strengths of your case; you must also know your weaknesses. Experts can help you find them.

Purely Consulting

Because discovery rules will ordinarily require you to disclose most experts, you have to be careful about what you tell your experts before you find out their opinions in order to avoid disclosing the identity of an expert who gives you an unfavorable report. Unfavorable reports are valuable, particularly if you find out before opposing counsel does and can still negotiate a reasonable settlement before they've hired an expert to find out the same thing. You lose the leverage, though, if you have to disclose those experts.

A **purely consulting expert** is one who will not testify at trial. A purely consulting expert generally will not have to be disclosed. This is the status you want to keep your expert in until you know what the expert is going to say. As soon as you know what the expert is going to say, then the attorney will decide whether he will be testifying. If your expert is going to rake you over the coals, you don't really want him, right?

Once a decision is made to have an expert testify, all discovery should be supplemented promptly. In order to preserve this option, experts should be found long before the deadline to disclose all experts or you will be in the position of disclosing your expert before you know what he will say.

Consulting/Testifying

A purely consulting expert may lose his non-disclosable status, however, if the testifying expert relies in any way on what the consulting expert said or did. You must make sure to segregate all reports of consulting experts that you decide not to use from any other papers, and be sure not to disclose those purely consulting reports to contaminate the studies of the testifying expert unless you want the other side to find out about your consultant and his opinions.

The **testifying expert** is just what it sounds like: the expert you plan to have testify at trial. Ordinarily, the opponent is entitled to question him and to have his opinions reduced to writing prior to trial by a certain date, depending on whether there is a specific docket control order or whether general discovery rules apply as to when that report is due. Failure to comply will result in the exclusion of the expert's testimony at trial—something that can be fatal to a case.

In-House Experts

In commercial litigation, or in personal injury where the defendant is a business entity, there is often a desire on the part of the client to limit expenses by using its own **in-house experts.** After all, the business's experts know more about what happens and what should happen than anyone else, right? Aside from the relatively obvious problem of bias on the part of these in-house experts, the client runs a substantial risk in taking this option. If the client wishes to take this route, she should be warned.

Along the same lines as discovery, the evidence rules address what must be disclosed about the bases of expert opinions.

> Rule 703. Bases of Opinion Testimony by Experts
>
> The facts or data in the particular case upon which an expert bases an opinion or inference may be those perceived by or made known to the expert at or before the hearing. If of a type reasonably relied upon by experts in the particular field in forming opinions or inferences upon the subject, the facts or data need not be admissible in evidence in order for the opinion or inference to be admitted. **Facts or data that are otherwise inadmissible shall not be disclosed to the jury by the proponent of the opinion or inference unless the court determines that their probative value in assisting the jury to evaluate the expert's opinion substantially outweighs their prejudicial effect.**
>
> Rule 705. Disclosure of Facts or Data Underlying Expert Opinion
>
> The expert may testify in terms of opinion or inference and give reasons therefor without first testifying to the underlying facts or data, unless the court requires otherwise. **The expert may in any event be required to disclose the underlying facts or data on cross-examination.**
>
> Fed. R. Evid. 703, 705 (emphasis mine).

In-house experts are often privy to information that you really do not want the jury to see. It's sad to watch a highly placed in-house expert start to crumble as he realizes that he's just let the other side find out about the memo or report that never was supposed to see daylight because that was the only source of his information. Usually the stumble is just obvious enough for the lawyer to seize on it and make the witness fall to pieces and begin thinking about updating his resume.

DISCOVERY AND OPPOSING EXPERTS

When attorneys and their paralegals get rushed, they sometimes do rash things. One of these rash things is to disclose an expert without knowing what he is going to say. This usually occurs when no one is paying attention to deadlines. The date for designation of experts draws near, and everyone panics. In your concern for having an expert available to testify (because you know that if you don't have one, you lose), you list any. And then, when the expert provides his report—horrors! His analysis supports the opposing side! You want to make it go away. But how?

If you are on the side that receives a gift of an opposing expert's beneficial report, you would celebrate. Except for one thing: How do you make sure that you keep the report and the expert for trial? An expert retained initially by one side and now desired by the other is a **Red Rover expert.**

Like many matters in law, the outcome in this situation depends on your jurisdiction. The first step, which sometimes helps, is to de-designate the expert. In some states, the courts will then view the Red Rover as a consulting-only expert, not subject to any use by the opposing side; others, however, will not allow that tactic to insulate the expert from depositions by the other side. The ultimate use of Red Rover testimony is all over the place, from leaving it in the hands of the trial judge to decide to absolutely, positively never letting opposing counsel use a Red Rover expert. In the following bankruptcy case, the judge honestly relates his problems with the issue.

In Re Vestavia Associates Limited Partnership, 105 B.R. 680 (1989).

THIS CAUSE came on for consideration upon the Motion to Strike Testimony of an Expert Witness filed by Centrust Savings Bank (Centrust), a mortgagee of the Debtor. The Debtor is a limited partnership owning two apartment houses. There are three mortgages on the property. Centrust has the first mortgage on one particular apartment house.

A number of lengthy hearings have been held on motions filed by all parties concerning the use of cash collateral and relief from the automatic stay. Throughout these hearings, a major issue has been the value of the two apartment houses. At an earlier hearing on the use of cash collateral, this Court determined the value of the two particular apartment complexes. Centrust had not participated in presenting evidence. At a later hearing on motions to lift the stay, Centrust was prepared to put on its expert appraisal witness, but withdrew the expert witness from testifying. Instead Centrust relied on the Court's previous determinations on value and cash collateral. Debtor's counsel, prepared to cross examine the expert as to value, sternly objected to the withdrawing of the expert witness. Throughout these hearings Debtor has called only its general partner to testify as to value by way of a form of the income approach. It is apparent Debtor was relying extensively on its cross examination of Centrust's expert witness to bring about a redetermination of value. Thus, the Debtor intended Centrust to be hoisted on its own petard.[1]

The Debtor did not have the opportunity at this hearing to examine Centrust's expert as the expert had conveniently left the courthouse. This Court ruled on the motions to lift the stay and for adequate protection, but scheduled an additional hearing to allow the Debtor to seek to elicit the testimony of Centrust's expert witness if permissible under the Federal Rules of Civil Procedure and Federal Rules of Evidence.

On June 7, 1989, the Debtor subpoenaed Centrust's expert witness retained to value the specific apartments subject to their mortgage. Upon service of the subpoena, Centrust filed a motion for protective order. Over Centrust's objection, the Court conditionally denied the motion for protective order and allowed the expert to testify as to value. This Court, however, at the time of hearing the expert witness' testimony reserved ruling on Centrust's motion to strike the expert's testimony. In order to decide the Motion to Strike, this Court must decide whether a party who would have had limited discovery of an opponent's expert witness under Fed. R. Civ. P. 26, may call that expert witness either as their own or as an adverse witness. Fed. R. Civ. P. 26(b)(4) establishes the parameters of discovering the opinions of opposing party's expert witnesses. Identity of an expert expected to be called at trial may be discovered through interrogatories. Through the same medium, the sum and substance of the expert's opinion may be gleaned . . . Further, limited discovery may be allowed thereafter by the Court . . . If the expert has been retained in anticipation of trial but will not be called as a witness, however, Rule 26 limits discovery to exceptional circumstances where the ability of the party to gather such information is impractical . . .

---

[1] *See*, W. Shakespeare, *Hamlet*, Act III, Scene IV, "For 'tis the sport to have the engineer hoist with his own petard."

Clearly, the Debtor has not utilized the mechanisms of Rule 26 to discover the substance of the expert's opinion. The expert witness, once withdrawn by Centrust, would have to be classified as an expert under Fed. R. Civ. P. 26(b)(4)(B), retained in anticipation of trial but not expected to testify . . . It is within Centrust's preogative to withdraw the witness and by its strategy limit Debtor's discovery . . .

In similar yet rare circumstances, federal courts have considered the issue at hand. In *Healy v. Counts*, 100 F.R.D. 493 (D. Colo. 1984), plaintiff's two experts had found no medical malpractice by the defendants. Defendants inadvertently learned of the expert witnesses opinion and sought to have them testify for the defense. The magistrate denied plaintiff's motion to strike these experts as defendant's witnesses. The district court reversed. The court considered a number of policy considerations espoused by the Tenth Circuit Court of Appeals in *Ager v. Jane C. Stormont Hospital and Training School for Nurses*, 622 F.2d 496 (10th Cir. 1980).

The Tenth Circuit Court of Appeals in *Ager* and the District Court in *Healy* were concerned that allowing the testimony of expert witnesses discovered by happenstance but who could not have been formally discovered would cause a distortion of the trial process. A jury might think evidence is being hidden if a party seeks to elicit testimony from an opponent regarding why experts were not produced at trial. Experts may be dissuaded from testifying if they thought they would be whipsawed between parties . . . Lastly, "the formal strictures of discovery" might be destroyed where the expert witness' identity had been determined by happenstance. . . .

The Tenth Circuit Court of Appeals had an additional occasion to consider this problem in *Durflinger v. Artiles*, 727 F.2d 888 (10th Cir. 1984). The plaintiff had retained an expert as a consultant, designated the expert as a witness for trial, and then changed its mind. Upon learning this information, the defendant contacted the expert requesting a copy of the report prepared for plaintiff's counsel. In *Durflinger*, unlike *Healy* and *Ager*, there was a specific violation of Fed. R. Civ. P. 26. The Court concluded, however, the expert would have been classified as "an expert who has been retained or specially employed by another party in anticipation of litigation." *Durflinger, supra* at 891; Fed. R. Civ. P. 26(b)(4)(B). "The rule is designed to promote fairness by precluding unreasonable access to an opposing party's diligent trial preparation." *Durflinger, supra* at 891. The Court hinted at the possibility a trial court might not have to exclude the testimony of such witness under different circumstances. Those circumstances were not eluded to by the Court.

The obverse side of these decisions begins with *Granger v. Wisner*, 134 Ariz. 377, 656 P.2d 1238 (Ariz. 1982). There, the trial court permitted the opposing party's expert to testify for the defense, but prohibited defense counsel from inquiring into the previous consultation. . . . Defense counsel appears to have obtained information about the expert during pretrial discovery. No impropriety as to the discovery rules was identified by the court. More germane to the court's decision was the defense's listing of the expert witness and plaintiff's waiting until the third day of trial before objecting to the expert being called as a defense witness.

In *Granger*, the concerns of the *Ager* and *Healy* court were acknowledged. The court specifically pointed out the concern in *Healy* that while restricted from exploring the expert's prior consultation, the plaintiff's ability to impeach this expert is distorted.

> While the risk of undue prejudice to a party in the position of plaintiff in this case is substantial and may make it proper in some situations for the court to entirely preclude the witness, Ariz. R. Evid. 403, we do not believe that the trial court's action in the case at bench was at all unreasonable. Plaintiff had numerous opportunities to raise an objection to the use of this expert.

. . . *Steele v. Seglie*, No. 84-2200, slip op. (D. Kan. Mar. 27, 1986), is similar to *Granger*. In *Steele*, plaintiff had contacted three doctors to examine plaintiff's daughter. At a deposition the defendant found out the child had undergone a physical examination at a hospital and thereafter requested the hospital to produce documents. Part of the documents produced were the expert witnesses' reports prepared for plaintiff's counsel. Plaintiff sought to suppress the testimony of the physicians. The defendant had taken the deposition of the expert witnesses. Rather than filing a motion for protective order prior to the depositions, plaintiff's counsel raised an objection at the time of taking of the deposition. There is no doubt plaintiff's counsel did nothing to curtail defense counsel's activities to elicit testimony from plaintiff's expert witnesses. In fact, plaintiff's counsel actually noticed the deposition of one of these experts. The District Court of Kansas acknowledged the factual similarities with *Healy* yet declined to follow *Healy*. The Court noted that in both *Granger* and *Ager*, the courts acknowledged that Fed. R. Civ. P. 26(b)(4)(B) "does not address itself to the admissibility at trial of the testimony of such an expert which is elicited by the opponent." *Steele, supra; Granger*, 134 Ariz. at 377, P.2d at 1242; *Ager* at

503. *Steele* further focuses on *Ager* where the Court "acknowledged this distinction and expressly reserved the question of whether a party 'may attempt to compel an expert retained or specially employed by an adverse party in anticipation of trial, but whom the adverse party did not intend to call, to testify at trial.'" . . .

The District Court in *Steele,* while agreeing with the *Healy* court's concerns, disagreed that identities and discovery of expert witnesses, whether through formal discovery or happenstance, should be treated differently. The Court reiterated the *Healy* court concerns, stating

> we [sic] are convinced that such difficulties can be avoided through careful limitations on the type of questions allowed to be posed to these experts. For example, the *Granger* court allowed a similar expert to testify only "with the restriction that defense counsel could not mention the fact of the previous consultation with plaintiff's counsel. This restriction was proper because the fact of the prior consultation for the plaintiff was irrelevant to the issue of negligence." . . .

. . . The District Court stated any problem could be resolved by requiring the defense to insure its expert did not mention the earlier consultations and restricting plaintiff from impeaching the expert witness by showing discrepancies between trial testimony and earlier written reports provided to plaintiff. The defense would also be prohibited from seeking to rehabilitate plaintiff's expert witnesses by showing that the plaintiff had retained the witness initially. Rule 403 of the Federal Rules of Evidence, said the District Court, would "prevent defendants from resorting to this rehabilitative technique.". . .

Clearly, the courts have come to two different policy conclusions regarding opponents calling opposing parties' expert witnesses. The first line of cases illustrated by *Healy* would require preservation of the policy behind Fed. R. Civ. P. 26(b)(4)(B) in order to prevent an aberration to the discovery and trial process under such a set of facts . . . It is quite apparent from review of the cases and treatises the concept of Fed. R. Civ. P. 26(b)(4)(B) was based on fairness. Notwithstanding the probable complexities suggested by *Healy*, its purpose was in the first instance to thwart the attempts of parties to use opponents' experts to establish their affirmative case.

The second line of decisions exhibited by *Steele* and *Granger* suggests a more open policy which discounts the application of Fed. R. Civ. P. 26(b)(4)(B), believing that once the horses are out of the barn, it is far better to build a new corral. Admittedly, in these cases counsel's failure to timely object to the use of experts reinforced this broad evidentiary policy.

Under the facts in this case, *Healy* is the better view. A jury trial is not the case at bar. Here there is something more fundamental. A debtor unwilling to expend available funds to obtain its own expert witness seeks to use the expert of an opposing party. Centrust's expert who originally may have been discoverable under Fed. R. Civ. P. 26(b)(4)(A) is not now discoverable. The Debtor is also seeking to impeach other parties' expert witnesses' testimony. In order for the Debtor to have utilized Centrust's expert witness even at the late stage of the hearing, it must prove exceptional circumstances as if Fed. R. Civ. P. 26(b)(4)(B) applied . . .

The Court finds under the facts in this case that the underlying policy of fairness does not allow the Debtor to use Centrust's expert to prove the Debtor's affirmative case as to value. Therefore, Centrust's Motion to Strike should be granted.

The failure to properly object to the utilization of such an expert, the violation of the rules of discovery, or the use of the expert during a jury trial may require a different analysis predicated on the concerns and solutions announced by the various courts mentioned herein.

Bottom line: Watch your deadlines and get your experts early.

CHAPTER SUMMARY

Experts are a necessary part of many trials, and most negative incidents relating to experts can be avoided with early planning. Find and evaluate needed experts early in the trial process so that you can determine whether you want to disclose them or not. Obtain the expert's credentials, references, fee schedule, and availability on first contact. Follow up on the references. Make sure the expert has no dirty laundry. Use the expert wisely—maximize his usefulness and limit the expense to your client.

FOR FURTHER READING

Stephen D. Easton, *"Red Rover, Red Rover, Send That Expert Right Over": Clearing the Way for Parties to Introduce the Testimony of Their Opponents' Expert Witnesses*, 55 SMU L. Rev. 142 (2002).

Stephen D. Easton, *Can We Talk?: Removing Counterproductive Ethical Restraints Upon Ex Parte Communication Between Attorneys and Adverse Expert Witnesses*, 76 Ind. L.J. 647 (2001).

George C. Harris, *Testimony for Sale: The Law and Ethics of Snitches and Experts*, 28 Pepp. L. Rev. 1 (2000).

Jeffrey L. Harrison, *Reconceptualizing the Expert Witness: Social Costs, Current Controls and Proposed Response*, 18 Yale J. on Reg. 253 (2001).

John V. Jansonius and Andrew M. Gould, *Expert Witnesses in Employment Litigation: The Role of Reliability in Assessing Admissibility*, 50 Baylor L. Rev. 267 (1998).

Eric Ilhyung Lee, *Expert Evidence in the Republic of Korea and Under the U.S. Federal Rules of Evidence: A Comparative Study*, 19 Loy. L.A. Int'l & Comp. L.J. 585 (1997).

Lee Mickus, *Discovery of Work Product Disclosed to a Testifying Expert Under the 1993 Amendments to the Federal Rules of Civil Procedure*, 27 Creighton L. Rev. 773 (1994).

CHAPTER REVIEW

KEY TERMS

American Lawyer	dueling experts	*Martindale-Hubbell*
bench trial	eminent domain	purely consulting expert
condemnation	expert witness	Red Rover expert
condemnee	fee schedule	testifying expert
condemnor	Findlaw	VerdictSearch
court-appointed expert	junk science	voir dire
curriculum vitae (c.v.)	in-house experts	
Daubert standard	inter alia	

FILL IN THE BLANKS

1. You always want to be careful to keep your _____ expert separate from your _____ expert, or they may both be disclosed to opposing counsel.

2. Although the term is mainly identified with the initial jury selection process, _____ also refers to the process of questioning an expert in order to establish his credentials.

3. When the judge, rather than the jury, makes findings of fact, the trial is referred to as a(n) _____.

4. One publication you can use to find a(n) _____ anywhere in the United States is _____.

5. When the government takes land for public use, in the exercise of its power of _____, the person who owned the land, or _____, has the opportunity to contest the value of the land in court, and does so by suing the _____, the governmental entity taking the property, in a(n) _____ action.

6. In family law cases, social studies are often done by a(n) _____ expert, such as a child psychologist.

7. Experts, instead of having a resume, have a(n) _____, the better to put all their accomplishments on.

8. Among other things, judges like to use the term _____ to show off their Latin skills.

9. A Web site you can use to find an expert witness is _____, but he probably won't post his _____ online because the prices might scare you off.

10.   It's easy to remember the name of a(n) _____ expert, one retained by one side and wanted by the other, because of the children's song and game of the same name.

11.   As well as being a good place to find out how much a particular type of case is worth if tried before a jury, a(n) _____ is an excellent source of leads for experts.

12.   Although _____ are an inexpensive source of good information, using them to testify easily backfires, for their opinions are often arguably based on privileged information, and having them testify can result in the disclosure of evidence.

13.   In order to get around the _____, or poorly established and widely criticized not-very-scientific theories out there, the United States Supreme Court established the _____ in place of the *Frye* standard, giving judges a list of flexible criteria upon which to evaluate the admissibility of scientific evidence.

WEB WORK

1.   Martindale-Hubble's online site at http://www.martindale.com has an area to look for experts. See if you can find an expert for each kind of case discussed in this chapter.

2.   The *National Law Journal* also has an online expert database at http://www.nljexperts.com/. Do you find the same experts there?

3.   West bought Findlaw and it became far more commercial—it also has a spot to find experts: http://marketcenter.findlaw.com/ More experts or repeats of earlier searches?

4.   You will not escape the marketing machine that is TASA if you join any professional organization, so you might as well check it out first at http://www.tasanet.com/. It provides some articles on communicating with your expert and such, but they are pretty much a rehash of the basics.

5.   The U.S. Access Board, a federal agency for promoting accessible design (yes, Virginia, there is a federal agency for everything) has a links page to professional organizations at http://www.access-board.gov/links/professional.htm. (You may already know this, but if the particular page you are looking for is missing, delete all of the Web address past the first single slash and that will usually take you to the home page of the Web site.) Look through the associations listed. For what kinds of cases might you want these organizations? What information do they have handy that is helpful? Can you find experts' names from the site?

WORKING THE BRAIN

1.   If the bases of an expert's opinion may be disclosed, does that include any attorney work product that may have been conveyed to the expert in the course of conversations with the attorney? Why or why not?

2.   What do you believe is the best solution for the Red Rover expert problem? Why?

3.   Evaluate the sample C.V. and fees for use in the *Haus* case. Which side would be thinking about this expert? Do you think this expert would be worth investigating or do you think you'd eliminate her right away? Why or why not?

4.   Given what you read of *T. K. v. Simpson County School Dist.*, what do you believe made the difference in the trial judge's opinion? Why do you think it went to a bench trial instead of a jury? Do you think the outcome would have been different with a jury?

5.   Do you believe the adversarial system of experts should be reformed? Why or why not?

PUTTING IT TO WORK

1.   What other experts are needed for each side for the *Haus* case? Using your available resources, make a list of potential experts and how to contact them. Select three and contact them for their C.V.s and fee schedules.

2.   Check your jurisdiction for the rules on disclosure and Red Rover experts.

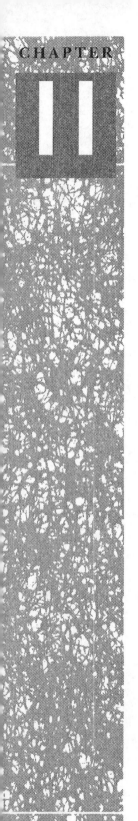

REAL AND DEMONSTRATIVE EVIDENCE

> "By a small sample, we may judge of the whole piece."
>
> *Miguel de Cervantes (1605)*
>
> "Example is always more efficacious than precept."
>
> *Samuel Johnson (1759)*
>
> "In the discovery of secret things and in the investigation of hidden causes, stronger reasons are obtained from sure experiments and demonstrated arguments than from probable conjectures and the opinions of philosophical speculators of the common sort."
>
> *William Gilbert (1600)*

REAL EVIDENCE

Physical objects used as evidence, or **real evidence**, fascinate the jury. "Show and tell" is always far more interesting to anyone than all the documents and talking, so if you can bring in tangible, three-dimensional "stuff," it makes an impression. If the case is about rebar, bring in rebar. If the case is about paint, bring in the paint. If it's about popcorn . . . well, the judge may not let you bring in the popcorn. The jurors might eat the evidence.

When you have real evidence, you need to show how it has been preserved since the time of the incident and how you know it is the actual item—authentication, again. If you have the chassis of the demolished vehicle, some witness will need to identify it and say it is in substantially the same condition—that it hasn't been left out in the rain or hammered or whatever. When your real evidence is too big to bring into the courtroom, you may want to consider using a model instead. As long as it is to scale and representative of every aspect of the actual item, the model should be admissible in lieu of, say, the two-hundred-foot-high crane that you're claiming was the cause of the accident.

It's also important to keep track of real evidence and make sure you take it home with you after the trial. One bailiff loved to show new lawyers what all he had in his closet—leftovers from prior trials. It looked like a very peculiar culling of a garage sale. Chief among the treasures was

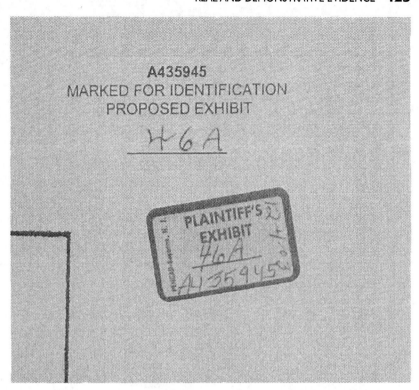

This exhibit tag is on a foam board upon which legal team has mounted an enlargement of a document.

a brown grocery bag full of pot that no one had ever come to get and that is probably still sitting in the closet—the bailiff doesn't have authority to dispose of it, and no one from the DA's office ever came back for it. No one really knew why it was in a civil courtroom to begin with.

As each exhibit is entered, whether a document or a piece of tangible evidence, it is tagged with a label marking it "Plaintiff's Ex. ___" or "Def's Ex. ___" or "State's Ex. ___." The space is filled in with the number assigned in the order each piece of evidence is admitted. At the end of the trial, the attorney should move to substitute any non-documentary, non-photographic evidence with a photograph. The motion is routinely granted; you simply hand the court reporter a photo of the widget with the same label as the widget had on it and then take the widget home. Everyone is happier that way.

DEMONSTRATIVE EVIDENCE

There is one type of evidence you can create: **demonstrative evidence**. This is evidence that you use to illustrate or summarize testimony of the witnesses. It may be taken from the testimony of one witness or from several; it must, however, accurately reflect the testimony of someone. Demonstrative evidence has been around for a long while, with references in cases from at least as far back as the nineteenth century of lawyers writing on chalkboards or paper tablets to list their points. The following case summarizes the general attitude toward demonstrative evidence in both criminal and civil trials.

People v. Burrows, 592 N.E.2d 997, 1002 (Ill. 1992).

The defendant, Joe Burrows, was indicted, along with Ralph Frye and Gayle Potter, by an Iroquois County grand jury for the murder and armed robbery of an 88-year-old man, William Dulin (Dulin). Defendant's motion for severance was allowed, and after his first trial resulted in a mistrial, he was retried and a jury found him guilty of murder and armed robbery. At his sentencing hearing, defendant waived his right to a jury and the court sentenced him to death . . . .

The State presented the following evidence at defendant's trial. Patricia Swan, Dulin's daughter, and her husband, Robert Swan, testified that on Tuesday, November 8, 1988, they traveled from their Indiana home to Dulin's home, which was located in Sheldon, Illinois. They arrived at Dulin's home, knocked on his front door, walked inside, and found Dulin lying face up on the living room floor. He appeared to be dead, so Robert Swan contacted the police. . . .

Gayle Potter, a codefendant who, at the time of defendant's trial, was awaiting trial on charges of murder, armed robbery, forgery, and attempted theft due to her involvement in Dulin's death, provided the following background information: she became acquainted with Dulin through her mother because her mother was Dulin's housekeeper and her mother also provided nursing care for his wife; Potter considered Dulin a friend and, over a two-year period, she had borrowed money from Dulin four times; on one occasion in August of 1988, defendant went with her to Dulin's home when she borrowed some money . . . Potter identified the gun that was used to kill Dulin as the same gun that was stolen from her trailer . . . she contacted Dulin that Sunday afternoon to see if he would be home during the evening because she intended to go to his home and ask for a loan (she did not notify Dulin of the purpose of her visit); and she then went to the Mobil station at . . . [the] request [of Poll, a drug dealer she owed $3,000 to].

Potter then testified that the following transpired between the time she arrived at the Mobil station and the time she visited Dulin's home: she saw defendant and Poll at the gas station; she was unsure whether she could come up with the money and Poll told defendant to "persuade" her that the money was needed; defendant then hit her with a piece of wood; defendant left the station and returned with Frye and an argument ensued over money; defendant then hit her in the head with a gun and she was shoved outside of the gas station office; she was called back inside and Poll told her that he "was going to send the guys," meaning defendant and Frye, up to Dulin's home in Iroquois County . . . they then followed her to Dulin's home.

Potter testified that the following occurred at Dulin's home: she walked across the front porch and knocked on the front door; Dulin recognized her, let her in, and defendant and Frye pushed their way in behind her; she asked Dulin for a $3,000 loan and he said that he did not have that kind of money; defendant then pulled out a gun from his waistband and told Dulin to write out a check; Dulin lunged for the gun and he began to struggle with defendant; Dulin reached for a BB gun but defendant quickly knocked it from his hands; shots went off and Dulin was shoved by defendant; Dulin was crying and out of breath, and said that there was no need to kill him; defendant smiled and shot Dulin in the head (she made an in-court identification of defendant as the person who shot Dulin); she became hysterical and defendant forced her head down onto the living room desk, hit her on the head and she began bleeding; she was shoved outside and forced into the truck. . . .

Frye . . . gave the following testimony about what had occurred . . . that evening: he and defendant went with Potter to the front door of a farmhouse after Potter "said there was no reason for us to sit in the truck"; Potter knocked on the door and an elderly man answered; she asked him for a $3,000 loan, but he said that he did not have that kind of money; he invited them inside his house and Dulin again refused Potter's loan request; defendant stepped in, shoved Dulin, and pulled a gun from his waistband; defendant and Dulin struggled over the gun; in the meantime, Potter tried to intervene and Frye knocked a lamp from her hands; shots were fired and Dulin was shoved backwards; defendant said, "you old son-of-a-bitch, you could have at least given us the money, we wouldn't have to go through all of this"; defendant then shot Dulin in the head; Potter became hysterical and she said she was going to call the police; defendant knocked the telephone out of her hands and had her on the top of the desk; defendant then hit Potter with the butt end of the gun on the left side of her face; defendant stopped hitting Potter and picked up a gold-colored check from the desk; defendant pulled off Dulin's pants and showed Frye a gold money clip that he had found; the three went outside and Frye put Potter in the truck . . . defendant told Potter to leave and threatened to kill her if she opened her mouth; defendant climbed into the truck . . . Frye was dropped off at his trailer and was arrested there at 4:30 A.M. on November 9, 1988; and between the time he returned to his trailer and the time he was arrested, he did not see or converse with either defendant or Potter.

On cross-examination, defense counsel elicited the following testimony from Frye . . . he was also convicted of the murder and armed robbery of Dulin and was waiting to be sentenced . . . he was arrested November 9, 1988, and he gave a taped statement shortly after his arrest; he admitted to making a mistake in that statement when he told the police that he traveled to Watseka with Potter and defendant in defendant's pickup truck; he gave a false statement to the police when he told the police that the pickup truck was left near an airport; in his post-arrest statement he also said that there was a hallway in Dulin's house and that defendant had a .38-caliber gun; he acknowledged that he can talk with Potter through a pan hole at the jail and that they talk to each other all the time; he admitted that after his conviction, he wrote a letter to a judge telling him that the taped statement he had given the police was a lie and that he was not at Dulin's home (on redirect, Frye said that Boyer (defendant's attorney) told him if he wrote the letter, he would try to represent him and get him out of jail); and he admitted that he lied when he stated at a hearing that his lawyer and the prosecuting attorney told him he would get life unless he testified against the defendant.

A tape was played of a statement Frye had given to defendant's attorneys, Ron Boyer and Mark Thompson. In the taped statement, Frye said that he was not present when Dulin was murdered and that he gave a post-arrest statement because police officers were jumping down his throat and telling him things.

The State also called Frye's attorney, Michael Jones, to the stand, and he testified that he was unaware that his client had given a taped statement to Boyer and Thompson, defendant's attorneys. Jones also stated that he informed Boyer that he did not have his permission to talk to his client . . .

Defendant . . . maintains that the prosecutor's use of a chart during closing argument suggested that defense counsel played a role in the case and, thus, the attention of the Jury was improperly shifted from the proper evidence presented at trial to the conduct of defense counsel. The State, on the other hand, believes that the chart was a proper piece of demonstrative evidence which showed the jury "how the many names in the evidence fit together . . . "

Courts look favorably upon the use of demonstrative evidence, because it helps the jury understand the issues raised at trial. "The overriding considerations in admitting demonstrative evidence are relevancy and fairness . . . The question of the admissibility of such exhibits is a matter within the trial court's discretion and will be disturbed only on a showing of clear abuse." . . . Defendant has failed to demonstrate that the use of Boyer's name on the chart was clearly irrelevant and unfair given the facts presented at trial.

Drawn on the right-hand side of the chart was an arrow leading from Frye's name to Boyer's name. It is clear that Boyer's name was displayed for the purpose of showing his involvement with Frye relative to Frye's decision to give recantation statements. The evidence at trial established that Frye communicated with Boyer on each of his recantation statements. . . .

For the reasons set forth above, we affirm the defendant's murder and armed robbery convictions and his sentence of death. The court directs the clerk of this court to enter an order setting Wednesday, September 16, 1992, as the date on which the sentence of death entered by the circuit court shall be carried out. The defendant shall be executed in the manner provided by section 119-5 of the Code of Criminal Procedure of 1963 (Ill. Rev. Stat. 1987, ch. 38, par. 119-5). The clerk of this court shall send a copy of the mandate to the Director of Corrections, the warden of Stateville Correctional Center, and the warden of the institution wherein the defendant is confined.

Judgment affirmed.

Generally, counsel is given fairly wide latitude with demonstrative evidence. This is an area in which you can be creative, and should be thinking about long before trial. How can you make the jury understand the case better? What portions will be difficult to visualize simply from testimony? Will it be hard to keep track of the players? The time frame? The places? People sometimes have difficulty carrying a lot of complex information in their mind, particularly when it is introduced in a non-linear way. In the courtroom, evidence is introduced witness by witness, and the information may not come in chronological order. To help the jury remember key points, various demonstrative summaries can be very helpful.

ETHICAL ISSUES

In keeping with the ethical duty to be fair to opposing counsel and to be truthful with the court, you should make sure that your demonstrative evidence does not distort the truth. Because you will generally be preparing it ahead of time, or at least thinking about it ahead of time, you need to make sure that all of the evidence it reflects is in the record or comes into the record. Make a list of the witnesses that will support each point and keep track of the list during the trial. If any of the points are omitted because any witness's testimony is not admitted for some reason, you must make sure you amend the demonstrative evidence or have a different witness make the point.

EVIDENTIARY ISSUES

As long as the type of evidence is perceived as demonstrative evidence, you are potentially looking at authentication, relevance, and Rule 403 issues. First, you may have to have someone say that the evidence represents what you say it does. This arises in videotape and photos that show an actual location or object. Someone must say that this is the place where the accident occurred, or this is the vehicle or the same type of vehicle, or same type of rebar, or whatever product or structure that may be in issue in the case. If the picture is of a deceased plaintiff, someone must identify the person. If the picture is of a plaintiff prior to scarring, someone must testify to those facts.

The attorney must also show that whatever he wants to show is relevant and that it won't be unfairly prejudicial, waste the court's time, or confuse the jury. If done right, demonstrative evidence should actually save time. The unfairly prejudicial issue is more of a problem, depending on the judge. It is absolutely true that people tend to remember things they see and hear better than things they just hear. Is that unfairly prejudicial or simply prejudicial in the sense of giving the better-prepared side (or more monied side) an edge? Many academics and philosophers out there argue that slickly produced demonstrative evidence, like jury consultants, widen the gap between justice for the poor versus justice for the rich. Some pundits even propose that demonstrative evidence be taxed as a court cost to be jointly shared by both parties. This could still potentially penalize the poor, for a rich opponent could spend the poor litigant out of the running unless there were a cap on what could be spent.

The items that truly violate Rule 403 are objects like bloody and gory pictures (e.g., the body of a victim of a train/car wreck hanging on the siding of one of the cars), or a photograph taken from an angle that exaggerates some aspect of the case (e.g., the amount of space a defendant had to react to a child who darted out from between parked cars). These types of pictures can and should be excluded from evidence. To avoid the expense of taking pictures, enlarging them, and mounting them on foam board just to have them excluded, make sure that they are accurate and free of any image that would tend to gross out the ordinary person.

Anything that is really disgusting or upsetting that can be demonstrated in some alternative way will probably be excluded. In criminal cases, truly gory pictures of the victim are routinely excluded from the guilt/innocence phase because of this **inflammatory** effect—the tendency (or so it is believed) that the pictures will make a jury so upset that it will want to find someone—anyone—guilty, and will not be as concerned about reasoning out whether this particular defendant is guilty. The pictures are admissible, though, once guilt has been determined, as the nastiness of the crime is relevant to the punishment phase, and how gross it was is not going to hurt the defendant in any unfair way at that point. The same sort of reasoning applies in civil law, although it is not usually as transparent.

Real evidence may also be arguably inflammatory, but if the physical evidence is demonstrative, it usually will rest in the court's discretion.

Davis v. Traylor, 530 S.E.2d 385 (S.C. Ct. App. 2000).

In this negligence case, Amanda Traylor appeals from a jury verdict for Regina Davis finding Traylor's negligence proximately caused serious injury to Davis. Traylor contends the trial court erred in . . . permitting the use of a rifle for demonstrative purposes.

On August 4, 1992, Amanda Traylor drove to a mall parking lot where teenagers often gathered. She was looking for her boyfriend, Brian Hammond. She found Hammond, who was highly intoxicated, and told him Art Garrett "wanted to jump on him." When Hammond approached Garrett and asked him "what the problem was," the two began fighting. Mall security eventually broke up the fight. Traylor witnessed the fight and overheard that Garrett intended to resume fighting at the Port Station. . .

Traylor later drove Hammond to his house and waited while he went inside. When Hammond emerged, he asked Traylor to drive him to the Port Station. Shortly before reaching the Port Station, Hammond asked Traylor to let him out at the Courtyard, a hotel on a hill overlooking the Port Station.

According to Traylor, before she let Hammond out of her car, he expressed his intention of killing a "n----." Traylor testified she understood this to refer to Garrett but did not take it seriously until Hammond stepped out of the car and Traylor saw he had a rifle.

Traylor left Hammond and went home to get her parents. They returned to the Courtyard and searched for Hammond. As they searched, they heard a shot. Hammond shot one bullet, which penetrated Garrett's throat, exited, and struck Regina Davis in the chest. Davis was seriously injured.

In her civil suit Davis contended Traylor was negligent in transporting Hammond, who was armed and highly intoxicated, to the Port Station. Davis also asserted Traylor was negligent in failing to contact police and failing to warn third parties. . . .

Traylor . . . argues the trial court erred in permitting Davis to use a rifle similar to the one used by Hammond for demonstrative purposes. At trial, Davis produced a rifle similar to the one used by Hammond for the purpose of showing Hammond could not have concealed the rifle from Traylor. The trial court refused to admit the rifle into evidence but allowed Davis to use it for demonstrative purposes only. After Hammond acknowledged the rifle was similar in size and appearance to the one he used on the night of the shooting, Davis asked Hammond to demonstrate how he entered the car with the rifle that night. Traylor contends the exhibition of the rifle was "unduly prejudicial and inflammatory.". . . We disagree.

We have found no South Carolina case in which the trial court refused to admit an object into evidence but allowed the use of the object for demonstrative purposes during trial. We believe the standard for merely showing or exhibiting demonstrative evidence, however, would not be higher than the standard for actually admitting demonstrative evidence. The trial court has broad discretion in the admission or rejection of evidence and will not be overturned unless it abuses that discretion. . . .

In this case, the demonstration was relevant to whether Traylor knew or should have known Hammond had a rifle. The size of the bolt-action rifle with a scope and strap aided the jury in determining whether Hammond could have successfully concealed the rifle from Traylor as he entered her compact car. We, therefore, conclude the trial court did not abuse its discretion in allowing Davis to exhibit this rifle to the jury.

AFFIRMED.

The **abuse of discretion** standard referred to in the case gives the trial court judge a good deal of power. This case and others that refer to this standard do not say that all judges in the same situation must do as this judge did. They simply say that it was within the range of choices the judge could legitimately make. Another judge who refused to allow the plaintiff to demonstrate the rifle might also be upheld under this same standard, which basically says that a trial judge can make many different decisions and still be within his authority and be upheld by the higher courts. In order to find a trial judge has abused his discretion, the appellate court will have to find that the judge made no reference to any standard, or that his decision was clearly arbitrary or capricious or without any reasonable basis. That is a fairly high burden to meet if you want to contest a discretionary matter on appeal.

OBTAINING AND AUTHENTICATING PHYSICAL EVIDENCE

One significant problem that plagues physical evidence is the need to retrieve it quickly after the time of an incident, something that ordinarily doesn't happen. At the time of an incident, particularly a serious one, the persons involved are usually far more interested in solving the immediate problem than preserving the evidence. If you have a building problem, such as a collapse, even if there are no personal injuries, the people at the scene will first think about saving any valuable possessions contained within the building, not about trying to find and preserve the source of the problem. If you have a man who falls from a bridge, you are more interested in getting him help than in finding what may have broken or what he may have slipped on. When people get around to looking for evidence, weather, animals, searches for other things, other work, and multiple other events can disturb the evidence. This is much different from a criminal scene, where the police will cordon off the area until they can process the evidence in its original state and position. Civil investigators are at a much greater disadvantage, often working with locations that have been compromised to a great extent.

If you are looking for physical evidence, you'll want to go to the site of the occurrence as soon as possible after the incident occurred if there was no prior criminal investigation. If there was a criminal investigation, you'll want to see what you can do to protect the law enforcement evidence from being released after the criminal trial and have it transferred to your custody. Normally when both criminal and civil cases arise out of the same incident, as in the case of a DWI accident, for example, the civil trial will be **abated**, or held in suspension, until after the criminal trial is concluded, mainly because it avoids the complication of Fifth Amendment privileges. Law enforcement is charged with taking care of the evidence and establishing a clear chain of custody in criminal prosecution, and they keep the physical evidence in designated locked facilities until the trial is concluded. At some point, evidence will either be released or, in the case of contraband such as illicit drugs, destroyed. To avoid the dispersal of evidence when you have a concurrent criminal case, you'll want to prepare a motion for a protective order instructing law enforcement not to dispose of the evidence, but to either hold it or transfer it pending the trial or settlement of the civil case. The attorney will be impressed you thought of it.

When you do not have a concurrent criminal case, which is more common, you'll have to find the physical evidence. Where there has been an insurance investigation, you may have the insurance adjuster and appraiser's file to go on, but you are left with any weaknesses or errors he or she may have made. There are both personal and commercial insurers for all sorts of things, so don't overlook the possibility that someone took a look at the claim early on and may have, at the very least, pictures of physical evidence, if not the evidence itself.

In an auto case, if the vehicle has been totaled and the property damage portion concluded, you may have some problems if you want your own examination of the damage to the vehicle. Pictures may be available from the insurance file; pray they are decent. For as soon as a totaled vehicle claim is concluded, the vehicle is issued a salvage title, and then it is usually sold for salvage, and either scrapped or stripped. If the car has been repaired, you have the same problem. Although pictures help, the real thing is far more instructive. And if you had any hope of bringing a **manufacturing defect** in a **products liability** suit, it is pretty much destroyed with the vehicle. Even if your cause of action is intact, it is still far more dramatic to have the vehicle available. Which would impress you more: a picture of a squashed Geo Storm or the actual vehicle that fits in the space between the counsel tables, the judge's desk, and the jury box? **Immediacy** is very powerful.

Other helpful bits of physical evidence to look for in automobile accidents are debris and skid marks. Was there glass at the site? Where did it fall? Where are the skid marks? Where do they begin and end? What other debris did you find and where? If there are contradictions in the witnesses' stories, sometimes the physical

Debris from an automobile accident can be crucial to explaining the way it happened.

evidence—particularly its placement on the roadway—can help eliminate some possibilities or, at least, make them highly unlikely.

If any property is damaged or destroyed, there is the possibility of insurance. **Homeowners' insurance** covers residential property and contents; **renters' coverage** takes care of private personalty. **Commercial policies** can cover all types of business property as well as all types of liability. If someone has been injured on the job, there may also have been a **worker's compensation** investigation, so you may want to look there for pictures or physical evidence. The problem with worker's compensation is that if you are aligned with a tort defendant, the insurer is not going to be terribly cooperative; the **comp carrier** will probably be looking to you for reimbursement for part of whatever it has paid. More on that topic will be discussed in Chapter Thirteen.

After investigating the site (where you will take pictures; more on that later), you will probably have a better idea of what sorts of things you may be looking for. Whenever you interview witnesses, make sure you ask about the existence of any physical evidence: "Was there any debris on the ground?" "What kind?" "Do you know what happened to it?" Once you find the real evidence, you'll have to establish some sort of chain of custody. Courts tend to be stricter about the specifics of chain of custody in criminal than in civil trials, but the proper foundation must still be laid.

Van Hattem v. Kmart Corp., 719 N.E.2d 212 (Ill. Ct. App. 1999).

Hazel Van Hattem (Hazel), Nancy Witvoet, Donna Jonkman and Marilyn Neumeyer, in their capacities as administrators of Ernest Van Hattem's estate (collectively, plaintiffs), brought a wrongful death and survival action against Dr. James S. Habib, alleging that he misdiagnosed and prescribed inappropriate medication to Ernest Van Hattem (Ernest); and against Kmart Corporation (Kmart), alleging that a Kmart pharmacy misfilled a prescription for Ernest, resulting in his death. A jury returned a verdict for plaintiffs against Kmart, but against plaintiffs and for Dr. Habib. The circuit court entered an $810,000 judgment for plaintiffs and against Kmart. Kmart appeals, contending that the court erred in. . . denying Kmart's motion *in limine* which sought to bar admission of the contents of a prescription bottle for failure to establish a proper chain of custody for that evidence . . .

The evidence adduced at trial established that, on June 15, 1995, 76-year-old Ernest died at St. James Hospital following an intracerebral hemorrhage, or massive brain bleed. At the time of his death, Ernest was taking several prescription medications, including Coumadin, a drug for reducing clotting factors and thinning the blood.

Dr. Habib, Ernest's physician, had first prescribed Coumadin for him during a three-month period in 1991 to prevent phlebitis, for which he had been hospitalized. Thereafter, in June 1994, after being hospitalized for acute thrombophlebitis, Ernest again was prescribed a two-milligram dosage (one pill) of Coumadin once per day by Dr. Habib. On July 15, 1994, Dr. Habib increased Ernest's dosage from six milligrams every three days to eight milligrams every three days. His specific instructions were for Ernest to take one pill on the first day, one pill on the second day and two pills on the third day, repeating that dosage, or a 1-1-2 regimen . . .

On October 14, 1994, Dr. Habib again prescribed a 1-1-2 regimen of two-milligram-strength Coumadin for Ernest. The prescription was filled at Kmart's Steger pharmacy, as it had been by the pharmacy previous times: on June 17, 1994; on July 29, 1994; and on September 7, 1994. Refills of the October 1994 Coumadin prescription also were filled by the Kmart pharmacy on December 29, 1994, March 10, 1995 and May 30, 1995.

Each time Dr. Habib prescribed Coumadin, he warned Ernest about the dangers associated with that drug, specifically abnormal bleeding. Upon his discharges from the hospital, Ernest also was warned about Coumadin and was told to report any unusual symptoms or bleeding to his doctor. In addition, each time the Kmart pharmacy filled Ernest's Coumadin prescription, written warnings were provided and stapled to the bag containing the prescription bottle.

According to Hazel, who picked up all Ernest's prescriptions at Kmart's Steger pharmacy, warnings were attached to each prescription bag, but she regularly removed those warnings before she gave Ernest the medication. . . Although she could not specifically remember picking up the May 30, 1995, Coumadin refill, Hazel testified that it was her custom to telephone a refill request to the Steger pharmacy whenever Ernest placed his pill bottle by the telephone. She then brought the prescription home, removed the warning labels and receipt and gave the bag containing the prescription bottle to Ernest. She believed she had done this for the

May 30, 1995 prescription, but could not remember specifically. After giving her husband his prescription, she did not monitor the manner in which he took his medication. Ernest took his own medicine and kept a "drug diary," entering a check mark each time he took medication.

While Ernest was on Coumadin, Dr. Habib checked his prothrombin time (the number of seconds it takes for a plasma sample to clot) monthly. From June 1994 until June 1995, Ernest's prothrombin time remained therapeutic. On June 14, 1995, after he was brought to the hospital, however, Ernest's prothrombin time was abnormally high and more than twice the previous result from a test taken on May 24, 1995.

On the afternoon of June 13, 1995, Hazel and Ernest were vacationing in Dowagiac, Michigan. There, Ernest remarked to a friend that he might have passed blood in his urine. Ernest's friend advised him to see his doctor. That evening, after returning to their home in Crete, Illinois, Hazel noticed spatters of blood in front of their toilet; Ernest told her he would see his doctor in the morning about his "prostate." Ernest, who suffered from migraines, also complained of a headache. The next morning, Hazel found her husband unconscious and bleeding from his mouth and nose. Paramedics were called and Ernest was transported to St. James Hospital.[3]

On June 15, 1995, while Ernest was in the hospital, Hazel remembered the warnings about Coumadin and bleeding. At home, she removed the Coumadin prescription bottle from the drawer in their home where her husband kept it, looked at its contents, and noticed the number "5" on the 79 pills remaining in the bottle, although the prescription label indicated that the dosage was two milligrams. While at the hospital, the Van Hattems' daughter Marilyn Neumeyer, a registered nurse since 1968, overheard her mother express concern that the Coumadin prescription bottle contained pills imprinted with a "5." Neumeyer then requested a Physician's Desk Reference and saw that the number "5" on the pills meant that they were five-milligram strength.

On June 16, 1995, after Ernest's death, one of his sons-in-law brought the subject Coumadin prescription bottle to his niece, Julie Witvoet, a pharmacist. Witvoet, who had been a licensed pharmacist for three years, identified the pills as five-milligrams in strength, not the two-milligram strength set forth on the prescription label.

Immediately, the Van Hattem family placed the prescription bottle containing the pills in a basement safe and contacted their attorney, who then placed the prescription bottle in a bank safe deposit box. On September 6, 1995, plaintiffs filed the present suit.

Prior to trial, Kmart sought to bar, *inter alia*, admission of the prescription bottle and its contents. Arguing plaintiffs could not establish that the 79 five-milligram strength pills contained in the prescription bottle were in substantially the same condition as when Kmart allegedly had given them to Hazel, Kmart asserted that a proper chain of custody could not be established. The circuit court denied Kmart's motion *in limine,* but allowed Kmart "free rein" at trial to argue that the pills were not provided by its pharmacy.

At trial, further evidence was presented as to Kmart's custom and practice in filling prescriptions. According to a Kmart pharmacist, when a new prescription is brought into Kmart, a review is done to establish that all the pertinent information is legible. Then, the pharmacist enters onto a computer the patient's name, the name of the medication, its quantity, its directions, the number of refills and the doctor's name. A second check is done by comparing the computer screen to the written prescription. The computer then generates a label, patient information, warnings and a receipt. To fill the prescription, a member of the pharmacy staff removes the indicated drug, which is labeled with a National Drug Code (NDC) number, from the shelf. The pharmacy staff consists of pharmacists and technicians . . .

A member of the pharmacy staff then matches the NDC, the name and the strength of the drug on the stock bottle to that on the prescription label. Thereafter, the pills from the stock bottle are poured into a tray, counted out, and then poured from the tray into the prescription bottle, which is capped and labeled. If the prescription is completed by a technician, the bottle is left to be checked by a pharmacist. Similar procedures are used for refills. None of the pharmacists or technicians on duty the day Ernest's May 30, 1995 refill was prepared remembered refilling that prescription.

Dr. Habib and two of plaintiffs' expert witnesses, Dr. Scott Kale and James O'Donnell, a pharmacologist, testified at trial that the Kmart pharmacy misfilled the May 30, 1995 prescription with five-milligram strength Coumadin instead of the prescribed two-milligram strength, resulting in Ernest's death. Dr. Harry Messmore, a hematologist testifying as Dr. Habib's expert, was of the opinion that Kmart misfilled the May 30, 1995

---

[3] Testimony was presented that, had Ernest sought medical attention immediately upon noticing blood in his urine or even that evening, the likelihood of successful treatment would have been greatly increased.

prescription, causing Ernest's cerebral hemorrhage. Dr. Robert Barkin, Kmart's expert and a pharmacy professor, believed the prescription was filled properly and characterized the source of the five-milligram pills as "not identified." Dr. Ashok Raojibhai Patel, a hematologist and oncologist, testified that the cause of Ernest's cerebral hemorrhage was unknown. Dr. Patel also suggested that a review of Ernest's medical charts indicated to him that Ernest had been taking a 5-5-10 regimen since February 15, 1995; he also acknowledged, however, that Kmart's pharmacy records never reflected a five-milligram dosage prescription being received or filled for Ernest Van Hattem. . . .

. . . Kmart contends that the circuit court abused its discretion in denying its motion *in limine* and allowing admission of the prescription bottle and its contents in evidence because plaintiffs did not establish a proper foundation for their admission, having been unable to prove a proper chain of custody.

Before real evidence may be admitted at trial, an adequate foundation must be laid establishing that the item sought to be introduced is the actual item involved in the alleged occurrence and that its condition is substantially unchanged. . . . A proper foundation for the introduction of an object may be laid either through identification of the object by a witness or through the establishment of a chain of custody. . . . The character of the object sought to be introduced will determine which method is required. . . . If the object is fairly unique, readily identifiable and impervious to change, it can be admitted merely on the basis of unimpeached testimony that it is the item in question and is in a substantially unchanged condition . . . if the offered evidence is not readily identifiable or is susceptible to alteration by tampering or contamination, a chain of custody must be proved. . . . This chain of custody must be of sufficient completeness to render it improbable that the object has either been exchanged with another or subjected to contamination or tampering. . . . A circuit court's determination as to the admissibility of evidence is discretionary and will be overturned only if the court's decision abuses its discretion. . . .

Kmart claims that the circuit court erred in allowing admission of the five-milligram Coumadin pills absent evidence that those pills remained "unchanged" or were in the same condition as when dispensed by Kmart. Kmart also asserts that "every person" in contact with those pills must testify and, since Ernest was clearly unable to testify as to the condition of the pills, they were inadmissible. For support, Kmart cites several cases for the proposition that testimony based on an inspection after the event is not competent unless evidence is also introduced to show that the conditions inspected had remained unchanged in the interim; those cases, however, primarily involved objects such as airplane engine parts, doors, automobiles, trains, and floors of which particular conditions were the subject of dispute. . . .

In the instant case, no evidence was adduced to suggest that the two-milligram pills had degenerated or somehow were converted into five-milligram pills. Kmart's contention is that the pills are inadmissible absent evidence proving that they were the exact pills Kmart dispensed on May 30, 1995. Kmart posits that Ernest somehow had an "alternate" source of the drug (maybe from a friend who was taking five-milligram Coumadin) and placed 79 or more five-milligram pills which he received elsewhere into the Kmart prescription bottle. Kmart specifically argues that plaintiffs presented "no evidence which eliminated the possibility that [Ernest] or someone else altered the contents of the prescription bottle."

To establish a sufficient chain of custody, every possibility that the evidence was tampered with or replaced need not be disproved; rather, plaintiffs needed to show only that it was reasonably probable the evidence remained unchanged in any important respect, or was not substituted . . . Unless defendant provided actual evidence of tampering or substitution, plaintiffs needed to establish only the probability that the evidence was not substituted. . . .

Here, evidence established that Hazel received the prescription for 100 two-milligram Coumadin pills on May 30, 1995, and gave that prescription to Ernest, who kept those pills in the same drawer in which they were found. Two weeks later, when the pills were located in that drawer, they totalled an amount diminished by the number of pills Ernest would have taken after following the 1-1-2 regimen. No family member other than Ernest used those pills or possessed them during those two weeks. Based on the unrebutted evidence of Ernest's meticulous habits, it is reasonably probable that those pills remained unchanged in the two-week period. Kmart's conjecture that Ernest substituted someone else's drugs for his own is not borne out by the record. Nor is support for Kmart's suggestion that some other family member substituted the five-milligram pills (presumably in order to support the lawsuit) apparent from the record.

It was within the discretion of the circuit court to rule on the admission of evidence. Based on this record, it cannot be said that the court erred. . . .

Don't overlook the possibility of real evidence on the person of your client. Scars, injuries, actual evidence of brain damage before the jury, missing limbs: these are also real evidence. Although the opposing side can not ordinarily compel a party to display himself, it is no problem to voluntarily do so. Animals are also real evidence and have been brought to trial; if you have a dogbite case, think about bringing Fluffy or Butch into the courtroom for the jurors to observe. Of course, you'd better make sure doing so will benefit you; check out Fluffy ahead of time in the context of a roomful of strangers before you introduce her to the courtroom. In environmental cases, various critters in jars, tanks, and other preservatives will also be part of the evidence, although you should make sure that the jury is forewarned to avoid a panic from a member who is, say, arachnophobic when you are bringing in spiders.

If you decide to use a model in lieu of the real thing, make sure that it conforms to the actual item. Examine the model carefully for any distortions and misleading details in color, size, texture, or materials. And make sure it can fit through the doors in the courthouse.

You should also ask about physical evidence in interrogatories and depositions. Physical evidence is crucial in products liability cases, where you really need to have the actual product in question, but in many others, it is simply one piece of the picture. However, as discussed before, physical items have a certain fascination that other evidence can't compete with very well.

What about the guy who fell off the bridge? It happened at the construction of the bridge, a type known as a segmental bridge, and he later claimed that he was straightening a piece of rebar that broke. By the time the suit was filed, that section of the bridge was finished, the rebar enclosed in concrete, and only other similar pieces were available. Neither he, nor anyone else, could produce the actual piece of rebar that he claimed had broken—a significant evidentiary problem for his case when the sample pieces all turned out to be up to the specifications required. He was able to obtain samples both from his employer, who had some others left over, and from the manufacturer, who had more. The only way that the actual piece could have been found would have been for someone to look for it immediately after the accident — not months to years later. But who was thinking about it at the time of the accident? He was well-liked by other workers and the management of the construction company, he had just fallen off a three- to four-story high bridge, and no one knew if he would live or not. He lived, but as a **partial quadriplegic**, and in the subsequent lawsuit was unable to obtain sufficient evidence to prove to a jury that it was the fault of anyone other than himself.

PRESERVATION, INSPECTION, TESTING, AND SPOLIATION ISSUES

If you are the keeper of physical evidence, you must take care to preserve it in the condition it was in, as we say in legalese, "at the time of the incident made the basis of the lawsuit." People have had to keep body parts in the law firm's refrigerator, car parts in the closet, burnt bits of building, various fixtures, and other oddments until time of trial to make sure they stayed secure and in shape. If the firm has a vault, that is an ideal place to keep these items. Temperature-controlled storage facilities are sometimes rented just to hold on to various items alleged to cause injuries—anything from vicious exercise bikes to deadly ATVs.

In most circumstances, the parties work out a mutually agreeable time to inspect these crucial pieces of evidence. If you do not possess the evidence, take still pictures and video footage as well as measurements of everything. If at all possible, take your expert along. Cost considerations may preclude the presence of your expert; in that case, you'll have to make sure you have adequately educated yourself so that you will obtain the necessary data for the expert to review later.

Parties are also allowed to perform nondestructive tests on the evidence or destructive tests on small samples if it will not substantially affect the evidence. For instance, if there is a claim that a fabric is not sufficiently flame retardant, the defendant is probably entitled to a sample of the fabric in question to run his own tests to determine whether it is flame retardant, even if the testing destroys the sample, as long as there is still sufficient fabric for the plaintiff to enter into evidence.

In Chapter Seven, we had the case of the disgruntled ex-employer. Here, gentle reader, is the case of the missing ladder.

Nichols v. State Farm Fire and Cas. Co., 6 P.3d 300 (Alaska 2000).

. . . Dallas Nichols sued his neighbor's insurance company for intentional and negligent spoliation based on the insurance company's failure to secure critical evidence in Nichols's case against the neighbor. The superior court granted summary judgment to the insurance company, and Nichols appealed. We affirm.

. . . On September 1, 1996, Dallas Nichols was assisting his neighbor, Richard Gittlein, with roof repairs when the ladder Nichols was standing on collapsed beneath him. Nichols fell eight or nine feet, tearing a rotator cuff. It is uncontested that the ladder was "old," "beat-up" and "had a lot of cracks in it." Gittlein left the broken ladder under the deck of his house.

Two months later, on December 5, 1996, a fire heavily damaged Gittlein's house. Nichols claims that the ladder was not destroyed in the fire . . . Shortly after the fire, on December 18, 1996, Nichols filed a claim with Gittlein's insurance company, State Farm, for his injuries suffered in the ladder accident. The claim was assigned to State Farm agent Janet Sperbeck. She contacted Gittlein on December 20th, who reported that he was not sure if he still had the ladder and that it may have been destroyed in the fire.

On January 2, 1997, Sperbeck met with Nichols for the first time. He told her that the ladder was still in existence on the property and that it should be preserved. Sperbeck went to Gittlein's premises on January 2, hoping to find him and ask about the ladder. When she arrived, she discovered that the house had been destroyed and all that was left was a shed. Sperbeck left without finding Gittlein or the ladder.

After this visit, Sperbeck wrote to Gittlein, asking whether he had found the ladder. She called him twice, without reaching him. But she did not contact the State Farm agent who was handling Gittlein's fire claim and who was in communication with Gittlein.

On January 15 Sperbeck called Nichols and spoke with Nichols's wife, Judy. Judy expressed concern that, if Sperbeck failed to collect the ladder, it would soon be too late. Sperbeck traveled to the premises on that date but did not find Gittlein there.

On January 27 Gittlein made contact with Sperbeck. He told her that he could not find the ladder and that it must have been thrown out with the fire debris.

Subsequently, in July 1997, State Farm wrote Nichols stating that its liability analysis was complete and that Gittlein was not negligent. State Farm therefore declined to make any payments under the liability coverage of its policy. . . .

On August 6, 1997, Nichols filed suit against Gittlein and State Farm. Nichols alleged that Gittlein was liable for negligently providing a ladder for use by Nichols that Gittlein knew or should have known was defective and unsafe for use. Nichols also alleged that Gittlein and State Farm "acted negligently, intentionally or recklessly in failing to preserve the ladder." These claims for intentional and negligent spoliation were the only claims alleged against State Farm. . . .

. . . [W]e recognized that acts of intentional spoliation of evidence can give rise to independent tort claims for intentional interference with a prospective civil action . . . [and] that intentional spoliation claims can be made against parties to the original action (called "first-party spoliators") and non-parties to the original action (called "third-party spoliators").

We have not recognized an independent tort for negligent spoliation of evidence. In *Sweet v. Sisters of Providence in Washington* . . . we were presented with a first-party negligent spoliation claim. The plaintiffs alleged that a hospital had negligently lost medical records that were critical to plaintiffs' medical malpractice claim against the hospital and others. We held that the jury should be instructed that the loss of the medical records raises a rebuttable presumption of negligence on the part of the hospital . . . This shifts the burden of proof to the hospital to prove that it was not negligent . . . We noted that the court should first determine whether the missing evidence "sufficiently hinders plaintiff's ability to proceed . . . If the spoliated evidence is important enough to meet this standard then the rebuttable presumption/burden-shifting remedy can be applied.

We concluded in *Sweet* that the burden-shifting remedy was a sufficient response to the problem of missing evidence under the circumstances presented . . . We did not decide whether negligent spoliation could ever form the basis for an independent suit and implicitly recognized that in cases of third-party spoliation the burden-shifting remedy might not be effective. . . .

Nichols ignores an important aspect of his claim for negligent spoliation by failing to focus on whether it is a claim of first-party or third-party spoliation . . . State Farm is not, to use the language of *Sweet,* a "third party not associated with the underlying lawsuit."

. . . We see no reason why the *Sweet* remedy would not be a sufficient response to negligent spoliation of the ladder, whether by Gittlein or State Farm, assuming the ladder's disappearance was found to be a sufficient hindrance to the prosecution of Nichols's claim. If the absence of the ladder were found not to be a sufficient hindrance, then no tort remedy would be needed. Thus here, as in *Sweet,* we conclude that a separate tort remedy for negligent spoliation may not be maintained.

For this reason, we uphold summary judgment dismissing the negligent spoliation claim against State Farm.

AFFIRMED.

This is a typical way of handling spoliation claims. If there is missing evidence, the party spoliating the evidence is penalized with an evidentiary **presumption**. Presumptions are what they sound like: if there is no evidence to the contrary, the fact will be found in favor of the presumption. So where evidence has been destroyed, it will be presumed that the evidence would have favored the opponent unless evidence is shown to the contrary.

This presumption is ordinarily accomplished through a jury instruction. The jury will be given an instruction that states that unless they believe there was sufficient evidence to overcome the presumption, they are to find that the spoliated evidence would have helped the other party.

WHAT, WHEN, AND HOW OF DEMONSTRATIVE EVIDENCE

As observed by Anthony Bocchino,

Most of the technical aspects of the use of . . . technology are easily learnable if the lawyer is so inclined and, if not by the lawyer, by a paralegal. Most people under the age of twenty-five already know what they need to know to accomplish . . . as a technical matter. . . . All the lawyer needs do is request that an exhibit be displayed. It is of no consequence whether the lawyer could actually accomplish the display on his own if called upon to do so. The same is true with regard to charts and graphs and timelines and relationship charts and all manner of persuasive graphics. All of this can be displayed by someone other than the lawyer.

Working back then, who is it that prepares the exhibits for their display? Again the lawyer need not have any talent whatsoever in putting exhibits onto a CD. They certainly do not need to know how to create a PowerPoint presentation in order to use one at trial. All that is necessary to run a sequence of graphic displays in a courtroom is the ability to press a space bar on a computer or the use of a remote electronic device to accomplish the same. So we have taken care of the technical. There are people who do this for a living and people already employed at most firms or law offices who can already accomplish technically what needs be done for most trials.

Anthony J. Bocchino, *Ten Touchstones for Trial Advocacy–2000,* 74 Temple L. Rev. 1 (2001).

What to use as demonstrative evidence is only limited by your creativity. The lawyer is given great latitude during closing, and pretty much anything that helps make her point can be used. Even so, some fairly common types of demonstrative evidence show up, and a discussion of each type, its uses, and its pitfalls is warranted. Remember, as in everything else, your mileage may vary; not only do things vary from state to state, they also vary from locale to locale within states. Always ask around, or, at the very least, go sit in on a few trials. All trials are public; you may always go in and watch. There are usually rules about attire, so make sure you don't wear shorts or a halter top; aside from that, you're probably okay. Go in quietly, don't talk, don't chew gum, don't eat or drink. If you observe those few rules, you'll be welcome. Many judges will even answer any questions you have if you explain who you are and why you're there during a break, particularly in jurisdictions where judges are elected.

While exercising your creativity in creating demonstrative evidence such as computer slides, you may want to keep in mind some of the principles that graphic artists use when preparing items to convey a message.

- Never use a sentence when a word will do.
- Use color to enhance your message, but make sure it does not detract.
- Make sure you use color consistently to create meaning for the colors.
- Be aware of the meanings that are tied together by design or color.
- Limit the variations of color and images and make sure that those you use create a flow that is harmonious.
- Link the demonstrative evidence to trial exhibits whenever possible.
- Order demonstrative evidence in a way that builds to a point or develops an argument in a way the jury can visualize.
- Make sure you do not overkill with demonstrative exhibits. Be selective.

When is a tougher issue than *what.* Judges have differing tolerances about when demonstrative evidence may be introduced. The safe assumption is that demonstrative evidence can't be introduced until after a witness has actually testified to the facts contained within the demonstrative evidence. Sometimes the demonstrative evidence may be shown to the jury immediately thereafter, while the witness is still there; sometimes not until after. When a witness makes his own demonstrative evidence, there's usually no problem having it displayed to the jury. This is the case when a witness draws a diagram in order to clarify testimony: Where was the couch? Where were the other witnesses? Where was the witness before he fell? Where did the witness land? Sometimes this is not technically considered demonstrative evidence. When the demonstrative evidence is a summary of the evidence from multiple sources, there is a greater likelihood that it will not be allowed before the jury until **closing arguments** (also known as **summation**).

Despite that, you will want to prepare the demonstrative evidence well ahead of time. You must plan in advance. Failure to do so will result in poorly presented demonstrative evidence. Whether you decide to go low tech or high tech, know what you need to have available in terms of equipment, props, accessories—whether it's simply a working black magic marker or a complex of computer equipment with power access.

One thing that will help you will be the Order on the **Motion in Limine.** As you may recall, a motion in limine is a preliminary motion on evidentiary issues at trial, and the order will require attorneys to approach the bench before broaching certain topics before the jury. Although it is only a preliminary order, and subject to change as the trial proceeds, more often than not the Order on the Motion in Limine is an accurate indicator of what will occur in trial. As a result, after the hearing on the motion in limine, you will want to look through your demonstrative evidence and **redact** anything that you need to in order to comply with the Order.

The issue of how to introduce demonstrative evidence varies with the type. Some things are ordinarily considered demonstrative evidence can sometimes be characterized as real or **substantive evidence.** The following case does a good job of distinguishing the two.

Anderson v. Anderson, 514 S.E.2d 369 (Va. Ct. App. 1999).

In this appeal, Daniel Lawson Anderson ("husband") argues the trial court erred by . . . classifying two IRA funds as marital property; 5) failing to order or address the issue of the division of tangible personal property in its equitable distribution award; and 6) failing to award him an equitable distribution exceeding one-half of the marital property. . . .

We review the evidence in the light most favorable to wife, the party prevailing below and grant all reasonable inferences fairly deducible therefrom. . . .

On May 28, 1997, the trial court issued a letter opinion granting wife a no-fault divorce. It also . . . ruled that husband's American Funds and Crestar IRA accounts were marital property; found that husband did not meet his burden of tracing as to the funds in these accounts; . . . and awarded an equal division of marital property. Upon motions to reconsider its initial ruling, the court issued a second letter opinion on October 13, 1997, again holding that the American Funds and Crestar IRA accounts were marital property and that husband had failed to satisfy his burden of proof on the retracing issue. The court entered a final decree of divorce, incorporating its previous findings, on February 26, 1998. . . .

Husband . . . contends the trial court erred by classifying two IRA accounts, one with American Funds and the other with Crestar, as marital property. Husband contends the American Funds account is entirely his separate property and the Crestar account is part marital and part separate property. Husband admits the American Funds and Crestar accounts were established during the parties' marriage and prior to their separation. Husband contends, however, he presented sufficient evidence to trace the funds in the American Funds and Crestar accounts back to two pre-marital Keogh accounts, which are presumed to be separate property . . . We disagree.

At trial, husband testified that he opened two Keogh accounts with Heritage Savings & Loan Association prior to marrying wife. Husband then testified to a series of post-marriage transfers and deposits involving the Heritage accounts. These transactions involved the creation of several new accounts and the movement of these funds from one account to the next before they ultimately reached the American Funds and Crestar accounts at issue here. Husband admitted commingling his allegedly separate funds with marital funds over the course of the marriage. In support of his testimony, husband relied on a flow chart, which the court received as demonstrative evidence, and certain financial documents to trace the source of his allegedly separate funds in the American Funds and Crestar accounts back to his pre-marital Keogh accounts. Husband introduced the chart and financial documents as Exhibit 8 at a deposition on April 9, 1997, explaining what they purported to show at that time.

We find no error in the trial court's conclusion that husband presented insufficient evidence of tracing and no error in the court's classification of the funds at issue as marital property. Husband failed to prove by a preponderance of the evidence that any portion of the funds in the American Funds and Crestar accounts are his separate property. . . .

We find it unnecessary to recite every step of the complicated series of transactions leading to the deposit of the funds at issue into the American Funds and Crestar accounts. For the purposes of our decision, it is sufficient to recite the following relevant evidence pertaining to each account.

As to the American Funds account, husband claims he established the account on May 23, 1986 with a roll over deposit of $5,000 of allegedly separate funds from another IRA account with Investors Savings. Husband contends he made no further deposits or contributions to the American Funds account after 1986 and claims its balance, $13,831.26, as separate property, the result of passive interest earnings. Assuming without deciding that appellant's claim regarding the deposit of $5,000 of separate property is true, the evidence does not support his assertion that the balance of the American Funds account is his separate property.

Before the trial court, husband offered only one financial statement showing the activity in the American Funds account after 1986. This statement shows the account's activities during 1996 and a balance of $13,831.26 on December 31, 1996. Husband presented no other statements regarding the activity in this account over the preceding nine years of its existence, including any statement showing the rate of interest that it may have earned. Thus, husband's claim that no other contributions were made to the account and that the account's growth was solely attributable to passive interest earnings rested on his testimony and the demonstrative flow chart alone. "It is well established that the trier of fact ascertains a witness' credibility, determines the weight to be given to their testimony, and has the discretion to accept or reject any of the witness' testimony." . . . Furthermore, the flow chart, as a demonstrative, or illustrative, exhibit that played no actual part in the events before the court and that husband offered to explain and clarify his testimony, had no independent probative value. *See Kehinde v. Commonwealth,* 1 Va. App. 342, 347, 338 S.E.2d 356, 358 (1986) (approving of the use of illustrative evidence "to clarify [a] witness' explanation and to insure a common understanding between the witness and [the trier of fact] as to the events which took place"); *Saunders v. Commonwealth,* 1 Va. App. 396, 397–98, 339 S.E.2d 550, 551 (1986) (indicating that photographs introduced for the purpose of illustrating a witness' testimony do not constitute substantive evidence in the case); Friend, *supra* at § 13.1 (defining illustrative evidence as that which "played no part in the events of the case but which is introduced to assist the jury in understanding what happened in the case" and "to demonstrate the meaning of a witness' testimony . . . "). *See also United States v. Paulino,* 935 F.2d 739, 752 (6th Cir.) (holding that charts summarizing documents or testimony may be admitted as demonstrative evidence under Rule 611(a) and "should be accompanied by a limiting instruction which informs the jury of the summary's purpose and that it does not constitute evidence"), *cert. denied,* 502 U.S. 914, 112 S. Ct. 315, 116 L. Ed. 2d 257 (1991); *Sykes v. Floyd,* 65 N.C. App. 172, 308 S.E.2d 498, 499 (N.C. Ct. App. 1983) (stating that photographs introduced to illustrate testimony are not admissible as substantive evidence); *Smith v. Ohio Oil Co.,* 10 Ill. App. 2d 67, 134 N.E.2d 526, 530 (Ill. App. Ct. 1956) ("Demonstrative evidence . . . is distinguished from real evidence in that it has no probative value in itself, but serves merely as a visual aid to the jury in comprehending the verbal testimony of a witness."). It follows that the trial court was also entitled to give the flow chart no weight. *See Jurado v. Jurado,* 119 N.M. 522, 892 P.2d 969, 975–76 (N.M. Ct. App. 1995) (finding that any error in the admission of demonstrative exhibits calculating the rates of return on two properties was harmless because the trial court did not rely on the exhibits in determining an award). In short, the trier of fact determines the credibility and weight of the evidence. It was therefore entitled to give no weight to husband's testimony that the funds in the American Funds account were maintained as separate property, particularly in the absence of documentary evidence establishing the integrity of the funds as separate property. We accordingly find no error in the court's refusal to classify the American Funds account as husband's separate property . . .

For the foregoing reasons, we affirm the trial court's finding that husband failed to meet his burden to trace the funds in the American Funds and Crestar accounts to a contribution of separate property and the court's classification of these funds as marital property. . . .

Charts and Timelines

You may use a variety of charts, graphs, or timelines. For numeric information, which many people have difficulty retaining, consider using graphs, whether a **pie chart**, a **bar graph**, or a **line graph**. If you are trying to demonstrate any type of business loss, you'll get into a number of accounting statements that will probably make the average juror begin contemplating the contents of the vending machines and his pocket to calculate what he'll get at the next break. Make it simple. Show them in nice, color-coded charts what you should have gotten under the contract and what you actually got due to the breach, or the loss of profits due to the tortuous actions of the dastardly defendant, or not, depending on whom you happen to be representing. If there are complicated family or business relations, make a tree demonstrating them, whether in a standard **organizational chart** or some other diagram. If you are trying to show the accumulation of bad decisions that resulted in the harm, or if you want to show all the decisions made to prevent it, you may want to make a **flow chart** that shows each choice and its place in the chain of events. Making these charts will be worth the time you put into them; make one based on each witness you have to speak to the issue so that if any one of them is excluded or doesn't show, you are not caught short.

Timelines have a similar function. Because evidence is not introduced chronologically, but rather witness by witness, it is easy for a jury to lose track of what happened when. A chart that delineates what witness explained what, and how it fits into the overall scheme of things, can be an invaluable aid to jury understanding of the case.

Documents

Documents have been discussed to a great extent as far as content, but the physical properties have not. At times, a key document, like a contract or the proverbial **smoking gun**, has language to which you want to bring the jury's attention. To do so, you can physically enlarge the document, mount it on **form board**, and highlight the key portions.

Price v. Mackner, 58 N.W.2d 260 (Minn. 1953).

This case arises out of a head-on collision between two automobiles which occurred about 12:30 A.M. on Sunday, June 18, 1950, about two miles northeast of Detroit Lakes, Minnesota, on Minnesota trunk highway No. 34, which runs east and west at the point of the collision. . . .

Plaintiff was 19 years of age at the time of the accident . . . [O]n Saturday, June 17, 1950, he met two friends, James J. Leitheiser and Dean O. Stilke . . . About 12:30 A.M. they left the [Erie C]lub and proceeded to drive west toward Detroit Lakes. Plaintiff was driving, Leitheiser was in the front seat with him, and Stilke was riding in the rear seat.

Defendant James Mackner was also 19 years of age when this accident happened. He . . . with Wallace I. Swedberg as a passenger . . . [at] about 12:20 A.M. decided to drive out to the Erie Club.

Minnesota trunk highway No. 34 is a tarvia-surfaced road 26 feet wide from shoulder to shoulder, and the center of the highway is marked with an intermittent white line. Immediately west of the Erie Club the road takes what was described as a medium curve to the southwest or to plaintiff's left as he drove west. This curve ends at the crest of a hill. According to the measurements of the sheriff, the accident occurred 822 feet west of the crest of the hill. This measurement was made by standing at the scene of the accident and observing the point to the east where the lights of an oncoming car first came into view. A similar measurement showed that the lights of an automobile approaching the accident scene from the west were visible 1,572 feet from that point. The accident occurred approximately half a mile from the Erie Club.

Both plaintiff and his passenger, Leitheiser, were rendered unconscious by the collision and were not able to testify with any degree of clarity regarding the circumstances of the accident. Plaintiff was only able to recall turning onto the highway and driving toward Detroit Lakes. He thought that he was not driving over 40 miles an hour and that at his last recollection he was on the right side of the road. Leitheiser recalled traveling a couple hundred yards down the road toward Detroit Lakes, during which time, according to his testimony, plaintiff's car was on the right-hand side of the road. As to anything that occurred after the time the car got 200 yards down the road and prior to the time of the accident, his mind was a blank.

Dean Stilke was riding in the middle of the rear seat of plaintiff's car. He testified that plaintiff's car was on the right-hand (north) side of the road and was traveling in a straight line. He said that he remembered suddenly seeing lights in front of the car and that he called to plaintiff to pull over. Only a very short space of time elapsed between his seeing the lights and the collision. Upon cross-examination, Stilke testified that he could not say whether the Price car was on the right-hand side of the road between the time he saw the lights and the collision.

Defendant testified that he was driving on his right-hand (south) side of the road, that he had been meeting a succession of cars coming from the opposite direction, and that approximately 100 feet in front of him he noticed a car on his side of the road "angling slightly toward my shoulder and I stepped on my brakes and froze at the wheel." He testified that he saw the oncoming car make a slight turn to the right about 15 feet from him and then the collision occurred. Defendant's passenger, Swedberg, who was riding in the front seat with him, testified that at the time of the accident he had turned his attention to tuning the car radio as it had just faded out. He said that for about a quarter of a mile before reaching the scene of the accident they were meeting oncoming cars about every two car lengths and that just before he looked at the radio defendant was driving on his right-hand side of the road. He said also that just before the accident he heard defendant yell "'Look out' or 'Look' or something like that."

. . . It is quite clear from the exhibits that this was a full head-on collision, or nearly so, and that, as stated by plaintiff, the verdict must rest upon a finding that plaintiff was traveling on the south side of highway No. 34 at the time of the collision. . . .

Plaintiff's exhibit 1 is a photograph taken with the camera facing west along highway No. 34. Plaintiff's automobile is in the foreground, sitting at an angle facing northeast and almost entirely on the north side of the highway. Defendant's car is behind plaintiff's and is partly obscured by it. It appears to be facing in a northwesterly direction, and both rear wheels appear to be on the south side of the highway. Plaintiff's exhibits 2 and 3 make it clear that the collision was almost completely head on, but they certainly are not conclusive, or even particularly illuminating, as to the side of the highway on which the accident occurred.

Patrolman Archie Northup was called to the scene of the accident. He testified that he observed droppings from the automobiles on the north side of the highway. He could identify the droppings because they were smooth on the side that had been clinging to the cars. He further testified that the breakage from the accident was on the north side of the pavement. On cross-examination, Northup testified that defendant's automobile caught fire after the collision and that quite a little sand had been shoveled on its front end in an effort to put out the fire. . . .

Plaintiff contends that the photograph showing the position of the automobiles following the accident and the testimony of patrolman Northup bring this case within the rules set out above. We cannot agree. The picture was far from being conclusive evidence that the accident occurred on the north side of the highway. In fact it is quite possible that it was of some aid to the jury in determining that the accident occurred on the south side. . . .

Certainly this court cannot determine that as a matter of law the collision occurred on the north side of the highway from an examination of plaintiff's photographs.

The testimony that the debris and droppings were on the north side of the highway, either considered alone or in conjunction with plaintiff's exhibits 1, 2, and 3, is not so conclusive or overwhelming that the evidence supporting the verdict must be disregarded. The testimony about the debris must be considered along with the evidence that dirt was shoveled onto the north side of the highway to put out the fire in defendant's automobile. . . .

While we consider that the evidence set out above in support of the verdict was a reasonable basis for the verdict in the face of plaintiff's contentions, it should also be pointed out that certain other evidence was offered tending to support the verdict. There was the testimony of Loraine Homcik that she was a passenger in another car which passed plaintiff's car near the Erie Club and that she observed plaintiff's car zigzagging down the road. There was also the testimony of Arthur J. Waldron, a deputy sheriff who was on duty that evening in the Erie Club, that between 11 and 11:30 P.M. he saw plaintiff leaning out of his car vomiting.

Under the circumstances as above set out, it is our opinion that the question whether this accident occurred on the north or south side of the road was for the jury to determine upon a consideration of all the evidence, including plaintiff's exhibits 1, 2, and 3 and the testimony about the location of the debris. The jury having evidently decided that the accident occurred on the south side of the highway and there being sufficient evidence to support that verdict, this court has no alternative except to affirm.

Affirmed.

You can also use something along the lines of Dataflight Software's **Opticon**™ or Adobe Acrobat's .pdf system to transfer the unaltered original into your computer system and then highlight and magnify the selections you are interested in for projection. Another option is to have a **video out card** on your laptop, which allows you to connect your computer directly to a television and use it as a monitor, a more economical solution for most people. Some devices on the market also will allow you to directly link from your computer to a television without the video out card. Be very careful of these—the picture quality on the television is often extremely poor because fewer pixels are needed to give a good picture on your laptop. When you spread these same little squares on the television, you may end up with boxy graphics. The video out card will let you make the graphic appropriate to the television; these other devices won't.

The most common way to integrate these types of computer files is to set them up in Microsoft **PowerPoint** presentation software, although there are certainly other types of presentation software out there. Whichever you choose, be ready to jettison slides as needed based on what witnesses and evidence are admitted or excluded.

If you have questions about the physical document, the paper, ink, or signature, you'll need to have a document examiner discuss the issue. Document examiners are more commonly used in criminal cases, but they do come into play in civil cases as well. In will contests, questions about the veracity of a signature or whether a testator had testamentary capacity at the time she signed often arise. Document examiners can conduct some interesting comparisons between normal signatures and the signature found on the questioned document, as well as test the paper and the ink used in the document.

Photographs and Videotapes

Photographs and videotapes present an interesting problem. On the one hand, in some states, "photographs" are automatically discoverable and not considered the same as documents. On the other hand, there are times when videotapes are used as part of the process of the attorney's preparation. In other states, and under the federal rules, photographs and videotapes are generally treated the same as any other document. Another verse, same as the first: Check your jurisdiction to find out what rules apply to you.

Photographs are not subject to many objections as long as nothing is exaggerated about the angle or point of view, or the subject matter is not inflammatory, either of which is subject to a Rule 403 objection. The photograph needs to be of whatever you are trying to portray in as close as a condition as it was at the time of the incident in order to be relevant, but aside from that, it is probably admissible. In this admittedly older case, photographs were even admissible when they tended to prove something different than they purported to prove.

Jensen v. Intermountain Power Agency, **977 P.2d 474 (Utah 1999).**

This case involves a negligence claim relating to damage caused by flooding of the Sevier Bridge Reservoir in 1983 and 1984 and an unrelated claim concerning certain water rights located under the reservoir. As to the disputed water rights, the trial court concluded, as a matter of law, that defendants had an easement to store water in the reservoir and that plaintiff's land and water rights were subject to the terms of that easement. As to claims that defendants' negligence resulted in the flooding of plaintiff's land, a jury found that defendants were not negligent. We affirm on both issues.

Defendants in this case, Delta Canal Co., Melville Irrigation Co., Abraham Irrigation Co., Deseret Irrigation Co., Central Utah Water Co., and Intermountain Power Agency . . . (collectively "IPA"), have appropriation rights in water from the Sevier River and storage easements in the Sevier Bridge Reservoir ("the reservoir") . . . These easements give IPA the right to store water up to the level of the reservoir's capacity of 80 feet, the height of the reservoir's spillway. Plaintiff L. Carl Jensen owns certain property, some parcels of which straddle the reservoir's 80-foot contour and some parcels of which lie completely below the contour.

In June of both 1983 and 1984, runoff flows were at unprecedentedly high levels and caused portions of Jensen's land to flood. Jensen claims that this flooding damaged his property straddling the contour by damaging fences, corrals, and roads and by leaving silt, alkali, and debris deposits. Jensen also claims that this flooding caused damage to his land lying below the contour and thereby interfered with his stock operation. . . Jensen filed an action against IPA, claiming that it was negligent in failing to adequately prepare for the excessive runoff. Jensen sought injunctive relief and damages in excess of twelve million dollars. Jensen also filed a quiet title action, alleging water rights in both water appurtenant to the reservoir and appropriated water from the reservoir . . . Jensen also sought damages for IPA's and its predecessor's expropriation and conversion of his water.

On February 2, 1994, the trial court granted a partial summary judgment in IPA's favor and dismissed Jensen's easement and water rights claims. The trial court conducted a jury trial on the flooding issues. The jury found that IPA was not negligent, and the court dismissed the remainder of Jensen's claims. Jensen moved for a judgment notwithstanding the verdict and for a new trial. The court denied both motions and entered a final judgment on August 10, 1995. Jensen appealed. . . .

Jensen . . . argues that the trial court erred by admitting certain statistical evidence regarding the level of runoff in both 1983 and 1984 and a videotape showing flooding of the Sevier River below the dam. The admissibility of an item of evidence is a legal question . . . However, in reviewing a trial court's decision to admit or exclude evidence, we allow for broad discretion. . . .

We address the admission of the statistical evidence first. Jensen objected to the admission of evidence of the Sevier River's historic flows suggesting that flooding of 1983's and 1984's magnitude likely would occur only once every 200 to 30,000 years. Jensen argues that the trial court should have excluded the evidence under rule 403 of the Utah Rules of Evidence because its prejudicial effect "outweighed" its probative value. We disagree. Rule 403 mandates admission of relevant evidence unless its prejudicial effect "substantially outweighs" its probative value. Utah R. Evid. 403. The probative value of the statement that flooding of 1983's and 1984's magnitude would occur only once every 200 to 30,000 years is not substantially outweighed by its prejudicial effect or its potential to mislead. This is especially true because Jensen, as the trial court acknowledged, could cross-examine the witness and establish that despite these predictions, the once-every-200- to 30,000-year flooding occurred in both 1983 and 1984.

Jensen also argues that the trial court should have excluded a videotape depicting the DMAD dam on the lower Sevier River collapsing as a result of the 1983 flooding. Jensen argued that this evidence was irrelevant or that, if relevant, its prejudicial effect outweighed its probative value. It is true that the video depicted flooding in an area far distant from Jensen's land. However, the runoff causing the collapse in the video was the same runoff that caused damage to Jensen's land. IPA introduced the evidence to support its theory that given the system-wide flooding, decisions related to the management of the Sevier River Reservoir necessarily had to consider the downstream effects of those decisions. This goes to IPA's defense against Jensen's claim that it acted negligently in operating the dam. Given IPA's theory, the video was very relevant, and Jensen has failed to show that its prejudicial effect substantially outweighed its probative value. Accordingly, we conclude that the trial court did not abuse its discretion in admitting either the statistical evidence or the video. . . .

In conclusion, we determine . . . that the trial court did not abuse its discretion in admitting either the statistical evidence or the videotape . . . Affirmed.

Digital cameras are popular for many reasons. For amateur photographers, one of the most attractive features is the opportunity to see the picture before leaving the site. In the context of litigation, this is a plus, as you are charging a client for your time or you are trying to maximize your efficiency to otherwise increase your profitability to the firm, and you must be away from the office to take photos of whatever scene is part of the case. If you don't find out until later that the pictures are unusable, you have to go back. The advantage of being able to see whether the pictures show what you need is definitely a selling point for digital cameras.

The problem for admissibility, if raised, is that digital photographs are easily manipulated, as is easily evidenced by any walk down an aisle of your favorite software store in the photo software area. You'll see people stretched, in the color of aliens, and in some very odd surroundings. As others have pointed out, all media have been open to manipulation; the problem with digital media is that the manipulation is so much more seamless and so much harder to detect. It is this capability of computers that worries some opponents and courts, although many don't know enough to raise the issue and others don't know enough to phrase it. As a result, digital photographs so far have been treated as any other photographs. However, as the computer literacy of all members of the legal community improves, this could change, and calls for reform in the treatment of digitally produced images have already been made. To get ahead of any possible changes, you may want to adopt methods that can not easily be impeached along these lines.

The first issue is the type of digital format in which you save your image file. If the file is **compressed** or compressible, such as a .jpeg, that means the size of the file is reduced when you are not viewing it to make more space on the computer. To shrink the file size, the computer removes bits of information, and when you reopen the file, it guesses what was there by extrapolating from what is left. This can lead to errors that can compound over time. To avoid that problem, you should save pictures you plan to use in litigation in .tiff, .bmp, or .gif format, and if asked if you want to compress, always say no.

You also want to make sure that when you blow up the picture to show the jury, it doesn't end up looking like a Pong game or a bunch of blocks. This means that you want a high density of **pixels.** Pixels are the little dots (actually, little squares/rectangles) the computer uses to make a picture. The more individual dots, the smaller they are, and the more you can blow up a picture without it looking like . . . a bunch of squares or rectangles of different colors. The bigger the number, the more pixels, and the greater the density of pixels in the pictures that the camera will take. Now, the problem is that the more pixels, the more memory required for each image, and the small memory cards in the digital camera won't be able to hold many pictures. Your solution is either to have several memory cards with you or to take a laptop and upload the pictures as they are finished.

This is not enough, though, to prove that the image was not manipulated. You can testify to the fact, but you really don't want to take the stand if you don't have to. Your client or other witnesses can testify that the picture looks right, but when it gets to fine details, they are likely to break down and say they can not remember. So how can you verify the time that the pictures were taken and that there have been no alterations?

There are several methods, but they still require some honesty on the part of the photographer at the outset, so the specter of alteration can not really ever be totally removed. What all these methods can do is prove that the digital images have not been altered from a given point, and although you can put time and date on the picture in many cameras, that, too, may be manipulated. First, you can store the digital images on a storage medium that assigns each image a unique serial number and does not allow alteration, known as a Write Once, Read Many [times] or **WORM** (an acronym I think is unfortunate, given viruses of the same name). If the image is put in such a medium and logged in at the same time with a serial number with a date and deposited with the court, then there is verification that the picture is a certain way on a certain date. This is probably the easiest way to take care of the problem, as you can not manipulate the images after this date without it being rather obvious. But it still begs the question as to whether you would have manipulated it to begin with to match your theory. If you have avoided compression, used a high-quality photograph with a high density of pixels, and made an attempt to show that you did not alter the picture, then there is little else the court could require from you in making a good faith effort to produce accurate, authenticated pictures.

The same types of issues attend videotapes. Digital videocams are attractive because you can pull out a still photograph with little difficulty if you need one, and editing is far easier once any evidentiary issues are resolved. Videotaped depositions need to be considered very carefully. If a witness does not present well physically, it may be better to simply read in the testimony rather than to play the videotape.

Videotapes can be demonstrative evidence; they can also be substantive evidence. There are things that the jury cannot be shown in the courtroom that can be shown through a videotape. If you have a medical malpractice case, an educational video demonstrating what should have been done in a surgery can help the jury see what you are talking about. If you have a contract case that is based on the performance of an amusement park ride, it would be far more useful to videotape the ride from various vantage points (e.g., the rider's, the operator's, the mechanic's) to show what the parties are arguing about. What is "too fast" or "too jerky"? It is much better to show a jury in that context than to try to describe it, and this would probably be treated as substantive rather than demonstrative evidence.

Sommervold v. Grevlos, 518 N.W.2d 733 (S.D. 1994).

Jon Sommervold (Sommervold) and Dave Grevlos (Grevlos) each appeal from adverse judgments entered after a jury awarded each of them nothing on their claims against each other for negligence. We affirm. . . .

On June 16, 1986, some time between 9:50 P.M. and 10:05 P.M . . . Grevlos . . . was riding a bicycle west on Tomar Road in Sioux Falls. Sommervold . . . was riding a bicycle east on Tomar Road. Sommervold and Grevlos collided at the bottom of two steep . . . grades where Tomar Road curves slightly just west of Cliff Avenue. The cyclists' speeds were estimated from 28 to 40 miles per hour.

Grevlos had the light on his bicycle turned on while Sommervold did not have a bicycle light. The sun set at 9:10 P.M. and the amount of light was disputed . . . Apparently, neither saw the other until the collision occurred. The location of the collision was also disputed. Sommervold claimed that the collision occurred in his lane and Grevlos claimed that the collision occurred near the center of the road. The location of the center of the road was also in dispute because Tomar Road is not banked around the particular curve in question and cars have tended to drive closer to the south side of the curve with the result that the apparent center of the road is farther south than the geometric center of the road. The only eye-witness, Ian Moquist, a junior high school student, first told authorities that the collision occurred in the center of the road but testified at trial that the collision occurred in the south (Sommervold's) lane. It is undisputed that the riders collided right side to right side . . . When help arrived. Sommervold was laying in the middle of the road and Grevlos was sitting near the south curb.

Sommervold sustained injuries which required medical attention that cost approximately $3,600.00. Grevlos' right shoulder was seriously injured and could not be repaired. Eventually, Grevlos' shoulder was fused to his arm resulting in the practical loss of use of his right arm . . .

The appeals . . . relate to rulings on exhibits offered at the trial . . . We will deal with the evidentiary questions first. . . .

Grevlos offered Exhibit E to show how dark it was on the evening of the collision. The photo was taken at 8:54 P.M. on August 30, 1992, more than six years after the collision. Testimony was offered to show that the light at 8:54 P.M. on August 30th approximated the light at 10:00 P.M. on June 16th (the date of the collision in 1986).

Generally photographs are admissible if they accurately portray something which a witness is competent to describe in words or where they are helpful to aid the verbal description of objects and conditions and provided they are relevant to a material issue . . . [P]hotographs taken at or near the time of collision were held to be admissible. Even if relevant, the probative value of the photographs must outweigh their prejudicial effect. . . .

Exhibit E was taken more than six years after the collision. Although it was offered to show how much light was available, the time and date were different. Particularly, the sun was 20% farther south on the horizon on August 30th in contrast to its location on June 16th. The trees in the area had six additional years of growth to obscure light. Cloud cover may have been different. The trial court noted that the photo was darker than the testimony indicated that the conditions were on the date and at the time of the collision. No foundation was laid to show that the aperture on the camera lens approximated what the eye would see.[1] Significantly, no eye-witness testified that Exhibit E approximated the light actually available on the date and at the time of the collision. In fact, Exhibit E was offered to impeach eye-witness Ian Moquist's description of the lighting conditions. The foundation for Exhibit E was not sufficient. A judicial mind could reasonably reach this conclusion. Therefore, the trial court exercised proper discretion in excluding Exhibit E. . . .

Grevlos offered Exhibits F1 and F2 to show how far a light on a bicycle could be seen on the roadway in the vicinity of the collision under similar light at the approximate time of the collision. These video tapes were taken starting at 8:52 P.M. and concluding at 9:16 P.M. on August 28, 1992, more than six years after the collision. Testimony was offered to show that the light at 8:52 P.M. on August 28th was equivalent to the light on June 16th (the date of the collision in 1986). F1 was taken from Sommervold's vantage and F2 from Grevlos' vantage. The trial court found that F1 was not consistent with Sommervold's testimony and was much darker than the testimony and that F2 did not adequately recreate what a particular individual's eyes could or could not see.

Demonstrative evidence must be relevant, probative and nearly identical. . . . In *Jenkins* the court noted that conditions can seldom be duplicated exactly. However, when demonstrative evidence attempts to recreate an event rather than illustrate physical properties, it must be more nearly identical. . . . The impact of video reenactment is substantial. When people see something on television, they think it is real even when it is not.

Exhibits F1 and F2 were taken more than six years after the collision. The time and date were different. F1 was much darker than the testimony indicated. Twenty-three minutes passed during the filming which would make the end of the tape equivalent to 10:23 P.M. on the date of the collision, much later than any testimony (from 9:50 P.M. to 10:05 P.M.). The trial court found that the videos were not similar enough to the testimony and therefore their prejudice outweighed their probative value. A judicial mind could reasonably reach this conclusion. Therefore, the trial court exercised proper discretion in excluding the video tapes . . .

Grevlos offered a computer generated video animation to illustrate his accident reconstruction expert's testimony. The exhibit consisted of four components. Two video components were offered to show what Grevlos saw and what Grevlos would have seen if Sommervold would have had a light on his bicycle. One video component was offered to show that Sommervold should have seen Grevlos. The animation component was offered to "illustrate" Grevlos' expert's testimony.

SDCL 19-17-1(9) requires the proponent of computer generated evidence to describe the system and show that the program produced an accurate result. Then the animation must be relevant, probative and nearly identical. . . . The animation must fairly and accurately reflect the oral testimony of the witness and be an aid to the jury in understanding the issues . . .

The animation is not similar enough to be admissible. The animation assumes that both bicycles were travelling 25 miles per hour but the evidence varied from 28 to 40 miles per hour. The animation also depicted the light from a streetlight cast clearly in a circle rather than diffused in an ellipse as shown by the evidence. The animation showed the wrong location (off center and west of the actual location) and the injuries to the riders were inaccurately depicted as being left side to left side when they were actually right side to right side . . . The trial court found that the exhibit added nothing to the testimony and would be more prejudicial than probative because "a video recreation of an accident . . . becomes in the nature of testimony and it stands out in the jury's mind. So it emphasizes that evidence substantially over . . . ordinary . . . spoken testimony." A judicial mind could reasonably reach this conclusion. Therefore, the trial court exercised proper discretion in excluding the computer generated video animation. . . .

---

[1] Photographs are usually taken through a lens. The amount of light to which the film is exposed depends on the amount of light which the lens admits into the camera. If the aperture is opened, more light reaches the film; if the aperture is constricted, less light reaches the film. Consequently, in the same lighting conditions, photographs can be made lighter or darker by manipulating the aperture. In addition, similar results can be achieved during the process of printing photographs by adjusting the light introduced through the enlarger lens. Finally, with color photographs, color balance can be manipulated to enhance lighter or darker colors, giving the photographs a lighter or darker appearance. When a photograph is used to establish how light or dark the conditions were at a given date and time, the foundation must include some evidence that the camera and printing faithfully reproduced the conditions that actually existed.

Sommervold offered Exhibit 21 to show where the collision occurred. The photo was taken the day after the collision by an insurance adjustor who was with Arlo Sommervold, Jon's father. The photo shows a very faint black mark on the street together with a tape measure in the vicinity of the collision. The trial court granted Grevlos' motion in limine made at the beginning of the trial, denied admission of the photo and precluded Arlo Sommervold from testifying to the length, width, color or location of the mark on the road or that he picked pieces of a rubber-like substance from the mark. The trial court also denied Sommervold's offer of proof during the trial. The trial court held that the foundation was inadequate and that the probative value was outweighed by the prejudicial effect because no one could say how or when the mark was made or what made the mark. . . .

Photographs were admitted without proving the skid marks came from the plaintiff's automobile in *Zinda v. Pavloski,* 29 Wis. 2d 640, 139 N.W.2d 563, 566–67 (Wis. 1966). In *Zinda,* the trial court decided that the foundation was adequate. Here the trial court did not and observed: "There is no foundation that it came from either of the bicycles . . ." and "there is no direct evidence foundation that the mark was left by a bicycle at all let alone a bicycle involved in the accident." In *Zinda,* the Wisconsin Supreme Court determined that the skid marks were probative. Here the trial court did not, stating: "But those facts don't prove anything unless the inference is [sic] that black line and the rubber or rubber-like substance that was found on the black line was left by one of the bicycles left in the accident." Finally, the trial court found the prejudicial effect of the evidence outweighed any probative value: "It would be unfairly prejudicial to the defendant to allow the jury to speculate that that mark was left by one of the bicycles involved in the accident." A judicial mind could reasonably reach this conclusion. Therefore, the trial court exercised proper discretion in excluding the photograph of a black mark in the road and the accompanying testimony of Arlo Sommervold . . .

. . . We affirm.

Computer Animation

Computer **animation** is a wonderfully effective way to demonstrate a theory of events. Depending on the quality desired and the talent of the people in the law office, it may be produced in house or be farmed out. The problem with using outside contractors is that they may not understand the need for the animation to be strictly based on the facts given—that it can not be altered "to make a better flow." We'd like that, but we can't do that if the evidence is not there.

Unlike the other types of demonstrative evidence, though, animation is far more difficult to redact at the last minute if evidence upon which it relies is excluded. To be admissible, every fact represented in the animation must reflect some evidence in the record. So a piece of evidence that cost the client thousands of dollars may have to be tossed at the last minute because the court rules against one piece of evidence used as the basis of some part of the animation. Therefore, clients must be apprised of the risk as well as the benefit of using an animation in the courtroom. The following case demonstrates how the courts analyze computer animation.

In the *Sommervold* case, some careless mistakes were made, such as the left side to left side collision in the animation. As this case shows, care must be taken to imitate the circumstances of the incident underlying the suit as nearly as possible, or you run the risk of losing all the hard work and the client's investment.

Another problem is that animation may be classified as expert or demonstrative evidence, depending on the content. If the animation merely reflects the testimony of the expert, it probably will be deemed demonstrative evidence, which is sometimes described as **pedagogical** evidence—that used to teach the jury. If, however, it reflects the use and application of formulas that are not fully (and painfully) explained by the expert, the animation may be considered substantive evidence, often under the label of **computer simulation**, and treated under the rules governing the admission of expert evidence rather than the rules governing those of demonstrative evidence.

Bledsoe v. Salt River Valley Water Users' Ass'n, 880 P.2d 689 (Ariz. Ct. App. 1994).

Salt River Valley Water Users' Association (SRP) appeals from a jury verdict and judgment in favor of plaintiff Joseph Bledsoe, who was seriously injured while riding his bicycle on SRP's property in the early morning hours of April 5, 1989. . .

SRP delivers irrigation water in the Phoenix area through a system of canals and dozens of "laterals," which are smaller, secondary canals that carry water from the main canals to various delivery points. The banks of the canals and laterals have dirt access roads which SRP's employees use to operate and maintain the irrigation system. The roads are also used by the general public for nonmotorized activities, such as walking, jogging, biking, etc. Motorized use is prevented by gates of various types, including "cable" gates. A cable gate consists of a length of cable stretched across the road between two steel posts. Bledsoe was injured by this type of gate.

At the time Bledsoe was injured, he worked for the Phoenix Fire Department in its health center. His duties included designing and implementing physical fitness programs. To set a fitness example for the other firefighters, Bledsoe decided to ride his bicycle to work. The route he chose was primarily on city streets, but part of it included an SRP lateral road with which he was unfamiliar.

Bledsoe's first ride began before sunrise. It was dark and his bicycle had no headlight. After traveling 16 to 18 miles on city streets, he came to the SRP lateral. Bledsoe saw that the lateral road was blocked by a cable gate, but he was able to pass through a gap at one end of the gate and continue riding. Some distance later, Bledsoe came to a locked ranch gate. He dismounted, picked up his bicycle, carried it around the gate, and resumed riding. Shortly thereafter, he struck a second cable gate, was thrown over the front of his bicycle, and was rendered a quadriplegic. Attached to this second cable gate was a two-foot wide, orange-and-white reflector, which became the primary focus of SRP's defense. . . .

SRP argued to the jury in closing that, based on the testimony of its experts from experiments they conducted under conditions similar to those on the morning of the accident, Bledsoe could have seen the reflector and avoided the cable gate had his bicycle been equipped with a $19.95 headlight. Bledsoe's counsel challenged SRP's position at the close of his rebuttal argument, contending that SRP's experts "never took any pictures of this . . . they just told you that this was the case. So let's see." Counsel then requested permission to use the previously admitted reflector and headlight to refute SRP's experts. Specifically, counsel wanted to show that they were wrong in concluding (1) that Bledsoe could have seen the reflector from a distance of 66 feet or more, a safe stopping distance, and (2) that he could have seen the reflector even if the headlight were not shining directly on it because the headlight had a 12-foot cone of light. After SRP's objection was overruled, Bledsoe's counsel proceeded to make the following argument to the jury while shining the headlight on and off the reflector in a partially darkened courtroom at a distance of 40 feet:

> Now, that's directly on it. Move it off and what do you see, and I want you to also recognize the fact that a bike is going to be going down a road like this, but where is the 12 foot [cone of light]? Which leads us to the last question, would the light have made a difference?
>
> I submit to you that it would not have made a difference. That's 40 feet. [SRP's experts] are talking about 100 feet. They were talking about 66 feet. They were talking about all sorts of distances that you can see this marvelous cone of light.
>
> This 19.95 marvel that Joe Bledsoe, if he had it on his bike would have avoided the accident. There is no cone of light that's available to Joe if he had it on his bike, if he was not directly on it and that's why they took all the photographs they took with the lights shined directly on the reflectorized sign.
>
> I think that weighs upon the evidence. Your verdict should clearly be for Joe.

SRP contends that it was error to permit this courtroom experiment because it differed substantially from SRP's own experiments in three respects: the headlight batteries were two years old, the courtroom was only partially darkened, and the jurors' eyes did not have time to adjust to the darkness. Bledsoe counters that these differences affect merely the weight the in-court experiment should be given, not its admissibility . . . in which we stated:

> Prior to the reception of evidence based on out-of-court experiments, it must ordinarily be shown that the experiments were conducted under substantially similar conditions to those prevailing during the occurrence in controversy. The conditions need not be identical and minor variations in conditions go to the weight rather than the admissibility. . . .

Because *Wagner* concerned the admissibility of an expert's testimony about his own out-of-court experiments, it is plainly distinguishable from this case and not controlling. Here, the experiment was conducted by counsel, not an expert, and we believe the variations were major, not minor . . .

Moreover, it is apparent from the circumstances that counsel was attempting to replicate SRP's out-of-court experiments rather than simply trying to illustrate the headlight's traits or characteristics. The distinction is important because replications require a greater degree of similarity than demonstrations . . .

Finally, because the experiment was conducted during counsel's rebuttal argument, the risk of misleading the jury was substantial. As SRP points out, the experiment "would not face cross-examination, explanation by the opposing experts, or even comments of opposing counsel." . . .

For the foregoing reasons, we hold that the trial court erred in permitting Bledsoe's counsel to conduct the in-court headlight experiment during rebuttal argument under conditions substantially different from the out-of-court experiments SRP's experts conducted . . . We also hold that the court erred in permitting Bledsoe's counsel to show the jury a videotaped computer simulation (VCS) of the accident during closing argument. Prior to trial, SRP moved in limine to preclude Bledsoe's use of the VCS, arguing that it would be unsupported by the evidence or by the testimony of the computer expert who prepared it because Bledsoe would not be calling him as a witness. Bledsoe countered that the expert's testimony was unnecessary because the VCS would not be offered in evidence, but used "merely for demonstrative purposes" in Bledsoe's closing argument to show counsel's "version of what happened." The trial court viewed the VCS and reserved its ruling, stating: "I've got to hear what comes in at the trial. I can't sit here and prejudge everything." After the evidentiary phase of the trial, the court ruled as follows:

> As to everything that is depicted in the videotape, [Bledsoe's counsel] could get up and draw it and this is just a more sophisticated way of presenting his theory as to how the accident happened.
>
> The fact that there's no foundation as [to] how it was prepared is completely immaterial.

We disagree.

The VCS is not, as Bledsoe contends, "the same as a chart or a diagram" drawn by counsel during closing argument. Such charts or diagrams are what one evidence treatise calls pedagogical devices: "Courts have permitted the use of [pedagogical devices] as an aid to the fact-finder in cases involving complicated or voluminous evidence . . . [because they] are particularly useful in showing time sequences, tying together much testimony and exhibits to show chronological and personal relationships.". . . Having viewed the VCS ourselves, we conclude that it is not a pedagogical device. The VCS depicts a computer expert's opinion of, among other things, how the accident happened, the location of lighted and darkened areas at the time, and the effect of alternate or additional lighting. Bledsoe was thus required to lay the appropriate foundation for those opinions, and SRP was entitled to cross-examine the expert about them . . . Without requiring such foundation and permitting the opportunity for cross-examination, the trial court erroneously "admitted" the VCS under the guise of closing argument.

. . . In *Szeliga*, the jury saw two films showing how an automobile accident had happened, and in *Datskow*, it saw a VCS showing how an aircraft accident had happened. Both cases are inapposite because in both, unlike the case at bar, the experts testified and were subject to cross-examination. In *Szeliga*, the court conducted extensive voir dire on the tests depicted before the films were shown to the jury and the "cross-examination of [the] expert was thorough and comprehensive." . . . In *Datskow*, the expert testified "that he had worked with an animator 'to reconstruct a Beechcraft Debonair,' and that 'the purpose of [the VCS] is to represent what I have reconstructed happened to this aircraft in the final few moments of flight.'" . . .

Accordingly, we hold that although the evidentiary use of computer simulations is generally permissible . . . their use is dependent on satisfying the usual foundational requirements for other demonstrative evidence . . . At a minimum, the proponent must show that the computer simulation fairly and accurately depicts what it represents, whether through the computer expert who prepared it or some other witness who is qualified to so testify, and the opposing party must be afforded an opportunity for cross-examination. In some instances, the proponent may also be required to show that:

> (1) the computer is functioning properly; (2) the input and underlying equations are sufficiently complete and accurate (and disclosed to the opposing party, so that they may challenge them); and
> (3) the program is generally accepted by the appropriate community of scientists.

. . . In this case, because Bledsoe elected not to satisfy even the minimal foundational requirements for the VCS, the trial court erred in allowing it to be shown to the jury. . . .

Bledsoe contends, however, that reversal is not required because the trial court's rulings were not an abuse of discretion or prejudicial to SRP. We disagree.

The trial court has great discretion in conducting a trial . . . That discretion will not be disturbed on appeal unless abused. . . Abuse occurs when the discretion is "exercised on untenable grounds, or for untenable reasons." . . . That abuse occurred here because, as discussed previously, the trial court's rulings are legally untenable.

Bledsoe nevertheless argues that reversal is not required under the standard of appellate review set forth [by] the supreme court['s] four factors for determining whether the trial court has abused its discretion. In this case, the first factor is present, that is, "there has been an error of law committed in the process of reaching the discretionary conclusion." . . .

The presence of that factor alone, however, does not end our inquiry. We must further determine whether the error influenced the verdict. "Reversal will be required only when there has been error or misconduct and it appears probable that the misconduct 'actually influenced the verdict.' ". . . Ordinarily, the determination whether the verdict was so influenced is made initially by the trial court, and when made, will not be reversed on appeal unless clearly erroneous. . . In this case, however, the record is silent regarding such a factual finding by the trial court and, thus, we must determine for ourselves whether its erroneous rulings influenced the verdict. To make that determination, we must decide "whether there is a reasonable probability a different verdict might have been reached if the error[s] had not occurred.". . .

As noted earlier, the crux of SRP's defense was that Bledsoe could have avoided the accident with the use of an inexpensive bicycle headlight. SRP's counsel thus argued to the jury in closing that Bledsoe was totally at fault for his own injuries. The jury, however, only found him 40 percent at fault. We believe that it is reasonably probable that a different verdict might have been reached had Bledsoe's counsel not been allowed to conduct his headlight experiment during rebuttal argument. But for this improper courtroom experiment, SRP's experiments were essentially unchallenged. Bledsoe's experts had conducted no headlight experiments of their own and could not say whether a headlight would have helped or not. Moreover, the courtroom experiment and accompanying argument came at the very end of the case just before the jury retired to deliberate.

We also believe that the jury's verdict might have been influenced by the improper showing of the VCS during Bledsoe's closing argument. A respected evidence treatise comments as follows regarding photographs and videotapes that represent such a staged reproduction of the facts:

> Here the extreme vividness and verisimilitude of pictorial evidence is truly a two-edged sword. For not only is the danger that the jury may confuse art with reality particularly great, but the impressions generated by the evidence may prove particularly difficult to limit. . . .

. . . Even Bledsoe's counsel recognized the persuasive impact of the VCS, explaining to the jury: "The reason why we did this was . . . because sometimes just looking at a simple little thing like a tape could make something clear, even more clear than it already is.". . . McCormick could not agree more: "Since 'seeing is believing,' and demonstrative evidence appeals directly to the senses of the trier of fact, it is today universally felt that this kind of evidence possesses an immediacy and reality which endow it with particularly persuasive effect.". . .

For the foregoing reasons, we reverse.

Courtroom experiments are dangerous, as you might expect. (Remember O.J. and the glove?) If a witness, usually an expert, or you as assistant to your attorney, are going to conduct one, make sure you have practiced it numerous times before and are absolutely sure it won't backfire in the courtroom. A courtroom experiment that ends up demonstrating the opposing party's position is not just damaging, it is almost always fatal.

CHAPTER SUMMARY

Physical and demonstrative evidence is compelling for jurors. Tangible, three-dimensional "stuff" helps jurors visualize the case brought before them. Asking each witness about the existence of physical evidence is important, and you must preserve any physical evidence in your care or run the risk of answering for spoliation. Plans for demonstrative evidence need to be made in advance so that the proper materials can be assembled. Where rules require exhibit exchanges, you need to have them ready well in advance. Be flexible in your use of demonstrative evidence, for admissibility determinations may affect what will be usable. Computer animation is a wonderful tool, but not easily modified, and clients must be informed of the possible loss of investment. When used by experts, animation can become computer simulation, which may be subject to *Daubert* analysis. Used properly, demonstrative and physical evidence can be the most persuasive evidence placed before the jury, as it aids both in recollection and in integration and understanding of your story.

FOR FURTHER READING

Margaret A. Berger, *Laboratory Error Seen Through the Lens of Science and Policy*, 30 U.C. Davis L. Rev. 1081 (1997).

Karen D. Butera, *Seeing Is Believing: A Practitioner's Guide to the Admissibility of Demonstrative Computer Evidence*, 46 Clev. St. L. Rev. 511 (1998).

Comment, Emilia A. Quesada, *Summarizing Prior Witness Testimony: Admissible Evidence, Pedagogical Device, or Violation of the Federal Rules of Evidence?*, 24 Fla. St. U.L. Rev. 161 (1996).

Kristin L. Fulcher, *The Jury as Witness: Forensic Computer Animation Transports Jurors to the Scene of a Crime or Automobile Accident*, 22 Dayton L. Rev. 55 (1996).

Fred Galves, *Where the Not-So-Wild Things Are: Computers in the Courtroom, the Federal Rules of Evidence, and the Need for Institutional Reform and More Judicial Acceptance*, 13 Harv. J. Law & Tech. 161 (2000).

Gregory T. Jones, *Lex, Lies & Videotape*, 18 U. Ark. Little Rock L.J. 613 (1996).

Note, Mario Borelli, *The Computer as Advocate: An Approach to Computer-Generated Displays in the Courtroom*, 71 Ind. L.J. 439 (1996).

Note, Elan E. Weinreb, *"Counselor, Proceed with Caution": The Use of Integrated Evidence Presentation Systems and Computer-Generated Evidence in the Courtroom*, 23 Cardozo L. Rev. 393 (2001).

Note, Jill Witkowski, *Can Juries Really Believe What They See? New Foundational Requirements for the Authentication of Digital Images*, 10 Wash. U. J.L. & Pol'y 267 (2002).

CHAPTER REVIEW

KEY TERMS

abate/abatement	homeowners' insurance	products liability
abuse of direction	immediacy	presumption
animation	inflammatory	real evidence
bar graph	line graph	redact
closing arguments	manufacturing defect	renters' coverage
commercial policy	Motion in Limine	smoking gun
comp carrier	Opticon	substantive evidence
compressed	organizational chart	summation
computer simulation	partial quadriplegic	video out card
courtroom experiment	pedagogical	worker's compensation
demonstrative evidence	pie chart	WORM
flow chart	pixels	
form board	PowerPoint	

FILL IN THE BLANKS

1. A computer storage medium that assigns serial numbers to files and does not allow overwriting is referred to by the unfortunate acronym of WORM, meaning _____.

2. The insurance company that covers employees during the course and scope of their employment is a(n) _____.

3. When image files are rewritten in such a way to make the data smaller, it is called _____.

4. Most evidentiary decisions made by the trial judge are reviewed under a(n) _____ standard, which gives the trial judge wide latitude in making those determinations.

5. A computer _____ is a re-creation used by an expert that usually involves mathematical formulas to get the results.

6. A(n) _____ card is used in a computer to make it compatible to project on video screens.

7. When an action is held in _____, it is temporarily put on hold.

8. A dangerous but effective form of demonstrative evidence is the _____, in which the party tries to re-create a part of the event in front of the jury.

9. Several computer programs can be useful in preparing demonstrative evidence, including _____ by Dataflight for processing and marking up documents and _____ by Microsoft for presentation.

10. A presentation used for teaching purposes is referred to as _____.

11. The squares that make up a digital picture are called _____.

12. A rule of evidence that requires the jury to find a certain fact unless it is overcome by at least a preponderance of the evidence is called a(n) _____.

13. A(n) _____ is a piece of evidence that is extremely damaging, as the image suggests; _____ evidence is that which would upset the jury to the extent that it would no longer be objective.

14. Editing out information that is privileged or otherwise cannot be released to the jury is the process of _____.

WEB WORK

1. Multimedia's Flash Shockwave is an animation program for the Web that is relatively easy to learn with an amazing range of outcomes. Look at the competition level for what the program is capable of at www.flashforward2004.com and click on the link for past winners to see the various categories and what won. Can you see any applications for demonstrative evidence?

2. The home for Flash is at www.macromedia.com. The Web site has tutorials and samples for developers. Do you think it is something you could learn? Or would you want to leave it to professionals?

3. One of the newer technologies for computer projections is the interactive computer whiteboard. Surf the Web to find out what it is, and compare it in terms of options and price to other forms of computer projection technology.

4. For a graphic illustration of what can happen in compression of files, check out what happened to the FBI's fingerprint files during attempts to compress them and what the FBI Fingerprint Impression Image Compression Standard is all about at http://www.c3.lanl.gov/~brislawn/FBI/FBI.html.

5. Designer-info.com at http://www.designer-info.com/ has articles and information about a wide range of computer graphics related issues, including bitmap standards. If you look around the page, you'll find a link to the articles archive. Click on it. What articles might be useful to you?

WORKING THE BRAIN

1. As a practical matter, how helpful is the evidentiary presumption as a cure for spoliation of evidence? Wouldn't this be something that the attorney would argue anyway and that the jury would think about without a jury instruction? Or do you think there is something significant to the jury instruction? Pick a position on the matter and make an argument for or against this as a remedy.

2. Look through the cases in this chapter. How many of them refer to the abuse of discretion standard? How often do the appellate courts decide that the trial court made the wrong decision? When the decision is against the trial court, what is the appellate court's explanation?

3. Evaluate the issues raised in authenticating digital images. Do you think there is a substantial enough difference between digital images to warrant additional safeguards, or do you think this is all much ado about nothing? Explain and defend your position.

4. Review the cases addressing the difference between computer simulation, computer animation, and courtroom experiments. Make a chart comparing and contrasting the distinctions in standards for each, to the extent they exist.

5. Can you articulate the difference between substantive and demonstrative photographic or video evidence? Try to explain the difference to someone who has never been tainted by introduction to the law or legal concepts—your frequent job as the translator of legalese.

PUTTING IT TO WORK

1. What physical evidence would you bring to the court in the *Haus* case as the plaintiff? As the defendant? Who would have it? Check your Department of Motor Vehicles for how to find salvage titles and make a list of your local salvage yards.

2. What other charts would you make for the *Haus* case? Download the free version of SmartDraw at www. smartdraw.com and prepare an appropriate demonstrative chart or illustration.

3. What was your story for the *Haus* case? Does this demonstrative evidence support your story? Review all your investigation plan documents and make sure you have everything up to date, including the various exhibits you've just prepared.

4. How do you redact something without making it, well, ugly? Often the traditional solution has been to simply take a big, fat black magic marker to it—if you make FOIA requests, you'll become very familiar with the process. Can you come up with creative ways to do the same thing?

WITNESS PREPARATION

"Short words are best and the old words when short are best of all."

—*Sir Winston S. Churchill (1952)*

"Not every truth is better for showing its face undisguised; and often silence is the wisest thing for a man to heed."

—*Heraclitus (c. 540-489 B.C.E)*

"I think the necessity of being ready increases. Look to it."

—*Abraham Lincoln (1861)*

"Airing one's dirty linen never makes for a masterpiece."

—*François Truffaut (1972)*

INTRODUCTION

If a case is not settled, witnesses will have to testify, whether by deposition, at trial, or both. Whether the witness is a client, a fact witness, or an expert, preparation is necessary. I remember being perplexed when one lawyer said he was off to "woodshed a client." I found that was one way of describing witness preparation; the idea is that you take the witness out to the woodshed and whip him into shape. Whether you call it **woodshedding**, **horseshedding**, coaching, preparing, or something else, it's still a necessary step in the process.

Witness preparation may be done by the attorney or the paralegal; it depends on the firm, the case, the particular witness, the budget, the client's preferences, and other such factors. Testifying is a scary experience, even for fact witnesses whose testimony is not likely to generate much in the way of attack by any of the attorneys.

ETHICAL ISSUES

Witness preparation should not be done unethically. **Coaching** is a term used to describe unethical preparation, although it is sometimes a neutral term; *preparation* is the most neutral term. It is one thing to assist a client or witness in presenting himself well; it is something else again to suggest in any way that the witness change his story. The ethical rules are quite clear.

A lawyer shall not knowingly offer evidence that the lawyer knows to be false. If a lawyer, the lawyer's client, or a witness called by the lawyer, has offered material evidence and the lawyer comes to know of its falsity, the lawyer shall take reasonable remedial measures, including, if necessary, disclosure to the tribunal. . .

A lawyer shall not:

b. falsify evidence, counsel or assist a witness to testify falsely, or offer an inducement to a witness that is prohibited by law;

. . .

f. request a person other than a client to refrain from voluntarily giving relevant information to another party unless:

   1. the person is a relative or an employee or other agent of a client; and

   2. the lawyer reasonably believes that the person's interests will not be adversely affected by refraining from giving such information.

Model Code Prof'l Cond. R. 3.3(a)(3), 3.4.

Therefore, there is no excuse for any lawyer or his staff to suggest, explicitly or implicitly, that a witness falsify anything. The point of witness preparation is just that: preparation. Usually time has passed, so the witness may need her memory refreshed. However, it needs to be *her* memory, not the memory of others. You must be very careful what you use to help her remember or she may substitute a false memory for a real one. Further, coaching witnesses can subject you to various sanctions, as the following case illustrates. To orient you a little to the procedural oddness in this case, the appellants are requesting extraordinary relief, called a **writ of mandamus** in most places, but a **prohibition** in Ohio (and presumably other states). Notice that the defendant is the judge; this is a big clue that you're looking at an appeal of a judge's decision before the case is over. (The original party to the case who benefited from the ruling is often called the **real party in interest.** In the following case, O.K.I. Supply Co. and Raymark Industries, Inc. are the real parties in interest.) The appellate court didn't think if was necessary to decide this case before trial, so it never gets around to deciding whether the judge made an acceptable decision. However, the discussion about the "extensive jurisdiction" of the trial court under those circumstances would not make me optimistic about the plaintiff's chances of winning that argument. The case is filed as a new case in the appellate court; that's why there's a discussion of **original jurisdiction.** What the appellants are seeking is an order from an appellate court before the case even goes to trial to avoid the effects of the judge's ruling. In many jurisdictions, if not most, there must be some sort of irreparable harm before the appellate courts will intervene before the matter has some sort of final, appealable order. This sort of pre-trial appeal is referred to as **interlocutory,** and appellate courts just don't like them, as this case also demonstrates.

Abner v. Elliott, 706 N.E.2d 765 (Ohio 1999) (per curiam).

Appellants, Donald Lee Abner and over eight hundred other persons, are workers and their representatives who filed actions in the Butler County Court of Common Pleas against various manufacturers, suppliers, installers, and distributors of products containing asbestos. Appellants claimed that they had been injured through exposure to asbestos. Respondent, Judge George Elliott, was assigned to hear all claims pending in these cases. Judge Elliott's orders governing discovery in any single case were binding in the proceedings in all of the cases.

In May 1997, Judge Elliott granted the motion of defendant O.K.I. Supply Co. for a protective order concerning appellants' attorneys' conduct during depositions in the asbestos cases. Among other things, Judge Elliott ordered that in future depositions in the asbestos litigation, counsel would refrain from making speaking objections or attempting to suggest answers or otherwise coach witnesses and that counsel would not confer with witnesses during depositions except to decide whether to assert a privilege.

In August 1997, a document entitled "Preparing for Your Deposition/Attorney Work Product" authored by Baron & Budd, P.C., a law firm representing appellants in the Butler County asbestos litigation, was disclosed during the deposition of a plaintiff represented by Baron & Budd in unrelated asbestos litigation in Texas. The document was purported to advise plaintiffs in asbestos personal-injury cases to testify in a manner that would not necessarily be consistent with the truth.

Defendant Raymark Industries, Inc. subsequently filed a motion to compel discovery, for a protective order, and for other relief based on its contention that the depositions in the Butler County asbestos litigation established that the plaintiffs had been improperly coached by either the same preparation document used by Baron & Budd in Texas or substantially similar advice. Judge Elliott held a hearing on Raymark's motion at which appellants' counsel conceded that some aspects of the Texas document were shocking and surprising and that the document should never have been used "in the first place." But appellants claimed that neither the Texas document nor anything similar had been used in the Butler County cases.

In September 1997, following the hearing, the court granted Raymark's motion in part and ordered the following:

1. Defendants may inquire into and obtain discovery respecting allegedly improper preparation or coaching of witnesses by plaintiffs' counsel, and, or plaintiffs' counsel's agents, representatives and employees. . . .

Despite Judge Elliott's September and October 1997 orders, appellants did not provide the defendants in the asbestos cases with any witness preparation documents . . .

Defendant North American Refractories Company filed a motion for sanctions. In December 1997, after a hearing, Judge Elliott issued an order in which he found that the Texas deposition preparation document constituted evidence of improper coaching of prospective deponents, that it was reasonable to infer that similar deposition materials had been used to coach clients and witnesses in asbestos litigation in Butler County that had been filed by the same law firm that prepared the Texas document, that the court thereby issued its September and October 1997 discovery orders, and that appellants had not complied with those orders. Judge Elliott consequently ordered the following:

". . . At the trial of this case . . . , the jury will be instructed to . . . consider the following as being conclusively proved facts. . . . :

3. During each of those meetings [of the plaintiff and his attorneys and paralegals the legal team] either gave to or showed plaintiff . . . certain lists, photographs, or other items which disclosed the product name, manufacturer name, product type, product description, packaging description, location of use, time of use, and typical trade or job of the Armco workers who used numerous products manufactured by defendants. . .

Before, during, or immediately after the disclosure of that information to plaintiff and, or, the coworkers, plaintiff's attorneys informed plaintiff . . . that it would be to his advantage . . . to name as many of the defendants' products as possible during their depositions.

"The foregoing instruction shall also be given to the jury in any other asbestos-related personal injury action in this county wherein court-ordered discovery of improper witness coaching techniques either has been or will be prevented by the objections of plaintiffs' counsel."

In February 1998 . . . appellants filed a complaint in the court of appeals for a writ of prohibition to prevent Judge Elliott from enforcing any of his discovery orders in the asbestos litigation. . .

. . . Appellants claim that dismissal was improper because Judge Elliott exercised unauthorized judicial power by ordering disclosure of privileged materials and issuing sanctions without first conducting an *in camera* inspection of the privileged matters. . . .

. . . Trial courts also have extensive jurisdiction over discovery, including inherent authority to direct an *in camera* inspection of alleged privileged materials and to impose sanctions for failure to comply with discovery orders, so a writ of prohibition will not generally issue to challenge these orders. . . .

. . . [A]ppellants have an adequate remedy by appeal to resolve any alleged error by Judge Elliott. . . In other words, an appeal from the discovery orders challenged by appellants provides an adequate legal remedy because if appellants are victorious on appeal, a new trial would remedy any potential harm to them from Judge Elliott's orders. The attorney-client privilege invoked here is peculiarly related to the underlying asbestos litigation. . . .

. . . Because the work-product exemption protects materials that are peculiarly related to litigation, any harm that might result from the disclosure of those materials will likewise be related to litigation. An appellate court review of such litigation will necessarily be able to provide relief from the erroneous disclosure of work-product materials. . .

Based on the foregoing, the court of appeals properly dismissed appellants' prohibition action pursuant to Civ.R. 12(B)(6). Accordingly, we affirm the judgment of the court of appeals.

Judgment affirmed.

If your witness is nervous about testifying or speaking in public, or about being among all those "educated people," she may need some coaching (in the neutral, not unethical sense) in terms of how to present herself in a formal situation. Given the importance of nonverbal cues, if she has some nervous tics, she'll need feedback on them and help in overcoming them. She may need help in overcoming the fear of testifying so that her anxiety doesn't make her appear untrustworthy. She needs to know what to expect, what the rules of the game are, and what the other side will try to do. None of these preparatory acts changes the facts; it simply affects presentation. However, if you are altering someone's behavior to make an untrustworthy witness seem trustworthy, is that ethical? There is some debate among the courts and among attorneys on that issue. When change simply involves appearance, there seems to be less inclination to call it unethical, even though those changes can be as significant to the outcome of the case as altering the content of witness testimony.

The ethical considerations become even more difficult when the witness is the client. As discussed before in the context of Rambo litigation, on the one hand, you have a duty to do the best job possible for the client. On the other hand, you have a duty of fairness to your opponent and a duty of honesty to the court. This is a much more subtle area, where it is easy to nudge clients into unethical behavior unintentionally if you do not keep your eyes open to the possibilities during the preparation process.

"The Lawyer and the Leopard's Spots"
by Ruth A. Kollman

Sex, lies and audiotapes. Presidential advisers and asbestos. Special prosecutors. Rogue paralegals. What do these very different subjects have in common besides grand juries? They each share a common genesis: the role of lawyers in witness preparation.

Rules of procedure and evidence dictate trial strategy and are familiar tools to lawyers. However, another set of rules also influences trial strategy—the rules of ethical conduct. In particular, ethical rules affect a major area of concern to trial counsel: witness preparation.

An apocryphal anecdote has a prominent trial attorney stressing the importance of direct examination to a group of young lawyers: "It is vital that the client get on the stand and tell your story." The lawyer then pauses for a moment, smiling slyly, and amends, "I mean, his story." The laughter that always follows illuminates the attitude trial lawyers take toward witness preparation.

Rule 3.03 of the Texas Disciplinary Rules of Professional Conduct prohibits a lawyer from offering or using false evidence. Rule 3.04 prohibits a lawyer from counseling a witness to testify falsely. Both of these disciplinary rules govern a lawyer's role in witness preparation, an ethical concern that is currently receiving statewide and national attention.

OFFERING OR USING FALSE EVIDENCE

Current headlines show that lawyers are having more and more difficulty recognizing when witness preparation produces false evidence. Most lawyers recognize an out-and-out lie as perjury. However, a more subtle form of perjury also occurs. A witness may commit perjury by swearing to a matter about which the witness consciously has no knowledge. If the witness is conscious of not having the knowledge required to testify about the subject and testifies anyway, the witness commits perjury. And the lawyer who provides the information with the intent that the witness testify about it and then presents the testimony has offered or used false evidence.

The catch, of course, comes in deciding whether an advocate merely aggressively prepares a witness or whether that aggressive behavior crosses the line into urging the witness to commit perjury. "It is one thing to ask a witness to swear to facts which are knowingly false. It is another thing, in an arms-length interview with a witness, for an attorney to attempt to persuade her, even aggressively, that her initial version of a certain fact situation is not complete or accurate." *Resolution Trust Corp. v. Bright*, 6 F.3d 336, 341 (5th Cir. 1993).

Surprisingly, because of a gap in the Texas Penal Code, the crime of "suborning perjury" (as that term is often used in the media to describe what a lawyer does in counseling a witness to commit perjury) is no longer an offense in Texas. Instead, since 1974, Texas has applied the criminal law of "parties" and "criminal conspiracy." Both make an actor criminally responsible for the conduct of others under certain circumstances. Case law on application of these criminal complicity concepts in Texas to lawyers who counsel witnesses to commit perjury is virtually nonexistent. On the other hand, Rule 3.04 directly prohibits a lawyer from counseling a witness to testify falsely. In its more subtle application as discussed above, a lawyer counsels a witness to testify falsely if the lawyer provides information to the witness about which the lawyer knows the witness has no independent knowledge or recollection, intending the witness to testify as if having personal knowledge.

THE LAWYER'S ROLE

A witness' function is to relate facts. A lawyer's job is to help the witness relate those facts within the limitations of the rules of evidence. Just how much help is permissible? Consider the following scenarios:

Lawyer takes witness to courtroom to familiarize witness with surroundings;

Lawyer advises witness to observe other trials;

Lawyer discusses testimony with witness in advance of trial;

Lawyer causes witness to improve personal appearance;

Lawyer coaches witness on diction and elocution;

Lawyer instructs witness on mannerisms jury equates with truthfulness; or

Lawyer instructs witness on material aspects of testimony.

This paradigm describes standard trial preparation tactics. The conduct is overtly taught in trial skills literature. But note the activity comes closer and closer to altering the truthfulness of the testimony of the witness in each cell of the paradigm.

Trial lawyers believe they can influence the outcome of a trial by changing a witness' spots. Trial lawyers even believe effective advocacy requires them to do so. However, the truth-finding nature of the judicial process and lawyers' roles as officers of the court within that process demand careful evaluation of the level of advocacy they reach. "An attorney owes his first duty to the court. He assumed his obligations toward it before he ever had a client. His oath requires him to be absolutely honest even though his client's interests may seem to require a contrary course. The [lawyer] cannot serve two masters and the one [he has] undertaken to serve primarily is the court." *In re Integration of Nebraska State Bar Association*, 133 Neb. 283, 289, 275 N.W. 265, 268 (1937). The adversarial system is designed to cover a multitude of sins. Alteration of the truth is not one of them.

The burden is on the lawyer to stop witness preparation short of counseling the client to commit perjury. How many clients will refuse to testify about information the lawyer provides? Will any client ever say, "Hold it, I don't know anything about that, I can't testify about that." We are the gatekeepers of truth. It is not a job to be taken lightly.

I am deeply disturbed, not entertained, by recent media reports of lawyers' dubious advocacy. Questionable witness preparation, even if it only flirts with the edges of permissible advocacy without actually stealing a kiss, demeans all lawyers. On a practical note, controversial witness preparation discredits all lawyers in front of the very jurors whose opinions we seek to influence, creating ever more skeptical audiences for our efforts.

It comes as no surprise that the rules of ethics prohibit a lawyer from offering or using false evidence. Less apparent is the careful consideration a trial lawyer must give to the ethics of changing our leopards' spots when preparing witnesses for trial. This is particularly the case when providing information to the witness that the witness does not already know or cannot remember. Zealous advocacy is not always ethical advocacy. Only by careful attention to the rules of ethics can lawyers appreciate the difference.

(continued)

EVIDENTIARY ISSUES

When preparing a witness, be careful of what you tell him and double check what he writes down. Although written statements are subject to an objection on the basis of hearsay, there is a hearsay exception covering any notes a witness relies on to testify.

A memorandum or record concerning a matter about which a witness once had knowledge but now has insufficient recollection to enable the witness to testify fully and accurately, shown to have been made or adopted by the witness when the matter was fresh in the witness' memory and to reflect that knowledge correctly. If admitted, the memorandum or record may be read into evidence but may not itself be received as an exhibit unless offered by an adverse party.

Fed. R. Evid. 803(5).

If the witness has such a document, such as notes or an earlier statement, that's fine. But if the witness takes notes on the record about what you say to him, those actions could potentially cause a problem:

Q: What is the document you're referring to there?

A: It's a statement I gave just after the accident. [Because he's been well-prepared, he doesn't mention that it was given to an insurance adjuster, which would put him in violation of the motion in limine.]

Q: May I look at it?

A: [after a glance at the attorney, who nods] Sure.

Q: [cocking his head quizzically] I don't remember the copy I have having these notes in the margins. Can you explain these to me?

A: Oh, those are the notes I took when the paralegal was telling me what to say. [He tries to look around the attorney, who also turns his head, towards the sound of a loud thud.]

Q: What was that?

Judge: I believe that was the aforementioned paralegal.

Although the content may be excluded on the basis of attorney work product, the damage is done. It looks as though the witness, who may have even been a neutral witness who happened to be favorable to the paralegal's client, has been "told what to say," rather than just telling the truth. No matter how an attorney tries to **rehabilitate** the witness by going back and asking, "But you really are just telling what you know and not what we tell you?" it won't work. It will just be a matter of whether the personality of the witness outweighs the damage of that statement. So watch what the witness writes on any documents he plans to take to the stand with him.

PREPARING WITNESSES TO TESTIFY

Witness preparation is one of the hardest things to get used to doing. You may have to tell people you barely know some fairly harsh things in an inoffensive way that will encourage their cooperation. To do so, you need to think very carefully about what you are going to say and how to approach it. Remember what you may have heard as a child, "It's not what you say, it's how you say it."

Most people don't take criticism well, even when it's meant for their benefit. By the time you are preparing a witness, usually a client (but not always), you have developed some rapport, so she should know that you have her best interests in mind. Even so, you may push some buttons when you start telling a witness or client that:

- He needs to improve his personal hygiene because he either has a bad odor or looks unkempt.
- She needs to wear longer skirts, more modest blouses, looser-fitting jeans.
- He needs to trim his hair, beard, or mustache.
- She needs to be less flirty.
- He needs to get rid of the saggy pants.
- She needs to wear less makeup.
- He needs to look less sullen.
- She needs to sit up straight.
- He needs to quit biting is nails.
- She needs to keep her hand away from her face.
- He needs to keep his fingers out of his mouth, ears, nose, armpits, or any other orifice.
- She needs to clean and trim her fingernails.
- He needs to brush his teeth.
- She needs to wear something other than that godawful bullet-proof polyester.
- He needs to stop fidgeting so much.
- She needs to watch her inappropriate or nervous laughter.
- He needs to stop the heavy sighs.
- She needs to watch her cursing anywhere within earshot of anyone else associated with the case.
- He needs to talk more quietly.

These little tidbits can be hard on a person's ego. As the authors of *Difficult Conversations* observe, these sorts of discussions can provoke **identity issues**: Am I a good person? Am I a competent person? You must frame the discussion in such a way as to focus on behaviors while affirming the person's identity. How do you do that?

Start by discussing the context. If you are preparing someone for trial, the preparation will be more intensive. If for deposition, then appearances generally don't matter; videotaped depositions are usually only for experts, who usually don't have appearance problems. (Even if they do, good luck convincing them. Experts take the independent in "independent contractor" very seriously.) You may have an exception that you will need to apply these principles to, but for the most part, the nastiest preparations are for trial.

At any rate, in trial preparation, you can explain that the jury will not have time to get to know the "real you" of the witness. Jurors can't talk to the witness directly or interact with her; therefore, they tend to make judgments based on superficialities. You might toll the witness, "Although you don't have to be a movie star, you have to make sure that there's nothing to distract the jury from seeing *you*, and it's my job to find the smallest thing that might possibly bother the jury. It may not bother them, but we don't want to take chances. It doesn't really mean anything about what you're going to say, or what kind of person you are, but people are so used to watching television and movies these days that they expect the witnesses in a trial to be like actors in one." Something along those lines tells the witness that he is okay the way he is, that you are aware this is a surface judgment, that it is not a judgment about him as a person, and that you are there to help. You still may have some problems from some witnesses, but an approach like this usually smoothes most feathers.

In the context of a deposition, you play it a little differently. You will still want your client, in particular, to clean up a bit, whether physically or figuratively. The approach would be similar, except instead of needing to play to the jury, you will need to explain that in addition to obtaining information, the lawyer will be assessing how the jury will evaluate the client's credibility and that the assessment will affect the possibility of settlement.

In addition to superficial issues you need to address the content of the testimony. First, you need to stress to the witness the need to be truthful. Because of the way the rules work with regard to character evidence and impeachment, it is better to confess than be caught. Confessions can be covered in motions in limine; getting caught usually can't. Moreover, a straightforward witness is one the jury will be more likely to believe. The witness doesn't need to embellish the story; just keep it simple. If the lawyer pushes the witness to remember details and she doesn't, tell her not to give in; simply say, "I don't know." However, "I don't know" or "I don't remember" is not permissible if it is not the truth. Consider the following case.

United States v. Barnhart, **889 F.2d 1374 (5th Cir. 1989).**

Wayne Barnhart was sentenced to 18 months imprisonment upon being convicted for making false declarations before a grand jury, in violation of 18 U.S.C. § 1623. . . . We find no error in his conviction or sentence and accordingly affirm. . . .

A detailed recitation of the evidence is necessary to a discussion of Barnhart's contentions.

In connection with a federal task force investigation of fraud in the savings and loan industry in Texas, Wayne Barnhart was contacted by telephone in early June of 1988 by Federal Bureau of Investigation ("FBI") agent John Dillon. Dillon asked Barnhart if he was familiar with a $ 19,300,000 loan from three Texas financial institutions, Meridian Savings, Security Savings and People Savings Association, which involved property in Corpus Christi, Texas, and a company known as Omni Interest (referred to generally as the "Omni-Corpus Christi transaction"). Barnhart responded that he was familiar with the transaction. Dillon requested a grand jury subpoena for Barnhart to testify on July 6, 1988.

On that date, prior to Barnhart's testimony, Dillon questioned Barnhart as to details of the transaction under investigation. When Barnhart would not provide the requested information Dillon asked why Barnhart was not cooperating. According to Dillon's testimony, Barnhart responded that an official of the Federal Savings & Loan Insurance Corporation ("FSLIC") had told him that he should "get dumb" regarding any information he was to provide the grand jury or the FBI. In an attempt to elicit some useful information from Barnhart, Dillon outlined what the investigation had uncovered concerning the transaction. Barnhart said to Dillon "there is only one thing wrong with what you have told me and with a little bit more work you should be able to figure that out." When asked for the missing information, Barnhart gave no answer. Barnhart's testimony before the grand jury reflected his reluctance to provide the information requested.

When Agent Dillon told Assistant U.S. Attorney David Jarvis about Barnhart's "get dumb" comment, Barnhart was subpoenaed for a second appearance before the grand jury. The second subpoena was to be served by FBI Special Agent John Wallace who was not associated with the investigation. Wallace was assigned to the FBI office in Waco, Texas, which was close to Barnhart's residence.

When Barnhart came to Wallace's office on July 12 to pick up the subpoena he asked Wallace why he was being called as a witness for a second time. Wallace told Barnhart some common reasons based upon his own experience and at that point Barnhart became "very nervous." Barnhart began to discuss the investigation even though Wallace had said that his role was merely to serve the subpoena. Barnhart said that the investigation of the Omni-Corpus Christi transaction "was really going the wrong way." Barnhart remarked that the FBI had thrown out a large net, but was only catching the small fish while allowing the big fish to get away.

Barnhart told Wallace that while vacationing in Mexico he had received a telephone call from a FSLIC official who had advised Barnhart to "get dumb" when he appeared before the grand jury. When asked by Wallace to identify the FSLIC official Barnhart clasped his hands, leaned back in his chair and said, "I've just got a real bad memory about those things. I just can't remember."

Barnhart then said that while working in the banking industry he became aware of two instances where large amounts of money ($50,000 and $1,000,000) had "slipped through the cracks." Wallace asked for details and Barnhart responded by again clasping his hands looking up at the ceiling, and with a "smirk on his face" he contended that he had a loss of memory.

Barnhart related to Wallace that $37 million was involved in the transaction under investigation. Barnhart told Wallace that he did not trust the government to maintain his confidentiality if he became an informant. When Wallace gave Barnhart a copy of the subpoena, Barnhart stated that if required to go before the grand jury a second time he would adhere to his previous testimony and continue to "get dumb" as he had been advised by a "close personal friend" in the FSLIC. Agent Wallace related to agent Dillon the substance of this conversation including the intentional ignorance or "playing dumb" remarks.

On July 19 Barnhart telephoned agent Wallace seeking his advice as to his upcoming appearance. Wallace told him to go before the grand jury and tell the truth. Barnhart remarked that "Bogota looked real good this time of year." Barnhart stated that if required to testify he would continue to "get dumb in this whole matter." Barnhart wanted to meet Wallace at a local restaurant. Wallace, not being involved in the investigation, asked Barnhart to call back after he had sought advice from agent Dillon. Wallace was told that Barnhart was expected to give his information to the grand jury rather than the FBI. Barnhart did not call back.

On July 21 Barnhart met with government attorneys Jarvis and Dillon prior to his grand jury appearance. They advised him that he was regarded as merely a witness rather than a target of the investigation, and that he should tell the truth. Barnhart stated that he knew where to look for information regarding the transaction in question and that he knew how the individuals involved operated.

Jarvis questioned Barnhart before the grand jury as to his first conversation with Dillon on the telephone, and whether he initially told Dillon that he was familiar with the details of the transaction. Barnhart recalled the conversation and that he had told Dillon that he "was basically familiar with the transaction." Barnhart was asked whether he remembered telling Dillon that the reason he suddenly changed his position, from remembering details of the transaction to being unwilling to disclose those details, was due to someone at the FSLIC advising him to "get dumb" as to any information he might provide. Barnhart replied, "I don't recall that. I may have said that to him, but I do not recall it."

Barnhart was asked whether he remembered telling agent Wallace on July 12 about the same "getting dumb" strategy. Barnhart said that he "didn't recall that conversation." After again warning Barnhart about the consequences of false testimony, Jarvis asked Barnhart if he remembered a statement he made to Wallace on July 19, two days prior to his grand jury appearance that a "'friend at FSLIC told me to get dumb,'" and that this was a longtime friend who reiterated this advice three or four times. Barnhart replied "No sir." Barnhart stated that he did not recall whether an FSLIC official had ever advised him to "get dumb" while testifying before the grand jury.

Jarvis asked, "You told two different agents on three different occasions that a FSLIC examiner told you to get dumb, you just can't explain that, can you?" Barnhart replied, "No sir." Jarvis asked, "They just kind of grabbed that out of the blue?" Barnhart replied, "Yes sir." Barnhart persisted after repeated questioning that he didn't remember any of the "get dumb" remarks.

After the testimony, Jarvis told Barnhart that he believed Barnhart had perjured himself. Jarvis asked Barnhart to identify the FSLIC examiner with whom he had spoken. Barnhart replied that he had already mentioned his name. Recalling that the name of Bill Strickland, an examiner for the FSLIC, had arisen during his grand jury testimony, Jarvis asked Barnhart whether Strickland was the one who had given the "get dumb" advice. Barnhart did not respond.

When Barnhart was eventually arrested for perjury on September 22, after he had failed to surrender as directed on September 19, Barnhart stated to his mother at the FBI office, "I tried to get invisible. I tried to run, but I couldn't run fast enough or far enough."

After a jury trial, Barnhart was convicted of making declarations at a grand jury proceeding in violation of 18 U.S.C. § 1623 . . .

To obtain a § 1623 conviction for perjury, the government must prove that the defendant's statements were material, that they were false, and that, at the time they were made, the defendant did not believe them to be true . . .

Barnhart urges only that the evidence was insufficient to demonstrate his knowledge of the falsity of his particular answers. This contention is without merit. The government could prove a false claim of a lack of recall through circumstantial evidence of any sort. . . The jury could reasonably have concluded that Barnhart knew the falsity of his answers based upon the testimony of the two FBI agents who testified in detail about Barnhart's numerous references to the advice to "get dumb," the memorable nature of such an occurrence, the proximity of those statements to the grand jury testimony, the testimony of the agents as to Barnhart's other knowledge of the transaction under investigation and as to Barnhart's attitude toward the investigation, the testimony of the agents and the government attorney regarding Barnhart's demeanor, the transcript of the grand jury testimony, and the audio tape of the grand jury testimony. . . The jury in the instant case could reasonably have found that Barnhart knowingly testified falsely. . .

For the foregoing reasons, the judgment of the trial court is *AFFIRMED*.

Smirking is always a bad thing.

Also tell the witness that if the lawyer makes her go over the same little bit over and over to try to trip her up, she should keep telling the same story; the lawyer is just trying to shake her. Other rules to convey to the witness include the following.

* Listen carefully to what is being asked and answer the question, not what you want to answer.
* Don't answer more than what is being asked for: don't volunteer additional information. However, you do need to "tell the truth and the whole truth."
* Don't look to "your" lawyer for an answer. If you don't understand the question, say, "I don't understand the question."
* Don't take any attack personally. Part of the strategy of the opposing counsel is to try to make you angry.
* If one of the lawyers makes you look bad, instead of arguing with him, getting flustered, or being upset, try to remember that one of the other lawyers probably will want to make you look good and will give you an opportunity to repair any damage. If no one gives you a chance to fix it, odds are it wasn't as bad as you felt it was.
* Look at the jury when you are answering questions. This may feel unnatural, as it is the lawyer who is asking the questions, but it is the jury that you want to communicate to.
* Don't be afraid to show emotions related to the story you are telling. Emotions are as much a part of the testimony as the facts.
* "I don't know" and "I don't remember" are legitimate answers if they are the truth.

Sometimes witnesses (and lawyers) have trouble with the line between simply answering the question and volunteering versus being evasive. The idea behind this instruction is to keep the witness from going off on a tangent, inadvertently offering up privileged or—up until this point—undiscovered information. The lawyer has to play his part of Go Fish: The witness does not have to tell him what he holds in his hand. However, once the lawyer asks the right question, the witness can't hide the card, pretend he can't read it, see it, or thinks "tuna" is actually "trout." Nor should the lawyer suggest that the witness testify that it is trout or that it would be better for the case if it were trout.

The bottom line: Credibility is the key to success for a witness, particularly a client, and false statements will come out. Never prepare a witness to lie. Prepare a witness to tell the truth in the most effective way possible.

One lawyer who had trouble with the distinction was a crusader for prosecuting a hate crime case that involved the murder of a Chinese-American. This case demonstrates how a good case can be messed up by getting too wrapped up in making things perfect instead of letting things be true.

United States v. Ebens, 800 F.2d 1422 (6th Cir. 1986).

Ronald Ebens appeals from a judgment of conviction and a twenty-five year sentence following his conviction by a jury . . . with violating the civil rights of Vincent Chin, a United States citizen of Chinese descent. Ebens had killed Chin in an altercation which occurred on June 19, 1982.

We cannot permit the judgment to stand because Ebens was denied a fair trial.

Ebens was originally prosecuted in the Wayne County, Michigan, Circuit Court and prior to trial pleaded guilty to the crime of manslaughter. When he was placed upon probation and fined $3,720, public outrage at the perceived lenity of the penalty was extensive, especially within the Chinese-American community. The case was accompanied by massive publicity at both the state and national levels and undoubtedly because of activity on behalf of the Chinese-American community, the United States Department of Justice, overruling the decision of the local United States Attorney not to prosecute, instituted proceedings under the Civil Rights Act in the United States District Court for the Eastern District of Michigan. . .

. . . A Detroit attorney, Lisa Chan, formed a group known as The American Citizens for Justice, and appears to have been instrumental in publicizing the killing, the handling of the case by the Wayne County Prosecutor's office and the sentences given to Ebens and Nitz in the state court. Rallies were held and the publicity generated much television coverage including at least two special news stories on the subject and a program over national television as well. The public excoriation of the state trial judge who placed Ebens and Nitz on probation was particularly severe. The headlines can only be described as scathing. One large cartoon, appearing in *The Detroit News*, even showed the trial judge putting a baseball bat in one ear, as if it were a pencil, and sharpening it with a pencil sharpener installed in the opposite ear. . . .

The incident giving rise to this litigation occurred on June 19, 1982, in Highland Park, a suburb of Detroit. Chin, then twenty-seven years old, lived with his mother in Oak Park, Michigan, another suburb of Detroit. He had come to this country from China in 1961 when he was adopted by a Chinese-American couple. He became a United States citizen in 1965.

To celebrate his upcoming wedding, Chin invited his friends Robert Sirosky and Gary Koivu to meet him at a topless bar at 7:00 P.M. that night. After about an hour there and after having several drinks the group went on to the Fancy Pants Lounge, a nude dancing establishment in Highland Park. En route they purchased a pint of vodka and it is rather apparent from the record that they were in a mood of elevated joviality in consequence. Koivu later left to pick up one Jimmy Choi, another of Chin's friends, and together they brought another bottle of vodka into the Fancy Pants. The group was laughing, tipping the dancers heavily, and generally celebrating. At that time Ronald Ebens and his stepson, Michael Nitz, were also at the Fancy Pants, sitting directly across the elevated dancing runway from Chin and his friends. Construing the evidence most favorably to the government, Ebens began making racial and obscene remarks toward Chin calling him a "Chink" and a "Nip" and making remarks about foreign car imports. It is apparent that Ebens seemed to believe that Chin was Japanese and he was quoted as having made the further comment that "it's because of you little mother f_ _ _ _ _ _ that we're out of work." Ebens may not have distinguished between Orientals of Japanese and Chinese descent since there is testimony to show he made references to both. After a further exchange of words Chin got out of his chair and walked up to the stage where Ebens was sitting and there was general jostling and fighting between Ebens and Chin in which Nitz then joined. The doorman and the parking lot attendant broke up the fight. The parking lot attendant took Chin outside and the doorman took Ebens and Nitz to the men's room. The doorman got a towel and some ice for Nitz who was bleeding from a cut on the head and later escorted Ebens and Nitz outside. The quarrel resumed outside the Fancy Pants Lounge. Chin challenged Ebens to finish the fight outside, calling him names. Ebens thereupon went to Nitz's car, opened the hatchback and removed a baseball bat. Seeing Ebens with a bat, Chin fled across Woodward Avenue and was pursued a short distance by both Ebens and Nitz.

While still in the Fancy Pants parking lot, Chin's three friends had decided that Choi would join Chin across Woodward Avenue and that Koivu and Sirosky would get their car and pick him up. Ebens and Nitz drove by in their car and, seeing Sirosky and Koivu, stopped and asked where their friend was. When they said they didn't know, Ebens then saw Choi and started after him. Nitz threw a glass bottle at Choi, and Ebens and Nitz returned to their car and drove off after Choi. After driving about a block from the Fancy Pants, Sirosky and Koivu stopped the car, removed a tire iron from the trunk and headed back toward the Fancy Pants. Unexpectedly they came upon Nitz's car which was parked on Woodward Avenue. Ebens got out of the car with the baseball bat and chased Sirosky and Koivu a short distance before getting back into Nitz's car. Meanwhile, after Choi had crossed Woodward Avenue he found Chin and suggested that they should flee. The two then ran south on Woodward Avenue for a few blocks until they stopped at a McDonald's restaurant where they apparently sought protection in the crowd, also hoping that Koivu and Sirosky would find them. Choi picked up a piece of wood for protection and handed Chin an unbroken bottle. Ebens and Nitz continued to look for Chin and upon meeting one Jimmy Perry, Nitz offered Perry $20 to help him find and catch a "Chinese guy."

According to Perry's testimony Ebens and Nitz talked during the ride about catching a "Chinese guy" and "busting his head" when they caught him.

The final confrontation occurred in the lot of a supermarket next to McDonald's. Ebens and Nitz approached Chin and Choi using a parked truck for cover. Ebens was still carrying the baseball bat. Chin saw them coming and yelled "Scram." Choi escaped but Nitz grabbed Chin in a bear hug from behind. Chin broke loose and ran onto Woodward Avenue. Ebens struck Chin several times with the bat on the back and head causing Chin to fall to the ground. While the precise circumstances of the assault are in dispute, especially whether Nitz was holding Chin at the time, it is undisputed that Ebens was the aggressor. Meanwhile, the Highland Park police officers who were working as security guards at McDonald's came up, drew their guns and ordered Ebens to drop his bat.

Chin was taken to Henry Ford Hospital, losing consciousness several times en route. He suffered two lacerations on the back left side of his head and abrasions on his shoulder, chest and neck and lapsed into a severe coma. After the performance of emergency surgery his brain ceased functioning entirely. At 9:50 P.M. June 23, 1982, a ventilator which had been employed to keep him breathing was removed and he was pronounced dead. . .

Ebens claims that the trial court committed reversible error in refusing to permit the admission of certain evidence which was offered by Ebens to impeach the government's witnesses. Specifically, two types of evidence are involved.

As we have stated, after the state court sentencing, Lisa Chan, a Detroit attorney, formed a group known as the American Citizens for Justice and appears to have been instrumental in publicizing the killing and the handling of the case by the Wayne County prosecutor's office. Ms. Chan traveled to Washington, D.C., to discuss the matter with William Bradford Reynolds, Assistant Attorney General in charge of the Civil Rights Division of the Department of Justice with respect to the possibility of federal prosecution. Rallies were held in Detroit, in which the protestors carried placards reading "Jail the racist killers" and "It's not fair," the latter a comment made by Chin before he lapsed into unconsciousness. It is undisputed that the events occurring after the state court sentencing received widespread publicity.

The three principal government witnesses were Choi, Sirosky, and Koivu. All testified, in one form or another, concerning the incident and the statements purportedly made by Ebens in the course of the evening from which racism could be found.

Ebens and codefendant Nitz sought to introduce into evidence tape recordings of interviews which had been conducted by Lisa Chan with these witnesses. The defense purpose was to demonstrate that the witnesses' testimony concerning Ebens' racist statements was false and that it was the result of improper coaching of them by Chan in preparation for the trial. He claimed that the tapes were admissible to show collusion, witness influence, and prior inconsistent statements. Each time the defendants sought to introduce the tapes, however, the court sustained the government objection on hearsay grounds, ruling however that the defense counsel could confront a witness who takes the stand with his own words on the tape but that the statements of Lisa Chan to the witness which elicited that witness' statement could only be introduced through her should she be called. The government concedes that these rulings were erroneous.

The government correctly notes in its brief on appeal that the definition of hearsay under the federal rules requires that the third party statement testified to by the witness in question be offered for the purpose of proving the truth of the matter asserted. . . .

Obviously the purpose of introducing the Chan tapes was to show the effect of Chan's statements on the testimony of Choi, Sirosky, and Koivu. Plainly, Chan's out of court utterances were admissible to show not the truth of what she said but the effect on Choi, Sirosky and Koivu as bearing on whether the witnesses' subsequent sworn testimony was coached and hence inaccurate. . . In this light, the tapes were highly relevant and important to the defense.

The defense did use the transcripts of the tapes to some extent during the trial. Counsel for Ebens examined Koivu concerning the purpose of his meeting with Chan. Koivu replied, "Well, she wanted to get an idea of what happened, just to get the flavor of the night, to get an idea of what happened." The defense also questioned Koivu about specific responses he had made to Chan's questions. In the interview, Koivu expressed fear that his testimony, as well as that of Choi and Sirosky, would sound too rehearsed. On cross-examination, defense counsel asked Koivu whether he had expressed this fear to which he replied, "In a way."

In cross-examining Robert Sirosky, the defense again attempted to prove two prior inconsistent statements by reciting questions asked by Ms. Chan and the responses given by Sirosky. However, the most extensive use of the Chan tapes was during the testimony of Jimmy Choi. Defense counsel sought to discredit Choi's testimony that he heard racial slurs by introducing a portion of the Chan tapes. In this portion Choi suggested to Lisa Chan that he did not hear any racial slurs made by Ebens on the night of the fight. When he denied making any such statement, defense counsel read Chan's questions and Choi's responses. Later in Choi's cross-examination, the defense used the transcript of the tapes to refresh Choi's recollection. . . .

Ebens should have been permitted to introduce into evidence the entire contents of the tapes at least insofar as they involved conversations occurring at the time the government witnesses were present. The three witnesses were the most crucial of all witnesses for the government. Each testified as to events inside the Fancy

Pants Lounge and to verbal exchanges between Ebens and Chin. The Chan tapes were offered to support Ebens' claim that Choi, Koivu and Sirosky did not tell the truth when they testified that they heard the racial statements. Since the physical facts of the assault were essentially undisputed, the entire defense hung upon Ebens' claim that the fight was not racially motivated. It is true that the district court permitted the defense to elicit the statements made in interviews and did allow a few of the statements, but it was not within the province of the court's proper discretion to prevent the jury from hearing the tapes themselves and judging for themselves the impact upon the witnesses which the purported conversation had and measuring that against the statements made in court by the witnesses. . . .

. . . We have appended to this opinion other statements made by Chan and others in these interviews. The content of these nonhearsay statements shows why their erroneous exclusion by the trial court was not harmless. . . .

. . . Had the jurors been permitted to hear the tapes of Lisa Chan's joint witness interview of May 17, . . . they would have had at least a means to determine whether the witnesses' testimony was in fact correct or the extent to which it was coached. Excerpts from that interview are appended hereto as appendix A and show the nature of the coaching which took place. . . .

REVERSED and REMANDED for a new trial.

APPENDIX A

Excerpts from joint witness interview of May 17, 1983:

Liza [sic] Chan: The purpose of this meeting tonight is so we can help each other remember exactly what happened, how it happened, when it happened and all the minor details. We were just going over—I was talking with Eddie Hollis this afternoon, the parking lot attendant, the black guy, I don't know when he came in. I think—but according to his version of the facts, it's quite different from what I have so far understood them to be. So, I would center on my facts on what you, three of you, say they are and somehow try to either fit all the facts around these, or if they don't fit, then I have to watch out, you know, there's something else, somebody's saying something else.

Liza [sic] Chan: We will agree this is the story, this is it. When it's a federal prosecution, h'm, we're all going to have to be agreeing on this is what happened. Now, if you don't agree, like I explained to them earlier, you definitely remembered certain things happened, say, it's a black car and you definitely remembered it's a white car and we kind of (inaudible), okay, other than that, let's all have it sort of down, have it down pat, is it five minutes or is it ten minutes. Is it more like eight minutes, let's all agree. Otherwise, you all look funny on the stand. You all supposedly were there. But one says two minutes, the other says eight and that's what robbed me before.

Gary Koivu: Is there any harm in getting too accurate, because they could say, well, you all rehersed [sic] this, like if you're in court and we all have exactly the same times.

Liza [sic] Chan: As long as you're within, you know, you could say 8:10, you could say 8:20, I mean, that doesn't matter.

Gary Koivu: Mm hmm. Right, but as long as they have example.

Liza [sic] Chan: Right. But as far as the crucial facts, the crucial ones are not conflicting. I'll give you an example. Like what you've people have been telling me and then what Eddie Hollis told me. Totally make me completely confused. That is going to be raising a question in the jury's mind: well, who's telling the truth? Or what actually happened. Maybe nobody's to be believed. Now, I don't mean exactly everybody agreed okay, everbody [sic] agree at 6:30 right on the dot.

Robert Siroskey [sic]: Mm hmm.

Liza [sic] Chan: This could have a little bit of leeway.

Robert Siroskey [sic]: Okay.

Liza [sic] Chan: Okay. H'm, but I mean, you know, you can't say that we stayed at Fancy Pants for two hours and then another person says we stayed at Fancy Pants for half an hour. I mean that's a big discrepancy there.

Robert Siroskey [sic]: Right. . . .

Liza [sic] Chan: Okay. We all remember our different lines, okay. There's no agreement that that's fine, just remember your different lines—

Robert Siroskey [sic]: Right.

Liza [sic] Chan: Chink, foreign car part, big f_ _ _ _ _, little f_ _ _ _ _, all f_ _ _ _ _ _, don't call me a f_ _ _ _ _, we all remember our lines, okay? Umm, then what happened? Go ahead.

Lisa Chan: Maybe you heard that before: don't call me a f_ _ _ _ _.

Robert Sirosky: See, I have to go with what he said. . . .

Lisa Chan: Then VINCENT could have said: don't call me a f_ _ _ _ _. Could be. I'm just saying—

Gary Koivu: No, I'm just saying what I—-like I said, I'm not saying I saw everything, but I did see—

Lisa Chan: But what you did hear or did hear, was after the words: don't call me a f_ _ _ _ _, I'm not a f_ _ _ _ _.

Gary Koivu: Mm hmm.

Lisa Chan: So, but you did remember hearing something about little f_ _ _ _ _ _ and big f_ _ _ _ _ _, we're all f_ _ _ _ _ _.

Jimmy Choi: Mm hmm.

Gary Koivu: Yeah.

Lisa Chan: And you, same thing?

Robert Sirosky: Yes. I remember hearing something to the effect that—

Lisa Chan: Coming from EBENS or NITZ. Coming from EBENS or NITZ?

Robert Sirosky: Who's EBENS? Who's NITZ? I don't—

Gary Koivu: EBENS was the big guy.

Lisa Chan: Is it the big guy?

Gary Koivu: The older guy.

Robert Sirosky: The older guy.

Lisa Chan: Okay.

Jimmy Choi: The blond haired guy. . .

Lisa Chan: Well, any suggestions? We're all sure what we heard? That's okay, I mean, that's fine, too. I just—

Robert Sirosky: I'm positive—

Lisa Chan: —while I have all three of you—

Robert Sirosky: I'm positive what I heard after VINCENT said that.

Gary Koivu: Yeah, what VINCENT said after that.

Lisa Chan: Okay. We rely on you whatever was said afterward.

Gary Koivu: Before that VINCENT said I'm not a f_ _ _ _ _—

Lisa Chan: Right.

Gary Koivu: I'm out of it, you know, these two.

Lisa Chan: You weren't paying attention.

Gary Koivu: See what they heard.

Lisa Chan: At some point you heard chink definitely, for sure.

Robert Sirosky: Right, right.

Lisa Chan: Could it be into the fight?

Robert Sirosky: Into the fight? No.

Robert Sirosky: We're all sitting—

Lisa Chan: Sitting.

Robert Sirosky: Yes.

Lisa Chan: Still things are going fine. The first thing you heard was something about chink.

Robert Sirosky: Mm hmm.

Lisa Chan: Fighting and all other words came later?

Robert Sirosky: Mm hmm.

Lisa Chan: You heard something about foreign cars; that's also the same situation, not in the middle of the fight or anything, or in the middle of an exchange?

Robert Sirosky: There's a lot of destractions [sic], too, because the music is loud—

Jimmy Choi: The people—

Robert Sirosky: —The people

Jimmy Choi: —were around, girl dancing—

Robert Sirosky: —girls dancing.

Jimmy Choi: —and then—he and I were talking.

Lisa Chan: All right, then, the next thing. We've got all these lines.

Gary Koivu: I told you I tapped VINCENT on the arm saying forget it, you know,—

Lisa Chan: Okay.

Gary Koivu: —I may have said, it's not important. . .

Gary Koivu: But after I tapped him and EBENS said, I just don't know if you're a big or little f_ _ _ _ _, that's when VINCENT said I told you I'm not a f_ _ _ _ _, friend.

Lisa Chan: Did anybody hear that?

Robert Sirosky: I didn't hear it, but, you know, he's talking to him and, you know, I might have saw him point out of the—no, I can't say something like that—

Jimmy Choi: I think I heard him say nobody calls me a mother f_ _ _ _ _.

Robert Sirosky: —I can't even say that.

Lisa Chan: Mm hmm.

Ms. Chan's discussion with the witnesses about how to resolve the testimony was improper; it suggested to them that they should have changed their stories accordingly. Her references to "lines" makes it sound scripted rather than real. Sirosky said, at one point, "No, I can't say something like that," resisting her suggestions, but there are other indications that Chan was leading the witnesses to align their stories with her version of reality or to conform to other accounts. These small differences could be accounted for, as raised by the witnesses, by the noise and distractions of the club. The discussion Chan was having with the witnesses should have been had with the other attorneys involved in the case. (By the way, as this case demonstrates graphically, get ready for shocking language if you are not used to it.)

The fact that the opposing side obtained this videotape is another consideration. It is becoming more common to videotape witnesses to give them feedback about their "performance." In jurisdictions where all prior statements and all photographs are discoverable, there is some question whether this would fall under attorney work product or not.

On the other hand, it is not impermissible to let a witness know of conflicting testimony after the witness has recounted his own. What is important is how you handle it. Part of preparation is preparing the witness to deal with the potential of being challenged by a conflict. If you tell the witness up front that you are confident in him and that you want him to recount what he saw truthfully and to the best of his memory, but you want him to be prepared for this possible problem, then you are empowering the witness to make his own decision rather than suggesting he change his story to conform. Should you let him know about conflicting testimony if you don't think there will be a direct challenge? Here's what one court had to say.

State v. Earp, 571 A.2d 1227 (Md. 1988).

In this case we. . . hold that the trial judge did not abuse his discretion when he permitted testimony by witnesses who, prior to trial, had been shown a videotape recording of the victim's deposition testimony. . . .

This case grows out of a melee that occurred in Montgomery County on the evening of 31 October 1985. The victim, Michael Dwayne Lawrence, was attending a Halloween party, together with more than 100 other people. When word spread that someone had been struck by a pick-up truck just outside the place where the party was being held, many of the persons in attendance, including Lawrence, went to the scene.

Lawrence testified[1] to the subsequent events as follows. When he arrived outside, he observed 40 or 50 people engaged in fights. Other people were attacking the truck with sticks, pipes, and shovels, breaking the headlights and attempting to get to the two occupants. Lawrence knew the passenger in the truck, and advised him to flee. Lawrence then questioned the driver, and upon learning that the driver had struck the pedestrian, Lawrence held him against the truck. At this point, while police officers were making their way through the crowd toward the truck, Randall Paul Earp grabbed Lawrence by the shoulder, attempted to hit the driver of the truck, and said, "let me have a piece of him." Lawrence told Earp that only the police were "going to get something from him." Earp responded with, "some slang words" and said, "well, I'll take a piece of you." Lawrence then felt a punch in his back, and looking over his shoulder saw a knife handle protruding from his back. He felt the knife being pulled down and saw it being withdrawn. Earp then lunged at Lawrence a second time, and as Lawrence was attempting to defend himself, he was cut on the thumb. Lawrence said Earp attempted "about 10 to 15 slices," but Lawrence was able to block most of them. Earp ran when the police officers reached the truck.

Other witnesses confirmed the attack by Earp on Lawrence, and the essential nature of the conversation between them. One witness described the knife used by Earp as a "Buck 110," having a blade three to four inches long. . .

[The court] found Earp guilty of attempted murder in the second degree and assault with intent to maim, and imposed concurrent sentences of imprisonment of 25 years and 9 years respectively. Earp appealed to the Court of Special Appeals. That court reversed the conviction of attempted murder in the second degree, but affirmed the conviction of assault with intent to maim. . . We affirm that judgment. . .

Aware that Lawrence was dying of cancer, the State obtained an Order of Court authorizing the perpetuation of his testimony by videotape deposition. . . Thereafter, but before trial, the defendant filed a "Motion to Exclude Testimony of Witnesses" alleging that certain state's witnesses had been shown the videotape of Lawrence's testimony. Earp. . . contended that allowing the testimony of the witnesses who had been influenced by the testimony of the victim would violate his constitutional guarantee of due process. . .

The question of just how far an attorney may go in preparing a witness for trial is a difficult one. It involves ethical considerations as well as the possibility of tainting a witness to the extent that due process and the necessity for reliable evidence may justify the exclusion of that witness's testimony.

Attorneys have not only the right but also the duty to fully investigate the case and to interview persons who may be witnesses. A prudent attorney will, whenever possible, meet with the witnesses he or she intends to call. The process of preparing a witness for trial, sometimes referred to as "horse-shedding the witness,"[2] takes many forms, and involves matters ranging from recommended attire to a review of the facts known by the witness. Because the line that exists between perfectly acceptable witness preparation on the one hand, and impermissible influencing of the witness on the other hand, may sometimes be

---

[1] Lawrence died of cancer before trial. His testimony was given by videotape deposition taken pursuant to Maryland Rule 4–261.

[2] The term "horse-shedding the witness" is said to have been coined by James Fenimore Cooper. *See* G. Fowler, *The Great Mouthpiece: A Life Story of William J. Fallon* 93 (1931). Fowler wrote that there were carriage sheds near the courthouse in Cooper's day, where attorneys lingered to rehearse witnesses. James McElhaney, in *McElhaney's Trial Notebook* (2d ed. 1987), published by the Section of Litigation, American Bar Association, says that "good taste demands that [the term] be spoken with unusual precision, and it is often accompanied by a short explanation, just to make sure the listener did not misunderstand." Perhaps to avoid misunderstandings, others have referred to "woodshedding" a witness. . .

fine and difficult to discern. . . attorneys are well advised to heed the sage advice of the Supreme Court of Rhode Island:

> [I]n the interviews with and examination of witnesses, out of court, and before the trial of the case, the examiner, whoever he may be, layman or lawyer, must exercise the utmost care and caution to extract and not to inject information, and by all means to resist the temptation to influence or bias the testimony of the witnesses. . .

It is permissible, in a pretrial meeting with a witness, to review statements, depositions, or prior testimony that a witness has given. It also may be necessary to test or refresh the recollection of the witness by reference to other facts of which the attorney has become aware during pretrial preparation, but in so doing the attorney should exercise great care to avoid suggesting to the witness what his or her testimony should be. In some instances, as in the case of an expert witness who will be asked to express an opinion based upon facts related by others, and who is not a factual witness whose testimony could be influenced by reading what others have said under oath, there is little danger in having the witness review the depositions of others. When, however, the testimony in the deposition bears directly on the facts that the reviewing witness will be asked to recount, and particularly when, as here, the testimony is known by the witness to be exactly that which will be used at trial, and is presented in its most graphic form by videotape, the potential for influencing the reviewing witness is great.

When there is evidence suggesting that a witness has been improperly influenced, the trial judge must decide whether the extraordinary action of excluding that witness's testimony at trial is required. Although a number of factors must be weighed in reaching that decision, the overriding consideration ordinarily will be whether the testimony in a particular case will likely be so unreliable that exclusion is justified. . . Quite often, as was the case here, the trial judge will determine that disclosure through cross-examination of a witness concerning the pretrial activity that created the potential for influencing the witness's testimony will allow the trier of fact to adequately assess the witness's testimony. . . The loss of the testimony of an otherwise competent witness carries with it its own danger of injustice and the subversion of the ultimate search for truth. It is not an action lightly to be taken. . .

In the case before us, the prosecutor was sensitive to the possibility that witnesses reviewing Lawrence's deposition might be influenced by Lawrence's identification of Earp as his attacker, and the witness who was to make an in-court identification was not permitted to see that part of the deposition.

The trial judge expressly found that full disclosure to the trier of fact was an effective remedy in this case. We conclude that the trial judge properly refused to exclude the testimony.

If your preparation has improperly influenced a witness to the point that he changes his story, then there's a problem. So a good deal of care has to be taken in deciding what to share with witnesses. A more difficult problem arises when the witness is the client, with whom the attorney will need to discuss problems in the case in order to discuss the status of the case and settlement value. Even though this knowledge is given for a different purpose, it still may influence testimony in an unethical way. Again, it is the approach to this problem that may make the difference to whether your client will change her story. If the client appears to be waffling, first you need to draw her attention to prior statements, and ask her why she believes she was wrong then. Usually that will get her attention without a need for you to get the attorney to advise her that it's a no-no that will make the case even worse. Then explain (probably for the umpteenth time, just like I have in this text) that the jury will decide who's telling the truth that day based only on what they see in this artificial situation; her job is just to tell the truth the best she can.

JURY CONSULTANTS

A whole cottage industry has sprung up around the issue of witness preparation as well as forecasting how juries will react. Some forensic psychologists, often with a Ph.D. in psychology, practicing in the area where law and psychology intersect, have moved into the area of researching specifically how psychological factors influence jurors, what demographic groups are more likely to accept certain types of jury arguments, and helping witnesses deal with their nonverbal reactions to questioning. These experts are referred to as *jury consultants* or **trial consultants.** These terms are interchangeable. Other trial consultants are sociologists or related behavioral scientists; a few are movie types (i.e. movie producers, scriptwriters, etc.) who simply help the lawyer shape a story.

Trial consultants have been instrumental in some very high-profile cases. The O.J. Simpson trial teams employed jury consultants, as did the Rodney King trial defense teams of the police officers. Although the trial was actually the state of California against the officers, it became known as the Rodney King trial for the victim of a videotaped beating by police. For instance, one of the recommendations from jury consultants was to show the tape over and over until it lost its capacity to shock. By the time the jury went to deliberate, they had seen the tape over a hundred times, all of it in slow motion as well as at regular speed, and were no longer emotionally affected by the content—a point that favored the police officers. Jury consultants also assisted the officers in stress reduction exercises to keep them from becoming angry under the provocation of cross-examination. The prosecution wanted to demonstrate for the jury that these officers were out of control and beat King in a frenzy. The defense wanted to portray the incident as one of controlled escalation of force according to regulations. The psychologists' work was successful; only one of the defendants was found guilty, and he was the one who showed evidence of temper (and had made racist remarks over the mobile data terminal [MDT] in his vehicle).

These are effective trial tactics. These are expensive trial tactics. Do they create justice? Are they ethical? This is the dilemma that is posed; it has largely been left to the discretion of the legal team to answer. Academics and polemicists argue about it; nothing has been done to eliminate such tactics from the legal scene. Newer research has supported the argument that jury consultants actually do no better than lawyers on their own, but that their value lies more in reassuring the lawyer. More important to the outcome of cases is the quality of the evidence as opposed to the makeup of the jury. Regardless, due to the expense of employing jury consultants, only cases in which much is at stake, as in very large dollar cases (or, as from the examples, life or liberty), will they be employed, although some attorneys fear that it may be malpractice *not* to use a jury consultant.

How is the trial consultant's advice treated with respect to privilege? Is he an expert, an agent of the attorney and part of the legal team, or something else? In the following case, the party hiring the jury consultant must have had a few bad moments after the ruling by the trial judge.

In re Cendant Corp. Securities Litigation, 343 F.3d 658 (3d. Cir. 2003).

At issue on appeal is whether the "work product" of a non-testifying trial consultant in this case is privileged and subject to only limited discovery. Ernst & Young, LLP, and Cendant Corporation are co-defendants in a federal securities class action involving Cendant's alleged accounting fraud. The class action claims were settled, leaving claims asserted by Cendant and Ernst & Young against each other as the focus of the remaining litigation. . .

Cendant deposed Simon Wood, a former Ernst & Young senior manager and auditor who prepared the Cendant financial statements at issue in the underlying litigation . . . At Wood's deposition, Cendant inquired into communications that took place between Wood, Ernst & Young's counsel who also represented Wood, and Dr. Phillip C. McGraw of Courtroom Sciences, Inc. Dr. McGraw is a consulting expert in trial strategy and deposition preparation who was retained as a non-testifying trial expert to assist Ernst & Young's counsel in anticipation of litigation.

Specifically, Cendant's counsel asked Wood: "Have you ever met Phil McGraw?"; "On how many occasions did you meet with Phil McGraw?"; "Did you understand Phil McGraw to be a jury consultant?"; "Did Mr. McGraw provide you with guidance in your conduct as a witness?"; "Did you rehearse any of your prospective testimony in the presence of Mr. McGraw?"; "In the course of preparing for this deposition . . . did you review any work papers?"; "Did you select the work papers that you reviewed?"; "Did you ask anyone for the opportunity to review any particular work papers?"; and "Did you ask to review work papers on any particular subject?" Ernst & Young's counsel objected, citing the work product doctrine and the attorney-client privilege and arguing the discovery sought related to private communications relayed in the presence of counsel and for the purpose of assisting counsel in rendering legal advice. In March 2002, the Special Discovery Master . . . held:

> Wood may be asked whether he has met with Dr. McGraw, the date and duration of any meetings, who was present and the purpose for same. He may not be asked what Dr. McGraw told the witness, whether testimony was practiced, whether any part of the meetings were recorded, whether the

witness took any notes, or whether Dr. McGraw provided the witness with any documents. In my view, answers to the latter questions would violate the work product doctrine.

From the information developed thus far, it appears that Dr. McGraw is an expert retained by Ernst & Young's counsel to assist in trial preparation. He is not expected to be called as a witness and no exceptional circumstances have been cited to justify the exploration Cendant seeks.

In November 2002, the District Court reversed the Special Discovery Master's determination, holding the work product doctrine and attorney-client privilege did not apply . . .

The work product doctrine is governed by a uniform federal standard set forth in Fed. R. Civ. P. 26(b)(3) n6 and "shelters the mental processes of the attorney, providing a privileged area within which he can analyze and prepare his client's case." . . . Under Rule 26(b)(3), the work product doctrine applies to "documents and tangible things . . . prepared in anticipation of litigation or for trial by or for another party or by or for that other party's representative (including the other party's attorney, consultant, surety, indemnitor, insurer, or agent)" . . . The Supreme Court articulated the essential nature of the doctrine in *Hickman v. Taylor*, 329 U.S. 495, 510–11, 91 L. Ed. 451, 67 S. Ct. 385 (1947):

In performing his various duties, it is essential that a lawyer work with a certain degree of privacy, free from unnecessary intrusion by opposing parties and their counsel. Proper preparation of a client's case demands that he assemble information, sift what he considers to be the relevant from the irrelevant facts, prepare his legal theories and plan his strategy without undue and needless interference. That is the historical and the necessary way in which lawyers act within the framework of our system of jurisprudence to promote justice and to protect their clients' interests. This work is reflected, of course, in interviews, statements, memoranda, correspondences, briefs, mental impressions, personal belief, and countless other tangible and intangible ways—aptly though roughly termed . . . as the "work product of the lawyer." Were such materials open to opposing counsel on mere demand, much of what is now put down in writing would remain unwritten. An attorney's thoughts, heretofore inviolate, would not be his own. Inefficiency, unfairness and sharp practices would inevitably develop in the giving of legal advice and in the preparation of cases for trial.

It is clear from *Hickman* that work product protection extends to both tangible and intangible work product . . . Furthermore, this protection extends beyond materials prepared by an attorney to include materials prepared by an attorney's agents and consultants. As the Supreme Court explained, "Attorneys often must rely on the assistance of investigators and other agents in the compilation of materials in preparation for trial. It is therefore necessary that the [work product] doctrine protect materials prepared by agents of the attorney as well as those prepared by the attorney himself." . . .

Courts have wrestled with the idea of affording opinion work product absolute immunity from discovery . . . In 1946, the Advisory Committee on Civil Rules proposed a rule that would create absolute protection against discovery into information at the core of the work product doctrine, but the Supreme Court declined to adopt it . . . .

. . . Cendant argues that Rule 26(b)(3)'s work product protection is superseded by Rule 26(b)(4)(B), which governs discovery of "facts known or opinions held by an expert who has been retained or specially employed by another party in anticipation of litigation or preparation for trial and who is not expected to be called as a witness at trial." . . . But Rule 26(b)(3) provides work product protection independently of Rule 26(b)(4)(B). In *Bogosian v. Gulf Oil Corp* . . . we held attorney opinion work product shown to experts in an antitrust case was not discoverable.

Litigation consultants retained to aid in witness preparation may qualify as non-attorneys who are protected by the work product doctrine . . . Moreover, a litigation consultant's advice that is based on information disclosed during private communications between a client, his attorney, and a litigation consultant may be considered "opinion" work product which requires a showing of exceptional circumstances in order for it to be discoverable. *Duplan Corp. v. Deering Milliken, Inc.*, 540 F.2d 1215, 1219 (4th Cir. 1976) ("Opinion work product immunity now applies equally to lawyers and non-lawyers alike."). . .

Cendant concedes "that the work product doctrine extends to materials compiled by a non-attorney, who, as the 'agent' of a party or a party's attorney, assists the attorney in trial preparation," and further, "that the doctrine also protects the 'intangible' work product of an attorney, such as testimony that would reveal counsel's mental impressions or trial strategy." . . . But Cendant contends that a non-attorney's advice regarding witness testimony does not fall under the work product doctrine. Cendant asserts that the jury is entitled to know the consultant's communications with the witness, in the same way it is entitled to know and assess all other factors that may have informed the witness's testimony and may affect credibility. The District Court held that the work product doctrine should be cabined to lawyers and be strictly limited when applied to a lawyer's agent. The District Court said:

> Work product deals with things legal, things with preparation, evaluation, strategies, tactics and it is at first limited to lawyers and then will strictly or rigidly expand it, or restrictively expand it to include people such as paralegals and maybe assistants to lawyers because of their intimacy with the lawyer.
>
> The privilege is really that of the lawyers. . . because he or she has a right to tell his or her client certain things. But, when we go beyond that into a person who is not dealing with the law but telling someone how to prepare it as *Blumenthal v. Drudge* indicates, one of the questions where the lawyer was telling this witness what to do, it's a question what this jury consultant [is] more or less telling that person what to do.

As noted, in reaching its decision, the District Court relied on *Blumenthal,* which held communications between a client and a political consultant were not protected by the attorney-client privilege when no attorney was involved in the communication . . . But the *Blumenthal* court never considered the work product doctrine because it was never raised . . . The District Court's reliance on *Blumenthal* therefore was misplaced because "the work product doctrine is distinct from and broader than the attorney-client privilege.". . .

As noted, the District Court held that the work product doctrine should be cabined to lawyers and be strictly limited when applied to a lawyer's agent. The District Court said:

> I admit that if an attorney had prepped his witness like I think all of us who are single or small firms have done without the need for a jury consultant X, you've got to shave, you've got to do this, you got to put this question, you've got to put that answer that way and all of that, I'm quite sure anyone in his right mind would consider that part of work product and attorney-client activity and no one even tries to find out what went on.
>
> But my problem is when you don't bring in a lawyer, you bring in someone who is not dealing with the law but dealing with the manner in which things are presented, then I think it may be a little bit much to expect that to be countenanced. . .

After the District Court made this determination, Cendant conceded that it was not accusing Ernst & Young of fabricating false testimony in the meetings between Wood, his attorney, and Dr. McGraw . . . But Cendant argued that, as a result of the District Court's conclusion that the work product doctrine did not extend to meetings with Dr. McGraw, they were entitled to inquire into the content of those meetings. Cendant said "We are not here now deciding what they did or accusing them of anything. But once it is not privileged . . . once that veil is no longer there, we are entitled . . . to show anybody, judge or jury, what went on as they practiced with the witness.". . .

We disagree and hold that the work product of Dr. McGraw is privileged and subject to only limited discovery. Ernst & Young contends that questioning into the content of advice Dr. McGraw gave to Wood during a private consultation with Wood's attorney clearly calls for attorney work product protection. In retaining Dr. McGraw, Ernst & Young expected all counsel's communications with him to be confidential and protected from discovery. Had Ernst & Young or its counsel anticipated that counsel's communications with this litigation consultant would be subject to discovery, Ernst & Young asserts Dr. McGraw would not have been retained or the nature and extent of the matters counsel communicated to him would have been severely curtailed.

Ernst & Young asserts that, based upon the expectation of confidentiality, Dr. McGraw participated in frank and open discussions with Ernst & Young's counsel regarding counsel's view of the important facts of the case, the contentions of the parties, and Ernst & Young's trial themes, theories, and strategies. These discussions were at all times understood and intended to be confidential by all participants. Furthermore, in connection with these discussions, Dr. McGraw was provided with documents prepared by Ernst & Young's counsel reflecting counsel's mental impressions, opinions, conclusions, and legal theories. In addition, Dr. McGraw's notes of these discussions may reflect the mental impressions, opinions, conclusions, and legal theories of Ernst & Young's counsel. Discovery of this information goes to the core of the work product doctrine and, therefore, is discoverable only upon a showing of extraordinary circumstances. Cendant has failed to cite any extraordinary circumstances that would justify discovery of the information sought. Thus, the private communications between Wood, Dr. McGraw, and counsel merit protection under the work product doctrine, as they reflect and implicate Ernst & Young's legal strategy regarding a deposition taken as part of this litigation. . .

We hold that the District Court erred and that the Special Discovery Master's ruling is essentially correct. These communications merit work product protection. The Special Discovery Master properly found that no exceptional circumstances were cited to justify the exploration sought by Cendant. Nonetheless, we believe Wood may be asked whether his anticipated testimony was practiced or rehearsed. But this inquiry should be circumscribed. As with all discovery matters, we leave much to the sound discretion of the District Court.

For the reasons outlined, we will reverse the order of the District Court and remand for proceedings consistent with this opinion.

Even if you do not use a jury consultant, reading materials by them and for them can help you in your own preparation for witnesses, so don't overlook those materials when you are working on cases. Check out the ***Psychological Abstracts*** under any heading starting with "Jury" or "Forensic." You'll find some interesting reading; although at first you may need a good dictionary handy.

GENERAL STRESS REDUCTION TECHNIQUES

One of the main barriers to effective communication by clients and witnesses is stress. There is no way that sitting in that stand is not stressful, and thinking about sitting there is just as scary. The events surrounding lawsuits are, by the nature of the beast, stressful. So reducing stress for the witness—client or other—is one significant way to assist him to testify clearly, coherently, and truthfully without managing the content of the testimony in any way.

Stress reduction techniques are something that trial consultants are very helpful with, as illustrated in the misnamed Rodney King case described earlier. There are times where the assistance of a psychologist with special experience in trial work is a necessity. But you don't need a high-priced trial consultant for a run-of-the-mill case, and you can use and teach the witness some of the same techniques.

How is it that you, a nonprofessional, can teach stress reduction techniques? Think about it. In order for this kind of behavior modification to be useful, it must be accessible to the ordinary person, not just Ph.D.s in psychology. It must be something that they can teach. Now some techniques, like biofeedback, necessitate special equipment and training, and you definitely want to refer anyone needing that level of intervention to a mental health care professional.

If you have a client with a diagnosed psychological condition, such as **depression**, **bipolar disorder** (also known as *manic depression*), **anxiety disorder**, or **obsessive compulsive disorder (OCD)** (and this is not an all encompassing list—these are just some of the most common **functional** but neurotic folks) you'll need to get permission from your client to discuss her condition with her therapist and/or psychiatrist. Work with the health care professional in a team approach: it serves both of your goals to keep the client in a functioning state.

The following lists have been based on diagnostic criteria in the *Diagnostic and Statistical Manual of Mental Disorders*, 4th ed. (DSM-IV). If you suspect a disorder, you should refer your concern to a properly trained and authorized medical expert.

Diagnostic Criteria for Depression

A. Five (or more) of the following symptoms have been present during the same 2-week period and represent a change from previous functioning; at least one of the symptoms is either (1) depressed mood or (2) loss of interest or pleasure.

Note: Do not include symptoms that are clearly due to a general medical condition, or mood-incongruent delusions or hallucinations.

1. depressed mood most of the day, nearly every day, as indicated by either subjective report (e.g., feels sad or empty) or observation made by others (e.g. appears tearful).
Note: In children and adolescents, can be irritable mood.

2. markedly diminished interest or pleasure in all, or almost all, activities most of the day, nearly every day (as indicated by either subjective account or observation made by others)
3. significant weight loss when not dieting or weight gain (e.g., a change of more than 5% of body weight in a month), or decrease or increase in appetite nearly every day. Note: In children, consider failure to make expected weight gains. Insomnia or hypersomnia nearly every day.
4. psychomotor agitation or retardation nearly every day (observable by others, not merely subjective feelings of restlessness or being slowed down)
5. fatigue or loss of energy nearly every day
6. feelings of worthlessness or excessive or inappropriate guilt (which may be delusional) nearly every day (not merely self-reproach or guilt about being sick)
7. diminished ability to think or concentrate, or indecisiveness, nearly every day (either by subjective account or as observed by others)
8. recurrent thoughts of death (not just fear of dying), recurrent suicidal ideation without a specific plan, or a suicide attempt or a specific plan for committing suicide
B. The symptoms do not meet criteria for a Mixed Episode.
C. The symptoms cause clinically significant distress or impairment in social, occupational, or other important areas of functioning.
D. The symptoms are not due to the direct physiological effects of a substance (e.g., a drug of abuse, a medication) or a general medical condition (e.g., hypothyroidism).
E. The symptoms are not better accounted for by bereavement, i.e., after the loss of a loved one, the symptoms persist for longer than 2 months or are characterized by marked functional impairment, morbid preoccupation with worthlessness, suicidal ideation, psychotic symptoms, or psychomotor retardation.

Detecting Generalized Anxiety Disorder

For on more days than not for at least six months:

- Excessive anxiety and worry.
- Difficulty controlling the worry.
- Three or more of the following six symptoms:
  - Feeling restless or keyed up.
  - Easily becoming fatigued.
  - Experiencing sleep disturbance.
  - Finding it hard to concentrate, mind going blank.
  - Acting irritably.
  - Experiencing muscle tension
  - Undergoing impairment of functioning or relationships.

Note: Make sure the symptoms are not due to substance abuse, prescribed medication, a medical condition, post-traumatic disorder.

Detecting Obsessive-Compulsive Disorder

- Person has either obsessions or compulsions—i.e., recurring and lasting impulses or images that result in marked anxiety or distress. (The impulses are *not* everyday worries about life's problems.)
- The person cannot ignore, neutralize, or suppress the impulses.
- At some point, the person realizes the impulses are of his or her own creation.
- The behaviors are time-consuming, i.e., more than an hour a day, and/or interferes with the person's normal routine.

Compulsions are defined one of the following:

- Repetitive behaviors or mental acts, often in accordance with rigid "rules."
- The person behaves or thinks in these ways so as to prevent distress or a dreaded event, when there is no realistic cause-and-effect relationship.

Source: Reprinted with permission from the *Diagnostic and Statistical Manual on Mental Disorders*, Fourth Edition, Text Revision, Copyright 2000. American Psychiatric Association.

Depressives can become so distressed that they will cease showing up for important appointments (like depositions); manic depressives may do that or may go through the hyperactive, fast-talking, manic stage that will exaggerate a particular aspect of their personality, such as a sense of invulnerability, that will distort the perceptions of who the person is when not manic. Clients and witnesses with anxiety disorders may be overcome with dread and experience all the symptoms of a heart attack; obsessive compulsives can become paralyzed if their routines are disrupted. If these conditions are not part of the litigation, you want to keep them from becoming an issue, and keeping the client steady is an important feature. Follow the recommendations of his therapist or psychiatrist over any other advice, and keep in mind that no matter what you do, the client can undermine your efforts by not staying current on his medication. Bipolars are noted for noncompliance with their medication regime; because of the enduring stigma of mental illnesses, many people want to get off "the drugs" as soon as their mood or mental state improves. It just isn't that easy. Encouraging compliance will go a long way with these clients.

At any rate, if you have the go-ahead from the doctor or a witness with no known mental illness issues, then you can proceed. (Think of this as the mental/emotional equivalent of the warnings before beginning exercising; for most folks, it's not a problem, but if you've got a heart condition, you really shouldn't start out with any ol' exercise program without talking to the cardiologist.)

We are all under stress all the time: Stress is simply a stimulus to which we respond. It is an *overload* of stress that causes problems, or stress of a type that we don't deal well with. When suffering from stress overload, an individual will begin to react in a number of ways, some of them physical, like sore or aching muscles in the jaw from clenching teeth. The individual has amassed so many **fight-or-flight** situations (circumstances the body perceives as threatening) that the side effects have not dispersed, and they are accumulated into a mass of nasty symptoms.

There are ways to make sure that people have adequate responses to particularly stressful situations. Some are general strategies that do not apply to any particular situation, but rather prepare the mind and body to handle stress better. These are those things that we hear all the time but ignore when we most should pay attention: eat right, take vitamins, exercise, and so on. Meditation is gaining adherents as more studies show its effectiveness in reducing stress levels. However, for any of these stress relievers to have any effect, they must be practiced regularly over a significant amount of time (at least six weeks in most cases) before any benefit will be seen.

SIGNS OF THE FIGHT-OR-FLIGHT RESPONSE

- Racing thoughts
- Rapid pulse
- Gritting of teeth
- Restlessness
- Tremors
- Rapid, shallow breathing
- Serious concerned expression
- Numbness
- Impulsive behavior
- Inability to concentrate
- Narrowed attention span
- Pounding heart
- Muscular tension
- Clenched jaw
- Tightened stomach
- Increased perspiration
- Narrowed field of vision
- Cold, clammy hands
- Gripping emotions
- Dry mouth

Source: Abascal, Juan R., Brucato, Laurel, and Brucato, Dominic, *Stress Mastery: The Art of Coping Gracefully (NetEffect Series)*, 1st Edition, ©2001. Reprinted by permission of Pearson Education, Inc., Upper Saddle River, NJ.

THE CUMULATIVE BENEFITS OF REGULAR EXERCISE

- Improved sense of well-being decreased depression
- Lowered anxiety and muscular tension
- Greater ability to handle domestic and job-related stress
- Increased endorphin production (endorphins are the body's natural painkillers and mood elevators)
- Decreased production of stress hormones such as adrenalin and cortisol
- Improved concentration and productivity

(continued)

- Increased metabolic rate, leading to decreases in setpoint and easier weight loss
- Quicker recovery from acute stress
- Less fatigue; more energy and stamina
- Higher levels of HDL relative to LDL cholesterol in blood
- Stronger heart muscle that works more efficiently
- Reduced blood pressure and resting heart rate
- Improved cardiopulmonary functioning; lower risk of heart disease
- More restful sleep
- Fewer physical complaints in general; boosts in immune functioning
- Better self-image and more self-confidence
- A more attractive physique; improved muscle-to-fat ratio

Source: Abascal, Juan R., Brucato, Laurel, and Brucato, Dominic, *Stress Mastery: The Art of Coping Gracefully (NetEffect Series)*, 1st Edition, ©2001. Reprinted by permission of Pearson Education, Inc., Upper Saddle River, NJ.

So how do we help Nellie and Ned Nervous get through the next hour of testimony? The simplest techniques to teach and use are variations of breathing and visualization exercises. Some are based in hypnosis, some in meditation, but they all have the effect of helping the user to relax and focus. Quick relaxation exercises, followed by these techniques, can do wonders.

First, teach the client a few easy stretching exercises. Many people build up a lot of tension in the face, neck, and shoulders. If you are tense, you may notice that one of the first things you do is pull up your shoulders. Simply forcing yourself to drop the shoulders back will do two things: it will lengthen and stretch the muscles from the neck to the top of your shoulder where the socket meets the top of your arm, and it will open up your throat. Many people cut off their ability to speak clearly simply by this one physical manifestation of tension. Dropping the shoulders will make you sound more relaxed and in command, and then maybe you will be. There's something to the old saying, "Fake it 'til you make it."

Source: Abascal, Juan R., Brucato, Laurel, and Brucato, Dominic, *Stress Mastery: The Art of Coping Gracefully (NetEffect Series)*, 1st Edition, ©2001. Reprinted by permission of Pearson Education, Inc., Upper Saddle River, NJ.

Neck rolls and stretches are also helpful. During these movements, make sure you keep breathing steadily. Drop your chin toward your chest, relaxing as far forward as you can go without straining. Roll your head around to your left shoulder, spine, right shoulder, and back, smoothly, several times, then reverse direction. Your earlobes should graze your collar (or almost, depending on what you're wearing), and the back of your skull should meet your spine on the trip.

The second stretch is from side to side. Stare straight ahead at a constant point. Try to touch your ear to your shoulder. Hold on each side for at least 20 seconds. Usually, if you're stressed, the muscle will start out very tight and not give much at first, but there's a point at which it seems to give in and relax. Try to hang in there for that moment when you feel the muscle release.

Source: Abascal, Juan R., Brucato, Laurel, and Brucato, Dominic, *Stress Mastery: The Art of Coping Gracefully (NetEffect Series)*, 1st Edition, ©2001. Reprinted by permission of Pearson Education, Inc., Upper Saddle River, NJ.

Now, simply look over your shoulder. Try not to use your waist. Although the pictures show hands on hips, I prefer to keep my arms down, trying to keep those shoulders from hiking back up. Again, hold the stretch for a minimum of 20 seconds, trying to get those muscles to relax.

The last stretch is the chicken walk, except without the walk. Stretch your chin straight out forward, not up or down, and hold. Then pull your chin straight back into your neck as far as you can. Repeat three times. You are now ready for your chicken impression.

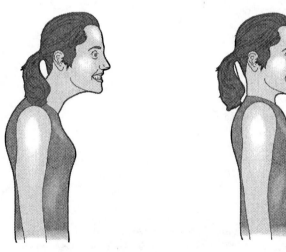

Source: Abascal, Juan R., Brucato, Laurel, and Brucato, Dominic, *Stress Mastery: The Art of Coping Gracefully (NetEffect Series)*, 1st Edition, ©2001. Reprinted by permission of Pearson Education, Inc., Upper Saddle River, NJ.

Raise both arms over your head. Grasp your left elbow with your right elbow, and pull gently toward your head, and hold for another 20 second count. Reverse arms and repeat. Now you should be ready for breathing exercises.

Unlike the stretching, which you would have a client do in private before testifying, breathing can be done both before and during the stressful event. Stress overload is caused, in part, by an accumulation of flight-or-fight responses that are not adequately dealt with. One of the first things that happens in flight-or-fight response is altered breathing. Controlling breathing, interestingly enough, can help control the rest of the response. So if you (or the client or witness) concentrate only on the breathing aspect (and keeping those shoulders down), much of the rest will take care of itself.

DIFFERENTIATING COMMUNICATION STYLES

	Passive	Assertive	Aggressive
Verbal Behaviors	Apologetic	Direct statements	Accusations, threats
	Indirect statements	Honest expression of feelings	Insults, put-downs
	Rambling	Describing objective behavior	Blaming
	Not saying what you really mean	I-statements	You-statements
	Giving up easily	Straightforward	Sarcasm
		Good listener	Failure to listen
		Talking slowly	Manipulative comments
		Emphasize key words	
Nonverbal Behaviors	Incongruencies	Actions congruent with words	Staring
	Poor eye contact	Good eye contact	Yelling, shouting
	Soft, timid voice	Firm, calm voice	Loud, hostile voice tone
	Looking down	Assured manner	Arms crossed over body
	Fidgeting	Gesturing	Finger pointing
	Leaning back	Leaning forward	Getting too close
	Stumped posture	Erect posture	Clenched fists
		Open arms	Breaking things
		Face person squarely	
You Are	Scared, anxious	Confident	Angry, full of rage
	Helpless	Effective	Indignant
	Manipulated	Respectful	Misunderstood
	Ignored	Valued	Controlling
	Resentful	Relieved	Guilty
Others Feel	Frustrated	Respected	Intimidated
	Puzzled	Valued	Alienated
	Unsure of your needs		Angry, resentful
			Humiliated, hurt
			Defensive
Results	Stress	Problem solving	Interpersonal stress
	Depression	High self-esteem	Guilt, remorse
	Low self-esteem	Self-respect	Low self-esteem
	Helplessness	Respect of others	Loss of self-respect
	Failure to solve problems	Satisfaction	Loss of respect from others
	Resentment	Good relationships	Passive-aggressive responses
	Lost opportunities	Less stress	Frustration
	Health problems	Improved health	Failure to solve problems
			Broken relationships
			Loneliness
			Hostility from others

Source: Abascal, Juan R., Brucato, Laurel, and Brucato, Dominic, *Stress Mastery: The Art of Coping Gracefully (NetEffect Series)*, 1st Edition, ©2001. Reprinted by permission of Pearson Education, Inc., Upper Saddle River, NJ.

The first thing to do is to take a long, full breath in through your nose until you feel as though you can not take in any more air. Do it slowly and steadily. Then let the air out at the same speed. Then deliberately breathe in and out at the same speed. Some say to breathe in through the nose and out through the mouth; I'd vary it when I no longer am concentrating on the breathing but am still stressed.

To calm immediate stress, you add a focus point—something to concentrate on. One favorite is to concentrate on one nostril breathing in and the other breathing out. You can also select a particular spot between your nostrils and concentrate on feeling the flow of air coming back and forth next to it. You can count. You can follow the flow of air all the way to your lungs and back out. The point is to focus on nothing but the act of breathing, which you are controlling. This tends to calm people and put them back into control of other things as well. Some people do well with focus objects—something that reminds them of a prior success, like a wedding ring or a watch given in appreciation of a job well done.

Visualization techniques add the component of envisioning some particular image to help in the calming process. Movies make jokes about "finding my happy place," but there is some merit to the idea of having a mental refuge where you can "zone off" when the stress is getting to you. Beach people like the waves; mountain people have their cozy cabins or alpine glens. Content doesn't matter; if it works, go for it. Mental rehearsing for the event is one way to handle the stress: imagining, in a relaxed state, testifying confidently and well, and how to handle the trouble areas.

The bottom line: Find a way to keep calm in the storm and focused on the job at hand. Non Illegitimi Carborundum. (Run it through **www.google.com** for a translation.)

CHAPTER SUMMARY

Clients and witnesses need to be prepared for testimony and deposition, although this can not be done to the point where the individual changes his testimony to conform to what the legal team wants the witness to say. Preparation includes a focus on physical appearance, presentation, content, and review of materials. In major cases, jury consultants (also known as *trial consultants*) may be used to assist in jury selection, witness preparation, and case material selection. One of the major barriers to testifying effectively is stress, and ordinary stress relief techniques can be helpful, although if the client or witness has mental health issues, you need to consult her mental health care provider before discussing any form of stress relief technique with her.

FOR FURTHER READING

Juan R. Abascal, Dominic Brucato, and Laurel Brucato, *Stress Mastery: The Art of Coping Gracefully* (Prentice Hall 2001). (Excellent, concise, practical resource on dealing with stress in personal and professional context).

W. William Hodes, *The Professional Duty to Horseshed Witnesses Zealously, Within the Bounds of the Law*, 30 Tex. Tech L. Rev. 1343 (1999).

Diana G. Ratcliff, *Using Trial Consultants: What Practitioners Need to Know*, 4 J. Legal Advoc. & Prac. 32 (2002).

Lisa Renee Salmi, *Don't Walk the Line: Ethical Considerations in Preparing Witnesses for Deposition and Trial*, 18 Rev. Litig. 135 (1999).

Charles Silver, *Preliminary Thoughts on the Economics of Witness Preparation*, 30 Tex. Tech L. Rev. 1383 (1999).

Franklin Strier & Donna Shestowsky, *Profiling the Profilers: A Study of the Trial Consulting Profession, Its Impact on Trial Justice and What, If Anything, to Do About It*, 1999 Wis. L. Rev. 441 (1999).

Richard C. Wydick, *The Ethics of Witness Coaching*, 17 Cardozo L. Rev. 1 (1995).

CHAPTER REVIEW

KEY TERMS

anxiety disorder	identity issues	real party in interest
bipolar disorder	interlocutory	rehabilitate
coaching	obsessive compulsive disorder	trial consultants
depression	original jurisdiction	visualization techniques
fight or flight	prohibition	writ of mandamus
functional	*Psychological Abstracts*	woodshedding
horseshedding		

FILL IN THE BLANKS

1. The _____ response evolved to protect humans from threats, as it gives us an immediate surge of energy to respond to the challenge.

2. Preparation of witnesses is often known as _____, because the older term must be said just so or it sounds like you might be cursing, but neither of the "shedding" terms do not have the same negative overtones as the term _____, which is often used to imply that the lawyer gave the witness the answer.

3. A person with a mental illness is said to be _____ when he is able to cope with normal life; the term is also used to indicate that the disorder emerges from life's circumstances, as opposed to being primarily organic, or biological, in nature.

4. Core questions that go to the issue of who a person thinks he is are called _____.

5. To ask for an order entered by an appellate court prior to the trial court entering its final appealable order, or a(n) _____ order, is a request for _____ relief.

6. When a witness has said something damaging, his attorney will try to "fix it" to make the witness look better. This is known as an attempt to _____ the witness.

7. Although often psychologists, _____ do not have to be, and may be sociologists, writers, or even movie producers.

8. _____ help you relax by giving you an image to focus on that helps you center and calm down.

9. An appellate court has _____ jurisdiction, meaning the case is filed in the court of appeals, when the petitioner requests a writ of _____, also known as a(n) _____ in some states.

10. A good source for articles on forensic psychology is _____.

11. A mood disorder characterized by "the blues"; _____ an anxiety disorder characterized by an extreme need for order; _____ a mood disorder formerly known as manic-depressive disease; and, _____ a disorder characterized by panic attacks, are some of the most common mental illnesses.

WEB WORK

1. The American Society for Trial Consultants has a Web site at http://www.astcweb.org/. What are its goals and codes? Do they answer any of the concerns about trial consultants? What publicly available information on the site is helpful for researching any of the topics addressed in this chapter?

2. Go to Dr. James Morrison's DSM-IV Made Easy site at http://www.geocities.com/morrison94/. What are the clinical criteria for each of the diagnoses mentioned in this chapter? Are there any other mental conditions that you have heard of listed in the Web site?

3. Perform a few searches on your favorite Web search engines for the term <stress relief> and you'll probably come up with a few thousand hits. Do some surfing and see if anything strikes you as useful. Don't buy into the stress-relief-in-a-pill; there are numerous scams out there.

4. Try surfing for the term <breathing exercises>. Note any useful sites.

5. Another big stress reliever is humor. Use it carefully with clients and bosses, and freely with everyone else. Find some Web sites that make you laugh. There are many lawyer joke sites out there; I don't find them funny anymore, not because I don't like lawyer jokes, but because I think I've heard them all . . . and heard them . . . and heard them. But if you find a spot that makes you laugh (I like www.theonion.com, a satirical version of, oh, *USA Today*, maybe), bookmark it and take a break to read it when you get stressed and need a laugh.

BRAIN WORK

1. One of the philosophical complaints raised against the use of jury consultants is that it tilts the system toward the wealthy. What is your response to that argument? How do you differentiate that from any other budget issue in litigation and investigation?

2. Do you think it is possible to prepare a client without affecting his story? Why or why not?

3.   Do you think there need to be more safeguards or rules regarding witness preparation, particularly nonclient witnesses? Why or why not?

4.   What other benefits can you see to the application of the stress alleviation techniques mentioned in this chapter other than for deposition or trial testimony?

5.   Another issue, not discussed in the text, that has some bearing on stress is the ability to act assertively, which is not the same as acting aggressively or passively. Why do you think this is so? What effect might it have in the context of witness testimony?

PUTTING IT TO WORK

1.   What would you say to the witnesses depicted in this chapter about their appearances? How would you go about counseling each to change his or her appearance?

2.   What would you expect to be issues in dealing with Jerry Smoker? If you were the one to prepare him for trial, how would you do so?

ENDING THE LITIGATION

> "The law is the last result of human wisdom acting upon human experience for the benefit of the public."
>
> —*Samuel Johnson (1786)*
>
> "Everyone has his day and some days last longer than others."
>
> —*Sir Winston S. Churchill (1952)*
>
> "Efficiency of a practically flawless kind may be reached naturally in the struggle for bread. But there is something beyond—a higher point, a subtle and unmistakable touch of love and pride beyond mere skill; almost an inspiration which gives to all work that finish which is almost art—which is art."
>
> —*Joseph Conrad (1906)*

INTRODUCTION

You've finished all the preliminary interviewing and investigating and discovery. What do you do with all of it? It depends on where you are taking it. There are different possibilities, depending on the type of case and the stage it is in. You may go to some form of **alternative dispute resolution: a settlement conference,** a **mediation,** or an **arbitration,** and you may choose to offer some evidence there—or, in the case of a binding arbitration, you may have to.

If you are going to a jury trial, you have multiple considerations both before and after trial that need to be considered: arranging for the presentation of the evidence, relaying instructions to witnesses, keeping track of exhibits, and helping to ensure the attempt at admission of all evidence and the preservation of error when evidence is excluded.

Regardless of when or how the case ends, you must be aware of other parties who are interested in the outcome of the litigation. Certain parties may have a financial stake that cannot be ignored, and if the investigation indicates their existence, you need to follow up and verify the extent and amount of the financial interest the party may have in your client's proceeds or payment.

ETHICAL ISSUES

In the film *A Civil Action,* the lawyers portrayed by John Travolta and Robert Duvall are shown awaiting the jury's decision on causation in the courthouse halls. During this period (and after making an offer of $20,000,000 in settlement), Duvall's character makes a statement to the effect that there's no need for anyone else to be there to make a decision about whether to settle—that attorneys are like kings in their ability to decide life-changing matters on their own.

After reading the book on which the film is based, I believe the words are those of a Hollywood writer—not those of the well-respected lawyer portrayed by Duvall, the late Jerry Facher. Hollywood has a legitimate reason for believing they're possible, though. Many lawyers act as though they need not consult their clients for settlement authority, although not usually the ones paying—they are very certain of their settlement range prior to making an offer. The lawyers on the receiving end tend to be the ones who reject or accept offers without asking their clients first.

This can be a problem. Another movie, *The Verdict,* which is horribly unrealistic in many details and has a laundry list of ethical violations, does a good job of showing why settlement without client consultation is a bad idea: the lawyer, portrayed by Paul Newman, is rounded on by the client, who demands to know why he was not told about and why the lawyer (Newman) did not accept a rather large settlement offer. The client remarks that he didn't want to have to find out about the offer from the other side, and comments that if the attorney doesn't win the case, it is he and his wife that will have to live with the error, not the lawyer.

This is the reason the client needs to be involved in the decision to settle. Although the lawyer's recommendation will weigh heavily with the client, it is still the client's cause of action. With the exception of repeat players, most clients have only one major piece of litigation (or maybe two, given the divorce rate in this country) in their lives; they need to feel that they have not wasted or missed their chance. Or, if they do settle later, they need to feel that the settlement was their call and their responsibility, or the lawyer may be facing a grievance.

Where do you come in as a paralegal? Two problems are apparent. First, the never-ending problem of "What-do-you-think?" is prone to be exacerbated because the client probably doesn't think of this as legal advice. To him, it is like asking if he got a good deal on a car. Your response to the question, however, is legal advice, so you will need to avoid commenting, even if your statement is nothing more than agreeing with the attorney. Defer and refer all questions to the boss with the license, even if the client growls. Sympathize with his anxiety, all you like, but don't give any advice about what to do.

Second, when negotiations are getting hot and heavy, make sure you know exactly where the client is so you can contact him within a few minutes. When the numbers are getting close, things seem to take on a frantic life of their own, and no one wants to lose the momentum. If you know there's a plan to begin negotiations, ask if the attorney wants the client on standby. This is not only practical, but also gently reminds the lawyer that the client needs to be involved.

Once you get to trial, you have a new set of people to whom you can't speak. You can speak to the judge and the judge's staff on your own about administrivia (Where do you want me to sit? Is it okay if I plug this in here? etc.), but anything that has any substantive bearing on the case must be addressed in the presence of a representative of the other litigants. This rule usually isn't too much of a problem, nor is the no contact rule described earlier. The party's counsel has probably told the litigant that you are the prince/ss of darkness, so other people's clients tend to avoid you.

The greater problem is avoiding casual contact with **veniremen.** *Veniremen* is the old term for anyone sitting on a panel either as a potential juror or once empanelled as a chosen juror. As a member of a legal team, you are not to improperly influence a juror; doing so can result in a mistrial as well as charges for ethical violations. It sounds easy enough to do, but when you're in a relatively small courthouse, taking the same restroom and lunch breaks, it's amazing how often you'll find yourself in close quarters with the jurors. Smiling, nodding, "excuse me," and "thank you" are fine to avoid being rude, but that's about the extent of safe interaction with jurors until a verdict is entered. Anything more is running the risk of an accusation of improper influence, not because you actually did anything wrong, but because someone will see you exchange a few words with a juror and *think* you did something wrong. Avoid putting yourself in any situation where you have to justify your actions. It's just not worth it.

EVIDENTIARY ISSUES

Just before trial, the motions in limine will be filed and argued, and you may have to prepare the brief in support of your motion and in reply to your opponent's, outlining the legal arguments for your position.

NO. <u>05-CI-101010</u>

PATTY HAUS,	§	**IN THE DISTRICT COURT**
Plaintiff	§	
	§	
V.	§	**225TH JUDICIAL DISTRICT**
	§	
JOHN JUSTICE AND VISTA LIBRE	§	
APARTMENTS,	§	
Defendants	§	**OF DUX COUNTY, CONFUSION**

<u>PLAINTIFF'S MOTION IN LIMINE</u>

To the Honorable Judge of Said Court:

Plaintiff, Patty Haus ("Movant"), prior to the voir dire examination of the jury panel and out of the presence and hearing of the panel, makes this Motion in Limine.

I.

Movant seeks to exclude matters that are irrelevant, inadmissible, or prejudicial to the material issues in this cause. If these matters are introduced into the trial through a party, a witness, or an attorney, the testimony will cause irreparable harm to Movant's, incurable by any jury instruction.

II.

Movant moves the Court to instruct all counsel and parties that violation of any of these instructions ordered by the Court may cause harm to Movant and deprive Movant of a fair and impartial trial, and the failure to abide by such instructions may constitute contempt of court.

III.

Should any of these matters be brought to the attention of the jury, either directly or indirectly, Movant will move for a mistrial. In an effort to avoid prejudice and a possible mistrial, Movant urges the Court to grant this Motion in Limine.

IV.

Movant requests the Court to enter the attached order prohibiting counsel or the parties from offering any of the evidence listed below, without first asking for a ruling from the Court, out of the hearing of the jury, on the admissibility of the evidence:

1. Any evidence that Non-Movants failed to produce in discovery or any evidence that Non-Movants failed to produce in response to requests for discovery or failed to supplement in response to Movant's discovery requests.

2. Any matters stated in the pleadings of the parties that have been superseded by amendment, in that prior pleadings have no force or effect, and matters stated therein are irrelevant to these proceedings.

3. Any reference to opposing counsel's "personal opinions" regarding the case.

4. The filing of this motion, or any ruling by the Court on this motion, suggesting or implying to the jury that Movant wrongfully and improperly moved to prohibit proof.

5. Any mention that the parties engaged in settlement negotiations of any kind or that a party did not negotiate.

6. That any actual damages awarded by the Jury in this cause under any special statute or acts will be increased by operation of law.

7. Any reference to incidents of alleged domestic violence between Plaintiff and Geronimo "Jerry" Smoker.

8. Any reference to alleged threats made by any party or witness to or about any person not a party to the litigation.

WHEREFORE, PREMISES CONSIDERED, Movant prays the Court grants this Motion in Limine, and for such other and further relief that may be awarded at law or in equity.

Respectfully submitted,

By: _____
Lisa St. Joan
100 Years War Lane, Suite 1412
Big City, Confusion 99999
(888) 555-0987
(888) 555-0986 (telefax)
State of Confusion Bar No. 0987676
Attorney for Plaintiff
Patti Haus

CERTIFICATE OF SERVICE

I certify that on March 27, 2004 a true and correct copy of Plaintiff's Motion in Limine was served by facsimile transmission on Thomas Battle at (888) 555-1231.

_____
Lisa St. Joan

NO. 05-CI-101010

PATTY HAUS	§	**IN THE DISTRICT COURT**
Plaintiff,	§	
	§	
V.	§	**225TH JUDICIAL DISTRICT**
	§	
JOHN JUSTICE AND VISTA LIBRE	§	
APARTMENTS	§	
Defendants.	§	**OF DUX COUNTY, CONFUSION**

ORDER GRANTING
PLAINTIFF'S MOTION IN LIMINE

On _____, the Court considered the PLAINTIFF'S MOTION IN LIMINE, and after reviewing the evidence and hearing the arguments, the Court hereby **ORDERS:**

Counsel for all parties herein, any and all witnesses called on their behalf, are to refrain from any mention or interrogation, directly or indirectly, in any manner whatsoever, regarding the subject matter in the paragraphs marked **GRANTED** below. This prohibition includes the offering of documentary evidence, without first requesting and obtaining a ruling from the Court, outside the presence and hearing of the jury or any prospective jury member.

1. Any evidence that Non-Movants failed to produce in discovery or any evidence that Non-Movants failed to produce in response to requests for discovery or failed to supplement in response to discovery requests.

GRANTED: ___X___

DENIED: _____

2. Any matters stated in the pleadings of the parties that have been superseded by amendment, in that prior pleadings have no force or effect, and matters stated therein are irrelevant to these proceedings.

GRANTED: ___X___

DENIED: _____

3. Any reference to opposing counsel's "personal opinions" regarding the case.

GRANTED: __X__

DENIED: _____

4. The filing of this motion, or any ruling by the Court on this motion, suggesting or implying to the jury that Movant wrongfully and improperly moved to prohibit proof.

GRANTED: __X__

DENIED: _____

5. Any mention that the parties engaged in settlement negotiations of any kind or that a party did not negotiate.

GRANTED: __X__

DENIED: _____

6. That any actual damages awarded by the Jury in this cause under any special statute or acts will be increased by operation of law.

GRANTED: __X__

DENIED: _____

7. Any reference to incidents of alleged domestic violence between Plaintiff and Geronimo "Jerry" Smoker.

GRANTED: __X__

DENIED: _____

8. Any reference to alleged threats made by any party or witness to or about any person not a party to the litigation.

GRANTED: _____

DENIED: __X__

SIGNED this _____ day of _____, 200__.

_____
JUDGE PRESIDING

Approved By:

_____
Lisa St. Joan
Attorney for Plaintiff Patty Haus
100 Years War Lane, Suite 1412
Big City, Confusion 99999
(888) 555-0987
(888) 555-0986 (fax)
State of Confusion Bar No. 0987676

_____
Thomas Battle
Attorney for John Justice and Vista Libre Apartments
2020 Slaughter Lane
Big City, Confusion 99999
(888) 555-1230
(888) 555-1231 (fax)
State of Confusion Bar No. 1230303

If the motion in limine is denied, and evidence is allowed in or is talked about before the jury without being introduced, the movant may appeal the denial of the motion. In order to preserve the issue for review by an appellate court, the movant may also need to object when the allowed evidence is introduced and mentioned.

Warren v. Sharp, Docket No. 28562, 2003 Ida. LEXIS 168 (November 21, 2003).

Two automobile accidents occurred on Highway 200 on January 7, 1997, in the late afternoon. The first was a one-car accident, which left Lily Sharp's vehicle in a snow bank with her vehicle facing traffic. The second involved Glenn Warren's vehicle striking Stephanie Waterman's vehicle, which resulted in Glenn Warren's death. Bonnie Warren, the widow, brought this action against Sharp alleging Sharp's negligence was a proximate cause of Glenn Warren's death. After trial, a jury found no negligence on the part of Sharp. This case comes before the Court following the district court's grant of a motion for new trial. We reverse and remand for further proceedings . . .

On January 7, 1997, Lily Sharp was traveling westbound on Highway 200. Sometime between 4:30 and 4:45 P.M., Sharp lost control of her vehicle and eventually came to rest facing eastbound in a snow bank on the westbound shoulder of the road. Shortly thereafter, Glenn Warren was traveling westbound on Highway 200. Warren's vehicle lost control and struck Stephanie Waterman's vehicle, which was traveling in the opposite eastbound lane. Glenn Warren died as a result of the accident.

Glenn Warren's wife, Bonnie Thompson Warren ("Warren"), filed a complaint alleging Lily Sharp's negligence was the proximate cause of her husband's death. Prior to trial, Sharp filed a motion in limine seeking to exclude the opinions of Warren's accident reconstruction expert. Following a hearing, the district court denied the motion. A five-day jury trial began on September 24, 2001, with the jury returning a verdict finding no negligence by Sharp.

On October 11, 2001, Warren filed a motion for new trial before judgment was entered. Judgment was entered on October 18, 2001, against Warren, dismissing the claims against Sharp. Later, on April 4, 2002, the district court granted the motion for new trial . . . Sharp appeals . . . the denial of her motion in limine. . . .

The standard of review which is to be exercised by an appellate court reviewing the grant or denial of a motion for new trial is well settled. Because the trial court is in a far better position to weigh the persuasiveness of all the evidence and the demeanor, credibility, and testimony of witnesses, this Court has consistently held that the trial court's grant or denial of such motions must be upheld unless the court has manifestly abused the wide discretion vested in it.

. . . When an exercise of discretion is reviewed on appeal, the Court inquires: (1) whether the lower court rightly perceived the issue as one of discretion; (2) whether the court acted within the boundaries of such discretion and consistently with any legal standards applicable to specific choices; and (3) whether the court reached its decision by exercise of reason . . .

Sharp contends that the district court abused its discretion in denying her motion in limine seeking to exclude the expert testimony of William Skelton, Warren's accident reconstruction expert. Sharp argues that Skelton's opinions were not supported by a reliable scientific foundation as required by I.R.E. 702 and were not based on physical evidence. Sharp contends that the expert's testimony was based upon impermissible assumptions and speculations. Sharp argues the district court's ruling allowed jurors to pick and choose which assumption they would rely upon or to just substitute their own common sense. By allowing jurors to pick and chose which expert opinions they accept or discard, Sharp contends the district court abused its discretion . . .

It is clear from the record that Dr. Skelton is an engineer and has expertise in the area of automobile accident reconstruction. In ruling on the motion in limine, the district court acknowledged that Dr. Skelton's testimony, in part, relied upon assumptions and speculation as to how the accident occurred. However, the district court found that there was a factual basis for the testimony and that "his opinion is in part based upon the reaction and perception time studies, time and distance calculations, and then the fundamental laws of physics with regard to objects at rest and objects in motion." The district court determined that the testimony was not based on junk science. The district court said "the lack of skid marks on the pavement should not preclude a party from attempting to put forward the best evidence that exists in explaining an event like this."

A motion in limine seeks an advance ruling on the admissibility of evidence . . . The motion in limine is based upon an alleged set of facts rather than the actual testimony in order to for the trial court to make its ruling and therefore is not a final order . . . The trial court may reconsider the issue at any time, including when the actual presentation of facts is made. . . .

There is nothing in the record to suggest that the district court acted outside the boundaries of its discretion in denying the motion in limine. This Court holds that the district court did not err in denying Sharp's motion in limine . . .

. . . We affirm the district court's ruling on Sharp's motion in limine. We hold that a portion of Dr. Skelton's expert testimony was inadmissible. No fees are awarded, however costs are awarded as a matter of right to Sharp as the prevailing party.

Preservation of evidence or **preservation of error** refers to taking the proper steps to ensure that the record of the trial reflects the attorney's argument, the judge's actions, and the content of the evidence. Ordinarily when evidence is excluded, the attorney must try to admit the evidence, and the judge must rule that it is inadmissible. When it is testomonial evidence, the attorney must then remember to make a record of the proffered evidence at some point when the jury is not in attendance. This record is usually called an **offer of proof.** In the midst of everything that goes on in a trial, it is easy for this to slip the attorney's mind; if you are there to keep track of the evidence, you need to make sure this is accomplished. If the offer of proof isn't made, you won't be able to complain about it on appeal.

Lozoya v. Sanchez, 66 P.3d 948 (N.M. 2003).

This case arises from two automobile collisions in which Ubaldo and Osbaldo Lozoya, father and son, were traveling together. The first of these collisions took place on June 21, 1999. Ubaldo and Osbaldo were stopped at a red light on Coors Boulevard in Albuquerque when another vehicle collided with them from behind. The other vehicle was driven by Defendant Diego Sanchez, an employee of Defendant Statkus Engines, LLC.

At the scene of the accident, neither of the Lozoyas complained of any injuries. Ubaldo began to experience pain shortly thereafter, however, in one of his arms, head, and legs. Father and son visited Presbyterian Occupational Medical Clinic eight days later. The doctor found that Ubaldo was experiencing tenderness in his neck and back, but that his range of motion in these areas was "pretty close to normal." An x-ray showed what appeared to be a compression of one of Ubaldo's vertebrae that "looked like it was old," but the doctor believed that the soreness Ubaldo was experiencing was a result of the accident. Ubaldo visited the same doctor again about a week later, and the doctor decided that Ubaldo could return to work on a light duty basis.

Osbaldo reported experiencing lower back pain. The doctor referred him to a physiatrist (muscle & bone specialist) to determine if anything further should be done. The physiatrist diagnosed him as having a soft tissue injury and sent him to physical therapy. Osbaldo did not show up for this third appointment with the physiatrist so he was released from care.

Ubaldo continued to experience pain, however, and he followed up with another doctor. This doctor ordered chiropractic care and physical therapy. Ubaldo went to one physical therapy appointment, then stopped. This doctor believed that Ubaldo would not be able to return to his former occupation because of the back problems he was experiencing. Ubaldo was presented with the options of either enduring the pain as it existed, taking medication, having "epidural blocks" performed, or surgery. Ubaldo decided that he did not want the injections or surgery.

On April 18, 2000, approximately ten months after the first accident, Ubaldo and Osbaldo were involved in another collision as they were driving toward a job site . . . This time, the other vehicle involved was a dump truck operated by Defendant Philip McWaters. . . . The impact of the McWaters vehicle pushed the Lozoya vehicle into the vehicle in front of it . . .

The Lozoyas' claims in both accidents were brought in a single lawsuit, and the case went to a jury trial in June 2001. During the course of the trial, the court did not allow Plaintiffs to present evidence that Ubaldo had one vehicle repossessed for failure to make the payments, and that foreclosure proceedings on the house had recently been initiated against him, although they were allowed to inform the jury that he had not been able to make the payments. . . .

Mr. Sanchez and Statkus Engines admitted negligence as to the first accident. The jury returned a verdict in favor of Plaintiffs as to that accident, assessing damages in favor of Ubaldo in the amount of $38,500, and in favor of Osbaldo in the amount of $1500. Although the court allowed the jury to consider Sara's [Ubaldo's live-in of 20 years] loss of household services by Ubaldo, the jury did not award any damages as to that claim. Mr. McWaters did not admit negligence as to the second accident, and the jury found that he was not negligent. Accordingly, no Plaintiff was awarded any damages as a result of the second accident. After the trial's conclusion, Plaintiffs moved for a new trial, based on the same asserted errors they bring before this Court, as well as some others. This motion was denied and the district court entered judgment according to the jury verdict. . . .

Plaintiffs . . . claim that the court should have allowed the jury to consider the fact that Ubaldo had one vehicle repossessed, and foreclosure proceedings on his house had been initiated. They also claim the court should have allowed the jury to learn the amount of social security payments that Ubaldo received . . . We address each argument in turn, and hold that the district court should be affirmed as to all issues. . . . .

. . . Plaintiffs argue that the district court erred by excluding evidence that Ubaldo's vehicle had been repossessed after the accidents, and that foreclosure proceedings had been initiated on his house. Plaintiffs contend that these circumstances were caused by the financial hardship Ubaldo and Sara experienced as a result of the accidents.

We will reverse the district court's decision to admit or exclude evidence only if it is clear that the court abused its discretion . . . Here, the district court excluded evidence of the foreclosure proceedings and repossession both because of their lack of relevancy and their propensity to confuse the issues . . . The district court properly instructed the jury to consider damages for lost earnings and earning capacity. We agree with the district court that this evidence was not relevant . . . The foreclosure proceedings and repossession are independent of Ubaldo's lost earnings claim, and they do not change the amount of economic damages. Further, the district court properly exercised its discretion in excluding the evidence . . . because evidence of the foreclosure proceedings and repossession may have given the jury the wrong impression that Plaintiffs should have been compensated for these events. . .

Plaintiffs also argue that the district court improperly excluded evidence of the amount of monthly payments that Ubaldo received from the Social Security Administration. They argue that the jury may have assumed that these payments fully compensated Ubaldo for his injuries, while in reality they were quite low. Plaintiffs never attempted to have this evidence brought before the jury, either through asking a witness, or through an offer of proof. In other words, this evidence was never excluded; it simply was not offered. Plaintiffs discussed the amount of the payments with the court, out of the presence of the jury. If anything, it appears that the court told Plaintiffs that they may go ahead and offer the evidence, but they decided not to do so. When Plaintiffs did put evidence before the jury that the Social Security Administration had determined that Ubaldo was totally disabled, over Defendants' objection, Plaintiffs never attempted to inform the jury of the amount of these payments. "[A] trial court can be expected to decide only the case presented under issues fairly invoked.". . . Thus, we require a party to invoke a ruling or decision by the district court to preserve a question for review . . . Because the district court did not rule on this issue, Plaintiffs may not raise it for the first time on appeal . . .

. . . [W]e hold that the district court did not abuse its discretion by excluding certain evidence at trial. . . .

PARTIES WITH INTEREST IN THE OUTCOME

Along with the actual parties to the case are those with a financial interest, usually some type of **lienholder.** A lienholder is generally someone who can enforce a debt against specific property interests. A **general creditor,** in contrast, is someone to whom money is owed, but who doesn't have the ability to directly enforce the debt against any particular property of the person owing the money.

How do you find out if these parties exist in your case? Follow the money. Ask the client appropriate questions to find out about the financial side of the case: What are your out-of-pocket damages? Who paid the bills for those things—medical care, income while out of work, and the like? While the deadbeat dad wasn't paying child support, how did you get along? If a business or the government took care of some portion of the legal damages or consequences, there's a good chance they'll want their money back.

Some lienholders' rights accrue under contract; others arise under statute. Also, the common law principle of **subrogation** states that when someone has a legal obligation to pay for damages done to another, that person may step into the shoes of the person for whom they paid and exercise his legal rights to the extent necessary to recover payment. For instance, if a homeowners' insurance company pays for your house that burns to the ground, it may sue the arsonist when he is found and recover as much as it paid. If the insurer gets more than it paid, it would have to give the money to you. (Some insurance defense firms take these kinds of files—ones with a very low probability of recovery—as a favor to their insurance clients. Usually new associates get stuck with them for "training"—that's what they're grumbling about when they talk about **subro files**.)

Royal Ins. Co. v. Roadarmel, 11 P.3d 105 (Mont. 2000).

The Royal Insurance Company ("Royal") initiated this subrogation action against Earl W. Roadarmel ("Roadarmel"), who had been injured in a workers' compensation accident in 1986, and the attorney who prosecuted his claim, Donald E. White ("White"). The Workers' Compensation Court, State of Montana ("the WCC"), granted summary judgment to Royal under the subrogation statute of the Workers' Compensation Act, § 39-71-414, MCA (1985), finding Roadarmel and White (collectively "Appellants") personally liable for Royal's share of third-party proceeds received as a result of litigation against two third parties, the Exxon Corporation and the Great Western Chemical Company. Roadarmel and White appeal the WCC's grant of summary judgment to Royal. We reverse and remand. . . .

Roadarmel suffered an industrial injury stemming from chemical exposure in September of 1986 while working as a heavy equipment operator on a highway project in Butte, Montana. Roadarmel filed a workers' compensation claim against his employer, Acme Concrete, which was defended by its insurance carrier, Royal. White represented Roadarmel and the case was tried before the WCC, resulting in a judgment for Roadarmel . . .

Roadarmel, represented by White, also filed a third-party action against the Exxon Corporation and the Great Western Chemical Company, alleging strict liability in tort for failure to warn of possible effects of the chemical agent which caused Roadarmel's injuries. Roadarmel, through White, provided notice to Royal, as required by the subrogation standard of § 39-71-414, MCA (1985), that a third-party action was being commenced. Pursuant to the subrogation statute, Roadarmel requested that Royal pay a portion of the costs of the third-party action. Royal agreed to participate in the costs rather than waive 50% of its subrogation rights under § 39-71-414, MCA (1985), and tendered a check for $5,000 towards the costs of the third-party action.

On March 10, 1992, at the conclusion of the jury trial in federal district court, White sent notice to Royal advising it of Roadarmel's successful third-party action and of the fact that the third parties had filed an appeal with the Ninth Circuit Court of Appeals. The Ninth Circuit subsequently upheld the verdict. On February 18, 1994, White sent another letter to Royal advising it of the resolution of the third-party appeal. This letter attached copies of the check received from Great Western Chemical and the jury verdict forms; provided a break-down of the actual costs of the third-party action; and requested that Royal determine its subrogation interest in a portion of the third-party proceeds.

Royal then independently computed the amount it contended it was owed, and by letters dated April 7 and October 3 of 1994, advised Roadarmel that it was going to file an action to determine its subrogation interest in the proceeds from the third-party action. White, acting on behalf of Roadarmel, did not respond to either of Royal's aforementioned letters. However, after receiving Roadarmel's February 18, 1994 notice of the successful third-party action, a period of three years passed before Royal filed, on October 29, 1997, a petition for hearing to determine its subrogation rights in the third-party proceeds.

Though discovery in the subrogation action, Royal learned that White had disbursed the third-party proceeds to Roadarmel on February 18, 1994, the same date that White had requested a computation of Royal's subrogation interest. White, upon disbursing the money, allegedly instructed Roadarmel to hold the funds pending a subrogation determination. Royal amended its petition, on November 17, 1997, to include a separate count against White for an alleged breach of the duty of trust owed Royal as a third-party beneficiary of the trust imposed on the third-party proceeds.

The WCC decided this case on cross-motions for summary judgment. The court determined that a "subrogation agreement" had been formed in the exchange of letters between White and Royal's attorney, James G. Edmiston (Edmiston), and that the statute of limitations on the contract had not expired. Therefore, the WCC issued judgment in the amount of $63,864.79 jointly and severally against Roadarmel and White for breaching the subrogation contract and failing to honor Royal's "first lien" on the judgment . . .

. . . Roadarmel and White contend that Royal's action to collect a portion of the third-party proceeds under the subrogation statute of the Workers' Compensation Act, § 39-71-414(1), MCA (1985), is time-barred by the two-year statute of limitations which governs actions based upon "a liability created by statute," § 27-2-211(1)(c), MCA. The basis for the position of Appellants is that the subrogation right of Royal constitutes a "statutory liability" which is entirely dependent upon § 39-71-414, MCA (1985). There is no common law right involved here, asserts Appellants, and without the statute there would be no liability as to the third party proceeds received by Roadarmel. Therefore, they argue that the two-year statute of limitations of § 27-2-211(1)(c), MCA, governs Royal's claim for reimbursement against Roadarmel. We agree with the position of Appellants.

Section 27-2-211, MCA, provides in pertinent part that "within 2 years is the period prescribed for the commencement of an action upon . . . a liability created by statute other than . . . a penalty or forfeiture; or . . . a statutory debt created by the payment of public assistance." Section 27-2-211(1)(c)(i)-(ii), MCA. It is not contended here that Royal's entitlement to a portion of the third-party proceeds pursuant to § 39-71-414(1), MCA (1985), is in the nature of a "penalty or forfeiture" or a "statutory debt created by the payment of public assistance." Thus, the question becomes whether Roadarmel's obligation to Royal amounts to a "liability created by statute" within the meaning of § 27-2-211(1)(c), MCA.

To begin with, there is no doubt that the insurer's "right of subrogation" provided for in § 39-71-414, MCA (1985), creates a statutory liability as to any recovery by the injured employee against a third party . . . The insurer's right of subrogation is a first lien on the claim, judgment, or recovery. . . .

However, that does not end our inquiry. As Appellants correctly contend, the phrase "liability created by statute" has a settled meaning in the law of Montana as well as other states. This Court has construed the phrase to mean "'a liability which would not exist but for the statute'". . . Put differently, the test is whether liability would exist absent the statute in question. . . .

. . . At this juncture, it becomes necessary to address Royal's contention, as accepted by the WCC, that the correspondence regarding the third-party action between the respective attorneys, White and Edmiston, created a "subrogation agreement" to which the statutes of limitations for contract actions apply. . . .

The problem with Royal's position is that . . . no contract was formed concerning Royal's subrogation interest in the third-party proceeds because all of the correspondence allegedly giving rise to the "subrogation agreement" took place in the context of the mandatory and self-executing right of subrogation . . . and, therefore, lacked the essential element of free and mutual consent. . . .

The correspondence in this case only confirmed in writing that which was required by the statute, from the initial notice that the third-party action was being filed up to the final accounting of the successful appeal before the Ninth Circuit. Thus, we hold that the WCC erred in concluding that the correspondence between the parties, which took place entirely in the context of the mandatory statutory procedure provided for in § 39-71-414, MCA (1985), gave rise to an enforceable contract. . . .

Our question now is whether an insurer's "first lien" under § 39-71-414(1), MCA (1985), against any proceeds recovered in a third-party action by an injured employee constitutes a "liability created by statute" governed by the two-year statute of limitations of § 27-2-211(1)(c), MCA. We conclude that it does . . .

While we recognize that rights of equitable subrogation exist at common law, we nevertheless determine that the insurer's "first lien" against any third-party proceeds recovered by the injured employee must be conceptually distinguished from the common law right of equitable subrogation. . . .

. . . "[T]he concept of subrogation merely gives the insurer the right to prosecute the cause of action which the insured possessed against anyone legally responsible for the latter's harm." . . . Therefore, an insurer's claim by subrogation, being purely derivative, is subject to the same statute of limitations as though the cause of action were sued upon by the insured. . . .

The Workers' Compensation Act provides for such a subrogation claim proper. *See* § 39-71-414(3), MCA (1985) (providing that insurer may institute third-party action if employee fails to do so within one year of date of injury). Though the statute as a whole is loosely phrased in terms of "subrogation," the insurer's right of subrogation *per se* provided for in subsection (3) must be distinguished from the insurer's "first lien" under § 39-71-414(1), MCA (1985), which amounts to a statutory right of "reimbursement" rather than a subrogation right in its classic sense. . . .

. . . Section 39-71-414(1), MCA (1985), though phrased in terms of an "insurer's right of subrogation," amounts to a statutory right to reimbursement or recoupment as against proceeds recovered from a third-party tortfeasor. For purposes of the relevant statute of limitations, this statutory right of reimbursement must be distinguished from the insurer's right of subrogation proper as provided for in § 39-71-414(3), MCA (1985). Subrogation, in its common law sense, is the substitution of one person in place of the other, so that the person substituted succeeds to the rights of the other in relation to the debt or claim at issue. . . .

Now we must determine when Royal's reimbursement claim accrued for purposes of determining whether it was timely filed. Under Montana law, a claim or cause of action accrues when all elements of the claim or cause exist or have occurred. . . .

. . . [T]he parties in this case are in agreement that Roadarmel's February 18, 1994 notice to Royal of the successful completion of the third-party action triggered the start of the two-year limitations period . . . To give Royal the benefit of the doubt, we assume without deciding that the statute of limitations began to run on February 18, 1994. From that date until the time Royal filed for determination of its statutory right to reimbursement, three years elapsed. Thus, we hold that Royal's claim against Roadarmel based on a liability created by statute is time-barred. . . .

. . . White contends that the three-year statute of limitations . . . bars any action Royal has against him based upon an alleged breach of trust. Before the WCC, Royal argued that White was personally liable for its subrogation interest since he was a "constructive trustee" of the third-party funds recovered by Roadarmel. . . .

While White's failure to respond may have been "discourteous and unprofessional," Royal provides no reasonable explanation as to why it waited several years, after informing Roadarmel that it was going to bring an action for determination of its subrogation interest, to file its claim. . . .

Royal's claim against Roadarmel based on the "first lien" created by § 39-71-414(1), MCA (1985), is time-barred. Put differently, Royal's statutory lien was "extinguished" as a matter of law two years after it received the notice of February 18, 1994 . . . Royal concedes this point on appeal: "the insurer's first lien is only extinguished by the running of the statute of limitations on the principal obligation." Therefore, even assuming that Royal is correct in asserting that the three-year statute of limitations of § 72-34-511(1)(a), MCA, did not begin to run until 1998, by that point in time White could no longer be characterized as a trustee, constructive or otherwise, of the third-party proceeds. Alternatively, if we assume that the three-year statute of limitations began to run in 1994, Royal's action against White was untimely as it was filed three years after Royal was put on notice of successful completion of Roadarmel's third-party action against Exxon and Great Western Chemical. . . .

Royal's reimbursement claim against Roadarmel is barred by the two-year statute of limitations of § 27-2-211(1)(c), MCA, and Royal's breach of trust claim against White is similarly barred by the three-year statute of limitations of § 72-34-511(1)(a), MCA. Where, as here, all of the facts bearing on the resolution of legal issues are before this Court, we have the authority to reverse the trial court's grant of summary judgment and direct it to enter summary judgment in favor of the other party . . . Reversed and remanded for entry of summary judgment in favor of Roadarmel and White.

Any kind of lienholder or person with a legal interest may have recourse in the underlying lawsuit. Some must join the case as an **intervenor,** which is a special kind of party who does not plan on arguing the facts but simply states that if one party prevails, they get something because of another set of facts. The pleading an intervenor uses to officially enter the litigation is a plea in intervention. Usually these are financial claims, but there are other sorts of intervenors, such as family members affected in child custody suits. Others may simply make a claim whenever they become aware that monies are to be paid or have been paid, whether for reimbursement, recoupment, or contribution.

PATTY HAUS	§	**IN THE DISTRICT COURT**
Plaintiff,	§	
	§	
v.	§	**225TH JUDICIAL DISTRICT**
	§	
JOHN JUSTICE AND VISTA LIBRE	§	
APARTMENTS	§	
Defendants.	§	**OF DUX COUNTY, TEXAS**

<u>**PLEA IN INTERVENTION**</u>

TO THE HONORABLE JUDGE OF SAID COURT:

NOW COMES MIKE'S MECHANICS ("Intervenor") and files this Plea in Intervention, and in support thereof would show the Court the following:

I. PARTIES AND SERVICE

1. Plaintiff, Patty Haus, has appeared in this action as an individual and may be served with notice of this Plea by sending a copy to her attorney, Lisa St. Joan, at 100 Years War Lane, Suite 1412, Big City, Confusion 99999.

2. Defendant, John Justice, has appeared in this action as an individual and may be served with notice of this Plea by sending a copy to his attorney, Thomas Battle, at 2020 Slaughter Lane, Big City, Confusion 99999.

3. Defendant, Vista Libre Apartments, has appeared in this action and may be served with notice of this Plea by sending a copy to its attorney, Thomas Battle, at 2020 Slaughter Lane, Big City, Confusion 99999.

II.

5. Intervenor MIKE'S MECHANICS has a justiciable interest in the matters in controversy in this litigation. MIKE'S MECHANICS provided repairs to the pick-up truck that was damaged in the incident mad the basis of this litigation, and has not been paid for said repairs.

III.

6. As a direct and proximate result of the occurrence made the basis of this claim, Intervenor has provided reasonable and necessary repairs to the pick-up truck owned by Geronimo "Jerry" Smoker to the extent of $5,623.

WHEREFORE, PREMISES CONSIDERED, Intervenor, MIKE'S MECHANICS, respectfully prays that the parties take notice of the filing of this Plea in Intervention, and that upon a final hearing of the cause, judgment be entered for the Intervenor and against Plaintiffs or Defendants for damages in an amount within the jurisdictional limits of the Court; together with pre-judgment interest at the maximum rate allowed by law; post-judgment interest at the legal rate, costs of court; and such other and further relief to which the Intervenor may be entitled at law or in equity.

Respectfully submitted,

By: _____
Fidel Semper
Confusion Bar No. 678910
117 Big Boulevard
Big City, Confusion 99999
Tel. (888) 555-4554
Fax (888) 555-4556
Attorney for Intervenor
MIKE'S MECHANICS

CERTIFICATE OF SERVICE

I certify that on March 27, 200X a true and correct copy of Plaintiff's Petition in Intervention was personally delivered to Lisa St. Joan, attorney for the plaintiff, Patti Haus, at 100 Years War Lane, Suite 1412, Big City, Confusion 99999 and to Thomas Battle, attorney for the defendants, John Justice and Vista Libre Apartments, at 2020 Slaughter Lane, Big City, Confusion 99999.

Sarah Miller

Physical or Mental Health Care Lienholders

One of the most common kinds of lienholders is health care insurers or governmental entities providing health care, whether physical or mental. If the injury occurred while the plaintiff was on the job, there is probably a **workers' compensation lien (comp lien)** somewhere. How draconian the lien is depends on your state's statute. Often comp liens are **first money liens,** meaning that the **workers' compensation insurance company (comp carrier)** will be paid what it is owed before the plaintiff sees any money. For example, if the plaintiff is awarded medical damages (past and future) of $20,000, lost wages of $5,000, and general damages of $25,000, but the defendant has no money that may be collected except the $25,000 automobile insurance liability policy, and the comp lien is $25,000, the comp carrier will get the entire amount to be paid.

Having a legal right, though, doesn't mean you have to use it. Comp carriers also often have the right to bring suit in the claimant's name. (In this context, **claimant** refers to the worker making the workers' compensation claim.) As you might imagine, as a practical matter it doesn't work well to file suit on behalf of an unwilling, unhappy claimant. A smart comp adjuster will go ahead and make some sort of compromise on the amount of the lien if only a limited amount of money is available in settlement. (You have probably gathered by now that *comp* is used as shorthand for everything referring to workers' compensation and that *carrier* is used interchangeably with *insurance company*.) You will, unfortunately, run into some not-so-smart ones who will stick to their guns and refuse to compromise. This puts the legal team in a bad situation, particularly in a contingency fee case if the comp lien is caught late. You've all put time into the case, and now even if you win, your client loses. Under either statute or case law, the attorney is usually entitled to fees. If under case law, the courts have generally paid the attorney under the theory of **quantum meruit** or some other justification, finding that is unfair for the carrier to profit at the expense of the attorney when he has worked on the case, and that it is also unfair for the injured party to bear all of the costs of recovery if there is some amount of recovery to share.

Alvarado v. Kiewit Pacific Co., 993 P.2d 549 (Haw. 2000).

We granted the petition for a writ of certiorari filed by petitioners-appellees Kiewit Pacific Company (Kiewit) and their workers' compensation insurance carrier, Aetna Casualty and Surety Company (Aetna), to review the decision of the Intermediate Court of Appeals (ICA) in *Alvarado v. Kiewit Pacific*, 92 Haw. 524, 993 P.2d 558 (Haw. Ct. App. April 8, 1998) (hereinafter the "ICA opinion"). In *Alvarado*, respondent-appellant Marcelo Alvarado (Alvarado) appealed the circuit court's July 9, 1996 judgment granting Kiewit and Aetna's motion for reimbursement of their lien. The ICA vacated and remanded the circuit court's judgment, holding, inter alia, that: (1) the employer and insurance carrier were entitled to first lien only in amount of workers' compensation expended less their share of attorney's fees and expenses and (2) the employer's and their carrier's "share" of attorney's fees and expenses was to be based upon the amount of benefits already paid and the amount of future benefits they were relieved from paying, as a result of the settlement. . . .

In September of 1991, Alvarado, a Kiewit employee, suffered a work-related injury, within the scope of his employment, when he was struck by a motor vehicle owned by Hygrade Electric Company (Hygrade). At the time of Alvarado's injury, Kiewit was insured by a policy of workers' compensation insurance through Aetna. Kiewit and Aetna accepted liability for Alvarado's workers' compensation claim and paid workers' compensation benefits to or on behalf of Alvarado.

Subsequently, on February 3, 1993, Alvarado filed a complaint against Hygrade seeking to recover damages resulting from the accident. On or about January 3, 1995, Hygrade made an offer of judgment to Alvarado in the amount of $110,000.00. On January 31, 1995, Kiewit and Aetna filed a motion for intervention, which the circuit court orally granted on February 8, 1995. Alvarado accepted Hygrade's offer and a judgment in favor of Alvarado was entered on April 5, 1995. Final judgment in favor of Kiewit and Aetna, against Alvarado, in the amount of $72,310.25 was entered on July 9, 1996.

The ICA's opinion outlined a method to distribute, between an employer and employee, the amount of a settlement recovered by an injured employee who prosecutes a third-party tortfeasor alone. The ICA determined that pursuant to HRS § 386-8, the starting point is: (1) the total amount of the judgment or settlement, less (2) the reasonable litigation expenses and attorneys' fees which are based solely upon the services rendered by the employee's attorney in effecting recovery both for the benefit of the employee and the employer, less (3) the amount of the employer's expenditure for compensation which is reduced by (4) the employer's "share" of expenses and attorney's fees.

The ICA held that the circuit court did not properly reduce the amount of the employer's expenditure for workers' compensation by the employer's share of the employee's attorney's fees and expenses. Thus, the ICA vacated in part the circuit court's August 4, 1995 order granting Kiewit's and Aetna's motion for reimbursement of workers' compensation lien and the July 9, 1996 circuit court judgment in favor of Kiewit and Aetna and against Alvarado, remanding the case for determination of Kiewit's and Aetna's share of Alvarado's attorney's fees and costs.

On May 5, 1998 Kiewit and Aetna applied for a writ of certiorari seeking review of the ICA opinion, which we granted on May 12, 1998 . . .

The interpretation of a statute is a question of law which the appellate courts review de novo . . .

When construing a statute, our foremost obligation is to ascertain and give effect to the intention of the legislature, which is to be obtained primarily from the language contained in the statute itself. And we must read statutory language in the context of the entire statute and construe it in a manner consistent with its purpose.

When there is doubt, doubleness of meaning, or indistinctiveness or uncertainty of an expression used in a statute, an ambiguity exists.

In construing an ambiguous statute, the meaning of the ambiguous words may be sought by examining the context, with which the ambiguous words, phrases, and sentences may be compared, in order to ascertain their true meaning . . . Moreover, the courts may resort to extrinsic aids in determining the legislative intent. One avenue is the use of legislative history as an interpretive tool. . . .

Also, this court is bound to construe statutes so as to avoid absurd results. . . .

HRS § 386-8 provides in relevant part that: If the action is prosecuted by the employee alone, the employee shall be entitled to apply out of the amount of the judgment for damages, or settlement in case the action is compromised before judgment, the reasonable litigation expenses incurred in preparation and prosecution of such action, together with a reasonable attorney's fee which shall be based solely upon the services rendered by the employee's attorney in effecting recovery both for the benefit of the employee and the employer. After the payment of such expenses and attorney's fee there shall be applied out of the amount of the judgment or settlement proceeds, the amount of the employer's expenditure for compensation, less his share of such expenses and attorney's fee. On application of the employer, the court shall allow as a first lien against the amount of the judgment for damages or settlement proceeds, the amount of the employer's expenditure for compensation, less his share of such expenses and attorney's fee.

. . . Inasmuch as HRS § 386-8 does not contain an express definition of "share," the term is ambiguous. However, legislative history provides us with explicit guidance of the legislature's intent when they amended HRS § 386-8. The current language of HRS § 386-8 was amended in 1973, with the addition of the language "less [the employer's] share of such expenses and attorney's fee." . . .

The House of Representatives specifically stated:

> This bill proposes to explicitly restate the intent of the legislature to require an employer or insurance carrier to share in the payment of attorney's fees and costs in cases where an injured employee brings a third party action and there is a recovery from a third person which benefits both the employee and the employer. The court's interpretation which created a windfall for the employer was not intended by the legislature and legislation to explicitly provide a sharing of attorney's fees and costs is presently required. . . .

Moreover, as the Senate stated in its evaluation of this issue:

> This bill proposes to explicitly restate the intent of the legislature to require an employer or insurance carrier to share in the payment of attorney's fees and costs in cases where an injured employee brings a third party action and there is a recovery from a third person which benefits both the employee and the employer. The effect of this bill will be to accord the worker a greater portion of the settlement as well as insure fairness to all parties. . . .

Therefore, under HRS § 386-8, the starting point to determine an employer's "share" is to be calculated as (1) the fraction equal to the amount of workers' compensation expended, plus calculable future benefits, divided by the total amount of the settlement . . . This fraction will then be (2) multiplied by the total amount of reasonable attorney's fees and costs incurred by the employee in the course of pursuing the recovery action. This "share" (computed in steps 1 and 2) should then be (3) subtracted from the total compensation already expended to date, by the employer . . . This results in a first lien that the employer may assert against the settlement amount. However, prior to the execution of the lien, the remainder of the attorney's fees and costs should be (4) deducted from the settlement corpus. Then, (5) the amount of the employer's first lien (already calculated as compensation expended minus share of the attorney's fees and costs) may be asserted against the settlement. If a portion of the settlement corpus remains after the employer's execution of the lien (6), the employee is entitled to that remainder, subject to the requirement that the employee first exhaust all necessary future workers' compensation payments from that remainder prior to requesting future compensatory payments from the employer or its insurance carrier for the compensable injuries arising out of the same incident. . . .

Therefore, we now adopt the rationale of state courts interpreting similar statutes, and require an employer to bear a pro rata share of the employee's reasonable attorney's fees and costs, because the attorney guarded the employer's interests, as well as the employee's, when the employer's attorney had not been active in litigation . . . *Cordell v. Chanhassen Auto Body*, 269 Minn. 103, 130 N.W.2d 362 (Minn. 1964) (dependents entitled to recover from the employer a pro-rata share of the costs and reasonable attorney's fees incurred in pursuing settlement); *Insurance Co. of N. Am. v. Wright*, 886 S.W.2d 337 (Tex. Ct. App. 1994) (workers' compensation insurance carrier properly chargeable with proportionate share of employee's costs and attorney's fees); *Quinn v. State*, 15 Cal. 3d 162, 539 P.2d 761, 124 Cal. Rptr. 1 (Cal. 1975) (employer should bear a proportionate share of reasonable litigation expenses incurred by employee in effecting tort recovery from third party); *Transport Indemnity Co. v. Garcia*, 89 N.M. 342, 552 P.2d 473 (N.M. Ct. App. 1976) (employer's workers' compensation insurance carrier's recovery of paid compensation was reduced by proportionate share of expenses incurred in prosecuting action against third party); *Davis v. Weyerhaeuser Co.*, 96 N.C. App. 584, 386 S.E.2d 740 (N.C. Ct. App. 1989) (upon employee's recovery from third party, employer reimbursed less employer's proportionate share of the employee's attorney's fees and then remainder of the recovery disbursed to the employee).

In the instant case the distribution of the $110,000 settlement from Hygrade should be as follows: (1) the $111,306.40 of the workers' compensation expenditures should be reduced by Kiewit's and Aetna's share of the attorney's fees and costs; (2) the share of Kiewit's and Aetna's attorney's fees and costs is the full $37,689.75, because the fraction of expenditures over the settlement total is greater than the whole number one (1); (3) the lien amount is $111,306.40 minus $37,689.75 or $73,616.65; (4) the $73,616.65 lien is then executed against the $110,000 settlement; finally resulting in (5) a $36,383.35 residuary to Alvarado.

Furthermore, we provide the following example to clarify the distribution of the settlement (or judgment) amount when the fraction resulting from the employer's share of attorney's fees and costs does not exceed the whole number one (1). Assume a settlement in the amount of $200,000, attorney's fees and costs totaling $60,000, workers' compensation expenditures to date equaling $100,000, and it is agreed that the injured employee will require $25,000 in future workers' compensation benefit payments. The fraction would be (1) $100,000 plus $25,000 divided by $200,000 or .625. This fraction should then be (2) multiplied by $60,000, or $37,500. This share should then be (3) subtracted from the $100,000 compensation paid, resulting in a lien of $62,500. The remaining $22,500 of the attorney's fees and costs should (4) be deducted from the settlement of $200,000, resulting in $177,500. Then, the $62,500 employer's lien should be (5) executed against the $177,500 resulting in a $115,000 remainder to the employee. However, the employee must still (6) draw his $25,000 in future workers' compensation benefits from the $115,000 remainder, with a net to the employee in the amount of $90,000, assuming that the $25,000 future benefits estimate is accurate.

As the two previous calculations exemplify, under HRS § 386-8, the employer must bear a proportionate share of the employee's attorney's fees and costs incurred while pursuing recovery from the third party tortfeasor. The circuit court is to utilize the aforementioned applicable formulae as starting points in determining an employer's share of reasonable attorney's fees and costs. However, if the circuit court determines that the employer's share of the attorney's fees and costs, as first computed under the applicable formula, is not reasonable in light of the particular circumstances of a case, we emphasize that the circuit court retains the discretion to consider each case on its merits. Thus, for example, if an employer does not cooperate and/or hinders an employee's attempt to pursue recovery, the employer's lien may be reduced by a greater share of the employee's attorney's fees and costs, at the circuit court's discretion. . . .

. . . [W]e emphasize that under HRS § 386-8, an employer, and/or its workers' compensation insurance carrier, must bear its share of the employee's attorney's fees and costs in proportion to the present and future benefits derived from a third party settlement or judgment.

. . . [W]e remand this case to the circuit court for entry of judgment consistent with the computations set forth in this opinion. . . .

The attorney is entitled to a reasonable fee for the work done. However, it's not enough for the attorney to get his due: He and his team owe a duty of loyalty to the client, and if the client is not getting anything, the ethical response would be to refuse to continue on the case unless the client shares in the recovery. The prudent action is to investigate for liens and find out totals early in the process.

If you fail to pay the comp carrier when you know (or, in many cases, should have known) of the existence of a lien, your firm and your client can be in serious trouble on either side of the docket. Many states have a statutory scheme requiring the plaintiff to give notice of settlement or of the suit and, in some statutes, the plaintiff must await the comp carrier or employer's permission before settling.

Because the plaintiff/claimant should know she received workers' comp and owes the carrier, the plaintiff will almost always be personally liable if the lien is not paid. However, there's an overwhelming tendency for the award to have vanished by the time the carrier comes calling for its share when it has been overlooked. If there's any evidence the plaintiff's attorney knew of the lien, she may be held personally liable for the lien as well. The defendant attorney is not ordinarily held personally liable for the lien, but if the attorney or his client had notice of the lien and failed to guarantee its payment by cutting a check directly to the lienholder or by having the check jointly signed by the lienholder and the plaintiff, the client may have to pay the amount of the lien a second time, having already paid it to the plaintiff. If this occurrence is attributable to the negligence of the lawyer's office, the client now has a malpractice claim against its lawyer.

In some jurisdictions, the lien extends to all of the recovery; in others, only to the amount attributable to the part of the recovery that corresponds to the damages covered by workers' comp. The following case illustrates the first point of view.

Perry v. Hartford Acc. & Ind. Co., 481 A.2d 133 (Me. 1984).

In his action in Superior Court (Cumberland County) against his employer's compensation carrier, plaintiff Robert Perry sought a declaration that the lien provided to his employer by section 68 of the Workers' Compensation Act . . . does not extend to the amounts plaintiff had recovered from a third party tortfeasor for pain and suffering and other damages not compensable under the Act . . . We . . . order summary judgment in favor of defendant Hartford because, as a matter of law, the section 68 lien does extend to the entire amount that plaintiff recovered from the third party tortfeasor for bodily injury, including that part recovered for pain and suffering and other damages not compensable under the Workers' Compensation Act.

On December 11, 1980, plaintiff sustained a back injury as a result of an automobile accident caused by the negligence of another driver. At the time of the accident plaintiff was an employee of NASCO, Inc., and was acting within the scope of his employment. NASCO was covered by a workers' compensation insurance policy issued by Hartford.

In his complaint and his subsequently filed affidavit, plaintiff Perry alleged that on February 20, 1981, he underwent back surgery for injuries sustained in the automobile accident. He was readmitted to the hospital on March 4, 1981, with massive gastro-intestinal bleeding, caused by medications administered for the back injury, and subsequently underwent a near total gastrectomy. As the result of his injuries Perry was totally disabled from December 11, 1980, until July 6, 1981. During that period Hartford paid Perry benefits of $284.38 per week and also paid medical bills on Perry's behalf totalling $43,176.85. On July 6, 1981, Perry agreed to a discontinuance of benefits. Then, on July 8, 1981, he entered into a settlement agreement with the driver of the other car involved in the accident that awarded plaintiff $100,000, apparently the limit of the other driver's insurance coverage. Of the $100,000 settlement, $51,555.64 was paid directly to Hartford in satisfaction of its section 68 lien for benefits and medical expenses previously paid to Perry or on his behalf, and $48,444.36 was paid to Perry himself.

Plaintiff's affidavit averred that following the discontinuation of benefits and the settlement of his third party claim, he continued to suffer "dumping syndrome[1] and reactive hypoglycemia, a result of the gastrectomy. However, he returned to work and continued working until June 25, 1982, when he was disabled for a period of six weeks by hypoglycemia secondary to the dumping syndrome. The affidavit further stated that since returning to work following the second period of disability he has continued to suffer from intestinal problems culminating in additional surgery in 1983. Despite plaintiff's petitions for payment of further compensation and medical expenses and for recovery for permanent impairment, Hartford made no payments after July 6, 1981, claiming a credit against plaintiff's third party recovery not already paid to it, in the amount of $48,444.36. Plaintiff claimed that as of August 1, 1983, the date of his affidavit, he was owed benefits under the Workers' Compensation Act in excess of $20,000.

Following commencement of this action, plaintiff filed a motion for partial summary judgment on his claim that a section 68 lien does not extend to portions of a third party recovery allocable to pain and suffering and other damages not compensable under the Workers' Compensation Act. . . .

. . . [T]he court in the case at bar denied declaratory relief by granting summary judgment of dismissal for defendant. Summary judgment is appropriate only when "'the facts before the court so conclusively preclude . . . [a party's] recovery' that a judgment in favor of the other party is the only possible result.". . . The undisputed facts before the Superior Court did not demonstrate that Perry's third party recovery for pain and suffering and other damages not compensable under the Workers' Compensation Act was nonexistent or so indeterminate as to preclude the presence of a "real controversy." On the contrary, in the present case, there is no doubt that plaintiff Perry sustained pain and suffering by reason of the injuries caused by the third party's tort. The settlement agreement between Perry and the tortfeasor specifically provided that in consideration for the amount received by plaintiff, he discharged the third party from "any and all claims, demands, rights, and causes of action . . . arising from . . . bodily and personal injuries" resulting from the accident. Thus . . . here it is clear that plaintiff Perry did in fact settle all his claims, including his very real claims for

---

[1] Dumping syndrome is a condition whereby food is prematurely dumped by the stomach into the small intestine prior to proper digestion.

pain and suffering. In his affidavit plaintiff states that at the time of settlement he was advised by the insurance carrier of the third party tortfeasor, "that the settlement included elements of pain and suffering." Defendant has not contested that averment. Although plaintiff did not indicate what amount of the third party settlement was allocable to pain and suffering, the amount of those damages could be determined through further litigation.

In determining that issue, as well as the other issues presented by this case, the court would be assisted by the advocacy of the parties, who are fighting hard for their respective positions. The adversarial relation of the parties is the direct result of the financial interest each has in the settlement fund. The uncontradicted affidavit of plaintiff recites:

Since the commencement of this action Defendant has agreed to stipulate to a 10% permanent impairment of back but asserts that payments of the same, amounting to approximately $5,687.60, is offset by its continuing lien. Benefits under the Workers' Compensation Act owed to me at this time including wage benefits, medical expenses and permanent impairment exceed $20,000.00.

The undisputed facts before the Superior Court by no means dictated a summary finding that no "real controversy" existed between the parties.

Furthermore, adjudication of plaintiff's claim would serve a useful purpose and would settle an issue of public importance. As noted above, each of the parties stood to gain or lose a substantial sum depending on the court's determination of the scope of the section 68 lien. Determination of that issue is of widespread concern, as the section 68 lien would potentially apply to any third party recovery obtained by a workers' compensation claimant that contained elements of pain and suffering and other damages not compensable under the Act. Under the totality of the circumstances presented by this case, the Superior Court erred in summarily denying for lack of a "real controversy" plaintiff's request for a declaration construing section 68.

Plaintiff thus prevails in his claim that the Superior Court should not have entered a summary judgment of dismissal in defendant Hartford's favor. However, that success on his first point on appeal avails him nothing in the end. On the merits of the question presented by his motion for partial summary judgment, we must order summary judgment for defendant Hartford . . . We hold that the employer's lien under 39 M.R.S.A. § 68 extends to the entire amount of an employee's recovery against a third party tortfeasor for bodily injury, including those portions allocable to pain and suffering and loss of wages not compensable under the Workers' Compensation Act.

In so holding, we need look no further than the statute itself. To determine the meaning of a statute this court first will consult the statutory language . . . Where that language is clear and unambiguous, "our duty is to give effect to the intent of the Legislature as evidenced by the language of the statute.". . . In those circumstances, it is unnecessary to resort to rules of statutory construction . . . 39 M.R.S.A. § 68 provides in pertinent part:

If the injured employee elects to claim compensation and benefits under this Act, any employer having paid such compensation or benefits or having become liable therefor under any compensation payment scheme shall have a lien for the value of compensation paid on *any damages subsequently recovered* against the third person liable for the injury.

If the employee or compensation beneficiary recovers damages from a third person, *he shall repay to the employer or compensation insurer,* out of the recovery against the third person, *the benefits paid to him* by the employer or compensation insurer under this Act, less said employer's or compensation insurer's proportionate share of cost of collection, including reasonable attorney's fees.

(Emphasis added) The highlighted portions of the statute make clear that the injured employee must "repay to the employer or compensation insurer," out of the third party recovery, "the benefits paid" (less the employer's or compensation insurer's proportionate share of cost of collection). The language also makes plain that the employer's lien "for the value of compensation paid" extends to "any damages" recovered. The statutory language does not delineate two categories of third party damages, one of which gives rise to the employer's lien and the other of which does not; it creates a general right of reimbursement and a lien that is coextensive with the right. By the plain meaning of the statutory language, the employer's lien extends to all of the third party recovery, including those portions attributable to pain and suffering and other damages not compensable under the Workers' Compensation Act.

Our interpretation of section 68 is in accord with the prevailing interpretation of comparable provisions in workers' compensation statutes across the country . . .

In the circumstance where a third party is liable for the employee's injury, section 68 allows the employee the additional right to proceed against the third party at the same time that he claims benefits under the Act. In providing the employer with a right to reimbursement out of the third party recovery for benefits paid, and in granting the employer a lien to enforce that right, section 68 assures only that the employee will recover under "the more generous of the two systems—tort or workers' compensation—but not both.". . . Section 68 does not deprive the employee of his common law cause of action against the third party; it only limits him to a single recovery, the more generous one. We see no constitutional infirmity in that limitation . . .

Remanded to the Superior Court for entry of declaratory judgment in accordance with the opinion herein.

One tactic sometimes used to keep more of the recovery in the hands of the plaintiff is to bring a derivative claim on the part of the spouse, or, when applicable, the children or parents. These claims for loss of consortium are not payable to the employee and thus, theoretically, are exempt from the lien. Before you rely on this strategy, though, check your state's case law—the courts may have closed this particular window.

Finding liens at the outset and remembering them at time of settlement is often delegated to staff, and often that staff member is the paralegal. Don't forget if you have that duty; be sure to remind the attorney about liens prior to finalizing any settlement and, if you get a chance, remind her before agreeing to a settlement. Set aside liens in a separate folder or section of the client's file to help you stay aware of them, or, on the plaintiff's side, use some sort of post-it on the client's contract (which you usually have in hand to review during settlement distribution to the client).

In other states, the law is not quite as friendly to workers' compensation insurers; instead of getting their money back, their payment works in favor of a later first-party coverage. Let's take the situation of an injured Kansas (for example) plaintiff who has an on-the-job automobile accident with an uninsured driver. If it is his personal vehicle and he was running an errand for the employer, he'd still be on the job. So whether it was a company or personal vehicle, workers' compensation would pay for his lost wages and medical expenses. For any other damages, the injured plaintiff could look to the **uninsured motorist (UIM)** part of the automobile insurance, which steps in to act as if the uninsured driver had insurance. In Kansas, the auto insurer gets credit for what the workers' compensation carrier paid, so it would only have to pay for general damages and specials not covered by workers' compensation. In that situation, it would behoove the legal team for the UIM carrier to make sure they know the coverages and payments of the comp carrier. This approach will not be uniform, so check your jurisdiction's statutes regarding comp liens to know how the lien payment will be handled.

Other types of insurance carriers, doctors, and hospitals have liens as well, but they are not nearly as formidable. **Hospital liens** are often created by statute, and may be filed in the county court. Check for your local procedure and then check the filing authority for any statutory liens against your client. Similar liens are created by statute for government-paid health care benefits like Medicare or Medicaid; large ones make a surprise bite into a settlement that a client very well may blame on your office if you haven't found out about the total and resolved it (or talked to the client about what can happen) prior to an agreement, as this unhappy woman found out.

Cargill v. State of Wyoming, 967 P.2d 999 (Wyo. 1998).

Appellant contests the district court's order awarding the Department of Health full reimbursement, from appellant's settlement with a third party, of benefits paid by Medicaid on her behalf . . . [W]e affirm . . .

Cargill was burned by a home health care provider employed by St. John's Hospital Home Care Services (St. John's). Medicaid paid the expenses of Cargill's medical treatment for her burns. Cargill filed a complaint against the health care provider and St. John's, and entered into settlement negotiations with them. Under the terms of the settlement reached, $70,000.00 was to be placed in a special needs trust for Cargill's benefit during her life, with the Department as remainderman. The settlement terms also provided that, in the event the trust was not established, the $70,000.00 was to be paid to Cargill immediately, "subject to the Medicaid lien claimed or which may be claimed by the State of Wyoming . . ."

Cargill and St. John's sought approval of their settlement agreement from the district court, and a hearing was scheduled. At this juncture, the Wyoming Attorney General was notified, for the first time, of Cargill's complaint and the settlement negotiations. The attorney general was invited to participate in the hearing to approve the proposed settlement . . . The Department moved to intervene in the case, seeking disapproval of the special needs trust. The complaint in intervention also alleges that the Department paid $13,579.69 for medical services related to Cargill's burns. Intervention was granted over Cargill's objection.

At the hearing, it was generally conceded that the law does not permit a special needs trust with a Medicaid recipient as lifetime beneficiary and the Department as remainderman. Cargill turned, instead, to argue that the Department should not be reimbursed because it had not filed a lien statement to perfect its lien. Cargill also argued that, even if the Department is entitled to reimbursement without having perfected its lien, Wyoming statutes require that attorney's fees and expenses be deducted from the lien amount, and since Cargill's fees and expenses were higher than the Department's lien, the Department should receive nothing.

The district court found that the special needs trust contemplated in the settlement agreement was not permitted by Wyoming law. The remainder of the settlement was approved. The district court also found that Wyoming statutes and Department rules and regulations require full reimbursement of Medicaid payments from the settlement proceeds, and ordered that the Department be fully reimbursed. Cargill appeals the reimbursement order . . .

The crux of this case is whether Cargill is required to reimburse the Department, out of her $70,000.00 settlement with St. John's, the $13,579.69 Medicaid paid for treatment of her burns. All three of Cargill's arguments against reimbursement require interpretation of statutory provisions enacted to ensure Medicaid benefit recovery when there is a liable third party . . . "We endeavor to interpret statutes in accordance with the Legislature's intent. We begin by making an "'inquiry respecting the ordinary and obvious meaning of the words employed according to their arrangement and connection.'"' . . .

Medicaid is funded jointly by the state and federal governments. Before a state can receive federal appropriations for Medicaid, a state plan must be approved by the federal Health Care Financing Administration . . . Under federal law, the state plan must include provisions for collecting payments from liable third parties and reimbursement of those payments to Medicaid. States must require recipients to assign to the state any rights to recovery of payment of medical care from a liable third party. This assignment is a condition of eligibility to receive Medicaid benefits. . . .

Wyoming's compliance with this federal mandate is found at Wyo. Stat. §§ 42-4-201 - 42-4-208 (1997). Wyo. Stat. § 42-4-201(a) clearly and succinctly reiterates federal law and states the intent of the Wyoming legislature:

> If a recipient covered by this chapter receives an injury under circumstances creating a legal liability in some third party, the recipient shall not be deprived of any medical assistance for which he is entitled under this chapter. He may also pursue his remedy at law against the third party. *If the recipient recovers from the third party in any manner, including judgment, compromise, settlement or release, the state is entitled to be reimbursed for all payments made, or to be made, on behalf of the recipient under this chapter.*

(Emphasis added.) There can be no clearer statement that Wyoming's legislature intended the Department be fully reimbursed for Medicaid payments made on behalf of a recipient who recovers those payments from a liable third party.

The statutes give the Department three methods for achieving reimbursement. Wyo. Stat. § 42-4-202 provides for a lien against the recipient's recovery. Wyo. Stat. § 42-4-204 makes the Department subrogated to the recipient's right of recovery and also grants the Department an assignment of "any entitlements from . . . a claim or action against any responsible third party for medical services, not to exceed the amount expended by the department . . ."

In her first issue, Cargill argues that the Department cannot be reimbursed unless it files and perfects a lien as permitted by Wyo. Stat. § 42-4-202, which states in part:

(a) When the department provides, pays for or becomes liable for medical care, it shall have a lien for the cost of the medical assistance provided upon any and all causes of action which accrue to the person to whom the care was furnished, or to the person's legal representatives, as a result of the injuries which necessitated the medical care.

(b) The department *may* perfect and enforce its lien by following the procedures set forth in W.S. 29-1-301 and 29-1-302. . . .

(Emphasis added.) Almost completely ignoring Wyo. Stat. § 42-4-204, Cargill contends that, since the Department did not file a lien statement, she is not required to reimburse the payments made to treat her injuries. The Department counters that it chose not to perfect and enforce its lien, preferring in this case to rely upon the statutory assignment of benefits . . . These statutes and rules provide for an automatic assignment of benefits upon application for Medicaid. This assignment is a condition of eligibility for receiving benefits, and is mandated by federal law. . . .

Cargill next argues that the Department's recovery should be reduced by the full amount of her attorney's fees and litigation costs, which are greater than $13,579.69, leading to a zero recovery. She relies upon Wyo. Stat. § 42-4-202(f), which provides:

Upon any judgment, award or settlement of an action under this section, or any part of it, **upon which the department has filed its lien,** an attorney may collect fees and expenses incurred, in an amount and in a manner which shall be established by department rule and regulation. The department's lien shall be reduced by the attorney's fees and expenses authorized pursuant to this section.

(Emphasis added.) This statute plainly applies only when the Department has exercised its option to file a lien statement. Here, since the Department did not file a lien, this section does not apply to Cargill's case and could not have been violated. The appropriate method for addressing the payment of attorney's fees and costs in this case is found in Chapter 35, Section 8 of the Department's rules and regulations:

(d) Amount of the Department's recovery. Except as provided in paragraph (ii), the Department shall recover the full amount of Medicaid funds paid to or on behalf of the recipient because of the injury, illness or disability involved in the cause of action.

(i) If the recipient's net recovery is greater than or equal to the Medicaid funds paid to or on behalf of the recipient, the Department shall recover the full amount of the Medicaid funds. . . .

(e) Determination of recipient's net recovery. The recipient's net recovery shall be:

(i) The recipient's gross recovery, minus

(ii) The necessary costs incurred in pursuing the judgment or settlement, minus

(iii) Attorney's fees not to exceed one-third of the amount determined by subtracting (ii) from (i).

These rules and regulations . . . give preference to attorney's fees and litigation expenses, providing Medicaid reimbursement only after payment of fees and costs. Here, Cargill's gross recovery of $70,000.00, minus costs and attorney's fees, leads to a net recovery greater than the amount of Medicaid funds paid on her behalf. The district court correctly ruled that the Department is entitled to full reimbursement, after Cargill's attorney's fees and costs are paid . . .

Cargill has put forth tremendous effort to deny the Department reimbursement for the medical expenses paid on her behalf. Her settlement with St. John's includes the amount of those expenses, and clearly recognizes that the Department is entitled to reimbursement. We are sympathetic to Cargill's plight and understand her need for future medical attention unrelated to this case. However, she has received medical treatment paid for by Medicaid, and she has also received from St. John's the money to pay for that treatment. To allow her to avoid reimbursing the Department would not only result in a windfall to Cargill, it would violate both state and federal law.

The statutes at issue are plain and unambiguous. The district court did not err in its interpretation of these statutes, and, accordingly, we affirm the district court's order.

Doctors and other health care providers try to create liens in the mass of paperwork they have patients sign; ordinarily they do no better than general creditors. A common practice in personal injury practices, though, is to sign a **letter of protection,** which is a letter agreement from the attorney stating that she will make sure this particular doctor is paid from the settlement proceeds, if any, if the doctor will continue to treat the patient/client.

March 27, 200-

Eloise Payne, Ph.D.
711 Freud Tower Circle, Suite 1313
Big City, Confusion 99999

RE: Patient's Name:	Patty Haus
Date of Injury:	[incident date]
Date of Birth:	04-01-1972
Social Security No.:	111-11-1111

Dear Dr. Payne:

    I represent Patty Haus in a claim for injuries and damages received in an accident which occurred on [incident date].

    By this letter, I agree to pay your office all outstanding medical expenses for Patty Haus's injury-related treatment directly out of any net settlement proceeds or payment resulting from a jury verdict otherwise payable to Patty Haus. Should the verdict be less than the total of medical expenses, I agree to pay your office first monies available which are not otherwise encumbered by statutory liens with priority.

    As consideration for this protection letter, you have agreed to refrain from taking any action to collect outstanding medical bills while Patty Haus's case is pending.

    Please forward copies of any and all medical records and bills pertaining to Patty Haus's treatment. Also, as Patty Haus continues to receive treatment for these injuries, please forward all medical records and bills as they accrue. I am enclosing a signed medical authorization permitting you to release this information to me.

    Thank you for your assistance in this matter.

Sincerely yours,

Lisa St. Joan

LSJ/jgm
cc: Patty Haus

Health insurers also try to create liens through the contract. The enforceability of these liens is up for grabs. Most of them do a good job of creating a lien against a **third-party tortfeasor,** someone with no contractual relationship to the plaintiff who has committed a tort against him, although not all states will allow enforcement of the contractual lien. The reasoning varies from state to state. The following New Jersey Supreme Court case bases its reason on the statutory abolition of the **collateral source rule.**

Perreira v. Rediger, 778 A.2d 429 (N.J. 2001).

The question presented in these consolidated appeals is whether the collateral source rule embodied in N.J.S.A. 2A:97-15 allows a health insurer, who expends funds on behalf of an insured, to recoup those payments through subrogation or contract reimbursement when the insured recovers a judgment against a tortfeasor. The answer is no.

    The purpose underlying N.J.S.A. 2A:15-97 is twofold: to eliminate the double recovery to plaintiffs that flowed from the common-law collateral source rule and to allocate the benefit of that change to liability carriers. Allowing health insurers to recover funds expended pursuant to an insurance contract either by way of subrogation or contract reimbursement would reallocate the benefit accorded by N.J.S.A. 2A:15-97 in contravention of the underlying legislative intent Accordingly, we hold such recovery to be interdicted by the statutory scheme. . . .

The *Beninato* case arose when Takako Beninato, a professional dog groomer, was seriously injured during a grooming session involving a dog owned by Lenore and Leonard Achor. Beninato's health insurer, Oxford Health Plans, Inc. ("Oxford"), paid $7,357 for her medical expenses. Beninato then sued the Achors, whose homeowner's insurance carrier, Preferred Mutual Insurance Company ("Preferred"), defended the suit.

While the underlying case was pending, the Achors and Preferred filed an action against Oxford, seeking a declaration that Oxford was barred by the collateral source statute, N.J.S.A. 2A:15-97, from asserting a subrogation or reimbursement remedy. That action was consolidated with the Beninatos' negligence action that settled for $95,000. The release expressly stated that "payment for medical bills and expenses incurred" are not included in that amount.

Oxford moved for summary judgment, arguing that if medical expenses were included in the settlement, it had a right to be reimbursed for what it expended on behalf of Beninato. If those expenses were not included in the settlement, then Oxford claimed a right to bring a subrogation action against the Achors for repayment. The Achors and Preferred argued that "the collateral source rule and the subrogation provision within [Oxford's] insurance contract conflict with each other." The trial court entered judgment for the Achors and Preferred, concluding that Oxford's claim was barred by the collateral source statute. Oxford appealed.

The *Perreira* case arose when Maria Perreira fell on the premises of the Columbia Savings Bank ("Columbia"). She sued Columbia along with its liability carrier Atlantic Mutual Insurance Company ("Atlantic"), Michael Rediger, the bank's snow removal contractor and Rediger's liability carrier, the Preserver Insurance Company ("Preserver"). In that case, Oxford, Perreira's health insurer, had paid about $13,000 for her medical expenses.

While that suit was pending, the Perreiras filed an action against Oxford, Columbia, Rediger, Atlantic, and Preserver, "seeking a declaration that Oxford was barred by the collateral source statute from either reimbursement or subrogation against the defendants." That action was consolidated with the Perreira's negligence action.

The Perreiras moved for summary judgment, arguing that under the collateral source rule, Oxford could not assert a lien on their recovery in the tort action. The trial court granted the motion and Oxford appealed. After the grant of summary judgment, the Perreiras entered into a settlement with Columbia and Rediger, the terms of which have not been disclosed. . . .

The collateral source rule, with deep roots in English common law, is firmly embedded in American common law as well. It was first cited in an American judicial decision in 1854 and has had continued currency in the centuries to follow . . . The common law collateral source rule "allows an injured party to recover the value of medical treatment from a culpable party, irrespective of payment of actual medical expenses by the injured party's insurance carrier. The purpose of the collateral source rule is to preserve an injured party's right to seek tort recovery from a tortfeasor without jeopardizing his or her right to receive insurance payments for medical care." . . . The rule "prohibits the tortfeasor from reducing payment of a tort judgment by the amount of money received by an injured party from other sources" and "bars the submission of evidence that the injured plaintiff received payment for any part of his damages, including medical expenses, from other sources." . . . It is thus a rule of damages as well as a rule of evidence. . . .

. . . The policy advanced by the rule is that "a benefit that is directed to the injured party should not be shifted so as to become a windfall for the tortfeasor." . . . Thus, if an injured party has the foresight to provide that his or her medical expenses will be paid by maintaining an insurance policy, the common law collateral source rule allows him or her to benefit from that foresight by recovering not only the insurance proceeds but also the full tort judgment . . .

However, in the early to mid-1980's, state legislatures began to revisit the collateral source rule based on the notion, advanced by insurance industry analysts, that the rule contributed "to the liability insurance availability and affordability crisis in this country. . . ." . . . Indeed, in 1986, a report commissioned by the Attorney General of the United States and prepared by a governmental inter-agency working group and the White House recommended a series of initiatives to address "the rapidly expanding crisis in liability insurance availability and affordability." . . . Included among those initiatives was the suggestion that tort judgments be reduced by collateral sources of compensation for the same injury . . .

In response, many state legislatures passed comprehensive tort reform legislation in the latter half of the 1980's. Statutory modification of the collateral source rule in one form or another was a common factor among those different legislative initiatives . . . No universal approach was adopted in all jurisdictions. One common legislative reform to avoid double recovery to plaintiffs requires a tort judgment to be reduced by the amount of collateral source payments but specifies that such reduction will not occur if a subrogation or reimbursement right exists . . . Alaska Stat. § 09.17.070(a)(Michie 1998); Colo. Rev. Stat. Ann. § 13-21-111.6 (West 2001); Conn. Gen. Stat. Ann. § 52-225a (West 1991); Fla. Stat. Ann. § 768.76(1) (West Supp. 2000); Haw. Rev. Stat. § 633-10 (1986), Idaho Code § 6-1606 (1998); 735 Ill. Comp. Stat. 5/2-1205.1 (West 1992); Me. Rev. Stat. Ann. tit. 24, § 2906 (West 2000); Mich. Comp. Laws Ann. § 600.6303 (West 2000); Minn. Stat. Ann. § 548.36 (West 2000); Mont. Code Ann. § 27-1-308 (West 2000), Utah Code Ann. § 78-14-4.5 (1953).

A second approach permits a plaintiff to introduce evidence at trial of collateral source benefits received, presumably to reduce the amount of the tort judgment and benefit liability carriers. Cal. Civil Code. Ann. § 3333.1 (West 2001); Ga. Code Ann. § 51-12-1 (West 2000). Within that category, contractual reimbursement is allowed and subrogation denied to the health insurers in some states. Ga. Code. Ann. § 33-24-56.1 (West 2000). In other states, contract reimbursement and subrogation are specifically prohibited. Cal. Civil Code. Ann. § 3333.1(b) (West 2001).

A third approach does not purport to tinker with the common-law collateral source rule at all, but simply creates a statutory right to subrogation for health insurers, thus eliminating double recovery to plaintiffs and benefitting the health insurance industry. S.C. Code Ann. § 38-71-190 (Law. Co-op. 2000).

Each of the aforementioned initiatives has the effect of avoiding double recovery to plaintiffs and thus altering the effect of the common-law collateral source rule. However, they differ dramatically regarding which segment of the insurance community will benefit from the change. Where subrogation or contract reimbursement rights are granted to health insurers, that industry is the beneficiary of the legislative modification. Where subrogation and reimbursement are prohibited, the liability carriers benefit.

Like other jurisdictions, New Jersey responded to the call for modification of the collateral source rule by enacting N.J.S.A. 2A:15-97 in 1987. Although, like the modifications enacted in other jurisdictions, its primary effect was to eliminate double recovery to plaintiffs, it was not modeled exactly on any of the other statutes. It provides:

> In any civil action brought for personal injury or death . . . if a plaintiff receives or is entitled to receive benefits for the injuries allegedly incurred from any other source other than a joint tortfeasor, the benefits, other than workers' compensation benefits or the proceeds from a life insurance policy, shall be disclosed to the court and the amount thereof which duplicates any benefit contained in the award shall be deducted from any award recovered by the plaintiff, less any premium paid to an insurer directly by the plaintiff or by any member of the plaintiff's family on behalf of the plaintiff of the policy period during which the benefits are payable. Any party to the action shall be permitted to introduce evidence regarding any of the matters described in this act. . . .

On its face, N.J.S.A. 2A:15-97 eliminates double recovery by directing the court to deduct from any tort judgment the amount received by plaintiff from collateral sources (other than workers' compensation and life insurance) less any insurance premiums plaintiff has paid . . . Unlike the out-of-state enactments, the statute is silent regarding any right to subrogation or reimbursement on the part of the health insurers.

The legislative history of the statute is instructive. . . .

That legislative history reaffirms the plain language of N.J.S.A. 2A:15-97 and underscores that it had more than one purpose. To be sure, its primary purpose was to disallow double recovery to plaintiffs, but a secondary goal was clearly the containment of spiraling insurance costs. The effectuation of no-double-recovery therefore required a separate legislative decision regarding which segment of the insurance industry would be the beneficiary of that disallowance. The Legislature had two choices: to benefit health insurers by allowing repayment of costs expended on a tort plaintiff, or to benefit liability carriers by reducing the tort judgment by the amount of health care benefits received.

As the legislative history reveals, the choice was made to favor liability carriers . . . That legislative determination took the form of a reduction from the tort judgment of the amount received from collateral sources. By that action, the Legislature eliminated double recovery to plaintiffs, reduced the burden on the tortfeasors' liability carriers and left health insurers in the same position as they were prior to the enactment of N.J.S.A. 2A:15-97. . . .

Although courts have identified an implied right of subrogation under certain contracts of insurance, such an implied equitable right has not been recognized with respect to all forms of insurance. Thus, for example, policies covering property damage such as fire insurance have regularly been held to include an implied right of subrogation . . . But the same has not been true in the area of personal insurance, a category that includes health and medical insurance. . . .

Among the courts that have addressed the question of the existence of a common-law equitable right of subrogation, the weight of authority concludes that no such right exists in the health insurance field . . . *American Pioneer Life Ins. v. Rogers*, 296 Ark. 254, 753 S.W.2d 530, 532-33 (Ark. 1988) (stating that absent specific subrogation clause medical insurer has no right to share in proceeds of insured's settlement or recover from tortfeasor); *Schultz v. Gotlund*, 138 Ill. 2d 171, 561 N.E.2d 652, 653-54, 149 Ill. Dec. 282 (Ill. 1990) (holding that because no common law or equitable right to subrogation is recognized in group health policies, absent express subrogation clause in policy, group health insurer had no right to share in proceeds of personal injury settlement between insured and tortfeasor); *Frost v. Porter Leasing Corp.*, 386 Mass. 425, 436 N.E.2d 387, 389-90 (Mass. 1982) (stating that insurer providing medical and hospital expense benefits had no right of subrogation in insured's recovery against tortfeasor or personal injuries when group policy contained no express provision entitling insurer to subrogation rights); *Michigan Hosp. Serv. v. Sharpe*, 339 Mich. 357, 63 N.W.2d 638, 641-42 (Mich. 1954) (holding that equitable subrogation not allowed for health insurance contract); *Ridge Tool Co. v. Silva*, 33 Ohio App. 3d 260, 515 N.E.2d 945, 946-47 (Ohio Ct. App. 1986) (denying reimbursement because health insurer's contract did not expressly provide for reimbursement in event of insured's recovery from tortfeasor); *Shumpert v. Time Ins. Co.*, 329 S.C. 605, 496 S.E.2d 653, 656-58 (S.C. Ct. App. 1998) (holding that health insurance provider cannot obtain equitable subrogation of insured's recovery against third-party tortfeasor when it fails to include subrogation provision in health insurance policy); *Cunningham v. Met Life Ins. Co.*, 121 Wis. 2d 437, 360 N.W.2d 33, 38 (Wis. 1985) (stating that group hospitalization and physician's services coverage contained in same contract with indemnity coverage is in nature of investment insurance and, absent subrogation clause, insurer who paid benefits under such policy was not equitably subrogated to insured's claims). . . .

The rationale behind the rule against finding equitable subrogation in personal insurance contracts is set forth in one treatise as follows:

> Subrogation rights are common under policies of property or casualty insurance, wherein the insured sustains a fixed financial loss, and the purpose is to place that loss ultimately on the wrongdoer. To permit the insured in such instances to recover from both the insurer and the wrongdoer would permit him to profit unduly thereby.

In personal insurance contracts, however, the exact loss is never capable of ascertainment. Life and death, health, physical well being, and such matters are incapable of exact financial estimation. There are, accordingly, not the same reasons militating against a double recovery. The general rule is, therefore, that the insurer is not subrogated to the insured's rights or to the beneficiary's rights under contracts of personal insurance, at least in the absence of a policy provision so providing. Nor would a settlement by the insured with the wrongdoer bar his cause of action against the insurer. However, if a subrogation provision were expressly contained in such contracts, it probably would be enforced quite uniformly. Such a provision cannot be read into a policy by calling it an indemnity contract, however. . . .

Thus, courts typically have not implied a non-contractual or non-statutory right to subrogation in health insurance.

We are satisfied that no equitable remedy of subrogation was available to health insurers in 1987, at the time N.J.S.A. 2A:15- 97 was enacted. We reach that conclusion based on learned treatises and the weight of cited out-of-state authority to that effect, and on the complete lack of evidence that such a right was ever exercised . . . Most significant to us, however, is that one of the core purposes of N.J.S.A. 2A:15-97, as conceded by all parties, was to avoid "double recovery" by plaintiffs. If, under the law existing prior to 1987 when the collateral source rule was amended, health insurers could equitably obtain repayment from tortfeasors for the health care costs they advanced to plaintiffs, then plaintiffs, in fact, would not have experienced double recovery and there would have been no point to N.J.S.A. 2A:15-97. In a word, double recovery occurs only when a plaintiff recovers not only the health insurance proceeds but also the full tort judgment. If health insurers had a common-law equitable right to be repaid out of a tort judgment for the health care costs they advanced to plaintiff, the entire notion of double recovery would not have existed . . . Thus, we have found no support for the proposition that health insurers had an equitable right of subrogation available under the common law. . . .

We turn next to contract reimbursement. Oxford's policies contained a reimbursement provision allowing it to recover expended health care costs "when payment is made directly to the member in third-party settlements or satisfied judgments." That contract provision was not authorized by law at the time the collateral source rule was amended in 1987. The Commissioner of Insurance refused to allow such provisions in health insurance contracts pursuant to his regulatory authority . . . Presumably, that decision mirrored the lack of a statutory or equitable right on the part of a health insurer to recover costs against a tortfeasor by way of subrogation.

In 1993, after years of declining to approve such provisions, the Department of Insurance allowed the inclusion of subrogation and reimbursement provisions in health insurance policies provided through the Small Employer Health Benefits Program and the Individual Health Coverage Program . . . Later, the Commissioner promulgated regulations that for the first time permitted such provisions in large group health insurance policies . . .

It is pursuant to that authority that the Oxford reimbursement provision was included in its contract. The question presented is whether, in light of N.J.S.A. 2A:15-97, the Commissioner's regulations exceeded his authority.

We generally accord a high degree of deference to administrative agency regulations that are consistent with the statutes and public policy of the state . . . However, "no administrative agency has inherent power, and none may arrogate to itself the authority to accomplish ends not envisioned by the legislative grant or to employ means not fairly within the powers that have been bestowed.". . . In short, an administrative code provision must give way if it is inconsistent with a state statute. . . .

The Commissioner's authorization of subrogation and reimbursement provisions in health insurance contracts must be tested against N.J.S.A. 2A:15-97. As we have indicated, in that statute the legislature eliminated double recovery to plaintiffs and allocated the benefit of what had previously been double recovery to the liability insurance industry. The Commissioner was not free to alter that scheme . . . Accordingly, the regulations authorizing the inclusion of subrogation and reimbursement provisions in health insurance contracts must be interpreted narrowly as limited to cases in which the collateral source rule does not apply, for example, a case in which choice of law principles require application of the law of a jurisdiction with a collateral source rule at variance from our own. The health insurance benefits at issue in this case clearly do not fall into that category. Such an interpretation, that narrowly limits the application of the regulations, fairly accords with their very language that earmarks for reimbursement health care sums "received" by the insured. Where the collateral source rule applies, those amounts are subtracted from the judgment, and the insured has no entitlement to "receive" them. Oxford therefore cannot invoke the contract provision as a basis for reimbursement. . . .

Health insurers have no common law equitable right to subrogation. Under the common-law collateral source rule, plaintiffs had the right to keep their health insurance proceeds and their full tort judgments. In amending the common-law collateral source rule, N.J.S.A. 2A:15-97 eliminated double recovery to plaintiffs, allocated the benefit of that elimination to liability carriers, and left health insurers in the same position they had been in before its enactment—with no right to recover paid benefits from the insured or from the tortfeasor. In allocating the benefit of no-double-recovery to liability carriers, N.J.S.A. 2A:15-97, in turn, barred the Commissioner of Insurance from enacting a different allocation scheme. Thus, the Commissioner's regulations empowering health insurers to include reimbursement and subrogation provisions in their contracts only apply to cases that do not involve the collateral source rule . . .

The judgment of the Appellate Division is reversed. The judgments of the trial court are reinstated.

The problem is that many of these insurance contracts try to collect against any other contracts the plaintiff may have entered into to protect himself, which is **first-party coverage** and arguably overreaching because the plaintiff has paid for those benefits, whether with labor or cash. The language in those insurance contracts follows the **Federal Medical Care Recovery Act,** which empowers the federal government to recover money from other sources when it pays for the medical care of military personnel or their dependents.

In any case in which the United States is authorized or required by law to furnish or pay for hospital, medical, surgical, or dental care and treatment (including prostheses and medical appliances) to a person who is injured or suffers a disease . . . under circumstances creating a tort liability upon some third person . . . to pay damages therefor, the United States shall have a right to recover (independent of the rights of the injured or diseased person) from said third person, or that person's insurer, the reasonable value of the care and treatment so furnished, to be furnished, paid for, or to be paid for and shall, as to this right be subrogated to any right or claim that the injured or diseased person, his guardian, personal representative, estate, dependents, or survivors has against such third person to the extent of the reasonable value of the care and treatment so furnished, to be furnished, paid for, or to be paid for. The head of the department or agency of the United States furnishing such care or treatment may also require the injured or diseased person, his guardian, personal representative, estate, dependents, or survivors, as appropriate, to assign his claim or cause of action against the third person to the extent of that right or claim.

42 U.S.C. § 2651(a) (2000).

Despite the fact the United States may be a real party in interest, this case does not have to be brought in federal court; the statute expressly allows for concurrent jurisdiction in state and federal courts. If the recovery of medical expenses is the only basis of federal jurisdiction, the case will probably stay in state court. The federal government's attempts to reach first-party benefits has been mixed.

Government Employees Ins. Co. v. Andujar, **773 F. Supp. 282 (D. Kan. 1991).**

This case arises out of an automobile accident caused by the negligence of Donald Good, an uninsured motorist. The accident resulted in the death of Good and all of the occupants of the car with which he collided. The other car, driven by Nereida Andujar, was covered by an automobile insurance policy issued by the Government Employees Insurance Co. (GEICO), which included uninsured motorist coverage. This action was filed by GEICO to determine its rights and obligations under the insurance contract.

As a result of injuries caused by the accident, the United States Army (United States), as authorized and required by law, furnished hospital, medical and surgical care and treatment to Nereida Andujar, Yaritza Andujar and Carmen Sara Alicea. The United States, under the Federal Medical Care Recovery Act, (FMCRA) . . . claims that it is entitled to recover from GEICO the reasonable value of the care and treatment it furnished . . .

The essential facts are uncontroverted; the United States's response adds additional facts to the defendants' statement of uncontroverted facts and controverts one statement of fact which is immaterial to the court's decision. A copy of the insurance policy issued by GEICO is included as an exhibit to the memoranda in support of the motions for summary judgment.

GEICO is a foreign insurance corporation duly qualified to do business in Kansas and having its principal place of business in Chevy Chase, Maryland. The United States of America administers the Civilian Health and Medical Program of the Uniform Services (CHAMPUS). . . . Nereida Andujar, David Andujar, and their children were covered by CHAMPUS as a military family for a specified portion of health care obtained by them from civilian hospitals and doctors.

GEICO issued a policy of automobile insurance to Roman David Andujar which afforded liability, medical payments and uninsured motorist coverage.

On October 3, 1987, Nereida Andujar was driving a 1981 Toyota, insured by GEICO, west-bound on U.S. Highway 24 in Pottawatomie County, Kansas when it was struck by an east-bound motor vehicle driven by Donald Good. Yaritza Andujar, Carmen Sara Alicea and Brenda Omayra Alicea were passengers in the vehicle driven by Nereida Andujar at the time of the accident.

Nereida Andujar, Yaritza Andujar, Carmen Sara Alicea, Brenda Omayra Alicea and Donald Good died as a result of injuries suffered in the accident. Donald Good's negligence was the sole cause of the accident. Donald Good had no motor vehicle insurance in effect at the time of the accident.

As a result of the automobile accident, the United States Army, as authorized and required by law, furnished hospital, medical and surgical care and treatment to Nereida Andujar, Yaritza Andujar and Carmen Sara Alicea for their injuries caused by the negligence of Donald Good.

On behalf of Nereida Andujar and Yaritza Andujar, Roman David Andujar, as administrator of the estates of Nereida Andujar and Yaritza Andujar, and as sole heir of Nereida Andujar and Yaritza Andujar, has made claim against the proceeds of the GEICO uninsured motorist coverage in the amount of $50,000 and bodily injury liability coverage in the amount of $50,000. Stephen Freed, as special administrator of the estates of Carmen Sara Alicea and Brenda Omayra Alicea, Jaun R. Alicea-Sanchez, and Jaun R. Alicea-Esteras, Jr., also claim an interest in the proceeds.

On November 13, 1989, GEICO filed this lawsuit for a declaration of its rights and obligations as against the various claims of the defendants filed herein. The government claims an interest in the policy in the amount of $76,155.29 for the value of the care furnished to Nereida Andujar, Yaritza Andujar and Carmen Sara Alicea on account of the injuries they sustained as a result of the careless and negligent acts of Donald Good.

On May 23, 1990, the GEICO deposited with this court the sum of $100,000 as the proceeds of its bodily injury and uninsured motorist coverage afforded under the Andujar policy of insurance. Pursuant to the agreement of the parties and the order and judgment of this court, the obligations of plaintiff under its policy of insurance are satisfied and discharged.

Roman David Andujar, individually and for and on behalf of the heirs at law of Nereida Andujar and Yaritza Andujar, has filed a separate action in this court against Toyota Motor Distributors, Inc., and others, for the wrongful death of Nereida Andujar and Yaritza Andujar; and a survivorship action on behalf of Nereida Andujar . . .

The aggregate of the claims of all the parties in the instant case exceed the maximum amount of GEICO's obligation under the policy—the $100,000 paid into the court.

The Andujars and the Aliceas have reached an agreement regarding the just and proper distribution of the proceeds of the GEICO policy: one-fifth (1/5) going to the heirs at law of the four (4) individuals for the wrongful death claims and another one-fifth (1/5) going to the heirs at law of Nereida Andujar for her survivorship claim. The United States acknowledges the existence of that agreement, but contends that its rights to the insurance proceeds are not affected by that agreement. . . .

The parties seeking summary judgment contend that the United States is not entitled to any portion of the proceeds of Andujar's insurance policy. They contend that under FMCRA, the United States is only entitled to recover the reasonable value of medical expenses from the tortfeasor, Donald Good. Because GEICO is not the tortfeasor, the United States is not entitled to the proceeds of the uninsured motorist policy under the FMCRA. The parties seeking summary judgment argue that allowing the United States to recover medical expenses from Andujar's insurance policy is a windfall to the government which is neither supported by the legislative history nor the express language of the statute. . . .

The United States acknowledges that GEICO is not the "tortfeasor," but argues that it is nevertheless entitled to compensation for the reasonable value of medical services rendered. The United States cites several cases in which the court has allowed the government to access the uninsured motorist coverage proceeds, notwithstanding the fact that the government was not directly entitled to recover under the FMCRA. The United States contends that those courts have looked to the express terms of the insurance agreement and concluded that the government was either an "insured" under the insurance policy or was otherwise entitled to recover as a third party beneficiary.

The parties seeking summary judgment respond that the cases cited by the United States are inapposite as none of the insurance policies at issue in those cases contained the same limitations found in Andujar's policy with GEICO. They contend that under the express terms of the insurance policy, the government's claim for the reasonable value of medical services is barred . . .

42 U.S.C. § 2651(a) provides in pertinent part:

In any case in which the United States is authorized or required by law to furnish hospital, medical, surgical, or dental care and treatment . . . to a person who is injured or suffers a disease, after the effective date of this Act, *under circumstances creating tort liability upon some third person . . . to pay damages therefor, the United States shall have right to recover from said third person the reasonable value of the care and treatment so furnished or to be furnished* and shall, as to this right be subrogated to any right or claim that the injured or diseased person, his guardian, personal representative, estate, dependents, or survivors has against such third person to the extent of the reasonable value of the care and treatment so furnished or to be furnished.

. . . This statute "creates no substantive law of negligence, and the courts must look to the applicable state law to determine whether the injured party has any rights or claims to which the government may be subrogated." . . . The primary thrust of FMCRA is to ensure that the cost of treating injured persons to whom the United States makes care available is borne by those legally responsible for the injury, not the taxpayer . . .

While not directly relevant to the case at bar, the court notes that in states which have adopted no-fault insurance (which basically substitutes a contractual claim for the traditional common law tort claim), courts have recognized that no FMCRA right exists. . . . The court also notes that Congress has amended the veteran's benefit statute to allow the Secretary of Veterans Affairs to recover for medical care provided to veterans in states with no-fault insurance. . . . Apparently, no comparable amendment has been made to 42 U.S.C. § 2651.

Under the facts of the case at bar, the FMCRA does not provide the United States with a direct right to the proceeds of Andujar's uninsured motorist policy. Nereida Andujar was not a "third person" nor was she the tortfeasor. GEICO is not liable in tort . . . Donald Good, the uninsured motorist, was the tortfeasor. The FMCRA only provides the United States with a right to recover from Donald Good.

This analysis does not, however, end the court's inquiry. As the United States argues, several courts have allowed the government to recover uninsured motorist proceeds for the reasonable value of the medical services provided notwithstanding the fact that the government was not entitled to recover directly under the FMCRA. In those cases, the courts have looked to the express terms of the insurance policy and applicable state law to determine whether the United States was an "insured" or otherwise able to claim an interest in the proceeds as a third party beneficiary.

As an example, in *GEICO v. United States,* 376 F.2d 836 (4th Cir. 1967), Raymond F. Krebs, III, the son of an Army officer, was in an automobile accident in which the car he was traveling was struck by a car not covered by liability insurance. The car in which Krebs traveled was insured by GEICO; Krebs entered a settlement agreement with GEICO under the uninsured motorist clause of that policy.

The United States apparently claimed a right to recover the medical expenses incurred by it in treating Krebs. The district court granted the United States summary judgment; the court of appeals affirmed.

The portion of the policy obligating GEICO to pay under the uninsured motorist provision defined "insured" to include "(a) the named insured and any relative; (b) any other person while occupying an insured automobile; and (c) any person, with respect to damages he is entitled to recover because of bodily injury to which this Part applies sustained by an insured under (a) or (b) above."

GEICO made essentially the same argument advanced by the parties moving for summary judgment in this case. The court commented:

> [GEICO argues] that the right of the United States to recover rests wholly upon the provisions of the Federal Medical Recovery Act, which gives a right of action solely against the third-person-tortfeasor, or, as in this case, the uninsured motorist, without any rights of subrogation, and that, since appellant is not such a third-person-tortfeasor, it is without liability. But this argument misapprehends that the right of the United States does not rest wholly on the Federal Medical Recovery Act. It relies on that Act merely to establish its right to recover of the uninsured motorist, a right apparently conceded by [GEICO]. But it plants its right to recover upon the express language of the policy, which provides that one entitled to recover of the uninsured third party is in turn entitled to payment under the policy as an insured as defined in [the policy]. . . .

. . . The policy issued by GEICO to Andujar (as amended) states in pertinent part:

SECTION IV

. . .

DEFINITIONS

. . .

2. *"Insured"* means:

   a. the individual named in the declarations and his or her spouse if a resident of the same household;

b. *relatives* of [a] above if residents of his household;

c. any other person while *occupying* an *insured auto;* or

d. any person who is entitled to recover damages because of *bodily injury* sustained by an *insured* under [a], [b], and [c] above.

. . .

EXCLUSIONS:

When Section IV Does Not Apply

. . .

4. We do not cover the United States of America or any of its agencies as an insured, a third party beneficiary or otherwise.

By the express terms of the insurance agreement the *United States* is not an insured or a third party beneficiary. In none of the cases cited by the United States did the insurance policy under which the government was allowed to recover contain a similar exclusion. The court, in its independent research of this issue, could find no case in which the United States claimed the status of "insured" or third party beneficiary where the uninsured motorist insurance policy contained an exclusion similar to the one contained in the Andujars' policy . . .

An insurance policy is a contract . . . Plain and unambiguous insurance policies must be given their plain meaning . . .

The court concludes that the United States is not entitled to any portion of the proceeds of the uninsured motorist coverage . . . By the express terms of the policy, the United States is not an insured or a third party beneficiary. . . .

IT IS THEREFORE ORDERED that the motions for summary judgment of defendants Roman David Andujar, Juan R. Alicea-Esteras, Jr., Juan R. Alicea-Sanchez, Carmen Sara Alicea, deceased, and Brenda Omayra Alicea, deceased are granted insofar as the court concludes that the United States does not have an interest the proceeds of the GEICO policy. This order does not determine the validity of the claims of the remaining defendants, Allstate and Dairyland.

The mechanism used by GEICO to deposit the funds into the registry of the court and to be relieved of all further liability is called an **interpleader.** It's tailored to these kinds of actions, where a party is in possession of funds that it knows it owes, but can't make a determination as to who should be paid. The party gives the funds to the court to dole out among the competing claimants.

This same first-party/third-party dichotomy arises in workers' comp situations, so beware. The outcome varies according to state law, like so many other issues.

Mechanics/Materialmen

When certain types of high-priced property is repaired or built, the person furnishing repairs or material automatically has a lien. In real property construction, the workers involved are usually **materialmen,** but a **mechanic** (in this sense) is also possible. (The other common kind is automobiles, but attorneys don't get involved in those disputes very often.) The lien involved is usually referred to orally as an **M&M lien,** the initials standing for the two types of services, but either kind are called a "mechanics' lien" for short. Statutes governing the liens explain what one must do before filing a lien, how to file one, and when to release a lien. The lien is against the property repaired or built. If you are involved in a construction dispute, you need to check for liens from the subcontractors to make sure they are take care of. It won't make a client (or your boss) happy if the main case is settled and then a new wave of problems arise. Such liens are easy to find, as the statutes usually require filing in the same place real estate records are filed.

In the following case, a construction project went bad, and after two subcontractors filed against the owner, the general contractor, the bank, and anyone else their lawyers could think of, the two cases were consolidated, probably on the motion of one of the defendants. Another subcontractor thought the lawsuit looked like a good idea, and he also had a claim, so he intervened. This tale of bankruptcy, multiple states, and mechanics' liens is not unusual when a large project folds.

Sachs Electric v. HS Construction,
86 S.W.3d 445 (Mo. Ct. App. 2002) (per curiam).

This appeal arises out of Amended Findings of Fact, Conclusions of Law, Order and Judgment (amended judgment) entered after a non-jury trial in consolidated cases to enforce mechanic's liens, for equitable liens, and for relief in quantum meruit and/or unjust enrichment. At issue in this appeal is the circuit court's decision regarding the liability of Anheuser-Busch, Incorporated, Anheuser-Busch Companies, Inc., and Metal Container Corporation . . . (collectively referred to as Anheuser-Busch) to Bazan Painting Company (Bazan) and Charles E. Jarrell Contracting Company, Inc. (Jarrell) for money due to Bazan and Jarrell for work they performed in Texas and Missouri under subcontracts they had with a now-bankrupt general contractor, HS Construction Company. We reverse in part, affirm in part, and remand.

Prior to January 18, 1999, HS Construction Co., as general contractor, and Anheuser-Busch, as owner, entered into contracts for construction and repair projects on various premises, including for this appeal's purposes, premises in the St. Louis, Missouri area, in Rome, Georgia, and in Houston, Texas. HS Construction Co. also entered into various subcontracts with Bazan and Jarrell for work pertaining to those projects. Bazan and Jarrell have not been paid in full for the work they performed under those subcontracts.

On January 18, 1999, an involuntary bankruptcy proceeding was filed against HS Construction Co. On February 16, 1999, Jarrell filed a mechanic's lien against Anheuser-Busch real estate. The bankruptcy court lifted the stay as to Bazan on February 2, 2000, as to Anheuser- Busch on June 21, 2000, and as to Jarrell on December 12, 2000. Bazan and Jarrell, among others, filed separate petitions against Anheuser-Busch, Inc., and others, seeking to recover the money allegedly due for the unpaid work. The circuit court consolidated those cases.

After the parties, other than Jarrell, had a non-jury trial, and after Jarrell's lawsuit was consolidated with the other consolidated cases and submitted on motions for summary judgment, the circuit court entered its amended judgment. In its amended judgment the circuit court:

> awarded Bazan $70,591.31 against Anheuser-Busch, Inc., together with interest at the legal rate;
>
> awarded Bazan $2,987.90 against Metal Container Corp., together with interest at the legal rate;
>
> awarded Jarrell $16,851.00 against Anheuser-Busch, Inc., together with interest at the legal rate;
>
> entered judgment in favor of Anheuser-Busch Companies, Inc., Anheuser-Busch, Inc., and Metal Container Corp., and against Jarrell on its mechanic's lien claim; and entered judgment in favor of Anheuser-Busch Companies, Inc., Anheuser-Busch, Inc., and Metal Container Corp. and against Bazan on its equitable lien and constructive trust claims.

The circuit court also expressly addressed certain other claims and then dismissed with prejudice any claim not "expressly determined or dismissed" in other parts of the judgment or proceedings . . .

In its three points on appeal, Jarrell urges the trial court erred (1) in dismissing its mechanic's lien count as not filed within six months because Anheuser-Busch was estopped from asserting this defense and no lawsuit would "be a complete action" in the absence of the bankrupt general contractor; (2) in dismissing its mechanic's lien count for untimeliness because Missouri law allows suspension or tolling of the time period for filing when Anheuser-Busch "has engaged in affirmative conduct unmistakeably likely to mislead" Jarrell; and (3) in denying Jarrell's claim for a declaration of and a disbursement from a "construction trust" fund because Missouri law permits unpaid subcontractors to recover surplus funds in the hands of an owner on such a theory . . .

On December 21, 2000, Jarrell filed its petition against Anheuser-Busch, Inc., as well as the now-bankrupt HS Construction Co., seeking a total of $16,851.00, "exclusive of interest, costs and attorneys' fees," due for work itemized in its mechanic's lien. Jarrell sought this relief through a mechanic's lien claim and an unjust enrichment claim. Those claims arise out of the unpaid subcontract work Jarrell performed for HS Construction Co. at Anheuser-Busch's St. Louis property . . .

Jarrell first challenges the circuit court's decision that its mechanic's lien claim was barred as untimely because Jarrell did not file a mechanic's lien lawsuit within six months after the filing of the mechanic's lien as required by Section 429.170 RSMo 1994. . . .

. . . Here there is no dispute that the automatic stay of 11 U.S.C. Section 362(a) went into effect when HS Construction Co.'s bankruptcy was filed on January 18, 1999, and that it was not lifted with respect to Jarrell's claims until December 12, 2000. . . Jarrell's period for filing a mechanic's lien action did not commence until the stay was lifted on December 12, 2000. Jarrell filed the mechanic's lien action against Anheuser-Busch, Inc. within nine days of the lifting of the stay. That action was timely filed. . . .

. . . Missouri also makes joinder of the general contractor and property owner in any mechanic's lien action a requirement of such an action. . . Thus, the general contractor is a necessary party to a mechanic's lien action in Missouri, and . . . its bankruptcy stay tolls or extends the time for filing of an action to enforce a mechanic's lien to a period after that stay is lifted. . . .

We conclude the circuit court erred in determining Jarrell's mechanic's lien claim was barred, because the automatic stay of the general contractor's bankruptcy tolled or extended the six-month period of time in which Jarrell had to file a mechanic's lien action and Jarrell timely filed such an action after the bankruptcy court lifted the stay. . . .

In summary: The circuit court's judgment that Jarrell's mechanic's lien claim is barred as untimely is reversed and remanded for further proceedings. By this remand, we are not authorizing Jarrell to obtain a double monetary recovery from Anheuser-Busch, Inc. for mechanic's lien relief and quantum meruit relief due to the same work and materials. . . .

Taxing Entities

The IRS is an earthly power to hold in awe and fear. It has enforcement powers that will supersede whatever your local structure is and can make clients miserable. If your client has any tax problems, again, try to find out early. It is possible to negotiate even with the IRS. The sooner you know what the problem is, the sooner your attorney can decide what to do about it. Other taxing entities—states, educational districts, water districts, counties, municipalities, and the like—are possible problems, but none is as fearsome as the IRS. If you have a construction issue, check for any tax delinquencies; they would show on the real property records. They can probably be deferred or negotiated until the case has been resolved if the client can stay current and **arrearages** (owed back payments) are the only problem.

What all of these various liens and subrogation rights mean to you as an investigator is that you must be alert to situations that create these rights in third parties. If you are working a case with personal injuries, find out who has paid for the medical care and what type of rights they have in your state. You may not want to volunteer to pay a health care insurer who is "sitting on its rights," but you need to be aware that a potential insurance lien out there (not doing anything) in case the company decides to do something about it. Conversely, in a case where you have an affirmative duty to pay, such as in a statutory scheme where you must notify and get permission from a workers' comp carrier for settlement, you need to do so. Check the medical bills for payment; see who paid.

In cases involving property, check the pertinent filing authority for liens. High-ticket personalty may have UCC filings; real property liens are found with the rest of real property filing. Make sure someone with an interest in the outcome is not awaiting settlement to pounce; your team will need to take the amount of lien into account for settlement.

ENFORCEMENT ACTIONS INITIATED

	FY96	FY97	FY98	FY99	FY00
Civil Injunctive Actions	180	189	214	198	223
Administrative Proceedings	239	285	248	298	244
Contempt Proceedings	32	14	15	29	36
Reports of Investigation	2	1	0	0	0
Total	453	489	477	525	503

Source: IRS website.

SETTLEMENT PRESENTATIONS

In a settlement presentation, the goal of each party is to convince the other to see the case from his point of view. Exactly how much evidence and which evidence to present are tactical decisions for the lawyer to make, but they usually want to just talk about the things that are their strongest points without giving away anything that may give them a surprise edge at trial, if there is such a thing. If both sides have done their jobs well, very little should be a surprise at a civil trial.

Usually settlement negotiations are conducted informally in phone calls hashing over issues after an initial formal settlement demand in writing has set forth the plaintiff's position. In a really large case, the plaintiff may call a settlement conference after initial discovery, or the court may order one. A defendant rarely calls a formal settlement conference. To use such a conference effectively, all of the attorneys need to come with **settlement authority,** meaning that they need to have a certain sum of money they can offer or accept, or that they have certain conditions they will accept to settle the case. Alternatively, the parties or their corporate representatives need to be present, and they need to have settlement authority.

In order to achieve settlement, investment in a "day-in-the-life" video is often effective. This is a film demonstrating how the injury at issue has affected the daily life of the plaintiff, and depicts key ordinary activities that the plaintiff has difficulty with on a regular basis. Other effective videos can be causation videos or reenactments of the event. One video that quickly settled a case was a reenactment of the stabbing of a woman who was working after hours at her desk. She was attacked and stabbed over twenty times by a member of the janitorial staff who had not been screened by the cleaning company under contract with the building. When the video was shown to a roomful of adjusters at a continuing education seminar, the group held its collective breath when the attacker returned after his first round of stabbing to resume his attack. The power of this video moved the adjuster to offer sufficient funds to close the case.

In the following case, the edited version of the plaintiff's last days had a considerable effect on the jury. (Too bad it hadn't influenced the defendant more—they could probably have settled for far less than the approximately $8.8 million verdict.) Although not designated as such, the videotape fits into the day-in-the-life genre.

Pittsburgh Corning Corp. v. Walters, 1 S.W.3d 759 (Tex. App.—Corpus Christi 1999, pet. denied).

This is a products liability and negligence case tried before a jury. Pittsburgh Corning Corporation ("PCC"), appellant, appeals the adverse judgment for damages under the Texas Wrongful Death and Survival Statute. . . .

Douglas F. Walters was a California resident. In the 1960's, Walters enlisted in the Navy. During his tour of duty, Walters was responsible for some degree of oversight in the process of constructing nuclear submarines. Such construction was done in both California and Virginia. At the time, the Navy used Unibestos, a product manufactured by PCC, in the construction process. As a result, Walters was exposed to Unibestos which contained asbestos. After his Naval career ended in 1971, Walters returned to California. In 1994, Walters sought medical attention for sharp chest pains. A doctor diagnosed Walters with mesothelioma, a cancer caused by asbestos exposure. Walters died in La Mesa, California on August 15, 1994. . . .

During the course of the trial, the court permitted Walters to introduce a four-and-a-half-minute videotape with statements from the victim, made approximately four days before his death. In the audio portions, the decedent discussed his overall condition. The parties dispute the underlying nature of the videotape. Both sides admit that the videotape presented at trial was an edited version of a one-and-a-half-hour tape in which counsel asked Walters many questions. PCC claims that the statements contained in the videotape are made in response to expurgated questions from counsel. The court nevertheless admitted the videotape. . . .

. . . PCC argues that the trial court erred by admitting an edited videotape with sound, depicting Douglas Walters in the hospital four days prior to his death, as evidence of Walters' then-existing physical and mental condition. Specifically, PCC claims that the court erred because Walters' counsel circumvented the rules regarding depositions and denied PCC any opportunity to cross-examine Walters. PCC also asserts that the videotape constitutes hearsay evidence not subject to any exception and that the presentation of the videotape was unfairly prejudicial.

The videotape in question was originally one-and-one-half-hour in length, but was edited by Walters' counsel down to a four-and-one-half-minute presentation. On the video, Walters appeared extremely gaunt, with sunken cheeks and protruding bones. The tape, in part, showed Walters slowly walking through hospital hallways and using an IV stand for support. In other parts, Walters was in bed. Throughout, Walters, whether prompted or not, made comments about his physical condition and the pain he was experiencing. PCC's only objection was to the audio portions of the videotape. Therefore, we will focus solely on that issue. . . .

PCC contends that the audio portion of the videotape constitutes a deposition to perpetuate testimony. Thus, they argue that Walters did not comply with the requirements of rule 187. We disagree. While the statements contained on the audio portion of the videotape are certainly testimonial evidence, not all admissible testimonial statements must be given during depositions. The mere fact that a witness or a party has given a statement which may be used in court does not automatically invoke the cross-examination protections provided by the rules of civil procedure, although such statements are clearly subject to the rules of evidence. A deposition may have been the preferable method of preserving this evidence, but it was not the exclusive method for doing so. We do not find any conflict with rule 187.

PCC further objected to this testimony as hearsay . . . The court admitted the testimony under rule 803(3), which provides that a statement is not excluded as hearsay if the statement is of "the declarant's then existing state of mind, emotion, sensation, or physical condition" . . . Statements admitted under the rule are "usually spontaneous remarks about pain or some other sensation, made by the declarant while the sensation, not readily observable by a third party, is being experienced." . . .

Here, the statements made by Walters fall within the exception in rule 803(3). Walters explained the pain he was enduring, the difficulties he was having, and the sensations he was feeling during the time that the tape was recorded. Without his descriptions, the finder of fact would have seen a videotape displaying a gaunt and dying man, but would not have been aware of the physical pain he was suffering. PCC's assertions that these statements were staged responses to questions from counsel are unpersuasive here. Were we to adopt that position, any statement ever made in response to even the simplest question would immediately become inadmissible hearsay. Rule 803(3) is not so dogmatic. We hold that in this instance, Walters' responses were sufficiently spontaneous and contain practically no danger of faulty perception or memory to vitiate exclusion.

Finally, PCC argues that presentation of the videotape was far more prejudicial than probative. The fact that evidence has some prejudicial effect is insufficient to warrant its exclusion. Instead, there must be a demonstration that introduction of the evidence would be *unfairly* prejudicial to the objecting party. *See* Tex. R. Evid. 403 (emphasis added). Moreover, to be excluded, "evidence must not only create a danger of unfair prejudice, but such danger must substantially outweigh its relevance." . . . A trial court's decision to admit evidence is committed to its sound discretion and we will reverse only if there is a demonstrable abuse of that discretion. . . .

The presentation of the tape may have had the ancillary effect of arousing the sympathy of the jury for Walters' plight, but the trial court did not err in concluding that this tape had sufficient probative value to overcome whatever prejudice it created. Douglas Walters' condition at or near the time of his death was a necessary part of his wife's case. The videotape used at trial was an effective means of presenting that condition in its unexpurgated form . . . PCC argues that the presentation of the video was needlessly cumulative of other testimony. We disagree. While there may have been some degree of repetition in the videotape, the tape was also Douglas Walters' only opportunity to inform the jury about his condition. Under those circumstances, we cannot say that the evidence contained on the tape was unnecessarily cumulative.

PCC cites this court to several federal cases which it claims support its position . . . However, our review of these cases has led us to a contrary conclusion. For instance, in *Thomas*, the plaintiff was badly burned in an automobile accident. *Thomas*, 465 F. Supp. at 567. During his stay in the hospital, he and his wife were videotaped during a physical therapy session. *Id.* After an extensive discussion of the tape's contents, the court held the tape was inadmissible because of the likelihood that it would prejudice the jury. *Id.* at 571. The court specifically noted that its decision was influenced by the fact that the plaintiff would be available to testify at trial. *Id.*

Similarly, in *Bolstridge,* the court rejected the plaintiff's attempts to introduce a day-in-the-life video. 621 F. Supp. at 1204. Importantly, the court held that "videotapes should be admitted . . . only when the tapes convey the observations of a witness to the jury more fully or accurately than for some specific, articulable reason the witness can convey to them through the medium of conventional, in-court examination." *Id.* The court again was influenced by the fact that the plaintiff was available to testify and could make the same demonstrations in court that were shown on the videotape. *Id.* Clearly, Douglas Walters was not available to testify in this case, and thus, *Bolstridge* and *Thomas* are distinguishable.

We hold that the trial court did not err by permitting the presentation of the videotape and its audio portion. . . .

. . . PCC complains that the trial court erred by admitting irrelevant and unfairly prejudicial documents. Specifically, PCC complains about the admission of an article published in the *New York Times* on March 2, 1966, and two excerpts from the *Federal Register.*

The *New York Times* article describes a report that autopsies of recently-deceased persons demonstrated that 25 percent had asbestos lodged in their lungs. When the article was initially presented during trial, PCC objected to the unauthenticated document as hearsay. However, the record reflects that after a conference, PCC withdrew its objection to the exhibit for notice purposes. When Walters moved to admit the exhibit, PCC again made no objection. Thus, any objection to the admission of this document was waived. . . .

Moreover, the article indicates that PCC had, at the very least, constructive notice of the dangers associated with asbestos-related products. We have noted in a similar context that whether or not "the manufacturer was aware of information regarding the dangers of asbestos use at the time of marketing is immaterial since an asbestos manufacturer is charged with the duty to know the dangers of asbestos products." . . . Thus, like Egilman's testimony, the article provides some evidence of what PCC should have known about its product.

PCC did object to the admission of two excerpts from the *Federal Register* dated June 20, 1986. Occupational Exposure to Asbestos, Tremolite, Anthophyllite, and Actinolite; Final Rules, 51 Fed. Reg. 22615 & 22628 (1986). The excerpts state that the Occupational Safety and Health Administration (OSHA) has found asbestos universally harmful. PCC argues that these excerpts are irrelevant because they describe findings which came at least twenty years after Walters' exposure to Unibestos. However, these documents were used during the testimony of Dr. Brody, who testified only to the inherent dangerousness of asbestos-containing products. Used in that context, the documents were used to support the underlying basis for Brody's testimony . . . The conclusions stated in the excerpts comported with Brody's independent assessment of the dangers associated with asbestos and, as such, were admissible . . .

Accordingly, the judgment of the trial court is AFFIRMED.

When attending a settlement conference, have all your arguments regarding the damages amounts in line. If you are arguing over **valuations** (value of a contract, a damaged/destroyed property, or cost of repairs), have yours ready. Be able to explain how they were calculated and why your figures are superior. Write a memo explaining it to the lawyer handling the case at least a week in advance of the settlement conference. Find out as far in advance as possible if he wants the expert who performed the valuation available by phone in case a question comes up that you'll need to counter (expect to pay for that service), preferably when the date is set so that you can make sure the expert's calendar is free that day before agreeing to a particular time.

Settlement conferences are often held at the plaintiff's office, but you can try for a neutral spot if you are the defendant and don't want the plaintiff to be on her home ground. As the plaintiff, you may soften up the defendant (or just make him wonder why) if you ask to meet somewhere other than your office or his. Sometimes parties think arguing about where to hold a settlement conference is just petty gamesmanship and became annoyed. Ask your attorney how he wants to handle the arrangements.

Dick Gilby Realty

16607 Blanco Road Suite 502
San Antonio, Texas 78232-1940

August 15, 2003

Mr. Kim M. Pettit
Attorney
411 Heimer
San Antonio, Texas 78232

                          Re: Brokers Price Opinion
                                 1700 Encino Crest
                                 San Antonio, Texas 78259

Dear Kim,

I have reviewed the comparable sold properties for the subject property. Following is
the data supporting my Price Opinion.

            Sold & Closed properties Averages $/sq ft $70.51

Based on the above average sold per square foot price range the property should
market for $148,000 to $152,000. The average number of days on the market for
closed properties was 80 days.

I would recommend a sales price of $152,000 and expect a marketing period of 90
days.

This price opinion is based upon the current sold/closed listings. I would want to
preview the property prior to establishing a firm sales price and placing the property
on the market for sale.

Thank you for the opportunity to assist you with a Brokers Price Opinion on the
subject property. I look forward to working with you again in the future

Sincerely,

Richard T. Gilby
Broker/Owner

RECEIVED
BY _____ | DATE 8/19/03

517

MEDIATION PRESENTATIONS

Mediation is a popular choice for alternative dispute resolution. Basically, it is facilitated negotiation—the parties can't negotiate for themselves, so a third party comes in to help them recognize their risks and to advocate for settlement. The mediator doesn't (or, at least, shouldn't) advocate for any particular settlement, just for a settlement. In some jurisdictions, mediation is required prior to a jury trial; in others, it's required before certain types of trials (e.g., divorces). The discussion before the mediator is confidential and cannot be used in trial; ordinarily the mediator is only to report that the case did or did not settle.

In mediation, the parties are required to attend along with their attorneys. The theory is that the parties are to have an opportunity to air their grievances and to fashion their own settlement of the problem. In practice, the attorneys often try to control much of what their clients say. The mediator will introduce himself, explain the process, and give each party and attorney a chance to speak. Depending on the jurisdiction, more or less time will be spent in this joint session. The majority practice is to spend most of the time in the joint session hammering things out; the minority practice is to break out relatively early into **caucus sessions.** In caucus sessions, the mediator practices shuttle diplomacy, going from one party and legal team to another, discussing positions, problems, and offers.

Many times the attorney only wants a synopsis of the key evidence, organized in a way that makes sense to her. Perhaps it will be chronological, perhaps it will be by elements of the cause of action—it all depends on the particular circumstances of the case and what is most at issue. Ordinarily no evidence, demonstrative or otherwise, is presented at mediation because the timing is such that everyone is usually pretty familiar with the evidence. It's usually a matter of shifting perspective by either allowing the parties to vent at each other or having a neutral party contribute a fresh point of view.

Arbitration usually comes about as a result of a contractual provision. Arbitration differs from mediation in that a third party, usually an expert, listens to the evidence and makes a decision about the case. The decision can be binding or nonbinding. Binding arbitration is similar in many ways to administrative hearings because of its "trial-like" nature, but the general inapplicability of the usual rules that apply to a trial turn the case into a good deal of guesswork. The major arbitration groups, like the **American Arbitration Association (AAA)** have their own rules, but the arbitrators are given wide latitude to make decisions about procedural and evidentiary issues.

TRIAL PREPARATION

The case just won't settle, so you have to go to trial. You don't usually know that until the Friday before you go to pick a jury on Monday, but that had better not be when you start your trial preparation in earnest. In one sense, you start trial preparation from the very first client interview. If you have kept up your investigation plans and organized your files well, it shouldn't be positively awful to get ready. But there is still a significant difference between cases that settle and those that go to trial.

The first early warning date is at ninety days pretrial. On that date, you should begin notifying witnesses of the trial date and making sure they are all available should the trial occur as scheduled. In some jurisdictions, this is more difficult to predict than it should be. Because there will always be a good percentage of cases that settle, trial dockets overbook, just like the airlines, so that someone will be present to go to trial. However, some courts habitually overbook to such an extent that you may go through six or seven jury settings when you know you need to go to trial; others don't overbook by much so you will almost always be assured of going on a first setting. It all depends. It's another one of those things that you not only have to know about the local area, but also about each particular judge, because you'll have to be able to warn the witnesses and the client accordingly when you start making contact to arrange for witness appearances at trial.

You'll also need to check pleadings and discovery to make sure that everything that you needed to disclose to the other side has been sent to them. In the process of investigation, you accrue pieces of information bit by bit, and sometimes supplementation occurs at times that are not the same as the time you found

OFFICIAL FEES FOR THE CLARK COUNTY DISTRICT COURT AND COUNTY CLERK
Effective October 1, 2003, (NRS 17.110, 19.013, 19.020 19.031, 19.0313, 19.0315, 19.033,33.030, 41.200, 108.2275, 125A.200, 146.070, 440.605)

Adoptions	When filing a new Adoption proceeding..	$101.00
Answer or Appearance	When any defendant, or number of defendants filing jointly, answer a complaint; to be paid upon the filing of the first paper in the action Civil, including UIFSA and Domestic Cases not contained in NRS 125..............	$86.00
	* For each additional defendant named in a civil answer or first appearance...............................	$30.00
	** For each additional party appearing in a civil action at the time the additional party appears	$30.00
	Divorce, Annulment, Separate Maintenance..	$80.00
	Child Custody..	$75.00
Appeal from a Justice or Municipal Court	When filing an appeal from a Justice Court or Municipal Court..	$47.00
Appeal/Supreme Court	When filing a Notice of Appeal (payable to the Clerk of the Supreme Court)...............................	$250.00
Complaints Annulment or Separate Maintenance	When filing a Complaint for Annulment or a Complaint for Separate Maintenance........................	$132.00
Child Custody	When filing a Complaint for Child Custody	$122.00
Civil	When filing a new Civil action or proceeding	$133.00
	***For each additional plaintiff named in a civil complaint or amended civil complaint...................	$30.00
Divorce	When filing for a Divorce..	$152.00
Domestic Not Specified Above	When filing a domestic case not specified above	$133.00
Confession of Judgment	For filing a Confession of Judgment...	$28.00
Demand for Jury Trial	**When filing a Demand for Jury Trial**..	**Deposit of $400.00**
Domestic Case-Reopen	When filing a motion or other paper that seeks to modify or adjust a final order issued pursuant to NRS 125, 125B and 125C and on filing any answer or response to such a motion or other paper, excluding those exceptions noted in NRS 19.0312. (effective 11/04/02)..	$25.00
Fictitious Firm Name	For filing the name of a Fictitious Firm...	$20.00
Foreign Child Custody	To register a foreign child custody Order	$25.00
Liens, Frivolous or Excessive	When filing an application regarding frivolous or excessive liens...	$162.00
Minor's Compromise	When filing a Petition to Compromise a Minor's Claim	NO FEE
Miscellaneous Filings	To file other papers to be kept by the clerk, except for papers filed in court or filed by public officers in their official capacity, and not otherwise provided for	$15.00
	For issuing any certificate under seal, not otherwise provided for	$6.00
Notary Public Bonds	When filing and recording a bond of a notary public...	$15.00
Notice of Appeal	For filing a Notice of Appeal to the Supreme Court	$24.00
Peremptory Challenge	**Peremptory challenge of a Judge (payable to the Clerk of the Supreme Court)**	**$300.00**
Petition to Seal Records	When filing a new Petition to Seal Records...	$133.00
Probate/Guardianship	When filing a petition for letters testamentary or administration or guardianship where the stated value of the estate is $2,500 or less	NO FEE
	OR	
	Where the stated value of the estate is $2,500 or more	$146.00
	When filing a petition to contest any will or codicil, objection or cross-petition to the appointment of an executor, administrator or guardian or an objection to the settlement of account in an estate or guardianship	$86.00
Transfer from another District Court or County	To transfer an action or proceeding from another District Court or County	$133.00
Transfer from a Justice or Municipal Court	When transferring a case from a Justice Court or Municipal Court	$42.00
Will	When filing an original Will..	$15.00
Copies For each page copied from any document(s)..		$1.00
Certify/Exemplify (Copy fees of $1.00 per page also apply)	To certify copies of any document(s) prepared by the clerk...	$3.00
	To exemplify any document(s) prepared by the clerk	$6.00
	To examine and certify a copy of any document(s) prepared by another	$5.00
	To examine and exemplify a copy of any document(s) prepared by another................................	$9.00
Searches	For performing a search of the records per year, per name..	$1.00

U:\Fee List\FEELIST-10-03.rtf Rev 10/03

A typical fee sheet from a trial court

1994CI06614	I W 11/10/2003	CHARLES LEE OAKES III VS LOUIS DAVID BOHLS ET AL
1997CI11728	I F 11/10/2003	FRANCES M KNUTSON VS. TIM L KNUTSON
1998CI01350	I W 11/10/2003	DAVID ROMO VS. TEXAS DEPARTMENT OF TRANSPORTATION
1998CI16713	I W 11/10/2003	PATRICIA MESCH ET AL VS. DIANA BLANK
1999CI04222	I W 11/10/2003	DELIA R ANGULO VS. RODOLFO R MARTINEZ
1999EM503298	I F 11/10/2003	INT OF ZOE REBECCA GRAVES A CHILD VS.
2000CI00683	I W 11/10/2003	HAYWOOD JORDAN MCCOWAN SAT INC VS. GOETTING A
2000CI03434	I W 11/10/2003	FROYLAN MURRILLO VS. NOE G GARCIA ET AL
2000CI04667	I W 11/10/2003	LIBRADA ALVARADO ET AL VS. ELISEO TALAMANTES
2000CI05808	I W 11/10/2003	BARTON E LEE VS. OSCAR GONZALEZ
2000CI08052	I W 11/10/2003	GARY GREGG ET UX VS. ANTONIO HERNANDEZ III ET AL
2000CI09563	I W 11/10/2003	EDWARD O ESCOBAR ET AL VS. STATE FARM LLOYD
2000CI14252	I W 11/10/2003	WILLIE G CEDILLO ET AL VS. TMS MORTGAGE INC ET AL
2000CI17241	I W 11/10/2003	DEAN TORREROS-CARTER VS. MELVIN L BRAZIEL ET
2000CI18221	I S 11/10/2003	EDWARD DRESSER ET AL VS. MARCUS BROUSSARD ET AL
2000CI18329	I W 11/10/2003	MARY L STANSBERRY VS. FAMILY DOLLAR STORES INC
2001CI00060	I W 11/10/2003	SHERYE THOMAS VS. SYLVIA HOPE
2001CI00396	I W 11/10/2003	OLGA R PEREZ VS. GREGORY A MCDOWELL
2001CI00899	I W 11/10/2003	THOMAS A SCHAFFER VS. WILLIAM A OHLEMUELLER
2001CI05139	I W 11/10/2003	ALLEN GOLDSMITH VS. JOHN C WINKLER ET AL
2001CI07662	I W 11/10/2003	CYNTHIA TREVINO VS. CHARLES E MCDONALD
2001CI10201	I W 11/10/2003	CELIA C SAMARRIPA VS. SARA N PURDUE ET AL
2001CI10498	I W 11/10/2003	RAUL GONZALES ET UX VS. STEVE MARIN
2001CI10602	I F 11/10/2003	VIVKI L LAVELLE VS. RICHARD J LAVELLE
2001CI11103	I W 11/10/2003	PCI TRANSPORTATION INC VS. GROCERY SUPPLY COMPANY
2001CI11713	I W 11/10/2003	DENZIL HALLMARK ET AL VS. ANCIRA GMC TRUCKS
2001CI12707	I W 11/10/2003	DWAIN A GROFF VS. JAMES V VISTUBA

This docket sheet is thumb-tacked to a billboard outside the jury setting clerk's office in this county.

the information or the time your attorney decided to use it. To use it, you have to disclose it. Make sure everything has been sent to the other side. If the investigation has led to new theories of the case requiring new causes of action, you also need to include those new causes of action in amended pleadings. Conversely, you may want to eliminate causes of action that have not really been supported by the evidence. Every cause of action will produce jury questions; jury questions always have the potential of confusing the jury, which may be to your benefit or detriment. Talk to the attorney about these issues and make sure you have lined up the paperwork well in advance insofar as possible. Does he want you to prepare the jury charge? Many states have pattern jury charges available; if yours does, use it.

Anything you can file under the rules for self-authenticating documents, file. Start contacting the various custodians of records to tell them to expect your letters, and then send them the affidavits, records, and cover letters with self-addressed, postage-paid return envelopes. File them at the courthouse as soon as they have been returned. Calendar them for a week after you have sent them so you can follow up with phone calls if they do not come back.

Both pictures depict mere sections of shelves on jury instructions for preparing the charge for the court.

Begin actively working on demonstrative evidence. Prepare a list of the exhibits you believe will be needed with projected time allocation and costs. Meet with the attorney to prioritize and set deadlines for the exhibits.

At sixty days, send follow-up letters to witnesses and clients regarding the trial and mention the need for witness preparation time prior to trial. Begin scheduling those times. Go through your evidence again and make sure every point you need to cover has supporting evidence. If it does not, and you are stuck, make sure you speak to your supervising attorney about the problem. Have a status meeting with the attorney about the state of the case and the demonstrative evidence.

Trial Notebook

The next step is to begin putting together a trial notebook for the attorney unless, of course, he wants to do it himself. A trial notebook is what it sounds like: a three-ring notebook with dividers and pocket inserts for every part of the trial, each witness, and the live pleadings. It should be a thumbnail of every hot document, every key statement, every important photograph, and reference the location of the documents in your files if they are too numerous or large to be contained within the notebook. As the person accompanying the attorney to trial, you will be responsible for locating the physical document when he refers to it and having it marked for entry into evidence if it has not yet been admitted. The trial notebook is his reference system and attack plan.

As with anything else, ask for a sample of a trial notebook the attorney has had in the past that he liked for a model. Just as all cars basically do the same things but people become passionately attached to different models, the same thing happens to different systems of trial notebooks. Be flexible enough to go with the model your attorney likes. If you see something that doesn't work, you can suggest improvements as you gain credibility with your attorney. Don't try to change too much too quickly.

[Today's Date]

Roxanne Spur
5067 Lincoln Street, Apartment 312
Big City, Confusion 99999

    RE: Patty Haus v. John Justice and Vista Libre Apartments

Dear Ms. Spur:

The trial date for Patty Haus's case against John Justice and the Vista Libre Apartments is approximately three months away: Monday, March 17, 200-. Please make arrangements to be available during that week and for at least one day in the week before.

In order to prepare for you to testify, I will need to discuss the case with you during the week prior to the trial so that you will have an opportunity to review the deposition you gave. I will discuss the probable time you will testify and try to answer any questions you may have.

Please contact me to make an appointment for the week of March 10. I look forward to hearing from you.

Sincerely,

Jennifer Edwards
Paralegal to Ms. St. Joan

JEE/jgm

cc: Patty Haus

THE FOLLOWING JUROR QUESTIONNAIRE IS MANDATED BY GOVERNMENT CODE, SECTION 62.0132.
PLEASE TYPE OR PRINT WITH INK ONLY   *JUROR QUESTIONNAIRE*

| ☐ Male ☐ Female | Race (required by State Law): | Age: | Religion: | U.S. Citizen? ☐Y ☐N | **0405 1948** |

How long have you been a resident of Bexar County? | Your Occupation: | Your Employer: | How Long?

Highest level of education completed: | Current Marital Status: | Number of children: _____ Ranges of Age: from ___ years to ___ years

Spouse's Name: | Spouse's Occupation: | Spouse's Employer: | How Long?

Has any accidental bodily injury requiring medical attention ever been sustained by you? ☐Y ☐N
If so, what type?   By your family? ☐Y ☐N   If so, what type?

Have you ever served on a: Civil Jury? ☐Y ☐N   Criminal Jury? ☐Y ☐N
Have you ever been party to a civil lawsuit? ☐Y ☐N If yes, what type?
Have you ever been accused, complainant, or witness in a criminal case? ☐Y ☐N
Are any of your relatives law enforcement officers? ☐Y ☐N

If the above mailing address is incorrect, make corrections here:

I CERTIFY THAT ALL ANSWERS ARE TRUE AND CORRECT.
Please sign here:

Similar forms are used in most jurisdictions for jurors to complete. The finished form is copied and given to attorney for use in voir dire.

You'll also need your own trial notebook, but yours serves other purposes. During trial, you will be first be keeping track of jurors during voir dire, and then keeping track of evidence and exhibits and witnesses. You will need checklists and indices—checklists for what you need to do and indices for finding what you have.

Jury Selection

Jury selection varies from state to state in terms of whether the judge or the attorneys actually ask the questions, but the predominant form in state court seems to be for the attorneys to pose their queries. In federal court, the judge also questions from those submitted by the attorneys. Ordinarily general and then specific questions are asked of the jury panel, who signify responses to general questions by raising their hands or a number. Specific questions are based either on responses to the general questions or to information contained in cards that the jurors fill out prior to coming into the panel. Notes on each juror need to be made, both of their oral responses and of their nonverbal reactions. The lawyer conducting voir dire has difficulty keeping track of all of this information at the same time he asks the questions and tries to charm the jury, so the assistance of the paralegal is invaluable. Even when the judge is asking the questions, an additional pair of eyes to watch the body language of the potential jurors is a plus.

After the questions are finished, the attorneys exercise their peremptory strikes, which may be used for any reason except race. Because peremptory strikes are limited in number, attorneys much prefer that questionable jurors are struck for cause, for which no limit exists. Even a paralegal's relationships can be dragged into this fight.

Carton v. Missouri Pacific RR Co., 865 S.W.2d 635 (Ark. 1993).

Appellant Carla Blakemore Carton, the operator of a diesel fuel delivery truck owned by Gulf Oil Corporation, slipped and fell in January of 1979, while unloading diesel fuel at Missouri Pacific's facility in North Little Rock.

The case was . . . tried [in August of 1992], and the jury returned a verdict in favor of appellee Missouri Pacific. Appellant appeals. . . . There was no reversible error, and we affirm the judgment. . . .

We . . . address appellant's assignment asserting error for failure to remove a seated juror from the panel and replacing her with an alternate juror. The argument is two-fold: First, she contends that the juror is related by affinity to a paralegal in the office of appellee's law firm, and therefore, was disqualified, and, second, she contends the juror should have been disqualified because she had a material interest in the outcome of the case. Neither argument has merit.

Section 16-31-102(b)(1) of the Arkansas Code Annotated of 1987 provides, in part, "Except by consent of all the parties, no person shall serve as a petit juror in any case who . . . is related to . . . an attorney in the cause within the forth degree of consanguinity or affinity." Relation by affinity is "that which arises from marriage between the husband and the blood relations of the wife, and the wife and the blood relations of the husband." . . . Degrees of relationship are counted by the number of degrees removed from the common ancestor . . . The statute provides for disqualification of a venireman who is related to an attorney within the fourth degree. In this case, a seated juror notified the bailiff that she realized she had a relationship with someone involved in the case. The bailiff notified the trial court. The court invited the juror into chambers in the presence of counsel. In chambers, the court questioned the juror, and she replied that her husband was a cousin of a paralegal working for appellee's law firm. However, she said that she barely knew the paralegal and did not even know her last name. The court then asked counsel if they had any questions. Appellant's counsel replied, "No." The record does not establish whether the juror was a first cousin of the paralegal or a cousin five times removed. In a similar case . . . we wrote:

> The challenging party should have made out a prima facie case of the juror's relationship within the prohibited degree by questions asked by the juror or by the offer of other proof. Failing to do this, there was no error in the ruling of the court pronouncing him a competent juror.

Similarly, no error is shown in the ruling in this case. Since the juror is not [closely related to the paralegal], it is not necessary for us to decide whether a paralegal should be construed to be an "attorney in the cause" as defined in the statute.

Appellant's second part of this argument is that the juror should have been replaced because she had a material interest in the outcome of the case. Again, the record refutes appellant's argument. Near the end of the trial, appellant's counsel stated that the juror's husband, who is a lawyer, had possibly worked in a law firm with another attorney who had represented the appellant in another matter and appellant still owed that other attorney some money. There was no evidence whatsoever in support of the argument, and we affirm on that basis.

Introduction of Evidence

Whenever a piece of evidence is introduced, it is first marked by the party introducing it. This can be done ahead of time by purchasing evidence tags and attaching them prior to trial. You just need to be sure that the tag is a different color than the other party will be using. You can also just wait and have the court reporter tag each piece as it comes up. Either way, the number will not be assigned until the lawyer hands it to the court reporter. From then on, it is referred to as "X's Exhibit No. n."

To make sure every bit of evidence you want admitted has made it into the record, you need to have a list of all the evidence organized in a way that makes it easy for you to find and that has a place to check off which party entered it and its exhibit number. You also need to know where it is filed so you can find it easily and a place to check if the evidence is excluded and if an offer of proof was made. Some people have a running list with the party name and exhibit numbers preprinted and then write in exhibits as they are entered. However, this system does not alleviate the problem of overlooking the entry of a piece of evidence, although it is a nice way to keep track of what number you're on. I'd do both before I'd give up the former.

As a paralegal, another of your responsibilities will be last-minute preparation and production. For any evidence requiring equipment—an easel, a projection screen, a computer—conduct a test run before you have to use the equipment. Do this when the jury is not around. Even low-tech stuff can collapse or fail. The jury may not hold lack of preparation against your lawyer, but your lawyer may hold it against you.

Other preparation is needed for testimonial evidence. You'll need to keep in touch with all witnesses on a daily basis from the week prior to trial until the day they testify. Advise the witness to show up at least an hour before the earliest you think you might possibly need him. The uncertainty of exactly when someone may testify is what has led to videotaped experts—due to the increased costs associated with making experts wait. When fact witnesses must come from out of town, the problem is compounded; pass that problem to the lawyer if at all possible, so that he can solve it early with a **special setting,** which means that the trial is set for a more certain date than most trials—it is guaranteed to go if it has not settled.

EXHIBIT LIST [THOS. BATTLE]

Exhibit Description	Location	Reason for Entry	Exhibit Number	Admitted?
Police Report from Arrest	Tab C [of Trial Notebook]	To establish the statements made to the arresting officers & real reason for arrest		
Eviction Notices	Tab B	To establish motive on part of Haus		
Entry and Detainer Suit	Tab B	To establish motive on part of Haus		
Apartment Lease	Tab B	To show contractual duties		
Smoker's Criminal Records	Tab D	To establish motive on part of Haus		
Haus's Medical Records	Tab E	To show alternative cause for Haus's claimed mental anguish damages		
Haus's Medical Bills	Tab E	Make sure they match ours		

π's Ex. No.	Δ's Ex. No.	Description	Admitted?
1		Police report	Y
2		Letter from A	Y
	1	Eviction notice	Y
	2	Smoker's criminal record	N

Excluded Testimony	Witness	Offer of Proof
Smoker's Prior Criminal Acts	Joe Cop	Y

When witnesses show up, make sure they don't come in to the courtroom before being called to testify. It is customary to put witnesses under **The Rule.** There doesn't seem to be any other name for it; we all just call it The Rule. It simply means that witnesses may not hear one another testify. So when a witness appears, he or she must wait in the hallway. Expert witnesses are the exception: They usually are not subject to The Rule.

When witnesses appear to testify, you must also instruct them on matters regarding the motion in limine. Once the judge orders the parties not to discuss certain topics in front of the jury without approaching the bench first, the expectation is that all the witnesses will know to stay away from those areas. If the legal team had planned to have the witness talk about the excluded evidence, and your witness does so in violation on the order on the motion in limine, the attorney or the client may be held in contempt or a mistrial can be declared. If your side didn't want to talk about the excluded evidence and your witness brings it up, the other side will say that you "opened the door," and that he now has free rein to discuss that nasty evidence you wanted to keep out—and he has a good chance of being allowed to do so.

So as witnesses show up, you need to tell them to get out of the courtroom (nicely) and to keep their mouths shut (nicely) as to subjects listed in the order on the motion in limine. Smile, give them an estimate of when you think they might testify, and then scurry back to keep track of the exhibits.

POST-TRIAL JURY CANVASSING

After the trial is over, you may want to talk to the jury about what made the difference to them in their decision. This is not to find evidence of jury tampering or to try to change the outcome of the trial. Your goal is feedback. The juror's names and contact information will be available to you, so you don't have to ask questions at the time of the verdict, but jurors are often most open to talking about the experience immediately after trial. They've been listening to your team for days, maybe even weeks, and they often are ready to talk back. So while you are awaiting the verdict, think about what questions you'd like to ask the jury.

Are there any pieces of evidence you and the attorney discussed leaving out or introducing that might have swayed juror opinion? Whom did jurors believe? Disbelieve? What parts of the story did or did not make sense to them? It is these kinds of questions you can explore with your jury—a real jury, not one you are trying to imagine, and one as well acquainted with the issues as you are, and often as interested in the outcome because of their responsibility in reaching a decision. The information you get will be invaluable, for although every jury is somewhat different, the way they view the evidence will give you insight into how to structure the next trial on which you work.

CHAPTER SUMMARY

Like its kindred skill, research, investigation is not complete until you have finished the analysis and application. In an investigation, the analysis and application is in disposing of the matter through settlement or trial. You can get to a settlement through negotiation, mediation, or arbitration, but you want to make sure you include all interested parties, including any lienholders, so that when it's over, it's really over. If there's no settling the case (and some cases aren't meant to be settled), it's time to get ready for trial, which means organizing all those people you've interviewed (and the notes, summaries, depositions, background checks, and any other impeachment evidence you have against them), all the documentary evidence you've obtained, all the physical evidence you've preserved or observed, and all the demonstrative evidence you've created, and getting it to the courthouse in a form that makes it look like a snap. Orchestrating the people, the papers, and the oddments that go with the trial is the both the worst and the best of the interviewing and investigating process. Good luck and go to it.

FOR FURTHER READING

Anthony J. Bocchino and Samuel H. Solomon, *What Juries Want to Hear: Methods for Developing Persuasive Case Theory,* 67 Tenn. L. Rev. 543 (2000).

Robert P. Burns, *Professional Responsibility in the Trial Court,* 44 S. Tex. L. Rev. 81 (2002).

H. Mitchell Caldwell, L. Timothy Perrin, Richard Gabriel, and Sharon R. Gross, *Primacy, Recency, Ethos, and Pathos: Integrating Principles of Communication into the Direct Examination,* 76 Notre Dame L. Rev. 423 (2001).

Steven I. Friedland, *On Common Sense and the Evaluation of Witness Credibility,* 40 Case W. Res. 165 (1990).

Michael H. Graham, *Application of the Rules of Evidence in Administrative Agency Formal Adversarial Adjudications: A New Approach,* 1991 U. Ill. L. Rev. 353 (1991).

Paula L. Hannaford, B. Michael Dann, and G. Thomas Munsterman, *How Judges View Civil Juries,* 48 DePaul L. Rev. 247 (1998).

Paul F. Kirgis, *The Problem of the Expert Juror,* 75 Temple L. Rev. 493 (2002).

Note, Joseph M. Herlihy, *Beyond Words: The Evidentiary Status of "Day in the Life" Films*, 66 B.U.L. Rev. 133 (1986).

Note, Constance R. Lindman, *Sources of Judicial Distrust of Social Science Evidence: A Comparison of Social Science and Jurisprudence*, 64 Ind. L.J. 755 (1989).

Henry H. Perritt, Jr., *Changing Litigation with Science and Technology: Video Depositions, Transcripts and Trials*, 43 Emory L.J. 1071 (1994).

CHAPTER REVIEW

KEY TERMS

alternative dispute resolution

American Arbitration Association (AAA)

arbitration

arrearages

caucus sessions

claimant

collateral source rule

comp lien

comp carrier

Federal Medical Care Recovery Act

first money liens

first-party coverage

general creditor

hospital liens

interpleader

intervenor

letter of protection

lienholder

M&M lien

materialmen

mechanics

mediation

offer of proof

preservation of era

preservation of evidence

quantum meruit

settlement authority

settlement conference

special setting

subro files

subrogation

The Rule

third-party tortfeasor

uninsured motorist (UIM)

valuations

veniremen

workers' compensation insurance company

workers' compensation lien

FILL IN THE BLANKS

1. When you are behind in payments, you start accruing _____ .

2. _____ , which is just a fancy name for a process other than trial to resolve a controversy, includes _____ , or direct discussion between the parties about how to settle the claim; _____, a facilitated discussion of settlement; and _____ , where a neutral third party makes a determination, which may or may not be binding.

3. The *M&M* in an M&M lien stands for _____ and _____ .

4. The part of an insurance contract that covers injuries to the person paying for the policy is referred to as _____ coverage, which includes _____ coverage on an automobile party when the driver of the other vehicle has no insurance.

5. The client gives the lawyer a range or a particular dollar amount for which he will settle the case as _____ .

6. The _____ is a statute that allows the government to recover for payment of federal health care benefits paid when there is third-party liability.

7. The portion of a mediation when the parties split up and the mediator engages in shuttle diplomacy is referred to as the _____ .

8. A(n) _____ is a party who gives money to the court to give away; a(n) _____ is a party who wants some of the money to be given away because it has a financial claim due to a relationship with one of the adversaries.

9. A(n) _____ is an assurance by an attorney that a particular service provider (usually a doctor) will be paid out of the proceeds of any settlement.

10. The _____ , who insures the employer for injuries to employees arising in the course and scope of their employment, usually has a(n) _____ lien under the applicable statute, meaning it is paid first, against any recovery from a(n) _____ , or individual outside of the workplace who is liable under a tort theory.

11. To _____ , or make it so you may appeal a bad call by the judge, you must object to the evidence with a clear basis and obtain a ruling from the judge if you want to complain about evidence that was admitted, or make a(n) _____ to show what the evidence would have been if you want to complain about evidence that was not admitted.

12. Most of the liens in these cases are not secured, or guaranteed by particular pieces of property, so the _____ , or person owed the money, is given the status of a _____ , which means he gets what is left over after property exemptions and secured creditors are paid.

13. The _____ is a common law concept that precludes the introduction of any resources that an injured party has that will keep him from actually suffering financially from the losses imposed on him by the defendant so that the defendant does not benefit from the plaintiff's foresight; e.g., the plaintiff's planning in paying premiums so that he had disability insurance coverage and therefore was actually receiving some income he would have gone without otherwise.

14. Under certain circumstances, some cases will receive a(n) _____ so that the case will actually begin trial on the scheduled date (unless, of course, it settles).

15. The rule that requires the absence of any witnesses in the courtroom while another witness is testifying is simply called _____ .

16. Some jurisdictions will schedule a formal _____ at a specific time prior to trial to try and force the parties to come to an agreement.

17. States sometimes have statutory allowances for _____ , which can be filed at the courthouse to protect the interest of the health care facility.

18. The Latin term _____ refers to an equitable doctrine that will allow a worker to be paid the value of his work even if there is a problem with the contract to prevent unjust enrichment on the part of the person receiving the benefit of the work.

WEB WORK

1. Mediate.com, at, surprisingly enough, www.mediate.com, is an excellent site with lots of interesting articles about mediation. Investigate the site and find an article that appeals to you. Summarize it.

2. Check out how arbitration works in another country: go to the French Commission on Arbitration, or Comité Français de l'Arbitrage at http://www.arbitrage-fr.org/html-gb/default.html. It has versions in both French and English (Anglais, if you end up on the French page). How does it compare to American arbitration in the sense described in this chapter?

3. In case you didn't get enough of what you can do with Flash in an earlier chapter, here's another Web site with cool applications using Flash: http://www.grownmencry.com/web/resguide_f.html.

4. Go to www.google.com and run <trial notebook as your search>. You'll find books, computer systems, and models online—all sorts of things to check out. See what looks most helpful to you.

5. Run a search for <electronic courtroom> on the Web. What does that mean? Narrow the search with terms for your locale. Is there one near you?

WORKING THE BRAIN

1. Along with the issues of how to deal with a motion in limine versus the introduction of testimony, *Warren v. Sharp* addresses standards for evaluating abuse of discretion. Does this discussion supplement, contradict, or repeat the information given earlier about abuse of discretion? How and why?

2. *Warren v. Sharp* also addresses the admissibility of expert witnesses. From reading this case, does Idaho follow the *Daubert* standard?

3. Several of the cases in this chapter dealt with statutory construction. What did you learn about how to interpret statutes from reading those cases?

4. The collateral source rule and double recovery tends to start arguments: Is it fair to allow the person who did something wrong to not have to pay for medical bills or such because the person she injured happened to have enough sense to get in a position to have them covered? Or is it immoral for the person who was injured to, in essence, get paid twice—the double recovery frequently mentioned? Does it matter to you if the injured party pays for the insurance or if it is a benefit of employment? Explain your answers.

5. What did you learn about contract law, equitable subrogation, and statutory enforcement rights from reading the cases in this chapter? How do they compare?

PUTTING IT TO WORK

1. Prepare a trial notebook for one of the parties in the *Haus v. Justice* case.

GLOSSARY

abate: to temporarily set aside; to lessen.

abuse of discretion: a standard of review often used to evaluate decisions of judges. If more than one decision can be reasonably reached, there is no abuse of discretion; if the decision is clearly wrong, arbitrary, capricious, not based on any facts or law, or outrageous, then it may be reversed under this standard.

active listening: a set of techniques to involve the listener in what the speaker is saying rather than focusing on the listener's own responses.

acute: in medicine, of recent origin or currently being experienced and of expected limited duration.

ad hoc: as needed for one specific situation.

admissible evidence: evidence that a court will allow to be introduced to a jury.

affiant: person swearing to an affidavit.

affidavit: sworn written statement.

affirmative defense: a defense that is not dependent on the allegations of the opposing party but relieves the defendant of liability for some independent reason.

alternative dispute resolution: way of settling conflict without trial.

AMA: American Medical Association.

ambient noise: environmental sound.

American Arbitration Association (AAA): national association of arbitrators.

American Lawyer Media: a legal periodical giant.

American Sign Language (ASL): gesturing language created for the deaf.

animation: some form of non-filmed moving picture.

answer: defendant's document setting forth his or her official contentions.

anxiety disorder: one of the psychological conditions characterized by excessive worry.

arbitration: an alternative dispute resolution in which a third party, often someone with expert knowledge of the subject to be decided, hears evidence and determines the outcome of a dispute; binding usually by contract.

arrearages: dollar amount of missed payments of an obligation.

associate: a lawyer at a firm who does not have an ownership interest in the firm (but probably hopes to).

assumed name certificate: official filing of a business name.

attachment: legal process of taking property to pay a debt.

attorney ad litem: lawyer appointed by the court to provide legal representation only for a minor or incompetent.

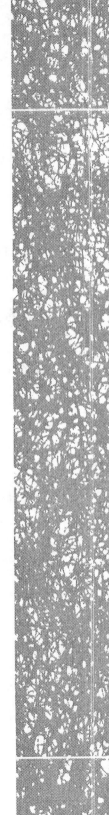

attorney-client privilege: a right to keep communications between a lawyer and his or her client confidential.

attorney work product: a right to keep information related to the strategy of a lawyer confidential.

authentication: proving that an item is what it is purported to be.

authority structure: the relationship of supervisors, management, and employees in decision making for a business.

autism: a psychological condition in which the sufferer has profound difficulty with social interaction.

baby lawyer: slang term for a new lawyer.

backup tapes: a general term referring to any back-up system; specifically relates to magnetic tape storage, which records all the information in the computer at a given time; not differentiated for use of searchers but set up for the use of the computer system as a whole; see **www.linktionary.com/b/backup.html**.

bar graph: a pictorial representation of information by using bars to indicate relative amounts.

bench trial: trial wherein judge is the factfinder.

billable hour system charging clients based on fractions of an hour. The hour may be divided into tenths (.1) or in quarters (.25). The client is charged for the entire fraction from the first moment it begins.

billing charges attributable to clients; this amount often is used as an evaluation tool for paralegals working in a firm that uses billable hours as its primary method of payment. The billable hours are those which were actually spent; collections (or collectible hours) are those which are actually paid by the client, occasionally after negotiation of the bill, but more often after the reviewing attorney cuts some of the time.

bipolar disorder: also called *manic depression,* a psychological condition in which depression alternates with periods of frantic, impulsive action.

blunderbuss: a wide-mouthed musket; when used as a metaphor, referring to a scatter-shot approach.

burden of proof: the duty of producing evidence in favor of the person's position.

Business Records Exception (BRE): a common exception to the hearsay rule for documents ordinarily kept by businesses.

calendar: to record events and deadlines on the schedules of all members of the legal team working on a case

capacity: ability to make legal decisions.

caucus sessions: part of a mediation in which the mediator visits with the parties separately.

cause of action: a recognized pattern of facts upon which a court may grant relief.

caveat: beware; warning.

Census Bureau: agency of the federal government charged with keeping statistical data on the United States population.

Centers for Disease Control (CDC): a federal agency charged with tracking causes of mortality and illness and with designing and implementing plans to reduce those causes.

CEO: Chief Executive Officer; the person responsible for the operations of a corporation.

cervical: pertaining to the neck.

Certified Legal Assistant (CLA): a designation awarded by National Association of Legal Assistants.

Certified Legal Assistant Specialist (CLAS): an individual who has passed both NALA's CLA exam and a subsequent exam in a particular subject area.

Certified Paralegal: the newer, alternative title for the CLA; an individual successfully passing the NALA national examination for paralegals/legal assistants.

chronic: ongoing; in medicine, a continuing or intermittent condition that did not originate from a recent occurrence.

Chinese wall: named for the Great Wall of China, this term refers to the practice of isolating certain members of the legal team from files upon which they formerly worked as a member of the opposing party's legal team. Also referred to as an ethical wall.

CLA Review: official study text for the Certified Legal Assistant exam.

claimant: insurance term for any person claiming payment under an insurance policy.

CLI: Certified Legal Investigator, a designation awarded by NALI.

closed question: inquiry that can only be answered with predetermined list of responses.

closing arguments: the attorneys' statements at the end of trial designed to persuade the jury to find for their clients; another term for *summation*.

coaching: a sometimes derogatory term for witness preparation.

coccyx: tailbone.

cognitive interviewing: an interviewing technique that attempts to mentally take an interviewee to the time and place of the incident under discussion.

collateral source rule: evidentiary rule excluding information about other resources a party has available to pay damages.

colorable: in law, usually found in conjunction with the word "claim," meaning roughly the same as a prima facie case—that the person with a burden of proof has sufficient evidence on each element of a claim so as to proceed to a jury.

commercial policy: insurance for a business entity that ordinarily includes protection for property and payment of attorneys fees and awards when the entity incurs legal liability.

comp carrier: insurance company providing workers' compensation insurance.

comp lien: a workers' compensation lien.

competency: condition of being competent.

complaint: document with which the plaintiff begins litigation, outlining the parties, factual basis of suit, causes of action, damages, and request for action by the court (prayer).

compressed: packed together more tightly; made to take up less space.

computer simulation: product of a computer based on inputted evidence and calculations by the computer

condemnation: court proceeding to transfer private property to a governmental entity for public use.

condemnee: person whose property is taken for public use.

condemnor: governmental entity exercising eminent domain.

confidentiality: in the context of legal ethics, the duty of a lawyer and his legal team to keep all aspects of a client's case, sometimes even including his identity, secret.

confirmation letter: document affirming an event, action, appointment, etc.

conflict check: the process of determining whether a conflict of interest exists.

conflict of interest (COI):   inability to represent a client due to circumstances that would cast doubt on the loyalty of the attorney to a present or past client.

conformed copies: copies of documents filed in a court that have the official stamp of the court or clerk indicating the time and date the documents were filed; also called *file-stamped* copies, although conformed copies may also include indications of actions by the court.

congenital: existing since birth.

contingency fee contract: an agreement for attorneys' fees that is based on a percentage of any recovery obtained for the client.

contract basis: being paid on an hourly or flat fee for designated work as an independent contractor as opposed to being an employee.

control group test: one of the tests used to determine which individuals in a corporation are represented by counsel for purposes of privilege and the no-contact rule. In this test, the individuals who have managerial responsibility over the area involved in the events of the litigation are the persons represented.

corporation: a business entity with perpetual duration that limits the liability of investors, created by filing the appropriate documents and paying the requisite fees to the state of incorporation.

coterminous: ending at the same point.

court-appointed expert: a neutral expert retained to assist the judge in making decisions but paid for by the parties.

Court Appointed Special Advocate (CASA): a specially trained representative for minors.

courtroom experiment: a live demonstration in front of a jury.

crime-fraud exception: an exception to the ethical duty of client confidentiality that allows disclosure of the commission of a crime or fraud with the attempted assistance of the attorney.

cultural defense: an argument that an individual acted in accordance with his or her culture and should be judged by the standards of that culture.

curriculum vitae: a report of one's professional history and accomplishments.

custodian: keeper.

Daubert standard: a principle enunciated by the United States Supreme Court requiring judges to evaluate expert evidence for reliability.

d.b.a.: doing business as.

Deaf culture: a societal group whose communication is based on American Sign Language.

deafness: condition of inability to hear or near-inability to hear.

death penalty sanction: a severe court-ordered sanction that "kills" the party's chance to prevail in the litigation; e.g., striking pleadings.

declarant: person making an out-of-court statement.

default judgment: a judgment entered for one party because the other party fails to appear.

defense attorney: in civil litigation, an attorney who ordinarily represents defendants of tort actions.

degenerative: a medical condition that worsens gradually.

demand letter: a request for a settlement sent by the attorney outlining the reasons supporting the request.

dementia: a condition found primarily in the elderly that makes them unable to reason rationally.

demonstrative evidence: displays for the purpose of illustrating or combining other admitted evidence.

deponent: the individual being deposed.

deposition: usually refers to an oral deposition.

deposition notice: the document filed with the court and served on all parties as well as the deponent which informs them of the person, time, and place of the deposition.

depositions by written questions: a discovery device used to obtain limited sworn information from a non-party, usually documents, through a court reporter.

depression: a mood disorder characterized by a complete lack of energy.

diary: an organizational device to ensure that files are reviewed on a regular basis; also called a *tickler system*.

directed verdict: an order entered in the midst of trial or an instruction to the jury that requires it to make a decision in a particular way.

discoverable evidence: any information or thing that will help lead to relevant, admissible evidence.

discovery: court-supported investigation.

discovery abuse: using discovery to harass another party.

discovery action plan: schedule and/or objectives for discovery.

discovery plan summary: a short statement of the results of discovery.

dispositive: determinative of the issue(s) or litigation.

docket control order: a court order requiring the parties to meet interim deadlines before trial; also called a *scheduling order*.

Dow Jones Industrial Average: a figure representing the average value of stocks taken from various industries.

DSM-IV (Diagnostic and Statistical Manual): manual for psychiatric diagnoses produced by the American Psychological Association.

dual representation: representation by an attorney of two (or more, in some usage) clients in the same matter

dueling experts: situation wherein hired experts for the parties dispute each other's analysis, opinion, etc.

Dun & Bradstreet: a commercial information company.

egregious: glaringly, obviously bad.

eminent domain: the power of the government to take private property for public use.

ephemeral: short-lived, brief; has a connotation of lightness.

ETH: medical abbreviation indicating the presence of alcohol.

ethical wall: this term refers to the practice of isolating certain members of the legal team from files upon which they formerly worked as a member of the opposing party's legal tem. Also referred to as a Chinese wall.

ex parte communications: communications with a court about litigation outside of the presence of opposing counsel.

exempt: excepted.

expert witness: an individual with specialized knowledge that qualifies him or her to render an opinion.

extension: in law, usually refers to additional time to meet a filing deadline.

extraordinary relief: a court-ordered remedy that is not payable in money and not entered in the ordinary course of litigation.

extremities: in anatomy, those parts of the body away from the trunk and head: arms, legs, knees, elbows, hands, feet, fingers, toes.

facilitated communication: a technique to assist autistic individuals to communicate utilizing a computer.

fact witness: an individual with information related to the litigation that is not dependent on opinion.

false memories: recall of events that were not actually experienced by the individual remembering.

Federal Medical Care Recovery Act: statute allowing the government to recover money for certain types of governmentally provided health care.

fee schedule: a list of rates charged for particular services.

field interview: an interview outside the office.

fight or flight: a primal human response to stress that physiologically prepares the individual to run from or combat a perceived threat.

file clerk: an employee of a law firm whose primary task is to maintain the internal filing system of the firm.

file-stamped copies: copies of documents filed in a court that have the official stamp of the court or clerk indicating the time and date the documents were filed; also called *conformed copies*.

Findlaw: a legal Web site; **www.findlaw.com.**

first money liens: debts that have first priority in payment from a financial source.

first-party coverage: insurance protections payable to the insured.

flow chart: a graphic representation of a chain of events, decisions, etc.

formboard: a large, sturdy, lightweight surface for mounting photos or enlargements with a polystyrene core covered by a smooth white surface.

foundation questions: inquiries required prior to the admission of evidence.

fragmented data: information that has been split into smaller pieces for routing purposes but should be together to make the data make sense.

framework of dealing: the circumstances and practices of ordinary interaction between persons or entities.

Freedom of Information Act (FOIA): a federal act requiring disclosure of governmental information upon proper request; states have similar statutes.

friendly witness: a person with information relevant to the litigation who is aligned with a party.

functional: in psychology, referring to a cause that is circumstantial rather than biological.

garnishment: process of setting aside a portion of a person's salary to pay a debt.

general creditor: a person owed money not chargeable against a particular asset.

Gray's Anatomy: a standard text on human anatomy.

guardian ad litem (GAL): a court-appointed representative for a child or incompetent person.

hearing loss: an inability to hear certain pitches or volumes of sound; usually refers to partial impairment rather than total inability to hear.

hearsay rule: evidentiary principle that excludes out-of-court statements offered to prove the truth of the matter asserted.

herniated: medical term when one part of the anatomy has a tear or hole that causes it to impinge on another part of the anatomy.

HIPAA: Health Insurance Portability and Accountability Act of 1996.

homeowners' insurance: an insurance policy providing protection for the realty and personalty of the insured as well as paying for damages and defense of nonbusiness, nonauto-related liabilities of the insured.

horseshedding: witness preparation.

hospital liens: statutory right of hospitals to recover for hospital bills.

hostile witness: (AKA hostile fact witness) a person with knowledge of the facts relevant to the litigation who does not want to cooperate with a particular party or with the litigation.

hourly billing: charging attorneys fees based on the time spent on a file; hours are often divided into tenths or quarters for time less than an hour.

identity issues: deep-seated psychological concerns related to how an individual perceives himself or herself.

immediacy: experience at the same time or close by.

impeach: show a person to be unbelievable or untrustworthy.

imputed: transferred from one to another, usually with the connotation of some sort of negative behavior being transferred to one who will take responsibility for the act even if not actually involved in the behavior (or even necessarily aware of it).

in camera: usually used to describe the situation in which a judge reviews items in private.

inapposite: not applicable.

incompetent: someone lacking legal capacity; an individual who by reason of physical or mental condition is unable to make reasoned decisions about his or her property or person.

indemnification agreement: contract or part of a contract wherein one party agrees to defend the other in litigation or to pay damages on behalf of the other under certain circumstances.

inflammatory: having the tendency to provoke anger, disgust, or other strong emotion.

in-house experts: employees of a party with specialized knowledge about a subject relevant to the litigation.

insurance defense: an area of legal practice in which the attorney is retained and paid by the defendant's insurance company.

insured: the customer of an insurance company.

insurer: an insurance company.

intake forms: questionnaires designed to gather basic information.

inter alia: among other things.

interlocutory order: a court order entered before the final decree or judgment.

interpleader: a suit in which a party owing funds but not knowing to whom the funds should be paid brings all possible claimants before the court for allocation of the monies.

interrogatories: discovery devices requesting information from a party; limited in number of questions and in writing.

intervenor: the name of a party who joins litigation because it has a legal interest in the outcome; e.g., a lienholder.

interviewing: the process of obtaining information from an individual.

investigating: finding facts about a particular matter.

investigation action plan: an outline scheduling or defining facts to be learned and potential sources.

investigation plan summary: short narrative tallying the current status of investigation.

ISP: Internet service provider; the company that provides an individual or entity with access to the Internet, whether through telephone, cable, or data stream lines.

JBOD: "just a bunch of disks"; electronic information storage without any organizing principle.

judgment non obstante veredicto: j.n.o.v.; a judgment entered contrary to the decision of the jury.

judicial notice: an evidentiary device in which a judge officially recognizes certain facts and admits them.

junk science: technical or scientific theories with little to no verifiable foundation; often highly subjective or dependent on practitioner.

law clerk: ordinarily a law student working in a law firm, usually with the primary duty of research; may also be used to designate an attorney working as an assistant to a judge or justice.

laying a foundation: taking the requisite procedural steps prior to introducing a piece of evidence; also called *laying a predicate.*

leading questions: inquiry that suggests the answer and requires only a yes or no answer.

learned treatise: secondary source for legal information written by a recognized expert or academician; may be one volume or multivolume set.

legal administrator: an individual responsible for the business aspects of the firm, particularly human resources; usually someone with management experience and/or training.

legal assistant: traditionally, synonymous with *paralegal;* currently in flux and can mean paralegal or legal secretary or some other person in a legal office.

legal assistant manager: a supervisor of legal assistants.

legal secretary: traditionally, a skilled assistant to a lawyer who performs high-level clerical and typographical tasks.

letter of nonrepresentation: a letter to a potential client making it clear that the attorney is not undertaking the potential client's legal matter.

letter of protection: a document agreeing to pay a treating physician out of settlement or award money to ensure continued care for a client and/or delay payment of medical bills.

lienholder: an individual with a verifiable, collectible claim for money against another.

line graph: a graphic representation of information on an *x-y* axis that connects plotted points.

litigator: an attorney involved in practice related to civil trials; usually on the defense side.

Legal Nurse Consultant (LNC):   a registered nurse with legal training. As opposed to nurse paralegals, a Legal Nurse Consultant is aligned more with medical than legal practice and usually meets a particular set of criteria.

lumbar: the lower back or small of the back.

M&M lien: mechanic's and materialman's lien; an enforceable claim for money owed to a mechanic or materialman; often requires compliance with extensive statutory requirements.

malpractice carrier: an insurance company providing a policy for professional negligence.

manufacturing defect: in strict liability for the manufacturers, retailers, and anyone else in the distribution chain, a condition of the product due to improper manufacture that renders the product unreasonably dangerous.

market reports exception: an exception to the hearsay rule allowing the introduction of evidence that is a business report ordinarily relied upon by participants in the business.

Martindale-Hubbell: the name of a legal publisher commonly used to refer to the multivolume attorney directory it publishes.

materialmen: persons providing supplies for construction of real estate or repair of real estate or expensive personal property.

mechanics: persons providing services for construction of real estate or repair of real estate or expensive personal property.

mediation: a non-binding form of alternative dispute resolution in which a neutral third party assists the parties in negotiation.

metadata: data about data.

motion for new trial: a request to start the trial over again because of some extreme circumstance that deprives the litigant of a fair trial; the request can be made during the trial or after the verdict.

motion in limine: a request to the court asking that certain matters not be discussed in front of the jury without the express permission of the judge.

NALI: National Association of Legal Investigators.

National Association of Legal Assistants (NALA):   www.nala.org.

National Federation of Paralegal Associations (NFPA):   one of the two major national professional paralegal organizations.

National Institutes of Health (NIH):   a federal agency tasked with research about diseases and education regarding disease.

near-line data: a large-capacity information storage system that has incremental information storage; data can be easily retrieved; see www.linktionary.com/b/backup.html.

neutral witness: a person with knowledge of matters related to the litigation who has no affiliation with any of the parties.

no-contact rule: ethical rule prohibiting an attorney from contacting a party represented by another attorney.

nomenclature: naming system.

nonverbal cues: actions or inflections that communicate information or emotions.

NTSB: National Transportation Safety Board, a federal agency.

nurse paralegal: an individual trained as a paralegal who also has nursing experience and training.

obfuscation: making something difficult to understand; has the connotation of being purposeful.

objection: an official complaint about or opposition to the offer or request for information or evidence stating the basis of the complaint.

obsessive compulsive disorder: an anxiety disorder characterized by repetitive rituals and rigid behavior.

offer of proof: presenting evidence to the judge for the record, outside the presence of the jury.

office administrator: see *legal administrator*.

official witness: a person with knowledge of the event in question who holds some sort of government position that bears on the event.

offline storage: saved data that is sent offsite for safekeeping; see www.linktionary.com/b/backup.html.

online data: information stored in a readily accessible portion of the computer.

open-ended question: an inquiry inviting the respondent to answer at length without suggesting a particular outcome; e.g., "What was your relationship with your husband like?" not "Did your husband abuse you?"

Opticon: software for integration of graphic images within a case management computer program.

oral deposition: a witness statement taken under oath before a court reporter and all attorneys to litigation for which the deposition is necessary; what people generally mean when they say "depo".

organizational chart: a graphic description of the hierarchical relationship within an entity where the supervisory power starts at the top and flows down.

original jurisdiction: the power to hear a matter at the outset.

OSHA: Occupational Safety and Health Administration, a federal agency.

ostensibly: with the apparent purpose of.

paralegal: an individual engaging in substantive legal work (as opposed to clerical work) under some level of supervision of an attorney. NFPA, NALA, and the ABA all have slightly different formulations, but this definition embraces the usual elements.

partial quadriplegic: someone mostly paralyzed in all limbs but with some limited ability to move his or her upper body or arms.

partner: a person who is one of the owners of an unincorporated law firm.

party-opponent admissions: statements made by the opposing party that are not in the party's best interest

PDR: *Physician's Desk Reference,* an annual publication listing information about drugs.

pedagogical: educational.

peer review committee privilege: a right to keep communications among the members of a medical reviewing group and any health care provider reviewed confidential.

personal jurisdiction: one of the elements necessary for a court to have the power to enter an enforceable decree; consists of official notice to the defendant (service) and geographical jurisdiction or the existence of at least minimum contacts over the defendant; can be waived.

physician-patient privilege: a right to keep communications between an individual and his or her medical care provider confidential.

PI lawyer: a "personal injury" attorney, usually on the plaintiff's side when so designated.

pie chart: a graphic display of information in the form of a segmented circle.

pixels: a unit of computer graphics measurement consisting of a very small square.

plea in intervention: a document that officially includes a party wishing to participate in the litigation because of a legal interest in the outcome.

pleading requirements: the rules regarding the form, contents, and deadlines of pleadings.

pleadings: documents setting forth the official positions of the parties; e.g., complaint, answer, plea in intervention.

policy limits: the maximum amount an insurance company must pay under an insurance policy; liability limits can be by incident or person.

PowerPoint: Microsoft Office's presentation software.

preservation of error/preservation of evidence: the formal process by which an attorney makes a record of what the judge has ruled about and, where applicable, omitted from the evidence in order to have the decision reviewed on appeal.

presumption: the default state of the facts—how the facts of a case will be found without some evidence to the contrary.

prevaricate: (to) lie; has the connotation of delay being involved.

priest-penitent privilege: a right to keep communications between an individual and his or her religious advisor confidential.

prior bad act: any wrongdoing on the part of a witness or party that is offered for admission into evidence.

privilege: a right to prohibit certain evidence from being disclosed.

pro se/pro per: an individual representing himself or herself in a legal matter.

probative: persuasive.

process of service: the procedure for giving a defendant formal notice of a suit, required to acquire jurisdiction over the person; the steps of the procedure are dictated by the jurisdiction.

products liability: a category of legal practice and issues revolving around manufactured products that cause injury; also used to describe strict liability for defective products.

progeny: offspring; children.

prohibition: forbidden action.

propensity evidence: evidence of prior bad acts in order to prove that the person acted the same way in the current situation in controversy.

proprietary function: action by a governmental entity that is not something ordinarily done by governments but is instead often a function of private entities; proprietary functions were exempt from sovereign immunity under common law.

prove up: obtain or turn in evidence in an admissible form.

Psychological Abstracts: a multivolume index summarizing published psychological research; available at most university libraries.

psychotherapist-patient privilege: an evidentiary/discovery principle that protects the records and testimony of a psychotherapist from disclosure.

public records exception: an exception to the hearsay rule that makes public reports or documents created and maintained pursuant to law admissible.

purchase money security interest (PMSI):   a lien created against a particular piece of tangible personal property by the loan of the purchase price.

purely consulting expert: an expert whom the legal team consults but does not use personally or by reference to any tests, results, etc. The status all experts should initially be in; their opinions and identity are not discoverable.

purport: (to) claim.

quantum meruit: an equitable remedy allowing a person to recover pay for work performed.

radiculopathy: a medical term for symptoms of radiating pain or numbness.

Rambo litigators: take-no-prisoner attorneys who turn every part of the trial into a battle, who delay progress as a matter of course, and who are devoid of professional courtesy.

real evidence: tangible, non-documentary, non-demonstrative evidence.

reasonable and necessary: a phrase referring to the requirement of showing that damages claimed by a party are both reasonable in price and type and are necessary under the circumstances.

recapitulate: repeat and summarize prior statements.

receptionist: an employee responsible for incoming calls and clients.

Red Rover expert: an expert previously retained by one party and now utilized by an opposing party.

redact: eliminate privileged, confidential, excluded, or identifying information from a document, film, videotape, audiotape, etc.

registered paralegal (RP): the designation for an individual who successfully passes the NFPA PACE examination.

registration number: one of the terms for the number assigned to persons convicted of a crime.

rehabilitate: in litigation, the attempt to make a witness recover from prior statements that impeach him or her or that demonstrate bias; used in reference to potential jurors as well as trial witnesses.

release: (1) a document by which the keeper of privileged or confidential information about the person signing the document may disclose it to another; (2) a document that relieves the defendant of liability signed in the course of settlement.

relevancy: the degree of relationship between offered evidence and the matter to be proved.

remainderman: the individual who has a property right after others who have it with less than a fee simple basis. For example, if Joe is given a life estate (ownership for the duration of his life) in Green Acres and then it is to go to Sue, Sue is the remainderman.

renters' coverage: insurance that covers a person who is renting his or her home. These policies usually reimburse the insured for destruction to the insured's property from named causes (less the deductible), protect the insured if he or she is sued, and sometimes make limited medical payments for injuries sustained on the insured's premises.

repeat players: parties, usually businesses, who, by the nature of their business or the extent of their holdings, will appear in court on a regular basis.

reporter's privilege: a rule that protects a reporter from disclosing sources in judicial proceedings; only available in states with statutes specifically granting such a privilege.

request for admissions: a discovery device asking another party to judicially admit to the truth of certain matters; once so admitted, the party ordinarily cannot withdraw the admission without a demonstration of good cause.

request for an independent medical exam: a request (which can also be a motion) to have an opposing party who is complaining of physical or mental injuries seen by a doctor of the requestor's choosing.

request for inspection of tangible evidence: a request (which can also be a motion) asking for permission to go onto the premises of a place controlled by an opposing party to see (and sometimes test) tangible evidence

request for production: a discovery device sent to a party asking for documents or tangibles.

request to reduce opinions to writing: a request made to a party to have the opinions of its testifying expert put in writing and disclosed.

res gestae: events or statements that make up the occurrence that is the basis of the lawsuit.

residual data: data/information left over when a file is deleted.

retainer: a money deposit given to an attorney to secure his or her services.

return of service: the document provided by the process server in which he or she certifies who was served, how, where, and when.

reverse look-up: finding the name of an individual or business using a telephone number or address.

review de novo: an appellate review of issues as if they were first presented to the appellate court rather than the court below.

runner: an employee of a law office whose job is to deliver files, file documents at the courthouse, and pick up documents from other offices.

sanction: a court-imposed punishment on a party or his or her lawyers.

scheduling order: a court order requiring the parties to meet interim deadlines before trial; also called a *docket control order.*

secondary gains: a term found in medical records to indicate the doctor's opinion that rather than having a physical malady, the patient is complaining in order to gain something other than medical care, such as damages or attention.

secretary of state: on the state level, an official who oversees required state filings, such as documents relating to incorporation.

self-authentication: the process by which some documents are admissible without a live witness testifying that the document is what it is purported to be.

settlement authority: an amount of money or specific terms of settlement that a client has specifically given the attorney permission for which to settle.

settlement conference: a formal meeting of the parties to discuss settlement, sometimes presided over by the judge in the case.

shareholder: an individual owning shares or stocks in a corporation; in legal practices, used to describe the owners of an incorporated practice instead of using the term *partner.*

skip trace: the process of finding someone whose whereabouts are no longer known; the person has "skipped," and now must be "traced."

smoking gun: a piece of evidence that condemns a party to losing.

sole practitioner: an attorney who engages in the practice of law without entering into a business relationship with any other attorneys.

special needs trust: a trust formulated so as not to violate the eligibility rules for government assistance for the elderly or disabled, usually excluding use of the funds for food, clothing, or shelter, so that supplemental assistance is available.

special setting: a fixed time for trial used when there are special circumstances justifying a non-flexible date, such as extremely long and complex litigation or witnesses traveling from out of state or out of the country. Granted at the discretion of the judge.

specious: weak, unsubstantiated.

spoliation: destruction of evidence by a party; depending on the jurisdiction, it may give rise to sanctions or an evidentiary presumption.

standard of care: the factual procedures or guidelines ordinarily used to determine the need for action in any particular industry, profession, etc.; used to establish breach of duty by demonstrating the difference between what actually occurred and the standard of care.

State Identification Number (SID): one of the terms used to refer to a tracking number assigned by a state to persons who have been arrested, convicted, or who have otherwise entered the criminal justice system. Some governmental employees are assigned SID numbers as well, even with no criminal record.

statute of limitations: the amount of time a plaintiff has to file suit after a cause of action has accrued. Times vary greatly from state to state. The equity version of a statute of limitations is called *laches.*

stipulations: matters agreed to by the parties and filed with the court. Stipulations can streamline trial by restricting the time and consideration of the court and the jury to contested matters and eliminating discussion of routine or undisputed matters.

structured interview: an interview using open and closed questions to control the topics and manner of the interview.

sua sponte: on its own motion; used to describe a court's action when it raises an issue not raised by attorneys to the litigation.

sub judice: under judgment.

subject matter test: one of the tests used to determine which individuals in a corporation are represented by counsel for purposes of privilege and the no-contact rule. In this test, the individuals who are involved in the events of the litigation are the persons represented.

subpoena: a court document ordering a non-party to appear at a stated place and time; used to compel attendance at depositions and at trial.

subpoena duces tecum: a court document ordering a non-party to appear at a stated place and time and to bring along documents or objects or minors; used to compel attendance at depositions and at trial.

subro files: insurance cases for collection against a tortfeasor after the insurer has paid the insured.

subrogation: a common law doctrine that states that when one party is legally obligated to pay on behalf of another, the paying party "steps into the shoes" of the one for whom he or she paid.

substantive evidence: any evidence that is not used simply to illustrate other evidence; see *real evidence*.

summation: the attorneys' statements at the end of trial designed to persuade the jury to find for their clients; another term for *closing arguments*.

surveillance: covertly watching (and usually videotaping) a witness or party with the objective of catching him or her in activities contrary to claims or testimony.

testifying expert: an expert retained by a party and expected to testify at trial, either live or by deposition; must be disclosed.

The Rule: the court rule prohibiting witnesses from listening to each other's testimony (and sometimes extended to prohibit witnesses from discussing their own testimony with anyone except the lawyers or judge).

third-party tortfeasor: in contracts, a reference to someone outside the contract who causes tort damages to a party to the contract.

thoracic: in anatomy, the part of the body covered by the ribcage.

tickler system: an organizational device to ensure that files are reviewed on a regular basis; also called a *diary* or *diary system*.

tort: a civil wrong resulting in loss or injury to an individual's person, property, reputation, or other intangible rights which is not dependent upon a contractual relationship. Fact situations resulting in criminal liability are often also torts.

tort claims act: a statute waiving sovereign immunity under specified conditions in which the plaintiff has a tort cause of action against a governmental entity.

tortfeasor: individual allegedly committing a tort.

traumatic: in medicine, an injury caused by an agent outside the body during a discrete period.

trial attorney: an attorney who primarily represents personal injury plaintiffs in court.

trial consultants: experts, often psychologists, who help determine what arguments juries will respond to and what types of jurors are best for a particular trial; they often work with witness preparation as well.

trial notebook: a tool for organizing notes and evidence in a trial, often a sectioned three-ring binder.

UIM: underinsured motorist coverage. Paired with UM (Uninsured Motorist Coverage), this is a section of most automobile insurance policies. In most (if not all) states, this coverage is required in personal policies (as opposed to commercial policies). The policy owner's insurance coverage will pay under this section if the legally responsible party has no insurance or is underinsured by that state's definition.

unauthorized practice of law (UPI): practicing law without a proper license from the state; may be a civil matter or a criminal act, depending on the jurisdiction and the particulars of the law practiced; includes giving legal advice, representing another in court, or signing pleadings and other court documents.

uncontroverted: undisputed; not challenged by any evidence to the contrary.

underinsured: for purposes of UIM coverage, there are two standard definitions used in different states: (1) the legally responsible person has a lower maximum number of dollars that can be paid than the policy owner, so the policy owner's policy will pay for the difference between the lower and higher amounts; or (2) the legally responsible person's insurance is insufficient to adequately compensate the policyholder for his or her damages and therefore the policyowner's insurance will pay for his or her damages that exceed the limits of the legally responsible person's policy up to the limits of the UIM policy.

unfair prejudice: a term ordinarily associated with Rule 403 in the Federal Rules of Evidence (and often numbered the same way in jurisdictions adopting the rules), this refers to situations in which otherwise admissible evidence may be excluded because its value in the case is low in relation to the effect it will have on the jurors' opinion of a party.

valuations: expert assessments of the value of any particular property.

veniremen: potential jurors; the jury panel.

vent: in conflict management, a term for expressing negative feelings.

verdict reporter: a publication that reports on the amount of jury awards; may also include other information about the trial, such as attorneys' and experts' names.

VerdictSearch: a national online verdict reporter database; also publishes regional trial reports, including names of parties, attorneys, experts, as well as the amount of the award.

video out card: a computer card that fits into a slot inside the main "box" of the computer to make it possible to play multimedia on a standard television.

vision impairment: some deficiency in eyesight that renders it difficult, if not impossible, to see things clearly or read. Some visual impairments can be overcome with various techniques and devices; some cannot.

visualization technique: an exercise used to reduce stress by imagining oneself successfully achieving the desired outcome.

voir dire: the questioning process used at the beginning of a trial to evaluate prospective jurors in the jury panel. In federal practice, this is done by the judge; in many states, the attorneys conduct voir dire. The term is pronounced differently in various areas of the country.

weight of the evidence: a common legal phrase, often paired with a discussion of admissibility, that refers to the quality of the evidence, either in whole or in reference to the particular item of evidence under discussion.

withdrawal: in legal contexts, usually refers to terminating employment with a client in litigation (as in Motion to Withdraw).

witness statements: any report of what fact witnesses to an incident said; more particularly, use of signed statements prepared by someone other than the witness.

woodshedding: preparing witnesses or clients for deposition or trial.

workers' compensation: a statutory system whereby injured workers receive benefits on a schedule or formula as long as they are injured in the course and scope of their employment, relieving them of the burden of proving fault but lessening recovery.

workers' compensation insurance company: an insurance company that pays for injuries sustained by workers in the course and scope of their employment.

workers' compensation lien: a claim for a portion of the proceeds of a cause of action on behalf of a workers' compensation carrier when the carrier has paid workers' compensation to a party, usually the plaintiff.

WORM: a type of digital recording that can only be recorded once, although it may be accessed many times; the acronym stands for Write Once, Read Many.

writ of mandamus: an order requiring a judge to change his or her actions. This remedy is used while the suit is still pending, and is available under limited circumstances, usually where the petitioner (the person filing the Application for a Writ of Mandamus) would suffer irreparable harm if the judge's decision is not changed. Frequently seen in discovery disputes.

zealously represent: a catch phrase from the original Canons of Ethics that has been used to justify a "win at any cost" ethos.

INDEX